W9-CUD-100

THE OXFORD ENCYCLOPEDIA OF
WOMEN IN WORLD HISTORY

EDITORIAL BOARD

THE OXFORD ENCYCLOPEDIA OF WOMEN IN WORLD HISTORY

Bonnie G. Smith

Editor in Chief

Volume 1

Abayomi–Czech Republic

2008

OXFORD
UNIVERSITY PRESS

Oxford University Press, Inc., publishes works that further
Oxford University's objective of excellence
in research, scholarship, and education.

Oxford New York
Auckland Cape Town Dar es Salaam Hong Kong Karachi
Kuala Lumpur Madrid Melbourne Mexico City Nairobi
New Delhi Shanghai Taipei Toronto

With offices in
Argentina Austria Brazil Chile Czech Republic France Greece
Guatemala Hungary Italy Japan Poland Portugal Singapore
South Korea Switzerland Thailand Turkey Ukraine Vietnam

Published by Oxford University Press, Inc.
198 Madison Avenue, New York, NY 10016
www.oup.com

Library of Congress Cataloging-in-Publication Data
The Oxford encyclopedia of women in world history / Bonnie G. Smith, editor in chief.
v. cm.
Includes bibliographical references and index.
ISBN-13: 978-0-19-514890-9
1. Women—History—Encyclopedias.
2. Women—Biography—Encyclopedias.
I. Title: Encyclopedia of women in world history.
II. Smith, Bonnie G., 1940
HQ1121.O93 2008
305.4203–dc22
2007034939

1 3 5 7 9 8 6 4 2
Printed in the United States of America
on acid-free paper

EDITORIAL AND PRODUCTION STAFF

Acquiring Editor
Ralph Carlson

Development Editors
Tanya Laplante   Timothy H. Sachs   Meera Vaidyanathan

Production Editor
Georgia Shepherd Maas

Editorial Assistants
Ryan Abrecht   Christina Carroll   Robert Repino   Shona Sequeira   Alycia Somers

EDP Coordinator
Nancy Tan

Copyeditors
Heidi Yerkes
Dorothy Bauhoff   Kerry Doyle   Richard Goodman   Gretchen Gordon
Jean Kaplan   Katherine H. Maas   Robin Perlow   Alan Thwaits

Proofreaders
Carol Holmes   Matthew Robison   Mary Hawkins Sachs   Kaari Ward

Art Research
Shira Bistricer

Chronology Prepared by
Darcie Fontaine   Rebecca Tuuri

Index Prepared by
Katharyn Dunham, ParaGraphs

Compositor
SPi

Manufacturing Controller
Genieve Shaw

Designer
Book Type

Cover Design
Rachel Perkins

Managing Editor
Martin Coleman

Editorial Director
Kim Robinson

Publisher
Casper Grathwohl

CONTENTS

THE OXFORD ENCYCLOPEDIA OF
WOMEN IN WORLD HISTORY

LIST OF ARTICLES

INTRODUCTION

This project began with a simple idea: to survey the history of women in the world. Rather than looking at women's history in any one nation, in any one culture, or on any one continent, we wanted to move beyond the parochial and familiar, and in the year 2000, as a new millennium began and as the idea of globalization became current, we were optimistic that the time was right for such a survey. We believed from the outset that *The Oxford Encyclopedia of Women in World History* should offer an up-to-date look at what was known on this vast topic—for world history, like women's history, was a field then breaking with many older models of how to understand the past. Confidence remained strong as some nine hundred authors, an editorial board of scholars in women's and world history, and more than a dozen editors at Oxford University Press worked to realize this vast survey of women's history in all parts of the world and at all times in the past. It looked as though a global encyclopedia about women would succeed.

Then, more recently, growing excitement replaced everyday confidence in the project as entries came in from some fifty countries around the world. We read essays from Palestine, Swaziland, Sri Lanka, and Argentina. Scholarship from Norway, the United States, and Italy was matched by contributions from Ghana, Cambodia, and Mexico. Reviewing the entries, we found ourselves learning about Chinese literary theory, Japanese divers, and women who throughout history had profited handsomely from engaging in regional and even global trade. Our essayists were producing extraordinary surveys of Muslim women's organizations, Pan-American conferences of feminists, and women's activities even in prehistoric times. The Encyclopedia's diversity was unparalleled. From writing about codes of laws in a dozen regions of the world to writing histories of sexuality, ethnicity, religion, and race, the Encyclopedia's authors were spreading a rich array of scholarship before our eyes. We had scoured the globe for contributors, and they were sending us the best the world had to offer in women's history.

The range of our contributors' expertise was astonishing, too. They wrote about health, malnutrition, diseases, and women's life-cycle experiences—or about women's participation in nongovernmental organizations (NGOs), the World Health Organization, and the United Nations. Their enthusiasm drove this project, especially when they suggested new approaches and topics that we had entirely missed. "I'm so happy about surveying this topic globally," said one author, "that I'm going to offer a new global course for my students." Because of her commitment, another leading scholar found us a team of experts in disability history and then coordinated an entry with unprecedented global reach. Thanks to our authors we soared to the heights of women's artistic and intellectual accomplishments—and sank as our essays detailed the horrors of genocide, war, and rape. All the while the world's scholars on women dazzled us with their erudition and good will. They have converted this survey of what is known about women in world history into a unique work of pathbreaking scholarship.

We Stand on the Shoulders of Giants. Anyone with knowledge of women's history knows that both the clarification of our task and our progress in this Encyclopedia are deeply indebted to generations of scholars. That debt goes back, in fact, centuries and even millennia. Writers have long written about the accomplishments, trials, and intellect of women, and equally readers have found the history of women fascinating and instructive. Over the centuries so many authors from around the world have mined written records and oral histories to produce their histories that scholars have not yet fully accounted for all of them.

In 1831 a learned Chinese woman, Wanyan Yun Zhu, published *Precious Record from the Maidens' Chambers*, a history of Chinese women from many walks of life. To produce this work Wanyan Yun Zhu relied in part on her collection of some three thousand women poets, for in that same year she also produced an annotated anthology of their works called *Correct Beginnings*, edited with the help of her three granddaughters. As readers sent more poems to the family, the granddaughters produced successive volumes—*Correct Beginnings Continued*. The books by Wanyan Yun Zhu and her granddaughters showed interest in women poets from all parts of China and Korea and in women from all times facing a variety of challenges. We might call their books an encyclopedia of women in the making, spurred by enthusiasm for producing a record of women's accomplishments and experience. We truly do stand on the shoulders of such scholarly giants.

This encyclopedia was born amid a similar snowballing of evidence from women's past. The Qing dynasty (1644–1912), during which Wanyan Yun Zhu and her granddaughters were swamped with materials on women, could boast thousands of women authors. Two centuries later a comparable sense that vast quantities of scholarship about women exist inspired Oxford University Press to undertake this Encyclopedia to survey that scholarship. Historians around the world today are writing histories of women that are meticulously researched. These histories are pouring forth in the tens of thousands, and it is the task of this Encyclopedia—like the very first encyclopedias ever compiled—to summarize the knowledge that has been amassed in order to give curious readers a sense of where we stand. We follow the lead of Wanyan Yun Zhu in producing this compilation.

Other historians in the past have taken a deep interest in the history of women around the world. At about the time of Wanyan

Yun Zhu's compilations, the American author and abolitionist Lydia Maria Child published her *History of the Condition of Women* (1835), a work rich in evidence of women's lives, including both the privileged and the poor, around the world. Going back several centuries, Christine de Pizan's *Book of the City of Ladies* (1405) celebrates the history of women in ancient and medieval times in Europe, the Middle East, and parts of the Mediterranean basin, even addressing such issues as violence against women and household abuse. More limited in their reach, late in the eighteenth century several Chinese men produced works on the long intellectual history of Chinese women. In 1797, Zhang Xuecheng published an extensive essay chronicling women's erudition in the ancient Chinese past and decrying women's gradual turn away from scholarly pursuits and toward poetry and the arts.

Even when women have not been the main topic of their investigations, some male authors have noted women's contributions. In writing his history of the French Revolution, for example, the historian Jules Michelet famously and accurately noted: "Men captured the Bastille, but women captured the king" (*Femmes de la révolution*, 1854). Michelet was full of bons mots about women in history. Meanwhile, sustained and serious investigations in women's history were building steam even as he wrote. Late in the nineteenth century erudite African American women turned their attention to compiling biographies of accomplished African American women, just as scholarly women in many parts of the world were bringing to light evidence of both women's distinction and the patterns of everyday life. Scholars in the academy, employing the new methods of professional history, studied a wide range of women from nuns to heads of state to ordinary people running households. During the reinvigoration of feminism and other forms of women's activism from the 1960s on, the flood of books and the breadth of information became somewhat overwhelming. Now is the time to try to organize this mass of information, taming what scholars of the first encyclopedias did when they tackled early instances of "information overload."

Joining Women's History and World History. This Encyclopedia allows its readers a look at women's history from an array of viewpoints. Over recent decades, world history alone has developed a range of perspectives from which to view the past. It looks at individual civilizations and cultures, while sometimes comparing and contrasting them. It also charts connections among peoples, seeing interactions and encounters as the true measure of what is important in the history of the world. We have merged these categories with those important to women's history, beginning with attention to the general terms that have become important to charting women's past—"patrilocality," "age grades," "class," and "gender" are a few examples. Some of these terms may be common across regions and through time, whereas others are specific to certain cultures. Our authors defined those terms according to the most recent scholarship or showed how the terms' meanings had evolved over time. When a term was pertinent to many groups of women, our authors tried to provide instances of its use in various societies. The authors addressed differences as well as commonalities in usage.

The Encyclopedia merges extensive general entries with biographies that give a more focused perspective on the broad history of regions and topical knowledge. Our biographical subjects come from all fields of endeavor, from the arts to the economy and politics, whose history they have helped create. Nonetheless, the Encyclopedia presents a mere sample of women throughout history who have led important lives. These entries are brief and selective, covering women in all regions of the world. We shied away from living women—though there is a scattering of these, too—and we allotted a certain percentage to each of the world's regions. So our biographical coverage, given that there are many biographical dictionaries, is representative rather than exhaustive. Yet biographies provide detail to general issues, and they can guide research, leading our readers to the friends, allies, families, contemporaries, and coworkers of these extraordinary women leaders.

Because world history itself has many strategies for describing the past, the outline designates all of those strategies as categories for coverage, including geographic coverage of topics, comparative coverage, and world coverage. Geographic coverage comprises the units of government in different parts of the world or different regions of the world down through time. The experience and achievements of women in such regional or national areas as North Africa since 1500, Chile since independence, Egypt since 1800, or the United States in the modern period are examples of what the reader will find covered in geographic entries. The Encyclopedia surveys the prehistory of each continent, while also investigating the early peoples and cultures that followed. Regional experts on the board of editors determined the appropriate time spans and the entities to be covered. The chronological breaks for the coverage of topics in South Asian history, for instance, are different from those in North America, and the determination of how regions would be designated differs from one part of the world to another—all as our scholars on the editorial and advisory boards judged most appropriate.

Women's lives in world history have comparative aspects that are treated in another category of entries. In these entries experts cover such topics as pregnancy and childbirth, civil disobedience, and codes of law. Comparative entries examine how women participated differently in monarchies across the globe and through time and how they created feminist movements in an array of times and places. Authors compare women's participation in religions and also consider the different attitudes toward women in those religions. Goddesses, priestesses, and other spiritual leaders are equally topics of investigation as seen through a comparative lens. Our authors write comparatively about economic systems such as agriculture, artisanal production, pastoralism, trapping and hunting, fishing, industry, and service work. We have not been able to provide examples from every part of the world, but our experts give examples of places that can be compared and discussed fruitfully together.

A final type of world history focuses on the connections among peoples, which we have approached by looking at the experience of women in wars, trading systems, international organizations, cultural exchange, and diasporas. The Encyclopedia provides the latest scholarship on the traffic in human beings, including the histories of slavery and prostitution. Women have moved around the world by the tens of millions, and never more so than in the present day—whether as refugees, migrants, or sex workers in global networks. Our entries thus consider some of the most pressing issues of our time, including the epidemics that have cut the life expectancy of women in Africa and the poverty that is part of the low value placed on women's and children's lives worldwide. We also present developments and institutions that have worldwide influence even on women who never move from their locale: the rise of tourism or the work of a variety of associations in which women play a part.

A World of Expertise. Unlike almost any other work on women, we have enlisted the world in making this Encyclopedia. Not only do we have a wide geographic range of contributors, but we have a range of expertise and experience. Some of our authors are the most practiced in their fields, while others are fresh, junior specialists in certain areas that historians of women like themselves are just beginning to open up. Our global authors have often expanded their research, made inquiries of colleagues, and taken on coauthors—all in the name of providing the most global scholarship possible for this compendium of women's history. The result is more than 1.6 million words and 450 illustrations on women's history in all regions of the world. We thank these contributors from Argentina, Bulgaria, Canada, Jordan, Korea, Mauritius, New Zealand, and dozens of other countries for their careful work. Sometimes we scoured the globe unsuccessfully for scholars who would undertake topics that we felt needed covering, but our disappointment and concern were kept in check by the expertise that informed the diversity of articles we did receive. We thank the authors for the dedication, skill, and cheerful revision that went into their entries.

An incomparable board of editors added to the world of expertise. The Encyclopedia's vision and reliability springs from their work, as the editors scrutinized the categories of knowledge that guided the selection of individual entries. They provided not only regional expertise but also a proven grasp of various subject fields and genres of history. They helped determine the list of articles and their contents, select authors (and in many cases search again and again for historians to provide just the right coverage), review and edit entries, and even add fresh material themselves to expand an essay's global treatment. On occasion the editors pooled their knowledge to compose several of the entries, and individually they wrote some of the entries themselves. These editors—Iris Berger, Indrani Chatterjee, Barbara Engel, Natalie Kampen, Asunción Lavrin, Chana Kai Lee, Paul Ropp, and Judith Tucker—are themselves among the world's leading scholars in women's history. As such, they imposed exacting standards and contributed their rich scholarly imagination to the creation of this work. They are the brains, heart, and soul of *The Oxford Encyclopedia of Women in World History*. An advisory board of other leading scholars in women's history oversaw the composition of the final list of entries and then themselves contributed some of the most knowledgeable of those entries. We thank Barbara Watson Andaya, Françoise Dussart, Theda Perdue, Anne Walthall, Merry Wiesner-Hanks, and Judith Zinsser for their invaluable advice. Sincere thanks to Professors Kathleen Keller and Sarah Hughes, who provided invaluable help in the early stages of the project.

Our skilled and dedicated editors at Oxford University Press backed this work from the very start. Special thanks go to Ralph Carlson, who enthusiastically commissioned this Encyclopedia, and to Meera Vaidyanathan, who helped finalize the list of entries. Tanya Laplante was the guiding spirit behind the bulk of the actual commissioning and writing of these 1.6 million words. Her patient, cheerful, and professional leadership, ably seconded by Robert Repino and Ryan Abrecht, made the Encyclopedia a reality. It would be hard to thank her enough. Many thanks go to Tim Sachs, who stepped in at the end to oversee the final details of completing the work, and to Georgia Maas for her generous help in guiding the complicated task of production and for her own knowledgeable contributions. Receiving manuscripts to revise was never a grim prospect because of cheerful communications from Nancy Tan. All authors owe her thanks, as they do Christina Carroll, who helped arrange and caption our many illustrations that Shira Bistricer diligently researched. It has been a pleasure and a learning experience to work with this team and with the many other editors and assistants at the press who contributed to the successful completion of *The Oxford Encyclopedia of Women in World History*.

My colleagues at Rutgers University, which has one of the leading women's history programs in the world, have also pitched in. Many sacrificed time from their own publishing to write an entry, find an author, or give advice. Dear friends and family members likewise contributed, not only with expert entries but also with good will and endless support. I hope these close companions will think the effort worth it when they see this final work, a work they have made possible.

Bonnie G. Smith
New Brunswick, N.J.

USING THE ENCYCLOPEDIA

There are nearly 1250 entries and subentries in *The Oxford Encyclopedia of Women in World History*, arranged in alphabetical order letter by letter. Composite entries gather together discussions of similar or related topics under one headword. For example, under the entry "West Asia" the reader will find four subentries: "Ancient Period," "Roman and Byzantine Periods," "Islamic Empires," and "Ottomans." A headnote listing the various subentries introduces each composite entry.

The contributors have sought to write in clear language with a minimum of technical vocabulary. The articles give important terms and titles in their original languages, with English translations when needed. A selective bibliography at the end of each article directs the reader who wishes to pursue a topic in greater detail to primary sources, the most useful works in English, and the most important scholarly works in any language.

To guide readers from one article to related discussions elsewhere in the Encyclopedia, end-references appear at the end of most articles. Blind entries direct the user from an alternate form of an entry term to the entry itself. For example, the blind entry for "Nutrition" tells the reader to look under "Health." The Encyclopedia includes nearly 450 illustrations.

A detailed chronology of women's history follows this note. Volume 4 contains the topical outline, the directory of contributors, and the index. Readers interested in finding all the articles on a particular subject may consult the topical outline, which shows how articles relate to one another and to the overall design of the Encyclopedia. The comprehensive index lists all the topics covered in the Encyclopedia, including those that are not headwords themselves.

CHRONOLOGY

Date	Global	Sub-Saharan Africa	North Africa and the Middle East	Europe	Central and South Asia
c. 2400 B.C.E.			Ku-Bau, a woman tavern-keeper who became an early Mesopotamian ruler of Kish, is possibly the earliest known woman ruler in the ancient Near East.		
2334 B.C.E.			Sargon of Akkad conquers the Sumerian city-states and installs his daughter Enheduanna, the world's first author known by name, as high priestess of the Sumerian moon god Nanna at the southern city-state of Ur.		
1750 B.C.E.			The Code of Hammurabi prescribes the death penalty for adultery in Babylon.		
c. 1500 B.C.E.					Hinduism begins in the Indus Valley–Sarasvati region of what is now Pakistan. It spreads gradually over the next millennium first to the Ganges valley and from there throughout the subcontinent.
mid-fourteenth century B.C.E.			Nefertiti rules as the powerful queen of Egypt (r. 1353–1336 B.C.E.) and is often depicted on equal footing with her husband Akhenaten.		
tenth century B.C.E.			Makeda, also known as Balqis, the Queen of Sheba (now variously identified as Yemen or Ethiopia), visits the court of Solomon, King of Israel.		
seventh and sixth centuries B.C.E.			Witchcraft, as the idea that some people have power over occult relationships among the human, animal, and natural worlds, is documented as a widespread belief around the Mediterranean.	The Greek poet Sappho, one of the great lyricists and one of the few known woman poets of ancient Greece, writes innovative lyric poetry; she refines the prevailing lyric meter such that the meter is now known as Sapphic meter. She is particularly known for representing lesbian relations in literature—called	

Southeast Asia	East Asia	Australia, New Zealand, Oceania, and the Polar Regions	The United States and Canada	Latin America and the Caribbean	Date
					c. 2400 B.C.E.
					2334 B.C.E.
					1750 B.C.E.
					c. 1500 B.C.E.
					mid-fourteenth century B.C.E.
					tenth century B.C.E.
					seventh and sixth centuries B.C.E.

Date	Global	Sub-Saharan Africa	North Africa and the Middle East	Europe	Central and South Asia
				"lesbian" after Sappho's home, the island of Lesbos.	
500 B.C.E.					In India the earliest prescriptive texts in Sanskrit, which lay down social norms, are compiled from this period onward and are connected to systematic attempts to enforce gender stratification because of a concern with controlling procreation. This period also witnesses attempts to consolidate *varna*, or caste, identities.
248 B.C.E.					
195 B.C.E.				Roman women participate in a collective action in favor of the repeal of the Lex Oppia, a law governing women's display of certain luxury items. This is the first, and perhaps only, example in Roman history of women participating in collective action on their own behalf.	
180 B.C.E.					
first century B.C.E.					Sati, the Hindu custom of widow immolation, is first mentioned by a Greek author describing instances from the fourth century B.C.E. in the Punjab (northwestern India, eastern Pakistan).
39 B.C.E.					

Southeast Asia	East Asia	Australia, New Zealand, Oceania, and the Polar Regions	The United States and Canada	Latin America and the Caribbean	Date
					500 B.C.E.
The Vietnamese woman warrior Trinh Trieu Thi, known as Lady Trieu or Elder Sister Trieu, rides astride an elephant to lead a band of courageous but ill-trained local rebels against Chinese troops.					248 B.C.E.
					195 B.C.E.
	Chinese Empress Dowager Lü Zhi, who was empress consort of the founding emperor of the Han dynasty, Gaozu, and regent after his death, dies. She is the first woman ruler in Chinese history to issue imperial edicts.				180 B.C.E.
					first century B.C.E.
The Trung sisters (d. 43 B.C.E.), two elite Vietnamese women, spark a rebellion against the Chinese, and					39 B.C.E.

Date	Global	Sub-Saharan Africa	North Africa and the Middle East	Europe	Central and South Asia
38 B.C.E.				Livia Drusilla (58 B.C.E.–29 C.E.) marries Octavian (later Augustus), the first emperor of Rome, becoming the foremost woman in ancient Rome. She plays a central role in the dynastic politics of the Julio-Claudian clan for more than fifty years.	
30 B.C.E.			Cleopatra VII (b. 69 B.C.E.), the final and best-known pharaoh of the Ptolemaic dynasty of ancient Egypt, commits suicide following the Battle of Actium (31 B.C.E.).		
62 C.E.				Queen Boudicca, leader of a rebellion against the Roman conquerors of Britain, commits suicide after the Romans defeat the Britons.	
second century					The Kama Sutra, a Sanskrit text attempting to codify desire in general and sexual desire in particular, is composed between about the second century and the fourth century C.E. in India.
203			The Christian martyr Perpetua (b. 182 C.E.), born near Carthage in North Africa, is imprisoned and sentenced to die in the arena for her refusal to reject her Christian beliefs.		
238					
251					
267			Zenobia, the second wife of Septimius Odaenathus, king of a short-lived empire		

Southeast Asia	East Asia	Australia, New Zealand, Oceania, and the Polar Regions	The United States and Canada	Latin America and the Caribbean	Date
although they both die in defeat, they remain symbols of Vietnamese national resistance.					
					38 B.C.E.
					30 B.C.E.
					62 C.E.
					second century
					203
	Himiko, queen of the Wa and a shaman in the Japanese kingdom of Yamatai, begins her reign, which lasts until 247.				238
	Lady Wei Huacun (d. 334 C.E.) founds the Shangqing school of Daoism in China.				251
					267

Date	Global	Sub-Saharan Africa	North Africa and the Middle East	Europe	Central and South Asia
			based in the city of Palmyra (in modern Syria), succeeds him on the throne after his death, ruling until the Roman conquest of Palmyra in 272.		
c. 360			Hypatia of Alexandria (d. 415/6), a philosopher and the first woman mathematician of whose life we have fairly detailed knowledge, is born.		
496				Clotilda (475–545), wife of Clovis, the king of the Franks, converts her husband from paganism to Roman Catholicism, establishing the first formal link between church and state that is typical of European kingship.	
mid-sixth century				Radegund (c. 525–587), queen of the Franks, founds the Convent of the Holy Cross in Poitiers, France, an influential monastery for women of all classes that often served as a refuge for aristocratic women escaping domestic violence and political persecution.	Hinduism develops a universalistic strand as it expands into new regions and thus competes with both Buddhism and Jainism. Women and low castes became the paradigmatic devotees. Some women, bypassing or leaving marriage to compose religious poetry in regional vernaculars, become acclaimed *bhakti* saints.
555			Khadijah (d. 619 or 620 C.E.), first wife of the prophet Muhammad, is born. She is the first person to accept Muhammad's status as a prophet and embrace Islam, and she supports him both emotionally and financially in the face of hostility from powerful Meccan opponents.		
seventh century C.E.					Princess Bhrikuti of the Licchavi dynasty brings Buddhism to Tibet when she marries King Songtsen Gampo (r. 618–641 C.E.).
622	The first Muslim community is				

Southeast Asia	East Asia	Australia, New Zealand, Oceania, and the Polar Regions	The United States and Canada	Latin America and the Caribbean	Date
					c. 360
					496
					mid-sixth century
					555
					seventh century C.E.
					622

Date	Global	Sub-Saharan Africa	North Africa and the Middle East	Europe	Central and South Asia
	founded in Medina, Arabia.				
632			Fatima bint Muhammad (b. 604), the daughter of the prophet Muhammad and his first wife Khadijah, dies. She is the mother of al-Hasan and al-Husayn, who are considered by Shia Muslims to be the legitimate imams (spiritual and temporal leaders) of the community of believers.		
634					
647			The Arab conquest of North Africa begins, leading to the Islamization of Berber societies. The transformation in the legal and social status of women from Berber to Muslim is a lengthy process that takes place following the conquest.		
656			ʿAʾisha (c. 614–678), the third and most controversial wife of the prophet Muhammad, rides to the Battle of the Camel where she surveys the first civil war in Islamic society. She and two male allies, now revered by Sunni Muslims, challenge the leadership of ʿAli ibn Abi Talib (d. 661), whose partisans, or Shia, become her political enemies.		
664				The influential Anglo-Saxon abbess Hild of Whitby (c. 614–680) hosts the ecclesiastical Synod of Whitby.	
690					

Southeast Asia	East Asia	Australia, New Zealand, Oceania, and the Polar Regions	The United States and Canada	Latin America and the Caribbean	Date
					632
	The Korean queen Sandok (r. 634–654) is the first of three women rulers of the Silla Kingdom in southern Korea. She keeps the kingdom intact and promotes scholarship, diplomacy, and research, introducing innovations in religion and administration.				634
					647
					656
					664
	Wu Zetian of the Chinese Tang dynasty (618–907) declares herself emperor of				690

Date	Global	Sub-Saharan Africa	North Africa and the Middle East	Europe	Central and South Asia
eighth century					
792					
801			Rabiʿah al-ʿAdawiyyah (b. c. 714), a noted ascetic and teacher and one of the three great Sufi women saints of Basra, Iraq, dies.		
tenth century		Gudit, Queen of Agao, known as the "queen of Damot," rebels against the Christian Ethiopian kingdom and becomes a representative of a tradition of female political rule in southern Ethiopia.			
early eleventh century					
1021			Sitt al-Mulk (970–1023), a princess belonging to the Shiʿa Ismaʿili Fatamid dynasty of Egypt, becomes the ruler of the Fatimid regime, serving as regent		

Southeast Asia	East Asia	Australia, New Zealand, Oceania, and the Polar Regions	The United States and Canada	Latin America and the Caribbean	Date
	China and rules for fifty years—the only woman ever to rule in her own name as sovereign of the Chinese Empire. She also chooses Buddhism over Daoism as the state religion.				
	The practice of foot-binding appears to have originated in China with a woman dancer in the court of the Tang emperor Daizong (r. 762–779). The common appeal of foot-binding reaches its pinnacle during the Ming (1368–1644) and Qing (1644–1912) dynasties.				eighth century
	Lu Meiniang (d. c. 820), the famous courtesan of the Tang dynasty (618–907) and the only Tang woman known as both a Daoist saint and a poet, is born in southern China.				792
					801
					tenth century
	The Japanese author, diarist, and poet Murasaki Shikibu (c. 973–c. 1014) writes *The Tale of Genji*, one of the world's earliest novels. Ever since, she has been considered one of Japan's greatest writers.				early eleventh century
					1021

Date	Global	Sub-Saharan Africa	North Africa and the Middle East	Europe	Central and South Asia
			for her nephew al-Zahir. There is extensive speculation about whether she was involved in the murder of her brother al-Hakim, the caliph, an event that led to her rule.		
1039					
1083			Anna Comnena (d. c. 1153), a Byzantine princess and author of the historical work *Alexiadis*, is born in Constantinople.		
twelfth century					Mahadevi Akka, a poet and the best-known woman saint in India, is one of the group of saints, both men and women, who congregate around Basavanna in southwestern India and come to be known as Veerashaivites.
1129				The French abbess Heloise (c. 1095/1100–1164) receives land near Troyes—from her husband Peter Abelard, to whom she wrote her three Latin letters—that becomes the Convent of the Paraclete.	
1147				Eleanor of Aquitaine (1122–1204), at that time wife of the French king Louis VII, accompanies her husband on the Second Crusade to Jerusalem. Their marriage is later annulled, leaving Eleanor free to marry the future English king Henry Plantagenet.	
1173				The German abbess and mystic Hildegard of Bingen (1098–1179) completes her final visionary work *Liber divinorum operum* (Book of Divine Works), which	

Southeast Asia	East Asia	Australia, New Zealand, Oceania, and the Polar Regions	The United States and Canada	Latin America and the Caribbean	Date
	Korean law states that slave status is hereditary and derived principally from the mother's status, regardless of the father's status.				1039
					1083
					twelfth century
					1129
					1147
					1173

Date	Global	Sub-Saharan Africa	North Africa and the Middle East	Europe	Central and South Asia
				represents her most sophisticated theological ideas.	
1218					
1236					Sultan Raziyya (r. 1236–1240) becomes the only woman sultan of Delhi, ascending the throne despite qualified male siblings, potential contenders to the throne.
1249			After the death of Sultan al-Salih Ayyub of Egypt, his widow Shajar al-Durr coordinates the successful Egyptian defense against the Crusade of King Louis IX of France.		
1262					Rudrama-devi (r. 1262–1289) inherits the throne of the Kakatiya kingdom from her father, becoming one of the most successful woman rulers in South Asia's medieval history.
1279					The Indian poet and ascetic Muktabai (d. 1298), who along with her siblings creates the foundation of what is known as Varkari *bhakti* poetry in Marathi, is born in the holy town of Alandi.
1298				The papal edict *Periculoso* enjoins strict enclosure on all Catholic nuns, although the edict was more discussed than enforced before the sixteenth century when it is reissued by the Council of Trent and is enforced in more strident tones by a Catholic Church threatened by the Protestant reformers.	
1380				Catherine of Siena (b. c. 1347)—Catholic	

Southeast Asia	East Asia	Australia, New Zealand, Oceania, and the Polar Regions	The United States and Canada	Latin America and the Caribbean	Date
	Hōjō Masako (1157–1225), administrator and stabilizer of Japan's first warrior government, the Kamakura Shogunate (c. 1183–1333), reaches the height of her prestige when she receives the Junior Second Rank from the imperial government.				1218
					1236
					1249
					1262
					1279
					1298
					1380

Date	Global	Sub-Saharan Africa	North Africa and the Middle East	Europe	Central and South Asia
				saint and mystic, Dominican Order tertiary, co-patron of Italy, and Doctor of the Church—dies at the age of thirty-three because of the severe regimen of self-starvation and bodily mortification that she practiced for years.	
1392					
1405				*The Book of the City of Ladies* by the French author Christine de Pizan (1365–c. 1430), which undercuts men's claims to intellectual superiority and argues for a place for women in the public sphere, first appears in France.	
1431				The French Catholic visionary Joan of Arc (b. c. 1412) is burned at the stake in Rouen after being condemned by the English as a heretic for her support of the French dauphin Charles VII during the Hundred Years' War (1337–1453).	
1453					
1474				Isabel I of Castile (1451–1504) becomes queen of Spain, where she rules as an	

Southeast Asia	East Asia	Australia, New Zealand, Oceania, and the Polar Regions	The United States and Canada	Latin America and the Caribbean	Date
	The Chosŏn dynasty of Korea (1392–1910) introduces the Confucian system, fundamentally altering gender relations. Confucian doctrine stresses patrilineal descent, draws a sharp distinction between public and private, and considers it a law of nature that women are accorded positions inferior to those of men.				1392
					1405
					1431
Shinsawbu (1395–1472?), also known as Shengtasambhu, becomes queen of the Mon Kingdom of Pegu (Hanthawaddy) in Burma.					1453
					1474

Date	Global	Sub-Saharan Africa	North Africa and the Middle East	Europe	Central and South Asia
				influential and proficient Renaissance monarch with her husband, Ferdinand II of Aragon.	
sixteenth century	The Atlantic slave trade begins.	Idia, the mother of the great warrior Oba Esigie (r. 1504–1550), ruler of the kingdom of Benin in southwest Nigeria, becomes the first woman to receive the title of *iyoba*, or queen mother, and is the only woman to go to war with an army that she raised to fight for her son.			
1519					
1523					Gulbadan Banu Begam (d. 1603), the daughter of the first Mughal king of India, Babur, and the author of *Ahval*, a memoir detailing the domestic life of the early Mughal kings, is born in Afghanistan.
1531					

Southeast Asia	East Asia	Australia, New Zealand, Oceania, and the Polar Regions	The United States and Canada	Latin America and the Caribbean	Date
Islam takes root in the islands of Southeast Asia in the fifteenth and sixteenth centuries.					sixteenth century
				Hernán Cortés takes Malinche (c. 1496–1531 or after 1551), an indigenous woman who could speak in the languages of both the Nahua people and the Maya, as his own mistress and companion during the conquest of Tenochtitlan (1519–1521).	1519
					1523
				According to tradition, a vision of the Virgin Mary appears to the Aztec peasant Juan Diego at Tepeyac Hill in northern Mexico City, telling him to build a church at Tepeyac for Indian converts to Catholicism. As a sign she leaves an image	1531

Date	Global	Sub-Saharan Africa	North Africa and the Middle East	Europe	Central and South Asia
1536					
1541					
1545–1563				The Council of Trent reaffirms the necessity of cloistering for all women religious.	
1558				Elizabeth I (1533–1603) becomes queen of England and Ireland, ruling alone until her death.	
1564					

Southeast Asia	East Asia	Australia, New Zealand, Oceania, and the Polar Regions	The United States and Canada	Latin America and the Caribbean	Date
				of a dark-skinned Mary, an icon that becomes known as the Virgin of Guadalupe.	
				The wife of the son of Christopher Columbus, María de Toledo (1490–1549), engages in a legal campaign in order to reconfirm economic benefits for her family. She wins her case when the royal councils of Spain ratify Columbus's entailed estate.	1536
				The Spanish woman Inés de Suárez (c. 1507–1580) helps the Spanish military leader Pedro de Valdivia found the city of Santiago, Chile. The same year, when Valdivia is away, Suárez helps fend off thousands of indigenous people from taking Santiago. As a reward for her actions, Spanish officials give her extensive landholdings, making her one of the richest Spaniards in colonial Chile.	1541
					1545–1563
					1558
					1564

Date	Global	Sub-Saharan Africa	North Africa and the Middle East	Europe	Central and South Asia
1576		Aminatu (1536–1610) becomes the queen of Zauzau in northern Nigeria, ruling for thirty-four years. Aminatu was known as a warrior queen who led her mounted troops into battle and united a large portion of Hausaland.			
1589				Catherine de Médicis (b. 1519), who ruled as regent of France from 1560 to 1574 and was an important figure in the French wars of religion, dies in France.	
1599					
1602					
1607				The Company of Mary, the Catholic female teaching order, is founded by Jeanne of Lestonnac (1557–1640) in Bordeaux, France. The Company of Mary follows a life dedicated to studying, as a	

Southeast Asia	East Asia	Australia, New Zealand, Oceania, and the Polar Regions	The United States and Canada	Latin America and the Caribbean	Date
The Thai queen Suriyothai disguises herself as a soldier and accompanies her husband to the battlefield after the Burmese attack Ayutthaya; she dies saving his life.					
					1576
					1589
			Marie de l'Incarnation (d. 1672), an Ursuline nun who taught both French and Indian women in the Quebec wilderness, is born in France.		1599
				Sor María de Agreda (d. 1665) is born. She becomes a Spanish nun, mystic, and author who is also a recurring figure in the folklore of the American Southwest.	1602
					1607

Date	Global	Sub-Saharan Africa	North Africa and the Middle East	Europe	Central and South Asia
				personal goal, and teaching women, as a social goal.	
1611					Nur Jahan (1577–1645), the most powerful of all Mughal women, marries the emperor Jahangir and then leads the dominant faction at court. In the years shortly before her husband's death in 1627, she even seems to have been the acting sovereign.
1617					
1624		Queen Njinga (1582–1663) becomes leader of the northern Angolan kingdoms of Ndongo and Matamba, ruling until her death. She is known for her resistance to Portuguese incursion, her conversion to Christianity, and her alleged gender ambiguity.			
1638					

Southeast Asia	East Asia	Australia, New Zealand, Oceania, and the Polar Regions	The United States and Canada	Latin America and the Caribbean	Date
					1611
			After visiting London with the financial backing of the Virginia Company, Chief Powhatan's daughter Pocahontas (b. c. 1596) dies and is buried in Gravesend, Kent. The truth of the story of Pocahontas remains largely unknown, but it is likely that Captain John Smith fabricated the story of his salvation by Pocahontas.		1617
					1624
			In March 1638, Anne Hutchinson (1591–1643) is tried by the Boston Puritan church, whose ministers worry about the influence that Hutchinson has on Boston's women. The congregation's men agree to excommunicate her for lying about how long she had held her heterodox opinions. That spring Hutchinson and other radicals leave Boston to found a colony in what later became Rhode Island.		1638

Date	Global	Sub-Saharan Africa	North Africa and the Middle East	Europe	Central and South Asia
1641					
1643					
1650					
1653					
1666				The Quaker leader Margaret Fell (1614–1702) publishes the well-known tract *Womens Speaking Justified, Proved and Allowed of by the Scriptures*, which argues for women's spiritual equality and for their voices to be heard in meetings and preaching.	
1671					
1677					

Southeast Asia	East Asia	Australia, New Zealand, Oceania, and the Polar Regions	The United States and Canada	Latin America and the Caribbean	Date
Taj al-Alam Safiyyat al-Din (r. 1641–1675) ascends the throne as sultana of Aceh in northern Sumatra, the first of four women rulers who govern Aceh consecutively in the seventeenth century.					1641
			For the first time, Virginia tax law distinguishes between African women—who are "tithable"—and white women.		1643
			In London, the brother-in-law of Anne Bradstreet, an English colonist in America, publishes Bradstreet's first volume of poetry, *The Tenth Muse, Lately Sprung Up in America*. This is the first volume of poetry written by a colonist.		1650
			Marguerite Bourgeois (1620–1700), a French nun born in Troyes, founds the first women's congregation in Canada for teaching young French and Native American girls.		1653
					1666
				Saint Rose of Lima, born Isabel Flores de Oliva in Peru (1586–1617), is canonized, becoming the first Catholic saint in the Americas.	1671
			The Puritan Mary Rowlandson (c. 1635–1711), a white woman who was captured by the Narragansett Indians in a raid on her town in		1677

Date	Global	Sub-Saharan Africa	North Africa and the Middle East	Europe	Central and South Asia
1678				The Venetian Elena Lucrezia Cornaro Piscopia (1646–1684) becomes the first woman university graduate when she receives a PhD from the University of Padua.	
1689					
1693					
eighteenth century	The Western intellectual and cultural movement known as the Enlightenment begins in Europe.				
1700					The Indian leader Tarabai (1675–1761) becomes regent of the Hindu state of Maratha, guarding Maratha independence from the Mughal Empire.
1704		Kimpa Vita (b. c. 1684), a Kongolese woman known as the Kongolese Joan of Arc, claims to be possessed by Saint Anthony. Because she is a threat to the			

Southeast Asia	East Asia	Australia, New Zealand, Oceania, and the Polar Regions	The United States and Canada	Latin America and the Caribbean	Date
			1676 during King Philip's War, publishes her book *A True History of the Captivity and Restoration of Mrs. Mary Rowlandson*.		
					1678
				Sor Juana Inés de la Cruz (1648–1695), the most famous nun from colonial Spanish America, known in her lifetime as the "Tenth Muse of America," publishes her first collection of poetry, *Inundación castálida* (Inundation of the Muses).	1689
			Fourteen women and five men are hanged and one man is pressed to death after 156 people are accused of practicing witchcraft during the Salem witch trials in Salem, Massachusetts.		1693
					eighteenth century
					1700
					1704

Date	Global	Sub-Saharan Africa	North Africa and the Middle East	Europe	Central and South Asia
		power of secular and religious leaders, in 1706 priests and the royal council condemn her as a heretic and burn her at the stake.			
1714					
1727					
1730		Empress Mentewwab (r. 1730–1768), a central figure in Ethiopian national politics, rules the country through a web of male kinsmen. She maintains power until the assassination of her grandson in 1768.			
1733					
1735					

Southeast Asia	East Asia	Australia, New Zealand, Oceania, and the Polar Regions	The United States and Canada	Latin America and the Caribbean	Date
				Sor María Anna Águeda de San Ignacio (1695–1756) enters a female lay religious institution called the Beaterio de Santa Rosa de Santa María in Puebla, and she later transforms it into the earliest colonial convent to venerate the Americas' first saint, Rose of Lima.	1714
			The Sisters of the Order of Saint Ursula open the Ursuline Academy, a girls' school in New Orleans. This academy is now the oldest continuously operating girls' school in the United States.		1727
					1730
				The Company of Mary, a Catholic religious order dedicated to teaching women, opens its first convent in the New World in Cap Français (today's Haiti), a French colony.	1733
	The Korean Lady Hyegyŏng (d. 1815), the wife of the crown prince				1735

Date	Global	Sub-Saharan Africa	North Africa and the Middle East	Europe	Central and South Asia
1740				The accession of Maria Theresa (1717–1780) to the throne of the Habsburg Monarchy leads to the War of the Austrian Succession (1740–1748).	
1742					
1751					
1753				The state senate, Russia's highest court, issues a ruling that allows married women to buy and sell property and enter contracts independent of their husbands, a right unique in Europe.	
1762				Catherine II (1729–1796) becomes empress of Russia. She makes women's education the responsibility of the state.	
1763					

Southeast Asia	East Asia	Australia, New Zealand, Oceania, and the Polar Regions	The United States and Canada	Latin America and the Caribbean	Date
	Sado and the author of *Hanjungnok* (The Memoirs of Lady Hyegyŏng), which gives extraordinary insights into eighteenth-century court life, is born.				
					1740
				Sor Francisca Josefa Castillo y Guevara (b. 1671), a colonial Colombian nun whose posthumously published spiritual autobiography becomes one of the world's most popular, dies.	1742
	The Chinese poet and *tanci* novelist Chen Duansheng (d. c. 1796) is born in Qiantang (Hangzhou), Zhejiang Province, China. She is known today for her *tanci* entitled *Zaisheng yuan* (Karmic Bonds of Reincarnation).				1751
					1753
					1762
Gabriela Silang, a "priestess" who became leader of an anti-Spanish rebellion in the Philippines following the death of her husband, is executed for	The Chinese novelist Cao Xueqin (b. c. 1715), author of the preeminent classic Chinese novel, *Hong lou meng* (Dream of the Red Chamber), dies. The				1763

Date	Global	Sub-Saharan Africa	North Africa and the Middle East	Europe	Central and South Asia
1773					
1774					
1776					
1781					
1788					
1789					

Southeast Asia	East Asia	Australia, New Zealand, Oceania, and the Polar Regions	The United States and Canada	Latin America and the Caribbean	Date
her opposition to colonization.	novel describes the Qing dynasty (1644–1912) family structure and how women and girls manage within this male-dominated structure.				
			Phillis Wheatley (1753–1784), an enslaved woman poet living in Boston, travels to Britain and publishes her verse under the title *Poems on Various Subjects, Religious and Moral*. This is the first book of poetry published by an African American.		1773
			The Shaking Quakers (or Shakers), an English religious group founded in 1772 by "Mother" Ann Lee, move to the North American colonies. They eventually settle in some nineteen communes across the United States.		1774
			Abigail Adams (1744–1818) urges her husband and the Continental Congress to "remember the ladies" when writing laws for the newly formed United States of America.		1776
				Micaela Bastidas (b. 1744), leader of resistance to Spanish colonial rule in the Andes, is executed in Cuzco by the Spanish colonial administration.	1781
		The first shiploads of British convicts, including women, arrive in Sydney, Australia, and from the 1790s small numbers of free women migrants begin arriving.			1788
				Leona Vicario (d. 1842), a key protagonist in the Mexican independence movement, is born in Mexico City to wealthy Spanish parents.	1789

Date	Global	Sub-Saharan Africa	North Africa and the Middle East	Europe	Central and South Asia
1792				The British author Mary Wollstonecraft (1759–1797) publishes *Vindication of the Rights of Woman*, voicing the early feminist argument of women's equality in response to the rhetoric of the French Revolution.	
1793				During the height of the French Revolution, the French queen Marie-Antoinette (b. 1755) is convicted of plotting against the French Republic and is guillotined in Paris, just months after her husband Louis XVI was executed for treason.	
1804				The Napoleonic Code is introduced throughout the French Empire and eventually becomes the basis of civil codes throughout the world.	
1805					
1807	Great Britain abolishes the slave trade; slavery is abolished in the British colonies in 1833.				
1810		The South African Sara Baartman is taken from Cape Town to London, where she is displayed as the "Hottentot Venus." She dies in Paris in 1815, having been		The French-Swiss woman of letters and political figure Germaine de Staël (1766–1817) publishes her most celebrated literary work, *On Germany*, which introduces German manners, letters, and	

Southeast Asia	East Asia	Australia, New Zealand, Oceania, and the Polar Regions	The United States and Canada	Latin America and the Caribbean	Date
			Sarah Pierce's Litchfield Female Academy is founded in Connecticut. More than three thousand women attended the school during its forty-one-year existence.		1792
					1793
					1804
			Mercy Otis Warren (1728–1814) publishes her *History of the Rise, Progress, and Termination of the American Revolution*. The three-volume tome was not only one of the earliest histories of the American Revolution but the first written by a woman.		1805
					1807
					1810

Date	Global	Sub-Saharan Africa	North Africa and the Middle East	Europe	Central and South Asia
		exhibited and owned by an animal trainer.		philosophy to the French.	
1811					
1815					
1817					
c. 1825		The Swahili poet Mwana Kupona (d. 1860) is born			

Southeast Asia	East Asia	Australia, New Zealand, Oceania, and the Polar Regions	The United States and Canada	Latin America and the Caribbean	Date
				The Company of Mary opens New Enseñanza, a convent in Mexico City for teaching Indian women. Previously the order had founded the houses of Mendoza (today's Argentina, 1780), Mexico City (1754), and Santa Fé de Bogotá (today's Colombia, 1783).	1811
				In the war for Bolivian independence, Juana Azurduy de Padilla (c. 1780–1862) and her husband Manuel mount a guerrilla war against Spanish royalists. She trains a group of women, known as the Amazons, who fight in sixteen battles, and she herself gains a reputation as a daring soldier who will not hesitate to kill the enemy or pursue them in battle.	1815
				Policarpa Salavarrieta (b. c. 1795) is executed by the Spanish government for helping try to liberate Colombia from Spain. She becomes a martyr for the Colombian independence movement.	1817
					c. 1825

Date	Global	Sub-Saharan Africa	North Africa and the Middle East	Europe	Central and South Asia
		in Siu, in the northern Kenyan Lamu archipelago. She is best known for the *Utenda Wa Mwana Kupona*, a 102-stanza poem in Arabic script, which gives advice to her daughter.			
1826					
1828					
1829					The British prohibit the practice of sati (widow immolation) in India.
1830s		The Asante stateswoman Yaa Kyaa (c. 1770–c. 1840) brokers peace between the Asante and the British, which brings about the opening of trade routes in the Gold Coast. She continues to lead Asante diplomatic missions in West Africa in the 1830s.			
1831					

Southeast Asia	East Asia	Australia, New Zealand, Oceania, and the Polar Regions	The United States and Canada	Latin America and the Caribbean	Date
		Eliza Darling founds the Female School of Industry and the Female Friendly Society in Australia.			1826
			The Oblate Sisters of Providence, a Catholic order for African American women, is founded in Baltimore, Maryland.		1828
				Josepha Ortiz de Domínguez (b. c. 1768), wife of Don Miguel Domínguez, a Spanish-appointed *corregidor* who was sympathetic to the Mexican independence movement, dies. Ortiz de Domínguez, or "La Corregidora," is also a key protagonist in the Mexican independence movement.	1829
		In Tasmania, Tarenorerer (c. 1800–1831) leads a band in armed warfare against European colonists.			1830s
			Mary Prince (c. 1788–?) publishes *The History of*		1831

Date	Global	Sub-Saharan Africa	North Africa and the Middle East	Europe	Central and South Asia
1833				The British Factory Act inaugurates hours regulation, barring children younger than nine from working in textile factories and reducing the working day to twelve hours for thirteen- to eighteen-year-olds. It was not until about a decade later that a bill was passed to include women under such legislation.	
1834					
1836					
1840					

Southeast Asia	East Asia	Australia, New Zealand, Oceania, and the Polar Regions	The United States and Canada	Latin America and the Caribbean	Date
			Mary Prince, a West Indian Slave, Related by Herself, becoming the first known self-emancipated slave woman to write an autobiography.		
			Lydia Maria Child (1802–1880) publishes her *Appeal in Favor of That Class of Americans Called Africans*, the first extensive study of slavery and emancipation. Widely read and debated, Child's *Appeal* is often credited with turning abolitionism into a movement.	Soledad Acosta de Samper (d. 1913), the Colombian writer and notable advocate for the education of women, is born.	1833
			Textile workers in Lowell, Massachusetts, go on strike (and again in 1836) to protest deteriorating conditions and speedups in the factories.		1834
			The American Anti-Slavery Society persuades both Angelina Emily Grimké (1805–1879) and Sarah Grimké (1792–1873)—two sisters who had spoken out against slavery after growing up in a wealthy slaveholding family in South Carolina—to move to New York and speak with women in private homes. The Grimkés thus become the first women abolitionist agents.		1836
			Lucretia Mott (1793–1880) and Elizabeth Cady Stanton (1815–1902) meet at the World Anti-Slavery Convention, where they are both refused seats because of their sex. Watching the meeting from the balcony, Mott and Stanton decide to form a convention devoted to achieving women's rights.		1840

Date	Global	Sub-Saharan Africa	North Africa and the Middle East	Europe	Central and South Asia
1841					
1845			In Algiers, the Frenchwoman Véronique Allix-Luce founds a Franco-Arab school for girls that receives government support and provides schooling to some one thousand young girls until 1861, when it is brought to an end by Muslim opposition.		
1847				The English writer Charlotte Brontë (1816–1855) publishes her novel *Jane Eyre* under the pseudonym Currer Bell; the novel immediately becomes a best seller.	
1848					
1849					
1850					

Southeast Asia	East Asia	Australia, New Zealand, Oceania, and the Polar Regions	The United States and Canada	Latin America and the Caribbean	Date
			Catherine Beecher (1800–1878), an educator and social reformer who promotes the concept of separate spheres, publishes her popular *Treatise on Domestic Economy*. The book seeks to recast women's gendered identity to give women greater power in their personal and family lives, as well as in their communities.	Gertrudis Gómez de Avellaneda (1814–1873), Cuban-Spanish Romantic poet, novelist, and dramatist, publishes her first and most famous novel, *Sab*. Like Harriet Beecher Stowe's *Uncle Tom's Cabin* (1852), *Sab* also draws a clear parallel between the evils of slavery and the powerlessness of women.	1841
					1845
					1847
			In July, the Seneca Falls Convention is held in Seneca Falls, New York. The convention is the first to call explicitly for women's educational, religious, social, economic, and political rights, and it has been considered the symbolic beginning of the nineteenth-century women's rights movement.		1848
			Elizabeth Blackwell (1821–1910) becomes the first woman to graduate from medical school in the United States.		1849
					1850

Date	Global	Sub-Saharan Africa	North Africa and the Middle East	Europe	Central and South Asia
1851					
1852			Qurrat al-ʿAyn (b. 1814), an early champion of women's equality in Iran—as well as an activist, intellectual, poet, and one of the first eighteen believers in the Babi movement—is put to death in Tehran.		
1853					
1856		Muganzirwazza (1817–1882) assumes the role of queen mother of Buganda on the accession of her son Mutesa I to power. Her influential role is something similar to that of a king and a prime minister, and she is among the first anti-imperialists of Buganda.			
1858			The first state schools for girls open in the Ottoman Empire. An		Lakshmi Bai, the only woman rebel leader of the revolt of 1857 in Jhansi,

Southeast Asia	East Asia	Australia, New Zealand, Oceania, and the Polar Regions	The United States and Canada	Latin America and the Caribbean	Date
			Sojourner Truth (c. 1797–1883), New York preacher, freed slave, and abolitionist, dictates *The Narrative of Sojourner Truth.*		
	The Taiping Rebellion (1851–1864) begins in China as an uprising against the ruling Manchu Qing dynasty (1644–1912). Women have often been seen as central to the Taiping ideology, and feminists and socialists alike have looked upon the Taiping movement as offering the first blossomings of gender and class equality in China, even though evidence of women's emancipation in the movement is slim.				1851
			The American author Harriet Beecher Stowe (1811–1896) publishes *Uncle Tom's Cabin.*		1852
				Marianita de Jesús (1618–1645), an Ecuadorian saint also known as the Lily of Quito, is beatified on 20 November 1853 and is canonized on 9 June 1950.	1853
					1856
					1858

Date	Global	Sub-Saharan Africa	North Africa and the Middle East	Europe	Central and South Asia
			1869 decree makes primary education compulsory for both boys and girls aged six to ten, though its implementation is limited.		India, dies fighting the British near Gwalior.
1860				Jewish women in France establish the Alliance Israélite Universelle to regenerate Jewish culture and identity through modern coeducational schools.	
1861					
1863	The International Red Cross is founded by Swiss citizen, Jean Henri Dunant (1828–1910), after the bloody battle at Solferino (24 June 1859) during the Austro-Sardinian War.				
1868					
1869					

Southeast Asia	East Asia	Australia, New Zealand, Oceania, and the Polar Regions	The United States and Canada	Latin America and the Caribbean	Date
		Between 1860 and 1900, nearly ninety thousand single British women, who were in demand both as domestic servants and as wives, arrive in Australia as assisted migrants. They are helped by such organizations as the Female Middle Class Emigration Society, founded in London in 1862 to help solve the problem of "surplus women."			1860
			A former slave who hid in a tiny garret for seven years to avoid capture, Harriet Jacobs, under the pseudonym Linda Brent, publishes her autobiography, *Incidents in the Life of a Slave Girl*.	Nuns are expelled from all convents in Colombia. Five years later, nuns are expelled from convents in Mexico. However, in both countries the nuns are able to refound their schools and resume their educational services in less than fifteen years.	1861
			A former slave and a conductor for the Underground Railroad, Harriet Tubman (1825–1913) engineers the Combahee River Raid on 2 June 1863, during which more than 750 slaves are freed.		1863
			Louisa May Alcott (1832–1888) publishes *Little Women*, a novel that has become a worldwide icon of American girlhood.	The Cuban war for independence from Spain begins. During the initial Ten Years War (1868–1878), Mariana Grajales sacrifices several sons to the war effort.	1868
					1869

DATE	GLOBAL	SUB-SAHARAN AFRICA	NORTH AFRICA AND THE MIDDLE EAST	EUROPE	CENTRAL AND SOUTH ASIA
	Pope Pius IX (r. 1846–1878) decrees that any interruption of pregnancy after conception is a grave sin and that anyone who participates in an act of abortion has excommunicated herself or himself from the Roman Catholic Church.				
1870					
1871				The French anarchist, feminist, and revolutionary Louise Michel (1830–1905) plays a central role in the Paris Commune. She is exiled to New Caledonia after her arrest but returns to France in 1880 and receives a hero's welcome.	
1872					
1873					

Southeast Asia	East Asia	Australia, New Zealand, Oceania, and the Polar Regions	The United States and Canada	Latin America and the Caribbean	Date
			Lucy Stone (1818–1893) helps establish the American Woman Suffrage Association (AWSA), which endorses the Fifteenth Amendment and focuses on winning a separate woman suffrage amendment.		
			Victoria Woodhull (1838–1927) and her sister Tennessee Claflin open the first Wall Street brokerage firm for women. Two years later, Woodhull runs for president and starts a newsletter, *Woodhull & Claflin's Weekly*, a forum for unconventional social thought.		1870
					1871
	The Japanese Education Ordinance institutes compulsory elementary education for boys and girls in coeducational schools. In 1899 the Girls' High School Law requires the opening of at least one high school for women in every prefecture. By 1904, 90 percent of Japanese women are enrolled in school.				1872
			Susan B. Anthony (1820–1906) is tried for voting in the 1872 election. Anthony was using the "New Departure" theory, first proposed by Victoria Woodhull in 1871, that she was already afforded the right to vote by existing laws.		1873

Date	Global	Sub-Saharan Africa	North Africa and the Middle East	Europe	Central and South Asia
1874				The Russian mathematician, writer, and social activist Sofia Kovalevskaia (1850–1891) becomes the first woman to earn a doctorate in mathematics, receiving her degree from Göttingen University in Germany.	
1875		The Luso-African Mãe Aurélia Correia (b. 1810?), a prominent slave trader and merchant in the Upper Guinea Coast, dies.			
1878				The Dutch physician, public health advocate, suffragist, and international peace activist Aletta Jacobs (1854–1929) earns her medical degree in Amsterdam. She opens a practice the next year. Jacobs also translated and wrote many essays on women's rights and peace, and she later became interested in the issue of contraception.	
1879				The Norwegian playwright Henrik Ibsen's play *A Doll's House* is first performed in Copenhagen. Ibsen's heroine Nora embodies the	

Southeast Asia	East Asia	Australia, New Zealand, Oceania, and the Polar Regions	The United States and Canada	Latin America and the Caribbean	Date
					1874
			The Supreme Court rules in *Minor v. Happersett* that voting is a privilege, not a right, of citizenship, thus striking down the "New Departure" theory that women already, under existing laws, had the right to vote.	Juana Paula Manso de Noronha (b. 1819), a pioneering women's rights advocate in a society in which the majority of women are illiterate, dies. Noronha spent her life defending women's education as necessary for women's social and financial emancipation and for the progress of Argentina as a nation.	1875
					1878
The Indonesian nationalist and pioneer of women's schooling Raden Ajeng Kartini (d. 1904) is born in Java. She is declared a national heroine by			Frances Willard (1839–1898) becomes president of the Woman's Christian Temperance Union (WCTU), holding the post until 1898. As president, Willard builds		1879

Date	Global	Sub-Saharan Africa	North Africa and the Middle East	Europe	Central and South Asia
				struggle associated with the First Wave of the women's movement in Europe.	
1882					
1883					Kadambini Ganguly (1861–1923) graduates from Bethune College in Calcutta (now Kolkata), becoming one of the first women to earn a bachelor's degree under British colonial rule. She later attends medical school in India.
1884					
1885					The Indian National Congress is founded and has women delegates by 1889. The public activism of bourgeois women for the nationalist cause does not come into its own, however, until the launching of the Swadeshi campaign in 1905 for the substitution of foreign with indigenous products.
1886				Britain's Contagious Diseases Acts are repealed as a result of a campaign led by the social reformer Josephine Butler (1828–1906).	

Southeast Asia	East Asia	Australia, New Zealand, Oceania, and the Polar Regions	The United States and Canada	Latin America and the Caribbean	Date
President Sukarno in 1963.			the WCTU into the largest women's organization in the nineteenth-century United States, thereby shaping the political, reform, and legislative goals of a generation of middle- and upper-class American women.		
			Clara Barton (1821–1912) becomes the first president of the American Red Cross, holding the post until 1904. Barton had led a difficult but successful campaign to have the United States sign the Geneva Convention and thus establish the American Red Cross.		1882
		Victoria, Australia, becomes the first British colony to give married women property rights with the Married Women's Property Acts.			1883
		Henrietta Dugdale founds the Victorian Women's Suffrage Society in Melbourne; it is one of the first suffrage organizations in Australia.			1884
	The Japanese feminist and socialist Fukuda Hideko (1865–1927) is imprisoned for her part in the Osaka Incident, making her the first woman in modern Japanese history to be jailed as a political prisoner. She is released in 1889.				1885
	The Ewha Womans University is founded in Korea by Mary F. Scranton, an American Methodist missionary. As one of the oldest modern higher educational institutions in Korea, Ewha has produced many firsts in a wide range of fields, including liberal arts, fine arts, Korean				1886

Date	Global	Sub-Saharan Africa	North Africa and the Middle East	Europe	Central and South Asia
1888					
1889		T'aitu Bitoul (c. 1850–1918) becomes empress of Ethiopia, working alongside her husband, Menelik II (r. 1889–1913), to preserve Ethiopia's political independence. An active participant in the Battle of Adwa in 1896, she is described as the real founder of Addis Ababa.			
1890					
1891					The Age of Consent Act is passed in India. Although it does not raise the age of marriage, the act raises the age of consent for penetrative sexual intercourse from ten to twelve for both married and unmarried girls.
1892					

Southeast Asia	East Asia	Australia, New Zealand, Oceania, and the Polar Regions	The United States and Canada	Latin America and the Caribbean	Date
	studies, music, dance, and physical education.				
				D. Isabel de Bragança (1846–1921), acting as a regent for her father Emperor Pedro II, signs a law outlawing slavery in the Brazilian empire, thus earning the title "the Redemptress."	1888
			Jane Addams (1860–1935) and Ellen Gates Starr found Hull House in Chicago, launching the settlement house movement.	The National Women's Exposition is held in Buenos Aires, Argentina.	1889
			The National Woman Suffrage Association (created by Elizabeth Cady Stanton and Susan B. Anthony in 1869) and the American Woman Suffrage Association (created by Lucy Stone and Henry Browne Blackwell in 1869) put aside their differences and create the conglomerate group the National American Woman Suffrage Association (NAWSA).		1890
					1891
			It becomes illegal to advertise or sell contraception in Canada.		1892

Date	Global	Sub-Saharan Africa	North Africa and the Middle East	Europe	Central and South Asia
1893					The first Jadid schools open in Turkestan, founded by the Tatar educator Ismail Bey Gaspirali, who believed that phonetic literacy and linguistic unity were the tools that would free Turkic peoples from Russian domination. The Jadids favored education for women, with the limited aim of training enlightened mothers to raise a new generation of Muslim patriots.
1894				Most German bourgeois women's organizations are united in the Bund Deutscher Frauenvereine (BDF; Federation of German Women's Organizations), and in response to the promulgation of the Bürgerliches Gesetzbuch (German Civil Code) in 1896, the BDF commits itself to fighting for the legal equality of women and men, including women's suffrage.	
1895					
1896				The film director Alice Guy shoots *The Cabbage Patch Fairy*, the first scripted film in France.	

Southeast Asia	East Asia	Australia, New Zealand, Oceania, and the Polar Regions	The United States and Canada	Latin America and the Caribbean	Date
		Women in New Zealand get the right to vote, followed by women in South Australia in 1894, and white women in Western Australia in 1899.	Sophia Hayden (1868–1953), the first academically trained woman architect in the United States, designs the Women's Building for the Chicago World's Columbian Exposition.		1893
	The Kabo Reform in Korea, the result of a campaign by reform-minded intellectuals, enhances women's position in society through promoting education and through abolishing concubinage and the prohibition of widow remarriage. It also eliminates the status distinctions between the *yangban* elite and commoners and ends slavery in Korea.		Elizabeth Peabody (b. 1804), New England transcendentalist educator, author, publisher, editor, and social reformer, dies.		1894
			Elizabeth Cady Stanton writes her controversial work *The Woman's Bible* (1895), which argues for the superiority of women and questions women's treatment by religion.	Soledad Acosta de Samper (1833–1913), the most important Colombian writer of the nineteenth century and a notable advocate for the education of women, publishes *La mujer en la sociedad moderna* (The Woman in Modern Society).	1895
			The National Association of Colored Women (NACW) forms from a merger of the National League of Colored Women (founded in 1892) of Washington, D.C., and Boston's National Federation of Afro-American Women (1895). With the motto		1896

Date	Global	Sub-Saharan Africa	North Africa and the Middle East	Europe	Central and South Asia
1897				The French feminist Marguerite Durand's journal *La Fronde* first appears in France.	
1898					
1899					
1900	Women first compete in the Olympic Games, held in Paris in 1900, in three sports—golf, tennis, and yachting—despite the vocal objections of the International Olympic Committee founder Pierre de Coubertin.	The Nigerian anticolonial and women's rights activist Funmilayo Ransome-Kuti (d. 1978) is born to Yoruba parents in Abeokuta. One of the best-known African women activists of the twentieth century, she became a significant figure		The Irish actress Maud Gonne (1866–1953), who was instrumental in the Gaelic revival and the struggle for Irish independence, founds Inghinidhe na hÉireann (Daughters of Ireland) in response to the exclusion of women from Irish nationalist groups.	

Southeast Asia	East Asia	Australia, New Zealand, Oceania, and the Polar Regions	The United States and Canada	Latin America and the Caribbean	Date
			"Lifting as We Climb," the organization aims at achieving self-protection, self-advancement, and justice for African Americans.		
					1897
			Despite the pleas of Queen Lili'uokalani (1838–1917), who travels to Washington, D.C., with a petition signed by nearly every native Hawai'ian alive, the United States annexes Hawai'i as a territory. Thus Lili'uokalani becomes the last monarch of Hawai'i.	Cuba and Spain sign the Treaty of Paris after Cuba wins its war for independence from Spain. Ana Betancourt demands that women's rights be incorporated into the new national agenda.	1898
				Cecilia Grierson (1859–1934) becomes the first woman in Argentina to earn a degree as a medical doctor. In 1891, Grierson had founded the first professional nursing school in Argentina, and she was an active founding member of the Argentine National Council of Women and the Argentine Association of University Women.	1899
			Margaret Abbott takes the gold medal for golf, one of three sports open to women, at the Paris Olympics.		1900

Date	Global	Sub-Saharan Africa	North Africa and the Middle East	Europe	Central and South Asia
		in human rights and independence struggles throughout the world.			
1901		The Asante queen mother Yaa Asantewaa (c. 1830–1921) surrenders to the British after leading the final Asante resistance to British rule. Defeated, she is exiled to the Seychelles, where she dies in October 1921.		Queen Victoria (b. 1819), England's longest-reigning monarch (r. 1837–1901), dies, ending the Victorian era, one of conservative values and customs but one that also saw a new technologically advanced and industrialized world begin.	
1902	The International Woman Suffrage Alliance (IWSA) is founded in Washington, D.C., by suffrage leaders including Carrie Chapman Catt and Anita Augspurg to promote the enfranchisement of women throughout the world.				
1903				Marie Curie and her husband Pierre win the Nobel Prize in Physics for their research on radioactivity. Marie Curie wins a second Nobel Prize, in Chemistry, in 1911.	
1904			The Swiss traveler and Islamic convert Isabelle Eberhardt (b. 1877) dies in a flash flood in the Sahara after spending decades traveling throughout North Africa disguised as "Si Mahmoud," a male Sufi.		
1905					

Southeast Asia	East Asia	Australia, New Zealand, Oceania, and the Polar Regions	The United States and Canada	Latin America and the Caribbean	Date
	Girls are finally included in the Chinese education system as a result of a campaign to promote women's education that emerges in the aftermath of China's defeat in the first Sino-Japanese War (1894–1895).			The Argentine feminist, activist, reformer, and author Elvira López publishes her groundbreaking doctoral thesis "El movimiento feminista." The thesis examines questions of gender equality and the preservation of difference, and it advocates access to education as a crucial factor in rectifying social and class inequities.	1901
		In Australia, women active in temperance campaigns from the 1880s become involved in the suffrage struggle, resulting in the 1902 Commonwealth Franchise Act, which extends federal political rights to all white women. Aboriginal women are excluded from citizenship and political rights until the 1960s.			1902
			The Women's Trade Union League (1903–1950) is founded by social reformers and trade unionists to organize wage-earning women into trade unions, provide education, and agitate for protective labor legislation in the United States.		1903
			Ida Minerva Tarbell (1857–1944), an American investigative journalist for *McClure's*, publishes some of her muckraking articles in a two-volume collection, *The History of the Standard Oil Company*.		1904
					1905

Date	Global	Sub-Saharan Africa	North Africa and the Middle East	Europe	Central and South Asia
				The British suffragist Christabel Pankhurst—daughter of Sylvia Pankhurst, who founded the Women's Social and Political Union (WSPU) in 1903—initiates the WSPU's "militant," or confrontational and extra-Parliamentary, tactics to campaign for the vote.	
1906				Finland becomes the first European nation to grant women full suffrage. The Scandinavian countries of Norway (1913) and Denmark and Iceland (1915) soon follow.	
1907	The member parties of the meeting of the Second (Socialist) International support a resolution calling for universal suffrage.			The Italian educator Maria Montessori (1870–1952) becomes the director of a primary school, Casa dei Bambini (Children's House), where she develops a method of early-childhood education that emphasizes individual development and self-motivation.	
1908					
1909	International Women's Day (IWD) is launched in the United States by socialist women calling for improved		The Muhammad Ali Benevolent Society, one of the first non-governmental women's charitable organizations, is	The Swedish novelist Selma Lagerlöf (1858–1940) becomes the first woman to win	

Southeast Asia	East Asia	Australia, New Zealand, Oceania, and the Polar Regions	The United States and Canada	Latin America and the Caribbean	Date
					1906
	The revolutionary Chinese feminist and writer Qiu Jin (b. 1875) is executed for her role in planning an uprising against the Qing dynasty (1644–1912). She becomes a martyr for the Chinese nationalist movement and is viewed as one of the great woman revolutionaries of modern times.		The Fédération Nationale St.-Jean-Baptiste is founded as an umbrella feminist organization in Quebec.		1907
	The Korean government legalizes women's higher education and builds the Capital School for Girls' Higher Education.			The Pan-American Scientific Congress is held in Santiago, Chile, in 1908–1909; among the two thousand teachers, scientists, and physicians in attendance are more than one hundred women who, according to accounts at the time, express their opinions openly.	1908
			Supported by the Women's Trade Union League, between twenty and thirty thousand Italian, Russian, and Jewish women take to		1909

Date	Global	Sub-Saharan Africa	North Africa and the Middle East	Europe	Central and South Asia
	wages and working conditions for women. The IWD, originally the idea of the German socialist Clara Zetkin (1857–1933), begins in Europe in 1911, and the United Nations proclaims the IWD (8 March) an official holiday in 1975.		founded in Cairo, Egypt, to instruct new mothers in child care.	the Nobel Prize in Literature.	
1910					
1911					
1912		Mekatilili Wa Menza, an elderly Kenyan woman, becomes a leading figure of the Giriama resistance, 1912–1914, in British-colonized Kenya. Under Mekatilili, the Giriama swear oaths and articulate grievances and noncooperation but do not declare war.			
1913			The Turkish feminist and novelist Halide Edib Adivar (1882–1964) publishes her famous novel *Yeni Turan* (New Turan), in which she envisions a democratic Turkey in which women enjoy political suffrage and wider employment opportunities.		
1914	The assassination of the Austro-				

Southeast Asia	East Asia	Australia, New Zealand, Oceania, and the Polar Regions	The United States and Canada	Latin America and the Caribbean	Date
			the streets to fight for union recognition, higher wages, shorter working hours, and better conditions at work.		
			Amid Progressive-era panic over "white slavery," the Mann Act is passed in the United States, prohibiting the transportation of women across state lines for "immoral purposes."	The First International Feminine Congress is held in Buenos Aires. It is organized by the Argentine Association of University Women and is the first conference of openly feminist leanings in Latin America.	1910
	The Japanese feminist, writer, and New Woman Hiratsuka Haruko (1886–1971) founds the women's literary magazine *Seit.*				1911
The first Indonesian women's organization, Putri Mardika (Free Women), is established, an event that is considered the start of Indonesia's national awakening.	Tang Qunying founds the Chinese Suffrage Society, and the Chinese Republican revolutionary government bans foot-binding. But only in the 1950s—after the Communist mobilization of Chinese peasants and workers—does foot-binding end.		Despite the International Olympic Committee's invitation to have women swimmers participate in the Stockholm Olympics, James Sullivan, the American Olympic administrator, bans American women from participating in the sport.		1912
			Willa Cather (1873–1947) publishes her second novel, *O Pioneers!* Featuring a Swedish immigrant heroine in Nebraska, the novel establishes Cather's reputation as a novelist of the American West.		1913
	Jiang Qing (d. 1991), Chinese actress,		The African American sculptor Meta Vaux	María Jesús Alvarado founds	1914

Date	Global	Sub-Saharan Africa	North Africa and the Middle East	Europe	Central and South Asia
	Hungarian archduke Franz Ferdinand and his wife Sophie in Sarajevo on 28 June sets in motion a chain of events the leads to the outbreak of World War I in Europe and the Middle East.				
1915	The Women's International League for Peace and Freedom (WILPF) is founded at the meeting of the International Council of Women in The Hague, Netherlands, to seek universal disarmament and permanent peace.				
1916		Empress Zewditu (1875–1930) ascends the throne of Ethiopia, ruling until her death. She is the only woman known to have ruled Ethiopia in her own right.		The Irish nationalist Constance Markievicz (1868–1927) serves as a commandant in the failed Easter Rising; she is sentenced to death but is released from prison in 1917.	The college professor Dhondo Keshav Karve (1858–1962), the husband of the remarried Brahman widow Anandibai Karve, founds India's first women's university, now known as S.N.D.T. Women's University.
1917				On International Women's Day (23 February), working-class women in Petrograd, Russia (formerly Saint Petersburg), stage an enormous demonstration calling for bread and peace, sparking the revolution that overthrows Tsar Nicholas II. Russia becomes the first major country to grant women full suffrage.	The Women's Indian Association (WIA) is formed in Adyar (part of Madras) by a diverse group of women, including Annie Besant and Margaret Cousins, the theosophist Dorothy Jinarajadasa, and Ammu Swaminathan, Malathi Patwardhan, Mrs. Dadabhoy, and Mrs. Ambujammal.
1918	World War I ends with the signing of the armistice on 11 November. The minimum number of battlefield deaths in the war is estimated	Initially known as the Bantu Women's League, the African National Congress (ANC) Women's League		Great Britain grants suffrage to women over thirty; in 1928 all women over twenty-one can vote. Poland also grants suffrage to women in	

Southeast Asia	East Asia	Australia, New Zealand, Oceania, and the Polar Regions	The United States and Canada	Latin America and the Caribbean	Date
	politician, and the wife of Mao Zedong, is born in Shandong Province.		Fuller (1877–1968) completes her work *Ethiopia Awakening*, in which she uses an Egyptian-style female figure to represent the growth of African self-awareness and desires for autonomy.	Evolución Femenina (Feminine Evolution), an institution that seeks legal equality for women in Peru.	
				The Chilean educator and feminist Amanda Labarca organizes the country's first women's organization, the Readers Club, to promote the cultural education of women.	1915
			Margaret Sanger (1879–1966) opens the nation's first contraceptive clinic in Brownsville, Brooklyn, and is promptly arrested and later imprisoned for thirty days. She first coins the term "birth control" in 1914 in *The Woman Rebel*, a militantly feminist journal published in New York by Sanger herself. She founds the American Birth Control League in 1921.		1916
					1917
			Federal suffrage is extended to women in Canada but excludes Japanese Canadians, Chinese Canadians, Doukhobors, and indigenous people.	Alicia Moreau de Justo (1885–1986), Argentine physician, socialist, and feminist, helps found the Unión	1918

Date	Global	Sub-Saharan Africa	North Africa and the Middle East	Europe	Central and South Asia
	at ten million, with thirty million wounded or incapacitated. The global influenza epidemic that follows leaves as many as one hundred million more dead.	is founded in South Africa. The league is formally acknowledged as part of the ANC in 1931, although women were not admitted as members of the ANC until 1943.		1918. The Netherlands follows in 1919, Austria in 1920, Spain in 1931, and France and Italy in 1945.	
1919	The Treaty of Versailles is signed at the Paris Peace Conference, emphasizing German war guilt and redrawing the map of Europe and the Middle East. In addition, the League of Nations is created, providing the foundation for international work on women's rights in the latter part of the twentieth century.		The Egyptian Uprising breaks out in early March, uniting Egyptians of all classes and religions in a common struggle against British colonial rule. Cairene women of all classes participate in demonstrations, and when a number of lower-class women are killed in demonstrations in Cairo, their funerals turn into further demonstrations of nationalist solidarity.	The Polish-German revolutionary Rosa Luxemburg (b. 1871) is brutally murdered in Berlin with her colleague Karl Liebknecht. Luxemburg was a founder—with Liebknecht, Clara Zetkin, and others—of the German Spartacist League, which becomes the German Communist Party in 1919.	
1920					
1921	The International League of Iberian and Hispanic-American Women (Liga Internacional de Mujeres Ibéricas			The first umbrella women's organization of the Kingdom of the Serbs, Croats, and Slovenians, Narodni	

Southeast Asia	East Asia	Australia, New Zealand, Oceania, and the Polar Regions	The United States and Canada	Latin America and the Caribbean	Date
				Feminista Nacional (National Feminist Union) and its journal, *Nuestra causa* (Our Cause), in which she publishes many of her articles on women's political rights.	
					1919
			The Nineteenth Amendment to the U.S. Constitution is ratified by three-quarters of the states, thus making the amendment law. The amendment bars states from denying suffrage to citizens on the basis of gender. However, the amendment does not extend to women in the American colonies, so women in Puerto Rico and the Philippines do not win the right to vote until the 1930s.	The Brazilian Bertha Lutz (1894–1976) founds her own women's rights organization, the Liga para a Emancipação Intelectual da Mulher (League for the Intellectual Emancipation of Women). Two years later this small local group is transformed into the Federação Brasileira pelo Progresso Feminino (FBPF; Brazilian Federation for Feminine Progress), affiliated with the International Woman Suffrage Alliance.	1920
	The Japanese poet, translator, social critic, and essayist Yosano Akiko (1878–1942) opens, with some progressive friends, the	Edith Cowan becomes the first woman elected to the state parliament of Western Australia. It is not until 1943 that Dame Enid Lyons of Tasmania	The Sheppard-Towner Maternity and Infancy Protection Act, the first federal social welfare measure in the United States, is passed. This		1921

Date	Global	Sub-Saharan Africa	North Africa and the Middle East	Europe	Central and South Asia
	e Hispano-americanas) is formed by Latin American liberal feminists with their Iberian counterparts.			Zenski Savez Srba, Hrvata, i Slovenaca (National Woman's Alliance of Serbs, Croats, and Slovenians), founded in 1919, brings together fifty thousand women from 205 organizations around the country.	
1922		Fearing social and political disruption after the 1921 Bulhoek massacre, South African officials declare the religious prophet Nontetha Nkwenkwe (c. 1875–1935) mad and incarcerate her in an asylum, where she remains—despite repeated appeals for her release—until her death from cancer.			
1923			The Egyptian feminist Huda Shaʿrawi (1879–1947), leader of the Women's Wafd, founds the Egyptian Feminist Union (EFU).	The French actress Sarah Bernhardt (b. 1844), the best-known and most highly regarded stage actress of the nineteenth century, dies.	The Afghan king Amanullah (r. 1919–1929) begins an ambitious reform program intended to make Afghanistan a modern nation while still respecting Islamic law. The reforms include restrictions on polygyny, banning child marriage, and opening public schools for girls. He abdicates in the midst of a civil war in 1929, and further reforms for women are delayed by decades.
1924					

Southeast Asia	East Asia	Australia, New Zealand, Oceania, and the Polar Regions	The United States and Canada	Latin America and the Caribbean	Date
	Bunka Gakuin (Cultural Academy), with a goal that Yosano had advocated in her essays: to foster women's individual talents and promote their economic self-sufficiency.	and Dorothy Tangney of Western Australia are elected to the federal legislature.	act provides federal matching grants to the states to combat infant and maternal mortality. In 1929, conservative and medical opposition force the program to shut down.		
	The Chinese Communist revolutionary Xiang Jingyu (1895–1928) is chosen to lead the Chinese Communist Women's Bureau, becoming its first director. She is arrested and executed by the Nationalist government in 1928, becoming the most famous woman revolutionary martyr of the Chinese Communist revolution.		The Equal Rights Amendment is introduced by the National Woman's Party.		1922
					1923
				Magda Portal, along with Raúl Haya de la Torre, founds the Alianza Popular Revolucionaria Americana (APRA), which is the formalized party of the Aprista movement that works on behalf of Peru's women and indigenous and poor people.	1924

Date	Global	Sub-Saharan Africa	North Africa and the Middle East	Europe	Central and South Asia
1926			Women in the Jewish community of Palestine achieve the rights to vote and to be elected to political office.	The Italian novelist and short-story writer Grazia Deledda (1871–1936) wins the Nobel Prize in Literature.	
1927					The Communist Party of the Soviet Union launches a massive assault against all "crimes of traditional life" (known in Russian as *byt* crimes), intended to liberate women and restructure Central Asian society. The Zhenotdel stages public demonstrations in the Uzbek, Tajik, and Kyrgyz regions, where women burn their veils and demand freedom.
1928					
1929	The stock market crash in the United states in October sets off the Great Depression, an economic disaster that affects the global economy.	In Nigeria, the Igbo "women's war" draws thousands of rural women to protest a census and rumored taxation of women.	The Arab Women's Union holds a congress in Jerusalem, bringing together more than two hundred women to form a Palestinian women's movement whose aims are to work toward an independent nation-state and to elevate the status of women and girls.	The British modernist writer Virginia Woolf (1882–1941) publishes the feminist classic *A Room of One's Own*.	The Child Marriage Restraint Act in India establishes the minimum age of marriage at fourteen for girls and eighteen for boys, abandoning the attempt to police consummation of marriage. Later acts in 1955 and 1978 raise the minimum age of marriage to eighteen for girls and twenty-one for boys.

Southeast Asia	East Asia	Australia, New Zealand, Oceania, and the Polar Regions	The United States and Canada	Latin America and the Caribbean	Date
				The Colombian socialist María Cano (1887–1967) takes an active role in the labor movement as vice president of the Third National Conference for Workers. On that occasion the conference declares her "La Flor del Trabajo de Colombia" (the flower of all workers of Colombia).	1926
					1927
				The Inter-American Commission of Women (IACW), or Comisión Interamericana de Mujeres (CIM), is established in Cuba and is the first intergovernmental organization in the world to be founded for the express purpose of working for the rights of women.	1928
					1929

Date	Global	Sub-Saharan Africa	North Africa and the Middle East	Europe	Central and South Asia
1930	The Roman Catholic Church's opposition to abortion becomes absolute with the publication of the papal encyclical *Casti connubii*, which also prohibits Roman Catholics from using any form of birth control and stresses the sanctity of marriage.	The Kenyan political activist Wambui Wangarama (1905–?) leads nationalist women to break from the Kikuyu Central Association and found the first women's political organization in Kenya, the Mumbi Central Association (MCA).		The Central Committee of the Soviet Communist Party announces the liquidation of the Women's Section, known as the Zhenotdel, which was formed in 1919 under the leadership of the Bolshevik women leaders Inessa Armand, Alexandra Kollontai, and Nadezhda Krupskaia.	The Indian nationalist Mahatma Gandhi organizes the Salt Satyagraha, in which he marches to the sea to make salt in defiance of the British monopoly over its manufacture. This campaign about a common kitchen item brings women of all classes in unprecedented numbers to the campaign.
1931			A new civil code in Iran, developed by the reformist leader Reza Shah, gives women the right to ask for divorce under certain conditions and raises the marriage age to fifteen for girls and eighteen for boys. Though demands for voting rights are refused, the shah implements reforms in girls' education and establishes a government office for women's affairs.		
1932					Pritilata Waddedar (b. 1911) becomes one of the first women martyrs for the Indian nationalist cause, marking a shift in women's involvement in revolutionary groups, from peripheral supportive roles to bearing arms and undertaking assassinations.
1933					

Southeast Asia	East Asia	Australia, New Zealand, Oceania, and the Polar Regions	The United States and Canada	Latin America and the Caribbean	Date
			The Liberal Cairine Reay Wilson becomes the first woman senator in Canada.	At the Third International Conference for Women in Bogotá, Colombia, Ofelia Uribe de Acosta (1900–1988) delivers a paper proposing full civil and economic rights for married women. This becomes the basis for a bill, passed by the Colombian parliament in 1932, that grants these privileges to women.	1930
			The American pacifist and feminist Jane Addams (1860–1935) wins the Nobel Peace Prize.		1931
			President Franklin D. Roosevelt names Frances Perkins (1880–1965) secretary of labor, thus making her the first woman to serve in the U.S. cabinet.	Women in Brazil get the same rights to vote as men. Illiterate women, like illiterate men, are still not allowed to vote. Literate Guatemalan women get the right to vote in 1945 (all women get the right to vote in 1966). Women get the vote in Chile in 1949, in Argentina in 1952, and in Peru in 1956.	1932
			Gertrude Stein publishes *The Autobiography of Alice B. Toklas*. This story of		1933

Date	Global	Sub-Saharan Africa	North Africa and the Middle East	Europe	Central and South Asia
1934			Women in Turkey get the rights to vote and to be elected, and eighteen women are elected as deputies in the February 1935 elections.		
1935				Irène Joliot-Curie (1897–1956), the daughter of the physicists Pierre and Marie Curie, wins the Nobel Prize in Physics with her husband Frédéric Joliot-Curie for their experiments that resulted in the first production of radioactivity in 1934.	
1936				The Spanish anarchist group Mujeres Libres, the only autonomous anarchist women's organization in Europe, is founded.	
1937–1938					

Southeast Asia	East Asia	Australia, New Zealand, Oceania, and the Polar Regions	The United States and Canada	Latin America and the Caribbean	Date
			Stein's life bears the name of her longtime companion Alice B. Toklas (1877–1967).		
				The postmodern Argentine feminist poet and playwright Alfonsina Storni (1892–1938) publishes *Mundo de siete pozos* (World of Seven Wells), which many regard as one of her two most accomplished works. The other work is *Mascarilla y trébol* (Mask and Shamrock, 1938).	1934
The Vietnamese Communist Nguyen Thi Minh Khai (1910–1941), the highest-ranking woman in the Indochinese Communist Party (ICP) in the 1930s, is the only woman selected to address the Seventh Congress of the Comintern in Moscow. She uses this platform to highlight issues of gender oppression within both the colonized societies and the West.					1935
			Mary McCleod Bethune (1875–1955) is appointed to the head of the Division of Negro Affairs, in the National Youth Administration, thus becoming the first black woman in U.S. history to hold such a high-level federal position.		1936
	The Rape of Nanjing—large-scale murder, plunder, and rape of Chinese soldiers, prisoners, and civilians—is committed by Japanese troops in and around Nanjing. Western observers in 1937 estimate that twenty thousand rapes occur; the People's				1937–1938

Date	Global	Sub-Saharan Africa	North Africa and the Middle East	Europe	Central and South Asia
1937				The Danish author Karen Blixen (1885–1962), under the pseudonym Isak Dinesen, publishes her memoir *Out of Africa* about her life as a coffee farmer in Kenya.	The Indian reformer Durgabai Deshmukh (1909–1981) starts the Andhra Mahila Sabha (Andhra Women's Conference) to generate funds for and set up educational and vocational training facilities for women in India.
1938		The black South African feminist and politician Cissie Gool (1897–1963) is elected to the Cape Town City Council. She remains active in local politics and resistance organizations in South Africa until her death.			
1939	World War II begins on 1 September when the German military, under the leadership of Adolf Hitler, invades Poland, causing Britain and France to declare war on Germany.			The Ravensbrück concentration camp, the only Nazi camp that incarcerated mostly women, is established in Brandenburg, Germany. Although Ravensbrück did not become an extermination camp until late 1944, around twenty-eight thousand people died there because it was a central site for the female slave market and for many medical experiments.	
1940					

Southeast Asia	East Asia	Australia, New Zealand, Oceania, and the Polar Regions	The United States and Canada	Latin America and the Caribbean	Date
	Republic of China claims eighty thousand.				
Women in the Philippines achieve the right to vote after extensive campaigning. In the same year, twenty-four women are elected to local offices, and in 1941 the first woman is voted into the House of Representatives.	The Socialist Party legislator and birth-control activist Katō Shidzue (1897–2001) opens a birth-control clinic in Tokyo. She is later arrested and forced to close the clinic, but she continues her work from her home and later runs successfully for political office.		The American Medical Association recognizes contraception as a legitimate service that should be included in the medical curriculum.		1937
					1938
			Ethel Waters (1896?–1977) becomes the first African American to star in her own show on television, NBC's *The Ethel Waters Show*. In 1962 she becomes the first African American actress to be nominated for an Emmy Award, for her portrayal of a dying jazz singer in "Good Night, Sweet Blues," an episode of the television drama series *Route 66*.	The Mexican artist Frida Kahlo (1907–1954) paints her classic piece *Las Dos Fridas*. Kahlo's systematic exploration of numerous alternative roles and her subsequent espousal of "nontraditional selves" reflect a deep understanding that identity is a complex, mutable, and multilayered configuration rather than a static and monolithic "given."	1939
			Emma Goldman (b. 1869), a Russian Jewish immigrant anarchist in the United States, dies in Toronto. Goldman's ideas resonated especially with women and with workers faced with the challenges and new	The Cuban constitution prohibits sexual discrimination in employment and guarantees women equal pay for equal work.	1940

Date	Global	Sub-Saharan Africa	North Africa and the Middle East	Europe	Central and South Asia
1942					
1944					
1945	World War II ends in Europe with the German surrender on 8 May. The war continues in the Pacific until the Japanese surrender on 14 August after the United States drops an atomic bomb on each of two Japanese cities, Hiroshima and Nagasaki.			Eleanor Rathbone (1872–1946), English feminist and member of Parliament, succeeds in getting the Family Allowances Act, central to the creation of the postwar welfare state, passed through Parliament.	The Pakistani politician, diplomat, and writer Begum Shaista S. Ikramullah (1915–2000) becomes the first Muslim woman to receive a PhD from the University of London. In Pakistan she is active in the women's rights movement and later becomes a delegate to the United Nations and ambassador to Morocco.
1946	The United Nations Commission on the Status of Women (CSW) is formed. The CSW focuses on mapping out the legal status and social positions of women in the member states and subsequently on the preparation of legislation and international conventions for the advancement of women.		The Berber peasant Fadhma Amrouche (1882–1967), the mother of the noted Algerian writers Taos Marie-Louise Amrouche and Jean Amrouche, writes *Histoire de ma vie*, the first autobiography written by an Algerian woman. It is not published, however, until 1968, a year after her death.		
1947		The Uganda Council of	The Iraqi poet and critic Nazik al-Malaʾika		India gains independence from Britain under the

Southeast Asia	East Asia	Australia, New Zealand, Oceania, and the Polar Regions	The United States and Canada	Latin America and the Caribbean	Date
			mobility of budding industrial capitalism.		
				Women in the Dominican Republic get the right to vote; women received the vote in Puerto Rico in 1932, in Cuba in 1934, and in the English-speaking Caribbean countries by 1964.	1942
			The U.S. Supreme Court rules in favor of Mitsuye Endo, a Japanese American who argues that the process of detention to an internment camp during World War II is illegal because of the violation of her citizen's rights of habeas corpus. This ruling enables Japanese Americans to return home, though often to lives shattered by internment.	Amelia Peláez (1896–1968), a modernist Cuban painter, becomes the most highly praised of the artists represented in the exhibition Modern Cuban Painters at the Museum of Modern Art in New York City.	1944
				Gabriela Mistral (1889–1957), a Chilean poet, journalist, educator, and diplomat, wins the Nobel Prize in Literature.	1945
Indonesia's largest Islamic organization, Nahdlatul Ulama (NU), establishes a women's section, Muslimat NU, at the same time that two women become ministers in early Sukarno cabinets: Maria Ulfah (minister for social affairs in 1946) and S. K. Trimurti (minister for labor in 1947–1948).	Under the new Japanese constitution of 3 November, women and men have equal rights. In 1945 Japanese women achieve the rights to vote and to run for office.		The American Babe Didrikson Zaharias (1911–1956) has a streak, lasting into 1947, during which she wins sixteen of seventeen golf tournaments. In 1932 she had won three medals at the Olympics.		1946
					1947

Date	Global	Sub-Saharan Africa	North Africa and the Middle East	Europe	Central and South Asia
		Women (UCW) is founded. Known for the multiracial character of its membership, which includes women of African, Indian, and European descent as well as women representing religious and community organizations, the UCW remains active until the early 1970s.	(b. 1923) launches free verse as a new form with her famous poem "Cholera," refashioning poetry from a strict masculine art in Arab culture by loosening its age-old strictures, incorporating social and psychological realities into it, and creating poetry with organic unity.		leadership of Mahatma Gandhi, who credits his strategy of active nonviolent resistance, or satyagraha, to the tradition of passive resistance of the women in his own family and British women's suffrage campaigns that he witnessed in London.
1948	The United Nations adopts the Universal Declaration of Human Rights, the first major international human rights covenant. The commission that creates the document is led by former American first lady Eleanor Roosevelt.	The system of racial discrimination known as apartheid formally begins in South Africa with the election of the National Party. Under apartheid a wide swath of laws are passed that restrict the movement, education, and labor opportunities of black South Africans.	The Israeli constitution, established after the creation of the state of Israel in 1948, is one of the earliest constitutional documents in the world to include sex as a group classification within a guarantee of equality and political rights.		
1949			Syrian women are granted the right to vote; women are granted political rights in Lebanon in 1953.	The French novelist and intellectual Simone de Beauvoir (1908–1986) publishes her influential book *Le deuxième sexe* (*The Second Sex*), widely considered to be a key text in the Second Wave feminist movement of the 1960s and 1970s.	
1950					
1952		The Kikuyu nationalist Rebecca Njeri Kairi (1895–?) is		Women in Greece are granted full voting rights, and then wider political	

Southeast Asia	East Asia	Australia, New Zealand, Oceania, and the Polar Regions	The United States and Canada	Latin America and the Caribbean	Date
	A new constitution is instituted with the establishment of the Republic of Korea (17 July 1948) in the southern half of the Korean peninsula, guaranteeing individual freedom, the equality of men and women, the right to education, and universal suffrage.		*Sexual Behavior in the Human Male*, the first of two scientific surveys of sexuality, is released (the second is released in 1953). Together known as the Kinsey Reports, the surveys attract widespread public interest and controversy.		1948
					1949
	The Marriage Law of 1 May 1950 guarantees rights for women in Communist China.		Gwendolyn Brooks (1917–2000) becomes the first African American to win the Pulitzer Prize in poetry for *Annie Allen*, published in 1949.		1950
The Singapore Council of Women, spearheaded by Shirin Fozdar, is formed as an umbrella				The Argentinean first lady and powerful political figure	1952

Date	Global	Sub-Saharan Africa	North Africa and the Middle East	Europe	Central and South Asia
		detained by British authorities in Kenya for her role in the Mau Mau uprising. After her release in 1960, Kairi leads the women's branch of the Kenya African National Union (KANU) and is elected to the KANU executive council in 1961.		rights in 1955 in an attempt to improve Greece's international reputation in the aftermath of the civil war (1944–1949). However, equality between women and men is not constitutionally established until 1975.	
1953					
1954		Mai (Mother) Chaza (d. 1960), a healer and prophet, leads an independent African church known as Guta re Jehova (City of God) in colonial Zimbabwe until her death. She fits into a tradition of strong women healers in Shona culture.			The Indian novelist Kamala Markandaya (1924–2004) publishes her renowned first novel *Nectar in a Sieve*, which highlights the experiences of lower-caste peasants in South India. Her work more generally focuses on the experiences of women and their resistance to patriarchal paradigms.
1955				The right to abortion is reinstated in the Soviet Union, two years after the death of Joseph Stalin. Although first made legal in 1920, abortion was abolished in 1936 in a governmental push to stabilize the family and birthrates.	The Hindu Marriage Act is passed in India, making polygamy illegal and legalizing divorce.
1956		Twenty thousand women from all over South Africa march to Pretoria to demand an end to pass laws for women in a demonstration sponsored by the	Djamila Bouhired (b. 1935) and many other Algerian women play key roles in the Battle of Algiers during the Algerian war of independence (1954–1962). Bouhired and two Algerian women dressed as Europeans place concealed bombs		

Southeast Asia	East Asia	Australia, New Zealand, Oceania, and the Polar Regions	The United States and Canada	Latin America and the Caribbean	Date
group for the more than thirty women's associations concerned with educational, racial, social, and professional affiliations in Singapore.				Eva Perón (b. 1919) dies at the age of thirty-three. She had become secretary of labor in 1946, and among the poor she became known as the Lady of Hope.	
	The Japanese feminist Ichikawa Fusae (1893–1981) is elected to the Japanese Diet, where she campaigns for women's issues. She remains active in politics until her death.				1953
The Vietnamese feminist and scholar Le Thi, who participated in the revolution against the French during the 1940s, becomes the director of the Center for Family and Women's Studies in the National Center for Social Sciences and Humanities, the foremost research facility of its kind in Vietnam; she serves until 1995.					1954
			Rosa Parks (1913–2005) refuses to give up her seat on a bus in Montgomery, Alabama, and is arrested, thus beginning the Montgomery bus boycott and the civil rights movement.		1955
					1956

Date	Global	Sub-Saharan Africa	North Africa and the Middle East	Europe	Central and South Asia
		Federation of South African Women (FSAW), a nonracial organization formed in 1954.	in the European sections of Algiers; Bouhired is captured in 1957 and becomes a cause célèbre for the French army's systematic use of torture.		
1957		Ghana becomes the first African nation to achieve independence from European colonial rule. In the coming years most African countries achieve independence, with the notable exceptions of the Portuguese colonies of Angola, Mozambique, Guinea-Bissau, and Cape Verde and the southern African settler nations of South Africa, Namibia, and Zimbabwe (then Rhodesia).			
1958	The International Labour Organization adopts the Convention on Discrimination (Employment and Occupation), with the aim of contributing to the elimination of discrimination on the basis of race, creed, or sex in employment and occupation.				Aruna Asaf Ali becomes the first elected mayor of Delhi.
1960		Aoua Kéita (1912–1980), midwife and feminist political activist, is the first woman elected deputy to the newly independent Republic of Mali's national assembly, following many years of anticolonial activism.			Sirimavo Bandaranaike (1916–2000) is elected prime minister of Sri Lanka, becoming the world's first woman prime minister.

Southeast Asia	East Asia	Australia, New Zealand, Oceania, and the Polar Regions	The United States and Canada	Latin America and the Caribbean	Date
			Ellen Louks Fairclough (1905–2004) is named secretary of state for Canada, thus becoming Canada's first woman federal cabinet minister.		1957
					1958
			The birth-control pill is introduced in the United States.	Vilma Espín (1930–2007) becomes president of the Federación de Mujeres Cubanas (FMC; Federation of Cuban Women), an organization created by her brother-in-law Fidel Castro.	1960

Date	Global	Sub-Saharan Africa	North Africa and the Middle East	Europe	Central and South Asia
1961					
1962				The British writer Doris Lessing (b. 1919) publishes *The Golden Notebook*.	
1963				The Russian cosmonaut Valentina Tereshkova (b. 1937) becomes the first woman in space during her mission in *Vostok 6*. She later becomes active in politics, including chairing the Soviet Committee for Women from 1968 to 1987.	
1964					Women in Afghanistan get the right to vote in the wake of reforms under Zahir Shah (r. 1933–1973).
1965	The World Health Organization (WHO), one of the main bodies of the United Nations, launches its own family-planning program in 1965, organizing symposia and conducting hundreds of studies on fertility control methods, including steroid contraception, the rhythm method, and abortion, and their health implications.				
1966		Constance Cummings-John (1918–2000), a nationalist leader who helped found the Sierra Leone Women's Movement (SLWM) in 1951, becomes mayor of	The Egyptian psychologist, writer, and activist Nawal el Saadawi (b. 1931) becomes Egypt's director of public health. She publishes *Women and Sex*, her groundbreaking book on mental health, sexuality, and women,	The German-Jewish writer Nelly Sachs (1891–1970)—who, together with Paul Celan, is considered to be the most important poet of the Holocaust—wins	Indira Gandhi (1917–1984) becomes prime minister of India, serving for four terms until her assassination in 1984.

Southeast Asia	East Asia	Australia, New Zealand, Oceania, and the Polar Regions	The United States and Canada	Latin America and the Caribbean	Date
			Elizabeth Gurley Flynn (1890–1964), agitator and organizer for the Industrial Workers of the World, becomes the first woman national party chair of the Communist Party.		1961
			Rachel Carson (1907–1964), an American biologist, writer, and environmentalist, publishes *Silent Spring*.		1962
					1963
			Title VII of the Civil Rights Act in the United States outlaws gender discrimination in employment by expanding the act to include "sex."		1964
			In Hawai'i, Patsy Takemoto Mink (1927–2002) becomes the first Asian American woman elected to the U.S. Congress.		1965
			Betty Friedan (1921–2006)—author of the influential *Feminine Mystique* (1963)—and other liberal feminists help form the National Organization for Women (NOW).		1966

DATE	GLOBAL	SUB-SAHARAN AFRICA	NORTH AFRICA AND THE MIDDLE EAST	EUROPE	CENTRAL AND SOUTH ASIA
		Freetown, Sierra Leone—the first woman to be mayor of an African city.	in 1969. At least in part because of controversy over the book, el Saadawi is dismissed from the ministry of health in 1972.	the Nobel Prize in Literature.	
1967				Illegal since the early nineteenth century, abortion becomes legal in England, Wales, and Scotland.	The Pakistani political activist Fatima Jinnah (b. 1893), sometimes called the *Mader-e-Millat* (Mother) of Pakistan, dies in Karachi. She is known both for her strong support of her brother Quaid-i-Azam (Muhammad Ali Jinnah), the founder of Pakistan, in achieving Pakistani independence and for her political activism, including an unsuccessful campaign for president in 1964.
1968	The successful marketing of the birth-control pill in 1960 arouses hopes among liberal Catholics that their church would accept hormonal methods of contraception, but the papal encyclical *Humanae vitae* confirms traditional Roman Catholic teachings against the use of contraception.		The Family Protection Law in Iran provides women with some rights to divorce, requires that a first wife give written consent before her husband can marry a second wife, and sets the marriage age for women at eighteen. The law is abolished in 1979 with the ascension of the Ayatollah Khomeini and the establishment of the Islamic Republic of Iran.		
1969			Golda Meir (1898–1978) becomes the first woman prime minister of Israel, holding this position until 1974.		
1971			Türkan Akyol (b. 1928) becomes the first woman prime minister of Turkey.		

Southeast Asia	East Asia	Australia, New Zealand, Oceania, and the Polar Regions	The United States and Canada	Latin America and the Caribbean	Date
					1967
			The activist Helen Keller (b. 1880), who at the age of nineteen months contracted an illness that left her totally deaf and blind, dies. In 1904, Keller graduated magna cum laude from Radcliffe College; while still a student she published her first book, *The Story of My Life* (1903).		1968
Nguyen Thi Dinh (1920–1992) serves as deputy commander of the armed forces of the National Liberation Front after 1969, the highest-ranking woman in the southern Communist forces during the Vietnam War. She later serves as president of the Vietnam Women's Union and continues to advocate for women's rights until her death.			The Canadian government legalizes birth control and makes limited provisions for abortion. Meanwhile, police raid New York City's Stonewall Inn, a popular gay bar, galvanizing the gay community. The early days of the post-Stonewall gay liberation movement (1969–1971) see calls to overturn monogamy, gender hierarchies, and other normalizing binaries; it is said that this will free heterosexuals as well as "sexual minorities" from such artificial and stifling conventions.		1969
			The feminist Gloria Steinem (b. 1934) founds, with Patricia Carbine as well as other		1971

Date	Global	Sub-Saharan Africa	North Africa and the Middle East	Europe	Central and South Asia
1972		The Nigerian-born British author Buchi Emecheta (b. 1944) publishes her first novel, *In the Ditch*, chronicling her own experiences of racial discrimination and poverty in London.		The West German author and radical Ulrike Meinhof (1934–1976) is captured after participating in several lethal bombings with the Red Army Faction, a guerilla group that she cofounded with Andreas Baader and Gudrun Ensslin.	Abortion is legalized in India.
1973					
1974					The Progressive Organization of Women (POW), founded in South India, is the first contemporary feminist group formed in India.
1975					

Southeast Asia	East Asia	Australia, New Zealand, Oceania, and the Polar Regions	The United States and Canada	Latin America and the Caribbean	Date
			feminist writers and editors, *Ms.*, a progressive commercial magazine for women. The completely woman-run magazine first appears as an insert in *New York* magazine; the first stand-alone issue is published in the spring 1972.		
		The principle of "equal pay for work of equal value" is adopted in Australia under the leadership of the Australian Labour Party. The federal government also begins funding child care, paid maternity leave is granted for Commonwealth public servants, and no-fault divorce is introduced.	The National Action Committee (NAC), Canada's leading organized feminist group, forms at a meeting of the Royal Commission on the Status of Women.		1972
	Yang Zhihua (b. 1900), an early Communist revolutionary, prominent party labor organizer, and high-ranking leader in the All-China Federation of Trade Unions and the All-China Women's Federation, dies of cancer in Beijing.		The U.S. Supreme Court rules 7 to 2 in favor of Jane Roe, a woman seeking to have an abortion in Texas. The court case, known as *Roe v. Wade*, sets the precedent for abortion legislation in the United States.	Incited by women's demonstrations, military men take control in Chile, overthrowing the democratically elected Salvadore Allende. Before the takeover, thousands of conservative women had marched in protest against Allende, banging empty pots and pans to symbolize that they lacked food because, they claimed, of government policies.	1973
			In the United States, the Women's Educational Equity Act is passed. It provides for federal financial and technical support to local efforts to remove barriers for women in all areas of education—through, for example, the development of model programs, training, and research.	Cuba passes the Working Women's Maternity Law, which grants working mothers eighteen months of paid leave.	1974
					1975

Date	Global	Sub-Saharan Africa	North Africa and the Middle East	Europe	Central and South Asia
	The United Nations names 1975 International Women's Year, and the first United Nations Conference on Women is held in Mexico City. The United Nations Decade for Women (1976–1985) is also the result of this conference.	Graça Machel (b. 1945), the first lady of Mozambique, is appointed minister of education and culture. Throughout her political career she worked for children's causes including increased access to education and the problems of child soldiers. In 1998 she married Nelson Mandela and became the first lady of South Africa.			
1976					The Grameen Bank is founded in Bangladesh. A world-renowned program known for its micro-credit activities on behalf of women, the bank, along with its founder Muhammad Yunus, wins the 2006 Nobel Peace Prize.
1977		The biology professor Wangari Maathai (b. 1940) launches the Green Belt Movement in Kenya, encouraging women to plant trees in rural areas to prevent deforestation and soil erosion.			The Mahila Dakshata Samiti (MDS), a socialist women's organization linked to the socialist political party Janata Dal, is founded in India.
1978	The International Lesbian and Gay Association (ILGA) is founded and focuses on sexual-orientation discrimination as a global issue.	The Zambian prophet and healer Alice Lenshina Mulenge (b. c. 1924), the founder of the Lumpa Church,		Contraception is legalized in Spain, followed by the legalization of divorce in 1981 and of abortion in the 1990s.	

Southeast Asia	East Asia	Australia, New Zealand, Oceania, and the Polar Regions	The United States and Canada	Latin America and the Caribbean	Date
		Pat O'Shane is admitted to the bar, becoming Australia's first Aboriginal barrister.		*Nós Mulheres* (We Women), the journal of Brazil's Associação de Mulheres (Women's Association), forms in São Paulo. The journal is one of the first feminist journals to emerge from the radical Second Wave feminist organizations.	1976
			Leslie Marmon Silko (b. 1948), an acclaimed novelist, poet, and storyteller of Mexican, Anglo-American, and American Indian ancestry, publishes her first major novel, *Ceremony*.	Las Madres de Plaza de Mayo (the Mothers of the Plaza de Mayo) meet for the first time in the Plaza de Mayo in Buenos Aires, Argentina, to protest the military dictatorship that does not acknowledge its role in the disappearance of the mothers' loved ones.	1977
	The Chinese novelist Zhang Jie (b. 1937), a pioneering Chinese feminist writer of the post-Mao era, wins the National Best Short Story Prize for her first story, "Cong senlin li lai		Lois Gibbs (b. 1952) discovers that her neighborhood of Love Canal, in Niagara Falls, New York, was built on a toxic waste dump. Now an environmental activist, in 1980 she sets		1978

Date	Global	Sub-Saharan Africa	North Africa and the Middle East	Europe	Central and South Asia
		dies in prison; she had been arrested and her settlements destroyed by the newly independent Zambian government.			
1979	The United Nations General Assembly adopts the Convention on the Elimination of All Forms of Discrimination against Women (CEDAW), the definitive international legal instrument for the protection of women's human rights.			Margaret Thatcher (b. 1925) becomes prime minister of Britain, the first woman to hold that office. She remains a controversial figure because of both her conservative policies and her hostility toward feminism.	The Albanian-born Catholic nun Mother Teresa (1910–1997) wins the Nobel Peace Prize in recognition of her work with the poor in India, where she founds the Missionaries of Charity and establishes hostels for AIDS patients, slum schools, dispensaries, and homes for the dying, lepers, and the mentally ill poor.
1980				The German feminist and peace activist Petra Kelly (1947–1992) helps found Die Grünen (the German Green Party, or "Greens"), a new political movement that links feminism, environmentalism, and pacifism.	
1981	The International Olympic Committee elects its first women members, Flor Isava-Fonseca of Venezuela and Pirjo Haggman of Finland, at its Baden-Baden meetings.			Abortion is legalized in the Netherlands.	
1982		The South African journalist and antiapartheid activist Ruth First (b. 1925) is killed by a letter bomb sent by a South African police death squad.		The Swedish social reformer, sociologist, author, and international politician Alva Myrdal (1902–1986) wins the Nobel Peace Prize for her work in nuclear disarmament. Along with her husband Gunnar Myrdal, she is a leading promoter for a woman-friendly welfare	

Southeast Asia	East Asia	Australia, New Zealand, Oceania, and the Polar Regions	The United States and Canada	Latin America and the Caribbean	Date
	de haizi" (The Music of the Forests).		up a national network called the Citizens' Clearinghouse for Hazardous Waste (CCHW), which helps local communities clean up toxic waste.		
				Lydia Gueiler Tejada (b. 1921) becomes the interim president of Bolivia—the first woman president in both Bolivia and South America.	1979
			Lois M. Wilson (b. 1927) becomes the first woman moderator of the United Church, Canada's largest Protestant denomination.		1980
			President Ronald Regan appoints Sandra Day O'Connor (b. 1930) as the first woman Supreme Court justice. She is confirmed by a unanimous vote in the Senate. She resigns from the court in 2005 but serves until her successor, Samuel Alito, is confirmed in January 2006.	Venezuela's Flor Isava-Fonseca (b. 1921) becomes one of two women to be elected for the first time to the International Olympic Committee at its Baden-Baden meetings.	1981
			Bertha Wilson (1923–2007) becomes the first woman judge on the Canadian Supreme Court.		1982

Date	Global	Sub-Saharan Africa	North Africa and the Middle East	Europe	Central and South Asia
				state, known as the Swedish model.	
1983					
1984					The Dowry Prohibition Act is passed in India, prohibiting the giving or taking of dowry in consideration of marriage; the act is seen as a major victory for the women's movement.
1985	DAWN (Development Alternatives with Women for a New Era), a network based in the global South that conducts research and advocacy on economic justice, gender justice, and democracy, is formed.		The Syrian Socialist National Party (SSNP) sends its first suicide bomber, a girl named Sana'a Mehaydali (Khyadali Sana, Sana'a Mehaidli), to attack an Israeli convoy in Lebanon. Between 1985 and 1987 the SSNP conducts six more suicide attacks using women.		
1986					The Indian prime minister Rajiv Gandhi enacts the Muslim Women's (Protection of Rights on Divorce) Act (MWA) in response to a divorce case in 1985—that of Shah Bano—in which the Indian Supreme Court argued that criminal law overrides personal law, causing uproar among Muslim religious leaders.
1988		The Zimbabwean writer and filmmaker Tsitsi Dangarembga			Benazir Bhutto (b. 1953) is elected prime minister of Pakistan at the age of thirty-five. She is removed in 1990 and reelected in 1993, only

Southeast Asia	East Asia	Australia, New Zealand, Oceania, and the Polar Regions	The United States and Canada	Latin America and the Caribbean	Date
			Alice Walker (b. 1944) wins the 1983 Pulitzer Prize in fiction for her book *The Color Purple* (1982). She is the first African American woman to be awarded the prize.		1983
In the Philippines, a proliferation of grassroots organizations leads to the establishment of GABRIELA (General Assembly Binding Women for Reforms, Integrity, Equality, Leadership, and Action), which comprises more than a hundred groups whose political ideologies differ but who are united in their desire to advance women's causes and redress social inequality.			Jeanne-Mathilde Benoît Sauvé (1922–1993) becomes Canada's first woman governor-general.	In Guatemala the Mutual Support Group for the Appearance, Alive, of Our Children, Spouses, Parents, Brothers, and Sisters is founded.	1984
					1985
Corazon Aquino, widow of Benigno Aquino, becomes president of the Philippines after the overthrow of Ferdinand Marcos; she holds the office until 1992.			The American modernist painter Georgia O'Keeffe (b. 1887) dies. O'Keeffe became most prominent during the 1970s when feminists rediscovered her art, promoting her as a woman artist who invented vaginal iconography. Although O'Keeffe rejected such interpretations, her art and life nevertheless became inextricably linked to Second Wave feminism.		1986
The Vietnamese dissident novelist Duong Thu Huong (b. 1947) publishes her third and most			The Canadian Supreme Court strikes down laws limiting access to abortion. Also, the Liberal Ethel Blondin-		1988

Date	Global	Sub-Saharan Africa	North Africa and the Middle East	Europe	Central and South Asia
		(b. 1959) publishes her most famous work, the novel *Nervous Conditions*; in 1989 it wins the African division of the Commonwealth Writers Prize.			to be dismissed by presidential decree in 1996, charged with corruption, laundering money, and taking bribes.
1989					
1990	The U.N. Convention on the Rights of the Child goes into effect.			Mary Robinson (b. 1944) becomes the first woman president of Ireland, a position that she holds until 1997. After leaving the presidency she serves as the U.N. high commissioner for human rights until 2002.	
1991		The South African writer Nadine Gordimer (b. 1923) receives the Nobel Prize in Literature for a body of work that addresses the racism and apartheid that have divided South Africa.			A young Tamil woman named Thenmuli Rajaratnam (Dhanu) assassinates the Indian prime minister Rajiv Gandhi, detonating a bomb that kills them both, along with sixteen others.

Southeast Asia	East Asia	Australia, New Zealand, Oceania, and the Polar Regions	The United States and Canada	Latin America and the Caribbean	Date
controversial novel, *Paradise of the Blind*. The book was later banned in Vietnam for its critical appraisal of both official misconduct and also the heartless interference in the public and private lives of ordinary people during the land reform of the 1950s.			Andrew (b. 1951) becomes the first Aboriginal woman to be a member of parliament in Canada.		
Aung San Suu Kyi (b. 1945) is put under house arrest, where she still remains in 2007. In 1988 she had cofounded the National League for Democracy (NLD) in Burma, becoming its secretary-general and rallying millions across Burma through her embrace of Buddhist and Gandhian tactics of nonviolence and her outspoken rejection of oppression. She received the Nobel Peace Prize in 1991.		Jenny Shipley becomes the first woman prime minister of New Zealand. Helen Clark becomes the deputy prime minister and then, in 1999–2006, the prime minister.			1989
				Violeta Barrios de Chamorro (b. 1929) becomes the first woman president of Nicaragua after defeating the left-wing revolutionary Daniel Ortega.	1990
In Cambodia, Khemara, the first non-governmental organization formed in the post-1989 liberal climate, is founded. Khemara aims at the advancement and empowerment of women in Cambodian society. It is established by a Cambodian woman, Mu Sochua, who later serves as Cambodia's minister of women's and veteran's affairs (1998–2003).				The thirteenth World Conference of the International Lesbian and Gay Association—founded in 1978 to focus on sexual-orientation discrimination as a global issue—is held in Acapulco, Mexico, after city officials in Guadalajara, Mexico, threaten to arrest attending individuals and then shut down the conference.	1991

Date	Global	Sub-Saharan Africa	North Africa and the Middle East	Europe	Central and South Asia
1992					
1993	The United Nations adopts the Declaration on the Elimination of Violence against Women.			Abortion is delegalized in Poland, forbidden except on the grounds of medical necessity or in the case of rape or incest. This legislation triggers women's political mobilization, helping to create one of the strongest feminist movements in Eastern Europe.	In the Chinese-controlled Central Asian province of Xinjiang, Rebiya Kadir, a Uyghur mother of eleven who built her own multimillion-dollar firm, founds the Thousand Mothers Association, a mutual aid society to promote women-owned businesses and combat drug abuse among Uyghur youth.
1994	The International Conference on Population and Development (ICPD) held in Cairo, Egypt, produces the first major international agreement recommending improved access to safe abortion.	At the age of eighty, the South African political activist Ellen Kuzwayo, or "Ma K" (1914–2006), is elected to South Africa's first nonracial parliament, representing the constituency of Dobsonville for the African National Congress.			Chandrika Bandaranaike Kumaratunga (b. 1945) becomes the president of Sri Lanka, a post that she holds until 2005. Both her parents were prime ministers of Sri Lanka, and her mother Sirimavo Bandaranaike (1916–2000) was the first woman prime minister in the world.
1995	The United Nations Fourth World Conference on Women in Beijing produces the Beijing Declaration and the Platform for Action that identifies twelve areas of continuing concern regarding women's status.				

Southeast Asia	East Asia	Australia, New Zealand, Oceania, and the Polar Regions	The United States and Canada	Latin America and the Caribbean	Date
				Rigoberta Menchú (b. 1959), a Maya social activist, receives the Nobel Peace Prize in recognition of her international efforts to defend indigenous people's rights and promote social justice. She is the first indigenous American to receive the award.	1992
			Toni Morrison (b. 1931), an African American novelist, wins the Nobel Prize in Literature. In Canada, the Conservative Kim Campbell (b. 1947) becomes Canada's first woman prime minister.		1993
			The U.S. Violence against Women Act is passed. With this act the U.S. Centers for Disease Control and Prevention establish the Rape Prevention and Education (RPE) Program, which provides funding for programs that help prevent sexual violence.	The Peruvian Commission of Congressional Women is organized. Four years later the commission realizes one of its main goals when the electoral law establishes that all political parties must include a minimum of twenty-five women candidates in all electoral races.	1994
					1995

Date	Global	Sub-Saharan Africa	North Africa and the Middle East	Europe	Central and South Asia
1996	The International Labour Organization adopts the Convention on Home Work, a major achievement for women in the informal sector worldwide.			The Polish poet Wislawa Szymborska (b. 1923), a member of the Polish school of poetry, wins the Nobel Prize in Literature.	The Taliban establishes control over Kabul in Afghanistan, instituting a version of extremist Islam that includes total seclusion of women from public places, a ban on women's education, and a dress code that requires women to wear the *chadri* (a sheetlike covering for the entire body) outside the home.
1997	The organization of the Women's International War Crimes Tribunal begins, through the collaboration of international women's groups. The movement emerges from a global initiative to address the Japanese army's sexual violence against more than two hundred thousand women in Asia during World War II.			In the European Union, a European Court of Justice decision, *Marschall v. Land Nordhein-Westfalen* (1 C.M.L. R. 547 [1997]), validates gender-based affirmative action.	
1999					
2000				France becomes the first country to institute a legal parity mandate requiring that all political parties present equal numbers of men and women candidates in most elections.	
2001					
2002					

Southeast Asia	East Asia	Australia, New Zealand, Oceania, and the Polar Regions	The United States and Canada	Latin America and the Caribbean	Date
			The Canadian Human Rights Act prohibits "sexual orientation" as a basis of discrimination.		1996
				El Salvador strikes down the only remaining legal grounds for abortion, to save a woman's life.	1997
			Beverley McLachlin (b. 1943) becomes the first woman chief justice of the Canadian Supreme Court.		1999
	Annette Hsiu-lien Liu, a political activist who was jailed in 1979, becomes Taiwan's first woman vice president in the first multiparty presidential election in Taiwan.				2000
Megawati Sukarnoputri (b. 1947) becomes Indonesia's first woman president, an office that she holds until 2004.					2001
			The U.S. State Department announces its decision to suspend $34 million in funding from the U.N. Population Fund, which it claims (without evidence) is supporting abortions in China.	The Afro-Brazilian political leader Benedita da Silva (b. 1943) becomes the first woman governor of the state of Rio de Janeiro. Silva had helped found the Partido dos Trabalhadores	2002

Date	Global	Sub-Saharan Africa	North Africa and the Middle East	Europe	Central and South Asia
2003			Hanan Ashwari (b. 1946), Palestinian politician and promoter of peace, receives the Sydney Peace Prize. Also, the Iranian human rights activist Shireen Ebadi (b. 1947) wins the Nobel Peace Prize. Both events are seen by many as hopeful signs of support for women's rights in Muslim societies.	Doris Lessing (b. 1919), a British novelist, wins the Nobel Prize in Literature.	
2004		Wangari Maathai (b. 1940) wins the Nobel Peace Prize for her work in the Green Belt Movement and her contributions to peace, democracy, and sustainable development.			
2005		Ellen Johnson-Sirleaf (b. 1938) is elected president of Liberia, becoming the first elected African woman head of state.	The National Assembly of Kuwait grants women the right to vote.	Angela Merkel (b. 1954) becomes the first woman chancellor of Germany.	
2006					
2007					

Southeast Asia	East Asia	Australia, New Zealand, Oceania, and the Polar Regions	The United States and Canada	Latin America and the Caribbean	Date
				(PT; Brazilian Workers' Party) in 1980. Silva also was, in 1994, the first woman elected to the Brazilian senate.	
	The Chinese politician Wu Yi (b. 1938), the only woman since the 1970s to assume a high level of prominence and authority in the People's Republic of China, is appointed minister of health.				2003
		Marion Scrymgour (b. 1960) becomes the first indigenous woman minister in Australia, having also served as the member for Arafura in the Northern Territory in 2001.	Susan Sontag (b. 1933), an American philosopher of culture, filmmaker, playwright, theater director, short-story writer, and novelist, dies of cancer.		2004
				Sister Dorothy Stang (b. 1940), an environmental activist of the Sisters of Notre Dame de Namur, is murdered in Brazil.	2005
			The Episcopal Church in the United States elects its first female presiding bishop, Katharine Jefferts Schori (b. 1954).		2006
			Congresswoman Nancy Pelosi (b. 1940) becomes the first woman elected to serve as Speaker of the U.S. House of Representatives.	Rigoberta Menchú tries to become Guatemala's first woman president.	2007

THE OXFORD ENCYCLOPEDIA OF

WOMEN IN WORLD HISTORY

ABAYOMI, OYINKAN (née Ajasa, 1897–1990), founder of the Nigerian Women's Party and advocate of woman suffrage. Abayomi was born to Sir Kitoyi Ajasa, a lawyer and newspaper founder, knighted in 1929, and Lady Lucretia Cornelia Olayinka Ajasa. Abayomi's early education took place in Nigeria, and then she studied in England during the years of World War I. On her return to Nigeria, she founded the first Nigerian branch of the Girl Guides and was the force behind their admission into the World Association of Girl Guides and Girl Scouts. She helped raise funds for the establishment of Queens College, the first nondenominational secondary-educational institution for girls in Nigeria. Active in one of the early protonationalist parties of the colonial period, the Nigerian Youth Movement, she subsequently became head of its Ladies' Section. In that capacity in 1935 she authored an article titled "Modern Womanhood," published in *The Service*, the newspaper of the Nigerian Youth Movement, in which she exhorted women to participate in the political processes that shape their futures and cautioned them not to see matrimony as the sole "career" to which they aspired. She also cautioned against elitism and encouraged Nigerian women to develop their leadership potential for the benefit of their sex and race.

None of the early protonationalist parties had women in policy-making positions, nor were women included in the limited franchise extended to men of the colony. Hence, on 10 May 1944 Abayomi convened a meeting in her home that resulted in the founding of the Nigerian Women's Party. Abayomi recalled in an interview of June 1976 that she called this meeting because women were being cheated by both the British-run colonial government and their own men. The party specified in its founding constitution that it was organized to demand women's rights. Among these it included the right to vote and representation on the Lagos Town Council and on the Legislative Council for the colony. The motto of the Nigerian Women's Party was "Aim High," and membership was open to women natives of Nigeria and to women residents of Nigeria of African descent. Though composed primarily of middle- and upper-class women, the Nigerian Women's Party explicitly expressed its desire to advocate for women of all classes and ethnic backgrounds within Nigeria. Thus it joined a handful of organizations that sought to organize across class and ethnicity. Active membership of the party was small (500–2,000 women at various times during its existence). In 1950, when limited woman suffrage was enacted, the Nigerian Women's Party fielded the first women political candidates of the colonial period in Nigeria. Abayomi and Tinuola Dedeke, secretary of the Nigerian Women's Party, both ran for seats on the Lagos Town Council, but neither was elected. By the mid-1950s the Nigerian Women's Party was on the wane. In 1959, when the National Council of Women's Societies, an umbrella group of Nigerian women's organizations, was founded, Abayomi became head of its Lagos branch. After her death, a major street in Lagos was named Oyinkan Abayomi Drive in her honor.

[*See also* Nigeria *and* West Africa, *subentry* Twentieth Century.]

BIBLIOGRAPHY

Johnson-Odim, Cheryl. "Lady Oyinkan Abayomi: A Profile." In *Nigerian Women in Historical Perspective*, edited by Bolanle Awe, pp. 149–163. Lagos, Nigeria: Sankore Press, 1993.

CHERYL JOHNSON-ODIM

ABELLA DE RAMÍREZ, MARÍA (1863–1925), the first notable feminist and freethinker in Argentina. Born in the province of San José, Uruguay, María Abella de Ramírez lived most of her adult life in La Plata, Argentina. Married twice and the mother of eleven children, Abella de Ramírez was also an elementary school teacher. Her family obligations may have been the reason for her delayed entrance into journalism and civic life in 1898 at age thirty-five.

From the beginning of her career as a writer and activist, Abella de Ramírez defined herself as a freethinker and a feminist, two radical positions for a woman living in a provincial Argentine city. In 1900 she attempted to found a women's club as a social center for women. It was probably unsuccessful, but it launched her career as an outspoken proponent of women's rights and social change. In July 1902 she founded *Nosotras* (We Women), defined as a literary and feminist magazine; it ran through 1904. In 1906 she attended the International Congress of Freethinkers in Buenos Aires with a list of demands to achieve gender equality which included divorce, equal footing for mothers and fathers in sharing control of the children, and equal education and employment opportunities for women. Many of Abella de Ramírez's newspaper and magazine articles were collected in 1908 in *En pos de la justicia* (In Quest of Justice).

Becoming progressively engaged in feminism, she founded the National Feminist League in La Plata in May 1910, at a time when most women hesitated to call themselves feminists. At that time she was in touch with most of the leading feminists in Argentina and participated in the First International Feminine Conference in Buenos Aires in 1910 as a representative of the Freethinkers Association. That same year, Abella de Ramírez launched *La nueva mujer* (The New Woman) as a mouthpiece of the National Feminist League. Another strong-willed feminist and freethinker, Julieta Lanteri (1873–1932), was her coeditor at *La nueva mujer*. In 1911, Abella de Ramírez organized the Feminist Athenaeum in Montevideo, and in October 1913 she participated in the First Congress on Childhood (Congreso del Niño) in Buenos Aires. After that year her activities become difficult to trace. In 1965 a collection of her essays was reprinted under the title *Ensayos feministas* (Feminist Essays).

Abella de Ramírez's ideas are unexpected for their boldness. She criticized the negative influence of the church on women's social status, and her advocacy of real divorce, not the ecclesiastic form of mere separation, distanced her from religious circles. Her main objective for women was freedom from all traditional and legal restrictions. She defended the rights of children born out of wedlock and promoted the need to understand female sexuality. Her argument was that if society condoned double standards of morality and did not punish male seduction, it had no right to stigmatize unwed mothers. Though she reasserted the positive contribution of mothers to the nation, she rejected the notion of special protection for working women, because not all women would be mothers, and she believed that working women should be on the same footing as male workers. Such ideas place Abella de Ramírez in a special niche among the first feminists of Latin America.

[*See also* Argentina *and* Feminism.]

BIBLIOGRAPHY

Abella de Ramírez, María. *Ensayos feministas*. Montevideo, Uruguay: El Siglo Ilustrado, 1965.

Lavrin, Asunción. *Women, Feminism, and Social Change in Argentina, Chile, and Uruguay, 1890–1940*. Lincoln: University of Nebraska Press, 1995.

ASUNCIÓN LAVRIN

ABOLITION AND ANTI-SLAVERY MOVEMENT.

Women played a significant part in the international campaign against the use of African slave labor in the New World, a cause humanitarians had urged since the eighteenth century. Individual women stand out, gaining fame as tractarians, public speakers, and organizers, but the majority worked privately through anti-slavery associations that were independent of male societies, by collecting signatures for petitions against black slavery, holding fairs to raise funds, and organizing protests against the use of black slave labor.

The European Anti-Slavery Movement. The most famous European savante, Germaine de Staël (1766–1817), wrote strongly against slavery, but the anti-slavery cause was less popular on the Continent than in Anglo-Saxon countries. Despite Enlightenment ideals and revolution, France, the major Continental nation using slave labor, did not end slavery in her colonies until 1848. French liberals were the backbone of such anti-slavery societies as the Amis des Noirs and gave significant help to a visiting family of American abolitionists, the Weston sisters, who lived in Paris between 1848 and 1855. The Americans were under police surveillance for their views, but French women collected goods for them to send to America for anti-slavery fairs, and leading intellectuals supported their Gift Book, the *Liberty Bell*.

The British Anti-Slavery Movement. Britain, a major slave-owning nation, opposed slavery actively, outlawing the slave trade in 1807 and emancipating the slaves in British colonies from 1833 to 1838. These campaigns were led by political liberals, often aided by such hostesses as Georgina, Duchess of Devonshire, and Lady Holland, both famous for their salons. The support of British Quaker and Unitarian abolitionists was even more important, for they encouraged women including Elizabeth Fry (1780–1845), who worked for many causes including anti-slavery, to support the abolition movement. Soon after the formation in Britain of the male Anti-Slavery Society in 1823, the first female abolition society began in 1825 and lasted until 1919, a unique example of longevity. Led initially by Lucy Townsend (1781–1847), a minister's wife, it became the Female Society for Birmingham and worked "for the relief of Negro slaves," especially female Negro slaves. Its example encouraged the formation of other female associations, and by 1831 at least seventy-three female societies had formed. These were mainly in towns and worked independently of male societies, by "diffusing information," fund-raising, and collecting signatures for petitions demanding complete emancipation of slaves in British colonies, a campaign that succeeded when Parliament passed the Emancipation Act of 1833. After this, numbers declined but female societies continued to campaign for the emancipation of black slaves internationally. They protested conditions on former slave plantations and worked with missionary organizations for "Negro improvement," such as education for the former slaves. Their work was of real value when the 1865 Morant Bay Riots in Jamaica showed that blacks were still little better off than under slavery.

Throughout these years, women, including the educationalists Hannah More (1745–1833) and Harriet Martineau (1800–1876), were noted propagandists, and their writings encouraged other women to think about the problem of slavery. During the Civil War the British actress Fanny Kemble (1809–1893) won public sympathy for the Union cause by describing the horror of living on a Southern slave plantation.

The Anglo-American Anti-Slavery Movement. Britain emancipated slaves in the 1830s but the United States not completely until 1863, and Anglo-American cooperation in the intervening years was very important. There was constant interchange of visiting abolitionists between the two countries. British workers sent letters of moral support and practical aid in the form of gifts for anti-slavery fairs, and lifelong Anglo-American friendships were forged, such as that between two bluestockings, Martineau of Britain and Maria Weston Chapman (1806–1885) of America. British Quakers and Unitarians continued to be the most active abolitionists, a noted example being Elizabeth Pease of Darlington, who gave generous financial aid.

British intervention was resented in republican America, however, while support for the American South grew in Britain, whose economy depended on raw cotton grown by Southern slave labor. Thanks to English, Irish, and Scottish women, and to such leaders as Amelia Chesson of London, daughter of the British abolitionist George Thompson; Hannah Webb of Dublin; and Eliza Wigham of Edinburgh, support for the North was maintained during the Civil War when a "cotton famine" caused many cotton mills in Lancashire to close. Having no vote and lacking status, these British women were nevertheless significant reformers. By virtue of their being women their views carried more weight in America, where revolutionary prejudices against Britain remained strong.

The American Anti-Slavery Movement. Because black slavery existed on U.S. soil, the American anti-slavery cause, unlike the European, became a major social and political movement. Slavery had been legal in all the British colonies, but following the Revolutionary War, the states of the North initiated processes of gradual emancipation. The anomaly of being "half free, half slave" angered many in the North, and with universal male suffrage by 1830, slavery became a political cause so controversial as to lead in 1861 to a split between North and South.

Not all anti-slavery societies formed between 1830 and 1860 were political pressure groups; some favored pacifism or were part of an evangelical crusade. The oldest, the Pennsylvania Abolition Society, was founded in 1775, but more traditionally, its auxiliary, the Philadelphia Female Anti-Slavery Society, which began in 1833 and disbanded in 1870, set the example. Philadelphia's female abolitionists, "the silent sisters" (many were Quakers), organized two anti-slavery conventions of American women in 1838 and 1839, following the first one held in New York in 1837. A proslavery mob, however, burnt the new Pennsylvania Hall in 1838 as the women delegates gathered there. Later, Pennsylvanians worked with the Underground Railroad to help fugitive slaves escape to freedom in Canada. New York female societies, on the other hand, were short-lived and conservative; those in Ohio lasted longer; but in Massachusetts, women's societies flourished until nearly 1850 and were radical. The Boston Female Anti-Slavery Society had an 1835 meeting broken up by a mob who thought that George Thompson, a visiting British lecturer, was present. When the Grimké sisters visited Massachusetts to lecture on the evils of slavery, not surprisingly their action provoked clerical protests throughout the state over women speaking in public. Sarah and Angelina Emily Grimké, "Carolina's high-souled daughters," had left their comfortable home on a slave plantation in South Carolina to settle in the North to write and lecture in public against slavery.

Worse division came when a minority of the Boston women abolitionists supported the controversial abolitionist William Lloyd Garrison, editor of Boston's anti-slavery weekly, the *Liberator*. Garrison had been attacked by the 1835 mob, and then opposed by conservative clergy and anti-slavery political activists alike. However, he depended on women as fund-raisers and in 1840 placed his ally, Abby Kelley, on the business committee of the national American Anti-Slavery Society based in New York, causing a section to break away, claiming to have the support of the national British anti-slavery society. Further division came internationally when Garrison and other American delegates declined to be seated at the 1840 World's Anti-Slavery Convention in London, because British organizers "ignored" the American women delegates. Now divided internationally by the "woman question," American female anti-slavery societies continued in Pennsylvania, New England, and Ohio until nearly 1850, but the work of these groups was mainly traditional. In America as in Britain women were the workhorses of the anti-slavery movement, fund-raising and collecting signatures for anti-slavery petitions presented to state legislatures and Congress despite gag rules, but they also defied convention. Kelley, now Kelley Foster of Massachusetts, became an agent of the Massachusetts

Anti-Slavery Society and for years spoke publicly throughout New England, helping to form female anti-slavery societies. More conventionally, Lydia Maria Child and Maria Weston Chapman, also from Massachusetts, won recognition as anti-slavery propagandists by editing journals or writing anti-slavery pamphlets, but their fame was eclipsed in 1852 when Harriet Beecher Stowe (1811–1896) published her novel *Uncle Tom's Cabin*, the most successful of all propaganda works. It enjoyed unprecedented circulation, and its sentimental but humanitarian appeal influenced many to oppose slavery. The book was so popular that President Abraham Lincoln is said to have described Beecher as "the little woman who made the great war." Significantly, by the 1840s women were the chief organizers of anti-slavery societies, men being more concerned with public protest, especially political—Ralph Waldo Emerson left the organization of the Concord anti-slavery society to his wife, preferring to write and lecture on the subject. A few outstanding women kept pace with the men: the anti-slavery lecturer Abby Kelley Foster campaigned tirelessly in New England, Child did yeoman work editing the national *Anti-Slavery Standard* in New York, Maria Weston Chapman took the anti-slavery cause to Paris, and Lucretia Mott kept abolition alive in Philadelphia.

Never to be forgotten were the black women abolitionists, especially in Boston; Salem, Massachusetts; and Philadelphia, where a few black families had gained place, creating what was later to be called "the talented tenth." In 1831 Maria Stewart of Boston became the first black woman abolitionist to speak in public, while Sarah Parker Remond and Charlotte Forten were active in anti-slavery work. Even poor black women played a significant part, and escaped slaves including Sojourner Truth (c. 1797–1883) and Harriet Brent Jacobs (c. 1815–1897) gave practical help to other fugitives, or won converts with tales of their own escape. All blacks were as conscious as Ellen Craft, who could "pass for white," how difficult it was to be an escaped slave, or simply a black in the free North. Stories told by many female abolitionists of the difficulty of running an integrated school underline the problem. In the 1830s Prudence Crandall of Connecticut, a white woman, was put in prison when she opened an integrated school; she eventually closed her school "for the girls' safety." Caroline Weston, who had been mobbed in Boston in 1835, said that integrated schools never worked. It took twenty more years for the city of Boston to legislate for integrated schools, and by then white anti-slavery women had on more than one occasion walked arm in arm with a black sister to protect her from abuse on the street. Without the vote women could protest only verbally or in written form, and their societies, some little more than sewing circles, had disbanded when the 1850 Fugitive Slave Law compelled the rendition of fugitives and forced the American anti-slavery movement into a new phase of violent confrontation with Southern conservatives.

The Legacy of Female Abolitionism. There is a clear link in Britain and America between the anti-slavery cause and the women's rights campaign demanding the right to vote. In 1848 Elizabeth Cady Stanton, wife of the prominent abolitionist Henry B. Stanton, helped organize the first woman's rights convention in Seneca Falls, New York, and the Philadelphia Female Anti-Slavery Society more cautiously followed her lead. Demands for female emancipation began in earnest after the American Civil War ended in 1865 and had the support of many former abolitionists, including Julia Ward Howe (1819–1910), author of the "Battle Hymn of the Republic." "Freedom for slaves and women" had by this date become meaningful, for women internationally had no vote, were unable to hold property if married, and were as subject to a male relation as any slave would be. Yet female abolitionists on both sides of the Atlantic were experienced organizers, speakers, and propagandists, and their protests symbolically ended when the Birmingham Society disbanded in 1919 with British women assured of the vote. The American author Henry James wrote *The Bostonians* in 1886 to illustrate "the situation of [American] women, the decline of the sentiment of sex, the agitation on their behalf." The novel highlights how Southern and Northern women worked together for female emancipation while the men were still divided. James knew that in Europe feminism and demands for political equality made slow headway. However, France's most important twentieth-century feminist, Simone de Beauvoir (1908–1986), later encouraged the "Deuxième Sexe" to seek to emancipate themselves. The experience and example of female abolitionists, irrespective of class or color, undeniably helped change attitudes toward civil rights and racial equality in the years that followed.

[*See also* Child, Lydia Maria; Civil War, *subentry* United States; France; Great Britain; Grimké, Angelina Emily; Grimké, Sarah; Jacobs, Harriet Brent; Seneca Falls Convention of 1848; Staël, Germaine de; Stanton, Elizabeth Cady; Stowe, Harriet Beecher; Truth, Sojourner; *and* United States, *subentry* Nineteenth Century.]

BIBLIOGRAPHY

Hansen, Debra Gold. *Strained Sisterhood: Gender and Class in the Boston Female Anti-Slavery Society*. Amherst: University of Massachusetts Press, 1993.

Jeffrey, Julie Roy. *The Great Silent Army of Abolitionism: Ordinary Women in the Antislavery Movement*. Chapel Hill: University of North Carolina Press, 1998.

Midgley, Clare. *Women against Slavery: The British Campaigns, 1780–1870*. London and New York: Routledge, 1993.

Salerno, Beth A. *Sister Societies, Women's Anti-Slavery Organizations in Antebellum America*. DeKalb: Northern Illinois University Press, 2005.

Sterling, Dorothy. *Ahead of Her Time: Abby Kelley and the Politics of Anti-Slavery*. New York: Norton, 1991.

Taylor, Clare. *British and American Abolitionists: An Episode in Transatlantic Understanding*. Edinburgh: Edinburgh University Press; Chicago: Aldine, 1974.

Taylor, Clare. *Women of the Anti-Slavery Movement: The Weston Sisters*. New York: St. Martin's Press, 1995.

Van Broekhoven, Deborah Bingham. *The Devotion of These Women: Rhode Island in the Antislavery Network*. Amherst: University of Massachusetts Press, 2002.

Yellin, Jean Fagan. *Harriet Jacobs: A Life*. New York: Basic Civitas Books, 2004.

Yellin, Jean Fagan, and John C. Van Horne, eds. *The Abolitionist Sisterhood: Women's Political Culture in Antebellum America*. Ithaca, N.Y.: Cornell University Press, 1994.

Zaeske, Susan. *Signatures of Citizenship: Petitioning, Antislavery, and Women's Political Identity*. Chapel Hill: University of North Carolina Press, 2003.

CLARE TAYLOR

ABORTION

This entry consists of three subentries:

Overview
Comparative History
Politics

Overview

Throughout time women have turned to abortion to terminate unwanted pregnancies, and religious, medical, and state authorities have sought to control women's access to the procedure. The role that authorities played in controlling access to abortion changed significantly over time. Physicians and medical writers, for instance, sometimes disseminated information about abortion and performed abortions; at other times they lobbied for criminalization. At various times and places state authorities permitted and regulated abortions or prohibited the practice and prosecuted those involved. Church authorities were slow to take a position on the issue but over time moved toward greater restriction of information about birth control and abortion. Eventually religious doctrine and the law of states converged to criminalize abortion. Only in recent decades has this trend begun to reverse.

Ancient World, Middle Ages, and Renaissance. In the ancient world abortions were available, albeit often dangerous. Hebrew, Greek, and Roman thought converged on the point that abortion prior to the formation of the fetus was not homicide. Early abortion was preferable to late, and abortion by herbs was preferable to surgical abortions. Medical writers consistently listed herbs that might terminate pregnancy. In his work on gynecology in the early second century, Soranus explained that if a woman wanted to destroy a fetus in the first thirty days she should follow the opposite of a regimen intended to prevent miscarriages. In particular, he recommended aerobic exercise, diuretic concoctions to bring on menstruation, daily baths, and poultices and plasters. Similarly, in the first century, Dioscorides, the foremost authority on ancient pharmacy, named fourteen of the fifteen drugs specified by Soranus. Egyptian writers, too, recognized that certain agents could prevent conception or cause an abortion. By the end of the second century, the ancients had reached a consensus about which drugs functioned as abortifacients.

Although drug abortions were the preferred means to end an unwanted pregnancy, Greco-Roman medical literature also described surgical and manipulated abortions. Because of the dangers, however, medical authorities cautioned against pregnancy termination. Abortions were not criminal per se, but courts could hold a second party liable if the mother was harmed in the process.

Arab medical writings that recorded and expanded on knowledge regarding abortifacients passed into thirteenth-century western Europe. In Muslim society there is abundant evidence of the ongoing use of early-stage abortifacients. Muslims believed that the soul entered the conceptus at the end of 120 days, but Muslim jurists differed on the length of gestation during which abortions were acceptable. Some permitted women to abort until 120 days after conception; others set the limit at 40 days.

Throughout the Middle Ages, physicians in Europe not only described abortion procedures but also provided a moral justification: to save the lives of women. But whereas physicians taught and justified abortion under certain conditions, the church's position and secular law increasingly focused on protecting the life of the fetus. This contributed to a view that simultaneously tolerated abortion but saw it as a sin with varying degrees of penalties attached. Nevertheless, even the church acknowledged that individual women might have problems that needed compassionate solutions. For example, the writings of Hildegard of Bingen, the author of *Liber simplicis medicinae* and a woman considered by some to be the first female physician in Germany, suggest that her attitude toward abortion was more sympathetic than the official church position. Nevertheless, although the knowledge of birth-control devices and abortifacients in the written record had never been greater than in the late Middle Ages, the Roman church took an increasingly militant stance against almost all nonprocreative sexual activity.

Over the next several centuries the church extended its influence into matters of sexuality and reproduction. Compared with those of classical and medieval times, Renaissance sources tell little about birth control and abortifacients. Transformations in the medical field contributed to the loss of medical information about abortion. By the twelfth century, medical training had shifted from the apprenticeship

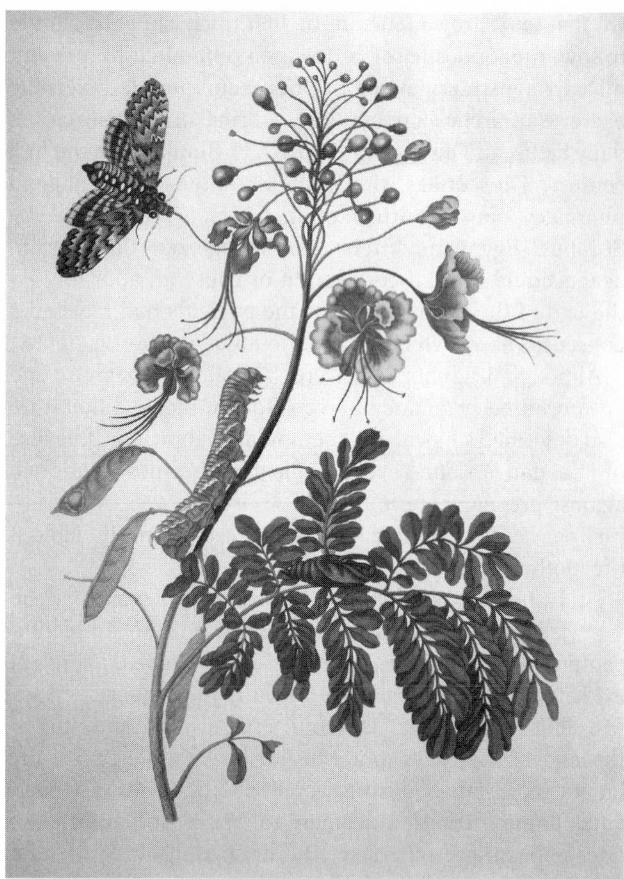

***Flos Pavonis*, or Peacock Flower.** A herbal abortifacient. Drawing by Maria Sibylla Merian, 1705. BILDARCHIV PREUSSISCHER KULTURBESITZ, STAATSBIBLIOTHEK ZU BERLIN/ART RESOURCE, NY

system to the universities. Because the university curriculum was geared more to medical theory than to the clinic, and the dispensing of drugs increasingly fell to pharmacists rather than to physicians, medical knowledge about abortifacients began to fade. By the fifteenth and sixteenth centuries few physicians knew about birth control and abortion, and there was no ready means by which they could gain this kind of information. Gynecology, the specialty most likely to be concerned with abortion, increasingly fell into the hands of midwives who received no formal training. Evidence suggests, however, that midwives retained knowledge about abortion. French midwives, a source from 1566 notes, came to private homes to provide abortions.

The Modern Period. Knowledge about contraceptives and abortifacients continued to decline in the seventeenth and eighteenth centuries as physicians increasingly excluded antifertility drugs from their realm. The greatest authority on gynecology and obstetrics at the time was Francis Mauriceau, who condemned abortion and would not write about contraception. The great herbalists of the time usually mentioned antifertility plants, but they did so not to educate about abortifacients but to warn about the plants' unwanted consequences.

Nevertheless, although evidence from other parts of the world has not been reported, documents from Europe and North America demonstrate that despite increasing religious and legal opposition to abortion, women continued to learn about the possibility of pregnancy termination and took advantage of this knowledge. A 1742 court case in the Connecticut village of Pomfret illustrates that knowledge of abortion was fairly widespread and extended to young people, who were familiar not only with the idea of abortion but also with its associated slang. If Pomfret's young people knew about abortion, so did many other people. Even in the seventeenth century, when books were not commonly available, many families owned the popular herbals compiled by John Gerard, John Parkinson, and Nicholas Culpeper, which list more than a dozen abortifacients common to English and New England gardens.

On the Continent, too, women knew about and practiced abortion. Despite the illegality of birth regulation in Hungary, for instance, women in western Hungary as well as in Warsaw (at that time part of Poland) were aware of a variety of herbs and chemicals that might induce abortion. In eighteenth-century France, abortion and contraception were so widespread that contemporary observers, including Charles-Louis de Secondat, the baron of Montesquieu, Jean-Jacques Rousseau, and the Marquis de Sade, commented on its availability. Indeed, French historians attribute a drastic decline of births to the availability of contraception and abortion in the second half of the eighteenth century.

In seventeenth- and eighteenth-century Malta, abortion was a serious offense in the eyes of the law and the church. Nevertheless, the Inquisitional Tribunal and the Bishop's Court heard cases relating to abortion, including the case of a seventeen-year-old woman who accused herself of having had carnal relations with men and animals brought to her by the devil. She became pregnant and procured several abortions. Although evidence from other parts of the world is scant, we know that in eighteenth-century India, Rajasthan society considered abortion a crime but, because of the region's rural and harsh natural conditions, enforced social restrictions against it less strictly than officials in other parts of the country did.

The Industrial Era. In the nineteenth century the advent of the printing press radically transformed the ways in which people learned about abortion. Abortion became a commercial business. Both England and the United States passed antiabortion legislation early in the century, but in neither country did criminalization lead to a significant number of indictments. Starting in the 1830s ideas about contraception and abortion were disseminated by books, newspapers, and advertisements, as well as in public lectures.

From 1840 on, advertisements informed women of a wide variety of drugs and instruments to induce abortion that were readily available through the mails.

By mid-century, cities in New England and the Middle Atlantic states had a growing number of professional abortionists who offered a variety of services. The most famous is probably Madame Restell, who operated abortion services in New York City from the 1840s through the 1870s. Restell—who charged $5 for an examination, from $1 to $5 for a box of pills, and $100 for an operation—combined compassion and competence with business shrewdness. In 1871 she reported spending approximately $60,000 per year on advertising alone. This included, among other things, numerous newspaper ads and handbills. France, too, saw the emergence of semilegendary figures who provided abortions. The very fact that they enjoyed such notoriety is one indication of the public's knowledge of their role.

With the commercialization of abortion came a significant shift in the kind of woman who had abortions. In the first half of the nineteenth century, abortion was primarily seen as an exceptional act—the last resort of unwed mothers, who sought the procedures from midwives and lower-level practitioners. During the latter half of the nineteenth century and the early twentieth century, abortion became a backup method of contraception for middle-class women. By the end of the nineteenth century French and British physicians themselves were responsible for making abortion an option. Many failed to consider abortion a crime, and French physicians began to differentiate between criminal abortions and therapeutic abortions to preserve the health of the mother. Indeed, in the late 1800s the French writer E. Adolph Spiral first fully articulated arguments for a woman's right to abortion. These developments transformed the very nature of abortion, which became one of several methods of birth control.

Increased access to birth control and abortion resulted in a drastic decline in birthrates across industrialized nations. Between the late nineteenth century and World War I, women in industrialized nations across the world began to restrict the number of children they bore. Regardless of its legal status, abortion played a significant role in the drop of fertility rates. In Norway, for instance, seeking an abortion was a capital crime until the mid-1800s. After the criminal code was revised in 1842, the punishment was no longer decapitation, but a woman was subject to imprisonment for up to six years. Despite the promise of such a severe penalty, abortion played a significant role in the decrease of Norwegian fertility rates after 1900. In France, rising abortion rates and declining birthrates were not simply attributed to industrial change but were taken as a symptom of an emerging feminism. The changing role of sexuality and women's determination to control childbearing, along with falling birthrates across the Western industrialized world, contributed to deep ambivalences about the role of abortion in modern society.

Twentieth-Century Legislation. As access to abortion led to worries about population decline, industrialized nations initiated a new wave of antiabortion legislation. Starting in the late nineteenth century, American social-purity reformers began to lobby for the regulation of abortion, contraception, and pornography. American physicians, less

TO MARRIED WOMEN—MADAME RESTELL, *Female Physician*, is happy to have it in her power to say that since the introduction into this country, about a year ago of her celebrated Preventive Powders for married ladies, whose health forbids a too rapid increase of family; hundreds have availed themselves of their use, with a success and satisfaction that has at once dispelled the fears and doubts of the most timid and skeptical; for, notwithstanding that for twenty years they have been used in Europe with invariable success, (first introduced by the celebrated Midwife and Female Physician. Madame Restell, the grandmother of the advertiser, who made this subject her particular and especial study,) still some were inclined to entertain some degree of distrust, until become convinced by their successful adoption in this country. The results of their adoption to the happiness, the health, nay, often the life of many an affectionate wife and a fond mother, are too vast to touch upon within the limits of an advertisement—results which affect not only the present well-being of parents, but the future happiness of their offspring. Is it not but too well known that the families of the married often increase beyond the happiness of those who give them birth would dictate? In how many instances does the hardworking father, and more especially the mother, of a poor family, remain slaves throughout their lives, tugging at the oar of incessant labor, toiling to live, and living but to toil; when they might have enjoyed comfort and comparative affluence; and if care and toil have weighed down the spirit, and at last broken the health of the father, how often is the widow left, unable, with the most virtuous intentions, to save her fatherless offspring from becoming degraded objects of charity or profligate votaries of vice? And even though competence and plenty smile upon us, how often, alas! are the days of the kind husband and father embittered in beholding the emaciated form and declining health of the companion of his bosom, ere she had scarce reached the age of thirty—fast sinking into a premature grave—with the certain prospect of himself being early bereft of the partner of his joys and sorrows, and his young and helpless children of the endearing attentions and watchful solicitude which a mother alone can bestow, not unfrequently at a time when least able to support the heart-rending affliction! Is it desirable then—is it moral for parents to increase their families, regardless of consequences to themselves or the well being of their offspring when a simple, easy healthy and CERTAIN remedy is within our control? The advertiser feeling the importance of this subject and estimating the vast benefits resulting to thousands by the adoption of means prescribed by her, would respectfully arouse the attention of the married, by all that they hold near and dear to its consideration. Is it not wise and virtuous to prevent evils to which we are subject by simple and healthy means within our control? Every dispassionate, virtuous, and enlightened mind will unhesitatingly answer in the affirmative. This is all that Madame Restell recommends or ever recommended. Price Five Dollars a package, accompanied with full and particular directions. For the convenience of those unable to call personally, "Circulars" more fully explanatory, will be sent free of expense (postage excepted) to any part of the United States. All letters must be post-paid, and addressed to MADAME RESTELL, Female Physician. Principal office, 148 Greenwich street, New-York. Office hours from 8 A. M. to 7 P. M. Philadelphia office, 30½ South Eighth street.

ap10 1m*

"To Married Women." Madame Restell, a female physician, advertises "preventative powders for married ladies, whose health forbids a too rapid increase of family," 13 April 1840. THE NEW YORK HERALD/NEWSPAPER AND PERIODICALS READING ROOM, LIBRARY OF CONGRESS tolerant than their French and British counterparts, associated abortion with strong-minded, married, middle-class women who were shirking their "natural" roles as wives and mothers. Between 1860 and 1880 they inaugurated a lobbying campaign through the American Medical Association that resulted in the criminalization of abortion across the nation.

By the end of the nineteenth century, abortion had become illegal in the United States. In Norway, revisions of the criminal code in 1902 called for the imprisonment of women seeking abortion for as long as three years. Moreover, for the first time, those who helped a woman obtain the procedure were subject to imprisonment, for six years—or for life if the woman died. In Germany, whose leaders worried about a dwindling birthrate and population losses during World War I, antiabortion laws were amended in 1926 to prohibit abortions that were not strictly medically indicated. The one exception to this trend was Russia, where a 1920 decree permitted free abortions at hospitals, reversing a tradition in line with the teaching of the Orthodox Church, which forbade abortion prior to the Bolshevik Revolution. In 1935, however, Joseph Stalin recriminalized abortion.

Driven underground in Western industrialized countries, abortion became far more difficult, expensive, and dangerous to obtain. Although the extent of prosecution and conviction varied over time and place, criminalization in the twentieth century led to the emergence of a two-class system: wealthy women found ways to obtain safe abortions from private physicians, and poor women were forced to seek help from underground abortion providers and were thus more likely to suffer ill effects or even die as a result of the procedure. Hospital emergency rooms were flooded with women who had obtained illegal abortions at the hands of incompetent providers. By the 1960s as many as five thousand women were dying annually in the United States as a direct consequence of criminalized abortion. Women of color were nearly four times as likely to die as a result of abortion as white women.

Abortion Today. By the late 1960s a number of factors had coalesced to bring about the liberalization of abortion laws in many parts of the world. The rise of the women's movement drew attention to issues of women's reproductive health nationally and internationally as women began to fight for the legalization of abortion. Physicians' experiences with botched abortions convinced many that legalization was necessary. At the same time, developments in medical technologies made abortions easier and safer, reducing physicians' objections. Finally, changing perceptions of the rights of individuals to bodily integrity and a right to privacy provided the legal foundation in a number of countries for the legalization of abortion.

Starting in the late 1960s and accelerating in the 1970s, the United States, Western Europe, Israel, and Japan liberalized their abortion laws. Although laws differed, and abortion did not become equally accessible in all these countries, women seeking to terminate pregnancies generally gained access to safe abortions. Legalization in industrialized countries was accompanied by legalization in a number of developing countries where there were concerns about burgeoning population growth. Vietnam, India, and China (in 1957), for instance, decriminalized abortion. In the 1970s passage of one-child programs in China and Vietnam resulted in coercive population policies and harsh international criticism. Cultural preference for male children in China and India led to the use of abortion for sex selection and thus to a growing gender imbalance in China. Laws enacted in the 1990s were intended to address issues of sex selection, but abortion for this purpose, along with female infanticide and the abandonment of female children, continues to be a problem.

The socialist countries of Central and Eastern Europe followed the example of the Soviet Union, which liberalized its abortion law in 1955 to promote the emancipation of women. Indeed, former Communist bloc countries have traditionally relied on abortion as the primary means of birth control, and abortion rates in these countries have thus been much higher than in the West. Concern over low birthrates, however, led Bulgaria, Czechoslovakia, Hungary, and Romania to pass new abortion restrictions in the 1960s and 1970s. With the collapse of most Communist governments in the early 1990s, the return of the Roman Catholic Church, and the rise of governments eager to undo previous Communist policies, abortion policies were again restricted in several Eastern European countries.

Indeed, religious doctrine results in the continued criminal status of abortion in many countries. The Catholic Church's opposition to abortion resulted in the criminalization of abortion not only in several former Soviet bloc countries but also in the Philippines and most countries in Latin America where the church has a strong influence. Most abortions in these countries are clandestine and are accompanied by a high risk of medical complications and maternal mortality rates. A conservative school of Islam in many Arab countries condemns abortion at any stage of pregnancy. There, as well as in most African countries where abortion is restricted under outdated colonial laws, the emergence of a black market has relegated poor women to unsafe abortions performed outside the law. In these countries abortions continue to be a major contributor to maternal mortality, with the treatment of incomplete and septic abortions severely taxing scarce health-care resources.

Even in the United States, access to abortion remains a contested issue. Although the 1973 U.S. Supreme Court decision *Roe v. Wade* legalized abortion, leading to the establishment of abortion services across the country, religious conservatives had launched a broad-scale attack on access to abortion services by the 1980s. State legislatures considered hundreds of bills intended to restrict, if not eliminate, the provision of abortions. Congress restricted funding for poor women seeking abortions, and in 2003 passed a ban on the late-term abortion procedure intact dilation and extraction (the so-called Partial Birth Abortion Ban Act). U.S. Supreme Court decisions since *Roe v. Wade* have upheld many of these restrictions, slowly eroding access to abortion care. In 2007 the Court upheld the ban on intact dilation in *Gonzales v. Planned Parenhood* in spite of the fact that the law lacked an exception to preserve the health of the woman. Many fear that this decision will lead to further erosion of women's access to abortion care.

[*See also* Contraception; Female Life Cycle; *and* Fertility and Infertility.]

BIBLIOGRAPHY

Brodie, Janet Farrell. *Contraception and Abortion in Nineteenth-Century America*. Ithaca, N.Y.: Cornell University Press, 1994.

Dayton, Cornelia Hughes. "Taking the Trade: Abortion and Gender Relations in an Eighteenth-Century New England Village." *William and Mary Quarterly* 48, no. 1 (1991): 19–49.

DiMauro, Diane, and Carole Joffe. "The Religious Right and the Reshaping of Sexual Policy: An Examination of Reproductive/Rights and Sexuality Education." *Sexuality Research and Social Policy* 4, no. 1 (March 2007): 67–92.

Grossmann, Atina. *Reforming Sex: The German Movement for Birth Control and Abortion Reform, 1920–1950*. New York: Oxford University Press, 1995.

Kligman, Gail. *The Politics of Duplicity: Controlling Reproduction in Ceausescu's Romania*. Berkeley: University of California Press, 1998.

McLaren, Angus. "Abortion in France: Women and the Regulation of Family Size, 1800–1914." *French Historical Studies* 10, no. 3 (1978): 461–485.

Michaels, Paula A. *Curative Powers: Medicine and Empire in Stalin's Central Asia*. Pittsburgh, Pa.: University of Pittsburgh Press, 2003.

Petchesky, Rosalind Pollack. *Abortion and Woman's Choice: The State, Sexuality, and Reproductive Freedom*. New York: Longman, 1984.

Reagan, Leslie J. *When Abortion Was a Crime: Women, Medicine, and Law in the United States, 1867–1973*. Berkeley: University of California Press, 1997.

Riddle, John M. *Contraception and Abortion from the Ancient World to the Renaissance*. Cambridge, Mass.: Harvard University Press, 1992.

Schoen, Johanna. *Choice and Coercion: Birth Control, Sterilization, and Abortion in Public Health and Welfare*. Chapel Hill: University of North Carolina Press, 2005.

Szreter, Simon, Robert A. Nye, and Frans van Poppel. "Fertility and Contraception during the Demographic Transition: Qualitative and Quantitative Approaches." *Journal of Interdisciplinary History* 34, no. 2 (2003): 141–154.

JOHANNA SCHOEN

Comparative History

In almost all times and places in human history, some forms of pregnancy termination have been illegal or highly stigmatized, but the type of pregnancy termination considered wrong varies a great deal from one context to another. The line separating abortion from contraception or menstrual regulation on the one hand, and from infanticide on the other, is not always clear. In any place and time, what counts as abortion depends on what counts as a real pregnancy, or, more accurately, what counts as the beginning of a sacred or rights-bearing human life. This beginning can be reckoned from many points: from the meeting of sperm and egg, from the implantation of the fertilized egg in the uterus, from the first perceptible movements of the fetus, or from a supernatural happening such as "ensoulment" or "the breath of life" entering the fetus. As a result, practices as diverse as using artificial hormones to prevent implantation of a fertilized egg or asphyxiating a premature infant at birth may be considered abortion by some people and be considered something quite different by others. Nonetheless, abortion of one form or another is ubiquitous in human history.

In the mid-1950s the anthropologist George Devereux argued that abortion has always existed, since the earliest formation of human societies, whether in the form of medicines that were ingested, objects inserted into the uterus, or the application of force to the abdomen. The earliest known written reference to abortion is an Egyptian papyrus scroll, the Ebers Papyrus, which is a compendium of medical prescriptions dating from 1550 B.C.E. It contains instructions for using acacia fruit and dates to induce abortion at any point in pregnancy and is probably a transcription of instructions that were at least a thousand years older. Instruments for terminating pregnancies have also been found at ancient archaeological digs, including Pompeii and Herculaneum.

Although the practice of abortion has existed for tens of thousands of years, the actual incidence of abortion throughout history is impossible to assess directly because the vast majority of abortions leave no trace in the historical record. Direct historical references to abortion are of dubious accuracy because the emotional power of abortion as a moral or political issue is such that vehement denunciations of the practice often bear little connection to the actual extent of abortion. Historians have attempted to discern the presence of abortion from sources as varied as religious tracts denouncing the practice to genealogies of prominent families but have come to no firm conclusion except that abortion has always existed.

Nonetheless, some historical evidence suggests that abortions were particularly common ways of controlling fertility

Antiabortion Movement in East Asia. Indonesian residents hold an antiabortion protest in front of a village clinic suspected of conducting abortions, December 1997. REUTERS/SUPRI

at certain times. For instance, demographic historians have pointed to the apparent discrepancy between rapidly falling birthrates in western Europe in the eighteenth and nineteenth centuries or in the Roman Empire in the first few centuries C.E. and the absence of effective contraception as evidence that abortion was increasingly being used to produce smaller families. Other historians have also assumed that prosecutions for infanticide indicated a high number of abortions, as in nineteenth-century England, on the grounds that infanticide acted as a backup plan for failed abortion, and so for every case of infanticide, the existence of many more successful abortions could be inferred (the exact ratio of infanticide to abortion is still not clear).

In the same period, prosecutions for the crime of "concealment of pregnancy" may also be an index of the prevalence of abortion because concealment-of-pregnancy laws were based on the premise that the only reason a woman would actively hide her pregnancy was that she intended to end it. In the early twentieth century in North America the proliferation of advertising for over-the-counter medications that claimed they would "regulate" menstruation or remove "obstructions" in the uterus may indicate that many women wanted to ensure that they were not pregnant and would use these medicines after missing one or more menstrual periods, even if they were unable to confirm whether they were pregnant.

Even literature has been drawn into the quest to understand the history of abortion. For example, scholars have pointed to several references to "rue," in contexts where Shakespeare's audience would have understood the word to have a double meaning, indicating both remorse or regret and the name of an herb known to produce abortion. The libertine literature of seventeenth- and eighteenth-century France has also been scoured for references to abortion as a way of dealing with the unwanted consequences of extramarital sex, although these references suggest that abortions were unusual and were mainly the province of the wealthy who could find reliable and discreet abortion providers. These historical studies suggest, but do not prove, that abortion has always been present even when officially suppressed or tabooed.

Religious and Political Regulation of Abortion. Most historical studies of abortion are actually studies of the prohibition of abortion, based on the strictures issued by religious, medical, or political leaders. Almost all regulation of abortion has been justified by religious convictions having to do with the moral status of the fetus, so the history of abortion prohibition is intrinsically connected to the history of religion. The strength of religion per se is not necessarily predictive of the status of abortion in a given society—what is crucial, in setting the terms under which women may lawfully terminate a pregnancy, is the extent to which religious hierarchies are entwined with state hierarchies. For example, abortion is much more restricted in the Philippines, a country in which the Catholic Church has historically been a powerful force in government, than in Brazil, a country with a comparably devout Catholic population but in which the separation of church and state has been much more pronounced.

In the Islamic world a similar correlation exists between the centrality of Sharia as a guiding principle of the state—in other words, the acknowledgment of religious influence on lawmaking—and the stringency of the conditions under which abortion is permissible. For instance, both Tunisia and Kuwait describe themselves in their constitutions as Islamic states, but the Kuwaiti constitution allows for a much greater role for Sharia in the administration of the state and also has much stronger regulations against abortion.

In a few historical periods, however, practices that would now be considered abortion were not taboo—for instance, in pre-Christian Rome, abortion for eugenic and therapeutic purposes is alluded to in the Utopian works of Plato and Aristotle. The earlier in the pregnancy the abortion occurred, the less objectionable it was considered to be, and many statements of classical philosophers that appear to condemn abortion may in fact have been referring to what we would now call infanticide. Abortion appears to have been more common than contraception and to have played a significant role in keeping the size of wealthy families small. Medical writings of the period contain descriptions not only of how to bring about abortions but also of how to care for women who have inflicted injuries on themselves through self-induced abortion.

Below, the perspectives of three major "state religions"—those that have had the greatest influence on the governance of societies—are presented. These three religious traditions have been particularly influential in the regulation of abortion because they have been aligned with powerful states or empires at different points in history and so have spread throughout much of the world.

Christianity. In the writings of the early church fathers, abortion is linked with fornication and adultery as part of a network of sexual sins that, taken together, signify immorality and social decay. However, this religious stance against abortion was nowhere near as absolute as the stances taken by many churches today. For instance, one of the first collections of canonical law in the twelfth century states that early abortion was a minor crime, not comparable to homicide. Pope Innocent II (r. 1130–1143) reflected the religious, legal, and medical opinion of the day when he said that interrupting a pregnancy before fetal movement could be felt (before "quickening") was not a grave sin, but interrupting a pregnancy after quickening was the moral equivalent of murder. These views paralleled secular legal codes of the time.

In 1591, Pope Gregory XIV rescinded a papal bull based on Thomas Aquinas's thirteenth-century theology of reproduction in which abortion and contraception were deemed crimes against nature and offenses against the sacrament of marriage. It was not until 1869 that Pope Pius IX (r. 1846–1878) decreed that any interruption of pregnancy after conception was a grave sin and that anyone who participated in an act of abortion, whether by terminating one's own pregnancy or by facilitating the termination of another person's pregnancy, had excommunicated oneself from the church. The exact reason for this change in the Catholic Church's stance is still debated, but some historians argue that it was a reaction to a decline in the church's power and influence in Europe and came from a desire by the Catholic hierarchy to reassert the church's moral authority in all aspects of the lives of believers and to increase the Catholic birthrate. Since then the Roman Catholic Church has been one of the strongest opponents of abortion and has had enormous influence on the regulation of abortion in countries with large Catholic populations.

Protestant positions on abortion have historically been more diverse, and often more liberal, than the absolute Catholic rejection of pregnancy termination. In general, those Protestant denominations that describe themselves as evangelical or that adhere to a literal interpretation of the Bible have been as strongly opposed to abortion as the Catholic Church has, while those that describe themselves as liberal or that reject the concept of Biblical inerrancy have been less stringent in their opposition. The latter denominations are the result of theological developments of the late nineteenth and early twentieth century, so for most of its history Protestantism has paralleled Catholicism in its disapproval of abortion.

During the nineteenth and early twentieth centuries, Christian church prohibitions on abortion dovetailed with pressure from secular sources to prohibit abortion. In particular, physicians who viewed lay practitioners of abortions as threats to their professional authority and politicians who feared that abortion was leading to a decrease in the birthrates of the "desirable" citizenry joined religious authorities in denouncing and restricting the practice in Christian countries. These countries later exported the restrictive regulation of abortion to parts of Asia, Africa, Oceania, and South America as western Europe expanded its colonial empires throughout the world.

Islam. Within the Islamic tradition, a similar approach to abortion held sway, in that the moral and legal status of abortion depended on the stage of the pregnancy. In all schools of Islamic jurisprudence, terminating a pregnancy during its first three months was considered relatively unproblematic, based on the chronology of pregnancy described in the Qur'an in which the spirit enters the fetus during the fourth month of pregnancy. However, this inspirited fetus was not yet the moral equivalent of a human being, so that later terminations were permissible (depending on the authority consulted) if the mother's life was at risk or if the life of a child already born was thought to be at risk, particularly if the pregnant woman was still breast-feeding. Medieval Islamic medical authorities held that continuing a pregnancy posed a danger to a nursing woman's milk supply and thus to the survival of her nursing child.

Whether or not an abortion before the ensoulment of the fetus in the fourth month would be morally acceptable depended largely on the reasons for which it was performed—abortion to avoid excess financial strain on the family was not permissible under any school of Islamic law, but abortion when the pregnancy was the result of rape might be permissible, depending on which authority was consulted. In general, Islamic interpretations of abortion were more liberal than the Christian counterparts were for most of the last millennium. In addition to religious writings on abortion, the writings of Islamic physicians (which also served as primary sources of medical knowledge outside the Islamic world) contain references and instructions for procedures to regulate or improve menstrual flow, procedures that might be abortifacient in their effects, if not in their (explicit) intentions. The more conservative tendencies within Islam that arose in the twentieth century were to be strongly opposed to abortion, as is the case with their Christian counterparts.

Hinduism. In societies under Hindu jurisprudence, abortion was often prohibited on the grounds that it interrupted the process of reincarnation and prevented a soul from being reborn into the body of an infant. At the same time, however, other Hindu authorities held that abortion was not as serious a sin as their Christian counterparts believed, on the grounds that terminating a pregnancy did not destroy or irreparably damage the soul in the fetus but merely diverted it into another body to be born. Tendencies within Hinduism that put great stress on nonviolence (*ahimsa*) as a primary religious principle were more likely to oppose all types of abortion as a form of violence against both the fetus and the pregnant woman. However, Ayurvedic medical texts also contain detailed directions for surgically terminating pregnancies in order to protect the health of the mother, suggesting that the knowledge and practice of abortion was more widespread and more sophisticated than in the Christian world.

Other religious worldviews. In other parts of the world where practices concerning abortion were not regulated by the major state religions, the status of pregnancy termination depended on the local understandings of the point at which a "social person" is said to come into existence. This point may come after the completion of a pregnancy, as in some Polynesian societies where the first cry of a newborn infant is said to mark the point at which the infant "inhales a soul" and becomes a human being, or in some African and Indian societies where a naming ritual marks the creation of a new person. In such contexts the termination of a pregnancy before birth may be unremarkable, because no human life is thought to have been ended. However, the spread of conservative forms of Christianity and Islam, coupled with technologies for diagnosing pregnancies at earlier and earlier points, is spreading new ideas about the commencement of social personhood, moving it to earlier and earlier points in pregnancy, with major implications for the status of pregnancy termination.

It is important to remember, in looking at the norms, codes, and beliefs that have regulated abortion over the centuries, that the majority of abortions have occurred outside the purview of state and religious authorities, by people whom we would now call lay medical practitioners—men and women with knowledge of abortion acquired not through formal training under the auspices of state or religious authorities but through its being passed on informally from person to person, usually through apprenticeship or intergenerational transmission of knowledge in families. People who had the skills for attending births—midwives, who are usually, but not always, women—were most often the same people who had the skills to prevent births. Abortion may thus be the only medical procedure that has been in the hands of laypeople for most of its history.

Impact of Abortion. Given that abortion has been ubiquitous in human history, what impact has it had on the world? How have current societies been affected by the long history of abortion? Looking at the consequences of abortion around the world at the start of the twenty-first century can provide an idea of how abortion has shaped the experiences of women across time and space. The impact of abortion can be divided into three categories: medical, manifested by maternal deaths or injuries due to abortion; demographic, manifested in effects on fertility rates or age structures of populations caused by the reduction in births as a result of abortion; and social, manifested by the psychological, cultural, and political phenomena associated with abortion around the world.

The World Health Organization estimates that approximately 52 million pregnancies end in abortion every year, more than a quarter of all pregnancies that occur. Of these, approximately 26 million are legal abortions. The remainder are illegal, meaning that they take place in circumstances in which abortion is not permitted by law; they are characterized by the absence of medical safeguards and support and by a clandestine atmosphere. The United Nations Fund for Population Activities estimates that in Latin America, the United States, and China, about 1 in every 4 pregnancies ends in abortion; in Africa and the Middle East, about 1 in 10; in South and Southeast Asia, about 1 in 5.

Legal abortion follows a somewhat different distribution pattern: the majority of legal abortions take place in Eastern Europe and China, and the majority of abortions in other regions, such as Africa and Latin America, are illegal. The last three decades of the twentieth century saw a broad worldwide trend toward the liberalization of abortion laws, particularly in those countries that had been under colonial domination. While some parts of the world, such as Latin America, are continuing to see the liberalization of abortion laws, that trend has slowed or even reversed elsewhere, with abortion access becoming more restricted, particularly in post-Soviet states and in the United States.

Historical trends in abortion are closely linked to trends in the availability of other ways to prevent unwanted births. The number of abortions in any given country is often inversely related to the availability of contraception: where contraception is widely accessible, abortion numbers decrease. For instance, in Kazakhstan, Uzbekistan, and the

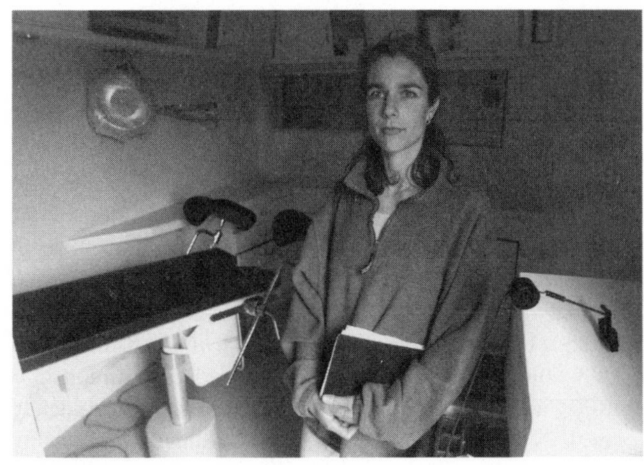

International Abortion Clinics. Rebecca Gomperts, the founder of Women on Waves, stands in an onboard abortion clinic on the ship *Sea of Change,* June 2001. REUTERS/JERRY LAMPEN

Kyrgyz Republic the use of modern contraception increased by 30 percent to 50 percent between 1990 and 1999, and abortion rates declined by half. Similarly, in Russia the number of abortions per year declined from a high of 4.6 million in 1988 to 1.7 million in 2002 after contraceptives became much more widely available, following the collapse of the Soviet Union.

Medical impact of abortion. The legal status of abortion has tremendous consequences for the safety of abortion because rates of morbidity and mortality from abortion are highest where abortion is least legal. For example, Africa, the continent with the greatest proportion of countries with no legal abortion, has 10 percent of the world's population and 40 percent of its abortion-linked deaths. When abortion is performed in safe, hygienic conditions, mortality rates are extremely low—less than 1 per 100,000 procedures, compared to a mortality rate of 6 to 25 per 100,000 for births under similar conditions. However, these safe and legal abortions account for only about half of all abortions. Where abortion is illegal, the mortality and morbidity rates are considerable higher—an estimated 330 deaths per 100,000 procedures in the developing world, where most illegal abortions take place.

In poor countries, abortion deaths are a significant subset of all deaths from pregnancy-related factors, the largest single cause of death for women. The United Nations Fund for Population Activities (UNFPA) estimates that abortion accounts for 13 percent of the half a million deaths due to pregnancy-related factors every year, and the World Health Organization estimates that seventy thousand women die from abortion-related causes every year. In some individual countries, the rates are even higher: in Ethiopia, 55 percent of maternal mortality is abortion related, in Nigeria, 50 percent. Abortion-related maternal mortality "represents the central drama of reproductive health in Africa," according to Christiane Welflens, director of obstetrics at Yopougon University Hospital Center, one of Abidjan's largest hospitals.

In addition to mortality, abortions can also produce injuries or health problems, most notably a perforated uterus, bladder, or bowel and septic shock. This abortion-related morbidity is more difficult to count than deaths because these injuries may not come to the attention of medical personnel with the same frequency that deaths do. However, UNFPA estimates that approximately four million deaths and injuries occur in Latin America alone as the result of abortion (Latin America represents about one-quarter of the world's abortions). Other estimates of abortion injuries suggest that for every death, twenty to thirty women suffer significant health complications.

One of the most detailed studies of the morbidity and mortality caused by abortion was carried out in Uganda, where abortion is illegal except when the mother's life is in danger. A team from the Alan Guttmacher Institute found that 21 percent of maternal deaths reported at three Kampala hospitals in 1992 and 1993 were the result of unsafe abortion and that complications from abortion resulted in more than half of all admissions to the gynecological emergency unit in another Kampala hospital. The majority of these abortions happen outside medical facilities, but even of those that are done legally or illegally by medical practitioners, the majority are surgical abortions, which usually have higher rates of complications than vacuum aspiration or medical abortions do.

When abortion is illegal or highly restricted, it poses significant dangers, but when restrictions on abortion are loosened, resulting in more abortions being performed by trained personnel in safe conditions, morbidity and mortality drop significantly. For instance, in Romania abortion was severely restricted between 1966 and 1989: during that period, abortion-related maternal deaths soared to 142 per hundred thousand live births. But in 1990, after restrictions on abortion had been eased and abortions could again be obtained safely and legally, abortion-related deaths dropped to one-third of the levels of 1989.

Demographic impact of abortion. Given that abortion, whether legal or illegal, is extremely common, how has it affected the shape of populations on a national or global scale? The evidence suggests that abortion has played an important, but often unrecognized, role in the reduction of the birthrate in many countries, despite being illegal in many of those places. Demographic analyses suggest that on a global scale, abortion has an impact on the live birthrate that is quantitatively similar to that of contraceptive use—that is, the existence of abortion has reduced the live birthrate from what it would be if abortion did not exist to a degree similar to the way that the use of contraception has decreased the birthrate from what it would be if contraception did not exist. This impact varies widely across countries and regions—in Latin American countries, abortion reduces fertility by 38 percent to 55 percent, while in the Middle East, abortion reduces fertility by only 6 percent to 19 percent. On a country-by-country basis, the demographic impact of abortion is highest where contraceptives are least accessible, suggesting that abortion substitutes for contraception as a means of fertility control.

In addition to reducing the number of births, abortion also has indirect effects on population growth because where abortion is available, women are able to postpone marriage and childbearing, rather than having to get married at a young age because of an unintended pregnancy. The result of these later marriages is that fewer children are born than would be the case if women married at a younger age. For instance, in Hong Kong, 29 percent of pregnancies are legally terminated, with an impact not only on declining birthrate but also on marriage rates, because abortions enable women to postpone marriage and childbearing.

Some governmental regimes have attempted to use abortion or the prohibition of abortion as a tool for achieving specific demographic goals, such as increasing or decreasing the size of the population. In these cases the prohibition of abortion usually goes hand in hand with other measures to restrict women to childbearing and maternal roles, such as restrictions on contraception or on women's involvement in the paid workforce.

For instance, abortion was severely restricted in Ceauşescu's Romania, as was contraception, because the ruling regime believed that the population of Romania was under threat by faster-growing neighboring countries. Although abortion was punishable by prison terms of one to five years, this restriction had a minimal effect on actual population growth rates because women resorted to illegal abortion and to folk medicine for the use of contraceptives. After the end of the Ceauşescu's regime, squalid orphanages containing more than two hundred thousand children were discovered, a legacy of pregnancies that could not be terminated.

During the late twentieth and early twenty-first centuries, the Chinese government's attempts to curb population growth through the one-child policy, according to which the majority of couples are restricted to having one child, have involved abortion, even though abortion is not specifically mentioned or promoted in the policy. International human rights groups have accused the Chinese government of turning a blind eye to local-level officials who force illegally pregnant women to have abortions, in an excess of zeal to reduce the population, although the Chinese government has recently begun to prosecute cases of forced abortion.

The most notorious case of using abortion as a political tool was Nazi Germany, where in 1943 the Nazis declared abortion by "Aryan" women a crime against the state, punishable by death. By contrast, abortions were forced on Jewish women and other women whom the Nazis considered undesirable.

Social impact of abortion. The existence and practice of abortion dramatically affects the lives of all women and men, even those who do not have abortions themselves, and the effects are cultural, political, and religious. One of the most profound effects of abortion is the extent to which abortion makes criminals, heretics, or social deviants of a vast number of women. The ubiquity of abortion means that women everywhere have good odds of coming into conflict with the laws or religious traditions of their society over the course of their reproductive lives. For many women, no other life event has the same power to put them at the center of moral and political debate. In Pakistan, where legal abortion is restricted to cases in which a pregnant woman's life or health is in grave danger, the Population Council estimates that women have on average about one induced abortion, legal or illegal, during their lifetime. Similarly, in Uganda, where abortion is legal only to save a woman's life, the average woman has a 50 percent chance of needing care for complications following an induced abortion in her lifetime.

Abortion has also had profound social consequences where it has been used selectively, to eliminate the births of particular types of children. The prohibition of abortion as a means to eliminate "undesirable" ethnic groups has been described; another (unintended) consequence of abortion as a means of reducing certain types of births is the sex imbalance among younger generations in India and China, where female fetuses have been aborted at much greater rates than male fetuses have. Although the practice of sex-selective abortion is illegal in India, demographers estimate that half a million female fetuses are aborted annually, producing a "deficit" of up to 10 million women. The pattern of sex selection varies greatly by province and region and can be as extreme as 79 girls being born for every 100 boys born in Punjab. (The natural ratio of female to male births is approximately 95 to 100.) Similar sex-ratio imbalances have been observed in China, on the order of 86 girls born for every 100 boys, although China has not taken as aggressive measures as India has to prohibit sex-selection in abortion. The long-term consequences of these ratios are still unknown—what will it mean for China or India to have many more men than women in their adult population? How will gender relations, to say nothing of national economic or political interests, be affected by a surplus of males and a deficit of females?

[*See also* Christianity; Contraception; Gender Preference in Children; Hinduism; Islam; *and* Midwifery.]

BIBLIOGRAPHY

Alan Guttmacher Institute. *Sharing Responsibility: Women, Society, and Abortion Worldwide.* New York: Alan Guttmacher Institute, 1999.

Asman, Oren. "Abortion in Islamic Countries: Legal and Religious Aspects." *Medicine and Law* 23 (2004): 73–89.

Baldwin, Katherine. "Britain Defies U.S. with World Abortion Funding." *Reuters*, 6 February 2006.

Devereux, George. "A Typological Study of Abortion in 350 Primitive, Ancient, and Pre-Industrial Societies." In *Therapeutic Abortion*, edited by Harold Rosen. New York: Julian Press, 1954.

Dugger, Celia W. "Modern Asia's Anomaly: Girls Who Don't Get Born." *New York Times*, 6 May 2001.

French, Howard. "On Africa's Back Streets, Abortions Take Heavy Toll." *New York Times*, 3 June 1998.

Johnston, Heidi Bart, and Kenneth H. Hill. "Induced Abortion in the Developing World: Indirect Estimates." *International Family Planning Perspectives* 22 (1996): 108–114.

Kligman, Gail. *The Politics of Duplicity: Controlling Reproduction in Ceauşescu's Romania.* Berkeley: University of California Press, 1998.

Myers, Steven Lee. "After Decades, Russia Narrows Grounds for Abortions." *New York Times*, 24 August 2003.

Nguyen, Katie. "Kenyan Women Take Risks with Backstreet Abortions." *Reuters*, 27 April 2005.

Petcheskey, Rosalind Pollack. *Global Prescriptions: Gendering Health and Human Rights.* London and New York: Zed Books; Geneva, Switzerland: U.N. Research Institute for Social Development, 2003.

Population Council. *Unwanted Pregnancy and Post-Abortion Complications: Pakistan.* Islamabad, Pakistan: Population Council, 2004.

Riddle, John M. *Eve's Herbs: A History of Contraception and Abortion in the West.* Cambridge, Mass.: Harvard University Press, 1997.

Sen, Amartya. "Missing Women—Revisited." *British Medical Journal* 327 (2003), 1297–1298.

Singh, Susheela, Elena Prada, Florence Mirembe, and Charles Kiggundu. "The Incidence of Induced Abortion in Uganda." *International Family Planning Perspectives* 31 (2005): 183–191.

United Nations Fund for Population Activities. *State of World Population 2005.* New York: UNFPA, 2005.

Van de Walle, Etienne. "Towards a Demographic History of Abortion." *Population: An English Selection* 11 (1999): 115–131.

Xinhua News Agency. "Population-Control Abuses in Shandong Confirmed." 20 September 2005.

AMY KALER

Politics

The World Health Organization (WHO) reports that every year about 25 percent of pregnancies worldwide—approximately 46 million—are terminated in induced abortion. Of these, at least 19 million occur under dangerous circumstances, when women turn to untrained providers often working in unhygienic conditions. As a result, an estimated seventy-eight thousand women die every year from unsafe abortion. An additional 5 million women experience serious complications, for which many do not receive proper treatment, leading to permanent injury. However, women do not suffer equally around the world. There is wide regional variation in mortality and morbidity rates from unsafe abortion. Ninety-five percent of women who die from abortion live in poor countries; a woman in Africa, for example, is at least seven hundred times more likely to die from an abortion than is a woman in the West. Indeed, disparities in reproductive health status, including rates of death and injury from dangerous abortion, constitute one of the greatest differences between women in rich and poor countries.

Since the 1960s women's health activists from all parts of the world have worked to make abortion safer, and they have won significant gains, though women continue to face tremendous obstacles. After World War II and until the end of the Cold War, women's need for safe, accessible abortion services was rarely discussed at the global level by members of international institutions such as the United Nations, WHO, and major donor agencies such as USAID funding "development" projects in the global South (or Third World). Instead, these agencies focused their attention and funds on population control and family planning programs in the colonized and other parts of the non-Western world.

Beginning in the 1960s reproductive rights activists in the West, gaining renewed strength from the resurgent women's movements in their respective countries, fought and won campaigns to liberalize national laws prohibiting abortion. Though these were important victories for women in the West, millions of women in Asia, Africa, the Middle East, and Latin America continued to terminate unwanted pregnancies under unsafe, often humiliating conditions. In the 1970s reproductive health activists began working together across regional divides to redress the global gap. By the late 1970s there was an international campaign for abortion rights that comprised members mainly from Europe and also representatives of groups working for safe abortion from North America and Latin America. The absence of abortion advocates from Africa and Asia reflected the intensely taboo nature of abortion in those regions: activists felt unable to associate themselves with the campaign.

After the Cold War ended in 1989, women's health advocates moved quickly to take advantage of the new, optimistic global climate in the early 1990s that made it possible to redirect military expenditure into social development. They promoted reproductive rights, including the right to safe abortion, through a series of international meetings convened by the United Nations to further social development at the global level, such as the 1993 World Conference on Human Rights in Vienna, the 1994 International Conference on Population and Development in Cairo, and the 1995 Fourth World Conference on

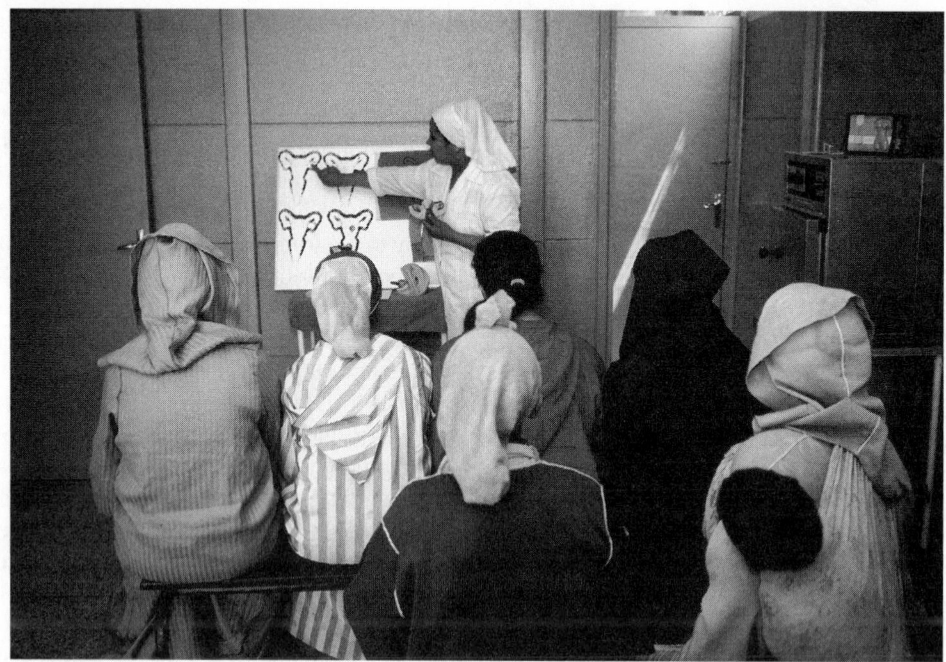

Family Planning. Women learn about the reproductive system at a UNICEF-assisted clinic, Settat, Morocco, July 1987. U.N. PHOTO/JOHN ISAAC

Women in Beijing. At these events they began liberalizing attitudes and government policy on abortion.

The Turning Point. The 1994 International Conference on Population and Development (ICPD) produced the first major international agreement recommending improved access to safe abortion. The conference's Programme of Action noted in paragraph 8.25 the public health impact of unsafe abortion, stated the need to reduce recourse to abortion by expanding family planning services, and recognized that women with unwanted pregnancies should be able to access reliable information, compassionate care, and safe abortions where the procedure is not against the law. Elsewhere in the document governments also agreed to support comprehensive reproductive health services, including the choice to regulate fertility, again with the proviso that access would be made available for services that "are not against the law."

The Programme of Action was a major step forward at the international level in overcoming the stigma of abortion and legitimizing the practice as a fundamental component of reproductive health care. However, it was not a full-fledged victory for women's health advocates because they were unable to persuade governments to recognize women's right to abortion. Their inability to do so was a result of the intensely controversial nature of the issue at the ICPD. In fact, endorsing safe abortion was one of the most difficult issues negotiated at the conference, given the strong opposition of religious and ideological conservatives—for instance, the Catholic Church and the governments of some Muslim nations.

These conservatives, benefiting from the general lack of political will to promote women's rights, health, and well-being, forced reproductive health activists to make a political compromise on abortion that left the Programme of Action with internal contradictions. While on the one hand the program recognized the dangers of unsafe abortion, on the other hand it stated that "in no case should abortion be promoted as a method of family planning." The latter statement belies the reality that every woman's decision to seek an abortion is integrally related to her desire to plan whether and when to have children.

In turn, the weakness of the Programme of Action has prevented it from providing governments with a clear directive for action. Today, even in countries where abortion is legal, many women still face many medical, political, and social barriers to obtaining the procedure safely. Nevertheless, by succeeding in having abortion recognized as a major public health threat, the ICPD was a turning point in the campaign for women's reproductive rights.

Post-1994 Global Policy and Advocacy. Since the ICPD, women's health activists have continued working through international conferences and institutions to end unsafe abortion around the world. In 1995 the Fourth World Conference on Women at Beijing produced a Platform for

Action, of which paragraph 106 reaffirmed the ICPD Programme of Action and called upon governments to consider reviewing restrictive laws that seek to punish women who obtain illegal abortions.

In 1999 the U.N. General Assembly held a Special Session to evaluate progress of the Programme of Action during which governments made further recommendations to make abortion safe and more accessible. For example, the Special Session agreed that "In circumstances where abortion is not against the law . . . health systems should train and equip health service providers."

In 2003 the WHO developed guidelines for the implementation of this recommendation, and in the following year it reaffirmed the call for safe abortion services in the Strategy to Accelerate Progress towards the Attainment of International Development Goals and Targets Related to Reproductive Health, which was passed by the World Health Assembly in May 2004 by a large majority. In addition, the U.N. Human Rights Committee and the Convention on the Elimination of All Forms of Discrimination against Women, among other U.N. committees, began in the 1990s to apply human rights law to reproductive rights, including abortion, which has resulted in calls on governments of states such as Chile, for example, to liberalize its draconian abortion legislation and in calls on others, such as Poland, to provide access where the law permits it.

In addition, women's health advocates have worked assiduously alongside health policymakers, health-care providers, social justice activists, and human rights advocates in regional networks to promote sexual and reproductive rights to raise public awareness within their countries and regions of the prevalence and cost (human and financial) of unsafe abortion, and also to press their governments to provide safe, accessible, legal abortion services. For example, in 2003 the African Partnership for the Sexual and Reproductive Health and Rights of Women and Girls co-convened the first regional conference on unsafe abortion in Africa. Held in Addis Ababa, Ethiopia, the conference was attended by more than one hundred medical providers, policy makers, public officials, women's health activists, and youth advocates who together called upon African governments to improve access to abortion services.

Similar regional networks have emerged in the Asia-Pacific region, central and eastern Europe, and Latin America. Together these and other groups operate through national and international institutions and conferences to strengthen and implement international agreements to address dangerous abortion. Currently, efforts to improve access to legal abortion services and reform restrictive laws are under way in at least nine countries, from Brazil to Thailand, and have already been achieved in at least another fourteen: Albania, Benin, Burkina Faso, Cambodia, Chad, Ethiopia, Germany, Guinea, Guyana, Mali, Nepal, Portugal, South Africa, and Switzerland.

These important developments have led most women's health advocates to conclude that there is a growing consensus among governments and public health policy makers that the goals of the ICPD require meaningful support. Though feminists lament that they have yet to have abortion legally recognized internationally as a woman's right, many agree that the strategy adopted at Cairo and pursued subsequently—framing abortion as a public health issue—has been effective in forging WHO policy and technical guidance and in various intergovernment negotiations where asserting a woman's right to abortion would doubtless have failed. Feminists continue attempting to link abortion to women's rights in national as well as international policy arenas.

Post-1994 Opposition to International Efforts. The growing international consensus among health policy makers and health-care providers that abortion should be made safe and accessible has emerged in spite of consistent attack by conservative religious, political, and economic forces. Indeed, since the success of the ICPD in enshrining in its Programme of Action the goal of making "reproductive health accessible through the primary health-care system to all individuals of appropriate age as soon as possible and no later than 2015," there has been an ongoing battle over reproductive health at the United Nations led by the Vatican, a small number of fundamentalist Muslim governments, American right-wing religious groups, and, more recently, the American government itself. These groups and governments have joined forces at the international level to block the implementation of the ICPD goal of reproductive health, including accessible safe abortion, for women around the world.

The Catholic Church's opposition to abortion has become almost absolute since 1930 with the publication of *Casti Conubii*, and the church has been especially active in undermining the gains made at the ICPD and subsequently. The Holy See has consistently opposed abortion at the international level and has brought pressure to bear on health-care providers and policy makers in Catholic countries, especially in Latin America, to withdraw support for safe abortion. In 1997, for example, El Salvador struck down the only legal grounds for abortion, to save a woman's life. The many other examples of the Vatican's intervention include the current efforts of the Slovakian government to negotiate a treaty with the Vatican on the unlimited right of health-care providers to conscientious objection on abortion, as well as on contraceptive prescription and the provision of sex education.

Joining forces with the Holy See to block international endorsements of safe abortion at the ICPD were a few conservative Muslim governments, most notably Iran,

Libya, and Sudan. Islamic fundamentalist governments entered into a marriage of convenience with the Vatican, not so much to oppose abortion per se but to prevent the weakening of patriarchal power that appeared likely to occur with the implementation of aspects of the conference's Programme of Action, such as, for example, the goal of providing advice or reproductive health care directly to wives or unmarried children rather than through a male authority figure. Indeed, most Muslim governments have refrained from antiabortion agitation, in large part because Islam, unlike the Catholic Church, does not have a single, hard-line policy on abortion; different Islamic legal schools have varying positions on the morality of abortion.

The U.S. government during the presidency of George W. Bush was also extremely proactive in attempting to undermine the ICPD's principles and recommendations concerning abortion, to the extent of taking on the role of international leader of the antiabortion movement. In 2001 the U.S. government, which had been a leader at the ICPD, reversed its support for the Programme of Action by implementing the Mexico City Policy, commonly called the Global Gag Rule. The Global Gag Rule, which is a reinstatement of Ronald Reagan's original Gag Rule of 1984 that was rescinded by the Clinton administration in 1993, restricts non-governmental organizations (NGOs) in developing countries from engaging in most abortion-related activities, regardless of the source of funds used in such activities. Specifically, NGOs outside the United States are not eligible for family planning assistance through USAID or the U.S. State Department if they use funds to perform abortions in cases other than rape, incest, or a threat to the life of the woman; provide counseling and referral for abortion; or lobby to make abortion legal or more available in their country.

Reinstatement of the Global Gag Rule led almost immediately to withdrawal of funds from the International Planned Parenthood Federation and a number of its member associations, as well as from the affiliates of Marie Stopes International, because they refused to abide by the new criteria for obtaining financial support from the U.S. government. The Global Gag Rule works in tandem with the Helms Amendment to the U.S. Foreign Assistance Act, adopted in 1973, which prevents any direct use of USAID funds for abortion-related activities by both governments and NGOs.

In 2002 the U.S. State Department announced its decision to suspend $34 million in funding to the U.N. Population Fund, which it claimed (without evidence) was supporting abortions in China. It is difficult to assess the effect of U.S. antiabortion measures on women's health in the developing world because in each country the impact is determined by national politics of reproductive health, the size of the role played by NGOs in providing abortions, and the presence of other donors to assist reproductive health programs.

The Struggle Continues. Though policy developments at the international level are very encouraging, real improvement for millions of women around the world in the form of safe abortion on demand can be realized only at the national level. And on this point the poorest countries are still lagging behind. In Africa, for example, almost all countries on the continent apart from South Africa still have restrictive abortion laws. Notably, in Africa (as well as elsewhere in the formerly colonized world) laws prohibiting abortion were originally put into place by European colonial powers in the nineteenth and early twentieth centuries. Though Africans and other non-Western citizens have rid themselves of imperialism in recent decades, millions of women remain colonized by these inherited laws. Thus much work remains to be done at the national level within many countries to decriminalize abortion and to press governments to make it accessible where it is legal.

Moreover, the opposition of the U.S. government and the Holy See appear to be unflagging as they continue to work together to undermine reproductive health efforts at the international level. In 2001, for example, they succeeded in having the goal of reproductive health, established at the ICPD, removed from the Millennium Development Goals during a closed session at the United Nations. Meanwhile, women's health advocates continue to create new ways to work across national boundaries to press for the provision of safe abortions. An example is Women on Waves, a Dutch nonprofit organization whose mission is to prevent unsafe abortions by, among other activities, working with women living in countries where abortion is illegal to organize the provision of medical abortions on board ships sailing in international waters.

[*See also* Contraception; Religion, *subentry* Contemporary Issues; *Roe v. Wade*; United Nations; *and* World Health Organization.]

BIBLIOGRAPHY

Basu, Alaka Malwade, ed. *The Sociocultural and Political Aspects of Abortion: Global Perspectives*. Westport, Conn.: Praeger, 2003. A collection of articles by experts on the cultural, demographic, and sociopolitical aspects of abortion from a global perspective.

Cook, Rebecca J., Bernard M. Dickens, and Mahmoud F. Fathalla. *Reproductive Health and Human Rights: Integrating Medicine, Ethics, and Law*. Oxford: Clarendon Press, 2003. This book is written by three of the leading experts on international reproductive health policy using a rights-based approach. It discusses the ethical, legal, and human rights dimensions of reproductive and sexual health from a global perspective. It also includes the texts and summaries of key international documents and guidelines, up-to-date reproductive health statistics, and countries' human rights treaty commitments.

Hartmann, Betsy. *Reproductive Rights and Wrongs: The Global Politics of Population Control*. Rev. ed. Boston: South End

Press, 1995. This classic is the standard text that traces the politics of population control post-1945 and analyzes the issue of global fertility control (including abortion) from a feminist, antiracist perspective.

Hessini, Leila. "Global Progress in Abortion Advocacy and Policy: An Assessment of the Decade since ICPD." *Reproductive Health Matters* 13 (2005): 88–100. This periodical is an excellent source of up-to-date information on efforts to improve access to safe abortion in all regions of the world, as well as on international advocacy efforts of reproductive health activists.

Kulczycki, Andrzej. *The Abortion Debate in the World Arena.* New York: Routledge, 1999. Examines the intersecting political, medical, health, and religious forces and institutions involved in abortion debates in Kenya, Poland, and Mexico and extrapolates insights from these three case studies to the international level.

SUSANNE M. KLAUSEN

ABRAHAMS, LIZ (b. 1925), South African activist and union organizer. Elizabeth Adrian Abrahams, known familiarly as Liz or Nana, devoted her life to fighting racism, economic exploitation, and apartheid on behalf of workers in South Africa. She was born in Paarl in the Western Cape. Her mother worked in a fruit-processing factory, and her father made bricks and worked in the wood industry until poor health left him unable to work. He died when Abrahams was very young. Her education ended before high school when she went to work with her mother in the fruit factory to help support her eight siblings. Her experiences in the factory, with its appalling work conditions, awakened her social consciousness. The hours were long and the pay low. Bosses often denied workers breaks, and there were no restrooms. Maternity leave was not an option; pregnant women were fired.

Determined to change these conditions, Abrahams became active in factory labor politics and was elected into the Food and Canning Workers' Union alongside leaders Ray Alexander and Oscar Mpetha. She served the union in many capacities, including as a member of the floor committee, a branch executive, treasurer, and general secretary. She organized union branches throughout both the Western Cape and the Eastern Cape and negotiated with employers for workers' rights. Her fight for social justice took its toll on her marriage; her husband felt neglected and often locked Liz out of the house when she came home late from union meetings. Her troubles grew worse when the 1955 Suppression of Communism Act was passed and Abrahams, who participated in the concealment of fugitives from the government, was banned from associating with union leaders and organizing further union activities. She was eventually detained without trial by the apartheid government.

After her release, Abrahams continued to carry on her work underground until the five-year ban was lifted and she openly resumed her work with the union. Soon afterward, she was involved with a series of campaigns intended to bolster progressive trade unionism. She commented: "In particular, Coloured workers in the Western Cape showed they were no longer prepared to put up with the injustices and insults which they are forced to suffer as third grade citizens" (cited from Luckhardt and Wall, p. 243). A year later she left her job at the fruit factory following a car accident in which she broke her leg and some ribs. Although she could no longer work with the union at the ground level, she used her experience to consult with other organizations, such as the Congress of South African Students and the African National Congress Women's League (ANCWL) on matters of racism, gender discrimination, and union organizing. She later became the chairperson of the Paarl branch of the ANCWL and was elected to Parliament, where she was able to continue the movement from within the government. Even after she retired from Parliament in 1999, Abrahams remained a dominant presence in the South African labor movement.

[*See also* Southern Africa, *subentry* Twentieth Century.]

BIBLIOGRAPHY

Abrahams, "Nana" Liz. In *Married to the Struggle.* Edited by Yusuf Patel and Philip Hirschsohn. Cape Town: Diane Ferrus Press and University of the Western Cape, 2005.

Berger, Iris. *Threads of Solidarity: Women in South African Industry, 1900–1980.* Bloomington: Indiana University Press, 1992.

Luckhart, Ken, and Brenda Wall. *Organize or Starve!: The History of the South African Congress of Trade Unions.* London: Lawrence and Wishart, 1980.

MacLean, Barbara Hutmacher. *Strike a Woman, Strike a Rock: Fighting for Freedom in South Africa.* Trenton, N.J.: Africa World Press, 2004.

DENISE BATES

ACKROYD, ANNETTE (1842–1929), British educator in India. Ackroyd became a significant figure in feminist historiography during the early 1990s, when she was the subject of several books proposing a radical reexamination of British women's lives in colonial India, and in particular the role of Western feminists in the Indian nationalist movement. An understanding of the complex mix of progressive, feminist views with more conventional white supremacist ideology offers a valuable sense of the contradictions that helped shape Victorian feminism at the heart of the empire and in the colonies.

Ackroyd first went to India as a teacher in response to a call from the social reform organization Brahmo-Somaj. However, her zeal for educating young women in order that they could resist colonial rule was short-lived. Just a few years later, her controversial stance on the Ilbert Bill (1884), a measure that gave native-born Indian judges jurisdiction over Europeans in certain types of courts, marked her as a women's rights activist whose resentment of Indian men for their dominant role in patriarchal society outweighed her critique of British colonial rule.

Ackroyd was born in Stourbridge, England, into a Nonconformist family headed by her Unitarian father, William, who believed that access to education was a pressing social issue. He encouraged his daughters to take their schooling seriously. Ackroyd's studies at Bedford College were followed by a brief period of social reform work in her hometown. She helped found a working-women's college in London, where she moved after her father's death in 1869 and where she encountered the Brahmo-Somaj, whose work had long been supported by the Unitarians. She heard the message that Indian women were clamoring for her kind of educational skills, and her enthusiasm was also kindled at many public meetings where she encountered other progressive Indians passing through London as they campaigned for reform in the colony.

Ackroyd arrived in Calcutta (now called Kolkata) in 1873 and spent several months trying to establish her school for young girls. The experience was to prove a complete failure. Ackroyd was alienated from British colonial society but unable to form lasting relationships with Indian women. She expressed horror at the state of gender relations among Indian couples, and her diaries indicate that she was not able to communicate with her pupils, a factor she also blamed on the behavior of Indian men. The school lasted until 1875, when she left to marry a British colonial administrator, Henry Beveridge.

Ackroyd's husband was a liberal who had expressed support for her project, but following the marriage she became a more conventional wife and mother. She maintained her view that Indian women were more oppressed by their own patriarchal social system than by British colonialism and urged them to rise up against their "enslavement" from their menfolk. Her copious diaries have been an invaluable resource for feminist historians interested in the gender dynamics of British colonialism, as well as the history of British feminism.

[*See also* Imperialism and Colonialism; India; *and* Nationalism.]

BIBLIOGRAPHY

Chaudhuri, Nupur, and Margaret Strobel, eds. *Western Women and Imperialism: Complicity and Resistance.* Bloomington: Indiana University Press, 1992.

Jayawardena, Kumari. *The White Woman's Other Burden: Western Women and South Asia during British Rule.* New York and London: Routledge, 1995.

Ware, Vron. *Beyond the Pale: White Women, Racism and History.* London and New York: Verso, 1992.

VRON WARE

ACOSTA DE SAMPER, SOLEDAD (1833–1913), the most important Colombian writer of the nineteenth century and a notable advocate for the education of women. She was born in Bogotá, the daughter of Joaquín Acosta, a military general and a historian, and Carolina Kemble Rou, an American citizen. Being born into a privileged milieu, the young Soledad Acosta received an extraordinary education compared to other Colombian girls of her era. At the age of twelve, after attending primary school in Bogotá, she moved to Halifax, Nova Scotia, with her family, and then to Paris. After several years of traveling and studying in France, she returned to Bogotá and in 1855 married the politician and writer José María Samper Agudelo. The couple lived in Europe from 1857 to 1862; then moved for a time to Lima, Peru, where they founded the magazine *Revista Americana* (American Magazine); then returned to Bogotá, where Acosta de Samper began her own prolific literary career. Among her writings are thirty-five novels, fifty short stories, and several biographies and essays. Her work deals with local themes, advice for women, and historical events. She also founded five journals, translated books and novels, and wrote widely for newspapers and journals under different pseudonyms, including "Aldebarán," "Andina," "Bertilda," "Olga," and "Renato."

In her most influential books, Acosta de Samper rejected the model of female passivity that prevailed in the society of her time. Nevertheless, she did not envision a path of autonomy for women and did not question her culture's ideal of a submissive woman who would obey her parents, serve her husband, and follow the teachings of the Catholic Church; she believed that only through piety could women tolerate suffering. In *La mujer en la sociedad moderna* (The Woman in Modern Society, 1895), she promoted positive female models meant to open new horizons beyond marriage but without embracing ideas of female "liberation."

Her commitment to women's education is best appreciated in her writing, *La Mujer* (The Woman, 1878–1881), a biweekly journal she founded that was targeted at women. After 1880, Acosta de Samper's literary work focused mainly on historical events and biographies, a genre not often cultivated by women. Among her works are *Biografía del General Joaquín Paris* (Biography of General Joaquin Paris), which received a literary prize in 1883, the year it appeared; *Biografías de hombres ilustres o notables* (Biographies of Notable Men, 1883); *Lecciones de historia de Colombia* (Colombian History Lectures, 1908); and *Catecismo de historia patria* (Catechism of Colombia, 1908).

In 1884 she founded a monthly magazine called *La Familia* (The Family). The weekly *El domingo de la familia cristiana* (Sunday of the Christian Family, founded in 1888) was her last literary enterprise in Colombia. After her husband's death, she moved (in 1889) to Paris. In France she continued writing about issues pertaining to women and family in a quasi-pedagogical manner, producing *Consejos a las mujeres* (Advice for Women, 1896) and *Conversaciones y lecturas familiares* (Family Conversations and Readings, 1896). Her last journalistic effort was *El domingo* (Sunday, 1889), a weekly magazine committed mainly to historical, scientific, and literary issues.

[*See also* Salavarrieta, Policarpa.]

BIBLIOGRAPHY

Acosta de Samper, Soledad. *Diario intimo y otros escritos de Soledad Acosta de Samper*. Edited by Carolina Alzate. Bogotá: Alcaldía Mayor de Bogotá, D.C., Instituto Destrital Cultura y Turismo, 2004.

Pratt, Mary Louise. "Soledad Acosta de Samper: Colombia, 1833–1913." In *Rereading the Spanish American Essay: Translation of 19th and 20th Century Women's Essays*, edited by Doris Meyer, pp. 67–69. Austin: University of Texas Press, 1995. Acosta de Samper's essay "The Mission of the Woman Writer in Spanish America" follows this biographical introduction.

Samper Trainer, Santiago. "Soledad Acosta de Samper. El eco de un grito." In *Las mujeres en la historia de Colombia*, edited by Magdala Velásquez. Vol. 1. Bogota: Presidencia de la República and Norma, 1995.

GUIOMAR DUEÑAS-VARGAS

ʿADAWIYYAH, RABIʿAH AL- (c. 714–801), one of the three great Sufi woman saints of Basra, Iraq, along with the female ascetics Muʾadhah al-ʿAdawiyyah (d. 702) and Umm al-Dardaʾ (d. 699). She lived and died in her native city of Basra. Little objective information is known about Rabiʿah. Information provided by the writers al-Jahiz (d. 868) and Ibn Abi Tahir Tayfur (d. 893) indicates that she was a member of Banu ʿAdi ibn Qays, one of the most important Arab clans of Basra. Later authors, starting with the Sufi writer Sulami (d. 1021), portray Rabiʿah as a client of ʿAdi ibn Qays, which adopted her and allowed her to use its name. In early Islam, a convert to Islam had to be adopted by a member of an Arab tribe, who served as the convert's patron. This is unlikely in Rabiʿah's case because Jahiz, the earliest writer to report about her, states that the leaders of her clan offered to buy her a slave. Ibn Abi Tahir Tayfur, who claims that the governor of Basra wanted to give her a house, called her Rabiʿah al-Musmiʿiyyah (Rabiʿah who must be heard).

Rabiʿah was a noted ascetic and teacher. Her most famous student was the jurist Sufyan al-Thawri (d. 778). Sufyan relied on Rabiʿah for personal guidance and practical wisdom. Rabiʿah followed a Basra tradition of women's asceticism that was started by Muʾadhah al-ʿAdawiyyah. This tradition stressed detachment from the world, absorption in the love of God, and inward and outward sincerity. Some of Rabiʿah's statements have ambiguous meanings. When asked whether she loved the prophet Muhammad, she replied, "Truly I love him. But love for the Creator has turned me away from love for created things." This may mean that nothing came between Rabiah and her love for God. Yet it may also mean that the words of God in the Qurʾan are more important than the words of the prophet Muhammad.

There are as many versions of Rabiʿah's legendary persona as there are accounts attributed to her. These accounts appear in the most influential collections of Sufi biography. ʿAttar (d. 1220) portrayed her as a second Mary. Sarraj (d. 988) highlighted her Sufi knowledge. Makki (d. 996) credited her with introducing the concept of love into Islamic asceticism. Hanbali scholars such as Ibn al-Jawzi (d. 1201) appreciated her for her asceticism and otherworldliness. Sulami portrayed her as the quintessential Sufi woman and female saint. Some biographers portrayed Rabiʿah as an antisocial recluse whose behavior bordered on hysteria. Others portrayed her as a perceptive critic of the world and of human weaknesses.

Accounts about Rabiʿah often confuse her with other Sufi women. Some of the statements attributed to her on love-of-God mysticism may actually have come from her student, Maryam of Basra. Rabiʿah is often confused with the Sufi woman poet Rabiʿah bint Ismaʿil, who lived in Damascus, Syria, and died about fifty years after her. Rabiʿah bint Ismail's tomb in Jerusalem is still thought to be that of Rabiʿah al-ʿAdawiyyah, and many of the Syrian woman's poems have been attributed to her Basra predecessor.

[*See also* Islam.]

BIBLIOGRAPHY

"Rabiʿah al-ʿAdawiyya." In *Arabic Literary Culture, 500–925*, edited by Michael Cooperson and Shawkat M. Toorawa. Detroit, Mich.: Thomson Gale, 2005.

Smith, Margaret. *Rābiʿa the Mystic and Her Fellow-Saints in Islām, Being the Life and Teachings of Rābiʿa al-ʿAdawiyya al-Qaysiyya of Basra Together with Some Account of the Place of the Women Saints in Islām*. Cambridge, U.K.: Cambridge University Press, 1928.

RKIA EL AROUI CORNELL

ADDAMS, JANE (1860–1935), a founder of the settlement house movement in the United States and the Nobel Peace Prize recipient in 1931. Addams was born on 6 September 1860 in Cedarville, Illinois, to a well-to-do miller family, the eighth of nine children. In 1877 she entered Rockford Female Seminary, and she received a collegiate certificate in 1881. She was granted a bachelor of arts degree in 1882 when the institution became Rockford College.

Addams met Ellen Gates Starr at Rockford Seminary and began a lifelong friendship. They later cofounded one of the first settlement houses in the United States. While traveling in Europe, Addams visited Toynbee Hall in London's East Side and was inspired to organize a settlement house in the United States that would serve poor communities and advance social reform activities. In 1889, Addams and Starr founded Hull House in Chicago in the Charles Hull mansion, built in 1856. The project included educational facilities, a public kitchen, a library, and one of the first night schools for adults. By 1890, Hull House regularly fed more than two thousand people every week.

Addams held administrative and leadership roles in several organizations and committees. In Chicago she was a founding member of the Chicago Federation of Settlements (1894), a garbage inspector of the Nineteenth Ward (1895), a member of the Board of Education (1905–1908), a founding member of the Chicago School of Civics and Philanthropy (1908), president of the National Conference of Charities and Corrections, later named the National Conference of Social Work (1909), and the first vice president of the National American Woman Suffrage Association (1911–1914). She was the first president of the Women's International League for Peace and Freedom, founded in 1915. That same year she chaired the Women's Peace Party and spoke out against U.S. participation in World War I.

Addams's work in social reform included witnessing and participating in several strikes and protests. She was a mediator in the Chicago garment workers' strike in 1910. She was also a formative figure in combating racist attitudes and practices as well as economic injustices. She participated in the founding of the National Association for the Advancement of Colored People in 1909 and in the founding of the American Civil Liberties Union in 1920. In 1931 she became the first woman to receive the Nobel Peace Prize.

Addams published several books and pamphlets, including *Democracy and Social Ethics* (1902), *Newer Ideals of Peace* (1907), *The Social Application of Religion*, with Charles Stelzle, Charles Patrick Neill, Graham Taylor, and G. P. Eckman (1908), *Twenty Years at Hull House* (1910), *Symposium: Child Labor on the Stage*, with Henry Baird Favill and Jean M. Gordon (1911), *The Long Road of Woman's Memory* (1916), *Peace and Bread in Time of War* (1922), and *The Excellent Becomes the Permanent* (1932).

The Jane Addams Peace Association was founded in 1945 as an educational affiliate of the Women's International League for Peace and Freedom. It sponsors the Jane Addams Children's Book Award each year, given to a book that promotes the ideals of peace, freedom, and equality. Addams died in Chicago on 21 May 1935 and was buried in Cedarville, Illinois.

[*See also* International League for Peace and Freedom *and* Settlement House Movement.]

BIBLIOGRAPHY

Berson, Robin K. *Jane Addams: A Biography*. Westport, Conn.: Greenwood Press, 2004. From the Greenwood Biographies series and intended for high school and college students.

Knight, Louise W. *Citizen: Jane Addams and the Struggle for Democracy*. Chicago: University of Chicago Press, 2005. Focuses mostly on the first half of Addams's life and the formation of her character.

TRISHA M. FAMISARAN

ADIVAR, HALIDE EDIB (1882–1964), a Turkish novelist, journalist, translator, social and political activist, and prominent feminist of the Second Constitutional and Republican periods. Immediately following the Young Turk revolution of 1908, Adivar became a columnist, writing prolifically on issues related to women's education, polygamy, motherhood, and Turkish nationalism. Her outspoken stance against polygamy was paralleled in her personal rebellion to refuse the second wife that her first husband, Salih Zeki, wanted her to accept, and to divorce Salih Zeki. In the Second Constitutional period she founded women's organizations that promoted women's education. Into the 1910s, Adivar propagated Turanism through her journalistic articles and her famous novel *Yeni Turan* (New Turan, 1913), envisioning a democratic Turkey in which women enjoyed political suffrage and wider employment opportunities.

Even though Adivar supported the Unionists because of their progressive stance toward women's emancipation, she was highly critical of their military strategies during World War I, particularly of the Armenian deportations in 1915–1916. Because of her outspoken criticism against the deportations, Adivar was sent into exile in Syria in 1916. In this period Adivar worked at and attempted to reform the curriculum of Dar al muʾallimat (Women's Teachers' Training College) in Jerusalem, a school that gave teaching credentials to women.

Returning to Istanbul in 1918, Adivar became an influential public speaker to a war-stricken nation. In 1920 she joined the nationalist army fighting against the Greeks in Anatolia. During the struggle for nationhood (the Greco-Turkish War, 1919–1922) Adivar served as journalist, translator, novelist, and nurse, being promoted to sergeant major in the nationalist army. *Ateşten Gömlek* (The Shirt of Flame, 1922), which depicts the struggles of the national army against the Greeks, was one of her most popular national romances and has been translated into six languages.

Adivar actively supported the Turkish women's suffrage movement and motivated Nezihe Muhittin, the leader of the movement, to establish the first political party in the Turkish Republic, the Republican Women's Party (1923). The party was closed and suffrage was not granted to women in the 1920s. Adivar's frustration with the newly founded republic and her irreconcilable split with Mustafa Kemal and his single-party regime led her to live in self-imposed exile in Paris and London between 1925 and 1939. Her first publication in English was her two-volume autobiography, *Memoirs of Halidé Edib* (1926) and *The Turkish Ordeal* (1928), which delineated her contribution to the different phases of the Turkish struggle for independence, ending with the military victory in 1922.

The first woman lecturer to be invited to the Williamstown Political Institute's roundtable conference (1928), Adivar delivered a series of lectures on the history of the Ottoman Empire and Turkey, which were published as *Turkey Faces West* in 1930. Her comparative analysis of the progress of nationalism and secularization—and of the role of women in these processes—in Turkey and India in *Inside India* (1937) was considered an eloquent statement on India in the 1930s.

Recipient of the Republican People's Party novel award in 1942, her novel *The Clown and His Daughter* (1935), which she translated into Turkish as *Sinekli Bakkal* (The Fly-Plagued Grocer), was a critique of the rapid-secularization policies of the Kemal regime and an exploration of the possibilities of women being emancipated within Islam. Her absurdist play *Maske ve Ruh* (Masks or Souls? 1938) was a bitter satire on dictatorships and totalitarian regimes, particularly the Kemal regime.

After returning to Istanbul in 1939, Adivar, working as professor of English literature at Istanbul University, published numerous academic works on the history of English literature. In 1950 she became an independent member of parliament, but she decided to leave politics altogether upon completing her four-year term, being disillusioned with the prevailing political parties and with politics in general. Adivar's critical stance against polygamy, her public activities and writings on the importance of women's education and the need to provide women with wider professional opportunities, and her public support of emancipation have been influential in the tribute paid to her as the most famous "Turkish feminist" in Turkey, the Middle East, and India.

[*See also* Turkey.]

BIBLIOGRAPHY

Adak, Hülya. "An Epic for Peace." Introduction to the *Memoirs of Halidé Edib*, by Halide Edib Adivar, pp. v–xxv. Piscataway, N.J.: Gorgias Press, 2004.

Adak, Hülya. "National Myths and Self-Na(rra)tions: Mustafa Kemal's Nutuk and Halide Edib's Memoirs and the Turkish Ordeal." *South Atlantic Quarterly* 102 (2003): 509–527.

Adivar, Halide Edib. *Inside India*. London: G. Allen and Unwin, 1937.

Adivar, Halide Edib. *Memoirs of Halidé Edib*. New York: Century, 1926.

Adivar, Halide Edib. *Turkish Ordeal: Being the Further Memoirs of Halidé Edib*. New York: Century, 1928.

HÜLYA ADAK

ADNAN, ETEL (b. 1925), a Lebanese-American educator, novelist, poet, and visual artist. She was born in Beirut to a Muslim Syrian father and a Christian Greek mother. Adnan worked for the French Information Bureau when she was sixteen. She attended the École Supérieure des Lettres and taught at the Ahliya School for Girls and then studied philosophy at the Sorbonne in Paris, the University of California at Berkeley, and Harvard University. She taught philosophy of art at the Dominican College of San Rafael, California, and has presented courses, classes, and lectures at over forty universities and colleges throughout the United States. She retired from a permanent teaching position in the late 1970s to devote herself to her art and writing.

Adnan creates oils, ceramics, and tapestry, and has had a number of solo exhibitions in the United States, Europe, and Lebanon. She has also written more than ten books of poetry and fiction, including *Sitt Marie Rose* (1978), her first novel, which has been translated into six languages. *Sitt Marie Rose* was written during the siege of the Palestinian camp of Tel al-Zaatar in the summer of 1976. Her most important message is one of love and peace. This message best speaks to the chaos and destruction brought by war. Adnan denounces the love of clan, which is the kind of love practiced by Arabs. For her, real love is not tribal, jealous, possessive, or exclusive, but rather reaches out to others. Love even goes so far as Sitt Marie Rose's loving her executioners and forgiving them: "I want to make my peace with everyone. Even with my captors, I want to make my peace. I can no longer sustain this hatred. It's what brought us to this apocalypse" (p. 86).

The ability to transform reality into metaphor is a key aspect of Adnan's creative genius. Yet her immense talent and lyrical fluency do not cease with poetry and fiction. Adnan has also crafted masterful essays. In "To Write in a Foreign Language" (1996), she discusses the history of her personal involvement with various languages and how these have affected her own poetry and prose. Adnan writes about her past resentment of expressing herself in French because of associations with political conflict and apartheid. She explains how important language is in every art form, whether it be writing or painting, but ultimately views painting as more neutral. A true cosmopolitan, Adnan divides her time between Lebanon, Paris, and California.

[*See also* Art and Architecture *and* Syria and Lebanon.]

BIBLIOGRAPHY

Abu-Jaber, D. Review of *Of Cities and Women*, by Etel Adnan, and of *Paris, When It's Naked*, by Etel Adnan. *Middle East Journal* 49 (1995): 686–687.

Accad, E. Review of *Of Cities and Women*, by Etel Adnan, and of *Paris, When It's Naked*, by Etel Adnan. *World Literature Today* 68 (1994): 421–422.

Adnan, Etel. *Sitt Marie Rose: A Novel.* Translated by Georgina Kleege. Sausalito, Calif.: Post-Apollo Press, 1982.

Booth, M. Review of *There: In the Light and Darkness of the Self and of the Other*, by Etel Adnan. *World Literature Today* 71 (1997): 857–858.

Dickison, S. Review of *Paris, When It's Naked*, by Etel Adnan. *Review of Contemporary Fiction* 14 (1994): 231.

Garden, N. "When We Were Young." *Lambda Book Report* 7 (1998): 14–15.

John, J. "Lebanon Gates of the City." *World Literature Today* 68 (1994): 208.

EVELYNE ACCAD

ADOPTION

This entry consists of two subentries:

Overview
United States

Overview

It is good to remember that modern legal adoption is a relatively recent phenomenon in world history but that the acceptance of nonrelated children into a family is a longstanding practice. In times of shorter life spans parents might have died at far younger ages than they do in the early twenty-first century, leaving children to the care of relatives or close friends. As for attitudes toward more formal adoption, those have been mixed throughout history and across cultures. Whereas infertile women in ancient Mesopotamia could adopt children, the early Christian Church condemned adoption as contrary to the laws of God and nature, and in the early twenty-first century in cultures with a Catholic heritage, such as in Latin America, reticence to adopt or talk about adoption is powerful.

In most early societies, from ancient Rome to India to China and Japan, the reasons for adoption were almost entirely for the sake of the adoptive family, to adopt an heir to ensure the survival of the patrilineal family. Only in the twentieth century did it become common anywhere for orphans to become the legal children of adoptive parents. In modern times the complexities of adoption have also become apparent, as adoptees, natural and adoptive parents, and an array of public and private institutions all debate the specific emotional, financial, and other ingredients of adoption. In an age when identity is of primary concern, cross-racial and transnational adoptions have provoked some adoptees to question who they are. As science advances, knowledge of one's parents' and ancestors' medical history is often a life-and-death concern, further prompting the search for biological parents. Advocacy groups with a broad definition of adoption work to resolve some of the conflicts and dilemmas that accompany adoption.

Famous women adoptees are legion, and they include such notables as the American poet Maya Angelou and the actress Marilyn Monroe. The Swedish actress Ingrid Bergman was brought up by relatives after the deaths of her parents, while Bessie Head, the famed Botswana author and daughter of a wealthy white South African and an African worker in the family, was adopted by a mixed-race couple. Head's important novel *Maru* (1971) is the story of a well-educated and conflicted young "bush" woman raised by missionaries who see themselves as her adoptive parents. Birth mothers and daughters in the United States have testified to the psychological effects of surrendering a child and growing up as an adoptee.

The Chinese Example of Adoption. In many early and patrilineal societies, only male children were adopted. However, poor Chinese families sometimes practiced a form of female adoption in what was called "minor marriage." Poor families who could not afford to raise a daughter, much less provide her with a dowry, sold her before the age of eight or ten so she could live and work in the family of her eventual husband, who was usually an infant at the time of her transfer. She worked in effect as a servant in her in-laws' household and helped raise and nurture her future husband.

Throughout imperial Chinese history (from 221 B.C.E. into the early twentieth century), in the patrilineal Chinese family the primary reason for adoption was to allow otherwise childless couples to fulfill their filial obligations, perpetuate their family line, and continue their ancestral sacrifices. It has long been common for childless Chinese couples formally to adopt a paternal or maternal nephew from a sibling who had more than one son. Although Chinese law generally forbade adoptions across surname groups, historians and anthropologists have discovered that many childless Chinese families have preferred to adopt the children of strangers rather than relatives on the presumption that the children of relatives are more likely to have mixed loyalties than the children of strangers. Ironically, it appears that in southern China, where lineage organizations are strongest and where lineage rules prescribe that any adoption occur only within the lineage, many families prefer to adopt outside the lineage precisely to prevent divided loyalties of an adoptive son with natal ties within the lineage. Where Chinese widows without sons were suddenly confronted with the need to find an heir to a recently deceased spouse, these widows often gained power over the choice of the adoptee.

Abuses. Some of the most chilling abuses in the tradition of adoption came during colonization and later, when Europeans and their descendants legalized the seizure of Aboriginal children from their families to civilize them by placing them either in orphanages or in adoptive families. These occurred in both Australia and Canada and have been well documented as the practice has been curtailed. As Aboriginal adoptees try to recoup their past histories and find their relatives, a huge archive is being created of the feelings and experiences of this kind of seizure and adoption. The video *Bringing Them Home* shows an Aboriginal mother saying over and over "We're family people! We're family people!" as her children are taken from her. Other testimonials come from the women who have taken in Aboriginal children, and obviously there exist the highly charged reports of adoptees themselves—both in Australia and Canada.

During Germany's Third Reich (1933–1945), abuses were equally severe. Both in Germany and in conquered countries such as Norway, women impregnated by German soldiers often delivered their children in an institution called *Lebensborn*, designated as care centers for women giving birth to so-called "Aryan" children—that is, people of supposedly superior and untainted German blood. Childless and other German families often adopted these children. German forces often simply took blond children from their mothers to be similarly adopted by Germans and raised as part of the master Aryan race. Finally, desperate Jewish parents sometimes sent their children via the *Kindertransport* or child removal to accepting families in safer parts of the world either to be adopted or raised temporarily until peace returned.

There remains in the early twenty-first century the situation in which parents in rural areas place their children with entrepreneurs or sex traffickers in exchange for money. In some parts of Africa desperate rural families unable to feed their children drop them off in cities to be taken in by families that need extra help in the house or extra workers for a family enterprise.

Transnational Adoption. Despite these cruelties, many cases of adoption in the twentieth century became focused more on the creation of close family bonds, completing the creation of an emotionally bonded family through the adoption of children. Improving the conditions of life for children who would otherwise be confined to orphanages also motivates adoption. Transnational adoptions have become frequent, as childless couples across the West seek out orphans from Romania, South Korea, China, Brazil, and other countries where for a variety of reasons children are warehoused. In some cases, such as China and India, the preference for sons made a glut of girls available for adoption after the 1970s. In the Maoist period the Chinese government forbade any adoption of Chinese children by foreigners, even though millions of Chinese starved in the late 1950s as a result of the Great Leap Forward. After the opening of China and the institution of a one-child policy in an effort to curb runaway population growth in the 1980s, some restrictions on transnational adoptions were eased, and the Chinese government took a much more pragmatic approach, permitting and even promoting the adoption of infant girls by foreign couples. The traditional Chinese preference for sons is exacerbated in the Chinese case by the one-child policy, which has resulted in Chinese orphanages being filled with mostly girls. Since the year 2000, American families have adopted from four to seven thousand Chinese children—nearly all girls—per year.

The Balance Sheet. Adoption advocates and support groups have sprung into being to monitor the situations of adoptees. In particular they have collected the testimonies of birth mothers and have traced the assorted, sometimes fraught connections between mothers and daughters. Health issues—both psychological and physical—have also been at the forefront of advocacy concerns, and feminist groups have lobbied for more protection of the well-being of girls who are sent outside their birth families under bad conditions. Finally, issues of identity—familial, transnational, racial, and class—shape the activism and fill the testimonials of the adoption community.

[*See also* Family; Gender Preference in Children; *and* Inheritance.]

BIBLIOGRAPHY

Clay, Catrine, and Michael Leapman. *Master Race: The Lebensborn Experiment in Nazi Germany*. London: Hodder and Stoughton, 1995.

Cuthbert, Denise. "Stolen Children, Invisible Mothers, and Unspeakable Stories: The Experiences of Non-Aboriginal Adoptive and Foster Mothers of Aboriginal Children," *Social Semiotics* 11, no. 2 (August 2001): 139–154.

Goody, Jack. "Adoption in Cross-Cultural Perspective." In *Production and Reproduction: A Comparative Study of the Domestic Domain*, pp. 66–85. Cambridge, U.K.: Cambridge University Press, 1976.

Wadia-Ells, Susan, ed. *The Adoption Reader: Birth Mothers, Adoptive Mothers, and Adopted Daughters Tell Their Stories*. Seattle, Wash.: Seal, 1995.

Waltner, Ann. *Getting an Heir: Adoption and the Construction of Kinship in Late Imperial China*. Honolulu: University of Hawai'i Press, 1990.

Wolf, Arthur P., and Chieh-shan Huang. *Marriage and Adoption in China, 1845–1945*. Stanford, Calif.: Stanford University Press, 1980.

BONNIE G. SMITH AND PAUL S. ROPP

United States

Adoption is anomalous in most human cultures, for kinship is pervasively defined by blood and marriage. Though many societies have practiced some kind of child exchange, formal legal adoption is less common. The earliest adoption laws in the United States regulated inheritance; only later were they focused on child nurture. Adoption that makes adoptive kinship the full legal and social equivalent of biological kinship is an American invention, first appearing in the nineteenth century and not fully elaborated until the twentieth century.

Adoption has been accepted more readily and practiced more widely in the United States than in any other comparable industrialized nation, a testament to the relative openness of American society, its fluid class and social structure, and its racial and ethnic diversity. American history itself is a history of adoption—of immigration and self-invention, upward mobility and escape from the past. And adoption is a quintessentially American institution, one that embodies the optimistic faith in self-construction and the confident, sometimes arrogant, social engineering that characterizes much of American history.

In the United States adoption took shape in relationship to earlier practices of child exchange. Outside the boundaries of formal legal institutions, children were raised by relatives or neighbors when economic pressures, desertion, or death left children without adequate means of support. Apprenticeship and indenture were systems of labor regulation that also provided for the care of children outside biological families, with reciprocal obligations stipulated by contract and long-standing social practice.

The first adoption law in the United States was passed in Massachusetts in 1851. Many early adoption statutes, however, were directed primarily to the regulation of inheritance. Even as they made provision for bequests to those outside the circle of blood kinship, they also explicitly preserved the rights of biological heirs. By contrast, the evolving institution of adoption in the twentieth century made adoptive families the full legal equivalent of families formed by biology. In some times and places adoption has established a new relationship between adults. In the United States adoption meant child adoption, and by decree of adoption, biological strangers became legal and social kin.

Growth. During the 1910s and 1920s adoption emerged as an ambitious new social transaction. It was crafted in the context of Progressive reform, as child welfare drew national attention and concern and as reformers criticized orphanages as inadequate and inhumane. In the social sciences the new paradigm of environmentalism influenced the developing profession of social work. On a popular level such ideas helped undermine long-standing fears of the "bad seed" and made adults less anxious about adopting children of unknown heredity. These changing conditions created an extraordinary groundswell of popular support for adoption. Initially reluctant to place children with unrelated adults, social workers gradually became advocates of adoption—in part influenced by pressure from eager prospective adopters.

Adoption reached its apex in the 1950s and 1960s. Social workers became ardent advocates of adoption, regarding it as the "best solution" for the growing numbers of children born out of wedlock. Once accepted as a useful and humane alternative for some dependent children, adoption assumed a prominent role as social policy. With the support of a broad white middle-class consensus, social workers supervised an exponential expansion of adoption. Their advocacy echoed larger social themes of postwar optimism and mobility. Adoption was a "second chance" for all involved. In one bold stroke it rescued children from illegitimacy, offered a "fresh start" to "girls in trouble," and conferred parenthood on infertile couples longing to join the postwar domestic idyll.

The decline of ethnic particularism facilitated the expansion of adoption. Post–World War II records show little concern about ethnic differences that had once loomed large. In another measure of the prevailing confidence in adoptive kinship, some adoptive families formed across racial and national boundaries that had been rarely breached before. Some white Americans adopted biracial or African American children, and a brief social experiment removed American Indian children from reservations to white adoptive homes. International adoption began with placement of children from Korea in the 1950s, and by the 1970s American adoptive families included children born in many nations around the world. These "unmatched" family groups were visible testament to the postwar confidence in melting-pot assimilation.

These years also ushered in the era of confidential adoption as state after state began to sequester adoption records and to issue amended birth certificates. The practice reflected social confidence in the family of adoption, proclaiming the power of law and love to forge kinship among strangers. And yet it also registered a telling insecurity and denial. The adoptive family could be real only if its true origins were minimized and concealed.

Decline. By 1970 the broad consensus supporting adoption began to erode. Further liberalization of sexual attitudes, improved birth-control technology, and then legal abortion made seeing adoption as the "best solution" seem anachronistic. The political ferment of the 1960s posed other challenges to the assumptions of the "best solution." Black nationalists protested transracial adoption of African American children by white adopters. Activists defending tribal autonomy challenged adoptions of American Indian children that removed them from their original communities. Critiques of American global hegemony sometimes found expression in challenges to international adoption, seen by some as a form of imperialism. The numbers of adoptions dropped sharply by 1975.

Adoptive persons themselves began to challenge the narrative of the "best solution," followed by women who had relinquished their children in earlier decades. The sunny optimism of the postwar consensus, they charged, denied the trauma of adoption—its rupture and erasure of biological kinship. In a growing movement they fought cultural and legal prohibitions to establish ties with biological kin. Women who had relinquished children for adoption began to speak out. Rejecting the shield of silence provided by confidential adoption, they claimed a new identity as "birth mothers," a neologism that repudiated the fundamental doctrine of adoption, that blood ties could be permanently severed by law. In state after state, adopted persons challenged laws that sealed adoption records. Informal networks and formal organizations developed to assist adopted persons and birth parents in finding one another. Search narratives became a familiar autobiographical subgenre, the stuff of popular memoirs, films, radio and television talk shows, and newspaper accounts.

These shifts had a chilling effect on adoption in many ways. Prospective adopters might well be daunted by vociferous critics of adoption, some of whom asserted that biological ties were primary and adoption was disruptive—even abusive. Few children were available for domestic adoption, and prospective adopters confronted a range of obstacles and new considerations if they pursued transnational adoption.

And yet even as the postwar consensus dissolved, by the early twenty-first century there were signs of an emerging new consensus—one that cautiously reaffirmed adoption as an alternative family form. This new paradigm asserted the importance of both biological and adoptive kinship, rejected adoption secrecy, and celebrated the diversity of adoptive families. Gay men and lesbians were increasingly accepted as adoptive parents. Older prospective parents were no longer automatically rejected. International adoption, often transracial, claimed a growing percentage of all adoptions. In domestic adoptions, birth mothers assumed a new role in placement. Often they were directly involved in selecting adoptive parents. In some cases they stayed in contact with children placed for adoption.

[*See also* Abortion; Family; Inheritance; *and* Kinship.]

BIBLIOGRAPHY

Adoption History Project, University of Oregon. http://darkwing.uoregon.edu/~adoption/about.html. Comprehensive and well-designed site, the best source on the Web for the history of adoption.

Berebitsky, Julie. *Like Our Very Own: Adoption and the Changing Culture of Motherhood, 1851–1950.* Lawrence: University Press of Kansas, 2000.

Carp, E. Wayne. *Family Matters: Secrecy and Disclosure in the History of Adoption.* Cambridge, Mass.: Harvard University Press, 1998. Excellent history of confidential adoption by the first historian to have access to twentieth-century adoption records.

Carp, E. Wayne, ed. *Adoption in America: Historical Perspectives.* Ann Arbor: University of Michigan Press, 2002.

Kunzel, Regina G. *Fallen Women, Problem Girls: Unmarried Mothers and the Professionalization of Social Work, 1890–1945.* New Haven, Conn.: Yale University Press, 1993.

Melosh, Barbara. *Strangers and Kin: The American Way of Adoption.* Cambridge, Mass.: Harvard University Press, 2002.

BARBARA MELOSH

ADULTERY

This entry consists of two subentries:

Overview
Comparative History

Overview

Adultery, the sexual infidelity of a husband or wife, has been viewed as a serious transgression in most societies across the world. From the earliest times adulterers have been subject to harsh punishment. The ancient Babylonian code of Hammurabi (c. 1750 B.C.E.) prescribed that a married woman caught in adultery should be drowned with her lover, and adultery by a wife also carried the death penalty in ancient Egypt, Greece, and Rome. In Jewish law adultery merited death by stoning for both the adulteress and her partner. Adultery was also prohibited in Islamic teaching. The Qurʾan banned adultery and prescribed that offenders be whipped with one hundred lashes. Sharia (Islamic law based on the Qurʾan) took a harsher line, prescribing death by stoning for married offenders, although this penalty rested on the act of adultery's being witnessed by four male witnesses, and in practice many cases may have been dealt with by families.

Christianity viewed adultery more as a spiritual failure than as a public crime, and in the medieval Catholic Church offenders were commonly dealt with by ecclesiastical courts. Adultery became a serious issue after the Reformation because Protestants placed new emphasis on marriage as a linchpin of the social and moral order. The sixteenth-century reformers Martin Luther (1483–1546) and John Calvin (1509–1564) both argued that a marriage was irreparably damaged by infidelity, and they advocated divorce in such cases. The death penalty was introduced by Puritans in the Massachusetts Bay Colony in 1631 and in England in 1650 during the short period of Puritan government (1649–1660) following the Civil War, although in both societies these laws seem to have resulted in few executions.

Although European travelers and colonists frequently cited the loose morals of native peoples as evidence of the inferiority of other civilizations—thereby providing a justification for conquest—adultery seems to have been treated seriously in many non-Western societies. Many indigenous

Conjugal Law. An adulterous wife appearing in court, fourteenth century. BIBLIOTECA REAL, MADRID/BRIDGEMAN-GIRAUDON/ART RESOURCE, NY

peoples of Central America, South America, and the Caribbean punished adultery severely before the arrival of Europeans in the sixteenth and seventeenth centuries. In China, Confucianism taught that the social and political order rested on order within the family, and Ming (1368–1644) and Qing (1644–1911) law allowed a man to kill his wife if she was caught in the act of adultery.

Sexual Double Standard. Throughout history the adultery of wives has been treated more seriously than the adultery of husbands. In the *Lex Julia de adulteriis* (18 B.C.E.), the basic statute on sexual offenses in ancient Rome, the definition of adultery rested on the status of the woman involved. Adultery involved sexual acts between a married woman and someone other than her husband, while a man's infidelity was treated as fornication. Islam, Judaism, and Christianity all attributed great importance to virginity in women before marriage and to absolute fidelity in wives. In biblical times, Jewish law defined adultery as sexual intercourse between two individuals who could not legally be married. Because ancient Jewish law permitted polygamy, men were not held to account for sexual relations with other women in the same way that their wives were punished for adultery.

Germanic and Celtic peoples of the early Middle Ages also defined adultery largely as a female crime. In contrast, some Christian writers sought to emphasize that husbands and wives shared an equal duty to be faithful to each other. Saint Augustine cited Saint Paul's words from 1 Corinthians 7:4—that a "wife does not have power over her body, but her husband does, and likewise the husband does not have the power over his body, but his wife does"—in arguing that men and women should be subject to the same penalties for adultery.

In seventeenth-century England, some religious moralists argued that because men supposedly possessed more reason than women did, they should bear the greater guilt for adultery. However, women's adultery remained much more heavily prosecuted than men's. As a corollary, many societies have made it easier for a man to divorce an adulterous wife than for a woman to divorce an adulterous husband. Eighteenth-century Englishmen could obtain divorces by private act of Parliament on the basis of their wives' adultery, but the same rights were not accorded to women. Similarly, although the Meiji Civil Code introduced in Japan in 1890 allowed women and men to sue for divorce, only a woman's adultery was accepted as grounds for annulment.

The apparent basis for this sexual double standard is adultery's threat to paternity and its implications for the inheritance of property. Similar concerns about the social impact of a wife's adultery may be found in different cultures around the world. In Roman and Jewish law and in Islam, adultery was condemned above all because it denied a legitimate heir his inheritance by introducing a spurious heir into the family. In late imperial China, adultery was viewed as a disruption of the descent order of another man's lineage. Adultery by a man did not threaten the family and lineage in the same way that adultery by a married woman did, so male adultery was viewed as less of a threat to community values or family alliances. Consequently, many societies have viewed chastity, together with related virtues such as modesty, as more central components of women's honor and reputation than of men's.

Private Act with Public Consequences. Adultery has been seen in many societies as a private act with public consequences. In the medieval and early modern period both Islamic and Christian moralists argued that toleration of adultery would incur divine wrath. The view that adultery betokens disaster has also been a popular theme in fiction and poetry. Homer's *Iliad* (c. eighth century B.C.E.) and Sir Thomas Malory's prose epic *Le morte d'Arthur* (1469–1470) both tell of disasters that come as a consequence of infidelity. The figure of the female adulteress has exercised a powerful hold on the imagination for centuries.

Medieval literature such as Boccaccio's *Decameron* (1349–1351) and *One Thousand and One Nights*, made up of stories from Persia, Egypt, Arabia, and India, contains many tales of promiscuous wives who outwitted their cuckolded husbands in ingenious ways. Such stories present adultery as comedy yet also warn of the dangers of uncontrolled female sexuality. Cuckoldry remained a staple theme in English comic drama until the end of the seventeenth century. Novels of female adultery, such as Gustave Flaubert's *Madame Bovary* (1857) and Leo Tolstoy's *Anna Karenina* (1875–1877), flourished in nineteenth-century Europe, presenting tragic stories in which passion was set against social convention.

From the eighteenth century onward, adultery has ceased to attract the attention of the courts in most Western societies. Among the middle classes in Europe and the United States in the nineteenth century, adultery was cast more as a private matter, albeit one with serious consequences. If a husband discovered his wife's infidelity it could lead to divorce, social ostracism, and the loss of child custody. Attitudes toward illicit sex have softened in many places in recent times. However, laws criminalizing adultery remained in force almost everywhere in the United States until the 1960s, while modern Islamist movements have sometimes called for the full force of Sharia law to be brought against adulterers.

[*See also* Divorce *and* Marriage.]

BIBLIOGRAPHY

Ahmed, Leila. *Women and Gender in Islam: Historical Roots of a Modern Debate*. New Haven, Conn.: Yale University Press, 1992.

Brundage, James A. *Law, Sex, and Christian Society in Medieval Europe*. Chicago: University of Chicago Press, 1987.

Burguière, André, Christine Klapisch-Zuber, Martine Segelam, and Françoise Zonabend, eds. *A History of the Family*. Translated by Sarah Hanbury Tenison, Rosemary Morris, and Andrew Wilson. 2 vols. Cambridge, U.K.: Polity Press, 1996. Translation of *Histoire de la famille* (1986). Multiauthored history of the family from ancient times to the modern period. Contains much useful information, although it might have benefited from a more thematic approach.

Carmody, Denise L. "Judaism." In *Women in World Religions*, edited by Arvind Sharma, pp. 183–207. Albany: State University of New York Press, 1987.

Cohen, David. *Law, Sexuality, and Society: The Enforcement of Morals in Classical Athens*. Cambridge, U.K.: Cambridge University Press, 1991. Borrowing effectively from anthropology, a detailed analysis of the regulation of morals in ancient Athenian society.

Nashat, Guity, and Judith E. Tucker. *Women in the Middle East and North Africa: Restoring Women to History*. Bloomington: University of Indiana Press, 1999.

Sommer, Matthew H. *Sex, Law, and Society in Late Imperial China*. Stanford, Calif.: Stanford University Press, 2000.

Turner, David M. *Fashioning Adultery: Gender, Sex, and Civility in England, 1660–1740*. Cambridge, U.K.: Cambridge University Press, 2002. Analysis of adultery's representation in early modern English culture and society.

Wiesner-Hanks, Merry E. *Christianity and Sexuality in the Early Modern World: Regulating Desire, Reforming Practice*. London and New York: Routledge, 1999.

David M. Turner

Comparative History

Adultery is understood today as the breaking of marriage monogamy vows by a person's having sex with someone who is not his or her husband or wife. However, understandings of adultery and its social implications have differed historically. Gender and social status have influenced perceptions of infidelity and governed how it has been dealt with. Different societies have treated infidelity as a religious transgression, as a crime deserving sometimes severe punishment, or as a private wrong (or as a mixture of these). The history of adultery reveals much about the history of the social importance of marriage, while contrasting attitudes toward male and female infidelity are a key indication of gender difference in past societies.

Adultery in the Ancient World. The first recorded injunctions against adultery are in the code of the Babylonian king Hammurabi, dating from about 1750 B.C.E.; the code prescribes that a married woman caught in adultery be bound to her lover and thrown into water so that they drown together. In Assyrian law, adultery was treated more as a private wrong for which the husband or father of the woman involved was entitled to compensation from the seducer. Across the ancient world there were reports of brutal personal justice against adulterous wives. A popular story from Egypt relates how a powerful man had his unfaithful wife burned at the stake and her paramour fed to crocodiles. Nevertheless, it seems that such cases were rare, and in Egypt wives could be exonerated if they swore an oath of innocence. Husbands who falsely accused their wives were forced to pay compensation to their families, and a wife also had the right to denounce an adulterous husband and force a divorce.

Many ancient societies, however, viewed male and female adultery in different terms. In biblical times, Jewish law prescribed that adulterous wives and their partners be stoned to death. Adultery was defined as sexual intercourse between two individuals who could not legally be married, and since ancient Jewish law permitted polygamy and concubinage, men were not held to account for infidelity in the same way that their wives were. In the principal Roman statute on sexual offenses, the *Lex Julia de adulteriis* (18 B.C.E.), a distinction was drawn between adultery and *stuprum* (fornication). The definition of adultery rested on the status of the woman involved: adultery was understood as sex between a married woman and someone other than her spouse, while *stuprum* consisted of unsanctioned sex between any man (married or not) and a woman under another man's legal power, including women and spinsters. Definitions of adultery were also influenced by social status. The wife of a slave could not commit adultery because all slave unions lacked the dignity of legitimate marriage in the eyes of the law.

A sexual double standard also existed in classical Athens, where adultery was understood primarily as the violation of a husband's exclusive sexual access to his wife. In both Greece and Rome acts of revenge were sanctioned by law. Under the *Lex Julia de adulteriis* a husband was permitted to kill his wife's lover, provided that he had caught the man in the act and did the killing immediately; the husband was not, however, allowed to kill his wife. It was expected that a cuckolded husband should repudiate his wife; otherwise he risked being accused of complicity in the affair. Athenian law also allowed the husband or appropriate magistrates to kill the adulterer caught in the act. The extent to which these sanctions were applied is, however, unclear. Reactions to adultery in all societies are complex, and some deceived husbands might have responded with silence, acquiescence, or extortion.

Adultery in Medieval and Early Modern Europe. With the advent of Christianity, perceptions of adultery and how it should be punished changed. In Christian thought, adultery was seen first and foremost as a moral failure rather than a public crime, and therefore the church advocated spiritual remedies against adulterers rather than execution. The church fathers widened the definition of adultery that had existed in Roman law to include the infidelity of husbands as well as wives. Adultery's meaning was also extended in 388 C.E. by a law of Valentinian II (r. 375–392) that defined marriage between Christian and Jew as adulterous.

The development of canon law in the twelfth century enshrined the perception of adultery as a spiritual misdemeanor. By the end of the twelfth century, church courts had established jurisdiction over marriage and morals both in England and on the Continent. Canonists repudiated the practice of taking personal revenge in adultery cases, warning deceived husbands that slaying their wives would be treated as murder. Some canonists argued that a man who discovered his wife in adultery was obliged to turn her out of his house. The key work of canon law, Gratian's *Decretum* of c. 1140, established that the adultery of men and women was equally culpable and that men found guilty of adultery were barred from entering the priesthood. Adulterers were punished by penance or even excommunication, and marital separation (though not full divorce) was allowed in cases of infidelity. However, various shaming punishments were adopted by local communities to make an example of offenders. These included shaving the heads of adulterous women and parading them through public places, and sometimes the secular authorities punished adulterers by whipping.

The Protestant Reformation brought about renewed interest in marriage and sexual morality. Protestants saw marriage as a linchpin of the social and moral order. At the beginning of the sixteenth century the Christian concept of marriage was vigorously debated by reformers. For Protestants such as Martin Luther (1483–1546) and John Calvin (1509–1564) marriage was a divine institution but not an indissoluble sacrament, as Catholics saw it. Condemning priestly celibacy, reformers placed greater importance on sex within marriage, and many viewed adultery as amounting to an irreparable breakdown of marriage. Accordingly, Protestant marital courts in Germany, Scotland, France, Switzerland, and Scandinavia allowed divorce for adultery.

At the same time, the Reformation was seen by its most fervent supporters as an opportunity for spiritual and moral renewal. Protestant moralists in early modern England saw the interests of church and state as inextricably linked. In the patriarchal political ideology of seventeenth-century England the family was cast as a "little commonwealth," a microcosm of the state at large, and disorder in the one betokened disorder in the other. Failure to punish adultery was thought to invite God's punishment on families, communities, and the nation at large. Across Protestant Europe there were calls for laws against sexual offenders to be tightened. An adultery law passed in Geneva, Switzerland, in 1566 called for capital punishment in cases of double adultery (that is, cases in which both parties were married). The death penalty for adultery was introduced by English Puritan settlers in the Massachusetts Bay Colony in 1631 and briefly in England itself during the period of Puritan rule (1649–1660) that followed the Civil War. These laws generally treated female adultery more harshly; in spite of the death penalty's applying to both male and female offenders in cases of double adultery, the Genevan law of 1566 punished sex between a married man and a single woman with a jail sentence, whereas all offenders who were married women could face execution. In practice, difficulties in securing adequate proof meant that there were few executions.

Marriage and Adultery beyond Europe. When Europeans began to explore and colonize other continents during the early modern period, sex and marriage became a means of judging the relative value of civilizations. In America, Roman Catholic missionaries in colonial New France and northern Mexico, together with Protestant settlers in New England, reported strong resistance to their efforts to impose monogamous marriage on natives. Western travelers to Islamic countries also drew attention to practices such as polygamy as evidence of alien sexual mores. Even the veil worn by Muslim women to preserve modesty was seen by some as giving women anonymity that allowed them to carry on adulterous affairs free from detection.

However, differences between European and non-European morals were often exaggerated, sometimes as a means of justifying conquest, and closer analysis reveals that laws and social sanctions against adultery existed in many parts of the world. In pre-Islamic Arabia adultery was not treated as a crime. However, with the advent of Islam in the seventh century C.E., adultery became outlawed and subject to severe punishment. Islam, like Judaism and Christianity, attributed great importance to virginity in girls prior to marriage and absolute fidelity in wives. The Qurʾan prohibited adultery and prescribed that offenders receive a hundred lashes. Sharia (Islamic law based on the Qurʾan) took a harsher line, prescribing death by stoning for married offenders. As was the case in Europe, prosecutions under Sharia were hindered by difficulties of securing evidence. Adultery needed to be witnessed directly by four reputable men, and it seems that many cases were dealt with by families. Since a woman's adultery jeopardized the honor of her own family, suspected adulteresses may have been killed by their male relatives. Like medieval and early modern Christian moralists, Muslims also saw adultery as a sin that invited divine retribution. When plague raged in Arabia in 1437 it was believed that the disease was sent by God as a punishment for adultery, and the Sultan ordered women to be confined to their homes.

In Inca societies and Mexico adultery was proscribed since it was believed that marriage was indissoluble until the death of one of the spouses. Such beliefs provided continuity with the marital practices imposed by the conquering Spanish in the sixteenth century. Confucianism in China maintained that order in the universe depended on order in the family. Thus as in patriarchal Western societies, the disorder caused in families by adultery had wider political implications. For the Chinese, as for ancient Romans, legal definitions of adultery were also determined by social status. In imperial China, though free women of either elite or commoner status were expected to remain chaste, female slaves and bondservants, whether married or not, were sexually available to their masters. Ming (1368–1644) and Qing (1644–1911) law allowed a husband who caught his wife in the act of adultery to kill her and her lover with impunity, provided that he acted at once. This was one of the few occasions when anyone other than the emperor was allowed to take life and thus testifies to the seriousness of adultery in Chinese society.

Gender, Property, and Honor. Thus although adultery has been treated as a significant matter in many societies, punishments were not meted out equally to all involved. Similar gender differences are apparent in practices of divorce and marital separation. In early modern England, for example, church courts allowed both husbands and wives to sue for separation on the grounds of adultery, but in practice the majority of cases concerned the adultery of wives, and women bringing cases often had to supplement their accusations of adultery with allegations of cruelty. When full divorce was permitted by an act of Parliament from the late seventeenth century, women were not allowed to sue for divorce on the basis of their husbands' infidelity. Similarly, although the Meiji Civil Code, introduced in Japan in 1890, allowed both men and women to sue for divorce, only a woman's adultery was accepted as grounds for annulment.

The key to this double standard is adultery's threat to paternity and its implications for the inheritance of property. Though Christian moralists of the Middle Ages and early modern period often acknowledged that adultery was a great sin in both men and women, many conceded that in practical terms a woman's infidelity had more serious practical consequences. In Islam, as in Jewish and Roman law, adultery was condemned because it denied a legitimate heir his inheritance, while in late imperial China adultery was viewed as a disruption of the descent order of another man's lineage. A husband's adultery with a single woman did not threaten the family and social order in the same way, and as such male adultery has historically carried fewer penalties. Recent research on early modern Britain has shown that there were circumstances in which adultery might threaten a man's public standing, but much evidence points to divergent treatment of male and female infidelity in both society and popular culture.

As a result, adultery in many societies was more risky for women. Aside from the risk of judicial punishment, adulterous wives have faced social ostracism and the loss of custody over their children. In many places (especially in Islamic and Mediterranean societies) the reputation of married women—and with it that of their whole family—has rested on chastity and fidelity. A man's sexual honor and reputation, in contrast, has rested more on the control of his spouse. Comic stories in which cuckolded husbands were mocked for their inability to satisfy their wives sexually were popular in classical drama, in medieval epics such as Boccaccio's *Decameron* (1349–1351), and in street ballads and plays in early modern England and Europe, warning men of the need to exercise their patriarchal authority. But in spite of adultery's risks for women, history provides examples of famous adulteresses—such as Barbara Palmer, Lady Castlemaine (1641–1709), the lover of King Charles II of England (r. 1660–1685)—who achieved status and influence through their relationships with powerful men. Women may have embarked on affairs looking for excitement and emotional fulfillment lacking in their own marriages, especially in societies where entry into marriage for the elite or middle class might have been regulated by family pressure and dynastic interests.

Adultery in the Modern Age. The sexual double standard remained a powerful adjunct of respectability in the Victorian period, a theme explored in popular novels of female adultery such as Gustave Flaubert's *Madame Bovary* (1857), in which the heroine's passion was set tragically against stultifying social convention. In 1843 the Louisiana Supreme Court gave child custody to the husband of an unfaithful wife even though he had abused her. By this time criminal prosecutions for adultery had disappeared in most Western societies. Adultery was cast as a private matter, but if affairs became public knowledge they could have a devastating effect. The career of the Irish nationalist politician Charles Stewart Parnell (1846–1891) was fatally damaged when his cohabitation with Kitty O'Shea, the wife of a member of Parliament, was exposed in 1889. In Britain in 1923, women were finally granted the right to sue for divorce on the basis of their husbands' adultery. Further reform of the law to allow divorce on the basis of incompatibility in Britain and elsewhere, together with the growth of cohabitation in Western societies in recent times, has further downgraded the significance of adultery. Nevertheless, adultery remained a criminal offense in most parts of the United States until the 1960s. Condemning the perceived liberal attitudes of the West, Islamist movements in Pakistan and Iran have also called for the full force of Sharia law to be brought against adulterers. As in the early modern period, practices concerning adultery remain an important means of comparing cultural values.

[*See also* Divorce *and* Marriage.]

BIBLIOGRAPHY

Ahmed, Leila. *Women and Gender in Islam: Historical Roots of a Modern Debate.* New Haven, Conn.: Yale University Press, 1992.

Brook, Stephen, ed. *The Penguin Book of Infidelities.* London: Viking, 1994. Anthology of writing on adultery from ancient Rome to the present.

Brundage, James A. *Law, Sex, and Christian Society in Medieval Europe.* Chicago: University of Chicago Press, 1987.

Burguière, André, Christine Klapisch-Zuber, Martine Segelam, and Françoise Zonabend, eds. *A History of the Family.* Translated by Sarah Hanbury Tenison, Rosemary Morris, and Andrew Wilson. 2 vols. Cambridge, U.K.: Polity Press, 1996. Translation of *Histoire de la famille* (1986). Multiauthored history of the family from ancient times to the modern period. Contains much useful information, although it might have benefited from a more thematic approach.

Capp, Bernard. "The Double Standard Revisited: Plebeian Women and Male Sexual Reputation in Early Modern England." *Past and Present* 162 (1999): 70–100. Reexamination of male sexual mores in sixteenth- and seventeenth-century England.

Carmody, Denise L. "Judaism." In *Women in World Religions,* edited by Arvind Sharma, pp. 183–207. Albany: State University of New York Press, 1987.

Cohen, David. *Law, Sexuality, and Society: The Enforcement of Morals in Classical Athens.* Cambridge, U.K.: Cambridge University Press, 1991. Borrowing effectively from anthropology, a detailed analysis of the regulation of morals in ancient Athenian society.

D'Emilio, John D., and Estelle B. Freedman. *Intimate Matters: A History of Sexuality in America.* New York: Harper & Row, 1988.

Keddie, Nikki R. "Introduction: Deciphering Middle Eastern Women's History." In *Women in Middle Eastern History: Shifting Boundaries in Sex and Gender,* edited by Nikki R. Keddie and Beth Baron, pp. 1–22. New Haven, Conn.: Yale University Press, 1991.

Nashat, Guity, and Judith E. Tucker. *Women in the Middle East and North Africa: Restoring Women to History.* Bloomington: University of Indiana Press, 1999.

Sommer, Matthew H. *Sex, Law, and Society in Late Imperial China.* Stanford, Calif.: Stanford University Press, 2000.

Stone, Lawrence. *Road to Divorce: England 1530–1987.* Oxford: Oxford University Press, 1990.

Weeks, Jeffrey. *Sex, Politics, and Society: The Regulation of Sexuality since 1880.* London: Longman, 1981. Classic study of sexuality in Victorian and modern Britain.

Wiesner-Hanks, Merry E. *Christianity and Sexuality in the Early Modern World: Regulating Desire, Reforming Practice.* London and New York: Routledge, 1999.

DAVID M. TURNER

AFFIRMATIVE ACTION. Affirmative action is one of the most successful policies for addressing gender inequality to appear in the late twentieth century. Although the details of affirmative action policies have varied, all call on employers and governments to take "affirmative" or proactive steps to ensure equal opportunity. The most commonly recognized kind of affirmative action mandates goals or even quotas in order to achieve this objective. As a result of new hiring, promotion, and admissions programs meant to remedy the deep structural inequality in the workplace and higher education, the number of women doctors, lawyers, professors, business executives, and high-ranking civil servants has multiplied significantly. Their changed economic and professional status has transformed work and family relations in far-reaching ways.

Women's historians have paid relatively little attention to affirmative action. There are three reasons for this. First, most scholarly attention has been on the contentious, sometimes violent history of race and ethnic-based affirmative action. Gender-based affirmative action is treated as marginal. Its existence is explained as almost accidental and without controversy. Second, feminist concerns about global issues, such as women's suffrage and legal rights,

Kenyan Affirmative Action. Beth Mugo, chairperson of the affirmative action street committee, protests Kenya's decision not to guarantee a quota of Kenyan women in the newly formed East African parliament, Nairobi, December 2001. REUTERS/Antony Njuguna

marriage laws and customs, and health and reproductive rights, often seems more pressing and dramatic in nature. Third, in the realm of equal employment opportunity, women's struggles for pay equity, improved pregnancy and maternity benefits, and strong sexual harassment laws have received more notice as dramatic issues affecting a large number of women across race and class lines. Women's historians understood affirmative action recipients to be primarily college-educated professional women.

Recently, however, historians have begun to consider affirmative action an important part of the long trajectory of struggle over women's rights that originated in the nineteenth century. Its more immediate origins date to the period after World War II, during which union women and other activists shifted their support away from protective measures for working women, such as special hours laws, and toward new gender-equality policies. Also, historians now acknowledge a broader definition of affirmative action that includes compensatory education and training as well as targeted recruitment of women. They incorporate affirmative action's development into their analyses of the ways ostensibly gender-neutral policies disproportionately affect women.

Political and legal structures have determined the shape and character of affirmative action in individual countries. In some countries, such as the United States, they originated in presidential orders and executive branch agency directives; in others, such as Australia and Italy, they had their beginning in parliamentary or legislative measures; and in yet others, such as India, they came about through constitutional amendments. Although scholars disagree about the extent of influence grassroots social protests had on affirmative action development, they understand the role of women activists, both in and out of government positions, as crucial to affirmative action's implementation and record of success.

Affirmative Action in the United States. The roots of gender-based affirmative action in the United States run deep, fed by civil rights and liberal currents of the 1950s and the early 1960s in support of equality. The Equal Pay Act of 1963 and Title VII of the Civil Rights Act of 1964 banned, among other things, race and sex employment discrimination, thereby manifesting the prevailing confidence that the problem of unfair treatment would soon disappear. Civil rights activists and feminists, along with academic and political allies, soon argued that the legal guarantees in place were insufficient. Where some saw steady, positive change, others believed weak enforcement mechanisms could not dismantle systematic barriers to inequality. New feminist organizations, such as the National Organization for Women (NOW) and the Women's Equity Action League (WEAL), worked with allies in government agencies, such as the Equal Employment Opportunity Commission, to promote affirmative action. By the early 1970s they were helping to draft consent decrees in the steel and telecommunications industries that brought dramatically new numbers of women of all races into the higher-paid workforce. Affirmative action often came from the centers of power, especially executive branch agencies, courts, and nation's boardrooms, but it also appeared in local contexts through protests, lobbying, and state and municipal governments. Americans were soon seeing women police officers, firefighters, bus drivers, construction workers, electricians, and high-ranking military officers on the job.

Feminists were instrumental in placing gender-based affirmative action on an equal footing with race-based affirmative action. In the area of faculty hiring in higher education, for example, NOW and WEAL leaders mobilized local members to file complaints about the lack of women faculty members, especially at the associate and full professor levels. By 1973 WEAL members alone had lodged over 360 class action complaints. The federal government soon revised executive orders to include women. Executive Order 11246, issued by President Lyndon B. Johnson in 1965, extended an earlier order by President John F. Kennedy banning discrimination by race, color, religion, and national origin in requiring businesses holding federal contracts to include "affirmative action" plans; President Johnson expanded his order in 1968 to include women. In 1971 the U.S. Office of Contract Compliance revised its Order No. 4, issued in 1970, mandating affirmative action hiring timetables for minorities to include women as well. College and university administrators instituted programs to admit more women into graduate and professional schools. In 1950, 5.3 percent of all students in medical schools were women; by 1972 the figure was 13.6 percent (Harvard's shot up to 20 percent). Women made up 40 to 50 percent of most law school classes by the mid-1970s. In the mid-1960s less than 1 percent of dentists were women, but women made up around 20 percent twenty years later.

Affirmative action's effectiveness has been limited. The highly paid union jobs that working-class women expected to receive in the 1970s as a result of consent decrees dried up in the wake of recessions and deindustrialization. Minority women's progress has lagged significantly behind that of white women. Even those who have benefited from affirmative action admissions and hiring have experienced the "glass ceiling" effect of being relegated to entry level or junior positions (only 11 percent of women, for example, are law firm partners).

Affirmative Action outside the United States. The history of affirmative action in other countries underscores the important effects of legal mandates on employer, union, and government policies. The United Nations Declaration of Human Rights (1948) as well as the subsequent United Nations conventions, commissions, and meetings served as an impetus for activism. They provided legal obligations for signatory nations to implement gender-based affirmative action. The U.N. declaration announced equal rights for men and women; it enumerated a wide range of social and economic rights that supporters later argued could only be realized through affirmative action. The U.N. General Assembly adopted the Convention on the Elimination of All Forms of Discrimination against Women (CEDAW) in 1979. It included specific language supporting affirmative action. By early 2006, 182 nations had ratified CEDAW, and another 98 (including the United States) were signatories but had not yet ratified it.

The role of the international agreements and networks of feminist activists is significant as well. In Australia the influential group of feminists in the civil service section (known as "femocrats") pushed the Australian Labor Party government in 1973 to ratify the International Labor Organization Convention No. 111, Discrimination in Employment and Occupation. Several state governments followed with sex discrimination bans. In 1983 Australia signed CEDAW; the next year parliament passed the Sex Discrimination Act, which outlawed discrimination on the grounds of sex, marital status, and pregnancy in employment, education, and provision of service. The Affirmative Action Act (1986) required that companies with more than one hundred employees and higher education institutions establish and report annually on their programs.

The effect of race- and ethnic-based affirmative action on gender-based programs has varied across countries. Supporters debate the significance of clustering targeted groups on feminist efforts to advocate for transforming gender relations, especially when some women look not to their gender but to their racial or ethnic identities in making affirmative action claims. In some countries gender-based affirmative action stands alone. Australia's gender-based programs developed independently of programs for Aborigines. Japan's Equal Employment Opportunity Law (1985) came about as a direct result of CEDAW. The history of affirmative action in Canada is more complex. It began in the early 1960s to address French Canadian economic, social, and educational marginalization. The Employment Equity Act of 1986 required implementation of proportional representation of women, Aborigines, the disabled, and "visible minorities" in organizations with over one hundred employees. Indian affirmative action is characterized by strong constitutional support dating to 1950 for members of the country's disadvantaged castes. Some Indian affirmative action policies benefit women (e.g., earmarking of seats for women in elected municipal councils), but the overwhelming focus of India's programs in not on gender.

Just as in the United States, the courts elsewhere have proven to be important avenues for promoting affirmative action. In the European Union (EU), a European Court of Justice decision, *Marschall v. Land Nordhein-Westfalen* (1 C.M.L.R. 547 [1997]), validated gender-based affirmative action. In the preceding four decades Europeans at the national and supranational levels embraced measures that laid the groundwork for this ruling. The authors of the Treaty of Rome (1957), the founding document of the European Economic Community (the forerunner of the EU), included specific prohibitions against discriminatory pay for women wage earners. Subsequent treaties and agreements, such as the European Social Charter (1961), the European Charter of the Fundamental Social Rights of Workers (1989), and the Maastricht Treaty (1992), strengthened the language of support for gender equality. They did so, however, only in general terms. In *Marschall* the court considered a case involving a male applicant who failed to obtain a German civil service promotion. They held that a preference for a woman applicant, where all of the applicants' qualifications were otherwise similar, merely served to ensure adherence to the nondiscrimination principle. The Treaty of Amsterdam (1997) specifically allowed member states to establish gender-based affirmative action programs.

Many European nations already had strong affirmative action programs, particularly in legislative and other political and governmental bodies. Belgium and Finland increased the number of female legislators by half; Denmark requires that all public committees and governmental agencies be gender-balanced. Most political parties have adopted internal regulations with specific quotas for female candidates. The German Social Democratic Party, for example, requires that at least 33 percent of its candidates be women and that they hold 40 percent of party positions; in Sweden the four largest parties mandate that one-half of their candidates be women.

Opposition to Affirmative Action. Opponents of affirmative action have influenced the shape and character of affirmative action. The reasons for their opposition vary. Business leaders fear governmental regulations, conservatives and disaffected liberals argue on behalf of race- and gender-blind merit, and there exists an anxiety about the effect of transformed gender relations on marriage and family relations that is difficult to quantify. Opponents have succeeded in limiting the range and effectiveness of affirmative action, not in eliminating it. The Australian conservative government, for example, passed the Equal Opportunity for Women in the Workplace Act (1999) that curtailed the use of affirmative action to achieve goals. The law reduced the annual reporting requirements to biennial reports and provided employers with flexibility in meeting their goals.

Opposition to affirmative action has been especially fierce in the United States. It exists elsewhere but to a lesser extent owing to the general acceptance of collective solutions and remedial programs to correct social and economic woes. This is clear from the names given to affirmative action laws, such as Italy's Measures for Positive Discrimination (1999). In the United States, with its strong tradition of individualism and weak social policies, such language would be unacceptable. From affirmative action's inception, its supporters have faced opposition, especially in the skilled trades, police and fire departments, and industrial workplaces. Colleges and universities have been the sites of some of the most significant opposition to what foes call "reverse discrimination." Disgruntled academic job seekers and applicants who failed to gain admission to increasingly competitive graduate and professional schools argued that they held qualifications (especially test scores) that were superior to those of affirmative action recipients.

Affirmative action opponents have used the legal system. The U.S. Supreme Court first considered a "reverse discrimination" claim in *DeFunis v. Odegaard* (1974). The case involved Marco DeFunis, a white man denied admission to the University of Washington Law School. Since DeFunis had nearly completed his legal studies (he entered law school as the result of a lower court ruling), the justices considered his case "moot." Four years later, in *Regents of the University of California v. Bakke*, a divided court decided that, while quotas or "set asides" for affirmative action recipients were unconstitutional, admissions committees could consider an individual's race as one of several factors in efforts to achieve diversity. It was a victory for the plaintiff, a white man named Allan Bakke, whom the court ordered enrolled in the University of California, Davis, Medical School since the university had set aside a specific number of seats for minority students. Since *Bakke* an increasingly conservative court has limited the range of affirmative action but has not rejected this reasoning.

Beginning in the 1980s opponents increasingly turned their attention to gender-based programs. The reasons for this are unclear. Some scholars contend that it was part of a general backlash to Second Wave feminism. Others suggest that it was a considered strategy to undermine affirmative action by challenging the validity of programs that were not race-based. These efforts failed. In *Johnson v. Santa Clara* (1987) the Supreme Court upheld a lower court decision involving a municipal worker who complained that a female coworker unfairly received a coveted road dispatcher position. In a 6-to-3 decision the justice wrote that it was not unreasonable to consider sex as one factor among many in making promotion decisions. Affirmative action supporters experienced defeats as well. In a much-publicized case involving Sears Roebuck and Company, for example, the Equal Employment Opportunity Commission (EEOC) filed a lawsuit in 1979 alleging that the company was guilty of sex discrimination in its promotion of women into commission sales positions. Sears prevailed in 1986 and 1987, when federal district and appellate courts ruled that statistical disparities were the result of "legitimate non-discriminatory reasons" having to do with women's individual career and family decisions.

The fresh challenges in the 1990s to higher education affirmative action in public universities in Maryland, Texas,

Georgia, Washington, and Michigan included a large number of women plaintiffs. Their actions and the fact that in public opinion polls white women oppose affirmative action as strongly as white men, even though they benefit from its policies, reveal the weakened state of equal employment opportunity in the early twenty-first century. Affirmative action opponents, however, are not able to claim victory. Polls indicate as well that a majority of Americans back at least some version of affirmative action, usually limited. This was true as far back as the 1970s, when liberal unionists in sympathy with affirmative action plans that included numerical goals balked at suggestions that layoff and termination practices, especially the union-defended "last hired, first fired," be modified to protect the jobs of recently hired affirmative action recipients. As the struggle over affirmative action continues in the twenty-first century, the lack of a common definition of what exactly constitutes affirmative action and who supports (and opposes) it will plague activists on all sides.

[*See also* Convention on the Elimination of All Forms of Discrimination against Women.]

BIBLIOGRAPHY

Anderson, Terry H. *The Pursuit of Fairness: A History of Affirmative Action*. New York: Oxford University Press, 2004.

Bacchi, Carol Lee. *The Politics of Affirmative Action: "Women," Equality, and Category Politics*. Thousand Oaks, Calif.: Sage Publications, 1996.

Ginsburg, Ruth Bader, and Deborah Jones Merritt. "Affirmative Action: An International Human Rights Dialogue." *Cardozo Law Review* 21 (1999): 253–282.

Hoff, Joan. *Law, Gender, and Injustice: A Legal History of U.S. Women*. New York: New York University Press, 1991.

Lake, Marilyn. *Getting Equal: The History of Australian Feminism*. Saint Leonards, New South Wales, Australia: Allen and Unwin, 1999.

MacLean, Nancy. *Freedom Is Not Enough: The Opening of the American Workplace*. Cambridge, Mass.: Harvard University Press, 2006.

Parikh, Sunita. *The Politics of Preference: Democratic Institutions and Affirmative Action in the United States and India*. Ann Arbor: University of Michigan Press, 1997.

Timpson, Annis May. *Driven Apart: Women's Employment Equality and Child Care in Canadian Public Policy*. Vancouver: UBC, 2001.

Urofsky, Melvin I. *Affirmative Action on Trial: Sex Discrimination in Johnson v. Santa Clara*. Lawrence: University Press of Kansas, 1997.

VanBurkleo, Sandra F. *"Belonging to the World": Women's Rights and American Constitutional Culture*. New York: Oxford University Press, 2001.

DENNIS DESLIPPE

AFGHANISTAN. A landlocked Islamic republic in South Asia, Afghanistan shares borders with the nation-states of Pakistan, Iran, Uzbekistan, Turkmenistan, Tajikistan, and China. Although the vast majority of Afghans are economically poor and are engaged in farming and raising sheep, the country is the world's largest producer of opium. Unstable governments since 1979, followed by the religious extremism of armed militia groups in the 1990s, have severely disrupted Afghan community life. Militarism and ethnic and religion-based violence have exacted a huge human toll. An estimated 1.5 million people have died, and thousands of refugees have fled to Pakistan, India, the United States, or European countries. The consequent social disruption, massive unemployment, and immense poverty have seriously affected the lives of Afghan women, who have been brutally oppressed at multiple levels. With low literacy rates among women and alarming maternal mortality rates, Afghanistan ranks near the bottom of the United Nations Gender Development Index (GDI). Nationalism and religion are contentious issues, and in recent decades Afghan women, politicized as symbols of community identity, have borne the brunt of oppression by armed groups, who have invoked notions of "Afghan culture" to restrict women's rights and freedom severely.

Politics, Nationalism, and the Taliban. Throughout the twentieth century, efforts at modernizing Afghanistan that have favored women-centered social reforms have bred resistance among ethnic tribal leaders whose power bases would be threatened if prevailing gender ideologies and customary practices were challenged. The efforts of King

Violin Lessons in Kabul. Frau Wenzlitzka, an Austrian violin teacher, gives a lesson at the School of Music in Afghanistan, 1963. AKG-IMAGES/PAUL ALMASY

Amanullah (r. 1919–1929), who finally defeated the British in the Anglo-Afghan war in 1919, to promote female education and discourage the veiling of women were opposed as "Western." After his exile in 1929, for the next two decades various Afghan rulers introduced conflicting laws for women—from total abrogation of gender-equality laws by Amir Habibullah II (r. 1929) to Nadir Shah (r. 1929–1933), who opened girls' schools but retained a cautious approach to avoid conflicts with religious and conservative tribal leaders. After Nadir Shah's assassination in 1933, under Zahir Shah (r. 1933–1973) a climate of reform ushered in significant changes in the 1950s and 1960s. Afghan women got franchise in 1964, and when the Soviet-backed organization PDPA (People's Democratic Party of Afghanistan) rose to power, Afghan women gained opportunities and social visibility.

After Communist rule was established in 1978, the PDPA initiated widespread literacy projects and women-centered reforms—raising the age of marriage and prohibiting traditional feudal practices such as forced seclusion, payment of bride-prices, and forced marriage. Afghan reformers supported these initiatives, and hundreds of urban middle-class Afghan women joined the workforce as teachers, physicians, and office workers; many women from elite families received Western-style education overseas. In the 1980s women in Kabul moved about freely without *hijab* (the veil). Women represented 50 percent of the students and 60 percent of the teachers at Kabul University, 70 percent of schoolteachers, 50 percent of civilian government workers, and 40 percent of doctors in Kabul.

However, conservative groups perceived such nontraditional roles as Western imports and threats to Afghan culture. Such rhetoric was used to rouse fervor in the name of "national identity" and to challenge the Soviet occupation of Afghanistan (1979–1989). As a result of the backlash, women's dress, behavior, and lifestyle came under surveillance. Following the Soviet withdrawal, factional fighting and civil war completely disrupted life in Afghanistan. The rule of the mujahideen (1992–1996) followed by the extremist Taliban militia ushered in lawlessness and untold human rights abuses. Intimidating communities and capturing cities, the Taliban established control over Kabul in 1996. The mujahideen version of strict Islam was replaced with extremist injunctions, including total seclusion of women from all public places, a ban on female education, and a stern dress code requiring the *chadri* (a sheetlike covering for the entire body) to be worn outside the home. Offenders were flogged, abducted, or killed.

These injunctions used Islamic rhetoric about "community honor" and religious identity to rationalize unbelievable atrocities on women, men, and children. Hundreds of women were raped by armed groups. Such rapes appear to have been condoned by leaders as methods to intimidate vanquished populations and reward soldiers. There were widespread reports of women and minors being sold into prostitution, pushed into coercive marriages, and stoned—without any legal recourse.

Despite severe constraints, some home-based schools and vocational training programs supported by the United Nations or other non-governmental organizations (NGOs) continued to function. In 1998 the head of Taliban's Department for the Promotion of Virtue and Prevention of Vice (DPVPV) accused the programs of spreading anti-Taliban propaganda and closed them down. Given that women teachers had been the backbone of the system, the national school system collapsed, and by 2000 literacy rates dropped severely. Although state infrastructure and institutions were largely destroyed by 2000, the Taliban obstructed humanitarian assistance from the United Nations and the international community from reaching those most in need. Aid workers carrying food and medicine to women and children were threatened with their lives. Without basic health care, thousands of Afghan children died from respiratory infections, and women succumbed to maternal mortality or other curable ailments. Through the 1990s millions of women were terrorized and violated physically and emotionally—while losing sons and husbands to intertribal warfare.

State Support, Activism, and International Aid since 2001. After a United States–led military alliance unseated the Taliban in 2001, there was some relief from the draconian regime. From Mazār-e Sharīf, Kabul, and elsewhere there were reports of women moving in public places without the previously mandated male relatives as escorts. Some women discarded burkas, *chadris*, or other forms of veiling, which would have garnered brutal punishments under the Taliban. However, as organizations such as the Human Rights Watch gained access to post-Taliban Afghanistan, shocking instances of violence against women came to light—for instance, about a woman's being stoned to death for suspected adultery or flogged for accidentally revealing her ankle beneath her burka. However, in a highly patriarchal society where rape is seen as a loss of community and personal honor, incriminating testimony was hard to come by. Like victims of rape and sexual abuse in most societies, Afghan women were reluctant to narrate their traumas.

These brutalities, however, spawned pockets of resistance and networking among Afghan women, such as the Revolutionary Association of the Women of Afghanistan, a radical multiobjective organization operated during the Taliban regime through clandestine consciousness-raising meetings and women's literacy classes. Their outreach work helped thousands of women in refugee camps in Pakistan. Since the establishment in 2003 of the first democratically elected government in Afghanistan, there has been a Ministry of Women Affairs (MWA) that has sponsored many new projects for women in crisis, including those previously detained in prison, and for women seeking refuge from domestic abuse, facing health problems, or aspiring to an education. Although hospitals and schools are scarce, there is no restriction on women's access to health care, employment, and participation in public life. In 2004, Afghanistan was represented by its first women Olympic competitors: Robina Muqimyar, a runner, and Friba Razayee, in judo.

Most local NGOs in Afghanistan are supported by U.N. agencies or women's organizations overseas, especially from the United States. They use multipronged strategies focusing on health, education, and livelihood programs. Despite many state and private initiatives for women's empowerment, norms of sex-segregation prevail in Afghan society. In 2005, reports from the U.N. Fund for Women, the World Health Organization, and Physicians for Human Rights showed that, of 4 million young Afghans going to school, only 25 percent were girls, and 40 percent of the 1,038 health-care facilities had no female health workers. Social prejudice against women entering public life remains strong—on 25 September 2006 the provincial director of the MWA in Qandahār was assassinated by two gunmen outside her home. A resurgence of sporadic Taliban-sponsored violence in 2006–2007 has caused concern.

Although international funds pouring into Afghanistan have brought much-needed financial resources for reconstruction, most NGO documentation and appeals for support lavishly use the figure of the "helpless" Afghan woman "victimized" by her own religion, thus echoing stereotypical Orientalist discourses that demonize Islam. It is important to underscore that Afghan society is not homogeneous, and the decrees of the Taliban cannot be seen as Qurʾanic injunctions. This would give extremist regimes the legitimacy they seek for brutal suppression. More important, this would overlook the courageous acts of resistance of Afghan women as they struggle with issues of livelihood, poverty, and violence that plague their lives.

[*See also* Islam.]

BIBLIOGRAPHY

Ahmed-Ghosh, Huma. "A History of Women in Afghanistan: Lessons Learnt for the Future; or, Yesterdays and Tomorrow: Women in Afghanistan." *Journal of International Women's Studies* 4, no. 3 (2003): 1–14.

Brodsky, Anne E. *With All Our Strength: The Revolutionary Association of the Women of Afghanistan.* New York: Routledge, 2003.

Latifa. *My Forbidden Face: Growing Up under the Taliban, a Young Woman's Story.* Translated by Linda Coverdale. New York: Hyperion, 2001.

Mehta, Sunita, ed. *Women for Afghan Women: Shattering Myths and Claiming the Future.* New York: Palgrave Macmillan, 2002.

Skaine, Rosemarie. *The Women of Afghanistan under the Taliban.* Jefferson, N.C.: McFarland, 2002.

Maina Chawla Singh

AFRICA

This entry consists of three subentries:

7000–5000 B.C.E.

This essay reviews the transition from foraging to farming and animal keeping in Africa from 7000 to 5000 B.C.E.—particularly in northern Africa, where the major changes occurred—with attention to gender relations. Addressing such a huge geographic expanse in ancient times presents challenges of scale and interpretation. Africa was probably as culturally diverse in prehistoric times as it has been historically, and this part of the prehistoric time span is documented solely by archaeological evidence, presenting its own interpretive challenges to studying gender relations.

Environmental Background: Tumultuous Times. Nine thousand years ago—around 7000 B.C.E.—northern Africa was very different than it is today. Paleoenvironmental evidence shows that at the end of the last Ice Age (12000 B.C.E.) northern Africa warmed rapidly. Rainfall increased to several times its modern levels, lakes were about 330–660 feet (100–200 meters) higher and much more extensive than today, and northern and eastern Africa were joined by a network of rivers over a huge area. Mediterranean vegetation and equatorial forests expanded into the Sahara, and deserts became savannas. These millennia of greening also held dangers: torrential rainfall in the Ethiopian highlands produced what geologists call the "wild Nile." Floods scoured the Nile Valley, which had been a human refuge in the hyperarid late Ice Age, driving groups into the green Sahara. By 7000 B.C.E., rainfall levels lessened, and the Nile Valley was again inhabitable, but lakes and rivers were still extensive throughout the Sahara, and true desert was restricted to the Sahara's central core. Rainfall became more erratic over the next two millennia. By 5000 B.C.E. the aquatic network linking northern and eastern Africa had been cut, and the Sahara reached its final desiccation by 3000 B.C.E.

Northern Africans coped with these environment dynamics by consistently innovating subsistence strategies.

Rock Engraving. *Fat Ladies*, Chad. DAVID COULSON/TRUST FOR AFRICAN ROCK ART

Some innovations led toward animal domestication and farming, but the details differ markedly from those of the better-known Southwest Asian (Near Eastern) Neolithic. Many early hunter-gatherers in the greening Sahara were not nomadic; instead, they settled for at least part of the year by lakes and rivers or in well-watered highlands. They did not farm but relied on abundant wild foods, including wild millet, sorghum, and other grains; fish, waterfowl, and aquatic reptiles such as crocodiles; and turtles and land mammals. Profuse grinding stones and grain storage pits in their settlements testify to intensive use of wild grains. Ceramic vessels, radiocarbon-dated to more than 9,500 years ago, appear in sites across the Sahara, antedating Southwest Asian pottery by two millennia. Saharan hunter-gatherers also left behind a rich corpus of rock art that testifies to their material and spiritual worlds and suggests something of gender relations.

As northern Africa desiccated during the period 7000–6000 B.C.E., evidence testifies to Africans' initiative in managing dwindling resources. Some in southern Libya penned wild Barbary sheep (aoudad), but the species was not fully domesticated, perhaps because domestic cattle, sheep, and goats appeared in the region at about the same time. Wild ancestors of sheep and goats live only in Southwest Asia, where they were domesticated, but wild cattle were widespread throughout temperate Eurasia and North Africa. Until the very late twentieth century, archaeologists thought that cattle were domesticated in Southwest Asia and introduced into northern Africa and Europe. However, genetic comparisons of living cattle from South Asia, Southwest Asia, Africa, and Europe suggest three independent cattle domestications: in the Indus Valley, in the Taurus Mountains of Syria and Turkey, and in northern Africa.

In the period 6000–5000 B.C.E., permanent settlements gave way to nomadic pastoralism in the Sahara's still widespread grasslands, where livestock provided a viable alternative to dwindling aquatic resources. Pastoralists prosper in savannas, where their herds convert grass into meat and milk, but people must move in rhythm with the availability of water and forage for their animals. Archaeological evidence from 6000–5000 B.C.E. reflects pastoralists' extensive communication networks: exotic stones and seashells were traded over thousands of kilometers, and rock art shows strong similarities in artistic conventions throughout the Sahara. African pastoralists continued to make pottery and harvest still profuse wild grains in an increasingly Sahelian semidesert environment.

In the Nile Valley and Egyptian oases, abundant water allowed the sedentary forager lifestyle to endure, and these groups incorporated cattle, sheep, goats, and domestic barley and wheat from southwest Asia rather late (4500–4000 B.C.E.). Predynastic Egypt probably represents a fusion of these communities, with pastoralists who moved into Lower Egypt during a fifth millennium B.C.E. Saharan drought. By 4000–3000 B.C.E., large sedentary communities near Khartoum, Sudan, added domestic sheep and goats to a

Rock Painting. *Women and Cattle*, Chad. DAVID COULSON/TRUST FOR AFRICAN ROCK ART

lifestyle heavily reliant on sorghum and fishing. Whether the Khartoum people farmed the sorghum is debated: it lacks the physical hallmarks of a domestic grain, but staggering numbers of storage pits and grinding stones suggest to some archaeologists that people were actively fostering its growth.

Pastoralists finally abandoned the Sahara for regions to the south during the third millennium B.C.E. Their long way of life in the Sahel apparently ended during a severe, prolonged drought in 800–0 B.C.E. Pastoralists and local hunter-gatherers alike were driven to seek refuge at the Niger River's inland delta and Lake Chad, where they developed new economic strategies to cope with very poor conditions. When climate improved in the first millennium C.E., Africa's first farming villages appeared, as well as specialized herding societies interdependent with farmers, and commodity-producing towns. Such economic innovations were basic to the rapid emergence of Central and West African cities and states.

Gendering Archaeological Narratives. How do gender relations fit into this story of ecological challenge and human response? Gender studies emerged in archaeology in the period 1985–1990, rather later than in anthropology. Though some approach this as a hunt for "women" and "men" in the archaeological record, more sophisticated research begins by questioning whether such dichotomous and universalized modern categories are useful to a gender-conscious archaeology.

Approaches to gender-conscious archaeological research vary, but two central ideas guide research on gender relations in the undocumented past. First, given the ethnographic evidence for great cross-cultural diversity in gender roles, one must avoid essentializing ancient gender roles. Thus specific crafts and occupations should not be assumed a priori to have been the province of prehistoric women or men; for example, it should not be assumed that women were invariably potters, or even that women were "the gatherers." Such linkages of gender and work are best seen as hypotheses, to be evaluated with data. As a corollary, a gender-conscious archaeology allows that ancient gender categories may have diverged from any known today, with more than two genders, differing relations of gender to sex, gender to sexuality, sex to sexuality, and so forth.

Second, feminist archaeologists assert that archaeological research is always an interpretive act, always historically situated, and always a mix of theory, method, and materials analysis. Margaret Conkey, Joan Gero, and Alison Wylie, for instance, have noted that although it is true that archaeologists cannot "dig up" gender, it is equally true that they cannot dig up ecosystems, a time-honored topic of archaeological study. The challenge, then, is to craft ways of thinking about scanty archaeological evidence that enables socially focused research, using the anthropological literature to enhance our awareness of gender diversity on the one hand and feminist perspectives on social inequality, control, and resistance on the other.

Concretely, what kinds of evidence can be used to explore gender relations? Archaeologists recover artifacts, food debris, structures, burials, and art. They can document how these vary across the landscape and over time. The next sections explore gender in the earlier hunter-gatherer and later pastoral phases of northern African history using such data.

Reproduction and Production. The earlier "green Sahara" hunter-gatherer phase saw a semisedentary lifestyle in many areas, with groups staying in one place and relying on stored grains and rich aquatic resources for a significant part of the year. This is unusual among foragers, who historically tended to be more mobile. Both sedentism and reliance on stored foods have implications for women in such groups. Cross-cultural studies of hunter-gatherers reveal that most groups divide work and gender roles in two, male and female, but that age distinctions are very important markers of status and of work obligations. We may imagine that earlier foragers probably divided work along generally dichotomous gender lines, with most females in their reproductive years forming households with one or more male partners serially or simultaneously, seeking to rear offspring, and dividing food-getting work with male partners. However, as with historically documented foragers, it is possible that persons of other genders, with variable social roles, may have existed.

A fundamental question is whether women in early sedentary forager communities lived in better or worse circumstances, in terms of workload, diet, and health, than did their more mobile counterparts. To explore this question, it is possible to study the regular and important changes that occur in modern foraging women's lives, regardless of where in the world they live, when nation-states press their groups to settle down. These are not all beneficial.

One result of shifting to a sedentary life is that women do not try so hard to space their children four to five years apart, as they did when following a mobile lifestyle. Mother's milk was a forager baby's sole sustenance until it was weaned to adult foods, often not until four to five years old. A physically active mother usually could not nourish two nursing children simultaneously. Moreover, mothers living on the move and foraging for food daily would have had literally to bear the extra burden of children born too close together. In settled communities, forager women relaxed their vigilance against pregnancies that come too soon after the birth of the previous child. Milk from domestic animals and cereal gruels enhanced the survival chances of babies born two to three years apart. This ultimately leads to rapid population growth, but in terms of women's everyday lives, more of their time must be devoted to infant care, though older children may help.

Storing grains extends the season in which they can be eaten, but this in turn presents novel labor allocation and management problems. Grains are digestible only after processing with grinding stones and cooking with water as porridge or bread. The profusion of wild grains and grinding stones in ancient northern African sites necessarily implies increased demands for firewood, water collection, and good grinding stones. Such increments in workload were undoubtedly points of tension and negotiation between ancient male and female foragers. Though female workload may have increased with grain use, new forms of female authority may also have emerged: in the majority of ethnographic cases, senior female household members manage stored plant foods, and only they can decide how to use them.

Older ethnographies of pastoralists often placed women at the periphery of male-dominated societies, but more recent, woman-focused studies show that they are neither passive nor sequestered. They build their own homes, sometimes engage in trade, milk livestock, care for young animals, and are especially involved in managing sheep and goat flocks. Male ethnographers tended to see "small stock" as insignificant "small change" in pastoral systems, but economic development studies have demonstrated that sheep and goats play a major role in feeding women and children.

Saharan Rock Art and Gender Relations. The rich array of Saharan rock art provides provocative insights into gender and sexuality in the hunter-gatherer and pastoralist times. Like Paleolithic cave art of western Europe, Saharan hunter-gatherer art is full of animals, but unlike European cave art, Saharans portrayed many people, too. Like South African rock artists, Saharans often depicted animal-headed, human-bodied beings, or "therioanthropes." South African rock-art analysts have interpreted these as shamans in trance states, and at least one student of the Saharan images (Jean-Loïc Le Quellec) accepts this interpretation, but they may be mythic beings.

Saharan therioanthropes are portrayed as carnivore-headed, many resembling African hunting dogs, and are often depicted killing or carrying huge wild game. Therioanthropes with gigantic phalli are shown engaging in sex with elephants and other animals, female therioanthropes, and human females. Human males and females are also depicted in sexual intercourse, and other representations depict wild animals in sexual states and activities, such as male elephants in musth, with dripping penises. An engraving from the Messak, southern Libya, depicts a human female and male having intercourse, while near them a Barbary sheep ram is shown sniffing a ewe's vulva, a prelude to copulation.

Female bodies are often shown in an "open woman" position, frontally with knees drawn up, sometimes receiving the erect penis of a male mate, sometimes giving birth, sometimes simply exposing a cavernous vagina. In other cases, women are depicted from the side in intercourse with human males, with therianthropes, or with beings that appear to be animals.

What do these images say about early Saharan hunter-gatherer gender relations and ideological systems? Three beings are commonly depicted: sexually active human females, sexually active human males, and persons with carnivore heads and human genitalia shown hunting or in heterosexual intercourse. Hunting and sex are privileged activities in this widespread art, and females join in the sex—but not the hunting—without appearing to be physically coerced. If the carnivore heads reflect African hunting dogs, the images assert a link between humans and a species that hunts cooperatively and shares food with everyone in its group. Children and babies are not portrayed, other than in birth scenes. Thus the central foci are adult, sexually active beings, mapped onto male and female by genital representation, in a dyadic heterosexual pattern, but one not species-restricted, because each gender is depicted having relations with other species.

Gendered Life Paths among Pastoralists. Saharan pastoralist rock art contrasts not in style but in subject matter with earlier hunter-gatherer representations. Sexual acts are seldom shown, and genitals depicted are not exaggerated in scale. Women, men, and, notably, children are shown, as are domestic and nondomestic animals, often in scenes that appear to portray daily routines. As in dynastic Egyptian art, pens and houses are shown from above, but humans, animals, containers, beds, and other objects are represented in profile. Cattle are shown tethered to a picket line and milked, being led out in herds from camp or in the field, and people forage or sit in small houses. Scenes showing men and dogs hunting are common, and therianthropes sometimes appear in them.

The Cameroon-born archaeologist Augustine Holl has presented a provocative view of gender among ancient North Africans, analyzing a painted panel at Tikadouine in Tassili, southern Algeria. He argued that the panel presents a narrative of a male's life history, from boyhood to elderhood, stages typical of modern pastoralist males. Holl asserts that signifiers of gender and age mark males in each panel segment. For example, hunting wild animals defines a phase of youth, whereas a different hairstyle and association with domestic herds, a house, a woman, and a child appear to mark elderhood.

Neither Holl nor others have discussed signifiers of adult womanhood or other female statuses, but associations of female figures with specific hairdo, dress, and activities should be explored systematically. Holl's idea that pastoral representations engender male individuals as men through multiple markers and activities may equally apply to gendering female persons as women by their hairdo, dress, and consistent association with children and a house. Paintings show female figures dancing, digging, harvesting wild grain, tying cattle on picket lines and milking, and resting inside houses, as well as interacting with men and children. In contrast with hunter-gatherer art, Saharan pastoral art shows children, and these are placed mainly with female figures, either as babes in arms or as freestanding small figures, apparently helping with tasks.

Westerners may be inclined to read the depictions of women in houses as reflecting an oppressive, woman-at-home ideology, but these may convey Saharan notions of adult female agency. In most ethnographically documented African pastoralist societies, adult women build and hold their own homes as property, and from early marriage women exercise a level of authority over household activities unknown in most Indo-European societies. Adult female status in such societies rises with the number of surviving children, and prehistoric depictions associating females with children may also reflect a positive mark of achieved status among ancient Saharans. Only systematic research will reveal if such representational associations hold up consistently.

Pastoralist burials provide insights into the equipment of womanhood and manhood. Adult pastoralist females in the south-central Sahara were interred with large, elegantly formed grinding stones, while males are not, perhaps attesting to female work and crafts during life. Ostrich eggshell beads, made almost exclusively by adolescent and adult females in historically documented times, are interred with female adults but seldom with males.

Other cultural practices in northern Africa are more alien to Westerners but nonetheless enduring in the region: for instance, pastoralists from Egypt to the western Sahara sometimes buried young cows near human interments or under monumental stones, a practice that continued into dynastic Egyptian times.

Thinking about gender in the ancient past challenges us to transcend modern categories of "woman" and "man." Sometimes, as with the burials and representations of cows and people, we might even need to entertain the idea that some significant creatures were thought of as persons, and thought of as gendered. Hathor, symbolic mother of all pharaohs, is depicted as a fusion of woman and cow, supporting the life-giving sun with her horns. Researchers would be well advised to be open to possibilities that ancient people could have defined personhood, gender, and difference in ways truly alien to our own, and to seek to understand traces of those systems of thought in their own terms.

[*See also* Agriculture; Gender Roles; Gender Theory; Hunting and Gathering; Nomads; Pastoralism; *and* Prehistory.]

BIBLIOGRAPHY

Bradley, Daniel G. "Genetic Hoofprints: The DNA Trail Leading Back to the Origins of Today's Cattle Has Taken Some Surprising Turns along the Way." *Natural History*, February 2003, pp. 36–42. A readable source on genetic research that has revolutionized Neolithic studies.

Conkey, Margaret W., and Joan M. Gero. "Programme to Practice: Gender and Feminism in Archaeology." *Annual Review of Anthropology* 26 (1997): 411–437. A key literature review and critical analysis of gender studies in archaeology and the role of feminist theory.

Coulson, David, and Alec Campbell. *African Rock Art: Paintings and Engravings on Stone.* New York: Harry N. Abrams, 2001. Lavishly illustrated compendium that includes good coverage of the Sahara, though little gender-conscious interpretation.

Di Lernia, Savino. "Dismantling Dung: Delayed Use of Food Resources among Early Holocene Forgers of the Libyan Sahara." *Journal of Anthropological Archaeology* 20, no. 4 (2001): 408–441. Discusses archaeological discovery of an early experiment in animal management by northern Africans.

Haaland, Randi. "Emergence of Sedentism: New Ways of Living, New Ways of Symbolizing." *Antiquity* 71, no. 272 (June 1997): 374–385. Among the few Africanist archaeologists to embed a discussion of gender in analysis of plant use and sedentism. Argues for Sudanese farming of "wild" sorghum.

Hassan, Fekri A. "The Predynastic of Egypt." *Journal of World Prehistory* 2, no. 2 (1988): 1–16. An Egyptian archaeologist's revisionist perspective: the roots of dynastic Egypt lie in a fusion of sedentary foragers and Saharan pastoralists.

Holl, Augustine. "Pathways to Elderhood: Research on Past Pastoral Iconography—the Paintings from Tikadourine (Tassili-n-Ajjer)." *Origini* 18 (1995): 69–113. A Cameroon-born archaeologist breaks with traditional interpretations of Saharan art, asserting that this panel shows the making of manhood.

Le Quellec, Jean-Loïc. *Art rupestre du Fezzan septentrional (Libye).* Oxford: B.A.R., 1987. Profusely illustrated compendium of hunter-gatherer and rock art from southern Libya.

Lewis-Williams, J. David. *Believing and Seeing: Symbolic Meanings in Southern San Rock Paintings.* London: Academic Press, 1981. On the basis of ethnographic linkages, asserts that southern African rock art represents rituals and shamanic trance states, not everyday life. Widely accepted as an interpretation of that corpus, but not of all prehistoric art.

Neumann, Katharina. "The Romance of Farming: Plant Cultivation and Domestication in Africa." In *African Archaeology: A Critical Introduction*, edited by Ann B. Stahl, pp. 249–275. Malden, Mass.: Blackwell, 2005. An updated overview of the emergence of farming, arguing that northern Africans did not have to develop farming until forced to during the so-called dark millennium.

Smith, Andrew B. *African Herders: Emergence of Pastoral Traditions.* Walnut Creek, Calif.: AltaMira Press, 2005. An overview of the archaeological evidence on pastoralism from the Sahara and elsewhere.

Wylie, Alison. "Gender, Theory, and the Archaeological Record: Why Is There No Archaeology of Gender?" In *Engendering Archaeology*, edited by Joan M. Gero and Margaret W. Conkey, pp. 31–54. Oxford: Basil Blackwell, 1991. A feminist philosopher assesses the conceptual and political issues implicated in the slow emergence of gender studies in archaeology.

DIANE GIFFORD-GONZALEZ

5000 B.C.E.–1000 C.E.

Most studies that have addressed the history of African women have examined the roles and status of women in the colonial and postcolonial periods, but because of the lack of evidence little is known of the history of women in ancient Africa. Most is known about women who lived in the region of the Nile River valley, especially Kemet (Egypt).

The period around 5000 B.C.E. was a turning point in ancient African history. It witnessed the transition from Paleolithic to Neolithic societies in different parts of the continent. As more societies settled down and attained food surpluses, they were able to engage in endeavors beyond the search for food. The origin of the Nile River valley civilizations has been traced to transformations in the region of what is now the Sahara Desert. Around 5000 B.C.E. the Sahara experienced desiccation and hence set off human migrations to the precincts of the Nile River valley in the east and southward toward the cluster of river valleys, including the Niger, the Senegal, and the Volta.

By 3500 B.C.E., viable Neolithic societies had emerged along the river valleys, including the Nile. The civilizations in the Nile Valley were the most flourishing. Overall, by the Postclassical millennial period of 1000 C.E., African societies had gone through much change. In the fourth millennium B.C.E., Egypt dominated the area around the first cataract, known as Nubia. The spread of Egyptian influence between 1700 and 1500 B.C.E. led to the creation of the Kingdom of Kush with its capital city Kerma around

Hunting and Gathering. Sitting women and returning hunter, frescoes of Tassili n'Ajjer, Algeria, 2000 B.C.E. MUSÉE DE L'HOMME, PARIS/ERICH LESSING/ART RESOURCE, NY

the third cataract of the Nile. The people of Axum settled the Ethiopian highlands around 500 B.C.E., and by the first century C.E. Axum was a thriving a metropolis in the Nile River valley. Kingship had emerged around 3100 B.C.E. among the Nile River valley societies. Ancient Egypt, Nubia, and Axum structured their societies to meet new challenges of political and social order, long-distance trade, cross-cultural communication and diffusion of ideas, cultural and religious worldviews, and social formation.

Women in Hunter-Gatherer Societies before 5000 B.C.E. Evidence on modern hunter-gatherer societies suggests that African hunter-gatherer women held as much status as men. Paleolithic women played equal roles with men in the survival of communities of about twenty-five people, mostly kin groups, who lived cooperatively together to survive. Cave art of Sahara desert communities depicts women foraging for plants, suggesting that they may have been the primary plant gatherers. By 3500 B.C.E., as Neolithic communities emerged along the Nile basin, women's roles in food gathering ensured the survival of the communities. Paleolithic Nile Valley communities depended more on plant food than on meat. This suggests that women's roles were invaluable in the acquisition of food, and thus for the survival of the group—which may have elevated women's status.

Archaeologists have mapped out the lives of women in hunter-gatherer societies. Probably the major difference between hunter-gatherer communities and other human communities was the dominance of the social institution known as the band over that of the communal family. Bands moved from one temporary camp to another and cooperated to forage for plant foods, hunt for animals, and share food, water, and shelter. African women played central roles in the band: they not only provided food but also made decisions that affected the survival of the groups—for instance, in matters of resource distribution and cooperative relationships with other groups.

Matrilineal kinship influenced the leadership of the communities in the Nile Valley: women were central to the institutions of political power and the political economy of resource sharing. Descent was traced through the mother's line; as a result, women influenced polytheistic religious, ontological, and eschatological worldviews. Women worked cooperatively to raise children, bringing normative socialization to their communities. Overall, the lifespan of Paleolithic women, about twenty-five to thirty years, was longer than men's and hence enabled matriarchs to play significantly greater roles in shaping family and communal affairs.

Paleolithic African women, like their counterparts in other areas of the ancient world, tended to space their children's births three to five years apart. The transient and insecure nature of a foraging lifestyle militated against having too many children spaced closely together. African women used lactation as an early type of birth control by nursing young children to suppress ovulation. The combination of early mortality and spacing of births had the effect of leaving many children motherless, to be raised by relatives. Overall, women played prominent roles in raising the community's children, and hence they were involved in making major decisions that influenced their communities, such as where to set up camp. It is very likely that after 3500 B.C.E., considerable transformation in child spacing occurred as roaming bands settled down and hence experienced fewer deprivations.

African Women in the Earliest Neolithic Communities. Neolithic African women's labor tended to be more gender specific than was their Paleolithic counterparts'. Nevertheless, the separation of work into mostly female versus mostly male occupations did not necessarily mean that Neolithic women's labor was valued less than men's. African women in the Nile Valley played pioneering roles in agricultural innovation and production. Archaeological and artistic evidence shows that Neolithic African women were engaged in a variety of economic tasks beyond the domestic sphere. For instance, tomb paintings illustrate women involved in clearing land, cultivating and tending plants, and harvesting and winnowing grain. Neolithic African women made many significant contributions to emerging agricultural societies. They were leaders in domesticating plants and some animals, and indeed the transition to agricultural societies in the Nile Valley by 3500 B.C.E. necessitated a great deal of experimentation with different varieties of plant species.

Although men first prepared the land, men and women planted, tended, and harvested crops together. Just as in other societies, African hunter-gatherer women systematically began to select the seeds and plants that would ensure their survival and ultimately paved the way for a sedentary lifestyle based on the cultivation of grains. Emerging Neolithic communities depended on women's domestication of sheep, goats, cattle, and dogs, as well as their trapping fish. Eventually the efforts of Neolithic African women advanced the technology of farming tools and food-processing techniques. Organizing and coordinating women's productive activities were probably the most essential contribution of women to the Iron Age advancements among African communities.

African women in the Neolithic period also took up weaving, like their pastoralist counterparts. In some regions adjacent to the Nile Valley where the environment did not support the domestication of crops, communities minimized foraging and began to control their food sources by innovations that resulted in the domestication of animals instead of plants. Such pastoralist communities traded with the sedentary agricultural communities for plant foods.

Women in the Nile Valley used grassy plants to weave cloth. Spinning was mostly the work of women, and it entailed the production of enormous amounts of yarn. The location of weaving depended on the season; during the summer months it occurred outdoors, and during the rainy seasons it occurred indoors. Increasingly, as weaving by women became a public activity, it attained more visibility and hence gained recognition. Women benefited from publicly weaving together because they could easily assist each other in their tasks, perhaps reinforcing matrifocal arrangements. Women were responsible for tending small stock and for other productive activities, such as making salt, soap, cloth, pots, and oils for cooking and cosmetics.

Another area of Neolithic African women's economic contribution was local and regional trade. Women merchants supplied milk, chickens, rice, cereal grains, lotus flour, and processed foods, and they traded metal and pottery products. The historical evidence suggests that women dominated the production of pottery by hand, while men dominated the specialized production and trade in wheel-turned pots. Kushite women cultivated fruit, grew cotton, spun and wove cloth, produced gold, and even smelted iron for trading purposes.

Many Neolithic communities valued women's work: women were often buried with the tools of their crafts or occupations. In ancient Egypt and in the Nubian Kingdom of Kush, increasing gender differentiation accompanied the rise of class-based urban civilization and a centralized political system. Yet women held positions of relative equality, and royal women played prominent roles in politics. The Neolithic communities that existed before the creation of the first urban centers around 3500 B.C.E. belonged to organized political states ruled by hereditary rulers.

The comparative isolation of the Old Kingdom (3100–2181 B.C.E.) of Egypt from serious military threat and the suitability of the Nile Valley for the production of agricultural surpluses suggest that ancient Egypt was not particularly militarized. As one result Egypt experienced relative gender equality in its social and economic hierarchies, and this minimized constraining conditions for women. Overall, even as social stratification increased, elite Egyptian women continued to exercise strong political influence. Collectively, the reigns of female pharaohs were marked by internal stability and external recognition and prestige.

Several female pharaohs ruled in Egypt. Ahmose-Nefertari (1570–1505 B.C.E.) was instrumental in the expulsion of the Hyksos who had conquered Egypt, and Hatshepsut (1503–1482 B.C.E.) was a highly successful ruler who strengthened Egypt's defenses and trade networks, initiated many construction projects, and enjoyed a stable, prosperous reign. She took male titles, dressed as a man, and even wore a beard. For her part, Cleopatra (69–30 B.C.E.) used diplomacy to buttress the independence of Egypt at a time when political instability was ravaging the Mediterranean basin.

Despite the increased militarization and weakened position of Egyptian women under the New Kingdom (1550–1070 B.C.E.), elite women continued to make important contributions to economic, cultural, and political life. Even as late as the fifth century B.C.E., as noted by the Greek historian Herodotus, Egyptian women had more independence than other women in the ancient world did.

Nubia (Kush) and Axum (Ethiopia) shared similar social and political characteristics with Egypt. Nubian or Kushite warrior queens, queen regents, and queen mothers, also known as *kentakes* (Greek, *candaces*) played crucial roles in the development of the state. In 332 C.E., Alexander the Great sought to conquer Nubia, but the unique military preparations under the *kentake* of Nubia weakened Alexander's resolve, so he attacked Egypt instead. The "black queens" of Kush were also significant political figures; indeed, research suggests that Nubian kingdoms had a greater number of queens than the Egyptians had.

Bas-reliefs depict *kentakes* attired in armor and wielding scepters of queen-motherhood and spears as symbols of power and authority. Evidence shows that in some cases the *kentakes* were co-rulers with sons and brothers, but the title "queen of queens" symbolized their unique autonomous leadership. In 23 C.E., an Axumite *kentake* led an army that marched up to Elephantine (part of modern Aswan) near the first cataract of the Nile. The origin myth of Axum, known as the Kebra Nagast, identifies Makeda, the first queen of Ethiopia, as the biblical queen of Sheba. Through the administrative skills of Makeda, by 1000 C.E. Axum had reached its apogee, with its influence felt not only along the basin of the Nile but also in the Middle East.

Axum had eight generations of queens. Apart from this, most Ethiopian kings had high priestess queens who assisted in religious and ritual performance. The elite women of Axum were given fitting burials. For instance, Queen Amanishaketo (35–20 B.C.E.) was buried in a pyramid entombed with treasures, including ten bracelets, nine shield rings, and sixty-seven signet rings. Even once the matrilineal descent systems had eroded during the advanced stage of Neolithic society, women retained ritual power in many African polities and served as founts of maternal wisdom. Queens were kingmakers and were occasionally expected to act as a necessary check on a male ruler's power.

Although lower-class Neolithic women in the Nile Valley certainly did not wield political power, they had rights and recognition. For many lower-class women, childbearing placed them in high esteem, as sedentary communities hoped for large supplies of labor to sustain themselves. The societies sometimes actually pressured women to have more children to increase the labor supply, and they valued women for their ability to foster population growth.

Motherhood was important among all African societies. Ancient Egyptian women celebrated pregnancy, and society showered respect and accolades on mothers, especially those who were able to have many children. Barrenness was a cause for divorce; infertile women sought medical help and were encouraged to adopt children.

Religion and ritual were significant aspects of life in the Nile River valley. Matriarchs practiced ancestor cults and maintained shrines to commemorate and supplicate deities, such as the Taweret goddess for health and fertility in both procreation and agriculture. Women served as priestesses of the goddess Hathor, and during the Old Kingdom, women were prophetesses of the deities Thoth and Ptah. Both Egyptian and Nubian women worshipped Isis, identified as the queen of all goddesses. By the time of the New Kingdom, however, women's roles as priestesses had been considerably reduced, as men increasingly took up priestly positions as career options with the Egyptian state. However, women continued to play important roles in religious and ritual performance; for example, royal women including the queens Ahhotep, Ahmose-Nefertari, and Hatshepsut held the title of God's Wife of Amun (the sun god).

Egyptian and Nubian women carried out a variety of occupations, some gender specific and others not. In Egypt, evidence exists of women working as scribes, bakers, prophets, and temple workers; none of these jobs was solely women's work. Additionally, Egyptian, Nubian, and Axumite women participated in the efflorescence of the sciences. Women were involved in astronomy and mathematics, medicine, and food processing, as well as in metallurgy, textile making, and pottery. In Egypt, astronomy, mathematics, and medicine flourished most during the Old Kingdom; in the Fourth Dynasty there was a body of female physicians led by a woman named Peseshet. Some women gained recognition as powerful healers in Neolithic Africa, perfecting the processing and use of indigenous minerals and herbal medicines.

Many of these occupations, of course, required literacy. Archaeological evidence suggests that women were more literate in the Old Kingdom than in the New Kingdom, and upper-class women were more likely to be literate than lower-class women were. The actual level of literacy among women probably never reached more than 10 percent.

Textile manufacturing, the most important industry in Egypt, was an occupation generally performed by women, enslaved and free, even when it took place on a large scale and outside the domain of households. Egyptian female spinners and weavers produced a highly valued primary commodity for export. Women were also in charge of storehouses and served as suppliers of food and other materials for industry.

Unlike their counterparts elsewhere, such as in Greece, Egyptian women had the right to inherit, will, and own property, as well as to sign contracts. Egyptian women supervised industrial work in textile, perfume, and fragrant oil factories. They worked alongside men and received the same wages. They took part in long-distance trade along the banks of the Nile to the southern reaches of Nubia. Women held private property and used it as they wished. Women acquired property through several means, including gifts, purchase, and marriage. Properties that accumulated from a woman's dowry in the course of marriage belonged to the woman in the case of divorce. In addition, ancient Egyptian law mandated that a wife inherited one-third of her deceased husband's property. Women also owned movable goods including livestock and slaves. Propertied women could independently administer and manage their wealth. They independently engaged in legal settlements, including marriage and divorce issues. Women could be sued, and they had the right to initiate suits on their own.

African women paid attention to their appearance by adopting fashions commensurate with their class and social standing. During the liberal phase of the New Kingdom, the fashions of wealthier men and of women—jewelry, wigs, and colorful robes—appeared to be similar. Upper-class women wore wigs, and commoner women curled or braided their hair. Unlike in other parts of the Mediterranean basin and Eurasia, where women's public appearance was restricted, Egyptian women could mingle with men in public and were allowed to hold their own in conversations and public discourse.

In spite of the relative equality that characterized the lives of Nile River valley women, they faced some challenges and experienced some constraints. For instance, Egyptian society was dominated by men. Husbands dominated their wives and could have multiple wives. Elite men like the pharaoh had their own harems. Although upper-class women could hold power, lower-class women held nonadministrative positions. Additionally, labor specialization allowed for the concentration of wealth in the hands of a few men. As land became more valued than labor, the tendency toward patrifocal families increased, as did the stratification of wealth among men. The extant evidence on non-elite women prior to the New Kingdom is not as rich as the evidence on upper-class women.

[*See also* Agriculture; Egypt, *subentry* Ancient Period; Hunting and Gathering; Monarchy; *and* Pastoralism.]

KWABENA O. AKURANG-PARRY AND CATHERINE B. CLAY

1000–1500

Historical writing about women in sub-Saharan Africa from 1000 to 1500 generally falls into two groups, one concerned with common women and the other with elites. Unfortunately there is little source material upon which to base studies of women in either group during this period. Traditionally historians have mined archives for written records compiled in the past, but for sub-Saharan Africa from 1000 to 1500 few written primary sources are available. With the exception of a small number of Sudanic and East African societies that employed scribes who knew Arabic, African societies did not keep written records during this period. A handful of observations recorded by Muslim travelers and, in the end of the period, European sailors have survived. However, travelers and sailors were most interested in the affairs of state and were generally attracted to those they thought wielded power—men. Hence they wrote little about African women, and what they did write was often tinged with cultural biases.

Since the 1960s Africanist historians have developed methodologies for collecting and analyzing African oral narratives, or oral traditions, that are remembered by specialists, the best known of which are the griots of Mali. However, these sources also reveal little about the lives of women in this early period in sub-Saharan African history. Oral narratives tend to compress events from the distant past, making periodization difficult. Further, since most traditions serve the purpose of lending legitimacy to existing structures of power, they focus on great leaders, most (but not all) of whom were men, and on events such as wars and migrations. They reveal little about the lives of common people, particularly women, and less about changes in women's lives over time. Finally, archaeological and linguistic analyses have provided much evidence of broad social and political transformations in early African history, but archaeologists and linguists have not always succeeded in differentiating what men and women did or in determining how gendered roles changed over time.

Models and Generalities. Presented with a dearth of sources through which to explore the place of women in Africa from 1000 to 1500, historians have often fallen back on models derived from studies of societies in other parts of the world and from known historic and present-day practices in Africa itself. Such models often begin with the assumption that lineage (or kin group) affiliations, which are important across Africa in the early twenty-first century, were important in the distant past and served as the basic building blocks of communities. As bearers of children, women were crucial for lineage survival. Since people produced subsistence crops and trade items, and were necessary for defense against enemies and for expansion into new territories, having children was one of the most important ways to extend a lineage's power and wealth. Polygynous marriages provided powerful men with more wives to bear more children. Wives also linked communities to one another, thereby fostering lasting alliances that were important in times of stress.

In patrilocal societies, men lived out their lives in the villages of their birth, marrying women from other villages who took up residence with them. In these societies, women were often important as arbiters in disputes, since they had strong ties in their husbands' communities and in the communities of their birth. As the bearers of the heaviest workloads, both in households and in fields, women were also valued in lineages as producers of goods needed for subsistence and trade. Within lineages, separate spheres for men and women were differentiated. Generally, it is argued, men dominated the exosphere, which included diplomacy, war, and long-distance trade, while women dominated the household, managing food supplies and watching children.

However, since African societies differed over time and space, there are many exceptions to these and other generalities. For example, Nupe and Yoruba women conducted long-distance trade. And the nature of marriage and residence patterns in many places made women the best choice as diplomats and trade negotiators. For example, following patterns developed before 1500, women from small-scale communities on the upper Guinean coast became the most important go-betweens in relations between European sailors and African slave dealers. Many women married whites who settled on the coast, and some rose to control commercial houses in important ports. Given this, models have to be applied with caution.

Incorporating outsiders was another important way to expand a lineage's numbers and therefore power. This was accomplished by purchasing, seizing, or adopting strangers who in the West might be considered slaves. However, across Africa the institution of slavery was different from its Western counterpart. Generally "slaves" in the African context, particularly in the period 1000–1500, were viewed as marginal members of lineages, and their marginality decreased over time. One of the easiest ways to incorporate an outsider or slave into a lineage was through marriage, and men often married slave women, who could then provide more children for the lineage. The ability to bear children, then, made female slaves particularly valuable. Their value was augmented by the fact that women did most of the agricultural work in societies across the continent. With the rise of the Atlantic slave trade after 1500, Africans, then, were often more willing to part with marginal male than with female slaves, which in part explains why about twice as many males than females were exported from the continent.

Of course the structures of African societies differed greatly. In matrilineal societies, a man did not have claim to his own children. They were claimed by his wives' lineages, and he and his brothers in turn claimed the children of their sisters. Under this system, men risked losing control over their sisters since they often lived far away. However, because slave wives had no relatives to claim their children, men in matrilineal societies recognized that acquiring slave women gave them more control over their offspring. In patrilineal systems, men controlled their wives' children, so both "free" and "slave" wives augmented a lineage's numbers. In both systems, free women had families to whom they could appeal if they were mistreated by their husbands. Slave wives had no family and so had no defenders.

Most African women, be they slave or free, labored in fields and households, where they processed and cooked food, the rhythm of their lives determined to a great extent by the crops they grew. When new crops were adopted as the result of ecological changes or contact with new groups of people, the patterns of women's work in particular were transformed. For example, prior to 1000 rice was an important crop in the Mande heartland of the Niger River basin. In about 1100 the Mande began to expand to the west and south. As they did so, they introduced rice and rice-growing technologies to coastal people. Everywhere the tasks required for rice growing and processing became gendered. However, the number of female tasks varied from place to place. The more central rice became to diets, the more males became involved in its production. In places where rice was somewhat marginal, women became responsible for everything from planting to harvesting to processing. In places where rice was central, planting and harvesting became male tasks. But everywhere women were responsible for seed selection, processing, and cooking. The processing of rice centered on milling, a laborious task requiring the use of a heavy handheld mortar and a pestle. The demands of crops grown elsewhere—other grains, yams, bananas—as well as the manner in which societies gendered tasks meant, then, that the patterns of women's lives across Africa varied greatly before 1500.

Women in Great African States. Oral narratives and scattered written sources from some of Africa's great states have allowed historians to explore other aspects of women's lives from 1000 to 1500. Founded in the early thirteenth century in the Niger River basin, the Mali Empire rose to prominence as the result of the Malinke controlling goldfields and desert side towns through which goods traded across the Sahara were funneled. Like most work in Africa, gold mining was organized along lines of gender and was performed by family groups. Men dug and women extracted ore. Though Islam was slowly embraced by some in the region, including most of Mali's rulers, in the thirteenth and fourteenth centuries, Islamic law was not strictly applied and had little impact on women's lives. In the mid-fourteenth century the Moroccan traveler Ibn Battuta, who was a devout Muslim, left the most thorough written account of the position of women in Mali's towns. In Iwalatan on the desert's edge, Battuta noted that in the presence of men women did not veil themselves; they seemed to marry whomever they pleased; and they had male companions outside what he saw as the prohibited degrees of marriage, something that did not bother their husbands. Women appear to have been responsible for supervising household food supplies. Women were also, according to Battuta, barred from traveling or going on long-distance trading journeys. The king himself had four wives and about one hundred concubines. Other women in the empire were slaves, and the trade in female slaves north over the desert was thriving, thousands each year following routes north. Battuta himself encountered a caravan leaving Mali that consisted of about six hundred females. Female slaves were highly desired in North African Muslim communities, so exporters responded to demand in their selection of slave exports. Elsewhere Battuta noted black slave women working beside men in copper mines.

In the late fourteenth century Mali's kings saw their power steadily decline as outlying chiefs claimed independence. Songhai, whose political center lay in the east of the empire, claimed independence in the early fifteenth century, becoming a formidable power by mid-century and controlling much of the territory that was the heart of the Mali Empire. Songhai was founded by pagan rulers, but in the late fifteenth century a Muslim named Muhammad Ture ascended to the throne with the help of religious leaders in Timbuktu, a center for Muslim scholarship. Though he did not force people in his empire to embrace a strict form of Islam, it is evident that Islam had had an impact on the region by this time and particularly on women. An early-sixteenth-century Moroccan visitor to the area named Leo Africanus noted that women covered their faces in public, not showing the same sort of "immodesty" that they had in Battuta's day. Though women did not travel to conduct long-distance trade, they did market goods locally. The daughters of elites, Africanus said, were given in marriage to other people holding power, often wealthy traders, likely as a way to ensure future business deals. Slavery continued to be an important institution, with locals keeping great numbers of slaves, particularly women slaves. At Songhai's capital Gao, Leo Africanus reported that the king had a large number of concubines. The slave trade across the Sahara continued under Songhai, and thousands of slaves, mainly women, were shipped north each year.

On the East African coast a string of city-states dominated by people known as Swahili became prominent around 1000. Swahili states traded goods among themselves in small sailing boats called dhows and had considerable contact with Arabs who sailed south down the coast and settled in towns for a period of time until winds allowed them to return north. Though Islam was the religion of the ruling elite, most Swahili women did not seclude themselves. Common women performed the same tasks as their sisters across the continent; they worked in fields, gathered wood, and fetched water. Men fished and traded. As elsewhere, lineages attempted to marry their daughters strategically, using them to form important alliances. Lineages were particularly keen to marry daughters to merchants who traded up and down the coast or to Arabs who could provide valuable trade links to the outside world. Swahili society was matrilineal and matrilocal, so when they married, men took up residence with the families of their wives. In the early sixteenth century the Portuguese writer Duarte Barbosa described Swahili women wearing many jewels of gold and silver and fine silk garments, all of which had been imported by Indian Ocean traders. Swahili also employed and traded slaves, most of whom were taken from communities to the interior. Between 800 and 1600 probably one thousand slaves, most of whom were women, left the East African coast per year. Swahili activity in the south sparked considerable economic activity on the Zimbabwe Plateau. From the eleventh to the sixteenth century the state's capital was an impressive city called Great Zimbabwe. Little is known about the nature of social structures in the state. Archaeologists have suggested that a great walled enclosure in the capital was an initiation center for girls. If it served the same function as such centers do in the early twenty-first century, girls of marriageable age went there for twelve months, working for the king in his fields and attending school, where they learned about proper etiquette and moral behavior and about sex, rituals, and dances. Some have suggested that the great walled enclosure itself was divided symbolically with structured male and female oppositions.

Elites and Individuals. In addition to allowing historians to chart some major shifts in women's lives in sub-Saharan African societies from 1000 to 1500, scattered sources provide insights into the roles of some individual women in shaping events during this period. Oral narratives and written sources frequently depict elite women as founders of states, leaders or supporters in wars, manipulators of men, and kingmakers whose political support was crucial during interregnums. In each of these roles, elite women held a central place in the exosphere of African societies. That place was often institutionalized, as in the position of the queen mother (mother of the ruler), who in many societies held a high status and was influential in politics. In some cases when a ruler's mother died, she was replaced with a successor since the official role had to be filled. In Kanem and Borno rulers' mothers were particularly influential, so much so that in the eleventh century a king was imprisoned for a year by the queen mother. In patrilineal societies, the formal recognition of the queen mother's place in government probably gave some assurance that the ruler's mother's lineage would lend its support to the ruler himself. Elsewhere rulers' sisters held important positions in government and were replaced when they died. Sometimes they managed to overstep the powers that were given to them by tradition, assuming the prerogatives of weak and ineffectual brothers. For example, in Borno in the sixteenth century Aisha, the sister of the king Idris Aloma, ruled in the young king's place.

Mossi oral narratives indicate that elite women played an important military and political role in Mossi states. For example, narratives claim that the Mossi kingdom of Ouagadougou was founded in the fifteenth century partly as the result of the actions of Princess Nyennenga, the daughter the king of Gambaga in modern-day northern Ghana. This princess was said to be a warrior who met Rialle, who is sometimes described as an elephant hunter and other times as a prince from Mali, during one of her adventures north of Gambaga. Defying the wishes of her father, Nyennenga married Rialle, eventually giving birth to a child named Ouedraogo, who eventually conquered the region of his birth. Ouedraogo and his sons established several Mossi states both through conquest and by marrying the daughters of important local leaders, thereby lending legitimacy to the sons born from these unions. Also important in Mossi narratives is Padre, the sister of the man who wanted to succeed Ouedraogo. During a succession struggle, Padre played a key role, taking the royal amulets and giving them not to her brother but to Yadega, who established the Mossi state of Yatenga.

Similarly Ibn Battuta described the centrality of women in Mali's most powerful political circles. At the time the king of Mali was Sulaiman and his senior wife was Qasa, which meant queen. Battuta said that Qasa was not subordinate to Sulaiman but was his equal in kingship, a custom, he emphasized, of the region. During Battuta's stay, Sulaiman became suspicious of his wife, so he brought one of her slave women to his court for interrogation. The slave reported that Qasa had been plotting his overthrow. Fearing for her life, Qasa then took refuge in a mosque. The event seemed peculiar to Battuta, who came from a part of the Muslim world in which women did not hold recognized positions of authority. Oral narratives from Mali also depict women as holding a central place in politics as well as in religion. Particularly important in narratives of the empire's founding is Sogolon Kedjou, a powerful sorceress who married the king of Niani and gave birth to the founder of the empire, Sundiata, in the thirteenth century. Sogolon protected her son, who, it is said, loved and respected her. At the king's death, Sogolon's co-wife is said to have maneuvered herself and her weak son into power, denying Sundiata his birthright, something he later claimed. Finally,

Sundiata's half sister Nana Triban is credited with having tricked Sundiata's enemy Soumaoro into revealing his weakness, knowledge of which allowed Sundiata to defeat him and vanquish his army.

Elite women are also prominent in oral narratives from other sub-Saharan African states. Hausaland narratives name women among the founders of important cities and say they led migrations and conquered kingdoms. Songhai narratives speak of female rulers, including Queen Amina in Katsina, who is said to have been responsible for conquests that stretched as far as Nupe in the fifteenth century. In addition to building many cities and receiving tribute from lesser male chiefs, she is said to have introduced kola nuts to the region. Bazao-Turunku, a woman from a neighboring state, is also praised for her success as a military commander, as are women in the traditions of the Lango in the Congo basin.

[*See also* Kinship; Marriage; Matriarchy; Monarchy; *and* Slavery.]

BIBLIOGRAPHY

Hall, Martin. *Farmers, Kings, and Traders: The People of Southern Africa, 200–1860.* Chicago: University of Chicago Press, 1990.

Hawthorne, Walter. *Planting Rice and Harvesting Slaves: Transformations along the Guinea-Bissau Coast, 1400–1900.* Portsmouth, N.H.: Heinemann, 2003.

Ibn Battuta. *Ibn Battuta in Black Africa.* Translated and edited by Said Hamdun and Noël King. Princeton, N.J.: Markus Wiener Publishers, 1994.

Lebeuf, Annie M. D. "The Role of Women in the Political Organization of African Societies." In *Women of Tropical Africa*, edited by Denise Paulme, translated by H. M. Wright, pp. 93–120. Berkeley: University of California Press, 1960.

Niane, D. T. *Sundiata: An Epic of Old Mali.* Translated by G. D. Pickett. London: Longmans, 1965.

Nurse, Derek, and Thomas Spear. *The Swahili: Reconstructing the History and Language of an African Society, 800–1500.* Philadelphia: University of Pennsylvania Press, 1985.

WALTER HAWTHORNE

AFRICAN LIBERATION AND NATIONALIST MOVEMENTS. Women played noteworthy roles in nationalist movements and liberation struggles across the continent of Africa during the twentieth century. They joined nationalist parties, organized women's associations, and worked both to liberate their nations and to improve the position of women within the liberation movements. In some areas of Africa women had held significant posts of authority prior to the colonial period, and their efforts in anticolonial and nationalist activities were in part an attempt to recapture their earlier positions. European colonizers brought their own preconceptions with them, assuming that men would be involved in government and that women would be concerned only with home and family. When they began to organize local governing bodies in the early decades of the twentieth century, women were excluded in nearly every African setting, with no recognition of what women's prior public political activities might have included. Thus women had a particular grievance against colonialism, which brought reductions in their previous roles in governing their own societies and also brought new restrictions on women's activities and freedom of movement.

Following the end of World War II, the African continent experienced a stepped-up pace in the movement toward independence. The French and British colonial powers, though initially reluctant to relinquish control, began to move toward granting independence to individual nations, with Ghana in West Africa the first in 1957. That was followed by the end of colonialism in most African countries, with the notable exceptions of the Portuguese colonies of Angola, Mozambique, Guinea-Bissau, and Cape Verde and the southern African settler nations of South Africa, Namibia, and Zimbabwe (then Rhodesia). In those countries Africans fought liberation wars to gain their freedom from European rule, and women were involved most often in women's organizations that were subject to the demands of the male-controlled nationalist parties. This entry provides an overview of the variety of activities in different regions of the continent and includes a number of biographical profiles of women who came to prominence as nationalist leaders.

Women's Motivations in West Africa. From the early years of colonialism women agitated to protect their own economic interests as farmers and market women. They protested the extension of taxes and the introduction of colonial controls over their agricultural decisions. They frequently formed women's organizations to achieve their goals. Some of the most visible actions by women after World War II were attempts to protect their work as farmers. The Anlu uprising in Cameroon in 1958–1961 was a prominent example of this type of organization and activity.

Anlu was a traditional method of protest used by Kom women in the Cameroon grass fields to ostracize community members, male or female, who transgressed behavioral norms, including those that protected women's authority in agriculture. Though the term describes a category of activity, it most commonly refers to one particular event, a widespread protest when the British colonial authorities tried to introduce agrarian reforms, including new methods of farming that undercut women's authority. In November 1958 an all-woman delegation marched to the government offices in Bamenda, where the Anlu leaders expressed fears about women's loss of control over food production and fertility. Although it began as an autonomous protest focused on women and agriculture, within a few months there were seven thousand

Universal Suffrage in South Africa. Women queue to vote in the Phola Park squatter camp in South Africa's first all-race elections outside Johannesburg, April 1994. REUTERS/JUDA NGWENYA

members meeting in branches throughout the region. The protest was eventually affiliated with the anticolonial political party Kameruns National Democratic Party, which was in the midst of a dispute about Cameroon's future as part of the British or French colonial sphere. The 1958 Anlu was noted for the disruption of both colonial and traditional authority in the region as roads were blocked and the women obstructed the rule of the *fon*, the traditional male ruler.

There were also protests throughout West Africa related to taxation, and frequently market women were involved in organizing to stop the extension of tax collection to women and their productive work. Nigerian women in Abeokuta and Lagos were at the forefront of these campaigns. One prominent organization was the Abeokuta Ladies' Club, founded by a group of Western-educated women in the 1930s, that initially focused on civic work with local youth. In the 1940s the club members began to include market women who were interested in learning to read. Through the presence of the market women, the club learned of the seizure of rice that women were taking to sell in the market, and the club's efforts to end the seizures were successful. The club was then transformed into a vibrant political organization that fought for market women's rights, and in 1946 it changed its name to the Abeokuta Women's Union. In one of its first campaigns, members criticized the local government for the misuse of funds and recommended that foreign companies pay more taxes in order to diminish the burden on market women. There were twenty thousand dues-paying members and another hundred thousand supporters who could be counted on to turn out when needed. After 1949 it was a chapter of the national organization the Nigerian Women's Union.

Funmilayo Ransome-Kuti (1900–1978), president of the Nigerian Women's Union from its founding until her death in 1978, was a pioneering leader in women's political action and in promoting girls' education. She was born in Abeokuta, Nigeria, to a family that was well known as Christian converts and community leaders. She was the first girl to enter the Abeokuta Grammar School, and after finishing there she went to England for further education. During the colonial period she began wearing Yoruba dress exclusively and made all of her public speeches in Yoruba, demonstrating her fervent nationalism. She was a leader for women throughout Nigeria and an advocate of Nigerian culture, but she also had a high profile on the international scene during and after the colonial period. She traveled to England in 1947 as the only woman in the delegation of the National Council of Nigeria and the Cameroons political party when they protested a proposed constitution. Of the role of women in gaining Nigerian independence, Ransome-Kuti wrote that "Women organized and broke down this power from its highest seat ... women faced the struggle fiercely and courageously with their men folks and they were victorious" ("The Status of Women in Nigeria," reprinted in Sutherland-Addy and Diaw, p. 244).

Women's political work often was allowed to flourish as an adjunct to male-dominated political parties. One of the first examples of this kind of female activism in the post–World War II era was the march on Grand Bassam prison outside of Abidjan, Côte d'Ivoire (Ivory Coast), in 1949. The male leaders of the Parti Démocratique de Côte d'Ivoire (Democratic Party of the Ivory Coast) had been jailed by the French colonial authorities, and in December 1949 they began a hunger strike. Five hundred women staged a dramatic march filled with songs and dance, traveling the thirty miles from the city to the prison. The women were attacked by French colonial troops, who injured forty women and arrested four of them. It was a pivotal event that played a role in the French decision to reach an agreement about ending African independence.

One of the leaders of the march on Grand Bassam was Célestine Ouezzin Coulibaly (b. 1914), an anticolonial leader in French West Africa in the 1940s from Côte d'Ivoire. Ouezzin Coulibaly helped institute the women's section of the Rassemblement Démocratique Africain in Côte d'Ivoire and Upper Volta (now Burkina Faso) and was elected general secretary of the women's section in 1948. She wrote a newspaper article, "We Women of the Upper Volta," which included the claim that women "must work compellingly to help create a climate truly favorable to the full development of the nation. No longer does the regime in power keep women in inferior status" (*Carrefour Africain*, 10 November 1961, reprinted in Sutherland-Addy and Diaw, pp. 225–227). After independence in 1958 she was appointed minister of social affairs, housing, and work in the new government of Upper Volta and served until 1959, when she was elected to represent Upper Volta in the French Community Senate (1959–1961). Ouezzin Coulibaly was probably the first female cabinet member of any Francophone West African government.

Another well-known political leader from West Africa was Constance Agatha Cummings-John (1918–2000). Born into the Horton family, an elite Creole (Krio) family in Sierra Leone, she was a leader in the nationalist movement in West Africa. She was educated at elite private schools in Freetown and at age seventeen went to England and participated in the West African Students' Union and the League of Coloured Peoples, both groups whose members actively worked to end colonialism. After she returned to Sierra Leone in 1937, she worked with the radical nationalist I. T. A. Wallace-Johnson in 1938 to found the Sierra Leone branch of the West African Youth League (WAYL), which claimed more than forty-two thousand members within a year. Cummings-John was the first woman elected to office in a colonial governing body when she was elected to the Freetown Municipal Council that same year at the age of twenty; she served until 1945. She also worked closely with women leaders from the markets and with them founded the Sierra Leone Women's Movement (SLWM) in 1951. Cummings-John was elected to the legislature in 1957 but did not take her seat as a result of internal factionalist conflicts. In 1966 she became the mayor of Freetown, the first woman to be a mayor of an African city, but she was forced to live in exile after a military coup in 1967.

The SLWM worked to include women in the early efforts at self-government in Sierra Leone. Based among the market women, it counted more than twenty thousand members, published a newspaper, held mass meetings, and focused attention on women's issues. In 1960, as Sierra Leone was about to gain its independence, the SLWM published a petition calling on the authorities to recognize the central role of women in Sierra Leone society and demanded that the new constitution protect women's rights, especially concerning marriage, property rights, and inheritance. It was not successful in bringing about legal reforms. The SLWM remained active until the coup d'état of 1967, and in the 1980s it owned a restaurant and a nursery but was not involved in political action.

Like Cummings-John, Mabel Dove Danquah (1905 or 1910–1984) was educated before World War II and became a leader in the postwar years. Dove Danquah was a writer and politician from Ghana, which was then called the Gold Coast. She went to England for further education and returned to Accra, Ghana, where she found work as a typist with the well-known trading firm Elder Dempster. Dove Danquah supported Kwame Nkrumah's Convention People's Party (CPP) by writing articles in the party publication, the *Accra Evening News*. In 1951 she was appointed editor of the newspaper, the first African woman to hold such a position, though she was dismissed after five months when she disagreed with Nkrumah over editorial methods. Dove Danquah was the first woman elected to the Ghanaian parliament in 1954, before independence, and possibly the first woman elected to an African legislature.

Hannah Cudjoe (1918–1986) was another Ghanaian political activist who was influenced by Nkrumah. Nkrumah depended on the crucial support of market women, who provided food and other materials that ensured his ability to lead the CPP. Cudjoe worked with the United Gold Coast Convention (UGCC) in developing nationalist propaganda. In 1948 she organized a mass demonstration to protest the arrest of UGCC leaders by the British colonial authorities, using her dressmaking work as a cover for visiting households to spread information about the protest. The women spread clay over their bodies and wore white cloth, possibly the first time that women dressed in a nationalist uniform. In the 1950s Cudjoe was a founding member of the CPP and was elected the party's national propaganda secretary. She was instrumental in founding the Conference of Women of Africa and African Descent that met in Accra in 1960 and evolved into the All African Women's Conference, and she was general director of the Ghana Women's League. She fell out of favor when Nkrumah was ousted by a coup in 1966, and though she returned to public life in the mid-1980s, she died soon after making a speech for International Women's Day in 1986.

East Africa. One of the first postwar actions to gain international attention was the Mau Mau struggle in Kenya. Mau Mau was the name given by the British to a nationalist revolt in Kenya in the 1950s that was led by the Land and Freedom Army. The goal was to end British colonialism and reclaim land that had been alienated by the colonial government. Though women played an important role, they have been neglected in the conventional histories of the movement. Studies have demonstrated that women had a history of political activism in Kenya, and their participation in Mau Mau was an extension of that experience. Women were present at the oath-taking ceremonies that marked membership in the Land and Freedom Army, they were recognized as district organizers, they were listed among the prisoners, and a small number rose to high positions within the organization. Their work was particularly crucial in the provision of food and supplies to the Mau Mau members who were living in the forests outside the urban areas.

Founded in 1952 with the support of Canadian and British charity groups, the Maendeleo Ya Wanawake Organisation (Women's Progress Organization) was an outgrowth of the Mau Mau years. Developing into the national Kenyan women's organization, it has a history of involvement in development projects, literacy programs, and political action for women. In the 1950s it published a newspaper in Luo, Kikamba, Swahili, and Kikuyu. For the most part its leaders worked to expand the membership while not angering male leaders of the ruling party, the Kenya African National Union (KANU).

Also in East Africa, Bibi Titi Mohamed (1926–2000) emerged as a nationalist leader in Tanzania and was responsible for bringing women into the Tanganyika African National Union (TANU) in the 1960s. A Muslim woman, she did not have a formal education, but she was involved in community dance groups, where she met women from around the city. Women had not been involved in TANU, and when John Hatch of the British Fabian Society visited in 1955 and asked where the women were, the male leaders turned to Bibi Titi to develop their women's section. Bibi Titi and her husband had two of the earliest TANU membership cards, but prior to 1955 there had not been a women's section. She called on the dance groups to recruit women in the community to the nationalist cause, and she became general secretary of the TANU Women's Section in 1959. In 1962 all women's groups were merged into the Umoja wa Wanawake wa Tanganyika (UWT; Tanzanian Women's Union), and Bibi Titi served as president of the UWT until 1967.

Another important women's organization in East Africa was the Uganda Council of Women (UCW), which was founded in 1947 and was active in the 1950s and 1960s. It was noted for the multiracial character of its membership, which included women of African, Indian, and European descent as well as women representing religious and community organizations. In the 1960s it focused on reforming marriage laws, publishing the pamphlet *Laws about Marriage in Uganda* (1961), though because of male opposition new legislation was not introduced until 1973. The UCW had difficulty working with the ruling party, however, and had ceased to exist by 1972.

One later area where women were involved in an independence struggle was the effort in the 1980s of women in Eritrea to free their country from rule by Ethiopia. The Eritrean war was not fought against a European colonial power or a white minority government, in contrast to all of the other events described in this entry. Eritrea had been an autonomous province in Ethiopia until 1962, when Emperor Haile Selassie of Ethiopia incorporated Eritrea as an integral part of his country. Eritreans fought for their independence under the leadership of the Eritrean People's Liberation Front, which promoted socialist policies and included a strong platform of support for women's liberation as well. Independence came in 1993 following the overthrow of the Ethiopian government. Eritrean women were visible in the struggle to end Ethiopian rule and to improve their own position in Eritrean society.

Armed Struggle in Southern Africa. The most prolonged and violent struggles to end colonialism were in southern Africa. The Portuguese colonies of Mozambique and Angola as well as the small West African colony of Guinea-Bissau and Cape Verde gained their independence in 1975 following more than a decade of armed struggle, and Guinea-Bissau and Cape Verde split into two nations in 1980. Zimbabwe suffered through an extended civil war following the 1965 Unilateral Declaration of Independence by the minority white government before becoming independent in 1980. Namibia (also called Southwest Africa) was under trusteeship to South Africa and gained its independence only in 1990. The last African nation to end white minority rule was South Africa, where Africans struggled for decades to end the racist apartheid system of government, finally achieving success in 1994 with the first open democratic elections. Typically the women's groups in these countries were formed as affiliates of the

Pan-African Antiapartheid Movement. An American poster for an African Liberation Day protest shows black workers revolting against apartheid and discrimination in Zimbabwe and also shows the Wilmington Ten in jail in the United States. PRINTS AND PHOTOGRAPHS DIVISION, LIBRARY OF CONGRESS

main nationalist organizations, though individual women did agitate for women's issues in particular. Their primary focus, however, was to gain political independence from the colonial powers.

One important aspect of the politics of these organizations was their adoption of socialist policies that included a component focused on women's liberation. Although the nationalist organizations continued to be dominated by men, they often developed analyses that aimed to understand the origins of women's oppression, encouraged women's political involvement, and developed strategies to support women. The analyses and the strategies were limited, yet they raised social awareness of women's condition in society and led to the introduction of many women-centered policies related to maternity leave, equal pay, and similar measures.

The Organização da Mulher Moçambicana (OMM; Organization of Mozambican Women) was founded in 1972 as a wing of the Frente de Libertação de Moçambique (FRELIMO; Mozambique Liberation Front). There had been two earlier women's organizations, the Liga Feminina Moçambicana (LIFEMO; League of Mozambican Women), which was disbanded by the male FRELIMO leaders, and the Destacamento Feminino (Female Detachment), which was essentially a department in the military. Male FRELIMO leaders believed that neither of those groups performed the kind of organizing work that was needed, and they encouraged the OMM's emergence as the primary organization for women. Women were included in combat activities but played a greater role in developing new social institutions, such as orphanages and schools.

The Organização da Mulher Angolana (Organization of Angolan Women) was established in 1962 as a part of the Movimento Popular de Libertação de Angola (MPLA; Popular Movement for the Liberation of Angola), one of the leading anticolonial organizations. The group's primary activities were to recruit more women and to improve the ability of women to participate in MPLA actions, as was common in political party organizations. Literacy classes and rural cooperative work were among the projects the group initiated. Some women were also involved in combat, and 2 March is Angolan Women's Day in recognition of the deaths at the hands of a rival organization on that day in 1967 of five female combatants, including Deolinda Rodrigues, a leading Angolan nationalist. Rodrigues was the only woman on the central committee of the MPLA.

The União Democrática das Mulheres (UDEMU; Democratic Union of Women) was established in 1960 as part of the Partido Africano de Independência da Guiné e Cabo Verde (PAIGC; African Party for the Independence of Guinea-Bissau and Cape Verde), the party fighting to end Portuguese colonialism in Guinea-Bissau and Cape Verde, with the mandate of representing women's issues. When Guinea-Bissau and Cape Verde split, UDEMU was replaced by the Organização das Mulheres de Cabo Verde (Organization of Women of Cape Verde).

In Zimbabwe—prior to independence the country was known as Rhodesia—there was not an organization of women, but women were integrated into the armed struggle that was eventually won by the Zimbabwe African National Union (ZANU) and its army, the Zimbabwe African National Liberation Army (ZANLA). Some estimates suggest that up to one-third of the guerrillas were women, and they clearly played a significant role. One of the best known was Joyce Mujuru Nhongo (b. 1955), who was given the honorary name "Teurai Ropa," or "Spill Blood." She joined the military wing of the liberation struggle in 1973 and rose to command the Women's Detachment of ZANLA. In 1977 she joined the central command of the army. She was an exception, however, because most women were relegated to child care and other more typically female endeavors. After independence Mujuru Nhongo served in a variety of government positions, including as minister of community and women's affairs in the 1980s.

In Southwest Africa, which became Namibia upon independence, the SWAPO Women's Council was the primary women's group. It was affiliated with the South West African People's Organization (SWAPO), the nationalist organization fighting for Namibian independence, and was founded in 1969 or 1970. The first congress, held in 1980 in neighboring Angola, was attended by sixty people who were primarily living in exile in Zambia and Angola. Women participated in the armed struggle chiefly as support staff rather than combatants. They published the *Namibian Woman* and focused on raising understanding of women's oppression and working to improve women's condition within the structures of SWAPO.

South Africa. Women in South Africa had protested racially restrictive policies from the early twentieth century. The post–World War II period was marked by the drastic intensification of apartheid laws following the 1948 election, which resulted in the victory of a government intent on expanding racial segregation. In response, women in the 1950s increased their organizing and visibility, particularly protesting the extension of restrictive pass laws to women. African men had carried detailed identity cards called passes for decades, and the passes were central to the apartheid system of racial oppression and control. After the election of 1948, women faced new attempts to force them to carry passes as well, though the government initially called them "reference books" and claimed that they were not actual passes. Those affected were primarily urban women who had moved into the cities looking for work after they lost access to rural land for cultivation.

Antiapartheid Activists. Winnie Madikizela Mandela greets supporters of the African National Congress (ANC) at an elections rally in Soweto, South Africa, March 1999. REUTERS/JUDA NGWENYA

Women responded by organizing the Federation of South African Women (FSAW) as a nonracial organization in 1954 and sponsoring demonstrations throughout the country. Within months the FSAW had more than ten thousand members, primarily urban African women. Though active in a variety of venues, the FSAW's focus was on bringing women into the efforts to end apartheid. After a number of smaller protests, the FSAW called for a massive demonstration in 1956 that brought twenty thousand women to Pretoria, where they handed in petitions opposing the new pass laws. Their actions focused on three primary objections to the passes: passes would restrict women from easily seeking work, women would be subject to sexual abuse by officials, and the inevitable arrest and detention of women for pass offenses (the most common cause of male arrests) would have a negative effect on their homes and families. Despite the massive response by women, they were obliged to carry passes.

As government repression escalated, it became increasingly difficult for the FSAW to organize, and the African National Congress (ANC) leadership also placed less emphasis on large-scale demonstrations. Some observers suggested that the male ANC leaders wanted to keep women from playing a central political role, though it is also true that the ANC did not have the resources to defend thousands of arrested activists, whether male or female. The FSAW ceased to be active after 1963. South African women continued to organize as women, including an unsuccessful revival of the Federation of South African Women in the early 1980s, a short-lived Women's Congress that was part of the United Democratic Front (UDF) in the 1980s, and the 1992 founding of the Women's National Coalition, which it was hoped would revive the broad-based appeal of the original FSAW. After the 1994 election that marked the end of apartheid, South African Women's Day was established to commemorate the 9 August date of the 1956 anti-pass march.

South African women were also active in the ANC Women's League formed in 1918, developing out of the anti–pass law demonstrations of 1913. Initially known as the Bantu Women's League (BWL), it was formally acknowledged as part of the ANC in 1931, though women were still not admitted as members. Women were finally welcomed as members of the ANC in 1943, and the ANC Women's League was then established with Madie Hall Xuma as its first president. The organization focused on recruiting women to the ANC and on raising issues of importance to women within the ANC. As was the case with many political party organizations, it took direction from the ANC and focused its organizing efforts on ANC priorities. It was part of the coalition of the FSAW and participated in the 1956 march.

Women came to prominence through their work to end apartheid. Among the best known were Winnie Mandela (b. 1936), who used her status as the wife of the imprisoned activist Nelson Mandela to agitate for change. She was born in Pondoland, South Africa, and trained as a medical social worker. She married Nelson Mandela in 1958, and he was imprisoned from 1962 to 1990. Winnie Mandela was herself subjected to repeated banning orders and imprisonment for her activities. She was active in the ANC and helped found the Black Women's Federation and the Black Parents' Association in response to the Soweto uprising of 1976. She later gained notoriety for the involvement of her associates in the beating death of Stompie Seipei, a young member of a soccer team she sponsored.

Another influential antiapartheid leader was Lilian Ngoyi (1911–1980), the daughter of a clergyman in Pretoria. Her family could not afford to keep her in school through high school. Widowed when her daughter was three, Ngoyi worked at a variety of difficult jobs, including in a garment factory. By 1952 she was deeply involved in the Garment Workers Union, and she was later elected to the executive committee of the union. A pivotal experience was a trip in 1954 to attend the World Congress of Women in Switzerland during which she visited several other European countries. The 1952 Defiance Campaign protesting the expansion of restrictive pass laws brought her into the ANC. She served as president of the ANC Women's League in 1953 and then as president of the FSAW in 1956. In her presidential speech to the 1956 FSAW annual meeting, she closed her comments with a rousing call to the members, saying that the racist South African government "will never stop the women of Africa in their forward march to FREEDOM IN OUR LIFETIME" (cited in Daymond et al., p. 244). Known to all as Ma Ngoyi, this powerful orator was also charged with treason as part of the infamous treason trial of the 1950s and spent most of the subsequent years under banning orders that restricted her public activities.

Another internationally known antiapartheid activist was Albertina Sisulu (b. 1918). Sisulu joined the ANC Youth League with her husband Walter Sisulu (1912–2003), a trade union activist and ANC leader. They married in 1944. Albertina Sisulu later was a top member of the ANC Women's League and a leader of the FSAW, where she was involved in the anti-pass Defiance Campaign. She was restricted by banning orders from 1964 to 1983, including ten years of house arrest. In 1983 she was elected as Transvaal president of the UDF. In 1990 she helped the ANC Women's League get reestablished inside South Africa, and she was elected to parliament in 1994.

Assessment. Although women were scarce in the leadership of national liberation movements, they were active members in every part of the African continent. They joined local and regional organizations, worked in groups that focused on improving women's position, and enlisted in women's auxiliaries. They made important contributions to tax protests, combat activities, and the hard day-to-day work of organizing individuals to come together in the efforts to end colonial and white minority rule. They were all eventually successful, though the post-struggle incorporation of women into newly independent governments remained an issue of contention.

In the post-independence era women across the continent have found it difficult to move into leadership positions despite their crucial roles in the various liberation struggles. In the 1990s the numbers of women announcing themselves as candidates in presidential races increased and drew renewed attention, and a growing number of women served as prime ministers. Gains have also been seen in the greater numbers of women elected to parliamentary seats and named to government ministries. Ellen Johnson Sirleaf was the first elected African female head of state, winning a widely publicized campaign for president of Liberia in 2005.

[*See also* African National Congress Women's League; Central Africa; East Africa; Imperialism and Colonialism, *subentry* Anticolonial Protests; Nationalism; North Africa; Southern Africa; West Africa; *and biographical entries on women mentioned in this article.*]

BIBLIOGRAPHY

ANC Women's League. *The ANC Women's League: Contributing to a Democratic, Non-racist, and Non-sexist South Africa.* Johannesburg, South Africa: ANC Women's League, 1993.

Aubrey, Lisa. *The Politics of Development Cooperation: NGOs, Gender, and Partnership in Kenya.* New York: Routledge, 1997. A history of the Kenyan women's organization Maendaleo Ya Wanawake.

Cleaver, Tessa, and Marion Wallace. *Namibia: Women in War.* London: Zed Books, 1990. An overview of women's involvement in the liberation struggle in Namibia.

Daymond, M. J., et al., eds. *Women Writing Africa: The Southern Region.* New York: Feminist Press, 2003. A comprehensive collection of women's writings on a wide range of topics.

Diabaté, Henriette. *La marche des femmes sur Grand-Bassam.* Abidjan, Côte d'Ivoire: Nouvelles Éditions Africaines, 1975. A brief history of an important demonstration in Côte d'Ivoire in 1949.

Geiger, Susan. *TANU Women: Gender and Culture in the Making of Tanganyikan Nationalism, 1955–1965.* Portsmouth, N.H.: Heinemann, 1997. A groundbreaking study of women in the Tanzanian nationalist movement that includes a biography of Bibi Titi Mohammed.

Hassim, Shireen. *Women's Organizations and Democracy in South Africa: Contesting Authority.* Madison: University of Wisconsin Press, 2006. Based on extensive interviews and primary research, this book provides a reliable discussion of the organizational histories and current issues facing South African women.

Johnson-Odim, Cheryl, and Nina Emma Mba. *For Women and the Nation: Funmilayo Ransome-Kuti of Nigeria.* Urbana: University of Illinois Press, 1997. An important biography that details the political activities of women in Nigeria in the post–World War II era.

Lyons, Tanya. "Guerrilla Girls and Women in the Zimbabwean National Liberation Struggle." In *Women in African Colonial Histories*, edited by Jean Allman, Susan Geiger, and Nakanyike Musisi, pp. 305–326. Bloomington: Indiana University Press, 2002. A useful overview of women's activities in the liberation movement in Zimbabwe.

Presley, Cora Ann. *Kikuyu Women, the Mau Mau Rebellion, and Social Change in Kenya.* Boulder, Colo.: Westview, 1992. Women's varied activities as militants in the freedom struggle in Kenya.

Schmidt, Elizabeth. *Mobilizing the Masses: Gender, Ethnicity, and Class in the Nationalist Movement in Guinea, 1939–1958.* Portsmouth, N.H.: Heinemann, 2005. A welcome contribution to studying nationalist movements from the grassroots level.

Scott, Catherine V. "'Men in Our Country Behave like Chiefs': Women and the Angolan Revolution." In *Women and Revolution in Africa, Asia, and the New World*, edited by Mary Ann Tétreault, pp. 89–108. Columbia: University of South Carolina

Press, 1994. Highlights the continuing obstacles women faced in Angola.

Sheldon, Kathleen E. *Pounders of Grain: A History of Women, Work, and Politics in Mozambique*. Portsmouth, N.H.: Heinemann, 2002. This wide-ranging study includes a chapter on the liberation struggle in Mozambique.

Sisulu, Elinor. *Walter and Albertina Sisulu: In Our Lifetime*. Claremont, South Africa: David Philip Publishers, 2002. A biography of a leading couple in the struggle to end apartheid in South Africa, written by their daughter-in-law.

Sutherland-Addy, Esi, and Aminata Diaw, eds. *Women Writing Africa: West Africa and the Sahel*. New York: Feminist Press, 2005. A wide-ranging selection of women's writings from across West Africa.

Urdang, Stephanie. *Fighting Two Colonialisms: Women in Guinea-Bissau*. New York: Monthly Review, 1979. A report from the front lines published during the armed struggle to end Portuguese colonialism in Guinea-Bissau.

Wilson, Amrit. *The Challenge Road: Women and the Eritrean Revolution*. Trenton, N.J.: Red Sea, 1991. A useful study of women's concerns and contributions to the revolutionary movement in Eritrea.

KATHLEEN SHELDON

AFRICAN NATIONAL CONGRESS WOMEN'S LEAGUE. The African National Congress Women's League (ANCWL) traces it origins to women's resistance to pass laws in the Orange Free State in 1913. This resistance arose among black women who had catered at the formation of the African National Congress (ANC) in 1912. Charlotte Maxeke (1874–1939) founded the Bantu Women's League in 1918 because women were not allowed formal membership in the ANC. Maxeke wanted to overcome the belief that women belonged on the periphery of political activity as helpers. In the early 1920s the Bantu Women's League consisted of only a few branches. The branch in Maxeke's Zoutpansburg district defended the rights of pregnant women farmworkers against excessive hard labor and torture.

In 1943 the ANC revived the Women's League and appointed Madie Hall Xuma (1894–1982) as its first president. She was the black United States–born wife of the ANC president, Alfred Xuma. Ida Mtwana (1903–1960) became the next president, in 1948, representing a surge of youthful participation in politics. The ANCWL built strong branch and provincial structures, mostly in working-class urban townships throughout the country.

During the 1950s the ANCWL primarily fought the introduction of pass laws to African women. They saw passes as a tool to prevent women from seeking desperately needed employment in towns and as something that exposed women to sexual harassment from the police. Many women first participated in political action during the ANC's Defiance Campaign against unjust laws in 1952. This gave them experience and confidence to build the ANCWL, which became the largest partner in a nonracial umbrella organization formed in 1954, the Federation of South African Women (FEDSAW). In 1955, FEDSAW canvassed women's opinion to produce a Women's Charter for the Congress of the People in Kliptown. Thereafter the ANCWL organized protest marches, petitions, and demonstrations against the new pass laws, from 1956 to 1959, in both urban and rural areas.

The largest marches were to the government in Pretoria in 1955, involving two thousand women, and again in 1956, involving twenty thousand women from all over the country. Led by Lilian Ngoyi, Helen Joseph, Rahima Moosa, and Sophie De Bruyn, the women delivered thousands of petitions, then stood silently for half an hour before dispersing. They composed a song that day addressed to the South African prime minister Johannes Gerhardus Strijdom (1954–1958): "When you touch a woman, you have touched a rock, / you have dislodged a boulder, you will be crushed." The march's anniversary, 9 August, is now the National Women's Day public holiday in South Africa.

The government outlawed the ANCWL in a clampdown on political resistance following massacres of protesters at Sharpeville in 1960. Women activists then organized clubs under the banner of FEDSAW, but these could not be sustained in the face of the severe restrictions on women leaders. When many activists went into exile, the ANC formed a women's section under Gertrude Shope, a former teacher living in exile in Lusaka, Zambia. The women's section formed alliances with international women's organizations and kept women's issues alive in ANC publications.

During the 1980s a new round of women's organizations emerged inside South Africa as resistance to apartheid escalated. These included the Federation of Transvaal Women, the Port Elizabeth Women's Organisation, the Natal Organisation of Women, the United Women's Congress (Western Cape), the Congress of Border Women (Eastern Cape), and the Eastern Transvaal Women's Union. When the ban against it was lifted by the government, the ANCWL formally relaunched itself in 1991, incorporating internal and external women's organizations. It successfully demanded that all political parties participating in peace negotiations to end apartheid include women in their delegations.

Starting in 1991 the ANCWL led the National Women's Coalition, which embraced women from all political and racial groupings. The coalition canvassed women's opinions from throughout the country to formulate a Women's Charter. Presented to the newly installed South African president Nelson Mandela in 1994, this document formed the basis of full gender equality in the South African constitution adopted in 1996.

In the early 1990s the ANCWL demanded that a third of all officeholders within the ANC be women, but the idea met with strong resistance. Over time, however, the concept of gender quotas prevailed. In the 2006 local government elections the ANC enforced a 50 percent quota of women as municipal councillors. In its 2003 constitution the ANCWL dedicated itself to promoting the implementation of full equality of women in all spheres of life, to lobbying for affirmative action programs, to rooting out patriarchy, and to working toward ending violence against women and children. Leadership in the ANCWL has often served as a stepping-stone for women into senior political offices as ministers, premiers of provinces, and provincial members of executive committees.

[*See also* African Liberation and Nationalist Movements; Apartheid; Feminism; Joseph, Helen; Maxeke, Charlotte; Nationalism, *subentry* Nationalist Movements; Ngoyi, Lilian; Southern Africa, *subentry* Twentieth Century; *and* Xuma, Madie Hall.]

BIBLIOGRAPHY

"ANC Women's League, 50 Years of Struggle: Malibongwe Igama Lamakhosikazi [Praise the Name of Women]." http://www.anc.org.za/wl/docs/50years.html.

Maclean, Barbara Hutmacher. *Strike a Woman, Strike a Rock: Fighting for Freedom in South Africa*. Trenton, N.J.: Africa World Press, 2003.

Walker, Cherryl. *Women and Resistance in South Africa*. London: Onyx Press, 1982.

Wells, Julia C. *We Now Demand! The History of Women's Resistance to Pass Laws in South Africa*. Johannesburg, South Africa: Witwatersrand University Press, 1993.

JULIA WELLS

AGE GRADES.

AGE GRADES. Age grades were the ritually marked life stages (such as junior, elder, and senior elder) through which groups of people of a similar age range (called age sets) moved together. In many regions of Africa, especially among pastoralists in East Africa, age grades were a key principle of social organization, clearly defining a person's rights, responsibilities, and relationships with other people. Although age grades were primarily male institutions, sparse evidence suggests the existence of female age grades among some groups before colonialism. Women were, however, central to the practices and rites that constituted age grades in many societies.

Age Grades and the Life Course. The recruitment of age sets and the promotion of members up the ladder of age grades followed a common pattern. Within a certain "open" period that was usually several years long, boys deemed mature enough—often between twelve and twenty years old—participated in initiation rituals at their homesteads that transformed them into "junior men." Many of these rituals included forms of hazing (such as being taunted with abusive songs), circumcision, feats of bravery, dances, feasts, and a liminal period of healing. Once the initiation period had been closed to new participants, junior men from the same area assembled for a collective ritual in which they were blessed and named by a selected group of elder men. The same unique age-set name was given to all junior men in a society, with some regional variations. Approximately fifteen years later these men came together for another collective ritual that marked their promotion to the age grade of "elders," and another group of boys began the process of forming a new age set of junior men. Thus, as each age set was promoted to a more senior age grade, all the age sets switched age grades accordingly, so that elders became "senior elders" and eventually "venerable elders."

Each age grade was associated with specific rights, responsibilities, and restrictions that shaped relationships among men and between men and women. These often included rules concerning food (for example, junior men were prohibited from eating alone or in front of women), sexual and marital relations (delaying marriage until junior men became elders or forbidding men of a certain age set from having sexual relations with their classificatory daughters, that is, the daughters of their fellow age-set members), respect behaviors (for example, the protocol for who greeted whom, and how), responsibilities for livestock (junior men guarded the herds from raiders and predators; elder men decided where to graze and water animals), and conflict resolution (perhaps the responsibility of senior elders). To facilitate easy recognition of a man's age grade, each grade was signified by distinct forms of dress, ornamentation, and weaponry (spears, swords, knives, and clubs).

Women and Age Grades. Although differences in women's age status were recognized in these societies, they were not marked by collective rituals or unique names. Instead, many aspects of women's lives were determined by their association—as daughters, wives, or mothers—with men of particular age sets. In addition to determining the appropriate practices and interactions, such as those described above, between different categories of women and different age grades of men, male age grades were a source of power and pleasure to many women. As young girls they danced, sang, and flirted with junior men. As wives some risked the anger of their husbands (who were often much older) to become the lovers of junior men. As mothers their status increased with each age-grade promotion of their sons, beginning with the boys' initiation into the age grade of junior men. Women young and old made beaded jewelry and other ornaments for men and themselves to symbolize these diverse relationships. Finally, as mothers and wives women were often key participants in age-grade rituals. Among Maasai, for example, the peak moment of the Eunoto ceremony occurred when a mother shaved her son's long hair to ritually transform him from a junior man into an elder. Sometime afterward, men drank milk alone in front of their wives to signal the transfer of their primary commitments from their age set to their households.

Past and Present. Documentary and linguistic evidence suggests that age grades existed in East Africa by at least the sixteenth century and perhaps even as early as the first millennium B.C.E. For pastoralist peoples who lacked centralized political systems, age grades facilitated social organization and political decision making among dispersed, mobile populations. In contrast to clans, which divided and organized communities along vertical lines, age grades joined together men (and women) of similar ages across clans and communities. As men traveled across the land, they could seek hospitality with their age mates, even if they were complete strangers. If an age mate was absent, his wife was expected to treat the visitor as she would treat her husband, providing food, shelter, and sometimes sex. Male age mates consulted with one another, especially about determining access to and use of range lands and resources. But age sets could also be divided by clan and homestead in times of conflict, when junior men of different areas were mobilized by age set to fight against one another. Although men, especially junior men, had strong loyalties to their age sets, their commitment usually lessened as they devoted more time and effort to the concerns of their families, livestock, and homesteads. However, their ties with their age mates were renewed at feasts and celebrations, where they sat together, eating, drinking, and sharing stories about their past feats.

Under colonialism age grades disappeared in some societies (including Pokot and Nandi) but flourished in others (Maasai). Reasons for these different outcomes include differential treatment by colonial administrators, efforts to outlaw livestock raiding, missionary evangelization, new economic opportunities for young men, the availability of alternative legal regimes, and shifting political structures. In some areas, colonial efforts to forcefully suppress the age-grade system backfired, leading to a fierce revitalization of the institution. In others, age grades simply faded away.

Age grades still exist among some societies, including Maasai, but their meaning, forms, and rituals have changed. For example, in many communities the liminal period has been drastically shortened to accommodate school calendars. Junior men now spend more time cultivating their fields or working in towns as guards than wandering the plains with their age mates. Educated junior men increasingly challenge the political power and prerogatives of senior elders. Nonetheless, age grades still guide respect relations, marriage decisions, and other forms of social interaction.

The effects on women of the changing nature of age grades are unclear, in light of the many other changes in their lives. Moreover, the influence of age grades differs by class, rural versus urban location, education, and other variables. Young women must still comply with fairly strict standards of respect behavior toward men of their father's age set and more senior age grades. Moreover, the age grade of a woman's father remains an important factor in determining eligible marriage partners. Married women, however, especially those who are educated and live in urban areas, are no longer expected to have sex with visiting age mates of their husband or even host them when their husband is away. (The spread of Christian principles of monogamy and sexual fidelity has also reshaped these expectations.) The changes in age grades have perhaps affected women most as mothers, as they have lost a key source of status and prestige.

[*See also* East Africa.]

BIBLIOGRAPHY

Bernardi, Bernardo. *Age Class Systems: Social Institutions and Polities Based on Age*. Translated by David I. Kertzer. Cambridge, U.K.: Cambridge University Press, 1985. Broad comparative study of age-grade systems, with attention to variations in models. One chapter examines women and age-grade systems.

Hodgson, Dorothy L. *The Church of Women: Gendered Encounters between Maasai and Missionaries*. Bloomington: Indiana University Press, 2005. Several chapters explore the centrality of women to male age grades and age sets.

Spencer, Paul. *The Maasai of Matapato: A Study of Rituals of Rebellion*. Bloomington: Indiana University Press, 1988. A thorough account of the rituals, responsibilities, rights, and relationships of male age grades among Maasai that downplays the roles of women.

Spencer, Paul. *Time, Space, and the Unknown: Maasai Configurations of Power and Providence*. London: Routledge, 2003. A comparative study of the meaning and function of age grades and age sets among Maa-speaking East African pastoralists.

DOROTHY L. HODGSON

AGE OF CONSENT AND CHILD MARRIAGE.

Debates over the age of consent and child marriage in the late nineteenth and early twentieth centuries attracted widespread attention in both India and Britain. This was the first reform issue around which Indian leaders mobilized mass opinion, the first intermixing of nationalism and social reform, and the last social legislative measure in India directly affected by influencing British public opinion.

By the nineteenth century a trend in favor of child marriages had become evident among Hindus. Sociologists and social historians attribute this to a combination of factors, including the restrictions on intercaste (*jati*) marriages as well as on those among subcastes (*gotra*) of the same larger caste. Another factor was a new and competitive assertion of higher social rank (*varna*) through the performance of textually prescribed rites such as the *garbhadhana* (after a girl's first menstruation). By the end of the nineteenth century, social prestige was attached to child and infant marriages; any deviation from it invited loss of ritual rank. The celebrated reformer Mahadev Govind Ranade from western India was married at the age of eight, and Ram Mohun Roy, from Bengal, was a reluctant nine-year-old bridegroom.

Nationalist restructuring of domestic sexual relations came to a head in the 1880s with two lawsuits: *Dadaji v. Rukhmabai* and the *Empress v. Hari Mohan Maiti* (Phulmoni Dasi) case. Rukhmabai was a twenty-six-year-old woman who had been married as a child but had not consummated the marriage. In 1884 she refused to do so on the grounds of her husband's immoral behavior, his failure to provide a home, and his ill health. Phulmoni was the eleven-year-old Bengali child bride of a thirty-eight-year-old husband whose sexual intercourse with her led to her death. At the heart of these legal cases were crucial issues such as the governance of Indian female sexuality and of Hindu conjugality. Among the questions debated were whether a girl could resist patriarchal marriage and remain Hindu and whether the institution of child marriage was sustainable in the light of sexual violence. These politicized the debates on child marriage and led to calls in Britain and India for a restructuring of heterosexual family norms.

Behramji Malabari, a Parsi reformer from Bombay, published two sensationalist political tracts, *Notes on Infant Marriage and Enforced Widowhood* (1884) and *An Appeal from the Daughters of India* (1890). The Indian response to *Notes* was divided: some welcomed Malabari's suggestions for reform, others resented intervention from a non-Hindu. Encouraged by British middle-class public opinion, shaped during the same years by the social-purity campaigns to raise the age of consent for sexual intercourse to sixteen, Malabari went to England in the late 1880s with the goal of influencing legislators and reform-minded Britons.

Notes coincided with the founding of the Indian National Congress in 1885. Nationalists aspired to greater political autonomy, and their goals collided with Malabari's proposal for greater British and colonial legislative intervention in reforming Hindu marriage customs. The hostility to social-reform issues expressed by a majority of nationalists in the congress led to the formation in 1887 of a separate organization, the Indian National Social Conference. In 1889 this conference resolved that the consummation of a marriage with a wife under the age of twelve should be deemed a criminal offense; it also called for educating Indian masses about the need to postpone sexual intercourse with wives younger than fourteen. Bal Gangadhar Tilak, the leader of a conservative faction of nationalists, characterized this as an alien government's attempt to emasculate Indians and interfere with private and religious customs. The opinion and participation of Muslims in the controversy over the Age of Consent Act of 1891 have not been studied in any great detail.

If Indians themselves showed great diversity in their perspectives on child marriage, the colonial government showed remarkable consistency in its approach. Contrary to the commonly accepted view that the British government was authoritarian and interventionist at all times, historical documents reveal colonial reluctance to interfere in Indian social and domestic issues in the later nineteenth century. The government urged caution until such time as Indian public opinion was unanimous in its call for legislation. Only in 1890, when Malabari took the agitation to Britain and successfully harnessed the support of influential Victorians and the British press, did the government solicit opinions from diverse groups representing India: orthodox Hindu priests, Indian princes, liberal reformers, provincial administrators, doctors, and lawyers.

Historiography. The historical significance of the age-of-consent debates was in providing revivalist nationalists with a consciousness-raising issue. The movements for social reform in the early nineteenth century had affected only a few elite groups. Whereas practices of widow immolation (sati) and female infanticide had been limited to regional groups, the practice of child marriage nullified differences in caste, religion, class, and status. It thus provided—for the first time—a common platform for the expression of Indian opinion on a national basis. The controversy over age of consent revealed the outline of a Hindu and nationalist position on conjugality and female sexuality.

In the 1960s and 1970s social historians interpreted the colonial rhetoric regarding the age of consent literally and thus understood the Age of Consent Act as a humanitarian attempt to ameliorate women's condition. Later scholarship, however, has argued that male Indian nationalists were ambivalent about Indian women, simultaneously needing them to be "modernized" by emulating middle-class British women and demanding that they retain a cultural identity distinct from that of the West. Consequently the nationalist rhetoric drew boundaries around the home, or private sphere, as a spiritual haven for Indians where they could exercise sovereign autonomy and remain undominated by the material West.

It is within this imperial context that the conservative Indian response can be comprehended. Dagmar Engels interpreted the debates as part of a larger global confrontation between two opposing systems of female sexuality—Victorian and Indian—unable to comprehend each other. Mrinalini Sinha has shown how Victorian notions of masculinity inhering in notions of athletic and bold sportsmanship denigrated Bengali male elites as effeminate in their inability to control sexual appetites, as demonstrated by the Hari

Mohan Maiti case. This absence of self-control demonstrated the inability of indigenous elites to govern themselves effectively in both the public and private spheres.

Indian women, whom the legislation affected most, were not formally invited to voice their opinions. Nevertheless, they participated in every aspect of the debate. A close analysis of various women's writing from the period, according to Padma Anagol, reveals that it was not only the matter of the minimum age at which a girl or boy could be married that caught the attention of Indian women supporting the Age of Consent Act, but it was also the physical and psychological harm done to the girl wife as well as the helplessness of the boy bridegroom. In their gendered critique of Indian social relations, feminists from western India faulted the socialization of girls and boys and the institution of arranged marriage, which resulted in conjugal unhappiness and domestic disorder. When Rukhmabai was imprisoned for defying the court's injunction to join her husband, Indian feminists condemned the government's act as a compromise with Indian male reactionaries at the cost of the welfare of Indian women and as a convenient linkage between the Victorian and Indian systems of patriarchy.

In the mid-1880s Indian women sought to collaborate with British feminists in order to negotiate more effectively with the colonial government. Such international alliances indicated that Indian women reformers had lost faith in their male counterparts. At the same time, many ordinary women had brought legal challenges to older practices of restitution of conjugal rights, alimony, and divorce. Thus the sense of siege articulated by Hindu male nationalists in the age-of-consent debates was a response not to the discourses of colonial masculinity but to the rebellions of ordinary Indian women.

The Age of Consent Act raised the age of consent for penetrative sexual intercourse from ten to twelve for both married and unmarried girls. It did not raise the age of marriage but changed the age at which a husband could claim conjugal sexual intimacy with his wife. In theory, men found guilty of having penetrative sex with girls younger than twelve years old could be punished with up to ten years in prison or banishment to a penal colony for life. In practice, however, enforcement of the act was virtually impossible because, given the secrecy surrounding such acts in a Hindu joint family system, the offense could not be verified. The scope of the act was limited even further when in negotiations with militant Indian nationalists the government ordered that only Indian magistrates, not the police, were to investigate suspects. Eventually the penalty of transportation for life was abrogated, and the offense was made a noncognizable (less serious) one.

Child marriage was addressed in the Child Marriage Restraint Act passed in 1929. It fixed the minimum age of marriage at fourteen for girls and eighteen for boys and ignored the age of consent entirely. Like the Age of Consent Act, this legislation was spurred by a debate in print. From the early 1920s liberals in reformist organizations such as the Arya Samaj had introduced bills in the legislative assembly to raise the marriageable age of girls. They had been ignored until an American journalist, Katherine Mayo, published *Mother India* in 1927. Mayo reiterated the charge of Indian unfitness for political self-determination on the grounds of a sexualized pathology characteristic of Hindus. The book provoked indignant reactions from many nationalists, including Mahatma Gandhi.

Liberals from the 1890s had evinced concerns about maternal and infant health to argue for a higher age for sexual intercourse. For instance, M. G. Rande, a famous reformer from Western India had argued in 1885 that "early marriage leads to early consummation and its results are the physical deterioration of the race ... and fills the country with pauperism, bred of over-population by wealdings and sickly people." These arguments were renewed by colonial officials and Indian male reformers alike in the 1920s owing to their internationalization in a postwar world by bodies such as the League of Nations. Judy Whitehead has touched on the increasing use of biomedicine and medical jurisprudence in the discourses of this period; it was widely believed that a healthy mother created a healthy child and thus a biologically fit society and nation. The three major women's organizations—the All India Women's Conference, the National Council of Women in India, and the Women's India Association—participated in this discourse and engaged in the new round of debates in 1929, with consensus on the need to eliminate child marriage. This participation also furthered women's political skills in organizational lobbying, petitioning, and bargaining with the government and Indian men.

Assessment. Some scholars interpret the Child Marriage Restraint Act as an improvement on the Age of Consent Act because the Child Marriage Restraint Act abandoned the attempt to police consummation of marriage for the more verifiable safeguard of a fixed minimum age of marriage. However, imprecise and uneven registration of births in India, as well as a generalized fear of social censure, negated the envisioned protection of girl wives. Furthermore, by omitting provisions related to the age of sexual consent, the 1929 act left vulnerable marginal groups such as unmarried young prostitutes. The act specified that prosecutions could take place only if initiated by a private individual, and only by a district magistrate, not by the law courts. Most scholars concur in characterizing both acts as "paper tigers."

In postindependence India, legislators and liberals have favored a higher marriage age for girls, impelled by the need to control overpopulation—hence the Child Marriage Restraint Act of 1955, followed by the Child Marriage

Restraint Act of 1978, which raised the minimum age of marriage to eighteen for girls and twenty-one for boys.

The long trajectory of debates over the age of consent and marriage clearly reflects two trends. In the first phase, up to 1929, it reflects the aspirations of male nationalists to thwart assertiveness in Indian women and defend patriarchy by regulating and controlling female sexuality. In the second, postindependence phase, it reflects the postcolonial state's commitment to modernity rather than to the advancement of women's welfare.

[*See also* Hinduism; India; Marriage, *subentry* Laws and Rituals; Sati; *and* Sexuality.]

BIBLIOGRAPHY

Anagol, Padma. *The Emergence of Feminism in India, 1850–1920*. Aldershot, U.K., and Burlington, Vt.: Ashgate, 2006. See especially pp. 181–218.

Banerji, Himani. "Age of Consent and Hegemonic Social Reform." In *Gender and Imperialism*, edited by Clare Midgley, pp. 21–44, Manchester, U.K.: Manchester University Press, 1998.

Engels, Dagmar. *Beyond Purdah? Women in Bengal, 1890–1939*. New Delhi, India, and Oxford: Oxford University Press, 1996. See especially pages 100–115.

Forbes, Geraldine. *Women in Modern India*. New Cambridge History of India, vol. 4, part 2. Cambridge, U.K.: Cambridge University Press, 1996. A highly readable synthesis of scholarship on the gender and women's history of India. See especially chapters 3 and 4.

Sarkar, Tanika. "Rhetoric against Age of Consent: Resisting Colonial Reason and Death of a Child Wife." *Economic and Political Weekly* 28, no. 36 (1993): 1869–1878.

Sinha, Mrinalini. *Colonial Masculinity: The "Manly Gentleman" and the "Effeminate Bengali" in the Late Nineteenth Century*. Manchester, U.K.: Manchester University Press, 1995.

Whitehead, Judy. "Modernising the Motherhood Archetype: Public Health Models and the Child Marriage Restraint Act of 1929." *Contributions to Indian Sociology* 29, nos. 1 and 2 (1995): 187–210.

PADMA ANAGOL

AGING. Any overview of the theme of aging must be, at best, very partial. The history of aging and old age is still in its early stages and is far from being explored or understood in all, or even most, times and places. This entry will focus on what is known about aging and old age as they relate to women in what is broadly defined as Western culture, beginning in the ancient Greek and Roman worlds, because only for this region of world culture does a sustained, reasonably comprehensive historiography exist.

Ancient Greece and Rome. People recognized to be "old" have been a substantial presence in all known societies. A high proportion—often a majority—of these old people have been female. But the further we go back in history the less we know about the history of old age and aging, and the more heavily reliant we are upon sources concerning the elite and, especially, elite males.

We do not have good age statistics for ancient Greece and Rome, or for elsewhere in the ancient world, but there is good evidence from tombstones and documents that some people survived into their nineties and beyond. In general, longer life was more probable among the wealthy than among the poor, though not with certainty, because the rich diets of the better-off and elite men's engagement in war diminished their life chances.

At any time or place before the twentieth century, life expectancy at birth was quite low, perhaps age thirty in ancient Rome. But such averages were greatly reduced by high infant mortality rates. At all times those who survived childhood had a good chance of surviving to their sixties at least. Even in classical times, literary evidence suggests that dying in one's sixties or beyond was regarded as natural, and to die younger was regarded as harsh and unnatural. The biblical "three score years and ten" was regarded as a fair description of a good age rather than one of exceptional length. It is estimated that around 6 percent of the population of the Roman Empire in the first century C.E. was age sixty or over. Perhaps 2 percent lived past seventy, though epidemics and wars caused variations across place and time. A very few would have survived to one hundred.

"Old age" in ancient Greece and Rome, and for long after, was defined physiologically and culturally as well as chronologically. It was popularly seen as occurring when people appeared too weak physically or mentally to perform their normal work on a regular basis. This was assumed to occur sometime in the earlier sixties, preceded by a period of gradual decline, though it was accepted that people were perceived as "old" at variable ages. Beyond age sixty, people—mainly men because women had few allowable public duties—might withdraw from public life. For women, menopause was believed to signal the approach of old age, and male writers assumed that this occurred around age fifty—but whether or not this was so is unknown.

Medical specialists were intrigued by the characteristics and meaning of aging. Medicine in classical times and for long after was dominated by the belief that all life processes could be explained in terms of the interaction of the four "humors": warmth, cold, moisture, and dryness. Aging was interpreted as a process of progressive drying and cooling of the body, which increased susceptibility to disease. These processes did not progress identically in all bodies, and Galen (129–c. 199 C.E.) in particular argued that with due care and moderation, especially of diet and exercise, the aging process could be slowed.

In ancient Rome a woman over age fifty could not make a legitimate marriage with a man under sixty because it was assumed that she could not bear children. In general, wives were about ten years younger than their husbands and in consequence were highly likely to spend their later years as widows. This brought better-off women a period of enhanced freedom to control their own lives. Normally, however, women of all classes and ages were subordinate, socially marginalized and confined to domestic roles.

Some old women and men sought to hide the signs of aging: plucking out or dyeing grey hairs or seeking to smooth away wrinkles with oils or asses' milk or hiding them with white lead. There is no sign that old women or men were automatically venerated for being old, or automatically denigrated. In satiric comedy, such as that of Aristophanes, old men and women might be pilloried as ludicrously sex-crazed, while in more serious drama (as of Euripides) or in statues or paintings, both might be represented as serene and powerful. Attitudes toward and experiences of old age were always diverse. Philosophers differed as to whether old age was a stage of life to be welcomed or feared. Cicero's essay *De senectute* (On Old Age), which was written in around 44 B.C.E. when Cicero was sixty-two and was read in Europe at least until the nineteenth century, draws on older Greek writers, including Plato. It stresses the wisdom and calm that comes with old age, when such distractions as sexual passion have died. As with all such writing the essay was addressed to men. Aristotle passed down a more ambivalent, perhaps more realistic message: "Beauty differs for each stage of life ... a good old age is slowness to age and freedom from pain ... it is a product both of the excellences of the body and of luck ... and none persists to old age without luck."

Medieval and Renaissance Europe. The themes of substantial numbers of women and men living to old age—in circumstances that varied according to gender, class, and place, but nowhere conferring automatic deference—form long continuous threads through the history of Western culture. It was as true in medieval Europe as in ancient Greece and Rome that people who survived to early adulthood had a fair chance of reaching the age of sixty or seventy, and some lived to eighty or even ninety. People over sixty normally constituted between 6 percent and 8 percent of the population, though in exceptional periods, such as following plagues, the proportion could rise. Plagues killed more young people than old people. Thus in Florence in 1427, 14.6 percent of the population was over sixty, and in Ravenna 15.9 percent. Among the nobility, women tended to outnumber men because of the frequency of violent deaths among males. Among poorer people the situation was often reversed. Childbirth killed some women, hard work killed others. Also, women looked after the sick and were more exposed to infections. Women still tended to marry older men, so more women than men were widows at the end of their lives.

Legislation still exempted people (mainly men) from public service, including military service, from the age of sixty or sometimes seventy. Women were, however, obliged to work until age sixty under the Statutes of Labourers of England, passed in 1349, and they could be punished for begging or vagrancy if they did not. Under the laws of the crusading kingdom of Jerusalem, a widow could not be compelled to remarry by her feudal lord once she passed the age of sixty. Such age regulations must have had some relationship to the contemporary experience of aging to have survived so long and been so widespread.

Old men or women were not necessarily venerated or even respected unless they merited it for their contribution to the community. Attitudes toward them were diverse. Postmenopausal women were regarded in some medical texts as particularly venomous once they were unable to expel the menstrual blood, which was believed to be impure and harmful. Or they were reviled as sexually predatory once the fear of pregnancy was past, especially if they sought to conceal their aging with lavish clothing and cosmetics.

Philosophical reflections on aging, as in the ancient world, give little attention to women, while recognizing the varied experience among men: for some a period of calm and wisdom, for others one of melancholy and a bitter sense of loss. No writings survive of women reflecting on their own old age, while those of men express this same dichotomy.

Marginal though women of all ages were in medieval Europe, a few elite older women exerted authority. Hildegard of Bingen (1098–1179) founded an independent community of nuns at Eibingen at age sixty-seven and remained at its head until her death. Ela, Countess of Salisbury (c. 1190–1261) in England, after her widowhood founded a Cistercian nunnery and became its abbess. She retired at age sixty-eight, two years before her death. Heloise (notorious for her relationship with Abelard) remained abbess of her nunnery until her death at sixty-three. Other women inherited wealth and power at their husband's deaths. Matilda of Tuscany (1046–1115), who died at sixty-nine, and Margaret of Flanders (1202–1279), who died at seventy-eight, inherited feudal principalities and ruled them until their deaths. In England, Elizabeth de Burgh, Lady of Clare, was born in 1295. Her first husband died in 1313 and her third in 1322 when she was twenty-six. All three left her with control of substantial amounts of land. Thereafter she was almost forty years a widow, until her death in 1360, still actively managing a large estate.

Katherine Neville married John Mowbray, Duke of Norfolk, in 1412. He died in 1432, leaving her a life interest in his substantial estates. She lived for a further fifty-one years, remarrying three times—on the third occasion, in her sixties, to a teenager, who was assumed to be at least partly in pursuit of her fortune. If so, he was unlucky, because she outlived him by fourteen years. She died in 1483 in her eighties. Her three younger sisters were also well-endowed widows for fifty, thirty-five, and twenty years. There is every sign that such women enjoyed wealth, independence, and power, which was rarely available to women with surviving husbands.

For women of the lower classes, widowhood more probably brought poverty. The widows of artisans were rarely allowed to carry on their husband's trade, even if they had worked together before his death. In northern Europe older men and women who had some land could trade it as they aged. They made formal agreement with younger people—relatives or not—who, for a share of the land and eventual inheritance, gave the older people shelter and support until death (a form of pension). Such arrangements continued in parts of northern Europe into the early twentieth century. In southern and parts of eastern Europe families were more likely to share landholdings, with control passing gradually to the younger generation. Women and men who had no such security struggled to work for survival for as long as they could.

Women were generally poorer in old age than men because their earnings were always lower and because they had less opportunity to save for old age, though they might be able to work a little later in life at such tasks as child-minding. When men and women could no longer work, they might be supported by family or by charity, but the families of the poor were often very poor themselves, and as many as one-third of people reaching sixty would have no surviving children. If they had children able to support them, the generations were often wary of the tensions that could result if they lived together, and it was not always a favored option, at least until the older person became physically unable to survive independently.

The Seventeenth Century. People over sixty were present in even greater numbers in seventeenth-century Europe, reaching around 10 percent in many regions later in the century. Greater prosperity and better diets improved survival rates. Women seemed more consistently than before to outlive men, perhaps again because of improved diets and lesser exposure to dangerous employments. Hence more older women, in the richer classes, enjoyed the independence of widowhood. More women than before did not marry at all, partly because they were a majority of the population, partly perhaps because even poor young women had improved employment opportunities as servants for a growing bourgeoisie. Single women over fifty accounted for more than 15 percent of all women in towns such as Lyons and Rheims.

It continued to be recognized that people aged at variable paces. Some would be addressed as "old" or "mother" or "father" in their forties, others not until their seventies, though most commonly in their sixties. Men continued in public office at least to their sixties, and women were still excluded, though as midwives or with some knowledge of medicine they could be valued in their communities—or persecuted as witches if something went wrong.

Postmenopausal women were still thought evil and dangerous because of the menstrual blood trapped within their drying bodies, though views increasingly diverged, and as the women's bodies aged, dried, and became more "male" in appearance, some thought the women more capable of reason, like men, and hence worthy of more respect. But old women could still be feared and pilloried for suspected lustfulness, though old men who aped the young fared little better, especially at the hands of satirists as in the Italian commedia dell'arte. The better-off could keep wrinkles and brittle bones at bay for longer than the poor with their harder-working lives and more limited diets, though the rich lost their teeth sooner as the liberal use of expensive sugar became a fashionable luxury. Doctors, as they had since ancient times, urged moderate habits of eating and drinking and gentle exercise, such as walking, in order to keep fit and keep decrepitude at bay. Moderation throughout life was urged by medical men and churchmen, especially upon men, as the key to successful aging.

By the seventeenth century we have the views of some women themselves on their aging—generally women of the upper class. The accomplished Italian painter Sofonisba Anguissola painted her own portrait as a dignified woman of seventy-eight in 1610. In England, Lady Sarah Cowper (1644–1720) recorded her aging and that of others in her diary, criticizing women who dressed to look young, though refusing to admit that she herself was old until she was sixty-five. She recorded how her favorite activities of reading, writing, and learned contemplation—which she regarded as better suited to the lives of older women than sociability was—gradually diminished as her health failed, and she ceased to write three years before her death at seventy-six.

Most old women were still poor and poorer than men, though as Europe became more prosperous they had greater access to charity and poor relief, in institutions or, more frequently, in their own homes. The aged, especially women, were generally regarded as the "worthy" poor, deserving relief when in need because of incapacity to work. But many of them preferred to struggle on in whatever employment they could find for as long as they were able, descending to begging and pawning or selling possessions before resorting to charity.

The Eighteenth Century. Through the eighteenth century the age composition of European populations remained roughly what it had been through the early modern era. Those aged sixty and above constituted anywhere from 6 percent to 10 percent. In France they averaged 8 percent, in England 9–10 percent in the early part of the century and below 8 percent at the end, when fertility was rising. But—especially toward the end of the century in some rural areas, where out-migration of younger people in search of work was high—as trade, industry, and urbanization expanded, people over sixty could constitute between 13 percent and 18 percent of all those over age twenty. At the same time, though infant mortality rates remained high, the life expectancy of those who survived childhood was rising thanks to economic improvements.

From the 1740s to the 1820s in France, the share of twenty-year-olds reaching age sixty rose from 41.9 percent of men and 43 percent of women to 59 percent and 58.1 percent, respectively. The age to which twenty-year-old females could expect to live rose from 54.2 to 60.2 years. Women now had a clear survival advantage over men, and the advantage was still greatest among elites. As people lived longer, it became more common for three generations of a family to be alive together. From the seventeenth century, grandparents—most often grandmothers, because they were normally younger at the birth of their children than their husbands were—became increasingly common figures in painting, literature, and everyday life.

Medicine paid more attention to understanding diseases of old age, observing with greater care the processes of bodily aging, especially in France with its exceptionally low birthrate and high proportion of older people, though medicine still had a very limited capacity to cure. A pioneering French specialist, Jean Goulin, claimed, contrary to centuries of assertion, that menopause benefited the health of women and contributed to their longevity. Philosophical works advised the elite on how to achieve a good old age, in the tradition of Cicero, who was frequently translated in an increasingly secular age.

A version of Cicero for women was published in France in the mid-eighteenth century by Anne, Marquise de Lambert. Against still current notions that as women aged their bodies became more masculine and they became more sexually voracious, Anne disputed the loss of a distinctive femaleness after menopause and advised, like Cicero, retreat to a contemplative life and avoidance of passion to achieve a calm, happy old age. As she herself aged, however, Anne's sentimental life continued, and she remained at the center of a busy Parisian salon. Elite older women were more often than before represented in portraiture holding the symbols of learned contemplation, books, though caricatures castigating the unseemly behavior of "old flirts" continued. Poorer old women, like poor old men, were represented as active, dignified workers, as servants, weavers, and street vendors, or as pathetic beggars.

By the eighteenth century more (elite) older women spoke for themselves. The letters of the writer Madame de Graffigny, Voltaire's friend, describe in detail the friendships, health, loves—even the first orgasm at age forty-eight—of an aging woman who continued to enjoy life. As she came closer to death, the descriptions of her ill health become increasingly frequent and sad. For more conventional women, later life could bring a period of personal fulfillment, no longer dominated and constrained by the demands of dependent children while they were themselves still physically fit.

For example, when Martha Ballard, a farmer's wife in Maine, born in 1735, reached her fifties, she left her daughters to do the housekeeping and weaving that had previously preoccupied her and became a busy midwife. Elizabeth Drinker, born in the same year, a wealthy merchant's wife in Philadelphia, did not need to work and used this period of life for reading, writing, spiritual development, and the development of medical skills, which she practiced on her family. In England around the same time the farmer's wife Sarah Savage and the wealthier Lady Sarah Cowper similarly devoted their later lives to their own intellectual and spiritual development, while the widowed Lady Russell managed her own and her late husband's estates highly successfully.

This phase of early, fulfilled old age passed as the women reached the older, weaker stage of life. When Ballard's daughters married, she had to take on housework again in her late sixties, which, together with her heavy midwifery work, she found hard. She had much responsibility for her many grandchildren, which she found stressful. A period of living with one of her sons and his family was not happy, though as she grew older still, her grandchildren and children were sources of support. Cowper's life was much eased by the death of her husband, with whom she had long been miserable. Those women whose chief activity in old age was the life of the mind could sustain such pleasures longer than the majority, who, like Ballard, worked hard in later life.

The Nineteenth Century. In much of Europe, other than France, the birthrate rose rapidly from the later eighteenth century to the mid-nineteenth century. Consequently, although adult life expectancy continued to rise, the proportions of older people in European countries overall fell to, for example, around 5 percent in Britain by the end of the century. As the white migrant populations of the New World grew, they were overwhelmingly young and male, the normal demography of migrants, though they gradually aged as their populations grew and matured. In Ontario, Canada, the balance shifted from a majority of older males in 1851 to a female majority in 1901. Three percent of its population was over age sixty in 1851, 4.6 percent in 1871, and 8.4 percent in 1901.

The age structures of the indigenous populations of North and South America, Australasia, and Africa are unknown, as are the precise demographic effects of their brutal treatment by the in-migrants. From the beginning of the century we have, for the first time, reliable official statistics of the populations of many European countries and their white colonies or former colonies. In the United States the

Elderly Roles. Children play with kittens as their grandmother watches. Painting by Joseph Clark, late nineteenth century. FINE ART PHOTOGRAPHIC LIBRARY, LONDON/ART RESOURCE, NY

percentage of white people aged sixty or above was 4 percent in 1830 and 6.4 percent by 1906. In France this age group made up 8.7 percent of the population in 1801, rising to 12.6 percent in 1906. In England its share remained around 6 percent throughout the century.

Migrants left behind aging populations in rural areas of Europe and majority-female populations everywhere, as migration often separated the generations permanently by thousands of miles. Sometimes older women migrated to towns or to other countries with their younger relatives, providing housekeeping and child care while the younger people worked. They themselves were rarely welcome in new industries requiring new skills, though many of them continued to work for as long as they could at marginal, poorly paid occupations. In 1861 just under a quarter of London's female workforce was aged forty-five or over, but nearly half its laundresses and charwomen came from that age group. The alternative to paid work was still charity or poor relief.

Only in 1889 were the first state pensions introduced, in Germany, but these provided mainly for better-paid male workers, rarely for women, and not for the very poor. The United States provided extensive pensions for veterans of the Civil War and their widows or other dependents, as did European governments for army and navy veterans and civil servants, but nowhere were official pensions provided for women in their own right. In the 1890s New Zealand and Denmark introduced pensions targeted at the very poor, which especially benefited women, who became the majority of pensioners in these countries. In increasingly prosperous Europe a growing middle class also meant increasing numbers growing old in comfort, alongside desperate poverty. The experience of aging became ever more varied as social and economic experience became more diverse.

A minority of medical specialists, especially in France, continued to study the aged, though this remained a marginal interest in the medical profession. In general, older people, especially poor older people, were less likely to receive medical care or hospital treatment than the young. Most simply did not seek the attention of doctors. The better-off, as ever, could buy medical care—such as it was, given the limited capacities of nineteenth-century medicine. The most helpful advice was still to avoid excess in food and drink and to maintain moderate exercise.

Older men and women remained objects of religious and philosophical injunctions that a virtuous life followed by a calm, virtuous, independent existence would bring a good, long, active, even pain-free, old age followed by an easy "natural" death. Unfortunately, the reality did not always match the ideal. Ministers of religion, at least in Protestant countries, increasingly saw the welfare of the elderly as their responsibility, which must have brought some comfort. For others, old people continued to be objects of caricature and ridicule. No more than at any previous time were they uniformly objects of respect.

Asian Comparisons. Although much less English-language scholarship has been done on Asian history than on Western history, we can offer a few generalizations. As in the West, there were always sharp differences in the treatment of the elderly depending on the social, economic, and political status of the women involved. Two factors in the Confucian cultures of China, Japan, Korea, and Vietnam—ancestor worship and the great emphasis placed on filial piety—often gave elderly women, particularly in the elite class of scholar-officials, considerable power and influence in the family. If a woman had sons, she could generally count on their solicitous obedience long after they became adults. And if she was widowed, and thus became the senior surviving member of the extended family, she often exercised authority over the entire household.

There were, to be sure, ambiguities in the status of elderly women throughout Asia. On the one hand, they had far more leisure time and far greater freedom than younger women did. They were much freer to roam outside the "inner quarters" than were premenopausal women. Consequently, they often engaged in matchmaking activities, in the arts of healing and midwifery, and in religious activities ranging from pilgrimages to temples to shamanistic rituals of communication with the spirit world. Such women were often criticized as meddlers or gossips, and conservative male Confucian moralizers warned against them, but even such warnings reveal the considerable power and influence elderly women could have.

The Twentieth Century. In the twentieth century, for the first time in history, it became normal to grow old. There was a rapid decline, from the later nineteenth century, in death rates at all ages. In Britain at the beginning of the twentieth century an average of seventy-four people each year reached the age of one hundred; by 2006, more than ten thousand did so. In Japan, with its later and very rapid economic development, even in 1960 there were only 144 centenarians; in October 2005 there were 25,606. In both countries and in most others, with the exception of a cluster of countries in South Asia (India, Pakistan, Bangladesh), most very old people were female. In Britain, to take a typical example, life expectation at birth in 1901 was fifty-one years for men and fifty-eight for women; in 1999 it was seventy-five and eighty years, respectively. This change was the result of both rising adult life expectancy and also the dramatic decline in infant mortality.

Not only death rates but also birthrates fell to historically low levels over the twentieth century. One consequence was that, in most developed and many less developed countries, the proportion of people age sixty or above rose to historically high levels. In the United States it reached 13.2 percent by 1960 and 17 percent by 1990, and in Germany and the United Kingdom it was 20 percent by 1990; in impoverished Angola, in contrast, it was static at both dates at 5 percent. Not only did women and men live longer, they remained healthy and active to later ages than before. In spite of this apparently greater capacity to support themselves, more now received state pensions. These spread to Australia (paid at sixty-five) and Britain (paid at seventy) in 1908. In Britain the pension age was reduced to sixty-five in 1925 and, for women only, to sixty in 1940. Pensions were introduced in Canada in 1927 and the United States in 1935, both from age seventy. By the end of the century minimum pension ages, and hence official definitions of when old age began, varied between fifty-five and seventy, but were most commonly sixty or sixty-five.

Pensions were initially everywhere paid to manual workers and the poor. Only after World War II did they become universal in most high-income countries. From the beginning it was widely acknowledged that incapacity due to old age afflicted people at differing ages, but administrative convenience and economy required that pensions be paid at common ages. The age chosen in each country was influenced by prevailing conceptions of the age at which most people were incapacitated from regular work and by considerations of cost—the later the age, the fewer survivors and the lower the cost. Those countries that initially chose higher ages later reduced them under pressure mainly from trade unions and other representatives of workers, who argued that payment at too late an age left many old people in poverty for too long before they could claim a pension. The pension age for British women was reduced to sixty in 1940 following demands from unmarried women who argued that they faced discrimination in the labor market from their late fifties, employers preferring to hire younger women whom they regarded as more "decorative." The pension age for men and women was gradually equalized again following a ruling by the European Union in 1990 that reversed a rare example of sex discrimination that favored women.

Insurance pensions such as those in Germany in 1889 tended to provide primarily for men because fewer women had regular or sufficient incomes to enable regular contributions. Noncontributory pensions, paid by redistribution through the tax system, as initially in Denmark, Britain, Australia, and New Zealand, favored women because the pensions were normally means-tested and confined to the poorest—and old women still tended to be poorer than old men. In Britain it was awareness of the greater poverty and need of older women that determined the choice of a noncontributory rather than an insurance pension system in 1908. Two-thirds of the first British pensioners were female. An insurance scheme favoring men was added onto the existing pension system in 1925, as it was in Denmark in 1933.

At the end of the century, old women had lower pensions and were in general still poorer than old men. Some acquired prosperity and independence as a result of marriage and widowhood, but many more lived on in poverty having never married (more common in the first half of the century), being left as widows by poor men, or, increasingly in the later twentieth century, following divorce, which normally left women poorer than men. Though more women had high-income jobs by the end of the century, they still tended to earn less and, consequently, to have lower pensions than men. Women in general had fewer opportunities than men to accumulate assets to protect them in later life, because of, above all, more limited opportunities for employment, interrupted employment related to family responsibilities, and lower earnings.

It was normally assumed that on receiving a pension, pensioners would cease paid work, though this was not always obligatory, especially in noncontributory systems, and pensions were generally so small that many older people struggled on in at least part-time employment in order to survive. It was only after World War II that pensions in most high-income countries became large enough to enable most pensioners to retire from work, the first time that poor people had such an opportunity.

Pension Payments. Pensions for the elderly and infirm, Hamburg, Germany. Print after a drawing by Karl Müller, c. 1865. AKG-IMAGES

The spread of retirement to become a norm in the mid-twentieth century created a new cultural barrier between the lives of older and younger people. Older people might lose the social status associated with paid work, though the degraded work at which many poor old people had previously struggled in reality conferred little status. Retirement affected the lives of women less comprehensively than those of men. Women's work, in the form of domestic responsibilities, whether or not they were previously in paid employment, continued unchanged across the life course. Women who retired from paid work had normally long carried the double burden of work in and outside the home. Continued responsibility for domestic work after "retirement" provided continuity in their everyday lives. For men, whose lives were often centered on their employment, retirement created disruption and sudden confrontation with old age, which many found shocking. Aging women generally experienced less of a loss of self.

Generally, toward the end of the century, a period of leisure between working life and physical decline created new possibilities in the later lives of many women and men. Faced with rising expectations and greater general affluence, more older people than ever before—though not all—could enjoy new possibilities for leisure, travel, and active retirement.

Yet influential older people in high-status occupations did not retire and relinquish power unless they wished to do so, and they were not necessarily publicly perceived as old. In Britain, Margaret Thatcher was not defined as weak and decrepit when she served as prime minister past the female pension age of sixty, and she remained formidable after her involuntary retirement as prime minister, at sixty-five, in 1990. Nor was Queen Elizabeth II described as feeble when she visited the United States at age eighty-one in 2007, the same age that her great-great-grandmother Queen Victoria was in 1900.

Nevertheless it was commonplace to represent people past their sixties as dependent and fragile. Even though "old people" were the most stereotyped of all age-groups, social, economic, and physical differentiation was greatest at later ages, in a "group" comprising people from their sixties to past one hundred. In terms of physical condition, "old" men and women varied from the very fit to the extremely frail, and in terms of income they varied from some of the richest to the very poorest, and they included some of the most and the least powerful.

However, improved living standards (including diet)—and consequently improved health for most of the population—improved medical knowledge and care, and improved access to it even for poor people in most high-income countries after World War II led to medical opinion by the 1980s placing the onset of serious debility associated with old age at around age seventy-six, in contrast to age sixty to sixty-five at the beginning of the century. Those who were fit and active in their mid-sixties were likely to remain so for at least another decade, though with some weakening, for many people, from the later sixties. The medical specialty geriatrics, beginning in the United States around 1909, sought to ensure that older people received suitable medical attention and were not marginalized in the health care system, though geriatrics retained a relatively low status within the medical profession.

In the second half of the century, medical advances such as hip replacements and heart bypasses improved the quality of life for many older people, despite the extraordinary neglect, until the very end of the century, of research into the effects upon old people of some of the diseases most likely to kill them, in particular cancer and heart disease. At the same time the last days and months of some old people were made miserable by the capacity of modern medical technology to sustain life past the point at which it was worth living.

Menopause was more extensively discussed as a medical problem than before, as indeed were many conditions during the century in which scientific medicine made unprecedented advances. Remedies such as hormone replacement therapy were introduced to counter menopause's ill effects, though its benefits were increasingly questioned. It remained unclear whether menopause caused women more discomfort than in earlier times and, if so, in what proportion of women and why.

Paradoxically, at the very time that women and men became physically old later in life than ever before, their formal social and economic roles during the years of added vigor appeared to be diminishing. It was widely assumed, in popular and political discourse and among some scholars, that families were not important providers for the support of older people in modern, highly mobile societies. This was reinforced by the conviction of economists that welfare states crowded out family support, that altruism and reciprocity were redundant in modern market-based societies. It was also assumed that the falling birthrate and falling family size in the later part of the century would leave old people with fewer children to support them. Such predictions seemed to be supported by the steadily growing numbers of old people, especially women, who lived alone. In the United States and Britain at the end of the century almost half of women (and about a fifth of men) over age sixty lived alone.

These statistics could be, and often were, interpreted as evidence of the increasing isolation of old people from their families. Yet there was also consistent evidence, especially in the second half of the century, that many old people lived alone (as did growing numbers of younger people) not because they were neglected, but as a positive choice. At last, more people had the resources to exercise the preference for independent living that older people had expressed for centuries. Some, sadly, as at all times, were isolated and neglected, sometimes because they had no surviving family. Many surveys show, however, that just because older people lived alone, they did not necessarily lack frequent and close contact with family and friends, who gave support when it was needed, just as old people themselves gave support to others. No more than in earlier centuries could old people be stereotyped as undifferentiated dependents upon others. It was often forgotten that they gave to as well as took from their communities—in the case of older women, often in the form of care for grandchildren or sick or disabled friends or relatives.

The speed and ease of late-twentieth-century communications—motor vehicles, airplanes, telephones, the Internet—compensated for the effects of greater spatial mobility. Not all old people had close relatives, though probably more did so at the end of the century than at the beginning. Though average family size fell over the century, rates of marriage and childbirth and survival rates of infants rose, so that by the end of the century, in most high-income countries, more older women had at least one surviving child than at the beginning of the century. In the twentieth century, as in earlier centuries, older women without close relatives often formed networks of friendship that provided the same supportive role as blood kin. Older women in general coped better than men with living alone, being better able to care for themselves and having stronger social networks.

The spread of industrialization and urbanization in the twentieth century has served to globalize many of these trends. Yet in East and South Asia, most elderly women (and men) continued to live with, and be supported by, at least one of their children. Though urban industrialized areas provided pensions and retirement incomes for retired workers, in all the rural parts of the developing world, families remained the primary, and often the only, source of support for the aged. And in return, grandmothers in these areas were the main source of child care for working mothers.

The growing affluence of many old people at all social levels in high-income societies, the availability of a new and wider range of consumer goods, plus the effects of medical and technological changes, profoundly influenced the experience of old age in the twentieth century. New technologies generated new and widely disseminated sources of images of older people, as of everything else, in magazines, advertisements, films, and television. Individuals, mostly female, could manipulate their own images through the use of a growing range of makeup items, hair dyes, and cosmetic surgery, together with increasingly widespread attention in the later part of the century to the long-known age retardants of diet and exercise. All of these techniques were, of course, most easily available to the most affluent, but the growth of the mass market made them more cheaply available to more people than before, and they became more widely socially acceptable in the second half of the century.

Disguising the visible signs of age by older women was condemned by some as obeisance to a cult of youth but was

Aging. A woman in Hong Kong. BURHAN DOGANÇAY/ART RESOURCE, NY

encouraged by the mass media, which was said to induce refusal to accept the "realities" of aging and to "grow old gracefully" and "naturally." This overlooked the reality experienced by women and men through the centuries that natural aging, unassisted by adornment or medical intervention, could be far from graceful. The assumption that at a certain age women should cease practices, such as use of makeup and hair dyes, that might have been a part of their everyday experience since their teens, or that sixty-year-olds who had worn jeans for forty years should abandon them because they had reached a certain age, suggested a new kind of stereotyping, which increasing numbers of assertive older people resisted.

A greater variety of personal documents than ever before in many countries—diaries, letters, social surveys—convey the experiences of older women. As in early centuries they express diversity. Some feel sad and marginalized. Many more express resistance to ageist stereotyping, recognize the variability of the aging process, and themselves lead active lives.

[*See also* Cosmetic Surgery; Demography; Female Life Cycle; Poverty; Welfare State; *and* Widows and Widowhood.]

BIBLIOGRAPHY

Achenbaum, W. Andrew. *Old Age in the New Land: The American Experience since 1790.* Baltimore: Johns Hopkins University Press, 1978. Valuable survey of the U.S. experience.

Botelho, Lynn, and Pat Thane, eds. *Women and Ageing in British Society since 1500.* Harlow, U.K., and New York: Pearson Education, 2001. A useful collection of essays on one country.

Bourdelais, Patrice. *Le nouvel âge de la vieillesse: Histoire du vieillissement de la population.* Paris: Éditions O. Jacob, 1993. Good demographic survey of France from the eighteenth to twentieth centuries.

Cass, Victoria. *Dangerous Women: Warriors, Grannies, and Geishas in the Ming.* Lanham, Md.: Rowman & Littlefield, 1999. Chapter 3, "Grannies," details the ambiguities of old age for women in Ming dynasty China (1368–1644).

Cole, Thomas R. *The Journey of Life: A Cultural History of Aging in America.* Cambridge, U.K., and New York: Cambridge University Press, 1992. Mainly nineteenth century.

Davis-Friedman, Deborah. *Long Lives: Chinese Elderly and the Communist Revolution.* Cambridge, Mass.: Harvard University Press, 1983. Pioneering study of aging in the People's Republic of China.

Day, Alice T. *Remarkable Survivors: Insights into Successful Aging among Women.* Washington, D.C.: Urban Institute Press, 1991. A study of older women in the United States in the late twentieth century.

Haber, Carole. *Beyond Sixty-Five: The Dilemma of Old Age in America's Past.* Cambridge, U.K., and New York: Cambridge University Press, 1983.

Haber, Carole, and Brian Gratton. *Old Age and the Search for Security: An American Social History.* Bloomington: Indiana University Press, 1994.

Johnson, Paul, and Pat Thane, eds. *Old Age from Antiquity to Post-Modernity.* London and New York: Routledge, 1998. Expert essays on old age in ancient Rome, medieval Europe, nineteenth- and twentieth-century Britain, Germany, France (eighteenth to twentieth centuries), and New Zealand.

Lamb, Sarah. *White Saris and Sweet Mangoes: Aging, Gender, and Body in North India.* Berkeley: University of California Press, 2000. Intimate anthropological study of gender and aging in a village in West Bengal.

Ottaway, Susannah, R. *The Decline of Life: Old Age in Eighteenth-Century England.* Cambridge, U.K., and New York: Cambridge University Press, 2004. Authoritative in its field.

Ottaway, Susannah R., L. A. Botelho, and Katharine Kittredge, eds. *Power and Poverty: Old Age in the Pre-Industrial Past.* Westport, Conn.: Greenwood Press, 2002. A good collection of essays on old age in Europe, covering the sixteenth to early nineteenth centuries.

Parkin, Tim G. *Old Age in the Roman World: A Cultural and Social History.* Baltimore: Johns Hopkins University Press, 2003. The most authoritative survey of the field.

Shahar, Shulamith. *Growing Old in the Middle Ages: "Winter Clothes Us in Shadow and Pain."* Translated by Yael Lotan. London and New York: Routledge, 1997. The best, and the only, survey of old age in medieval Europe.

Thane, Pat. "Geriatrics." In *Companion Encyclopedia of the History of Medicine,* 2 vols., edited by W. F. Bynum and Roy Porter, pp. 1092–1115. London: Routledge, 1993.

Thane, Pat. *Old Age in English History: Past Experiences, Present Issues.* Oxford and New York: Oxford University Press, 2000. Surveys old age in English history since medieval times, with a chapter also on the legacy of ancient Greece and Rome.

Thane, Pat, ed. *A History of Old Age.* Los Angeles: J. Paul Getty Museum, 2005. Also published as *A Long History of Old Age* (London: Thames and Hudson, 2005). Volume of essays by leading experts on old age in Western culture since ancient Greece and Rome, superbly illustrated with images of old women and men.

Troyansky, David G. *Old Age in the Old Regime: Image and Experience in Eighteenth-Century France.* Ithaca, N.Y.: Cornell University Press, 1989. Authoritative in its field.

PAT THANE

AGREDA, SOR MARÍA DE (1602–1665), Spanish nun, mystic, and author. Born María Coronel in the small Castilian town of Agreda near the border with Aragon, María de Agreda devoted her life to the church from an early age. First as nun and then as abbess of the Convento de la Purísima Concepción, Sor María de Jesús de Agreda was soon well known for her piety and mysticism. Sor María never left her small hometown during her lifetime, but she became a well-known and controversial figure on both sides of the Atlantic.

Sor María is perhaps most readily recognized as the author of *Mística ciudad de Dios* (English trans., *Mystical City of God*), an enormous work on the life and import of the Virgin Mary. It was first published in Madrid in 1670, with two more editions appearing before the end of the seventeenth century. The work was published many more times in Spanish, Latin, and other European languages over the course of the eighteenth, nineteenth, and twentieth centuries. The book sparked controversy during the seventeenth century because of the ongoing debates surrounding the idea of the Immaculate Conception of Mary, which had not yet been fully accepted as official church doctrine. The book was harshly criticized by a number of Catholic theologians before being banned for a time by the pope. Since the early eighteenth century, however, the book has been cited as evidence of Sor María's contribution to church doctrine during repeated attempts to promote her case for canonization.

During her lifetime, the appearance of this controversial work only intensified the scrutiny that Sor María received from the Inquisition because of her reported bilocations to the New World. During her twenties, Sor María reportedly entered trances during which she traveled to the region of New Mexico and communicated with the indigenous population there in their own language. Thus she was said to be bodily present in two locations at the same time. This mystical experience was corroborated by the Franciscan friar Alonso de Benavides, who was working in the missions of New Mexico at that time. He reported in his chronicle that a delegation of Jumano Indians arrived every spring at the mission, requesting friars and baptism and claiming to have been sent by a beautiful young woman in blue. Upon his return to Spain, Benavides heard of Sor María's bilocations and concluded that she was indeed the Lady in Blue. New Mexican and Texan folklore tell of numerous other sightings of this figure long after Sor María's death in 1665.

Though she was undoubtedly concerned about the unwanted attention from ecclesiastical authorities surrounding her mystical experiences and writings, Sor María found protection in her close friendship with King Philip IV of Spain. The more than six hundred letters exchanged between nun and monarch have interested Spanish historians for the light that they shed on the king's personal life and thoughts, as well as on seventeenth-century political theory. The king often sought spiritual and sometimes political advice from the nun in Agreda and, in turn, encouraged her in her writing and in her dealings with the Inquisition. Though Sor María was admired by her fellow Spaniards during her lifetime for her piety, mysticism, and friendship with the king of Spain, it is her contribution to doctrine through her account of the life of the Virgin Mary that has gained her renown in the Catholic world.

[*See also* Spiritual Leaders, *subentry* Nuns and Abbesses.]

BIBLIOGRAPHY

Baranda, Consolación. "Introducción." In *Correspondencia con Felipe IV: Religión y razón de estado,* by María de Agreda, pp. 9–48. Madrid: Editorial Castalia, 1991. A useful introduction to Baranda's selection, in Spanish, of María de Agreda's correspondence with Philip IV of Spain.

Colahan, Clark. "María de Jesús de Agreda: The Sweetheart of the Holy Office." In *Women in the Inquisition: Spain and the New World,* edited by Mary E. Giles, pp. 155–170. Baltimore: Johns Hopkins University Press, 1999.

Colahan, Clark. *The Visions of Sor María de Agreda: Writing, Knowledge, and Power.* Tucson: University of Arizona Press, 1994. An important contribution to the secular scholarship on María de Agreda.

Kendrick, T. D. *Mary of Agreda: The Life and Legend of a Spanish Nun.* London: Routledge and Kegan Paul, 1967. A thorough biography of both the Spanish nun and the figure of Southwestern folklore.

KATIE G. MACLEAN

AGRICULTURE

This entry consists of four subentries:

Overview
Early History
Methods of Farming
Peasantry

Overview

The economics of farming looks at access and control of the economic factors of production: land, labor, and capital. Over time, these have been increasingly privatized and separated. That separation has tended to lead to accumulation of control of the factors of production in the hands of fewer and fewer people and organizations, which increasingly tend to be corporations with male management. However, the process of global accumulation is complex, and women's economic role is not linear over time. Further, women's access to and control of other resources (natural, cultural, human, social, political, and financial) have to a degree balanced men's domination of agricultural production, distribution, and consumption. Who has access to and control of such resources in turn influences what is farmed, where it is farmed, how it is farmed, and who farms it.

As human groups became settled—planting crops and taming animals, which allowed them to stay in one place throughout the year—women were active as farmers. Early archaeological data suggest that women were the first to domesticate plants, systematically bringing the seeds they had gathered to plant near to their dwellings to ensure a regular food supply. Women were also crucial in the domestication of animals, which in turn contributed toward creating agricultural surplus by making available draft animals and manure to increase productivity, as well as the milk, fiber, and meat provided by the animals themselves. Even with nomadic people, who migrated with their animals seeking seasonal pastures, women provided critical knowledge and labor in managing the animals and processing their by-products. Sami women in northern Europe, for example, tamed and milked the reindeer that provided the base of their diet, as well as processed every part of the animal for household use and trade from at least 500 B.C.E. to the present.

The existence of food surpluses, the result of selection of better-producing crops, in turn supported more elaborate forms of social organization that built and managed irrigation systems in such civilizations as the Fertile Crescent, the Nile Valley, and the Inca Empire. That is, the existence of surplus led to the creation of more surplus. Though some researchers attribute the agricultural revolution to the use of the plow and animal production, societies such as those in Central and South America managed to generate large agricultural surpluses through more biologically based technologies such as complex crop rotations and management of water systems through building terraces and ditches.

The result was that fewer people were needed to produce food. Individuals freed from the demands of food production maintained and expanded the system as rulers, priests, and warriors. In the more hierarchical societies, women and men farmers had limited choices in what they could produce and how, because they had fewer resources to use in food production, storage, and processing.

Traditional Division of Labor. Historical accounts of Europe, Africa, Asia, and Latin America all suggest the importance of women in agricultural production. Evidence from drawings and farm records illuminates women's complementary activities within the European feudal system. Women in the Inca Empire were critical in the selection of seeds, while men did the digging for planting, and women managed livestock reproduction while men worked with livestock in the pastures.

Complementary roles. Current anthropological accounts stress that women and men played complementary roles in traditional agriculture. In most agriculturally based households, it was crucial that everyone work—young, old, male, and female. The division of labor was based in part on the physical abilities of the individuals, so that the old were spared from extremely heavy work, as were the very young. In large measure, culture determined the way that work was allocated according to age and gender. What was men's work in one culture, such as the care of milk cows, was women's work in another culture. Almost always, land clearing and plowing, which were viewed as heavy work, were male-dominated, but there are cultures in which women engaged in these activities as well. For example, men milk cows in the mountains of the Dominican Republic, but women milk cows in parts of Europe.

Roles in agriculture were learned through apprenticeship, which was often gender specific. Some knowledge was specific to women, and other knowledge to men. Women would know how to choose the best seed to save over the hungry season in order to plant for the next harvest, as well as the way to care for small animals to ensure survival of the

Inca Agriculture. Inca men breaking soil with a *taccla* or foot plow, while a woman behind them sows seeds. Facsimile of a drawing from "El primer nueva corónica y buen gobierno," by Felipe Guaman, c. 1565. Nick Saunders/Barbara Heller Photo Library/Art Resource, NY

healthiest when food supply was limited. In Honduras, in an area of recurrent drought where feed is limited, women's practice in hog rearing is to let shoats suckle from the sow for the first month. The strongest survive, while two-thirds of the shoats die. The shoats that survive the first few months then receive supplemental feed and care. Given the limited resources available, the high shoat mortality is not a problem and, in fact, helps ensure that those shoats in which the family invests survive to adulthood and serve as a source of savings for the family. Instead of being consumed on a regular basis, hogs could be sold or slaughtered at any age, making them available for emergencies or investment. Animal husbandry and the knowledge necessary to maximize local resources are often women's responsibility.

Further, women often gather herbs and medicines from forested areas. Studies in a variety of areas have suggested that women are able to identify nearly six times as many different species of indigenous plants than are men. This contributes to maintaining genetic diversity.

Social capital and farming. Trust, reciprocity, shared norms and values, formal and informal groups, and working together—social capital—have been critical in the success of farming operations over time. In more traditional communities, much of agriculture was based on a community division of labor, not just on a family division of labor. Complicated labor exchanges were negotiated by men and by women, often with members of the same sex. Such exchanges involved direct exchanges of labor at times of particularly high labor demand, as well as simple gifts, particularly food, seed, and plant cuttings, that could be used to maintain agricultural productivity. Very often women were in charge of the less-formal exchange relationships that were vital in maintaining communities and protecting them from the necessity of becoming totally dependent on wage labor. Such informal exchanges helped maintain agricultural production in small-scale operations.

Integration into the World System. Traditional communities were based on subsistence production with very little for sale. As world markets penetrated these communities, the division of labor in agriculture changed dramatically, and the surplus generated was taken ever farther from where it was produced.

In much of the colonized world, particularly Africa and Latin America, the first major change that impacted traditional farming systems was the removal of male labor to work in mining and in seasonal plantation agriculture. Men were needed for the sugar harvest and the banana harvest. A few women followed to provide domestic services such as cooking and doing laundry. But generally, women remained at home in charge of subsistence production plots and animal care and breeding.

That disruption in traditional farming systems intensified as harvests of export crops such as coffee and cotton used entire families as laborers. Perhaps the most disruption to the complementary division of labor by gender occurred in those areas in Africa, Latin America, and parts of Asia where male labor was drawn into mining activities. When men worked at harvesting seasonal plantation crops, they could return home for plowing and land clearing, but when they worked in the mines they were often gone for years at a time, which left women in charge of the farm. Particularly in parts of southern Africa, where strict rules regulated the movement of people across national boundaries, agriculture became an almost entirely female occupation.

Integration into a world economic system changed land use—from subsistence crops and those destined for domestic markets to export crops. In much of Latin America, for example, large areas of very good land had been given out as Spanish or Portuguese land grants in return for service to the crown in the sixteenth and seventeenth centuries and were farmed extensively with livestock, predominantly cattle. Indigenous peoples and mestizos—those of mixed European and native descent—had use rights to land, on which they raised subsistence crops in exchange for the labor they provided to the hacienda owner. In these systems, both women and men provided labor as part of the encomienda, or land grant.

Economic Impacts of the Shift to Export Crops: Plantation Systems. Colonization was in part a project to provide raw materials produced by cheap labor and a market for manufactured goods. The land either was property of the Crown or was given to male proprietors or male-owned corporations in order to ensure loyalty and steady production. But labor was always a problem in colonized areas. In the Americas, the indigenous people made poor plantation workers, particularly because the plantations tended to be established in malarial areas where the land was relatively flat and water relatively abundant. Two different ways of providing labor from Africa were attempted, one in English colonies and the other in Iberian New World colonies. The Iberian colonies, particularly Brazil, depended on a steady supply of male slaves. But in North America, particularly as England began to limit the slave trade, women and men were brought as slaves from Africa in order to provide a local supply of cheap and easily exploited labor.

Different areas of North America, Latin America, Asia, and Africa entered the export crop market at different times. For example, in the sixteenth and seventeenth centuries the islands of the Caribbean were settled by colonists from several nations primarily because of their suitability for sugar production and were almost always export oriented. As a result, particularly in the English-speaking Caribbean, women produced most of the food crops. In parts of Africa and Asia, male labor has dominated in the harvest of the plantation crops, particularly sugarcane, since the fifteenth century. However, developments such as the mechanization of sugarcane production in Hawai‘i and of pineapple production in the Dominican Republic introduced selective use of women in plantation fields, as well as in packing sheds, when male workers found better-paid work.

For example, in the wake of disastrous hurricanes in Florida, Louisiana, Mississippi, and Alabama in 2004 and 2005, male workers previously employed in harvesting fruits and vegetables and in the cultivation of ornamentals instead found employment in construction as rebuilding took place, leaving field work to women. The vulnerability of agricultural labor has increased as workers no longer are hired directly by the farm operator (and thus no longer protected by labor laws) but instead are hired by labor contractors, who often recruit them from their home countries and receive the money that may or may not be given to them as wages. As these men and women are often unauthorized, employers view them as valuable employees (they do not complain, despite long hours, low pay, and unsafe conditions), and despite increasing anti-immigrant sentiments, specialty crop employers find ways to keep a constant migration stream coming from the south both to Europe and the United States.

In plantation systems, such as that of sugar and pineapple in Hawai‘i and cotton in the South of the United States, and in the neo-plantation systems of fruit and vegetable production, the combination of gender and nationality made women the cheapest and most vulnerable workforce. Women migrant workers from other countries are at the bottom of the scale in a foreign workplace, exploited both economically and sexually.

In parts of Latin America, few export crops were planted until the era of land reform, beginning in the early 1960s. Most land reforms promulgated during that period were intended to make land more productive, not to redistribute land. Under the threat of expropriation, many large landowners shifted from extensive agricultural systems to more intensive ones, planting soybeans, cotton, and even more sugarcane—all crops aimed at foreign markets. As a result, people who had previously farmed the land based on customary rights of use granted to local populations were displaced. Many moved to the cities, whereas others moved to less-desirable highland areas where they found that the traditional practices that worked well on flat ground tended to erode hillside lands. Others moved to jungle and rain forest areas, with equally disastrous results. In the new colonization schemes that governments in Latin America and Asia are pursuing to ease the pressures of urban population, women's labor is critical yet undervalued. Women's ability to maintain social connections provides access to land and labor for subsistence and market production.

In the new cropping systems that emerged in the fragile highland and jungle areas, there is a marked difference between "his" crops and "her" crops. She raises vegetables and tree crops around the house, and he cultivates row crops and commercial tree crops farther away from the household living area. There is also an increase in the division of labor in animal raising, varying by area. Men are in charge of raising large animals, an enterprise that requires a certain capital investment, and women maintain the production of small animals, using them for both household consumption and sale in times of economic stress.

Impacts of Land Privatization. A third important trend that has affected the division of labor by gender worldwide has been the movement toward the privatization of land. In traditional agricultural communities, much land was controlled in common, with village leaders assigning land use on a year-by-year basis. In this system, women had access to land through traditional use rights. As land became titled, moving from common access to private control and the legal right to buy and sell, it was almost always titled in the name of the man in the household rather than the man and woman. The new private plots in the reformed areas and in new colonization and seasonal grazing areas favored men's crops, which tend to be sold outside the community, while women's crops are used for domestic consumption. Although women's gardens might be vital for household nutrition and even survival, little land was left for them. Women's collective production efforts were eliminated entirely. Often the animals that women would pasture, such as small ruminants, also were not allocated land for grazing.

The trends in world agriculture away from subsistence and toward a focus on export crops and the privatization of land have tended to break down the role complementarity previously present in traditional systems. One can no longer assume what men will do or women will do in agriculture. A lot depends on the differential costs of land, labor, and capital. For example, if there is a destination where male labor pays more, the men may migrate. On the other hand, if women will work for less, exporters will hire primarily women to do the field work. Thus subsistence-oriented family and community-based agricultural programs have deteriorated. Because women and men tend to spend their income in different ways, and women tend to direct theirs toward household and children's needs, the welfare of children is disproportionately affected when women lose access either to land to cultivate or to labor markets.

Current Characteristics of Women in Agriculture Worldwide. Not only has the traditional division of labor by gender in agricultural production varied enormously over time and space, so have the amount and allocation of resources within households. Different members of farming households have different sources of income, and men and women use those sources of income differently. In pre–World War II American agriculture, women earned egg and butter money by raising chickens or milking the cows and marketing the product in local markets. The same was true in Europe during the same time period. Women either bartered their products at the local store for other kinds of food the family needed, such as coffee or salt, or sold them if cash was needed for other family necessities. Very often they used such cash for special items of household consumption or even set it aside for children's schooling. Men's income was more likely to be reinvested in production.

How income is used by gender. Intra-household income streams vary widely in farming households. In some areas household income is pooled. In other areas, particularly in parts of Africa and Asia, women lend their husbands money at interest. Different members of the family decide whether to sell different crops or to consume them at home.

Income that goes directly to women in agricultural households is more likely to be used for household necessities, particularly children's food, clothing, and schooling. Men's income is often used for a variety of male bonding activities, such as drinking, that may contribute to community solidarity but not to household well-being. As a result of these different uses of income, increasing a farm family's income does not equally benefit all family members. The existence of patriarchy—that is, the dominance of the oldest male in the household—tends to mean unequal and sometimes arbitrary distribution of income within any particular household.

Resource access by gender. The impact of unequal access to resources combined with heavy workloads for all household members can be judged by looking at the sex ratio in rural farm areas in developed countries. There are generally many more men than women, despite the overall tendency of women to outnumber men as adults. Women are more likely to leave farm areas, because they feel that the hard work they put in on a farm, particularly in livestock operations such as dairy, is not worth the limited return in cash and respect that they receive. Thus the reason that women in advanced industrial societies are reluctant to participate in agricultural production is that farm women have too much work to do at home, at their jobs, and in the community, little chance of leisure, and little control over resources for production. Although figures for many developed countries show women as major landowners, this gives a distorted picture. Women who own land are very often widows who simply hold land title as placeholders for their sons, who take on the major decision making and control of the agricultural production practices.

Increasingly in industrialized countries, ownership is separated from management. This hastens the industrialization of agriculture. The goal of industrial agriculture is to produce effectively and efficiently, as judged by short-term profit. Issues such as justice to farmworkers or environmental degradation are not included in the calculation of costs and benefits. Standards are based on the qualities of a specific product, not how a crop is grown. Research on farm-owning women in the United States suggests that they feel at the mercy of their farm managers, who may be relatives, neighbors, or a land-management company and who practice the industrial model of agriculture without seeing that there are choices.

On the other hand, women are disproportionately represented in civic agriculture, which includes organic agriculture. In civic agriculture, the standards are based on

Agriculture in World War I. Three women harnessed to a plow, Oise, France, 1917. PRINTS AND PHOTOGRAPHS DIVISION, LIBRARY OF CONGRESS

such things as environmental sustainability or fair trade and are enforced through attention on process rather than simply on the end product. This is a small but growing part of the economics of agriculture worldwide.

Technology and Women. Agricultural technology has been developed to make both labor and land produce more per unit. However, most of that technology has been channeled toward men. For example, when chicken production became highly technical and market oriented, the technology was brought to the males of the family by the extension service, a government-funded educational and technical-assistance institution based at agricultural universities in all states of the United States. As a result, women lost their source of separate income, although they would often continue to do the work. Men enjoyed greater access to the credit needed to employ technology to expand the chicken production, as well as almost exclusive access to the technical assistance offered by either the agricultural extension service or, later, the poultry integrators (large multinational corporations who purchased the chickens). And the milk check, the chicken check, or the egg check would be written in the name of the male head of household. Yet women provide crucial labor in contract chicken production, particularly in the South of the United States.

In the developing world as well, technological innovation has tended to disadvantage women compared to men. That women's sources of income were not recognized often meant that income-producing activities moved from female hands to male hands. As more official marketing channels were put into place, such as milk production in the high plateau of Bolivia, women milkers lost control of the milk, and male community leaders sold it to dairies. Further, the income-producing labor that women did, such as rice hulling in parts of Africa and Asia, was, when mechanized, taken over by men, leaving women without the hard work but also without the important income that it generated.

A number of studies in different parts of the world have shown that farm women produce as much as farm men when they have access to similar resources. This includes education, access to markets, access to credit, and access to technical assistance. New technologies, such as biotechnology and pesticides, and marketing contracts are gendered, and they are biased almost always toward men and away from women.

Gendered Patterns of Production. Despite the gendering of access and control of the land, labor, and capital necessary for production, a number of different gender patterns in agriculture have emerged and can be seen in different areas and in different proportions. The first pattern is one of men and women having separate and different agricultural enterprises. This occurs most often in Africa but also in parts of Latin America and the Caribbean, where men will have particular crops for particular markets and women will have quite different crops for quite different markets.

The second pattern is one of separate but similar agricultural enterprises. For example, both men and women may raise vegetables. In the Caribbean, men may raise vegetables for a world market, whereas women may raise vegetables for the local market. The first pattern has implications for agricultural research and extension in that there is a tendency to focus only on the crops that men produce. The second pattern has implications for agricultural research and extension in that, particularly if fruits and vegetables are being raised, those for a local market can have different characteristics than those for markets where extensive shipping is required. Thus men and women will use different varieties of the same species.

A third pattern involves having separate tasks within the same enterprise. This often occurs in developed countries, as well as in developing countries, where men will be in charge of plowing, women will be in charge of seed selection, both do planting and harvesting, men do tilling, and women do postharvest processing.

A fourth pattern, much less common, is that of men and women sharing tasks in the same enterprise. Although such ungendered task sharing occurs in Canada, the United States, and Europe, this pattern was actually decreasing in the early years of the twenty-first century as increasing stress on farm incomes forced men and women off the farm to seek outside income. In many rural areas, women have an advantage in terms of off-farm employment, taking jobs in government-supported service industries, such as health care and education, that offer health insurance (which in the United States is uniquely linked to employment). Thus men take over many of the jobs that they once shared with their wives.

A final pattern, which is increasing in many developing countries and in certain parts of the developed world, is that of female-run enterprises, a category that comprises both de facto female-headed enterprises (in which the enterprise has a male head of household but a woman actually runs it because the male is gone for all or most of the year) and de jure female-headed enterprises (in which the land and resources are legally in the woman's name). De jure female farms are much less common. They tend to be present in developed countries, where an increasing number of women choose to engage in agriculture on their own.

Implications for Agricultural Change. The recognition of the role of women in agriculture, as landowners, agricultural managers, and agricultural workers, is extremely important to understanding how agriculture will change over time. For example, women agricultural workers are prevalent in the production of export crops in many developing countries, especially in harvesting and immediate postharvest processing. Defining jobs as suitable for specific populations—migrant women, white men, and so forth (categorization that is often referred to as "segmented labor markets")—reduces female wages and limits their employment possibilities. In many developed countries, male migrant laborers serve the same function and may displace female local workers.

Agricultural research would be much different if it were to look more carefully at the role of women in the economics of farming. This recognition of women's roles might lead to changes in the types of crops or animal enterprises that are researched, and it might guide changes in the plant and animal characteristics that are bred for or the type of farming practices that are developed, depending on recognition of the differential needs of different types of producers. Rather than reinforcing the conventions of industrial agriculture, it also might lead to more attention to rewarding production that contributes to the greater good.

Agricultural extension would be transformed by a recognition of the types of agricultural work that women actually do and acknowledgment of the fact that if women carry out particular tasks, then technical-assistance providers need to train women, not their husbands, to perform those tasks.

Agricultural marketing would also change if there were an awareness of what women actually do in agriculture. For example, if women do the work, agricultural marketing that allows them to receive the cash for the product would enable them to better recognize the product characteristics that get a higher price and change their production practices accordingly. Using women's groups for marketing or including women in existing agricultural marketing cooperatives as a specific policy might be very important. For example, women are more effective in identifying new markets for new products, such as in linking to chefs or specialty retailers. In the twenty-first century, women have difficulty achieving leadership positions in producer organizations, although they are more likely to have a voice in sustainable agricultural groups in Australia, Europe, and the United States.

In value-added agriculture—that is, the enterprise of creating a more valuable secondary product from a primary agricultural product, such as making cheese from cow and goat milk—understanding who does what when can be extremely important. Mechanizing a process and turning it over to men often takes away from the work that women traditionally did to earn income. Artisanry or rustic development projects, such as weaving traditional baskets from reeds grown on the farm or home canning (where women use traditional means to process food after it is produced), may add to women's work but not to their incomes. Thus value-added strategies must include awareness of not only who does what but also who has control over which resources in agricultural production.

Redistributing Land. Members of Celina's Settlement—a contingent of the Landless Workers' Movement (MST), whose goal is the redistribution of land among the poor—weed between crops, Pernambuco, Brazil, June 2003. REUTERS/Bruno Domingos

Finally, recognizing the role of women in agriculture has enormous implications for how agricultural communities are organized. It is important to recognize women's role as wage laborers and their need for the kinds of services that facilitate their participation in the labor force, such as health care and child care. It is also very important to include women in natural-resource management, because they often have particular interests in common property as well as in individual property.

Civic Agriculture and Women. Industrial conventions—the norms and values of efficiency, the rules and regulations to define efficiency, and the regulatory mechanisms to enforce those rules and regulations—have tended to be controlled by men. Women for the most part have been more active in setting civic conventions—that is, conventions around norms and values of maintaining community, sustaining a health ecosystem, and providing a fair return to producers and workers. Women have been leaders in setting rules and regulations for such civic conventions as organic agriculture and fair trade, as well as in setting up alternative certification mechanisms.

Civic agriculture often uses a wide variety of new technologies in new ways. To be successful, it must be aware of the gendered division of labor, as well as of the control over resources by gender. Civic agriculture demands a community commitment as well as an individual commitment to social change. The skill set for engaging in civic agriculture includes human capital (the individual skills and abilities), political capital (to make sure that the type of agriculture practiced is rewarded through state mechanisms such as subsidies—direct for crops, or indirect by access to water or payment for conservation measures), tax incentives, and marketing rules. Women's tendency to have a liberal, as opposed to a technical, education helps create and enforce new standards by using cultural capital and social capital as well.

Ecofeminist theory proposes that women have a particular concern and linkage to the soil and animals and thus an inbred desire to sustain and protect them. That essentialist position is critiqued by structuralists, who point out that there are cultural reasons why women would be more concerned about civic agriculture than would men, who often have a shorter time frame in seeking profits because the standard for profitability in male-dominated enterprises is more typically based on income and capital accumulation. Certainly, much of the degradation of once-fertile cropland can be attributed to aggressive agricultural practices, such as the decades of suitcase farming that in the 1930s turned much of the Great Plains of the United States into a literal dust bowl. But such catastrophes may simply be coincident with men having control over the land and may not be evidence that men are inherently less oriented to sustainability than women are. Women might have brought about similar results if they had had the access and control of the land and money.

Assessment. Women have been, and continue to be, active in agriculture as workers, owners, and managers of both common agricultural land and individually held agricultural resources. Understanding the specificity of women's access and control of the factors of production, including their own labor, can help make agriculture more efficient and effective as resources are developed and targeted to the part of the population that can best use them, enhancing the conventions of industrial agriculture. Women's economic clout can also bring civic conventions into greater prominence, emphasizing issues of social justice and ecosystem health. But because gender is a social phenomenon, it must be understood in context.

[*See also* Ecofeminism; Gardens and Gardening; Imperialism and Colonialism, *subentry* Modern Period; Labor; Patriarchy; *and* Slavery.]

BIBLIOGRAPHY

Anderson, Anna. *Women and Sustainable Agriculture: Interviews with Fourteen Agents of Change.* Jefferson, N.C.: McFarland, 2004.

Barndt, Deborah. *Tangled Routes: Women, Work, and Globalization on the Tomato Trail.* Lanham, Md.: Rowman and Littlefield, 2002.

Deere, Carmen Diana. *Household and Class Relations: Peasants and Landlords in Northern Peru.* Berkeley: University of California Press, 1990.

Feldstein, Hilary Sims, and Susan V. Poats, eds. *Working Together: Gender Analysis in Agriculture.* West Hartford, Conn.: Kumarian Press, 1989.

Fink, Deborah. *Open Country, Iowa: Rural Women, Tradition, and Change.* Albany: State University of New York Press, 1986.

Gladwin, Christina H., ed. *Structural Adjustment and African Women Farmers.* Gainesville: University of Florida Press, 1991.

Guthman, Julie. *Agrarian Dreams: The Paradox of Organic Farming in California.* Berkeley: University of California Press, 2004.

Haney, Wava G., and Jane B. Knowles, eds. *Women and Farming: Changing Roles, Changing Structures.* Boulder, Colo.: Westview Press, 1988.

Lyson, Thomas A. *Civic Agriculture: Reconnecting Farm, Food, and Community.* Medford, Mass.: Tufts University Press, 2004.

Sachs, Carolyn E. *The Invisible Farmers: Women in Agricultural Production.* Totowa, N.J.: Rowman and Allanheld, 1983.

Spring, Anita, ed. *Women Farmers and Commercial Ventures: Increasing Food Security in Developing Countries.* Boulder, Colo.: Lynne Rienner, 2000.

CORNELIA BUTLER FLORA

Early History

Until about thirteen thousand years ago, all humans made their living by some combination of plant collecting, hunting, scavenging, and fishing. The beginnings of farming, including the domestication of both plants and animals, led to changes in many aspects of human life, including settlement patterns, demography, technology, and, of course, diet. The social and economic changes that resulted from the adoption of farming are so widespread that the beginning of farming is often termed the Agricultural Revolution, on analogy with the nineteenth-century Industrial Revolution. In addition, farming provided the economic basis for the development of complex, urban societies in many parts of the ancient world.

The beginning of food production involves the domestication of both plants and animals. Domesticates are morphologically different from their wild ancestors. Wild sheep, for example, are not woolly. The differences between domestic plants and animals and their wild forebears resulted from conscious or unconscious human selection.

Archaeological Evidence for Early Farming. The earliest experiments with agriculture took place nearly eight thousand years before the appearance of writing, so we have no historical evidence of the first human farming societies. All our data come from archaeological excavations of early farming villages and, in particular, from studies of the plant and animal remains recovered from archaeological sites. Archaeological researchers have identified a number of regions of the world where plants, animals, or both, were independently domesticated. These centers include the Near East, South Asia, sub-Saharan Africa, China, highland New Guinea, the southeastern United States, southern Mexico, and several areas of South America.

Near East. Since the middle of the twentieth century, archaeologists have focused their research on the beginnings of farming in the ancient Near East. As a result we know more about agricultural origins in the Near East than those in any other region on the globe. Late Ice Age hunter-gatherers in Syria may have begun to experiment with the cultivation of rye about 11,000 B.C.E. However, the bulk of the archaeological evidence suggests that Near Eastern foragers began to cultivate barley and wheat shortly after the end of the Ice Age. Archaeological evidence from the Pre-Pottery Neolithic A (PPNA; approximately 9700–8500 B.C.E.) sites suggests that farmers may have begun to cultivate barley at this time. Morphologically domesticated wheat and barley appear during the late PPNA or early Pre-Pottery Neolithic B (PPNB), around 8500 B.C.E.

In the Near East animal domestication did not appear until the middle PPNB, approximately 8100–7300 B.C.E. The earliest known domestic goats were recovered from the site of Ganj Dareh in western Iran, dated to 7900 B.C.E. Shortly thereafter, domesticated goats were found in PPNB sites in the southern Levant. Sheep appear to have been domesticated slightly later in northern Syria and southeastern Anatolia. Pigs and cattle were domesticated somewhat later in the Near East. The earliest domesticated cattle and pigs appeared during the late PPNB, approximately 7300–6750 B.C.E.

East Asia. Dogs were initially domesticated in East Asia about fifteen thousand years ago. From there, domesticated dogs spread throughout the Old World and the Americas. Dogs are the only domesticated animals that are commonly found with hunter-gatherer populations, and the domestication of the dog predates the domestication of all other plants and animals by at least two thousand years.

China is home to two independent centers of plant domestication. Rice was initially domesticated around the Chang (Yangtze) River valley, near the northern end of the distribution of wild rice, around 7000 B.C.E. Foxtail and broomcorn millets were domesticated farther north, in the central and western regions of the Yellow River (Huang) valley beginning around 6500 B.C.E. At early Chinese farming sites, rice and millet are often accompanied by domesticated pigs, dogs, and chickens.

Other centers of plant and animal domestication in the Old World. Cattle were among several animals domesticated in the Near East during the early Neolithic and were also domesticated in two other locations in the Eastern Hemisphere. Zebu, or humped cattle (*Bos indicus*), were initially domesticated in South Asia. Cattle were also domesticated in Africa just south of the Sahara beginning about ten thousand years ago. Unlike the Near East, where plant domestication clearly preceded animal domestication, in sub-Saharan Africa animal domestication preceded plant domestication by several millennia. Domesticated plants did not appear in sub-Saharan Africa until about 2000 B.C.E. Early African domesticates include sorghum, pearl millet, yams, watermelons, and African rice.

Archaeological research in New Guinea in the late twentieth and early twenty-first centuries has demonstrated that highland New Guinea was another independent center of plant domestication. Widespread cultivation of taro and bananas was established there by 4500 B.C.E.

Plant and animal domestication in the Americas. Domesticated plants such as maize, squash, and beans provided the economic background for the development of complex urban societies, including the Aztecs, Incas, and their predecessors, in the Americas. Since the early 1960s archaeological researchers have attempted to identify the initial domestication of these staples as well as other economically important animals and plants, including llamas, alpacas, and potatoes.

The site of Guilá Naquitz in Oaxaca has yielded the remains of early domesticated squash and gourds dated to between eight thousand and ten thousand years ago. The Guilá Naquitz plant remains are the earliest evidence of plant domestication in the Americas. Later levels at the site have produced the world's earliest examples of domesticated maize cobs. These maize remains have been dated to about 4300 B.C.E. Later Mesoamerican domesticates include beans, tomatoes, and avocados.

South America is another independent center of plant and animal domestication. Both potatoes and quinoa were domesticated in highland South America by the fifth millennium B.C.E. The llama and the alpaca were domesticated in the puna—the highest elevations in the Andes that are suitable for human habitation—beginning in the fifth millennium B.C.E. Alpacas were kept primarily for their wool, and llamas were used for both meat and transport. Manioc, a starchy root crop, was initially domesticated in the forested tropical lowlands of South America.

Native Americans in the southeastern and midwestern United States domesticated a range of plants long before maize, beans, and squash were introduced into the region from Mesoamerica. Native Americans began to domesticate plants, including goosefoot and sumpweed, between 2500 and 1200 B.C.E.

The Social Context of Plant Domestication. The reasons that humans began to domesticate animals and plants and the social context in which early domestication took place are matters of considerable debate. Since the beginning of plant domestication took place around or shortly after the end of the Pleistocene (about 11,500 years ago) in many parts of the world, many scholars have suggested that the beginnings of farming may be related to the widespread climatic changes that occurred at the end of the ice age. Others have suggested that the development of farming was a response to worldwide population growth. Social factors, such as the need for food surpluses for ritual feasting, may also have played a role in the adoption of agriculture. Keeping livestock and growing crop plants require more labor than hunting and gathering do, but farming can provide a higher yield per acre than foraging can. In some cases, farming may also provide more predictable access to plant and animal resources.

In many parts of the world, including the ancient Near East and North America, the predecessors of the earliest farming communities were sedentary or semisedentary hunters and gatherers. These foragers built permanent houses and cemeteries and may have had territorial control over important plant and animal resources. For example, the Natufian culture of the southern Levant (approximately 13,000–10,000 B.C.E.) is ancestral to the early farmers of the PPNA. The Natufians collected wild cereals and hunted animals such as gazelles. They built houses with circular stone foundations, which were occupied on a year-round basis. Natufian cemeteries appear to have been used by family groups. Sedentary foraging villages that controlled access to valuable resources may have provided the social context in which early farming communities developed.

Until the early 1980s archaeologists often viewed early farming communities through a distinctly androcentric lens. Men were seen as playing active roles in these societies as farmers, herders, and hunters, while women were relegated to domestic tasks. Even archaeologists who argued that women may have played a role in early plant cultivation saw women's roles as essentially domestic in nature. Andrew Sherratt, for example, suggested in a 1981 essay that women may have served as hoe cultivators in Europe and the Near East during the early Neolithic period. He argued, however, that the introduction of the plow in the fourth millennium B.C.E. led men to take over most agricultural tasks. This in turn caused women to return to the home and engage in craft activities such as weaving. Underlying these early models is the assumption that women's activities in early farming communities were centered in and around the home, while men were more active and carried out a wider range of tasks outside the home.

A call for an archaeology of gender by the researchers Margaret Conkey and Janet Spector in 1984 changed the ways that archaeologists looked at early farming communities in both the Old World and the Americas. For example, in 1991 Patty Jo Watson and Mary C. Kennedy described their reexamination of the archaeological evidence for early farming communities in the eastern United States. They noted that ethnohistorical documents from the southeastern United States describe the important roles that women played in traditional Native American farming activities, and they also noted that many ethnographically known hunting and gathering societies have a division of labor based on men's hunting and women's gathering. Using these data, Watson and Kennedy proposed that women may have initially domesticated plants, including goosefoot, sumpweed, and sunflowers. Their research suggests that women played an active and creative role in the transition from foraging to farming in the Eastern Woodlands of the United States.

Archaeological research, such as that cataloged by Jane Peterson in her 2006 survey "Gender and Early Farming Societies," has also shed light on women's and men's roles in early agricultural societies in the American Southwest. Maize agriculture was introduced to the region from southern Mexico around 1400 B.C.E. Archaeological data and human skeletal remains suggest that men in the Southwest hunted with bows and arrows, while women ground corn to make maize meal. Ethnographic and historical data suggest that weaving (using looms) was a men's activity; women were engaged in pottery production. However, the production and distribution of maize, the staple crop for early farming communities in the Southwest, have not yet been successfully engendered. Skeletal data indicate that women and men in the Southwest had physically demanding lifestyles, and it is likely that men and women either shared farming tasks or controlled different, but equally demanding, aspects of maize cultivation and distribution.

Similar studies are also being carried out in the Old World. For example, in her 2002 volume *Sexual Revolutions: Gender and Labor at the Dawn of Agriculture*, Jane Peterson discusses the evidence of human skeletal remains from Natufian and Neolithic sites in the southern Levant and how this may help us understand the pre-Neolithic sexual division of labor and the ways in which it may have changed with the adoption of agriculture. Her data suggest some sexual division of labor during the Natufian. Males seem to have engaged in activities that involved overhand throwing motions, such as hunting with spears. These differences decreased during the early Neolithic, suggesting that many early agricultural activities were shared by men and women. Both women and men appear to have worked harder during the Neolithic, indicating that farming was a labor-intensive activity during the early Neolithic. In addition, skeletal remains from the Neolithic site of Abu Hureyra in Syria suggest that women were involved in the arduous task of grinding grain on a daily basis. Although the data on women's activities in early farming communities are still relatively limited, the new archaeological evidence suggests that women played much more active roles in early farming societies than many archaeologists had traditionally assumed.

Prospect. Archaeologists have successfully identified a number of centers of early food production in the Eastern and Western Hemispheres, but until the late twentieth century less attention was paid to the social and political contexts in which plant and animal domestication first appeared. The analysis of human skeletal remains provides one line of evidence on the roles that men and women may have played in early farming communities. However, archaeologists will need to make use of multiple lines of evidence, including plant and animal remains, human skeletons, and a wide range of artifactual data, in order to more fully understand the social contexts of early farming societies.

[*See also* Africa, *subentry* 5000 B.C.E.–1000 C.E.; Indigenous Cultures; *and* Prehistory.]

BIBLIOGRAPHY

Bar-Yosef, Ofer, and Avi Gopher, eds. *An Early Neolithic Village in the Jordan Valley*. Part 1: *The Archaeology of Netiv Hagdud*. Cambridge, Mass.: Harvard University Press, 1994. The site report volume for this important PPNA site in the Jordan Valley.

Bellwood, Peter. *First Farmers: The Origins of Agricultural Societies*. Oxford, U.K.: Blackwell, 2005. An up-to-date review of the beginnings of farming on a worldwide basis that considers the relationship between the spread of farming and language change.

Childe, V. Gordon. *Man Makes Himself*. London: Watts, 1936. A classic account of the Neolithic Revolution and its relations to the development of urban, literate societies in the Eastern Hemisphere.

Conkey, Margaret, and Janet Spector. "Archaeology and the Study of Gender." In *Advances in Archaeological Method and Theory*, edited by Michael B. Schiffer, vol. 7, pp. 1–38. New York: Academic Press, 1984. A classic essay criticizing traditional androcentric interpretations in archaeology and calling for a theoretically informed archaeology of gender.

Cowan, C. Wesley, and Patty Jo Watson, eds. *The Origins of Agriculture: An International Perspective*. Washington, D.C.: Smithsonian Institution Press, 1992. Region summaries of the archaeological evidence for the beginnings of farming. The chapters on Africa and eastern North America are particularly useful.

Crabtree, Pam J. "Early Animal Domestication in the Middle East and Europe." In *Archaeological Method and Theory*, edited by Michael B. Schiffer, vol. 5, pp. 201–245. Tucson: University of Arizona Press, 1993. Includes a discussion of the criteria that archaeologists use to identify animal domestication in the archaeological record.

Crabtree, Pam J. "Gender Hierarchies and the Sexual Division of Labor in the Natufian Culture of the Southern Levant." In *The Archaeology of Gender*, edited by Dale Walde and Noreen D. Willows, pp. 384–391. Calgary, Alberta, Canada: The Association, 1991. A critique of androcentric models of preagricultural societies in the southern Levant and an attempt to use archaeology to understand the sexual division of labor in the Natufian culture. The volume as a whole is a classic study of the archaeology of gender.

Flannery, Kent V., ed. *Guilá Naquitz: Archaic Foraging and Early Agriculture in Oaxaca, Mexico*. Orlando, Fla.: Academic Press, 1986. A complete description of the excavation of this important Mesoamerican site.

Kuijt, Ian, and Nigel Goring-Morris. "Foraging, Farming, and Social Complexity in the Pre-Pottery Neolithic of the Southern Levant: A Review and Synthesis." *Journal of World Prehistory* 16, no. 4 (December 2002): 363–440. The most comprehensive summary of the PPNA and PPNB in the southern Levant.

Marshall, Fiona, and E. Hildebrand. "Cattle before Crops: The Beginnings of Food Production in Africa." *Journal of World Prehistory* 16, no. 2 (June 2002): 99–143. The most up-to-date summary of the beginnings of farming in Africa.

Moore, Andrew M. T., Gordon C. Hillman, and Anthony J. Legge. *Village on the Euphrates: From Foraging to Farming at Abu Hureyra*. London: Oxford University Press, 2000. The site-report volume for this important Syrian site. It includes detailed studies of the plant and animal remains and the human skeletons.

Peterson, Jane. "Gender and Early Farming Societies." In *Handbook of Gender in Archaeology*, edited by Sarah Milledge Nelson, pp. 537–570. Lanham, Md.: AltaMira Press, 2006. Provides an up-to-date survey of gender studies of early farming communities in several parts of the world. Crabtree's chapter in this volume may also be of interest.

Peterson, Jane. *Sexual Revolutions: Gender and Labor at the Dawn of Agriculture*. Walnut Creek, Calif.: AltaMira Press, 2002. A pioneering study that uses human skeletal remains to examine changes in the sexual division of labor that may have accompanied the transition from hunting and gathering to farming in the southern Levant.

Price, T. Douglas, and Anne Birgitte Gebauer, eds. *Last Hunters, First Farmers: New Perspectives on the Prehistoric Transition to Agriculture*. Santa Fe, N.Mex.: School of American Research Press, 1995. The articles provide regional summaries on the transition from foraging to farming. The chapters on the Near East and Europe north of the Alps are especially recommended.

Sherratt, A. G. "Plough and Pastoralism: Aspects of the Secondary Products Revolution." In *Pattern of the Past: Studies in Honour of David Clarke*, edited by Ian Hodder, Glynn Isaac, and Norman Hammond, pp. 261–305. Cambridge, U.K.: Cambridge University Press, 1981. Sherratt argues here that the introduction of the plow (a major part of the Secondary Products Revolution) led men to take over most farming tasks, leading women to return to the home and engage in tasks such as weaving.

Watson, Patty Jo, and Mary C. Kennedy. "The Development of Horticulture in Eastern North America: Women's Role." In *Engendering Archaeology: Women and Prehistory*, edited by Joan M. Gero and Margaret W. Conkey, pp. 255–275. Oxford: Blackwell, 1991. On the basis of ethnographic, archaeological, and ethnohistorical evidence, the authors suggest that women may have domesticated plants in eastern North America.

Pam J. Crabtree

Methods of Farming

Women have been involved in farming in all regions of the world. Their substantial contribution to agricultural production has shaped farming and provided food for many families and communities. With changes in global agricultural systems, women's work in farming is taking new shapes and directions with particular emphasis on the long-term social, economic, and environmental sustainability of agriculture and food production.

As hunter-gatherer societies shifted to agriculture, women in many locations were certainly the first agriculturalists as they made the transition from observing plant behavior to selecting, saving, and replanting seeds, roots, and tubers. As agriculture developed differently in various regions of the world, women and men took on particular responsibilities in farming activities. The agricultural economist Ester Boserup characterized the shifting hoe cultivation—a type of land-extensive agriculture in which fields change from season to season and for which hoes and other hand tools are used for land preparation, planting, and cultivation—in many regions of Africa as a female farming system because women did the bulk of the work. By contrast, farming systems in Latin America that used plow cultivation were designated as male farming systems, in which men did a significant amount of the work. This distinction between female and male farming systems has been critiqued as being too simplistic and overlooking the complex interplay among class, race, and caste in determining who does what agricultural work with what types of technology. Nevertheless, regardless of region of the world and historical period, gendered divisions of labor clearly exist in farming systems and agricultural methods.

Crop Production. In the agricultural cycle, from land preparation to seed selection, planting, caring for plants, harvesting, and processing, most societies have clear gender divisions of labor. Whether with water buffalo in South Asia, tractors in Australia, or oxen in Kenya, men often have responsibility for plowing and land preparation. This work is often physically demanding but is limited in time to the beginning of the agricultural season. Although the physical demands of land preparation lessen as technologies become increasingly mechanized, men continue to perform the bulk of these activities.

Selection and conservation of seeds in many regions have historically been the work of women. These seed-selection and conservation activities have been the key to preserving the biodiversity of crops. Seed saving avoids the expense of buying seeds from commercial seed companies, but in the current global crop production system, seed companies and international agriculture research centers now control and produce the vast majority of seeds that most farmers use. In South and Southeast Asia, women have selected and saved numerous rice varieties that they favor because of a number of characteristics, including cooking quality, storage capacity, and plant characteristics.

Rice is usually harvested by hand, and after the rice is harvested, women spread their rice (paddy) crop on the ground for drying, sorting, and selecting the seeds for next year's crop. They have preserved rice varieties that are drought tolerant, pest resistant, and tasty. In the Andes, women have long saved multiple varieties of potatoes and other tuber crops such as *oca*, *mashua*, and *ulloco*. As seed selection and crop improvement increasingly shift to the province of plant breeders and agribusinesses, the value of women's knowledge in preserving biodiversity in crops has often been overlooked.

Hybrid and genetically modified varieties of crops cannot be saved by farmers because the next generation of seeds from these crops will not produce plants the same as those from which they are collected; thus in many locations seed saving is now practiced only by small farmers and gardeners. In many regions of the world, a renewed interest exists in maintaining local varieties of crops in the face of declining biodiversity. Women in many regions continue to lead this effort in saving seeds and preserving crop diversity in their fields and gardens. They have unique knowledge about the value and diversity of genetic resources.

Caring for crops in fields, gardens, and orchards involves labor-intensive work throughout the growing season. Women have often been responsible for weeding and pest-control activities. Compared to planting, which usually occurs once at the beginning of the growing season, weeding is an ongoing labor-intensive activity that must be performed constantly throughout the growing season. However, over time, as these activities have become more capital intensive and chemical intensive, men have often assumed responsibility for controlling weeds and pests. For example, in labor-intensive irrigated rice production in South and Southeast Asia, women traditionally transplanted and weeded in the rice paddies. With the adoption of herbicides for weed control, the task of spraying pesticides has generally gone to men.

Harvesting crops, which often must occur within a specified and limited time frame, has historically been the work of every available set of hands: men, women, and children. With the increasing mechanization of harvesting, especially of agronomic crops such as wheat and maize, these tasks are now usually the work of fewer men operating larger harvesting equipment. Women often continue to perform the labor-intensive work of harvesting fragile horticulture crops such as fruits, vegetables, and flowers. As the commercial production of these crops moves to southern countries for export to Europe and North America, larger producers are relying on women's labor for harvesting. Justifying their use of women by the argument that women have nimble fingers and are more careful with produce than men are, producers hire women who work long hours for low wages to supply the growing European and North American market for year-round fresh fruits and vegetables. For example, in Mexico, women provide the bulk of the labor in picking, grading, and packaging strawberries for the North American market. Women also provide the bulk of the labor in greenhouse production of fresh flowers in countries ranging from Kenya to Colombia.

Postharvest activities including the storage and processing of crops have historically been the province of women in many types of farming systems. In sub-Saharan Africa, women often had responsibility for grinding millet, sorghum, and maize. Grinding typically occurred by hand, with women grinding the grain in large containers using wood or stone pestles. Husking rice has been women's work in many regions of Asia and in West Africa. These labor-intensive activities have largely been mechanized, with electric grinders now available in most rural communities. However, processing crops for family consumption, especially on small farms, remains the work of women in many areas of the world. Storing crops to last throughout the year has traditionally been women's responsibility. Postharvest crop losses are particularly problematic for small, subsistence farmers. Women's knowledge and practices to protect stored crops from water damage, frost, disease, and insects often makes the difference between food adequate for subsistence and hunger.

Animal Husbandry. Women have also historically been quite involved in livestock production. Though some women are involved in large-scale livestock enterprises, the majority of women farmers are engaged in small-scale livestock production. With large livestock such as cattle, horses, and buffalo, women often play key roles in feeding, watering, and caring for calves and foals. In many regions of the world, women have had and continue to maintain responsibility for poultry production and small ruminant production including sheep and goats. As poultry production became commercialized and concentrated, in the early to mid-twentieth century women's small-scale poultry enterprises disappeared on many farms, especially in North America. However, as consumers since the late twentieth century have become more concerned about meat safety and animal health and welfare, new markets have developed for free-range chickens and turkeys and eggs from free-range chickens. Women farmers, often with smaller and less capital-intensive operations, have quickly stepped into this market.

In dairy production, women in Europe and North America have historically provided much of the care of dairy cows and calves and have provided much of the labor in milking small herds by hand. With increasing scale and mechanization of dairy production, men now provide the majority of labor in large-scale dairies. In many regions of Africa, Latin America, and Asia, women maintain responsibility for small-scale livestock production for the market or for family consumption. Women in many locations keep chickens or ducks, which provide eggs and meat. In the Andes, women often raise guinea pigs that provide meat for their families or cash income when sold in the market. Raising small ruminants like goats and sheep for meat and milk also contributes to household food security. Women's efforts in livestock production often provide the much-needed protein for family food security or a quick source of income to meet family emergencies.

New Approaches to Agriculture. As agriculture has become increasingly mechanized and capital intensive, with the majority of farmers producing for export in global markets, fewer and fewer people are involved in producing food. In some regions of the world, such as the United States, the decline in the number of farmers is accompanied by a steady growth in the number of women farmers. Green Revolution technologies, which include hybrid seeds, increased chemical fertilizer use, and increased reliance on chemical pesticides, favored large farmers and contributed to the decreased number of farmers worldwide. Other production practices, such as no-till farming, reduce labor demands in land preparation and crop production. In the early twenty-first century, women farmers are using new types of farming methods and techniques to craft new local types of agricultural production. Compared to men farmers, women often have smaller farms with less capital equipment.

On these smaller operations, many new women farmers are adopting sustainable or organic methods of agricultural production. Sustainable production systems focus on the economic, social, and environmental aspects of farming and attach importance to preserving long-term environmental amenities such as soil quality and water quality. Organic production strictly requires biological rather than chemical strategies for enhancing production and controlling weeds, insects, and diseases, but sustainable agriculture likewise promotes biodiversity and the use of biologically based systems such as integrated pest management, crop rotation, companion planting, and fertilizing with compost and animal manure. For example, integrated pest management (IPM) uses a combination of biological and chemical methods to control insects and diseases. In contrast to chemical-intensive production systems in which spraying occurs on a predetermined timetable, IPM involves regular scouting of crops for insects and diseases before spraying. These methods usually reduce insecticide and fungicide use, thus reducing the impact of chemicals on the environment and limiting insect and disease resistance to chemicals.

Rather than growing a single commodity, such as corn or soybeans, many sustainable and organic women farmers produce a wide diversity of crops and crop varieties. Many women compensate for the lack of volume of their crops and livestock by adding value to their products. For example, rather than selling goat milk, women are making specialty goat cheeses with their milk. Herbs may be sold directly or made into tinctures or lotions. Similarly, many women's small livestock operations raise and breed heritage varieties of chickens, cattle, or sheep. These production methods are practiced by both men and women farmers, but farms where women are involved as decision makers are more likely to be diversified operations using organic and sustainable practices.

Another major contribution of women to food security is their use of home gardens for producing food for their families. In many regions of the world, women maintain gardens near their homes to provide vegetables, fruits, herbs, and spices for their families' consumption. In tropical regions these multistoried gardens of fruits, vegetables, and herbs are often the source of much-needed nutrients and hold the key to household food security. These spaces are much more biologically diverse than other agricultural holdings. Though women in rural households have typically maintained gardens and small-scale livestock or animal enterprises, these efforts are now following women to urban and peri-urban areas. Women are taking the lead in urban and peri-urban agriculture as they supply their households and neighboring communities with food grown on small plots of land.

Women's use of farming methods is tied to a number of factors, but clearly one key factor is their limited access to resources. Compared to men, they have limited access to land, credit, and capital. In places where government and extension services are unavailable to women, they often also have limited access to improved seeds, fertilizers, and irrigation. Commonly their production practices and methods are attempts to cope with limited resources. Nevertheless, their farming methods and practices are the key to food security for many households and communities throughout the world.

[*See also* Food; Gardens and Gardening; Household, *subentry* Production; Labor, *subentry* Globalization and Its Impact; *and* Pastoralism.]

BIBLIOGRAPHY

Alston, Margaret. *Women on the Land: The Hidden Heart of Rural Australia*. Kensington, Australia: University of New South Wales Press, 1995.

Boserup, Ester. *Women's Role in Economic Development*. New edition. London: Earthscan, 2007.

Brandth, Berit. "Gender Identity in European Family Farming: A Literature Review." *Sociologia Ruralis* 42, no. 3: 181–200.

Jellison, Katherine. *Entitled to Power: Farm Women and Technology, 1913–1963*. Chapel Hill: University of North Carolina Press, 1993.

Sachs, Carolyn E. *Gendered Fields: Rural Women, Agriculture, and Environment*. Boulder, Colo.: Westview Press, 1996.

Shortall, Sally. *Women and Farming: Property and Power*. Houndmills, U.K.: Macmillan, 1999.

Whatmore, Sarah. *Farming Women: Gender, Work, and Family Enterprise*. Houndmills, U.K.: Palgrave Macmillan, 1991.

CAROLYN E. SACHS

Peasantry

The adage that "a woman's work is never done" applies to peasant societies across time and place. In preindustrial subsistence economies in which labor was essential for survival and reproduction, although not a guarantee against famine, women had to work from before dawn until well after dusk at various tasks. Because their labors were critical to maintaining a viable household economy, their productive roles took precedence over child-rearing. Though women's productive responsibilities complemented those of men, their domestic tasks constituted extra burdens that men generally did not share. Changes in peasant economies resulting from the growth of markets only increased women's obligations.

Gendered Divisions of Labor. In preindustrial agrarian societies, patriarchal and patrilineal systems everywhere denoted specific crops as women's as opposed to men's—although women were expected to help out with the men's—and delineated work in gender-specific terms. Whereas men were in charge of grain (Europe, Russia, and northern China) and rice cultivation (Asia), women grew vegetables, roots (sugar beets and turnips), and fruits. The foodstuffs produced by women not only supplemented the monotonous peasant diet but also served as items to be bartered or sold at market or used as gifts or payment of taxes to landlords in feudal or semifeudal economic systems. In the same type of gender-determined arrangement, men prepared the land for field crop cultivation—plowing with or without the aid of horse, ox, or water buffalo—and did the sowing, while women assumed the labor-intensive and low-status work of weeding, spreading dung on land closest to home, gleaning grain, and processing crops by such methods as threshing and winnowing (grain), as well as cleaning and beating (flax).

In Europe and Russia, pulling turnips, digging potatoes, cultivating sugar beets, and harvesting hay constituted the most arduous female agricultural tasks. Short harvest seasons somewhat blurred gender roles; yet in European and Russian grain-growing areas the implements used in harvesting—the scythe (for men) and sickle (for women)—remained gender defined. While men tended field animals during the agricultural season, women were in charge of domestic animals, especially the cow and goat, whose milk was critical for children's nutrition as well as for butter and cheese making. Women also fed all livestock during the winter.

Such distinct divisions of labor collapsed, however, when men went off to war or when market expansion resulted in men hiring out during the sowing and harvest seasons (as in late imperial China) or encouraged seasonal male out-migration to distant but prosperous agricultural areas (for example, from the German lands to Holland and Saxony in the eighteenth and nineteenth centuries) and cities (in nineteenth-century Russia and late-nineteenth- and early-twentieth-century Japan). In their menfolk's absence, women shouldered the burdens of agricultural production, even if this meant hiring a male laborer to do the heavier work or, in the event of war, scaling back on the amount of land farmed. Changes in cultivation systems as well as the introduction of new crops and technology also modified divisions of labor, but gendered-determined arrangements continued to exist and still prevail among contemporary agrarian sectors of the global economy.

Those societies that had a cultural predisposition to separation of the sexes restricted women's agricultural labors, although economic exigencies and ecological conditions sometimes superseded cultural taboos. In China's fertile Chang (Yangtze) Delta, foot-bound women of prosperous peasant families followed strict Confucian gender norms and limited their work to the domestic sphere, whereas their poorer sisters had no choice but to labor or supervise work in the rice fields, even if they broke the taboo against women baring their bound feet in public. Bengali Hindus, who segregated women from men who were not close relatives, barred even poor rural women from participating in agricultural work. Where the threat of economic crises demanded that women labor in the fields, such as in the drought-prone Punjabi region of Haryana, women maintained gender seclusion by wearing a veil that concealed their faces from their spouses when out of doors.

In addition to agricultural work, peasant women also had substantial household responsibilities that were generally shunned by men and were, accordingly, less valued than

East Asian Peasantry. A peasant woman washes lettuce on the shore of Lake Motosu, Japan, 1904. PRINTS AND PHOTOGRAPHS DIVISION, LIBRARY OF CONGRESS

men's work. With the exception of Japanese husbands, who helped their wives with cooking, cleaning, and child-rearing, male peasants relegated the domestic sphere to women. Food preparation—the transformation of the raw into the cooked—constituted a woman's task, for which she could take pride. Beyond cooking and baking, peasant women gathered firewood or peat; built and tended precious fires; hauled water; did laundry; made beer, soap, candles, yarn, and thread; wove and embroidered cloth and linens; and sewed clothes for family members. These tasks required many hours and, in the cases of hauling, laundering, spinning, and weaving, also called for considerable physical strength before mechanization eased at least the processes of thread and cloth production.

Effects of Commercialization. Women's labors expanded and became more diversified once commercialization forced households to produce handmade goods for the market. The textile industry, in particular, provided an outlet for women's skills. In China during the Song dynasty (960–1279), silk production expanded from the towns to villages in the southeastern provinces and Sichuan. In China, Japan, and later in Italy, the intensive and unglamorous work of sericulture—the feeding of silkworms multiple times at night and the harvesting of silk—fell entirely on women's shoulders. During the Song, Chinese women did much of the silk weaving for income that helped families weather periods of drought and famine. Later, silk weaving, as it gained prestige, often became the preserve of men.

Similarly, the development of the Chinese cotton industry from the fourteenth through seventeenth centuries attracted women household laborers. Cotton picking around the world was relegated to women and children. Women involved in regionally specialized Chinese cloth production worked with raw cotton, which they purchased at local markets; having spun and woven the cloth, they returned to the markets to sell their wares. Textile production in Japan from the late eighteenth century onward was decidedly women's work alone.

In the early stages of European cotton cloth production in the eighteenth century, a gendered division of labor, similar to the one in agriculture, developed in the putting-out system, whereby merchants paid peasants for processing raw materials in their homes, largely because land shortages forced noninheriting sons to find alternative sources of income. In the cottage textile industry, women spun yarn, while men dominated weaving on heavier looms. Mechanization in Europe opened up weaving to women, and as market demand increased specialization, women who became dependent upon the cash remittances in the putting-out textile system began to abandon their farm tasks. When workshops and factories developed to mass-produce cotton (also in nineteenth-century Russia and Japan), the lure of wages—even though they were half of men's wages—drew single women out of agricultural households. In China, in contrast, the putting-out system strengthened rather than eroded the household as a productive unit, with Confucian notions restricting women's work outside the household economy.

As commercialization and then industrialization developed in Asia, Europe, and Russia between the 1750s and 1880s, peasant women participated in other market-oriented handicrafts, such as papermaking and lacquerware production (China); knitting, basket weaving, lace making, and glove making (Europe and Russia); and the fashioning of cigarette mouthpieces (Russia). Most of these trades were distinctly female occupations—in Europe and Russia, women could also earn income through wet-nursing—that received lower payments than men's work and were held to be less valuable, though necessary in supporting a family.

Around the globe, so long as men controlled family budgets in patriarchal systems, women's economic purchasing power was either nil or limited. However, in Europe and Russia women did keep the proceeds from the sale of agricultural goods such as eggs, butter, cheese, and mushrooms that they produced, tended, or picked.

Women's Status. Ultimately, the gendered division of labor in a patriarchal agricultural society endowed men's work with greater prestige and authority because men controlled access to technological knowledge and economic resources. It also deprived women of access to the public sphere. Women's extra labors in the household, in essence, left men free to engage in their community's politics and governance. Only when men were absent for substantial periods, or when women had become widows, did women represent their households in village politics. Otherwise they ventured into the political sphere infrequently—for instance, as participants in rice and grain riots when their families' sustenance was threatened by perceived unfair market practices, such as landlords' selling foodstuffs for profit when harvests were poor. In Japan, however, the maintenance of family prosperity and village harmony took precedence over assigned gender roles. Older Japanese women, respected for their wisdom, frequently sat on village councils. Only prosperous peasants followed the strict Confucian gender norm of the samurai elites that reserved the public domain for men.

Women's status within their communities depended upon both their productive and their reproductive abilities. As childbearers, they also had the privilege and responsibility of overseeing their children's early upbringing and arranging their children's marriages—until the eighteenth century in Europe, late nineteenth century in Russia, World War II in Japan, and present-day India. Their authority also extended to policing other women's activities through gossip and, in some cultures, ritual shaming. In societies with extended families (including kin outside of a nuclear family of parents and children), such as those of Japan, Russia, China, and India, authority over the household's other women accrued to the senior woman. Here low-status daughters-in-law labored the hardest and were often accused of sowing family discord in order to persuade their spouses to establish independent households. Finally, some peasant cultures (in Haryana, Malaya, Laos, and central and northern Russia) endowed women's work with greater significance through the institution of the bride-price, which transferred property from a groom's to a bride's family as compensation for a laborer's loss. A bride-price did not necessarily translate into greater respect for women, however. In Haryana, for example, it coexisted with female infanticide, female seclusion, and the custom of wearing the veil.

[*See also* China, *subentry* Imperial; Dower Systems; Family; Feudalism; Food, *subentry* Preparation and Work; Footbinding; Gender Roles; Household, *subentry* Production; India; Italy; Japan; Labor; Patriarchy; Prehistory; *and* Religion, *subentry* Contemporary Issues.]

BIBLIOGRAPHY

Chowdhry, Prem. "Customs in a Peasant Economy: Women in Colonial Haryana." In *Recasting Women: Essays in Colonial History*, edited by Kumkum Sangari and Sudesh Vaid, pp. 302–336. New Delhi, India: Kali for Women, 1989. Discusses the perceptions of British officials as well as the realities of agricultural women's lives among different castes.

Engel, Barbara Alpern. *Between the Fields and the City: Women, Work, and Family in Russia, 1861–1914*. Cambridge, U.K.: Cambridge University Press, 1994. Particularly strong on the effects of male out-migration on women, the protections that patriarchalism afforded women in the countryside, and the economic opportunities that the city provided peasant women.

Hane, Mikiso. *Peasants, Rebels, Women, and Outcastes: The Underside of Modern Japan*. 2nd ed. Lanham, Md.: Rowman & Littlefield, 2003.

Huang, Philip C. C. *The Peasant Family and Rural Development in the Yangzi Delta, 1350–1988*. Stanford, Calif.: Stanford University Press, 1990.

Hudson, Pat, and W. R. Lee, eds. *Women's Work and the Family Economy in Historical Perspective*. Manchester, U.K.: Manchester University Press, 1990. Focuses on western Europe. The introduction and Lee's chapter on nineteenth-century Germany are most relevant to the subject of peasant women's labor.

Sachs, Carolyn E. *Gendered Fields: Rural Women, Agriculture, and Environment*. Boulder, Colo.: Westview Press, 1996. Excellent overview of the sexual division of labor and women's worsening position in contemporary agriculture across the globe.

CHRISTINE D. WOROBEC

AIDOO, AMA ATA (b. 1942?), African writer and activist. The versatile Ghanaian Ama Ata Aidoo, a distinguished playwright, award-winning novelist, poet, writer of short and children's stories, essayist, lecturer, and activist, is energized by her matrilineal Akan culture. She graduated from the University of Ghana in 1964 during the heady days of Kwame Nkrumah's cultural and political revolution, which attracted the likes of W. E. B. Du Bois, the African American luminary. Nkrumah's and Du Bois's Pan-Africanism influenced Aidoo's works, particularly her inaugural play, *The Dilemma of a Ghost* (1965), which reestablishes links between Africa and the diaspora. While tackling black gender matters, she promotes discourses on the ambivalent relationship between Africans and African Americans, responding tangentially to Lorraine Hansberry's *A Raisin in the Sun*.

Issues of gender, economics, and race dominate Aidoo's oeuvre, demonstrating her concern for the place of black men, women, and children globally. Her womanism positions her to explore blackness and whiteness, male and female cultural constructions, and the poverty of people of color resulting from the slave trade, slavery, and colonialism.

Aidoo's play *Anowa* (1970), considered by some one of the best hundred literary works of twentieth-century Africa, with its audacious psychic excavation of Africa's undoing, refreshingly reexamines history. It challenges memory by revisiting African participation in and resistance to the slave trade and slavery, with their demographic, capitalist, gendered, and psychological fallout. Aidoo uses the photograph of a widowed, brooding Queen Victoria, a distorted mirror image of the powerful yet vulnerable Anowa, to dramatize women's complicity in the reproduction of empire. Power reversals that disadvantage women and the helpless and women's inability to dismantle barriers of status, race, geography, and economic affiliations stand in the way of a drive for equity in global governance. In addition, Aidoo intimates that lack of black solidarity is suicidal for Africa.

Our Sister Killjoy; or, Reflections from a Black-Eyed Squint (1966) is Aidoo's experimental mix of traditional storytelling and the novel. Using her female-centered Akan culture to advantage, she promotes women as griots (postmodernist performance storytellers), a liberating move that enables the central character, Sissie, to comment on the blatant global imbalance of power and the failure of African men to right matters.

In the award-winning *Changes: A Love Story* (1991), Aidoo posits women's untenable position in different versions of the family as the root of the African problem. With its Scheherazadean aura, the novel draws on West African Islamic tentacles, women's subject/abject positions in marriage as currently constituted, and the womanist possibilities of female empowerment through storytelling and career independence. She reconfigures male-female relationships to benefit family, nation, and continent.

Beyond her writing, Aidoo broadened the scope of her activism with her reforming zeal as Ghana's minister of education (1982–1983) under the presidency of Jerry Rawlings. She resigned in frustration and fled to Robert Mugabe's revolutionary Zimbabwe, which inspired several of her publications. Her global influence has been felt elsewhere through visiting professorships at Oberlin College and Brown University and lectures at Stony Brook University, Sarah Lawrence College, and Barnard College.

Priding herself that her works have never been out of print, Aidoo projects her wit, resilience, and analytical acuity in essays, lectures, short stories, children's stories, and poetry, as well as in other genres, invigorating qualities that propel her to the forefront of Ghanaian, African, and women's literature.

[*See also* Literature.]

BIBLIOGRAPHY

Azodo, Ada, and Gay Wilentz, eds. *Emerging Perspectives on Ama Ata Aidoo*. Trenton, N.J.: Africa World Press, 1998.

Davies, Carole Boyce, and Anne Adams Graves, eds. *Ngambika: Studies of Women in African Literature*. Trenton, N.J.: Africa World Press, 1986.

James, Adeola. *In Their Own Voices: African Women Writers Talk*. Portsmouth, N.H.: Heinemann, 1990.

Odamtten, Vincent O. *The Art of Ama Ata Aidoo: Polylectics and Reading against Neocolonialism*. Gainesville: University Press of Florida, 1994.

CHIKWENYE OKONJO OGUNYEMI

AIDS. The HIV/AIDS pandemic has emerged as the principal public health crisis of the modern period. With more than 40 million infected and more than 25 million dead by 2005, the disease has expanded from its original pockets to become a worldwide epidemic. It is arguably the first disease of globalization, one that links major urban hubs, such as New York, Kinshasa, and Bangkok, as well as remote villages in Equatorial Africa with their counterparts in the New Guinea highlands. Although HIV/AIDS shares with many other infectious diseases a powerful discrimination against the world's poorest and most marginalized populations, it also contrasts with other diseases in its choice of victims. Whereas diarrheal diseases and malaria principally target children and influenza is most dangerous for the elderly, HIV, by virtue of sexual transmission, strikes populations in the prime of their lives. It is therefore a disease that has menaced families, societies, economies, and entire states by cutting great swaths through first one and now a second generation, leaving millions of orphans and their grandparents in its wake.

Although AIDS initially appeared to plague communities of gay men in the United States and Europe, it is now principally a disease spread through heterosexual contact, with some three-fourths of its victims in sub-Saharan Africa. It is also increasingly imperiling women in the developing world, who are now its fastest-growing population at risk.

HIV/AIDS: Social and Natural History. In the summer of 1981 small clusters of patients appeared in clinics in Los Angeles, New York, and San Francisco with unique symptoms. Although ranging in age from their twenties to their forties, the patients, all men, were ravaged by conditions usually seen only among elderly and immune-compromised patients, including *Pneumocystis carinii pneumonia*, a common bacterium that is harmless in most healthy populations. The only apparent connection among these initial patients was their claim to having had sex with multiple men, some of whom suffered from like symptoms. The U.S. Centers for Disease Control and Prevention noted this connection in the *Morbidity and Mortality Weekly Report*, signaling physicians to "be alert" to these sorts of "opportunistic infections associated with immunosuppression in homosexual men."

The idea of a disease linked to male homosexuality gave rise to intense speculation over what factors placed this

ACT-UP. Members of the French AIDS action group ACT-UP protest Coca-Cola's refusal to pay for AIDS treatment for its employees in developing countries, Barcelona, Spain, July 2002. REUTERS/Gustau Nacarino

population at risk. Investigators explored the possible culpability of practices that they imagined to be prevalent among gay men, including drug use and sexual promiscuity leading to an "immune system overload." It also gave the syndrome its first colloquial name among epidemiologists: gay-related immunodeficiency disease or GRID. But the quick recognition of similar symptoms in other groups, including drug users who injected drugs, hemophiliacs, and Haitians living in the United States, pushed the development of a new name, *a*cquired *i*mmuno *d*eficiency *s*yndrome, or AIDS, which better captured the threat's reach.

The new risk groups suggested that an infectious agent transmitted through semen or blood products was at play in the spread of the disease. In 1983 researchers at the Pasteur Institute in Paris successfully isolated an unknown virus from the blood of a man "at risk for AIDS." Scientists soon concluded that this was the agent responsible for AIDS, and in 1984 an international scientific panel named the new pathogen *h*uman *i*mmunodeficiency *v*irus or HIV. The virus binds to T4 helper cells and macrophages, critical elements of the body's immune system. As a member of the family of retroviruses, HIV contains its genetic material in RNA rather than DNA and replicates by incorporating its genetic material into the host cell's genome. It then generates new viruses while also replicating along with infected cells as they divide. As new viruses bud from the cells, they eventually kill the cell in the process, thereby reducing the body's immunological capacities and leaving it vulnerable to opportunistic infections. HIV's incubation period is slow, meaning that its victims often harbor the virus—and infect others—for years before they are even aware that they are ill.

Although the virus's natural history is hotly contested, a general consensus points to Central Africa as its geographic origin. HIV-1, the most prominent strain of the virus in the AIDS pandemic, is closely related to the simian immunodeficiency virus that afflicts chimpanzees. Most scientists agree that the virus crossed the species barrier from chimpanzees to humans through hunting and butchering of chimpanzees in the early twentieth century. As colonial rule and the transitions to independence disrupted land use and local ecologies, urbanization and new social patterns favored the disease's spread from small enclaves to population hubs by the 1970s. Global travel and human migration then brought the virus into sustained contact with European and American populations, where it took hold among its initial risk groups.

Social transformations in the late twentieth century provided an ideal ecology for HIV's establishment in the West. The sexual revolution of the 1960s, fostered by the introduction of reliable contraception and changing social attitudes, apparently freed casual sexual contact from the consequences of pregnancy, while new antibiotics made diseases such as gonorrhea or syphilis nuisances rather than the public health scourges they had been in earlier periods. Yet widening circles of sexual contact also provided the perfect environment for the introduction of a new disease into the sexually active population. Simultaneously the decay of America's urban infrastructure that followed the mass suburbanization of the 1950s and 1960s, as well as the introduction of cheap heroin through soldiers returning from Vietnam, created an inner-city epidemic of addiction that facilitated HIV's spread through communities of injecting drug users. Meanwhile devastating poverty and unemployment contributed to the rise of sex work as well as a market for sex tourism in Haiti and other developing countries, allowing the disease to establish a strong foothold there, and HIV's introduction into the blood supply placed anyone receiving a transfusion at risk.

Women and HIV/AIDS: An Unseen Epidemic? Despite women's equal risk for transmission in each of these categories—through unprotected sex, injection, and transfusions—scientists and public health officials initially saw women as largely exempt from risk. This is surprising given the historical tendency to label women as reservoirs of sexually transmitted diseases; the Contagious Diseases Acts passed in Britain in the 1860s, for example, placed women suspected of prostitution under close epidemiological surveillance and left their clients unexamined. Yet an almost exclusive focus on men who have sex with men guided much of AIDS research during the epidemic's early years, which led many AIDS researchers to dismiss the idea of heterosexual transmission altogether. Nearly 1-to-1 ratios of male-female infections among Haitians and sub-Saharan Africans did not disrupt these views; instead, researchers concocted elaborate justifications for why such ratios were impossible in the West. Haiti's high infection rates were linked in publications including the *New York Times* and the *Journal of the American Medical Association* to Vodoun rituals involving the ingestion of human blood, while medical and social scientists claimed that a culture of violent intercourse akin to rape that marked normal sexual relations among Africans was responsible for women's infections there.

A general dismissal of women's risk for contracting HIV was therefore pervasive in the medical and popular press for much of the 1980s. This idea reached a peak in the popular press with the publication of an article by Robert Gould in *Cosmopolitan* magazine in 1988. Millions of women readers learned through this article that they had nothing to fear from "normal" sexual intercourse. Whereas the fragile tissues of the anus were not able to withstand penetration without tearing, the "rugged vagina," capable of withstanding childbirth, was far more resilient and therefore immune to infection in most cases. A range of articles and books, such as Michael Fumento's *The Myth of Heterosexual AIDS*, published in 1990, agreed with this premise, claiming that despite occasional anomalies, HIV was a significant threat only for its original risk groups.

More than reflecting widespread homophobia and prejudice about foreign cultures in Western scientific circles, these ideas gave many women a false sense of security despite their grave risk for infection. Such claims were both epidemiologically and biologically mistaken. Cases of women with AIDS who fit none of the basic risk profiles appeared within a year of the epidemic's emergence. Moreover, the "normal" sexual intercourse deemed safe in *Cosmopolitan* places women at high risk for contracting the disease—indeed, at greater risk than their male partners. High concentrations of HIV in semen and an easy entryway through the vaginal and cervical mucous membranes render heterosexual intercourse an effective mechanism of transmission. Moreover, in certain stages of the menstrual cycle and during pregnancy, women's immune systems are naturally suppressed, while breast-feeding and malnutrition both lower estrogen levels, thinning vaginal mucosa and making certain women more vulnerable to infection. As a result, by 1990 heterosexual transmission was the fastest-growing means of infection with HIV in the West and by far the leading means of infection in the developing world.

Despite the marginalization of women in much epidemiological and medical research on HIV risk, social scientists and humanists have begun to explore the complexities of this problem, particularly in the developing world. An emerging consensus has pointed toward the acute intersections of economic and gender inequality that have undermined women's autonomy in many societies and have placed women at increased risk for a range of health problems, including HIV/AIDS. For example, in many southern African societies, patterns of land tenure and inheritance that privilege a decedent's male relatives have exacerbated women's precarious economic circumstances, leaving widows with no economic resources. A turn to sex work and its dramatic increase in HIV risk is a frequent outcome for many women. Women in these situations may also find themselves forced to marry again, thereby introducing them into a new network of sexual contact and also increasing risk.

Steep gradients of economic inequality combined with the entrenchment of the dowry system in some regions in India has also predestined many women and girls to become infected with HIV, because many indebted rural families who cannot afford to marry their daughters have been forced to sell them to sex traffickers to supply a thriving urban sex trade. Finally, political disorder and the collapse of civil society in many developing countries amount to other important factors shaping a gendered AIDS pandemic. The use of rape as a weapon in conflict zones, as well as widespread sexual violence and the explosion of sex work as a backbone of the informal economy in many megacities in the developing world, has proved to be an efficient conduit for the transmission of HIV to women.

Knowledge, Power, and Activism. Women have been critical actors in the world of AIDS research and activism. They have contributed dramatically to medical, biological, and social knowledge about the epidemic in a wide range of fields. At the epidemic's beginning, Françoise Barré-Sinoussi, a woman virologist working at the Pasteur Institute, was the initial discoverer of the virus; subsequently the primatologist Beatrice Hahn has been at the forefront of research linking HIV's origins to specific simian viruses in Central Africa. In the humanities and social sciences, theorists such as Susan Sontag and Paula Treichler have provided deep insight into the ways in which AIDS is also, in Treichler's words, "an epidemic of signification," while anthropologists such as Brooke Schoepf have pioneered new methods for studying the social and cultural dimensions of the pandemic.

Whereas gay men dominated AIDS activism in the United States in the early part of the epidemic, women have been central to AIDS politics since the late 1980s. Upon the publication of Gould's article in *Cosmopolitan*, women members of the New York chapter of the AIDS Coalition to Unleash Power (ACT-UP) staged a protest at the magazine's Manhattan offices and launched a boycott campaign. The protest and subsequent actions and teach-ins led to the benchmark volume *Women, AIDS, and Activism* published by ACT-UP New York in 1990, as well as to the establishment of the Women's AIDS Video Enterprise (WAVE), a group founded by the filmmaker Alexandra Juhasz to encourage the empowerment of women living with AIDS through documentary video projects.

Women have also been at the forefront of AIDS activism in the developing world. Many have lauded the Brazilian government's efforts to provide antiretroviral therapy to every AIDS patient in the country. But this project was largely initiated by the HIV-positive schoolteacher Nair Brito who sued the government in the mid-1990s claiming that she and other AIDS patients were entitled to treatment under the nation's constitution, which guaranteed health as a right for all Brazilians. In Uganda, Noerine Kaleeba, the widow of an AIDS patient, founded The AIDS Support Organisation (TASO). Distressed by the stigma that surrounded her husband's illness, Kaleeba launched an informal network in 1987 to provide emotional and social support for AIDS victims and their families. TASO has grown from its modest beginnings to become one of the largest AIDS non-governmental organizations (NGOs) in the developing world in the early twenty-first century, providing medical treatment and support for more than twenty thousand Ugandans and playing no small role in that country's dramatic reduction in AIDS prevalence.

A Bleak Outlook. By 2005, women in many regions had become the leading risk category. In the Caribbean, for example, the female-to-male ratio of cases of HIV infection was 2 to 1, and in sub-Saharan Africa women and girls represented nearly three-fifths of all adult cases and three-quarters of juvenile cases. The West did not remain untouched by such discrepancies, at least in certain circles. In the United States in 2001, for example, AIDS was the leading cause of death for African American women aged twenty-five to thirty-four. These figures did not merely reflect women's increased biological vulnerability for infection. Instead, they reflected wider economic, social, and political inequalities that placed certain categories of women in positions of extreme vulnerability. From the disease of gay men, which it appeared to be in 1981, AIDS has become a powerful killer of women in the developing world and in lower economic sectors in the industrialized world, leading some to rename the disease "acquired income deficiency syndrome."

Despite the efforts of NGOs such as TASO and government policies like those in Brazil, most of the world's women affected by HIV lack access to effective treatment for the disease. Where this treatment exists, women are most often merely conduits of medication destined to help their children. Most antiretroviral treatment available to women consists in short-course therapy designed to prevent the transmission of HIV from mother to child in the course of birth. Such treatment has been a boon to the developing world's children, reducing the rate of perinatal transmission of HIV by two-thirds. At the same time it has left mothers untreated, meaning that many of these children who avoid contracting HIV in childbirth are destined for early orphanhood.

Action to quell the pandemic—especially among its most deeply afflicted populations—has been painfully slow. Yet researchers have demonstrated that a comprehensive treatment strategy that aims at both the economic inequalities that have allowed AIDS to become a global catastrophe in the making and also the biological ravages of the disease in individual bodies holds the promise of alleviating the physical, social, and political burdens of the pandemic, if only the resources can be found.

[*See also* Disease and Illnesses *and* Healing and Medicine.]

BIBLIOGRAPHY

ACT-UP New York. *Women, AIDS, and Activism*. Boston: South End, 1990. A collection of texts marking the launch of women's AIDS activism; a critical document in the history of women and HIV/AIDS.

Barré-Sinoussi, Françoise, J. C. Chermann, F. Rey, M. T. Nugeyre, S. Chamaret, J. Gruest, C. Dauguet, C. Axler-Blin, F. Vezinet-Brun, C. Rouzious, W. Rosenbaum, and L. Montagnier. "Isolation of a T-Lymphotropic Retrovirus from a Patient at Risk for Acquired Immune Deficiency Syndrome." *Science* 220, no. 4599 (1983): 868–871. The original publication marking the discovery of what came to be known as HIV.

Farmer, Paul. *Infections and Inequalities: The Modern Plagues.* Berkeley: University of California Press, 1999. A sweeping indictment of the economic inequalities that have placed the global poor and especially women at risk for AIDS and other health problems.

Fassin, Didier. *When Bodies Remember: Experiences and Politics of AIDS in South Africa.* Berkeley: University of California Press, 2007. A rich case study of economic inequality, violence, and politics in the world's most devastated AIDS zone.

Friedman, Robert. "India's Shame." *Nation*, 8 April 1996, pp. 11–20. An investigation of the sex-trafficking circles that have placed many South Asian girls and women at risk for HIV.

Fumento, Michael. *The Myth of Heterosexual AIDS.* New York: Basic Books, 1990. The view of a "denialist" of AIDS as an exclusively homosexual disease.

Hahn, Beatrice H., George M. Shaw, K. M. De Cock, and P. M. Sharp. "AIDS as a Zoonosis: Scientific and Public Health Implications." *Science* 287, no. 5453 (2000): 607–614. Paper pointing to the ecological meanings of the links between HIV and simian viruses.

Mukherjee, J. S., P. E. Farmer, D. Niyizonkiza, L. McCorkle, C. Vanderwarker, P. Teixeira, and J. Y. Kim. "Tackling HIV in Resource Poor Countries." *British Medical Journal* 327 (2003): 1104–1106. A plan for engaging with AIDS in the countries hit hardest by the pandemic.

Schoepf, Brooke G. *Gender, Sex, and Power: A Social History of AIDS in Mobutu's Zaire.* Oxford: Blackwell, 2004. Among the most important assessments of the gendered dimensions of AIDS in sub-Saharan Africa.

Sontag, Susan. *Illness as Metaphor and AIDS and Its Metaphors.* New York: Doubleday, 1990. A critical document in the history of the pandemic.

Treichler, Paula A. *How to Have Theory in an Epidemic: Cultural Chronicles of AIDS.* Durham, N.C.: Duke University Press, 1999. A description of AIDS and its meanings and an important engagement with the meaning of AIDS for gender and sexuality.

RICHARD C. KELLER

ʿAʾISHA (c. 614–678), the third and most controversial wife of the prophet Muhammad. ʿAʾisha bint Abi Bakr lived during the critical founding era of Islamic society, to which all Muslims continue to look for precedent in their daily lives. ʿAʾisha's life contained powerful lessons for later generations of Muslims in matters of sexuality, politics, and religion. One of the Prophet's twelve wives, she became his recognized favorite during her lifetime owing to her charm, beauty, and intelligence. Married at nine, accused of adultery at fourteen, and widowed at eighteen, ʿAʾisha led a life that continues to be read differently according to the sectarian interests of Sunni Muslims (the majority of believers, who revere her) and Shia Muslims (the minority, who revile her). The charged nature of her legacy demarcates contemporary fault lines within Islamic society regarding definitions of gender and rights for Muslim women.

The first controversy with which ʿAʾisha's name became synonymous was an accusation of adultery. Her reputation was impugned when she was accidentally stranded alone in the desert, and doubt was cast on her faithfulness to the Prophet. Although she denied these allegations, her ultimate defense, according to Islamic tradition, was provided by the revelation of Qurʾanic verses, which established the penalty for false accusation of adultery. Sunni Muslims still celebrate her exoneration; they argue that no other Muslim woman was ever the object of divine intervention. Shia Muslims believe that these verses, which do not mention her by name, never referred to her. This variation in Qurʾanic interpretation thus retains great significance in determining communal divisions.

As a widow of forty-two, ʿAʾisha participated in the first civil war in Islamic society. Together with two male allies she challenged the leadership of ʿAli ibn Abi Talib (d. 661), whose partisans, or Shia, became her political enemies ever after. In 656 she rode to the Battle of the Camel, an event named after the magnificent mount from which she surveyed the conflict. She did not fight in the battle, nor did she ever attempt to claim power, but in defeat her name became synonymous with communal strife. Thereafter Sunni and Shia male scholars applied her example to deny all Muslim women access to political participation. This negative legacy lingers but has been challenged in our era by women throughout the Sunni Muslim world, including Saudi Arabia and Afghanistan, who interpret ʿAʾisha's activism as a precedent for their own.

ʿAʾisha's last years were spent preserving and transmitting the traditions of the Prophet's life, which became the basis for later legal codes. Although her expertise was rejected by Shia legal scholars, Sunni jurists placed her contributions to the legal corpus above those of all other women and many men. Islamist women look to her contributions as the precedent for their own right to study and interpret the religious sources of their faith. ʿAʾisha's relevance continues to evolve: she is the inspiration for an award for exemplary Muslim women in the United States, and her life inspired an opera in the Netherlands about the rights of women in the first Islamic community. It was canceled after Muslim clerics claimed that it was disrespectful to portray ʿAʾisha on stage.

[*See also* Fatima bint Muhammad *and* Islam.]

BIBLIOGRAPHY

Abbot, Nabia. *ʿAʾishah: The Beloved of Mohammed.* Chicago: University of Chicago Press, 1942. The first and only scholarly biography of ʿAʾisha in English.

Spellberg, Denise A. *Politics, Gender, and the Islamic Past: The Legacy of ʿAʾisha bint Abi Bakr*. New York: Columbia University Press, 1994. Delineates ʿAʾisha's centrality to Muslim historiography in communal debates and sectarian identity.

DENISE A. SPELLBERG

AKHMATOVA, ANNA (1889–1966), modern Russian poet. Born Anna Gorenko, Akhmatova won great fame in the 1910s for her beautifully crafted love lyrics in the genre of the "erotic diary." From 1912 to 1922 she published five slim volumes of poems praised for their clarity, restraint, and economy. Anchored in the realities of everyday life, they reflect the period's cataclysmic events and express the poet's response to the 1917 Revolution. Akhmatova firmly identified herself with prerevolutionary Russia, yet she adamantly refused to emigrate, linking her fate with that of her homeland.

Russia's new rulers, viewing her poetry as ideologically incorrect, banned it from publication in 1925. Over the next decade Akhmatova composed few poems and mainly wrote scholarly articles exploring how the poet Aleksander Pushkin (1799–1837) had coped with persecution and censorship. Under Joseph Stalin, Russian writers experienced far worse persecution, peaking during the mass arrests and executions of the Terror (1936–1938). Akhmatova herself was not arrested, but her loved ones were, including her son Lev Gumilev, who was sent to Siberia's labor camps, and her friend the poet Osip Mandelstam, who perished in the camps. In her masterpiece *Requiem* (1935–1940), Akhmatova courageously protests against the Terror, commemorating its victims and chronicling its toll on both the individual and the nation.

The year 1940 was a creative high point for Akhmatova and saw the birth of a new poetic style informed with what she called an "acute sense of history." New themes relating to the poet's role, fate, and craft found expression in new rhythms and in larger, more complex poetic forms; literary quotations and allusions abounded. Akhmatova began her magnum opus *Poem without a Hero* (1940–1962), in which a swarm of apparitions from 1913 Saint Petersburg visit the poet in 1940 Leningrad and reenact events that culminated in the suicide of a young poet over unrequited love. Akhmatova contrasts his "senseless death" with the manifold deaths the future held for Russia's poets—on the battlefield, at the hands of the secret police, in Siberia's camps. The themes of memory, guilt, and retribution loom large.

During World War II some of Akhmatova's poems were published, but in August 1946 she was viciously denounced for her "decadent, bourgeois, harmful" poems in an official campaign. Stripped of her small pension and kept under constant surveillance, she supported herself through literary translations. Her son, who had been freed during the war, was rearrested in 1949. His release came only in 1956, three years after Stalin's death.

In Akhmatova's last decade (1956–1966) the official abuse ceased. Her poems gradually began to be published, and she was allowed to travel abroad twice to receive literary awards. She wrote many new poems and completed *Poem without a Hero* and the sublime cycle "The Sweetbrier Blooms." When she died in 1966, the full scope of her later work was unknown, and much of it, including *Requiem* and parts of *Poem without a Hero*, remained unpublished in Russia until 1989—just two years before the Soviet Union's fall. In this work she inveighs against the state for hounding and killing Russia's poets, laments having lived "under perdition's wing" for three decades, mourns the work that she burned to keep it from the secret police, and proclaims the indestructibility of the inspired poetic word and the triumph of spirit over matter.

[*See also* Literature *and* Russia and Soviet Union.]

BIBLIOGRAPHY

Akhmatova, Anna. *The Complete Poems of Anna Akhmatova*. Translated by Judith Hemschemeyer and edited by Roberta Reeder. 2 vols. Somerville, Mass.: Zephyr Press, 1990. A bilingual edition of the complete poetry, with helpful scholarly notes.

Akhmatova, Anna. *The Word That Causes Death's Defeat: Poems of Memory*. Translated and with critical essays and commentary by Nancy K. Anderson. New Haven, Conn., and London: Yale University Press, 2004. Outstanding English-language versions of *Requiem* and *Poem without a Hero*, accompanied by perceptive essays.

Amert, Susan. *In a Shattered Mirror: The Later Poetry of Anna Akhmatova*. Stanford, Calif.: Stanford University Press, 1992. An insightful study that illuminates the entire oeuvre.

Reeder, Roberta. *Anna Akhmatova: Poet and Prophet*. New York: St. Martin's Press; London: Allison and Busby, 1994. The best biography to date, equipped with a full bibliography.

SUSAN AMERT

AKHTAR, BEGUM (1914–1974), Indian *ghazal* singer. Born Akhtari Bai Faizabadi but better known as Begum Akhtar, she is remembered by music lovers in India as the Queen of Ghazals. Little is documented about her early life except that she was born in Faizabad, Uttar Pradesh (northern India), into a Muslim family of modest means. From an early age Akhtari Bai displayed an ardent interest in learning music, at a time when issues of respectability deeply constrained the lives of professional women singers.

In the tradition of Indian classical music, Akhtari Bai spent extended periods of time in Lucknow and Kolkata (formerly Calcutta) being individually tutored by masters like Ustad Imdad Khan, Ata Mohammed Khan, Abdul Waheed Khan, and Ustad Jhande Khan. She gave her first public performance when she was fifteen. This was followed by the release by the Megaphone Record company of her first disk, which brought Akhtari Bai much acclaim for her renditions of *ghazals*, *thumris*, and *dadras*. *Thumri* and *dadra* are forms of semiclassical Indian music that use devotional or romantic poems set to *ragas* (classical music forms). The *ghazal*, a musical rendering of often highly romantic Urdu poetry splashed with Persian words, is widely appreciated in India and Pakistan. Sung with little musical accompaniment, *ghazal* singing emphasizes the creation of a mood through lyrical rendition, or *adayegi*. It is this special type of singing that became the hallmark of Akhtari Bai's performances.

After the advent of films in India, Akhtari Bai acted in some Hindi films, including *Ameena* (1934), *Mumtaz Begum* (1934), *Naseeb ka Chakkar* (1936), and *Roti* (1942), directed by the renowned producer-director Mehboob Khan. Akhtari Bai lent her voice to songs in her films, a practice that has subsequently given way to playback singing.

In 1945, Akhtari Bai married Ishtiaq Ahmed Abbasi, a wealthy, reputable barrister in Lucknow and an ardent admirer of her music; henceforth she was known as Begum Akhtar—a title that brought both social prestige and professional constraints. Reflecting the social prejudice toward female public entertainers widely shared by many Hindu and Muslim elites at the time, Abbasi restrained his wife from performing in public. Begum Akhtar's withdrawal from singing continued for five years. But according to popular lore, when her health deteriorated she was advised to return to her performances as a cure.

Although she resumed recordings in 1949, sang frequently for the national radio, cut records for the films *Daana Paani* (1953) and *Ehsaan* (1954), and gave riveting performances throughout India and overseas, Begum Akhtar never performed again in her home city of Lucknow. Her last public concert was in Ahmedabad, soon after which she fell ill; she died on 30 October 1974. Begum Akhtar brought to *ghazal* singing a haunting romance and a definitive style for which she received the Padma Shri and Padma Bhushan national awards. Her best-known disciples include Shanti Hiranand, Anjali Banerjee, and Rita Ganguly.

A woman of great personal charm, Begum Akhtar shone best in *mehfils*, small informal concerts often hosted in the homes of her many admirers spread across India. For many who still recall her live performances, her recorded *ghazal* renditions bring to mind her sensitive facial expressions and the dazzle of the diamond nose-ring she always wore.

[*See also* India *and* Performing Arts, *subentry* Performers.]

BIBLIOGRAPHY

Chatterjee, Partha. "Memories of Akhtar." *Hindu*, 2 April 2006.

Hiranand, Shanti. *Begum Akhtar: The Story of My Ammi.* New Delhi, India: Viva Books, 2005. A mostly anecdotal biography, based on personal reminiscences.

MAINA CHAWLA SINGH

AKKA, MAHADEVI, twelfth-century poet and perhaps the best known of woman saints in India. Akka belonged to the medieval religious tradition called bhakti in India. She was one of the group of saints, both men and women, who congregated around Basavanna in southwestern India and came to be known as Veerashaivites. Their poems are known as *vacanas*—literally "utterances." The Veerashaivite saints had many women *bhaktas*, or devotees, unlike many other cults. Like the men in the group, the women came from a wide range of social and occupational categories, including seamstresses, grain grinders, and prostitutes. The *vacanas* often noted the poets' occupations as well as their names.

Akka is known for *vacanas* that depict Shiva as Chennamallika, "the Lord of the white jasmine," and for her use of strong sexual imagery. Among the women saints Akka alone refused to be constrained by the female body and conventional notions of modesty. She did not treat her body as an impediment in her search for salvation. Instead, her body was the instrument through which she expressed the intensity of her love for the object of her devotion: Chennamallika. In one of her *vacanas* she wrote:

He bartered my heart
looted my flesh
claimed as tribute
my pleasure,
took over
all of me
I'm the woman of love
For my lord, white as jasmine

A number of hagiographies of Akka have been written, one of which suggests that she was briefly married to a chieftain who was besotted with her. According to one tradition, when he violated a rule that she had made before she married him—that he would not take her against her will—she left him and wandered around naked: if one is not safe within the home, what is there to fear from the world outside, whether or not one is clothed? Having made her choices, she says with stunning contempt:

Take these husbands who die, decay,
and feed them to your kitchen fires!

Nudity was the specific marker of Akka's religious persona. She was both criticized—often by the women saints of her own tradition—and defended, by some of the followers of

Basavanna. An important philosophical text called the *Sunyasampadane* includes a segment in which a male philosopher questions Akka on the issue of nudity to test her level of mystical development. In one of her *vacanas* she said:

> To the shameless girl
> Wearing the white jasmine . . .
> Where is the need for cover and jewel?

Akka remains alive in popular memory and folklore in the region where she lived. Some women followers recognize that her image has been sanitized through omission of the challenge she mounted against social conventions and acceptable limits for women's manifestations of religious devotion. She continues to inspire feminists who have returned to her *vacanas* in search of indigenous sources of strength for their own lives.

[*See also* Europe, *subentry* Medieval Period; Hinduism; India; Literature, *subentry* Fiction and Poetry; *and* South Asia, *subentry* Medieval Period.]

BIBLIOGRAPHY

Datta, Madhusree, dir. *Scribbles on Akka*. 2000. A documentary film.

Kishwar, Madhu, and Ruth Vanita, eds. *Manushi* 50–52 (January–June 1989). Special issue: Women Bhakta Poets.

Ramanujam, A. K. *Speaking of Shiva*, pp. 125, 134, 129. London: Penguin, 1973. The source of the poems cited above.

Ramaswamy, Vijaya. *Divinity and Deviance: Women in Virasaivism*. Delhi: Oxford University Press, 1996.

UMA CHAKRAVARTI

ALBRIGHT, MADELEINE (b. 1937), diplomat and the first woman to serve as U.S. secretary of state. Madeleine Korbel Albright was born Marie Jana Korbel in Prague on 15 May 1937, to Josef Korbel and Anna Spiegel. Known as Madlenka during her childhood, Albright would later say that understanding her required knowing about her father, a man she emulated in becoming a university professor and diplomat. Albright's life was dramatically shaped by the rise of Nazi Fascism and Soviet Communism, and her personal and professional outlook on foreign affairs reflected the impact of those events. Though she later served as U.S. secretary of state, her career trajectory was not unlike that of many other women of her generation who attended elite colleges and universities and were oriented for success, but who found their public lives and professional careers delayed by raising children and gained formative experience through community activism and volunteer work.

Albright fled with her family to England in 1939, returning briefly to Prague after the war before leaving permanently, this time for the United States, after the Communist coup in 1948. While in England, Albright's parents converted the family to Catholicism. Albright did not discover her Jewish heritage until the 1990s and only then learned that many of her relatives had been killed in the Holocaust. Albright graduated from Wellesley College in 1959; several days later she married Joseph Medill Albright, of the prominent Chicago publishing family, from whom she was divorced in 1983. She worked briefly as a journalist before the birth of her children: twins Alice and Anne (1961) and Katharine (1967). While active in community affairs, she began graduate studies at Columbia University, receiving a doctorate in political science in 1976. Her professional political life began shortly thereafter, when she was nearly forty years old.

Madeleine Albright. U.S. Secretary of State Madeleine Albright listens as President Bill Clinton opens the NATO North Atlantic Council meeting, Washington, D.C., April 1999. REUTERS/WIN MCNAMEE

Albright became increasingly active in Democratic Party circles as a foreign policy expert. She served as Edmund Muskie's chief legislative assistant, worked as a National Security Agency aide under her mentor Zbigniew Brzezinski during the Carter administration, and was a chief foreign policy adviser to the 1984 vice-presidential nominee Geraldine Ferraro and the 1988 presidential nominee Michael Dukakis. From 1982 to 1992 she also held a position at Georgetown University's School of Foreign Service, where she was celebrated for her teaching style and cultivated many connections in Washington. Those relationships ultimately translated into greater policy influence, culminating in the senior positions she held in the 1990s.

In 1992, Albright was named U.S. ambassador to the United Nations by President Bill Clinton and served simultaneously in the National Security Council. As U.N. ambassador, a position that was elevated to the cabinet during her tenure, Albright faced difficult crises in Somalia, Rwanda, and Bosnia, and her encouragement of active military involvement reflected fears of appeasement born of her personal experiences as a child in Europe in the 1940s. Upon Clinton's reelection in 1996, Albright was tapped to serve as secretary of state, becoming the first woman to hold that post and one of the most influential women to serve in any American president's inner circle. In 2001, with the election of a Republican White House, Albright returned to her life as a student of foreign affairs, working in think tanks and similar venues and writing editorial pieces expressing her views on international policy.

[*See also* United Nations *and* United States, *subentry* Modern Period.]

BIBLIOGRAPHY

Albright, Madeleine, with Bill Woodward. *Madam Secretary*. New York: Miramax Books, 2003.

Blackman, Ann. *Seasons of Her Life: A Biography of Madeleine Korbel Albright*. New York: Scribner, 1998.

Blood, Thomas. *Madam Secretary: A Biography of Madeleine Albright*. Rev. ed. New York: St. Martin's Griffin, 1999.

Dobbs, Michael. *Madeleine Albright: A Twentieth-Century Odyssey*. New York: Henry Holt and Company, 1999. New ed. with afterword on the Balkan War. New York: Owl Books, 2000.

KIMBERLY A. BRODKIN

ALCOTT, LOUISA MAY (1832–1888), American fiction writer best known as the author of the girls' novel *Little Women* (1868–1869). Alcott was born in Germantown, Pennsylvania, to Abigail May Alcott and the progressive educator Bronson Alcott. The March family of *Little Women* was an idealized version of her own family, which was far less stable and more mobile. Alcott's father's idealistic education and reform ventures regularly failed, necessitating the family's frequent moves, and she and her mother increasingly provided the family's economic support. Her childhood and adolescence were split primarily between Concord and Boston, Massachusetts, where she was deeply influenced by members of her father's transcendentalist circle, including reform-minded writers and thinkers such as Margaret Fuller, Elizabeth Peabody, Ralph Waldo Emerson, and Henry David Thoreau.

Alcott's high rate of productivity and the extraordinary variety of literary forms in which she wrote, as well as the range of audiences she addressed, have challenged and intrigued scholars and leisure readers alike. Her first published story appeared in 1852 in the *Olive Branch*, a Boston story paper (an inexpensive weekly magazine published in newspaper format), and she continued to publish anonymous and pseudonymous tales in story papers intermittently throughout her career. These sensational melodramas featuring subversive heroines—"blood and thunder" tales, as Alcott called them—have kept twentieth-century scholars busy locating and reprinting them. Her first book, published in 1854 under her own name, was *Flower Fables*, a collection of fairy stories. She also published short fiction in elite venues such as the *Atlantic Monthly* magazine, plays, autobiographical Civil War sketches based on her wartime nursing experiences, and an adult novel, *Moods* (1864), all before *Little Women*, a novel that has become a worldwide icon of American girlhood. In Japan, *Little Women* was a perennial favorite for teaching good behavior, although occasionally young women admired Jo's individualism and rebelliousness.

Although *Little Women* and the stream of juvenile fiction that followed made Alcott and her family financially secure, she sometimes chafed at her new public fame as a writer of girls' books. Some critics read her body of work as unified by a feminist analysis of women's place in society; others emphasize the divisions between Alcott's literary personae. Whatever the politics of her fiction, she was active throughout her life in reform movements typically supported by white, middle-class women in the northern states, such as antislavery, women's suffrage, and temperance. Her public support of women's rights actually increased after *Little Women*. When Concord allowed women to vote in local school elections, Alcott led an initiative to educate women as voters and was the town's first woman to register to vote, in 1879. She also used her writing to offer explicit support to feminist reform. Between 1874 and 1888 she contributed frequently to the *Woman's Journal*, a women's-rights periodical, and her semiautobiographical adult novel *Work: A Story of Experience* (1873) traces its heroine's attempts to find meaningful work and make a home, ending with the widowed heroine becoming a lecturer on women's rights.

Mercury poisoning from medicine administered to treat the typhoid pneumonia that Alcott had contracted during the Civil War was the likely cause of years of pain and bad health and of her early death.

[*See also* Literature *and* Transcendentalism.]

BIBLIOGRAPHY

Eiselein, Gregory, and Anne K. Phillips. *The Louisa May Alcott Encyclopedia*. Westport, Conn.: Greenwood Press, 2001. Provides a detailed chronology of Alcott's life, alphabetical entries on her life and works, and an extensive bibliography.

Stern, Madeleine B. *Louisa May Alcott: A Biography* (1950). Reprint. Boston: Northeastern University Press, 1999. A thorough treatment of Alcott's life and works by the woman most responsible for recovering Alcott's anonymous and pseudonymous works.

MELISSA J. HOMESTEAD

ALI, ARUNA ASAF (1909–1996), activist in India's independence movement and the first elected mayor of Delhi. Aruna Asaf Ali's public life spanned nearly seven decades of the twentieth century. Born into a Brahmin family that migrated from East Bengal (Bangladesh) to Calcutta (now Kolkata), Aruna was the eldest of five children. Together with her sister Purnima, she received her early education at the Sacred Heart Convent in Lahore, where her father, Upendranath Ganguly, worked as a journalist. Thwarted in her wish to become a nun, Aruna eventually became a teacher at a girls' school in Calcutta. While visiting her sister in Allahabad, she met and fell in love with Asaf Ali, a barrister and a leader of the Indian National Congress in Delhi. They wished to marry, but Aruna's parents objected because he was a Muslim and twice her age. After Aruna's father died in 1928, she married Asaf Ali.

After her marriage, Aruna moved to Delhi and was drawn to the Congress Socialist Party. She joined the Salt Satyagraha, a protest march against imperialist laws, and was imprisoned for a year. This was the first of several times Aruna was imprisoned over the next decade, a common pattern for those in anticolonial resistance movements.

The turning point in Aruna's life was her participation in the Quit India movement launched by Mahatma Gandhi in August 1942. Following the arrest of all the leaders of the Indian National Congress, Aruna presided over the historic Congress session in Bombay (Mumbai) and hoisted the national flag. Outraged by the trampling of the flag by a British soldier, she renounced nonviolence and went underground to guide the movement, moving from city to city to escape arrest. Along with Ram Manohar Lohia, she edited *Inquilab*, a revolutionary monthly. The government announced an award of five thousand rupees for her capture, but she successfully remained underground until 1946, when the warrants against her were canceled.

Her experiences and compassion for the underprivileged led Aruna to regard the 1947 transfer of power from the British to the Congress as a sham. She broke away from the Congress and later joined the Left Socialist Group; she also took an active interest in the trade union movement. This group merged with the Communist Party of India (CPI) in 1955, and Aruna became a member of the central committee and vice president of the All India Trade Union Congress. In 1954 she established the National Federation of Indian Women, the women's wing of the CPI. In 1958 she left the CPI and became Delhi's first elected mayor. She was a leading member of the Indo-Soviet Cultural Society and the All India Peace Council. She was associated with two left-wing journals: *Link*, a weekly started in 1958, and *Patriot*, a daily founded in 1962.

Aruna was awarded several national and international awards, including the Lenin Peace Prize, the Indira Gandhi Award for National Integration, the Jawaharlal Nehru Award for International Understanding, the Padma Vibhushan, and, posthumously, the Bharat Ratna.

[*See also* India; Nationalism; *and* Socialism.]

BIBLIOGRAPHY

Grover, Verinder, and Ranjana Arora, eds. *Great Women of Modern India*. Vol. 8, *Aruna Asaf Ali*. New Delhi: Deep & Deep, 1993.

Kaul, T. N., ed. *Aruna Asaf Ali: A Profile*. New Delhi: Lancer International, 1999.

Raghavan, G. N. S. *Aruna Asaf Ali: A Compassionate Radical*. New Delhi: National Book Trust, India, 1999.

APARNA BASU

ALLENDE, ISABEL (b. 1942), widely read writer in Latin America; acclaimed author of seven novels, two memoirs, a collection of stories, and a book on aphrodisiacs. Allende's fiction capitalizes on the rich cultural tradition and baroque exuberance of her native Chile to create tales of love, mystery, and adventure in which she interweaves densely layered tales of passion with the stuff of history and legend.

Allende was born on 2 August 1942, in Lima, Peru, where her father, a Chilean diplomat, was posted. After her parents separated in 1945, Allende's mother took her three children back to Chile. She began her career as a journalist writing humorous, satirical articles for the radical women's magazine *Paula* and hosting a weekly television program. On 11 September 1973 her uncle, Chilean president Salvador Allende, was assassinated and a military government came into power. As a result of her involvement in underground political activities, Isabel Allende and her family were forced to flee to Venezuela in 1975 to escape death threats. In 1988 she moved to California.

Her first novel, *La casa de los espíritus* (1982; *The House of the Spirits*, 1985), established her as a significant voice in the previously exclusively male pantheon of Latin American fiction. In this compelling family saga, set against the backdrop of contemporary Latin American politics, Allende artfully combines the sordid realities of recent Chilean history with the magical world of the imagination through four generations of women who share their legacy of creativity, clairvoyance, and political activism. This novel, like most of Allende's works, is overtly feminist.

The novels *De amor y de sombra* (1984; *Of Love and Shadows*, 1987) and *Eva Luna* (1987; *Eva Luna*, 1988) examine a woman's evolution to greater self-, social, and political awareness. *De amor y de sombra* is a tale of the political awakening of a journalist who discovers mutilated bodies buried in a mine. Allende creates suspense as she reveals the lives of those touched by the brutal killings. *Eva Luna*, a modern, picaresque narrative of a storyteller who tells tales in order to survive, chronicles the transformation of a young girl from the lowest social class into a popular writer of a television soap opera.

Allende's ninth book, *Hija de la fortuna* (1999; *Daughter of Fortune,* 1999), a sumptuous nineteenth-century epic, narrates the life of a young girl of mysterious origins. In this historical romance the heroine follows the man she loves from Chile to California during the Gold Rush, and, disguised in men's clothing, embarks on a series of adventures that teach her the consequences and rewards of freedom.

Retrato en sepia (2000; *Portrait in Sepia*, 2001), a sweeping historical novel set in Chile at the end of the nineteenth century, is a marvelous family story peopled by characters from previous novels. The story develops primarily as the bildungsroman of a liberal-minded young woman, Aurora del Valle, a photographer who finds herself alone at the end of an unhappy relationship. Haunted by terrible nightmares, she decides to explore the mystery of her past to discover the hidden secret that has so affected her young life.

The transforming power of love, and its ability to withstand the vicissitudes of war, political repression, and even death, are recurring themes in Allende's work and are treated in a variety of ways, ranging from the fantastical to the elegiac. *Paula* (1994; *Paula*, 1995) is an anguished memoir dedicated to Allende's daughter, who died in 1992 of a rare hereditary disorder. When her daughter fell into a coma, Allende began writing her a letter, so that when she awoke she would learn what had happened while she slept. In this autobiographical narrative Allende traces her family history from the end of the nineteenth century to her own life in the United States. In her more recent work *Mi país inventado* (2003; *My Invented Country*, 2003), she continues the exploration of the role that memory and nostalgia have played in shaping her life and her fiction.

Afrodita: Cuentos, recetas y otros afrodisíacos (1997; *Aphrodite: A Memoir of the Senses*, 1998) is an illustrated, nonfiction but tongue-in-cheek book about sex and food. It contains a hodgepodge of memories, lore, poetry, stories, and recipes, interlaced with humorous anecdotes about aphrodisiacs. In *Zorro* (2005; *Zorro*, 2005), a historical novel, Allende imaginatively recreates the legend of Zorro, the famous Robin Hood of eighteenth-century colonial California, with a feminine twist.

A gifted storyteller who believes in the power and the magical quality of the word, Allende is best known for feminist novels that blend historical fact and family drama with uplifting fantasy. The strong, independent women whose loves and destinies shape her fiction are the hallmark of her literary production.

[*See also* Chile *and* Literature.]

BIBLIOGRAPHY

Allende, Isabel. *Conversations with Isabel Allende.* Edited by John E. Rodden and translated by Virginia Invernizzi and John E. Rodden. Austin: University of Texas Press, 1999.

Cox, Karen Castellucci. *Isabel Allende: A Critical Companion.* Westport, Conn.: Greenwood Press, 2003.

Hart, Patricia. *Narrative Magic in the Fiction of Isabel Allende.* Rutherford, N.J.: Fairleigh Dickinson University Press; London: Associated University Presses, 1989.

Ramblado-Minero, María de la Cinta. *Isabel Allende's Writing of the Self: Trespassing the Boundaries of Fiction and Autobiography.* Lewiston, N.Y.: Edwin Mellen Press, 2003.

NORA ERRO-PERALTA

ALONSO, ALICIA (b. 1921), prima ballerina and founder of the National Ballet of Cuba. Alicia Martínez began her formal dance training in 1931 at Havana's Pro-Arte Musical dance school under the direction of the Russian choreographer Nikolai Yavorsky. By the age of fifteen the young ballerina had already distinguished herself in Cuba and, in order to continue developing her craft, departed for New York with fellow dancer (now former husband) Fernando Alonso. Upon her arrival in New York she enrolled in the School of American Ballet and began training with the famed choreographers Enrico Zanfretta and Alexandra Fedorova. Alonso made her Broadway debut in 1938 and began touring extensively with the American Ballet Caravan, the predecessor of the New York City Ballet. She also became a charter member of the American Ballet Theater in 1940. Noted for the technical precision and emotional range of her performances, Alonso earned special acclaim for her work in *Billy the Kid* (1939), *Undertow* (1945), *Theme and Variations* (1947), and *Fall River Legend* (1948). At the age of nineteen, Alonso had suffered a detached retina and underwent the first of several painful surgeries to repair her rapidly deteriorating vision. Left virtually blind, Alonso defied her physicians' bleak prognosis when she returned to New York in 1943 and earned clamorous praise for her interpretation of the notoriously demanding role of Giselle in the opera of the same name. Alonso is still hailed as one of the great Giselles of all time.

During her extensive career, Alonso worked with many of the most celebrated dancers and choreographers of the twentieth century, including Mikhail Fokine, George Balanchine, Léonid Massine, and Agnes de Mille. Furthermore, her partnering with the Russian danseur noble Igor Youskevitch remains one of the most celebrated pairings in ballet history. Between 1938 and 1960, Alonso toured extensively with the American Ballet Theater and the Ballet Russe de Monte Carlo. She was also the first ballerina from the Americas invited to dance at the Bolshoi in Moscow (1957). Singularly influential internationally, Alonso also championed ballet in Cuba and established the island's first ballet company, the Ballet Alicia Alonso (now National Ballet of Cuba), in 1948. Admired for the rigor of its training and recruiting programs, the National Ballet of Cuba is widely considered the premier Latin American classical ballet troupe. The company has performed in more than fifty-eight countries and has garnered hundreds of international awards.

Alonso has received many of the highest commendations granted to an international cultural figure, including Cuba's Carlos Manuel de Céspedes decoration (1947), a Silver Trophy award from *Dance Magazine* (1959), a Premio Max Hispanoamericano de las Artes Escénicas (1998), and the prestigious Nijinsky Award from the International Dance Council of the United Nations Educational, Scientific, and Cultural Organization (2002). In June 2002, she was appointed UNESCO Goodwill Ambassador for her contribution to the development, preservation, and popularization of classical dance. Alonso's exceptional talent has also earned her the honorific title *prima ballerina assoluta*, a rank reserved for a ballerina able to perform any role in the classical repertoire. As a result of Alonso's influence, Cuba now boasts five professional ballet troupes, and each province features its own ballet school. Alonso ceased to perform in 1995, but she continued to direct the National Ballet of Cuba and the National School of Ballet.

[*See also* Cuba *and* Dance, *subentry* Modern and Professional.]

BIBLIOGRAPHY

Durbin, Paula. "Alicia Alonso: Legend of Spirit and Style." *Américas* 56, no. 4 (July–August 2004): 49–53. A brief yet detailed discussion of the trajectory and international impact of Alonso's career that includes photographs and excerpts of interviews with the ballerina herself.

Siegel, Beatrice. *Alicia Alonso: The Story of a Ballerina*. New York: Warne, 1979. A general overview of Alonso's personal and professional life through the late 1970s that includes a limited number of photographs and a glossary of related dance terms.

TIFFANY A. THOMAS-WOODARD

AMA. *See* Divers.

AMAZONS. In ancient Greek mythology, the Amazons were a people of warrior women living on the borders of the world. Combining manly valor with a female body implying sexuality, they are bewildering and redoutable foes of their male opponents. Epic stories focus on Greek heroes who prove their valor by vanquishing the Amazons (Homer, *Iliad*, III, 186–189; VI, 178–190). The mythical protagonists are sometimes individual heroes, such as Heracles, Bellerophon, Achilles, and Theseus, and they are sometimes groups: for instance the Greek army defeats the Amazons when the Amazons side with the Trojans in the Trojan War, and the collective Athenians defeat them in the early days of history when the Amazons invade their country (Apollodorus, *The Library*, II, v, 9; V, 1–2; [Ps.–] Lysias, *Funerary Oration*, 4–6).

A second group of stories features the Amazons as heroines who confer legitimacy to Greek settlements in newly won land, foremost in Asia Minor, by granting their names to Greek cities and their cults to Greek sanctuaries. The Amazon stories over time were enriched with new episodes and details: Achilles first slaying his opponent Penthesileia and in later versions falling in love with her; Heracles first fighting the Amazons but later expected to get the girdle of the Amazon queen, Hippolyta, by more peaceful means as the ninth of his twelve labors. In the course of time, encounters with Amazons changed from deadly battles to adventures with a mixture of love and death.

Convinced that the Amazons once had really existed, ancient Greek scholars created explanations of their (non-Greek) name, elaborating the common beliefs of what "Amazons" would have been like. Thus their name was either taken to mean *a-mazon*, "without breasts," suggesting that the Amazons removed one breast to improve their archery; or *a-maza*, "without cereal food," indicating a life of hunting rather than farming. Greek historians furthermore endowed the Amazons with a life of their own, including a city to live in on the eastern border of the Greek world ("Themiscyra," on the river Thermodon, in northern Turkey); other accounts give them a country of their own, sometimes in the north (Scythia, in southern Russia and Ukraine) and sometimes to the southwest (Libya, occasionally associated with Atlantis). The repertoire of Amazons' names expanded likewise, with Greek names recalling warfare and femininity.

Throughout classical antiquity, the Amazons were a favorite topic not only of stories but also of the visual arts. Numerous vase paintings and sculptures reflect scenes from the myths, showing the battles of Greeks with Amazons and the mythical heroes fighting duels with the Amazon queens. The visual representations underscored the similarity of the Amazons to male heroes, by dressing them in warriors' armor, and their difference, by making clear the femaleness of their bodies. Non-Greek costumes were added to emphasize the Amazons' foreign origins. The speculation about the removal of a breast, however, was not reflected in the visual repertoire, which always featured the Amazons with two breasts. The sculptures of wounded Amazons finding asylum in the temple of Artemis at Ephesus, of the fourth century B.C.E., are among the most celebrated works of ancient art.

From classical antiquity well into modern times, the Amazons represented a provocative and attractive alternative to regular gender patterns. Defying the traditional territories of male privilege by using weapons and by living on their own instead of under male dominance, the Amazons

Amazons in Battle. A battle between mythical Greek heroes and female warriors is engraved on the side of an Amazonian sarcophagus, Greece, c. 400 B.C.E. KUNSTHISTORISCHES MUSEUM, VIENNA/ERICH LESSING/ART RESOURCE, NY

provided a notable case of female independence, often but erroneously associated with a matriarchal society.

Valiant women all over the world have famously invoked the idea of Amazons. In prehistoric Scythia and in the Mongolian Altai mountains, prominent women of the nomad peoples were buried with weapons indicating their prowess. Wrestling contests between pubescent girls among several indigenous peoples in Latin America, notably the Xingu, gave the river dominating the area its name, Amazon, as the first European explorers there associated these warrior women with the ones they knew from classical literature. In the former African kingdom of Dahomey, the ruler maintained a distinguished guard of female warriors, notable for their challenging combination of fighting capacity and femininity. Belligerent women (for instance in the French Revolution), independent women, and women on horseback in western Europe have all proudly accepted the name of the classical Amazons. These modern-day cases, however, involve women crossing traditional gender boundaries but belonging to historically well-known societies comprising both men and women. The mythical Amazons, by contrast, were imagined to be an exclusively female society, whose territories have been searched for time and again in vain.

[*See also* Androgyny; Europe, *subentry* Ancient Greece; *and* Matriarchy.]

BIBLIOGRAPHY

Blok, Josine H. *The Early Amazons: Modern and Ancient Perspectives on a Persistent Myth.* Leiden, The Netherlands: Brill, 1995.

Blok, Josine H. "A Tale of Many Cities: Amazons in the Mythical Past of Greek Cities of Asia Minor." In *Proof and Persuasion: Essays on Authority, Objectivity and Evidence*, edited by Elizabeth Lunbeck and Suzanne Marchand, pp. 81–99. Turnhout, Belgium: Brepols, 1996.

Von Bothmer, Dietrich. *Amazons in Greek Art.* Oxford: Clarendon Press, 1957.

JOSINE H. BLOK

AMES, JESSIE DANIEL (1883–1972), early white advocate of African American rights. Born in rural east Texas to James and Laura Daniel in 1883, Jessie Daniel graduated from the "Ladies Annex" of Southwestern University in Georgetown, Texas, when she was nineteen. Having no prospect of marriage—a disaster for a Southern woman at that time—she continued to live with her family until she met and married Roger Post Ames, thirteen years her elder, in 1905. Ames was a friend of Jessie's father and an army surgeon. They had a son and two daughters, although they mostly lived apart. Jessie found marriage a loveless affair. Roger Ames spent most of their marriage in Central America while Jessie helped her mother run the telephone company in Georgetown. Roger's death in 1914 indirectly opened the way for a lifetime of paid employment and female activism. Almost immediately, Jessie Daniel Ames threw her energies behind the flourishing movement for woman suffrage and became the first president of the Georgetown Equal Suffrage League. She wrote a weekly column on women's issues for the *Williamson County Sun* and soon found herself serving as treasurer of the Texas Woman Suffrage Association. Once the Nineteenth Amendment to the U.S. Constitution was ratified, Ames turned to organizing the Texas League of Women Voters, the activist organization that was created in the wake of the suffragist effort. In 1920, and again in 1924, she served as a delegate-at-large to the national Democratic Party conventions. Her organizational skills and statewide connections led to the presidency of the state American Association of University Women and the Texas Federation of Women's Clubs.

Much of Ames's leadership developed through work as a Methodist laywoman. She served on the Board of Education (Women's Division) of the Methodist Church and became increasingly convinced that women's Christian duties included racial justice. Joining the small but vocal white critics of racial discrimination, in 1924 she became the director of the Texas Council of the Commission on Interracial Cooperation (CIC), an organization devoted to biracial, Christian social change. In 1929, she moved to Atlanta to become the national director of the CIC Women's Committee. She gradually wearied of the CIC's tentativeness on what she considered the most pressing racial problem: lynching. Reaching out to churchwomen beyond her Methodist networks, she created the national Association of Southern Women for the Prevention of Lynching (ASWPL). By targeting white women, she hoped to achieve what black women alone had not been able to; that is, legislation that made lynching a federal crime. Crisscrossing the South by train and bus, she taught members in her local affiliates how to investigate purported racial crimes and pressure law enforcement officials to make sure the accused received a trial, not vigilante justice. She continued to work with the CIC and the ASWPL until her retirement in 1942, mentoring numerous women and men in grassroots organizing. Congress never adopted the antilynching law, but many others took up the fight for civil rights in postwar America. Ames died in Austin, Texas, on 21 February 1972.

BIBLIOGRAPHY

Hall, Jacquelyn Dowd. "Jessie Daniel Ames." In *American Reformers: An H. W. Wilson Biographical Dictionary*. Edited by Alden Whitman. New York: H. W. Wilson, 1985.

Hall, Jacquelyn Dowd. *Revolt Against Chivalry: Jessie Daniel Ames and the Women's Campaign Against Lynching*. New York: Columbia University Press, 1979.

GAIL S. MURRAY

AMINATU, QUEEN OF ZARIA (1536–1610), ruler of a large state in northern Nigeria. In 1576 a young woman named Aminatu became the ruler of Zauzau in what is today northern Nigeria. She ruled for nearly forty years and is the only female ruler in the nine hundred years of the recorded history of Zauzau. In the early twentieth century, Zauzau was renamed Zaria by the British, and it is a province in the north of present-day Nigeria.

Zauzau, or Zaria, was a very important trade center and one of a series of Hausa states established after the fall of the Songhai empire, which covered most of northern and western Africa into the ninth century. Zaria came to dominate the north–south trans-Saharan trade between northern and western Africa and the Middle East from the ninth through the nineteenth centuries.

By the beginning of the thirteenth century, the rulers of Hausaland had converted to Islam. Although women had held public titles and played public roles in the early Hausa states, after Islam was introduced into the area women largely disappeared from public view. The reign of Aminatu is thus all the more remarkable.

Aminatu was the daughter of Sarkin (King) Nikatau, the twenty-second ruler of Zauzau, and Queen Bakwa Turunku (r. 1536–c. 1566). After her parents died, Aminatu's brother became the sarkin of Zaria. By the age of sixteen Aminatu had emerged as a leading warrior in her brother's cavalry. She became famous for her military skills, and she is still celebrated in traditional Hausa praise songs as "Amina daughter of Nikatau, a woman as capable as a man." When her brother died, Aminatu became queen, and according to the *Kano Chronicle*, Queen Aminatu continued to "wage war in the Hausa lands and conquered them all, so that the men of Katsina and the men of Kano brought her tribute" (Hogben and Kirk-Green, p. 217). As queen, she expanded Zaria to its largest size ever. As she conquered new lands and cities, she fortified them with earthen walls. These walls became the prototype for the walls used in all the Hausa states until the British conquest of the area in 1904. Many of these walls survive to the present day and are known as *ganuwar Amina* (Amina's walls).

The purposes of Aminatu's conquests were to extend the borders of Zaria and to reduce the other Hausa states to the status of vassal states paying tribute to Zaria. In this she succeeded. It is not clear whether Aminatu ever married, but according to Sultan Bello's *Infak al Maisuri* (translated into English by Hogben and Kirk-Greene), Aminatu took a lover in every town she conquered and had him beheaded the next morning. It is not clear how her reign of thirty-six years ended, but today schoolchildren in northern Nigeria cite Queen Aminatu as one of the greatest of all Hausa rulers.

[*See also* Africa *and* West Africa.]

BIBLIOGRAPHY

Callaway, Barbara. *Muslim Hausa Women in Nigeria*. Syracuse, N.Y.: Syracuse University Press, 1987.

Crowder, Michael. *The Story of Nigeria*. London: Faber and Faber, 1962.

Hogben, S. T., and Anthony Kirk-Greene. *The Emirates of Northern Nigeria*. London: Oxford University Press, 1966.

Palmer, Herbert. *Sudanese Memoirs: Being Mainly Translations from a Number of Arabic Manuscripts Relating to the Central and Western Sudan*. 3 vols. Lagos, Nigeria: Government Printer, 1928. Includes the *Kano Chronicle*, a collection of oral traditions from the area around present-day Kano in northern Nigeria, including Zaria, recorded between 1883 and 1893.

BARBARA J. CALLAWAY

AMMAIYAR, KARAIKAL (fifth–sixth century), poet-saint of southern India. Considered to be the earliest of the sixty-three Tamil Nayanmar, or devotees of Shiva, Karaikal Ammaiyar is also one of the very few women among the Nayanmar. Her life and poems are representative of the hagiography and development of the *bhakti* (devotion) movement of early Hinduism, which had its center in the far south of the subcontinent. The Vedas, the source of Hinduism, revolved around the maintenance of the world and prosperity within it by means of ritual sacrifices, which were performed by priests. Ammaiyar represents the rise of a religious movement revolving around individual devotion to a god who can provide everything from material benefits to liberation from the laws of karma and the cycle of rebirth. One of the earliest documents of the *bhakti* movement is the *Bhagavad Gītā* (The Song of God), a section of the *Mahābārata*, in which the god Krishna promises the warrior Arjuna absolution of his sins for having killed his relatives in war. *Bhakti* removed the need for the mediation of the priests and also mitigated the privilege of caste in obtaining religious benefits.

According to the earliest account of her life, in the *Periya Puranam* of Sekkizhaar (992–1042), Ammaiyar was born as Punithavathiar (Punitavati), the daughter of the merchant Thanathaththanar, in the town of Karaikal in Tamil Nadu. She married Paramadhaththan (Paramatattan), son of a great merchant of Nagappattinam. According to legend, her spiritual powers were revealed when, having given one of two mangoes to a mendicant, she gave the other to her husband. When he asked for the second, she prayed to Shiva; another mango appeared in her hand. Asked where she had gotten it, she told him the truth; he required her to prove it. She prayed again and placed in his hands another, which then disappeared. Her husband, sure she was a goddess, ran off to the kingdom of Pandya, where he married the daughter of a local merchant.

Some time later, her husband returned, asking forgiveness. She made a pilgrimage to the abode of Shiva, progressing up Mount Kailasa on her hands and head, lest she tread on holy ground. For her devotion, Shiva granted her wish to stay with him and ordered her to Tiruvalangadu to sing for him when he danced there. Again she made her way on her head and hands.

Ammaiyar's biography is a model of *bhakti* hagiography. She is a wife who becomes chaste in devotion to her god. She performs a pilgrimage to the dwelling of her god. Finally, her devotion is rewarded by a miracle. At the time of her metamorphosis and in the bliss of witnessing Shiva's dance, she utters poems.

[*See also Bhakti* Movement *and* India.]

BIBLIOGRAPHY

McGlashan, Alastair. *The History of the Holy Servants of the Lord Siva: A Translation of the "Periya Puranam" of Cekkilar*. Victoria, British Columbia: Trafford, 2006.

Smith, David. *The Dance of Siva: Religion, Art, and Poetry in South India*. Cambridge Studies in Religious Traditions, no. 7. Cambridge, U.K.: Cambridge University Press, 2002.

S. A. THORNTON

AMORÓS PUENTE, CELIA (b. 1944), a philosopher and feminist theorist, was born in Valencia, Spain, and completed her university studies in philosophy there. She was a guest professor and researcher at various international academic centers, a participant in the seminars of Sheila Benhabib, and for many years was a professor in the Department of Theory of Knowledge and History of Thought at the Universidad Nacional de Educación a Distancia (UNED; National University of Distance Education) in Madrid.

In her 1997 book *Tiempo de Feminismo* (Time of Feminism), Amorós describes the founding in 1987 of the Instituto de Investigaciones Feministas (Institute of Feminist Studies) at the Universidad Complutense de Madrid, which she directed for its first four years. On the basis of their shared interests, she says, a group of academics formed a group for systematic research into the relation between feminism and the Enlightenment, which constituted a permanent seminar to address academic and research interests in the field of feminism.

Although she has been a leading figure in promoting and defending the developing field of feminist studies in the academic sphere in Spain—going up against colleagues who consider the subject banal or second-rate—her commitment to feminism has not been merely intellectual. Her real-world militancy began in 1977 with activism as part of the Frente de Liberación del Mujer (Women's Liberation Front) in Madrid; since that time, she has participated in a multitude of feminist initiatives, including the creation in 1978 of the Librería de Mujeres, a women's bookstore in

Madrid, which served as a meeting place for feminist activists. The bookstore, which still existed in the early twenty-first century, organized expositions, diverse workshops, and discussion groups.

Amorós writes and lectures from a broad theoretical scope. Her feminist philosophy and her philosophical criticism arise from study of the Enlightenment philosophers of the eighteenth century and the Romantic philosophers of the nineteenth century, demonstrating how enlightened reason, the culmination of the emancipation of all human beings, transforms into a patriarchal discourse. Her 1985 book *Hacia una crítica de la razón patriarcal* (Toward a Criticism of Patriarchal Reason) constituted a new approach to philosophy from the perspective of gender, bringing androcentric biases to light. In *Tiempo de feminismo: Sobre feminismo, proyecto ilustrado y postmodernidad* (Time of Feminism: On Feminism, the Enlightenment Project, and Postmodernity; 1997), she reintroduced her theory of enlightened feminism, proposing it as the only way to achieve women's emancipation: feminism should be understood, she says—in keeping with a three-centuries-long tradition—as being a type of anthropological, moral, and political thought that has as its referent the rationalist and enlightened idea of the equality of the sexes. Her other books include *Søren Kierkegaard; o, La subjetividad del caballero* (Søren Kierkegaard; or, The Subjectivity of the Gentleman, 1987), and *Mujer, participación, y cultura política* (Woman, Participation, and Political Culture, 1990), reissued in 1994 with the title *Feminismo: Igualdad y diferencia* (Feminism: Equality and Difference). In 2006 Amorós won the National Prize for Essays with her book *La gran diferencia y sus escasas consecuencia para la lucha de las mujeres*. This was the first time the prize was awarded to a woman.

In discussing the "feminism of difference" (the school of thought that holds that the demand for equality of the genders is obsolete), she suggests that the celebration of feminine values in this form of feminism (that is, insisting on the feminine identity), runs the risk of celebrating the very product of domination. Celia Amorós, by contrast, has been a foremost voice for the "feminism of equality," playing a crucial part in a central debate within the current panorama of feminist theory.

In addition to being one of the most important feminist thinkers of the late twentieth and early twenty-first centuries, Amorós enjoys considerable academic acclaim, attending national and international congresses, directing important research projects, and traveling on the strength of her interest in Latin America to teach courses in countries including Chile and Guatemala. By the early 2000s she had directed roughly twenty doctoral theses on gender questions in philosophical thought. In 1980 she was honored with the María Espinosa prize for the best published article on feminist themes for her essay "Feminismo y Partidos Políticos" (Feminism and Political Parties).

[*See also* Feminism, *subentry* Overview; *and* Spain and Portugal.]

BIBLIOGRAPHY

Femenías, Luisa, and Amy A. Oliver, eds. *Feminist Philosophy in Latin America and Spain*. New York: Rodopi, 2007.

Posada Kubissa, Luisa. *Celia Amorós*. Madrid: Del Orto, 2000.

MARIA ISABEL CABRERA BOSCH

Translated from the Spanish by Matthew Miller

ANACAONA (1474–1503), a legendary Taíno queen, famed as a poet among the indigenous peoples of the West Indies and remembered as the ruler whose chiefdom was the last to fall to Spanish conquest on Hispaniola. She was the wife of Caonabo, the cacique of the Maguana people on Hispaniola, and she was the sister of, and successor to, the cacique Behechío of the Jaraguá people on the same island.

According to chronicles of the time, Anacaona was a kindhearted, cultured woman of great beauty. Her compositions, in the form of songs and poems, were performed in the *areitos*, communal festivals in which, under the cacique's direction, the myths of creation were sung and re-created. The name and glory of the queen of Jaraguá became a symbol in Taíno poetry; in the aboriginal language, her name meant "Golden Flower." She was forced to marry the fierce cacique Caonabo, but it seems she lived near her husband only for short periods. She usually accompanied her brother Behechío, helping him govern the prosperous neighboring kingdom of Jaraguá.

Anacaona exercised a degree of authority that manifested most clearly in the pressure she exerted on her brother to join the general revolt against Guacanaric, the cacique of Marien, who had imprudently welcomed the Spaniards. Anacaona seems to have taken the initiative in all the affairs of the kingdom (in league with other women of the time), from presiding over festivals (in 1496 she arranged a splendid reception for Christopher Columbus's brother Bartholomeo) to issuing the orders of government. Evidently her brother Behechío let her reign in his stead, perhaps enacting early the succession that would otherwise have taken place upon his death, since he left no descendants.

Anacaona's intelligence, grace, and beauty attracted the attention of the first Spanish conquistadores, who settled on Hispaniola in 1492. At first she expressed admiration and awe toward the Spaniards, but their continued abuses against the indigenous people converted that admiration into hatred and antipathy. Upon the death of her brother, Anacaona became the official cacique of the kingdom of Jaraguá, the only indigenous bastion on the island that had not yet submitted to the conquistadores. When Nicolás de Ovando came to the island to govern it on behalf of Spain in 1502, he announced a "peaceful visit" to Jaraguá but brought with him a well-armed contingent of three hundred infantry and seventy cavalry. The visit turned into a massacre in which the many dozens of Taíno dignitaries that Anacaona had assembled as a reception party were burned alive or lanced to death. Anacaona herself was declared guilty of instigating native rebellion against the Spaniards. In *A Short Account of the Destruction of the Indies* (1542), a firsthand and denunciatory chronicle of the Spanish abuses of the Taíno, the Spanish bishop Bartolomé de las Casas records that Queen Anacaona—whom he called a "a noble person and a great lady"—was put to death by hanging, "as a mark of respect and out of deference to her rank." The Spaniards then thoroughly ravaged the kingdom of Jaraguá, and the native people who were able to save themselves were reduced to slavery.

[*See also* Caribbean Region.]

BIBLIOGRAPHY

Vidal, Pedro L. Vergés. *Anacaona (1474–1503)*. Ciudad Trujillo, Dominican Republic: Editora Montalvo, 1947.

MARIA ISABEL CABRERA BOSCH
Translated from the Spanish by Matthew Miller

ANARCHISM. Anarchism is a theory and a practice aimed at creating a society free of hierarchy and structured relations of domination and subordination. Although the first major theorist of anarchism, William Godwin (1756–1836), published his *Enquiry Concerning Political Justice* in England at the end of the eighteenth century, anarchism as a social movement gained prominence only during the nineteenth century, especially in Russia, the United States, and Spain. Anarchist movements also existed, and played significant roles, in Argentina, Brazil, Chile, France, Italy, and Japan. In their opposition to hierarchy in all its forms, not simply to capitalism, many of these anarchist movements provided fertile ground for women activists who challenged male dominance as well as the authorities of church, state, and capital. Nevertheless, because they called on their male colleagues to live up to their egalitarian ideals, women anarchists frequently found themselves in a complex relationship with their movement brothers, struggling to find a place for themselves within the larger movement.

Two Forms of Anarchism. Anarchism has shown itself in two major forms, generally referred to as individualist and collectivist/communist, although both shared origins in the works of Godwin and Pierre-Joseph Proudhon (1809–1865). The individualist tendency is best exemplified in the writings of Max Stirner (pseudonym of Johann Kaspar Schmidt, 1806–1856) and Benjamin R. Tucker (1854–1939). With the exception of those in the United States who refer to themselves as Libertarians, however, this strand has had rather limited implications for social movements. As the label implies, individualists tended to focus on opposition to authority of all sorts, and they were wary of any form of collective organization. By far the more influential form of anarchism was the collectivist/communalist school usually associated with Mikhail Bakunin (1814–1876), Peter Kropotkin (1842–1921), Errico Malatesta (1853–1932), and Emma Goldman (1869–1940), among others. It is this collectivist/communalist (sometimes referred to as libertarian socialist) tradition that provided the intellectual basis for most of the major anarchist social movements.

Anarchism of this tendency aims to create a society based on equality, mutuality, and reciprocity. Anarchists conceive of humans as fundamentally social beings who can realize themselves fully only in relationship with others and as participants in societies organized so as to maximize mutuality and cooperation. Power is corrupting; therefore,

Emma Goldman. This bust of Emma Goldman appeared in her first published book, *Anarchism and Other Essays* (1910). PRINTS AND PHOTOGRAPHS DIVISION, LIBRARY OF CONGRESS

the ideal society is one in which hierarchical power relationships are kept to an absolute minimum. This social vision is combined with a theory of social change that insists that means must be consistent with ends, that people cannot be directed or coerced into a future society, but must create it themselves, recognizing thereby their own abilities and capacities. The process of creating a new society thus must be one of personal as well as social transformation. For some anarchists, a focus on total transformation has been accompanied by a willingness to use violence to overthrow existing social and political structures, while others have rejected violence as inconsistent with the goal of a mutualist, egalitarian society. Finally, many anarchist writers and activists recognized the particular relevance to women of such broad-based opposition to hierarchical relationships, and they insisted that full human emancipation required not just the abolition of capitalism and of authoritarian political and religious institutions, but also the overcoming of women's cultural and economic subordination, both inside and outside the home.

There have been libertarian, antiauthoritarian aspects to many revolutionary moments, but anarchism as a social movement arose in Europe in the last third of the nineteenth century. Many scholars root it in the experience of and reactions to the Paris Commune, a community- and worker-based uprising in Paris from 18 March to 28 May 1871, at the end of the Franco-Prussian War, which rejected centralized authority and experimented with local autonomy, workers' control, free popular education, and women's rights. This experiment in popular empowerment is credited with giving rise to the concept of "propaganda by the deed," which originally meant not individual acts of terror, but seizing a town or community as a base for social revolution or, more generally, gaining adherents by the power of a positive example. Indeed, although the Commune was crushed by the forces of the central government, and many thousands of Communards were killed, deported, or imprisoned, the Commune inspired many, including Kropotkin and Malatesta, with the vision of a communally based, egalitarian society, and it created its own martyrs, among them Louise Michel (1830–1905). It also provided impetus for anarchist movements in Russia, Italy, and Spain, as well as in France.

Anarchists differed from Marxists—their main antagonists as theorists and organizers of social revolutionary activity—both with respect to the place of authority in a revolutionary movement and on the centrality of economic conflict to social change. As opposed to Marx, who treated economic class relations as the motive force of history and insisted that overcoming capitalism was key to human emancipation, Bakunin and his followers argued that the state and the church, among other institutions, had a power apart from capitalism and would need to be addressed directly. Thus anarchist movements tended to differ from socialist organizations by including a focus on struggles involving community-based mobilizations, cultural activities, and opposition to political authorities and the state, as well as on more traditional workplace-based union organizing.

Anarchism in Spain. Within Europe, Spain proved the context where anarchism had its greatest impact, broadest influence, and most significant consequences for women. Between 1874 (with the arrival of Bakunin's emissary, Giuseppi Fanelli) and 1939 (which marked the victory of the rebel generals in the Spanish civil war) anarchism flourished in many areas in Spain; indeed, Spain boasted the largest mass-based anarchist movement in the world. Though it is true that a major focus of the anarcho-syndicalist labor confederation (CNT, founded in 1910) was to organize workers into unions, workplace organizing was never the sole focus of the movement. Practically from the beginning, Spanish anarchists insisted that a truly revolutionary movement must speak to the variety of contexts in which people live and work. Thus the movement in Spain committed itself to education—both the education of young children and the adult education of workers—sending organizers into the fields to teach agricultural day laborers while they worked and organizing storefront schools and cultural centers to provide educational opportunities for workers in cities and villages. In addition, movement organizers supported various forms of community-based activism—for example, cost-of-living protests—in which women played major roles. Further, anarchist congresses beginning in 1872 declared that women ought to be fully the equals of men in the home and in the workplace. This goal was repeated frequently at subsequent congresses—even if male-dominated movement organizations rarely made women's equality a priority of their organizing. Additionally, an extensive network of anarchist journals, newspapers, books, and pamphlets addressed issues of sexual repression, the sexual double standard, and free love, issues to which women contributed actively along with men.

Impelled by the tension between these visions of equality and the reality of their status within Spanish society and within their movement, anarchist women in Madrid and Barcelona began forming groups of their own in the years between 1934 and 1936. Just before the outbreak of the Spanish civil war in July 1936, representatives began the process of forming what was to become Mujeres Libres, an organization devoted to overcoming women's "triple enslavement to capitalism, to ignorance, and as women." Although it lasted for less than three years, Mujeres Libres mobilized more than twenty thousand women and developed an extensive network of activities designed to empower individual women while building a sense of community.

Mujeres Libres insisted that the full development of women's individuality was dependent upon the development of a strong sense of connection with others. Its programs were based in a commitment to education, broadly speaking, demonstrating again its roots in the larger anarchist movement.

Mujeres Libres established literacy programs and schools on a variety of levels (located both in major centers in central Barcelona and Madrid and in storefronts in towns and villages throughout republican Spain); organized programs on health care, sexuality, and child care, for which there was tremendous need; worked together with unions to set up apprenticeship programs in a variety of industrial settings, designed to enable women to move into industry and to overcome the extreme sexual division of labor; mounted an extensive program of publications, including fourteen issues of a magazine (*Mujeres Libres*) directed to women both inside and outside the movement, regular contributions to anarchist movement newspapers and journals, and the publishing of a series of pamphlets and books on women's history and activism, child rearing, and other topics of interest to women; and worked with women, both individually and in small groups (analogous to consciousness-raising groups), to enable participants to gain confidence speaking in public. The women of Mujeres Libres attempted to maintain a delicate balance (one repeated in the experience of countless other anarchist and socialist women) between working together with the male-dominated organizations of the larger movement and simultaneously acting together with other women to address their specific needs as women. Although Mujeres Libres's insistence on its organizational autonomy was neither understood nor appreciated by most mainstream organizations, Mujeres Libres considered itself to be acting in consonance with long-standing anarchist traditions: a commitment to nonhierarchy (in the family and community, as well as at work) and sexual equality, and a recognition that "direct action" means taking action in whatever contexts are meaningful to people—if women were to recognize themselves, and be recognized by others, as fully equal members of a revolutionary community, they had to be free to determine for themselves their goals and strategies.

Mujeres Libres, however, stood alone in Europe as an autonomous anarchist women's organization. In Italy and in France, for example, both anarchist and socialist women too often found themselves forced to choose between male-dominated working-class organizations that insisted that women's subordination was only a secondary issue that would have to await the "morrow of the revolution" and a largely bourgeois feminist movement that ignored or minimized issues of class. In the United States, Emma Goldman and Voltairine de Cleyre (1866–1912) were exceptions: they offered specifically feminist/women's perspectives on the issues confronting working people and women in general and the U.S. anarchist movement in particular. But they were exceptions: Goldman and de Cleyre both struggled throughout their lives to have their ideas about women and about the importance of gender issues taken seriously by their male colleagues. Nevertheless, it is also the case that they worked closely with other radical women—such as Victoria Woodhull (1838–1927) and Margaret Sanger (1879–1966)—to address issues such as birth control and repressive notions of sexuality and to argue for free speech in a variety of arenas. In addition, women were very influential in the IWW, the anarcho-syndicalist Industrial Workers of the World, and women's community-based activism played a critical role in the IWW-led Lawrence (Massachusetts) strike in 1912. Thus, especially when organizing reached beyond the workplace, anarchist women played crucial roles.

Anarchism in Russia, Japan, and Latin America. The situation in Russia, site of a radical/populist movement in the last half of the nineteenth century, was both similar and different. The "woman question" had been on the agenda of Russian radicals since midcentury. In the 1860s and 1870s women participated along with men in the radical populist movement, although they struggled to be considered (or treated) fully as equals of the men. When Russian populists, some of them inspired by Bakunin, went to the peasantry in the 1870s, women were among those who dressed as peasants, worked in professional positions such as teachers, and engaged in "flying propaganda." And when the movement, frustrated with the lack of freedom to organize either peasants or urban workers, turned to terrorism—in the hope of wresting concessions from the state or sparking a peasant uprising—women like Sofia Perovskaia (1853–1881) and Vera Figner (1852–1942) were prominent among them. Anarchist women also played a substantial role in the revolutionary movements of 1905 and 1917. Nevertheless, these radicals were ruthlessly suppressed when the Bolsheviks consolidated power, most notably after the anarchist-inspired Kronstadt rebellion of 1921.

In Japan, although women were active participants in anarchist activities in the first third of the twentieth century, they also struggled with their comrades (as well as with the state) to be taken seriously as militant activists. Kanno Suga (1881–1911) and Ito Noe (1895–1923) were both involved in anarchist activism, although as journalists their involvement in politics mainly took the form of published political commentary on issues from a feminist perspective or on issues of particular concern to women. Both participated in revolutionary activities: Suga conspired with comrades to inspire a rebellion that would include an attempt to assassinate the Meiji emperor, and Noe was engaged with others in activism during a period of martial law after the Great Kanto Earthquake of 1923. They were not, however, considered as dangerous to the powers that be as were their male comrades. Instead, they were frequently belittled as "mad." Nevertheless, despite the efforts of many international anarchists (including Emma Goldman) to come to their defense, each insisted on her equal culpability (along with her male comrades), and each was executed for engaging in terrorist activities, Suga in 1911 and Noe in 1923.

The other major arena for anarchist women's activism (especially between 1880 and 1920, inspired by the Haymarket events in Chicago) was Latin America. The largest and most significant of these movements was in Argentina. Beginning roughly in the 1880s, European (largely Italian and Russian, but also Spanish) immigrants carried anarchist ideas and practices to Argentina. As in Spain, the movement developed a broad range of activities, including educational programs and cultural activities, along with workplace-based activism, that engaged women as well as men. Women orators were prominent among those speaking at major conferences, and women often outnumbered men at public meetings. By 1904, at least 4,000 of the 33,000 members of Argentina's anarchist movement (FORA, Federación Obrera Regional de Argentina) were women. Between 1896 and 1899 anarchist women published their own newspaper, *La voz de la mujer*, and in 1907 a feminist-anarchist league was established, representing one of the first instances in Latin America of the integration of feminist and revolutionary ideas and practices. As would *Mujeres Libres* some decades later, *La voz de la mujer* called on women to mobilize to overcome their oppression both as workers and as women. Anarchist women activists such as Anna María Mozzoni (1837–1920) drew connections among and between the various forms of male power—in the priesthood, the legislature, the factory, the home, and the brothel. Anarchist feminist agitators criticized marriage and advocated free love, for both women and men.

Workers' movements in Brazil and Chile were likewise heavily influenced by anarchist perspectives, and in Chile, activism extended considerably beyond union- and workplace-based organizing. As was the case elsewhere, anarchist attention to the cultural dimensions of workers' subordination made these movements particularly open to a focus on women's issues. Thus in Chile, particularly during the first decade of the twentieth century, anarchist organizations focused explicitly on women's subordination, and women often spoke along with men in some of the major gatherings and cultural festivals sponsored by the movement. Attention to the sexual double standard and the uses of sexuality to control both women and men were prominent features of their analyses. Conversely, the decline of radicalism in the 1920s, prompted by increased governmental repression as well as competition from Marxist unions, resulted in a retreat from gender radicalism and a decline in women's participation.

[*See also* Feminism; Free Love; Japan; Russia and Soviet Union; Spain and Portugal; *and biographical entries on women mentioned in this article.*]

BIBLIOGRAPHY

Ackelsberg, Martha. *Free Women of Spain: Anarchism and the Struggle for the Emancipation of Women*. Bloomington: Indiana University Press, 1991. 2d ed., Oakland, Calif.: AK Press, 2005. Examines the history and activities of Mujeres Libres within the context of the Spanish anarchist movement.

Avrich, Paul. *An American Anarchist: The Life of Voltairine de Cleyre*. Princeton, N.J.: Princeton University Press, 1978.

Avrich, Paul. *Anarchist Portraits*. Princeton, N.J.: Princeton University Press, 1988. Thoughtful essays on major anarchist figures, primarily from the United States and Europe.

Avrich, Paul. *The Russian Anarchists*. Princeton, N.J.: Princeton University Press, 1967. Discusses both the historical and the philosophical contexts of anarchist activism in Russia.

Bowen Raddeker, Hélene. *Treacherous Women of Imperial Japan: Patriarchal Fictions, Patricidal Fantasies*. London and New York: Routledge, 1997.

Delamotte, Eugenia. *Gates of Freedom: Voltairine de Cleyre and the Revolution of the Mind*. Ann Arbor: University of Michigan Press, 2004. Extended biographical essay accompanies an extensive selection of Cleyre's writings related to women, feminism, and sexuality.

Engel, Barbara Alpern, and Clifford N. Rosenthal, eds. *Five Sisters: Women against the Tsar*. New York: Alfred A. Knopf, 1975.

Falk, Candace. *Love, Anarchy, and Emma Goldman*. New York: Holt, Rinehart and Winston, 1984. A biography that focuses specifically on the tensions in Goldman's own life between her beliefs about equality and her complicated relationships with men.

Gomez, Alfredo. *Anarquismo y anarcosindicalismo en América Latina*. Paris: Ruedo Ibérico, 1980.

Moya, José. "Italians in Buenos Aires' Anarchist Movement: Gender Ideology and Women's Participation." In *Women, Gender, and Transnational Lives*, edited by Donna Gabaccia and Franca Iacovetta. Toronto: University of Toronto Press, 2002. Thoughtful discussion of the anarchist movement and women's place within it.

Wexler, Alice. *Emma Goldman in Exile: From the Russian Revolution to the Spanish Civil War*. Boston: Beacon Press, 1989.

MARTHA A. ACKELSBERG

ANDERSON, MARIAN (1897–1993), African American recitalist, opera singer, and diplomat. The contralto Marian Anderson was born on 27 February 1897 in Philadelphia, Pennsylvania. Her mother was a former teacher, and her father was an ice and coal salesman. With the aid of the tenor Roland Hayes, Anderson embarked on a concert singing career. Numerous concert and operatic singers of various races and generations have hailed Marian Anderson as their primary influence and inspiration for entering the world of music and seeking a singing career.

In her prime her contralto voice was deep and rich. Anderson was not the first African American to embark on a career as a concert singer. She was, however, the first to achieve true celebrity status across the Western world.

She studied with Giuseppe Boghetti and made her New York Town Hall debut in 1924. Her discomfort with foreign languages was apparent during her recital. When she contemplated ending her career before it had fully begun, Boghetti convinced her to continue her training. Anderson went to London in 1925, and she studied and performed throughout Europe for the next ten years. She sang before many of Europe's leading dignitaries and musicians. Numbered among them were the Archbishop of Salzburg, the conductor Arturo Toscanini, the Finnish composer Jean Sibelius, and the English composer Roger Quilter. Her return to New York's Town Hall in 1935 was a critical success.

Anderson attempted to perform at Constitution Hall in Washington, D.C. The Daughters of the American Revolution, as owners of the hall, refused to grant permission for Anderson's appearance. First Lady Eleanor Roosevelt resigned as a member of the Daughters of the American Revolution in protest, and the resulting media frenzy was a major embarrassment for the highly respected organization. With the aid of the Department of the Interior and Mrs. Roosevelt, the recital took place on the steps of the Lincoln Memorial on 9 April 1939. When Anderson stood in front of the Lincoln statue, her first piece was "My Country, 'Tis of Thee, Sweet Land of Liberty."

In 1954, although past her prime, Anderson debuted at the Metropolitan Opera as Ulrica in Verdi's *Un ballo in maschera*. Even though a younger artist of color might have had a better vocal facility, Anderson's presence gave the historic event more meaning and greater significance.

Anderson was awarded the Spingarn Award for outstanding achievement by an African American in 1938 by President Franklin Roosevelt and received the Presidential Medal of Freedom in 1963 from President Lyndon Johnson. She performed at the inaugurations of Presidents Eisenhower and Kennedy. She also served as a goodwill ambassador for the U.S. State Department from 1957 to 1958. She died on 8 April 1993 in Portland, Oregon, of congestive heart failure.

[*See also* Performing Arts *and* Roosevelt, Eleanor.]

BIBLIOGRAPHY

Abdul, Raoul. *Blacks in Classical Music: A Personal History*. New York: Dodd, Mead, 1977.

Anderson, Marian. *My Lord, What a Morning*. New York: Viking Press, 1956.

Story, Rosalyn M. *And So I Sing: African-American Divas of Opera and Concert*. New York: Warner Books, 1990.

DARRYL GLENN NETTLES

ANDROGYNY. Stemming from the Greek words for "male" and "female," the term "androgyny" is commonly designated as the union of sexes in one individual or a personality with a balance of masculine and feminine attributes, although variations from these common definitions occurred even in ancient Greece, where it was occasionally used in reference to cowardly, impotent, or even castrated men. The tendency to associate the term with gender rather than sex becomes more prominent in its modern usage.

The concept of androgyny has pervaded religions all over the world since ancient times. Divinities in numerous religions are called "Father and Mother," embodying an incorporation of both paternal and maternal instincts. Such "divine androgyny" is often projected in the imagery of bisexuality: in ancient Caria people worshiped a bearded Zeus with six breasts, in Cyprus there emerged a cult of bearded Aphrodite, and in Italy tribute was paid to a bald Venus. Such androgynous gods can be traced to numerous religions in the world from ancient Germany to Polynesia. Although Judeo-Christian religion is often taken as patriarchal, with its worship of an omnipresent male god as the prototype for all human beings, the androgynous motif abounds in Gnosticism and the religious stories outside the official Scriptures. In one such tale the Lord proclaims the arrival of his kingdom when the male and female become one. Likewise, several ancient rabbinical explanatory notes on the Scriptures take Adam as an archetype of androgyny, being born back to back with Eve.

Ancient China. Philosophically, androgyny is most akin to some Asian thinking, particularly to Taoism, a philosophy that preached a nonaggressive approach to life and politics during the Warring States period (475–221 B.C.E). Incorporating the feminine principle to redress a predominance of masculine attitudes in an age of war, Taoism preaches a union of the masculine and the feminine in molding one's identity. A quintessential Taoist image is water, which yields to anything it encounters and yet wears down the most solid stone. Ostensibly a self-effacing force, but essentially an energy loaded with power, water encapsulates the hidden strength in femininity, the yang substance in a yin entity. Although Confucianism is partially responsible for the misogyny in ancient China, it upholds some holistic values, particularly the doctrine of the Mean, which stipulates a yin-yang balance in a person. Thus an ideal Confucian ruler should be endowed with both paternal and maternal attributes, combining the female gentleness and compassion with male strength and intellect. Although the traditional Buddhist attitude regards women as temptresses or evil incarnate, challenge to such prejudice is visible in a theme popular in Mahayana Buddhist texts, where female apostles often achieve Buddhahood through metaphorical sexual transformation. The Buddhist conviction in the ultimate insubstantiality of the phenomenal world

Androgyny. An Amazon with a bow, Greece, c. 300 B.C.E. MUSEI CAPITOLINI, ROME/ALINARI/ART RESOURCE, NY

gives rise to a more egalitarian outlook that takes all notions of sexuality as mental attachment and ascertains potentials for enlightenment in every sentient being, thus transcending the culturally dictated gender dichotomy.

Greece. The most direct expression of androgyny in world philosophy is found in the writings of the Greek philosopher Plato. In the *Symposium*, Plato, through Aristophanes, mentions the existence of three primordial races, one of which is made of the union between men and women. Although the united body is later split by God into halves of different sexes, each seeks the other, yearning for the original whole. The chase after androgyny that Plato projects here turns out to be one of the most powerful inspirations in stimulating the ideal of androgyny in human history.

Just as in Plato's philosophical writings, androgyny emerges as a recurrent motif in Greek mythology, although with varying degrees of acceptance. Praise of the androgynous ideal is prominent in the characterization of Athena, an important Olympian deity from whose name is derived that of the city of Athens. With her multiple identity as a goddess of war, a goddess of peace, and a patron of crafts, especially spinning and weaving, Athena personifies strength and power as well as mercy and domestic art, a sublime union of the masculine and the feminine. The fact that the Parthenon, a masterpiece of Greek architecture, was erected in Athens as her temple in the fifth century B.C.E. testifies to the general acceptance of the dual-gender role that she embodies. A less sympathetic attitude, however, is revealed in the attitude toward the Amazons, a tribe of warlike women who repeatedly appear in ancient Geek art and literature. Amazons are believed to have once invaded Athens, although it remains an open question whether this happened in history or merely in myth. The Amazon's affinity to androgyny lies in the fact that she is beautiful and seductive, yet dominant over men and thirsty for conquest. The general belief that as an archer she cuts off her right breast to accommodate the bow bespeaks a symbolic rejection of a pure feminine identity and an incorporation of a masculine element as her dominant principle. Although often taken as a reflection of Athena, unlike Athena, who becomes an instrument of her father, Zeus, the Amazons refuse to submit to the male will. They are finally defeated in Greek mythology, most likely because the gender inversion that they embody poses a threat to the patriarchal social order. In contemporary thinking the Amazon is often associated with radical feminism or with women who adopt the masculine principle but reject their native femininity.

Mulan. A mortal version of androgyny is celebrated in the characterization of Hua Mulan, the heroine in a Chinese ballad of the Six Dynasties (450–589), whose validity in history some scholars have tried to establish. To help her aging father fulfill a military duty, Mulan joins the army masquerading as a man. When she returns home after years of military service she puts on her female clothes and happily marries her man. Her smooth transition between masculine and feminine roles that are both endorsed by a patriarchal culture establishes Mulan as the prototype of Chinese androgyne. Nearly every dynasty in Chinese history produced women warriors, but Mulan remains the best-known hero among women. Moreover, as a male impersonator she has transcended in the Chinese mind the role of a female soldier to personify deviations from sexual norms in virtually any aspect of female life. In literature and art, therefore, Mulan's imagery can be associated with a woman warrior on the battlefield, a female scholar often donning male garments and competing with men in the exam halls, or a frantic maiden who defies patriarchal decrees of boudoir confinement in reckless pursuit of love. Mulan thus has become a symbol of androgyny par excellence.

Cross-dressing masquerade, as a vehicle for gender freedom, was historically adopted by Chinese women in premodern society when they were barred from serving in officialdom. Unofficial histories from the third to the fifth centuries repeatedly record cases of women masquerading as men to serve in the court. Their examples inspired women of later generations to break the cultural codes of boudoir confinement in search of a fuller life.

Elizabethan England. In the West, England witnessed a trend of gender ambiguity akin to androgyny in the late sixteenth century, when Elizabeth I (r. 1558–1603) wielded authority that traditionally belonged to men. It is said that when she visited her troops in 1584 Elizabeth remarked that she knew she had the body of a weak and feeble woman, but she had the heart and stomach of a king. As if to respond to the gender ambiguity in the court, some Elizabethan women took the liberty of dressing in men's clothing and roamed the London streets. It may not be a coincidence that Shakespeare, writing during this period, created such androgynous characters in his plays as Portia in *The Merchant of Venice*, Rosalind in *As You Like It*, and Viola in *Twelfth Night*.

Seventeenth-Century China. A cult of androgyny emerged in the courtesan culture of seventeenth-century China. Providing spiritual companionship to the literati scholars outside their arranged marriages, Chinese courtesans were expected to master the skills that traditionally belonged to men, such as poetry, calligraphy, painting, and chess. Their close companionship with male scholars further fostered in them a male value, political enthusiasm, which blazed in their heroic martyrdom in the patriotic movement against an alien regime in the mid-seventeenth century. A prominent case can be found in Liu Rushi (1618–1664), one of the most accomplished courtesans of the time. Donning male garments and rubbing elbows with the most renowned literati of the day, she drank and composed poems with them, romantically courting them, often passing as a man. After a dynastic change when China was subjugated to alien rule, she urged her husband to die a martyr's death. Failing that, she engaged herself in the patriotic movement of resistance. Talented in poetic skills, active in romantic pursuit, and heroic in political action, the glamorous courtesans embody in women the most admirable male qualities and epitomize the ideal of androgyny in late imperial China. They became a cultural icon frequently eulogized in Chinese literature during this period.

Twentieth-Century Theories and Practices. It was not until the first decade of the twentieth century that scientific study in the West began to explore and theorize androgyny. Based on the biological science of his time, the Austrian psychiatrist and neurologist Sigmund Freud (1856–1939) asserted the biological origin of bisexuality in human beings, namely, there exist both maleness and femaleness in everybody. Applying his theory to psychology, his student Carl Gustav Jung (1875–1961), a Swiss psychologist and psychiatrist, postulated feminine elements (*anima*) in the male unconscious and masculine elements (*animas*) in the female, and that a combination of both gender attributes makes a fuller personality. In divorcing gender from sex Jung became a pioneer theoretician on androgyny.

Among Freud's and Jung's contemporaries a modern version of androgyny was practiced by the Bloomsbury group, a circle of liberal-minded and talented English writers during the 1920s and 1930s. The members of this group shared a common belief in the value of androgyny, which they consciously applied to their lives and literary creations. To reject conventional sex-typed norms and sexual taboos, nearly all the members of this group involved themselves in both homosexual and heterosexual relationships. The Bloomsbury group demonstrated a high degree of intellectual rationality in its moral rejection of World War I amid a nationalistic war fever, but it was a rationality that rejected violence, not passion. The group's affirmation of both rationality and emotionality constitutes a salient inclination of androgyny. At the center of this group was Virginia Woolf (1882–1941) whose famous remarks in *A Room of One's Own* (1929) on a writer's androgynous mind—that a writer must "be woman-manly or man-womanly" before the act of creation—virtually serve as an androgynous aesthetic principle for this group. Not surprisingly, androgynous characters emerge in Woolf's writings as well as those of the other members of the group.

America experienced a new, intense awareness of androgyny upon the publication of June Singer's influential book *Androgyny: Toward a New Theory of Sexuality* (1976), which researched the whole sphere of human knowledge to reaffirm androgyny in the human psyche. Inspired by the feminist thinking of her time, Singer drew from Jung's theory a possible vehicle to rectify the gender polarization in contemporary society. The book triggered widespread interest in androgyny; in the ten years after its publication hundreds of monographs were written in the English language examining androgyny in various aspects of human life. Although the androgyny craze met with objection from the antifeminist camp with its insistence on sexual dichotomy as well as from some feminists who saw a presupposed sexual differentiation in the very notion of androgyny, many feminists perceived in androgyny a potential movement toward gender equality. They have modified Singer's notion of androgyny and then incorporated it into their cause as a feminist ideal. Yet most feminists are aware that to realize an androgynous society calls for a radical reorganization of domestic, political, and other institutions, and they do not see this reorganization on the horizon.

[*See also* Amazons; Elizabeth I of England; Femininity/Masculinity; Feminism; Mulan; Transgender/Transsexual; *and* Woolf, Virginia.]

BIBLIOGRAPHY

Eliade, Mircea. *The Two and the One*. Translated by J. M. Cohen. Chicago: University of Chicago Press, 1979.

Heilbrun, Carolyn G. *Toward a Recognition of Androgyny*. New York: Knopf, 1973.
Singer, June. *Androgyny: Toward a New Theory of Sexuality*. Garden City, N.Y.: Anchor Press, 1976.
Zhou, Zuyan. *Androgyny in Late Ming and Early Qing Literature*. Honolulu: University of Hawai'i Press, 2003.

ZUYAN ZHOU

ANGELOU, MAYA (b. 1928), critically acclaimed autobiographer, playwright, poet, and director. Born Marguerite Johnson on 4 April 1928, Maya Angelou is the only daughter of Bailey and Vivian Johnson. Revered for transcending the limitations and restrictions placed upon black women throughout her life, Angelou has created a model worthy of emulation by her readers. Although Angelou is known primarily for her success as the author of five autobiographies, she has also been recognized for her various significant historical contributions, including her service in the civil rights movement as northern coordinator of the Southern Christian Leadership Conference at the invitation of Dr. Martin Luther King Jr. Angelou's autobiographical series highlights her experiences as a black woman working to define herself as a poet and autobiographer; as a dancer, actress, director, screenwriter, and member of the Director's Guild of the American Film Institute; as a journalist and playwright.

Among many firsts, Angelou was San Francisco's first black streetcar conductor, Hollywood's first black woman director, and the United States' first woman and first African American to recite her own work at a presidential inauguration (in 1993). Angelou's career as a playwright and stage entertainer has included Off-Broadway performances, a Broadway debut in 1973's *Look Away*, and the direction of her own play *And Still I Rise* in 1976. Angelou, who has taught at the University of California and the University of Kansas, as well as the University of Ghana, among other places, has been a Rockefeller Foundation Scholar and a Yale University Fellow. She currently holds the lifetime position of Z. Smith Reynolds Professor of American Studies at Wake Forest University in Winston-Salem, North Carolina.

Angelou was once quoted as saying, "I speak to the black experience, but I am always talking about the human condition—about what we can endure, dream, fail at, and still survive." In her first and best-known autobiography, *I Know Why the Caged Bird Sings* (1969), "the Maya character" traverses the razor-sharp ironies of her black and female childhood, including abandonment by her parents, being raped by her mother's boyfriend at eight years of age, and the wounds inflicted by everyday racism and poverty. Yet even after an unwanted teenage pregnancy, Angelou emerges as a "formidable character." In addition to *Caged Bird*, she is also the author of *Gather Together in My Name* (1974), *Singin' and Swingin' and Gettin' Merry Like Christmas* (1976), *The Heart of a Woman* (1981), *All God's Children Need Traveling Shoes* (1986), as well as volumes of poetry and essays, and even a cookbook.

Angelou has suggested that she belongs to "a generation of women writers, writing in desperation to identify themselves and their times, to provide encouragement and direction." The body of her work speaks to the importance of remembering one's past, healing one's pain, and looking toward one's future. Consciously aware of her role as a phenomenal female image maker, Angelou presents her readers with the opportunity to meet the real joys and sorrows that are a part of the black female experience—and indeed, the human experience. More broadly, Angelou continually uses her creativity to celebrate her personal mantra, "I believe all things are possible for a human being, and I don't think there's anything in the world I can't do." Taken all together, the body of Maya Angelou's work lifts, inspires, and motivates other women, and especially African American women, to transcend the mundane and celebrate their "phenomenal" spirits and "formidable" characters. Her works have been translated into many languages.

[*See also* Brooks, Gwendolyn; Hurston, Zora Neale; Literature; Morrison, Toni; *and* Walker, Alice.]

BIBLIOGRAPHY

Braxton, Joanne M. "Maya Angelou." In *Modern American Women Writers*, edited by Elaine Showalter, Lea Baechler, and A. Walton Litz, pp. 1–8. New York: Scribner's, 1991.
Braxton, Joanne M. "A Song of Transcendence: Maya Angelou." In her *Black Women Writing Autobiography: A Tradition within a Tradition*, pp. 181–201. Philadelphia: Temple University Press, 1989.
Braxton, Joanne M. "Symbolic Geography and Psychic Landscapes: A Conversation with Maya Angelou." In *Maya Angelou's "I Know Why the Caged Bird Sings": A Casebook*, edited by Joanne M. Braxton, pp. 3–20. New York: Oxford University Press, 1999.
Tate, Claudia. "Maya Angelou: An Interview." In *Maya Angelou's "I Know Why the Caged Bird Sings": A Casebook*, edited by Joanne M. Braxton, pp. 149–158. New York: Oxford University Press, 1999.

JOANNE M. BRAXTON AND COURTNEY M. O'REILLY

ANGUISSOLA, SOFONISBA (c. 1532–1625), Italian portraitist at the Spanish court of Philip II. Widely celebrated in Renaissance Europe for her lifelike portraits, Anguissola fell into obscurity for more than three hundred years. The seminal 1976 exhibition "Women Artists, 1550–1950" at the Los Angeles County Museum of Art ignited a strong interest in Anguissola. Since then, she has been the subject of many journal articles, a book-length biography, and an exhibition seen in both Italy and the United States. She is often credited with introducing scenes of daily life into Italian portraiture and with helping to establish painting as a respectable pursuit for upper-class women.

Anguissola's elite status gave her privileged access to invaluable educational and social opportunities. One of seven children born to a family of minor nobility in the Italian city of Cremona, Anguissola acquired elegant social graces and studied both liberal and fine arts. Although her gender barred her from the workshop and apprentice system that shaped most painters' educations, the adolescent Anguissola studied drawing and oil painting with Bernardino Campi (1522–1591) and other local artists. Later, she sketched antique and contemporary treasures in Rome, where she met and exchanged drawings with Michelangelo.

Respecting conventions of domestic femininity, Anguissola spent her twenties painting primarily self-portraits and portraits of members of her family circle. Despite this limited range of sitters, her best-known early work, *The Chess Game* (1555), broke new ground in Italian portraiture by enlivening its formal traditions with a playful conceit. This group portrait depicts in painstaking detail the rich clothes, ornate embroidery, and fine jewelry of three elaborately dressed Anguissola sisters standing around a chessboard, accompanied by a servant. In a rare mention of a female artist, Giorgio Vasari, the first biographer of Renaissance artists, praised this painting in the second (1568) version of his *Le vite de' più eccellenti architetti, pittori, et scultori italiani* (translated centuries later as *Lives of the Most Excellent Painters, Sculptors, and Architects*).

Anguissola reached the apex of her career in 1559, when she was invited to join the court of Philip II of Spain as lady-in-waiting to Queen Isabel of Valois and attendant to Princess Isabella. Anguissola served as art tutor to the queen until Isabel's death in 1568, and as court artist for nearly twenty years. Her portraits of the Spanish royal family and members of their court are, fittingly, more formal than her renderings of friends and relatives. Many feature standing frontal poses and achieve stunning levels of sartorial detail.

After the death of her first husband, whom she had married in 1570 or 1571, Anguissola returned to Italy around 1580. There, in addition to painting members of the Italian and Spanish nobility, she took up serious religious painting for the first time. She remarried in 1584 and lived the remainder of her life in Genoa and then in the Sicilian city of Palermo. In 1624 the Flemish painter Anthony Van Dyck met and sketched the elderly Anguissola at her Sicilian home. Van Dyck's notebooks record his impressions as a young artist paying homage to an esteemed predecessor.

[*See also* Art and Architecture.]

Family Portrait. The painter's three sisters and a servant play chess. Painting by Sofonisba Anguissola, 1555. Muzeum Narodowe, Poland/Erich Lessing/Art Resource, NY

BIBLIOGRAPHY

Ferino-Pagden, Sylvia, and Maria Kusche. *Sofonisba Anguissola: A Renaissance Woman.* Washington, D.C.: National Museum of Women in the Arts, 1995. This slender publication accompanied the exhibition of the same name at the National Museum of Women in the Arts in 1995. It derives from the significantly larger catalog *Sofonisba Anguissola e le Sorelle*, published in conjunction with the exhibition's original appearance in Italy, which is the most extensive volume on the artist.

Perlingieri, Ilya Sandra. *Sofonisba Anguissola: The First Great Woman Artist of the Renaissance.* New York: Rizzoli, 1992. This biography, intended for nonspecialist readers, offers close analyses of many paintings and thorough discussions of the art, culture, and politics of Renaissance Italy. The result of sixteen years of research, this book is the first to incorporate many archival documents concerning Anguissola's twenty-year stay at the court of Philip II in Spain.

LAURA AURICCHIO

ANSCOMBE, ELIZABETH (1919–2001), English philosopher. Gertrude Elizabeth Mary Anscombe was the daughter of Gertrude Elizabeth Anscombe and Alan Wells Anscombe, who taught science at Dulwich College in London. Like Dulwich College, Sydenham High School, where Elizabeth Anscombe received her initial schooling, is a privately financed, competitive admissions, sex-segregated institution. From the beginning, then, Anscombe benefited from privileged educational opportunities. After Sydenham, Anscombe went on to St. Hugh's College, Oxford. There she studied classics and philosophy and graduated with First Class Honors in 1941. As a postgraduate student she started as a research fellow at St. Hugh's and went on to a research fellowship at Newnham College, Cambridge, in 1942.

During her student years Anscombe formed two relationships that were decisive for her personal and professional life. Having converted to Roman Catholicism, she not coincidentally met Peter Geach (b. 1916), also a Catholic convert and a philosopher. They married in 1941 and had seven children. While at Newnham College, Anscombe attended Ludwig Wittgenstein's lectures (he was professor of philosophy at Cambridge from 1939 to 1947). Convinced of the importance of his novel philosophical method, Anscombe commuted from Oxford to Cambridge to attend Wittgenstein's classes after returning to Oxford to take up a research fellowship at Somerville College. She became Wittgenstein's lifelong friend, the trusted translator of a number of his works, and ultimately one of his literary executors. Anscombe held a series of fellowships at Somerville College, Oxford, from 1946 until 1970 when she was appointed to the chair in philosophy at Cambridge University, the same position that Wittgenstein had held.

In 1953, two years after Wittgenstein's death, Anscombe's superb translation of his watershed book, *Philosophical Investigations*, appeared. Additional translations of Wittgenstein's work appeared regularly for the next fifteen years. In 1959, Anscombe published *An Introduction to Wittgenstein's Tractatus*, an examination of Wittgenstein's first philosophical position, which was superseded by the views propounded in the *Philosophical Investigations*.

In 1957, Anscombe published her most important book. *Intention* is a classic that is widely credited with founding the field of philosophy of action. Anscombe applies Wittgenstein's method of analyzing "language games"—the way words are used in ordinary conversation—to the problem of distinguishing intentional action from other forms of behavior, such as involuntary reflexes and idle movements. In the case of intentional action, it is always appropriate to pose the question, "Why?", because actions are intentional when the people acting have reasons for what they are doing. In addition, Anscombe points out that the "direction of fit" between thought and action differs depending on whether one is acting or observing action. For the agent, the aim is to change the world in order to bring it into alignment with one's desire. For the observer, the aim is to ensure that one's representation is in alignment with the way the world is, and one must change one's representation if there is a discrepancy. Another key contribution is Anscombe's observation that action is "intentional under a description." There are many ways to characterize any act, but it does not follow that the agent intended what is implied in all of those characterizations. It is only under the description that captures one's reasons for acting that one's action is intentional. *Intention* concludes with a trenchant critical commentary on Aristotle's cryptic account of practical reasoning.

"Modern Moral Philosophy" (*Philosophy* 33, no. 124 [January 1958]) is Anscombe's principal contribution to ethics. Once again, Aristotle is her touchstone. This essay rejects the Kantian and Utilitarian focus on duty and obligation together with their project of codifying morality in definitive standards of right and wrong. It argues that philosophers ought to be asking how to live well and to that end ought to be centering on issues concerning character, virtue, flourishing, and moral psychology.

As a teacher, Anscombe was renowned for her formidable intellect, combative style, and dauntingly high standards. Philippa Foot (b. 1920), a distinguished philosopher who was first a student and then a colleague of Anscombe's at Somerville College, describes what it was like to talk philosophy with Anscombe: "Naturally, I was regularly defeated. But I would be there objecting away, the next week. It was like in those old children's comics where a steamroller runs over a character who becomes flattened—an outline on the ground—but is there all right in the next episode."

Anscombe was intimidating to students, yet they appreciated the long hours that she spent discussing philosophy with them in their common room. Bearing in mind that most of Anscombe's academic career predated the women's liberation movement of the late 1960s and the 1970s, her success both as a mother and as a scholar was exceptional and provided a role model for a number of her female students. Anscombe's nonconformity with respect to social mores was remarkable as well. At a time when gender norms were narrow and rigid—for example, women were required to wear skirts when dining in the men's colleges at Oxford—she usually dressed in pants and smoked cigars and pipes. Altogether, she cut a uniquely gender-bending figure in the English academic world of her time.

As a social activist, Anscombe was guided by her religious beliefs, which were not necessarily congruent with official Catholic doctrine. She opposed Britain's entry into World War II on the grounds that fighting the war would certainly involve killing noncombatants. When Oxford decided to award the U.S. president Harry Truman an honorary degree in 1956, Anscombe protested vigorously, arguing that the atomic bombing of innocent civilians at Hiroshima and Nagasaki disqualified him for such an honor. In 1961, Anscombe collaborated with five other Catholic scholars to publish *Nuclear Weapons and the Christian Conscience.* This collection of essays launches a sustained critique of the Cold War arms race and the policy of mutually assured destruction (MAD) that the United States and the Soviet Union maintained. Stridently anti-Communist, the Roman Catholic Church did not advocate disarmament, and no Catholic press would publish this volume.

Anscombe's other great cause was sexual and reproductive morality. Her 1972 essay "Contraception and Chastity" is well known among conservative Catholics and has inspired a group of Princeton University students to form the Anscombe Society, which is dedicated to opposing campus promiscuity and advocating sexual abstinence outside of marriage. The same belief in the sanctity of human life that fueled Anscombe's opposition to war and nuclear weapons led to her antiabortion activism in the early 1990s. Convinced that life begins at conception, she participated in sit-ins at abortion clinics and was arrested.

Anscombe retired from her chair at Cambridge University in 1986. She died in Cambridge in 2001. Her standing among the great twentieth-century philosophers is beyond question.

[*See also* Education; Philosophy; *and* Scholars and Scholarship.]

BIBLIOGRAPHY

Anscombe, G. E. M. *Collected Papers.* 3 vols. Oxford: Oxford University Press, 2002.

Anscombe, G. E. M. *Intention.* 2d edition. Cambridge, Mass.: Harvard University Press, 2000.

Anscombe, G. E. M. *An Introduction to Wittgenstein's Tractatus.* London: Hutchinson, 1959.

Dolan, John M. "G.E.M. Anscombe: Living the Truth." http://www.firstthings.com/ftissues/ft0105/opinion/dolan.html. 2001.

Foot, Philippa. "The Grammar of Goodness: An Interview with Philippa Foot." http://personal.lse.ac.uk/voorhoev/Foot.pdf. 2003.

Monk, Ray. *Ludwig Wittgenstein: The Duty of Genius.* New York: Free Press, 1990. Biography that documents Anscombe's relationship to Wittgenstein.

O'Grady, June. "Obituary: Elizabeth Anscombe." http://www.guardian.co.uk/Archive/Article/0,4273,4115443,00.html. 2001.

Wittgenstein, Ludwig. *Philosophical Investigations.* Translated by G. E. M. Anscombe. 3d edition. London: Sheed and Ward, 2001.

DIANA TIETJENS MEYERS

ANTHONY, SUSAN B. (1820–1906), leading American woman suffragist. Susan B. Anthony was born in Massachusetts, the second of eight children. In 1826 her father moved the family to New York, eventually settling in Rochester. The children were raised with Quaker beliefs and were well educated.

Anthony initially used her education in the teaching profession. Her work experiences, especially the differential treatment of men and women as teachers, aroused her interest in labor issues and women's rights. After ten years in teaching she left the profession and returned to Rochester. Through acquaintances there such as Frederick Douglass and William Lloyd Garrison, she became involved in reform.

Her first public speech, in 1849, was for a temperance group. In 1856 she was recruited by Garrison to speak in New York City on behalf of the abolitionist movement. However, frustrated by the fact that women's roles were limited in these groups, she became increasingly interested in women's rights.

In 1851 Anthony met Elizabeth Cady Stanton. The two formed a partnership that was invaluable to the women's rights movement in the United States. Stanton was the writer of the pair; she said that she crafted the thunderbolts and Anthony threw them. Anthony proved to be a politic organizer and tireless speaker, described as the Napoleon of the woman suffrage movement.

At the close of the Civil War Anthony joined with other reformers to pursue civil rights for both freed African Americans and women. She published the newspaper the *Revolution.* However, while Anthony reminded men to "remember the women by your side, and secure to them all you claim for yourselves," by 1869 many were focusing on suffrage rights only for freedmen and setting aside efforts for women. In response, Anthony and Stanton founded the National Woman Suffrage Association (NWSA). The group held annual conventions in Washington, D.C., and sought a federal amendment for the enfranchisement of women.

Susan B. Anthony. Photograph by Mrs. L. Condon, c. 1900. PRINTS AND PHOTOGRAPHS DIVISION, LIBRARY OF CONGRESS

Through extensive travel to lecturing engagements throughout the country, Anthony became a celebrity. In a federal criminal case, brought after Anthony voted in 1872, the judge—without consulting the jury—handed down a guilty verdict that upheld states' rights to disfranchise women. In her courtroom response, Anthony said the verdict "trampled under foot every vital principle of our government."

In later years Anthony worked to consolidate national and international efforts to expand women's rights. With Stanton and others, she compiled the monumental *History of Woman Suffrage*. She helped organize the International Council of Women in 1888. In 1890 Anthony worked to mend post–Civil War rifts with the union of the NWSA and the American Woman Suffrage Association. She became president of the resultant National American Woman Suffrage Association (NAWSA) in 1892, a position she held until 1900.

Although Anthony never had children, she served as a mentor to younger women in the woman suffrage movement. In later years she faced criticism from both radicals and conservatives, but dedication to "Aunt Susan" often united the movement. Attending her final NAWSA convention in 1906, she left members with the message "failure is impossible." The Nineteenth Amendment, which gave all American women the vote, was later called the Susan B. Anthony amendment.

[*See also* Feminism, *subentry* Comparative History; Nineteenth Amendment; Stanton, Elizabeth Cady; Suffrage; *and* Suffragettes.]

BIBLIOGRAPHY

Barry, Kathleen. *Susan B. Anthony: A Biography of a Singular Feminist.* New York: New York University Press, 1988.

Gordon, Ann D., ed. *Selected Papers of Elizabeth Cady Stanton and Susan B. Anthony.* 4 vols. New Brunswick, N.J.: Rutgers University Press, 1997– . Meticulously edited work that discusses both the history of Anthony's role in the suffrage movement and her partnership with Stanton.

Harper, Ida Husted. *The Life and Work of Susan B. Anthony.* 3 vols. 1898–1908. Reprint. Salem, N.H.: Ayer, 1983.

Stanton, Elizabeth Cady, Susan B. Anthony, and Matilda Joslyn Gage, eds. *History of Woman Suffrage.* 6 vols. New York: Fowler and Wells, 1881–1922. Reprint. New York: Source Book Press, 1970. Still one of the richest histories of the movement.

LESLEY L. DOIG

ANTIFEMINISM. Antifeminism was the response to changes or threats of change that resulted from feminist reform movements. Antifeminism included the articulation of theories, as well as efforts to shape and enforce public policy, that would perpetuate the patriarchal gender system prevalent throughout developed and developing nations from the nineteenth century to the present. In developing nations in the twentieth century the debate over women's status and rights produced a variety of feminisms appropriate to the diversity among cultures; advocates of women's equality in colonized nations struggled to maintain the integrity of their nationalism. Antifeminists in developing nations indicted Third World feminists as dupes or subversive agents of colonialism for wanting Western-style rights. Some antifeminists argued that biology was destiny for women, or that women's subordination was a religious or cultural value essential to the nation. They argued that traditional women's roles within the gender system of their culture were sacrosanct aspects of a historical identity. Thus, although many feminists joined movements for national liberation, at independence they found themselves without either the promised vote or equal rights.

The history of antifeminism in modern Europe was influenced by the French Revolution, the aftermath of World War I—specifically the rise of fascism—and the devastating impact of World War II. The political and economic effects of the major events of this era created a hazardous

Anti-Suffrage Movement. An early-twentieth-century British poster portrays the house of a suffragette who has neglected her family. MUSEUM OF LONDON/HIP/ART RESOURCE, NY

landscape for the advocates of women's rights. Leaders of the French Revolution oversaw the execution of outspoken women such as Olympe de Gouges, and the subsequent Napoleonic Code stripped women of a whole range of rights, including the right to their own wages. The loss of men in World War I accompanied the increased presence of women in education and the civilian labor force, in the professions as well as in particular occupations on the military front.

In many countries women had received the vote by the 1920s. The interwar period produced a fleeting presence of women in politics, and activist women in Europe increased their participation in international movements for peace and workers' rights, just as feminists in the United States had done before World War I. Fascist governments were based on trouncing women's activism and feminist activities in the 1920s. They reasserted the domestic role for women and generally removed women from good jobs such as those in the civil service. Under fascism, defense of the gender system made it women's patriotic duty to subordinate themselves to men.

Many of these values persisted in Europe after World War II, even though there was a brief and temporary upsurge of women in government. During the Cold War, paralleling the contemporary antifeminism of the 1950s in the United States, removing women from public life and the workforce became a symbol of democracy; only in Communist countries, it was said, were women found in the workplace. Antifeminism was particularly strong in West Germany, where the fundamental laws and policies of the new state actually mirrored those of fascism when it came to reviving domesticity. Laws about grocery stores, for instance, restricted the times they could be open, making it impossible for working women to shop for their families. States opposed contraception and reproductive rights, women's sexual autonomy and sexual preference, and reform of married women's legal rights, and they failed to protect women against violence in the home and on the streets. They also opposed international ecofeminism and peace and antinuclear movements. State socialism masked the presence of feminist issues in the Eastern bloc until the fall of Communism brought the shift to capitalist democracy. The gender system endured all such changes in Europe and prompted feminist criticism and activism in the 1990s with varied results.

Antifeminist Activism. Antifeminism was distinguishable from the pervasive misogyny that supported patriarchal assumptions about women as different and lesser than men. Antifeminism emerged specifically in response to feminism and feminist reform movements. Antifeminists generally championed the maintenance of patriarchy and the perpetuation of the gender system in response to social change or modernization that enabled or promoted women's autonomy, most vividly from the last third of the nineteenth century. Reform activity that challenged either the subordination of women to men or the patriarchal limitation of women's status provoked an antifeminist response that included an intellectual and political campaign to halt progress toward women's rights and equality. Regardless of particular historical context, antifeminist campaign spokespersons were women and men who represented the spectrum of society, but especially the pious and the elite: academics, writers, members of conservative think tanks, popular authors, religious leaders and local politicians, middle- and upper-class women who were dabbling in the activism that they decried when feminists entered the public discourse or activism.

Various movements for women's rights in the nineteenth century had produced organized and concerted feminist group activity that in turn incited antifeminist response from individuals and organized groups. Contemporary popularity of few antifeminist leaders, advocates or organizations seldom brought lasting historical notoriety to their efforts to ridicule proposed feminist reforms or their arguments that divine ordinance of the gender system was bolstered by significant biological gender differences, or an a priori assertion of baneful consequences to society should feminist challenges to patriarchal authority prevail. Among the well-published nineteenth-century antifeminists, the clergyman Samuel Warren Dike (1839–1913) defended the gender system in his efforts to preserve the family and through his New England Divorce Reform League; the Roman Catholic Cardinal James Gibbons (1834–1921) advanced his public proclamations that women's public activities outside the home constituted their abandonment of their families. The English journalist and novelist and frequent contributor to the *Saturday Review* Eliza Litton (1822–1898) launched a campaign in 1883 with the publication of a collection of her essays that attacked the New Woman and feminism.

Feminist reform efforts tried to develop women's self-consciousness, encouraged women's questioning of (male) authority, and promoted the establishment of a sense of and commitment to community among women as the means of fostering women's autonomy and emancipation. Provoked by this prospect, opponents voiced their concerns about the particular nineteenth-century issues of the women's rights movement and all topics related to the social discernment, articulation, and enforcement of the proper role and status of women.

In the United States and Britain, feminism addressed the impact of married women's status under coverture, which rendered each married woman "civilly dead" and without legal identity, women's economic dependence on men, and the lack of a separate identity for each woman; these issues as well as woman suffrage and dress reform all challenged the status quo of the Victorian gender system. Nineteenth-century public discourse over such topics extended into the twentieth century as opponents refurbished nineteenth-century arguments against increased opportunities in women's paid employment outside the home or women's increased access to education. Antifeminists criminalized the practice of family planning and admonished against women's involvement in political issues and activities.

Despite consensus regarding the necessity and propriety of suppressing the assertion of women's rights, antifeminism nonetheless fostered diversity of opinion and perspective among proponents of its fundamental idea, that women's biological role of reproduction was central and inescapable. In each historical era, whenever feminist consciousness developed, antifeminism resisted proposed reforms that challenged the concepts and institutions of patriarchy as well as the gender system that supported and perpetuated a gender-defined, limited, and segregated existence for women; a constellation of conservative definitions of proper womanhood varied widely in approach, intent, and intensity without significantly deviating from the fundamental idea that maternity dominated women's existence.

From ancient times to the Middle Ages, leaders of the institutions of patriarchal religions in cultures throughout the world articulated as godly and righteous their opposition to the development of women's equality. Economic, political, and educational advances for men during the Renaissance, the Reformation, and the Enlightenment produced the concepts and language of crafted academic and scientific arguments that echoed the ancient antifeminism of the standard male-centered religions. Into the twentieth century, antifeminists continued to cite Aristotle's assertion of the inadequacy of women's intellectual capacity and Saint Thomas Aquinas's caution that women were unholy seductresses of righteous men as a basis for their defense of patriarchy and its subjugation of women. Nineteenth-century male physicians and psychiatrists such as S. Mitchell Weir (1829–1914) prescribed a gender-specific rest cure of enforced mental and physical inactivity for so-called hysteria and neurosis in women, especially intellectual and professional women. The well-known mid-twentieth-century psychiatrist Marynia Farnham (1899–1979) underscored the danger to women who forsook full-time homemaking in the post–World War II antifeminist publication *The Modern Woman: The Lost Sex* (1947).

The suppression of women's history, as well as the history of their contributions to and participation in events and significant historical movements deemed important by male elites and leaders, aided the subjugation of women; the presence of extraordinary women, such as Joan of Arc (c. 1412–1431), from age to age became the exceptions that proved the rule of women's exclusion from the historical record of nations. Unacknowledged, obscured, or discounted were the works of writers such as Hildegard of Bingen (1098–1179) and later Germaine de Staël (1766–1817). The pioneering career of Aphra Behn (1640–1689) established the possibility of careers for published and paid women writers. The presence and literature of writers like Behn contradicted the assertions of a fundamental argument of misogyny and antifeminism—that women could not think, learn, read, or write; however, the successful writing of women such as Jane Austen (1775–1817) or Harriet Beecher Stowe (1811–1896) was quickly defined as distinctly women's literature or children's literature and was segregated from the "real" literature of men's works.

Since 1800 the critics of feminism have had to absorb changes in the status of middle-class women in particular because of advances in women's rights and increased opportunity in education and employment for women in Western societies. These critics therefore have co-opted and

Antifeminist Cartoon. An American postcard caricaturing the suffrage movement, 1909. Sophia Smith Collection, Smith College

redefined some of the fait accompli changes to maintain that contemporary practices uphold the primary limitation for women in any century, that for women "biology is destiny," even into the twenty-first century. Opponents of sexual equality ultimately assert that an inescapable possibility of maternal duty grounds every woman's identity in her relationships to others, and especially to men, and limits her identity as an individual.

The pattern of antifeminist opposition to changes in women's status began with a bland dismissal or condescending ridicule that obviated the need for formal argument or specification of particular flaws in the feminist position on any particular issue. Once public discourse on feminism was engaged, opponents relied on assertions of divine ordination and natural law, as well as on scare tactics to arouse public fear of social disintegration without the continued existence and support of the patriarchal family as the essential unit of society.

Acknowledging neither the propriety nor the necessity of any changes in the gender system that were proposed by advocates of women's rights, antifeminists attempted to use and emphasize the existing separation of women by race or ethnic group, religion, and economic class. To obstruct any discussion based on facts of women's subordination and status, critics used guilt by association and subsequent ostracism to establish that the women's rights movement attracted only disreputable practitioners of lesbianism, Communism, and Socialism, or antifeminists castigated individual members and leaders of feminist organizations as deviant personalities or failed or disappointed women.

In non-Western cultures, antifeminists added the charge of treason to the tradition and cultural heritage of formerly colonized developing nations in their criticism of Third World feminists. As defenders of social order, antifeminists decried even the conservative efforts to promote limited advances and improvements that extended women's presence from the domestic sphere into the public sphere of mainstream political, economic, and social reform. Fear-mongering antifeminist leaders bullied the public to support maintenance of women's subordination in the home and on the job in their reaction to the consequences of advances and alterations that created ongoing social, economic, and political changes beyond their control.

The United States. Viewed over time, in an almost dialectical fashion, marked by achievements in legislative reform or a general increase in women's presence in the paid labor force, the end of a period of feminism has been marked by a burst of antifeminism. In U.S. women's history, the First Wave of feminism developed between the 1840s and 1920, the year the Nineteenth Amendment that enfranchised women was ratified. The decade that followed, the Roaring Twenties, was characterized by extreme and oppressive political fundamentalism that attempted to repeal and expunge the memory of the social feminist protective legislation—the same fundamentalism that supported the rise of the Ku Klux Klan.

Following the repression of women during the Great Depression of the 1930s, the changes in women's lives wrought by the conditions of the home front of World War II precipitated a postwar decade of enforced domesticity that brought on the Second Wave of U.S. feminism, from the 1960s into the 1980s, an era that included the so-called sexual revolution made possible by the oral contraceptive, "the pill." The Second Wave witnessed the passage of federal legislation that established women's economic, legal, civil, and reproductive rights; those accomplishments were threatened by the so-called backlash of the 1980s, which blamed feminism for the consequences of the unreformed gender system that had worsened women's lot at the end of the twentieth century. The backlash created and disseminated as "news" and "scientific fact" misinformation about women and their lives to add the considerable and ever-increasing body of urban myth. Documented in Susan Faludi's *Backlash: The Undeclared War Against American Women* (1991), unsubstantiated antifeminist claims in the media asserted that equality for women in employment produced "stress induced disorders" and implied among many dire consequences of advances toward equality in education and employment for women that working outside the home fostered an "infertility epidemic" among women, married or single, the latter of whom over 35 years of age also faced a "man shortage."

The Third Wave began in the 1990s with a focus on defending and extending the women's rights previously attained; in response to legal rights gained for women, neoconservatism in politics increased the difficulty of effective political influence or action. However, in the twenty-first century, the proponents of antifeminism used race and class to divide women who were still struggling with the second shift (working at home in the evening after working outside the home during the day), triple jeopardy (the particular difficulties of people discriminated against for being a certain race, a woman, and a woman of a certain race), and a more subtle and virulent form of sex discrimination that undermined implementation of civil rights and women's rights.

[*See also* Equal Rights Amendment; Feminism; Imperialism and Colonialism; Misogyny; *and* Nationalism.]

BIBLIOGRAPHY

Bard, Christine, ed. *Un siècle d'antiféminisme*. Paris: Fayard, 1999. Antifeminism in France since the turn of the twentieth century.

Bock, Gisela. *Women in European History*. Translated by Allison Brown. Oxford and Malden, Mass.: Blackwell, 2002. See Chapter 5, "Between Extremes," pp. 174–232. A concise history of women's issues in Europe during the interwar era.

Butler, Judith, and Joan W. Scott, eds. *Feminists Theorize the Political*. New York: Routledge, 1992. A collection of articles, some of which include analysis of international antifeminism.

Einhorn, Barbara. "Where Have All the Women Gone: Women and the Women's Movement in East Central Europe." *Feminist Review* 39 (Autumn 1991): 16–36. Changes in conditions for women since 1989, after the end of state socialism.

Ezekiel, Judith. "Le Women's Lib: Made in France." *European Journal of Women's Studies* 9, no. 3 (2002): 345–361. An instructive article that charts the development of French anti-amér-féminisme and its impact on French women's lives.

Gallagher, Sally K. "Where Are the Antifeminist Evangelicals? Evangelical Identity, Subcultural Location, and Attitudes toward Feminism." *Gender & Society* 18, no. 4 (2004): 451–472. A study of religiously committed Protestants that suggests that evangelicals are not uniformly antifeminist but are wary of feminism that promotes an individualism harmful to women's family and community relationships.

Howard, Angela, and Sasha Ranaé Adams Tarrant, eds. *Antifeminism in America, a Reader: A Collection of Readings from the Literature of the Opponents to U.S. Feminism, 1848 to the Present*. New York: Garland, 2000.

Kinnard, Cynthia D. *Antifeminism in American Thought: An Annotated Bibliography*. Boston: G. K. Hall, 1986.

Kishwar, Madhu. "Why I Do Not Call Myself a Feminist." *Manushi* 61 (November–December 1990): 2–8. A useful essay that considers feminism and antifeminism in terms of Indian women's issues.

Moraga, Cherrie. "From a Long Line of Vendidas: Chicanas and Feminism." In *Theorizing Feminism: Parallel Trends in the Humanities and Social Sciences*, 2d ed., edited by Anne C. Herrmann and Abigail J. Stewart, pp. 38–55. Boulder, Colo.: Westview Press, 2001. Analysis of the dismissal of feminists of color at home and abroad.

Narayan, Uma. "Contesting Cultures: 'Westernization,' Respect for Cultures, and Third-World Feminists." In *The Second Wave: A Reader in Feminist Theory*, edited by Linda Nicholson, pp. 394–414. New York: Routledge, 1997. Author includes analysis of antifeminism in response to Third World feminists.

Oakley, Ann, and Juliet Mitchell, eds. *Who's Afraid of Feminism? Seeing through the Backlash*. London: Hamish Hamilton, 1997. An international collection of articles that inform the reader's understanding of the sources and impact of the backlash.

Planert, Ute. *Antifeminismus im Kaiserreich: Diskurs, soziale Formation, und politische Mentalität*. Göttingen, Germany: Vandenhoeck & Ruprecht, 1998. A history of prewar antifeminism in the Wilhelmine empire from the 1890s to 1918, with reference to a link between antifeminism and anti-Semitism.

Pujol, Michèle A. *Feminism and Anti-feminism in Early Economic Thought*. Cheltenham, U.K.: E. Elgar, 1992. A consideration of feminism in an economic and historical context.

Sinha, Mrinalini. *Specters of Mother India: The Global Restructuring of an Empire*. Durham, N.C.: Duke University Press, 2006.

Angela Marie Howard

ANTIGONE. In ancient Greek mythology, Antigone was the daughter of Oedipus and Jocasta. The Athenian tragic playwright Sophocles (c. 496–406 B.C.E.) established the key features of Antigone's story for subsequent millennia. After Oedipus's death his son Polynices waged war on the family's native city of Thebes in an attempt to claim the throne but was killed in battle by his brother Eteocles. In Sophocles' *Antigone* (first produced c. 442 B.C.E.) their uncle Creon, now King of Thebes, forbids anyone to bury Polynices' body; Antigone defies his decree, buries her brother, and is punished with death. She shows no interest in the affairs of state with which Creon concerns himself; she is driven rather by loyalty to the family (which demands the burial of dead kin) together with a powerful sense of religious obligation (an unburied corpse is offensive to the gods).

Sophocles' famous drama has given rise to many hundreds of productions, adaptations, and reinventions in various artistic media. One of its most influential readers was the early-nineteenth-century German philosopher Georg

Wilhelm Friedrich Hegel, for whom the opposition between Antigone and Creon crystallized the tragic conflict between two claims that are both legitimate yet also both narrow and extreme. In modern times Antigone continues to serve as a vehicle for explorations of ethical, legal, psychoanalytic, and feminist theory, often in explicit counterpoint with her famous father.

Among literary critics, Hegel's legacy lives on in those who see legitimacy in Creon's position as well as Antigone's, and view both of them as at fault, if not equally so. Others see the conflict as more one-sided, with Antigone the play's indisputable hero for her courageous opposition to Creon's tyrannical decree. In ancient Greek terms, a hero need not be straightforwardly virtuous or appealing. Antigone's anger, intransigence, and sensitivity to insult are typical of Sophocles' heroes in particular. Yet these qualities are more often associated with heroic males; in Greek ideology, silence, self-restraint, and public invisibility are the proper virtues of women. Antigone thus becomes a site for problematic questions regarding the gendering of heroism. These questions have changed their shape along with shifting cultural mores. In Victorian times Antigone became the incarnation of dutiful Christian womanhood, but her resistance to masculine authority has also made her a feminist icon (Winterer).

Despite the complications presented by her gender, Sophocles' Antigone clearly has right on her side. And his play as a whole is almost obsessively preoccupied with the ideology and proper functioning of the democratic city-state, that is, with politics in a broad, albeit peculiarly Athenian, sense. These factors have made Antigone's story a fruitful dramatic outlet for the politically oppressed. Though her character as portrayed by Sophocles is fundamentally apolitical, her defiance of political authority has made her a poster-child for civil disobedience and free speech, and her death consecrated her as a martyr to state oppression. She has stood for political resistance in wildly divergent cultural conditions, from Nazi-occupied Europe to South Africa under apartheid, from the European student uprisings in May 1968 to the Irish "Troubles."

BIBLIOGRAPHY

Douzinas, Costas, and Ronnie Warrington. *Justice Miscarried: Ethics and Aesthetics in Law*. New York and London: Harvester Wheatsheaf, 1994. Treats *Antigone* as "the foundational myth of legality," comparable in importance to the Oedipus myth for psychoanalysis.

Foley, Helene P. *Female Acts in Greek Tragedy*. Princeton, N.J.: Princeton University Press, 2001. Stands out among the many scholarly discussions of gender and agency in Athenian tragedy.

Knox, Bernard M. W. *The Heroic Temper: Studies in Sophoclean Tragedy*. Berkeley: University of California Press, 1964. Influential account of the "Sophoclean hero," especially Antigone.

Sjöholm, Cecilia. *The Antigone Complex: Ethics and the Invention of Feminine Desire*. Stanford, Calif.: Stanford University Press, 2004. Uses Antigone as a focal point for questions about feminine desire; includes discussions of Hegel, Heidegger, Lacan, Butler, and other modern theorists.

Steiner, George. *Antigones*. Oxford: Clarendon Press; New York: Oxford University Press, 1984. Useful survey of post-Sophoclean Antigones, although there have been many more interpretations of her character since 1984.

Winterer, Caroline. "Victorian Antigone: Classicism and Women's Education in America, 1840–1900." *American Quarterly* 53, no. 1 (March 2001): 70–93.

RUBY BLONDELL

AOKO, GAUDENCIA (1943–1988), known as Mama Mtakatifu (Holy Mother), cofounder with Simeo Ondeto of the Legio Maria (Legion of Mary), the largest independent church in Africa to break away from the Roman Catholic Church. Largely made up of Luo people of western Kenya, but with a multiethnic membership, the Legio Maria emerged between 1962 and 1963 and was part of a larger movement in colonial Africa that saw the emergence of African Independent Churches (AICs). The AICs rose in opposition to mainstream European missionary churches, which were accused of broad discriminatory practices including denying or limiting African ascendancy into clerical positions, condemning and criminalizing many African cultural practices and sensibilities, and generally reproducing many of the grievances that Africans experienced under colonial regimes.

Aoko was born in 1943 in Awasi on the outskirts of the city of Kisumu in Nyanza Province, Kenya. She was married in 1957 to Simeo Ondeto, and the couple had two children who died young. Aoko's religious career was preceded by a series of dreams and visions in which she encountered the Virgin Mary and Jesus Christ, from whom she claims to have received the commission and power to heal the sick, cast out evil spirits, free the faithful from the debilitating power of witchcraft, and preach.

Largely based on Catholic rituals and liturgy, the Legio Maria differed from Roman Catholicism in such fundamental ways as to earn the accusation of being heretic. Aoko was strongly opposed to gender discrimination within the Catholic Church, especially the exclusion of women from clerical positions. She was also against the hierarchical organizational structure of the Catholic Church. Within the Legio Maria, Aoko performed various priestly duties including baptizing, conducting masses, and serving Holy Communion. She baptized large numbers of women who had previously been excommunicated by the Catholic Church for being in polygamous or leviratic marriages; she also baptized individuals denied the rite by the Catholic Church because of lack of the necessary fees. The masses she conducted included healing and exorcism activities.

The Legio Maria ultimately adopted an official structure that reproduced the same hierarchical leadership structure that it had sought escape when it seceded from the Roman Catholic Church. The new structure also forbade women to serve as priests, though it ordained them as church mothers. Aoko was opposed to the adoption of a hierarchical structure in the Legio Mario, and she rejected the offer of the position of cardinal or bishop. By 1967 she had been eliminated from the leadership of the Legio Maria, and she went on to establish a new church, the Communion Church of Africa.

Gaudencia Aoko was a charismatic religious leader who challenged indigenous African male authority, sexism, and gender hierarchy in the Catholic Church and then in the Legio Maria church that she cofounded. Her work can be viewed as representing Third World liberation theology with a feminist twist.

[*See also* African Liberation and Nationalist Movements; East Africa, *subentry* Twentieth Century; Religion; *and* Spirit Possession.]

BIBLIOGRAPHY

Schwartz, Nancy. "Active Dead or Alive: Some Kenyan Views about the Agency of Luo and Luyia Women Pre- and Post-Mortem." *Journal of Religion in Africa* 30, no. 4 (November 2000): 433–467.

Schwartz, Nancy. "Charismatic Christianity and the Construction of Global History: The Example of Legio Maria." In *Charismatic Christianity as a Global Culture*, edited by Karla Poewe, pp. 134–174. Columbia: University of South Carolina Press, 1994.

TABITHA KANOGO

APARTHEID. "Apartheid" refers to the system of racial domination and rule through which a white minority led by the Afrikaner National Party government oppressed and exploited the vast majority of black South Africans. Apartheid law decreed that the country's population be divided into four race groups: white (descendants of European settlers), African (indigenous groups), "coloured" (mixed race), and Indian (mainly descendants of indentured laborers brought by the British from India).

The vote was the preserve of white South Africans alone, and all three of the other race groups were thus denied access to the political and social institutions of the country. Apartheid law decreed that there was to be no marriage or sexual relations between black and white and that each of the four race groups was to live in separate areas, attend separate schools, and use separate amenities. However, it was the African people of South Africa who suffered apartheid's hardships most severely. All aspects of their lives were controlled by laws that decreed where they could work and live and that forbade them to work in skilled jobs and to form trade unions. The education policy of the apartheid government was bent on ensuring the place of African people as cheap labor. Apartheid's Bantustan, or homeland, policy crowded millions of African people onto inaccessible nonarable tracts of land in so-called independent states, depriving them of citizenship in the country of their birth. This was a vicious, inhuman system that not only denied basic rights to the vast majority of South Africans but also tore apart the very fabric of community and individual dignity.

From Segregation to Apartheid. The roots of apartheid lie in the history of imperialism and in the systems of legal discrimination and racial segregation established by early Dutch and British rule in the Cape of Good Hope in 1652 and 1845, respectively. Although these early forms of rule laid the administrative ground for a comprehensive system of segregation, it was the Afrikaners (mostly descendants of the Dutch) who perfected the system, rationalizing it on notions of racial superiority and on their being a chosen people. Though racism had flourished within—and even fueled—the imperial project of Europe in preceding decades, the Afrikaner national philosophy of racism took shape in the 1940s, a postwar era when the rest of the world, reeling from Nazi atrocities to Jews, declared racism morally objectionable. However, despite pronouncements by the United Nations against apartheid, international and local English capital used apartheid policies to ensure a supply of cheap labor.

Migrant Labor and the Bantustans. Policies of segregation suited the colonial project of rule as well as the project of capital accumulation from the early years of agriculture in the Cape and Natal colonies in the 1800s. As mining and industry developed in the early 1900s, the demand for labor increased dramatically, and employers and successive governments used and adapted instruments of control developed by the colonial and settler governments, translating the violence of colonial rule into the regimentation of labor in the compound or reserve, on farms, and in factories. For example, the British colonial reserve policy of demarcating separate living areas for the African people became entrenched in the Bantustans of the apartheid era, and pass laws, first enacted in the Cape Colony in the early nineteenth century to control the movement of African people, were perfected as a means of policing African people in the 1950s.

The movement of African people from the reserves was controlled by a system of migrancy in which the unskilled male labor required by the mines and industry was allowed to enter the mining compounds. Initially contracts were for the duration of a year, and although industries' needs were ensured through the imposition of taxes, it also suited the interests of local chiefs to send young men whose labor they could spare to the mines to earn cash with which to buy guns. Migrancy changed household relations, particularly when greater reliance on a cash economy made it a

South African Antiapartheid Movement. Black nurses protest segregation and their exclusion from the all-white South Africa Nursing Association, Johannesburg, 1958. Bob Gosani/Bailey's African History Archives

more protracted feature of life. The removal of men from the rural base for prolonged periods resulted in an increasing burden on the rural economy and, more particularly, on women.

In addition, the British codification of African traditional law, which strengthened the hand of chiefs loyal to the British, allowed for greater control of African people and additional disadvantages for women, preventing their ownership of land, restricting their status to that of minors, and making it impossible for them to enter into contracts without the consent of male relatives.

The majority of African women remained in the reserves while their men went to work in the towns, but increasing numbers of women migrated to urban settlements to look for husbands, brothers, or fathers or to escape the increasing devastation of the rural economies. Given the preference for African male labor in industry and many urban centers, even in domestic service, the only economic options open to African women were washing clothes, making and selling liquor, and working as prostitutes. In the 1910s the white-settler establishment saw African women as undesirable, unreliable, and immoral. However, as more labor was needed in the mines, domestic service began opening up for African women.

When it came into power in 1948, the National Party established apartheid as a legal system. Laws classified all South Africans by race, prevented sexual relations between black people and white people, and reserved all but the most menial jobs for whites. Black people were further dispossessed of land and removed from urban areas, and measures were introduced to restrict and police their movements.

In the 1960s the apartheid government forcibly removed some two to three million African people from urban areas and white farms in a bid to remove "black spots" from what they intended to preserve as white South Africa. The move served both to consolidate the spatial division of black people in the Bantustans and to contain the political threat of a black-majority population. The Bantustans, comprising territories dispersed across nonarable land without mineral wealth, covered roughly 13 percent of South Africa's land area but at the time held 85 percent of the country's population. Because cultivation of this land was difficult, the primary source of subsistence became wage earnings. Women who had previously been engaged in subsistence agriculture were now dependent on the wages of men. The economic recession of the 1970s and 1980s resulted in layoffs at the mines, and women were faced with loss of income and increasing numbers to feed as men returned to the Bantustans.

Until the 1950s, pass laws were sometimes used leniently by white municipalities, but they nonetheless entailed the indignity of being stopped to produce a pass and, if unable to produce one, being arrested. From the 1950s to the mid-1970s, passes were more vehemently policed, and many thousands went to jail daily for not having the correct documentation. In addition to the basic human indignity, this weakened workers' bargaining power and increased the likelihood of losing a job, striking, joining a union, or demanding better working conditions.

Job-reservation laws held jobs for whites following the 1922 strike by white mine workers. White workers used their political power, their skills, and their seats on industrial councils to have employers agree to exclude African workers from skilled jobs. Because African workers were untrained, employers could easily replace them if they went on strike, and because they were kept out of the electoral system they had no political leverage. Locked in the reserves, where overcrowding made subsistence farming more and more difficult, their families were increasingly reliant on their meager earnings.

African people resisted processes of colonization and conquest through wars, protest, and political organizations such as the African National Congress (ANC), the Pan-Africanist Congress (PAC), the South African Communist Party (SACP), the South African Congress of Democrats, the Indian Congresses, and trade unions such as the Industrial and Commercial Workers Union (ICU) and the South African Congress of Trade Unions (SACTU). Struggles in both urban and rural areas took place in the early 1900s. Participants in the Pondoland revolt in 1960 resisted government authority and demanded local control over local resources. Women were active in all these struggles, and in 1956 twenty thousand women from all over South Africa marched to Pretoria to demand an end to pass laws for women.

In the early 1900s the resistance organizations tended to fall along racial lines, but in the 1940s there was a greater coming-together of South Africans of all races in opposition to apartheid. Still, the resisters were no match for the might of the government, and in the 1960s resistance organizations were forced underground. Many leaders went into exile. The ANC decided to take up armed struggle against the apartheid state, whose use of violence to impose apartheid policies for decades through township administrations, control over housing, pass laws, and the police, as well as its exclusion of black people from national democratic processes, had legitimized violence as a means to effect social change.

For a time there was an absence of open political opposition to the government, but this changed with the watershed 1973 strikes by black workers, the formation of black-consciousness organizations such as the South African Students' Organisation (SASO) and the Black People's Convention in the early 1970s, and the uprising of school children in Soweto in 1976. As a result of pressure from workers' organizations, coupled with industries' need for more skilled laborers, the state embarked on legal reform that enabled African workers to join and form trade unions. This gave rise to a burgeoning trade-union movement that culminated in the formation of the largest federation of workers, the Congress of South African Trade Unions (COSATU), in 1985. Struggles with management gave factory workers a chance to wield power and brought a sense of dignity, self-respect, self-confidence, and control. The factory struggles were carried into communities, and the 1980s saw defiance in townships all over South Africa around issues such as discrimination in rents, bus fares, and education.

Women Challenging Apartheid. Women made their voices heard in these movements. Discussions of their roles in the liberation movements linked community and home struggles and brought attention to conflicts over sharing work in the home, maternity-leave policies, sexual harassment, and violence at the hands of male partners. Women in trade unions extended the challenge to their bosses to men in their homes and in their organizations. They set up separate women's forums in the unions, and women in communities set up separate women's organizations under the umbrella of the United Democratic Front, an alliance of community-based antiapartheid organizations. However, although they were able to put their concerns on the agendas of the male-dominated antiapartheid organizations, women found that they had to safeguard these gains because they were always under threat.

Under pressure from the antiapartheid movement—both within South Africa and internationally—and faced with increasing economic pressure that made apartheid increasingly unviable, the apartheid state undertook reforms and entered into negotiation with the main liberation movements in 1990. The bans on key liberation movements were lifted, political prisoners were released, and exiles were allowed to return to the country. Discussions between the National Party and the main liberation organization, the ANC, paved the way for negotiations in December 1991 and the country's first democratic election in April 1994.

Women in the ANC and in church and community organizations established the Women's National Coalition to ensure that women's concerns were addressed in the negotiations and in the country's constitution. Significant gains were made toward ensuring that the gender-equality clause in the constitution take precedence over culture and tradition and that an office on the status of women and a commission on gender equality would be set up.

In the period preceding the negotiations, women mobilized within the ANC to raise their concerns and were able to secure from the organization a commitment to gender equity. The women pushed the party to ensure that at least one-third of their list of parliamentary candidates would be women. Other political parties, not wanting to lose women's votes, adopted a similar policy, and the result was that women occupied 101 of the 400 seats in the first democratic parliament.

Assessment. Although the end of apartheid was a certain victory for democracy, apartheid left a painful legacy, with the oppression suffered under apartheid shaping present-day inequality. Poverty and vulnerability are experienced most deeply by black South Africans, particularly by those in the former Bantustans. That South Africa achieved democracy in the 1990s, an era of market fundamentalism, has seriously impaired the ability of the democratic government to redress the socioeconomic hardships faced by the majority of South Africans. New struggles are seen in the movements of landless people, community groups organized to demand access to basic services, and groups that campaign for greater access to HIV/AIDS treatment.

[*See also* African Liberation and Nationalist Movements; African National Congress Women's League; Racism; *and* Southern Africa, *subentry* Twentieth Century.]

BIBLIOGRAPHY

Lodge, Tom. *Black Politics in South Africa since 1945.* Johannesburg, South Africa: Raven Press, 1987.

Meer, Shamim. "Which Workers, Which Women, What Interests? Race Class and Gender in Post Apartheid South Africa." Presented at Project CES/MacArthur Symposium on Reinventing Social Emancipation, Coimbra, Portugal, 23–26 November 2000.

Meer, Shamim. "Women's Access to Productive Resources in South Africa's Rural Bantustans." MA thesis, Massachusetts Institute of Technology, 1994.

Morris, Mike, and Doug Hindson. "The Disintegration of Apartheid: From Violence to Reconstruction." In *South African Review*, edited by Glen Moss and Ingrid Obery. Vol. 6: *From Red Friday to Codesa*. Johannesburg, South Africa: Raven Press, 1992.

Sparks, Allister. *The Mind of South Africa*. New York: Alfred A. Knopf, 1990.

SHAMIM MEER

AQUINO, CORAZON (b. 1933), president of the Philippines from 1986 to 1992. Corazon Cojuangco Aquino made political history when she became the first woman president in Southeast Asia. The regime of Ferdinand Marcos had been ousted after four days of tumult in what is now known as the original "People Power Revolution" in the Philippines. As the widow of the assassinated Benigno "Ninoy" Aquino Jr., Marcos's archrival, Aquino immediately became the rallying symbol for the forces opposing Marcos's dictatorship. She was a reluctant heir to the leadership mantle—by her own admission she was "only a housewife," and she insisted that "it was Ninoy who knew everything about politics."

But Aquino's lack of political experience was compensated by her moral authority and widespread popularity as the logical leader of the opposition. In the 1986 "snap election" that Marcos had called, which was marked by massive cheating by the regime, Aquino was proclaimed the real winner and Marcos fled to Hawaii in exile.

As "transition president" Aquino's major task was to restore democratic rights and institutions by convening a representative group of Filipinos to draft a new constitution. Ratified by an overwhelming majority in 1987, the new charter mandated the first post-Marcos free elections, in which Aquino's ruling coalition won twenty-two of twenty-four senate seats. She also overhauled the country's local government system by appointing "officers in charge" for the provinces, cities, and municipalities. She released hundreds of political prisoners who had been held by the regime for years, and she restored freedom of expression and other fundamental rights. A law creating the Comprehensive Agrarian Reform Program (CARP) was passed while she was in office.

Aquino's true legacy is the restoration of what Filipinos have called "democratic space." Ironically, it was this restoration that would cause her many political problems during her six-year incumbency. Her presidency was wracked by a series of military coup and destabilization attempts by politicized elements whose members had previously plotted against Marcos. They thought Aquino was soft on communism and unequipped to govern. The attempts almost succeeded in 1987 and 1989. A combination of U.S. protection, the plotters' ineptness, and the long Filipino tradition of civilian supremacy saved Aquino's beleaguered government. Also, her chief of staff and later national defense secretary Fidel Ramos remained loyal. She would reward him later by "anointing" him her successor to the presidency.

The country's two long-term insurgencies, led by the Communist Party of the Philippines and New People's Army (CPP-NPA) and by the Muslims in Mindanao, continued throughout Aquino's tenure. Vigilante groups proliferated, and lawlessness and military abuses escalated. The media also turned against her, calling her presidency one of "lost opportunities." People expected her to deliver results overnight. She was also criticized for her failure to set an example for land reform by subdividing Hacienda Luisita, a property owned by her very wealthy family for thousands of tenants. On 6 November 2004, some five thousand mill and farm workers of the Hacienda held a demonstration protesting measures that had laid off one thousand of them since 1989. The protest led to a violent confrontation with the police; fourteen protesters were killed and at least thirty-five people were injured. No one has been charged with the killings.

After the end of her term in 1992, Aquino remained active politically and socially. She and Jaime Cardinal Sin were instrumental in the ouster of President Joseph Estrada by "People Power II" in January 2001. Estrada had been impeached following charges of corruption, bribery, and betrayal of the public trust. However, his followers in the senate suppressed evidence that would have convicted him, and forces led by Aquino, Cardinal Sin, and various civil society groups took to the streets and forced Estrada out.

During the July 2005 political crisis that hounded President Gloria Macapagal Arroyo, Aquino supported the latter by admonishing the people not to resort to extraconstitutional means; that is, street power. The crisis arose from charges of corruption against President Arroyo's family, particularly her husband and son, a member of the Philippine Congress. The president herself was accused of "rigging" the 2004 presidential elections in her favor, as revealed by her "taped" conversations with an election official. Morever, the Supreme Court had nullified the EVAT (expanded value added tax) law, and some of her cabinet and staff resigned en masse over loss of confidence in their chief executive. Various civil society and left-wing groups demonstrated in the streets calling for Arroyo's resignation.

As the crisis intensified, Aquino changed her mind and eventually called on Arroyo to "make the supreme sacrifice" of resigning to save the country. But Aquino was not supported by the influential church hierarchy, the Catholic Bishops' Conference of the Philippines, which refused to heed the call for Arroyo's resignation. The former president Fidel Ramos also parted ways with Aquino and pledged his support to Arroyo, calling for constitutional change in the country's political system.

Aquino has assumed the role of elder stateswoman devoted mostly to civic and community affairs. Her main legacy in Philippine history is having brought singular honor to a country long known for its strong women by becoming its first female president. She will long be remembered as having restored democracy to the country after the dark years of the Marcos dictatorship.

[*See also* Philippines.]

BIBLIOGRAPHY

Aquino, Belinda A., ed. *Presidential Leadership and Cory Aquino.* Quezon City: University of the Philippines, Center for Integrative and Development Studies, 1990.

Burton, Sandra. *Impossible Dream: The Marcoses, the Aquinos, and the Unfinished Revolution.* New York: Warner Books, 1989.

Joaquin, Nick. *The Aquinos of Tarlac: An Essay on History as Three Generations.* Manila, The Philippines: Cacho Hermanos, 1983.

Komisar, Lucy. *Corazon Aquino: The Story of a Revolution.* Scranton, Pa.: George Braziller, 1987.

Richburg, Keith B. *Reform or Revolution? The Aquino Government and Prospects for the Philippines.* Honolulu, Hawai'i: East-West Center Special Report, 1991.

BELINDA A. AQUINO

ARANGO, DÉBORA (1910–2005), Colombian painter. Born in Medellín, Colombia, the seventh of eleven children, Débora Arango Pérez attended Catholic schools during her childhood. Through her first exhibition at the Club Unión in 1939 she emerged as a controversial figure into the public sphere of a predominantly Catholic, conservative Medellín. She was then working in the orbit of the progressive Bachúe group, formed around her former teacher from Medellín's Instituto de Bellas Artes, Pedro Nel Gómez.

Paintings by Arango and the Bachúe group focused on the lives of Medellín's marginalized underclass and contrasted dramatically with the more conservatively academic works by artists represented by Arango's first instructor at the institute, Eladio Vélez. Arango's boldly executed images express a critical view of a society whose fractures only increased with Colombia's slow engagement with modernization. Arango's famously controversial nudes exhibited in the 1939 show, exemplified by *La amiga* (1939), scandalized Medellín's conservative viewers. The rarity of nudes in Colombian art, combined with the gender of the artist, the nudes' monumental presence in the composition, the unusual medium of watercolor on sheets of paper glued together, and the paintings' expressionism—similar to that seen in early twentieth-century Germany—galvanized opinion and set the stage for the censorship of her works through the 1950s. Arango restaged both the academic nude and traditional Catholic iconography in a context of contemporary urban labor, including prostitution, and the violence of urban society, especially as directed toward women, exemplified by *Trata de blancas* (White Slave Trade, 1940) and *La primera communion* (The First Communion, 1942).

Arango, who saw herself as both a Colombian and a Latin American artist, signed the Manifesto of Independent Artists issued in conjunction with their 1944 exposition. She lived in Mexico in 1946–1947, and her subsequent work showed the impact of the expressionistic painting and biting graphics of the Mexican artist José Clemente Orozco. From 1948 to 1960 her paintings deployed these tools toward the increasingly repressive and violent Colombian state, using images that unambiguously referred to specific contemporary events and people, such as *Plebiscito* (Plebiscite, 1958). Testimony to the political threat of Arango's art was the closure by the Francisco Franco regime of her 1955 exhibition at Madrid's Instituto de Cultura Hispánica.

Arango's 1984 retrospective at the Museum of Modern Art in Medellín and a well-funded prize from Colombia's secretary of culture marked her acceptance into the country's cultural establishment and a return to the public arena after a long period of retreat into private life. The exhibition and catalog attested to her unique place in Latin America's twentieth-century avant-garde. Her closest contemporaries in Mexico—for example, Frida Kahlo, María Izquierdo, and Nahui Ollin—often produced images characterized by a recognizable vocabulary of pre-Hispanic and/or popular imagery simultaneously worked through the strategies of contemporary painting. Arango's imagery is not articulated through a similarly national lexicon. Nor did she explore the more universal subjects of the Argentine painter Raquel Forner. Arango trained her eye on local conditions through the lens of an edgy, threatening realism. Her work was outside the centrifugal pull of Mexican muralism, emerging abstraction, and the disconcerting ambiguities of surrealism. Rather, Arango's paintings challenged the traditional categories into which twentieth-century Latin American art has been organized.

[*See also* Art and Architecture *and* Kahlo, Frida.]

BIBLIOGRAPHY

Arango, Débora. *Exposición retrospectiva.* Medellín, Colombia: Museo de Arte Moderno de Medellín, 1984.

Londoño Vélez, Santiago. *Débora Arango: Vida de pintora.* Bogotá, Colombia: Ministerio de Cultura, 1997.

STACIE G. WIDDIFIELD

ARENAL, CONCEPCIÓN (1820–1893), Spanish writer, jurist, and social activist. Concepción Arenal y Ponte was born in Galicia, the daughter of Ángel del Arenal, a military officer allied with Spain's liberal reformers who spent time in prison for his opposition to the absolutist monarchy of the Bourbon king Ferdinand VII (r. 1813–1833). Her father died when she was eight, and Arenal moved with her mother and sisters to Madrid, where she received an education in a prestigious school for young women. She viewed her education there as deficient, and she set out to rectify the situation by reading and attending public classes at the Universidad Central. The first woman to attend a university in Spain, she wore male attire in order to gain entrance. In 1848 she married the journalist and lawyer Fernando García Carrasco, a kindred spirit with whom she collaborated on the newspaper *La Iberia* until García died in 1857.

Arenal's criticism of the social injustices of her time was founded on a philosophy of social reformism with Catholic roots. As a jurist and activist, Arenal was an advocate for the most vulnerable elements of Spanish society and a proponent of the necessity for an effective system of public welfare. To this end, she founded a women's branch of the Catholic charity the Society of Saint Vincent de Paul and wrote *La beneficencia, la filantropía, y la caridad* (Welfare, Philanthropy, and Charity, 1861). She held positions as a social worker in a women's prison (in 1864) and as an inspector of women's houses of correction (in 1868), and her concern with the penitentiary system—especially her belief that prisons should be a venue for reeducating prisoners—are reflected in several books, including *El visitador del preso* (The Prisoner's Social Worker, 1894) and *Cartas a los delicuentes* (Letters to the Criminals, 1865). *La cárcel llamada modelo* (The So-Called Model Jail) and *Estudios penitenciarios* (Penitentiary Studies) appeared in 1877.

Arenal was an academic feminist who resisted the marginalization of women in her era and the purportedly scientific theory asserting that women were intellectually inferior to men. In Arenal's opinion, the actual limitations existed within, and were created by, the education system itself. Her seminal writings—*La mujer del porvenir* (The Woman of the Future, 1869), "El estado actual de la mujer en España" (1882; English trans., "The Woman Question in Europe"), and "La educación de la mujer" (The Education of Women, 1892)—reflect her insistence on the necessity of making education available to women and her interest in promoting the political, economic, and social rights of her sex.

Concepción Arenal fills the Spanish nineteenth century. As the foremost intellectual woman of her era, she lived a life deeply committed to the transformation and modernization of Spanish society. Dedicated to the path of European humanism, she was the first proponent of feminism in Spain, and her death elicited numerous public tributes, including accolades from Spain's male intellectuals, who emphasized the universal value of her work on penitentiary science, human rights, sociology, and literature. Appreciation for her work through the twentieth century sometimes coincided with the reinterpretation of her image for diverse political purposes, but in the twenty-first century Arenal is still extolled for the vigor with which she questioned the dominant social models of the epoch in which she lived.

[*See also* Spain and Portugal.]

BIBLIOGRAPHY

Irizarry, Estelle. "Weighing the Evidence: Legal Discourse in the 19th-century Spanish Feminist Concepción Arenal." *Computer and the Humanities* 29, no. 5 (October 1995): 363–374.

Lacalzada de Mateo, Maria José. *Mentalidad y proyección social de Concepción Arenal*. Madrid: Cámara de Comercio, 1994.

Maria Isabel Cabrera Bosch

Translated from the Spanish by Matthew Miller

ARENDT, HANNAH (1906–1975), German-born political theorist and author. Arendt spent her childhood in Königsberg, Prussia (now Kaliningrad, Russia), birthplace of the philosopher Immanuel Kant. She began higher education in 1924 at the University of Marburg, under the tutelage of the existentialist philosopher Martin Heidegger. From there she moved to the University of Heidelberg, where she wrote—under the guidance of the eminent psychologist and philosopher of "being at home in the world," Karl Jaspers—a dissertation on the concept of love in the works of Saint Augustine. Unable to find academic employment in an atmosphere parlous for European Jews, Arendt left Germany for Paris in 1933, only to be interned in a French prison camp as an enemy alien in 1940. A stateless person, she emigrated to the United States in 1941, along with her husband Heinrich Blücher. During the war she wrote columns for a New York German-language weekly on the prospects for a Jewish homeland, while becoming increasingly disenchanted with Zionism. Arendt's career shifted toward academia in 1951, the year she became an American citizen. From that time on she held distinguished positions at numerous universities. She was the first woman in the history of Princeton University to be accorded the rank of full professor.

The experience of being vulnerable to world alienation as a Jew, pariah, and refugee remained a powerful touchstone in Arendt's thinking, starting with the first major work after her dissertation, *Rahel Varnhagen*: *The Life of a Jewess* (1958). The unprecedented character of totalitarianism was also a pivotal point in her thought, most notably addressed in the *Origins of Totalitarianism* (1951). Arendt wrote as a public intellectual on Rosa Luxemburg, Isak Dinesen, and Bertolt Brecht, among others (*Men in Dark Times*, 1968) and on issues of contemporary politics from school integration to the war in Vietnam (*Crises of the Republic*, 1972). Her writings often generated intense controversy and misunderstanding, perhaps none more so than *Eichmann in Jerusalem: A Report on the Banality of Evil* (1963), in which she portrayed Eichmann as terrifyingly "banal"—an ordinary perpetrator of absolute evil.

Arendt's major theoretical works, including *The Human Condition* (1958), *Between Past and Future* (1961), *On Revolution* (1963), and *The Life of the Mind* (1978), brought new insights to an old vocabulary of theorizing politics. At their core is a persistent concern about modern world alienation and the loss of freedom, which Arendt symbolically associated with the Greek polis and thought was experienced primarily as political action in the "space of appearances" of the public realm. To be free and to act are one and the same. Political action, she argued, is the collective initiation of new beginnings ("natality") by distinctive and unique individuals and cannot be reduced to causal explanation or instrumental motivation. Its outcome is power: the capacity of people acting mutually in concert through shared "self-revelation" as speech and deed. Although Arendt called the linkage between politics and freedom an "old truism," she also sensed a falling away of humanity from politics with the rise of mass culture and society. With this bleak prospect in mind, Arendt persistently forwarded the invitation for human beings to "think what we are doing" as political actors and citizens, so that we might regain some semblance of freedom in the modern world.

[*See also* Scholars and Scholarship *and biographies of women mentioned in this article.*]

BIBLIOGRAPHY

Canovan, Margaret. *Hannah Arendt: A Reinterpretation of Her Political Thought*. Cambridge, U.K.: Cambridge University Press, 1992. A comprehensive interpretation and critique of major themes in Arendt's political thought.

Honig, Bonnie, ed. *Feminist Interpretations of Hannah Arendt*. University Park: Pennsylvania State University Press, 1995. A diverse collection of essays that consider the meaning and significance of Arendt's thinking for feminist politics and theory.

Pitkin, Hanna Fenichel. *The Attack of the Blob: Hannah Arendt's Concept of the Social*. Chicago: University of Chicago Press, 1998. A bold, in-depth analysis of Arendt's critique of the emergence of the "social" and the privileging of "society" in modernity, concluding with an Arendt-inspired call to political action.

Young-Bruehl, Elisabeth. *Hannah Arendt: For Love of the World*. 2nd ed. New Haven, Conn.: Yale University Press, 2004. The definitive biography; includes a complete chronological bibliography of works published by Arendt during her lifetime.

MARY DIETZ

ARGENTINA. At the time of the Spanish conquest in the late sixteenth century, the region of present-day Argentina was not inhabited by highly organized indigenous civilizations such as those of Peru or Mexico. Even so, the conquest meant a sexual subjugation of available indigenous women that began a process of *mestizaje* (miscegenation), although the racial mixing was never as extensive as that of other areas and did not have similar demographic consequences. Between the sixteenth and the eighteenth centuries several important urban centers developed in the northwest, such as the cities of Córdoba and Tucumán, which were closer to the Andes, especially the Andean city of Potosí, the hub of the Andean mining area. Buenos Aires did not develop in full until the eighteenth century, when (in 1776) the region became the Viceroyalty of the Río de la Plata, comprising territory that later became the nations of Argentina, Uruguay, and Paraguay.

The Colonial Era. Women of full Spanish descent were highly valued in the first century of settlement and expansion and enjoyed a better social position than the mestizas (mix of white and Indian) and indigenous women. Iberian law prescribed a patriarchal society and favored the elite's "purity" of blood. However, the sexual behavior of the lower classes was not guided by such directives, and although demographic evolution was slow, it pointed to a multiethnic society with a diverse racial heritage.

During the colonial period, women's role in society was circumscribed, confined to home, motherhood, and family. Some women received a basic education provided by private teachers and tutoring at home. However, it was only toward the end of the eighteenth century that a significant number of schools became available for women. Spanish legislation gave women several protective rights in family law, such as the equitable partition of property among all siblings and conjugal economic benefits for married women. Some women achieved significant economic roles as owners of private property and small businesses. The Catholic Church had a powerful role in the formation of a gender ideology. It promoted a type of patriarchal family that sometimes resembled conventual life. Elite or women of Spanish descent also had the option of entering monastic life as nuns. The church demanded dowries from those entering religious orders, and the inhabitants of these institutions formed a social and racial elite of their own. Less fortunate women and those of mixed racial descent formed a body of unskilled workers and servants. While African slavery never reached a high profile in the Argentine interior, it was visible in the urban centers. Slave women were mostly employed in domestic work and could even be part of the dowry of rich women.

Buenos Aires women participated in the struggle against the English invasion in 1806 that preceded the viceroyalty's

Eva Perón. Eva Perón, wife of the Argentinean presidential candidate Juan Perón, passes out campaign buttons, February 1946. THOMAS D. MCAVOY/TIME LIFE PICTURES/GETTY IMAGES

movement for independence, which began in 1810. During the wars of independence, some women joined the rebel forces in peripheral areas of the viceroyalty such as the northwest. Juana Azurduy de Padilla and Magdalena Güemes achieved notoriety as warring women who organized women guerrilla insurgents in the 1810s, while others played supportive roles. Once the region declared its independence from Spain, the former viceroyalty of La Plata took several decades to become a nation, and it was a fragmented state in which the city of Buenos Aires played the most significant national and international role. In that city, some women played a public role as social hostesses. Among them the most astute was Mariquita Sánchez de Thompson, who held a liberal salon and left her impressions of the early Argentine Republic in her correspondence. Manuelita Rosas, the daughter of the Buenos Aires dictator Juan Manuel de Rosas, was another well-known figure in her time. In these early republican years women's roles did not change significantly, although the fathers of the nation assigned a small group of elite women the task of developing the Beneficence Society, an organization that reigned supreme over the administration of the welfare activities of the nation throughout the nineteenth century.

The Republican Era. In 1853 Argentina finally became a unified republic under a federal constitution, and the first elected president of the nation, Domingo F. Sarmiento, began his administration in 1868. With the rise of liberalism, the national economy of Argentina began a process of fast transformation. The nation's first public educational system was put in place by Sarmiento, who was keenly interested in the education of women. Rosa Guerra and Juana Manso wrote on women's education. Guerra wrote a book titled *Julia o la educación* (Julia or Education) in 1863, and Manso edited *El album de señoritas* (Misses'Album) in the 1860s. By 1880 Argentina had transformed itself into a rich agrarian economy based on the export of cereals and beef, and the country had attracted a large number of immigrants who changed the social and racial profile of the nation. Men and women predominantly from southern Europe reached its shores, strengthening and enriching the cultural development of the nation. While most of the late-nineteenth-century immigrants formed part of the laboring masses, the second generation of settlers would help reshape Argentine politics in the early twentieth century.

Argentina's new Civil Code, adopted in 1869 and inspired by the Napoleonic Code, increased the subordination of married women to their husbands. Married women lacked juridical personality and had very little control over their children. For all intents and purposes they were subject to the will of their husbands. By the end of the nineteenth century, however, an improved educational system had produced a cadre of well-educated professional women who were conscious of their abilities as well as of the limitations imposed upon them by the legal system. Feminism had an early beginning in Argentina. A lecture by the scholar Ernesto Quesada praising the advancement of women under feminist guidelines in other parts of the world and the success of the National Women's Exposition in Buenos Aires in 1898 launched the discussion of feminism in Argentina. Elvira López's 1901 doctoral thesis, "El movimiento feminista," described the state of feminism in Argentina and gave this ideology a solid intellectual base as an academic topic.

The first women professional graduates of Argentine and foreign universities in general endorsed feminism. Among them were Elvira Rawson de Dellepianc, Cecilia Grierson, and Petrona Eyle. Grierson, who had participated in the International Congress of Women in London in 1899, was instrumental in the foundation of Argentina's National Council of Women (1901), which was affiliated with the international organizations of the same name. The influence of Socialism among organized urban labor also broadened the meaning and discussion of feminism; Socialists organized their own feminist groups. Among the notable

Socialist feminists were Fenia Chertkoff, Carolina Muzzilli, Raquel Messina, and Justa Burgos de Meyer. The Socialist Cecilia Baldovinos, among others, helped to organize women workers. At the same time, anarchism was also taking root in Argentina among the laboring classes, and although anarchist ideology proscribed an organized society, anarchists supported a change in domestic gender relations. They backed birth control and "free unions," instead of legal marriage, a position far from that of other activist groups.

Modern Feminism. In 1910 a group of reformist and feminist Argentine women organized the First International Feminine Congress in Buenos Aires to campaign on behalf of women's rights. Notable among the supporting organizations were the Association of Argentine University Women and the Socialist Feminine Center. Among the most important measures adopted were the promotion of the legislation to end juridical restrictions on women, the promotion of divorce and suffrage, and the adoption of "maternalist" measures of welfare for the protection of mothers and their children. Argentine women of the period as well as those participating in the First Feminine Congress endorsed maternalism—that is, the support of motherhood—as the axis of all other reforms affecting women and children. This ideological position would become central to Argentine feminism thereafter.

During the first decade of the twentieth century some feminists defined themselves as "freethinkers" who opposed the hegemony of the church and rejected adherence to any political party. Among the most notable freethinkers were the Uruguayan-born María Abella de Ramírez and Julieta Lanteri, who together published a feminist journal called *Nosotras* and organized a League of Women Freethinkers. Lanteri, who was born in Italy, challenged Argentina's policy of denying citizenship to women by applying for it on several occasions, and she became an unofficial candidate to the Argentine congress in 1920 after she organized the National Feminist Party. The Socialist physician Alicia Moreau was an ardent supporter of female workers' rights, suffrage, and the reform of the Civil Codes. She became the leader of Argentina's Feminist National Union, and after a trip to the United States she organized the Argentine Association for Women's Suffrage. Other notable women of this generation were Rawson de Dellepianc, also a physician, who headed the Women's Rights Association, and Adelia di Carlo, who founded a Humanist Party that also promoted women's rights. None of these parties was validated by the political system, but they became venues for training women in civic activism. At the end of the 1920s Carmela Horne organized the Pro-Women's Suffrage Committee that in the 1930s became highly visible in its advocacy for women's right to vote.

Until this time, Argentine society had rigid standards for women's behavior. Women faced strict disapproval for going out alone at night or being unaccompanied in public places such as cafés and restaurants. Hotels would not book rooms for unaccompanied women—a custom that endured into the 1930s. In general, however, during the 1920s Argentina experienced profound social changes. An oil boom supported a flourishing economy. Urban growth advanced the expansion of a middle class, the unionization of workers, and greater access to educational institutions for both sexes. Illiteracy declined rapidly, and women gained a significant presence in the teaching profession. (Female teachers, despite being professionals, still represented to most minds an extension of women's maternal duties to the schools. They also suited the objectives of the Argentine nation by inculcating an "Argentine identity" in immigrant children.)

The development and modernization of the country did not change the general opposition to female suffrage, although in 1926 the reform of the Civil Code reduced women's legal dependence from men. Even "liberal" personalities thought that, if given the vote, women, under the influence of the Catholic Church, would vote for conservative parties. However, as time passed some members of the church began to support a restricted women's vote.

Among other important developments in this period was the campaign to combat prostitution, a trade that often involved the importation of European women for that purpose under false promises. Known as the campaign against "white slavery," this was one of the battlegrounds of Paulina Luisi, a Uruguayan physician who had been born in Argentina, who was also an advocate of sex education and suffrage. Luisi fought the "regulation" of prostitution, which put these establishments under municipal regulation as taxpayers for the city. Under those premises, prostitutes had to undergo medical inspection, presumably to prevent the spread of sexually transmitted disease. Regulation in Argentina lasted until 1936, when prostitution was officially proscribed and brothels closed down.

Although the 1930s began with a constitutional breakdown and a military coup d'état, feminists continued their suffragist campaign. The Chamber of Deputies approved women's suffrage in 1932, but the project was shelved by the Senate. During this decade, many feminists turned their energies to working on behalf of the Spanish Republic and in opposition to the rise of fascism. Many feminists and reformers were also pacifists. Women continued to benefit from a more flexible moral code, while among the working classes the number of women involved in blue-collar work and domestic service continued to grow. Argentina, given its overall sympathy for Italian Fascism, only joined the Allies in 1945.

The early 1940s saw the rise of the military that had made its first bid for power in 1930. A coup d'état in 1943 put a cluster of right-wing military men into power. Among them,

Juan Domingo Perón emerged in 1945 as the leader, despite several attempts to curtail both his power and his growing popularity among the urban workers. Having married his mistress Eva, he was elected president in 1946, and he monopolized the political life of the nation until 1954.

Peronismo, the official name for Perón's ideology, was a mixture of populism and nationalism that was received enthusiastically by the working classes, to whom he catered with the support of economic nationalism and a vast array of social welfare measures. Eva Perón was a decisive force in the construction of Peronismo. No friend of feminism but a woman conscious of her humble origins, she adamantly opposed the landed and industrial aristocracy of Argentina. She became an advocate of the poor, and with a large amount of political leverage she organized the Eva Perón Foundation, which built a vast network of social welfare support for the nation's workers. The Peronist regime, conscious of its need for stronger legitimacy, approved legislation granting divorce, the recognition of the rights of children born out of wedlock, protective labor legislation for working women, and female suffrage. Perón was reelected in 1952, the year women first voted in national elections, and he won the presidency with massive women's support. Forced by new legislation promoting women's candidacies, women were elected in large numbers for the first time in the nation's history, supported by Perón's Justicialist Party. Eva Perón, meanwhile, succumbed prematurely to cancer in 1952.

Perón was deposed by the military in 1954, and Argentina plunged into a succession of weak governments until Perón's return in 1972. Throughout that period Argentines were torn between right-wing and left-wing ideologies in an atmosphere of growing instability. Despite this situation women continued to join educational institutions and the labor market, although many dropped out to raise their children because even among the most progressive elements, the task of raising children was regarded as natural for women. Argentina reached demographic stability prior to the 1960s, when female fertility declined and the national birthrate was slightly more than two children per family. Feminism languished during this period of polarization between the Right and the Left. However, in the 1960s the Movimento de Liberación de las Mujeres (Women's Liberation Movement) became active, and a National Feminist Union formed in the 1970s claimed among its members the influential cinema director María Luisa Bemberg.

Perón died in 1974, and his third wife, Isabel Perón, who was his vice president at that time, assumed the presidency. She lasted only two years in command of a government tottering on the brink of internal disorder. In 1977 the military took over, instituting a suffocating coercive regime that terrorized the population with its policy of eliminating its political enemies, most of whom were young and leftist. This brutal domestic policing known as the "dirty war" involved thousands of men and women (some say as many as thirty thousand) who were "disappeared," that is, kidnapped, tortured, and murdered. Opposition to this regime was organized by a group of mothers of the disappeared, who came to be known as the Mothers of the Plaza de Mayo. Their peaceful but dramatic resistance attracted world attention. Another organization known as the Grandmothers of the Plaza de Mayo began to rescue grandchildren who had been kidnapped by some members of the military and given up for adoption among their supporters. Defeated in its attempt to recapture for Argentina the English Falkland Islands, the military regime collapsed and a surge of popular support backed the return to democracy in 1984.

Amid democratic rebirth, women's organizations flourished, and they demanded a female political presence in the reconstruction of the nation. For the first time national universities offered a women's history curriculum. Argentines pioneered legislation known as the *ley del cupo* (the law of fixed quotas) that guarantees a minimum of 30 percent female candidates in the electoral list of candidates in all parties participating in national elections. In the first years of the twentieth-first century, women constituted 30 percent of the members in the Chamber of Deputies, thanks to the effective enforcement of the *ley del cupo*. While not all of these politicians were feminists, greater attention was paid to issues related to women such as the reduction of domestic violence and enforcing legal processes against men who fail to pay child support after divorce. Unfortunately economic setbacks to the once-rich nation have forced many women into low-level jobs in search of extra domestic income. Nearly 40 percent of women are members of the labor force, a notable jump from the nearly 30 percent of earlier decades. They are mostly employed as elementary and secondary education teachers, office workers, and domestics. Their industrial employment is mostly in textile and garment, meat-packing and canning factories, and pharmaceutical production. In comparison, rural employment is very small.

In the 1990s Argentine feminists were fighting for the decriminalization of abortion (still illegal owing to the influence of the Catholic Church) and the recognition of women's rights as human rights. While a greater equity for women had been achieved, there were still many rights to be accomplished. The number of women heading universities or in the higher echelons of public administration was very small. However, in 2006 the national Ministries of Defense and Economy, which had long been masculine enclaves, were both headed by women. Argentine women have an important and visible place in all fields of the humanities and the arts. Distinguished visual artists include Procesa Sarmiento de Lenoir (the sister of the educator Domingo F. Sarmiento), Eugenia Belin Sarmiento, Emilia Bertolé, Lía Correa Morales, Ana Weiss de Rossi, Aída Carvallo, Raquel Forner, and Lola Mora. They were respected painters and sculptors and opened the field for younger artists. Among the notable writers of the nineteenth century were Eduarda Mansilla and Juana Manuela Gorriti, whose novels and essays were widely read in their time. In the twentieth century Alfonsina Storni, Victoria and Silvina Ocampo, Norah Lange, and Luisa Valenzuela stood out as writers of poetry, novels and essays. Their works have received national and international recognition and have been translated into several languages. Alejandra Pizarnik and Olga Orozco are well-known contemporary poets of great linguistic and philosophical originality.

[*See also* Abella de Ramírez, María; Azurduy de Padilla, Juana; Eyle, Petrona; First Feminine Congress of the Pan-American League; First International Feminine Congress in Buenos Aires; Grierson, Cecilia; Luisi, Paulina; Mothers of the Plaza de Mayo; *and* Perón, Eva.]

BIBLIOGRAPHY

Barrancos, Dora. *Inclusión/exclusión: Historia con mujeres.* Buenos Aires: Fondo de Cultura Económico, 2002.

Bianchi, Susana, and Norma Sanchís. *El partido peronista femenino.* Buenos Aires: Centro Editor de América Latina, 1988.

Gil Lozano, Fernanda, Valeria Silvina Pita, and María Gabriela Ini, eds. *Historia de las mujeres en la Argentina: Colonia y siglo XIX.* Madrid: Taurus, 2000.

Guy, Donna J. *Sex and Danger in Buenos Aires: Prostitution, Family, and Nation in Argentina.* Lincoln: University of Nebraska Press, 1991.

Lavrin, Asunción. *Women, Feminism, and Social Change in Argentina, Chile, and Uruguay.* Lincoln: University of Nebraska Press, 1995.

Masiello, Francine. *Between Civilization and Barbarism: Women, Nation, and Literary Culture in Modern Argentina.* Lincoln: University of Nebraska Press, 1992.

Morgade, Graciela, ed. *Mujeres en la educación: género y docencia en Argentina, 1870–1930.* Buenos Aires: Miño y Dávila, 1977.

Nari, Marcela. *Políticas de maternidad y maternalismo político: Buenos Aires 1890–1940.* Buenos Aires: Biblos, 2004.

Ruggiero, Kristin. "Not Guilty: Abortion and Infanticide in Nineteenth Century Argentina." In *Reconstructing Criminality in Latin America,* edited by Carlos A. Aguirre and Robert Buffington, pp. 1469–1466. Wilmington, Del.: Scholarly Resources, 2000.

Shumway, Jeffrey M. *The Case of the Ugly Suitor and Other Histories of Love, Gender, and Nation in Buenos Aires, 1776–1870.* Lincoln: University of Nebraska Press, 2005.

Sosa de Newton, Lily. *Diccionario biográfico de mujeres argentinas.* 2nd ed. Buenos Aires: Ediciones Plus Ultra, 1980.

Zabaleta, Marta Raquel. *Feminine Stereotypes and Roles in Theory and Practice in Argentina Before and After the First Lady Eva Perón.* Lewiston, N.Y.: Edwin Mellen Press, 2000.

DORA BARRANCOS

ARISTOCRACY

This entry consists of three subentries:

Overview
Comparative History
Modern Period

Overview

Aristocracies thrive where social inequalities are viewed as natural and constructive. The rationales for this view differ so broadly across world populations—in construction, attendant privileges, and the capacity to hand on aristocratic status—that, historically speaking, aristocracies seldom resemble each other except in enjoying substantial advantages over others. Aristocratic status may derive from state-enforced privilege, a respected house- or kin-based group, claims of ancestry and careful selection of marriage partners, mythic tales of energy, life, and fertility, or of worth and honor, or merely from a monopoly of resources obtained through force, like the Vandal settlement in North Africa after the fall of Rome. Aristocracies are most secure where they rely on deference to maintain ascendancy; aristocratic women tend to profit from deference and may wield considerable authority and power where deference flourishes.

China, housing ancient and secure ruling classes, distinguished its officialdom from its landholding classes through use of examinations that tested advanced literacy. In practice a proportion of the privileged classes in China were clansmen of earlier royal dynasties, thus they were called the sons of the Son of Heaven. While other elite families arranged their own marriages, royal clan marriages were the affairs of state. Women would appear to have no role in such a ruling class structure, but through family and marriage they sometimes managed to play directing roles.

With the triumph of Islam in the eighth and ninth centuries, North Africa, southern Spain, and the Middle East were brought within the sphere of the Sharia (Islamic legal code), which asserted radical equality among the faithful. Hypothetically no "natural" aristocracy existed, although the early Islamic caliphates relied on a fighting force of Arabs, who became an intermarrying ruling elite within newly conquered lands. By the eleventh century court societies existed throughout Islamic lands, and the *Qabus Nama* (English trans., *A Mirror for Princes,* 1951) provided this advice: "nobody, and particularly so the rich man, requires a friend who is poor. Choose friends of your own degree . . ." (Kai Ka'us ibn Iskandar, p. 131). With the harem system the numbers of the wellborn proliferated, which abetted the tendency of great Islamic states to form power cliques, fragment, and hive off to form new principalities. While a ruler might elevate any woman he wished to the status of wife or concubine, in practice noble families competed to place their daughters within the royal harem. This assured privileges and access to power to offspring, natal kin, and often great influence for the heir's mother.

The ancient Greeks had defined an aristocracy as a polity where the best men ruled, a gendered definition. During the age of settlement in Europe another notion came into play. In the early barbarian kingdoms an aristocracy by birth was believed to descend from great ancestors who might include divinities. Blood conveyed the inherited traits that justified elite status such as those enjoyed by the long-haired Merovingians, who descended from the Great Sea Warrior. Intermarriage among elites united pools of superior traits. While the Greek definition of aristocracy might be interpreted to exclude women, barbarian practices of the intermarriage of powerful families relied on women to perpetuate the "natural" aristocracy. These two dissimilar concepts combined by the eleventh and twelfth centuries in western Europe to create a nobility, that is, a class of noble warriors who fought and therefore governed alongside a ruling monarch. The strength of the barbarian notion of aristocracy was sufficiently compelling that noble women participated in this power nexus, assuming governing roles. JoAnn McNamara and Suzanne Wemple state:

> profiting from the almost unlimited power of their families, women for two centuries [tenth and eleventh] were able to play central political roles . . . as chatelaines, mistresses of landed property and castles with attendant rights of justice and military command, proprietors of churches, and participants in both secular and ecclesiastical assemblies" (p. 108).

The greatest continuity with antique civilization occurred in Byzantium, which maintained unbroken lines of officialdom and was sustained by powerful old landholding families. Court society afforded at least some aristocratic women the opportunity to wield power. Royal princesses wed powerful lords within the empire or were sent off to Christianize and influence neighboring rulers: Theophano (959–991) wed the German Otto II (r. 961–983) of the Holy Roman Empire and Sofia Paleologue (1440s–1503) brought both Byzantine and western European influences to the Russian court after she wed Ivan III, grand prince of Russia (r. 1462–1505) in 1472. Olga of Russia (c. 890–969), wife of Prince Igor I of Kiev (r. 912–945) and later named a saint, visited Constantinople in 957 and converted to Christianity under the influence of the Byzantine court. Women held titles such as "Augusta" and figured in court ceremony.

Aristocratic Women in Western Europe. While everywhere intermarriage among aristocratic families and court society created opportunities for women, the West, more subject to weak centralized power, probably allowed women the most diverse opportunities. Ruthlessness, or great sanctity, or inheritance in lieu of male heirs all figured in the mix. The triumph of the principle of primogeniture (inheritance by the eldest male offspring) was not guaranteed for aristocratic and royal families in this era. By the thirteenth century first sons had gained inheritance rights and titles, leading women of highborn families to prefer marriage to first sons. Once primogeniture was established, aristocratic women exerted authority through guardianship of minors and influence over powerful and titled fathers, husbands, or offspring. Nevertheless, well into modern times aristocratic women continued to send their vassals off to war or led armies. They administered lands and defended castles under siege. A number of women in the upper echelons of society learned to read and write; some even learned Latin. Taking religious vows meant joining forces with another elite group: the clergy. Hildegard of Bingen (1098–1179) was the tenth child of a German family of the minor nobility when she was dedicated to the church as a young child; thus she served as a family tithe from among her noble siblings.

Massimo Livi-Bacci argues that the European small-family pattern emerged among the Italian nobility during the early modern centuries (pp. 182–200). Whereas medieval families of the upper classes had tended to be large, noble families now shrank adaptively, among other reasons in response to the emergence of paid royal armies. The inheritance of titles and understanding of patrilineage differed by time and place. As a result, aristocratic practices varied; for example, all offspring of counts in France received titles whereas in England only the eldest received title along with an entailed estate.

The early modern centuries saw aristocrats at a pinnacle of their power in Europe. Military roles diminished, but noblemen received significant state privileges, the most important of which was exemption from the tax burdens through which rulers protected privilege rather than private property rights. In landed realms most aristocracies were not closed systems. For example, the Habsburgs elevated an entrepreneurial family from Bergamo in Italy to the title of counts of Thurn und Taxis with letters of nobility in 1512 because they had created an excellent postal system for the empire. The family became enormously wealthy, and they were made princes of the Spanish court in 1681. Illustrious marriages to German princesses built their fame and increased their opportunities to acquire even greater wealth. For the Habsburgs the aphorism "Bella gerunt alii, Tu Felix Austria, nubes" (Let others wage war, Let thou, Happy Austria, marry) applied; it was just as apt for the princes of Thurn und Taxis.

Those fortunate enough to be given a dowry to enter into the religious life were almost exclusively noble by birth. By escaping the gender expectations imposed on married women, nuns wielded remarkable influence on occasion. In secular society aristocratic women enjoyed certain freedoms from gender restraints as well. They hunted and learned archery, allowing them to pursue noble field sports along with noblemen. At court they played chess and cards, gambled, danced, and learned the sport of tennis, assuring them access to circles of influence and power. Highborn women were the love objects of troubadours in the convention of courtly love in a broadly popular literary genre that assumes, rather than argues for, the natural superiority of highborn persons. Aristocratic women had found their way into universities as early as the seventeenth century; the Venetian patrician Elena Lucrezia Cornaro Piscopia (1646–1684) became the first woman university graduate in 1678, when she received a PhD from the University of Padua. Among the wealthiest in the land, women at court consumed to the limit of their resources—or, more likely, to the limit of the sumptuary laws that were written to curb spending (*sumptus* means "spending"). Nevertheless the privileges enjoyed by noble women were rarely sanctioned by laws of the realm, resting primarily instead on ancient custom and the community's disposition to pay deference. However, when in England William Blackstone (1723–1780), in his *Commentaries on the Laws of England* (1765–1769), advocated consistent application of common-law strictures on women's legal rights, women bearing titles did not escape the reach of laws pertaining to property, suing in court, marriage, and divorce.

[*See also* China; Europe, *subentry* Ancient Greece; Hildegard of Bingen; Marriage, *subentry* Comparative History; North Africa, *subentry* 700–1500; Paleologue, Sofia; Primogeniture; Property Rights; Spiritual Leaders, *subentry* Nuns and Abbesses; *and* West Asia, *subentries* Roman and Byzantine Periods *and* Islamic Empires.]

BIBLIOGRAPHY

PRIMARY WORKS

Aristotle. *The Politics, and the Constitution of Athens.* Rev. ed. Edited by Stephen Everson. Cambridge, U.K., and New York: Cambridge University Press, 1996.

Blackstone, William. *Commentaries on the Laws of England.* Vol. 4, *Of Public Wrongs (1765–1769).* Adapted by Robert Malcolm Kerr. 4 vols. Boston: Beacon Press, 1962.

Kai Ka'us ibn Iskandar. *A Mirror for Princes; the Qabus Nama.* Translated by Reuben Levy. New York: Dutton, 1951.

Smith, Adam. *An Inquiry into the Nature and Causes of the Wealth of Nations.* Edited by Edwin Cannan. New York: Modern Library, 1937.

SECONDARY WORKS

Bellomo, Manlio. *La condizione giuridica della donna in Italia: Vicende antiche e moderne.* Turin, Italy: Eri, 1970.

Dewald, Jonathan. *The European Nobility, 1400–1800.* Cambridge, U.K., and New York: Cambridge University Press, 1996.

Helms, Mary W. *Access to Origins: Affines, Ancestors, and Aristocrats.* Austin: University of Texas Press, 1998.

Livi-Bacci, Massimo. "Social-Group Forerunners of Fertility Control in Europe." In *The Decline of Fertility in Europe: The Revised Proceedings of a Conference on the Princeton European Fertility Project,* edited by Ansley J. Coale and Susan Cotts Watkins, pp. 182–200. Princeton, N.J.: Princeton University Press, 1986.

McNamara, JoAnn, and Suzanne Wemple. "Sanctity and Power: The Dual Pursuit of Medieval Women." In *Becoming Visible: Women in European History,* edited by Renate Bridenthal and Claudia Koonz, pp. 90–118. Boston: Houghton Mifflin, 1977.

Mohlo, Anthony. *Marriage Alliance in Late Medieval Florence.* Cambridge, Mass.: Harvard University Press, 1994.

SUSAN MOSHER STUARD

Comparative History

This article discusses the role of aristocratic women in the Byzantine Empire and Japan with reference to their access to economic power, literacy, and political power.

Byzantine Empire. The Byzantine Empire was, in its origins, the eastern part of the Roman Empire with a new capital, Constantinople, dedicated in 330. Formally, it lasted until the conquest of Constantinople by the Ottoman Turks in 1453. An important break occurred in the seventh century, when the eastern provinces fell to the Arabs and the Balkans were invaded by Slavs. Thereafter, the Empire grew considerably to include the Balkans and Asia Minor. But it changed significantly, though by no means completely, from what it was in the sixth century, as many of its structures became medieval.

The Byzantine aristocracy was, until the eleventh century, an aristocracy of service, comprising civil and military officials. Starting with the ninth century, aristocratic families began to solidify. The great ninth- and tenth-century families were weakened by imperial action; from the eleventh century on, there developed an aristocracy of blood, one of office, and a mixture of the two. There never was a nobility in the sense of a formally constituted aristocratic class. Thus, the aristocracy, and aristocratic women within it, ranged from fairly modest officials to the highest aristocracy, including the imperial family. Its composition and practices changed over time, with the eleventh century constituting a watershed. Within the aristocracy, the position and role of aristocratic women differed according to their place in the hierarchy.

The role of aristocratic women in society was connected with property ownership and control. According to Byzantine law, inheritance was bilateral and equal partible, so female children and male children inherited equal amounts. A woman's share of her parents' property was in part (or wholly) given to her in the form of a dowry. The dowry was owned by the woman but administered by the husband, unless it was proven that he was a poor administrator, as a woman of the minor aristocracy argued in the early twelfth

Empress Theodora. Theodora's Court, Byzantine mosaic, c. 600 C.E. S. VITALE, ITALY/SCALA/ART RESOURCE, NY

century. The dowry was highly protected; a woman could alienate her dowry only in extreme cases of need, and only with her husband's assent. Aristocratic women also owned property outside the dowry, and this they could manage and alienate at will. The known examples of rich or very rich aristocratic women must be but the tip of the iceberg. In the late ninth century, a woman named Danielis held vast estates in the Peloponnese and also a fabulous amount of movable property. She was a king-maker, financing the career of the future emperor Basil I and leaving a large part of her property to his son. It is not known whether she was a widow. In any case, widows were in a privileged position to administer family property. There are attested examples from the tenth century that aristocratic women, while married, administered household economic affairs (for example, Saint Mary the Young). This role became more important in the eleventh century and after, when women of the high aristocracy managed large fortunes. In this period the women of this class owned extensive properties, some of which they donated to monasteries. Their skills in administration and financial management are visible in the foundation charters of nunneries, for example, that of Kecharitomene, founded by Empress Irene Doukaina (c. 1066–1123), in which all but one of the officials charged with finances were women. Empress Theodora (d. after 867), daughter of a provincial middle-level official, extended these skills to the administration of the empire: during her brief regency, the Treasury showed a considerable surplus.

The question of the literacy of aristocratic women cannot be answered for the period from the mid-seventh century until the second half of the eighth century. At that point, there is evidence of literate women in the upper rungs of the elite. In the ninth and tenth centuries, it seems, aristocratic women, including those lower down in the hierarchy, were literate to some degree, if only enough to read religious texts. Two ninth-century ladies who later became saints (Saint Athanasia and Saint Theodora of Thessalonike) learned their letters on the small island of Aigina. Kassia (c. 800/10–843/67), daughter of a minor official, was a highly competent poet and hymnographer. Saint Irene of Chrysobalanton (c. 845–c. 940), from an aristocratic family in Asia Minor, was a well-known preacher to other aristocratic women. In the eleventh century and after, while women of the minor aristocracy were functionally literate, some members of the high aristocracy were truly erudite. Thus Anna Comnena (1083–c. 1153/4), the daughter of Emperor Alexios I Komnenos (r. 1081–1118), was a promoter of Aristotelian studies and the only secular woman historian of the Middle Ages. Other examples include the Sebastokratorissa Irene (twelfth century), Theodora Raoulaina (thirteenth century), and Irene Choumnaina (fourteenth century). In the last hundred years of the empire the literacy of women of this class may have declined.

The social status of aristocratic women was formally determined by that of their fathers or husbands, since there were very few court offices specifically for women. To the degree, however, that status meant worth, power, and independence, such determination varied with time and with place in the hierarchy. Women were important in the matrimonial strategies of the aristocracy ever since the ninth century. In the eleventh century this role increased tremendously as the new high aristocracy solidified itself through multiple and extensive matrimonial alliances often uniting the same families. From the eleventh century, women in this group proudly proclaimed their own aristocratic lineages, especially if their lineages were greater than those of their husbands. Young girls of the provincial aristocracy were pawns in this marriage game. Yet some provincial aristocratic women wielded extraordinary power over the people under their control.

Women's public powers were severely limited by law. They could not hold civil, military, or ecclesiastical offices. In practice, the women of the imperial family participated actively in religious controversies, in the ninth century as in the fourteenth. It was two empresses who restored the cult of icons: Irene in 787 and Theodora in 843. As patrons of clerics and monks and as founders of monasteries, women of somewhat lower aristocratic rank also had influence in ecclesiastical matters. As regents for their sons, empresses exercised more or less power, depending on the circumstances and the personalities involved. Some women of the imperial family held real power. For example, the Empress Irene (r. 797–802), or the mother of Alexios Komnenos, Anna Dalassene (c. 1025–1100/02), to whom he delegated all his powers and authority when he went on campaign, or his wife, Irene Doukaina, to whom he owed the throne as much as to his mother. In the lower ranks of the aristocracy, women's exercise of public power is much less visible. Indeed, in these social levels women seem most to have conformed to the social norm that limited them to the private sphere, although there were always exceptions.

Japan. In premodern Japan, the aristocracy emerged along with the forms and concepts of government itself. Between the fourth and seventh centuries, the early Japanese ruling elites refashioned the ranks and offices of the Chinese imperial bureaucracy to fit better the society and politics of early Japan. As a result of these alterations, the Japanese imperial aristocracy was defined solely in terms of lineage (imperial and noble status); access to official rank and office was acquired only through birth or adoption, and the right to rule was vested only in the lineal descendants of families and clans designated as imperial or noble on account of their ancestral heritage. Over time, especially during the Heian period (794–1185), the hereditary aristocracy developed an insular and highly refined culture whose rituals, language, and lifestyle became the model of civilized life itself for both men and women for centuries thereafter.

The exclusive emphasis on lineage as the determinant of aristocratic status in early Japan both hindered aristocratic women and endowed them with a particular type of power. Although aristocratic women themselves could not hold office or rank, they clearly were indispensable for perpetuating the aristocracy in their roles as wives of nobles and mothers of future heirs. Daughters were key assets in the strategic marriage alliances that bound noble families to each other and to the imperial house. The example of the statesman Fujiwara Michinaga (966–1027), scion of the main branch of the Fujiwara, the highest-ranking nonimperial noble clan, shows how aristocratic clans used marriage alliances to secure and maintain high status. By marrying four of his daughters to reigning emperors or imperial princes destined to become emperors, Michinaga became father-in-law to four emperors and grandfather to five. Michinaga thus exerted power at the highest level of imperial politics not only through the considerable prestige of his own official rank and office, but also by means of the personal influence he exerted over emperors and emperors-to-be through his close blood or marriage ties to them, which he secured through his daughters.

Men such as Michinaga also gained power through the women in their families by means of matrilocal residence, which was prevalent among the court nobility. Aristocratic women in the classical period could inherit property and financial assets, and although descent was reckoned patrilineally, once married, couples frequently resided together at the wife's family's compound in a separate residence, usually provided by the wife's family, or they lived apart, with the man residing only temporarily with his wife and their children, usually in her natal home or a separate residence. This pattern of residence allowed the woman's relatives, primarily her father and uncles, to exert significant influence on, among other things, the raising of heirs.

During this time, many highly literate elite women found their voices as writers and poets and were celebrated in their time and for long after as major literary talents, cultural chroniclers, and trendsetters. Indeed, women's writing produced at the height of court culture in the tenth and eleventh centuries forms the mainstay of the classical literary canon. For example, Murasaki Shikibu, a lady-in-waiting to the Empress Shōshi, wife of Emperor Ichijō (r. 986–1011), wrote *The Tale of Genji*, one of the great works of world literature.

While the imperial-court aristocracy maintained its unassailable status as the arbiter of high culture, its political power had waned considerably by the late twelfth century, and a new set of political actors emerged in the form of the *bushi*, or warrior class. With the establishment of the first shogunate, or military government, in 1192, a bifurcated form of rule emerged in which the emperor and imperial court continued to reign in theory while the shogun and samurai warriors took control over most practical matters of governance. This tandem rule continued until the restoration of unified imperial government in 1868.

The rise of the warrior class in the medieval period led to a military aristocracy whose wealth and power rivaled and more often than not outstripped that of the imperial court. In matters of culture, political symbolism, and legitimacy, however, even high-ranking warriors tended to defer to the imperial court. The interdependence of the court and military aristocracies was cemented by frequent intermarriage between high-ranking houses of the warrior and court nobilities and subsequent appointment of the male children born of these unions to official positions in both military and court bureaucracies. Women of elite military families, like their counterparts in the imperial aristocracy, thus came to play important roles in securing alliances within and beyond the military elite itself. But while women of the military class undoubtedly enjoyed privileges denied to the common folk, they lacked some key political and social advantages of court noblewomen. Matrilocal residence was never widely practiced within the warrior class, and women's inheritance rights were restricted under warrior rule.

As the size and power of the military aristocracy began to exceed greatly the small imperial court aristocracy in the late medieval and early modern periods (fourteenth to early nineteenth centuries), considerable divisions emerged within the warrior elite itself. Whereas women in high-ranking military families had retinues of servants to perform even the smallest tasks, women in low-ranking military families personally managed their households and worked at a variety of domestic chores. Daughters of such families often served as maids or attendants in higher-ranking warrior households to earn income and acquire the skills and knowledge of elite lifestyles that might enable them to marry above their own rank. Interestingly, female literary and artistic talents of the late medieval and early modern periods tended to come from the fringes of the warrior class: highly educated daughters of doctors, scholars, and literati of various sorts. Paradoxically, the status of these women on the margins of the elite may have freed them to exercise their literary and artistic imaginations, and to go beyond the confines of gender norms in their creative lives.

[*See also* Comnena, Anna; Japan; Marriage, *subentry* Comparative History; Matrilocality and Patrilocality; Murasaki Shikibu; Theodora; *and* West Asia, *subentry* Roman and Byzantine Periods.]

BIBLIOGRAPHY

Garland, Lynda. *Byzantine Empresses: Women and Power in Byzantium,* AD *527–1204*. London: Routledge, 1999.

Gouma-Peterson, Thalia, ed. *Anna Komnene and Her Times*. New York: Garland Publishing, 2000.

Hill, Barbara. "Imperial Women and the Ideology of Womanhood in the Eleventh and Twelfth Centuries." In *Women, Men, and Eunuchs: Gender in Byzantium*, edited by Liz James, pp. 76–99. London: Routledge, 1997.

Laiou, Angeliki E. "The Role of Women in Byzantine Society." In *Gender, Society, and Economic Life in Byzantium*, edited by Angeliki E. Laiou. Aldershot, Hampshire, U.K.: Variorum, 1992. First published in 1981.

Lebra, Takie Sugiyama. *Above the Clouds: Status Culture of the Modern Japanese Nobility*. Berkeley: University of California Press, 1993.

McCullough, William. "Japanese Marriage Institutions in the Heian Period." *Harvard Journal of Asiatic Studies* 27 (1967): 103–167.

Nicol, Donald M. *The Byzantine Lady: Ten Portraits 1250–1500*. Cambridge, U.K.: Cambridge University Press, 1994.

ANGELIKI E. LAIOU AND MARCIA YONEMOTO

Modern Period

Modernization in political and economic life generally weakened the hold of aristocracies, as they were gradually supplanted by businessmen and upwardly mobile politicians with commercial and industrial financial backing. The slow downward course for the world's nobility was evident in Europe beginning in the eighteenth century. As part of the Enlightenment, for example, women of the upper—though not necessarily noble—ranks held salons for the dissemination of new ideas and thus rivaled the social leadership of aristocratic women. The subsequent outbreak of the French Revolution in 1789 sent many noblewomen into exile or into counterrevolutionary movements such as that in the Vendée (in western France). Aristocratic women also lost their lives during the Terror. When Napoleon set up his empire in 1804 he called on the aristocracy to return in order to fill the imperial household with experienced courtiers. Stéphanie de Genlis, for instance, once prominent in the household of the duke d'Orléans, joined the Napoleonic court and became a favored social arbiter and author. For most of the nineteenth century European women of the court aristocracy held similarly important places as attendants to queens and empresses, as breeders of the next generations of the social elite, and as arbiters of taste. In Russia, the Habsburg Monarchy, and imperial Germany, where the middle classes enjoyed far less power, aristocratic women played an important role in court ceremonials that served to cement the regime's cultural power.

Despite the decline of aristocracy, aristocratic lifestyles for women remained distinctive. Before World War II, aristocratic women led more secluded lives than did their husbands and brothers, often being confined to home estates and going out only with chaperones, even on their honeymoon, as one Japanese woman reported. They attended schools primarily for children of the aristocracy. Many aristocratic women never had access to kitchens, servants' quarters, and other service parts of the house, all of which were seen as shameful places. Women also married according to the wishes of their parents to cement political and economic alliances. They might have no knowledge of a potential match until after the engagement, though some parents would tip their daughters off: "You are going, it seems, to marry Prince K, because his father visited us," one Japanese young woman was told (Lebra, p. 235). Others were offered virtually for sale to men of lower status but large fortune to bring money to the family.

In the nineteenth and twentieth centuries, the European imperial powers used and abused local aristocracies in countries they sought to rule. The British notoriously confiscated the wealth of women aristocrats in India, who were forced to surrender gold and jewelry in exchange for an allowance from the colonial state. Little wonder that in the Indian revolt of 1857 (also known as the Great Mutiny) many of these elite women joined in the uprising against the British. In Africa, imperial governors similarly bypassed women with traditional power such as queen mothers and chose to favor male royalty and aristocracy as local leaders. Simultaneously, aristocratic women were notoriously rebellious even in the imperial European powers, often joining underground movements and political opposition. In Russia, the emancipation of the serfs in 1861, which weakened the local nobility's hold over both people and institutions, saw young women and men of the high nobility rebelling against the power of their noble families. They joined communes, changed their appearance, and often worked for the cause of reform and revolution.

Notions of noble honor survived during the transition from social domination by a landed aristocracy to the empowerment of wealthy capitalists. For instance, women of noble samurai families in Japan were often sent by their parents to work in the developing textile factories late in the nineteenth century to show the family's sense of honor and to display its loyalty to the new national goal of modernization. In fact, the nobility owed much to the new Meiji regime (begun in 1868 with the crowning of the emperor Meiji) because it had confirmed the nobility's position by law even after the new, modernizing government had come into being. In Europe, even as agrarian power diminished, noblewomen also displayed their sense of family honor through social activism, especially toward the worthy poor, whose lives were made harder by industrialization. Aristocratic women became proponents of traditional religions in the face of campaigns to secularize society in the name of making it more modern. They were often staunch monarchists in the midst of democratizing societies.

World Wars I and II had a devastating effect on aristocracies. The decline in the number of servants left many aristocrats struggling to cope, as they came to live without cooks, chauffeurs, and the customary array of personal servants. Arranged marriages also decreased in number, but there were also far more extreme changes. After 1917 the Soviet government went directly after the aristocratic class, among other propertied groups, as an enemy, forcing its members into exile to save their lives. Knowing multiple languages, some aristocratic women became flexible translators, office workers, and even high-quality personal attendants in other areas of the world.

In 1947, Japan, under the occupation of the United States, abolished its aristocracy, yet insofar as the royalty remained a center of attraction the aristocracy kept a good deal of allure. In particular the aristocracy of birth helped the moneyed elites learn the consumer symbols and behavioral standards of high status. In some regions, including Japan, from the middle of the nineteenth century aristocratic women gained national and even international renown as models of fashion and beauty. Their escapades and love lives fed the media, making them, like film stars, leaders of celebrity culture. In contrast, other aristocratic women around the world emphasized what they called the traditional values of honor and plain living, dressing sensibly and exemplifying austere manners. Some worked hard on behalf of good causes, but as patrons for high-profile philanthropic events they promoted elite society indirectly, helping to unify such society by their mere presence.

Although monarchs around the world increasingly chose to marry commoners, the spotlight shone on aristocratic women whenever a male heir to the throne began searching for a wife, for the aristocrat might be the most eligible consort—even though popular opinion sometimes ran in favor of commoners. Despite the majority of nations being republics, fantasy life continues to engage with the aristocratic past—the most popular historical novels from Japan to the United States feature aristocratic women from past centuries as heroines. Nonetheless, more silently, other levels of the former aristocracy lead more ordinary lives in the workforce, as students, businesswomen, professionals, and housewives.

[*See also* Dual-Sex Political Systems; Enlightenment; Monarchy; Salon; *and entries on countries and regions mentioned in this article.*]

BIBLIOGRAPHY

Cannadine, David. *Ornamentalism: How the British Saw Their Empire.* Oxford and New York: Oxford University Press, 2001.

Engel, Barbara Alpern. *Mothers and Daughters: Women of the Intelligentsia in Nineteenth-Century Russia.* Cambridge, U.K., and New York: Cambridge University Press, 1983.

Kuper, Hilda. *An African Aristocracy: Rank among the Swazi* (1947). London and New York: Oxford University Press for the International African Institute, 1961.

Lebra, Takie Sugiyama. *Above the Clouds: Status Culture of the Modern Japanese Nobility.* Berkeley: University of California Press, 1993.

BONNIE G. SMITH

ARMAND, INESSA (1874–1920), Russian revolutionary and feminist. Inessa Armand has the distinction of being the first woman to be buried in the "Red Graveyard" next to the wall of the Kremlin. Her road to the pantheon of communism was not a straight one. She started off as a Tolstoyan when at the age of nineteen she opened a school for peasant children on her husband's estate. Five years of teaching left her disillusioned with a lack of measurable progress and rural bureaucratic obstructionism. In 1899 she moved to Moscow and became involved in the Society for Improving the Lot of Women. Within a year she was the society's president and the driving force behind its Shelter for Downtrodden Women. In addition to rehabilitating prostitutes, she sought to establish a Sunday school for working women and to edit a newspaper that could discuss broader aspects of the "woman question." Suspicious authorities thwarted both of these ventures.

In frustration Armand turned from upper-class philanthropy to Marxian radicalism in 1903, when she joined the

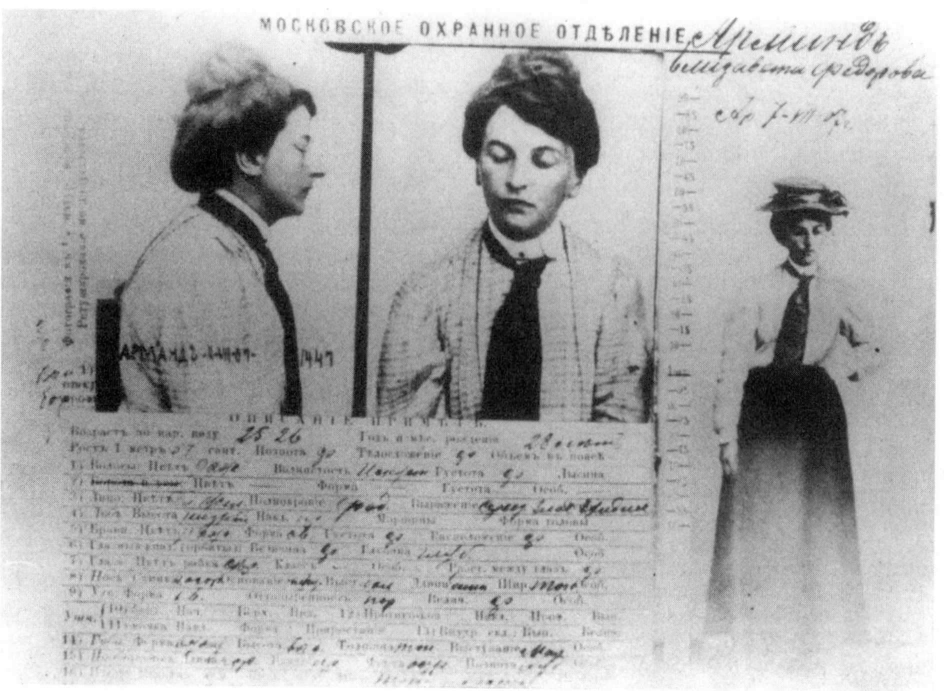

Inessa Armand. Mug shot, 1907. COURTESY OF CARTER ELWOOD

illegal Russian Social Democratic Labor Party. Four years as an underground propagandist led to three arrests and ultimately to exile north of Arkhangel'sk. She fled Russia in December 1908 and settled in Paris, where she was attracted to Bolshevism and its leader, V. I. Lenin. She lectured at his party school, ran his Committee of Foreign Organizations, and served as his contact with the French Socialist Party. As she later admitted, she also fell in love with him. In July 1912, at his behest, she returned to Russia on party business and was arrested. After six months in jail, she fled Russia a second time and rejoined Lenin's entourage. Soon thereafter she combined her earlier interest in feminism with her newer commitment to Marxism when she helped edit *Rabotnitsa* (Woman Worker), the Bolsheviks' first journalistic attempt to address issues of interest to proletarian women.

Armand spent the war in neutral Switzerland organizing the Third International Conference of Socialist Women (March 1915) and representing her party at three other antiwar conferences. At Lenin's insistence, she devoted much of her time to translating his articles and speeches into French or German. Increasingly, however, she sought to assert her intellectual and personal independence, daring to criticize his theoretical formulations and insisting on living elsewhere in the country. Her own efforts at writing a brochure on marriage and the family as well as articles on political themes were greeted with disdain or condescension by her paternalistic mentor.

Following the abdication of Tsar Nicholas II in March 1917, Armand returned to Russia on the famous "sealed" train. After the October Revolution, in which she played a minor role, she joined the Left Communists in opposing Lenin's peace of Brest-Litovsk with Germany. This opposition did not prevent her from serving as chair of the Moscow Provincial Economic Council or from sitting on the Soviets' Central Executive Committee. Nor did it keep her from being named the first director of Zhenotdel (the Women's Section of the Central Committee) in August 1919. For the last year of her life, she sought to increase female participation in the labor force by relieving many of the household responsibilities that normally fell to women, and she fought for female equality in the party and the workforce. Almost single-handedly, she edited Zhenotdel's theoretical journal *Kommunistka* (Female communist) and organized the First International Conference of Communist Women in the summer of 1920.

[*See also* Communism, *subentry* Comparative History; Russia and Soviet Union; Socialism; *and* Zhenotdel.]

BIBLIOGRAPHY

Elwood, Carter. "Lenin and Armand: New Evidence on an Old Affair." *Canadian Slavonic Papers* 43 (2001): 49–65. A review of recently published archival information.

Elwood, R. C. *Inessa Armand: Revolutionary and Feminist.* Cambridge, U.K.: Cambridge University Press, 1992. Paperback ed., 2002.

CARTER ELWOOD

ART AND ARCHITECTURE

This entry consists of six subentries:

Overview
Art History
Artists and Architects
Erotica and Pornography
Folk Art
Space and Gender

Overview

Throughout the centuries, women have scarcely been recognized as makers of art or architecture. Yet women have always been artists and builders, and there have always been glimpses of women's art within patriarchal society. No one knows if small stone carvings, such as the so-called *Venus of Willendorf* (25,000 B.C.E.), found in Austria, and other objects associated with women that seem to suggest fecundity, were made by women or men nor whether ideas for the first houses were generated by one sex. In nomadic and agrarian preindustrial societies throughout the world and throughout history, the secrecy of initiates' religious practice has made it difficult to take note of women's painting, carving, pottery, and metalwork, as well as of the kinds of spaces women used in their own rituals, but clearly such ritual needs were often met by women's skills. From the beginning, women have made fabric. Homer praised Penelope's courageous weaving in *The Odyssey* (800 B.C.E.). In pre-Columbian South America and Mesoamerica, temple carvings depicted women weaving on looms, and in these societies, woven cloth measured wealth. In Europe the eleventh-century Bayeux Tapestry, with a narrative embroidered by elite women, is a surviving monument of early secular art known to have been made by women. Women's clothing choice was an art with political and cosmic resonance in Japan in the late Heian court, as attested by the *Tale of Genji*, the novel written by Lady Murasaki in the tenth century.

Women have always used built space, but again they have often done so in ways that were marked by gendered attitudes and customs in their societies. Thus evidence for many early Mediterranean cultures, including the Greeks of classical Athens (fifth–fourth centuries B.C.E.), reveals the existence of houses with areas customarily used by men and distinguished by location and names from those associated with women. Strict separation of men's and women's areas is known from a number of societies in which wealth was marked by a man's ability to keep his women and children unseen and their honor unthreatened by outsiders—for example, the grand houses of nineteenth-century Rajasthan. Peasant women have rarely had the wealth required to provide strict spatial separation from men, but in North Africa, in a case famously discussed by the sociologist Pierre Bourdieu, areas of even simple houses have gendered associations. The customs associated with the built environment are thus often markers of status and power, and they may help to shape the very structures in which they are practiced.

Women prior to the modern period have seldom had the luxury of being freed from the work of making houses and furnishing them. Although women entered the profession of architect only after the mid-nineteenth century, they had already been taking important roles in the construction of habitations. This is especially true of societies in which housing is made of skins and fabrics, which many

"Nyrmla's Wedding II." The henna ceremony of the artist's elder sister's wedding. The painting asserts the continuing validity of traditional cultures against the threat of globalization. At the same time, symbols relating to the artist's British Indian identity offer an optimistic image of a workable coexistence of modernity and tradition. AMRIT K. D. KAUR SINGH/THE SINGH TWINS peoples associate with women's labor. Nomadic groups, for example in Central Asia and Mongolia, have often assigned women the role of builders and maintainers of the tents that are put up and taken down on a regular basis. Even though poor women have worked as the breakers and haulers of building stones, the makers of bricks or manure-based building materials, and the plasterers and painters of buildings—as in the case of the houses painted by Ndebele women in South Africa—their work has seldom entered the written history of architecture. So too the work of women in making the rugs for floors and walls, the pots for cooking and the dishes for eating, and the clothes for wearing were women's work long before art became a profession.

Elite women have been important patrons of art and architecture, and in this capacity many have played major roles in determining how buildings and other kinds of objects would look. Women of the Ottoman court, such as Mihrimah Sultan (d. 1578), often made major gifts to the public in the form of mosques and other buildings designed by the most important architects of the day. More individual motives can be seen in the patronage of Bess of Hardwick, Countess of Shrewsbury (1518–1608), who directed her architect Robert Smythson to construct for her a magnificent house, Hardwick Hall (completed 1597), whose facade was an absolutely untraditional wall of glass. And glass became crucial to the revolutionary Sun House of Dover, Massachusetts, designed in 1948 by Eleanor Raymond, whose work involved collaboration with women engineers and scientists as well as patronage by women.

Among the female patrons of paintings in Europe, Marie Antoinette is perhaps the best known today, but women of the courts in China and Japan also commanded the wealth to have books, scrolls, and other works of art made for them. Other kinds of art patronage have also allowed women agency, as is the case of the Mende women of Sierra Leone who commission men to make masks for the rituals of the Sande women's society or the many women throughout history who have ordered tombs, tombstones, and caskets for themselves and their kinfolk. The famous Mausoleum of Halicarnassus, in modern Turkey, was ordered as a tomb for the king Mausolus by his widow Artemisia in 353 B.C.E., but many women have been responsible for much simpler commemorations, including temporary roadside shrines to loved ones lost to car crashes in modern America.

Twentieth-century feminist historians of art and architecture took the measure of historical circumstances in western Europe and of the conditions that permit painting, sculpture, and architecture to be practiced at all. Among these are access to education and materials, to models, patrons, and commissions. Medieval nuns learned to paint manuscript illuminations in church scriptoria in ninth-century Spain and Germany, and the twelfth-century Christian scholars Herrad of Landsberg and Hildegard of Bingen probably supervised the illustrations in their encyclopedic religious treatises. How they were taught and by whom remains unclear, but outside the convents women artists in Europe and Asia were often the daughters of artists.

New images of women who are active agents appear in European Renaissance paintings by Sofonisba Anguissola, Artemisia Gentileschi, and Judith Leyster, and in the Netherlands, women painters such as Maria Sibylla Merian re-made the still-life genre in the service of scientific inquiry. The history and portrait painter Angelica Kauffmann was a founding member of the Royal Academy in London; in the late eighteenth and early nineteenth centuries a small number of women were made members of the French Academy, which then set the maximum number of women at four. A trickle of women students began to find admission into the new Continental and American art academies in the late 1770s, but the majority pursued portraiture and still-life rather than painting the historical and mythological subjects most favored by critics in this period in Europe.

In China and Japan, the women of elite families and those from the families of scholarly officials found encouragement as artists, often because they began in the acceptable mode of poetry writing and calligraphy, both genteel activities and evidence of intellectual and social status. Making paintings for their scrolls and books was considered acceptable, as was collecting and knowledge of the history of art. One of the most famous of the women painters of the gentry, Kuan Tao-sheng (1262–1319), was married to an equally well-known painter and remained a role model for later women artists such as Ch'en Shu (1660–1736). The famous calligrapher and painter Ryonen Genso was a Zen Buddhist nun, but she came from an upper-class family in seventeenth-century Japan and served at court before her marriage; she would have learned poetry and painting as part of the usual accomplishments of the men and women of her rank. Other Japanese women followed this path to a more independent life and earned a living through their art-making. Interestingly, at the same time, some of the well-known artists of the past in Japan and China were courtesans from the lower strata for whom the ability to write and paint was as important as the ability to sing and play musical instruments. The seventeenth-century painter Liu Yin is among the best known of the Chinese courtesan artists; she painted landscapes as well as flower and bird pictures.

Women's entry into the profession of architecture came much later than their participation in the other arts, although work with hard materials such as wood or metal also was often seen as men's purview, with the result that women began to make sculpture rather late as well. At the end of the nineteenth century, women started to be trained as architects despite resistance from men in the profession. Among the earliest are women in the United States, such as the California architect Julia Morgan (1872–1957) and the African American architect Amaza Lee Meredith (1895–1984), who built a number of houses in Virginia. From the end of World War II a number of women entered the profession of architecture in Asia as well; in Japan one of the earliest women's architectural firms was Hayashi-Yamada-Nakahara-Sekkei Doujin, founded in 1958. Testimony to the changing status of women architects is the increase in their numbers internationally, but also the fact that in 2004—for the first time in its history of almost thirty years—the prestigious Pritzker Architecture Prize went to a woman, the Baghdad-born Zaha Hadid. Women architects have also worked as critics and theoreticians, among the earliest of whom was the architect Minette de Silva of Sri Lanka, one of the founders of the important Indian arts magazine *MARG (Modern Architectural Research Group)*, which began publication in 1946.

An overview of women artists in Europe and the Americas in the modern era also begins in the nineteenth century with the achievements of painters and sculptors who had the economic resources to study and to travel (Edmonia Lewis, Mary Cassatt, Berthe Morisot). By the end of the nineteenth century, women had begun to flourish in the nascent field of photography, where new technologies allowed them to bypass traditional art school training. Women artists, among them Liubov Popova, Alexandra Exter, and Varvara Stepanova were central in early Russian revolutionary and European avant-garde movements. Twentieth-century bohemian oppositional culture offered unprecedented opportunities and subject matter to emancipated "New Women" who developed as artists (Paula Modersohn-Becker, Käthe Kollwitz, Hannah Höch, Sonia Delaunay, Georgia O'Keeffe), art world activists, critics, gallery and museum curators and directors, and influential collectors (Lizzie P. Bliss, Katherine Dreier). Surrealist women painters in Europe, Mexico, and the United States were iconoclasts in their explorations of mind and body. Louise Bourgeois has continued to develop fluidly sexual subject matter.

In different ways, because of different societal and developmental contexts since the 1960s, many women artists currently address personal and transnational issues of identity and explore global and diasporic politics. In Britain, Amrit and Rabindra KD Kaur Singh paint their own contemporary lives set in traditional Indian miniaturist settings, and performance artist Sonia Boyce's films and photographs of mouths, heads, and singers pinpoint racist stereotypes. The "in-between" exilic works of artists such as Mona Hatoum, a Palestinian artist born in Beirut and living in London, New York-based Shirin Neshat, born in Iran, and Emily Jacir, born in Bethlehem, tell of loss and insight and conflicting countries, cultures, and gender roles.

Beginning in the 1960s, many women taught and studied at art schools in the United States and Europe. These institutions became the sites of feminist activity, which in turn resulted in increased gallery and museum representation. Since then, a large and transformative body of theory, methodology, and information about women artists has emerged, and a diverse anti-hegemonic practice has revealed that conventional definitions of a universal male subject and of genius—as well as the formalist aesthetics of twentieth-century modernism—are historically specific notions. Seeking out past women artists has quickly led to a radical redefinition of past and present art to include nonmainstream art, the so-called decorative arts, installation art, and performance art sited in artists' bodies. A sudden and dramatic increase in the number of women artists throughout the world has made it nearly impossible to count them now, and the increase has revealed that there is no innate or singular female art. Rather, we see that the visual and symbolic languages of art—its imagery, materials, forms, and leaps of the imagination—shape and are shaped by culture, and that they transmit particular cultural ideas about beauty, power, desire, sexual difference, gender, race, and class.

[*See also* Anguissola, Sofonisba; Bess of Hardwick; Cassatt, Mary; Gentileschi, Artemisia; Hildegard of Bingen; Kollwitz, Käthe; Leyster, Judith; Modersohn-Becker, Paula; Morisot, Berthe; *and* O'Keeffe, Georgia.]

BIBLIOGRAPHY

Agrest, Diana, Patricia Conway, and Leslie Kanes Weisman, eds. *The Sex of Architecture*. New York: Harry N. Abrams, 1996.

Bates, Ulku U. "The Architectural Patronage of Ottoman Women." *Asian Art* 6 (Spring 1993): 50–65.

Bourdieu, Pierre, "The Berber House, or, The World Reversed." *Social Science Information* 9, no. 2 (April 1970): 151–170.

Chadwick, Whitney. *Women, Art, and Society*. London and New York: Thames and Hudson, 2002.

Heresies Magazine: A Feminist Publication on Art and Politics, 1976–1993.

Hooks, Bell. *Art on My Mind: Visual Politics*. New York: New Press, 1995.

Jones, Amelia, ed. *The Feminism and Visual Culture Reader*. London: Routledge, 2003.

Nochlin, Linda. "Why Have There Been No Great Women Artists?" In *Art and Sexual Politics*, edited by Thomas Hess and Elizabeth Baker. New York: Macmillan, 1973.

Pollock, Griselda. *Vision and Difference: Femininity, Feminism, and the Histories of Art*. London: Routledge, 1988.

Rendell, Jane, et al., eds. *Gender Space Architecture: An Interdisciplinary Introduction*. New York: Routledge, 2000.

Weidner, Marsha, ed. *Flowering in the Shadows: Women in the History of Chinese and Japanese Painting*. Honolulu: University of Hawai'i Press, 1990.

SUSAN FILLIN-YEH AND NATALIE BOYMEL KAMPEN

Art History

Gender studies in art history arose directly from the development of feminist art history within the modern and contemporary fields and its engagement with critical theory from deconstruction to discourse theory. The earliest manifestations of feminist art history in the 1970s had already announced some of the themes that were to figure prominently in later studies. In Linda Nochlin's article, "Why Have There Been No Great Women Artists?" from 1971, she discussed the social and cultural restrictions on women artists of the past; Carol Duncan's "Virility and Domination in Early Twentieth-Century Vanguard Painting," from 1973, is still an influential critique of masculine avant-garde artists' representation of the female nude. However, the implications of these early analyses could not be explored until the work of neglected women artists was brought to light. This inquiry was jump-started by the momentous exhibition organized in 1976 by Nochlin and Ann Sutherland Harris, Women Artists, 1550 to 1950.

Documentation of the work of women artists, in the form of monographs, articles, and surveys, followed. In 1980, Elsa Honig Fine established *Woman's Art Journal*, which she ran until her retirement; Joan Marter and Margaret Barlow subsequently became its coeditors. This journal has played a significant role in feminist art history and gender analysis through the rediscovery of women artists, critical essays, and book reviews. In a series of anthologies, the art historians Mary Garrard and Norma Broude have reproduced some of the best feminist art history and gender analysis in the field. Whitney Chadwick wrote the definitive survey of women artists from the eighteenth to the twentieth centuries, *Women, Art, and Society* (1990).

The late 1970s and the 1980s saw an increase in the publication of articles on the history of feminism in art and art history. Thalia Gouma-Peterson and Patricia Mathews wrote an overview, "The Feminist Critique of Art History," for *The Art Bulletin* in 1987, followed by the British art historian Lisa Tickner's "Feminism, Art History, and Sexual Difference" in *Genders* in 1988. These and other sources have allowed art historians, especially modernists, to begin to add information on women artists to their curricula. However, it soon became apparent that one cannot simply add women to the traditional male canon of artists. Rather, as the British art historian Griselda Pollock stated in her 1983 article, "Women, Art and Ideology: Questions for Feminist Art Historians," the authority of the structures and values of art and its histories must be questioned, and art history rewritten. Two years earlier she and Roszika Parker wrote a survey of a different sort, *Old Mistresses: Women, Art, and Ideology*, which they described not as "a history of women artists, but an analysis of the relations between women, art and ideology" (pp. 132–133).

By the 1980s Nochlin's earlier discussion of social and cultural roles and constraints on women artists had become central to a debate on gender difference, especially in contemporary art and art history. The historical hierarchies constructing women as the inferior "other" in both mind and body to the superior male were brought into question. The turning point for this debate is most evident in the work of two feminist artists of the late 1970s, Judy Chicago and Mary Kelly. Chicago, one of the most important initiators of the feminist movement in art, was interested in what she termed the "central core imagery" of the female body; her *Dinner Party* (1974–1979) used vaginal motifs in her representations of historical women. Kelly's more conceptual artwork, *The Post-Partum Document* (1973–1979), used Lacanian theory to talk about the construction of motherhood and of the child, based on her own experience. Kelly also wrote serious art theory and condemned the essentialist notions, so central to Chicago's work, of an absolute difference between genders, which originates in the body.

Feminists also addressed issues of the social construction of race—for example, bell hooks, Judith Wilson, Michelle Wallace, Lowery Sims, Sharon Patton, Samella Lewis, Lucy Lippard, and Anne Gibson—because race, too, was configured almost completely through a hierarchy of the physical.

Gender theory arose out of a conjunction of the rise of critical theory and the need to move beyond such essentialist formulations. Feminists had already deployed social construction theory, and the British especially had turned to a feminist form of Marxism. The 1980s entry into art criticism and art history of sophisticated critical models and methods of interpretation, such as poststructuralism, psychoanalytic theory, and discourse theory, provided a new model for the move to gender analysis. Feminist art historians were among the first to embrace critical theory and its methodologies. Issues included women's social roles, class, race, patriarchy, and the domination of women through history. Queer theory, recognition of transgender, gender performance as posited by the theorist Judith Butler, and the crossing of gender boundaries also arose largely out of this conjunction. Now gender was understood as a fluid field, as opposed to the more fixed and rigid notions of male and female, masculine and feminine.

Feminist film theory also had a major impact on gender analysis in art history. Laura Mulvey's article, "Visual Pleasure and Narrative Cinema," published in *Screen* in 1975, is still read today for its early and sophisticated formulation of desire, power, and the male gaze. Themes of voyeurism, scopophilia, and the passive role of women in a society in which they are the spectacle emerged during the 1980s, based largely on this and other feminist film theorists' work. However, the idea of women as passive victims of masculine difference arose much earlier. The British

Marxist critic John Berger wrote in 1972 the small but surprisingly influential volume *Ways of Seeing*, in which he critiques the passive role of the female nude in art and masculinist culture generally and makes the prescient statement that, in our culture, "men act, women appear."

The role of art and art history in contemporary thought and theory became exceptionally important for cultural studies—not only because we live in a society permeated by images but also because cultural theory embraced studies of images from film to media, and art criticism picked up these cues very early. Feminism was part of these early critiques in all areas, and art became increasingly seen as a language that produces culture as much as it represents it. Numerous academic disciplines have turned to art to speak about meaning within their own areas.

Also in the 1980s, partially as a result of the move to theory, feminism became passé, especially for the younger generation. The term "post-feminist" began to appear. Pollock decried this, noting that there is a sense that feminism has become irrelevant, its politics "contaminating" and "unmarketable" for both women art history scholars and artists (in Armstrong and Zegher, pp. 57–58). Along with many other art historians, Pollock rejected this notion.

More recently, several feminist art historians have returned to gender difference, not in its original and long-rejected essentialist incarnation, but through critical theory— in this case, psychoanalytic theory. Once again, the interest was preceded by artists in the early 1980s, as evidenced by Kelly's *Post-Partum Document*. Its widespread advocacy and critical interpretation by cultural theorists as well as psychoanalytic practitioners and theorists, especially feminist thinkers, have begun to recuperate the idea of difference, based on the role of a psychic space outside of Jacques Lacan's symbolic order of language.

Freud and Lacan's assumption that women could reach sexual differentiation and sexual maturity only through the rejection of the mother—the castration complex—and the notion of their own castration was strongly contested by the work of the so-called French feminist psychoanalytic theorists Luce Irigaray, Julia Kristeva, and Hélène Cixous. A number of art-historical writers have embraced their ideas. The British writers have been particularly influential here. Pollock advocated a "matrixial critique of phallocentrism" (in Armstrong and Zegher, p. 62) based on the Israeli-French artist and psychoanalytic theorist Bracha Ettinger's notion of the matrix, an order of the psyche that interacts and intervenes within and stands alongside Lacan's symbolic order.

There are three general forms of feminist art-historical practice within the Western tradition. All three remain important, and all are a form of gender analysis. The first, "a feminist politics that focuses on recuperating the experience of women and women artists," has become more critically directed. The second remains within the realm of critique and deconstruction and resistances. The third still involves "strategies concerned to rethink the cultural and psychological spaces traditionally assigned to women and consequently to reenvision the subject/self, particularly from a psychoanalytic perspective" (Mathews, p. 95). Although gender analysis has entered all areas of art-historical analysis, as a form of advanced theory it is still strongest where it began, in modern and contemporary art writing. However, it is a growing and flourishing field that now permeates all levels of art history.

[*See also* Cinema, *subentry* Feminist Theory and Criticism; Gender Theory; Literary Theory; *and biographies of women mentioned in this article.*]

BIBLIOGRAPHY

Armstrong, Carol, and Catherine de Zegher, eds. *Women Artists at the Millennium*. Cambridge, Mass., and London: MIT Press, 2006.

Cameron, Dan. "Post-Feminism." *Flash Art* 132 (February–March 1987): 80–83.

Chadwick, Whitney. *Women, Art, and Society*. London: Thames and Hudson, 1990.

Davis, Whitney. "Gender." *Critical Terms for Art History*, edited by Robert S. Nelson and Richard Shiff, pp. 330–344. Chicago: University of Chicago Press, 2003.

Duncan, Carol. "Virility and Domination in Early Twentieth-Century Vanguard Painting." *Artforum* 12, no. 4 (December 1973): 30–39.

Ettinger, Bracha Lichtenberg. "Matrix and Metamorphosis." *Differences* 4 (Fall 1992): 176–208.

Mathews, Patricia. "The Politics of Feminist Art History." In *The Subject of Art History: Historical Objects in Contemporary Perspectives*, edited by Mark Cheetham, Michael Ann Holly, and Keith Moxey. Cambridge, U.K.: Cambridge University Press, 1998.

Nochlin, Linda. "Why Have There Been No Great Women Artists?" *Art News* 69, no. 9 (January 1971): 22–39.

Parker, Roszika, and Griselda Pollock. *Old Mistresses: Women, Art, and Ideology*. New York: Pantheon, 1981.

Pollock, Griselda. "Women, Art, and Ideology: Questions for Feminist Art Historians." *Woman's Art Journal* 4, no.1 (1983): 39–47.

Robinson, Hilary. *Reading Art, Reading Irigaray: The Politics of Art by Women*. London and New York: Tauris, 2006.

PATRICIA MATHEWS

Artists and Architects

Since Linda Nochlin launched the discipline of feminist art history in 1971 with her groundbreaking article "Why Have There Been No Great Women Artists?" scholars have uncovered the lives and works of countless female cultural producers throughout time and around the world. They not only have resurrected the names and oeuvres of forgotten women but also have called attention to the historical circumstances that shaped these women's experiences and

Adélaïde Labille-Guiard. *Self-Portrait with Two Pupils*, 1785. THE METROPOLITAN MUSEUM OF ART, NEW YORK

reputations, identifying strategies that enabled them to negotiate their circumstances.

Though no single paradigm can explain the varied experiences of female artists and architects across cultures, this article explores several key issues that often play important roles in women's careers, productions, and receptions in the realms of art and architecture. These include access to required training; the social and economic circumstances of artists and architects; perceptions of styles, subjects, and media as gendered; the historical transmission of women's cultural contributions; and, perhaps most basically, the very definitions of art and architecture, which are now being rethought to include practices traditionally associated with women.

Training and Professional Status: Artists. Women's ability to pursue careers as artists depends, first, on access to education, for serious art-making generally requires years of specialized training. Yet many educational systems, from the apprenticeships of medieval Europe to the academies that flourished in Europe from the seventeenth to the nineteenth centuries, excluded female students. Women have historically fared better in cultures and fields in which skills are acquired through private or informal systems of education, systems that may not lead to professional status.

Most of the literature on women's artistic education focuses on the European academies' ban on female students before the late nineteenth century. Many scholars have pinpointed these institutions' focus on life drawing (studying from the nude male model) as the most significant obstacle to women's artistic education in the Renaissance and Baroque eras. Certainly, male anatomy was required for the most prestigious type of artistic production—the large-scale figural scenes known as history paintings that recounted moral tales from classical, biblical, or literary sources. However, the academies banned women not only from studying nude models but from all courses of study, in keeping with the system of single-sex education that was the norm of the era. Women therefore sought training elsewhere.

The form of this alternative training varied with students' class and family backgrounds. Daughters of artists and craftsmen might learn to draw, mix paints, prepare canvases, and master other necessary skills in the workshops of their fathers or other family members. Young women of the bourgeois classes could take lessons in the private studios of male teachers, some of whom also taught in the more prestigious academies, or with female teachers who were forbidden to teach in those schools. Upper-class women frequently studied drawing and watercolors, along with music, dancing, and other graceful skills, at home with private tutors.

The rules of local professional associations also shaped women's art careers. The trade guilds that regulated the production and sale of art in many European cities from the Middle Ages through the eighteenth century were frequent stumbling blocks. For instance, the painters' guild in Amsterdam did not admit women, so female artists could not sell their works in that city. Instead, some contributed to their family businesses by working alongside the journeymen and apprentices under their fathers' or brothers' supervision. Others joined guilds in neighboring regions, which became their official places of business. A handful of women, such as Rosalba Carriera, Angelika Kauffmann, and Adélaïde Labille-Guiard, became academicians in London, Paris, and other capitals in the seventeenth and eighteenth centuries, yet until late in the nineteenth century many academies accepted women, if at all, in limited numbers or with restrictions on their status. Finally, elite European women who wished to paint professionally might establish careers as court artists, although most pursued art as amateurs.

Indeed, women artists have often flourished in cultures that value amateur art traditions. For instance, although China from the tenth century onward supported a class of professional artists, the art produced by members of the literati—male and female scholar-amateurs who practiced both painting and poetry—was often more prestigious. The Yuan dynasty painter Guan Daosheng (or Kuan Tao-sheng, 1260–1368), one of the best-known female literati artists, is often credited with initiating a new style of landscape painting. Even during the early years of the Qing dynasty (1644–1911), when Neo-Confucian ideals increasingly relegated women to the domestic sphere, many noblewomen became well-known painters and influential teachers.

The relatively high status of women artists around the world today reflects a gradual opening of the field to women and to members of marginalized classes, races, and ethnicities. Since the late nineteenth century, women have worked in every medium and technique and have contributed to every major art movement. Groups as diverse as the Russian constructivists, the surrealists, and the abstract expressionists have counted women, however uncomfortably or unequally, among their members. Women now participate actively in the international exhibitions that have shaped the global art market since the early 1990s, although they consistently constitute less than half of the artists on view in major group shows.

Training and Professional Status: Architects. In terms of both education and professional access, architecture was even more restrictive than the art fields in Europe and the United States. Indeed, women were barred from all architecture schools and professional societies until the end of the nineteenth century. In 1898, Julia Morgan, best known for designing the San Simeon mansion of William Randolph Hearst, became the first woman to study architecture at the École des Beaux-Arts in Paris. In the same year, the Royal Institute of British Architects, the United Kingdom's leading professional architectural organization, admitted its first woman. The American Institute of Architects had welcomed women just ten years earlier.

Nevertheless, women have been involved with designing and constructing buildings for centuries. The first European women to make substantial architectural contributions were members of the upper classes who designed homes and chapels for their families or public institutions for the needy. Many had read the architectural treatises of the Renaissance as part of their private education or had visited architectural masterpieces on the Grand Tour of continental Europe. In the nineteenth century, middle-class women could find employment in architectural firms. But with neither the design training nor the professional status granted to their male counterparts, they were often assigned less creative duties, such as copying plans.

In the twenty-first century, women remain underrepresented in the field at large, yet they are among its best-known practitioners. The profession's governing bodies have been slow to recognize women; the first female winner of the prestigious Pritzker Prize came in 2004 when the Baghdad-born, London-educated Zaha Hadid received the honor. Even the most successful female architects generally enjoy less fame than their male counterparts. Some, like Denise Scott Brown and Liz Diller, are known primarily through their collaborations with male partners.

Gendered Definitions: Subject, Style, Medium. Although gender does not naturally correspond to any type of art or architecture, cultural norms often prescribe different practices for men and women. In many instances, the subjects, styles, and media deemed appropriate for women garner comparatively little prestige. In other cases, such as the "women's painting" (*onna-e*) that flourished at court in twelfth-century Japan, styles that may have originated with women were later adopted by male artists but retained their associations with female practitioners and viewers.

In the hierarchy of genres that prevailed in Europe from the Renaissance through the nineteenth century, the gendering of genres fell along a continuum of public (masculine) to private (feminine). History painting, which occupied the highest place in the hierarchy, was understood as a masculine endeavor. This reflected not only women's

La Pittura. Artemisia Gentileschi's self-portrait as the allegory of painting, c. 1630. The Royal Collection © 2006 Her Majesty Queen Elizabeth II

absence from life-drawing classes but also the superior intellectual and moral faculties attributed to history painters and their roles in representing a shared history for a public audience. Although some women did achieve fame as history painters—the Italian Baroque artist Artemisia Gentileschi built her reputation on biblical narratives—most pursued the lower-ranked and more intimate genres of portraiture, still life, and scenes of everyday life. Of these, still life was often the most acceptable option for women because it did not require venturing beyond the home.

Even when working within the same genres as men, women have sometimes carved their own niches with great success. In the 1870s and 1880s, the Impressionist Mary Cassatt painted primarily domestic scenes of women and children, while her friend and colleague Edgar Degas ventured into the public realm to observe the nightclubs, racetracks, and theaters. Since the 1960s, women have claimed as their own subjects those historically painted by men. For instance, the female nude, a traditional vehicle for the aesthetic experimentations of male artists from Titian through Picasso, changed significantly in the hands of feminist artists working with the female body; a very different nude emerges from the explicitly politicized performance art of Carolee Schneeman and the abject sculptures of Kiki Smith.

Media that can be used in the home are often deemed particularly appropriate for women. Whereas oil is the most prestigious painting medium in the European tradition, watercolors and pastels have been seen as more suitable for women. Unlike oil painting, which exudes an odor, requires lengthy drying time, and causes stains, these media are odorless, easily cleaned, and can be picked up and put down again as domestic duties require. Other forms of artistic production are so closely associated with female domesticity that they have been overlooked by the history of art. Embroidery, quilting, and other skills usually learned and practiced at home are among the crafts now entering the art history discourse. Art museums are beginning to include these media in collections and exhibitions; for example, in 2002 the Houston Museum of Fine Arts organized a touring exhibition of quilts made by African American women in Gee's Bend, Alabama. Moreover, feminist artists since the 1960s have reminded us of art history's exclusions by reclaiming overlooked media, such as the story quilts of the African American artist Faith Ringgold.

The notion of home as the locus of women's work resonates in architecture as well. In cultures around the world, women have made important contributions to domestic architecture. Yet many of these women do not claim the title of architect, and their works are sometimes overlooked by traditional architectural history. In the nineteenth-century United States, for instance, the popular home economics manual by Catharine Beecher and Harriet Beecher Stowe, *The American Women's Home* (1869), included not only guidelines for keeping house, tips on child-rearing, and dinner recipes but also ideal floor plans and interior designs for morally and physically sound homes for middle-class Christian families. The design of homes and home furnishings is, in fact, strictly women's work in many of Africa's nomadic cultures, including the Tuareg of the western Sahara, where women design and construct most of their family tents as part of the traditional wedding ceremony. The association of women with domesticity influences the work and reception of professional architects as well. Many women have followed the lead of Eileen Gray, the early twentieth-century modernist who started her career designing domestic furniture and later turned to house design.

Recognition and Social Status. Like women breaking into other predominantly male professions, female artists and architects have often struggled for both recognition and respectability. The social and economic contexts in which they work have played important roles in the outcomes of these struggles. Factors such as whether they display their works in public and sell their wares on the open market or whether they work within domestic or ritual confines may contribute to women's artistic and moral reputations.

In societies where art functions as a commodity, women artists may find themselves caught in a double bind, for acquiring professional acknowledgment may jeopardize personal reputations. In Europe this tension was particularly strong in the late eighteenth and early nineteenth centuries, when the system of court and church patronage that had long constituted the highest echelons of artistic practice was on the wane, and artists were being redefined as entrepreneurial figures whose income was directly linked to attracting attention in public exhibitions. This increasing reliance on public acclaim as a marker of artistic success emerged at a time when ideals of domestic femininity, which praised women for modesty above all, were taking root among the middle and upper classes. Bourgeois women who transgressed these norms by exhibiting and selling their art in public thereby jeopardized both their class and their moral standing by affiliating themselves with the lower-status market women who sometimes sold their bodies as well as their wares.

When serious art-making is divorced from both commercial dealings and public display, women have sometimes enhanced their virtue through artistic practice. In European history the women artists accorded the least fame but the greatest virtue might be medieval nuns who worked in seclusion. For instance, several works by Hildegard of Bingen, a twelfth-century nun, composer, and author of both visionary and scientific texts, were illustrated by sisters in her convent. Turning to the Renaissance, Jeffrey

Hamburger's book *Nuns as Artists* presents a group of manuscript drawings created by the nuns in the German convent of Saint Walburg in Eichstätt around 1500. These cloistered nuns developed a unique iconography and style that stand apart from the dominant mode of their era. Deriving most of their inspiration from their immediate surroundings, the sisters incorporated motifs from the furnishings, art, architecture, and gardens of their convent into books made for communal devotion.

Historical Transmission. Although Western mythology cites a woman—Dibutatis, who traced the silhouette of her soon-to-depart lover—as the first painter, her female successors received little attention from historians until the late twentieth century. From antiquity forward, most tales of great artists and litanies of notable women included a small sampling of women artists, some of whom received monographic studies. Yet they were often described as unusually talented women who overcame the limitations of their sex to excel in a masculine endeavor. Women who worked in convents or at home were rarely mentioned. Asian women whose names were remembered by their own cultures often fell through the cracks of European and American art history. The Second Wave feminists of the late 1960s and early 1970s encouraged scholars to seek out these forgotten women, and this project continues today. Courses on the history of women artists are taught routinely, and their students may read an increasingly large assortment of books on the subject, which are now opening up to include women of color from around the world.

Now that the process of recovery is well under way, many feminists are turning their attention to the ways in which these once-forgotten stories are told. One concern is that courses, books, and museums dedicated solely to women may relegate female cultural producers to a gender-based historical ghetto. Another is that the act of labeling "women artists" might unwittingly establish misleading links between biology or biography and artistic output. Finally, some argue that adding women's names to the canons only replicates the "great master" approach to art and architecture history, without challenging its basic tenets. With so many women having produced art outside the public realm, in styles and media generally overlooked by histories, a more profound rethinking of the discipline might be required if we are to account adequately for the full range of women's cultural contributions.

[*See also* Gardens and Gardening *and biographical entries on women mentioned in this article.*]

BIBLIOGRAPHY

Broude, Norma, and Mary D. Garrard. *The Power of Feminist Art.* New York: Harry N. Abrams, 1994. This amply illustrated collection of essays focusing on the feminist art of the 1970s provides a helpful introduction to the major figures and issues of the era.

Chadwick, Whitney. *Women, Art, and Society.* 3rd ed. New York: Thames and Hudson, 2002. Discusses female painters and sculptors working in Europe and the United States from the Middle Ages to the present; the nearly five-hundred-page third edition includes a final chapter on contemporary art that includes women from around the globe, focusing on international exhibitions.

Hamburger, Jeffrey. *Nuns as Artists: The Visual Culture of a Medieval Convent.* Berkeley: University of California Press, 1997. Hamburger's in-depth study of manuscript pages produced by the convent of Saint Walburg around 1500 provides a model for studying women artists working in ritual contexts.

Martin, Brenda, and Penny Sparke, eds. *Women's Places: Architecture and Design, 1860–1960.* London and New York: Routledge, 2003. Focusing on the United States and the United Kingdom, this collection of eight case studies, plus an introduction and a thorough bibliography, examines intersections among clients, architects, and interior designers in their historical and material contexts.

Nochlin, Linda. "Why Have There Been No Great Women Artists?" In *Women, Art, and Power and Other Essays,* pp. 145–178. New York: Harper and Row, 1988.

Nochlin, Linda, and Ann Sutherland Harris. *Women Artists: 1550–1950.* Los Angeles: Los Angeles County Museum of Art, 1976. This exhibition catalog inspired a great deal of research on European and American women artists; includes short biographies and bibliographies for each artist.

Parker, Rozsika. *The Subversive Stitch: Embroidery and the Making of the Feminine.* London: Women's Press, 1984. Offers a historical survey of needlework practices in Europe and America, focusing on the contexts and attitudes of women embroiderers.

Prussin, Labelle, ed. *African Nomadic Architecture: Space, Place, and Gender.* Washington, D.C.: National Museum of African Art, 1995. Examines tents and other impermanent structures made by women in several African cultures, focusing on their cultural and ritual contexts.

Rendell, Jane, Barbara Penner, and Iain Borden, eds. *Gender, Space, and Architecture: An Interdisciplinary Introduction.* London and New York: E. and F. N. Spon, 2000. Forty-two major essays, many in excerpted form, are reprinted in this wide-ranging reader.

Slatkin, Wendy. *Women Artists in History: From Antiquity to the Present.* 3rd ed. Upper Saddle River, N.J.: Prentice Hall, 1996. Of the readily available surveys of women artists, this is the only one to include discussions of women's art before the Middle Ages.

Torre, Susan, ed. *Women in American Architecture: A Historic and Contemporary Perspective: A Publication and Exhibition Organized by the Architectural League of New York.* New York: Whitney Library of Design, 1977. Looks beyond the history of professional architects to contextualize and explore women's uses of and influences on architecture, especially housing.

Weidner, Marsha, ed. *Flowering in the Shadows: Women in the History of Chinese and Japanese Painting.* Honolulu: University of Hawai'i Press, 1990. Includes ten essays (five devoted to China, five to Japan) and an introductory chapter, providing a valuable overview of the subject as well as in-depth studies of particular figures and eras.

LAURA AURICCHIO

Erotica and Pornography

The question of what constitutes pornography and whether or how it differs from erotic art is a troubled one, not least because it depends first on a fraught relationship with the depiction of sexual behavior, and second because the category of art is itself utterly unstable. Thus, some cultures depict explicit sexual activity without having a category of "art" (for example, the scene of copulation on the walls of the Paleolithic caves at Lascaux in southwestern France), and others depict it in sacred settings where "art" is less important than religious or ritual concerns. Neither art nor pornography would be relevant categories for the sculpture that covers the temples at Khajuraho in central India (ninth to fourteenth century). There divinities and their followers enjoy sex in endless variations, and the luxuriance and generative power of the gods is understood by viewers whether or not they experience comparable sexual arousal in the process of ritual gazing. By comparison, the sight of a real man and woman kissing in a Bollywood movie shown in India might well be considered by those same viewers as scandalously close to pornography.

Genres, categories, and functions shape the way viewers interpret what they see and feel, and the abstract concepts of art or pornography that attempt to crystallize and control those feelings seldom succeed even in making stable definitions that hold from one community to another. This becomes vivid when we look at the carved column capitals so frequently used in the cloisters of medieval French monasteries. Here monsters and humans and animals take grotesque and "obscene" poses, copulate, and in other ways give visual form to the problem of the temptations of the body that haunted and strengthened the faith of the monks for whom the images were designed. Should we label these images pornography or erotic art, or are they religious art with religious purposes?

Gendered Representation and Experience. Within this unstable set of discourses, gender is a frequently fixed point because of the rarity of documentable female artists and patrons. Regardless of how one defines erotic art or pornography, the fact remains that few societies have produced visual images known to be specifically for women or by women, and few have left any records documenting the responses of women to such imagery. It may be that those groups which believed that conception of a child could only occur if both man and woman experienced orgasm did indeed have visual images meant for the excitement and enjoyment of women. It has been suggested that some of the famous Italian Renaissance paintings of reclining nude women, such as Giorgione's *Sleeping Venus* (c. 1510) or Titian's many equally languorous Venuses (also from the sixteenth century), were meant to hang in the bedrooms of the rich and to help arouse the sexual interest of wives and husbands. A more enigmatic but equally provocative case is that of the little terracotta statuettes from ancient Greece that show Baubo, a woman raising her skirt to reveal her genitals. The story to which these images may refer concerns the goddess Demeter whose daughter was abducted by Hades. Her sorrow over her loss was so deep that only Baubo's gesture could make her laugh. What the laugh means and how the statuettes were connected to it remains mysterious, but it seems at the least to have to do with women's genitals as a source of joy or humor.

In the later twentieth century, as some feminists began to claim the right to express their sexuality both in their behavior and in representation, at least three issues emerged as locations for debate. The first was the question of whether there was a particularly gendered experience of erotic pleasure, the second whether women can make and enjoy pornography, and the third whether pornography is inherently inimical to the interests of women.

The first issue, women's pleasure, has been debated since antiquity, when the mythic Greek seer Tiresias, who experienced life as both a woman and a man, claimed that women experienced greater pleasure. Victorian rhetoric, by contrast, insisted on men's greater and less controllable erotic desire, and it tied pleasure both to gender and to moralizing judgments about ethnicity, race, and class, imagining women's pleasure normally only through men's eyes. Feminist artists, engaged by these debates about women's pleasure, sometimes took on the exploration of gendered experience in their work. Both abstraction, as in the work of Judy Chicago—whose central-focus pictures of the 1970s such as *Through the Flower* (1973) created an imagery of orgasmic radiance as particularly feminine—and figuration, as in work of Nicole Eisenman since the 1990s—with its ironic and historically referential paintings and installations—found ways to represent women's experience. The question of essentialism, which asked whether there was something inherently female or feminine about certain kinds of sexual responses or desires, accompanied efforts by artists to develop a visual language to express posited particularities of sexuality.

The circumstance of women as makers and users of pornography is always the flip side of women as makers and users of erotic art, the two separated by culturally specific definitions and discourses. The interest of a number of performance artists in a feminist body art, as with the work of Carolee Schneemann or Yoko Ono in the 1970s, opened one path to an exploration of the explicit depiction of women's pleasure, while a second path involved the movement by women performers and makers of commercial pornography to legitimate their work. Some performers located themselves in both sites; Annie Sprinkle, for example, since the 1980s has made films and videos and performance pieces that are usually indistinguishable from commercial pornography and combined the exploration of sexuality with a challenge toward conservative cultural standards of behavior and art making.

Debates and Redefinitions. Meanwhile, some feminists have debated whether commercial pornography should be viewed as inherently inimical to women and exploitative, even dangerous, to them. Even as "sex-positive" feminists in the 1970s and 1980s were arguing for the free-speech right to make explicit representations of women's sexual activity and as organizations such as Prostitutes of New York (PONY) were fighting for the rights of prostitutes, a group of feminists organized together with the writer Andrea Dworkin (1945–2005) and the legal theorist Catharine MacKinnon to place restrictions on commercial pornography. The polarization and public nature of these debates seems to have been part of a larger U.S. discussion of the nature of sexuality as well as of feminism's politics of sexuality, but by the 1990s some of the energy that had gone into the issue had faded as had discussions of women's pornography.

For feminists attentive to the growth of transnational theory and activism, the locally specific nature of the sexuality debates and art practices needed to be seen on a much larger stage and in relation to other, radically different, representational practices and norms. In this vein, a 2007 exhibition at the Brooklyn Museum called "Global Feminisms" included work by several artists for whom sexuality is central but for whom neither pornography nor erotic art are operative terms. A photo series included in the exhibition and dating from 2001 titled "Static Drift," for instance, by the Kenyan artist Ingrid Mwangi, uses the female body as a surface on which to map nation, race, and gender, while a 2001 photo series by Ryoko Suzuki, "Bind," explores the notion of binding the female body as a way to explore a gendered identity and sexuality. In all of these cases, notions of pornography and the erotic are always in the background but not in the foreground of the art.

International struggles around the exploitation of the bodies of the economically and socially vulnerable have begun to reconfigure representations of sexuality, although commercial pornography remains remarkably tradition-bound and prone to see only through the eyes of men as well as to see violence as profoundly connected to sex. Photographs released in 2004 from the Abu Ghraib prison in Iraq, showing U.S. soldiers using the sexual humiliation of detainees as a form of torture, reveal a conjunction of sex and violence and power that also constitutes a vivid form of pornography; the notorious incident suggested a possible location for further debate about how we define pornography and what the privileged position of the notions of "erotic" and "art" have to do, themselves, with power.

[*See also* Chicago, Judy; *and* Sexuality, *subentry* Overview.]

BIBLIOGRAPHY

Bertholet, Ferdinand. *Gardens of Pleasure: Eroticism and Art in China*. Translated by David Radzinowicz. New York: Prestel, 2003.

Broude, Norma, and Mary Garrard, eds. *The Power of Feminist Art: The American Movement of the 1970s, History and Impact*. New York: Abrams, 1994.

Cornell, Drusilla, ed. *Feminism and Pornography*. New York: Oxford University Press, 2000.

Desai, Devangana. *Erotic Sculpture of India: A Socio-Cultural Study*. New Delhi: Tata McGraw-Hill, 1975.

Doyle, Jennifer. *Sex Objects: Art and the Dialectics of Desire*. Minneapolis: University of Minnesota Press, 2006.

Eisenman, Stephen. *The Abu Ghraib Effect*. London: Reaktion, 2007.

Porter, James I., ed. *Constructions of the Classical Body*. Ann Arbor: University of Michigan Press, 1999.

Schneemann, Carolee. *Imaging Her Erotics*. Cambridge, Mass.: MIT Press, 2002.

Screech, Timon. *Sex and the Floating World: Erotic Images in Japan, 1700–1820*. Honolulu: University of Hawai'i Press, 1999.

NATALIE BOYMEL KAMPEN

Folk Art

The definition of folk art has long been debated among art historians and cultural critics. In its strictest sense "folk art" describes the artwork of traditional societies, often utilitarian or ritual in nature, reflecting traditional practices that have developed and endured over time. Once popularly called "primitive"—a description that is now generally avoided—it includes a wide range of art forms, such as ceramics, textiles, and baskets, as well as various forms of drawing, painting, and sculpture. The feminist art critic Lucy Lippard has suggested that the term "vernacular art" may be more appropriate in this context.

Folk art also includes the work of so-called outsiders—self-taught artists who work outside (often with little knowledge of or interest in) the echelons of "high art." This description suggests that folk art is necessarily amateur in nature and that it exists as an aesthetically inferior form of "low art," in opposition to the formalistic requirements of "high art." But this definition is also fluid. For example, affluent young American women of the early nineteenth century were taught to draw and paint in the female seminaries and day schools popular at the time, yet their work—the result of formal schooling—is widely identified as folk art. In all cases, the definition of folk art, although ambivalent and sometimes contradictory, appears to be driven by a sense of exclusion from the mainstream of fine art. Perhaps not surprisingly, much of the art so defined has been created by women.

Folk art made by women is of immense variety, encompassing a multitude of categories and media across the globe. One category consists of art created within traditional roles strictly defined by gender in media considered the domain of women (for example, the production of ceramics in Oaxaca in southern Mexico). A second category of folk art by women is in areas not strictly considered women's work; this art, whether decorative, narrative, or expressions of an otherwise undefined creative impulse, is nevertheless considered, for the most part, as existing outside the formal definitions of fine art.

Gender-Defined Art Production. Folk art made by women across the globe includes both utilitarian and ritual objects, and these objects are often produced within spheres specifically limited to women. In some cases this designation derived from an ancient definition of female power and fertility. For example, among various Native American groups, clay was considered a powerful substance that was linked to a female spirit, and the gathering of clay and the fashioning of pots were ritualized activities that were strictly limited to women. Quillwork—the complex splitting and sewing of porcupine quills to decorate clothing, moccasins, and other objects—was also the exclusive domain of women. Among the Cheyenne, the skill was passed from older women to younger ones in ritualized ceremony, and men were forbidden to touch the quillwork while it was being made. Women were the weavers of the Navajo people; the art was revered as a gift of the mythical Spider Woman to her daughters. This gendered production of art objects by Native Americans varied widely, largely corresponding to other divisions of labor. In tribes in which men were hunters, women usually dominated the craft production; in more settled tribes—for example, the Pueblo—men controlled some of the art forms, including weaving.

Other folk art objects made by women are tied to the female reproductive and life cycles. The women of the historical Mithila district of Bihar in northern India practice a distinct form of traditional folk painting that has survived from undocumented times to the present and that centers on marriage and reproduction. A young woman, taught by her mother or other female family members, creates a stylized "marriage proposal" painting that is presented to her prospective husband; the painting depicts both a lingam and a lotus, signifying the male and female union. She will paint the same image on the wall of the room in which the marriage will be consummated. As a married woman she will continue to paint images on the interior walls of her home, usually in celebration of Hindu religious festivals, and she will create designs in rice paste on the floors as part of the ritual of a householder.

The production of a wide range of utilitarian objects for personal and domestic use—such as pots, baskets, and clothing—has been part of women's labor across time and cultures. Textile production in particular has been the work of women in societies ranging from ancient Greece to Africa to the preindustrial societies of the West, as well as in present-day traditional cultures in Asia, Africa, and Latin America. Although in many cases the fiber arts have transcended utility—for example, the embroidery of twelfth- and thirteenth-century England known as *opus anglicanum*—and have involved highly skilled artistic practice, their domestic history has relegated them to the category of "lesser" arts. This link with the domestic sphere functioned to solidify the definition of textile art as "craft," but it simultaneously distanced women weavers, seamstresses, and embroiderers from the public, professional sphere of fine art. However, there were female members of craft guilds—for example, in medieval France, where embroiderers had public identities.

Outsider Artists. Some of the art production by women that has occurred outside the household, in more formal settings, is also described as folk art. American art provides significant examples of work of this type. In the early nineteenth century the daughters of relatively affluent American families, particularly in New England, were sent to day schools for young women, where the mastery of "handiwork" was considered an important part of their education. Although handiwork was originally defined as needlework, it expanded to include a wide range of art forms. As early as the colonial period, girls were taught at a young age to create an embroidered sampler, usually including the letters of the alphabet, as a demonstration of their skill. The schools for young ladies elevated this work to a more formal level, progressing beyond samplers to detailed embroidered scenes, often on silk. In addition to needlework, the schools taught drawing, painting, and cut-paper work. The students produced "theorem paintings," usually still lifes on velvet or paper, according to a formula; stencils were often used (either ready-made or created by the artist), but many were painted freehand. Existing examples of nineteenth-century "lady's painting" portfolios demonstrate a painstaking and serious approach.

Another element of the art curriculum for young American women, particularly in the early nineteenth century, was the mourning picture, or memorial painting. Following the death of George Washington in 1799, there was a surge of American interest in commemorative art—an interest that soon extended to the memorializing of deceased family members, usually through a painting made by a female relative. Some early forms of the mourning picture were embroidered; some combined needlework and paint; others were painted, in watercolor or ink, on paper. Most of the works depicted grieving family members gathered around a tomb or other marker, often topped by an urn; recurring motifs included garlands and the weeping willow. *Memorial for Polly Botsford and Her Children*, for example, a watercolor, was painted in Connecticut around 1815 by an unidentified artist (although the widespread practice of this art form by women suggests that the artist was female). *Sacred to the Memory of Abner Clapp* (embroidery and watercolor, c. 1809) is signed by Hannah Clapp. Some scholars speculate that young mothers and wives of the period may have painted their own mourning pictures, anticipating the possibility of an early death from disease or childbirth.

Other paintings by nineteenth-century American women, which are today part of folk art collections in museums and private ownership, commemorate family or community events. *Fourth of July Picnic at Weymouth Landing* (watercolor and cut paper, c. 1845; Art Institute of Chicago) is a detailed, naturalistic work that uses a collage technique; it is signed by Susan Merrett. Allegories were also popular, such as Betsy Lathrop's *Venus Drawn by Doves* (c. 1815; Abby Aldrich Rockefeller Collection), a small work—only fifteen inches square—rendered in watercolor and cut paper on silk.

Several women artists have become well known despite their designation as folk artists. Grandma Moses (Anna Mary Robertson Moses), perhaps the most famous American self-taught artist, began painting in her seventies and produced more than sixteen hundred works before her death at age 101. Typical of the self-taught artist, she apparently began painting as a form of creative expression, for her own pleasure.

Other folk artists, such as Missionary Mary Proctor, Sister Gertrude Morgan, and Bessie Harvey, claim a spiritual inspiration. Harvey, whose sculptural pieces are fashioned from roots and branches, describes her work as a visionary process in which the spirit of the wood speaks to her, suggesting a link to African tradition. Harvey, Morgan, and Proctor all use a multitude of found objects in their work, another commonality among outsider artists, whose access to traditional art materials is often limited. In many cases this break with traditional materials results in a flexible, innovative approach and a visual energy that some collectors and critics have praised as the distinguishing hallmark of folk art.

Folk Art and Feminist Art. The feminist art movement of the 1960s and 1970s, in its efforts to reexamine the arts and to create a nongendered definition of "artist," embraced folk art made by women throughout the ages. Linda Nochlin, Griselda Pollock, and other art and cultural historians pointed to a male-centered hierarchy of the arts that excluded art forms made by women, particularly those linked to the domestic sphere; Alice Walker's book *In Search of Our Mothers' Gardens* (1983) suggested a new definition of art that would include the everyday artistic practices of women. Judy Chicago, Miriam Schapiro, and other artists deliberately employed "women's crafts" in fine art pieces and installations that sought to address the exclusion of art forms such as quilting, embroidering, and china painting. Chicago's *The Dinner Party* (1974–1979), now considered an icon of feminist art, is a massive installation that honors historical and mythical women. A collaborative piece that centers on table settings, using ceramics, embroidery, and other "domestic arts," the work subverts prefeminist definitions of both art and artist.

The intersection of folk art and feminist art seems appropriate to the postmodern era, in which formalism has been overturned and definitions of art have broadened and in which new media proliferate. Nevertheless, "folk art" continues to function as a broad category for various forms of artwork that exist outside the historical walls of "high art." As such, it includes much of the art, from prehistory to the present, made by women.

[*See also* Artisanal Production; Chicago, Judy; Moses, Grandma; *and* Textiles.]

BIBLIOGRAPHY

Bank, Mirra. *Anonymous Was a Woman.* New York: St. Martin's Press, 1979.

LaDuke, Betty. "Traditional Women Artists in Borneo, Indonesia, and India." *Woman's Art Journal* 2, no. 1 (Spring–Summer 1981): 17–20.

Lipman, Jean, and Alice Winchester. *The Flowering of American Folk Art, 1776–1876.* New York: Viking Press and the Whitney Museum of American Art, 1974.

Lippard, Lucy R. "Crossing into Uncommon Grounds." In *Common Ground/Uncommon Vision: The Michael and Julie Hall Collection of American Folk Art*, pp. 56–67. Milwaukee, Wis.: Milwaukee Art Museum, 1993.

Parker, Rozsika, and Griselda Pollock, eds. *Framing Feminism: Art and the Women's Movement, 1970–85.* London: Pandora, 1987.

Rubinstein, Charlotte Streiffer. "The First American Women Artists." *Woman's Art Journal* 3, no. 1 (Spring–Summer 1982): 6–9.

Walker, Alice. *In Search of Our Mother's Gardens: Womanist Prose.* San Diego, Calif.: Harcourt Brace Jovanovich, 1983.

DOROTHY BAUHOFF

Space and Gender

Built environments are shaped by social relationships, economics, and cultural values, and as such they are indices of social hierarchies and relationships of power. Control over resources such as food, land, shelter, raw materials, and reproduction and status differences among individuals and groups are frequently enacted through conventions of spatial access and by ritual behaviors and ceremonies, notably those concerned with approach, departure, and boundary definition. Thus the use of space in buildings, cities, and landscapes by men and women in various regions of the world and in diverse cultures reflects and reinforces core definitions of male and female, public and private, identity and difference, propriety and transgression. These values also find expression in laws and regulations concerning building usage, in forms and materials, and in legislation relating to men's and women's behaviors in private and public, by rules of etiquette and by normative concepts of gender and sexuality.

Viewed in cross-cultural perspective and in historical context, it is clear that women's interventions in architecture and the built environment encompass a rich and varied array of activities. These range from public to private and can be observed in both indigenous cultures and industrialized, modern societies; in the latter cases, professional and political activism by women architects and planners since the 1970s and feminist challenges to the institutional cultures and professional practices both within specialized areas and among the public at large have created far-reaching changes in both the environment and the ways in which it is discussed and analyzed.

In the industrialized societies of North America, Europe, and Asia, profound changes in thinking about two key areas of spatial occupation have taken place. Although the effects of these changes clearly vary by location and culture, these shifts in cultural geography and spatial relations have had profound effects on individual lives and collective experience. In the first place, ideas about the home, housework, and the gendering of domestic space increasingly emphasize shared responsibility and power among men and women, as well as new patterns of living and working both in the home and in public or institutional workplaces. Second, increasing unencumbered use of city streets, parks, and public transportation by women has had far-reaching consequences for women's access to economic resources, organizations, and institutions. These shifts in spatial access, circulation, and movement have in turn increased spatial awareness and activism on the part of women, particularly among traditionally disempowered groups such as women of color, working-class women, and older women.

Overview. Women's use of architectural space and their roles in shaping the built environment can be divided into five principal categories:

1. professional activity in the fields of architecture and planning;
2. participation in and contributions to the building crafts and trades;
3. patronage of architecture and urban form through service on advisory boards or community planning groups, or through private activities as being architectural clients, home builders, or consumers of architecture or interior design;
4. publication of architectural criticism, journalism, history, and theory; research and writing in urban studies and cultural geography; participation in public debates;
5. environmental and urban activism, such as housing or tenant organization; participation in union and/or management decisions relating to the use of workplace or to the conduct of work by men and women; participation in grassroots organizations relating to safety and health in cities.

Recognizing that debates about access to and control over space often encode struggles over fundamental definitions of gender, sexuality, and individual rights, women have frequently focused on the built environment as a stage for spectacle and struggle, and they have long sought ways to intervene in its shape and character. Through small, seemingly personal, decisions—such as decisions about where to walk or shop, or whether to sit in a garden or on a rooftop—and in unconscious and traditional ways as much as in large, public debates or displays, women's use of space expresses cultural values that touch every aspect of their lives. Given the enmeshed relationship among gender values, relationships of power, and spatial negotiations, it is not surprising to discover either the wide variety of ways in which questions of spatial access and control have been approached throughout history and in different cultures, or the difficulty of documenting and analyzing these phenomena.

Architects and Planners. In the industrialized world, where specialized education and certification have become the norm for most professions since the nineteenth century, women have measured their success through rates of acceptance by professional schools and certification by professional organizations. Early-twentieth-century pioneers in the field, such as Sophia Hayden, Julia Morgan, and Marion Mahoney Griffin, whether working as individual practitioners or in collaboration with men, paved the way by securing important commissions for both houses and public buildings and by ensuring that the critical response to their work enhanced their reputations. For these women professionals, the collaborative contributions of other women—notably as clients or patrons (for example, Phoebe Hearst, who expedited Julia Morgan's relationship with the University of California and also with her son, William Randolph Hearst, builder of Morgan's best-known work, San Simeon) or as critics—was, and remains, essential. Moreover, access to essential educational, social, and professional networks is strongly affected by economics, ethnicity, and race, as well as gender. Though women have increasingly gained entrance to the professions of architecture and urban planning over the last century, their participation as a group has been limited; for women of color generally, and for women outside North America and Europe, professional access has been severely limited.

Craftswomen. The above observations hold true for the building trades as well. Yet, though women's entry into the professionalized trades and crafts has often been hampered by political and cultural prejudice, they have nonetheless played a significant role in interior design and decoration and in the furnishing of buildings, especially at times when handicraft and ornament are particularly valued: working as painters, ceramicists, metalworkers, furniture designers, and upholsters, women have thus had a notable impact on the built environment. It is also significant to note that among some indigenous groups, such as the Anasazi in the North American Southwest or the Ndebele of South Africa, women play a principal role in building trades, particularly as house builders.

Patronage. Though some might wish that questions of design and aesthetic choice among architects and their clients could be decided within a separate realm of artistic freedom and creativity, in practice most decisions about the built environment take place elsewhere and are beyond the control of individual designers or users. Limited access to money and material resources, as well as an inherited lexicon of building types and uses, severely narrows the scope of building and design imagination, reinforcing the primacy of existing models. Yet the opposite is also true: because of the enmeshed relationships between cultural values such as gender and their representation in spatial behaviors and conditions, even the smallest shift or change in practice can have far-reaching consequences. Feminists and other activists have long recognized the necessity and the potential ramifications of environmental change, whether this relates to the home, public buildings, workplaces, or city streets.

Changes in the use of rooms, in the relationships between public and private functions (such as bringing the public into one's home for meetings, child care, or food service), or in minor architectural interventions—like enclosing a porch or balcony to create a safe and private extension of the home—can easily remain invisible to all but local or privileged observers. Yet this is where some of the most profound shifts in the gendering of space can and have occurred. Whether through prominent, high-budget building programs—such as those undertaken by Bess of Hardwick in sixteenth-century England, or by Madam C. J. Walker (whose home and factory buildings represent significant works by African American architects), or by Frank Lloyd Wright's women clients of the 1920s—or in more modest, contingent actions by tenants in private homes and multi-unit urban housing developments, women's roles as users of space have offered opportunities to challenge spatial and gender values, as well as other social norms.

Moreover, the complex sequences of spaces within the courtyard houses and compounds historically found in agricultural settlements throughout the world, and still today in the urban settlements of the Middle East and much of Africa, offer myriad opportunities—described in literature, personal anecdotes, and increasingly by historians and social ethnographers—for women to find ways to take control of space and/or to contest normative values. These activities and their cultural ramifications are more difficult to document, but they are no less significant in the shaping of spaces or for the gender relationships negotiated and enacted within them.

Architectural Criticism, Historical Writing, and Journalism. Women have played a prominent public role as critics and historians of the built environment throughout history, resulting at first from their special identification with the home, family, and domestic realm, and later expanding as a result of feminist awareness of the signal role of space in shaping women's experience. Whether we cite prominent, well-published writers such as Marina Griswold Van Rensselaer or Ada Louise Huxtable, or turn to private letters, memoirs, or household accounts, it is clear that women have long focused on the built environment in their writings and that their critical observations have had a profound effect.

Urban and Environmental Activism. Access to urban space, adequate housing, and workplace health and safety remain primary concerns of women in general and feminist activists in particular. Through tenant organizations, grassroots groups, and many other forms of community service, activists strive to make the concerns of women public and to improve the lives of women, children, and men. This activism, which is often public and confrontational, is in and of itself an example of the critical linkage between spatial and gender norms since by its very nature it contravenes the traditional notion that women should remain out of sight, avoid controversy, and not speak out in public. Thus women activists—from the suffragettes of the early twentieth century, to civil rights protesters of the 1950s and 1960s, to the women who strove to "take back the night" by walking together through poorly lit or crime-ridden neighborhoods in the 1970s, to women students gathering together in the plazas and common spaces of universities throughout the world—have long recognized that their visibility and their very presence in public places carry a message of strength and solidarity, whatever their particular politics or message.

[*See also* Bess of Hardwick; Gardens and Gardening; *and* Houses and Housing.]

BIBLIOGRAPHY

Celik, Zeynep. "Gendered Spaces in Colonial Algiers." In *The Sex of Architecture*, edited by Diana Agrest, Patricia Conway, and Leslie Kanes Weisman. New York: Harry N. Abrams, 1996.

Colomina, Beatriz, ed. *Sexuality and Space*. New York: Princeton Architectural Press, 1992.

Franck, Karen A., and Sherry Ahrentzen. *New Households, New Housing*. New York: Van Nostrand Reinhold, 1991.

Hayden, Dolores. *The Grand Domestic Revolution: A History of Feminist Designs for American Homes, Neighborhoods, and Cities*. Cambridge, Mass.: MIT Press, 1981.

Torre, Susana, ed. *Women in American Architecture: A Historic and Contemporary Perspective.* New York: Whitney Library of Design, 1977.

Wekerle, Gerda R., Rebecca Peterson, and David Morely, eds. *New Space for Women.* Boulder, Colo.: Westview Press, 1980.

Wright, Gwendolyn. *Building the Dream: A Social History of Housing in America.* Cambridge, Mass.: MIT Press, 1981.

ALICE T. FRIEDMAN

ARTISANAL PRODUCTION

This entry consists of three subentries:

Overview
Marketing
Types of Artisanal Production

Overview

Over the centuries, woman's roles in artisanal production, otherwise known as handicraft production, have varied widely with respect to broader economic, cultural, and social conditions. These conditions have influenced women's abilities to be autonomous in the process of making artisanal products, to get and control the resources necessary for making their handicrafts, and to gain access to viable markets for their products.

Defining Artisanal Production. Artisanal production is the labor-intensive process of making something—cloth, shoes, silverware, furniture, pottery, and many other items—for self-consumption and for the market. Typically, the artisan, or craft maker, controls the tools and has all the knowledge necessary for production. This work tends to use low or specialized technology, but it should not be considered simple by any means. Many handicrafts such as weaving are not just labor-intensive: they are knowledge intensive, and they can also require a great deal creativity on the part of the artisan. Ideally, the artisan controls the raw materials and the marketing of the product but often is somewhat beholden to suppliers of the raw materials and middlepersons and vendors. Compared to other workers, artisans take pride in their relative independence.

Although artisans throughout the world have fabricated similar products, items are not universally associated with any one gender; the artisans identified with particular items or categories of production vary from culture to culture. If craft specialization is house-based, then it is generally considered a part-time occupation that complements other subsistence strategies. Crafts may be the product of the labor of all members of the household, each taking a distinct role in the process. When the product goes to the market, however, all participants in the process are not recognized.

Artisanal products differ dramatically from mass-produced industrial products in that no two products are the same. Each item reveals the manner in which it was produced and even the identity of the maker. Imperfections and innovations are also present in the final product. Prior to industrialization this was considered the norm, and some individual artisans became well known to their clients. Since industrialization, judgments of the aesthetic qualities of handicrafts range from criticisms of their flaws to praises for their distinctive characteristics.

Artisanal Production in Cultural and Historical Context. Anthropologists have long recognized that craft production has been part of many diverse societal and economic configurations, including peasant households and ranging from precapitalist, nonindustrial societies throughout the world to post-Fordist, late-capitalist societies of the twenty-first century.

Artisanal production has been associated most often with peasant economies. The handicrafts produced were part of the overall household economy, just one element of the peasant mode of production, which was based on the labor of all members of the household: female and male, children and adults. Because of women's place in the peasant household and their relationship to its other members, their artisanal work has often been overlooked because their labor was subsumed by males and sometimes by more senior female members. Women's labor was largely hidden in the peasant household when it came to craft production, especially if women did not have access to the market.

In precapitalist economies worldwide, labor was divided by gender and was considered complementary, involving separate control of the respective economic resources. Most craft production was part of a household's subsistence regime; only surpluses or those objects associated with ritual would become part of exchange relations among individuals, households, or kin groups. As individuals within societies became more differentiated by role and status, artisans also made specialty luxury items for elites and ritual specialists.

Where women's artisanal production in precapitalist non-Western societies was prestigious and ritually important—even lucrative—women artisans had high status. For example, in Tonga, woven mats were prestige items made by high-status women who controlled the mulberry bark needed to make them. In contrast, Malaysian women wove, but theirs was a housebound form of labor; men were the merchants and traders, and women did not control the cloth they made, nor did they achieve high status.

In Mesoamerican and Andean societies prior to the sixteenth-century Spanish conquest, women weavers were accorded at great deal of prestige, wealth, and symbolic importance. As each respective region developed state societies, female artisans were affected differently. During the rise of Inca civilization, male weavers usurped female weavers' power in the transition from kin-based society to state society. In Maya and Aztec societies, by contrast, women weavers resisted political and economic domination, maintaining their status and wealth.

In West Africa, women artisans were accorded significant social, ritual, and economic roles. Artisans in lineage-based groups were specialists differentiated by gender, with female and male artisans complimenting each other. Women who made pottery complemented men who made brass, and women who made ritual baskets complemented the male blacksmiths. Both men and women artisans had access to community forms of ritual, as well as to political and economic power. Both women and men wove, but the cloth that was made differed by gender in design and style. Women's economic and social power in precolonial Mesoamerican and African societies was supported by their access to markets, a cultural ideology of gender complementarity, and the relative autonomy of women's wealth.

Not all preindustrial societies afforded women artisans prestige, status, or wealth. During the Song dynasty (960–1279) women were treated as commodities, and their labor was controlled by the patriarch of the patrilineage of which they were members or into which they married. Although embroidery itself was highly valued, the Chinese women who did the work were not. Foot binding could be viewed as a mechanism that immobilized women and helped control them as they performed the homebound embroidery work. Finished products were made for consumption by household members or were marketed by the men of the household lineage.

Women artisans living in medieval Europe also had access to markets, were recognized as skilled craft-makers, and could accrue wealth and property. In the sixteenth and seventeenth centuries, societal gender dynamics began to shift, favoring patriarchal arrangements from the level of household to the state. At roughly the same time, capitalism began to develop in this region. This combination of patriarchy and capitalism put constraints on women's abilities to establish themselves as independent artisans. During this period men consolidated their economic and political power through the creation of guilds and by restricting craft knowledge to an apprentice system. Women and girls tended to provide unskilled or semiskilled labor to the male master artisan of the household of which they were members. Women rarely received credit for this work; women who were orphaned or widowed were exploited workers who were restricted from the knowledge, materials, and markets that would allow them to establish themselves outright. Some women, especially those in the homes of successful male artisans, were recognized as artisans in their own right, but this was a rare occurrence and usually involved the textile arts (spinning, weaving, lace making) and pin making.

In the first wave of European colonialism, indigenous women in the Spanish-colonized Americas (1492–1821) resisted the patriarchal impositions placed on them that restricted them from markets, put economic control in the hands of men, and devalued their social and political contributions. Indigenous society countered colonialism by maintaining traditional gender complementary values and by persisting in recognizing women's high-status roles in producing cloth and pottery for ritual and utilitarian use.

With industrialization, women artisans in Europe suffered even greater blows to their economic autonomy and their status as artisans. Artisans in general became marginalized mobile members of society, and women were in particularly precarious positions because the industrialization of textiles directly threatened their livelihood. Though lace makers were able to compete with industrially produced lace, most women's labor was not recognized, and when poor women worked, their wages were devalued.

The second wave of European colonialism and the spread of industrialism worldwide had a generally negative effect on women artisans. For example, both women and men in Maraka Sudanese households also wove cloth that was used by the household. Women produced indigo-dyed cloth, and men produced white cloth. When this cloth entered traditional, noncapitalist markets, the earnings went to the respective artisan according to gender. As capitalism penetrated the region and the indigo cloth gained greater market value beyond the household economy than white cloth, men seized control of its production and sale.

Similarly, in the late 1980s Maya men in Chiapas Mexico tried to seize control of women's pottery production, which had become popular in craft and tourism markets. This traditional, gender-specific occupation was based on women's control of the raw materials, kin-based knowledge of production, and access to local markets. When global capital markets became more integrated in the local economy, women's newfound wealth was considered a threat to male power. Among indigenous Philippine women, weavers were esteemed and ranked high in the sacred social hierarchy, but commoditization has resulted in the decline of women weavers' social and economic status.

Contemporary Female Artisans. Although capitalism has had a generally negative effect on women artisans, women have found economic niches in the period of late capitalism, or globalization. Contemporary economic development organizations have especially targeted women in parts of Africa, Asia, and Latin America to develop artisanal products for regional, national, and international markets. These projects have had varying degrees of success. Women themselves have devised some creative solutions of their own to develop and market handicrafts.

With the improvement of communication networks, market infrastructure, and international tourism, women artisans have found consumers for their handicrafts and have even developed new products and markets. Indigenous women weavers in Chiapas (Mexico), highland Guatemala, the Andes, Ifugao (Philippines), and Bali have been particularly successful in such endeavors by drawing on tradition and catering to their consumers' gendered conceptualizations of craft production.

The long-term success of development organizations or self-initiated projects ultimately is related to global fashion, consumption trends, and women's abilities to find markets for their products. Given these parameters, some women artisans, both individually and collectively through cooperatives, have improved their material conditions and have renegotiated more favorable social and economic roles.

[*See also* Capitalism; Indigenous Cultures; *and* Markets and Trade.]

BIBLIOGRAPHY

Braudel, Fernand. *Civilization and Capitalism, 15th–18th Century Vol. 2: The Wheels of Commerce.* Translated by Siân Reynolds. New York: Harper and Row, 1982.

Grimes, Kimberly M., B. Lynne Milgram, eds. *Artisans and Cooperatives: Developing Alternative Trade for the Global Economy.* Tucson: University of Arizona Press, 2000.

Hanawalt, Barbara, ed. *Women and Work in Preindustrial Europe.* Bloomington: Indiana University Press, 1986.

Moore, Henrietta L. *Feminism and Anthropology.* Minneapolis: University of Minnesota Press, 1988.

Nash, June, ed. *Crafts in the World Market: The Impact of Global Exchange on Middle American Artisans.* Albany: State University of New York Press, 1993.

Schevill, Margot Blum, Janet Catherine Berlo, and Edward B. Dwyer, eds. *Textile Traditions of Mesoamerican and the Andes: An Anthology.* Austin: University of Texas Press, 1991.

WALTER E. LITTLE

Crafts. A manuscript illustration of women sewing in a tailor shop, c. 1400. BIBLIOTHÈQUE NATIONALE, PARIS/SNARK/ART RESOURCE, NY

Marketing

Women throughout the world have been involved across time and space in various types of artisanal activities, as well as in trade and commercial endeavors. Women's work activities have been affected by the time periods in which they lived, cultural norms and values, and economic incentives, as well as by barriers that were developed to control women's economic activities. They were also affected by the various types of collective organizations and guilds that evolved to support particular trade and craft endeavors, which often reflected a gendered division of labor.

Urban Guilds. Urban guilds existed during the Middle Ages in Europe, and they exercised significant levels of power. When women were able to participate in guilds, their involvement exercised a positive influence on their lives. Guild membership provided women entrance into an important part of community life in which they were able to acquire some degree of economic security and social privileges, as well as various types of spiritual support. Although some available data on the Middle Ages indicate that most medieval women did not participate in guilds even when they performed skilled work, as in the case of the silk workers in London, in a few instances women actually dominated some of the guilds in Rouen, Paris, and Cologne. According to Maryanne Kowaleski and Judith Bennett, about five guilds in medieval Rouen were dominated by women.

These guilds focused primarily on textile trades, especially in the production of luxury goods and linen, one of the major export products produced in Rouen. During the latter part of the thirteenth century, seven of the more than one hundred guilds in Paris were women only or were dominated by women. Specializing in luxury textiles and intricate and detailed handwork, these guilds were able successfully to produce different kinds of fancy headgear and purses with gold thread, pearls, and silk, as well as to engage in the process of spinning silk and weaving silk ribbons.

Three women's guilds operated in late medieval Cologne: the linen yarn finishers, the gold thread spinners, and the silk makers. Like the women's guilds located in Paris and Rouen, these guilds focused on the production of textiles and luxury goods. Women in charge of the guilds had considerable economic power. They were able to operate profitable business enterprises, provide training to apprentices, and oversee the more technical aspects of their crafts.

During the late seventeenth and early eighteenth centuries in New England in the United States, women's relationships to the marketplace were being reconfigured within the context of the growing needs of a developing capitalist society and the expansion of the wage sector economy. Consequently, work performed by women in several of the clothing and textile trades increased as the overall number of wage sector occupations available to them decreased because of more competition from men. Though some previously female-dominated areas such as agriculture, brewing, and dairying began to be taken over by men, other occupations such as cloth making became dominated by women.

Market Women Traders. West African women have become legendary for their involvement in various types of artisanal production and trade activities. In this region as well, the role of culture and the sexual division of labor are important. Men and women among the Esan ethnic group of northern Nigeria (Edo) developed separate spheres of male and female craft and manufacturing work. Within the prevailing sexual division of labor in Esan society, men were very much involved in the craft activity of wood carving, creating various objects for spiritual and secular needs. One of the well-known female craft industries of the precolonial period was cloth weaving and dyeing. The women of Ohordua and Uromi achieved great fame as weavers, even though cloth weaving was commonplace in all of the Esan chiefdoms. Nevertheless, not all women were versed in this particular trade area. Women's work was very specialized; some women did the weaving, while others dyed the cloth.

The *ukpon-ododo*, a multicolored cloth, was clearly considered the most important product produced by the weavers. The cloth was also popular with the Benin traders and subsequently became a major article of trade with the Europeans—French, Portuguese, English and Dutch—from about 1500 to 1700. Women's involvement and dominance in the cloth-weaving industry provided them with an important means of attaining economic independence. Esan women also were involved in the production of ceramic products, including vessels for ritual use. Women who produced these ceramic products were held in high esteem in their various communities. Other important trades of women included palm-oil processing, soap making, and food processing.

With regard to the historical and cultural involvement of Yoruba women in trade and commercial activities in

Potters. Bambara women making pottery, Kalabougou, Mali, February 2007. REUTERS/Florin Iorganda

southwest Nigeria, they long participated in trade activities in both the precolonial and colonial periods. Women traders were versatile and participated in both buying and selling products. They also were involved in hawking their merchandise and traveling around to acquire goods and materials from farmers and producers, and they engaged in commercial transactions with other traders in order to acquire cheap products. Not only were women able participants in the regional trade networks, but they also participated in long-distance trade activities, which in some cases took them far away from their homes. They had to endure the physical demands of long-distance trade along with their male counterparts and even had to protect themselves in times of political instability. Yoruba women have remained actively engaged in trade and commercial activities into the postcolonial era.

Women have also been engaged in trade and commercial endeavors in other parts of Africa as well. For example, Kikuyu women in Kenya have been very much involved in trade activities. Their involvement is related to their central roles in agricultural production and the provisioning of fuel. This may explain in part why so many of the Kikuyu women in the Mathare Valley, a poor squatter community in the capital city of Nairobi, are involved in selling vegetables and charcoal. Indeed, the vast majority of the women derive their livelihood from some form of participation in the informal sector as petty traders. Most of the people who sell vegetables in the Mathare Valley are Kikuyu women. They operate very basic facilities, usually a market stall or a simple table with a piece of awning spread over the merchandise. Sometimes they place the merchandise on a plastic sheet on the ground. Even though the women are not able to generate a large profit, they still derive some economic benefit and enhance their possibilities for gaining some economic independence.

Kenyan women's organizations have also played an important role in helping to elevate and empower women. Among the approximately sixteen thousand women's organizations in Kenya, Maendeleo ya Wanawake (meaning, in Kiswahili, Women's Progress) is clearly one of the most important in the early twenty-first century. Established in the 1950s, it has helped women secure credit to enhance their entrepreneurial activities.

Another organization that has provided assistance to Kenyan women is the Kenyan Women's Finance Trust (KWFT), which was originally an affiliate of Women's World Banking, an outgrowth of the World Plan of Action (1975). It has provided economic assistance by helping Kenyan women to become traders and entrepreneurs. It has also provided training, especially for women who reside in rural areas, concerning business management and strategies to provide access to economic institutions. The organization has also provided loans to women entrepreneurs. Women's World Banking guarantees 50 percent of the loan amount, KWFT guarantees 25 percent, and the local bank guarantees 25 percent. The KWFT has been an important vehicle through which women have received financial capital for their businesses because many financial lending institutions will not readily provide loans to women, particularly in cases where they have no collateral or other tangible resources.

Credit rotation organizations and savings clubs exist and operate largely on the basic premises that it is through collective efforts that all members can participate and receive economic assistance. The number of participants differs from one organization to the next, as well as the rotational cycles and amount of funds dispersed. In Nairobi, many entrepreneurs and traders use industry-wide associations. Individuals who sell fruits and vegetables are able to join a general traders' union that represents them in negotiations with the municipal government. Unions help with a number of different issues, including policy matters and regulations, as well as lead discussions on how market stalls should be allocated and how police patrols work with the local traders.

[*See also* Capitalism; Indigenous Cultures; International and Regional Trade Systems; Markets and Trade; *and* Money, Banking, and Credit.]

BIBLIOGRAPHY

Dale, Marian K. "The London Silkwomen of the Fifteenth Century." *Economic History Review* 4, no. 3 (October 1933): 324–335.

House-Midamba, Bessie, and Felix K. Ekechi, eds. *African Market Women and Economic Power: The Role of Women in African Economic Development.* Westport, Conn.: Greenwood Press, 1995. See in particular Toyin Falola, "Gender, Business, and Space Control: Yoruba Market Women and Power" (pp. 23–40); Bessie House-Midamba, "Kikuyu Market Women Traders and the Struggle for Economic Empowerment in Kenya" (pp. 81–98); and Onaiwu W. Ogbomo, "Esan Women Traders and Precolonial Economic Power" (pp. 1–22).

Kowaleski, Maryanne, and Judith M. Bennett. "Crafts, Guilds, and Women in the Middle Ages: Fifty Years after Marian K. Dale." *Signs* 14, no. 2 (Winter 1989): 474–501.

Miller, Marla R. "Women's Artisanal Work in the Changing New England Marketplace." In *The Needle's Eye: Women and Work in the Age of Revolution*, pp. 185–210. Amherst: University of Massachusetts Press, 2006.

Nelson, Nici. "How Women and Men Get By: The Sexual Division of Labour in the Informal Sector of a Nairobi Squatter Settlement." In *Casual Work and Poverty in Third World Cities*, edited by Ray Bromley and Chris Gerry, pp. 283–302. New York: Wiley, 1979.

Ulrich, Laurel Thatcher. "Martha Ballard and Her Girls: Women's Work in Eighteenth-Century Maine." In *Work and Labor in Early America*, edited by Stephen Innes, pp. 70–105. Chapel Hill: University of North Carolina Press, 1988.

Bessie House-Soremekun

Types of Artisanal Production

Over time and across many different societies, women have participated in a wide variety of types of artisanal production. It would appear that they have had a great deal of freedom with respect to what they make and the management of resources, knowledge, and marketing of these products. More often than not, however, the factors limiting what women make and their control over the products has related to the specific cultural values, as well as the political system, in which they live. Tempered by cultural attitudes about appropriate gender roles, female artisans have established themselves in numerous productive arenas and have used artisanal production to surmount difficult economic, political, and social barriers.

Production Types and Activities. The kinds of artisanal production and the activities associated with women are vast. Depending on social conditions, need, and conditions of the market, women continually develop new products, as other products cease to have utility or economic value. A number of artisanal products, however, are economically and politically significant. These include a number of activities related to the production of cloth and items of apparel, such as spinning, weaving, cloth dyeing, embroidery, crocheting, knitting, and sewing, and making lace, mantuas, dresses, wigs, and hats. Although men are known to participate in these productive activities, women across the globe and throughout many cultural settings predominate in this arena.

With regard to many other artisanal production activities, the cultural, political, and economic contexts influence who produces a particular item. Depending on the cultural or economic system, women or men may dominate particular industries. Some examples include making fabric or paper flowers, basket making, bead and jewelry making, pottery making, calabash carving, carpentry, knotting carpets, metalworking, paper cutting, toy making, wall painting, printing, woodcarving, metalworking, baking, and brewing.

It would be a mistake to categorize the items produced from these activities as exclusively for domestic use or for the market. Furthermore, relegating an artisanal product or artisanal activity to exclusively one socioeconomic domain—household or market—belies the networks that women have established among themselves, alliances across genders, and abilities to mobilize beyond the domestic sphere. In fact, women have used their artisanal skills to help secure their domestic base at the same time they have extended their economic and political reach via the market and trade. For example, in pre-Columbian Mexico and Guatemala (prior to 1519), women were the central producers of thread and cloth for self-consumption in the household, but their weavings were also used to make clothing for warriors and were sold and traded as luxury goods. Women weavers were recognized for their talents, and their weaving designs were incorporated into the facades of public architecture. Likewise, in China, beginning in the Five Dynasties Period (907–960), but especially during the Ming dynasty (1368–1644), women's decorative paper-cutting skills were widely appreciated; their elaborate designs were used in public ceremonies and as decorations on public buildings. However, unlike women weavers in Mexico and Guatemala, who became highly respected and relatively autonomous due to their weaving skills, Chinese women seldom were able to use paper cutting as an avenue to wealth, prestige, or autonomy; it was instead considered an acceptable activity for women bound to a rigid patriarchal system.

Organization of Production. All artisanal production entails the special knowledge of fabrication techniques, the ability to procure materials, and access to the market, if production is not specifically directed to household consumption. To what degree women control this knowledge varies cross-culturally and from one political-economic system to another. Historically, most artisanal production by women has been organized at the household level and, in contemporary times, the household continues to be the primary locus for production, regardless of whether or not women's access to materials and market are restricted.

Typically, the household is the arena in which women employ their own and their kin's labor to make items for domestic use and the market. A woman and her offspring form a production unit. The mother teaches her children, especially the girls, how to fabricate the household artisanal product. The confines of the house constitute the actual space of production. As such, the labor to produce the item and the item itself are relegated to gender-specific social and economic domains. One of the enduring strengths of the household as a unit of production is its flexibility and its ability to harness labor, especially in preindustrial societies but also in the modern day for ethnic tourism, in which handicrafts are prized. The successful household, whether built upon patriarchal social control, autonomous female kin, or complementary relationships between women and men, has been a unit that responds to new materials and changes in the market.

In the case of West African food sellers, women enlist their daughters to assist them at all levels of the production process, as they make specialty foods and beer for the market. Knowledge of recipes, of procuring ingredients, and of marketing is passed from mothers to daughters. Girls learn from their mothers not only how to make these products, but also how to market them. Skill in both areas—fabrication and market—can lead to greater economic and social autonomy, and equality. In rural Kenya, for example, Kitui men are known to spend 60 percent of their weekly

Basketmaking. Native women weaving baskets, Sitka, Alaska, c. 1897. Winter & Pond/Library of Congress

income on beer made and sold by women. Likewise, in the late Middle Ages in England and Scotland, brewing was considered a female vocation, which may have grown out of baking. Similar to African women, some of these women became independent brewers, running their own alehouses with a large degree of social and economic autonomy. In pre-Columbian indigenous societies in the Andes, including the Wari, Inca, and others, elite women were brewers and are thought to have been socially equal to their male peers.

In indigenous households in Mesoamerica and the Andes, women and offspring form a household-based unit of production. Household production begins with spinning cotton by hand (less so today than in the past), continues by weaving it into cloth on a back strap hand loom, and ends by sewing it into clothing. Appearing deceptively simple, these various interrelated activities involve high levels of skill, creativity, and technical knowledge.

Women's artisanal production has not been exclusively limited to the household. During the 1500s in France, England, and Germany, seamstresses formed craft guilds, which interlinked non-kin women as artisans. Here the unit of production consisted of a hierarchy of specialists from apprentice to master. Novice sewers entered the workshop and were trained. The workshop, while serving as a site of production, was also linked to the market as the head seamstress took orders from clients. Today, artisanal production can be organized at the level of the household, the guild, and the cooperative, which may produce handicrafts for large multinational retailers, international tourists, and local consumers.

Production Types and Activities. One of the oldest types of artisanal production is basket weaving. Predating pottery, baskets were produced around twelve thousand years ago. Basket weaving, a handicraft that can be found throughout the world, exemplifies high utilitarian and artistic qualities. Basically, any pliable but sturdy material (bark, reeds, roots, cane, wood, and even plastic) can be used to weave baskets. Among Native Americans, weaving was elevated to a high skill that mothers taught their daughters. For, example, women in the Tohono O'odham tribe in Arizona weave baskets that are sturdy enough to haul grain and tight enough to hold water or liquor. Their baskets are highly collectable today, as are those produced by Hopi, Cherokee, Yup'ik Eskimo, and other Native American women.

An artisanal practice now thousands of years old, the spinning of cotton, wool, and other fibers into thread, is a technology that is found throughout the world. Spinning began with a simple spindle whirl, which is usually spun in a shallow dish. After 500 C.E. the earliest spinning wheels were developed in India and by the Middle Ages had spread to Europe and Asia. The spinning wheel allowed women to spin higher volumes of thread in less time than the spindle whirl. In the 1800s the spinning wheel was largely displaced by industrial spinning mills, which employed women and children—often working in dangerous, exploitive conditions—but both the spindle whirl and the spinning wheel continue to have a place in contemporary world culture. In Europe and North America, hand-spun thread and yarn are used to make specialty clothing, and spinning is a feature of living history museums and handicraft fairs. In Mesoamerica, women spin specialty thread for use in clothing for the tourism market and for ritual purposes. In India, however, spinning thread and making clothing was a form of resistance to British colonial rule.

In Mali, household cloth production is a polygamous household-based activity in which Bamana men and women work in complementary roles. Men grow cotton and weave it into cloth, which is then passed to the women for dyeing. Whereas weaving is a mundane utilitarian activity, cloth dyeing is considered a specialized skill intertwined with Bamana aesthetic ideals and economic strategies. The dyed cloth is called *bogolanfini*, which means "mud cloth." The art of dyeing, passed generation to generation from mother to daughter, begins with strips of cloth being soaked in a solution of stems and leaves. The result is yellow-stained cloth to which fermented, iron-rich mud is applied in an artistic fashion. The final step involves bleaching parts of the fabric to highlight the design motif. This process can take a year to complete, and co-wives are known to compete with each other in producing this prized fabric. Skilled cloth dyers are recognized as artists and can rise to fame beyond the community.

Similarly, in the Congo region, Kuba men weave raffia cloth, which is finished by women. The women are responsible for softening the stiff cloth and then decorating it with embroidery, appliqué, reverse appliqué, and tie-dyeing, among other techniques. Batik dyeing in China, on the other hand, which first developed during the Han Dynasty (206 B.C.E.–220 C.E.), has become a women's craft specialization that is not specifically linked to men's textile production or the household. Women draw decorative designs on fabric with molten wax and then the fabric is dyed blue. Once cleaned of the wax, the patterns of birds, insects, and other motifs can be seen. In Oaxaca, Mexico, Zapotec rug weavers use cochineal dye. This prized red dye is important to Zapotecs as a cultural identity marker and to Mexicans in general as a symbol of nationality. Unlike the above cases, however, men and women work together, often in interchangeable roles from harvesting and processing the cochineal, to spinning wool, to weaving the rugs, and finally to selling the rugs in the market.

Pottery is another artisanal product with a long history that has been produced by men and women for millennia. In the ancient Mediterranean and Middle Eastern societies, men played the central-most roles in pottery production. In the Americas, however, there is more gender variation with respect to pottery. Women potters in the southwestern United States, Mexico, and Guatemala have passed knowledge of clay and pottery-making techniques through their daughters for hundreds of years. What is impressive about these women is that they are continually innovating new pottery styles for aesthetic and utilitarian purposes. In 1964 Helen Codero, a Cochiti Pueblo woman, created "storyteller pots," which are elaborate sculptures. Her techniques have been imitated by hundreds of Pueblo women and are appreciated by modern-day pottery aficionados. Maya women from Amatenango, Chiapas, in Mexico, and the municipality of Chinautla, in Guatemala, have responded to changes in the market by developing decorative pottery for national and international consumption. By the 1960s, these women altered the basic utilitarian pottery—water urns, grain-storage vessels, and earthenware—that they had been making for hundreds of years, as a response to the influx of tourists. Knowing that these consumers were not likely to purchase heavy utilitarian ware, they created new decorative designs, including vases for flowers, small ceramic animals, and candleholders, among other objects.

Economic and Creative Opportunities. The above examples illustrate that women have made good use of artisanal production in order to be creative and to explore and exploit economic opportunities. Crafts can be prestige items that, in turn, elevate women's own social status and provide economic autonomy. They can also be the center of conflict between men and women.

For example, in the Amatenango case, in the 1980s Maya men tried to co-opt women's pottery production and to limit their autonomy by impeding women's ability to market their goods, taking over distribution and physically threatening the women. The women, however, maintained control of their clay sources and fabrication techniques, while forging ties with tourist organizations, churches, and fair trade networks to keep control of their craft.

In the late 1600s in France, seamstresses came head-to-head with tailors over similar issues. Where they competed over some consumers, the primary conflict revolved around the women's autonomy. Tailors expected to draw on household labor for their business, while seamstresses forged female-based alliances that were considered to threaten the male-dominated household base of production. Gender in this case became a locus of economic and social organization.

Women weavers in pre-Columbian Mesoamerica, however, enjoyed a high degree of social and economic autonomy, as well as prestige, for the work they performed as weavers. Despite Spanish colonialism, late-nineteenth-century national initiatives, and twentieth-century trends of industrialization and globalization, indigenous female hand-loom weavers have tended to maintain economic autonomy and are respected artisans within their respective communities.

Industrialization and Globalization. As the above examples suggest, over time female artisans have had to contend with profound political and economic changes. It would be a gross overstatement to conclude that industrialization and globalization have had only a negative impact on female artisans. However, some observations can be made. There has been a tendency for men to, in some way, co-opt women's craft production when it becomes lucrative, for instance, by controlling trade routes and distribution centers and by taking over sources for materials and even production itself. Despite these negative examples, women have responded creatively to these global economic and political processes and, even, to technological changes.

The sewing machine is one such technological innovation through which the impact of industrialization and globalization on women can be traced. When Elias Howe first patented the sewing machine in 1846, and with improved models patented in 1851 by Isaac Singer and others, women spinners, sewers, seamstresses, and fabric cutters faced increased threats to their incomes, which were being undermined by the mechanization of clothing production. In this process, many women were relegated to factory work or contracted labor through a "putting-out" system in which they were paid low wages. Such sweatshop conditions in the mid-1800s have persisted into modern times in much of the developing world and even in large global cities with large immigrant populations, such as New York and Los Angeles.

In the beginning, the sewing machine was considered an expensive, complex machine that women were not capable of operating. As sewing machines in the United States and Europe became more affordable and factory-made clothing was still not a viable economic option for many families, women became their primary users, making clothing for themselves and their families. From the 1920s onward, the sewing machine has had a less central role in American and European households. For some women, sewing machines are used for making specialty clothing and art. Such creative practices suggest that the sewing machine can symbolize femininity, family, and aesthetics from a distinctively gendered position.

Sewing machines have been part of global grassroots development strategies in which women in developing countries like Ecuador, Iraq, Mauritania, Pakistan, and other countries have been given sewing machines. Although the goal is to provide women with a resource to generate income, some women have embraced the sewing machine as a means to create art and to transform their clothing into forms of artistic and individual expression. Like those women described above, working in pottery and hand-woven textiles, Cuna women from Panama have taken their sewing to high artistic and creative levels as they make *molas*, which are panels of cloth in a layered appliqué style, for personal use and for trade with tourists and collectors. These are sewn onto women's blouses but have become a popular art in which fantastic animals, political slogans, and advertisements are depicted.

[*See also* Art and Architecture, *subentry* Folk Art; *and* Textiles.]

BIBLIOGRAPHY

Bartra, Eli, ed. *Crafting Gender: Women and Folk Art in Latin America and the Caribbean.* Durham, N.C.: Duke University Press, 2003.

Coffin, Judith G. *The Politics of Women's Work: The Paris Garment Trades, 1750–1915.* Princeton, N.J.: Princeton University Press, 1996.

Hecht, Ann. *The Art of the Loom: Weaving, Spinning, and Dyeing across the World.* Seattle: University of Washington Press, 2001.

Helms, Mary W. *Craft and the Kingly Ideal: Art, Trade, and Power.* Austin: University of Texas Press, 1993.

Schneider, Jane. "The Anthropology of Cloth." *Annual Review of Anthropology* 16 (1987): 409–448.

Wosk, Julie. *Women and the Machine: Representations from the Spinning Wheel to the Electronic Age.* Baltimore: Johns Hopkins University Press, 2001.

WALTER E. LITTLE

ARWA, QUEEN OF YEMEN (1045–1138), the only woman of any Islamic dynasty to have held both temporal and, allegedly, religious authority. Arwa, queen consort and then queen in her own right, is one of the few Muslim women extensively referred to by chroniclers of her own time and later not only on her own merit but also to legitimize religious-genealogical claims.

Arwa, daughter of Ahmad of the Yemeni Sulayhi clan, was born around 1045 and, after her father's death, was brought up in the capital Sanaa at the palace of her uncle ʿAli, the Sulayhi king, and her aunt Asmaʾ. Chroniclers describe her as well educated with an excellent knowledge of the Qurʾan and well versed in history and poetry. Upon her marriage to ʿAli's son al-Mukarram, Arwa received as dowry the yearly revenue of the port city of Aden. Around 1066 ʿAli appointed al-Mukarram as his successor and, shortly afterward, was murdered. Less than ten years later, King al-Mukarram became incapacitated by paraplegia. This event marks the beginning of Arwa's effective takeover of power in Yemen as queen consort. Ostensibly for medical reasons related to her husband's condition but more likely as a result of local rebellions, Arwa moved out of Sanaa to the hill town of Dhu Jibla in central Yemen, which she made the new Sulayhid capital.

The Sulayhid dynasty recognized the authority of the Fatimid imam-caliphs in Cairo and ruled over southern Yemen in their name for almost a century. For the Fatimids, Yemen was an important military, political, and commercial outpost but also a strategic location for the eastward spread of the Ismaʿili *daʿwa* (mission). To this end, after the death of al-Mukarram in 1084, the Fatimid imam-caliph al-Mustansir officially asked Arwa to oversee the missionary affairs in the eastern regions. As queen mother, Arwa ruled in the name of her son until he died in 1090. Now queen in her own right, Arwa continued to rule until 1138, when her long life came to an end and with it the Sulayhid dynasty as a whole.

Arwa's life was not without difficulties, first with a disabled husband and then as sole ruler. Her two main challenges were constant tribal fighting in Yemen and genealogical disputes within the Fatimid caliphate. The first she handled via diplomacy rather than military confrontation, and it eventually resulted in the rise of autonomous dynasties in cities such as Sanaa and Aden. The second arose after the death of the imam-caliph al-Mustansir, whom she had loyally supported, when succession to the Fatimid caliphate was disputed between the Mustaʿlis and the Nizaris. From 1130 onward further disputes arose among the Mustaʿlis themselves between the supporters of two claimants, al-Tayyib and al-Hafiz. Queen Arwa endorsed the legitimacy of al-Tayyib.

It is in light of such genealogical disputes that the extent of Arwa's spiritual authority can be best assessed. The queen received correspondence from the imam-caliph in Cairo announcing the birth of his son al-Tayyib, and according to the Tayyibis, she was invested with the spiritual rank of *hujja* (the highest rank after the imam-caliph). In this capacity, they assert, she appointed the first *daʿi mutlaq* (highest missionary), who initiated the chain of spiritual leaders of Yemeni Tayyibi Ismaʿilis that continues in the early twenty-first century. In Yemen, Queen Arwa is still remembered as a great and much loved sovereign, as attested in Yemeni historiography, literature, and popular lore, where she is referred to as *Bilqis al-Sughra*, that is, "the junior queen of Sheba."

[*See also* Islam.]

BIBLIOGRAPHY

Cortese, Delia, and Simonetta Calderini. *Women and the Fatimids in the World of Islam*. Edinburgh: Edinburgh University Press, 2006.

Daftary, Farhad. "Sayyida Hurra: The Ismaʿili Sulayhid Queen of Yemen." In *Women in the Medieval Islamic World: Power, Patronage, and Piety*, edited by Gavin R. G. Hambly, pp. 117–130. New York: St. Martin's, 1998.

Hamdani, Husayn F. al-. "The Life and Times of Queen Saiyidah Arwa the Sulaihid of the Yemen." *Journal of the Royal Central Asian Society* 18 (1931): 505–517.

Imad, Leila al-. "Women and Religion in the Fatimid Caliphate: The Case of al-Sayyidah al-Hurrah, Queen of Yemen." In *Intellectual Studies on Islam: Essays Written in Honor of Martin B. Dickson*, edited by Michael M. Mazzaoui and Vera B. Moreen, pp. 137–144. Salt Lake City: University of Utah Press, 1990.

Mernissi, Fatima. *The Forgotten Queens of Islam*. Cambridge, U.K.: Polity, 1993.

Simonetta Calderini

ASHRAWI, HANAN (b. 1946), a citizen of Jerusalem, scholar of literature, Palestinian politician, and promoter of peace. Born in Nablus, she received her bachelor's and master's degrees in literature in the Department of English at the American University of Beirut. After earning her PhD in medieval and comparative literature from the University of Virginia in the United States, Ashrawi returned to her homeland in 1973 to establish the department of English at Birzeit University on the West Bank just as the university was transforming itself from a two-year college to a four-year institution of higher learning. She served as chair of that department from 1973 to 1978 and again from 1981 to 1984. From 1986 to 1990 she served the university as dean of the Faculty of Arts. She remained a faculty member at Birzeit University until 1995, writing and editing numerous poems, short stories, books, and articles on Palestinian culture, literature, and politics.

Ashrawi's political career began as early as her days at the American University of Beirut, where she was actively involved in student and women's politics. In 1988, Ashrawi, still unknown to the world at large, grabbed the limelight when she was invited to appear on ABC's *Nightline* as part of a three-hour discussion among four Palestinians and four Israelis. Her fluent English and clarity of argument drew the attention of the Western world, and she was immediately in demand by other broadcasters. She successfully presented the Palestinian cause in a sympathetic light, humanizing the Palestinians' plight and giving them a voice that appealed to the world. Appointed by Yasser Arafat, from 1991 to 1993 she served as official spokesperson of the Palestinian delegation to the Madrid Conference, which started the Middle East peace process.

In 1993, with the Oslo Peace Accords signed by Arafat and Yitzhak Rabin and Palestinian self-rule established, Ashrawi headed the Preparatory Committee of the Palestinian Independent Commission for Citizen's Rights in Jerusalem, and she was founder and commissioner of that committee until 1995. From 1996 through 1998 she served as minister of higher education and research and became a member of the Palestinian Legislative Council. However, in 1998, when she was nominated as minister of tourism, Ashrawi resigned from government in protest against political corruption. At that time she founded MIFTAH, the Palestinian Initiative for the Promotion of Global Dialogue and Democracy, whose ultimate goal is democracy, peace, and a respect for human rights.

In the elections of January 2006, Ashrawi was reelected to the Palestinian Legislative Council. Ashrawi's party, the Third Way, is a newly created political faction that won two seats in the 132-seat council.

Ashrawi is a member of the Independent International Commission on Kosovo and of numerous international advisory boards, including the Council on Foreign Relations, the Middle East and North Africa Region group of the World Bank, and the United Nations Research Institute for Social Development. In 2003, Ashrawi was awarded the Sydney Peace Prize.

[*See also* Palestine.]

BIBLIOGRAPHY

Ashrawi, Hanan. *This Side of Peace: A Personal Account.* New York: Simon and Schuster, 1995.

Victor, Barbara. *A Voice of Reason: Hanan Ashrawi and Peace in the Middle East.* New York: Harcourt Brace, 1994.

ISLAH JAD

ATHAVALE, PARVATIBAI (1870–1955), champion of the education of Indian women, especially widows. Born into a poor and largely conventional Brahman family of coastal Maharashtra (the Marathi-speaking part of western India), Parvatibai Athavale (born Krishna Joshi) was married at the age of eleven in accordance with the custom of prepubertal marriage for girls. At fifteen she had her first child, who soon died. When she was twenty-one and the mother of one surviving son, her husband, employed in the customs department in Goa, died. According to the prevalent practice for Brahman widows, she was "ritually purified" at once, her head shaved and her ornaments removed as a mark of permanent renunciation. A widow was regarded as inauspicious to the sight and was reduced to a household drudge; her ritual disfigurement was intended to render her unattractive to the male gaze and protect her chastity. Brahman women could marry only once in their lifetime, although Brahman men were allowed to marry as many times as they wished.

After returning to her parents, Parvatibai took her son for his education to Poona (now Pune) where her remarried sister Anandibai Karve lived with her social reformer husband D. K. Karve (1858–1962). Parvatibai was socially conservative and was only gradually persuaded by the Karves to acquire an education and work as a teacher in the widows' home opened in 1896 by Mr. Karve. As her views evolved and became more progressive, she attempted to reduce the marginalization of widows within the family, introducing a more acceptable mode of dressing—in a plain white sari instead of a drab maroon one—and also the custom of letting the hair grow again. She also popularized education for widows during her public talks at various places in Maharashtra.

In 1918, Parvatibai went to the United States to study the conditions of women there and to raise funds for the widows' home while also learning English. But her plans went awry and she ended up earning a meager living as a domestic servant, occasionally staying with compatriots from Maharashtra, while making her way from California to the East Coast. Finally she made the acquaintance of Leonora O'Reilly and her mother, labor leaders in New York who taught her better English and made her aware of the conditions of workers. She also met Indian nationalists in New York, especially Lala Lajpat Rai (1865–1928) and the Young India group. Parvatibai returned home after two years to work at Karve's widows' home for the rest of her life.

Parvatibai's thoughts about what Indians should learn from American society and what they should avoid, as expressed in the concluding chapters of her autobiography, reveal her conventional mindset, albeit with a modern touch, about a woman's primary role as a wife, mother, and homemaker. This contrasted sharply with the progressive views of Pandita Ramabai (1858–1922), her compatriot who had visited the United States three decades earlier. But mainstream society had marginalized Ramabai, while privileging Parvatibai as a role model for widows and as an advocate of women's education.

[*See also* India; Karve, Anandibai; Ramabai, Pandita; *and* Widows and Widowhood.]

BIBLIOGRAPHY

Athavale, Parvatibai. *My Story: The Autobiography of a Hindu Widow.* Translated by Justin E. Abbot. New York: G. P. Putnam's, 1930.

Kosambi, Meera. "Women for All Seasons: Anandibai Karve and Parvatibai Athavale." In *Crossing Thresholds: Feminist Essays in Social History*, pp. 338–368. Delhi: Permanent Black, 2007. An outline of Parvatibai's life and an assessment of her contribution to social reform.

MEERA KOSAMBI

AUNG SAN SUU KYI (b. 1945), leader of Burma's democracy movement and recipient of the 1991 Nobel Peace Prize. Aung San Suu Kyi has campaigned for democracy and human rights in Burma through nonviolent tactics and civil disobedience. Despite repeated harassment and detention by Burma's military government, Suu Kyi continues her struggle and is recognized globally as a symbol of peaceful resistance against authoritarian rule.

Born in Rangoon, Burma, on 19 June 1945 to one of the country's leading families, Suu Kyi grew up in a politically oriented environment. Her father, Aung San, served as the head of Burma's independence movement during World War II and negotiated its independence from Britain. He was assassinated by political rivals in 1947. Suu Kyi's mother, Khin Kyi, received a diplomatic posting to India in 1960 and became the first Burmese woman to serve as an ambassador.

While Suu Kyi spent much of her early life abroad, she maintained her connections with Burma through regular trips home. She attended high school in New Delhi before moving to England, where she received a degree in 1967 from St. Hugh's College of Oxford University. She worked at the United Nations in New York and in 1972 married Michael Aris, a British academic. After working in Bhutan, the couple returned to England and had two sons. In 1977

Suu Kyi returned to academia and published several works on Burmese history, including *Burma and India: Some Aspects of Intellectual Life in Colonialism* (1990). In 1988 she began postgraduate study at the School of Oriental and African Studies in London.

Suu Kyi interrupted her studies in April 1988 to return to Burma to care for her mother, who had suffered a stroke. Her return coincided with the largest antigovernment protests in Burma's twenty-six years of military rule. She entered the political arena by writing an open letter to the government calling for multiparty elections. Later, in August 1988, Suu Kyi gave her first public speech in support of democratic reform to a crowd of over 300,000 people. While her initial popularity stemmed from her position as the daughter of Aung San, she developed a large following in part due to her engaging speeches and charisma. Suu Kyi emerged as the democracy movement's most popular and capable leader. After the government announced plans to hold multiparty elections, she helped found Burma's largest opposition party, the National League for Democracy (NLD), on 24 September 1988. As general secretary of the party, she campaigned throughout Burma despite military harassment. The government placed her under house arrest for the first time from July 1989 to July 1995. In the election of May 1990 the NLD won 392 of the 485 seats in the elections, but the government refused to transfer power and instead convened a national convention to draft a new constitution ensuring the continuation of military power. After Suu Kyi's release from house arrest in July 1995, the NLD withdrew from the convention on the grounds that it was not sufficiently democratic.

As general secretary of the NLD, Suu Kyi has repeatedly called for dialogue with the government to negotiate a peaceful transition to democracy. Influenced by the nonviolent tactics of Martin Luther King Jr. and Mahatma Gandhi, she has pressed the military to engage in national reconciliation and has mobilized popular support through civil disobedience. Yet the military has refused the NLD's requests for substantive political dialogue and continues to suppress Suu Kyi and the NLD through detention and harassment. On 27 March 1999 Suu Kyi's husband died of cancer in England. The government refused his earlier requests for a visa to enter Burma to visit his wife. The government placed Suu Kyi under house arrest for the second time from September 2000 until May 2002 for violating travel restrictions. On 30 May 2003, while she and her supporters were traveling near Depayin in northern Burma, a mob supported by the military government attacked her convoy, killing over seventy NLD supporters. After she recovered from her injuries, Suu Kyi was placed under house arrest for the third time.

Suu Kyi continues to receive overwhelming popular support in Burma and remains a powerful symbol of democratic opposition. Despite the continuing detentions and arrests of several of her top advisers, she has kept Burma's political opposition alive. Although the government has offered her the opportunity to go abroad on the condition that she not return, she has remained in Burma. In recognition of her work, she has received several awards, including the 1991 Nobel Peace Prize for her struggle for human rights and democracy.

[*See also* Burma *and* Dictatorship and Single-Party States.]

BIBLIOGRAPHY

Aung San Suu Kyi. *Freedom from Fear and Other Writings*. Edited with an introduction by Michael Aris. 2d ed. New York: Penguin Books, 1995.

Lintner, Bertil. *Aung San Suu Kyi and Burma's Unfinished Renaissance*. Bangkok: White Lotus, 1991.

Victor, Barbara. *The Lady: Aung San Suu Kyi, Nobel Laureate and Burma's Prisoner*. Boston: Faber and Faber, 1998.

JOHN BUCHANAN

AUSTEN, JANE (1775–1817), British author whose six novels quietly revolutionized world literature, and who is considered one of the greatest writers of all time. Austen has been compared to Shakespeare and hailed as the first woman to earn inclusion in the established canon of English literature. Although she lived most of her forty-one years in relative obscurity among the minor landed gentry of rural England, she transformed her limited domestic environs into a microcosm for humanity. Over two centuries after her birth, Austen continues to attract worldwide academic and popular interest.

Jane Austen was born in Steventon, a small Hampshire village in southern England, on 16 December 1775, the daughter of a clergyman. Austen's closest companion was her sister Cassandra, who later destroyed Austen's most personal letters in order to protect her privacy, leaving biographers to conjecture ever after about certain episodes in Austen's life. Despite declining health, Austen continued to write in the last months of her life. She died on 18 July 1817 and was buried in Winchester Cathedral. In keeping with Austen's very private life, the first inscription on her gravestone made no mention of her writing or her growing fame.

Relatives rapidly began to manufacture the image of "dear Jane," a bland maiden aunt who dabbled in writing as a hobby and never made sharp remarks. They added ruffles and ringlets to her portrait, censored biting portions of her letters, and suppressed the publication of her outrageous adolescent works. Early biographers presented Austen as an embittered old maid writing romances as a consolation for not having married, and early encyclopedia articles emphasized Austen's "little" life "barren of events" rather than her devotion to her craft and keen insight into human nature. Austen had warned in *Northanger Abbey* that a woman's work might be dismissed as

> "only a novel": or, in short, only some work in which the greatest powers of the mind are displayed, in which the most thorough knowledge of human nature, the happiest delineation of its varieties, the liveliest effusions of wit and humour are conveyed to the world in the best-chosen language.
>
> (Chapman edition, p. 38)

All six of Jane Austen's completed novels—*Northanger Abbey*, *Sense and Sensibility*, *Pride and Prejudice*, *Mansfield Park*, *Emma*, and *Persuasion*—have been hailed as major works and successfully filmed. Recurrent themes include the discrepancy between appearance and reality, the horror of loveless or inequitable marriages, the need to balance reason and emotion, the devastating effects of materialism and snobbery, and the inadequacy of female education. Irony laces Austen's descriptions of guardians without wisdom, clergymen without mercy, and aristocrats without civility.

Each novel tackles a different fictional problem. *Northanger Abbey* (published in 1818 but, like the next two novels, written in the late 1790s) satirizes the unrealistic gothic novels of Austen's day and presents a plain, down-to-earth heroine. *Sense and Sensibility* (published 1811) describes two temperamentally different sisters who survive disappointments in love and frustrations with cold-hearted relatives. *Pride and Prejudice* (published 1813) focuses on a family of five unmarried daughters struggling against unfair inheritance laws and introduces a radiantly healthy, witty, and outspoken heroine (Elizabeth Bennet) who finds her mate not through her beauty or title but through her character and "liveliness of mind." In *Mansfield Park* (published 1814), Austen suggests through her portrayal of Fanny Price that even a shy young woman can come of age through quiet courage and steadfast integrity. *Emma* (published 1815) presents a heroine who learns that being "handsome, clever, and rich" does not make her a lady unless she adds kindness, tolerance, and morality. An older heroine, Anne Elliot of *Persuasion* (published 1818), discovers the advantage of "maturity of mind." A startlingly revolutionary passage occurs in this final Austen novel when Anne exclaims, "Men have had every advantage . . . in telling their own story. Education has been theirs in so much higher degree; the pen has been in their hands" (Chapman edition, p. 234). By taking pen in hand and turning her rapierlike wit on society, Austen challenged many assumptions of her age.

Austen's impact on literature and culture has been profound. Women novelists in particular have built on her creation of heroines whose worth comes from their minds rather than their looks. Critics have revealed the underlying politics of Austen's seriously comic novels, whereas others have delineated their linguistic complexity and psychological realism. Austen's popular following has burgeoned, sprouting Jane Austen societies in Great Britain, North America, and Australia, thousands of Austen-related Web sites, scores of movies, and a whole business in Austen goods, whether T-shirts or tea towels. Over two hundred years after Austen's birth, popular and academic interest in her has never been higher. Jane Austen's six novels are hailed as classics and also widely read.

[*See also* Literature, *subentry* Fiction and Poetry.]

BIBLIOGRAPHY

Auerbach, Emily. *Searching for Jane Austen*. Madison: University of Wisconsin Press, 2004. Discusses two centuries of censorship and explores Austen in relation to other pioneering women writers.

Austen, Jane. *Jane Austen's Letters*. 3d ed. Edited by Deirdre Le Faye. Oxford and New York: Oxford University Press, 1995. The standard edition of Austen's letters and the source for quotations from Austen's letters in this entry.

Austen, Jane. *The Oxford Illustrated Jane Austen*. Edited by R. W. Chapman. 3d ed. Oxford: Oxford University Press, 1933.

Fergus, Jan. *Jane Austen: A Literary Life*. New York: St. Martin's Press, 1991. Delineates Austen's struggles with publishers and focuses on her craft.

Honan, Park. *Jane Austen: Her Life*. New York: St. Martin's Press, 1987. Rev. ed. London: Phoenix Giant, 1997. A balanced biographical study not superseded by later accounts by Claire Tomalin, David Nokes, and others.

Johnson, Claudia L. *Jane Austen: Women, Politics, and the Novel*. Chicago: University of Chicago Press, 1988. A provocative study of Austen's relationship to early feminists and revolutionary thinkers.

Shields, Carol. *Jane Austen*. New York: Viking, 2001. An excellent biography for lay readers written by a Pulitzer Prize–winning novelist.

EMILY AUERBACH

AUSTRALIA

This entry consists of two subentries:

Ancient and Indigenous
Modern Period

Ancient and Indigenous

It is now widely agreed that the first modern humans arrived in Australia as far back as 60,000 years ago; they were among the very first human groups to have left Africa. The subsequent occupation of the whole of the Australian continent, which then included Tasmania and what is now Papua New Guinea (east and west), was equally rapid, with all parts occupied by around 15,000 to 20,000 years ago, including deserts and snowy mountains. This indicates an extraordinarily robust people, capable of innovation and rapid adaptation to new environments. The women among them were capable nurturers, fertile and healthy, able to reproduce successfully in the complete absence of medical technologies and artificial feeding for infants.

The reconstruction of the world of Aboriginal Australians in the very distant past is naturally problematic. However, if we assume some level of continuity from past to present, it seems likely that gender relations in the earliest human communities were organized around kinship relationships that stressed the mutual recognition of kin groups related to one another across generations, through both men and women. Women supported themselves and their children significantly through their everyday subsistence activities, and valued foodstuffs and other material goods were exchanged by men and women in accordance with the subsistence strategies of the place and time. Systems of rule or law associated people with places and with each other; parents nurtured and valued their children and placed a high importance on their well-being. Ideas of ancestral power connected people to the natural world in a relationship of mutual support and recognition.

The indigenous Australians are unique in having remained largely isolated, because of rising sea levels, from all other human groups and societies. Certainly there were visitors from Southeast Asia who left some material, cultural, and biological traces in northern Australia, but only the arrival of Europeans in the eighteenth and nineteenth centuries brought to an end the customs, cultures, and practices of ancient Australia, the oldest continuous culture in human history. Most scholars believe that the kinds of social and environmental relationships evident in Australia at the time of first Western contact are at least indicative of practices and understandings common among the earliest human groups prior to the development of domestication and horticulture/agriculture. This makes the study of gender relationships particularly compelling in the light of common presuppositions about relations between the sexes in early human societies.

Indigenous Life and Gender Relations. In most regions Aboriginal people lived in small groups traveling across a familiar landscape exploiting its natural resources. They did not cultivate the ground or have any domestic animals, other than dogs (dingoes), which were not really "tamed" or domesticated but attached themselves temporarily to human encampments until reaching adulthood. Knowledge of the landscape, its resources, and its characteristics, including the location of water sources, was encoded in song, dance, and rite and passed on to new generations by both sexes, along with a powerful sense of connection through spiritual ideas linking humans to significant places and natural species, and past to present generations.

Women and men followed different patterns of subsistence occupation. While men hunted large game, in most parts of Australia it was women's labor that provided the most enduring and reliable food sources, including many varieties of small protein sources (eggs, shellfish, birds, reptiles, grubs) and a full range of edible vegetable foods (wild grains and fruits, berries, tubers). As is the case in most

Aboriginal Living Arrangements. Single women's *mia-mia*, South Yarra, Australia, 1884. NICHOLAS CAIRE/THE NATIONAL LIBRARY OF AUSTRALIA

hunter-gatherer subsistence economies, the colder the climate the more important male hunting became. Women generally provided firewood and water and helped in the building of shelters. Men helped care for children and were generally indulgent and nurturing toward them. The importance of Aboriginal women's subsistence activities lies in the fact that they provided the most consistent, certain, and reliable food sources across the annual cycle, even though the product of hunting was more highly valued socially. In marine and estuarine environments, a high reliance on fish and shellfish resulted in a comparable level of input for men and women.

Indigenous Women in the Early Years of Settlement. During the first two hundred years of European settlement, attitudes to the indigenous people were profoundly affected by popular stereotypes. They were thought to be "primitive." Because their economy did not rely on cultivation, they were considered little more than roaming animals, without property or law. The first Western explorers who left records concerning Australia's indigenous people said little about the women among them. In part this was because women and children usually hid from the alarming intruders, but also because "natives" usually appeared only as traces in explorers' journals and diaries unless violent confrontations took place. As white settlement proceeded, attitudes to indigenous people changed from indifference to hostility when resistance to loss of land intensified.

Although many early observers found much to admire in individuals, and many missionary groups believed it was possible to bring Aborigines to "civilization" through the gospel, there was little public sympathy for their plight among early settlers, and in many cases massacres and "dispersals" took place on a lawless frontier.

Aboriginal women were of great importance during the period of early settlement, a fact only slowly being accepted in modern Australia. In early decades both pardoned convicts and free settlers put pressure on land and waters. Most were single men. From 1790 until the 1840s there were very few available British or European women in the Australian colonies; although convict women were brought by the shipload, men far outnumbered nonindigenous women, especially in the remote regions.

An unspoken aspect of many violent encounters along the frontiers was the appropriation of Aboriginal women and girls by the settlers. In a few cases the men married the women and acknowledged the children, but it was far more common for the Aboriginal women to be treated as concubines or prostitutes. Many women bore children and undertook heavy labor on the newly claimed lands. But after a house was built and the lands cultivated, they were replaced by white women. By the mid-nineteenth century, in most of settled Australia large populations of "half caste" people sprang up, almost all children of white men and Aboriginal women. There are few written records of these periods, other than those from missionaries who were established behind the line of settlement and tried to care for the children in mission institutions, where they hoped to "civilize" them and to prevent frontier men from taking the girls and women from their care. As the frontier pushed farther north and west, toward the end of the nineteenth century and into the twentieth, there are many more accurate records of these activities and the conditions they produced. Such records include censuses, police records and court cases, diaries of settlers and their wives, and missionary letters and reports.

Many indigenous families today have taken the name of the white man they believe to have been their ancestor, and although white families in the remote regions may dispute this, the Aboriginal descendants today are firm in their views. In the far north also many white men willingly acknowledged their Aboriginal partners and children but until the early twentieth century some state laws actually prevented them from marrying Aborigines or passing on legal inheritance to their children. It is likely that many "white" Australians today, especially those from rural areas, have Aboriginal ancestry.

The Life of Aboriginal Women, Past and Present. The life of Aboriginal women in pre-Western times must be inferred from the practices and customs found in their communities by early white observers, who were mostly untrained and often exhibited common prejudices and misconceptions. Australia was very fortunate, however, to have some early scientists with a relatively high awareness of custom, tradition, and practices who worked closely among Aboriginal groups little affected by Western contact. In southern and eastern Australia several noted writers gathered systematic information on Aboriginal life from the middle of the nineteenth century on, even while that life was inevitably changing. In the first part of the twentieth century, trained anthropologists lived and worked in many remote communities, and their writings, photographs, and reports provide an invaluable record of indigenous lives and worlds, even if they are sometimes disputed in details and subject to interpretation. It is on the basis of this anthropological work that Australian laws were changed finally to recognize the land rights of the indigenous inhabitants and that many contemporary claims to land have been able to succeed in Australian courts.

It is impossible to generalize now about the lives of Aboriginal women across the whole continent. In many regions today Aboriginal women live in large towns and cities and are employed in the usual occupations for non-Aboriginal people in their areas. Their families speak only English, and although the maintenance of Aboriginal identity continues to be very important for many, the practices and customs of the "traditional times" are no longer observed.

For others, in the remote regions, their connection with their former lifestyles, beliefs, and practices is much stronger; many continue to live in very small, very remote settlements, utilizing traditional food sources as well as introduced ones, speaking their own languages, and observing their own distinctive cultural practices.

In Aboriginal communities the position of women is a complex matter. Cultural divisions clearly mark men from women, but there is no simple equation with ideas of "masculinity" and "femininity" as is common in the Western world. To be a "man" or a "woman" is more than being an adult person of one sex or the other. The life cycle is marked and named, and the expectations and responsibilities of people differ according to both age and sex. For men, initiation is a necessary aspect of adulthood; in some communities a parallel recognition is given to girls, but it is generally much less marked. Initiated men and adult women are equally expected to preserve and maintain the law of their communities. Women undertake essential economic tasks, holding important knowledge of subsistence and landscape resources, playing important roles in decision-making, and in some areas possessing a separate ritual life that in some respects parallels that of men.

Marriage and Kinship. Marriage arrangements and Aboriginal kinship systems have long been among the most difficult aspects for Westerners to understand. In most regions, girls were betrothed to their future husbands at or even before birth. Choice of partner was never considered an individual matter but one deriving from the operations of Aboriginal law, which prescribed the social groups into which persons married and the type of relative they would marry. For example, in many systems people married spouses classified as their mother's brother's daughter (from a man's point of view) or their father's sister's son (from a woman's point of view). This did not mean they had to be actual biological first cousins as we would understand it; but their preceding kinship relationships determined how they were grouped and who the appropriate partner would be based on patterns of marriage going back generations. There was no choice in this and no expectation of "romantic love." However, if spouses for any reason could not get along with one another, it was common for them to separate. A woman could then marry any man classified as a "brother" to her husband. Many men had more than one wife, and in some communities the mark of a man's success was having a great many wives of widely differing ages. Some men aged fifty would take a new wife aged twelve or thirteen if she had been previously bestowed to him. These marriage arrangements have caused a great deal of conflict and difficulty in contemporary Australia, where laws are intended to apply to everyone, and where marriage to a girl of this age is considered child abuse. While many contemporary feminists argue that all girls are entitled to protection under Australian law, it is apparent that destruction of the indigenous marriage system rapidly results in the breakdown of indigenous law and society.

Myths. Although the relationships between men and women can be analyzed in terms of economic and marital arrangements, interesting insights emerge when considering the mythological foundations on which Aboriginal belief and practices depend. In central Australian mythology, women are depicted in ways that seem very strange to a contemporary eye. Vast myth cycles cross the country and lay out a network of sacred places, water holes, resource-rich areas, and sites of mythic events where ancestral forces and powers left their imprints on the landscape. Among these cycles are two notable ones that can be traced from northern South Australia across the central desert and into northern Australia. "The Two Women Dreaming" tells of the travels of two sisters who pass from place to place singing and creating natural features of the landscape, encountering animal species and human beings as they travel. They are ceaselessly followed across the landscape by a male figure who attempts to catch them for intercourse. The sisters pause and menstruate at various sites, which are today the locations of highly valued red ochre, a substance required for use in almost all rituals that is believed to convey strength and beauty as it shimmers on human skin, forming a canvas on which other ritual designs can be traced.

A second important myth cycle tells of the "Seven Sisters," identified with the constellations known in the West as the Pleiades and Orion. The narrative concerning them is similar across vast areas, differing only in the identification of the particular tract of territory. The sisters travel across the country in a group, followed by a male with a rampant penis capable of detaching itself from his body and operating with a mind of its own. This penis sometimes attempts to have intercourse with the sisters by traveling underneath the ground and coming up beneath them while they are urinating. The male owner of the penis is incessantly obliged to follow it and to suffer punishment when local people discover he is the owner of the irrepressible organ. The male is related to the women in such a way as to make his sexual desire for them inappropriate (usually he is a "nephew"). Hundreds of localities feature in the song cycles relating to these stories, which reflect an inherent conflict in gender relations in that groups of women are subject to illicit male desire that transgresses the norms of kinship.

In the central regions of Australia the Pleiades are associated with the coldest time of the year. In tropical northern Australia the sisters are seen as wives of the stars in the constellation Orion and are associated with fishing and canoeing. Other sets of ancestral stories in the north and northeast also focus on pairs of sisters, who moved across the country naming clan areas and the animals found there. These ancestral women possessed ritual power because of the sacred objects they possessed, but they lost that power as a result of the men stealing the objects and rituals. In one narrative, incestuous male desire also appears, together with a giant python whose waterhole is polluted by the sisters' menstruation and who finally swallows them.

Many other mythic tales are embedded in ceremonies marking significant events of the life cycle, such as male initiation and particularly death. By contrast, little attention is paid to birth or marriage, which are rarely ritually marked and pass with little formal note. The management and organization of ceremonial life is integrally supported by both men and women, who have specific roles to play that arise from the kinship relationship between clans, families, and individuals. Persons related to an individual through the maternal line have particularly important responsibilities, often referred to by terms implying that "flesh" arises from the maternal line and "bones" from the fathers. These and other concepts stress the need for mutual support and complementarity between the sexes, even though in some contexts males dominate and control women's activities.

Indigenous Women Today. Today's indigenous women occupy a wide variety of activities and roles. Many are strong leaders within their communities, and the basis of female solidarity is highly supported in contemporary organizations such as Women's Councils and other collective activities. Indigenous women have risen to national prominence as political representatives in indigenous bodies such as Land Councils, and many are highly regarded professionals, including lawyers, professors, medical specialists, and educators. Young indigenous women are taking advantage of educational opportunities all over the country and entering a variety of employments and professions in ever-increasing numbers. Finally, women are among the most famous of the extraordinarily talented indigenous artists, with their work internationally recognized and selling for astronomical prices. The efflorescence of creative talent among indigenous women, urban and rural, young and old, is one of the most remarkable phenomena of contemporary Australia.

[*See also* Prehistory.]

BIBLIOGRAPHY

Bell, Diane. *Daughters of the Dreaming*. Melbourne: McPhee Gribble; North Sydney, N.S.W., Australia: Allen & Unwin, 1983. A highly influential study of the position of women in a remote central Australian community, this work argues strongly that indigenous women enjoyed a high position of autonomy and equality, with their own distinctive ritual spheres and rights in land.

Brock, Peggy, ed. *Women, Rites, and Sites: Aboriginal Women's Cultural Knowledge*. Sydney, Australia, and Boston: Allen & Unwin, 1989. In some respects an update of the volume edited by Fay Gale and published in 1970, this set of articles focuses on women's ritual knowledge and their activities as cultural custodians.

Gale, Fay, ed. *Women's Role in Aboriginal Society*. Canberra: Australian Institute of Aboriginal Studies, 1970. A very important first attempt to analyze indigenous Australian women's role from a variety of disciplines (anthropology, sociology, linguistics) informed by fresh research and postwar theoretical interests.

Hamilton, Annette. "Bond-slaves of Satan: Aboriginal Women and the Missionary." In *Family and Gender in the Pacific: Domestic Contradictions and the Colonial Impact*, edited by Margaret Jolly and Martha Macintyre, pp. 236–258. Cambridge, U.K., and New York: Cambridge University Press, 1989. An exploration of Aboriginal women on the frontier, their importance for early settlement, and the role of missions based on official reports, missionary correspondence, papers, and pamphlets of the time.

Hamilton, Annette. "Descended from Father, Belonging to Country." In *Politics and History in Band Societies*, edited by Eleanor Leacock and Richard Lee, pp. 85–108. Cambridge, U.K., and New York: Cambridge University Press, 1982. Based on extensive fieldwork in the Western Desert of Australia, this paper discusses the way in which rights to land and resources are passed on in desert communities and the frequent claim that males dominate due to their possession of religious, symbolic, and ritual knowledge. The argument presented in it has become central to current highly contested native title claims.

Kaberry, Phyllis M. *Aboriginal Woman: Sacred and Profane*. London: G. Routledge, 1939. The earliest comprehensive ethnographic study of Aboriginal women's lives in Australia, Kaberry's account introduces the key issues that have dominated the subsequent analysis of the position of indigenous women in Australia.

Kleinert, Sylvia, and Margo Neale, eds. *The Oxford Companion to Aboriginal Art and Culture*. Melbourne and New York: Oxford University Press, 2000. Section 3, "Kinship and Gender," covers a variety of issues with regard to indigenous women and kinship and gender practices as they relate to aesthetics, performance, and representation.

White, Isobel, Diane Barwick, and Betty Meehan, eds. *Fighters and Singers: The Lives of Some Australian Aboriginal Women*. Sydney and Boston: G. Allen & Unwin, 1985.

ANNETTE HAMILTON

Modern Period

Since 1788, when the first shiploads of British convicts arrived in Sydney, women's life experiences have been variously shaped by Australia's position as a colonial and supposedly postcolonial society and by the women's diverse ethnic origins. Though Australian history has focused on the Anglo-Saxon majority who swiftly re-created the country as white, prior to British arrival Aboriginal women and men had lived on the land for sixty thousand years or more. The arrival of refugee and migrant women—directly after World War II, from southern and eastern Europe, predominantly Greece and Italy, and later from Asia, the Pacific Islands, Africa, and the Middle East—also diversified Australian women's history.

Colonization. From the beginning of white settlement the fortunes of Aboriginal women and white women were intimately intertwined but radically different. In 1788 the number of Aboriginal women and girls was possibly two hundred thousand. British women, convicts and families of accompanying personnel, numbered about two hundred. As white settlement spread out eventually to encompass the island continent, with new colonies in Tasmania (1803), Western Australia (1828), South Australia and Victoria (1836), and Queensland (1859), the indigenous population shrank tragically. The British signed no treaties with indigenous communities but cleared them, forcibly if necessary, from their lands.

In the early days indigenous women often interacted with the new arrivals in nonviolent ways, such as bartering, and in 1791 a local woman, Warreweer, gave birth in the settler's encampment. But with the spread of settlement and the high number of single men on the frontiers, indigenous women's lives along with their communities' were severely disrupted. Murders on a violent frontier and deaths from introduced European diseases catastrophically reduced indigenous numbers, while sexual exploitation became a continuing feature of relations between indigenous women and white men.

As the frontiers stabilized, Aboriginal women entered the white workforce, though they were often paid by barter rather than in cash. Indigenous women worked both at outdoor labor and as nursemaids and domestic helpers on large cattle and sheep stations in the outback. In many areas indigenous workers, as the only labor available, were essential for the properties' survival. In areas of close settlement in the southeast, most indigenous people were forced off their land completely, many driven to seek refuge in Christian missions. Beginning in Victoria in 1869, the indigenous population of the southeastern colonies was increasingly controlled by so-called protection boards that determined everything from place of residence and employment to marriage and child custody. By 1901, when the colonies federated, white Australians numbered more than 3 million, and the indigenous people numbered perhaps ninety-five thousand. Although nominally British citizens, indigenous women in practice enjoyed few rights.

Australian National Council of Women. Members of the council with the Scottish geologist Dame Maria Ogilvie Gordon *(center)*, Melbourne, c. 1930. THE NATIONAL LIBRARY OF AUSTRALIA

The convict colonies were also harsh for the women who arrived in official disgrace. By 1852 around twenty-five thousand women, predominantly first offenders from England or Ireland, had been transported to Australian colonies, commonly under a sentence of seven years' hard labor for theft. These forced migrants faced lives of surveillance and control, with harsh punishments for infractions of discipline. Most convict women arriving in Sydney were sent to the Parramatta Female Factory to live and work or were assigned to work for military personnel or free settlers. Despite the common perception that most were hardened prostitutes, many were skilled in trades and rural labor and worked as seamstresses, servants, and dairymaids. They had an acceptable escape route: if they married they were effectively freed from their sentence. Governors promoted marriage as a route to redemption for these "fallen" women and as an aid to further white settlement. Ex-convict families furthered colonization when they took up small land grants on land wrenched without compensation from Aborigines.

By the mid-nineteenth century free migration was gradually changing the convict and military character of the colonies. From the late 1790s small numbers of free women migrants began arriving. Free migration increased in the 1820s as settlements shored up and particularly from 1830 with the introduction of assisted passages. From 1860 to 1900 about ninety thousand single British women, who were in demand both as domestic servants and as wives, arrived as assisted migrants. Organizations such as the Female Middle Class Emigration Society, founded in London in 1862 to help solve the problem of "surplus women," helped many middle-class women migrate in search of employment. Most found marriage. An imbalance of the sexes that persisted until the later nineteenth century meant extremely high marriage rates—approaching 95 percent. Families were generally large, averaging between five and six children.

Better-off free migrant women and officers' wives constituted a colonial elite who sought to replicate the norms of British genteel femininity. From the early years they engaged in various philanthropic activities, supporting orphanages and other endeavors for women and children. In every community, charitable parish organizations and Ladies' Benevolent Societies ministered to the "deserving" poor. Such activities created an influential place for middle- and upper-class women. Governors' wives often enjoyed considerable social and cultural influence. Anna King played a significant role in the Female Orphan School in Sydney from 1800, controlling its daily operations and making key managerial decisions, and Eliza Darling founded the Female School of Industry and the Female Friendly Society in 1826.

These highly placed wives were not, however, expected to take part in political affairs. Lady Jane Franklin, the wife of the Tasmanian governor Sir John Franklin, attracted considerable censure for her perceived meddling in state affairs and for her extensive solo travels. Caroline Chisholm, known as the "emigrants' friend" because of her association with early schemes to assist single female migrants, was atypical in her fame and influence in colonial Australia. She established the Female Immigrants Home in Sydney in 1841 and the Family Colonization Loan Society in 1849 in London, which helped thousands of emigrating families buy land. She was invited to give evidence to government committees in both Australia and Britain and spent considerable energy lobbying the Colonial Office to support her schemes to aid colonization.

High marriage rates meant that women had low visibility in the paid labor force; in the second half of the nineteenth century estimates ranged from 15 to 25 percent. Domestic service represented the largest sphere of women's employment, with almost half employed in this area. The statistics, however, did not include women who contributed substantially to family enterprises—for example, on large stations and small farms, which could barely survive without the labor of wives and daughters—or women who worked alongside husbands in businesses—for example, as hoteliers, shopkeepers, and other tradesmen.

A small number of women ran their own businesses, most commonly hotels, inns, boardinghouses, and shops of various kinds. For middle-class women a safely respectable form of employment was teaching, ranging from working as governesses to running their own schools. A small number tried their fortune at writing journalism and fiction, but only the talented and fortunate, such as the Tasmanian Louisa Meredith and New South Wales's Miles Franklin, enjoyed much commercial success. Though varied and difficult to quantify, women's labor, including their significant routine domestic work, was vital to the success of the colonial project.

Women's and Aboriginal Activism. In the nineteenth-century colonies, women's civil rights were restricted under the prevailing British law, which colonial legislatures slowly modified. In 1883, Victoria became the first colony to give married women property rights, and beginning in the late 1880s more equal divorce laws were passed. Groups specifically dedicated to campaigning for women's rights formed only in the 1880s—the first was Henrietta Dugdale's Victorian Women's Suffrage Society in Melbourne in 1884. Notable suffrage leaders rose to prominence in every colony, such as Rose Scott, a wealthy member of Sydney society who founded the Womanhood Suffrage League of New South Wales in 1891, and the working mother Louisa Lawson, who founded the *Dawn* (1888–1904), Australia's first feminist newspaper.

The campaign was strengthened at the grassroots level by the Woman's Christian Temperance Union, which combined temperance goals with support for women's rights. The movement quickly made remarkable gains. In 1894, just a year after the New Zealand precedent, women in South Australia gained the vote, joined in 1899 by white women of Western Australia. In 1902 the Commonwealth Franchise Act extended federal political rights to all white women. New South Wales, Tasmania, Queensland, and Victoria followed the Commonwealth's leadership successively in 1902, 1903, 1905, and 1908. The long-running campaign in Victoria gained momentum again when Vida Goldstein became secretary of the United Council for Woman Suffrage and established the paper the *Australian Woman's Sphere*. In 1903 she was among the first four women to stand for election to the federal parliament; all, however, were independents, and all were unsuccessful.

For Aboriginal women and men, however, the absence of political rights allowed further legislation restricting indigenous people's freedom. In the north and west, Aborigines faced even more draconian pressure to shift to reserves, where their human rights were disgracefully abrogated through expanding government control and surveillance. Educational opportunities were severely limited, and many girls were forced in early adolescence into domestic service for extremely low wages. This was part of the broader policy of child removal, the "stolen generations," which saw children in many parts of the country separated from their mothers, particularly those classified as "half-caste." Some policy makers promoted child removal as a means of biological absorption of the indigenous population, of "breeding out the color." It was not until the 1960s that indigenous Australians had their citizenship rights reinstated, the decade that saw Charles Perkins and Margaret Valadian become the first indigenous university graduates; in 1976, Pat O'Shane was admitted to the bar, becoming Australia's first Aboriginal barrister.

Meanwhile political emancipation widened white women's horizons in many ways. Middle-class women made significant gains in education, though this was slowly realized for working-class women. Even into the 1930s less than a tenth of students completed the final year of secondary school. But from the 1880s middle-class girls' secondary education expanded considerably, and some private and state girls' secondary schools, generally run by women, trained middle-class girls for entry to the universities. Women were first admitted to the University of Melbourne in 1880, with the Universities of Sydney and Adelaide quickly following suit, and in 1883, Bella Guerin became Australia's first woman graduate. From 1900 to 1940 women constituted from 20 to 30 percent of students in Australian universities.

During World War I some women formed patriotic organizations to support the war effort, while others joined the peace movement. Most single middle-class women joined the workforce rather than assist mothers at home, and they awaited marriage, a permanent outcome. Professional employment for women expanded considerably with increased education. By 1901 women constituted around half of all teachers, and nursing—which had been established only in the 1870s—attracted large numbers of girls from the middle and lower classes by the late 1880s. In 1890, Constance Stone, having studied and trained overseas, became Australia's first woman doctor; in 1902, Ada Emily Evans was the first woman to receive a law degree from Sydney University, although she was unable to practice until 1921 after the enactment of the Women's Legal Status Act of New South Wales. Working-class women began to desert domestic work in favor of work in factories, shops, and offices. During the Depression, when men lost their jobs in greater numbers, many working-class women found themselves as the main breadwinners for their families, although there was also somewhat of a backlash against working women.

The first decades of the twentieth century also saw declines both in marriage rates and in family sizes. The fertility rate fell from about 6 babies per woman in the mid-nineteenth century to 3.9 in 1901. It subsequently declined to 3.1 by 1921 and, associated with the Depression, to 2.1 in 1934. Marriage also became less common. Of women reaching marriageable age from the 1890s to the 1930s, 15 to 22 percent remained single, with even higher rates in the major cities. For women university graduates this trend was even more pronounced. Perhaps half of women graduating before 1920 remained single and worked throughout their lives. Women were still confined to a narrow range of occupations deemed suitable for women and were paid only 50 to 60 percent of male wages. For the whole period from 1901 to 1961, women represented 20 to 25 percent of the total labor force, only rising above 30 percent in the 1970s. They were barred from some areas of employment, and a marriage bar was also strictly enforced in public service. Even where this was not the case, social convention strongly dictated that married women should not formally be seen to engage in paid work.

Many married middle-class women in particular found an avenue for public service in flourishing volunteer and activist women's organizations. The active voluntary arena was not matched by entry of women into mainstream politics. After their early political emancipation, few women succeeded in gaining election. Women did join political parties but seldom had more than behind-the-scenes influence. The Australian Labor Party set up a women's auxiliary, and conservative women themselves formed the Australian Women's National League that in 1945 merged with the Liberal Party. But it was not until 1921 that the first woman, Edith Cowan, was elected to the state parliament of Western Australia and not until 1943 that Dame Enid Lyons of Tasmania and Dorothy Tangney of Western Australia were elected to the federal legislature. Women's representation in Australian parliaments remained below 5 percent until the 1970s.

During World War II, women were strongly involved in the workforce and in auxiliary services, indeed subject from 1942 to manpower regulations. Some women temporarily received equal pay, although this was primarily intended to protect men's wages in their absence. With the postwar marriage boom, marriage once again became the destiny of the great majority of women, and women tended to marry younger. The fertility rate also rose again to a high of 3.5 births per woman in 1961 before commencing a decline that continued into the twenty-first century.

Although women's representation in the paid labor force initially dropped, it began to rise again steadily from the early 1950s. The proportion of married women working rose significantly, reaching 29 percent by 1966 and 41 percent by 1975. This was largely because of the influx of refugee women and migrants from southern and eastern Europe, predominantly from Greece and Italy, and later from Asia, indicative of a relaxation of the White Australia Policy (introduced in 1901 and finally abandoned in 1973), leading to a greater cultural diversity. The economy boomed after the war, and Australian industry and the service sector, traditionally women's work, expanded rapidly. Migrant women, who had sacrificed living in their homelands to improve the life chances of their children, took full-time factory jobs, often under oppressive conditions, and made what arrangements they could for child care.

The 1970s saw the reemergence of a strong women's movement. A first clarion call in 1969 was the unionist Zelda D'Aprano's protest against the adverse decisions on equal pay; she chained herself to the Commonwealth Building in Melbourne. The Women's Liberation movement, which attracted radical young women, including many university students, and the more moderate Women's Electoral Lobby, which attracted mainly professional women, pursued a range of issues from the legalization of abortion to supporting women's entry into mainstream politics.

There were victories especially when the Australian Labor Party was in office in 1972–1975. In 1972 the principle of "equal pay for work of equal value" was adopted, although because most females and males worked under different awards, the outcomes were slight. The federal government began funding child care, paid maternity leave was granted for Commonwealth public servants, and no-fault divorce was introduced. In 1973, Elizabeth Reid was appointed women's adviser to the prime minister, the first such position in the world. In 1984, Senator Susan Ryan, the minister assisting the prime minister for the status of women, introduced the Sex Discrimination Act, followed in 1986 by the Equal Employment (Affirmative Action) Act. By the end of the 1990s, 43 percent of the workforce was women, and almost two in three of these women were married.

Australian women, nonindigenous and indigenous, became increasingly visible in Australian political life during the 1990s and the early 2000s. In 1986, Senator Janine Haines became the first woman in Australia to lead a political party, the Australian Democratic Party, and several other women subsequently led this party. By 2003 three states had appointed women as governors: Marjorie Jackson-Nelson in South Australia, Marie Bashir in New South Wales, and Quentin Bryce in Queensland. In 2006, 64 of the 226 members of the federal parliament (28 percent) were women. Five women held ministerial appointments in John Howard's coalition government, three of them in the cabinet. This somewhat remarkable reordering of the gender balance in politics did not occur by chance. Inside the Liberal Party, feminist sympathizers organized support groups to identify women of talent and offer mentoring for preselection and campaigning. In 1994 the Australian Labor Party adopted an affirmative action policy, setting the target ratio of 35 percent women members within eight years, lifted to 40 percent by 2012.

Indigenous women, too, rose to prominence. By 2006 indigenous people constituted about 2 percent of Australia's some 20 million people. During the 1990s some indigenous women sat on indigenous governing bodies at national, state, or local levels, most notably the South Australian Lowitja O'Donoghue, who was the inaugural chairperson of the Aboriginal and Torres Strait Islander Development Corporation and served on bodies such as the Council for Aboriginal Reconciliation and the Indigenous Land Corporation. Four Aboriginal women, all Labor representatives, were elected to state and territory legislatures. Marion Scrymgour, first elected as the member for Arafura in the Northern Territory in 2001, in 2004 became the first indigenous female minister in Australia. Indigenous women artists, writers, and performers have had enormous success both in Australia and internationally for their striking creativity in historical, political, cultural, and personal themes. These talented Australians have brought indigenous experiences to the fore of national consciousness.

Aboriginal people, however, still await social justice in this "postcolonial" society because of white racism, the legacies of dispossession and broken families, the consequent poverty and dislocation, and inadequate education and training. Nevertheless, Aboriginal women offer outstanding community leadership in both rural and urban areas in the fight at the personal and political levels against continuing social disadvantage.

[*See also* Democracy; Imperialism and Colonialism; *and* Racism.]

BIBLIOGRAPHY

Alford, Katrina. *Production or Reproduction? An Economic History of Women in Australia, 1788–1850*. Melbourne, Australia: Oxford University Press, 1984.

Caine, Barbara, ed. *Australian Feminism: A Companion*. Melbourne, Australia: Oxford University Press, 1998.

Gothard, Jan. *Blue China: Single Female Migration to Colonial Australia*. Carlton South, Australia: Melbourne University Press, 2001.

Grimshaw, Patricia, Marilyn Lake, Ann McGrath, and Marian Quartly. *Creating a Nation*. Rev. ed. Perth, Australia: API Network 2006.

Kingston, Beverley. *My Wife, My Daughter, and Poor Mary Ann: Women and Work in Australia*. Melbourne, Australia: Thomas Nelson, 1975.

Lake, Marilyn. *Getting Equal: The History of Australian Feminism*. Saint Leonards, Australia: Allen and Unwin, 1999.

Mackinnon, Alison. *Love and Freedom: Professional Women and the Reshaping of Personal Life*. Cambridge, U.K.: Cambridge University Press, 1997.

McCalman, Janet. *Sex and Suffering: Women's Health and a Women's Hospital, the Royal Women's Hospital, Melbourne, 1856–1996*. Carlton, Australia: Melbourne University Press, 1999.

McDonald, Peter. *Marriage in Australia: Age at First Marriage and Proportions Marrying, 1860–1971*. Canberra, Australia: Department of Demography, Australian National University, 1974.

McGrath, Ann. *"Born in the Cattle": Aborigines in Cattle Country*. Sydney, Australia: Allen and Unwin, 1987.

Oxley, Deborah. *Convict Maids: The Forced Migration of Women to Australia*. Cambridge, U.K., and New York: Cambridge University Press, 1996.

Reiger, Kerreen M. *The Disenchantment of the Home: Modernizing the Australian Family, 1880–1940*. Melbourne, Australia: Oxford University Press, 1985.

Saunders, Kay, and Raymond Evans, eds. *Gender Relations in Australia: Domination and Negotiation*. Sydney, Australia: Harcourt, Brace, Jovanovich, 1992.

Sawer, Marian, and Marian Simms. *A Woman's Place: Women and Politics in Australia*. Saint Leonards, Australia: Allen and Unwin, 1993.

Swain, Shurlee, with Renate Howe. *Single Mothers and Their Children: Disposal, Punishment, and Survival in Australia*. Cambridge, U.K.: Cambridge University Press, 1995.

JANE CAREY AND PATRICIA GRIMSHAW

AUSTRIA AND AUSTRIA-HUNGARY. In the early modern period, women's lives were largely conditioned by their political and economic relationships to men. Peasant women worked the land as part of rural, male-centered households, for example. Women in towns and cities often participated in informal or subsistence economic activity to support husbands, fathers, and children. At the time of the French Revolution, Austrian women had few political rights, and their economic roles were largely defined for them by the state and society. Cultural norms kept most women firmly enmeshed in family and religious life. Important exceptions existed to these broad characterizations, but in general Austrian women led highly restricted lives at the outset of the modern period. This was not true of aristocratic women or those from the dynastic household such as Maria Theresa (r. 1740–1780), Austrian archduchess and queen of Hungary and Bohemia, who did exercise direct and indirect political influence, but it was true for the majority of Austrian women.

Changes to Women's Work and the Development of Political Activism. At the end of the eighteenth century, some of these patterns changed and began to transform Austrian women's lives in several important ways. In some areas of the Austrian Habsburg Monarchy, which spread over large parts of central Europe, early industrialization took place. This development often changed the relationship of women to work; in addition to labor within the family and in agriculture, women began to work in textile and other forms of industrial production. Much of this work was done in the countryside or in small towns, and it changed the day-to-day patterns of life for those women involved. Austrian women, like women throughout Europe and in the United States, tended to have multiple and simultaneous economic roles: domestic labor within their own families, agricultural labor for their own kin or nonrelated landowners, and other types of hand or industrial work.

Women were involved in unorganized, but important, demonstrations against the economic burdens they endured in the first half of the nineteenth century. As early as the pre-1848 period, some Austrian women had become politically active. Most often, their demonstrations were protests related to the rising price of bread or other basic foodstuffs. In the revolutionary year of 1848, women's discontent became more widespread and vocal, as shown by the large-scale assembly of women in Vienna on 26 March 1848, at a time of great volatility in the empire's capital city. The fluid situation of that mid-century uprising allowed both working- and middle-class women to become politically active and to air some of their grievances. An example of middle-class activism in 1848 was the foundation of the Viennese Democratic Women's Organization (Wiener Demokratischer Frauenverein). As with many early European women's organizations, this one met stiff opposition from men's groups and from the state, and it was short lived, but it did represent a significant moment in early feminist political agitation.

In the second half of the nineteenth century, women's work and political activities continued to expand. Industrialization, which came later to Austria and Austria-Hungary than to England, France, and northwestern Europe, increased the potential work roles of women. The term "Austria-Hungary" was used after the Compromise of 1867 to show the relative political autonomy in domestic affairs of the eastern half, "Hungary," from the western half of the Austrian Empire.

Mobilization in Austria, World War I. Women on the roadside watch troops depart for the front, Vienna, 31 July 1914. AKG-IMAGES/JEAN-PIERRE VERNEY

Moreover, industrialization created new sites of production and new economic and social patterns in some Austrian towns and cities, all of which forced Austrian women (and men) to deal with a large array of changes to their day-to-day lives. For example, Vienna and the Vienna Basin region south of the Austrian capital city were transformed by industrial growth in the nineteenth century. A wide variety of factories were established in these areas, which provided new places of work. Thus in certain parts of the empire, Austrian women experienced social and economic dislocation brought on by the demands of industrial labor discipline and urban growth. By the turn of the nineteenth into the twentieth century, some low-ranking clerical and white-collar occupations—secretaries, bookkeepers, telegraph operators—also become largely feminine in character. Women in Austria also traditionally held other occupations—midwives, hairdressers, and the like—such that the association between these positions and women became an economic and cultural stereotype.

Clubs, Feminist Organizations, and the Suffrage Movement. In Austria, women participated in a wide variety of clubs at the end of the nineteenth and beginning of the twentieth centuries, the period about which perhaps more is known than about any other in the country's history. So well developed were these organizations that separate movements for middle-class and working-class women existed. In addition, a Catholic women's organization, the Katholische Reichs-Frauenorganisation, was founded in 1907.

These clubs and organizations also published a number of newspapers and critiqued contemporary Austrian society from a wide number of feminist perspectives. One of the most celebrated Austrian feminists, Adelheid Popp (1869–1939), was involved in such journalistic activities. Popp, the daughter of a weaver and a worker herself, became active in socialist politics early in life. She took over editorial responsibilities for the *Arbeiterinnen-Zeitung* (the Women Workers' Newspaper) and wrote or edited a number of controversial articles on marriage laws and practices, such as "Free Love and Civil Marriage" and "Women and Property." Her memoir of her early years in the factory, *Die Jugendgeschichte einer Arbeiterin* (Early Years of a Female Worker, 1909; English trans., *The Autobiography of a Working Woman*, 1913), became highly popular and was translated into several languages. After World War I she became a member of parliament and remains one of Austria's best-known feminists.

Movements in support of woman suffrage developed later in Austria than in England and the United States, where constitutional forms of government had longer histories than in Central Europe. Under older forms of voting, some women property owners had been enfranchised in Austria. As property qualifications diminished and notions of political liberalism centered on the individual took hold, however, more well-to-do women tended to lose their right to vote, since this was now primarily defined along gender lines—that is, men could vote and women could not. This situation, along with the growing influence of feminist agitation, helped create the suffrage movement in Austria.

In 1893 the General Austrian Women's Organization (Allgemeiner Österreichischer Frauenverein) was founded and became perhaps the most forward-looking feminist organization of the day. It not only pressed for women's right to vote but also critiqued existing laws governing marriage and family life, which it held were discriminatory toward women. Nevertheless, this club, and most of the feminist organizations in the late nineteenth and first half of the twentieth centuries, tended to accept prevailing notions of the biological and social differences between men and women. Despite their rhetoric, which was challenging in its day, these clubs generally agreed that there were real, and primarily sex-based, differences between men and women that conditioned the way both groups did and should relate to work, marriage, family, and sexuality.

More fundamental questioning of the defining relationships between the sexes and analyzing of gender roles in a modern feminist sense came in Austria only in the 1960s and 1970s. But as these important debates about the nature of women and their relationship to men took place over earlier decades, Austrian women acquired the basic right to vote with some restrictions in 1918, in the immediate aftermath of World War I. The franchise for women was gradually extended in the course of the twentieth century.

Education. One area in which Austrian women did make considerable progress in the late nineteenth and early twentieth centuries was in the field of education. Between the 1860s and World War I, educational opportunities for women, at least in the western, Austrian half of the empire, might have been greater than in other parts of central Europe. Women were allowed into the professionalized teaching professions during the course of the nineteenth century, for example. By the 1870s and 1880s, their compensation for work in the elementary schools was generally equal to that of men. Beginning in 1897, women were allowed to enroll in university courses and gradually gained more rights at Austria's institutions of higher education. Also in 1897, Gabriele Possaner (1860–1940) became the first Austrian woman to earn a doctorate; she had done her studies in Geneva and Zurich and struggled successfully with Austrian authorities to acknowledge her work and grant her the advanced degree. She did so in the field of medicine and is a notable figure in Austrian history for her tenacity in pursuing her education.

Middle-class feminist activism had helped to create these educational opportunities, which met with strong resistance in certain circles. In Austria, women from ethnic minorities, which were always of great importance in the polyglot empire, took advantage of these progressive educational measures in significant numbers; Jewish women, for instance, were well represented at Austrian universities.

World Wars I and II. World War I also brought other important changes in Austrian women's lives. Their participation in industries and economic activities increased. Thus women's labor was an important part of the overall Austrian war effort. Moreover, many Austrian women's organizations, which had formed in the last decades of the nineteenth century around a wide variety of interests and which were populated by women from various social classes, supported Austria's military activities with enthusiasm. The political outcome of the war was disastrous for the old empire, however, and it was split up into a number of successor states, with only a small and uncertain country remaining around the capital city of Vienna. Many former citizens of the empire, men and women alike, now resided in Czechoslovakia, Hungary, Yugoslavia, and other Central and Eastern European nations.

For Austria in general, the interwar period was tumultuous. The newly established republic struggled to maintain its democratic balance, but by the mid-1930s it was under severe pressure from authoritarian and fascist groups. Ultimately, Austria became annexed by Nazi Germany in March 1938. For Austria's women, the era brought debates about political participation, economic roles, and cultural values. As in many parts of Europe, women were sometimes forced out of jobs that they had held during World War I.

The fracturing and fissuring of Austrian politics in the interwar period also splintered women into various camps. Women, for example, could be found across the political spectrum in the 1920s and 1930s, particularly in the Social Democratic and Christian Social political camps. Women's political aims ranged from extending the social activism and welfare programs associated with the Red Vienna experiment to rolling back these same programs to create a far more conservative, corporatist structure for Austrian society. Finally, Austrian women were not immune to the promises and rhetoric of fascism in the 1930s, and they supported it even before the Nazi seizure of power.

As women did virtually everywhere in Europe, Austria's women experienced or participated in Nazism in radically different ways. On the one hand, there were strong ideological supporters of fascism in Austria and complacent citizens who preferred the strong fascist state to the chaotic situation of the 1920s and early 1930s. Some women worked within the Nazi apparatus or benefited directly from the fascist seizure of power in Austria. Some women benefited from the "aryanization"—that is, the expropriation—of Jewish property; others joined and worked in Nazi organizations.

On the other hand, some Austrian women were active in formal and informal networks of resistance to Nazism, which dominated the country from 1938 to 1945. Some of these women were caught and sent into the notorious camp system of the Fascists. Of course, Jewish women and women from other targeted ethnic, social, or political groups were particularly vulnerable in Austria and often found their lives cut short.

A good example of this was the case of Käthe Leichter (1895–1942), a middle-class Jewish woman and socialist activist. She was arrested by the Gestapo, the German secret police, in 1938 and held in custody at several locations, including Ravensbrück, the infamous concentration camp for women. She was executed by the Nazis in March 1942. Therese Schlesinger (1863–1940), another significant socialist feminist who had been very active during the interwar period, was able to flee from the Nazis into France, where she died in June 1940.

Women under Fascism also often found their work, family, and sexual lives altered in fundamental ways. Scholars, however, are just beginning to understand these developments. An important aspect of post-1945 Austrian history has been the ongoing challenge not to suppress the memory of the difficult Nazi years and instead to understand what went wrong in the political and social realms for both women and men.

The Postwar Period. In the post-1945 period, the position of women in Austrian politics and society shifted yet again. Women, directly confronted with the immediate consequences of the war, often had to rebuild their families and their homes. Women could be found repairing towns, cities, and farms across Austria. Male casualties during the war also meant that the influence of women in Austrian society grew proportionally. For example, the number of women voters in Austria expanded relative to men in the aftermath of the war. Theoretically, this development increased the political influence of women.

In the postwar period, a large number of women were widowed or remained unmarried, which raised important social, sexual, and economic debates in Austria, which in turn might have expanded the acceptable roles for women. Nevertheless, the post-1945 period in Austria has not brought as many benefits to women as might have been expected. The work that women did in the post-1945 period was not always highly valued by either men or women. It was seen as survival labor and did not usually lead to expanded economic opportunities for women. The "economic miracle," a general period of remarkable economic recovery in Europe from the 1940s to the early 1970s, meant that some Austrian women could afford to give up their positions or were pressured out of them, and lower-paying jobs were increasingly given to foreign workers.

Perhaps most significant for women in the post-1945 period was the creation of the so-called social partnership in Austria. This arrangement, which largely governs the relationship between business and labor, has been dominant in recent decades in Austria. It owes its origins to the perceived need for economic and social stability in Austria after the misfortunes of the 1930s and 1940s. Following the informal rules of the social partnership, many of the country's political and policy decisions are not made in the arena of participatory democracy but are made in negotiations between large institutional blocs and in closed-door committees. These blocs and committees have been largely the reserve of powerful men from the government, business concerns, and trade unions.

Thus even as women have gained seats in Austria's parliament and government in increasing numbers—following the November 2002 elections, for example, there were 62 women out of 183 representatives in Austria's lower and 13 of 62 in its upper chamber—they have not necessarily been allowed into the most important political negotiations, the early stages in which legislation is first crafted and amended. In the last decade or so, this situation may be breaking down in Austria, but it is too early for scholars to make any meaningful interpretations about these changes and what they might mean for women.

Austria's women have gained much in formal political rights and economic opportunities. The Equal Treatment Law of 1979 prohibits discrimination against women, for example. Culturally, Austria has in recent decades become a highly secularized and modern society, which has created important new cultural possibilities for women. Women have become more visible in Austrian society as authors (Elfriede Jelinek is the only Austrian ever to win the Nobel Prize), as artists, as university professors, and in other professional or cultural capacities.

The growth of the welfare state in the twentieth century has provided real benefits to women and especially to working women and mothers. Nevertheless, Austrian women still often feel that they are excluded from the arenas in which real power and influence is wielded and that gender equality is still a goal for the future.

[*See also* Fascism; Maria Theresa; Suffrage; World War I; *and* World War II.]

BIBLIOGRAPHY

Anderson, Harriet. *Utopian Feminism: Women's Movements in Fin de Siècle Vienna.* New Haven, Conn.: Yale University Press, 1992. The standard work on the specialized topic of women's organizational activity in the late nineteenth and early twentieth centuries.

Ariadne Project of the Austrian National Library. http://www.onb.ac.at/ariadne. An extensive online site maintained by the Austrian National Library. The Ariadne Project has much basic information, and entries can be translated into English.

Bischof, Günter, Anton Pelinka, and Erika Thurner, eds. *Women in Austria.* New Brunswick, N.J.: Transaction Publishers, 1998. A collection of essays that focuses on women's social and political positions in Austria, with an emphasis on the modern era.

Fodor, Eva. *Working Difference: Women's Working Lives in Hungary and Austria, 1945–1995.* Durham, N.C.: Duke University Press, 2003. A comparative look at women's work in the Austrian Second Republic and Communist Hungary.

Good, David F., Margarete Grandner, and Mary Jo Maynes, eds. *Austrian Women in the Nineteenth and Twentieth Centuries: Cross-Disciplinary Perspectives.* Providence, R.I.: Berghahn Books, 1996. An excellent collection of theoretically sophisticated essays that concentrate on the themes of women and politics, work, and identity.

L'Homme: Zeitschrift für feministische Geschichtswissenschaft. Vienna: 1990– . The premier journal for serious feminist scholarship in Austria; available only in German.

Weiss, Sabine. *Die Österreicherin: Die Rolle der Frau in 1000 Jahren Geschichte.* Graz, Austria: Styria, 1996. This German-language text is a good overview of women's history in Austria.

WILLIAM D. BOWMAN

AVRIL DE SAINTE-CROIX, GHÉNIA (1855–1939), Swiss-born French and international women's rights activist. Adrienne-Pierette-Eugénie Glaisette Avril de Sainte-Croix, known as Ghénia Avril de Sainte-Croix, was a founding member (1900), secretary-general (1901–1922), and then president (1922–1932) of the Conseil National des Femmes Françaises (CNFF). Under the pen name "Savioz" she was a journalist for the all-woman daily newspaper *La Fronde*, and after her marriage in 1900 at the age of forty-five she became an important political player in France and an energetic citizen-participant in global civil society—through both the International Council of Women (ICW) and the League of Nations—despite never having exercised political rights in her own country. Her organizational, reportorial, and diplomatic skills were legendary, and she was recognized internationally in the 1920s and 1930s as France's foremost feminist.

A fervent foe of government-regulated prostitution and the traffic in women and children, and a partisan of a single sexual standard for women and men, Avril de Sainte-Croix was regarded by many as the Josephine Butler of France. She viewed prostitution as primarily an economic issue, best addressed by raising working women's wages. In 1900 she founded the Œuvre Libératrice in Paris, a halfway house for rescuing and rehabilitating young prostitutes by providing them with a fresh start through education, job skills, and long-term counseling. Her contributions were highly appreciated by the French government; she was the first woman to serve on a French government committee (investigating the morals police), and during World War I she was appointed to the armaments ministry's Comité du travail féminin. Her honors included being named *chevalier* and *officier* of the Légion d'Honneur and being awarded medals from the ministries of public health and hygiene.

A professed feminist from 1896 and a self-identified freethinker, Avril de Sainte-Croix devoted her life to pro-woman philanthropy and politics, holding positions in many organizations such as the Ligue des Droits de l'Homme, the Fédération International Abolitionniste, and the Musée Social, where she organized and headed a women's section. In the 1920s she campaigned actively for women police. In 1929, 1930, and 1931 she presided over the CNFF's États-Généraux du Féminisme (Estates General of Feminism), congresses that comprehensively examined issues concerning (in 1929) women's legal rights, (in 1930) their economic standing, and (in 1931) their situation in the colonies.

Throughout the early twentieth century the widely traveled, multilingual Avril de Sainte-Croix regularly reported to the ICW on developments in France. She also chaired the 1904 ICW committee on White Slave Traffic and Equal Moral Standard. In 1920 she was elected an international vice president of the ICW, and in 1922 the League of Nations appointed her as the official representative of seven international women's organizations to the league's Advisory Committee on the Traffic in Women and Children; from 1925 she served as a delegate to the League of Nations for the Joint Standing Committee of Women's International Organizations. Her questionnaires directed to national councils, investigating various issues of concern to these organizations, are of considerable historical importance, as are her reports on the responses.

Avril de Sainte-Croix's publications include the book *Le Féminisme* (1907) and many longer topical articles concerning such topics as the traffic in women, women's work, and sex education, as well as a series of short stories concerning the peoples of eastern Europe, which appeared primarily in the French and Swiss press. Her reports on feminist activities can be found in the publications and proceedings of the International Council of Women, the League of Nations, and the International Abolitionist Federation, among others.

[*See also* Butler, Josephine; Feminism; *and* France.]

BIBLIOGRAPHY

Bard, Christine. *Les filles de Marianne: Histoire des féminismes 1914–1940*. Paris: Fayard, 1995.

Hause, Steven C., with Anne R. Kenney. *Women's Suffrage and Social Politics in the French Third Republic*. Princeton, N.J.: Princeton University Press, 1984.

Klejman, Laurence, and Florence Rochefort. *L'égalité en marche: Le féminisme sous la Troisième République*. Paris: Presses de la Fondation Nationale des Sciences Politiques, des Femmes, 1989. More essential background on the pre-1914 period; supplements Bard's book.

Offen, Karen. "Intrepid Crusader: Ghénia Avril de Sainte-Croix Takes on the Prostitution Issue," In *Proceedings of the Western Society for French History*, vol. 33 (2005), edited by Carol E. Harrison and Kathryn Edwards.

Offen, Karen. "'La plus grande féministe de France': Mais qui est donc Madame Avril de Sainte-Croix?" *Archives du Féminisme*, bulletin no. 9 (December 2005).

KAREN OFFEN

AZURDUY DE PADILLA, JUANA (c. 1780–1862), Bolivian insurgent during the wars of South American independence. Juana Azurduy was born near the city of Chuquisaca (also known as Charcas) in what was then known as Alto Peru (now Bolivia). Her family had a comfortable life. During her childhood she learned the Quechua and Aymara languages, and after the death of her parents she was sent to finish her education in a convent. Her rebellious nature prompted her expulsion after eight months. She was already an ardent supporter of republican ideas inspired by the French Revolution. In 1805 she married Manuel Padilla, son of a Creole (American-born) family, with whom she had four children.

In May 1809 Alto Peru declared its independence and experienced a series of resistance uprisings among indigenous people. The rebels received some help from Buenos Aires. Juana and Manuel were among the combatants. The revolutionaries occupied the key mining city of Potosí in 1813, and Manuel was in charge of organizing a proper revolutionary army. Juana joined him in this effort and persuaded many women to participate in the armed struggle. She also persuaded many Indian chiefs to join the war against Spain and was held in the highest regard by them. The revolutionary struggle had an uneven history of victories and defeats, and by 1814 Juana and Manuel had to separate their troops. She took refuge in a swamp area with her four children. By the following year all of them had died. This did not deter her patriotic ardor. In 1814 she was expecting her fifth child in the midst of a battle. After delivering the baby she faced a group of insubordinate officials and escaped with the troop's treasury.

In 1815 the royalists recovered a large area of Alto Peru and waged a bloody campaign against the insurgents. This obliged Juana and Manuel to mount a guerrilla war, in which they led more than six thousand indigenous troops. She trained a group of women, known as the Amazons, who fought in sixteen battles, and she gained a personal reputation as a daring soldier who would not hesitate to kill the enemy or pursue them in battle.

While trying to rescue his wounded wife, Manuel was taken prisoner and put to death. General Manuel Belgrano, an Argentine patriot, praised Juana's valor and appointed her lieutenant colonel, but she received no further help from Buenos Aires. She and her troops joined those of the insurgent leader Martín Güemez in the province of Salta (Argentina), under whose orders she fought for another three years until his murder in 1821. Depressed by the events, Azurduy wandered for several years in the remote province of Chaco. After rejoining her daughter, she requested funds to return to the newly minted nation of Bolivia, named after Venezuela-born general Simón Bolívar. The latter visited her in 1825, after the country became independent, and raised her rank to colonel. The new nation granted her a small pension, which lasted through 1852; Azurduy lived the rest of her life in extreme poverty. She is recognized as a national hero in Bolivia, and many streets and institutions, including an airport in the city of Sucre, bear her name.

BIBLIOGRAPHY

Batticuore, Graciela. "Juana Azurduy." In *Mujeres Argentinas: El lado femenino de nuestra historia*, edited by María Esther de Miguel. Buenos Aires, Argentina: Editorial Extra Alfaguara, 1998.

Asunción Lavrin

BÂ, MARIAMA (1929–1981), award-winning Senegalese novelist. Although Mariama Bâ was the author of only two novels published in Dakar, Senegal, her reputation and impact have extended worldwide. Her first novel, *Une si longue lettre* (1979; English trans., *So Long a Letter*, 1981), won the first Noma Prize for publishing in Africa and quickly became a classic, garnering praise for its depiction of contemporary urban women's experiences. Its epistolary form captures the fervent emotions of the narrator Ramatoulaye, who, upon her husband's death, reflects on her own life. Because the long letter to her best friend Aïssatou is never sent, the text resembles and functions as a diary. The broad impact of *Une si longue lettre* is also demonstrated by its selection as one of the top twelve among Africa's One Hundred Best Books of the Twentieth Century; inclusion on the required reading list for many master's and doctoral qualifying examinations and high school Advanced Placement tests in the United States; translation into more than a dozen languages, including Czech, Finnish, and Turkish; and adaptation into a stage play and television film in Wolof, Senegal's main spoken language. A local secondary boarding school for girls on Gorée Island and a children's library in an immigrant neighborhood in Italy are named for Bâ as well. Bâ is, without a doubt, one of Africa's most read, studied, and respected authors.

Une si longue lettre was not the first text published by an African woman, but it was responsible for launching and shaping Francophone African women's written tradition, complementing their rich oral heritage. In this groundbreaking novel, Bâ creates a variety of characters, privileging mothers, daughters, mothers-in-law, co-wives, and friends whose lives are not only disrupted by polygamy but whose interactions vary from supportive to deleterious. The novel is at once an elegy to women's friendship and a condemnation of those who are complicit in women's oppression. Embodying changing gender roles is Ramatoulaye, who, abandoned by her husband for a much younger woman, learns to negotiate city traffic (driving a gift from Aïssatou), a metaphor for her newfound mobility and entry into a male space. At the same time her primary concern is raising and educating her children, a distinctive characteristic of African feminism and a task made more difficult in a consumer society. Anchored in the past and opportunistic, Dame Belle-Mère and Tante Nabou make decisions that are harmful to girls and women. The former marries her high school-aged daughter to Ramatoulaye's husband Modou, in effect ending her formal education, precisely because he has the means to raise their social standing by lavishing material goods on her family. The aristocratic Tante Nabou rejects her daughter-in-law Aïssatou because her father is a goldsmith, a low-caste status trade. Bâ skillfully avoids stereotypes, illustrating instead the characters' complexities: a lawyer and a doctor who hide their midlife crises behind a Muslim religious practice that proves out of place in an urban setting and mothers who interfere in their children's marriages but also play important roles as oral educators and transmitters of culture.

Published posthumously, *Un chant écarlate* (1981; English trans., *Scarlet Song*, 1986) is also innovative. Centered on the French college student Mireille de la Vallée, who challenges her father's authority by secretly marrying Ousmane Guèye and returning to Senegal with him, the novel should not be interpreted as an indictment against interracial unions because both families' racial prejudices surface and Mireille descends into madness, killing her son in response to Ousmane's infidelity. It is rather an examination of culture clashes, betrayal, abandonment, displacement, and return as they intersect with race, class, and gender.

Bâ's training as a teacher informs her essay "La fonction politique des littératures africaines écrites" (The Political Function of Written African Literatures), which reads like a feminist manifesto. Articulating themes illustrated in Bâ's novels, it addresses women's condition in contemporary Africa, which Bâ says is characterized by inequality and injustice in the home and the workplace. Contrary to literary representations of women by *Négritude* writers who idealize "traditional" women, Bâ explains how in real life, patriarchal customs, practices, attitudes, and laws are responsible for their continued oppression. She urges women to use writing as a peaceful weapon to bring about societal change. It is no coincidence, then, that Bâ was a member of several women's organizations in Senegal.

[*See also* Literature, *subentry* Fiction and Poetry.]

BIBLIOGRAPHY

Bâ, Mariama. "La fonction politique des littératures africaines écrites." *Ecriture française dans le monde* 3, no. 5 (1981): 3–7. An articulation of her philosophy.

D'Almeida, Irène Assiba. *Francophone African Women Writers: Destroying the Emptiness of Silence.* Gainesville: University of Florida Press, 1994. Contains a detailed section on *Scarlet Song,* 98–122.

Nnaemeka, Obioma. "Urban Spaces, Women's Spaces: Polygamy as Sign in Mariama Bâ's Novels." In *The Politics of (M)Othering: Womanhood, Identity, and Resistance in African Literature,* edited by Obioma Nnaemeka, pp. 162–191. London and New York: Routledge, 1997. Excellent analysis of Bâ's treatment of polygamy.

RENÉE LARRIER

BAARD, FRANCES (c. 1908–1997), antiapartheid activist and labor leader in South Africa. Baard was born in the mining town of Kimberley, South Africa. Her earliest jobs included domestic work and a teaching post from which she was fired because a man was preferred in the one-teacher school. Following her marriage and the birth of her children, she took a job in a food and canning factory—an industry that employed many women during the 1940s. When a union was formed at her factory in 1948, she was elected organizing secretary. After her shock at the sight of people forced to sleep outside on a cold, rainy night for lack of accommodation, Baard attended a meeting of the African National Congress (ANC) and soon became involved in the ANC Women's League. When her husband died in 1952 she assumed sole responsibility for raising her four children.

Baard's leadership role in both union and women's struggles resulted, in part, from the close ties between the Food and Canning Workers' Union, its African affiliate, and the broader political movements against apartheid during the 1950s. Thus, Baard took part in the ANC's Defiance Campaign against apartheid laws, became a member of the National Executive Committee of the South African Congress of Trade Unions, and was a founding member of the Federation of South African Women (now known as FSAW or FEDSAW). Launched in 1954, this multiracial organization spearheaded women's opposition against the new requirement that African women as well as men carry identity documents known as passes, a requirement that would restrict their freedom of movement and subject them to the constant threat of arrest. The group also adopted a "women's charter" that called for gender and racial equality as well as improved living and working conditions. In 1955 Baard's union was formally affiliated with the Women's Federation, thereby encouraging politically aware women to combine labor organizing and political work. As part of this effort she led campaigns of union women in Port Elizabeth, South Africa, going from door to door and organizing in the factories to persuade women to refuse to take out passes.

In 1956, when the South African government intensified its campaign against resistance movements, Baard was among 156 people arrested in the famous Treason Trial. Among those released before the end of the trial (in 1961, when all defendants were acquitted), she continued her trade union and women's organizing until she was rearrested and banned in 1963. She spent a difficult year in solitary confinement, followed by five years in prison. Recalling this ordeal, she reflected, "I think they were trying to kill me somehow, but my spirit was too strong."

Rather than allow her to return to her home in Port Elizabeth at the end of her incarceration, authorities banished her to Mabopane, a township an hour outside the city of Pretoria, far from her home and family. There, she worked for a time in a newly established textile factory. During the 1980s, when the United Democratic Front, a new antigovernment coalition, was organized, Baard resumed her political activities; she also continued her work on a variety of local community projects.

[*See also* African National Congress Women's League; Apartheid; Labor; *and* Southern Africa, *subentry* Twentieth Century.]

BIBLIOGRAPHY

Baard, Frances, as told to Barbie Schreiner. *My Spirit is Not Banned.* Harare, Zimbabwe: Zimbabwe, 1986. An account of Baard's life based on lengthy oral interviews.

Berger, Iris. *Threads of Solidarity: Women in South African Industry, 1900–1980.* Bloomington: Indiana University Press; London: Currey, 1992. Includes material on Baard in the context of her union and women's organizing.

Walker, Cherryl. *Women and Resistance in South Africa.* New York: Monthly Review Press, 1991. First published 1982 by Onyx Press. Includes material on Baard's involvement in women's struggles.

IRIS BERGER

BACHELET, MICHELLE (b. 1951), the first female president of Chile and the third woman to be directly elected president in Latin America. Bachelet was elected president of Chile in January 2007, winning a runoff election with 53.5 percent of votes and all but one of the country's thirteen regions (provinces). Bachelet won with the support of a political alliance (*concertación*) of the Christian Democratic Party, the Party for Democracy, the Social Democrat Radical Party, and the Socialist Party. She has three children, Sebastián and Francisca, from her first marriage, and Sofia, from a second free union (because Chilean law did not at that time permit divorce). Bachelet is currently separated, a single mother, and professes no religion.

Bachelet was born in Santiago in 1951, the daughter of Angela Jeria, an archaeologist, and Alberto Bachelet, a member of the Chilean air force who achieved the rank of brigadier general. Bachelet is a physician who also took graduate courses in military science and speaks four languages in addition to her native Spanish.

While a student in the 1970s Bachelet joined the Unidad Popular Youth. Unidad Popular was an ideologically Socialist alliance. In the Unidad Popular the PC (Communists), the PS (Socialists), the PR (Social Democrats), and the radical Christian parties, MAPU and IC, worked together and backed president Salvador Allende (1908–1973). Bachelet's father, who served in Allende's government, was immediately imprisoned after a military coup d'état toppled the government in September 1973; he died of a heart attack in March 1974. Michelle and her mother were imprisoned in January 1975 but were allowed to go into exile to Australia in early February.

From Australia, Bachelet traveled to the Deutsche Demokratische Republik or DDR (German Democratic Republic or GDR) and began her medical studies at Humboldt University in Berlin. There she married Jorge Dávalos, the father of Sebastián and Francisca. She returned to Chile in 1979, receiving her degree in medicine in 1982 and specializing in pediatrics and public health. After Chile became a democratic regime again in 1990, she served in the ministry of health. She was elected a member of the central committee of the Socialist Party in 1995 and became actively engaged in politics.

Her interest in politics and the military led her to study military strategy in Chile's National Academy of Politics and Strategy. Having graduated first in her class, she obtained a fellowship to take a course in the Inter-American Defense School in Washington, D.C., in 1997. At her return she served as assistant to the minister of defense. After the election of the Socialist Ricardo Lagos in 2000, she was appointed minister of health, and in January 2002 she became Chile's first woman minister of defense. She was released from that position in October 2004 to allow her to launch her presidential campaign.

In 2004 she used her gender to claim that as a mother and a doctor she understood the needs of her country. Bachelet launched a successful presidential campaign promising to give women equal representation in her cabinet, a promise that she has fulfilled. In a cabinet with ten positions, among them the key ministries of defense, economy, planning, and health, all ten went to women. She has promised to maintain a stable economy, not to attempt any radical socialization of production or services, and to bring more justice and a better standard of living to the general population.

[*See also* Chile.]

BIBLIOGRAPHY

Angell, Alan, and Cristóbal Reig. "Change or Continuity? The Chilean Elections of 2005/2006." *Bulletin of Latin American Research* 25, no. 4 (2006): 481–502.

"Biographía: Michelle Bachelet." http://www.gobiernodechile.cl/biogra_bachelet/. Spanish-language biography of Bachelet on the Chilean government Web site. An English-language version is also available.

"Chile's President-Elect: Michelle Bachelet." http://www.pbs.org/newshour/bb/latin_america/jan-june06/chile_1-25.html. A transcript from the *NewsHour* with Jim Lehrer from 25 January 2006.

Rohter, Larry. "Woman in the News: A Leader Making Peace with Chile's Past." *New York Times*, 16 January 2006, late edition, section 1.

ASUNCIÓN LAVRIN

BAHINABAI (1628–1700), Indian poet-saint. Bahinabai was born in Devagaon in western Maharashtra to Brahman parents who had remained childless for many years. Bahinabai's early years were marked by frequent pilgrimages to temples of Rama and Vithoba, a localized form of the god Vishnu. Bahinabai's guru, Tukaram (c. 1608–1650), a sudra poet-saint, is credited with the crystallization of the Varkari movement, an instance of the revitalized devotionalism (*bhakti*) characteristic of the seventeenth and eighteenth centuries. Bahinabai was married at the age of five to Gangadhar Pathak, a thirty-year-old Brahman astrologer and distant relative. She became a mother at the age of eleven, first giving birth to a daughter and later to a son. Despite her husband's disdain for devotional practice and strict adherence to orthodox principles, Bahinabai's autobiography celebrates her unwavering commitment to *bhakti*. Indeed, her devotional practices often incited her husband's rage and, ultimately, his physical violence against her. Bahinabai's literary works envision this suffering as a test of her *bhakti*, and as inspiration for seeking refuge in Vithoba's grace.

Bahinabai's literary output, central to the elaboration of the Varkari movement and recited to her son during the last years of her life, included 473 devotional songs written in the genre known as *abhanga* (lyrical compositions produced in Marathi, the local vernacular). Her *abhangas* extol the virtue of *bhakti* and the saints, glorify Vithoba, redefine the criteria for Brahmanhood, and praise the role of the dutiful wife. In her autobiography, *Atmanivedana*, she articulated the tension between devotion and domesticity, which was her primary intellectual and spiritual concern.

Bahinabai's contribution as a poet-saint differed from that of other female saints of the period. Despite her criticism of the restrictions placed upon her religious practice, Bahinabai ultimately upheld the authority of the orthodox tradition, its reliance on Sanskrit, and its limited religious roles for women. In fact, her compositions venerate aspects of this culture, including the patriarchal ideal of the obedient wife, or *pativrata*. Though she interrogated the norms that limited female spirituality, she never provided a direct solution to the dilemmas female devotees (*bhaktas*) encountered. Instead, Bahinabai's contribution to *bhakti* culture generally, and the Varkari Panth in particular, was her ability to incorporate the role of the *pativrata* into the ethos of *bhakti*, thereby providing high-caste women with a new model for religious living.

Bahinabai's memorial (*samadhi*) is found in the town of Dehu, where she died a widow at the age of seventy-two.

[*See also* India *and* Literature.]

BIBLIOGRAPHY

Abbott, Justin E. *Bahina Bai: A Translation of Her Autobiography and Verses*. Poona, India: Scottish Mission Industries Co. Ltd, 1929.

Feldhaus, Anne. "Bahina Bai: Wife and Saint." *Journal of the American Academy of Religion* 50 (1982): 591–604.

McGee, Mary. "Bahinabai: The Ordinary Life of an Exceptional Woman, or, the Exceptional Life of an Ordinary Woman." In *Vaisnavi: Women and the Worship of Krishna*, edited by Steven J. Rosen. Delhi, India: Motilal Banarsidass, 1996.

Ramanujan, A. K. "On Women Saints." In *The Divine Consort: Rādhā and the Goddesses of India*, edited by John Stratton Hawley and Donna Marie Wulff, pp. 316–324. Berkeley, Calif.: Berkeley Religious Studies Series, 1982.

Vanita, Ruth. "Three Women Saints of Maharashtra: Muktabai, Janabai, BahinaBai." In *Manushi* 50–52 (January–June 1989): 45–61.

PREETI ASHOK PARASHARAMI

BAKER, ELLA (1903–1986), American civil rights activist. Ella Baker was a major architect of the modern civil rights movement. Born in 1903, she was raised in rural North Carolina and nurtured by a strong black community. She attended Shaw University in Raleigh, graduating in 1927. While the Depression derailed her formal academic career after her move to New York, her political education flourished as she immersed herself in the intellectual and cultural life of Harlem, an epicenter of black radical and progressive thought.

In 1938 Baker started working for the National Association for the Advancement of Colored People. As both field secretary and director of branches, she traveled widely, building local branches and creating an extensive personal network of civil rights activists. Unsatisfied with the top-down management style of the association, Baker resigned in 1946.

In an effort to raise money for the growing civil rights movement, Baker cofounded In Friendship in 1956. The group sponsored several important fund-raisers for the Montgomery bus boycott and other local initiatives. In 1958 Baker became the executive director of the Southern Christian Leadership Conference (SCLC), headed by Martin Luther King Jr. The male-dominated SCLC marginalized her because of her gender and outspoken nature. Furthermore, Baker's frustration with the organization grew as she realized that instead of building local leadership in the spirit of the bus boycott, SCLC relied heavily upon the public utterances and actions of its leader to advance civil rights efforts. For Baker, this overreliance on King highlighted reluctance to value grassroots movements and the leaders they produced.

When the sit-in movement began in 1960, Baker moved to support student protesters. She brought young activists from across the country to Shaw University, encouraged them to network, and helped them strategize. In an effort to bolster student autonomy, she helped form the Student Nonviolent Coordinating Committee (SNCC). For the duration of SNCC's existence, she served as the group's mentor, helping to guide the organization throughout the civil rights movement.

SNCC adopted many of Baker's philosophies: a belief in the power of indigenous movements, decentralized leadership, and a willingness to value the disenfranchised, particularly women of color. These beliefs made SNCC one of the most influential civil rights groups in the nation. Guided by these values, SNCC, along with Baker, created the Mississippi Freedom Democratic Party (MFDP) in 1964. At the Democratic National Convention, the MFDP challenged the regular (segregated) Democratic contingent for its official seat, a daring, nationally televised act that led to substantial reforms within the Democratic Party and laid bare the depth of the party's (and country's) unwillingness to share power with the dispossessed.

After the 1960s, Baker continued to work for numerous progressive organizations, such as the Puerto Rican Solidarity Committee and the Commission for Social and Racial Justice of the Episcopal Church. At her funeral in 1986, friends, colleagues, and movement "children" reflecting on her life concluded that, in her work as a bridge-builder, strategist, and organizer, "Ms. Baker" was one of the cornerstones of the civil and human rights movements of the last half of the twentieth century.

[*See also* Civil Rights Movement; Hamer, Fanny Lou; *and* Parks, Rosa.]

BIBLIOGRAPHY

Payne, Charles. *I've Got the Light of Freedom: The Organizing Tradition and the Mississippi Freedom Struggle.* Berkeley: University of California Press, 1995.

Ransby, Barbara. *Ella Baker and the Black Freedom Movement: A Radical Democratic Vision.* Chapel Hill: University of North Carolina Press, 2003.

CHARLES W. MCKINNEY JR.

BAKER, JOSEPHINE (1906–1975), American-born Parisian dancer, singer, and film star, who was arguably the most famous African American expatriate to settle in Paris during the twentieth century. Culturally and geographically she "belonged" to what she called her two loves—the United States and Paris. By the 1950s she had become a worldwide cultural phenomenon, civil rights advocate, and renowned humanitarian.

Born Freda J. McDonald in Saint Louis, Missouri, Baker had the all-too-common hard life of an African American girl growing up amid deprivation and racial violence. Witnessing the 1917 race riot in Saint Louis traumatized her, and poverty limited her opportunities. Baker's father, the vaudeville performer, left soon after her birth, and her mother, Carrie McDonald, forced her to work as a child domestic for wealthy whites. To cope, Baker ran away repeatedly.

A job as a nightclub waitress introduced Baker to the professional world of music and dance. Eventually she joined a local vaudeville group, the Jones Family Band, and later toured with the Dixie Steppers, a traveling troupe. While on tour in Philadelphia, Baker met the railway porter William Howard Baker, who became her second husband. (She had had a short-lived marriage at age thirteen.) Baker's vaudeville circuit breakthrough came in 1922 when she joined the road cast of *Shuffle Along*, the hit all-black Broadway musical produced by Noble Sissle and Eubie Blake. Two years later, on Broadway, she performed the lead in Sissle and Blake's *The Chocolate Dandies*, and the critics raved.

In 1925, Baker traveled to Paris with the company La Revue Nègre and caused a stir when she performed the "Danse sauvage" at the Théâtre des Champs Elysées. With only feathers covering her bottom, the topless Baker played the primitive exotic much to the delight of an approving crowd. Within two years, her music hall performances made her a Paris sensation. Her image remained the draw: she was a primal and sexy modernist creation—France's "new woman." Photography and fashion took note as French women yearned to imitate every aspect of her appearance—her brown skin, her hairstyles, and her dress. She soon became the highest paid entertainer in the world. The material fruits of international popularity notwithstanding, some, of course, were troubled by her exploitation of racial stereotypes and intimidated by her sophisticated command of the stage.

Baker also focused on film and recordings. Her movies included the silent *La sirène des tropiques* (1927), followed by the talkies *Zou-Zou* (1934) and *Princesse Tam-Tam* (1935). In 1934, she won critical acclaim for the lead role in the comic operetta *La Créole*, staged at the Parisian Marigny Theatre.

Social and political crises held Baker's attention throughout her career. During World War II, she spied for the French Resistance, for which the government awarded her the Médaille de La Résistance (Medal of the Resistance). Subsequently, in words and deeds, she supported the African American civil rights movement, thereby attracting the attention of the Federal Bureau of Investigation (FBI), which opened a file on her in 1951. She also fashioned herself a humanitarian, adopting twelve children of various nationalities—her "Rainbow Tribe"—to prove that people of different backgrounds could live together harmoniously.

Baker retired briefly in 1956, but financial difficulties led her back to the stage on and off until her death from a cerebral hemorrhage in 1975. Befitting her impact on national culture, the French held a funeral with full military honors. The American actress Grace Kelly, then princess of Monaco, a supporter during critical moments in Baker's career and private life, held a private ceremony for Baker in Monaco, where she is buried.

[*See also* Civil Rights Movement; Dance; France; Music; United States, *subentry* Modern Period; *and* World War II.]

BIBLIOGRAPHY

Josephine Baker. Compilation by Bryan Hammond based on his personal collection; theatrical biography by Patrick O'Connor. London: Cape, 1988.

Jules-Rosette, Bennetta. *Josephine Baker in Art and Life: The Icon and the Image.* Urbana-Champaign: University of Illinois Press, 2007.

CHANA KAI LEE

BALKANS. The modern history of the Balkans began later than in the West, with the formation of several small nation-states during the long nineteenth century. Serbia (1815), Greece (1830), Romania (1859), Bulgaria (1878), and later Albania (1912) emerged through secession from the Ottoman Empire. The Balkan states adopted not only Western-type constitutions but, sooner or later, Western law (civil codes) as well. As in the West, citizenship did not arrive at the same moment for men and women. Women in the Balkans gained some fraction of citizenship, depending on the social, cultural, and political conditions in their countries. As elsewhere, after their establishment the

Balkan states institutionalized gender hierarchy, based on the conveniently propagated discourse of an essential "natural" difference. Women, considered a particular category of noncitizens, had limited presence in the public realm and legally gained full social and political rights equal to those of men only after World War II.

Discourses on Women. During the nineteenth and twentieth centuries there were three main discourses on women's roles in the Balkans: old traditionalist, neotraditionalist, and emancipatory. The roots of old traditionalist discourse can be traced back to medieval Christian culture, but it gained strength and visibility with the birth of the periodical press and modern Balkan literatures within the process of nation forming. The press spread an image of womanhood (and concomitant normative elements) that was pretty universal: women were relegated to domestic and family spaces and roles (looking after the household, childbearing and child-rearing, cooking, sewing, and so on), qualities such as modesty and obedience were posited as women's virtues, and women's skills were demanded of women.

Women's subordination was emotionally reinforced by creating a culture of shame to reinforce certain norms and attitudes. Characteristically, the appearance of educated women in public life was presented as their "losing the redness of shame." Women's emancipation was viewed as part of a general trend of decay and deterioration, whose other manifestations were industrialization, the Westernization of lifestyles, and the decline of morals. Because the aspirations of the New Woman were argued for and partly legitimated by pointing to the more advanced West, one would expect conservatives to find fault with the morally contaminating influence of Western civilization. However, because the prestige of Western civilization was rather high and uncontested in Balkan societies, conservatives referred rather to a "false understanding" of it. Positively, the affirmation of the traditional image of womanhood—for instance, in the folk psychology popular at the beginning of the twentieth century—assumed the form of idealized past bucolic Balkan societies.

After World War I, in tune with the fashionable right-wing ideological currents of the day, a neotraditionalist discourse appeared. It was characterized by gender and ethnic essentialism, antimodernism, and extreme nationalism. This traditionalism did not change the notion of womanhood (though one may find new traits), but it had a different style of argumentation: more aggressive, pseudoscientific, constantly ideological, and manipulative. Some authors (both women and men) claimed the authority of biology and physiology in justifying misogynist notions of womanhood and presenting woman as "eternal Mother Nature." In pseudoscientific essentializing texts, women were presented as more loving of peace and disarmament, as appropriate for housekeeping and cooking, as entirely subordinated to reproductive functions, as primarily sexual creatures, as intuitive, irrational, and impulsive, and as intellectually inferior to men—all this allegedly dictated by biology and sexuality.

In pro-natalist views, giving birth to children was imputed as women's contribution to the nation, while any decrease of the fertility rate was seen as threatening the future of the nation, conceived of as an organism. Well-known male intellectuals misrepresented and caricatured women's emancipatory actions; Branišlav Nusić, in his

Balkan Conflict. Serbian refugees return home, early twentieth century. PRINTS AND PHOTOGRAPHS DIVISION, LIBRARY OF CONGRESS

1935 comedy *Ujež*, satirized the public activities of women as destroying their families and the natural order—an argument and strategy used by his Bulgarian colleague Stefan L. Kostov in his 1914 comedy *Muzhemrazka*, or Man-hater. They portrayed modern women as trying to escape from their natural duties and attributed to them the use of alcohol and tobacco and indulgence in fashion and luxuries. Feminism and women's struggles for emancipation, equality, and independence were depicted as sins of modernism. Even some women's organizations and their periodicals insisted on special education for girls that would better prepare them for their "mission" to "raise good sons for the fatherland" and to become dutiful wives, mothers, and housekeepers. Some writings asserted a double standard for men and women in marital life, derived prostitution from such intrinsic qualities as natural sinfulness and stigmatized it as a source of evil, and caricatured spinsters as deviations from the norm. Such traditional, misogynist views were defended by evoking the authority of "science."

In the nineteenth century the Balkans witnessed a transition from tradition to modernity. This transition included the spread not only of a new, modern, dynamic urban material culture but also of a new mentality comprising such liberal ideas as freedom, progress, the emancipation of the human spirit, the development of objective science, universal law, and morality, and the rational organization of everyday public life. Nationalism, the main ideological discourse of the nineteenth century, sought to break off with the Ottoman past and implement a Western model of a civilized nation-state. Thus Christianity was juxtaposed with Islam in the Balkans, and Hellenism was juxtaposed with Islam in Greece. Schools became an important means for achieving cultural emancipation and attaining political independence from the Ottoman and Austrian-Hungarian empires.

One result of nationalist efforts and the modernization process was growing social differentiation and mobility within the nation-states. In the discussions of nationalism and modernization, arguments in favor of women's emancipation were developed. It is there that one finds the roots of women's self-consciousness in the Balkans. The arguments of this emancipatory discourse came from two main sources: liberal and socialist. Gender as much as class was a locus of power struggles and social tensions. Balkan societies witnessed the mobilization of women seeking to break the limited space in which they were confined and find a legitimate place as citizens within the modern nation-states. Women's movements in the Balkans, as elsewhere, got their first impulses from education and social work—not surprisingly, because education was a priority in the classical women's movement. Although in the nineteenth century few Balkan women were literate and even fewer had access to printed media, some men and women of letters expressed a sort of literary feminism in the periodical press by arguing for the need to educate women on various grounds.

Greece. Already in his constitution of 1797, Rigas Velestinlis supported the idea that schools for children of both sexes should be established in each village. However, it was only after the Greek revolution of 1821 and subsequent independence that specific (though totally inspired by Western Enlightenment) Greek discourse on women's education arose. In the 1820s there were two views concerning girls' education among Greeks: the coeducation of girls and boys in the elementary schools and the establishment of separate schools for girls. The most visible differences among Greek regions were between the traditional, continental part of Greece and the more developed and urbanized ports and administrative centers. In general, only the urbanized regions participated in the educational debates and were receptive to separate education for girls. In the second half of the 1820s, there were a few girls' schools supported by Protestant missionaries and municipalities and a few schools of the Bell-Lancaster (mutual) type supported by the private initiative of Greek women and Protestant missionaries and by the municipalities. In the 1830s the first Hellenic schools for girls were established in Ermoúpolis (the Cyclades) and in Athens. In 1834 the Greek government introduced obligatory primary education for both boys and girls between five and twelve years of age. The law of 1834 ideologically justified separate education for girls and boys, though it did not openly oppose mixed elementary schools. This happened a bit later, in 1852, when the Greek state forbade coeducation in primary schools.

During the nineteenth century the idea that women should serve as mother-educators for spreading the national ideology reinforced opinions in support of women's education. Yet the two important fields for women's education—secondary education and the formation of women teachers—were abandoned to private initiatives, while the state devoted considerable resources to education for boys. Women's education was a privilege of the urban regions, and secondary education was reserved for girls of well-to-do families. Yet secondary education for boys was free. During the nineteenth century—in Athens, Ermoúpolis, Patras, and other urban centers—several superior women's private schools were established. Especially popular were those run by the Society of Friends of Education. Until 1860 this society had only one school in Athens, known as Arsakeion. In 1866 another Arsakeion was established in Corfu, and in 1890 another in Patras. Apart from giving girls formal secondary education, the Arsakeions were important for preparing future women teachers and for women's socialization and identity building.

Nineteenth-century educators of the Balkan nation-states, like their Western counterparts, believed in what

Thomas Laqueur calls the "two-sex model," that women and men have completely different abilities and intellectual potential. Accordingly, they insisted on different types of education and socialization for women and men, which would presumably correspond more properly to their "natural" dispositions. Such opinions were reflected in the schools' curricula. In modern Greece it was Grēgorios G. Pappadopoulos, a Westernized Greek philologist and pedagogue, who for the first time explicitly claimed that though women are different from men (psychically, mentally, and psychologically), they are not inferior. The ideal of the mother-educator reinforced the notion of women teachers and their mission in serving the nation. The 1870s witnessed the establishment of several new schools for Greek girls, thanks to the activity of the Association for Women's Education (founded in Constantinople in 1871), the Association of Ladies for Female Education (established in Athens in 1872), and various educational associations, and also thanks to the financial support of rich Greeks of the diaspora.

Greek women published articles on education and pedagogical works, gave public lectures, and edited the first women's periodicals. Two of the first Greek women's journals—*Thaleia*, published 1867–1868 in Athens by Penelope Lazaridou, and *Eurydice*, published 1870–1873 in Constantinople by Emilie Ktena-Leondias—united and made heard women's reflections on the "vocation" and education of the female sex. In 1887 a new women's periodical, *Efimeris ton Kyrion* (Ladies' Journal), appeared. The journal was the outcome of the growing gender consciousness among middle-class women at the time. During its thirty years of existence, *Efimeris ton Kyrion* had print runs of five thousand copies and enjoyed a vast readership, first as a weekly (1887–1907) and then as a biweekly (1907–1917). It was edited by Callirhoe Parren, a literary woman and journalist, the first to introduce feminism to Greece and to engage in emancipatory discourse. Her journal represented a moderate call for emancipating women intellectually and morally by means of education and paid work. *Efimeris ton Kyrion* was suspended in 1917 after Parren's exile, imposed by the Venizelos administration as a result of Parren's opposition to Greece's participation on the side of the Entente during World War I. In 1890 the first woman was accepted at a Greek University, and women's demands for equal pay for equal work were widespread.

Apart from her work as a journalist, Callirhoe Parren was also among the founders of the Enosis ton Ellinidon (Union of Greek Women, 1896). This union, the first mass mobilization of women in the public realm, coordinated women's patriotic involvement in the Greco-Turkish War of 1897. Women's active participation in this military event was significant not only because it proved their skills in fields previously unknown or forbidden to them but also because during that short but traumatic war, women managed partly to overcome the suspicion and rejection of women's collective actions, so typical of conservative Greek intelligentsia and politicians of the time.

In 1908, owing to Parren's efforts, the Ethniko Symvoulio ton Ellinidon (National Council of Greek Women) was founded and affiliated with the International Council of Women. In 1911, again with her participation, the Lykeion ton Ellinidon (Lyceum of Greek Women) was established to fight various forms of existing injustices in Greek society. Later on, Parren also chaired the Greek Section of the Women's International League for Peace and Freedom (affiliated with the league in 1921). During the interwar period the leaders of the newly established feminist organizations attacked Parren and her lyceum for being too conservative and well behind the current feminist agenda. An organization in tune with this agenda, the Syndesmos gia ta Dikaiomata tis Gynaikas (League for Woman's Rights), was founded in 1920 and affiliated with the International Woman Suffrage Alliance and its successor, the International Alliance of Women for Suffrage and Equal Citizenship. Avra Theodōropoulou was the leader of this organization for about thirty years (1921–1936 and 1944–1958) and was also a board member of the alliance (1923–1935).

Feminist activism in the interwar period, apart from traditional philanthropic work, focused on the struggle for more social and political rights. Though neither the Greek constitution of 1864 nor the subsequent electoral legislation mentioned male gender as a necessary condition for suffrage, women were not granted the right to vote. Greek women insisted first and foremost on the right to vote, but also on equal rights for mothers and fathers over the custody of their children, on the right to have an abortion, on free education, and on many other demands conforming to the agenda of the international women's movement at the time.

Between 1928 and 1932, Greek feminists of every persuasion collaborated in the struggle for women's franchise. In February 1930 women gained a limited right to elect local authorities, though restricted on the basis of age and education to no more than 10 percent of the Greek female population. After 1934 and just before the Metaxas dictatorship (1936–1941), some factions of feminist organizations collaborated with the leftist women's movement, in tune with the democratic, antifascist Popular Front, initiated by the Kommounistik Komma Elladas (Communist Party of Greece).

Ioannis Metaxas banned most women's organizations. Some of them, such as the National Council of Greek Women, turned to philanthropic activities to survive. Some leaders of the liberal feminist movement—such as Maria Svolou, general secretary of the League for Woman's Rights—turned toward socialism in the belief that gender equality could be reached only after fundamental changes in the economy and society. After World War II the League for Woman's Rights was revived, but its activities were limited in the political climate created by the civil war (1946–1949).

Greek women were granted full voting rights in 1952 and wider political rights in 1955 in an attempt to improve Greece's international reputation in the aftermath of the civil war. Yet under the civil code of 1946, Greek men were officially declared heads of their families. Equality between women and men was constitutionally established in 1975.

Yugoslavia/Serbia. Dositej Obradović (1742–1811), an early Serbian advocate of women's emancipation, urged the coeducation of boys and girls and saw overcoming women's ignorance as an important step for Serbian development. During the 1840s the first schools for girls were opened in Belgrade and subsequently in most territories of what later became Yugoslavia (the Kingdom of Serbs, Croats, and Slovenes). In 1863 the first women's high school in the Balkans was established in the Serbian capital. Despite substantial educational development in the late nineteenth and early twentieth centuries, as well as the introduction of compulsory primary education in 1882, the 1921 national census showed a national illiteracy rate of 51.5 percent. Women's literacy even in the early 1930s remained limited, about 44 percent. The Yugoslav government attempted to reduce illiteracy by opening new schools, but in 1940 the national illiteracy rate still remained high, at slightly above 40 percent.

Women have always worked in the fields in the Balkan countryside. Yet during this time women engaged in more diversified work outside their homes, and substantially more women engaged in paid work. In 1922 women made up about 20 percent of the nonagricultural workforce, and by 1940 their share reached 28 percent. In 1910, Serbia introduced legislation for labor protection and social benefits. Such laws banned women from the mining industry and other activities considered harmful. In 1922 the government also introduced four months' paid maternity leave for women workers. Yet most Yugoslav women, who worked in agriculture or as domestic servants, were not at all protected by the laws.

The first Serbian civil code, adopted in 1844 and effective in Serbia and part of Yugoslavia until 1946, privileged men over women. According to this legislation, after marriage women lose the right to be teachers and to be employed in general without their husbands' permission. As Thomas Emmert has pointed out, "Legally and by custom, Serb women were among the most oppressed of European women" (in Ramet). Yet a new generation of emancipated and professionally active women appeared in the course of time. Among them were Draga Ljocic-Milošević, the first woman medical doctor in Serbia and a women's rights activist; Isidora Sekulić, the first Serbian woman writer and activist of Kolo Srpskih Sestara (Circle of Serbian Sisters, 1903–1944); and Ksenija Atanasijević, the first Serbian woman PhD and first female university professor (in the department of philosophy at Belgrade University), editor of the first feminist journal in the country, *Ženski pokret* (1920–1938), and board member of the Skupštine Lige Žena za Mir i Slobodu (Serbian Women's League for Peace and Freedom).

The intensified struggle for women's emancipation in Serbia in the 1870s continued through the interwar period. Already in the 1860s some Serbian literati publicly expressed their ideas concerning women's situation and education. Among them was Draga Dejanović, feminist, actress, and poet. In 1866 the early Serbian socialists and liberals Svetozar Marković, Svetozar Miletić, and Vladimir Jovanović founded the Ujedinjena Omladina Srpska (United Serbian Youth, 1866–1872). This organization, modeled after Giuseppe Mazzini's Giovine Italia, was one of the first organizations to raise the question of women's emancipation. The first Serbian women's society was established in Hungarian-controlled Vojvodina (Novi Sad) in 1864. In 1875 in Belgrade, the Žensko Društvo (Women's Society), the first women's organization in Serbia itself, was founded. This was followed by the feminist organization established by the prominent journalist and translator Milica Ninković in Novi Sad in 1880. Other organizations active at the turn of the century were the Društvo "Kneginja Ljubica" (Society of Princess Ljubica), established in 1899, and the Kolo Srpskih Sestara (Circle of Serbian Sisters, 1903), the largest Serbian organization before World War I. To coordinate the activities of Serbian women's organizations, the Srpski Ženski Savez (Serbian Women's Alliance) was established in 1906. In 1911 this umbrella organization joined the International Council of Women and the International Alliance of Women.

In 1897 the first Slovenian women's journal, *Slovenka* (Slovene Woman, 1897–1902), was founded. It published materials on women's education—especially women's access to universities—paid work for women, women's suffrage, women's political and social rights, civil marriage and divorce, the need for women's organizations, and so on. The first two professional women's organizations in Slovenia, founded in 1898, were for women teachers and women lace-makers. Apart from their professional agenda, the two organizations supported the struggle for women's suffrage. The real beginning of the organized mass women's movement was in 1901 when the Splošno Slovensko Žensko Društvo (General Slovenian Women's Association) was founded in Ljubljana. In the next four decades more than twenty other women's organizations appeared, most of them established in the interwar period. These organizations united women of different social backgrounds, education, professional affiliations, religious beliefs, and visions for the future.

With the establishment of Yugoslavia in 1919, the first umbrella organization of the women's movement, the Narodni Ženski Savez Srba, Hrvata i Slovenaca (National Woman's Alliance of Serbs, Croats, and Slovenians), was founded. In 1921 this alliance united fifty thousand women grouped in two hundred and five organizations around the country. After 1929 it was known as the Jugoslavenski Žhenski Savez (Yugoslav Women's Alliance). Another important women's organization in the interwar period was the Društvo za Prosvećivanje Žene i Zaštitu Njenih Prava (Society for the Enlightenment of Woman and the Defense of Her Rights), founded in April 1919 in Belgrade and in September 1919 in Sarajevo. It aimed at educating women and struggling for women's voting rights and gender equality in all aspects of social life. In 1923 this organization changed its name to the Zhenski Pokret (Women's Movement), and by the end of the 1920s it established close contacts with the Jugoslavenski Žhenski Savez (Yugoslav Women's Alliance).

Although women had been promised voting rights within the new Yugoslav state and during the 1930s the women's movement organized strong campaigns in support of the vote for women, they did not get it. This fact and many other inequalities vis-à-vis men led women in interwar Yugoslavia to voice their concerns regarding women's limited legal property rights and lack of guardianship over their own children. They protested against the laws covering fathers of illegitimate children that did not permit paternity investigations, and they questioned patriarchal laws that excluded women from land inheritances. Most women's organizations in interwar Yugoslavia, however, considered women's emancipation a secondary goal and focused mainly on humanitarian and social work. It is not at all surprising, then, that in 1926 some of the more conservative groups of the Yugoslav Women's Alliance left it and created the Narodna Ženska Zajednica (National Women's Union).

From the beginning of World War II, women's organizations took part in the preparations for an armed uprising. In the military forces and in the new civil government, women were accepted as equals. After the establishment of the socialist system, the 1946 constitution confirmed women's economic, social, and political equality in the country—something that women had already achieved during the war. In 1961, however, the Yugoslav Women's Alliance was abolished and was replaced by the Conference for a Social Activity of Women. With the disappearance of women's organizations in Yugoslavia, the strong interest in changing the existing gender contract vanished. Yet some left-wing interwar activists continued their political careers under state socialism. For example, there was Vida Tomšič, who found it difficult to persuade her male party comrades to accept her ideas on issues such as family planning when drafting woman-friendly state gender policies in general.

Romania. In 1868, soon after the establishment of the Romanian nation-state, Constanta Dunca was the first to express publicly at the Bucharest Atheneum her gender-sensitive concerns regarding women's paid work and equality within the family. During the next twenty-five years the few existing women's organizations discussed the social role of Romanian women using arguments based on distinct gender identities and roles.

Although women's situation was discussed in earlier Romanian publications, it was during the 1870s that the ideas about women's emancipation and the "woman question" became a hot topic of discussion in the Romanian periodicals published both in the capital Bucharest and in other urban centers. Thus in 1879, Sofia Nădejde published in *Femeia Romana* (Romanian Woman) a polemical text criticizing the widespread opinion that women are incapable of any development. In her debate with the well-known intellectual Titu Maiorescu in the newspaper *Contemporanul* (The Contemporary) in the 1880s, Nădejde condemned prejudices regarding women as inferior while demonstrating profound knowledge of the scientific debates of her time. In 1894 the restructuring of an older organization gave birth to the Liga Femeilor din România (League of Romanian Women), which in 1896 addressed a petition to the parliament insisting on revision of legislation concerning paternity rights and women's administration of their own wealth.

Women's organizations set up to fight various forms of gender injustices proliferated in the early twentieth century. In 1908 the Reuniunea Femeilor Române din Braşov (Romanian Women's Society of Brasov) was established with Maria Baiulescu as its president. In 1910 in Bucharest another important organization appeared, the Societatea Ortodoxă Naţională a Femeilor Române (National Orthodox Society of Romanian Women). Its president between 1918 and 1938 was Princess Alexandrina Cantacuzino. In November 1911, Eugenia de Reuss Ianculescu founded the first Romanian women's suffrage association, the Asociatiaţ Drepturile Femeii (Woman's Rights Association), renamed in 1913 to the Liga Drepturilor si Datoriilor Femeilor (League for Women's Rights and Duties).

Already in 1912, Ianculescu tried to build a coalition with the newly established Cercul Feminin Socialist (Socialist Feminine Circle) but failed because socialist women believed that Ianculescu's organization of educated middle-class women was not truly interested in the problems of working-class and peasant women. In 1914 when some changes to the constitution were debated, the League for Women's Rights and Duties supported a petition to the Romanian parliament insisting on women's voting rights for local elections. *Drepturile femeii* (Woman's Rights), the publishing organ of this organization from 1912, supported women's rights to practice professions, insisted on equal pay for equal work, advocated changing family and marriage legislation in favor of women, condemned child prostitution, pleaded for equal political rights, and so on. In 1913 the Uniunea Femeilor Române (Union of Romanian Women) was established in Bucharest, headed by Maria Baiulescu until 1935. It united more than a hundred women's organizations with the aim to create a space where women could meet, talk, and exchange ideas about their common aims and activities. Baiulescu's feminism, however, was subordinated to her nationalism.

In 1919, Romania emerged on the redesigned map of postwar Europe as a victorious nation with its population almost doubled and with borders that satisfied the most daring nationalist expectations. Romania's ethnic diversity became a political challenge, however, and ethnic nationalism affected women's organizations as well. Also, though prior to World War I there was no unified women's movement in Romania and the existing organizations were not strongly committed to universal suffrage, the situation started to change during the war.

In 1917 a group of women petitioned the government to extend political and civil rights to all ethnically Romanian women. To help prepare such women for their political rights and duties, during 1917–1918 a group of prominent Romanian women's activists—among them Sofia Nădejde, Maria Baiulescu, Ella Negruzzi, Calypso Botez, and Elena Meissner—established the Asociația pentru Emanciparea Civilăşi Politică a Femeilor Române (Association for the Civil and Political Emancipation of Romanian Women). A year after its foundation the association already had branches in Bucharest, Cernauti, Brasov, and Sibiu. Leaders of this organization throughout the interwar period were Meissner and Negruzzi. They had to struggle with both the patriarchal establishment and with other women's organizations in the country.

In 1921 an umbrella federation of women's organizations, the Consiliul National al Femeilor Romane (National Council of Romanian Women), was created to coordinate the activities of the women's movement, increase women's public visibility, and build a platform for Romanian women to voice their concerns. After 1922 the council represented Romanian women in the International Council of Women. In 1925, Alexandrina Cantacuzino was elected one of the vice presidents of the council and became a leading figure in the nationalist-reformist branch of interwar Romanian feminism, which sought "a gender-based, but egalitarian, vision of social organization" (Offen). Cantacuzino became the second president of the National Council of Romanian Women responsible for the external relations of the organization, while Calypso Botez, as president, dealt with internal affairs. In 1925 there appeared a new organization called Solidaritatea (Solidarity), led from 1926 by Cantacuzino. After the League for Women's Rights and Duties (in 1913) and the Association for the Civil and Political Emancipation of Romanian Women (in 1924), Solidarity in 1929 became the third Romanian organization to be affiliated with the International Alliance of Women for Suffrage and Equal Citizenship.

Some tensions within the Romanian women's movement appeared in the course of time. Older feminists from the Association for the Civil and Political Emancipation of Romanian Women and the League for Women's Rights and Duties accused Cantacuzino of monopolizing and misrepresenting the Romanian women's movement, both in the country and abroad. After Botez resigned from the presidency (1930) and after other activists withdrew from the National Council of Romanian Women, Cantacuzino remained the only council leader and forced those who did not agree with her position to leave the organization.

In 1923, when it became clear that women would not be enfranchised under the new constitution, the leaders of the national council mobilized women to protest against new neglect of their rights by powerful Romanian statesmen. With the 1929 reform of electoral legislation, part of the Romanian female population gained the right to elect and be elected to local councils: those age twenty-five or older who had a secondary education, had vocational training, were bureaucrats, were members of leading cultural and charity societies, were war widows, or were women with war decorations. In 1929, Botez, Negruzzi, and Cantacuzino were among the first six women city councillors. Women members of the Bucharest and other municipal councils worked energetically to improve and protect employment opportunities for young women, especially for those from the villages. Women activists were very concerned about these vulnerable young people, who often became prey to abusive arrangements. To help such poor girls coming from the provinces to the capital, several training schools for female workers were founded. One such home economics school was Vojvode Radu, which provided orphans with the necessary skills for paid employment.

To mobilize women for work at the municipal level, Cantacuzino in 1929 established and became the leader of the Gruparea Femeilor Române (Association of Romanian Women). She forbade the members of association to enroll in male-dominated political parties. This regulation reflected the split within the Romanian women's movement in the 1920s over differences regarding women's participation in political parties. Unlike Cantacuzino, who opposed women's joining the existing parties, such women leaders as Meissner, Baiulescu, Botez, and Negruzzi thought that women should actively participate in political life to gain experience and prominence and thus shorten the path to winning full political and civil rights.

In the interwar period, Romanian women participated also in the debates organized by the women's section of the intellectually prominent Institutul Social Român (Romanian Social Institute), among them the debate over women's civil rights and enfranchisement led by Calypso Botez. Though in tune with the nationalistic discourse of the time, Botez's lecture at the institute was an elaborated and convincing argument in support of women's enfranchisement that skillfully deployed arguments from John Stuart Mill's liberal philosophy. Romanian liberals, however, had little truck with liberal ideas on gender equality and women's rights. During the debates over the new constitution in the late 1920s, several members of the National Liberal Party even adopted an openly negative stance toward Botez's plea for women's voting rights. Only the National Peasant Party had a limited positive agenda concerning women's rights, and after coming into power in 1929 it gave women the vote in local elections. In 1938 the new Romanian constitution introduced women's voting rights for the two legislative bodies, the house and senate, and the first women members of parliament were elected. During World War II, Romania elected its first woman senator, and Turkey elected fourteen women to its national assembly.

Romanian feminists of the interwar period also supported professionalizing women's social work. In 1926 the nationalist organization Astra (founded in Transylvania in 1861) created its Feminine and Biopolitical Subsection, which turned into one of the most active local women's organizations in the interwar period, with a strong emphasis on women's social duties. In 1929 women's organizations opened the first Romanian school for women social workers, which in 1930 became affiliated with the National Council of Romanian Women. Women's activists of the time addressed the double moral standard for women and men, worked in support of women's education (especially in the countryside), and promoted women's employment rights. In the 1920s Romanian women gained the right to be defense lawyers, and Ella Negruzzi became the first Romanian woman to practice law in Bucharest. During the unemployment crisis in the 1930s when the government started a campaign against women's rights to paid work and social benefits, women's organizations and professional women raised their voices in support of women's interests.

In 1932 the civil code was revised to grant all women almost full civil equality with men. Women activists, such as Elena Meissner, then pleaded to women's organizations to focus more actively on the education of peasant women. The main purpose of such educational activities was to encourage women to be responsible toward their families and to develop a strong work ethic, as well as to discourage the migration of vulnerable young peasant women to towns. Ethnic minorities in Romania established their own women's organizations. The activities of Hungarian, German, and Jewish women's organizations reflected such women's specific positions within Romanian society, with aims not always coinciding with those of mainstream Romanian women's organizations.

Full legal gender equality in Romania was introduced after World War II with the establishment of the Communist regime, which introduced measures to improve women's social position—especially in the realm of education and paid work—while at the same time treating them as biological machines for reproducing the Romanian nation.

Bulgaria. During the nineteenth century many literary men in the Balkans used traditionalist arguments to favor women's education but preached Jean-Jacques Rousseau's idea that women should be educated to serve individual men personally. Women, the thinking went, should be educated to become useful and entertaining companions for their husbands, better housewives, and well-prepared mother-educators of their children and the future citizens of the (Bulgarian) nation. With the increasing discourse on the need for women's education, there appeared translations of mostly French and German moral works encouraging a taste for good reading among young girls.

Though some Balkan male intellectuals declared their belief that women possessed the same intellectual faculties as men, only a few conceived of women's education in terms of a natural right. One of them was Lyuben Karavelov, a Bulgarian national revolutionary and man of letters who fiercely criticized special training for girls, which, according to him, "does not develop but incapacitates the mind of women and kills their independence" (quoted in Daskalova, *Ot siankata na istoriata*). He harshly attacked the European (mostly French) educational system because, according to him, it made women "trained slaves" and "beautiful dolls," to be used by "old children" and "whiskered masters" (Daskalova, in Jovanović and Naumović).

The Bulgarian movement for women's emancipation began in the 1840s with the opening of several dozen secular schools for girls, materially supported by some rich Bulgarian émigré merchants and local women's initiatives. The first such school was established in 1841. Already in 1850, thirty-five secular schools existed, their number rising to ninety in 1878 when the Bulgarian nation-state was established. The only intellectual profession opened to women under Ottoman rule was that of teacher. There were about four hundred women teachers prior to liberation in 1878. In the late 1850s the first women's benevolent, philanthropic, and educational organizations were set up, their number reaching sixty-one, with more than six thousand members, during the next two decades. Women's organizations opened women's reading clubs and libraries, organized public lectures, and sent articles to periodicals. Some women participated in amateur theaters as well. After the uprising against Ottoman rule in April 1876, many women's activists wrote to Russian diplomats in Constantinople, Bucharest, and Plovdiv, to foreign missionaries, to women's organizations and schools in Russia, Romania, and Prague, and to famous intellectuals and politicians abroad, trying to attract attention to the tragic events in the Balkans.

The government of the new Bulgarian state did not ensure the same rights and resources for its male and female citizens. Bulgarian nationalism institutionalized a gender hierarchy. Although after 1878 the state opened several new middle and secondary schools for girls and the number of girls who went through elementary schooling rose, women were still less educated than men. The total illiteracy rate in 1900 was around 70 percent, with huge differences between men and women, townspeople and peasants, and Bulgarians and ethnic minorities, the most illiterate being Turks and Roma (Gypsies).

In keeping with the two-sex model, statesmen of the time supported differential policies for girls' and boys' education. From elementary schools to high schools, girls and boys were made to study different subjects believed to be more suitable for their "nature" and social roles. This differential education was used as a convenient pretext to deprive girls of the benefits of a university education. In 1895 several hundred Bulgarian girls petitioned parliament and applied to Sofia University (established in 1888), insisting that the university open its doors to women as well. This was achieved only in 1901, when the first women were admitted. Women still faced numerous injustices. For example, those educated in the law did not have the right to work as defense lawyers or judges until 1945. Ironically, they won this right precisely when the rule of law became a travesty. Women's applications for positions in state administration were usually rejected on the grounds that there were enough male candidates for the position. According to the Sofia University statutes of the 1930s, women could apply for university teaching positions only when there were no male candidates. During years of crises, women were often ousted from positions and were deprived of benefits already gained to allow room for men. In addition, Bulgarian female citizens were long excluded from holding political office.

The twentieth-century Bulgarian women's movement was born out of the need to counter various forms of gender injustices. In 1901 there arose the first large national organization, Bulgarski Zhenski Sujuz (Bulgarian Women's Union), headed by the writer Anna Karima. She was also an editor of the newspaper *Zhenski glas* (Women's Voice, 1899–1944), which became the official publishing organ of the union. The Bulgarian Women's Union, an umbrella organization, united twenty-seven women's associations from around the country with the aim of working for the intellectual and spiritual uplifting of Bulgarian woman.

In the course of time two opposing views developed within the union: that of the more traditional, "bourgeois" feminists (who sympathized with the Social Democratic ideas of the broad socialists) and that of the orthodox (narrow) socialists. Tensions between these two factions within the international and Bulgarian socialist movement led to several internal splits: first in 1903 when the most radical women socialists left the Bulgarian Women's Union, and then in 1908 when the "true" feminists, led by Anna Karima, left it and set up a new organization, Ravnopravie (Equal Rights, known also as the Union of Progressive Women), devoted specifically to the pursuit of civil and political rights for women. In the organization's newspaper, *Ravnopravie*, Karima tried to justify her decision and argued that her new group sought not to divide but to strengthen the women's movement in the country. During the next years the Bulgarian Women's Union gradually evolved into a truly feminist organization, making equality—including political equality—the core goal of its activities.

Another important organization prior to World War II was the Zhenski Sotsialdemokraticheski Sujuz (Women's Social Democratic Union), established in 1921 to work for the civic and political education of working women. As is visible in the socialist newspaper *Blagodenstvie* (Prosperity), the publishing organ of the Women's Social Democratic Union, it differed from the Communist women's organization only in the methods for achieving the same goal. Women Social Democrats of the interwar period insisted on equal pay for equal work, on state measures to improve health and hygiene, on state support of the unemployed and poor, on educational and cultural facilities for all Bulgarian citizens, on the protection of children from child labor, and on the abolishment of prostitution.

In 1924, Bulgarian women with university degrees formed an organization of their own, the Druzhestvo na Bulgarkite s Visshe Obrazovanie (Association of Bulgarian Women University Graduates, later renamed the Bulgarian Association of University Women). The idea for this association came from the historian Ekaterina Zlatoustova. In 1925 the association was affiliated with the International Federation of University Women. It had four sections, formed over the years: one for women lawyers, one for women artists, one for women writers, and one for women students. After 1944 the association's board was changed, and its organizational life, after becoming politicized, gradually declined. The organization was closed down by the Communists in the middle of 1950.

Apart from their specific goals, all these women's organizations struggled for women's enfranchisement. Although

Bulgarian women were not specifically excluded from suffrage by the Bulgarian constitution of 1879 and electoral law, by patriarchal custom and tradition only men were regarded as citizens. All men, minority groups included, were granted voting rights. Already in the first decade of the twentieth century, women's activists petitioned parliament to give women political rights. They were supported by the radical democratic and peasant parties, which had put the civil and political rights of women in their programs, and also by the two socialist parties, at least by their rhetoric.

But fighting tradition proved more difficult than amending laws. The first small victory was the admission of women to the elections for school boards in 1909. A law granting women voting rights in local (communal) elections was passed only on 18 January 1937. According to this law, women were accorded voting rights if they were legally married mothers, and though voting was obligatory for male voters, it was optional for women. With the restoration of the constitution in 1937 (it had been suspended after the coup d'état in 1934), a new electoral law was drafted that defined voters as "all Bulgarian subjects, who have completed 21 years of age, men and women; the latter if married, divorced or widowed." In addition, the new electoral law gave women only the right to vote, not the right to be elected. Bulgarian women were granted full electoral rights by the Communist regime in the program of the Communist-dominated Fatherland's Front of 17 October 1944 and the electoral law of 15 June 1945, and then in the new Dimitrov's Constitution of 1947, yet the same regime emptied these rights of meaning.

Regional Initiatives. Women's movements in the Balkans established local networks to fight their marginalization within the international women's organizations and to articulate and defend their national interests against the conflicting interests of some neighboring countries. In May 1923 women activists from several Balkan countries—Yugoslavia, Bulgaria, Romania, Greece, Poland, and Czechoslovakia—created in Rome (during the congress of the International Woman Suffrage Alliance) the Little Entente of Women, modeled after the male political and military Little Entente established in 1920–1921.

The entente was established on the initiative of Alexandrina Cantacuzino, who became its first president (1923–1924). Bulgarian participation at this founding meeting, represented by the national branch of the Women's International League for Peace and Freedom, is somewhat ambiguous and against the logic of the regional political unions. The entente held conferences—in Belgrade in 1924, in Athens in 1925, in Prague in 1927, and in Warsaw in 1929—to monitor progress on women's issues in the member countries. These encouraged joint actions on a variety of issues, such as equalizing voting rights, protecting children and minorities in the workplace, reforming the treatment of children born out of wedlock, abolishing capital punishment, and favoring the teaching of civilization over war in history classes. The 1927 congress of the Little Entente of Women voted, against the strong opposition of Cantacuzino, to open the organization to women's organizations from Bulgaria, Turkey, and Albania. This decision of the entente was never implemented, however, because the entente gradually became inactive after 1929. Among the leaders of the Little Entente of Women were several activists from the Balkan countries: Alexandrina Cantacuzino, the Serbian activist Mileva Petrovitch, and the Greek feminist Avra Theodōropoulou, who was in charge of the organization between 1925 and 1927.

During the interwar period, women from the Balkan countries also participated in other local initiatives, such as several Balkan conferences held in the region in the 1930s, the Balkan Women's Conferences for Peace (the first one held in Belgrade in May 1931), and meetings organized by the Slavic Women's Committee. Balkan feminists also increasingly attended the international conferences of the International Council of Women, the International Woman Suffrage Alliance or International Alliance of Women for Suffrage and Equal Citizenship, and the Women's International League for Peace and Freedom, and some of them were elected to the governing bodies of these organizations. Among them, the Romanian Alexandrina Cantacuzino served as a vice president of the International Council of Women for many years (1925–1936) and the Greek feminist Avra Theodōropoulou served as a board member of the International Woman Suffrage Alliance and its successor, the International Alliance of Women for Suffrage and Equal Citizenship (1923–1935), as did the Romanian activist Eugenia de Reuss Ianculescu between 1926 and 1935 and the Bulgarian feminist Dimitrana Ivanova between 1935 and 1940.

[*See also* Europe, *subentry* Renaissance and Early Modern Period; Roma; Turkey; West Asia, *subentry* Ottomans; World War I; *and* World War II.]

BIBLIOGRAPHY

Avdela, Efi. "Between Duties and Rights: Gender and Citizenship in Greece, 1864-1952." In *Citizenship and the Nation-State in Greece and Turkey*, edited by Faruk Birtek and Thalia Dragonas. London: Routledge, 2005.

Avdela, Efi, and Angelika Psarra. "Engendering 'Greekness': Women's Emancipation and Irredentist Politics in Nineteenth-Century Greece." *Mediterranean Historical Review* 20, no. 1 (June 2005): 67–79.

Bock, Gisela. *Women in European History*. Oxford: Blackwell, 2002.

Bozinovic, Neda. *Žhensko pitanje u Serbiji u XIX i XX veku* (The Woman Question in Serbia in the Ninetieth and Twentieth Centuries). Belgrade, Serbia, 1996.

Bucur, Maria. "Calipso Botez: A Feminism Critique of Interwar Romanian Politics." *Jahrbücher für Geschichte und Kultur Suedosteuropas* 3 (2001): 63–78.
Bucur, Maria. *Eugenics and Modernization in Interwar Romania*. Pittsburgh, Pa.: University of Pittsburgh Press, 2001.
Budna Kodric, Natasha, and Alexandra Serse, eds. *Splosno Zensko Drstvo, 1901–1945*. Ljubljana, Slovenia, 2003.
Daskalova, Krassimira. "A Life in History (Fani Popova-Mutafova)." *Gender and History* 14, no. 2 (2002): 321–339.
Daskalova, Krassimira. "The Women's Movement in Bulgaria in a Life Story." *Women's History Review* 13, no. 1 (2004): 91–103.
Daskalova, Krassimira, ed. *Ot siankata na istoriata: Zhenite v bulgarskoto obshtestvo i kultura* (From the Shadow of History: Women in the Bulgarian Society and Culture). Sofia, Bulgaria: LIK, 1998.
Fournaraki, Eleni. "'Institutrice, femme et mère': Idées sur l'éducation des femmes Grecques au XIXème siècle (1830–1880)." PhD diss., Université de Paris VII, 1992.
Haan, Francisca de , Krassimira Daskalova, and Anna Loutfi, eds. *A Biographical Dictionary of Women's Movements and Feminisms: Central, Eastern, and South Eastern Europe, 19th and 20th Centuries*. New York: Central European University Press, 2006.
Jovanović, Miroslav, and Slobodan Naumović, eds. *Gender Relations in South Eastern Europe: Historical Perspectives on Womanhood and Manhood in 19th and 20th Century*. Graz, Austria: Institut für Geschichte der Universität Graz, 2002. Includes Krassimira Daskalova, "Women, Nationalism, and Nation-State in Bulgaria (1840s–1940s)," pp. 15–38; Ana Stolic, "Vocation or Hobby: The Social Identity of Female Teachers in the Nineteenth Century Serbia," pp. 55–90; and Radina Vucetic, "The Emancipation of Women in Interwar Belgrade and the 'Cvijeta Zuzuric' Society," pp. 143–166.
Offen, Karen. *European Feminisms, 1700–1950: A Political History*. Stanford, Calif.: Stanford University Press, 2000.
Paletschek, Sylvia, and Bianka Pietrow-Ennker, eds. *Women's Emancipation Movements in the Nineteenth Century: A European Perspective*. Stanford, Calif.: Stanford University Press, 2004. Includes Eleni Varikas, "National and Gender Identity in Turn-of-the-Century Greece."
Passmore, Kevin, ed. *Women, Gender, and Fascism in Europe, 1919–45*. Manchester, U.K.: Manchester University Press, 2003. Includes Maria Bucur, "Romania," pp. 57–78, and Carol Lilly and Melissa Bokovoy, "Serbia, Croatia, and Yugoslavia," pp. 91–123.
Ramet, Sabrina, ed. *Gender Politics in the Western Balkans*. University Park: Pennsylvania State University Press, 1999. Includes Thomas A. Emmert, "Ženski Pokret: The Feminist Movement in Serbia in the 1920s," pp. 33–49.
Saurer, Edith, Margareth Lanzinger, and Elisabeth Frysak, eds. *Women's Movements: Networks and Debates in Post-Communist Countries in the 19th and 20th Centuries*. Cologne, Germany: Böhlau, 2006. Includes Krassimira Daskalova, "Bulgarian Women's Movement, 1850s–1940s," pp. 413–437.
Schilde, Kurt, and Dagmar Schulte, eds. *Need and Care: Glimpses into the Beginnings of Eastern Europe's Professional Welfare*. Opladen, Germany: Barbara Budrich, 2005.
Stavrianos, Leften S. *The Balkans since 1453*. New York: Rinehart, 1958.
Wingfield, Nancy, and Maria Bucur, eds. *Gender and War in Twentieth-Century Eastern* Europe. Bloomington: Indiana University Press, 2006.

KRASSIMIRA DASKALOVA

BALL, LUCILLE (1911–1989), American actress and television executive. Many critics of popular culture would rate Lucille Ball the most successful female entertainer of the twentieth century. A former model, Ball began her movie career in 1933 as a Goldwyn Girl in *Roman Scandals*. Over the next twenty years she worked steadily in comedies and musicals, marrying Cuban bandleader and singer Desi Arnaz in 1940. But it took her 1951 debut on the small screen as Lucy Ricardo in *I Love Lucy* to turn Ball into the world's most famous comedienne, a part she perfected in nearly twenty years of hit television shows. Co-starring Arnaz, *I Love Lucy* placed among the top ten in the national ratings from its first episode until the last original episode aired in 1957. The success of the show, produced by Desilu, the production company created by Ball and Arnaz, financed their purchase of the ailing film studio RKO in 1957. Initially, Ball oversaw the details of the shows in which she starred while Arnaz supervised most of Desilu's other operations. However, in 1962, two years after the couple divorced, Ball bought out Arnaz and became the first woman to head a major production company since Mary Pickford's involvement with United Artists. In addition to producing *The Lucy Show* and *Here's Lucy*, Ball backed two of the most successful television series ever made by Desilu: *Mission: Impossible* and *Star Trek*.

In the early 1970s, Lucille Ball categorically denied any sympathy with the women's liberation movement. And certainly the persona of Lucy Ricardo would have expressed befuddled confusion over the ideologies associated with the second wave of feminism. Nevertheless, feminist cultural critics and media scholars have fruitfully explored how Ball's life and art—particularly *I Love Lucy*—displayed and shaped ideas about both women's abilities and gender roles in the 1950s. Ball's tremendous success left no doubt that a female performer could be at once beautiful and an irrepressible clown with physical comedy skills on a par with Charlie Chaplin's; this aspect of her career not only challenged the period's gender conventions, but also paved the way for a future generation of comics, including Carol Burnett and Goldie Hawn. Criticism of *I Love Lucy* suggests how the show offered fans a funhouse-mirror view of the conservative ideology that attempted to reinstate domesticity and the cult of motherhood as the ideal arrangement between the sexes. Fans could enjoy Lucy-the-zany-housewife and the glamorous Ricardos as a kind of idealized expression of this ideology. And on 19 January 1953, forty-four million Americans watched Lucy Ricardo give birth to Little Ricky on TV while Ball simultaneously delivered her son, Ricky Jr., by cesarean section. Yet both the show and the lives of its stars displayed signs of the contradictions and tensions surrounding this ideology. Domestic life never fully satisfies either Lucy or Ricky; Ball and Arnaz's marriage ended in a bitter divorce.

Most episodes display Lucy's failed attempt to break into her husband's public world of show business, but the show's success depended upon the brilliance of Ball's failures.

[*See also* Popular Culture.]

BIBLIOGRAPHY

Kanfer, Stefan. *Ball of Fire: The Tumultuous Life and Comic Art of Lucille Ball.* New York: Knopf, 2003. The best biography of Ball, it focuses more on her life than her art and includes a good bibliography.

Mellencamp, Patricia. *High Anxiety: Catastrophe, Scandal, Age, and Comedy.* Bloomington: Indiana University Press, 1992. The author offers an insightful reading of *I Love Lucy*'s reflection of postwar gender roles.

HILARY A. HALLETT

BALTIC STATES. Although the three Baltic countries—Estonia, Latvia, and Lithuania—are frequently referred to as a coherent sociopolitical unit, they constitute three distinct nations joined by geography but divided by language and culture. However, shared history, especially after annexation into the Soviet Union in the 1940s, has contributed to the emergence of a common identity. Baltic women's experience was thus complex from its historical roots up through the contemporary processes in which these women are constructing new ideologies of gender and nation while integrating themselves into transnational political and economic networks.

Historical Background before the Twentieth Century. The political histories of the three Baltic countries have been very different. Estonia and Latvia had no independent statehood until 1918 while Lithuania was a sovereign nation (from the sixteenth century in union with Poland) until 1795 and had considerable power in the region. From the thirteenth century Estonia and Latvia were ruled by Baltic-German gentry who retained control over the lands regardless of the crown to which the territories belonged. The indigenous population was concentrated in rural areas, while landed aristocracy and most citizens of towns were of German origin. In Lithuania class distinction did not automatically translate into ethnic difference, although there was a clear contrast between Lithuanian peasants and Polish-Lithuanian gentry. Gender ideologies that developed in the region were thus based on ethnicity and class. Thus local women, as peasants or, in more limited numbers, members of an urban artisan class, worked alongside men, helping to sustain family farms or family businesses, whereas the lives of Baltic-German, Polish, or Lithuanian noblewomen or middle-class women were characterized by a stricter gender segregation.

All three countries were Christianized relatively late (during the thirteenth through the sixteenth centuries), and remnants of distinctive pagan religions with powerful goddess figures can still be observed in Lithuania and Latvia. Estonia, and, to a large extent, Latvia, became Lutheran in the sixteenth century while Lithuania remained predominantly Roman Catholic, and the variation in the dominant religion in each region contributed to a differentiation of women's experiences. For example, the prevalence of Lutheranism led to a relatively high rate of literacy among Estonian peasantry, and also among women, especially after the Swedish crown made village schools compulsory in the seventeenth century. However, because the historical records were kept by people of nonlocal extraction, reliable information about Baltic peasants, let alone women, is scanty; more authentic insight about their life world can be

Industry in the Baltic States. Women working in a potato cannery, Latvia, 1950s. PRINTS AND PHOTOGRAPHS DIVISION, LIBRARY OF CONGRESS

gleaned from the rich oral traditions of each country, such as Estonian *runosong* and Latvian and Lithuanian *dainas*.

As traditional peasant societies, the Baltic countries were characterized by a patriarchal gender order but also a tradition of strong women. In a peasant community, what made a woman valuable was her physical health, important for both childbearing and farm work. The woman was subordinated to the man, but it was impossible to maintain a strict division of male and female spheres of existence: men's and women's tasks were clearly differentiated in peasant households, but women's physical labor was necessary for the survival of the family, and thus patriarchal ideology within the peasant community did not introduce a clear public-private split. The separation of gender roles was characteristic of Baltic-German or Polish upper classes and coveted by the indigenous populations as a sign of prestige, although largely unattainable for them. As a result, it can be argued that the local societies that tried to emulate the elites were more conservative about the aspirations of women than were other European nations of the same period.

Although literacy was increasingly common among Baltic women, it was difficult, especially for women of a peasant background, to gain further education. Special schools for girls were established in the nineteenth century, mostly with German or Russian as the language of tuition. Women could attend courses at the University of Tartu, the leading institution of higher education in Estonia and Latvia, from 1905; they were admitted as full students only in 1917. Prior to that, women had obtained their degrees in Zurich, Bern, or London. The preferred disciplines for the pioneering women were medicine and sciences that facilitated women's entry into professions where there was a shortage of specialists. Nevertheless, the numbers of women engaged in professions remained low, especially for Estonian, Latvian, and Lithuanian women who, in addition to the disadvantage of gender, had to overcome class barriers as well. (While women of German origin dominated in the professions, local women played an increasingly significant role in industrial labor, for example in the textile industry.) Many prominent women academics from the region achieved fame abroad; for example, Margarethe von Wrangell (1877–1932) in 1923 became the first woman granted full professorship by a German university.

A few women from the Baltic countries achieved considerable political prominence, among them were Barbora Radvilaitė, known as Barbara Radziwill in German and Barbara Radziwiłłówna in Polish (c. 1520–1551), grand duchess of Lithuania and queen of Poland, and Anna Ivanovna (1693–1740), duchess of Courland and empress of Russia (r. 1730–1740). These exceptions did not bestow rights on other women, however. Most men in Estonia and Latvia also lacked suffrage until the twentieth century, and therefore women's rights did not emerge as a topic of discussion prior to the early twentieth century. Lithuania, notably, had given women considerable rights already in the first Statute of Lithuania (adopted in 1529 and, in different versions, in force until 1840), which granted noblewomen the right to inherit property and attend public meetings, as well as to seek divorce, child custody, and protection against violence. Although the law was very advanced for the time, it did not extend to all women or grant women voting rights. These were acquired only after the achievement of national sovereignty in 1918, the same time as in Estonia and Latvia.

National Movements and Period of Independence. None of the three nations developed an active suffrage movement in the late nineteenth and early twentieth centuries when such activism started to emerge in many countries. Instead, the energies of the emerging national intelligentsia were channeled into national liberation. The national movements, imbued with an organic nationalism, endowed women with the sacralized duty of maintaining the spirit of the nation and guaranteeing its physical regeneration. Women became romanticized symbols of the nations' aspirations—notable are such authors as Lydia Koidula (Lydia Emilie Florentine Jannsen; 1843–1886) in Estonia, Aspazija (Elza Rozenberga Pliekšāne; 1865–1943) in Latvia, and Žemaitė (Julija Beniuševičiūte Žymantienė; 1845–1921) in Lithuania—but the movements remained patriarchal in all three countries. The first national song festival in Estonia, one of the key symbolic events of national awakening, organized in 1869, involved only male choirs and orchestras. The first Latvian song festival, however, organized in 1873, had women among its participants.

Despite the prevalent patriarchal ethos, feminist sentiment was voiced in all three countries. For example, in Latvia, the emergence of women's rights as distinct from the rights of the nation can be dated to 1870 when Karolīne Kronvalde (1836–1913) published a letter in which she spoke for women's right to education and personal freedom. The first Estonian feminist, Lilli Suburg (1841–1923) raised the issue of women's suffrage and women's rights in her magazine that first appeared in 1887. The first women's organization in Lithuania, the Union of Lithuanian Women for the Protection of Women's Rights (Lietuvos moterų susivienijimas moterų teisėms ginti), was founded in 1905, and although its primary aim was national liberation, it also raised the question of equal rights for women. Similar organizations appeared in all three countries, playing an important role in furthering women's social participation although they were at best skeptical about feminism.

The short period of independence that the Baltic countries enjoyed from 1918 to 1940 did not encourage the emergence of women's activism because of the focus on the national project. National constitutions (1920–1922) granted equal political rights to men and women, but women's participation in politics remained limited. For example, while 10 of the 112 delegates of the founding parliament of Lithuania were women, there were no women in the fourth parliament. Similarly, in Estonia, there were seven women in the constituent assembly but only one in the second parliament. A few women were elected to positions of political power, for example, Valērija Seile (1891–1970), who was appointed the assistant minister of education in Latvia in 1921. Many filled symbolic roles, such as Gabrielė Petkevičaitė-Bitė (1861–1943), who opened the first session of the Lithuanian parliament in 1920. Estonia had a number of women parliamentarians and high-ranking officials in municipal governments, such as Marie Reisik (1887–1941) and Alma Ostra-Oinas (1886–1960), but none reached a ministerial level. Nevertheless, some women used their prominence to advance women's causes. Berta Pīpiņa (1883–1942), the first woman elected to the Latvian parliament in 1931, consistently argued for legislation to support women's rights.

Attempts to provide legislative guarantees to women's rights found little support in all Baltic countries, with the exception of protective legislation for working mothers. Lithuania achieved the greatest progress by not just including gender equality guarantees in its constitution and civil code in 1922 but also granting equal rights of ownership and inheritance. However, the constitution of 1938 no longer explicitly mentioned gender equality. An attempt to free Estonian women from the financial and personal guardianship of their husbands through a revised marriage law prepared by women lawyers never became effective. It can be concluded that the period of independence gave Baltic women suffrage but that women's rights were backgrounded in an era dedicated to national self-construction that saw women as mothers of the nation, rather than as independent political actors. Gender was central to national debate, but in ways that curtailed women's agency. Despite the ideology of domesticity, however, both middle-class and working-class women increasingly worked outside the home.

Soviet Legacy. The three Baltic countries share the experience of forcible incorporation into the Soviet Union in 1940, the Nazi occupation, and the reinstatement of Soviet power in 1944. The gendered dimension of the hardships of Soviet deportations to Siberia, Nazi persecutions that eliminated most of the local Jewish population, forced Soviet collectivization, and mass emigration have remained regrettably unexplored. The postwar era was characterized by the implementation of the official Soviet gender ideology, encapsulated in the image of the working mother as a doubly productive member of society. Indeed, the Soviet system provided the infrastructure to support women's full labor force participation by guaranteeing services such as free and accessible child- and health-care services. However, the rationale for such measures was not the well-being of women but macroeconomic considerations: women were freed from the guardianship of men to become the wards of state. Such equality often proved to be constraining since, as a result of massive shortages in the Soviet Union, the double duty of paid and unpaid labor was onerous. The state-mandated equality was thus seen as a burden rather than a privilege, especially as women, with some token exceptions, had limited access to positions of authority. The domestic sphere, in fact, became a site of resistance, valorized as a haven from the ideologies of the public sphere, a locus of indigenous nationhood, and a site of preservation of the now sentimentalized 1930s values. When the public sphere was a prison, the private sphere came to symbolize freedom.

Women had divergent experiences depending on their different situations, their ethnic backgrounds, whether they were deported to Siberia during Stalinist purges, or were forced to emigrate. The richest resources about the complexities of women's experience in the period can be found in women's life stories that were actively collected in all three countries beginning at the end of the twentieth century.

Post-Soviet Situation. The end of the Soviet Union was in many ways reminiscent of the period of national awakening: women actively participated in a transformation process that did not translate into greater equality. In fact, because of the stigmatization of gender equality through its Soviet associations, the regained independence "liberated" women only for consumerism and domesticity. The early 1990s saw the revival of romanticized discourses of femininity focusing on the woman as a mother, endowed with the responsibility for the regeneration of the nation, and marginalizing minority women. The nationalist motherhood discourse was poorly matched with social realities, where families needed two incomes and women could not afford to leave the labor force to dedicate themselves to full-time motherhood. The nostalgic natalist gender ideology was challenged by the transnational business of femininity that emerged as a result of a rapid adoption of neoliberalism. Although this discursive shift did not result in an adjustment of gender balance in positions of authority, some women reached high political office: for example, Kazimira Prunskienė (b. 1943) acted as the first prime minister of Lithuania; Vaira Vīķe-Freiberga (b. 1937) has twice been elected the president of Latvia; and Ene Ergma (b. 1944) served as the president of the parliament. However, these few women have not reconfigured the masculinist gender order of the Baltic countries.

Despite the calls to redomesticate women, women's labor force participation rates have remained high because of economic necessities. Although women constitute the strong majority of university graduates, gender-based wage disparities have increased during the years of independence. Women also face new problems, such as prostitution and trafficking or, on a cultural level, commodification of femininity and sexualization of the public space. The feminization of poverty has been especially stark among minority women who have borne the brunt of the collapse of Soviet industries. The health-care system is increasingly privatized and the old network of day-care centers is being dismantled, making combining family and work responsibilities increasingly difficult, especially as women also face neonatalist public rhetoric, resurrected by low birth rates and fears of national survival. Although women have a prominent role in all spheres of life, political discourse that focuses on women still resembles that of the early twentieth century, treating women as an object of debate rather than as full political subjects.

One of the most notable features of postsocialist societies in general is the absence of feminist or women's movements, despite the many problems women face. This pattern is also repeated in the Baltic countries. All three countries ratified the U.N. Convention on the Elimination of All Forms of Discrimination against Women (CEDAW) in the early 1990s but this led to no noticeable change in women's lives. Since that time, the European Union (EU) has been the main engine of activities related to gender equality in the Baltic countries. The constitutions of all three countries adopted in the early 1990s declare the equality of all citizens, but specific laws related to gender equality were prepared only prior to EU accession: in 1998 the Lithuanian parliament adopted the Law on Equal Opportunities for Women and Men; Estonia passed the Gender Equality Act in 2004. Latvia has no specific gender equality law but equality is guaranteed by other legislation.

However, these legislative measures have not nurtured grassroots feminist activities. As occurred at the beginning of the twentieth century, the national cause has taken precedence over women's issues. Because most women's groups from the first period of independence were nonfeminist, there is no feminist tradition to be revived. Moreover, equality discourses have been discredited by their misuse in the Soviet Union. Paradoxically, the societies in the Baltic States believe that gender equality has been achieved and that, if anything, it is men who need protection. The denial of the need for gender equality measures has been deepened by neoliberalist emphasis on individual achievement and the weakness of civil society in the Baltic countries. Feminism continues to be demonized in the region in an ironical "frontlash" where antifeminist discourse precedes a feminist one. However, the gender policies of the European Union have legitimized many activities formerly branded Soviet, and the mainstreaming of gender policies could encourage more gender-inclusive policies.

[*See also* Antifeminism; Convention on the Elimination of All Forms of Discrimination against Women; Feminism; Gender Roles; Germany; Literacy and Numeracy; Russia and Soviet Union; United Nations; World War I; *and* World War II.]

BIBLIOGRAPHY

There are very few widely available English-language sources dedicated to the women in the Baltic countries. Western research into post-Soviet societies has tended to focus either on Russia or on central Europe, leaving the Baltic countries in a gap in between them. Local research, on the other hand, has neglected gender as a category for analysis, and the works produced have not always reached an international audience. Thus the resources listed here do not cover all areas of women's history systematically, but an attempt has been made to include most recent publications that have analyzed Baltic women and their experience.

Domsch, Michel E., Désirée H. Ladwing, and Eliane Tenten. *Gender Equality in Central and Eastern European Countries*. New York: Peter Lang, 2003. The collection includes articles on different aspects of gender in postsocialist states of central and eastern Europe, including articles on women on the Estonian, Latvian, and Lithuanian labor market by leading local scholars.

Gal, Susan, and Gail Kligman. *The Politics of Gender after Socialism: A Comparative-Historical Essay*. Princeton, N.J.: Princeton University Press, 2000. Although not explicitly dedicated to the Baltic countries, this perspicacious book analyzes how gender is intertwined with the processes of transformation that have enveloped the post-Soviet space (including the Baltic countries), for example the impact of marketization in the formerly state-managed field of gender relations.

Haan, Francisca de, Krassmira Daskalova, and Anna Loutfi, eds. *A Biographical Dictionary of Women's Movements and Feminisms: Central, Eastern, and South Eastern Europe, Nineteenth and Twentieth Centuries*. Budapest and New York: Central European University Press, 2006. This up-to-date dictionary includes articles on some leading women active in Estonia, Latvia, and Lithuania written by scholars from the region, although the brief articles cannot provide a comprehensive overview of the historical developments in the countries.

Kirss, Tiina, Ene Kõresaar, and Marju Lauristin, eds. *She Who Remembers Survives: Interpreting Estonian Women's Post-Soviet Life Stories*. Tartu, Estonia: Tartu University Press, 2004. The collection gathers life stories of nine Estonian women from the period that spans from World War II to the beginning of the twenty-first century, with added analysis by leading Estonian scholars who have worked with women's life writing.

Krupavičius, Algis, and Irmina Matonytė. "Women in Lithuanian Politics: From Nomenklatura Selection to Representation." In *Women's Access to Political Power in Post-Communist Europe*, edited by Richard E. Matland and Kathleen A. Montgomery, pp. 81–104. Oxford and New York: Oxford University Press, 2003. The article traces the situation of women in the transition from Soviet-style elections to a democratic model of political participation.

Lace, Tana, Irina Novikova, and Giedre Purvaneckiene. "Women's Social Rights and Entitlements in Latvia and Lithuania:

Transformations and Challenges." In *Women's Social Rights and Entitlements*, edited by Audrey Guichon, Christien L. van der Anker, and Irina Novikova pp. 180–202. Basingstoke, U.K., and New York: Palgrave Macmillan, 2006. The article surveys the state of affairs of women's social rights in Latvia and Lithuania, with theoretical analysis and comparative insights.

LaFont, Suzanne, ed. *Women in Transition: Voices from Lithuania*. Albany: State University of New York Press, 1998. The wide-ranging articles by Lithuanian scholars analyze social, economic, political, religious, and cultural influences on Lithuanian women in the past and present through descriptive materials and empirical studies.

Novikova, Irina. "Constructing National Identity in Latvia: Gender and Representation during the Period of the National Awakening." In *Gendered Nations: Nationalisms and Gender Order in the Long Nineteenth Century*, edited by Ida Blom, Karen Hagemann, and Catherine Hall, pp. 311–334. Oxford and New York: Berg, 2000. Novikova demonstrates how the male-dominated national movement rhetorically incorporated women (in their roles as educators of children and preservers of the national lore) into the new imaginary nationhood. Many of the insights about Latvia can also be extended to the formation of national identity in Estonia.

Walter, Lynn, ed. *The Greenwood Encyclopedia of Women's Issues Worldwide*. Vol. 3, *Europe*, edited by Lynn Walter. Westport, Conn.: Greenwood Press, 2003. This wide-ranging encyclopedia includes articles on all three Baltic countries that give an overview of women's issues, economy and employment, family, health, politics, law, and other aspects of life. The book is useful to scholars but also accessible to general readers.

White, Nijole. "Women in Changing Societies: Latvia and Lithuania." In *Post-Soviet Women: From the Baltic to Central Asia*, edited by Mary Buckley, pp. 203–218. Cambridge, U.K., and New York: Cambridge University Press, 1997. The collection analyzes societies that have emerged after the collapse of the Soviet Union and women's experience in them, on the basis of interviews with women that are complemented by a diversity of interdisciplinary perspectives. White, among other things, provides an interesting analysis of the abortion issue in the Baltic countries.

RAILI PÕLDSAAR

BANDARANAIKE, SIRIMAVO (1916–2000), the world's first woman prime minister. Elected prime minister of Sri Lanka on 21 July 1960, Sirimavo Ratwatte Bandaranaike not only placed her country on the map but also became a role model for women around the world. "Mathini" (Madam), as she was fondly known to the masses, and "Mrs. B.," as she was known to the English-speaking bourgeoisie, was a formidable political force to be reckoned with until her death in August 2000.

Thrust onto the political stage after the assassination in 1959 of her prime minister husband, S. W. R. D. Bandaranaike (1899–1959), this shy, convent-educated, forty-four-year-old mother of three drew upon her experiences running feudal land holdings and engagement in social development work through the Lanka Mahila Samiti to govern the country with the aid of what was derisively called her "kitchen cabinet." Valiantly battling sexism, sexualization, and political machinations, this "weeping widow" was described a decade later as "the only man in her cabinet." Bandaranaike successfully headed two coalition governments (1960–1965 and 1970–1977), withstood an attempted military coup (1963), crushed a youth insurgency (1971), and retained the leadership of the Sri Lanka Freedom Party until her death. Through special legislation drafted by her political opponents in 1980, she was stripped of her civic rights for seven years for alleged abuses while prime minister. She returned to political office, however, when her daughter, Chandrika Kumaratunga, was elected president in 1994 and nominated her as prime minister.

Influenced by her left coalition partners, "Mrs. B." nationalized key sectors of the economy such as banking, insurance, and foreign businesses, as well as many private and missionary schools; introduced land and housing reforms to enable a more equitable distribution of private property; and broke all links with Sri Lanka's former colonizer, Britain, by unveiling a republican constitution in 1972. Also during her time Ceylon was renamed Sri Lanka and Buddhism was made the de facto state religion. Her dispensing with English as an official language and her order to conduct all government business in Sinhala led to a civil disobedience campaign by minority Tamils. Bandaranaike's deportation of many Indian plantation workers, basing university entrance on population quotas, brutally crushing the 1971 insurgency, imposing rationing after the 1973 world oil crisis, and intolerance of criticism resulting in a seizure of the Lake House newspaper group severely eroded her popularity, leading to her party's being decisively defeated in the 1977 general elections.

However, Bandaranaike's international standing remained undiminished, and her contribution to the Non-Aligned Movement remained a lasting legacy. During her time as chair in 1976 she hosted the largest ever heads of state conference—attended by an impressive array of leaders such as Josip Broz Tito, Indira Gandhi, Julius Nyerere, and Anwar Sadat—that Sri Lanka has ever witnessed. Bandaranaike's close alliance with both India and China also enabled her to play a crucial role in defusing the Sino-India border dispute in 1962. An icon of the feminist movement, more for her unique achievement than for her policies, "Mathini" was feted in 1975 at the first U.N.-sponsored International Women's Conference in Mexico. Though many wives of world leaders participated, she alone attended as a woman prime minister and leader in her own right.

[*See also* Kumaratunga, Chandrika Bandaranaike; *and* Sri Lanka.]

BIBLIOGRAPHY

Bandutilleke, Malalgoda, ed. *Sirilaka Sirikatha* (in Sinhala). Colombo, Sri Lanka: Mahajana Prakasakayo, 1988.

de Alwis, Malathi. "Gender, Politics and the 'Respectable Lady.'" In *Unmaking the Nation: The Politics of Identity and History in Modern Sri Lanka*, edited by Pradeep Jeganathan and Qadri Ismail. Colombo, Sri Lanka: Social Scientists' Association, 1995.

Dhanapala, D. B. *Madam Premier*. Colombo, Sri Lanka: M. D. Gunasena, 1960.

Seneviratne, Maureen. *Sirimavo Bandaranaike*. Colombo, Sri Lanka: Hansa Publishers, 1975.

MALATHI DE ALWIS

BANGLADESH. Women in modern Bangladeshi history do not constitute a monolithic category; class, religion, and ethnicity fracture women's experiences, actions, and identities. Key moments in national and international history have shaped the lives of different groups of women in Bangladesh.

Gender and Nation. The late 1960s marked the crystallization of an autonomy movement in East Pakistan (now Bangladesh). This movement aimed at overturning the neocolonial government by West Pakistan of the eastern regions, established during the partition of the subcontinent in 1947. In the course of the new resistance, middle-class women became critical to the nationalist struggle both as activists and as symbols of cultural resistance. Bengali women's bodily practices—their clothes, the bindis on their foreheads, the music they openly embraced despite state prohibition—functioned as powerful markers of secular Bengali resistance to West Pakistan's economic and cultural imperialism.

Bangladesh came into being as an independent nation after a bloody war with the occupying Pakistani army in 1971. The nine-month struggle proved to be a critical turning point for all women in independent Bangladesh. Women's bodies came to be significant in various ways in the formation of the nation. Some women took up arms, while others hid arms and protected male freedom fighters. The mass rape of Bengali women by the Pakistani army during the liberation war exposed the vulnerability of women of all classes to sexual violence and patriarchal regulation. Women's bodies continued to be foregrounded as sites of honor and shame in the postwar social period, when many raped women found themselves rejected by families and communities.

Feminist consciousness was forged in Bangladesh at this time, when individuals from the middle and upper classes mobilized to assist women whose lives had been ravaged by the war and its aftermath. The institutionalization of postwar relief and rehabilitation efforts subsequently led to a blurring of boundaries between the women's movement and other social movements, including the nongovernmental organization (NGO) sector. The Bangladesh Mahila Parishad (BMP; Women's Council of Bangladesh), established in the late 1960s as part of the nationalist movement, participated in the liberation war by publicizing atrocities against women by the Pakistani army. The BMP moved into full gear after the war, taking up the task of grassroots mobilization. By the early twenty-first century it was the largest women's organization in the country, with more than thirty thousand members. Grameen Bank, world-renowned for its microcredit activities on behalf of women, was set up in Bangladesh in the early 1970s. In 2006, Grameen Bank and its founder Muhammad Yunus were awarded the Nobel Peace Prize in recognition of their efforts to improve poor people's and women's lives.

Women and women's groups have also been the most vocal in challenging state-sponsored Islamization and the militarization of society. The period of military rule between 1975 and 1990 coincided with an efflorescence of both women's activities and also the human rights movement. Naripokkho (On the Side of Women) mounted a legal challenge to the military government's efforts to declare Islam the state religion.

Although the momentum for activism was high in the 1980s, brutal state repression put an end to many initiatives. This led to a reconsideration of strategies. Instead of being part of a separate women's movement, many feminists preferred to work with a broader movement for democracy. Women's groups played a visible and popular role in the protest movement against the military regime of General H. M. Ershad in 1990. Later, despite considerable intimidation, the eminent writer Jahanara Imam (1929–1994) spearheaded a campaign to bring to justice wartime collaborators who had been rehabilitated into mainstream politics by successive military regimes. The mock trial or people's court she organized in the capital galvanized civil society into a more active stance against wartime collaborators.

Consequent to these struggles, some of the most prominent advocates of women's rights in contemporary Bangladesh do not focus exclusively on women's issues but rather on human rights and social justice as a whole. For instance, Nijera Kori (We Do It Ourselves) mobilizes landless women and men to fight for their rights. Ain o Salish Kendra (ASK; Law and Mediation Center) is a legal aid organization that aims to promote a holistic democratic environment within which all rights, including women's rights, can flourish. ASK was established specifically in response to authoritarian military rule. Both organizations have been at the cutting edge of the women's movement in Bangladesh. Accordingly, when in the early 1990s Islamist extremists charged the feminist poet and writer Taslima Nasrin (b. 1962) with apostasy, it was lawyers at ASK who immediately came to her defense. Bangladeshi feminists often work at the intersections of international and national politics. For instance, Salma Sobhan (1937–2003), a cofounder of ASK, was also a cofounder of the international network Women Living under Muslim Laws (WLUML).

Women are also active in the electoral process. During parliamentary elections in 1991 and 1996, more than 70 percent of women exercised their right to vote. This was to a great extent the result of successful NGO mobilization at the grassroots level. At the national level the leaders of both main political parties are women.

Thus high levels of activism characterize Bangladeshi civil society. Feminism is no exception, and women have been involved in all social and political movements. However, activist histories must be contextualized because their impact is necessarily limited. Bangladesh is a country with a population of more than 140 million. It is simply impossible for NGOs and women's activists to reach everyone. Moreover, activism is also limited by the extent of poverty that most Bangladeshis, including women, must negotiate every day.

Global Forces. Global and external forces of change have also shaped women's lives in Bangladesh. With the encouragement of the United Nations and its development partners, Bangladesh set up one of the earliest women's affairs ministries in Asia. Bangladeshi women have been active participants at the United Nations. The Fourth World Conference in Beijing in 1995 mobilized women's groups across the country. After Beijing, women's groups collaborated with the government to produce an impressive National Policy on the Advancement of Women, which remains a blueprint for gender-related public policies. Local women's groups often work with support from many international NGOs as well as the United Nations. Women's rights advocates frequently use international instruments such as the U.N. Convention on the Elimination of All Forms of Discrimination against Women (CEDAW) to press for their rights at home.

Liberalization and globalization since the late twentieth century have rendered Bangladesh dependent on external trade regimes. Insertion in the new global economy has opened up opportunities as well as dangers for women. The flourishing apparel export industry turns on the labor of almost 2 million young women, whose presence on the streets and on factories floors has reshaped the gendered landscape of urban Bangladesh. These young women have transformed gender relations at home and at the workplace. New ways of making a living have produced new ways of living. The daily presence of women workers in such large numbers in public spaces has thrown older social equations into disarray. Gendered relations are being contested and renegotiated on the streets every day, quite literally. For women workers, the other side of their newly found visibility and autonomy is poor job security, low pay, and the risk of exploitation in an environment in which casual labor relations are the norm.

[*See also* India; Pakistan; *and* South Asia.]

BIBLIOGRAPHY

Chowdhury, Najma. "The Politics of Implementing Women's Rights in Bangladesh." In *Globalization, Gender, and Religion: The Politics of Women's Rights in Catholic and Muslim Contexts*, edited by Jane H. Bayes and Nayereh Tohidi, pp. 203–230. Houndmills, U.K., and New York: Palgrave, 2001.

Jahan, Roushan. "Men in Seclusion, Women in Public: Rokeya's Dream and Women's Struggles in Bangladesh." In *The Challenge of Local Feminisms: Women's Movements in Global Perspective*, edited by Amrita Basu, pp. 87–109. Boulder, Colo.: Westview Press, 1995.

Siddiqi, Dina M. "In the Name of Islam? Gender, Politics, and Women's Rights in Bangladesh." *Harvard Asia Quarterly* 10, no. 1 (winter 2006).

Siddiqi, Dina M. "Taslima Nasreen and Others: The Contest over Gender in Bangladesh." In *Women in Muslim Societies: Diversity within Unity*, edited by Herbert L. Bodman and Nayereh Tohidi, pp. 205–227. Boulder, Colo.: Lynne Rienner, 1998.

DINA M. SIDDIQI

BAN ZHAO (c. 44–116), the daughter and sister of the Han-dynasty historians Ban Biao and Ban Gu, and with them a coauthor of the *Han shu* (Han Dynastic History). After her brother Ban Gu was imprisoned and executed in 92, Emperor He (r. 88–105) commanded Ban Zhao to complete several unfinished chapters, including the Eight Tables and Treatise on Astronomy. He also brought her to court to teach the empress and court ladies. (She continued in this role during both his reign and the regency of Empress Dowager Deng, after his death.)

There is also a tradition that Ban Zhao rearranged, edited, and supplemented the *Lienü zhuan* (Biographies of Exemplary Women). She is listed as an annotator in the bibliographic chapters of the dynastic histories of the Sui (581–618) and Tang (618–907) dynasties and in Song-dynasty prefaces to the *Biographies of Exemplary Women* (c. 1020–1050).

An extensive biography of Ban Zhao appears in the "virtuous women" (*lienü*) section of the *Hou Han shu 84* (Standard History of the Later Han, summarized in Swann 1932, pp. 40–42). The biography describes her as learned, talented, and a model of widowly rectitude. It includes in its entirety her *Nüjie* (Admonitions for Women), for which Ban Zhao is also known.

Admonitions for Women, the oldest extant text of female instruction in China, raises many questions. On the surface, it is a conservative text that instructs young women in how to be models of wifely submission. It contains many quotations from the classics (the *Classic of Poetry*, the *Book of Changes*, and the *Book of Rites*) justifying or exemplifying the admonitions presented in each chapter. Ban Zhao uses these quotations to illustrate and define a wife's proper roles and priorities in daily life. These include chastity, correct behavior, and circumspect language. It also discusses a woman's primary economic activity: textile work (sewing, weaving, and sericulture) and the preparation of food and drink for feasts or ancestral sacrifices.

Despite her own erudition, the *Admonitions* never refers to learned women and seems to express the view that womanly virtue requires no exceptional talent or intellectual skill. These conservative prescriptions seem at odds with Ban Zhao's own life as a historian, scholar, teacher, and court figure. The *Admonitions* also includes what may be the earliest known argument for female literacy, a careful argument that girls should have the same education as boys. Ban Zhao uses yin-yang theory to argue that the practice of educating only boys ignores the essential connection between the sexes, which is based on the analogy between women and men and yin and yang. Therefore, girls should study the same things as boys, at the same ages: "When they teach boys and do not teach girls, do they not ignore the connection between the one and the other? According to the *Rites* they begin teaching reading at the age of eight, and by fifteen they reach the point of [textual] study. So why can we not have these [girls] conform to the same principle?" (*Hou Han shu*).

Ban Zhao argues that the *Book of Rites* (*Li ji*) did not restrict education to boys, and her own family seems to have put this view into practice. Not only was she herself both literate and erudite; education seems to have been the norm for women in her family. The preface to the *Admonitions* specifically instructs each of her female relatives to make a personal copy. This injunction clearly assumes that they can read and write.

Ban Zhao's preface states that the *Admonitions* was written for her "daughters," that is, the female members of her family, but it has been argued that the work was also written for a larger audience, both to advocate propriety and to argue for female literacy, in terms acceptable to a conservative male audience. This interpretation would reconcile the inconsistency between the conservative formulations of the *Admonitions* and Ban Zhao's own prominence as a scholar and teacher.

Despite these intriguing possibilities, conservative readings of Ban Zhao's *Admonitions* influenced many later generations of writing about women, beginning with such works on family instruction as Yan Zhitui's *Yan shi jiaxun* (sixth century; *Admonitions for the Yan Clan*) and various works by the great Song-dynasty philosopher Zhu Xi (1130–1200). Ironically, Ban Zhao herself would become an exemplar of respectability for seventeenth-century women who functioned as "honorary men," teachers and writers who were esteemed both for their activities and accomplishments and for their morality and virtue.

[*See also* China, *subentries* Ancient Period *and* Imperial Period.]

BIBLIOGRAPHY

Raphals, Lisa. *Sharing the Light: Representations of Women and Virtue in Early China*. Albany: State University of New York Press, 1998.

Swann, Nancy Lee. *Pan Chao: Foremost Woman Scholar of China, First Century A.D.* New York: Century 1932.

LISA RAPHALS

BARRIOS DE CHAMORRO, VIOLETA (b. 1929), former president of Nicaragua. Violeta Barrios was born in 1929 to a well-to-do family in a cattle-ranching region south of Managua, Nicaragua. In 1951 she married Pedro Joaquín Chamorro, a member of a prominent Conservative family and a vocal critic of the dictator Anastasio Somoza. They had four children together, and she became a homemaker.

In 1952 Pedro Joaquín Chamorro became editor of *La Prensa*, an anti-Somoza newspaper owned by his family. *La Prensa* was often censored and shut down, and Pedro Joaquín Chamorro himself was arrested and jailed many times by the Somoza government. He was assassinated in 1978. His death precipitated the insurrection that brought about the end of the Somoza dictorship in 1979.

Violeta Barrios de Chamorro, like her husband, was ardently anti-Somoza. After Pedro Joaquín's death, *La Prensa*, under Violeta Barrios de Chamorro's leadership, continued its attacks on the Somoza family regime until the Sandinista National Liberation Front (Frente Sandinista de Liberación Nacional, known as the FSLN) finally toppled the last Somoza on 19 July 1979.

Given her political credentials, Chamorro was invited to join the junta that governed Nicaragua immediately after the Sandinista triumph. However, she soon became dissatisfied with the direction in which the revolution was going and resigned from the junta in 1980. She remained at the helm of *La Prensa* throughout the 1980s and turned the newspaper into an anti-Sandinista mouthpiece. During the 1980s *La Prensa* was constantly censored and shut down.

Chamorro's opposition to the Somozas and the Sandinistas made her an ideal candidate to represent the U.S.-supported anti-Sandinista UNO Coalition (Unión Nacional Opositora) in Nicaragua's 1990 presidential election. She campaigned as a mother and a widow and successfully appealed to those who did not want to send their sons off to fight against the U.S.-backed counterrevolutionary ("Contra") forces. Her victory over Daniel Ortega, the FSLN candidate, was unexpected. In retrospect, however, it makes sense that, after a decade of war, so many Nicaraguans would vote for a woman who campaigned on a platform of reconciliation and peace. Thus Chamorro became Nicaragua's first woman president, serving from 1990 to 1997.

A nonfeminist, she presided over a key moment in the expansion of second-wave feminism in Nicaragua. Feminist organizing flourished during the 1990s, in part as a response to the Conservative policies enacted under Chamorro's administration. During her years in power, Chamorro confronted difficult issues including a 40 percent unemployment rate, a 60 percent rate of poverty, struggles over property ownership, and extremely high inflation rates in a highly militarized and polarized society. She succeeded at depoliticizing the army, bringing inflation down, and dismantling the Contra army. Just as important, she oversaw the first peaceful turnover of power from one political party to another in twentieth-century Nicaragua, and she governed without widespread reprisals against Sandinistas. On the economic front Chamorro opened Nicaragua to neoliberal economic measures under the International Monetary Fund and the World Bank.

In the early twenty-first century, Chamorro headed a nonprofit organization with her children while her family continued to run *La Prensa*. One of two major newspapers in Nicaragua, *La Prensa* continued to play a major role in politics and maintained an anti-Sandinista position.

BIBLIOGRAPHY

Barrios de Chamorro, Violeta, with Sonia Cruz de Baltodano and Guido Fernández. *Dreams of the Heart: The Autobiography of President Violeta Barrios de Chamorro of Nicaragua*. New York: Simon and Schuster, 1996.

Kampwirth, Karen. "The Mother of the Nicaraguans" Doña Violeta and the UNO's Gender Agenda." *Latin American Perspectives* 23, no. 1 (Winter 1996): 67–86.

"Violetta B de Chamorro Fundacion." http://www.violetachamorro.org.ni/

VICTORIA GONZÁLEZ-RIVERA

BARRIOS DE CHUNGARA, DOMITILA (b. 1937), Bolivian union and social activist. Domitila Barrios was born in 1937 in the Bolivian mining district of Potosí. At the age of ten, she was left in charge of her siblings after her mother's death. Her formal schooling was short, and she married the miner René Chungara in 1957. She had seven children who survived early in the twenty-first century. During the turbulent early 1960s, when economic adjustment plans led to the closing of mines and the worsening of the already bad living conditions in Bolivia, Barrios de Chungara joined the Housewives' Committee of the Siglo XX mining district and was elected its speaker. The miners' struggle was brutally suppressed by the military governments of René Barrientos Ortuño (1964–1969), and Barrios de Chungara was jailed and tortured several times. She continued her struggle, and in December 1977, she and a few other "housewives," accompanied by several children, began a hunger strike, which eventually contributed to the fall of the military dictatorship of Hugo Banzer.

By the mid-1970s Barrios de Chungara had become a well-known figure, nationally and internationally. A film about the resistance of the housewives' organization had made them famous, and Barrios de Chungara was invited to attend the International Women's Year Conference summoned by the United Nations in Mexico in 1975. Shocked by the completely different agenda of North American and European feminists, Barrios de Chungara soon became the voice of lower-class women from the Third World. She maintained that the women's struggle had to be against capitalism and imperialism, and that it had to be carried out alongside men.

After the Mexico conference, a Brazilian sociologist helped her to write down the story of her life, and the testimony was published under the title *Si me permiten hablar* (If You Would Let Me Speak, 1978). It was soon translated into several languages and became one of the most widely read examples of the new genre of testimonial literature. Her second book, which appeared in 1985 under the title of *Aquí También, Domitila*, did not receive the same attention.

Barrios de Chungara continued her work on behalf of the mining families and ran for vice president in the 1978 elections, which were later annulled and followed by another military coup. After a short democratic interval in 1979, a coup d'état in 1980 forced her into exile for more than two years. In 1986 an economic crisis led to the closing of most of the state-owned mines, among them Siglo XX. Barrios de Chungara participated in the "March for Life and Peace," which yielded no political results. In the end, most of the miners and their families were obliged to migrate to other regions in order to make a living. Barrios de Chungara and her children moved to the city of Cochabamba, where she worked actively until health problems forced her to retire. Early in the twenty-first century she still believes that the solution to the situation of women lies within a socialist society. Her lasting achievement is to have brought lower-class and uneducated "housewives" into the public sphere and thus to have laid the foundation for the new social movements in Bolivia. Internationally, her testimony drew attention to the diversity of women's problems and political attitudes, especially in the Third World.

[*See also* Labor *and* Socialism.]

BIBLIOGRAPHY

Barrios de Chungara, Domitila, with Moema Viezzer. *Let Me Speak!: Testimony of Domitila, a Woman of the Bolivian Mines*. Translated by Victoria Ortiz. New York: Monthly Review Press, 1978.

Queiser Morales, Waltraud. "Class, Culture, and Identity: Women and Feminism in Latin America as Interpreted by Domitila Barrios de Chungara." *SECOLAS Annals*, 32 (2000): 38–50.

BARBARA POTTHAST

BARTON, CLARA (1821–1912), American humanitarian who pioneered aid to war victims, both military and civilian, founded the American Red Cross, and promoted feminist causes. Born 25 December 1821 to middle-class parents in North Oxford, Massachusetts, Clara Barton had a checkered career and was often a controversial figure. Largely taught at home, she began teaching at fifteen, but dissatisfaction with the organization of the American school system led her to abandon teaching and enter into government service in 1854 as a clerk in the U.S. Patent Office in Washington, D.C. The insults and discrimination she faced as the first woman in this position contributed to her subsequent feminism.

When the Civil War broke out in 1861, Barton enthusiastically embraced the Union cause. Taking a leave of absence from her job, she devoted her efforts to supplying the Union troops with medical supplies, food, and clothing to supplement the government's inadequate supply of such provisions. At great personal risk, she attended to the medical and emotional needs of the troops who served in the Army of the Potomac and in the Army of the James. She was greatly beloved by the common troops, but the officers were less appreciative of her efforts. Although many groups, especially women's organizations, provided Barton with financial and moral support, she was not the spokesperson for any one institution. Except for her appointment as superintendent of nurses for the Army of the James in June 1864, she did not hold any official position. She was instrumental in locating hundreds of missing soldiers, and in the course of this work she helped to bring to the public's attention the horrors of the prison at Andersonville, Georgia.

In Europe during the Franco-Prussian War (1870), Barton became interested in the International Red Cross, which had been established in 1863. After she returned to the United States, Barton embarked on a difficult but successful campaign to have the United States sign the Geneva Convention and thus establish an American Red Cross. She served as president from 1882 to 1904. At the Third International Conference of the Red Cross in Geneva in 1884 she strongly supported an amendment to the Geneva Convention that endorsed Red Cross humanitarian activities in natural disasters in peacetime.

Barton became famous not only for her humanitarian activities in the United States and abroad but also for espousing feminist causes. She supported equal rights for women in politics and in socioeconomic matters. She was opposed to marriage for herself, but she enjoyed the company of men. She had a brief affair with an army officer, John Elwell, who was married and had children.

With a volatile personality, mood swings, and bouts of depression, Barton was often perceived as a difficult person. Her fiercely independent spirit led to allegations that she was self-serving and authoritarian. Despite whatever undesirable personality traits she may have had, her contributions to humanitarianism and to the mitigation of the horrors of war earned for her a major place in the history of women globally.

[*See also* Healing and Medicine *and* International Red Cross.]

BIBLIOGRAPHY

Barton, Clara. *The Red Cross: A History of This Remarkable International Movement in the Interest of Humanity*. Washington, D.C.: American National Red Cross, 1898.

Burton, David H. *Clara Barton: In the Service of Humanity*. Westport, Conn.: Greenwood Press, 1995.

Oakes, Stephen B. *A Woman of Valor: Clara Barton and the Civil War*. New York: Free Press, 1994.

Pryor, Elizabeth Brown. *Clara Barton: Professional Angel*. Philadelphia: University of Pennsylvania Press, 1987.

ELISA A. CARRILLO

BASTIDAS, MICAELA (1744–1781), leader in the events that led to the end of Spanish colonial power in the Andes in the late eighteenth century. Micaela Bastidas Puyuqawua was born on 23 June 1744 (or on 24 June 1742 in some sources) in Pampamarca, district of Tamburco, Abancay, Peru, the daughter of Manuel Bastidas, who is alleged to have had some African blood in his veins, and Josefa Puyuqawua, a native woman. Little is known of her childhood, except that, like many young girls, she had no access to formal education, and she had two brothers, Antonio and Miguel. On 25 May 1760, one month shy of her sixteenth birthday, Micaela married the cacique of Pampamarca, Tungasuca, and Surimana, José Gabriel Condorcanqui, later known as Tupac Amaru II, in Surimana at the Church of Our Lady of the Purification before the priest Antonio López de Sosa. The couple had three children, Hipólito, born in 1761; Mariano, born in 1762; and Fernando, born in 1768. The family established its residence in Tinta, near Cuzco.

By 1780 Condorcanqui as a native authority had to contend with increasing native complaints about the excesses of the Spanish. The natives' obligation to serve the Potosí mita, a higher tribute, and the increasing costs of essential goods were especially irksome. After exhausting the avenues of legal protest, Condorcanqui issued a proclamation and took the Corregidor Antonio de Arriaga prisoner, setting off the largest and most serious native revolt against the colonial system of that century.

Micaela Bastidas, a slight woman, became a principal adviser to and driving force behind her husband. She was part of the famous Council of Five, participating in the summary judgment against Arriaga. Throughout the potentially revolutionary struggle, this energetic and enterprising woman of strong character and critical outlook aided her husband. She helped him organize, she pushed him, and at times she even chided him for his inaction. In one letter (dictated on 6 December 1780) she told him that he was "wasting time": "pues andas muy despacio paseanote en los pueblos, y más en Yauri, tardándote dos días con grande descuido, pues los soldados tienen razón de aburrirse e irse cada uno a sus pueblos" (as you move about slowly promenading through the towns, and especially in Yauri, lingering two days with great carelessness, no wonder the soldiers are right in being bored and returning each one to his home [quoted in Cornejo Bouroncle, pp. 53–54]). She accused him of doing the wrong thing, and she asked him why he did not march on Cuzco. His hesitation was one reason that the movement failed.

For their actions Bastidas, her husband, and their associates were executed by the Spanish colonial administration in Cuzco on 18 May 1781. Bastidas went to the scaffold, where before her husband's eyes her tongue was cut out and she was garroted. Her agony was prolonged because her neck was too slender for the screw to strangle her. The executioners finally succeeded by tying ropes around her neck and each pulling in a different direction. Her body and that of her husband were later carried to Picchu, where they were burned. Their ashes were thrown into a nearby river.

Bastidas's image in the early twenty-first century is of a woman who broke the molds and social prescriptions of women of the epoch. This uncommon companion, wife, and mother serves as a model and example of womanhood and is hailed as a pioneer and precursor of the independence of the Spanish colonies from Spain in the early nineteenth century.

[*See also* Indigenous Cultures, *subentry* South America.]

BIBLIOGRAPHY

Brewster, Claire. "Women and the Spanish American Wars of Independence: An Overview." *Feminist Review* 79 (2005): 20–35.

Campbell, Leon G. "Women and the Great Rebellion in Peru, 1780–1783." *The Americas* 42, no. 2 (1985): 163–196.

Cornejo Bouroncle, Jorge. *Sangre Andina: diez mujeres cuzqueñas*. Cuzco, Peru: Rozas, 1949. See pp. 48–54.

Susan Elizabeth Ramírez

BEARD, MARY RITTER (1876–1958), U.S. suffragist and historian. Beard grew up in middle-class comfort in Indianapolis, Indiana. She earned a PhB in 1897 from DePauw University in Greencastle, Indiana, where she met fellow student Charles Austin Beard. Immediately after their marriage in 1900, they went to Oxford, England, where Charles was studying. There Mary Beard first confronted working-class poverty and became committed to workers' education and the cause of votes for women workers.

After returning to the United States in 1901, Beard briefly enrolled in graduate school but found that volunteer reform work was more adaptable to family demands. (By 1907 the Beards had two children.) While working for the vote—first with the wage earners' wing of the Woman Suffrage Party of New York and then in the inner circle of the new militant Congressional Union—she teamed with her husband to write *American Citizenship* (1914), a civics textbook intended to prepare both girls and boys for political life. She then wrote *Women's Work in Municipalities* (1915), a hefty survey of contemporary civic efforts. Its subject forecast her lifelong emphasis on women's constructive, world-building endeavors.

A persistent maverick, Beard left suffrage activism behind after New York women gained the vote in 1917. Embarking on her vocation as a historian, she remained skeptical about academic expertise, sought no university affiliation, and found an all-important partner in her husband, whose outstanding originality and productivity brought him great influence. Together the couple wrote *A Short History of the American Labor Movement* (1920) for the Workers' Education Bureau (which they had helped to found). Then, after travel to war-ravaged Europe, Japan, and China, the Beards collaborated on *The Rise of American Civilization* (1927). This panoramic history, which stressed the nation's natural and industrial resources and its literature and arts, gave more attention to women than any other survey written prior to the 1970s. It was an extraordinary public (as well as academic) success, selling hundreds of thousands of copies. *America in Midpassage* (1939), on the 1920s and 1930s, followed, and then *The American Spirit; A Study of the Idea of Civilization in the United States* (1942), which especially showed Mary Beard's hand.

Charles Beard credited his wife with the distinctive broad-ranging "civilization" concept, although he received almost all the renown for these works. Mary Beard believed it necessary to "widen the frames" of history and "comprehend the wide course of civilization," in order to achieve a fully human history that included women. Building on acclaim for *The Rise*, she reached her peak of productivity and influence during the 1930s. She explored women's part in Western civilization in *On Understanding Women* (1931), created two anthologies of women's documents, *America through Women's Eyes* (1933) and *Laughing Their Way* (1934); and wrote articles on women's relation to the Depression, sharply criticizing capitalist individualism. To highlight and preserve knowledge of women's social contributions, Beard gathered sponsors and materials for a World Center for Women's Archives, which failed by 1940 from infighting and lack of funds.

Admittedly "obsessed" with women, Beard had an ambivalent relation to feminism. Her friends were activists but she did not join women's organizations. She was infuriated by a feminist version of history that viewed women simply as the subordinated sex. She instead believed that women shared an underacknowledged but highly creative partnership with men throughout world history. Beard's most ambitious work, *Woman as Force in History* (1946), elaborated that view, while acidly criticizing male historians for disregarding women. It was one of the first works consulted when the "new women's history" began in the 1960s and 1970s.

A founder of twentieth-century women's history, Beard left an awkward legacy. Her critique of feminism was disconcerting to later historians. Yet, alone in her generation, she centered women on the historical record, refusing to see in men's works the full measure of human accomplishment. Late in life she wrote *The Force of Women in Japanese History* (1953). Beard died in Arizona in 1958.

[*See also* History and Historiography; History of Women; Suffrage; United States, *subentry* Modern Period.]

BIBLIOGRAPHY

Cott, Nancy F. "Two Beards: Coauthorship and the Concept of Civilization." *American Quarterly* 42 (1990): 274–300. A historical analysis re-crediting Mary Beard in the couple's collaborative work.

Cott, Nancy F. *A Woman Making History: Mary Ritter Beard through Her Letters*. New Haven, Conn.: Yale University Press, 1991. Previously unpublished letters illuminating Beard's thought, introduced by an intellectual biography.

Lane, Ann J. *Mary Ritter Beard: A Sourcebook*. New York: Schocken Books, 1977. A compilation of Beard's published writings, framed so as to showcase her accomplishments.

Smith, Bonnie G. "Seeing Mary Beard." *Feminist Studies* 10 (1984): 399–416. A highly original analysis of Beard's viewpoint as historian.

Turoff, Barbara K. *Mary Beard as Force in History*. Dayton, Ohio: Wright State University, 1979. The principal biography.

NANCY F. COTT

BEAUTY PAGEANTS. From their beginnings in the raucous carnival atmosphere of the 1850s to their status today as corporate-sponsored major media events, beauty pageants hold a contradictory and problematic place in women's history. Contests selecting an individual to represent community standards of beauty and morality go back to the judgment of Paris of Greek mythology and to medieval calendrical festivals such as the Queen of the May. But the Miss America and Miss Universe competitions that exemplify modern beauty pageants developed more directly from the contests put on in the 1850s by the American showman P. T. Barnum, as an extension of his sideshow of curiosities, than from the contests of ancient Greece or medieval Europe.

Barnum's "beauty" contests put on display everything from birds to babies, and their popularity and profitability inspired newspapers throughout the country to run photo contests featuring young women. By the end of the nineteenth century, newspaper beauty contests were regular features of American life, with one twelve-city contest attracting more than forty thousand entries. The Miss United States pageant held in 1880 in Rehoboth Beach, Delaware, is the first "bathing beauty" contest of record and marks a growing acceptance of female public bathing. The first Miss America beauty pageant was held in 1920 on the boardwalk in Atlantic City, New Jersey, using a parade of women in bathing suits to promote tourism.

From Bathing Beauty to Model Citizen. During the 1920s and 1930s the Miss America pageant remained little more than a swimsuit contest to entice tourists to Atlantic City after Labor Day, and the bathing beauties of these decades used beauty pageants to signal their emancipation from Victorian mores and sometimes as a stepping-stone to a Hollywood career. Not until World War II—during which Miss America sold more war bonds than any other celebrity—did American beauty pageants begin to move into the mainstream of American culture as reputable civic events.

In the mid 1940s the Miss America contest added talent and evening gown components to the competition and began to offer scholarships as prizes. By the late 1940s Miss America had been transformed from a bathing beauty of questionable repute into a model of upright American womanhood: well-mannered, well-groomed, a good citizen of strong moral fiber. In addition to the Miss America pageant, today's American beauty pageants of note include the Miss USA pageant, the America's Junior Miss pageant, the Miss Teenage America pageant, and the Cinderella pageant (a leading children's pageant). Sponsored by civic associations such as the Rotary Club, the Lions Club, and chambers of commerce, American pageants by the end of the twentieth century had become both a focus of civic pride and major contributors to college scholarships for women. The Academy Award winner Halle Berry was a runner-up in the 1986 Miss USA pageant, and the television news anchorwoman Diane Sawyer was America's Junior Miss of 1962.

Throughout the 1920s and 1930s the idea of beauty contests as a popular form of entertainment spread from the United States to other parts of the world. With decolonization and the nationalist movements that followed World War II, these local and regional contests became a

"Bathing Beauties." Miss America Pageant, Atlantic City, New Jersey, September 1953. PRINTS AND PHOTOGRAPHS DIVISION, LIBRARY OF CONGRESS

focus for nationalist sentiments and pride. In the Caribbean, for example, beauty contests became an important mechanism for emerging island nations to differentiate themselves as tourist destinations; throughout Latin America and Africa beauty contests demonstrated a country's commitment to modernization; and in the Soviet Union in 1989, the first-ever Miss Moscow beauty contest made concrete the ideals of glasnost and signaled a move toward democratization.

In 1951 the Miss America Corporation created the Miss World franchise; in 1952 the Miss Universe pageant created its own franchise, partnered with the Miss USA pageant. By the end of the twentieth century most national beauty contests around the world were carried out under either the Miss World or the Miss Universe franchise; the Miss Universe pageant, which features contestants from seventy-eight countries, attracted a global television audience of close to one billion people.

Critiques of Beauty Pageants. The beauty queen is the representative of her community's notion of what is beautiful, and even though this notion of beauty may include deportment, leadership, and talent, a limited standard is nonetheless being applied. Until the late twentieth century in the United States, this meant that beauty pageant contestants were white, thin, able-bodied, and heterosexual—without being overly sexual. International pageants such as Miss Universe and Miss World conventionally select contestants who embody similar norms, thereby imposing a white Western standard of beauty upon diverse cultures and people.

Although ethnic beauty pageants have been held in the United States since the 1930s and the court of an early Miss America included a Miss Indian America, it was not until the coronation of Vanessa Williams in 1983 that an African American became Miss America. In 1985, Laura Martinez Herring, a naturalized Mexican American, was crowned Miss USA; in 1990 both the Miss America title and the Miss USA title were won by African Americans; and in 1994 a hearing-impaired woman, Heather Whitestone, became the first disabled Miss America. Though specialized beauty contests range from the Snake Charmer Queen contest of Sweetwater, Texas, to the National Indigenous Queen contest of Guatemala, to the Transvestite Beauty contests of the southern Philippines (see Cohen, Wilk, and Stoeltje, *Beauty Queens on the Global Stages*, for descriptions of these and other beauty pageants around the world), as alternatives to mainstream pageants, they tend to underscore, rather than dislodge, standards of normative femininity.

In 1968, to protest the absence of African Americans in the Miss America contest, civil rights activists staged a Miss Black America pageant in Atlantic City the same day that the Miss America pageant was held. That same year, the New York Radical Women organized a protest of more than four hundred feminists on the boardwalk outside the Miss America pageant. Waving placards that read, "No More Beauty Standards," and tossing cosmetics, high heels, and copies of *Ladies' Home Journal* and *Playboy* into a "Freedom Trash Can," the protesters objected to the role played by the Miss America pageant in promulgating limited and oppressive roles for women. These and subsequent protests of the Miss American pageant drew attention to the larger concerns of the civil rights and feminist movements and also brought about changes in the pageant itself. By the early twenty-first century the Miss America pageant was more ethnically and racially diverse, and it promoted itself as an advocate of women's professional achievement and of socially progressive programs such as AIDS education and campaigns against domestic violence.

Assessment. Prior to 1972, when the Title IX Education Amendment to the 1964 Civil Rights Act mandated equal opportunities for women in high school and college sports, beauty pageants were one of very few public forums available to American women to display their physical attributes, talents, and social skills and were one of few sources of nonacademic college scholarships for women. Since then, women around the world have continued to use beauty pageants as stepping-stones to careers and college. Meanwhile, child beauty pageants have become a billion-dollar business, and Miss Universe contestants readily admit to having cosmetic surgery in order to attain crown-winning physiques and faces.

Similarly, as much as beauty contests outside of the United States play important roles in nationalist struggles for recognition and international legitimacy, they are also politically charged events. In 2002 in Nigeria, where the Miss World pageant was to be held, protests that focused on the conflict between Islamic law and public display of women's bodies resulted in more than two hundred deaths; in the Miss Universe pageant that same year, Miss Lebanon withdrew, refusing to compete with Miss Israel. Worldwide, beauty pageants continued to be serious business, economically and politically, in the twenty-first century; as bellwethers of women's positions and roles, as sites of protests for change and claims for emancipation, they are also an important feature of women's history.

[*See also* Cosmetic Surgery *and* Cosmetics.]

BIBLIOGRAPHY

Banner, Lois. *American Beauty*. Chicago: University of Chicago Press, 1983. A feminist assessment of the place of beauty contests in the lives of American women.

Bivans, Ann-Marie. *Miss America, in Pursuit of the Crown: The Complete Guide to the Miss America Pageant*. New York: MasterMedia, 1991. The authorized history of the Miss America pageant, including interviews with contestants and winners.

Cohen, Colleen, Richard Wilk, and Beverly Stoeltje, eds. *Beauty Queens on the Global Stage: Gender, Contests, and Power*. New York: Routledge, 1995. A collection of essays analyzing the role of beauty contests in cultures around the world, with an emphasis on the relations among beauty contests, nationalism, and identity.

Deford, Frank. *There She Is: The Life and Times of Miss America*. New York: Viking, 1971. An early study of the Miss America pageant, with a popular culture approach.

Savage, Candace. *Beauty Queens: A Playful History*. New York: Abbeville Press, 1998. A lively account of the history of American beauty contests, with many historical photographs.

Watson, Elwood D., ed. *"There She Is, Miss America": The Politics of Sex, Beauty, and Race in America's Most Famous Pageant*. New York: Palgrave Macmillan, 2004. A collection of critical essays on the Miss America pageant.

COLLEEN BALLERINO COHEN

BEAUVOIR, SIMONE DE (1908–1986), French novelist and intellectual. Simone de Beauvoir is best known globally as the author of *Le deuxième sexe* (English trans., *The Second Sex*, 1953), first published in 1949, and widely considered to be a key text in the Second Wave feminist movement of the 1960s and 1970s. Beauvoir is also renowned as the lifetime partner of the French philosopher Jean-Paul Sartre (1905–1980), with whom she lived for fifty-one years. She was born to a solidly middle-class Parisian family in 1908, the daughter of the lawyer Georges Bertrand de Beauvoir and Françoise Brasseur, a devout Catholic from a very wealthy family. After a happy childhood, Beauvoir began to rebel against her bourgeois origins by declaring herself an atheist, determining to become a philosopher, and reading books deemed inappropriate for a young girl. By the time she was eighteen, Beauvoir was leaving the house unchaperoned to attend classes and counted men among her best friends. As a result of the financial catastrophe of World War I, the Beauvoir family's wealth was depleted by the 1920s. Like many other middle-class girls of the era, Beauvoir could no longer rely on the dowry system for her future, which jeopardized her chances for marriage. Instead, as her father solemnly informed her, she would have to prepare herself to make a living. Beauvoir took this change of fortune as an opportunity to do what she had always wanted to do anyway: become a teacher and a writer. At a time when higher education was just opening up to French women, she earned a degree from the Sorbonne. When she was twenty-one, she became the

Simone de Beauvoir. Paris, c. 1955. AKG-IMAGES

ninth woman to obtain the prestigious *agrégation* from the École Normale Supérieur, the youngest person of either sex ever to do so in philosophy. It was at the École Normale that Beauvoir met the young philosophy student Jean-Paul Sartre, who would soon become famous as the founder of existentialist philosophy. The two quickly became inseparable, although they never married or had children. Throughout their lifetime partnership, they collaborated on several joint projects, including the establishment of the French journal *Les Temps Modernes*.

Beauvoir taught intermittently during the years from 1931 to 1943, after which she concentrated on her writing. She was the author of several novels, including *L'invitée* (1943; English trans., *She Came to Stay,* 1949), *Le sang des autres* (1945; English trans., *The Blood of Others,* 1948), and, most famously, *Les mandarins* (1954; English trans., *The Mandarins,* 1956), for which she won the prestigious Prix Goncourt. She also wrote philosophical treatises such as *Pour une morale de l'ambiguïté* (1947; English trans., *The Ethics of Ambiguity,* 1948), a multivolume autobiography, travelogues, and the feminist treatise, *The Second Sex,* which became her most famous book. Although Beauvoir's relationship to the organized feminist movement had been nonexistent before the writing of *The Second Sex,* and afterwards remained ambiguous at best, the global success of this book transformed her into an emblem of the feminist intellectual. Influenced by Sartre's philosophy of existentialism, the main argument of *The Second Sex* is that throughout modern history, woman has acted as an "Other" to man's "Self." By this, Beauvoir meant that woman is always defined by man in relationship to him; in her words, she is the "incidental, the inessential, as opposed to the essential." Beauvoir's most famous dictum in *The Second Sex* is "one is not born, but rather becomes, a woman." This statement distinguishes between a woman's sex, to which she is born, and her gender, which she becomes. For Beauvoir, to be born a woman was to be definitively of the female sex. To become a woman was to be defined culturally as an Other by man. As an existentialist, Beauvoir conceived of freedom in terms of creative engagement and fulfillment in chosen projects. As long as woman was defined as an Other to man, this kind of freedom was not possible. A woman's inability to define her own subjectivity and ambitions constituted the primary source of her oppression because it forced her into a passivity and an alienation from herself that she could not overcome. A woman gained freedom by rebelling against her objectification as an Other and by defining herself through such creative projects as writing and art.

Beauvoir's main insight in *The Second Sex,* that gender is a cultural construction, became a central theme of the feminist movement in the 1970s. While Beauvoir, somewhat ironically, was hesitant to label herself a feminist, she did contribute to the French Women's Liberation Movement, most famously by signing a manifesto for abortion rights in 1970, and she was a strong believer in women's economic independence and equal education.

[*See also* Feminism *and* France.]

BIBLIOGRAPHY

Bair, Deirdre. *Simone de Beauvoir: A Biography*. New York: Summit Books, 1990.

Bauer, Nancy. *Simone de Beauvoir, Philosophy & Feminism*. New York: Columbia University Press, 2001.

Francis, Claude and Fernande Gontier. *Simone de Beauvoir*: A Life, a Love Story. Translated by Lisa Nesselson. New York: St. Martin's Press, 1987.

Moi, Toril. *Feminist Theory & Simone de Beauvoir*. Oxford and Cambridge, Mass.: Blackwell, 1990.

Moi, Toril. *Simone de Beauvoir: The Making of an Intellectual Woman*. Oxford, U.K., and Cambridge, Mass.: Blackwell, 1994.

MARY LOUISE ROBERTS

BEECHER, CATHARINE (1800–1878), educator and social reformer. Catharine Esther Beecher was born on 6 September 1800 in East Hampton, New York, the oldest child of Lyman Beecher (1775–1863), prominent Evangelical clergyman, and the sister of Harriet Beecher Stowe (1811–1896) and Henry Ward Beecher (1813–1887). Catharine Beecher's writings gained a wide public readership in the decades before the Civil War because they so cogently expressed new views about the expanded power of women in modern family life.

Beecher's many books and her promotion of women as educators consolidated trends generated in New England between 1820 and 1860. In 1823 she founded one of the new nation's most rigorous academies for higher education for women, the Hartford Female Seminary, in Hartford, Connecticut, and hitched her own star to the rising status of women teachers. In 1832 she followed her father and siblings to Cincinnati, where, like them, she championed the dominance of New England evangelism in the multicultural environment of the American West.

Beecher became an important figure in the New England cultural diaspora, the movement of people and ideas that dominated the expansion of the European-American population into the Northwest Territory, a region that later included the states of Ohio, Michigan, and Illinois. In these new regions she promoted gains in the status of women that had been developing in New England, such as public funding for the schooling of girls and the emergence of independent women's organizations like female moral reform societies, which existed in nearly every New England town by 1840. Moral reform societies denounced male sexual predators and promoted new notions of sexuality that encouraged women to control their own bodies. Later called

"Victorian," these new notions were essentially modern in the way they encouraged women to act independently of their husbands.

In this moment of fundamental transition from pre-modern to modern life, Beecher's writings recast women's gendered identity to give women greater power in their personal and family lives, and in their communities. She drew these three dimensions of women's lives together in a series of popular books. Her best-known publication was *Treatise on Domestic Economy*, first published in 1841, reprinted multiple times through 1856, and greatly expanded in a version coauthored with her sister Harriet, *The American Woman's Home; or Principles of Domestic Science*, which was widely reprinted between 1869 and 1873. In other books she challenged eighteenth-century notions of female dependency and urged young women to become self-supporting teachers. Beecher's advice to women reflected contemporary economic changes that were relocating male labor, and much of what had formerly been household production, outside the household. She advised married women to exercise greater control over domestic life, including family finances, and to value their work as an honorable calling that was shaping the future of American democracy.

Beecher's ideas were carried across the North American continent in covered wagons to Oregon and California. And they traveled abroad through the efforts of American women missionaries, especially the graduates of Mount Holyoke Seminary, who conveyed Beecher's ideas to women in India, China, and the Ottoman Empire.

[*See also* Feminism; Home Economics; Stowe, Harriet Beecher; *and* United States, *subentry* Nineteenth Century.]

BIBLIOGRAPHY

Caskey, Marie. *Chariot of Fire: Religion and the Beecher Family*. New Haven, Conn.: Yale University Press, 1978.

Leavitt, Sarah A. *From Catharine Beecher to Martha Stewart; A Cultural History of Domestic Advice*. Chapel Hill: University of North Carolina Press, 2002.

Sklar, Kathryn Kish. *Catharine Beecher: A Study in American Domesticity*. New Haven, Conn.: Yale University Press, 1973.

KATHRYN KISH SKLAR

BEGAM SAMRU (1741/53–1836), ruler of Sardhana, a 240-square-mile (about 620 square kilometers) *jagir* (assigned revenue land), later a virtually independent kingdom, in northern India near Delhi. Rising from slavery through personal charisma, astute political maneuvering, and eclectic patronage, she made her court in Sardhana the center for a rich composite culture during the transition to British colonialism in India. Evidently childless herself, she created diverse familial relationships with a variety of people over the course of her lifetime.

A Muslim slave in her youth with the personal name Farzana, around 1770 she became (either by her choice or his purchase) the consort of Walter Reinhardt (c. 1720–1778), a Catholic, German-speaking mercenary who had carved his domain of Sardhana out of the crumbling Mughal Empire (1526–1858). She adopted Reinhardt's epithet "Samru" (also spelled by her Somru, Sombre, Somroo, and Somer) and the Muslim honorific *begam* ("woman of rank"). On Reinhardt's death, she established her own control over Sardhana (whose annual revenues were 2.5 million rupees, the equivalent of £17,666,000 or $35 million today), over his army of some three or four thousand soldiers, and over his senior wife and his biological son, Nawab Zafaryab Khan, Muzaffar al-Daula (1769/70–1801/03). In 1781, three years after Reinhardt's death, she and his son converted to Roman Catholicism; she took the christening name Joanna Nobilis and he Louis (or Aloysius) Balthazar.

Begam Samru fought on behalf of various contending powers, including Maratha warlords and the Mughal emperor, who bestowed on her the grand titles of honor by which trusted courtiers were distinguished from others. In 1794, she secretly wedded, under Catholic rites, one of the French mercenary officers under her command, Le Vassoult. Her army opposed this union: he was murdered soon thereafter. In 1803, she strategically shifted her political alignment to the British East India Company, as the Mughal emperor himself had recently done. In exchange for her submission, the British guaranteed her relatively autonomous rule over Sardhana for the rest of her life, but expected to annex it into British rule on her death.

Under Begam Samru, Sardhana emerged as a highly cosmopolitan capital. Courtiers and distinguished visitors from across India and Europe attended upon her and enjoyed her largesse. She built a grand Catholic cathedral, modeled on Saint Peter's in the Vatican, and corresponded with the pope but also made generous donations to a range of Anglican, Hindu, and Muslim charitable causes. She adopted David Octerlony Dyce Sombre (1808–1851), a biological descendant of Reinhardt, as her personal heir, giving him £800,000 (worth £52,524,000 or $105 million today). After her death and the consequent British annexation of Sardhana, Dyce Sombre traveled to China before settling in England, marrying in 1840 Mary Anne Jervis (1812–1893), the daughter of Viscount St. Vincent, and purchasing a seat in the British Parliament in 1841–1842. After Dyce Sombre's death in 1851, his widow inherited Begam Samru's fortune, a part of which she used to build a school in Sardhana.

[*See also* Begams of Awadh *and* Begams of Bhopal.]

BIBLIOGRAPHY

Fisher, Michael H. "Becoming and Making 'Family' in Hindustan." In *Unfamiliar Relations: Family and History in South Asia*, edited by Indrani Chatterjee, pp. 95–121. New Brunswick, N.J.: Rutgers University Press, 2004.

Sharma, Mahendra Narain. *Life and Times of Begam Samru of Sardhana, A.D. 1750–1836*. Sahibabad, India: Vibhu Prakashan, 1985.

MICHAEL H. FISHER

BEGAMS OF AWADH. The Muslim title *begam* means "woman of rank," and the two women who became known as the "Begams of Awadh" were wives of successive Shiite Muslim nawabs (rulers) of that large north Indian kingdom. As chief consorts and then widows, Nawab ᶜAliya Begam and Bahu Begam used their wealth, charisma, and personal connections to exert strong influence over politics in north India from 1754 until 1815.

Awadh (formerly, Oudh and Oude) was a province and then a relatively autonomous kingdom covering about 24,000 square miles (about 62,000 square kilometers) with a population of about 11 million when it was annexed by the British in 1856. Sadr-i Jehan, Sadr al-Nisaʾ, known as "Nawab ᶜAliya Begam" (c. 1712–1796; *ᶜaliya* means "high"), was the eldest daughter of Saᶜadat Khan (1680–1739) who emigrated from Nishapur, Iran, and rose in service to the Mughal Empire to be the first nawab of Awadh (c. 1722, and ruling until his death). In 1724 she married her paternal cross-cousin, Safdar Jang (c. 1708–1754), who had also emigrated from Iran, risen as his father-in-law's deputy, and then secured rule over Awadh for himself as second nawab (1739–1754). Educated in the Qurʾan and its commentaries, she developed effective administrative and diplomatic experience through participation in contested politics of the age. At her husband's death, Nawab ᶜAliya Begam guided the succession and administration of their only son, Shujaᶜ al-Daula (1738–1775), the third nawab (1754–1775).

Ummat al-Zahra, Janab ᶜAliya Muta ᶜAliya, known as "Bahu Begam" (1728/29–1815; *bahu* means "daughter-in-law") was the nominally adopted daughter of the Mughal emperor Muhammad Shah and the biological daughter of a high Shiite Iranian family in the imperial administration. She entered a political marriage with Shujaᶜ al-Daula in 1745, becoming preeminent among his many wives and concubines. Although illiterate, she shrewdly guided her husband's policies and secured the succession of her only son, Asaf al-Daula (1748–1797) as fourth nawab (1775–1797).

Both begams established their courts in the earlier Awadh capital of Faizabad and controlled a vast fortune, estimated at 20 million rupees (the equivalent of £166,530,000 or $333 million today). They developed independent political relations with the East India Company through its resident political agent stationed in the newer Awadh capital, Lucknow. Indeed, the East India Company under Governor General Warren Hastings guaranteed in 1775 a contract between the begams and Asaf al-Daula that, in exchange for 5.6 million rupees, secured the rest of their fortune. Nonetheless, they allegedly supported anti-British insurrection in Benaras by Raja Chait Singh in 1781. Asaf al-Daula violated his contract with the begams, with the backing of East India Company troops, by seizing from them another 12 million rupees in addition to landholdings. Although their landholdings were reinstated in 1784, Hastings was indicted in the British House of Commons and put through a seven-year trial in the House of Lords (1788–1795), with this looting of the begams and the torturing of their entourage as part of the major charges against him. At her death in 1796, Nawab ᶜAliya Begam disbursed her fortune to her followers. In 1815, Bahu Begam left part of her fortune to relatives and charitable religious endowments, with the East India Company as trustee; her remaining 7.1 million rupees she left to the company itself.

[*See also* Begam Samru *and* Begams of Bhopal.]

BIBLIOGRAPHY

Barnett, Richard B. *North India between Empires: Awadh, the Mughals, and the British, 1720–1801*. Berkeley: University of California Press, 1980.

Santha, Kidambi Srinivasa. *Begums of Awadh*. Varanasi, India: Bharati Prakashan, 1980.

MICHAEL H. FISHER

BEGAMS OF BHOPAL. A series of women rulers (nawabs) and regents of Bhopal, a kingdom in central India (6,900 square miles, or 17,900 square kilometers, with a population of about 800,000), were collectively identified by the honorific *begam* ("woman of rank"). Their dynasty of Sunni Muslim Mirzai-khel clan Orakzai Pathans from Afghanistan ruled in Bhopal from 1715 until Bhopal merged into the Republic of India in 1949.

Mamola Bai (1715–1792), a local Hindu, converted to Islam on becoming the consort of the current nawab. She rejected purdah. From about 1742 until her death she established the distinctive Bhopal tradition of strong women rulers. From 1778, she made Bhopal an early supporter of the British East India Company's colonial rule in the region. (In 1818, Bhopal signed an official treaty of subordination and remained loyal to the British thereafter.)

Nawab Gauhar, Qudsiya Begam (1801–1881), the daughter of one nawab and the widow of another, convinced British and Islamic authorities and power brokers in Bhopal that she should rule as regent on behalf of her only child, Sikandar Begam, from 1819. Qudsia Begam left purdah and commissioned extensive public works, including aqueducts, a railway, and a grand mosque.

Her daughter, Sikandar Begam (1817–1868), served as regent from 1847 until 1860 on behalf of her only child, Shah Jehan Begam. She supported the British in the 1857 rebellion eventually known as the First War of Indian Independence. Invoking the precedent of Queen Victoria, she claimed to rule in her own right. The British agreed and awarded her the Grand Cross of the Star of India in 1863. She continued the building programs of her mother (including the Bhopal railroad line), reformed the state army and administration, appointed a *majlis-i-shura* (consultative assembly), replaced courtly Persian with vernacular Urdu as the official state language, and supported women's education. The first Indian woman ruler to make the Hajj (1863–1864), her account of the journey was published in English as *Pilgrimage to Mecca* (1870).

Shah Jehan Begam (1828–1901) had married an older man in 1855 (he died in 1867) on the insistence her mother, Sikandar Begam, and then deferred to her as nawab in 1859. After years of conflict with her mother, Shah Jehan Begam finally succeeded as nawab in 1868, with her only surviving child, Sultan Jahan Begam, as heir apparent. In 1871, Shah Jehan Begam married her chief minister, a widely published Islamist scholar, Syed Siddiq Hassan Khan (1832–1890), and adopted purdah. However, due to his perceived anti-British and pro-Islamic policies and publications, the British stripped him of power in 1884. She recorded her family's history in her book *Taj-ul Iqbal Tarikh Bhopal: or the History of Bhopal* (1876). She completed the railroad that linked Bhopal with the rest of India in 1884 and continued her mother's support for women's education.

Sultan Jahan Begam (1858–1930) succeeded Shah Jehan Begam in 1901. She was widowed six months later. She fostered social and educational reforms, especially for women, serving as the first chancellor of the Muhammadan Anglo-Oriental University at Aligarh, president of the All-India Women's Conference on Educational Reform, and founder of the All India Ladies' Association. Like her grandmother, she made the Hajj, which she described in *The Story of a Pilgrimage to Hijaz* (1909). She also wrote other books that were translated into English for publication: her autobiography, *Gohur-i Iqbal: An Account of My Life* (three volumes, 1910–1927), and commemorations of the lives of her great-grandmother and mother respectively in *Hayat-i Qudsi: Life of Nawab Gauhar Begum* (1918) and *Hayat-i Shahjehani: Life of Her Highness the Late Nawab Shahjehan Begum of Bhopal* (1926). She traveled to Europe in 1911 and then again in 1925–1926 (the latter for a protracted succession dispute through which she finally gained British recognition of her son, Hamidullah Khan [1894–1960], as heir apparent; she immediately abdicated to him as nawab). Having written extensively in defense of the moral advantages of purdah for Indian Muslim women, including *Al Hijab; or, Why Purdah Is Necessary* (1922), she reversed herself and discarded her own purdah as an act of reform in 1928, at age seventy.

After Bhopal merged into the Republic of India, Sajida Sultan Begam (1915–1995) succeeded her father in 1960 as nominal nawab of Bhopal but retained no official status as ruler.

[*See also* Begams of Awadh *and* Begam Samru.]

BIBLIOGRAPHY

Khan, Shaharyar M. *The Begums of Bhopal: A Dynasty of Women Rulers in Raj India.* London: I. B. Tauris, 2000. Historical narrative of his family by a grandson of the last official nawab.

Lambert-Hurley, Siobhan. "Out of India: The Journeys of the Begams of Bhopal, 1901–1930." In *Bodies in Contact: Rethinking Colonial Encounters in World History*, edited by Tony Ballantyne and Antoinette Burton, pp. 293–309. Durham, N.C.: Duke University Press, 2005. Scholarly study of the lives and writings of these women.

Preckel, Claudia. *Begums of Bhopal.* New Delhi: Roli Books, 2000. Accessible scholarly narrative of this dynasty.

Sultaan, Abida. *Memoirs of a Rebel Princess.* Edited by Siobhan Lambert-Hurley. Karachi: Oxford University Press, 2004. Autobiography of the heir apparent to the last official nawab until she emigrated to Pakistan, thereby forfeiting her inheritance.

MICHAEL H. FISHER

BEGUINES. Beguines were religious women whose movement flourished in northern Europe, particularly in the Low Countries, from the thirteenth century through the end of the Middle Ages. The term "beguine" (Latin, *beguina*; Dutch or Flemish, *begijn*) is of uncertain origin and may have been pejorative. Beguines first appeared in the late twelfth century and in 1216 obtained approval from Pope Honorius III for their way of life. (Beghards, the parallel group for men, probably had far fewer members.) "Beguines" generally refers to women who were not nuns, that is, they did not take formal vows of poverty, chastity, and obedience. Yet they were not quite laypersons either. Although they promised not to marry "as long as they lived as beguines," to quote one of the early rules, they were free to leave at any time because they did not take permanent vows of chastity. Beguines were part of a larger spiritual revival movement of the thirteenth century that stressed imitation of Christ's life through voluntary poverty, care of the poor and sick, and religious devotion.

Beguines tended to live in communal spaces, either by renting houses in urban spaces or by constructing a complex of buildings, called beguinages, in city centers. In these formal beguinages (Dutch and Flemish, *begijnhoven*) women generally selected a housemistress from among the membership. The bishop of Liège established a rule for beguines in his diocese in 1246 that became a model for other beguinages (reproduced in Nimal).

The origin of the beguine movement, like that of its name, continues to be debated. Groups of women pursuing similar goals in a variety of ways can be found in many areas of the Low Countries from the twelfth century onward. Secular canonesses, recluses, hospital workers, women who lived at home, and small devotional groups all provided impetus for a new type of religious laity.

Beguines represented all social classes in Europe. Some were quite wealthy and used rental income to support other, poorer beguines, who may have joined the movement out of economic necessity as much as out of a religious calling. Beguines lived in urban areas and were never isolated in rural convents as were nuns. They worked like other townspeople, generally in some aspect of the cloth trade, ran schools and infirmaries, and attended local parish churches. Because their devotional life also took place in urban and communal settings, beguines were much more visible in public than were nuns, who lived in monasteries far from town centers. The beguinages of most Flemish cities, such as Lier, Ghent, Mechelen, Dendermonde, and Antwerp, were located in the centers of these towns. Some beguinages, such as that at Lier, had gates located right off the commercial centers of towns and were constructed as "towns within towns." Others, such as the one Ghent, had a more formal square courtyard setting around which the beguine apartments were built.

Beguines were most prominent in the area now known as the southern Low Countries, a very heterogeneous cultural landscape. Regional norms were such that neither gender nor religious affiliation strictly limited anyone to a particular sphere of action. The active commercial life in this region encouraged a high degree of literacy across gender and class lines. Both girls and boys, rich and poor, received a basic education that included reading and writing. Indeed, it was common for the city to provide a free education to children whose parents or guardians were unable to afford it. A high rate of literacy, heritability of both sons and daughters, and the preference for public, oral testimony (in which women participated) contributed to the integration of women at almost all levels of the region's society. Women ruled Flanders as countesses for most of the thirteenth century and as duchesses of Brabant in the fourteenth. They were regents for the Habsburgs in the sixteenth century. They could be found in county administration, bargaining in the markets of the major towns, baking bread, tanning hides, retailing, growing wheat, butchering meat, selling cloth, and warping loom threads. Thus, the beguine movement cannot be separated from the larger cultural and historical context in which it developed, especially the general conditions for women in the Low Countries in that period.

Another propelling force in the development of beguine life was the late medieval devotional impulse toward simplicity and admiration for voluntary poverty, exemplified in such diverse religious groups as the Waldenses, the Franciscans, and, much later, the Brethren of the Common Life. Disenchantment with the urban mercantile way of life, its excessive wealth, and the disparity between rich and poor formed a common pattern in the lives of devout beguine women. The movement represented a social experiment in which all social classes could participate, and in which richer beguines and their admirers could pool their resources for the common good. In practice, of course, poorer beguines often complained of second-class treatment in living arrangements, but the ideal is evident in early rules.

The beguine movement was thus religious, social, and economic in nature. Some beguines acquired reputations in their communities for "holiness," primarily through their spectacular visionary experiences. The Latin term *mulieres sanctae* (holy women) is properly reserved for this small group of beguines rather than the movement as a whole. Such women enhanced the reputation of the movement through the admiration they elicited from townspeople and churchmen. Cistercians, Dominicans, and Franciscans were especially closely associated with beguines in their roles as confessors, biographers, and preachers. A few of these holy women, such as Hadewijch of Antwerp (thirteenth century), even wrote their own works. Such literature, either by or about beguines, is notable because it forms some of the earliest vernacular (non-Latin) devotional writing. Vernacular writing made devotional piety, formerly a monastic preserve, more accessible to laypeople.

By 1300 these groups of women, who were under the control of neither fathers, husbands, nor the church, became increasingly vulnerable to accusations of heresy. As early as the mid-thirteenth century Hadewijch referred to a woman executed by the Dominican inquisitor in her region. The most spectacular example of this changed attitude was the condemnation and execution of the beguine Marguerite Porete at Paris in 1310. The papal Council of Vienne in 1311–1312 condemned beliefs spread by "an abominable sect of wicked men called beghards and faithless women called beguines."

This change in attitude coincided with the economic crisis in parts of the Low Countries, which must have caused great financial difficulty for both beguinages and the communities in which they were located. By the mid-fourteenth century, the variety of beguine lifestyles had narrowed to include only the most formal types of beguinages. Such beguinages continued to exist in the southern Low Countries throughout the modern period, but the beguine movement as a widespread, influential, and, most important, experimental devotional way of life had faded from the European landscape.

The beguine movement in northern Europe is significant in three very important ways. First, beguines represented one of the earliest movements in European history in which women successfully controlled their own lives and dedicated themselves to self-chosen goals. Second, beguines provided clear spiritual and leadership roles for women, largely accepted within their society, outside of formal convents. Finally, beguines were at the forefront of the drive to increase lay participation in religion, a movement that culminated in the Protestant Reformation of the sixteenth century.

[*See also* Christianity; Codes of Law and Laws, *subentry* Medieval Roman and Canon Law; Europe, *subentry* Medieval Period; *and* Religion.]

BIBLIOGRAPHY

Kittell, Ellen E., and Mary A. Suydam, eds. *The Texture of Society: Medieval Women in the Southern Low Countries*. New York: Palgrave Macmillan, 2004.

McDonnell, Ernest W. *The Beguines and Beghards in Medieval Culture, with Special Emphasis on the Belgian Scene*. New Brunswick, N.J.: Rutgers University Press, 1954. The standard work in English on beguines.

Mulder-Bakker, Anneke B. *Lives of the Anchoresses: The Rise of the Urban Recluse in Medieval Europe*, translated by Myra Heerspink Scholz. Philadelphia: University of Pennsylvania Press, 2005.

Nimal, H. *Les beguinages*, pp. 43–50. Nivelles, Belgium: Lanneau et Despret, 1908. Contains reproductions of early rules.

Philippen, L. J. M. *De Begijnhoven: Ooorspong, Geschiedenis, Inrichting*. Antwerp, Belgium: Ch. and H. Courtin, 1918. An early introduction to the beguine movement.

Simons, Walter. *Cities of Ladies: Beguine Communities in the Medieval Low Countries, 1200–1565*. Philadelphia: University of Pennsylvania Press, 2001. An updated overview of the movement.

Ziegler, Joanna. "Secular Canonesses as Antecedent of the Beguines in the Southern Low Countries: An Introduction to Some Older Views." *Studies in Medieval and Renaissance History* 13 (1991): 114–135.

MARY SUYDAM

BEHN, APHRA (1640?–1689), the first female professional writer, the only woman playwright of the Restoration, and a pioneer novelist, poet, and translator, on whose grave, as Virginia Woolf put it in *A Room of One's Own* (1929), all women ought to strew flowers. The still incomplete accounts of her life tell us that she was born Aphra Johnson in Canterbury, England, and when she was very young she lived in Surinam, West Indies, later the scene of her most famous novel, *Oroonoko; or, The History of the Royal Slave* (1688). Back in London and soon a young widow after the death of her husband—a Mr. Behn who died of plague in 1666—she worked for a time (1666–1667) in Flanders as a spy for Charles II (r. 1660–1685) during the second Anglo-Dutch War. Her difficult financial situation drove her toward writing for the theater, the most popular form of entertainment at that time. In 1670, *The Forc'd Marriage*, a comedy, was staged, starting a career that was to establish her as the only female voice of Restoration theater, to whom more than a dozen plays can be attributed.

In a world dominated by male writers with misogynistic attitudes, Behn produced a vibrant *j'accuse* against the rules of a society that condemned a woman's voice to silence; her female characters are always acting out roles and using disguises that reveal their sense of entrapment in a patriarchal society where their bodies are objects of exchange. Her plays, such as *The Rover* (1677) or *The Luckey Chance* (1686), two of her most celebrated comedies, articulate a strong resistance to seventeenth-century denial and control of feminine desire.

The difference between the woman as a cultural imago constructed by others and her real life experience determines the plot in the three-volume *Love-Letters between a Nobleman and His Sister* (1684), the first epistolary novel of European literature. The story of the female protagonist who elopes with her sister's husband portrays the realism of the inner life, only much later developed by other novelists, and marks the rise of a new literary genre. Moving away from the cultural tradition of the time, the heroine openly recognizes her desire for the man she loves and questions family life and strategies of marriage. The first part of the novel is remarkable for the narrative technique that lets the characters speak for themselves, showing their different points of view.

Oroonoko, Behn's most celebrated prose work, was published the year preceding her premature death in 1689. The story of prince Oroonoko and his beautiful princess Imoinda, both sold into slavery, is important for its critical denunciation of the slave trade as well as for the technique that places the author-narrator inside the text together with her fictional characters, a device that anticipates the eyewitness of later realistic prose fiction.

In her own times esteemed mostly as a poet (*Poems upon Several Occasions*, 1684), Behn also translated works from French and was the author of the "Essay on Translated Prose" (1688) concerning the problems of translation, the first such essay written by a woman.

[*See also* Great Britain; Literature; *and* Performing Arts.]

BIBLIOGRAPHY

Goreau, Angeline. *Reconstructing Aphra: A Social Biography of Aphra Behn*. New York: Dial Press, 1980.

O'Donnell, Mary Ann. *Aphra Behn: An Annotated Bibliography of Primary and Secondary Sources*. 2nd ed. Aldershot, U.K.: Ashgate, 2004.

Todd, Janet, ed. *The Works of Aphra Behn*. 7 vols. London: Pickering and Chatto, 1992–1996.

ANNAMARIA LAMARRA

BELL, GERTRUDE (1868–1926), British archaeologist, writer, and government official. Bell was born into an upper-class British family but defied many of the restrictions imposed on women of her class. She was the first woman to earn a first-class degree in modern history at Oxford University. When she failed to attract a husband on the marriage market, her parents allowed her to travel to Mesopotamia to visit friends. This trip would be the turning point in her personal and professional life. She then embarked on a journey around the world, studying archaeology and languages, including Arabic, Persian, French, and Turkish.

Disguised as a male Bedouin, Bell traveled to Jerusalem in 1900 in search of the Druzes (a small Arab, non-Muslim religious community), and she befriended the Druze king Yahya Beg. Her sex proved a surprising asset, as did her cultural sensitivity and knowledge of languages, and in subsequent travels to the Middle East she met many Arab chieftains, who dubbed her the "daughter of the desert." Throughout the early 1900s she conducted archaeological digs in the Middle East, and in 1907 she published the first of several accounts of her observations in *The Desert and the Sown*. Despite her own independent spirit and political ambitions, Bell was not an advocate of feminism; she was even named an honorary member of the Women's National Anti-Suffrage League in Britain.

When World War I broke out, Bell volunteered for the Red Cross in France, but in 1915 she was summoned to Cairo to work for the Arab Bureau. It was her responsibility to encourage Arabic forces to join the British in the fight against the Turks and to draw maps to help the British army reach Baghdad. The only female political officer in the British forces, Bell received the title of liaison officer, correspondent to Cairo. At the end of the war, with the collapse of the Ottoman Empire, she was assigned to write a report on who should lead the new Iraq. Favoring Arabic leadership, she persuaded the British colonial secretary, Winston Churchill, to endorse Faisal, the recently deposed king of Syria. She not only supervised other appointments in the new government but helped determine the borders of the new nation, earning her the title "the uncrowned Queen of Iraq."

Bell's influence has been overshadowed by that of T. E. Lawrence ("Lawrence of Arabia"), who received most of the credit for the creation of Iraq, but Bell's advice and knowledge were equally instrumental in 1918. Some male critics, resentful of her influence, referred to her as "the terror of the desert." Bell has been unfairly blamed by some for indirectly causing the current troubles in the Middle East because of the boundaries she proposed in 1918. What cannot be questioned is her intense love of the region, where she rightly believed "things are happening."

During the 1920s Bell returned to her true passion—archaeology—and helped create the Baghdad Archaeological Museum. She became its director of antiquities in 1926, the year of her death. She was buried in Iraq, the place she called "the real East."

[*See also* Iraq.]

BIBLIOGRAPHY

Wallach, Janet. *Desert Queen: The Extraordinary Life of Gertrude Bell, Adventurer, Adviser to Kings, Ally of Lawrence of Arabia.* New York: Anchor, 1999.

Winstone, H. V. F. *Gertrude Bell.* London: Cape, 1978. Rev. ed. London: Barzan, 2004.

JULIE ANNE TADDEO

BERNHARDT, SARAH (1844–1923), French actress and international stage star. "La divine Sarah," as she was called, was the most well-known and highly regarded stage actress of the nineteenth century. During the peak of her career in the 1880s and 1890s, she not only commanded Parisian theater, but was arguably the most famous woman in the world. Her international tours, beginning in 1880, wrote the book on public relations for the early twentieth century. She was born Henriette-Rosine Bernhard in Paris in 1844 to a Dutch Jewish courtesan; the identity of her father remains uncertain. Educated away from home in a convent near Versailles, Bernhardt first wanted to become a nun but became enamored with the stage when the Duc de Morny, Napoleon III's half-brother and her mother's lover at the time, took her to her first theatrical performance. With Morny's help, she entered the Parisian Conservatory of Dramatic Arts, but she floundered in her early stage training and career. Her breakthrough role was in 1867 as Zanetto in *Le passant* by François Coppée. Her subsequent triumph in 1872 as Doña Maria in Victor Hugo's *Ruy Blas* solidified her reputation; soon after, she joined the Comédie-Française, France's premier theater, where she earned growing fame. Beginning in 1880, however, Bernhardt began to find the classical roles and traditional atmosphere of the Comédie to be stifling to her creativity. The actress was also no doubt aware that the theater world was rapidly changing from a form of elite culture to one of mass entertainment. With the playwright Victorien Sardou (1831–1908), Bernhardt staged several lavish and exotic productions, among them *Fédora* (1882), *Théodora* (1884), and *Cléopâtre* (1894); these spectacles made Bernhardt a star of the boulevards. In addition, guided by the whiz impresario Edward Jarrett, Bernhardt began a series of international tours to Europe, the United States, Australia, and South America. These tours both transformed Bernhardt into an international celebrity and pioneered new marketing and advertising techniques.

As a celebrity, Bernhardt became much more than a stage actress. At the peak of her career, she was a true phenomenon, representing many different things to many different people. For her fans, she became a commodity fetish—something to be consumed like a tourist attraction. The French daily *Le Figaro* once noted that tourists came to Paris to see two things: the Eiffel Tower and Sarah Bernhardt. For a Parisian cultural elite, Bernhardt and her adventures in boulevard drama symbolized the despicable conversion of theater—and art generally—into a commercial enterprise. For lesbians and "new women" trying to craft subversive identities on the borders of Parisian culture, Bernhardt was a role model, a woman who cross-dressed on stage and led what appeared to be a free and independent life. (She married only once, to Jacques Damala in 1882; he died soon after from drug addiction). For anti-Semites, particularly during the Dreyfus Affair (1894–1899) Bernhardt was stereotyped as a "Jewess"—greedy, wildly promiscuous, and dubious in her morality. In this one woman, fin de siècle fears concerning commodity culture, changing roles for women, and new racial hatreds in the West reached their most fully realized form. No wonder that Bernhardt inspired all the adoration and revulsion, love and hatred, of the era.

[*See also* Theater.]

BIBLIOGRAPHY

Berlanstein, Lenard. *Daughters of Eve: A Cultural History of French Theater Women from the Old Regime to the Fin-de-Siècle*. Cambridge, Mass.: Harvard University Press, 2001.

Gold, Arthur, and Robert Fizdale. *The Divine Sarah: A Life of Sarah Bernhardt*. New York: Knopf, 1991.

Skinner, Cornelia Otis. *Madame Sarah*. Boston: Houghton Mifflin, 1967.

Stokes, John, Michael R. Booth, and Susan Bassnett. *Bernhardt, Terry, Duse: The Actress in Her Time*. Cambridge, U.K., and New York: Cambridge University Press, 1988.

Vicinus, Martha. *Intimate Friends: Women Who Loved Women, 1778–1928*. Chicago: University of Chicago Press, 2004.

MARY LOUISE ROBERTS

BESANT, ANNIE (1847–1933), British writer and activist on behalf of free thought, birth control, socialism, theosophy, and Indian independence. Perhaps the most successful woman orator before the suffrage movement in Britain, Annie Besant is best known for her advocacy of secularism and birth control, her role in organizing the famous strike of the match girls employed by Bryant and May in 1888, and her work on behalf of Indian independence.

Annie Wood was born in London on 1 October 1847, the only surviving child of Emily Roche Morris and William Persse Wood, an underwriter. Her father died when she was five and, whether for financial or other reasons, when she was eight the precocious girl was handed over to a wealthy, unmarried woman, Ellen Marryat, for private schooling in Dorset. The arrangement provided a rich and unusually liberal education while also introducing Annie to a strict brand of evangelicalism, the rigor of which marked her for life. At the age of twenty, when living in Harrow with her widowed mother, she married a rigid evangelical minister, the Reverend Frank Besant, and gave birth to a son, Digby, in 1869 and a daughter, Mabel, in 1870. The couple settled in Sibsey, Lincolnshire, where Frank Besant took up a living at the parish church. Unhappiness in marriage and her reaction to motherhood generated a spiritual crisis as well as her first published work, informed by free thought, which questioned the divinity of Christ. This remarkably brazen act by the wife of a clergyman resulted in his demand that she either publicly avow her faith by taking Holy Communion or leave their household. She chose the latter and

Annie Besant. PRINTS AND PHOTOGRAPHS DIVISION, LIBRARY OF CONGRESS

moved to London with her daughter in 1874. Thus began her extraordinary public career.

As the first woman in Britain to endorse publicly the use of contraception, Besant achieved instant notoriety. She and Charles Bradlaugh, famed free-thought agitator, reprinted Charles Knowlton's pamphlet on birth control, *The Fruits of Philosophy*, in 1877. A passionate and charismatic speaker for the cause, she had already attracted large audiences across England. Brought to trial with Bradlaugh under a law against obscene publications, Besant argued and won their case in court on the grounds that advice on contraception would relieve poverty. She followed up with a highly successful tract of her own (*The Law of Population*, 1878), which contributed to the loss of custody of her daughter. Her next associations, with the socialists Edward Aveling and George Bernard Shaw, led to her participation in the Fabian Society and increasing involvement in Marxist and socialist groups. In 1888 she published her famous defense of the strike of the Bryant and May match girls in *The Link*, bringing their plight to the attention of the nation. Her efforts contributed to the success of "new unionism," through which unskilled workers were brought into the trade union movement. Prohibited as a woman from running for the London county council, she won a position on the London school board for Tower Hamlets as a socialist in 1889.

By this time Besant's disaffection from political and social reform led her in a search for what she regarded as a deeper, hidden power, a quest promoted by widespread enthusiasm for spiritualism at the end of the nineteenth century. From 1889 on, she devoted herself to the Theosophical Society and its leader, Madame Helena Petrovna Blavatsky, in a crusade for spiritual regeneration based largely on Eastern religious belief. Repudiating her former friends and even her own publications, Besant traveled to India and ultimately threw herself into Hindu culture. She founded the Central Hindu College in 1897, published her own translation of the *Bhagavad Gita*, and effectively assumed leadership of the Theosophy Society. The final phase of Besant's life, however, was political. Agitating on behalf of Indian independence, she was elected the first woman president of the thirty-second Indian National Congress in 1917 at Calcutta (now Kolkata). Throughout the 1920s she participated in debates over India's future. Besant died at Adyar, India, on 20 September 1933.

[*See also* Feminism; Great Britain; *and* India.]

BIBLIOGRAPHY

Besant, Annie W. *Autobiographical Sketches*. London: Freethought Publishing, 1885.

Besant, Annie W. *An Autobiography*. 2nd ed. London: T. Fisher Unwin, 1908.

Dinnage, Rosemary. *Annie Besant*. Harmondsworth, U.K.: Penguin, 1986.

Nethercot, Arthur Hobart. *The First Five Lives of Annie Besant*. Chicago: University of Chicago Press, 1960.

Nethercot, Arthur Hobart. *The Last Four Lives of Annie Besant*. Chicago: University of Chicago Press, 1963.

Taylor, Anne. *Annie Besant: A Biography*. Oxford: Oxford University Press, 1992.

DEBORAH VALENZE

BESS OF HARDWICK (1527–1608), Countess of Shrewsbury, builder and courtier who used her power and influence to build Hardwick Hall, Derbyshire, and to introduce significant innovations to architectural culture in England. Born Elizabeth Talbot, Bess of Hardwick holds a distinguished place in women's history for her role in helping to shape both the outcome of political events and the direction of architectural culture in Elizabethan England.

Notable both as a builder of country houses and as the founder of one of England's most prominent dynasties, Bess of Hardwick rose from humble beginnings to a position of power unrivaled by any woman except the queen herself. Through a series of four strategic marriages, as well as brilliant political maneuvering, she amassed a huge fortune; through clever diplomacy she gained power for herself and ensured that her descendants would remain among the richest and most influential families in England.

As a builder, Bess of Hardwick joins a handful of women patrons whose influence and economic power shifted the course of architectural design in her own time. Because the majority of such women builders were active in the nineteenth and twentieth centuries, Bess stands out as a particularly distinctive and unusual figure. Moreover, unlike the queen, who remained throughout her life uninterested in architecture and content to enjoy the fruits of her courtiers' labors in this arena, Bess of Hardwick was dedicated to architecture throughout her life.

Following their marriage in 1547, Bess's second husband, Sir William Cavendish, began to acquire vast landholdings in Derbyshire and Nottinghamshire, and together the couple set about the project of building a country house at Chatsworth. When Cavendish died in 1557, Bess retained a life interest in the estate and continued work on the house; all of her holdings eventually passed to her children, for whom she made strategic marriages. The pattern was repeated in her third marriage, to Sir William St. Loe, the captain of the Queen's Guard and butler of the royal household, in 1559. The most brilliant of Bess's marriages was her fourth and last, to the Earl of Shrewsbury in 1568; while married to him, she began work on the first of her country houses at Hardwick, Derbyshire, which amounted to a renovation and addition to an existing manor house left to her by her father.

Following Shrewsbury's death—and the consolidation of Bess's fortune once again—she shifted her attention to the building of an even larger and more architecturally innovative house, abandoning her work on the still-unfinished first Hardwick Hall. For the second Hardwick Hall, Bess hired London-based craftsmen to create a cutting-edge design and to construct the house from the finest materials; her architect, Robert Smythson, had recently completed work on Wollaton Hall, the home of Sir Francis Willoughby in Nottinghamshire, which Bess had visited and no doubt studied with particular interest.

At Hardwick, Bess and Smythson followed an entirely original architectural plan, derived from designs by Andrea Palladio, then virtually unknown in England. Although the exterior of the house bears little relationship to the Palladianism that became fashionable at court through the work of Inigo Jones, it is nonetheless significant as the first evidence of Palladio's influence in England. Moreover, since the building represents a significant departure not only in design but also in the use of rooms by its inhabitants—it effectively turned the great hall, traditionally the center of ceremony and symbolic status in the male-dominated household, into an entrance lobby, shifting operations to the traditionally more gender-neutral great chamber—it can be viewed as a milestone in the history of women's patronage and evidence of a forward-looking approach to planning and design, particularly in terms of the politics and gendering of space.

[*See also* Art and Architecture *and* Elizabeth I of England.]

BIBLIOGRAPHY

Friedman, Alice T. "Architecture, Authority, and the Female Gaze: Planning and Representation in the Early Modern Country House." *Assemblage* 18 (Fall 1992): 40–61.

Girouard, Mark. *Hardwick Hall*. London: National Trust, 1989.

Girouard, Mark. *Robert Smythson and the Elizabethan Country House*. New Haven, Conn.: Yale University Press, 1983.

ALICE T. FRIEDMAN

BETHUNE, MARY McLEOD (1875–1955), educator and leader of black Americans. Often described as a female Booker T. Washington, Bethune was born in Mayesville, South Carolina, the fifteenth of the seventeen children of Samuel and Patsy McLeod, former slaves. As a child she worked in the cotton fields with her family. In an age when the blacks in America had no opportunity for education, Mary was fortunate in being able to go to a Presbyterian mission school in Mayesville. As the most motivated pupil, she was chosen to study at the Scotia Seminary (now Barber-Scotia College) in North Carolina. She moved on to spend a year at Dwight Moody's evangelical Institute for Home and Foreign Missions in Chicago. In 1898 she married Albertus Bethune, a salesman. They had a son, but the marriage was not a happy one, and her husband left her in 1907.

Bethune initially wanted to be a missionary in Africa but, after being rejected because of her color, she turned to education, as she believed that education had transformed her own life and was the key to the advancement of black Americans. She founded the Daytona Normal and Industrial Institute for Training Negro Girls in Daytona, Florida, with $1.50 in capital and four or five pupils. The school expanded as a result of Bethune's tireless efforts and charismatic personality. She was its president for many years.

In the first half of the twentieth century Bethune epitomized black women's battle for racial and gender equality and was referred to as the First Lady of American black women. She established various black women's organizations, including the National Association of Colored Women and the National Council of Negro Women. Bethune forged a coalition of hundreds of black women's organizations across the country.

Bethune was also involved in national politics and public affairs. During the New Deal era, the National Youth Administration was set up to inculcate democratic ideals in young people and give them vocational training. Bethune became its director of Negro affairs, the first black woman in U.S. history to hold such a high-level federal position. As the leading race representative in the administration of Franklin D. Roosevelt, she worked for black empowerment through education and employment.

During her years in Washington, D.C., Bethune organized a small but influential group of black officials who came to be known as the Black Cabinet, which put forward an agenda for social change beginning with the demand for equal opportunities for blacks. During World War II Bethune was special assistant to the secretary of war and assistant director of the Women's Army Corps. She became a close friend of Eleanor Roosevelt and was the only woman to be included in the U.S. delegation to the conference to draft the United Nations charter in San Francisco in 1946. Bethune was awarded the Haitian Medal of Honor and Merit and the Liberian Commander of the Order of the Star of Africa. She died of a heart attack in Daytona Beach on 18 May 1955.

In her multiple roles as educator, black woman activist, and stateswoman, Bethune held to her belief in the "unalienable right of citizenship for black America." In 1974 a memorial to her was constructed in Lincoln Park in Washington, D.C., the first statue on federal land to honor an African American man or woman.

[*See also* National Association of Colored Women; Roosevelt, Eleanor; *and* Terrell, Mary Church.]

BIBLIOGRAPHY

Hicks, Florence, ed. *Mary McLeod Bethune: Her Own Words of Inspiration.* Washington, D.C.: DARE Books, 1975.

Holt, Rackham. *Mary McLeod Bethune: A Biography.* Garden City, N.Y.: Doubleday, 1964.

McClusky, Audrey Thomas, and Elaine M. Smith, eds. *Mary McLeod Bethune: Building a Better World.* Bloomington and Indianapolis: Indiana University Press, 1999.

Smith, Elaine M. "Mary McLeod Bethune and the National Youth Administration." In *Clio Was a Woman: Studies in the History of American Women,* edited by Mabel E. Deutrich and Virginia C. Purdy. Washington, D.C.: Howard University Press, 1980.

APARNA BASU

BETROTHAL

This entry consists of two subentries:

Overview
Comparative History

Overview

Betrothal is essentially a promise that two people will be married at a later date. Derived from the Old English *treowth,* meaning "truth," the word "betrothal" and the archaic expression "to give one's troth" signify a pledge of marriage enacted in good faith. From classical antiquity through the early modern period, betrothal was considered a binding commitment. If one party broke the engagement, he or she or the person's family had to return the gifts received at the time of engagement and lose those one had given, and sometimes face even greater penalties. Depending on the time and place, a promise of marriage could be effected between a man and a woman, or between their families on behalf of the intended spouses.

In ancient Greece, betrothal was essentially an oral contract made between the woman's father and the bridegroom. The father would say, "I pledge [woman's name] for the purpose of producing legitimate children." The groom replied: "I accept." The bride was not even present.

In ancient Rome, a father often negotiated the *sponsalia* (betrothal) when his daughter was quite young, as young as six or seven. Once the girl's father and the prospective bridegroom had settled matters between them, the groom would give the bride a ring to wear on the third finger of her left hand—a custom we have preserved in the form of the traditional engagement ring. The young woman's father was expected to throw an engagement party.

In ancien régime France (that is, prior to the Revolution in 1789), children were often pledged by their families at an early age, with the understanding that they would wed after puberty. With the aim of uniting two high-status families among the nobility, or two properties among the peasantry, these long engagements and subsequent marriages often paid scant attention to the desires of the marriageable children.

A countertradition that required the mutual consent of the marrying couple had roots in both Roman and canon law. Although the father or father surrogate always had a say in Roman marriages, Roman law held that consent of both the bride and the groom was the primary determinant of a valid union. When the church took over the jurisdiction of marriage during the early Middle Ages, it downplayed the need for parental consent and foregrounded the dual will of the intended spouses.

The church was always favorable to betrothal. Saint Augustine of Hippo (354–430) had argued that its purpose was to stimulate affection while the couple waited for the actual union. Although betrothal was never made mandatory by canon law, by the beginning of the thirteenth century it was customary for banns to be read in church during three successive weeks, a period of time considered sufficient for public objections to be made, or for the couple to withdraw if either party had serious last-minute misgivings. Two different interpretations of the promise of marriage were expounded by twelfth-century canonists Gratian (Franciscus Gratianus; d. before 1159) and Peter Lombard (c. 1095–1160). In his *Decretum Gratiani* (c. 1140), also called the *Concordia discordantium canonum,* Gratian considered betrothal an irrevocable commitment. The words of betrothal initiated the marriage process. Lombard assigned less weight to the promise of marriage in his *Sententiae* (written 1145–1151), writing that only the promise stated at the wedding constituted matrimonial vows. Pope Alexander III (r. 1159–1181) accepted the promise of marriage in the future as unconsummated marriage. In medieval and Renaissance Spain Gratian's interpretation was the most popular and betrothal with mutual consent carried legal consequences.

Ancient Germanic law also included betrothal as a way station to marriage. Both were secular events arranged without the benefit of clergy. In the Latin narrative *Ruodleib,* written in Bavaria around 1050–1070, a spirited young lady had already prepared a pair of golden rings to give to her betrothed, whoever he might be. When she fell in love with a knight during the course of a banquet, she gave him the ring and before long they were "burning with love for one another" and desirous of being joined in the bond of marriage (Grocock, p. 147). Her widowed mother's consent and leave for the pair to spend time together constituted a form of betrothal. Much of their short engagement seems to have been whiled away playing dice, with the rings moving back and forth between the lovers whenever one of them won three games in a row.

The wedding was a public ceremony presided over by the knight's uncle, Ruodlieb. All present were asked to witness the couple's vows and the customary exchange of dowries. A gold ring affixed to the hilt of the bridegroom's sword was offered to the bride. She accepted it but only after he swore he would be as faithful to her as she would be to him. Such a forced declaration was undoubtedly at odds with prevailing norms, but it suggests that a new form of gender relations was already germinating in the eleventh century. It would take another hundred years for the courtly epic to carry the idea of romantic love throughout Europe, at least for members of the nobility.

In the Germanic regions betrothal was a much-honored practice, often on a par with the wedding itself. In fact, the couple were called bride (*Braut*) and groom (*Bräutigam*) from the day of betrothal until their marriage.

When Martin Luther (1483–1546) and Katharina von Bora (1499–1552) decided on their union in 1525, defying Catholic dictates for monks and nuns, their betrothal was considered the official marriage. It took place in the presence of four witnesses and was followed two weeks later by a public celebration attended by Luther's father and mother. By the second quarter of the sixteenth century, following Luther and other reformers, the right of the clergy to marry and the nonsacramental status of marriage became common Protestant doctrine.

In Great Britain a different set of betrothal customs had prevailed for centuries. Engagement centered on the ancient ritual of joining hands and vowing to wed, known as "handfasting." It was a popular practice that did not disappear with the religious innovations of the Reformation. Indeed, it lasted into the mid-eighteenth century, and in Scotland into the twentieth.

Handfasting was essentially a solemn, binding contract, and for many people it was the equivalent of marriage. Whether it occurred in the presence of two or three witnesses, as church courts insisted it should for the sake of verification, and by a clergyman, as the church strongly recommended, or whether it took place with no human witnesses, the handfasting ritual could not escape the eye of God. English men and women did not take their vows lightly because they believed that God was witness to their words.

There was no set formula for the betrothal vows. It was enough to promise, in words still in use today, to take the other person as one's "handfast" or "wedded" wife or husband. The Anglican Book of Common Prayer (1549) offered a version of betrothal that some couples used, although many continued to invent their own ceremonies, sometimes impulsively and without witnesses, which could cause trouble later if one of the parties tried to back out of the commitment.

Many prudent women asked their fathers, kinsmen, friends, employers, or clergymen to act as intermediaries in public handfasting ceremonies held in homes and inns and attended by numerous witnesses. A ring or coin was often given as a sign of betrothal, although any gift would suffice. Often the couple would pledge their troth over a cup of wine.

It was relatively common for country folk to consider themselves married from the moment of betrothal and to begin living together. Communities tended to be tolerant of postbetrothal sexual activity, as long as the couple wed before a baby's birth. For this reason a couple was expected to solemnize their nuptials not more than six months after betrothal. Handfasting may have been sufficient to bind the couple, but only a religious service could make the baby legitimate.

Although betrothal has subsisted into the twenty-first century—commonly called "engagement" in English, *fiançailles* in French, *Verlobung* in German, and *desposorios* in Spanish—it began to lose some of its binding quality about two hundred years ago. In France since 1804 the breaking of an engagement has been without legal sanction. Anglo-American "breach of promise" suits are now little more than a quaint memory. Today in the Western world, when even marriage vows are broken with relative ease, many people do not consider engagement a lifelong commitment.

[*See also* Codes of Law and Laws, *subentry* Medieval Roman and Canon Law; Europe; *and* Marriage.]

BIBLIOGRAPHY

Carlson, Eric Josef. *Marriage and the English Reformation.* Oxford and Cambridge, Mass.: Blackwell, 1994.

Hufton, Olwen. *The Prospect before Her: A History of Women in Western Europe.* New York: Knopf, 1996.

Grocock, C. W., ed. *The Ruodlieb.* Chicago: Bolchazy-Carducci; Warminster, U.K.: Aris and Phillips, 1985.

Treggiari, Susan. *Roman Marriage: Iusti Coniuges from the Time of Cicero to the Time of Ulpian.* Oxford: Clarendon Press; New York: Oxford University Press, 1991.

Yalom, Marilyn. *A History of the Wife.* New York: HarperCollins, 2001.

MARILYN YALOM

Comparative History

A betrothal is a promise to marry. As marriage customs differ from time to time and place to place, so do betrothal customs. In some cultures, young people have participated in marriage plans while other cultures may include only the parents in negotiations. The requirements for an acceptable match also differ according to cultural norms.

Betrothal before the Modern Era. In the ancient world, only free people could marry. In Rome, betrothal and marriage involved only a contract for the bride's dowry. In pre-Christian Scandinavia, the process of marriage began with the betrothal, which was simply a formal

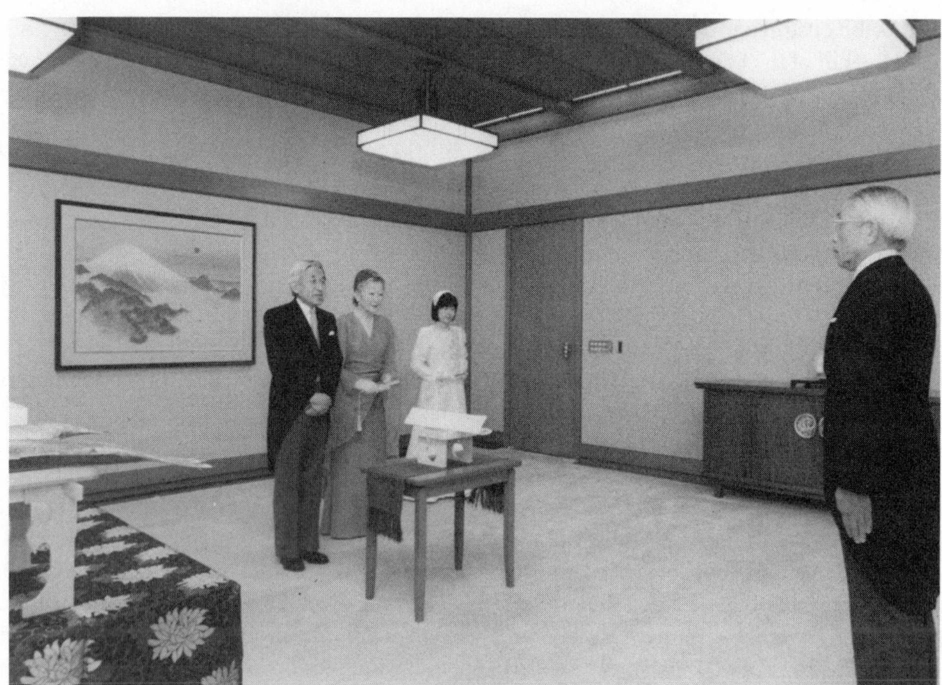

Betrothal. The Japanese princess Nori stands with Emperor Akihito and Empress Michiko during her betrothal ceremony in Tokyo, March 2005. REUTERS/Ho New

announcement of the engagement for a couple to marry soon. Among the Saami, or Laplanders, in northern Scandinavia, marriage customs included a long period of betrothal while gifts were exchanged between the families involved and the young man worked for his future in-laws. This delay of a year or more before marriage aimed to test the compatibility of the union. The entire process of marriage remained relatively informal.

With the coming of Christianity, matters changed. In Byzantium, the law required parents to find spouses for their children, but the wishes of the children were often considered. One legal case involved a girl who objected to her betrothal to a man whom she did not wish to marry. Accordingly, she alerted her beloved, who spirited her away. The girl was not unique and many abductions of brides were presumed to be the results of secret agreements. Conversely, a Byzantine woman who remained unmarried at twenty-five had the right to insist that her parents find her a husband.

By the Middle Ages, marriage contracts among the nobility involved detailed planning. Sometimes betrothals would be planned far in advance, with earnest money put down toward ensuring the terms were kept. The delicate negotiations could come to naught if the young man had sexual relations with a kinswoman of his intended bride. Because each family made as generous provisions as they could toward the marriage of their children and attempted to provide the new couple with the standard of living to which they had become accustomed at home, most young people consented to the arrangements and probably took part in them. Very few medieval ecclesiastical court cases cite force and fear as grounds for divorce.

Most betrothed girls in medieval France and England remained at home until they were old enough to marry. Potential brides were most often sent away to the groom's household as part of a peace treaty or when a girl's family was in a weak bargaining position—for example, if the groom's family was wealthier or more powerful, or if other candidates were competing for the marriage alliance. The same was not usually true for boys. This exchange could happen early in a child's life, as both boys and girls of the nobility were frequently betrothed at a very young age, despite twelfth-century papal decrees that set a minimum age of seven.

Not all young Europeans, however, had marriages arranged for them. Some were from poor families who had nothing to negotiate and, as a result, would either not marry or marry whom they pleased. Others were younger sons and daughters of wealthy families who were not part of their family's economic strategy. As a result, these children had greater independence. It is possible that in times of land shortage, family involvement in betrothal was less common because families had nothing with which to bargain. Accordingly, Irish peasants before the potato famine of the 1840s did not make elaborate arrangements for marriages because they had little property. After the migrations and deaths resulting from the famine, elaborate negotiations for marriage became more common.

Betrothal in the Middle East. While some European betrothal customs reflected Christian religious and legal traditions, some Middle Eastern betrothal customs were based on the rulings of the Talmud and of Maimonides (Moses ben Maimon; 1135–1204). Among the Jews of Yemen, before their migration to Israel upon its formation in 1948, minor girls were often betrothed in order to ensure them a good match. Once the parents had found a suitable husband, they betrothed their daughter while she was still a minor to forestall the possibility that someone else might marry her.

According to Jewish law, or Halacha, a woman is defined as a minor until she is twelve years old, as an adolescent for six months after her twelfth birthday, and thereafter as an adult. A minor girl cannot herself receive the money by which *kiddushin*, or betrothal, is accomplished, but a father has the authority to betroth his minor or adolescent daughter to anyone he wishes, and the betrothal is considered binding by law of the Torah (*de-oraita*, the highest and most absolute degree of religious authority). If the girl's father has died, her mother and brothers may betroth her as a minor only with her agreement. This betrothal is binding by rabbinic law. When she reaches adulthood, she comes under her own authority, as long as she is unmarried. At this time, she may be betrothed only with her consent.

According to Halacha, males are defined as minors until the age of thirteen. A male minor may not betroth a woman, and if he does, the betrothal is invalid. One 1778 case in Yemen involved a twelve-year-old boy who had betrothed a female minor on the condition that the agreement would be valid only if he desired her when the time for marriage came. At that point, he had lost interest and did not marry her. Sometime later, he sought to marry the girl's divorced sister. Had his earlier betrothal been considered valid, the second woman would have been considered his former wife's sister and so forbidden to him by a prohibition of the Torah. However, the betrothal was decreed to be not valid and the marriage was permitted.

The custom of separating the betrothal and the wedding was observed in the time of the Talmud and was continued in many places in Yemen throughout the history of the Jewish community there. In the first half of the twentieth century, however, the custom in Yemen was to hold the wedding the day after the betrothal ceremony, which took place in the evening. In modern Israel, most of these customs have disappeared because of the different social conditions prevailing in this nation. Today, the ordinances of the chief rabbinate forbid the betrothal of girls under the age of sixteen.

Within the Muslim-majority communities of the Middle East, betrothal practices varied. There is no betrothal, strictly speaking, under Islamic law because marriage is a contract that takes legal effect at the time of agreement, oral or written. In practice, however, it was common for a period of time to elapse between the agreement to the contract and the consummation of the marriage so that the contract could function as an article of betrothal. Guardians were empowered to arrange marriage contracts for their minor wards, both female and male, so that the practice of contracting minors in marriage, particularly girls, did occur; usually the marriage would be consummated when the girl came of age, as measured by puberty, or was otherwise deemed to be ready for marriage. Minors did not have the legal capacity to refuse such marriage arrangements. Once a girl came of age, however, some legal schools accorded her a "choice of puberty" as to whether she wished to remain in the marriage. Most Islamic legal schools agreed that women or men in their legal majority could not be contracted without their consent.

In the course of the twentieth century, most states in the Middle East have enacted minimum age of marriage laws that have eliminated the formal contracting of minor children in marriage. In many regions, it is common for a period of time to pass (anywhere from a few days to several years) between the signing of the marriage contract and the holding of a wedding party and consummation of the marriage, a period during which the couple is considered to be betrothed.

Betrothal in Asia. In Asia, gifts play an important role in betrothal customs. In Korea, an ornate gift box bearing goods from the groom's family is delivered by the groom's friends to the bride's family. Upon reaching the bride's house, an elaborate and often frustrating back-and-forth negotiation takes place between the man's friends and the woman's family. Eventually, the bride's family provides the groom's friends with money and food. At this point, the betrothal gifts are unwrapped and publicly displayed in the woman's house. While gifts from the groom's families are privileged and lavishly praised, gifts from the bride's side are assumed. This practice of long and drawn-out demand-and-resistance negotiations between the groom's friends and the bride's family is a new phenomenon in Korea and reflects the consumerist culture of the modern world.

When Mao Zedong took control of China, he sought a cultural revolution. In the 1950s and 1960s dowries and bride-price feasts were condemned as part of Mao's determination to destroy the economic-backed authority of the older generation over the younger one. The emancipated younger Chinese were thought to be more likely to embrace the Communist revolution. Accordingly, dowries and bride-price feasts disappeared while the age at marriage increased, but only because of the enforcement of government policies and law; Chinese culture did not fundamentally change. In the wake of Mao's death and as China has become increasingly capitalist, traditional rituals have resurged. Dowries and child betrothals are part of the response to the post-Mao economy, but this return to age-old customs is not uniform across the country. In the absence of state-imposed homogeneity, there emerge no set patterns, but rather piecemeal adaptations to local economic conditions.

One of these adaptations can be found in southern China. The opening of China has led a number of poor Chinese men to marry Vietnamese women. In southern China's autonomous region of Guangxi Zhuangzu, tradition demands that a would-be groom pay eight to ten thousand yuan to the bride's parents as a betrothal gift. Men who lack this money but who want the status and other benefits of marriage purchase a Vietnamese bride. Demand has led to a steady increase in the illegal trafficking of Vietnamese women to China as forced brides, volunteer brides, or prostitutes since the 1989 normalization of diplomatic relations between Vietnam and China. The anticipated shortage of marriageable Chinese women as a side effect of the government's one-child policy will likely increase both the price of betrothal gifts and the demand for foreign brides.

The consumer society has not reached Rajgarh, one of the poorest districts of the state of Madhya Pradesh in India. The position of women has been weakened in this region by the custom of child marriage. A survey conducted by the district administration between 1994 and 1996 showed the average age for betrothal for girls in the area as being 7.33 years; the age for boys was 9.17. *Sagai*, or betrothal, is usually accompanied by payment of some money by the girl's family to the boy's relatives. The marriage ceremony is conducted within a few years when the girl's family has collected sufficient money, usually following a good harvest. This practice is the same for different castes.

Early betrothal typically means that girls are still very young when they get married and when they bear their first child. Early birth has attendant poor effects on the health of the mother and the baby. As a result, the Rajgarh government undertook a public health campaign against child betrothal in 1996 that targeted the Dangi, Chamar, Sondhwadi, and Dhakkad caste communities. Caste-based *sammelans*, or public meetings, were successful. There has subsequently been a substantial reduction in child betrothals and, correspondingly, the number of child marriages.

Betrothal in Africa. Child marriage remains an issue in Africa. While Islamic law requires the consent of both parties, a girl's marriage is often arranged by her parents as part of tribal tradition. The groom pays a bride-price in cash or livestock, typically cattle, to the parents. As the girl is not present at the betrothal ceremony, she may not even know of it until afterwards. In Nigeria, girls may be betrothed from the age of nine to older men. Among the aristocracy, girls are given as gifts to the rich in order to cement the bond between families. In this highly patriarchal society, women do not have a say in marriage agreements.

African child marriages are complicated by the spread of HIV/AIDS throughout the continent. In Tanzania, a girl and her parents are expected to be honored when a man proposes marriage. It is not uncommon for men, having settled elsewhere, to order brides from their native community. The parents are paid for the bride. Often, the young woman, typically a girl, has very little say in the matter, especially if she has not previously been married. Since she is presumed to be a virgin, her parents can do as they please, regardless of her opinion. Islamic legal principles dictate that a woman cannot be forced into a union but, in practice, it does occur. In some cases, the Tanzanian would-be bride is not even asked for her consent. *Kadhis*, or marriage brokers, are empowered to contract marriages for Tanzanians and they are supposed to protect the woman's interests. However, at the start of the twenty-first century, *kadhis* have not yet instituted a premarital screening process of the man's health, background, or disposition. As a result, marriages are arranged in which HIV is spread to the unsuspecting woman. In cases of an older bride, women sometimes take a more active part in the betrothal. However, requesting an HIV test as part of the marriage arrangements can be seen as an attempt to shame the would-be groom and, as such, is discouraged by parents eager for the match.

Betrothal precedes and cements the intention to marry. When marriage is viewed as the union of two families as well as two people, betrothal has been a complex ritual. When marriage is seen as simply the joining together of two individuals for their own benefit, betrothal has been a simple matter. Yet the effects of betrothal have historically been very different for men and women. As the English jurist William Blackstone noted in the eighteenth century, husband and wife become one and that one is the husband. With her entire identity and future in the body of her husband, betrothal has historically been a far riskier proposition for a woman than for a man.

[*See also* Age of Consent and Child Marriage; AIDS; Christianity; Honor and Shame; Islam; Judaism; Marriage; Marriage Brokers; Religion; *and entries on countries and regions mentioned in this article.*]

BIBLIOGRAPHY

Ariès, Philippe, and Georges Duby, eds. *A History of Private Life*. Vol. 1, *From Pagan Rome to Byzantium*, edited by Paul Veyne. Cambridge, Mass.: Belknap Press of Harvard University Press, 1987.

Clare, Anthony. *Lovelaw: Love, Sex, and Marriage around the World*. London: BBC Publications, 1986.

Davis, Deborah, and Stevan Harrell, eds. *Chinese Families in the Post-Mao Era*. Berkeley, Calif.: University of California Press, 1993.

Gaimani, Aharon. "Marriage and Divorce Customs in Yemen and Eretz Israel." *Nashim: A Journal of Jewish Women's Studies and Gender Issues* no. 11 (Spring 2006): 43–83.

Greenstein, Amy Lila. "The Betrothal Fiasco." *Lilith* 20, no. 3 (September 1995): 4.
Hanawalt, Barbara A. *The Ties That Bound: Peasant Families in Medieval England*. New York: Oxford University Press, 1986.
Kendall, Laurel. *Getting Married in Korea: Of Gender, Morality, and Modernity*. Berkeley: University of California Press, 1996.
Maoulidi, Salma. "HIV/AIDS in Tanzania: Why Are Girls Still Being Buried Alive in Muslim Communities?" *Women in Action* (March 31, 2003): 25–27.
Monsarrat, Ann. *And the Bride Wore... : The Story of the White Wedding*. London: Gentry, 1973.
Murray, Jacqueline, ed. *Love, Marriage, and Family in the Middle Ages: A Reader*. Peterborough, Ontario: Broadview Press, 2001.
Rapoport, Jossef. *Marriage, Money, and Divorce in Medieval Islamic Society*. Cambridge, U.K., and New York: Cambridge University Press, 2005.

CARYN E. NEUMANN

BEYALA, CALIXTHE (b. 1961), Cameroonian novelist, essayist, and feminist. Calixthe Beyala was born shortly after Cameroon became independent from France. The sixth of twelve children, she obtained her early education in Cameroon, spending her childhood in Douala and the Central African Republic. She is of the Eton ethnic group and considers French her mother tongue. She completed her secondary and university studies in France and Spain and has lived in Europe since she was seventeen. She lives in France with her daughter, having resided longer in France than in Cameroon, and writes for major French publishing houses, mainly for a French and transnational audience. Beyala's career breaks with convention.

She is one of the rare African writers who earns her living by writing full-time and has made a name for herself as an African feminist in Paris's highly competitive environment. She has produced a steady stream of novels since 1987 at the rate of at least one every two years. In the media limelight because of controversy that resulted from two plagiarism trials, she has also been a spokesperson for greater racial inclusiveness in the French media through the group she founded, Collectif Egalité (Equality Collective). She has published two influential essays, one on her feminist struggle, "*Lettre d'une africaine à ses soeurs occidentals*" (Letter from an African Woman to Her Western Sisters, 1995), the other on racism in French society, "*Lettre d'une afro-française à ses compatriotes*" (Letter from an Afro-French Woman to Her Compatriots, 2000).

Beyala is an icon of literary success despite the controversy surrounding her work. She won the Grand Prix Littéraire de l'Afrique Noire in 1993; the Prix François Mauriac in 1994; and France's premier literary award, the Grand Prix du Roman de l'Academie Française, for her novel *Les honneurs perdus* (Lost Honors) in 1996. Her success reflects the change that has occurred in African literature, originally considered a male province even though women began to write in the 1960s (for example, Ama Atta Aidoo, Flora Nwapa, and Thérèse Kuoh-Moukoury). The women's movement, and the increased scholarly emphasis on gender issues that resulted from that movement, stimulated greater interest in works by women—for example, Mariama Bâ's *Une si longue lettre* (1978; Eng. trans., *So Long a Letter*, 1981). Beyala's work initially drew the attention of feminist critics because it pushed the patriarchal boundaries of African literature, breaking with conventional portrayals of women, the family, childhood, sexuality, eroticism, and Africa. Critics later questioned Beyala's seemingly opportunistic portrayal of Africa and Africans, which appeared to play into Western stereotypes. However, portraying "authentic" Africa and Africans has never been her aim.

In her novels Beyala has experimented with aspects of the French language as well as a wide range of settings, narrative perspectives, and subjects—some of them taboo—to portray African women in a new light. Her works include her early African trilogy, *C'est le soleil qui m'a brûlée* (1987; English trans., *The Sun Hath Looked upon Me*, 1996), *Tu t'appelleras Tanga* (1988; English trans., *Your Name Shall Be Tanga*, 1996), and *Seul le diable le savait* (Only the Devil Knew, 1990); followed by two "Parisian novels," *Le petit prince de Belleville* (1992; English trans., *Loukoum: The "Little Prince" of Belleville*, 1995) and *Maman a un amant* (Mommy Has a Lover, 1993); and four novels portraying naive African women who eventually find their way to France and to autonomy. Three more novels are set in Africa. In *La petite fille du réverbère* (The Little Girl under the Street Light, 1998), the setting is once again Beyala's childhood urban neighborhood, as it is in her erotic novel *Femme nue, femme noire* (Nude Woman, Black Woman, 2003). *La plantation* (The Plantation, 2005) is set in Zimbabwe's white community. With the publication of *L'homme qui m'offrait le ciel* (The Man Who Offered Me Heaven) in 2007, Beyala further explores the impact of exile. The failure of postcolonial African societies and the new identities that Africans in exile must forge are central to her work.

Beyala's African trilogy offers one of the earliest portrayals of postcolonial urban poverty and its impact on women. New family dynamics emerge, particularly as incest and prostitution transform mother-daughter relationships and cause her young female protagonists to desperately seek agency in a patriarchal society that exploits them. In her Parisian novels Beyala's gaze shifts to the African immigrant community as she continues to explore childhood, family dynamics, and female autonomy. In this context immigration empowers women and their children, who gain new identities, while the old African patriarchy seems to progressively fade away. At the same time Beyala's innocent African child narrator subverts the French Republic's claims regarding race and class. Among the novels that use an emancipatory journey motif that leads female protagonists from Africa to France, *Les honneurs perdus* is the best known and most controversial, having won the French Academy's highest award despite its author's use of plagiarism.

In spite of the controversy surrounding her writing, Beyala continues to explore the ways women survive the contemporary clash of cultures and class that ultimately result from colonization and that continue to have multiple impacts on Africa and Africans. Her novels follow a pattern that offers survival to African women who manage to extricate themselves from the clutches of what Beyala views as the failure of Africa.

[*See also* Feminism *and* Literature.]

BIBLIOGRAPHY

Cazenave, Odile M. *Rebellious Women: The New Generation of Female African Novelists.* Boulder, Colo.: Lynne Reinner, 2000. In-depth analysis of Beyala's early novels.

D'Almeida, Irène Assiba. *Francophone African Women Writers: Destroying the Emptiness of Silence.* Gainesville: University of Florida Press, 1994. Chapter on early novels.

Gallimore, Rangira Béatrice. *L'oeuvre romanesque de Calixthe Beyala: Le renouveau de l'écriture féminine en Afrique francophone sub-saharienne.* Paris: L'Harmattan, 1997. A complete study of Beyala's early works; includes an interview with the writer.

Harrow, Kenneth W. *Less Than One and Double: A Feminist Reading of African Women's Writing.* Portsmouth, N.H.: Heinemann, 2002. Chapters on *Tu t'appelleras Tanga* and *Le petit prince de Belleville.*

Hitchcott, Nicki. *Calixthe Beyala: Performances of Migration.* Liverpool, U.K.: Liverpool University Press, 2006. Thorough analysis of Beyala's Parisian novels; includes an examination of the relationship between her fictional characters and the character that Beyala herself projects upon the French literary and social scene.

Hitchcott, Nicki. "Calixthe Beyala: Prizes, Plagiarism, and 'Authenticity.'" *Research in African Literatures* 37, no. 1 (Spring 2006): 100–109. Details contradictions of Beyala the "fake" (convicted plagiarist) and "authentic" African writer and winner of literary prizes.

Mortimer, Mildred. "Whose House Is This? Space and Place in Calixthe Beyala's *C'est le soleil qui m'a brûlée* and *La petite fille du réverbère.*" *World Literature Today* 73, no. 3 (Summer 1999): 467–474. Compares Mariama Bâ and Beyala, applying Bhaba's concept of home to two novels.

Nfah-Abbenyi, Juliana Makuchi. *Gender in African Women's Writing.* Bloomington: Indiana University Press, 1997. Chapter discusses Beyala's use of sexuality and lesbianism.

ELOISE A. BRIÈRE

BHAGO, MAI (fl. 1699–1708), Sikh soldier and bodyguard for Guru Gobind Singh. Mai Bhago was born the daughter of Malo Shah in Jhabal village in what is now the Amritsar district of Punjab. Hers was a family of the Dhillon clan of the *jat* (peasant proprietors) of what is now northern India and Pakistan. She was married to Nidhan Singh of the Varaich clan who lived in Patti village.

Because her family had a close relationship with the founders of the Sikh faith—a religion that syncretizes Hinduism and Islam—Bhago was received twice by Guru Tegh Bahadur (1621–1675), who established the city of Anandpur Sahib in 1665. Here in 1699 his son, the next guru, Gobind Singh (1666–1708), formally established the casteless and militant community of the pure, the Khalsa. Bhago was in attendance with her family, received baptism, and was afterward known as Bhago Kaur ("Lioness"), the name taken by all Sikh women.

Bhago next makes an appearance in 1705. The Sikhs had long been under siege by the Mughal emperors and by the hill tribes. Alarmed by the rapid expansion of the Sikh army, the Rajput Raja of Bilaspur appealed to the Mughal emperor Aurangzeb, whose forces began the siege of Anandpur Sahib in May 1705. In December the Sikhs evacuated under a promise of safe escort; in the confusion that followed, Gobind Singh fled with two sons and some forty Sikhs. Pursued by the Mughal army and attacked at Chamkaur, Gobind Singh lost his two sons and all but five followers; two stayed behind to cover his escape.

At Dina, Gobind Singh gathered followers and then marched to Khidrana (Ferozepur); there he took a position on a hillock overlooking a water hole. Bhago and the *jathedar* (leader of volunteers) Mahan Singh arrived at the head of some forty Sikhs from her home district of Majha who had deserted during the siege of Anandpur and whom she and the other women persuaded to go back to the guru and apologize. They managed to intercept the Mughal troops at the water hole and, supported by fire from the hill, drove them off (on 29 December). Although badly wounded, Bhago was the only one to survive the skirmish. At her request, she became a bodyguard to Guru Gobind Singh until he was assassinated at Nanded in 1708.

She settled in the town of Jinvara, eleven kilometers from Bidar (Karnataka), and eventually died there. Her house, a shrine since her death, is now maintained by a committee as Gurdwara Tap Asthan Mai Bhago. She is revered as a saint and as a representative of martial women of the Sikhs, who respect women as spiritual equals. Her role as a cross-dresser and soldier was unusual for both her time and her religion, since Sikh women were not supposed to participate in the martial arts.

[*See also* Hinduism; India; *and* Islam.]

BIBLIOGRAPHY

Madra, Amandeep Singh, and Parmijit Singh, eds. *Sicques, Tigers, or Thieves: Eyewitness Accounts of the Sikhs, 1606–1809.* New York: Palgrave Macmillan, 2004.

Ralhan, O. P., ed. *Great Gurus of the Sikhs 4: Guru Tegh Bahadur and Govind Singh.* Delhi, India: Anmol, 1997.

S. A. THORNTON

***BHAKTI* MOVEMENT.** The *bhakti* movement, based on intense personal devotion, was an unequaled cultural and spiritual movement of dissent in India. It spanned many centuries, starting in South India as early as the sixth century and continuing right up to the seventeenth century in North India. The movement's power lay in the fact that the relationship established with God was unmediated by priest, temple, or sacred text, drawing in individuals from all walks of life. The movement enriched and deepened vernacular regional cultures and has left a lasting legacy in the vivid and inspiring works of the people—both women and men—who claimed the truth of the heart and lived by this. Women from all strata of life, from the aristocratic to the ostracized, who had before been denied access to scriptural knowledge and to a legitimate spiritual expression, were drawn into the cultural efflorescence of this devotional upsurge.

The *bhakti* movement has been variously interpreted. It has been identified as socially radical because artisan groups—often seen as "untouchables"—who were growing in strength in the southern region as well as in the expansion of the Delhi sultanate (and after) asserted their direct relationships with God in his manifold manifestations, insisting that the Brahmans had no prior or sole claim to this. The movement has been characterized as a cultural efflorescence because a vernacular and popular religion eroded the edifice of a ritualistic Brahmanism. It has been hailed as the beginning of a humanist movement in which the individual's worth and dignity lay outside the inscriptions of caste, gender, sect and arid, intellectual knowledge. It has also been considered the philosophical foundation of principles of individual rights and individual worth, and thus the perfect medium through which individual women *bhaktas* declared themselves—in striking words and imagery—loved by a lord of their choice.

The significance of the *bhakti* movement lies in its heterogeneous social base. In the south it included women such as Mahadevi Akka and Karaikalammaiyar, both of whom were of the Virashaiva tradition and who, defying social taboos, discarded the codes of female modesty, left their husbands, and wandered naked throughout the land. The renunciation of family and community for the life of a peripatetic devotee granted women mobility and hitherto unknown freedoms. Wedded princesses such as Mirabai, female servants such as Janabai, and skilled courtesans such as Kanhopatra all formed part of a movement that drew in many from ostracized social groups. The tenacity of each of these women in cultivating a life of the spirit in the face of tremendous odds is a moving testimony to their quest.

There are many historical questions that require further scholarship—the relationship between *bhakti* and Sufi mysticism, which came together at times in a person such as Lal Ded in Kashmir; the relationship between the women *bhaktas'* spiritual transgressions and the experiences of their female audiences and followers; and the relationships between the lives of the women *bhaktas* and the hagiographies that were later consolidated. There still remains the writing of a history that foregrounds the women *bhaktas'* inner desires and imaginings rather than using their lives and sayings as positivistic social texts. There also remains the writing of a history that shows how the nature of the supreme and the immutable was radically transformed by the women's remarkable imaginary and visionary relationships.

[*See also* Akka, Mahadevi; Hinduism; India; Mirabai; *and* Spiritualism.]

BIBLIOGRAPHY

Manushi, Tenth Anniversary Issue: Women Bhakta Poets, nos. 50–52 (1989). An insightful collection of essays by scholars; includes translations of song verses.

Tharu, Susie, and K. Lalita, eds. *Women Writing in India, 600 B.C. to the Present*. Vol. 1: *600 B.C. to the Early Twentieth Century*. New York: Feminist Press at the City University of New York, 1991. A valuable and accessible introduction to the creativity of the women in the *bhakti* movement, containing verse translations from the original.

PARITA MUKTA

BHUTTO, BENAZIR (b. 1953), prime minister of Pakistan and leader of the Pakistan People's Party. Bhutto was elected prime minister of Pakistan in 1988, at the age of thirty-five. She succeeded Mohammad Zia-ul-Haq, who had ruled from 1977. Bhutto is the eldest daughter of another former prime minister, the late Zulfikar Ali Bhutto, and Begum Nusrat Bhutto. Zulfikar Bhutto belonged to a Sunni Muslim landed family of Sind, and Nusrat was a Shia of Iranian origin. Bhutto was born on 21 June 1953 in Karachi. She attended the Convent of Jesus and Mary in Karachi and a boarding school in Muree. She then went to Harvard and Oxford universities. She was an excellent speaker and became president of the famed Oxford Union, a stepping-stone for many British prime ministers.

Within a fortnight of her return to Pakistan in 1977, her father was overthrown by his army chief of staff, General Zia-ul-Haq, arrested, tried for criminal conspiracy, and found guilty. He was finally hanged in 1979. Bhutto and her mother were tortured by Zia's regime, imprisoned, and exiled for nine years. In 1984, in London, Bhutto organized the Pakistan People's Party (PPP), with her mother as president. She mobilized world opinion against Zia's violation of human rights, and the PPP forged an alliance with its earlier adversary to form the Movement for the Restoration of Democracy.

On her return to Lahore in 1986, after Zia had lifted martial law, Bhutto received a tumultuous welcome. Crowds thronged to see her and hear her speak. In deference to Pakistan's social ethos, she agreed to an arranged marriage to Asif Zardai, a businessman, in 1987. Zia, along with his senior military aides, died in an airplane crash in August 1988, paving the way for national elections. The election dates were deliberately fixed for November in the hope that Bhutto's pregnancy would prevent her from campaigning. Various other attempts were made to keep her out of the election. The PPP did not get a majority in the National Assembly but managed to emerge as the single largest party. On 2 December 1988 Bhutto was sworn in as prime minister.

Bhutto faced enormous domestic and international challenges, and the domination of the army, revivalist theologians, and bureaucracy allowed her little leeway to make significant changes in economic or foreign policies. Her government was accused of being corrupt and incompetent, and she was removed from her position as prime minister by a presidential decree in 1990. She was reelected in 1993 but again dismissed by a presidential decree in 1996, and the supreme court upheld the dismissal. She was charged with corruption, laundering money, and taking bribes. In 1999 she and her husband were sentenced to five years' imprisonment and disqualified from participating in political activities for five years. She voluntarily went into exile in Dubai and has since lived there and in London.

[*See also* Pakistan.]

BIBLIOGRAPHY

Bhutto, Benazir. *Daughter of Destiny: An Autobiography.* New York: Simon and Schuster, 1989.

Hughes, Libby. *Benazir Bhutto: From Prison to Prime Minister.* Minneapolis: Dillon Press, 1990.

Zakaria, Rafiq. *The Trial of Benazir Bhutto: An Insight into the Status of Women in Islam.* Petaling Jaya, Selangor Darul Ehsan, Malaysia: Pelanduk Publications, 1990.

APARNA BASU

BIAN DONGXUAN (628–711), a Chinese Daoist woman saint of the Tang dynasty (618–907). Bian was born near what is now Beijing, an unimportant town at the time. As a child she secretly fed starving animals, showing "hidden virtue," highly prized in Daoist ethics. Later she performed acts of physical self-discipline, refused to marry, and cared for her aging parents. After their deaths she entered a convent, adopting the name Dongxuan (Grotto Mystery). She helped support the convent with her fantastic weaving, and her kindness to animals was said to have protected her convent from rats. She followed two Daoist paths to immortality: self-starvation and constant ingestion of elixir medicines, practices that fall squarely within Daoist traditions of asceticism and alchemy. Her extremes alarmed her sisters, but she persevered. Legend has it that Daoist deities rewarded her by sending her an elixir of immortality, delivered by a comical old man whom only she recognized as a Daoist immortal. Her followers believed that she ended her life by flying up to the heavens on a fragrant cloud, in front of a huge audience of reverent admirers.

Bian's life resonates with modern medical issues as well as with medieval religious issues. An example of severe asceticism, Bian embodies the current debate about predominantly female disorders such as anorexia nervosa and self-mutilation, behaviors that some psychologists have interpreted as attempts on the part of practitioners to heal themselves and exercise some self-determination in their own lives. We might understand both medieval religious practices and modern women better if we compare them. Bian Dongxuan's fasting and ingesting drugs that led directly to her death might look at first like deranged self-destruction. But her own interpretation of her behavior makes sense. She believed that she was approaching perfection and transcendence through her rigorous physical practices.

Bian Dongxuan's life also sheds light on distinctions between Daoist religious practice for women and that for men in medieval China. Bian Dongxuan, as part of her austerities, fasted and remained celibate. In general, Daoist women gave what they could give up and controlled what they could control: their bodies and the bodily functions of eating and childbearing. Chinese male ascetics tended to give up wealth, public position, and family ties, their own arena of action and so their biggest sacrifices. But we must not make too much of this distinction because many male Daoist practitioners also fasted and remained celibate. Apparently, the normal family activities of eating and reproducing were harmful to the religious aspirations of both male and female Daoists.

Bian Dongxuan's biography illustrates competition between medieval Chinese Buddhists and Daoists. In writing about her, Daoist writers take back virtues, such as compassion, that Mahāyāna Buddhists had claimed as exclusively theirs. Bian's "hidden virtue" was the Daoist version of compassion. Bian herself was a model Daoist saint, compelling enough to rival any Buddhist cult figure.

Bian is also associated with the Tang royal family and its mandate to rule. Bian's biographers imply that the deep interest of Emperor Xuanzong (r. 712–756) in Daoism and the ordination of his sister Yuzhen were both a result of Bian Dongxuan's influence.

Bian Dongxuan's life also affirms the Confucian family values held by Tang royalty and literati officials. She showed filial piety in caring for her aging parents and mourning them passionately. Her skill in weaving reveals her womanly virtue and discipline. In these ways she fulfilled the ideals of Confucian female propriety even as her fasting and refusing to marry flew in the face of everything that the traditional patrilineal family holds dear. Yet Bian is also one of the rare Daoists and even rarer women who were believed to have attained the highest form of transcendence available to human beings: ascending to heaven in broad daylight. She represents female perfection from the Daoist perspective.

[*See also* China, *subentry* Imperial Period; Li Ye; Lu Meiniang; World Religions; *and* Wu Zetian, Empress.]

BIBLIOGRAPHY

Cahill, Suzanne. "Pien Tung-hsuan: A Taoist Woman Saint of the Tang Dynasty (618–907)." In *Women Saints in World Religions*, edited by Arvind Sharma, pp. 205–220. Albany: State University of New York Press, 2000. Includes translations of biographies from the Tang and Song dynasties.

Du Guangting. *Divine Traces of the Daoist Sisterhood: "Records of the Assembled Transcendents of the Fortified Walled City."* Translated by Suzanne Cahill. Magdalena, N.M.: Three Pines Press, 2006. Translated and annotated biographies of female Daoist saints from the Tang and Song dynasties, with an introduction.

SUZANNE CAHILL

BIBI KHANUM (1858/59–1921), Iranian writer, educator, and women's rights activist. Also known as Bibi Khanum Astarabadi, her father, Muhammad Baqir, was the chief of Astarabad brigade. Her mother, Khadijeh Khanum, was a tutor in the royal household of Shukuh al-Saltaneh (1837–1891), one of the permanent wives of Nasir al-Din Shah (r. 1848–1896). Bibi Khanum was educated at home by her mother and became an educator herself, establishing in 1906 in her Tehran residence one of the first modern schools for girls. She also wrote numerous articles advocating women's rights, especially in education and family relations. When she was twenty-two or twenty-three, Bibi Khanum and Musá Vaziri (c. 1862–1925), a young immigrant four years her junior who was from the Caucasus and was later an army officer, fell in love. Because of opposition from Bibi Khanum's family, it was another four years before they married. They had five sons and two daughters. Their two daughters, Mawlud (d. 1952) and Afzal (1891–1980), became educators and writers for women's rights. Two of their sons are also well known: Hasan'ali Vaziri (d. 1954) became a prominent painter, and 'Alinaqi Vaziri (1897–1979) is known as the father of modern Iranian music.

Much of what we know about Bibi Khanum, including her marital life, its troubles, and her husband's taking a temporary wife—which she relates as a tale of warning for other women—comes from autobiographical sections in her manuscript *Ma'ayib al-rijal* (Vices of Men). Written in 1894 and not published until 1992, it must have had a fair circulation at the time—four manuscript copies, including one in her own handwriting, exist in archival collections. *Vices of Men* was Bibi Khanum's response to *Ta'dib al-niswan* (Disciplining Women), a male-centered, often misogynous text written in the mid-1880s in the tradition of satirical books of advice to men about how to treat their wives and train their daughters.

Bibi Khanum begins her text autobiographically, explaining her social and educational background. The text is made up of two sections; the first is a direct, wittily angry response to *Disciplining Women*. The second is addressed to other women ("my sisters," as she calls them) and is her advice and warnings about men, in particular as husbands. Bibi Khanum interweaves her text with classical poetry and composes her own occasional verses. Drawing at once on Islamic sources and Persian high poetry, polite and coarse language, and oral and written traditions, Bibi Khanum produces a text grounded in several cultural contexts. As a text conceived in a female homosocial space and addressed to other women, it connects us to the language of that cultural space, a language of feminine transgressive irony that was later to be rescripted as vulgar and rejected as backward.

Vices of Men is a consistently and remarkably female-centered text. Although Bibi Khanum's narrative, rhetorical, and intertextual ties with classical literary and religious sources transfer the authority of past culture to her text, her particular rewritings and reinterpretive gestures produce a highly subversive and innovative text. Aside from the significance of the text as a woman's response to a popular misogynous tract, it is also important because of its composition at a time when women's literacy was on the rise and women were beginning to publish in more public domains, such as newspapers—a process that had enormous repercussions in changing women's language.

[*See also* Iran *and* Literature.]

BIBLIOGRAPHY

Astarabadi, Bibi Khanum. *Ma'ayib al-rijal* (Vices of Men). Edited by Afsaneh Najmabadi. Chicago: Midland Printers, 1992.

Javadi, Hasan, Manijeh Marashi, and Simin Shekarloo, eds. *Ruyaru'i-i zan va mard dar 'asr-i Qajar* (Confrontations between Men and Women in the Qajar Period). Evanston, Ill.: Kānūn-i Pizhūhish-i Tārīkh-i Zanān-i Īrān; Bethesda, Md.: Shirkat-i Jahān, 1992.

Najmabadi, Afsaneh. "Veiled Discourse—Unveiled Bodies." *Feminist Studies* 19, no. 3 (Fall 1993): 487–518.

Powys Mathers, E., trans. *The Education of Wives*. Vol. 3 of *Eastern Love*. London: John Rodker, 1927. An English translation of *Vices of Men*.

Vaziri, Afzal, and Narjis Mihrangiz Mallah. *Bibi Khanum Astarabadi and Khanum Afzal Vaziri*. Edited by Afsaneh Najmabadi. New York: Scripting and Visaging Women Series, 1996. A collection of autobiographical essays, articles, and historical notes by and about these two women, in Persian.

AFSANEH NAJMABADI

BINODINI DASI (1863–c. 1941), Indian actress. Called by contemporary newspapers the "Star of the Native Stage" for her excellence as an actress in the fledgling Bengali public theater, Binodini Dasi now circulates in cultural memory as an icon of the redeemed sinner.

Born in a poor, low-caste, woman-headed household in colonial Calcutta (now Kolkata), Binodini was a precocious child who was recruited to the stage at age ten in order to support her family. She was catapulted into a heroine's role in only her second play with the Bengal Theatre company. Subsequently mentored at the National Theatre by Girishchandra Ghosh (1844–1912)—one of the foremost dramaturges of the time, with whom she was to have a close if turbulent relationship—she was also encouraged to write and publish poetry. Her extraordinary versatility as a heroine of light operatic pieces, mythological plays, and literary historical romances matched her comic roles in farces and pantomimes. It is an indication of the exigencies of the native actress performing in colonial India that she played Britannia in the historical *Palashir Juddho* (Battle of Plassey, 1878).

Binodini's career coincided with a period of Hindu revivalism, and she was applauded for a range of roles in a series of successful devotional (*bhakti*) plays. Contemporary accounts singled out her highly charged performance as Chaitanya (1486–1533), the charismatic (male) saint whose advocacy of devotionalism as the mode of salvation had broken down existing caste hierarchies. Binodini as Chaitanya was blessed by an equally charismatic sage, Ramakrishna (1836–1886), after a performance of *Chaitanya-Lila, Part I* in 1884. This incident has since acquired status as a legend in all discourse on the actress and her times.

Binodini's own narratives, written at different points of her long life after she abruptly left the theater at age twenty-three in 1886, offer a more complex and passionate articulation of her own location and the material conditions of performance. "Abhinetrir Atmakatha" (An Actress's Autobiography, 1910) and "Amar Abhinetri Jiban" (My Life as an Actress, 1924–1925) were originally serialized in contemporary theater magazines; the former was the nucleus of *Amar Katha* (My Story) brought out in two books by Binodini in 1912–1913. In these remarkable testaments of the pleasures and perils of performance as experienced by a first-generation professional actress in colonial India, Binodini charts the betrayals within the theater world, the death of her beloved daughter, and the companionship and loss of the upper-class patron whose death left her isolated once again, alongside humorous accounts of her tours with the company to places as distant as Delhi and Lahore (now in Pakistan).

Performing at a time when wages, mobility, and public display marked a woman as a prostitute, Binodini was given the hyphenated identity of a prostitute–actress (*beshya-abhinetri*). Aware of the talent and status of her Western compatriots (Ellen Terry and Sarah Bernhardt in particular), she recorded her achievements and her aspirations, her crises of faith and her professional pride. Besides providing an invaluable account of the formative decades of professional proscenium theater in Bengal, Binodini Dasi's writings stand outside the corpus of the fairly extensive range of women's personal narratives that have come to us from various parts of the subcontinent from the mid-eighteenth century.

[*See also* India *and* Performing Arts.]

BIBLIOGRAPHY

Acharya, N., and Chattopadhyay Soumitra, eds. *Binodini Dasi: Amar Katha o Anyano Rachana.* Calcutta, India: Subarnorekha, 1987.

Bhattacharya, Rimli, ed. and trans. *Binodini Dasi: "My Story" and "My Life as an Actress."* New Delhi, India: Kali for Women, 1998.

Dasi, Binodini. *Amar Katha* (My Story). Part 1. Calcutta, India: Great Eden Press, 1912.

RIMLI BHATTACHARYA

BIOLOGY. Biology is living physical reality: the material substances and processes that enable human beings and other creatures to exist. The question of how women's biology affected women throughout history is, however, quite controversial. Many people intuitively believe that the characteristics they associate with women are biological in origin and therefore immutable. In 1935, however, Margaret Mead, in *Sex and Temperament*, demonstrated that any characteristic that one culture considers feminine, such as being nurturing or warlike, is considered unfeminine by another culture.

Many feminist thinkers have therefore distinguished between sex (the biological difference between men and women) and gender (the cultural interpretation of sex). Because gender varies enormously among different cultures, they argue, both women and men must possess the full range of human potential, the expression of which is shaped by cultural beliefs and practices.

Focusing exclusively on cultural constructions, however, risks a disembodied worldview. Women's history lacks a significant dimension if it ignores women's experience of sexuality, pregnancy, childbirth, and breast-feeding. Many women's lives have been shaped, or even ended, by the demands of reproduction.

Europeans traditionally saw men and women as having effectively the same body plan, which in women was considered defective. According to the Greek physician Galen (129–c. 199/216), women lacked vital heat and therefore kept internally what should be external.

Seventeenth-century anatomists drew women's reproductive organs as if they were internal versions of male genitalia.

By 1800 European society had become fascinated by differences between the sexes. Scientists and writers catalogued these differences and used them to prescribe different activities for men and women. For example, many people believed that women's ovaries are easily damaged by intellectual or physical work. Women therefore had to be protected from too much education and from entering the professions, though no one applied the same logic to women who worked as servants or factory laborers.

Many twentieth-century feminists attributed such beliefs about biology to a cultural desire to make gender seem innate. If anatomy is destiny—if women's biology affects every aspect of their being and predestines them for certain social roles—then a woman who defies those social roles is abnormal. If, on the contrary, the belief that anatomy is destiny is a cultural ideology, a belief promulgated because it justifies the status quo, then challenging that belief will help women break out of sexist constrictions.

In the 1980s several female professional biologists argued that ideas about gender had deformed the science of biology. Ruth Hubbard, Anne Fausto-Sterling, and Ruth Bleier critiqued scientific studies that supported popular beliefs about gender differences. These studies, they claimed, were methodologically flawed and deeply skewed in their assumptions and analyses. The resulting bad science not only reinforced gender ideologies, but also retarded scientific progress. For example, the assumption that sperm are active and eggs are passive delayed studies of the role of eggs in fertilization.

These critiques echoed a larger controversy often dubbed the "nature-nurture debate." How much are human beings the product of their biology, especially their genetics? How much are they a product of their environment? People who preferred environmental answers were often quite optimistic about the human capacity for change, while those who preferred biological answers tended to see the potential for behavioral and cultural change as limited.

Evelyn Fox Keller's *A Feeling for the Organism: The Life and Work of Barbara McClintock* (1983) deepened the argument. McClintock discovered that genes can change location. This fact both challenged the prevailing biological orthodoxy and suggested that the nature-nurture debate was moot: if genes not only create proteins and then a body, but are themselves also subject to change, then the division between nature and environment is a false polarity.

Keller suggested that McClintock was predisposed to question the paradigms of molecular biology because she was female. She had "a feeling for the organism"—an intuitive understanding that led her in new and more productive directions. This suggestion disturbed many female scientists, who had fought for professional legitimacy by denying the age-old belief that women think differently from men.

Recent years have seen an explosion of research on sex differences. In the 1980s the National Women's Health Network pointed out that almost all medical research was done on men, and that medications and surgical procedures were used on women with no attempt to determine whether they had the same effects on women. Medical researchers now enroll both women and men in their studies and look for differences between them. One result has been better medical care for women.

Carol Gilligan's *In a Different Voice: Psychological Theory and Women's Development* (1982) suggested that a similar blindness had infected research on human psychology. Women, she argued, develop a sense of morality differently from men, and women's ethics of relationship is not inferior to men's ethics of rules. Many of her readers concluded that these ethical differences are innate.

Research on sex differences currently receives much financial support, and the popular media regularly contain reports on new findings of differences in the brain, heart, and other body systems. It is almost impossible, however, to receive funding for research on sex similarities or publicity about how women and men are similar. Some people believe that the new research offers useful insights into human behavior, evolution, and history. Others consider it an unfortunate preoccupation with making gender, a cultural phenomenon, seem biological and therefore inevitable.

[*See also* Evolution; Sciences, *subentry* Natural Sciences; *and* Scientific Revolution.]

BIBLIOGRAPHY

Fausto-Sterling, Anne. *Myths of Gender: Biological Theories about Women and Men*. 2d ed. New York: Basic Books, 1992. Evaluates (mostly critically) scientific studies that claim to find innate differences in women's and men's aptitudes and behavior.

Gilligan, Carol. *In a Different Voice: Psychological Theory and Women's Development*. Cambridge, Mass.: Harvard University Press, 1982.

Hubbard, Ruth. *The Politics of Women's Biology*. New Brunswick, N.J.: Rutgers University Press, 1990. Aimed at nonscientists. Introduces the process of scientific truth seeking; scientific thinking about genes, evolution, and sex differences; and the politics of prenatal technologies around 1988.

Keller, Evelyn Fox. *A Feeling for the Organism: The Life and Work of Barbara McClintock*. New York: W. H. Freeman, 1983.

Laqueur, Thomas. *Making Sex: Body and Gender from the Greeks to Freud*. Cambridge, Mass.: Harvard University Press, 1990. A fascinating study of how Europeans thought about anatomy: how the "one sex" model turned into a "two sex" model, and how belief in female orgasm almost disappeared in the process.

Mead, Margaret. *Sex and Temperament in Three Primitive Societies*. New York: HarperCollins, 2001. An anthropological study of sex and gender throughout the life cycle in three New Guinea tribes. Suggests that gender differences are caused by cultural conditioning.

LORI KENSCHAFT

BIRTH CONTROL. *See* Contraception.

BISEXUALITY. *See* Sexuality.

BLACKWELL, ELIZABETH (1821–1910), the first woman to graduate from medical school in the United States. Born in England, Blackwell moved to the United States in 1832 with her family. Her social activism stemmed from that of her parents, who were abolitionists and believed in equal education of the sexes. Unfortunately, her father's failed business ventures and then his death left his wife and daughters without financial support. Like most single middle-class women, Elizabeth resorted to teaching, but her real passion was medicine.

Before the mid-nineteenth century no medical school had admitted a woman. In 1847, however, the Geneva Medical College (now Hobart College) in New York State accepted Blackwell's application after students voted in her favor, partly as a joke. When she enrolled, she was treated as an outsider and even kept out of classes that were deemed inappropriate for women. Despite these obstacles, she graduated first in her class in 1849 and then traveled to Europe to further her training in women's medicine. That same year *Punch* magazine celebrated the triumph of the "excellent Miss Blackwell" in a set of verses. Sadly, an eye infection left her blind in one eye and unable to pursue a career in surgery. When she returned to New York City, hospitals refused to hire her and landlords would not rent office space to her. She therefore treated women and children in her own home and in 1853 opened a dispensary in the slums of New York. With financial support from liberal reformers, she founded the New York Infirmary for Indigent Women and Children in 1857. She also helped train nurses during the Civil War. In 1868, with her sister Emily, she opened the Women's Medical College at the infirmary; it remained in operation for thirty-one years. In 1869 Blackwell returned to England, where she helped to found the London School of Medicine for Women.

Blackwell devoted much of her time to giving public lectures and writing about women's health. She regarded her pursuit of a medical degree as a "great moral struggle," not only for herself but for all women. She also recognized the many social and professional obstacles that faced female medical practitioners. In her writings, considered controversial at the time, she discussed the need for sex education for children and rejected the Victorian notion of female "passionlessness." She also knew that many women were reluctant to seek medical attention because of ignorance about their own bodies as well as fears of "indecency"; hence she promoted the study of obstetrics and gynecology as "the true ennoblement of women." However, she did not completely reject Victorian notions of sexuality; she disapproved of masturbation and believed that women were more emotional and spiritual than men.

Blackwell was active in many social reform movements in the late nineteenth century. She advocated female suffrage and higher education for women, and she joined Josephine Butler's campaign to repeal Britain's contagious diseases acts (1864, 1866, and 1869). Like other Victorian women who devoted themselves to their careers, she rejected the convention of marriage, but she adopted a seven-year-old orphan in 1854. By the time of her death in 1910 there were more than seven thousand female doctors in the United States alone, and the hospital she founded in New York City is still in operation on East Fifteenth Street.

[*See also* Contagious Diseases Acts *and* Healing and Medicine.]

BIBLIOGRAPHY

Blackwell, Elizabeth. *Pioneer Work in Opening the Medical Profession to Women: Autobiographical Sketches.* London: Longmans, Green, 1895.

Hays, Elinor Rice. *Those Extraordinary Blackwells: The Story of a Journey to a Better World.* New York: Harcourt, Brace and World, 1967.

Morantz-Sanchez, Regina. *Sympathy and Science: Women Physicians in American Medicine.* New York: Oxford University Press, 1985.

JULIE ANNE TADDEO

BLATCH, HARRIOT STANTON (1856–1940), American suffrage leader. Harriot Eaton Stanton Blatch was the daughter of nineteenth-century American feminism's greatest thinker, Elizabeth Cady Stanton, but she was also much more. She was an innovative leader of American suffrage in its final decades, and an independent voice in the charting of the future of women's rights past the ratification of the Nineteenth Amendment.

Born on 20 January 1856, Stanton's sixth child and second daughter, Harriot inherited her mother's legacy of involvement in reform and commitment to feminism. An early graduate of Vassar College, she spent her young adulthood in Europe, going first to Germany and France in search of advanced education. From 1882 on, she lived in England, raising and educating her daughter Nora, and absorbing the new social democratic perspective of the Fabian movement there. In the 1880s, she debated the impact on women workers of sex-based ("protective") labor legislation with Beatrice Potter Webb (1858–1943). Blatch argued that state regulation of labor conditions was a positive good, but that such laws should apply to all workers, not just to women. She held to this position all her life, even when the debate between proponents and opponents of female-only labor legislation in the United States split the 1920s women's movement.

Blatch returned to the United States permanently in 1906, after the death of Susan B. Anthony (1820–1906), to take up suffrage leadership. Along with other modern suffragists, she helped to rebuild the movement around a combination of industrial women workers and college-educated professional women, thus linking the unfinished task of political rights to a future agenda of economic independence for women.

Her other great contribution as a suffrage leader was her ability to situate the movement's prospects in the context of partisan political developments. Especially in her home state of New York, she brilliantly maneuvered between suffrage's traditional Republican allies and rising forces in the Democratic party to get the legislature to call a 1915 voters' referendum on amending the state constitution to enfranchise women and then to organize a propaganda campaign among voters on its behalf. The referendum failed, but two years later, in 1917, when a second referendum passed, the electorate and Congressional delegation of the most populous state in the union joined the pro-suffrage side of the political tally.

By this time, however, frustrated at the effort expended on state-by-state referenda, Blatch had moved on to the revived campaign for a federal suffrage amendment. In this, the last phase of the American suffrage movement, she collaborated with the young militant leader Alice Paul (1885–1977). She introduced Paul to the leaders of the National American Woman Suffrage Association (NAWSA) and endorsed Paul's efforts to bring the dramatic new protest methods of the British suffrage movement to the national U.S. stage. When Paul broke with the mainstream suffragists, Blatch remained her ally, serving as the senior suffrage veteran in the leadership of the National Woman's Party that Paul formed in 1916.

Finally, Blatch has historical significance because of her diverse writings on the impact that World War I had on women. She wrote two radically different books on the war. The first, written at the height of the war, in the wake of an extended visit she paid to friends and family in England, extolled the possibilities of righteous military engagement for democracy and for women's civic engagement in particular. Two years later, after a trip to Paris when she and other women failed to get their opinions on international reconciliation heard by the male leaders who were negotiating the peace, she wrote a very different second book. In this later work, she argued that war in general, and World War I in particular, could never contribute to human progress or women's advancement.

Blatch remained opinionated and active in labor, peace, and feminist movements until her death on 20 November 1940.

[*See also* Anthony, Susan B.; Feminism; Stanton, Elizabeth Cady; Suffrage; *and* Suffragettes.]

BIBLIOGRAPHY

Blatch, Harriot Stanton, and Alma Lutz. *Challenging Years: The Memoirs of Harriot Stanton Blatch*. New York: G. P. Putnam's Sons, 1940.

DuBois, Ellen Carol. *Harriot Stanton Blatch and the Winning of Woman Suffrage*. New Haven, Conn.: Yale University Press, 1997.

ELLEN CAROL DUBOIS

BLAVATSKY, HELENA PETROVNA (1831–1891), also known as Madame Blavatsky and HPB, founder of the Theosophical Society, occultist, and writer. Blavatsky was born Elena Petrovna Gan in Ekaterinoslav (now Dnipropetrovsk, Ukraine). Her father was a military officer, and her mother, a writer descended from the aristocratic Dolgoruky family, died when Helena was only eleven. Helena and her younger sister Vera were raised in a privileged and intellectual, albeit provincial, environment by their maternal grandmother. Helena grew up well-read, imaginative, and headstrong. In 1849 she unexpectedly married Nikifor Blavatsky, vice governor of Erevan, who was twenty-two years her senior; she left him three months later.

Between 1849, when she first left Russia, and 1873, when she arrived in New York, Madame Blavatsky traveled in Turkey, Greece, Egypt, England, and France, supporting herself by holding spiritualist séances. She returned to Russia at least once during this time. Later she added that she had been in the Far East, India, and even Tibet, receiving occult training from a secret brotherhood of mahatmas in a lodge hidden in the Himalayas. She claimed that these mahatmas directed her occult work and channeled her writings.

In 1873, Madame Blavatsky settled in New York City, where she wrote for the sensationalistic press and practiced spiritualism. On 17 November 1875 she and Colonel Henry S. Olcott (1832–1907) founded the Theosophical Society to promote Theosophy, a neo-Buddhistic occult doctrine that claimed to synthesize science, philosophy, and religion. Her first major Theosophical work, *Isis Unveiled*, a syncretic blend of occult doctrines past and present, appeared in 1877. In 1878 she and Olcott traveled to India to form the World Headquarters of the Theosophical Society in Adyar. Madame Blavatsky's journeys became the subject of several lively and engaging travelogues. In 1884 she returned to Europe, going first to Paris and then to London.

In May 1887, Madame Blavatsky settled in London. Writers, painters, scholars, aristocrats, and occultists (including W. B. Yeats, George Russell, A. E. Waite, and Ernest Rhys) sought audience with this large, exotically dressed, hypnotic, acid-tongued, chain-smoking Russian woman at her house on Lansdowne Road. There Madame Blavatsky wrote her second occult opus, *The Secret Doctrine* (1888), and there she died on 8 May 1891 after a long illness.

In the early twenty-first century Madame Blavatsky is best known as the founder of Theosophy and the author of its massive core texts. But this unusual woman was also known as an adventuress, author, spirit medium, world traveler, esotericist, and charlatan. In her colorful lifetime she fended off accusations of bigamy, fraud, plagiarism, and even spying. After investigating her alleged psychic powers, the British Society for Psychical Research concluded in its *Proceedings* for December 1885 that she was neither the "mouthpiece of hidden seers" nor a "mere vulgar adventuress" but "one of the most accomplished, ingenious, and interesting impostors in history." A completely accurate biography of Blavatsky will never be written, although some have tried. Highly intelligent, fiercely independent, manipulative, and private, Blavatsky expended great effort to ensure that the facts of her unusual life would never be extracted from the extravagant personal mythology she wove around herself.

[*See also* Spiritualism.]

BIBLIOGRAPHY

Blavatsky's works include *Isis Unveiled* (New York, 1877), *The Secret Doctrine* (London, 1888), and *The Voice of the Silence* (London, 1889). These and other major writings are available in many editions and languages as well as on the Web. *From the Caves and Jungles of Hindustan*, translated from the Russian (London, 1892), includes Blavatsky's travel writings.

Cranston, Sylvia. *HPB: The Extraordinary Life and Influence of Helena Blavatsky, Founder of the Modern Theosophical Movement*. New York: Putnam, 1993. Written by an adherent of Theosophy; now the Theosophical Society's standard.

Meade, Marion. *Madame Blavatsky: The Woman behind the Myth*. New York: Putnam, 1980. Popular biography by a nonadherent.

MARIA CARLSON

BLIXEN, KAREN (1885–1962), Danish writer who published under the pseudonym Isak Dinesen. Blixen was born in Rungsted, Denmark, to Wilhelm Dinesen and Ingeborg Westenholz Dinesen. Dinesen, a soldier, landowner, writer, and Danish parliamentarian, committed suicide in 1895 reportedly after being diagnosed with syphilis. Her mother, Westenholz Dinesen, the daughter of a rich shipbuilder, a Unitarian, feminist, and activist, was the first woman elected to the local council of Rungsted. Blixen studied French in Switzerland with her sisters and mother and later attended the Academy of Art in Copenhagen. She began writing short plays and poetry as a teenager, and in 1907 published her first stories in Danish under the pseudonym Osceola.

In 1914 Blixen departed with her cousin Baron Bror von Blixen-Finecke (1886–1946) for then British-ruled Kenya, where they soon married and purchased a coffee plantation just outside Nairobi. Shortly thereafter she contracted syphilis from her husband. In 1916, the Karen Coffee Company was established with the financial backing of Blixen's relatives. In 1918, Blixen began what would become a long-lasting relationship with the British hunter and adventurer Denys Finch Hatton (1887–1931). After separating from her husband in 1921 (the divorce was finalized in 1925), she took over management of the plantation—first with her brother Thomas Dinesen (1892–1979) and later alone. During the 1920s Blixen was considered "pro-native," favoring independent native production and decreased taxes for indigenous farmers and opening a school for tenant squatters on her estate in 1923. In 1931, when, after years of continuous economic decline, her plantation was sold, Blixen was able to obtain territory in the Kikuyu Reserve for her tenant farmers before returning permanently to Denmark.

Blixen's health deteriorated throughout her fifties and sixties, during which time she began writing under the pseudonym Isak Dinesen. *Seven Gothic Tales*, her first publication to receive international acclaim, was published in the United States in 1934 and later translated by Blixen into Danish. In 1937–1938 Blixen published her most famous work, *Out of Africa*, in the United States, Sweden, and Denmark. This memoir about her years in Kenya achieved both critical and commercial success in the United States and Europe. During the German occupation of Denmark, Blixen completed *Winter's Tales*, which focuses on the landscape and peoples of Denmark. In 1944, Blixen published *The Angelic Avengers* under the pseudonym Pierre Andrézel. She also published numerous stories, articles, and essays including many posthumous works. In 1947, Blixen became involved with the journal *Heretica*, along with a group of avant-garde intellectual writers.

Blixen's works explore the conflict between tradition and modernity and highlight the aristocratic themes of romanticism, heroism, and honor along with feelings of alienation from modern bourgeois life. She was twice named a candidate for the Nobel Prize in Literature, but lost to Ernest Hemingway in 1954 and to Albert Camus in 1957. In 1959, she made a notable trip to the United States where prominent members of American society welcomed her as a renowned author. Suffering severe malnutrition as the result of an earlier stomach surgery, Blixen died at her family's estate in Rungsted in 1962.

[*See also* Literature.]

BIBLIOGRAPHY

Dinesen, Isak. *Letters from Africa 1914–1931*. Edited for the Rungstedlund Foundation by Frans Lasson. Translated by Anne Born.

Chicago: Chicago University Press, 1981. English translation of *Breve fra Afrika 1914–24* and *Breve fra Afrika 1925–31*, first published in 1978. This collection of Blixen's correspondence shows the realities of her life in Africa as opposed to the semifictional events conveyed in *Out of Africa* and *Shadows on the Grass*.

Thurman, Judith. *Isak Dinesen: The Life of a Storyteller*. New York: St. Martin's Press, 1982. Thorough biography that makes extensive use of previously unexplored archival and unpublished materials.

KRIS ALEXANDERSON

BLUESTOCKINGS. A group of men and women drawn together for intellectual conversation by the hostesses Elizabeth Montagu, Elizabeth Vesey, and Frances Boscawen in the 1750s, the Bluestockings represented an influential, widely discussed milestone in women's history. According to a much-repeated story, Benjamin Stillingfleet, whose *Miscellaneous Tracts* (1759) brought the work of the Swedish botanist Carolus Linnaeus (Carl Linné) to English attention, responded to an invitation with an apology that he had no suitably elegant clothes. He was told to come in his everyday coarse blue stockings; Admiral Boscawen with wry but symbolic humor began calling the group the Bluestockings, and Vesey created a blue room for the meetings. The term quickly assumed its modern usage. Today it is synonymous with "intellectual woman," whether that be a compliment to the hard work of becoming an educated person with judicious, informed opinions or a term of ridicule meaning a pedantic, assertive, snobbish, learned woman.

Rather than following the well-known examples of the French salons, Samuel Richardson's North End Circle, and Samuel Johnson's Club, the hostesses modeled their gatherings on the comparatively informal style of the Tunbridge Wells spa and country house parties. They outlawed cards, dancing, alcoholic beverages, and other detriments to intelligent discussion. Perhaps as much a gracious gesture to the less affluent members of the group as a sign of their commitment to ease and familiarity, dress at the gatherings was unpretentious, even informal. One guest even described the refreshments as "scanty" (Myers). There was never fixed membership, and Montagu once summarized the goals as "to inspire candour, a social spirit, and gentle manners; to teach a disdain of frivolous amusements, injurious censoriousness, and foolish animosities" (Pohl and Schellenberg). Among the men who regularly attended were David Garrick, Horace Walpole, and Edmund Burke, and, at first, "Bluestocking" referred to the men alone and then to the mixed group. By 1770, in spite of the group's usage of the term that continued into the 1790s, outsiders restricted it to the women.

The original Bluestockings were all impressive intellects, elegant letter writers, superb conversationalists, and women of impeccable reputations. Many were wealthy, and all were Church of England women from prominent, sometimes even aristocratic, families. Montagu knew French, Italian, and classical languages and wrote *Essay on the Writings and Genius of Shakespear* (1769), perhaps the only direct reply to Voltaire's criticisms of Shakespeare. Elizabeth Carter once published a reply to Samuel Johnson in Greek and Latin in *The Gentleman's Magazine*, and her *All the Works of Epictetus* (1758) remained a standard English translation at least through 1966, the last year it was reprinted in the Dent Everyman's Library series. Other prominent Bluestockings were Hester Chapone, whose *Letters on the Improvement of the Mind* (1773) required twenty-five editions by 1844, and Mary Delany, who wrote *A Catalogue of Plants* (1778). They displayed talent in the decorative arts; Delany invented "paper mosaics," now preserved in the British Library, and connoisseurs admired Montagu's elaborate feather screens. Some, including Vesey, Boscawen, Catherine Talbot, and Margaret Harley, Duchess of Portland, had no literary ambitions, but their published letters testify to their acute judgment, wide interests, and lively writing styles. Many of the women's letters were published after the French Revolution backlash, perhaps in an attempt to show that

Bluestockings. Elizabeth Montagu, the founder of the Bluestockings Society. Painting by John Raphael Smith, 1776. COURTESY OF THE DR. JOHNSON'S HOUSE TRUSTEES

women could be models of both domesticity and informed citizenship (Kelly).

Feminist Commitments. A dense network of varying relationships existed among the women. As Moyra Haslett says, in spite of the mixed company, "their most deeply felt association was as a kind of virtual community, meeting and conversing through exchanged letters" (2003). The women strongly supported each other's lifestyles and publication efforts and followed what they called the bluestocking philosophy. From the beginning, the women were recognized for their philanthropy and as patrons of the arts, but there were also specific, sustained commitments to women's causes. They subscribed to a very large number of books written by women, even by obscure women whose books were not conservative in form or content. Montagu and others patronized Elizabeth Carter, brought her into their circle, and later provided her an annuity. Elizabeth Elstob, the groundbreaking Old English scholar, came to Chapone's attention, and the Duchess of Portland employed her as a governess, keeping her in the family for eighteen years. The women sought deserving women for whom they found employment, distributed food to the laboring class, and founded and supported educational projects that benefited women and the poor.

Carter praised Chapone for having all of the qualities that characterized the ideal member of the group: "She has an uncommon exactness of understanding and a lively agreeable turn of conversation, and her conduct seems to be governed by the best and noblest principles" (12 August 1752 to Talbot, 2:89). They passed these values on to the next generation of Blues, whose members included Hannah More, Hester Thrale, and Mary Hamilton, and to provincial circles modeled after theirs that were led by prominent women including Anna Seward in Lichfield.

The eighteenth century was characterized by a vigorous debate over the nature, capacity, and duties of the female sex. Intellectual women are perpetual social problems, and their status was a major issue in these discussions. Ridiculed, feared, and sometimes declared mad, such women had occasionally come to widespread public attention or been cast as ludicrous figures in poems, plays, and novels, as were Katherine Philips and Lady Mary Wortley Montagu. Even Mary Astell was the object of a sustained journalistic attack. The Bluestockings recast the terms and perceptions that had defined, marginalized, and circumscribed intellectual women and their work. As a contemporary of the second generation of Bluestockings, Amelia Opie wrote, "I think it incumbent on all those women who are really bluestockings, to dare to be *themselves*, and to shew . . . that all females of cultivated minds are not pedants or *precieuses*, and that they love information for its own sake, and not for the sake of display" (*Detraction Displayed*, 1828, p. 264).

Women and the Republic of Letters. The Bluestocking women made the educated woman a respectable member of society. Like Carter, they set a powerful example for women, daring to display learning and yet maintaining the reputation of domestic, social, and moral paragons. Men approvingly mentioned Carter's pudding and Montagu's marmalade. Their conversation came to be seen as good for the nation, for they offered an ideal of modest, restrained, female patriotic virtue and a model of a civil society where public opponents could converse freely. Montagu's *Essay on . . . Shakespear*, for instance, was acclaimed as a perfect "blend of literary taste and national zeal" (Guest). As the years passed and the women's activities received more recognition, they attracted more criticism. Some of the second generation of Bluestockings were far more aggressive, and effusions such as Hannah More's poems about the circle helped create today's negative sense of the word and, unfairly, the entire group. The French Revolution polarized thought about women, and the exclusiveness, the social class, and the chauvinistic Anglicanism of the Bluestockings made them seem part of a discredited ideology.

It was, however, the generation of fully professional women writers in the last fifteen years of the century that made them seem old-fashioned curiosities. Charlotte Smith, Mary Robinson, Anna Barbauld, Helen Maria Williams, Joanna Baillie, and Maria Edgeworth construct themselves in the public consciousness through their excellent literary works, not in the mystique of the drawing room. The Bluestockings' promotion and support of women and the lasting image of their intense friendships with each other, their wide learning, and their interest in public affairs, however, created the possibilities of such lifestyles and careers. Their sense of themselves in terms of a collective gender identity and as representatives of women devoted to the life of the mind cast a long, enabling shadow, one that women of the generation after the first group of Blues recognized, in Opie's words, as allowing an intelligent woman to be herself. As Sylvia Myers, the best scholar of the movement, says, they created a satisfying way of life for themselves and "brought into public notice the idea that respectable women could study, write, and publish."

[*See also* Great Britain; Literature, *subentry* Personal and Private Narratives; *and* Salon.]

BIBLIOGRAPHY

Guest, Harriet. *Small Change: Women, Learning, Patriotism, 1750–1810*. Chicago: University of Chicago Press, 2000.

Haslett, Moyra. *Pope to Burney, 1714–1779: Scriblerians to Bluestockings*. Houndmills, U.K., and New York: Palgrave Macmillan, 2003.

Heller, Deborah. "Bluestocking Salons and the Public Sphere." *Eighteenth-Century Life* 22 (1998), 59–82.

Kelly, Gary, ed. *Bluestocking Feminism: Writings of the Bluestocking Circle, 1738–1785*. 6 vols. London and Brookfield, Vt.: Pickering & Chatto, 1999.

Myers, Sylvia Harcstark. *The Bluestocking Circle: Women, Friendship, and the Life of the Mind in Eighteenth-Century England.* Oxford: Clarendon Press; New York: Oxford University Press, 1990.

Pohl, Nicole, and Betty A. Schellenberg, eds. *Reconsidering the Bluestockings.* San Marino, Calif.: Huntington Library, 2003.

Ready, Kathryn J. "Hannah More and the Bluestocking Salons: Commerce, Virtue, Sensibility, and Conversation." *Age of Johnson* 15 (2004): 197–222.

Todd, Janet. *A Dictionary of British and American Women Writers, 1660–1800.* Totowa, N.J.: Rowman & Allanheld, 1985.

PAULA R. BACKSCHEIDER

BOARDINGHOUSES. Boardinghouses have existed in many parts of the world to shelter migrants, travelers, and various kinds of temporary residents in cities and towns. As global commerce and industrialization advanced after the sixteenth century, boardinghouses contained salesmen, students, soldiers, and working men and women newly arrived from the country. Single people in various walks of life also depended on boardinghouses for extended periods of time. The women and men who ran boardinghouses provided not only lodging but meals and sometimes laundry services, while those who inhabited them often enjoyed sociability with other boarders. The famed boardinghouse owner Mary Seacole of Kingston, Jamaica, profited so much from the stay of doctors in her establishment that she was able to become a skilled health worker herself, providing medical as well as other services. She eventually used those skills to care for British soldiers in the Crimean War (1853–1856). Running a boardinghouse was a business where one could find widows and married women working on their own to earn their livelihood.

Types of Boardinghouses. Individual women took migrants into their homes as boarders, renting out a room or two and sometimes providing meals. Eighteenth-century Paris was a city with an increasing number of migrants and with an abundance of hotels and boardinghouses, large and small. Women, and especially widows, were most often associated with the smallest of these, facilities that accommodated only individuals, not horses or large contingents of servants. Widowed proprietors of these establishments had a tendency to remarry reliable male servants to help them with the hard work of repairs, portage, and complaints. In Paris the owner of a small boardinghouse, unlike in other places such as the U.S. West, generally provided meals in rooms rather than in a central dining room.

Boardinghouses flourished with the global migration of the nineteenth century onward. Migrants to Australia, the North American West, and Latin America found their initial grounding by finding lodgings with women who were running boardinghouses. Chinese migrants hoping to make their fortunes in mining settled with people of their own ethnicity in boardinghouses. Some of the male proprietors latched on to local women to make these boardinghouses more appealing. Taking migrants in on a small scale, the women proprietors supplemented the family income, whereas women who ran larger boardinghouses often provided a substantial part of the family livelihood while their husbands worked outside the home. Where strapped for funds, women also rented out a room to a single migrant or to students—a practice of women in several countries after World War II when American students and scholars began studying and researching abroad. For women, taking in lodgers—whether individuals or on a larger scale—could provide security and even upward mobility.

Women also ran boardinghouses either directly connected to factories and department stores or less formally attached to them. During industrialization in the United States and Japan, factories explicitly sought out young single women from the countryside for work in new industries such as textiles. Mill workers from the countryside around Lowell, Massachusetts, lived in boardinghouses in the 1840s in conditions that the British writer Anthony Trollope called "utopian." The workers slept four to a room, two to a bed, in an establishment usually run by a "discreet widow," a married woman, or a married woman and her husband. The workers were well fed, but their conduct was strictly monitored for church attendance and sobriety. The workers paid between a third and half of their wages for room and board, including washing.

In Japan, where textile industrialization took place late in the nineteenth century, the competition for young women workers was so intense that employers often set up dormitories supervised by women where the young boarders were virtually imprisoned behind tall walls topped with barbed wire and glass and surrounded by moats so that they could not run away. In smaller silk-weaving establishments, the wife of the owner would board the dozen or so young girl workers—often in abysmal conditions. In Japan the board received was meager: small bowls of rice, sometimes with pickles and watery soup.

> More than a bird in a cage,
> More than a prison,
> Dormitory life is hateful.
>
> (quoted in Tsurumi, p. 70)

Women as Lodgers. As white-collar jobs opened up for educated women in such fields as librarianship, teaching, secretarial work, and telegraph and telephone work, single lower-middle- and middle-class women also left their homes for rooms in others' apartments, boardinghouses, and other accommodations—usually highly unsatisfactory. In principle they led independent lives in these spaces, apart from what were the often intricate and demanding rules of family and household. However, where service jobs for women developed, as in London from the mid-nineteenth century onward, the feminist press was quick to seize on the fact that there was little really suitable housing for single women, whether working or middle class. Far from the longed-for independence, boardinghouses often had strict rules such as curfews and obligatory attendance at morning prayers. Some were not respectable, leading the *Englishwoman's Review* in 1889 to call for "Suitable house accommodation at reasonable rents to ladies of small incomes, where, while retaining their entire independence, they may lie with greater comfort and economy than in lodging houses of the ordinary type" (quoted in Vicinus, p. 295).

Philanthropists sometimes bought up boardinghouses and converted them into model communities where women could have both independence and the longed-for community that came from the boardinghouse experience of eating together in common. Young working women enjoyed time away from the city of London in the House of the Good Shepherd by the sea in Whitstable. The House of the Good Shepherd subtitled itself "A Temperance Hotel and Boarding House," suggesting some of the features that single women often sought in lodgings. Some of these avowed utopian homes for women housed their occupants for decades, until they became stigmatized as homes for those who could simply not attract men and who continually and grimly had to earn a living.

Representations and Lore of Boardinghouses. Notable novels and documentaries have evoked the life in a boardinghouse or pensione. E. M. Forster's *Room with a View* (1908) captures the unpredictable relationships that could occur in a pensione where visitors could board for extended periods of time. In this pensione in Florence, frequented by the well-to-do and not-so-well-to-do traveler, love inappropriately blossoms because of conversations and glances exchanged around the boardinghouse table. In the 1920s and 1930s Sax Rohmer's Fu Manchu novels and others about Chinese life depicted the seamy lives of immigrants in London's boardinghouses and underworld neighborhoods, which included white Englishmen's encounters with Chinese femmes fatales. The film *Hester Street* (1975), directed by Joan Micklin Silver, is a story of Jewish migrants to the Lower East Side in New York; it describes the romance between a woman and one of her boarders that springs up because of cultural affinities and a shared concern between proprietor and boarder for preserving traditional customs.

The story of Mary Surratt provides one of the most sensational but true episodes in the history of women and boardinghouse life. Surratt's son John was a friend of John Wilkes Booth, a lodger at her boardinghouse in Washington, D.C., and the assassin of the U.S. president Abraham Lincoln in 1865. Though believed by many to be totally innocent of the conspiracy to assassinate Lincoln, Surratt was convicted of participating in the crime and was hanged in 1865.

[*See also* Domestic Service; Household; *and* Houses and Housing.]

BIBLIOGRAPHY

Dublin, Thomas, ed. *Farm to Factory: Women's Letters, 1830–1860.* New York: Columbia University Press, 1981.

Roche, Daniel, ed. *La ville promise: Mobilité et accueil à Paris (fin XVIIe siècle–début XIXe siècle.* Paris: Fayard, 2000.

Tsurumi, E. Patricia. *Factory Girls: Women in the Thread Mills of Meiji Japan.* Princeton, N.J.: Princeton University Press, 1990.

Vicinus, Martha. *Independent Women: Work and Community for Single Women, 1850–1920.* London: Virago, 1985.

BONNIE G. SMITH

BOCHKAREVA, MARIA (1889–1920), a woman combat soldier in the Russian Imperial Army in World War I and founder in 1917 of the first governmentally approved female combat unit of modern times. Daughter of a former serf, Leonty S. Frolkov, Maria "Yashka" Leontevna Bochkareva was born in July 1889 and grew up illiterate and in great poverty in Tomsk, Siberia. At age fifteen she married Afanasy Bochkarev, a peasant, but after four years fled his drunkenness and abuse. With the outbreak of war in Russia in July 1914 she was caught up in the initial wave of popular patriotism and resolved to sacrifice herself defending "Mother Russia." In November she successfully petitioned Tsar Nicholas II to be allowed to enlist as an infantry soldier and was assigned to the Fifth Siberian Corps. Known by the nickname Yashka, she soon managed to win her fellow soldiers' acceptance. She took part in a number of campaigns, being wounded three times and twice decorated for valor.

Bochkareva initially rejoiced at the revolutionary events of March 1917 and the abdication of the tsar, believing they brought freedom to Russia's long-suffering peasants, but she became outraged by the rapid breakdown of discipline and fighting capacity in the army. In response she conceived the idea of forming a unit of women soldiers both to inspire and to shame male soldiers into doing their duty; the women's unit would do this by leading them into battle. She found backing for this idea from several prominent political and military figures. Her public appeal for volunteers for what was called the First Women's Battalion of Death, issued in Petrograd on 29 May 1917, immediately drew nearly two thousand women. The new recruits were issued men's uniforms, had their hair cut off, and underwent a hasty basic training. Bochkareva became an international celebrity, often referred to in the allied press as the Russian Joan of Arc. Her example inspired formation of further women's combat units in Russia as some five to six thousand women, coming from all classes and educational levels, volunteered to fight.

Thanks to her severe discipline, Bochkareva had reduced her Women's Battalion of Death to three hundred soldiers by the time it was assigned to the 172d division of the Tenth Army in late June. On 8 July, near Molodechno, the battalion went into combat, joined by seven hundred male troops in leading an attack on the German positions. Though the women acquitted themselves well, helping take hundreds of prisoners and sustaining thirty-six casualties, their example did not inspire the majority of Russia's demoralized soldiers, and the action eventually turned into a rout. Male soldiers became increasingly hostile to her unit, seeing its zeal as prolonging the fighting. In September the army command quietly transferred the battalion to an inactive sector of the front.

Shortly after taking power on 26 October 1917, the Bolsheviks initiated peace negotiations with Germany and deactivated all women's combat units. In 1918, with Russia in the throes of civil war, Bochkareva visited the United States to muster support for the anti-Bolshevik ("White") cause. She met with President Woodrow Wilson and members of Congress, also finding time to dictate her memoirs. She returned to Russia in 1919, organizing a women's paramedic unit in Siberia to aid the White forces of Admiral Alexander Kolchak. Following his defeat she returned to her parents' home in Tomsk, where she was arrested by the special police, the *cheka*. After several months' imprisonment and interrogation, Maria Bochkareva was declared an enemy of the workers' regime and was shot on 16 May 1920, at the age of thirty. She and Russia's women soldiers were then virtually forgotten for more than half a century. In 1992, after the collapse of the Soviet Union, she was posthumously rehabilitated.

[*See also* Joan of Arc; Military; *and* Russia and Soviet Union.]

BIBLIOGRAPHY

Abraham, Richard. "Mariia L. Bochkareva and the Russian Amazons of 1917." In *Women and Society in Russia and the Soviet Union*, edited by Linda Edmondson, pp. 124–144. Cambridge, U.K.: Cambridge University Press, 1992.

Botchkareva, Maria. *Yashka: My Life as Peasant, Officer, and Exile*, as set down by Isaac Don Levine. New York: Frederick A. Stokes, 1919.

Stockdale, Melissa K. "'My Death for the Motherland Is Happiness': Women, Patriotism, and Soldiering in Russia's Great War, 1914–1918." *American Historical Review* 109, no. 1 (February 2004): 78–116.

Melissa Kirschke Stockdale

BODY ADORNMENT AND CLOTHING

This entry consists of two subentries:

Overview

Mark Twain famously quipped that "clothes make the man," but even a brief glance at a fashion magazine or a visit to the costume collection of a major museum would certainly suggest that clothes "make" women as well. The second part of Twain's remark—that "naked people have little or no influence on society"—is equally telling. Clothing and adornment in their various forms are centrally important in human cultures as ways to express and shape individual and collective identities—of gender, religion, family, social status, sexuality, and age, for example. Clothing and adornment are central to economic, religious, social, and political practices and institutions in a variety of cultures. By their very visibility—and their intimate, bodily association with the self—clothing and adornment become potent markers of subjectivity and power.

Native American Clothing. A woman's dress made of deer hides and beads by the Warm Springs Tribe, United States, nineteenth century. The Newark Museum, N.J./Art Resource, NY

Body adornment and clothing comprise a wide range of forms and practices: garments; footwear; hats, veils, and other headgear; jewelry; accessories and accoutrements like bags and belts; cosmetics; coiffure; and even alterations of the skin or body like tattooing, piercing, and tooth filing. Clothing and adornment may be permanent or impermanent, spectacular or plain, homemade or mass-produced, new or secondhand. This variety reinforces the reality that in many cultures and across human history, body adornment and clothing are often elaborated far beyond the simple utilitarian requirements of protection.

Scholarship. Scholars use several terms more or less interchangeably to encompass this range of forms, materials, and practices, including "dress," "costume," "clothing," and "adornment." One widely cited definition of the term "dress" identifies it as an assemblage of body modifications and/or supplements displayed by a person in communicating with other human beings. The idea of bodily adornment is closely linked to the idea of fashion, which can be defined as a prevailing style of dress or adornment in a particular cultural or time period—although there are also fashions in other arenas of human behavior and material culture. It is worth noting that the term "fashion" is most often applied to Western culture, but that many cultures—both large and small—exhibit the heightened interest in adornment and changing tastes that characterize fashion.

Philosophers and others have long commented on fashion and clothing—Michel de Montaigne's 1575 essay "Of the Custom of Wearing Clothes" is a notable example—but until relatively recently, many scholars viewed clothing and other forms of adornment as merely reflecting other aspects of human experience such as social relations, religion, and politics. Within many disciplines, attention to clothing and adornment was superficial or minimal, and women's contributions to the economic, aesthetic, and social value of clothing and adornment were often dismissed or ignored. For example, in a landmark publication, the anthropologist Annette Weiner focused on the fiber skirts made by women in the Trobriand Islands of Papua New Guinea. She drew attention to the ways that women's exchange and display of these skirts complemented and amplified the social relationships developed by men in their *kula* trading of shell ornaments. Although the *kula* trade had been made famous by the anthropologist Branislaw Malinowski in the early twentieth century, he—and the discipline as a whole—had overlooked the value of women's skirts.

Since the 1980s there has been a sharp increase in research on clothing and adornment, and gender is a central concern of this scholarly literature. This new scholarship of clothing and adornment draws on many disciplines, including archaeology, cultural anthropology, cultural geography, economics, sociology, history, art history, and cultural studies. A number of scholars have examined the ways that gender identity is expressed and shaped through dress and the different ways that gendered beings may claim social, political, spiritual, reproductive, and other forms of power through adornment. These explorations have focused on women's agency around clothing and adornment in terms of production and consumption; on the development of styles and what they signify; and on the control that women exercise over the clothing and adornment choices of others, such as children or spouses. For example, women in medieval Europe often managed household expenditures around clothing, a role that provided them with considerable access to money as well as power over the display of wealth and the expression of the family's social status.

Indeed, in many cultures at various times, the making and trading of clothing and adornment has been economically significant on a large scale, not just for the individual or family unit. Since the beginnings of industrialization, the production of clothing and adornment has tended to rely on the underpaid labor of the most vulnerable workers: working-class women, children, and new immigrant populations. These exploitative structures are remarkably resistant to change, and labor patterns that emerged in the nineteenth century in Britain and the United States have proliferated worldwide with the globalization of clothing production; these labor patterns are marked by inequalities of race as well as of class and gender. Women sweatshop workers in China, Thailand, Mexico, and other countries—as well as the urban centers of the United States and other developed nations—endure low wages, long hours, and unsafe working conditions.

In social interactions, clothing and adornment often play a primary role in establishing an individual's gender identity in social situations and in setting up expectations for gendered behavior; it is worth noting that clothing and adornment provide visual communication that may well precede verbal communication—we see a person before being introduced, for example—and that they may convey information that is not easily translatable into words. Clothing and adornment may draw attention to bodily differences between men and women. A tuxedo, for example, emphasizes a man's broad shoulders, while a cocktail dress may emphasize a woman's bust, hips, and legs; paradoxically, the enveloping cloak called a chador worn by some women in the Middle East draws attention to gender differences by completely obscuring the curves of their bodies. Particular articles of clothing can so strongly connote gender that they stand in for gender: the common expression "she wears the pants in the family" suggests that a woman has usurped male power and authority, even though women often wear pants in everyday life. The gender identities expressed and shaped through clothing and adornment intersect with identities of age, class, ethnicity, and sexuality. For example, a short haircut may signal a lesbian identity.

Cultural Meaning. However, clothing does more than simply draw attention to an already gendered body: clothing adds layers of cultural meaning that, because they are so close to the body, can be mistaken as "natural." In addition to reinforcing and expressing normative gender expectations, dress and adornment can also be used to subvert, challenge, and expand gender categories. Though cross-dressing and transgender practices in the United States and Europe have often met with hostility, fear, or scorn, they can also be culturally accepted practices, as in the "sworn virgins" of the Balkans region, women who dress and live as men, or the *mahu* of Tahiti, men who dress and live as women.

Clothing and adornment help us to enact gender and other identities. Particular forms of clothing or adornment enable or restrict particular kinds of movements and gestures and therefore particular kinds of social interactions: stiletto heels prompt a strutting, sexualized walk; the raising and lowering of a veil enables a subtle flirtation with the eyes. Judith Butler has noted that we learn gender roles through repetition and copying within a dominant heterosexual framework, and clothing and adornment play a key role in this process. A little girl may dress like her mother and receive positive reinforcement; if she dressed like her father, it would be a different story. Repeatedly compelled by adults to wear a skirt, a little girl may well grow up feeling more comfortable in a skirt than pants; constantly reminded never to leave the house without a handbag, she may feel naked without one. Through clothing and adornment, gender distinctions that are cultural begin to feel natural.

[*See also* Dress Reform; Gender Roles; *and* Personal Services.]

BIBLIOGRAPHY

Barnes, Ruth, and Joanne B. Eicher, eds. *Dress and Gender: Making and Meaning in Cultural Context*. London: Berg, 1992. See in particular Joanne B. Eicher and Mary E. Roach-Higgins, "Describing Dress: A System of Classifying and Defining."

Besnier, Niko. "Polynesian Gender Liminality through Time and Space." In *Third Sex, Third Gender: Beyond Sexual Dimorphism in Culture and History*, edited by Gilbert Herdt, pp. 285–328. New York: Zone Books, 1993.

Breward, Chistopher. *The Culture of Fashion*. Manchester, U.K.: Manchester University Press, 1994.

Butler, Judith. *Bodies That Matter: On the Discursive Limits of Sex*. New York: Routledge, 1993.

Entwistle, Joanne. *The Fashioned Body: Fashion, Dress and Modern Social Theory*. Cambridge, U.K.: Polity Press, 2000.

Garber, Marjorie. *Vested Interests: Cross-Dressing and Cultural Anxiety*. New York: Routledge, 1992.

Grémaux, René. "Woman Becomes Man in the Balkans." In *Third Sex, Third Gender: Beyond Sexual Dimorphism in Culture and History*, edited by Gilbert Herdt, pp. 241–281. New York: Zone Books, 1993.

Hansen, Karen Tranberg. "The World in Dress: Anthropological Perspectives on Clothing, Fashion, and Culture." *Annual Review of Anthropology* 33 (2004): 369–392.

Hollander, Anne. *Sex and Suits*. New York: Alfred A. Knopf, 1994.

Howard, Alan. "Labor History and Sweatshops in the New Global Economy." In *No Sweat: Fashion, Free Trade, and the Rights of Garment Workers*, edited by Andrew Ross, pp. 151–172. London: Verso, 1997.

Johnson, Kim K. P., Susan J. Torntore, and Joanne B. Eicher, eds. *Fashion Foundations: Early Writing on Fashion and Dress*. London: Berg, 2003.

Kidwell, Claudia Brush, and Valerie Steele, eds. *Men and Women: Dressing the Part*. Washington, D.C.: Smithsonian Institution Press, 1989.

Steele, Valerie. *Fashion and Eroticism*. New York: Oxford University Press, 1985.

Weiner, Annette B. *Women of Value, Men of Renown: New Perspectives in Trobriand Exchange*. Austin: University of Texas Press, 1983.

Weiner, Annette B., and Jane Schneider, eds. *Cloth and Human Experience*. Washington, D.C.: Smithsonian Institution Press, 1992.

Woodhouse, Annie. *Fantastic Women: Sex, Gender, and Transvestism*. London: Macmillan, 1989.

ANNE D'ALLEVA

Comparative History

Women's bodily adornment and clothing take an astonishing variety of forms, including garments; footwear; hats, veils, and other headgear; jewelry; accessories, and accoutrements like bags and belts; cosmetics; coiffure; and even alterations of the skin or body like tattooing, piercing, and tooth filing. This variety reinforces the reality that in many cultures and across human history, body adornment and clothing are often elaborated far beyond the simple utilitarian requirements of protection. Clothing and adornment in their various forms are centrally important in human cultures as ways to express and shape various individual and collective identities—of gender, religion, family, social status, sexuality, and age, for example. Clothing and adornment are central to economic, religious, social, and political practices and institutions in a variety of cultures.

Presenting a complete chronological history of dress and adornment around the globe is beyond the scope of this essay. This entry will instead focus on three forms of clothing and adornment—trousers, veils, and tattoos—that have been invested with multiple meanings at different times and in different places and that have been the focus of some controversy. These will serve as examples of the ways that clothing and adornment are central to the cultural construction of social and political life and gender identity.

Trousers. In the early twenty-first century, in many countries, it is common to see women wearing trousers to work as well as for physical and social activities. In fact, women wear an enormous variety of trouser styles. A woman may wear a business suit with a tailored jacket and pants during the day; baggy cotton-knit sweatpants for a workout; denim jeans at home or when running errands; or flowing silk palazzo pants for an evening out. Indeed, in Europe and its settler societies in the Americas, New Zealand, and Australia, trousers are hardly thought of as male attire at all, and there is little or no sense of shame or censure connected with them. While the trouser in the West has become a unisex garment, the same cannot be said for the skirt, despite the efforts of avant-garde couturiers. With the exception of ethnic costumes like the kilt, the skirt in the West remains a resolutely feminine garment. (At the same time, it is important to remember that men in South and Southeast Asian cultures often wear skirts, such as the *lunghi* and the sarong.) Dress reformers of the nineteenth and early twentieth centuries, however, struggled long and hard to achieve the changes that brought a general acceptance of women's trousers.

Historically, trousers developed as male garments in northern Europe. Romans adopted them as the stylish—and rather outré and daring—clothing of the barbarians. Essentially, however, the basic dress for both men and women at this time was a gown, with men wearing somewhat shorter tunics for war and leisure activities. During the early Middle Ages, leg coverings—not exactly trousers but two individual coverings attached to a waist band—became a common form of dress worn by men under their tunics. This soon became codified, gender-differentiated wear: women in long skirts and men in some kind of pants. Through the later Middle Ages, the Renaissance, and the early modern period, daring upper-class women occasionally flouted these conventions and wore trousers. In fact, "Turkish" trousers became quite popular as fancy dress and leisure wear among fashionable young men and women in eighteenth-century Europe. (Similarly, in Tang China, aristocratic young women shocked their elders by wearing "Turkish" style jackets and trousers with boots for riding.)

Although women in Europe and its settler societies struggled with the issues of trousers, in many cultures of Asia and the Middle East trousers have historically been considered appropriate clothing for women. The traditional Punjabi costume *shalwar kameez* is worn by Muslim women throughout Pakistan and India, for example. It consists of a long tunic (*kameez*) and loose trousers (*shalwar*). It is typically worn with a *dupatta*, a scarf that can be worn on the head as a veil or draped around the chest and shoulders. In fact, unmarried Hindu women have also adopted this style of dress, although once married they wear the traditional sari. Similarly, women in the Middle East have often worn loose trousers—and during the Qing Dynasty (1644–1912), Chinese women began to wear long tunics or jackets with either a skirt or loose trousers. By the late Qing period, unmarried women typically wore the tunic over trousers, while married women wore, in addition, a long, wraparound, pleated skirt that covered their trousers.

In the early nineteenth century, when the modern era of dress reform began in Europe and settler societies, trousers were clearly a publicly unacceptable garment for respectable women. Despite the rigidly enforced gender differences in clothing styles in the nineteenth century, there were individual women who flouted these conventions. Perhaps the most famous trousered woman of the nineteenth century was the French writer George Sand (born Amandine-Aurore-Lucile Dupin). Sand adopted both a male name and a masculine suit of tailored jacket and trousers, in which she was frequently photographed. Notably, she did not cut her hair or disguise the curves of her body. In fact, her well-tailored suits emphasized her female form—she was not engaged in drag, in creating the illusion of being of another gender. Sand's suit therefore signaled not a change of gender identity but a remarkable expansion of the notion of femininity; Sand was indicating that she was not interested in traditional female concerns of child-bearing and domesticity or the alluring submissiveness signaled by the display. Her masculine clothes signaled her interest in an assertive feminine sexuality, a life of the mind, and an ability to move freely in the world. Although some aristocratic country women wore trousers for riding, Sand's wearing of trousers in public and urban settings—and her change of name—represented a radical challenge to conventional gender roles.

Nineteenth-century dress reformers in Europe and North America argued that women's clothing styles were unhealthy and unsanitary. They pointed out that corsets restricted the internal organs, long skirts picked up dirt and debris in the streets, and the construction of dresses constrained movement. Some of the first dress reformers were associated with the American Utopian movements of the 1820s to the 1860s. The members of the New Harmony settlement in Indiana, for instance, believed that marriage was an equal partnership between men and women—a radical, minority view at the time—and also considered trousers to be a practical dress form for women. For the general public, this reinforced the association of women's trousers with sexual impropriety. Sensationalizing critics of women's rights used the connection between women's trousers, communal socialism, and sexual unorthodoxy to discredit women's struggle for political rights.

Perhaps the most famous of the nineteenth-century dress reformers was Amelia Bloomer, an American women's rights and temperance activist. She proposed a costume for women that included a full, calf-length skirt worn over pantaloons. Bloomers were associated with women's rights campaigns, which limited their appeal to mainstream women. Bloomers seemed to prompt both outrage and hilarity. Humor magazines like *Punch* did not hesitate to lampoon these unorthodox costumes. At the same time, clergymen criticized this form of dress in their sermons, invoking the need to preserve the God-given distinction between the sexes through clothing. Bloomer herself dropped the issue of dress reform in the late 1850s, arguing that the introduction of the crinoline, a stiffened petticoat designed to support the skirt, made further reform unnecessary.

Working-class women in the nineteenth century did sometimes wear trousers. There is little documentation of working-class women's clothing, but one of the best records comes from the photographs and journals of Edward Munby, an English gentleman who developed an unusual fascination with working-class women. For example, he documented women brewery workers wearing trousers and photographed a woman pit worker wearing trousers in the 1870s. Munby described one such pit worker as "a woman in flannel trousers, waistcoat (with livery buttons in this case) and pink shirt and lilac cotton bonnet. . . . A quite respectable woman. . . . Her dress was not noticed in the streets: in Wigan, a woman in trousers is not half so odd as a woman in a crinoline. Barbarous locality" (quoted in Hudson, p. 76). Despite his own preoccupation with working-class women, Munby could not help but take an upper-class attitude about this style of dress and its general acceptance in the local community. At the same time, it is worth noting that the woman in the photograph he describes wears a feminine bonnet with her trousers, not a man's hat. This suggests that she thinks of herself as feminine, even when wearing trousers for work, and that she is interested in expressing this publicly and perhaps even in exercising a certain level of womanly charm.

The popularity of bicycles in the late nineteenth century in Europe and the United States furthered the development of bifurcated lower garments for middle-class women. Bicycles and their forerunners, like velocipedes, were mass-produced in the 1860s and 1870s, but they did not become popular among women until the 1880s, when Queen Victoria ordered bicycles for her daughters and the new drop frame facilitated women riders by accommodating the volume of their skirts. (The drop frame survives today: instead of a straight bar between handles and seat frame, a lowered rod connects the two.) Manufacturers patented several ill-fated attempts to deal with the skirt problem, including a cage-like dress guard and a screen to attach to the bicycle and hide the rider's legs. Initially, women shortened their skirts to avoid catching them in the mechanisms. There were also straps, cords, and clips to elevate skirts or tether them to the legs. Divided skirts designed expressly for cycling incorporated fullness and pleats or panels and aprons to conceal the bifurcation. By the 1890s, women often wore bloomers, sometimes called knickerbockers, for cycling. Although these garments were quite full, some still considered them insufficiently modest and inappropriate, although women had been wearing bloomers for swimming and gymnastics since the early nineteenth century with little controversy. In these situations, bloomers may have been considered acceptable because beaches and gymnasia were sex-segregated and so were not considered truly public spaces.

In the late nineteenth and early twentieth centuries, dress codes for women began to loosen. These changes can partly be attributed to women's increasing presence in the workforce—the "New Woman" was someone who might well have a career and more of a public life than her mother or grandmother. Although they invariably wore skirts, the new professional women often adopted elements of men's clothing, including tailored jackets and neckties. By the 1920s, the growth in casual sportswear for women meant that there was no longer a need for specific cycling garments.

The second half of the twentieth century was marked by the proliferation of trouser styles for women, many of which were invested with particular meanings and associations. In part, this era of women's pants was ushered in by World War II, as middle- and working-class American women took jobs in factories vacated by men. Under these circumstances, jeans and work pants became common feminine weekday attire and carried patriotic associations. Inspirational wartime posters of Rosie the Riveter depicted her in bib overalls, and retailers quickly renovated their work-clothes departments to include women as well as men. In the postwar period, this experience helped to make jeans acceptable attire for women—not just women working on farms or ranches or mines. In the 1960s, couturiers like André Courrèges began to design pantsuits, which further brought women's trousers into fashionable acceptability.

The countercultural revolution of the 1960s extended the fashion for jeans and pants for women and invested them with new meaning. Women began to wear men's jeans as an anti-fashion statement (ignoring the fact that a pair of jeans is just as "designed" as a dress or skirt). Still, wearing jeans felt provocative, a way of breaking boundaries of gender and class. Jeans had the look of practical, unpretentious clothing, worn in protest against the idea of any fashionable strictures at all. Jeans became associated with feminism, women's rights, and lesbian identity—in the same way that bloomers had in the nineteenth century. When middle-class women pursued corporate careers in increasing numbers in the 1980s, they adapted the men's suit—including trousers—as a mode of "power dressing." Crisp trousers and jackets with padded shoulders expressed women's desire to join the corporate world. Far from expressing a countercultural sensibility, women's trousers in this context expressed the desire to join the establishment.

Veils. Since the late twentieth century, with the emergence of Islamic fundamentalism as a powerful political force on the world stage, the veiling of Muslim women has become a hotly contested subject. Some argue that practices of veiling are a sign of the subjugation of Muslim women—others, the opposite. Veiling gets caught up in larger political debates and becomes a medium for discussing multiple issues of gender identity, nationality, religion, and politics.

Whether Islam actually requires the veiling of women is open to debate. The feminist theorist Bronwyn Winter demonstrates that only three verses in the Qurʾan mention body covering in relation to women, and none of them prescribes punishment for women who do not cover their bodies. For example, verse 53 of Sura 33 exhorts the Prophet's wives to "lengthen their garments" so as not to be insulted; it also advises those talking to the Prophet's wives to address them, for modesty's sake, from behind a barrier or curtain, a recommendation that is extended to other female believers in verse 59. Sura 34 recommends that women draw "a veil across their chests" so as not to sexually excite men. Among the Hadith, which are reports by others of what the Prophet said or wished, only one, written by Muhammad's wife ʿAishah, reports that the Prophet told her sister that once a girl reaches puberty only her face and hands should he seen. But the Hadith are not law in Muslim terms and often present conflicting recommendations.

Nonetheless, covering for women has long been practiced by Muslim communities and expresses important cultural, religious, and political values. It is important to note that the English word "veil" has no counterpart in Arabic, and the use of the term in the Western press tends to conflate a variety of distinct, but related, covering practices among a range of Muslim communities. The term *hijab* indicates a women's headscarf that covers the hair and the neck. It originally meant "curtain" and is worn once women reach puberty, although prepubescent girls are now often dressed in some form of headscarf in more conservative communities. Women in more conservative communities may also wear the *jilbab*. This outer garment takes the form of a long, loose tunic or coat that covers the body except for the face and hands. The *burqa* is a heavy garment that entirely covers a woman's head, face, and body, leaving only a small mesh screen for her to see through; it is often associated with the women of Afghanistan. In Pakistan, the *dupatta* is a light scarf worn around the shoulders or pulled over the head; a woman may also opt to wear the *chador*, a large shawl draped around the head and upper body. The term *chador* is sometimes mistakenly used as a synonym for both *hijab* and *jilbab*.

Muslim veiling practices have long been associated with women's modesty, as suggested even by the few Qurʾanic texts and Hadith that address it. Again, just as the form of veiling varies through time and from culture to culture, so do the places and actions that constitute veiling as a practice. Women may engage in veiling practices in front of certain older male relatives, strangers, or when praying. In Afghanistan, under the Taliban and even afterward, a woman would not leave the house unless wearing the total covering of a burqa, whereas Punjabi women, whether in Pakistan or abroad, wear the much-less-enveloping *dupatta* in various ways to signal differing degrees of intimacy, distance, and respect. Nonetheless, both forms of covering address issues of honor, shame, and the control of both women's and men's sexuality, as this covering is meant to remove a powerful sexual temptation to men. Ultimately, it is this association with modesty that may link veiling to the idea of piety, as two elements in the set of ideal feminine qualities, rather than any explicit connection made in Islam's holy texts.

The idea of a required or customary women's head covering may seem foreign to Europe and its settler societies. Modern Western women typically wear headgear by choice for practical reasons—as protection against cold, rain, or sun—or as an expression of individual taste. In parts of Europe it is customary, and stylish, for women to wear hats to weddings. (The British royal family may include the only women who still regard hats as *de rigueur* for all public engagements.) The one occasion on which veils still appear as customary attire with powerful symbolic value is of course the wedding day. The bride wears a veil that covers her face as she walks to the altar; when she arrives there, her father (or other escort), who is "giving" her away, will uncover her face and present her to her future husband.

In fact, head-covering practices were common until the second half of the twentieth century in the West. For example, until the Second Vatican Council of the early 1960s, Roman Catholic women had to wear a hat or veil to church. In Europe and the Mediterranean world, there is a long history of veiling or head and body covering for women. In her 1992 book *Women and Gender in Islam*, Leila Ahmed notes that Islam did not invent the veiling of women; it was a practice widespread in the Mediterranean and Middle East. In ancient Greece and Byzantium, for example, women were veiled, and respectable women sometimes lived in seclusion; in ancient Mesopotamia, the rules around veiling for women were detailed in law. In Europe in the Middle Ages, married women covered their hair for modesty's sake with veils, wimples, or other headgear (the wimple survives today in certain traditional nuns' habits). Among Jewish women, it was important to cover the hair, and women in different Jewish communities might wear hoods, scarves, or caps. These practices continue among some modern-day Jewish communities and are often inflected by local customs; Jewish women of the southern coast of Morocco, for example, wear the spectacular *mahdour* headgear fashioned of intricately worked silver interwoven with horsehair. Jewish women in sixteenth-century Europe began to wear wigs when they became fashionable, and this has survived as a head covering among some Jewish orthodox groups.

A focus on women's veiling and covering practices in general can obscure the fact that men have historically engaged in comparable practices. For example, there is evidence in pre-Islamic Arabia for veiling by men, which the scholar Fadwa El Guindi suggests may have served as protection against the harm resulting from envy. In ancient Rome, the men's toga was drawn over the head during certain religious observances. And many cultures require head coverings of various kinds—even if not veils per se—for men in order to observe propriety; until the second half of the twentieth century in the West, for example, a respectable man would not have left home without his hat, whether a worker's cloth cap or a businessman's homburg or fedora. Since the sixteenth century, men's head covering has become obligatory among observant Jews (it is thus a much more recent phenomenon than Jewish women's head covering) and the yarmulke (or *kippah*), a kind of skullcap, is a familiar visual symbol of Judaism. In Christian countries, where men uncover their heads at religious worship, covering the head for worship became a sign of Jewish spirituality and identity.

For some young women since the 1970s, especially emigrants living outside Muslim-majority countries, coverings like the *hijab* have become a powerful emblem, and a complex one. For some women, wearing the *hijab* is understood as an expression not of religion but of "ethnic identity." Especially when worn abroad, the *hijab* may express a "new" identity, part of a deterritorialized global movement of Islamic culture and religion. Pnina Werbner writes that wearing the *hijab* asserts identification broadly with the Middle East, the heartland of Islam, and with Arabic, the sacred language of the Qurʾan, and thus with Islam as a universal religion. In this sense, wearing the *hijab* is not particularly radical, although some young Muslim associations do deploy a radical, anti-Western rhetoric. In wearing head scarves and other coverings, young women may also well be setting themselves apart from their parents and grandparents, rather than following their precepts. The sociologist Ernest Gellner argued that "contrary to what outsiders generally suppose, the typical Muslim woman in a Muslim city doesn't wear the veil because her grandmother did so, but because her grandmother did *not*" (cited in Werbner, p. 173). Veiling has complex and shifting situational meanings in Muslim society, both as a cultural institution and as part of the wider honor and shame complex, pointing to different, and perhaps contradictory, social, and institutional processes.

All this has become further complicated by the rise of political fundamentalist Islam, which includes covering for women as part of its agenda, and with the aftermath of the terror attacks of 11 September 2001. In this new global politics, the kinds of values and identities expressed above through the head scarf and other coverings become directly linked to politics of the most volatile kind. The burqa, for example, has become the universal symbol of the Taliban's oppression of women in Afghanistan. Many feminists have critiqued the paternalism informing the typical Western media representation of women wearing the burqa as voiceless victims who have to be spoken for. In some ways, as Leila Ahmed notes, this representation is but the latest manifestation of a long tradition of colonizing powers in the Middle East and South Asia, focusing on veiling as the prime symbol of the "degradation of women" and "the backwardness of Islam."

This is not to deny the clear and obvious abuses of power that the Taliban exercised in relation to compulsory wearing of the burqa, through laws that were enforced with harsh punishments. However, it is important to remember that the burqa was only part of a continuum of oppression exercised by the Taliban. The enforcement of the burqa objectified women and interlocked with their lack of education, health care, and economic opportunity under the Taliban. However, the media, by setting up a stark contrast between the burqa as evil and unveiling as good, offers no possibility for women to *choose* to wear the burqa out of personal preference or cultural tradition. In fact, after the fall of the Taliban, a significant number of Afghani women continued to wear the burqa (although it was no longer compulsory) or other forms of covering.

The debates around veiling have become particularly heated in Europe, North America, and Australia, as Christian-dominated countries try to come to terms with Muslim populations within their borders. Perhaps the most prolonged—and bitter—of these debates surrounded the enactment of a French law in 2004 forbidding the wearing of prominent religious insignia by teachers or students in schools. Although this law could obviously apply to crucifixes or yarmulkes, it was widely perceived as being directed primarily at Muslim girls and teachers wearing *hijab*. Two widely divergent reactions to this law emerged among feminists. Many French feminists, in their support of a secular society and equal rights for women, opposed the *hijab* as a sign of religious conservatism and women's oppression. At the same time, a number of French and Muslim feminists, including the prominent Christine Delphy, have opposed the law, pointing to its colonialist and racist overtones. They believe that Muslim girls and women in France should be free to wear head coverings as part of a multicultural society. They also point out that schools are precisely the places where citizens may be educated and where debates about clothing, beliefs, and values can be freely undertaken.

In thinking about veiling, it is important to remember that oppression is not necessarily intrinsic to Islamic covering

Ceremonial Dress. Woman with a feathered headdress, Papua New Guinea. Courtesy of Jim Steinhart of www.TravelPhotoBase.com

practices but is instead socially constructed through the religious, cultural, and political actions and ideas that inform these practices. Veiling practices raise a series of essential questions about gender, identity, agency, cultural difference, globalization, diaspora, and religion that will only grow in importance in the twenty-first century.

Tattoo. Toward the end of the twentieth century, the number of people wearing tattoos in Australia, the United States, and Europe increased significantly; a 2001 survey detailing the use of body art by undergraduate students at Pace University in New York State, for example, estimated that 22 percent of the men and 26 percent of the women were tattooed. Where tattoos were once considered the province of marginalized populations—sailors, bikers, gang members, circus performers—they now have become mainstream, even a rather common middle-class rite of passage for young people in the Western world. The change has been most remarkable when it comes to women, who are getting tattoos in increasing numbers. This shift in tattoo practice expresses new values invested in tattoos.

The English word "tattoo," which is used in variations in many European languages, actually derives from the Tahitian word *tatau*. Eighteenth-century European explorers discovered tattooing practices in many of the Pacific cultures they encountered, including Tonga, Tahiti and the Society Islands, and Aotearoa/New Zealand. Tattooing practices in these cultures were often class- and gender-specific; in Aotearoa/New Zealand, for example, high-ranking women wore a special tattoo around the mouth and chin, while high-ranking men wore a full-face tattoo. Tattoos often expressed social rank, genealogy, and spiritual and protective values. Despite pressure from missionaries and colonizers through the nineteenth and early twentieth centuries, tattooing practices continued in many Pacific cultures and since the 1970s have experienced a revival. Although the Pacific may have provided the immediate source for modern Western tattoo practice, tattoo has a long history in many cultures, and there is evidence for tattoo among ancient Egyptians and Celts, among others.

Eighteenth-century explorers brought back scientific knowledge, plants, animals, ethnographic objects—and their own tattooed bodies—from their voyages to the Pacific. Tattoo from the eighteenth through the early twentieth centuries followed a strongly class-based pattern. Tattoos were simultaneously the province of both aristocrats and also the lower classes. Aristocrats could "afford" to get tattoos because of their social preeminence; tattooing did not put them at risk of ostracization, while the very lowest classes had little to lose. It was the broad middle class that shunned tattoo as a marginal practice that might damage their social status. There was a clear association between loss of respectability and tattoo for women, especially: in the 1920s a rape conviction was overturned because the woman had a small tattoo on her body, which was interpreted as a sign of sexual promiscuity. In many ways these attitudes held fast through the post–World War II period, and negative attitudes toward women with tattoos were remarkably strong, even among the tattoo community.

Interest in and attitudes toward tattoo, and women's tattoo in particular, began to change with the countercultural revolution of the 1960s. Many young people were less interested in conforming to social expectations or preserving bourgeois or middle-class values. Through the 1970s and 1980s, the punk and rock music scenes continued to popularize tattoo, and their fan bases brought tattoo to more mainstream audiences. Tattooed female rockers like Janis Joplin set an example for adventurous women to follow. By the early years of the twenty-first century, many more young women were getting tattoos than ever before. In the United States, where the drinking age is usually twenty-one but tattoo is legal at eighteen or even earlier, it has become an important rite of passage, a way of marking separation from parents (who themselves may find tattoos distasteful) and celebrating the ability to make one's own choices.

Parallel to this tattoo revival, and intersecting with it in some ways, is the renaissance of traditional forms of tattooing (and related forms of body art, including scarification and piercing) among indigenous peoples. As noted above, this tattoo renaissance has been particularly vibrant in the Pacific since the 1970s. In New Zealand, for example, it is now possible to see in Auckland and Wellington, as well as on tribal lands, young Maori women, who are entitled by descent to do so, wearing the chin and lip tattoo. In Tahiti and the Society Islands, where strong missionary prohibitions virtually eradicated tattoo practice for over a hundred years, many young women, especially those involved in dance troupes and other cultural groups, now wear tattoos inspired by traditional patterns. Tattoos in these contexts may take on new layers of meaning, signifying not only the social and spiritual values traditionally located in these practices but also the celebration of indigenous history, commitment to cultural continuity, and resistance to colonialist politics and racism. Although historically tattoo artists in Pacific cultures practicing tattoo were almost always male, today some women have also trained as tattooists and practice traditional forms.

While such tattoo practices may connect Maori and other indigenous women to cultural traditions, young women in Western cultures who engage in body art practices such as tattoo and piercing (beyond the earlobes—including nose, lip, tongue, navel, and other piercings) say that they believe these actions mark them as independent, brave, adventurous, and unique. A 2005 paper by Sarah C. E. Riley and Sharon Cahill suggests that young women often see tattoo or piercing as a way of distancing themselves from the traditional feminine ideal of being a "nice" girl in the sense of being obedient, passive, dependent, or fragile. At the same time, it is possible to see tattoo and related body art practices as just another example of women undertaking dangerous activities to fulfill an external standard of beauty—even if, in this case, it is a peer group standard of beauty and not a parental or societal standard of beauty. (Dyes and other ingredients in tattoo pigments are unregulated.) The feminist scholar Sheila Jeffreys suggests that tattoo can therefore be put on a continuum, in this view, with cosmetic surgery, breast augmentation, and the use of harmful ingredients in cosmetics. Research suggests that some young women engage in tattoo only if it underscores and enhances the ways that they meet these cultural ideals of feminine beauty—a tattoo on the stomach, for example, to highlight well-toned abdominal muscles.

Some young women do see the practice of tattoo as personally transformational, rather than being simply about appearance or sex appeal—as something that helps them change who they are and, for example, overcome shyness or express themselves fully. While many young women may get a small shoulder or hip tattoo and think nothing more about it, others become part of a subculture dedicated to body art practices and gain a sense of identity in this context. Riley and Cahill note that body art devotees are often quite dismissive of those who get an inconspicuous butterfly or unicorn tattoo; to devotees of body art, such young women are victims of a faddish consumer culture with little understanding of these art forms. Some young women will also get tattoos to mark meaningful events in their lives: recovery from abuse or the death of a loved one, for instance.

Despite the prevalence of tattoo, negative attitudes toward women with tattoos still persist, and some research suggests that men have more strongly negative reactions toward women with tattoos than other women do. As a new generation of children is now growing up with tattooed parents, it will be interesting to see how the values expressed by women's tattoo practice, and the responses to it, change over the coming decades.

[*See also* Dress Reform; Gender Roles; *and* Personal Services.]

BIBLIOGRAPHY

Ahmed, Leila. *Women and Gender in Islam: Historical Roots of a Modern Debate*. New Haven, Conn.: Yale University Press, 1992.

Atkinson, Michael. "Pretty in Ink: Conformity, Resistance, and Negotiation in Women's Tattooing." *Sex Roles* 47 (2002): 219–235.

Boucher, Francois. *20,000 Years of Fashion*. London: Thames and Hudson, 1987.

Byrde, Penelope. *The Male Image: Men's Fashion in England, 1300–1970*. London: Batsford, 1979.

Caplan, Jane, ed. *Written on the Body: The Tattoo in European and American History*. Princeton, N.J.: Princeton University Press, 2000.

Cunningham, Patricia A. *Reforming Women's Fashion, 1850–1920: Politics, Health, and Art*. Kent, Ohio: Kent State University Press, 2003.

DeMello, Margo. *Bodies of Inscription: A Cultural History of the Modern Tattoo Community*. Durham, N.C.: Duke University Press, 2000.

El Guindi, Fadwa. *Veil: Modesty, Privacy and Resistance*. Oxford: Berg, 1999.

Gray, Sally Helvenston, and Mihaela C. Peteu. "Invention, the Angel of the Nineteenth Century: Patents for Women's Cycling Attire in the 1890s." *Dress (USA)* 32 (2005): 27–42.

Hawkes, Daina, Charlene Y. Senn, and Chantal Thorn. "Factors That Influence Attitudes toward Women with Tattoos." *Sex Roles* 50 (2005): 593–604.

Hollander, Anne. *Sex and Suits*. New York: Knopf, 1994.

Hudson, Derek. *Munby, Man of Two Worlds: The Life and Diaries of A. J. Munby, 1828–1920*. London: Abacus, 1974.

Jeffreys, Sheila. "'Body Art' and Social Status: Cutting, Tattooing, and Piercing from a Feminist Perspective." *Feminism & Psychology* 10, no. 4 (2000): 409–429.
Keinlen, Alexis. "Skin Deep." *Herizons* 19, no. 2 (2005): 24–27.
Kidwell, Claudia B. *Women's Bathing and Swimming Costume in the United States*. Washington, D.C.: Smithsonian Institution Press, 1968.
Kuwahara, Makiko. *Tattoo: An Anthropology*. Oxford: Berg, 2005.
Joshi, O. "Continuity and Change in Hindu Women's Dress." In *Dress and Gender: Making and Meaning*, edited by Ruth Barnes and Joanne B. Eicher, pp. 214–231. Oxford: Berg, 1992.
Laing, Ellen Johnston. "Visual Evidence for the Evolution of 'Politically Correct' Dress for Women in Early Twentieth Century Shanghai." *Nan Nu: Men, Women, and Gender in Early and Imperial China* 5, no. 1 (2003): 69–114.
Luck, Kate. "Trouble in Eden, Trouble with Eve: Women, Trousers, and Utopian Socialism in Nineteenth-Century America." In *Chic Thrills: A Fashion Reader*, edited by Juliet Ash and Elizabeth Wilson. London: Pandora, 1992.
Marly, Diana de. *Working Dress: A History of Occupational Dress*. London: Batsford, 1986.
Mayers, Lester B., Daniel A. Judelson, Barry W. Moriarity, and Kenneth W. Rundell. "Prevalence of Body Art (Body Piercing and Tattooing) in University Undergraduates and Incidence of Medical Complications." *Mayo Clinic Proceedings* 77 (2002): 29.
Pipponnier, F., and P. Mane. *Dress in the Middle Ages*. New Haven, Conn.: Yale University Press, 1997.
Ribeiro, Aileen. *The Art of Dress: Fashion in England and France, 1750–1820*. New Haven, Conn.: Yale University Press, 1995.
Riley, Sarah C. E., and Sharon Cahill. "Managing Meaning and Belonging: Young Women's Negotiation of Authenticity in Body Art." *Journal of Youth Studies* 8 (2005): 261–279.
Schreier, Barbara A. "Sporting Wear." In *Men and Women: Dressing the Part*, edited by Claudia Bruch Kidwell and Valerie Stele. Washington, D.C.: Smithsonian Institution Press, 1989.
Scott, Joan Wallach. "Symptomatic Politics: The Banning of Islamic Headscarves in French Public Schools." *French Politics, Culture & Society* 23 (2005): 106–127.
Steele, Valerie. *The Corset: A Cultural History*. New Haven, Conn.: Yale University Press, 2001.
Strawn, Susan, Jane Farrell-Beck, and Ann R. Hemken. "Bib Overalls: Function and Fashion." *Dress* 32 (2005): 43–55.
Thomas, Nicholas, Anna Cole, and Bronwen Douglas, eds. *Tattoo: Bodies, Art, and Exchange in the Pacific and the West*. Durham, N.C.: Duke University Press, 2005.
Tortora, Phyllis G., and Keith Eubank. *Survey of Historic Costume: A History of Western Dress*. New York: Fairchild, 1998.
Werbner, Pnina. "Veiled Interventions in Pure Space: Honor, Shame, and Embodied Struggles among Muslims in Britain and France." *Theory, Culture & Society* 24, no. 2 (2007): 161–186.
Winter, Bronwyn. "Secularism aboard the Titanic: Feminists and the Debate over the Hijab in France." *Feminist Studies* 32, no. 2 (2006): 279–298.

ANNE D'ALLEVA

BOOK OF MARGERY KEMPE, THE, a medieval religious manuscript. *The Book of Margery Kempe*, written in the late 1430s, is a single manuscript in the British Library (Additional 61823) that was copied probably just before 1450 by a scribe who signed himself "Salthows" on the lower part of the final page. The first page of the manuscript is marked "Liber Montis Gracie. This boke is of Mountegrace," the important Carthusian priory in northeastern Yorkshire. The Carthusians were an order of silence, prayer, and contemplation whose scholarly inclinations link them to the collection and preservation of many devotional texts. Excerpts from the book were printed by Wynken de Worde around 1501 and reprinted by Henry Pepwell in 1521. However, the latter printing, which describes Kempe as an anchoress, comprised only seven pages drawn from the purely devotional sections of the book. The manuscript remained unknown until 1934, when it was discovered among the family papers of Colonel William Erdeswick Ignatius Butler-Bowden and was identified and announced in the *London Times* by Hope Emily Allen, the first notable scholar to study the work.

A narrative of the spiritual and physical journeys of Margery Kempe of King's Lynn in Norfolk, *The Book of Margery Kempe* is radical in its persistent quizzing of the institutions of late medieval civil and ecclesiastical life. Kempe was the wife and daughter of prosperous merchants in a prosperous port town and the mother of fourteen children. *The Book* recounts her conversion from a preoccupation with fashion and profit to a personal relationship with Jesus and, in so doing, explores the very nature of an English community whose ideals are Christian but whose practices are far more worldly and delimiting. Kempe was castigated and revered for her penitential weeping, devotion to Christ, idiosyncratic clothing, and holy conversation, but her story can be seen as an attempt to write the life of the holy woman—with all its inevitable conflicts—in English prose. Like Continental accounts of Mary d'Oignies, Christina Mirabilis, and Brigit of Sweden, *The Book* presents Kempe in a social milieu that venerates her holiness while it chastises her for her unwillingness to fit in with communal expectations regarding her gender and social status and suspects her faith as a manifestation of heterodoxy.

Though the prefaces to *The Book* as well as some sections within it insist on Kempe's need for a scribe to write her life, there are grounds for thinking about her as not illiterate. By this time women of her station were frequently literate in English, and there are moments in *The Book* when Margery suggests her own textuality. Whether or not Kempe is the author, *The Book* should be thought of as "authored," as a text that is concerned with the terms of late medieval English urban life, the formation of individual identity, and the nature of female authority even as it offers a map of the world conceived of as a series of interlocking pilgrim routes leading to the Holy Land and to shrines in Italy, Germany, Spain, and England. Its author has the ambitious agenda of the true writer.

[*See also* Literature, *subentry* Personal and Private Narratives.]

BIBLIOGRAPHY

Goodman, Anthony. *Margery Kempe and Her World*. Harlow, U.K.: Longman, 2002.

Staley, Lynn, trans. and ed. *The Book of Margery Kempe*. Norton Critical Editions. New York: Norton, 2001.

Windeatt, Barry, ed. *The Book of Margery Kempe*. Longman Annotated Texts. London: Pearson Education, 2000.

LYNN STALEY

BORETSKAIA, MARFA (15th century), one of the wealthiest members of the nobility of the northwest Russian city of Novgorod. Marfa Boretskaia was reputedly a leader of the resistance to annexation of Novgorod by the Russian state of Muscovy.

The daughter of Ivan Loshinskii and sister of Ivan Ivanovich Loshinskii, Marfa married Isaak Andreevich Boretskii, a boyar and *posadnik* (mayor) of Novgorod, who died in the 1460s. They had two sons: Dmitrii, who also served as mayor, and Fedor. Until Grand Prince Ivan III annexed Novgorod (1478), arrested her, and confiscated her extensive landed estates, which produced valuable products ranging from flax to fur, Marfa was one of the wealthiest individuals in Novgorod.

Boretskaia is known for her alleged political role in the events that led to Moscow's subjugation of Novgorod, a wealthy commercial center in northwestern Russia that controlled vast territories and valuable resources. Although Novgorod recognized the Moscow ruler as its prince, tensions over borders, taxes, and autonomy had strained relations between Novgorod and Moscow for decades. They reached a critical point when Ivan III and Metropolitan Filipp became convinced that Novgorod was planning to transfer its political and ecclesiastical allegiance to Lithuania. To prevent what they perceived as a treasonous and heretical act, Ivan III waged war and defeated Novgorod in the Battle of the Shelon' River (1471). Boretskaia's sons were leaders of the pro-Lithuanian faction in Novgorod. Dmitrii, mayor of Novgorod in 1471, led Novgorod's army against the Muscovite forces. After the battle, Ivan III ordered his execution. Although boretskaia's second son, Fedor, and her brother subsequently paid homage to Ivan, the grand prince arrested them in 1475 and held them prisoner in distant Murom. Boretskaia and one of her grandsons, Vasilii Fedorov, were arrested on 7 February 1478 and exiled to Moscow. The date of her death is unknown.

An anonymous essay, incorporated first in one late-fifteenth-century copy of the *Sophia First Chronicle*, identifies Boretskaia as the "evil woman" and traitor responsible for Novgorod's proposed alliance with Lithuania. It charges that she plotted to marry a Lithuanian nobleman with whom she would rule Novgorod under Lithuanian suzerainty and conspired with Pimen, steward to the late archbishop of Novgorod and unsuccessful candidate to replace him, to subordinate the Novgorodian eparchy to the Metropolitan of Kiev, a supporter of union between the Orthodox and Catholic Churches.

Although no other sources corroborate these assertions or register any political activism on her part, this account became the basis of her personal reputation as a leading political figure as well as the more general conclusion that women played influential public, political roles in Novgorod before its subordination to Moscow. Historical studies and fictional literature of the nineteenth and twentieth centuries also drew upon this account but transformed the characterization of Marfa "Posadnitsa" from an "agent of the devil" into that of a tragic figure who heroically defended Novgorodian independence.

[*See also* Russia and Soviet Union.]

BIBLIOGRAPHY

Lenhoff, Gail, and Janet Martin. "Marfa Boretskaia, *Posadnitsa* of Novgorod: A Reconsideration of Her Legend and Her Life." *Slavic Review* 59 (2000): 343–368. Compilation of biographical, economic, and political data on Marfa with an analysis of the sources and a reassessment of her reputation as an influential political figure.

Pushkareva, Natalia. *Women in Russian History: From the Tenth to the Twentieth Century*. Translated and edited by Eve Levin. Armonk, N.Y., and London: M. E. Sharpe, 1997. Contains a brief, traditional summary of Marfa Boretskaia's life and political significance.

JANET MARTIN

BOUCICAUT, MARGUERITE (1816–1887), entrepreneur, philanthropist, and cofounder of the first department store in Paris. Marguerite Guérin was born 3 January 1816, in Saône-et-Loire, southeast of Paris. Of peasant origin, she moved to Paris at thirteen upon the death of her single mother. She first acquired a position as a laundress and later worked in a restaurant, where she met Aristide Boucicaut. She and Aristide married in 1836; their only child, a son, was born in 1839 and died at a young age. In 1852, Aristide borrowed the money to form a partnership with Paul Videau, as coproprietor of the Bon Marché. At that time, the Bon Marché was a small store on the Left Bank with just four departments and twelve employees. In 1863, Boucicaut bought out Videau (who had been alarmed by Boucicaut's innovative marketing strategies), and by 1877 when Aristide died, he and his wife were the coproprietors of one of the largest retail enterprises in the world. Unlike small, specialized shops, the Bon Marché sold a variety of "novelties" (draperies and "fine goods"), allowed exchanges, and boosted sales with advertising and extravagant "white sales." To promote the idea that shopping could be an enjoyable experience, the interior of the Bon Marché was dedicated to elegance, glamour, and excess, complete with ornate metalwork, glowing lamps, flowing ribbons, and frescoed ceilings. Throngs of immaculately dressed middle-class shoppers visited the store for the aesthetic and social experience as well as the shopping.

The Boucicauts envisioned the Bon Marché as a "grand family," with Marguerite as the mother and Aristide as the stern but just authority figure. In this paternalistic relationship the couple provided free health care, meals, and schooling in return for the employees' dedication and loyalty. As in a strict family, however, employee morality was closely regulated, and workers were dismissed for proven infractions of the (bourgeois) moral code, such as infidelity or sleeping with a coworker. By providing for their employees' subsistence and occupying their free time with parties, recitals, and fencing lessons, the Boucicauts also hoped to shape their character and stem their impulse to unionize.

After her husband's death in 1877, Marguerite Boucicaut managed the store, attempting to carry out his wishes for its growth and mission. Under her direction the store expanded several times, eventually occupying an immense quadrilateral. In 1876 the Boucicauts had implemented a "provident" plan at the company's expense, which provided each employee a lump sum upon retirement. The widow continued this dedication to her employees' well-being (and commitment to the store) by establishing a pension plan in 1886. Concerned about the future of the store, in 1880 she had formed a partnership of her closest business associates to purchase shares in the company. Showing inspired business acumen, Boucicaut integrated statutes that allowed her to maintain control of the Bon Marché while she was still alive and ensured that the store would be directed by those "intimately associated with the firm" after her death. Her deepest wish was to guarantee the future unity, solidity, and traditions of the "Bon Marché family."

Having never forgotten her humble beginnings, Boucicaut left her entire fortune to her employees and benevolent organizations. Some suggest that, being childless, she developed deep maternal ties of responsibility to her employees and they therefore became her heirs. However, she also bequeathed donations to scientific, religious, artistic, and educational organizations and directed that the remainder of her estate be used to build a hospital and, because she had never known her own father, found centers for unwed mothers. By the time she died in 1887, Boucicaut had played an essential role in the consumer revolution inspired by the Bon Marché and had set an impressive precedent of benevolence towards both her employees and her fellow man.

[*See also* Consumption.]

BIBLIOGRAPHY

Very few sources on Marguerite Boucicaut are available, in French or English. Secondary sources in French are based on archival documents or rare books from the nineteenth century.

Miller, Michael B. *The Bon Marché: Bourgeois Culture and the Department Store, 1869–1920.* Princeton, N.J.: Princeton University Press, 1981. The only readily available source that discusses Boucicaut, the Bon Marché, and the bourgeois society in which the Boucicauts lived. Although Miller assumes that Madame Boucicaut did not participate equally in business decisions, he fairly portrays her important contributions to the well-being of the store's employees and her philanthropic and benevolent works.

CYNTHIA SHARRER KREISEL

BOUDICCA (d. 62 C.E.), leader of a rebellion against the Roman conquerors of Britain. Boudicca is usually referred to as the queen of the Iceni, whom scholars describe as a tribe. Prior to the conquest of Britain in 43 C.E., however, it is not clear that the various peoples who lived on the island saw themselves as tribes or their leaders as kings and queens. What we know of Boudicca and other local leaders in this period comes from archaeological evidence, which lacks information on the words Iceni used for their social structures, and from the early second century C.E. writings of the Roman historian Tacitus (*Annals* XIV.29–37), who uses terms familiar to him from his own world. The spelling of her name also appears as Boadicea or as Boudica.

Boudicca's husband Prasutagus had been made the client king of the Iceni by the Romans. This process of designating or approving a local leader was a normal part of Roman efforts to follow military conquest with pacification. Prasutagus was clearly a willing participant because his will left half of his considerable property to his two daughters and half to the Romans. But the loot was not enough to guarantee peace, and when Prasutagus died and Boudicca assumed leadership over the Iceni, Tacitus reports that the Roman authorities and the soldiers pillaged their property, abused their families, and raped Boudicca's daughters. Tacitus sees this as reason enough for rebellion and describes Boudicca as heroic, although he portrays the Iceni and their allies as bloodthirsty and without a sense of "the laws of war" (Tacitus, *Annals* XIV.33). The Romans failed to prevent the sacking of three of their cities, including London, before a final battle between Boudicca and Suetonius Paulinus, the commander of the Roman troops in Britain, resulted in the defeat of the Britons and led to Boudicca's suicide.

Two aspects of Boudicca's story are especially interesting. One is the way in which Tacitus uses gender to create an image of Roman moral failings. The second is his use of gender to characterize the barbarism of these uncivilized non-Romans. He gives Boudicca a rallying speech worthy of any leader of a modern national liberation movement (Tacitus, *Annals* XIV.35). He has her say that, though women have led the Britons into battle before, this time it is "to assert the cause of public liberty, and to seek revenge for her body seamed with ignominious stripes, and her two daughters infamously ravished. From the pride and arrogance of the Romans nothing is sacred; all are subject to violation; the old endure the scourge, and the virgins are deflowered.... Though a woman, my resolution is fixed: the men, if they please, may survive with infamy, and live in bondage."

Suetonius Paullinus then follows her speech with his own to the Roman troops (Tacitus, *Annals* XIV.36). He tells them "Despise the savage uproar, the yells and shouts of undisciplined Barbarians. In that mixed multitude, the women out-number the men. Void of spirit, unprovided with arms, they are not soldiers who come to offer battle; they are bastards, runaways, the refuse of your swords.... " The remark that the women outnumber the men is predicted in Tacitus's reports of Suetonius Paullinus's earlier battles with the Britons (Tacitus, *Annals* XIV.30).

Tacitus uses women as a vehicle both to criticize Roman conduct and morality and, at the same time, to describe Roman attitudes toward the people they view as barbarians. Boudicca thus became for the Roman writer a vehicle for larger political and moral concerns, just as for the English of a later era she became a signifier of British heroism and desire for liberty. For some feminists she has also taken on the role of signifier of women's heroism and is combined with such other premodern elements of women's culture as Wicca.

BIBLIOGRAPHY

Hingley, Richard. *Boudica: Iron Age Warrior Queen*. London: Hambledon and London, 2005.

Mikalachki, Jodi. *The Legacy of Boadicea: Gender and Nation in Early Modern England*. London and New York: Routledge, 1998.

Tacitus. *Annals* XIV.30–37; Agricola 16.1–2; Cassius Dio 62.1–12.

Webster, Graham. *Boudica: The British Revolt against Rome AD 60*. London: B. T. Batsford, 1978.

NATALIE B. KAMPEN

BOUHIRED, DJAMILA (b. 1935), a member of the Front de Libération Nationale during Algeria's war for independence from France. Djamila Bouhired is regarded as a leading heroine of the Algerian war of national liberation (1954–1962) and as a vocal activist in the movement for women's rights in independent Algeria.

Born in 1935, Bouhired came from a bourgeois Arab Muslim family from Algiers and was educated in a European-type school. Her story can be understood only within the larger matrix of colonial Algeria. By the revolution's eve, when Bouhired was in her late teens, Algerian demands for limited political and civil rights had been repeatedly rebuffed by the French regime and the nearly one million European settlers in the country. The nationalist struggle thus evolved into armed conflict, mainly in the form of guerrilla operations overseen by the revolutionary Front de Libération Nationale (National Liberation Movement, or FLN), in rural areas from 1954 until 1956, when the FLN's military strategy shifted to the cities.

Bouhired and other young women played a critical role during the battle for Algiers, which began in September 1956. Bouhired assisted the FLN leader, Saadi Yacef, in recruiting young Muslim women from the capital who could pass as Europeans. Dressed as Frenchwomen, Bouhired and two other female militants placed concealed bombs in the European sections of Algiers. Two bombs exploded, causing civilian casualties; Bouhired's bomb failed to detonate. This event and others unleashed the Battle of Algiers, which raged until 1957. Bouhired eluded the French military and police until April 1957, when she was arrested, imprisoned, and subjected to appalling torture; in July she was sentenced to death by the guillotine after a trial deemed a travesty of justice. However, Bouhired became a cause célèbre because of international media coverage of the French army's systematic use of torture, and she was eventually released.

After the 1962 peace treaty with France was signed, the newly independent Algerian government registered nearly eleven thousand women as war veterans; but this greatly undervalued the actual number of women who contributed to the war effort, often with their lives. To assert political authority as well as to restore their masculine pride, so badly bruised by colonial rule, male nationalists resisted demands for full female emancipation. Over the course of 132 years of colonial rule, Algerian woman had been the symbol of the nation's Islamic traditions and cultural authenticity. After independence, the problem of appropriate models for emancipation arose because it was unthinkable that Algeria's women would emulate French or other European women in terms of dress, public behavior, and legal rights. The struggle between modernists and traditionalists centered around family law and personal status codes that govern the lives of women and men. Legal rights for married women in particular were bitterly contested because under the body of family law enacted after 1962, women enjoyed greatly reduced rights when it came to marriage, divorce, inheritance, child support and custody, and so on. Thus a cruel irony emerged. If the role of activist heroine had been created largely by nationalism as well as by wartime violence and bloodshed, in the postcolonial era female public activism was delegitimized by the male leaders of that same nation.

In the early twenty-first century Djamila Bouhired continued to be actively involved in feminist politics, advocating fundamental transformations in the legal, political, and social status of Algeria's women.

[*See also* Nationalism, *subentry* Nationalist Movements.]

BIBLIOGRAPHY

Clancy-Smith, Julia. "The Colonial Gaze: Sex and Gender in the Discourses of French North Africa." In *Franco-Arab Encounters*, edited by L. Carl Brown and Matthew Gordon, pp. 201–228. Beirut, Lebanon: American University of Beirut Press, 1996. Traces the French colonial image of Algerian women from 1830 until the eve of the independence struggle.

Lazreg, Marnia. *The Eloquence of Silence: Algerian Women in Question*. New York: Routledge, 1994. A comprehensive study of gender relations in Algeria from the precolonial (prior to 1830) period to the Islamist resurgence of the 1990s.

JULIA CLANCY-SMITH

BOXER UPRISING. The Boxer movement (*Yihetuan yundong*) emerged along the provincial boundary of Shandong and Zhili (now called Hebei) in late 1898. Employing a range of martial-arts practices that Westerners referred to as "boxing," as well as deep-breathing exercises (*qigong*) and invulnerability rituals, groups composed mainly of young peasants and unemployed drifters spread rapidly across much of North China, attacking primarily foreign missionaries and Chinese Christians. The origins of the Boxer Uprising are to be found in a conjuncture of circumstances: deteriorating socioeconomic conditions, breakdown of public order, increasing assertiveness of Christian converts, fear of foreign invasion, and, most crucially, the onset of a prolonged drought in the fall of 1898. By the spring of 1900 Boxer groups had reached Tianjin and Beijing, by then (having adopted such slogans as "Protect the Qing! Destroy the foreign!") manifesting more general antiforeign and prodynastic tendencies. Tensions increased dramatically when the Boxers besieged the foreign communities in these cities, culminating in a declaration of war by the imperial court on 21 June. The siege of the legations in Beijing was not lifted by foreign troops until 14 August 1900. Afterward the Allied Expeditionary Force launched punitive expeditions to suppress the Boxer movement in the provinces.

The principal protagonists in this conflict (local self-defense forces, martial arts brotherhoods, Chinese and foreign armies) were all male-dominated. Nevertheless, women were involved, primarily as victims, but to some extent also as actors. In Beijing, Western women, including the women of the diplomatic corps, contributed to the defense of the international community during the sieges of the legations and the Northern Cathedral (*Beitang*) and distinguished themselves by active bravery and hospital work under siege. In the surrounding provinces, foreign women were more vulnerable. In an atmosphere marked by fear and anxiety, fed by rumors conducive to producing mass hysteria at a time of severe drought, Boxers attacked Christian villages and mission stations, killing over two hundred missionaries and about thirty thousand Chinese converts. The most notorious incident occurred at Taiyuan, the capital of Shanxi province. There the antiforeign Manchu governor Yuxian is said to have personally supervised the killing of Catholic and Protestant missionaries. Several reports assert that the women, including seven recently arrived Catholic sisters of the Franciscan Missionaries of Mary, suffered barbaric indignities prior to decapitation.

A significantly greater number of Chinese women suffered at the hands of the Boxers, Chinese troops, and/or foreign soldiers, yet far less is known about their ordeals. As far as female Catholic martyrs are concerned, some details can be gleaned from the subsequent investigations preceding the processes of beatification and canonization. Also, some Western eyewitnesses reported terrible atrocities committed by soldiers of the Allied Expeditionary Force, including looting and destruction of property as well as the indiscriminate killing of Chinese men, women, and children. Following the relief of Beijing, the legendary courtesan Sai Jinhua (1874–1936), said to have been the mistress of Field Marshall Count Alfred von Waldersee, mediated between foreign troops and the Chinese people.

In the Tianjin and Beijing region the Boxer cause was actively supported by a female organization called the "Red Lanterns" (*Hongdengzhao*), composed for the most part of teenage girls and young unmarried women with allegedly remarkable magical powers. While it was feared that the ritual uncleanliness of adult women was harmful to the efficacy of Boxer magic, the powerful magic of virginal, mostly prepubescent youngsters of the Red Lanterns was eagerly accepted by Boxer groups as essential to the successful conclusion of the antiforeign campaign. It was believed, for example, that these young women, appearing suspended in the sky, could send swords flying through the air to cut off enemies' heads. Lin Hei'er, known as the Holy Mother of the Yellow Lotus, the leading Red Lantern in Tianjin, was thought to be able to restore the dead to life. While these females in fact constituted a marginal element of the Boxer Uprising, they were subsequently assigned a prominent place in the Cultural Revolution mythologization of the movement.

It was Empress Dowager Cixi (1835–1908) who played the most prominent role in the fateful events of 1900. She retained full control at court and, some vacillation notwithstanding, it was she who declared war on the foreign powers and encouraged the Boxers to fight against them. As a consequence of this catastrophe, the empress dowager soon thereafter took the first tentative steps to improve the lot of Chinese women by issuing edicts to abolish foot binding and to establish educational facilities for girls.

[*See also* Cixi, Empress Dowager.]

BIBLIOGRAPHY

Brandt, Nat. *Massacre in Shansi.* Syracuse, N.Y.: Syracuse University Press, 1994. A detailed popular history of the Boxer attacks on missionaries in Shanxi province.

Cohen, Paul A. *History in Three Keys: The Boxers as Event, Experience, and Myth.* New York: Columbia University Press, 1997. A seminal work, focusing on the significance of drought and rumors as crucial factors, followed by a historiographical discussion.

Esherick, Joseph W. *The Origins of the Boxer Uprising.* Berkeley: University of California Press, 1987. The most comprehensive and convincing work. Essential for understanding the origins of the Boxer movement.

Hoe, Susanna. *Women at the Siege, Peking 1900.* Oxford: Women's History Press, 2000.

R. G. Tiedemann

BRAZIL. In Brazil—one of the most highly stratified societies in the world—the radically unequal possibilities for rich and poor, white and black, urban and rural have shaped women's identities, their relationships with one another, and the possibilities for their political mobilization and collaboration. The abolition of slavery in 1888 left poor black women in largely unchanged positions as domestic servants to their richer, whiter employers. Although modernizing elites introduced into the 1934 constitution the principle of equality before the law without distinction of sex, women were not able to mobilize into movements that could effectively insist on implementation of the constitutional principle. Despite their success in organizing across party lines to gain strong wording in the 1988 constitution affirming formal equality of rights and duties between men and women, discrimination continues to exist not only in practice but also in law. Implementation of women's rights has been difficult to achieve in a society whose economy did not incorporate large numbers of women into the formal labor force until recently and still does not produce services such as education and health care on a scale sufficient to empower the majority of Brazil's women.

Legacies of Slavery and Colonialism. In Brazil's nineteenth-century slave society, male property owners controlled the labor and sexuality of their wives, children, and various dependents. Because family honor depended on female honor, elite women were generally cloistered within their homes, where they tended to household production, the administration of health care, and the education of children. Until the second half of the nineteenth century, when sons gained autonomy through medical and legal training and the use of the dowry declined, marriages were carefully arranged to preserve families' wealth and social standing. Only widowhood freed wives from the legal incapacity of married women, and it empowered those who inherited plantations or family enterprises to assume larger social and economic roles. At the other end of the social ladder, slave women labored as field workers, domestic servants, street vendors, seamstresses, prostitutes, and so forth. Vulnerable to sexual exploitation, they struggled to create community life and intimate familial relationships.

Situated in between were the racially heterogeneous lower-class women who competed with slave women as domestic servants, producers of home crafts, and small-scale itinerant traders. As precarious as their employment was, it gave them a measure of personal independence and financial autonomy. Marriage was uncommon among the lower classes, and many women headed households. Highly sexualized in popular culture, the stereotypically beautiful and sensual mulatta was simultaneously valorized as a coveted object of desire, with the power to seduce and manipulate, and demonized as the carrier of the supposed

Brazilian Feminist Movement. Bertha Lutz, a prominent Brazilian feminist, speaks at the Brazilian conference to adopt the U.N. Charter, December 1944. Gjon Mili/Time Life Pictures/Getty Images

vices of poverty and racial mixture. According to the well-known racist and sexist maxim popularized by the twentieth-century Brazilian sociologist Gilberto Freyre, "the white woman is for marriage, the mulatta is for sex, and the black woman is for work."

The Modernization of Gender Hierarchy. Change came gradually with the acceleration of urbanization after 1870 and abolition of slavery in 1888. The center of economic dynamism and population density shifted south to the states and capital cities of Rio de Janeiro and later São Paulo, where elites introduced European technological innovations while they welcomed European immigrants and imported the latest fashions, fads, and ideas. Between 1872 and 1920, Rio de Janeiro's population more than quadrupled, to more than 1.2 million, and São Paulo's population increased twentyfold, to 579,000, creating new social classes, new markets for periodical literature and manufactured goods, and new forms of political mobilization. One novelty for Brazil was the high degree of visibility that "decent" (elite) women achieved in the urban abolitionist movement during the 1870s and 1880s. Nevertheless, incorporated as nonpolitical, moral agents, these women when transgressing into the male public realm did not give rise to a movement for women's rights; nor did more than a few isolated women activists dare openly to challenge male domination.

A less contentious cause was female education. Woefully inadequate public and private schools, along with national female literacy rates of less than 12 percent in 1872 and 1890 (compared to 19 to 20 percent for men), mobilized male reformers to join women activists in advocating the extension of public education to girls as well as boys. Although most demanded education tailored to prepare women to fulfill their "sacred mission" of educating their children, the expansion of schooling opened employment opportunities for female schoolteachers, who were heralded for bringing "civilization" to the larger Brazilian nation. Brazil's major cities, where literacy had always been highest, led the way. Between 1872 and 1920, female literacy in Rio de Janeiro and São Paulo rose from 29.3 percent to 55.8 percent and from 17.1 percent to 52.1 percent, respectively; moreover, women made up more than three-quarters of the schoolteachers in these cities by 1920.

Limited and uneven economic growth, combined with marked social stratification, created bifurcated opportunities for employment and social participation. Following the opening of Brazil's institutions of higher learning to women in 1879, a few women secured degrees in medicine, law, pharmacy, dentistry, architecture, and engineering. Although they remained a tiny elite even into the 1920s, they formed a vocal and well-connected leadership for the suffrage campaign that secured the female vote in 1932. Within the emerging urban middle classes, women's access to normal-school education prepared them not just to work as schoolteachers but also to fill new white-collar positions in growing government bureaus and commercial enterprises. Despite low wages, they participated to some degree in the new urban consumer culture of the late 1910s to 1920s, attending movies, listening to the radio, and shopping for fashionable readymade clothing in downtown department stores.

Rural women and women of the urban lower classes enjoyed few such opportunities. Domestic service continued to be the most common occupation for women through most of the twentieth century. In 1920, 82 percent of all domestic servants in Rio de Janeiro were women, and fully half of the city's female labor force was employed in domestic service. Others toiled for meager wages as street vendors, prostitutes, or pieceworkers or in unsafe factories. Family responsibilities, the sexism of male trade unionists, high turnover in many female jobs, illiteracy, and the isolation of many women workers in private homes made it unusual for women to join unions. Nevertheless, in industries such as textiles where women and girls made up the majority of the workforce, they participated actively in protest movements and strikes.

The difficulty of building interclass linkages among women whose life prospects differed so radically undermined progressive reform efforts. The fact that respectable women from "good" families led the Federação Brasileira pelo Progresso Feminino (Brazilian Federation for the Progress of Women), or FBPF, founded in 1922, contributed to the success of the organization's suffrage campaign, which relied on political connections rather than on shocking public spectacles. Also key to minimizing opposition was Brazil's electoral law that limited suffrage to literates, thereby excluding the majority of Brazil's adult women as well as men. Although the FBPF's founder and leader, the biologist Bertha Lutz (1894–1976), was a firm believer in women's employment and economic autonomy, and although the FBPF concerned itself with issues of equal opportunity, equal pay, and safe working conditions, the organization never succeeded in forging strong ties with lower-class women.

During the 1920s and 1930s the FBPF rank and file—including professionals, members of illustrious families, charity women, and more modest typists, shop clerks, and schoolteachers—tended to be socially conservative. Even those who worked for wages often made a point of emphasizing their devotion to domesticity. Using rhetoric that stressed women's altruism and moralizing mission, they supported formal legal and constitutional reforms, not radical changes in family relations. Radicals including the Brazilian Communist Party member Patricia Galvão (popularly known as Pagú) and the free-love advocate Maria Lacerda de Moura scorned Brazil's feminist movement as bourgeois and irrelevant, but they were at odds with one another and found no constituency for a socialist feminist movement.

In 1937, President Getúlio Vargas imposed the authoritarian Estado Novo (New State), which abolished elections, congress, and all forms of popular protest including feminist activism. The 1937 constitution eliminated the principle of equality before the law without distinction of sex that had been introduced in the 1934 constitution, and the government closed various high-level civil service positions to women, including in the foreign service. When a new political party system was formed after 1945, women remained marginal, relegated to women's auxiliaries to the parties. Though they continued to make progress in securing employment in "female" occupations in the commercial sector, social services, education, and health care, only two women were elected to congress before the 1964 military coup.

Between 1940 and 1970, technological change and the mechanization of production dramatically reduced the percentage of women in the agricultural sector, while women also lost ground to men in the manufacturing sector. With men favored to operate increasingly sophisticated machinery in the garment industry as well as in newer industries, many women were squeezed out of factories. They worked instead in putting-out systems or intermediary sweatshops, and until 1970 nearly a third of all employed women in Brazil still labored as domestic servants. Marked sex segregation in the labor market led to a wide gap between male and female wages. In 1973, 54.8 percent of working women earned the minimum wage or less, compared to 19.4 percent of working men.

In the politically polarized climate of the early 1960s in Brazil, right-wing groups successfully mobilized middle- and upper-class women to oppose the nationalistic and radical populist reform proposals of President João Belchior Marques Goulart. Anti-Communist and pro-family slogans helped to legitimize a military coup in 1964 that brought a dictatorship of generals to power for two decades. Their program of capital-intensive, export-oriented growth provided consumer goods for the expanding urban middle classes while it dramatically eroded the health and living standards of the majority of the population. In Brazil's strongly sex-segregated workforce, lower-class women suffered chronic unemployment, underemployment, and wage discrimination.

Paradoxically, the military government's rhetorical celebration of women's traditional familial roles was contradicted by policies that drove women into the public sphere. While poverty forced poor and middle-class women to seek employment, many middle- and upper-class women benefited from expanded educational and job opportunities, although still in predominantly female disciplines and occupations. Between 1969 and 1975 the number of women attending universities grew fivefold. By 1980, women made up more than half of all university students in Brazil. However, in pursuing careers, this small, privileged elite of well-educated women depended on and reinforced the structure of domestic service.

Brazil's sparse indigenous population—and indigenous women in particular—has been the most adversely affected by accelerated economic growth since the 1960s and by the concomitants of disease, violence, and cultural assaults. Modernization has resulted in growing dependence of women on male wage earners. As road construction, the gold rush of the 1980s, and steadily expanding ranching and agribusinesses drew indigenous men into the cash economy, the value of women's unremunerated contributions to the household declined. Men—who were further empowered by the acquisition of technical skills, access to schooling, and fluency in Portuguese—also consolidated their political authority over women within indigenous communities, and they represented community interests to the agencies and bureaucracies of the Brazilian state. The inadequacy of efforts to protect and empower indigenous women has fueled female out-migration to cities, where these displaced women eke out livings as maids and prostitutes and suffer devastating loss of cultural identity.

Second Wave Feminism. Beginning in 1974 the military initiated a gradual process of political liberalization that culminated in the installation of the New Brazilian Republic in 1985. Among the earliest and most vocal opposition forces were neighborhood-based groups of poor and working-class women who drew on a language of family well-being to protest the military's regressive wage policies and the rising costs of living caused by structural adjustment. The crucial support that many of these groups received from progressive sectors of the Catholic Church legitimated their demands for human and social rights but constrained discussion of sexuality, reproductive rights, and gender inequality within the family. At the same time, the United Nations–proclaimed International Women's Year of 1975 provided protection for a broader range of new women's organizations when much other political activity was still illegal and dangerous. During the late 1970s and 1980s a highly diverse women's movement brought women to the forefront of the larger movement for political democracy, which it enriched by adding feminist demands for the democratization of daily life.

According to Sonia Alvarez, Brazil's women's movements of the late 1970s and 1980s were "arguably the largest, most diverse, most radical, and most successful" in Latin America (p. 3). In addition to their early demands for political amnesty, urban infrastructure, social services, and employment opportunities, women's organizations began to focus on gender-specific issues such as day care, violence against women, divorce, sexuality, and reproductive rights. Among the most notable successes, the women's health movement pressured state governments to implement non-coercive family-planning policies, and beginning in 1985 various states opened women's police stations staffed exclusively by female police officers specially trained to process cases of rape, sexual abuse, and domestic violence. Mobilizing to achieve and to institutionalize these victories created meaningful interaction and alliances across racial and class lines as well as between feminists and those who did not self-identify as feminists. New organizations of black women, women trade unionists, landless rural women, indigenous women, academic and professional women, and lesbians further vitalized and broadened the horizons of the movement. By the 1980s Brazilian feminists were articulating a vision of democracy that required cultural as well as political and economic transformation.

With new political parties courting the female vote, women activists made rapid institutional gains. Core demands of the feminist agenda appeared in the platforms of all the major parties, and the first state councils on women's rights were followed by the creation of the Conselho Nacional dos Direitos da Mulher (National Council of Women's Rights) in 1985. Concerted efforts of the CNDM in coordination with other women activists led to the strengthening of the principle of equality without discrimination on the basis of sex in the 1988 constitution.

The constitution also finally explicitly revoked the husband's rights as head of the conjugal unit, specifying that husbands and wives have equal rights and duties. It also requires that the civil code, the penal code, and all ordinary legislation contradicting this principle of equality be altered or revoked, a project that is ongoing. The extension of social rights includes the lengthening of paid maternity leave from ninety to a hundred and twenty days and the introduction of paternity leave, a promise of specific incentives for the hiring and retention of women in the workforce, increased rights and social benefits for domestic workers, and a commitment by the state to provide free nurseries and preschools for children under the age of six. The constitution facilitates divorce—which was legalized in 1977 but is allowed only once in a person's lifetime—and specifies that access to family planning in state-funded health clinics is a constitutional right. However, because of the opposition of the Catholic Church, abortion remains illegal except in cases where pregnancy results from rape or incest or presents a risk to a woman's life.

Challenges of the Present and Future. Egalitarian law, though crucial, is insufficient to eradicate deeply rooted discrimination. A lack of political will and public funding has hindered implementation of constitutional principles on many fronts including equal pay, occupational opportunities, and guarantees of access to family planning and child care. In a frequently cited example, employers reluctant to assume the costs of pregnant employees monitor female employees' fertility, requiring pregnancy tests or a certificate of sterilization (which was legalized in 1994) as a condition of employment. Despite the need for intense mobilization and monitoring to ensure enforcement of the law, the CNDM fell prey to partisan manipulation and budget cuts in the 1990s. At the same time, women's grassroots movements lost momentum, although this was partially compensated for by the rise of feminist non-governmental organizations.

The 2002 election of President Luís Inácio "Lula" da Silva of the Partido dos Trabalhadores (Workers' Party, or PT) brought to power the Brazilian party with the most progressive platform on gender issues and the largest number of female officeholders. Among the most popular PT candidates have been women of modest backgrounds who, like the black governor of Rio de Janeiro, Benedita da Silva, have risen through activism in grassroots organizations or unions to national political office. Nevertheless, the most powerful factions of the PT—organized labor, the Left, and the Catholic Church—remain ambivalent about aggressively promoting a feminist agenda.

World Bank statistics show that women are making gains in Brazil. Between 1980 and 2004, women's life expectancy increased from sixty-six to seventy-five, the percentage of women in the labor force increased from 31 to 42, and women surpassed men in school enrollment and literacy rates. With increasing education and employment, fertility dropped from 4.0 births per woman to 2.3, and infant mortality declined from 67 per 1,000 live births to 32. Nevertheless, the wage gap persists, with the differential greater among those who have the most education. Among Brazilians with up to four years of schooling, women earn 80.8 percent of what men earn; among Brazilians with twelve or more years of schooling, women earn 61.6 percent of what men earn. In addition, compared to the rest of Latin America and world averages, women's representation in Brazilian politics is lamentably low. Despite the 1996 passage of a quota law requiring political parties to reserve a minimum of 30 percent of slots for women candidates, women still made up only 9 percent of the Chamber of Deputies in 2004. Loopholes in the law, weak institutionalization of Brazilian parties, and the persistence of masculine personality cults hinder women's advancement.

[*See also* International Women's Year; Nós Mulheres; Race; *and biographies of women mentioned in this article.*]

BIBLIOGRAPHY

Alvarez, Sonia. *Engendering Democracy in Brazil: Women's Movements in Transition Politics*. Princeton, N.J.: Princeton University Press, 1990.

Besse, Susan K. *Restructuring Patriarchy: The Modernization of Gender Inequality in Brazil, 1914–1940*. Chapel Hill, N.C.: University of North Carolina Press, 1996.

Caulfield, Sueann. In *Defense of Honor: Sexual Morality, Modernity, and Nation in Early-Twentieth-Century Brazil*. Durham, N.C.: Duke University Press, 2000.

Centro Feminista de Estudos e Assessoria (Feminist Center for Research and Consulting). http://www.cfemea.org.br. CFEMEA is a feminist lobby located in Brazil that conducts and publishes research, tracks progress on women's rights legislation, circulates a monthly newsletter, organizes conferences, and advises women in congress.

Dias, Maria Odila Silva. *Power and Everyday Life: The Lives of Working Women in Nineteenth Century Brazil*. Translated by Ann Frost. New Brunswick, N.J.: Rutgers University Press, 1995.

Drogus, Carol Ann. *Women, Religion, and Social Change in Brazil's Popular Church*. Notre Dame, Ind.: University of Notre Dame Press, 1997.

French, John D., and Daniel James, eds. *The Gendered Worlds of Latin American Women Workers: From Household and Factory to the Union Hall and Ballot Box*. Durham, N.C.: Duke University Press, 1997. Includes several articles on Brazil: Theresa R. Veccia, "'My Duty as a Woman': Gender Ideology, Work, and Working-Class Women's Lives in São Paulo, Brazil, 1900–1950"; Barbara Weinstein, "Unskilled Worker, Skilled Housewife: Constructing the Working-Class Woman in São Paulo, Brazil"; and John D. French with Mary Lynn Pedersen Cluff, "Women and Working Class Mobilization in Post-War São Paulo, 1945–1948."

Hahner, June E. *Emancipating the Female Sex: The Struggle for Women's Rights in Brazil, 1850–1940*. Durham, N.C.: Duke University Press, 1990.

Jaquette, Jane S., ed. *The Women's Movement in Latin America: Participation and Democracy*. 2nd ed. Boulder, Colo.: Westview Press, 1994. An anthology covering the 1970s and 1980s, including a chapter on Brazil written by Sonia Alvarez.

Levine, Robert M., and José Carlos Sebe Bom Meihy. *The Life and Death of Carolina Maria de Jesus*. Albuquerque: University of New Mexico Press, 1995. Study of the life and work of a destitute black woman who wrote a best-selling diary about her life in São Paulo's slums during the 1950s.

Nazzari, Muriel. *Disappearance of the Dowry: Women, Families, and Social Change in São Paulo, Brazil, 1600–1900*. Stanford, Calif.: Stanford University Press, 1991.

Patai, Daphne. *Brazilian Women Speak: Contemporary Life Stories*. New Brunswick, N.J.: Rutgers University Press, 1988.

SUSAN K. BESSE

BREMER, FREDRIKA (1801–1865), Swedish novelist, travel writer, and social critic. Fredrika Bremer was born in Åbo, Finland (then owned by Sweden), but lived most of her life just outside Stockholm. An international networker and social critic who traveled and corresponded in several languages with women and men in Europe, the Middle East, and the United States, Bremer began as a novelist and later became an important spokesperson for women's rights, especially those of single women—she never married. Her own travels, begun after she was well known in Sweden and after her novels had been translated, were undertaken so that she could observe evidence of Christian worship and the position of women.

In the United States from 1849 to 1851, Bremer visited notable women, including Lucretia Mott and Harriet Beecher Stowe. She met Indian women in Wisconsin, slave women in the South, and abolitionist women in the North. At one point she spent several days with her fellow countrywoman Jenny Lind in Cuba. An accomplished artist, Bremer sketched and painted many of those she met, as well as the flora and fauna she came across in her travels. In a long letter to Queen Carolina Amelia of Denmark (April 1851), she discussed the superior position of women in the United States, especially in education.

Bremer's novel *Hertha* (1855) attacked the Swedish law of patriarchal guardianship over daughters. The novel influenced public debate and helped foster changes in the law. In the novel, Bremer used her favorable impressions of the relative freedom of American women, just as in her earlier novel *Brothers and Sisters* (1848) she had drawn inspiration from Saint-Simonian and Fourierist communities in France, England, and the United States.

In 1854, Bremer and a group of philanthropic Swedish women recommended organizing an international alliance of women for the promotion of peace and welfare. The alliance would ask each country to organize all female societies in that country and send out a newsletter describing their work to the central committee of all other countries. Bremer's proposal was sent to the *Times* of London and was published on 28 August 1854, during the buildup to the Crimean War. The letter was belittled by the editors, who asserted that such a scheme would be not only expensive but useless. "Besides," they continued, "if universal womanhood is to turn itself to the organization of charitable associations, what is to become of our *homes*?" Although Bremer couched her argument in terms of the Christian responsibility of women, her organizational strategy was still quite radical: she called all women sisters, reaching for commonality beyond diversity.

Fredrika Bremer did not return home from her next trip for five years, traveling from Belgium to Turkey, Syria, Palestine, Greece, and Italy between 1856 and 1861. Everywhere she visited the important women, sought out information on the "average" woman, resurrected women's history, and worried about the state of the souls and bodies of her interlocutors. She visited schools, convents, hospitals, orphanages, harems, and villages—and was entertained by royalty and aristocratic expatriates. She made astute observations about national character and worried about the position of women, especially unmarried women. She used an early form of the participant-observer method to carry out a monthlong retreat at a convent in Italy to learn more about Catholicism, although she was passionately Protestant.

Bremer, despite her enthusiasm for sisterhood, remained an "equality in difference" feminist. Her position is squarely in the separate-spheres camp: she believed, as she wrote in a letter in December 1837, that women are given "something higher than law, something more important than legislation, that is the moral spirit."

[*See also* Feminism; Literature; *and* Scandinavia.]

BIBLIOGRAPHY

Bremer, Fredrika. *Appeal to the Women of the World to Form a Peace Alliance* (1854). Reprint. Stockholm: Swedish National Council of Women, 1915.

Rooth, Signe Alice. *Seeress of the Northland: Fredrika Bremer's American Journey, 1849–1851*. Philadelphia: American Swedish Historical Foundation, 1955. Quotes extensively from Bremer's *The Homes of the New World: Impressions of America* (1853).

Stendahl, Brita K. *The Education of a Self-Made Woman: Fredrika Bremer, 1801–1865*. Lewiston, N.Y.: E. Mellen, 1994.

MARGARET H. MCFADDEN

BRONTË, CHARLOTTE (1816–1855), English writer noted for her novel *Jane Eyre* (1847). The daughter of the Reverend Patrick Brontë and his wife, Maria, Charlotte Brontë spent most of her childhood and adult life at the remote Haworth Parsonage in Yorkshire. There she and her siblings roamed the moors and wrote stories and poetry. Before becoming a published author, she taught school and worked as a private governess, experiencing firsthand the hardships of the middle-class unmarried Victorian woman that she would later write about in her novels.

Despite her father's insistence that she concentrate on domesticity, Brontë was determined to make a career as a writer. In 1846 she and her sisters, Emily and Anne, published a volume of poetry under the pseudonyms of Currer, Ellis, and Acton Bell, respectively. Although critically acclaimed, the book sold very few copies. In 1847 a novel by "Currer Bell" about a penniless orphan who becomes a governess and marries her tormented employer became an immediate best seller. Critics hailed the novel, and even Queen Victoria called *Jane Eyre* a "really wonderful book." When Brontë later revealed the true identity of all the "Bells," she explained that they had feared that "authoresses are liable to be looked on with prejudice." Her belief was justified when critics reevaluated *Jane Eyre*'s author as "unwomanly" and its subject matter as "coarse."

In 1854 Brontë married her father's curate, Arthur Bell Nicholls. She died from complications of pregnancy on 31 March 1855 in Haworth, Yorkshire, having outlived all her siblings. Her other novels include *Shirley* (1849), *Villette* (1853), and *The Professor* (1857).

After Elizabeth Gaskell's biography, *The Life of Charlotte Brontë*, was published in 1857, Brontë, along with Emily and Anne, quickly became a cultural icon. Gaskell told a dramatic tale of three lonely sisters, dominated by a tyrannical father, playing out their tragic destiny on the isolated moors of northern England. Gaskell thus assuaged Victorian critics by attributing *Jane Eyre*'s "coarseness" to the misery its author endured. The Brontës soon became the center of a great romantic legend, portrayed as gothic creatures doomed to early deaths, their unhappy lives overshadowing their novels. Since Gaskell's biography, the Brontë myth has evolved to reflect changing attitudes about the role of the woman writer. Lyndall Gordon, for example, sees Brontë as ahead of her time, having to hide her true self (daring and articulate) under an acceptable public image of the modest woman writer.

Literary critics all over the world continue to debate the feminist elements of Brontë's novels. Jane Eyre's passion, intelligence, and physical plainness subvert the image of the angelic Victorian heroine, but the novel is not a plea for economic or legal equality of the sexes. Jane does, however, lament women's confinement "to making pudding and knitting stockings, to playing on the piano and embroidering bags" (chapter 12). Overall, Charlotte Brontë was not the martyr depicted in Gaskell's biography but a complex and intelligent woman, acutely aware of the precarious position of the single middle-class woman in Victorian society.

[*See also* Literature.]

BIBLIOGRAPHY

Gaskell, Elizabeth. *The Life of Charlotte Brontë*. London: Smith and Elder, 1857.

Gordon, Lyndall. *Charlotte Brontë: A Passionate Life*. London: Chatto and Windus, 1994.

Miller, Lucasta. *The Brontë Myth*. London: Jonathan Cape, 2001.

Moglen, Helene. *Charlotte Brontë: The Self Conceived*. New York: Norton, 1976.

JULIE ANNE TADDEO

BROOKS, GWENDOLYN (1917–2000), poet and novelist. Gwendolyn Brooks was born on 7 June 1917 in Topeka, Kansas, to Keziah and David Brooks. When she was an infant, the family moved to Chicago, where Brooks resided until her death on 3 December 2000. Chicago's South Side became Brooks's lifelong home, and its diverse black community served as a source of literary inspiration for her. Brooks graduated from Wilson Junior College in 1936. Two years later, she met Henry Blakely, whom she married in 1939. The couple had two children, a son, Henry III, in 1940 and a daughter, Nora, in 1951.

Encouraged to read and write by her parents, Brooks was accomplished enough by age thirteen to publish her first poem in *American Childhood* magazine. In her teens, she met Langston Hughes (1902–1967), who complimented her efforts and suggested that she study the work of modernist poets such as T. S. Eliot (1888–1965) and e. e. cummings (1894–1962). By the time she graduated from high school in 1934, Brooks had published nearly a hundred poems in "Lights and Shadows," a weekly column in the *Chicago Defender*. Following high school, Brooks worked briefly as a maid, an experience she would later depict in her autobiographical novel *Maud Martha*. She was also employed as a secretary to a spiritual adviser who operated a Chicago apartment building known as the Mecca, which would become inspiration for *In the Mecca*, a collection of poems.

When Brooks joined the NAACP Youth Council in 1937, she met young people who shared her interest in writing. She later participated in a poetry class where she was further exposed to modernist poetry. During this time Brooks wrote many of the poems included in her first collection, *A Street in Bronzeville* (1945). In the wake of positive critical responses to *Bronzeville*, Brooks won a number of awards, including two Guggenheim fellowships in 1946 and 1947.

In 1950, Brooks became the first African American to win the Pulitzer Prize in poetry for *Annie Allen*, published in 1949. With the publication of *Annie*, Brooks's arrival as a new and compelling woman's voice was confirmed. A highly complex mock-heroic narrative poem, *Annie* is significant historically for its representation of Brooks's working-class black heroine's experience—her dreams, courtship, marriage, abandonment, and ultimate survival in the urban environment. At a time when black Americans, and black women in particular, were socially invisible, Brooks gave them voice and visibility through her poetry.

In the early 1950s, Brooks turned her hand to prose and published *Maud Martha* in 1953. In *Maud*, Brooks depicts the triple jeopardy of race, gender, and class faced by black women in American society. Maud, the dark-skinned heroine, confronts a standard of beauty that places her, literally, beyond the pale. Brooks is the first black woman writer to explicitly address the devastating psychological impact an exclusionary Western standard of beauty can have on black women. This theme is echoed in the work of subsequent generations of black women writers, including Toni Morrison in *The Bluest Eye* (1970) and Alice Walker in her Pulitzer Prize–winning *The Color Purple* (1982).

The literary achievements of Brooks were well honored during her lifetime. The state of Illinois acknowledged her work by naming her poet laureate for the state in 1968. In 1985 she became the first black woman appointed poetry consultant to the Library of Congress. She also received a prestigious Lifetime Achievement Award from the National Endowment for the Arts in 1989. In 1990 Brooks became the first American to receive the Society of Literature Award from the University of Thessaloniki in Athens, Greece, and the National Endowment for the Humanities named her its Jefferson Lecturer for Distinguished Intellectual Achievement in the Humanities in 1994. In addition to numerous other awards and prizes, Brooks was awarded more than seventy honorary doctoral degrees.

Brooks influenced at least three generations of writers during a career that spanned sixty years. She produced over twenty books of poetry, a novel, two memoirs, essays, children's books, and book reviews. Her writing served as the eloquent voice of a silenced and oppressed black America during the 1940s and 1950s, and in later decades she wrote as a consciousness-raising poet of the black poor and powerless. Brooks's work also honors and validates women's experiences in the private and public spheres. Over time, her writing has become the ubiquitous voice of blacks, women, and working-class people, inspiring and empowering new generations of poets and writers. Brooks's contribution to the tradition of women's writing is evident in the republication and ongoing critical appreciation of her life's work. The homage accorded Brooks for her accomplishments as a poet and writer suggests but cannot fully measure her profound contributions to arts and letters and to the struggles of ordinary people for justice and dignity in America and the world.

[*See also* Literature; Morrison, Toni; *and* Walker, Alice.]

BIBLIOGRAPHY

Christian, Barbara. *Black Women Novelists: The Development of a Tradition, 1892–1976*. Westport, Conn.: Greenwood Press, 1980.

Mootry, Maria K., and Gary Smith, eds. *A Life Distilled: Gwendolyn Brooks, Her Poetry and Fiction*. Urbana: University of Illinois Press, 1987.

PAULETTE CHILDRESS

BROWN, CHARLOTTE HAWKINS (1883–1961), African American educator, fund-raiser, women's leader, and public speaker. Brown was born in Henderson, North Carolina. Her seventeen-year-old unmarried mother, Caroline Hawkins Willis, later became a laundress and business owner. Her absent father was never identified. The extended family moved to Boston in 1889 to escape Jim Crow and seek economic and social opportunities. Charlotte attended school in Cambridge and in 1900 graduated from the prestigious English High School after changing her name from Lottie to Charlotte Eugenia, which she perceived as far more dignified for a young lady. In high school she attracted the attention of the Massachusetts educational leader Alice Freeman Palmer, who offered to finance Charlotte's education at normal school. In 1901 after a year at the Massachusetts State Normal School in Salem, the eighteen-year-old Charlotte moved from cosmopolitan Boston to rural North Carolina to teach at the

Bethany Institute, one of hundreds of small American Missionary Association (AMA) schools for African Americans in the state. She found a bleak community in a segregated Jim Crow society of illiteracy, intolerance, and some danger. State public schools for both races were woefully inadequate. When Bethany closed in a few months, Brown began her own school, Palmer Memorial Institute, in Sedalia, North Carolina, without any material resources. Fifty years later she retired as head of Palmer, which by then was acclaimed as the school of choice for upper-class African Americans along the eastern seaboard. With perseverance, intellect, active faith in God, persuasiveness, and good luck, Brown blended racial accommodation with some activism in a formula based on education, hard work, propriety, and social graces. Of the many black schools in the state, only Palmer gained national renown, and it outlasted virtually all of them.

Brown's career at Palmer exemplified several themes in African American history. Prizing education, she represented rising middle-class womanhood, a group who hoped that blacks would achieve respectability through education and then progress to full economic, social, and civil rights and freedoms. She espoused racial uplift, dignity, and propriety. In her life the formula had practical merit, and she spread her philosophy tirelessly.

Unlike most African American schools, Palmer resulted directly from one able black woman rather than from white paternalism. Over seventy years, primarily under half a century of Brown's leadership, the institute became a preparatory school attracting students from many states and overseas while producing more than a thousand graduates, including many professionals and leaders in society. Brown was greatly influenced by her strong mother and grandmother, both determined, able women who wanted their respective daughters to be achievers and ladies of propriety and culture. She was a zealous crusader, sacrificing health, two marriages, and economic security. A marriage to the teacher Edward S. Brown in 1911 ended in divorce in 1916; a hasty union in 1923 with the promoter John W. Moses was annulled within a year. The childless Brown helped raise several children of relatives and friends.

Brown developed the Palmer Memorial Institute with biracial support and help from national figures, especially the Boston philanthropist Galen Stone. Initially teaching industrial skills, she maintained a parallel liberal arts curriculum. She energetically obtained funds in the North and the South, often from women. Seeking stability, Brown raised $300,000 in the 1920s and reunited with the AMA until 1934. Wooing statewide leaders and attracting more money, she made Palmer an independent residential school and junior college.

Having spoken in thirty-five states by 1930, Brown stressed cultural education for racial uplift, was known as the "first lady of social graces" after a national network radio appearance and publication of an etiquette book, and received honorary degrees. She pioneered state women's movements. She was a founder of the North Carolina Federation of Negro Women's Clubs and its president for two decades, president of the North Carolina Teachers Association, and a national officer in various women's groups.

After Brown retired, her chosen successor, Wilhelmina Crosson, ran Palmer for fifteen years. Then, after Crosson's tenure, inexperienced new leadership and competition from public schools proved fatal within five years. Eventually the campus became a state-run historic site.

[*See also* Bethune, Mary McLeod; Clark, Septima Poinsette; Cooper, Anna Julia; *and* National Association of Colored Women.]

BIBLIOGRAPHY

Hunter, Tera. "The Correct Thing: Charlotte H. Brown and the Palmer Memorial Institute." *Southern Exposure* 11, no. 51 (September–October 1983): 37–43.

Wadelington, Charles W., and Richard F. Knapp. *Charlotte Hawkins Brown and Palmer Memorial Institute: What One Young African American Woman Could Do.* Chapel Hill: University of North Carolina Press, 1999.

RICHARD F. KNAPP

BRUNDTLAND, GRO HARLEM (b. 1939), a Norwegian physician, politician, environmentalist, and global health authority. Gro Harlem Brundtland has had a powerful impact in each of these fields and in the lives of European women. Her influence has also transcended the boundaries of her fields of expertise, indicating the important intersections of health, politics, environmentalism, and feminism, as well as the transdisciplinary reach of her personality and accomplishments.

Born 20 April 1939, Brundtland was the daughter of Gudmund Harlem, a physician and political figure in his own right. After graduating with a medical degree from the University of Oslo, Brundtland earned a master of public health degree from Harvard University in 1965, where she focused on the health impact of pollution and other environmental problems. She returned to Norway as a specialist in preventive medicine as well as in maternal and child health.

Her political career began in 1974 when she was named Norway's minister for environmental affairs, a position she held until 1979. A prominent member of the Labor Party, she was elected to Parliament in 1977 and became Norway's youngest and first female prime minister at the age of forty-one in 1981. She returned to the position twice, serving from 1986 to 1989 and from 1990 to 1996. Brundtland did much to enhance women's political influence in Norway, in 1983 establishing a widely imitated requirement that women constitute at least 40 percent of the Labor Party's candidates in every election. She also greatly enhanced women's political visibility as prime minister, appointing women to nearly half of her cabinet positions. These moves had a pronounced effect in Norway and throughout Scandinavia, where Sweden, Finland, and Denmark rapidly established similar systems.

Brundtland rose quickly to international prominence as an environmentalist as well. From 1984 to 1987 she headed the World Commission on Environment and Development, colloquially known as the Brundtland Commission. This group produced the 1987 report *Our Common Future*, which introduced the concept of sustainable development. Merging her interests in maternal and child health and in environmental health, the report illustrated the direct relationships between population health and environmental degradation as linked to global development.

In 1998, Brundtland was elected director of the World Health Organization (WHO). Among her principal concerns in this post was promotion of awareness about the global relationship between poverty and health. Although poverty had long been recognized as a determinant of ill health, Brundtland argued that poor health also stifled economic growth in the developing world. She therefore forged new relationships between WHO and other U.N. organizations, such as the World Bank, to promote a symbiotic understanding of health and development. Although some criticized Brundtland for developing partnerships between WHO and pharmaceutical conglomerates—thereby fostering the organization's dependency on private corporations while simultaneously enriching them—she was also the first WHO director to persuade drug companies to lower prices for the developing world. Brundtland also placed violence on the WHO agenda as a critical determinant of health in the developing world—one that has disproportionately affected women and children.

After leaving WHO in 2003, she continued her work with the United Nations as an Environmental Envoy, and in 2007 the U.N. secretary general Ban Ki-Moon named her one of three Special Envoys for Climate Change. Among other awards and honors, Brundtland was recognized by *Scientific American* as Policy Leader of the Year in 2003 for her coordination of WHO's response to the SARS epidemic. The following year the *Financial Times* ranked Brundtland the fourth most influential European of the previous quarter-century.

[*See also* Ecofeminism; Health; *and* World Health Organization.]

BIBLIOGRAPHY

Altman, Lawrence K. "The Doctor's World: Next W.H.O. Chief Will Brave Politics in Name of Science." *New York Times*, 3 February 1998, p. 3. A profile of Brundtland emphasizing her agenda as WHO director.

Mathews, Jessica. "Norway's Woman of Influence." *Washington Post*, 28 October 1996, p. A21. A biographical profile emphasizing Brundtland's political and environmental careers.

Naím, Moisés, and Gro Harlem Brundtland. "The FP Interview: The Global War for Public Health." *Foreign Policy* 128 (2002): 24–36. A feature interview highlighting a range of WHO programs implemented under Brundtland's watch, including the Roll Back Malaria campaign, anti-tobacco initiatives, and reproductive health programs.

Richard C. Keller

BUDDHISM. Buddhism is unique among major religions in that it originates from a philosophical argument: that belief in a substantial self is at the root of desire, and that we will suffer if and only if we have desires. Despite this logical spine, tensions in fundamental attitudes have been persistent within Buddhism, as within many religious movements. Scholars such as Diana Paul have commented on the tension, running through Buddhist discussions of women, between two contrary attitudes. One is gender discrimination, part of the cultural baggage that has been placed on Buddhism in most societies it has reached. The other is that humans, both women and men, generally have the capacity for Buddhist enlightenment. Often both attitudes run together in the same text.

The central ideas in early Buddhism (emphasized especially in the centuries before the Common Era, B.C.E.) were as follows. The self—the "me" that pervades virtually everyone's thoughts—has no fundamental reality. This illusion of a real self lends itself to a habit of desiring. This often (although not always) takes the form of desiring things for "me." Because desires are often frustrated, and also (even if they are attained) lead to further desires (and ultimately boredom or frustration), desire is the source of suffering. The only cure is to lose all of one's desires, even unselfish ones, and to have only mild preferences. The early texts generally assumed that this requires freeing oneself from the illusion of having a fundamentally real self.

Some early Buddhist texts, while denying that there is a substance of self deep within us, left room for the notion of a constructed self, built out of our thoughts and habits of mind. Like the Scottish philosopher David Hume (1711–1776) two millennia later, these texts insisted that the self of social intercourse is conventional, built out of bundles of psychological processes. There is no deep reality to it. Realization of this was treated as being liberating.

Once it was realized that the deeply real substantial self was an illusion, one could appreciate that our positive or negative experiences could just as easily have been someone else's. This left room for a low-key compassion, which preferred

Tibetan Buddhism. Sita Tara, a female Buddha associated with Buddhist Tantric practice. She represents compassion, long life, healing, and serenity. Tibet, fifteenth century. RUBIN MUSEUM OF ART

that sentient beings not suffer. This compassion lacked the intensity and attachment characteristic of what we would term "desire." To desire something is to have a very strong preference, so that you really are attached to the idea of getting (or not losing) what is desired. Desires, whether entirely satisfied or not, lead to other desires. Inevitably some will not be satisfied, leading to keen frustration and to suffering.

Suffering goes beyond pain, in that it includes also a sense that something else is in control: if you have to have something, that thing is in control. The frustration of desire can occur at any time, but such experiences are especially likely during sickness or in old age. The shock of finding out about sickness, old age, and death was a large element in the legends of the early life of Siddharta Gautama (Buddha; c. 500 B.C.E.), which were the story of how he became convinced that there was a pandemic of suffering. Buddha's search for a cure led him to the idea of the loss of desire, linked to the loss of a sense of an ultimately real self.

These interconnections were the logic of Buddhism, and it was assumed that anyone who can think rationally could see the logic. Thus, in the earliest period, enlightenment and liberation were thought to be possible in this lifetime for anyone, regardless of status in the traditional Indian castes, and also regardless of gender. There were nunneries as well as monasteries for those who wanted to make a concentrated effort.

Because Buddhism, like other religions, took root in particular social and cultural contexts, its practices varied accordingly. The forms of Buddhism to be encountered in China and Japan were not exactly like those of Sri Lanka (formerly Ceylon) or Southeast Asia. As one small example: meditation in charnel areas or graveyards appears to have been far less common in Japan than it has been in some other Buddhist countries. Similarly, attitudes toward women in Buddhism have varied from place to place, from time to time; even in a given place at a given time they could vary from one sect to another. Further, even the same writer might express conflicting attitudes. There was considerable ambivalence about women within Buddhist philosophy and thought.

The Roots of Ambivalence. The positive attitude appeared clearly to rest on the sense that women, like men, are generally capable of rational thought and also of self-discipline. The root of the negative attitude might at first seem equally clear. The societies in which Buddhism took root were all to some degree patriarchal, so that often women were denied both educational opportunities and much control over their lives. Discrimination breeds its own supporting prejudices.

There also was a widespread sense that women were necessary for family life. Buddhism early on held that family life (with its distractions and emotional tugs) conflicted with serious work on personal enlightenment. The first step toward liberation and enlightenment was to leave one's family. Reportedly that was Buddha's first step. However, there would be real social costs if many women left their families in search of enlightenment. Hence there were fewer nuns than monks.

One response to all of this was to emphasize different positive features in the two genders. The fertility and contribution to family life of women could be extolled, along with men's capacity for the self-discipline of purification. In the Buddha story, much positive light falls on Queen Maya, who died shortly after giving birth to the Buddha. Because a dream, rather than an actual sex act, is supposed to have led to her pregnancy, the positive light is enhanced: she represents a combination of purity and fertility.

All the same, there were Buddhist nuns, and they had some major accomplishments, even within the early periods. These include the *Therigatha*, a group of songs meant to be chanted (Susan Murcott, 2006). Despite the quality of such achievements, however, nuns were viewed as being less central to the Buddhist mission than were monks, thus reflecting attitudes of the surrounding society. Some further factors were involved in the tendency to assign lower spiritual potential to women than to men. Liz Wilson, in her ironically titled *Charming Cadavers* (1996), provides a very clear and convincing account of one factor. The Buddhist goal of loss of desire prominently included loss of sexual desire. Because of what Wilson calls the primacy of the "male gaze," this focused on the importance of men losing their sexual desires with seemingly not much attention paid to women losing theirs. Monks, required to wander, begging for food, had to train themselves to find women in their "natural state" unattractive; there appeared not to have been a similar program for nuns.

The context of this was a set of practices that developed in Buddhism for those making a serious effort to gain enlightenment and free the mind from desires. The practices centered on promoting a keener, more persistent sense of the unattractive features of the world. The realities of old age and death, and especially of old women and female corpses, were prominent among these unattractive features.

Meditation could focus on these unattractive features. Scholars have observed that the nature of meditation varies greatly among the religious movements in which it is important. A good deal of Christian meditation has focused on a sense of closeness to Jesus or God. Within Islam, Sufi meditation is concerned principally with a sense of something verging on identity with the divine. Hindu meditation is built around the fundamental doctrine that the substantial self (*atman*) deep within us is identical with Brahman (the universe viewed as divine). Hence much meditation has been oriented toward overcoming one's sense of the distinctions among things, and arriving instead at a unified spiritual reality of which the individual is a part.

Buddha denied that there was an *atman*, propounding the doctrine of *anatman*—that there exists no substantial self. Buddhist meditation often was and is designed to provide a calm but heightened sense of important realities. Because of this, in some Buddhist countries charnel areas (strewn with human remains) or graveyards (especially if skulls and bones were in evidence) were frequent places of meditation. The gender of corpses or human remains can serve the more specific purpose of freeing the mind of lustful desires. Hence the importance of the "charming cadavers." They were supposed to provide a frame within which the vision of women ceases to be alluring.

Having said this, one can add that as Buddhism developed in many different forms, attitudes toward sexuality (especially male sexuality) became less uniform. A stringently negative view did persist in some quarters. Edward Conze reports that a major schism in Buddhism (c. third century B.C.E.) grew out of Mahadeva's allegations that his fellow monks had lustful thoughts while asleep. This might have suggested that the do-it-yourself program of personal purification dominant in the early centuries had its limitations, and that even monks needed additional spiritual help.

On the other hand, some of the tantric forms (especially "left hand" trantrism, which emphasized transgressive routes to enlightenment) of Buddhism that developed in the early centuries of the Common Era (C.E.) allowed and even encouraged sexuality. Serinity Young depicts tantric Buddhism as connecting with earlier representations of women's fertility and sexuality. One recurrent idea in tantrism is that it is the attitude that matters, so that what might seem transgressive to some could be life-enhancing if done in the right spirit; and more particularly what normally involves desire could be done with detachment.

Sex Change in Early Buddhism. Two scholars of early Buddhism, Janice D. Willis and Nancy Schuster (in essays for the 1985 volume *Women, Religion, and Social Change*, 1985), have provided modulated accounts of Buddhist attitudes toward women in the period from its beginnings through the first few centuries of the Common Era. Schuster reports texts in which enlightenment was accompanied by sex change. In Willis's account, five years after establishing the male order of followers, Buddha not only attacked the caste system and traditional practices of animal sacrifice but also allowed for the "going forth" of women into the community of enrobed religious practitioners. Nuns, however, were not treated as being equal to monks. This gave a somewhat negative tilt to the Buddhist view of women. But Buddha in the early days of his mission was given material support by a number of wealthy women, mainly from the rising merchant groups. Buddhism on the whole provided a more favorable environment for women than generally existed elsewhere. In this sense, Buddhism can be argued to have been a progressive force for women in southern, southeastern, and eastern Asia. This has arguably been true for Buddhism in any of its settings, and in societies such as those of western Europe and the United States it can amount to a stance of gender equality.

The fact that nuns were expected to defer to monks suggests a status (separate and unequal) that did not deter some women from becoming nuns. Some early Buddhist sutras describe nuns preaching or having discussions with the Buddha. The most famous of these nuns was Mahaprajapati, the aunt and foster mother of the Buddha. Later on, there were stories of women who had attained enlightenment. But some of these stories also involved gender change: a female attained enlightenment and became male—or (as in some early Mahayana texts) the female must become male and then attain enlightenment. Also there was a goddess in the Vimalakirti Sutra who used her powers to change back and forth from female to male in order to demonstrate the superficiality of such things. In this literature there was an uneasy oscillation between the view, on the one hand, that gender is superficial in relation to enlightenment and, on the other hand, an affirmation of the primacy of the male.

Celestial Females. Perhaps there was often a greater degree of comfort with extremely powerful females if they were in exalted celestial regions, rather than being flesh and blood creatures in our own world. As unearthly objects of veneration they would not trigger lust among wandering monks. As inhabitants of celestial regions, also, they scarcely represented a drain on what is necessary to support family life on this planet. It helped also that the celestial females that were important in some forms of Buddhism had very specific roles, which included conferring benefits and protections against various evils.

The Buddhism that developed in Nepal and Tibet had an especially prominent role for such celestial females. These are the Taras, enlightened beings who play important roles in the running of the universe. They sometimes have been termed "female buddhas," and this makes sense, in that the title "buddha" simply means "awakened one." On the other hand, it can be argued that the historic Buddha was awakened in relation to an unenlightened starting point; and that a "back story" of having been unenlightened is required if we are to call the Taras buddhas.

Arya Tara (usually represented as green) was especially prominent in Tibet. She was an important source of enlightenment and also of energy. The first Dalai Lama, in a commentary on *In Praise of the Twenty-one Taras* (fifteenth century C.E.), spoke of Arya Tara as "swift and fearless." It should be noted that in Potala Palace, traditionally the home of the Dalai Lamas, there are numerous chapels dedicated to Taras.

Meditation on Arya Tara was encouraged, and the meditator, who often would have been male, was encouraged to identify with her. One of the possible rewards of this, besides greater clarity about the emptiness of "self," was thought to be greater energy. The Taras in general were thought of as being extremely dynamic and deeply involved in struggles between good and evil. There are some elegant statues and paintings of Taras. But visual representations of Taras often are not, in any conventional sense, pretty. Many paintings in particular replicate the vision of the world that might be gained in a charnel ground. The images of these fierce female protectors were therefore simultaneously distinctive and positive.

Other Regional Variations. The influence of aristocratic women in the imperial court was an important factor in the development of Buddhism in Japan. Clever, cultivated women were conspicuous in the formative periods of early and medieval Japanese culture. These include Lady Murasaki, who wrote one of the world's greatest novels, *The Tale of Genji*, in the early eleventh century, and the great mid-ninth-century poet Ono no Komachi.

A prime supporter of Buddhist causes was the empress Konyo (eighth century C.E.), who sponsored projects for copying sutras (Buddhist sacred texts) both before and after she became empress. Some of the sutras had been brought back from China by a Japanese monk, who was then appointed to the highest rank in the state-sponsored system for the supervision of the priesthood. It has been suggested that the imperial chapel that was his residence was located within the empress's quarters. She is also credited with influencing the project of constructing state-sponsored nunneries and monasteries in each province.

The role of women in Zen Buddhism throughout its history is comparable to that in other Buddhist cultures. There are nuns as well as monks, but clearly the monks had the more important role and maintained more respect than did nuns. However, the literature of Zen Buddhism collected by Paul Reps and Nyogen Senzaki in *Zen Flesh, Zen Bones* (1998) reveals outlines of well-informed commoner women who interrogated learned monks, for example in number 28 in the "Gateless Gate" section. This is a story of a monk in China who considered himself learned but traveled to the south in search of further learning. He stopped somewhere where an old lady offered tea and refreshments. She asked what he was carrying, and he replied that it was a commentary he had written on a sutra. To this she remarked, "I have read that sutra that said 'the past mind cannot be held, the present mind cannot be held, the future mind cannot be held.' You wish some tea and refreshments. Which mind do you propose to use for them?" The monk was stunned, and realized he needed more basic teaching. There are other examples presented of sharp women, including the nun who, having received secret love notes from a monk, invited him during a general meeting to discuss the subject.

Even the attitude that monks should take toward women was put into question, in the story of two traveling monks who encountered a beautiful woman standing on the edge of a muddy intersection. One of the monks carried her across, then put her down, and the two monks continued on their way. The second monk now was fuming at his companion for having carried the woman—and was told "I just carried her for a short while. Are you still carrying her?" There is a point here about attitudes toward women, and a more general point about how Buddhist detachment does not have to follow general rules.

[*See also* Central Asia, *subentry* Ancient Period; China, *subentries* Ancient Period *and* Imperial Period; Japan; Nepal; Religion; South Asia, *subentries* Ancient Period *and* Medieval Period; Southeast Asia, *subentries* Ancient Period *and* Medieval Period; Spiritual Leaders, *subentry* Nuns and Abbesses; Sri Lanka; *and* Tibet and Bhutan.]

BIBLIOGRAPHY

PRIMARY WORKS

Buddhist Scriptures. Edited and translated by Edward Conze. Harmondsworth, U.K., and Baltimore: Penguin, 1959.

The Dhammapada. This is a basic text of early Buddhism. There are many good translations, including *The Dhammapada: The Path to Perfection*, translated by Juan Mascaro. Harmondsworth, U.K.: Penguin, 1973.

The Questions of King Milinda. Translated by T. W. Rhys Davids. Vols. 35–36 of the series Sacred Books of the East. Originally published 1890–1894. Reprint, New York: Dover, 1963. The first volume includes a nuanced discussion of personal identity (including the putative identity between you and a reincarnation of you).

Reps, Paul, and Nyogen Senzaki, eds. *Zen Flesh, Zen Bones: A Collection of Zen and Pre-Zen Writings*. Boston: Tuttle, 1998.

SECONDARY WORKS

Collins, Steven. *Selfless Persons: Imagery and Thought in Theravāda Buddhism*. Cambridge, U.K., and New York: Cambridge University Press, 1982. A careful analysis of the Buddhist denial of self.

Conze, Edward. *Buddhism: Its Essence and Development*. Oxford: Cassirer, 1951.

Haddad, Yvonne Yazbeck, and Ellison Banks Findly, eds. *Women, Religion, and Social Change*. Albany: State University of New York Press, 1985.

Hongo, Masatsugu. "State Buddhism and Court Buddhism: The Role of Court Women in the Development of Buddhism from the Seventh to the Ninth Centuries." Translated and adapted by Massayo Kaneko. In *Engendering Faith: Women and Buddhism in Premodern Japan*, edited by Barbara Ruch, pp. 41–61. Ann Arbor: Center for Japanese Studies, University of Michigan, 2002.

Mullin, Glenn H., with Jeff J. Watt. *Female Buddhas: Women of Enlightenment in Tibetan Mystical Art*. Santa Fe, N.Mex.: Clear Light, 2003.

Murcott, Susan. *The First Buddhist Women: Poems and Stories of Awakening*. Berkeley, Calif.: Parallax Press, 2006. A new edition of Murcott's 1991 *The First Buddhist Women: Translations and Commentaries on the "Therigatha."*

Paul, Diana Y. *Women in Buddhism: Images of the Feminine in Mahāyāna Tradition*. 2nd ed. Berkeley: University of California Press, 1985.

Schuster, Nancy. "Striking a Balance: Women and Images of Women in Early Chinese Buddhism." In *Women, Religion, and Social Change*, edited by Yvonne Yazbeck Haddad and Ellison Banks Findly, pp. 87–112. Albany: State University of New York Press, 1985.

Willis, Janice D. "Nuns and Benefactresses: The Role of Women in the Development of Buddhism." In *Women, Religion, and Social Change*, edited by Yvonne Yazbeck Haddad and Ellison Banks Findly, pp. 59–85. Albany: State University of New York Press, 1985.

Wilson, Liz. *Charming Cadavers: Horrific Figurations of the Feminine in Indian Buddhist Hagiographic Literature*. Chicago and London: University of Chicago Press, 1996.

Young, Serinity. *Courtesans and Tantric Consort: Sexualities in Buddhist Narrative, Iconography, and Ritual*. New York: Routledge, 2004.

JOEL J. KUPPERMAN

BUI THI XUAN (d. 1802), a woman from Ninh Dinh Province who led Vietnamese peasant rebels called the Tay Son in the late eighteenth century. She is said to have learned martial arts using swords and sticks in her youth. The Tay Son rebellion, fueled by perceived injustices in the countryside, was against the corrupt Vietnamese ruling elite. During the rebellion, Bui Thi Xuan commanded a unit of five thousand men. At one point, the Tay Son controlled most of Vietnam and established their own dynasty, but in the end the Nguyen repressed the Tay Son in 1799–1802 with the aid of the French colonial forces. Elephants figure prominently in tales about Bui Thi Xuan: she was famous for training the beasts for war and was trampled to death by them when her enemies conquered her forces. The legend of Bui Thi Xuan has served as a useful symbol to level indirect criticism against corrupt officials in subsequent regimes.

[*See also* Duong Thu Huong; Le Thi; Nguyen Thi Dinh; Nguyen Thi Min Khai; Southeast Asia, *subentry* Modern Period; *and* Trung Sisters.]

BIBLIOGRAPHY

Mai Thi Tu and Le Thi Nham Tuyet. *Women in Viet Nam*. Hanoi: Foreign Languages Publishing House, 1978.

Marr, David. *Vietnamese Tradition on Trial: 1920–1945*. Berkeley: University of California Press, 1981.

KAREN TURNER

BUNINA, ANNA PETROVNA (1774–1829), poet and the first female writer in Russia to live by the pen. Anna Petrovna Bunina, who came from an impoverished family of provincial gentry, was the first major female writer in Russia. Her verse is original and offers observations of lasting appeal about women's experience, particularly of conflict with male peers, and of illness. Her life was unconventional. Unmarried but independent of her male relatives, she achieved a high public profile and economic autonomy. Her mother's early death deprived her of education, and she would not have achieved literary skill had she not used the small inheritance from her father to move from the provinces to Saint Petersburg (1802), where she studied literature, languages, and other subjects, principally with P. I. Sokolov, of the Russian Academy. Literary life was conducted in informal groups of amateur writers, almost exclusively male, and Bunina was fortunate that family connections led her to a literary mentor, A. S. Shishkov, who was a leading light in the Colloquium of Admirers of Russian Writing, probably the sole group that admitted women. Bunina was invited to join, though on inferior conditions: she was not allowed to present her works in person or to engage in discussion of their qualities. She found the protégée-mentor relationship oppressive but indispensable.

Bunina's first book was titled *The Inexperienced Muse* (1809), and a second volume under the same title appeared in 1812, followed by *Collected Works* (1819). She had greater thematic, stylistic, and metrical range than her female predecessors and contemporaries. Publishing by women in Russia began late, probably in 1759. Women took opportunities to publish in journals with well-disposed editors and especially cultivated poetry; by the beginning of the nineteenth century they were writing, as was deemed natural, about virtue, love, and nature in elegiac and pastoral genres and presented themselves as writing artlessly from the heart. The first collection of poems by a woman was published in 1798. Bunina, however, was at ease with civic verse for public occasions, fables, and mock epics; did not hesitate to write of love as unrequited passion or to show herself at odds with nature; and demonstrated a sophisticated knowledge of verse form. One of her most remarkable poems is "A Sick Woman's May Walk," inspired by her experience with breast cancer, the eventual cause of her death. The poem shows her feeling of exclusion from God's benevolent universe, her alienation from those who still enjoyed it, and the urge to escape overwhelming pain in annihilation.

Bunina's poems were well received, and she lived principally through pensions awarded her by imperial patrons. In her last years she raised funds by translating the sermons of Hugh Blair.

Bunina acquired considerable fame and suffered the brickbats of satirical epigrams from the rivals of the colloquium, notably the Arzamas circle. As often befalls women writers, she was soon forgotten, not least because Arzamas determined the canon of Russian literature. She was therefore not influential for subsequent poets. Her work has been rediscovered by Western scholars but has yet to reach the general Russian reader.

[*See also* Russia and Soviet Union.]

BIBLIOGRAPHY

An annotated translation of letters and prose works, edited by Cathy Frierson, has been commissioned by the University of Chicago Press. Translations of Bunina's poems into English by W. E. Brown and Sibelan Forrester, respectively, are in *Russian Literature Triquarterly* 9 (1974): 29–33 and *An Anthology of Russian Women's Writing, 1772–1992,* edited by Catriona Kelly, pp. 3–11 (Oxford: Oxford University Press, 1994).

Marshall, Bonnie. "Anna Bunina." In *Russian Women Writers,* edited by Christine D. Tomei, vol. 1, pp. 43–59. New York: Garland, 1999.

Rosslyn, Wendy. *Anna Bunina (1774–1829) and the Origins of Women's Poetry in Russia.* Lewiston, N.Y.: Edwin Mellen, 1997.

Rosslyn, Wendy. "Anna Bunina's 'Unchaste Relationship with the Muses': Patronage, the Market, and the Woman Writer in Early Nineteenth-Century Russia." *Slavonic and East European Review* 74 (1996): 223–242.

Rosslyn, Wendy. "Conflicts about Gender and Status in Early Nineteenth-Century Russian Literature: The Case of Anna Bunina and Her 'Padenie Faetona.'" In *Gender and Russian Literature: New Perspectives,* translated and edited by Rosalind Marsh, pp. 55–74. Cambridge, U.K.: Cambridge University Press, 1996.

WENDY ROSSLYN

BURMA. Early European accounts note the active participation of women in the Burmese (Myanmar) economy and their high social status relative to women in India and Europe. The 1911 census recorded 1,167 female traders for every 1,000 male traders. Burmese women enjoyed property rights equal to those of men, and marriage was a civil contract and divorce easily obtained. Colonial rule from 1824 to 1947 brought new encounters between Western women and the women of Burma. The new government excluded women from Burma's civil service, restricting their employment to schools and hospitals. Under colonialism the establishment of state and missionary schools for girls increased female literacy. Although a 1911 census recorded only nineteen women for every thousand men in the professional and liberal arts, most of the preeminent women in Burmese politics in the twentieth century were scholars and published authors.

Women in Philanthropy and Social Organization. Missionaries, nurses, and schoolteachers became particularly active in such organizations as the Women's Christian Temperance Union, which was well represented in Burma. The National Council of Women in Burma (NCWB), founded in 1926, was affiliated with the National Council of Women in India and the International Council of Women. Its aims were to promote sympathy among women of all races in Burma, train women in citizenship, improve the welfare of women and children, and coordinate and supplement existing women's societies. Noted philanthropists from this period include Daw Tee Tee, who established the Home for Waifs and Strays in Rangoon (now Yangon); five thousand boys passed through the

Democratic Movement in Burma. The Nobel Peace Prize laureate Aung San Suu Kyi under house arrest enforced by the junta government, Yangon, September 1994. She stands with Burma's defense minister General Than Shwe (center) and former prime minister Khin Nyunt. REUTERS

home during the thirty years after its founding in 1928. Other socially active forums were the Women's League of Burma and the Burmese Women's Council Co-operative.

After the country gained independence, these organizations played an active role in public life, establishing women's homes, cooperative stores, and schools and clinics for orphaned and destitute children. In 1962, General Ne Win assumed power, beginning more than fifty years of uninterrupted military rule. From 1962 to 1964 his government requisitioned the women's institutions.

More recent women's associations in Myanmar—as Burma has been known since 1989—include the Maternal and Child Welfare Association and the Myanmar Women's Entrepreneurial Association, founded in 1995. The government has demanded that the first group urge girls to "preserve traditional culture . . . and national lineage" and that the second encourage women to be "patriotic and safeguard the race" (*New Light of Myanmar*, 5 April, 6 April, and 24 May 1998), statements consistent with the regime's exclusion of women from politics and its denigration of Burma's most famous figure of late-twentieth-century history, Aung San Suu Kyi.

A narco-economy, corruption, and porous borders, combined with the regional growth in transnational trafficking syndicates, have all stimulated the sex trade in Burma and across its borders. An estimated forty thousand Burmese women of the total population of fifty million are employed in the sex trade in Thailand; many are from minority groups. Many others have joined the transnational Burmese diaspora or such forums as the Women's Association of Shan State, the Mon Women's Organisation, and the Karen Women's Organisation.

Women in Politics and Protest. In the 1920s women held offices in the Rangoon Municipal Corporation, and the students' union at Rangoon University included women in its leadership. In 1927 the NCWB, in its first political crusade for women's rights, organized a march of a hundred women in Rangoon to protest the Reforms Act of 1919, which barred women from the legislature. Two years later the act's sex-discrimination clause was revoked, and the sister of the nationalist leader U Chit Hlaing became the first woman to take a seat in the national legislature. The respected scholar and writer Daw Mya Sein was appointed in 1931 to represent Burmese women at the special Burma Round Table Conference in London. In 1936 the lone female candidate, Daw Hnin Mya, won a seat in Burma's first legislative assembly.

Amid rising nationalist sentiment in the 1920s and 1930s, many women joined the movement known as Dobama Asiayone (We Burmans Association); these female nationalists were known as Thakin-ma. They included the writer Khin Myo Chit, who in 1936 joined thirty-five other young women in a student strike at Rangoon University, camping alongside male strikers on the slopes of Burma's most sacred monument, the Shwe Dagon Pagoda. Women also emerged as a key force in the labor rights movement. In 1938 a hundred women led a strike at the Chauk oil field, forming a human blockade against police. When two hundred women workers in Rangoon went on strike in sympathy, they were publicly supported by the Thakin-ma. This period also saw the emergence of the noted novelist Daw Ma Ma Lay, a Thakin-ma whose later works linked gender and nationalism and who was imprisoned in 1962. Other significant modern women writers from this period include Dagon Khin Khin Lay, who founded the women's magazine *Yuwadi* in 1945.

After independence, organizations such as the Women's Freedom League became attached to political parties, but their function was largely administrative. In 1953, Ba Maung Chien became the first woman to reach cabinet rank in Burma; she later led the Karen opposition movement. There were sporadic elections of Burmese women to parliament in the 1970s, but no woman has since reached cabinet rank. In the early twenty-first century Burma had one of the world's lowest rates of female representation in government.

In 1988 the daughter of Burma's architect of independence, General Aung San, entered the political fray. A highly articulate scholar and author who was educated at Oxford and London universities, Aung San Suu Kyi cofounded the National League for Democracy (NLD). She became its general secretary and soon rallied millions across Burma through her embrace of Buddhist and Gandhian tactics of nonviolence and her outspoken rejection of oppression. The NLD's landslide victory in elections in 1989 left the military with only 10 of 392 seats. The government reacted by punishing the victors. Opposition parties were imprisoned and intimidated, and Aung San Suu Kyi was placed under house arrest. Her popularity intensified the government's insistence that the first duty of women should be to uphold the home and nation. From 1996 to 1997 state propaganda questioned Aung San Suu Kyi's fitness to rule and likened her to a prostitute and a "bad daughter" (quoted in Skidmore). For many Burmese and outside observers, however, Aung San Suu Kyi remains Burma's "woman of destiny" (Silverstein).

Although in 1997 the government became a signatory to the Convention on the Elimination of All Forms of Discrimination against Women, Suu Kyi spent much time under house arrest after 1989, and there is significant testimonial evidence that the military unofficially sanctions rape as a form of punishment for women political prisoners and women in insurgent areas. Because of this political climate and sociocultural pressure on young women not to stray far from their domestic nest, many families try to insulate their daughters from political reality. Excluded from the political sphere by cultural norms and the oppressive regime, women have emerged as the primary exponents of Burma's most popular contemporary genre, the short story, and the power of their pens is a source of fear to the military regime. Ma Thida served ten years in prison for the crime of good writing, and Ataram and other authors have faced censorship for critiquing reproductive-health policies.

[*See also* Aung San Suu Kyi.]

BIBLIOGRAPHY

Allott, Anna J. *Inked Over, Ripped Out: Burmese Storytellers and the Censors*. Chiang Mai, Thailand: Silkworm Press, 1994.

Daw Mya Sein. "Towards Independence in Burma: The Role of Women." *Asian Affairs* 59 (1972): 288–299.

Fink, Christina. *Living Silence: Burma under Military Rule*. New York: Zed Books, 2001.

Khaing, Mi Mi. *The World of Burmese Women*. London: Zed Books, 1984.

Silverstein, Josef. "Aung San Suu Kyi: Is She Burma's Woman of Destiny?" In *Freedom from Fear and Other Writings: Aung San Suu Kyi*, edited by Michael Aris, pp. 267–283. London: Viking, 1991.

Skidmore, Monique. *Karaoke Fascism: Burma and the Politics of Fear*. Philadelphia: University of Pennsylvania Press, 2004.

PENNY EDWARDS

BURROUGHS, NANNIE HELEN (1879–1961), African American educator, orator, activist, and religious leader. Known mostly for founding the National Training School for Women and Girls, Incorporated (NTSWG), Burroughs dedicated her life to the betterment of women by educating them, preparing them for the world of work in both traditional and nontraditional fields, and supporting them in their places of worship. Through her work as president of the NTSWG, her dedication to the National Association of Wage Earners, and her position in the women's auxiliary of the National Baptist Convention (NBC), Burroughs was an advocate and activist for women's rights in the United States and abroad.

Establishing a school for girls and women was a significant achievement, and an atypical one for African Americans at the time. Burroughs wrote in the school "Circular of Information" that girls should be educated in their own setting during their adolescent years. This, she felt, would help them to grow. Burroughs wanted a private school where she could develop women as leaders and teach them a sense of equality. The students were expected to see the all-women staff as exemplars and role models.

The National Association of Wage Earners, with Burroughs as president and Mary McLeod Bethune as vice president, supported and worked to protect the rights of women, migrant workers, and African Americans. Burroughs was actively involved in the women's-club movement. Viewed as being no-nonsense, and even harsh by some, she fought relentlessly for the rights of women. She understood that many women needed to work and that they often held leadership roles in their communities. It was her desire that they be well suited for both responsibilities.

The NBC played a very important role in Burroughs's life; she was a devout Baptist and served on the women's auxiliary for several decades. She first presented her idea to begin a school for women and girls to the NBC, and the women's auxiliary supported its inception and expansion. Within the church, Burroughs did not want women to settle for a place of submission but rather to have a voice and use it.

Burroughs wholeheartedly endorsed the idea of the need for African Americans to feel God's presence in their lives. She also understood the oppression and sexism that existed within religious entities. In establishing and developing the NTSWG, she faced a considerable amount of opposition. She fought racism and other types of discrimination, including blatant sexism and control by male ministers.

Often noted for her work with and contributions to the African American educational and religious communities, Burroughs worked in venues both on U.S. soil and abroad to enhance the lives of women and girls. To her, one of the most powerful ways of protest was through education.

[*See also* Bethune, Mary McLeod; Cooper, Anna Julia; *and* National Association of Colored Women.]

BIBLIOGRAPHY

"Circular of Information for the Seventeenth Annual Session of the National Training School for Women and Girls Incorporated, 1925–26." Nannie Helen Burroughs Papers, Manuscripts Division, Library of Congress, Washington, D.C.

Higginbotham, Evelyn Brooks. *Righteous Discontent: The Women's Movement in the Black Baptist Church, 1880–1920*. Cambridge, Mass.: Harvard University Press, 1993.

TRAKI TAYLOR-WEBB

BUTLER, JOSEPHINE (1828–1906), a principal in the campaign to end government regulation of prostitution in Britain and a leading feminist reformer and writer. Her family included prominent Whigs who were active in liberal causes, most notably the abolition of slavery and the reform of parliamentary franchise.

On 8 January 1852 Josephine Grey married George Butler, an Oxford-educated university instructor and Anglican clergyman. The couple settled in Oxford, where George taught and Josephine began raising their four children, born in the 1850s. She and George were evangelicals, regarding themselves as "Christian revolutionaries" seeking active work in Christ's service. In 1864 her only daughter, Eva, died in an accidental fall from a staircase. It was a turning point in Butler's life. She wrote, "Never can I lose that

Josephine Butler. New York Public Library, Astor, Lenox and Tilden Foundations, Manuscripts and Archives Division, Benjamin R. Tucker Papers

memory,—the fall, the sudden cry, and then the silence." In 1866 her husband was appointed to Liverpool College, and Butler began to seek out women "with pain keener than my own." She visited women in workhouses and jails. Soon Butler was opening her home to dying "magdalens" (reformed prostitutes), many of them destitute and consumptive. In 1867, with the financial support of wealthy Liverpool benefactors, Butler opened an industrial home for girls. She also became active in broader women's rights campaigns. In 1866 she signed a petition to Parliament calling for woman suffrage. She served as president of the North of England Council for Promoting the Higher Education of Women. In 1868 she published a pamphlet, *The Education and Employment of Women*, advocating improved education for women and the end to restrictions on women's employment.

In 1869 Butler was asked to lead the Ladies National Association for the Repeal of the Contagious Diseases Acts. The acts were enforced in eighteen garrison towns and ports to curtail the spread of venereal disease. They allowed the police to identify and detain suspected prostitutes, force the women to undergo medical examination, and confine to a hospital those found to have venereal disease. Butler said that she had a call from God to undertake the campaign to repeal the acts. She objected to them because they penalized women heavily and men not at all and provided for state-sanctioned and state-regulated vice. Butler called the medical examinations "instrumental rape." She also argued that the acts violated the constitutional rights of women because an accused woman had neither the right of appeal nor a trial by jury.

Butler was a compelling speaker as well as an effective organizer and fund-raiser. Her daring public addresses, particularly during election campaigns, resulted in attacks by angry crowds and the condemnation of those who believed women had no place in this debate. Her work expanded the range of feminist agitation activities, and her arguments against the acts brought women's sexuality to the forefront of feminist discussion. She campaigned against state-regulated prostitution in Europe and led the formation of the British, Continental, and General Federation for the Abolition of Government Regulation of Prostitution. After the repeal of the Acts in 1886, Butler worked for the repeal campaigns in the British Empire and for the reclamation of prostitutes. She wrote more than ninety books, pamphlets, and articles, many of them with wide influence. Butler died in 1906.

[*See also* Contagious Diseases Acts *and* Prostitution.]

BIBLIOGRAPHY

Daggers, Jenny, and Diana Neal, eds. *Sex, Gender, and Religion: Josephine Butler Revisited.* New York: Peter Lang, 2006. Articles on Butler's life and work.

Jordon, Jane. *Josephine Butler.* London: John Murray, 2001. A full biography of Butler.

Summers, Anne. "The Constitution Violated: The Female Body and the Female Subject in the Campaigns of Josephine Butler." *History Workshop Journal* 48 (1999):1–15. An examination of one of Butler's most important publications.

Walkowitz, Judith R. *Prostitution and Victorian Society: Women, Class and the State.* Cambridge, U.K.: Cambridge University Press, 1980. A history of the contagious diseases acts that examines the work of Josephine Butler.

Pamela J. Walker

CABALLÉ, MONTSERRAT (b. 1933), world-famous Catalan Spanish soprano. Born Maria de Montserrat Viviana Concepción Caballé i Folc in Barcelona to a humble family, Caballé struggled to finish her degree in singing during the twelve years that she was at the Conservatori Superior de Música del Liceu. She continued her training in Italy and eventually moved to Switzerland, where she joined the company of the Ópera de Basilea. She made her operatic debut in 1957 as Mimi in *La Bohème*. Between 1960 and 1961 she was under contract with the opera of Bremen, Germany, and specialized in bel canto roles. In 1962 she signed her first contract with the Gran Teatre del Liceu in Barcelona, where she sang the title role in Richard Strauss's *Arabella* to such acclaim that the Liceu offered her two more roles, as the protagonists of Mozart's *Don Giovanni* and Puccini's *Madame Butterfly*. In 1964 she married the tenor Bernabé Martí.

Caballé's first major international success was in 1965 when she performed in Donizetti's *Lucrezcia Borgia* at Carnegie Hall in New York. After this she made her debut in the most important opera houses in the world, including Covent Garden in London, the Paris opera, and the Metropolitan Opera House in New York. She has played many characters in a wide repertoire of around 130 titles, and her enormous success in singing works ranging from Verdi, Wagner, and Puccini to Richard Strauss lies in the remarkable purity and power of her voice as well as in her marvelous technical ability.

Caballé has also made excursions into pop music, performing as a duo with the rock singer Freddy Mercury in the song "Barcelona," which became the anthem of the 1992 Olympic games. With Liza Minelli she recorded "There's No Business like Show Business," and in a 2003 Christmas show she sang with Placido Domingo, José Carreras, Michael Jackson, Tina Turner, and Joe Cocker, among others.

Caballé has also participated in benefit events and has given recitals to support child victims of the Balkan war, victims of Chernobyl, and AIDS victims. She is a goodwill ambassador for UNESCO and has created a foundation for needy children in Barcelona. She has received multiple awards, such as the ribbon of Isabel la Católica in 1966, one of the highest Spanish merit awards, the gold medal of the Beaux Arts in 1973, and the Príncipe de Asturias de las Artes Prize in 1991. She is also a knight of the National Legion of Honor in recognition of her talent. She holds an honorary doctorate from the Universidad Politécnica de Valencia, and in 1988 she won the National Prize for Music.

Caballé is a universal diva. In her interpretations she favors innovation and likes the work of the new generations of singers. As she has said to encourage those who are starting out, "Solitude is one of the great enemies of this profession. When you are sad, the music consoles you and when you are alone it accompanies you" (*La Prensa*, 2 January 2005).

[*See also* Performing Arts *and* Spain and Portugal.]

BIBLIOGRAPHY

Pullen, Robert, and Stephen Jay Taylor. *Monserrat Caballé: Casta diva*. Boston: Northeastern University Press, 1995.

Maria Isabel Cabrera Bosch

Translated from the Spanish by Matthew Miller

CAI YAN (courtesy name, Wenji; 176–early third century), a famous poetess of the Three Kingdoms period. Cai Yan was erudite, talented, eloquent, and accomplished in music. Her biography appears in the *Hou Han shu* (Standard History of the Later Han). Her father, the Later Han scholar, poet, and statesman Cai Yong (133–192) of Chenliu prefecture in what is now Henan, was a scholar of the classics, mathematics, astronomy, and music. He held several court offices and died in prison after supporting an unsuccessful rebellion.

Cai Yan was initially married to Wei Zhongdao of Hedong. He died, and since she had no children, she returned to her parents' home. During the invasion of the nomadic Xiongnu tribes from the north after the death of the Ling emperor (r. 168–189), she was captured and was given in marriage to King Zuoxian of the southern branch of the Xiongnu. She lived with him for twelve years and bore him two sons. She was forced to leave them in 206 when she was ransomed by Cao Cao (155–220), who had come to power after the fall of the Han. Cao Cao's motives are not entirely clear. An acquaintance or friend of Cai Yan's father Cai Yong, Cao Cao may have grieved at his lack of (Chinese) descendants. Or he may have felt the need to placate the spirits of Cai Yan's ancestors by elevating the last descendant of the Cai family. In any event, he gave her in marriage to a new Chinese husband, the garrison commander Dong Si of Chenliu, even though her Xiongnu husband and sons were still living (*Hou Han shu* 84).

Like Ban Zhao, Cai Yan is a striking example of a woman scholar who mastered her father's occupation. Cai Yong had had a large library, which was lost during the wars following the death of the Ling emperor. On Cai Yan's return to court, Cao Cao summoned her and asked her whether she could remember any of her father's books, and she wrote down the titles of several thousand lost texts at his request (*Hou Han shu* 84). Later, her husband incurred Cao Cao's wrath and was sentenced to death. She successfully argued for her husband's life, asking Cao Cao if he intended to provide her with yet another husband.

Cai Yan is the author of three extant poems. The first two, which appear in her biography, express her grief at abandoning her sons and describe her life among the Xiongnu. The third, "Hujia shibapai" (Eighteen Songs for a Nomad Flute), appears in the eleventh-century anthology *Yuefu shiji* (Collection of Folk Songs) of Guo Maoqian, though her authorship of this poem is debated. In any case, the strong female voice it expresses gave rise to many subsequent imitations.

[*See also* Ban Zhao *and* China, *subentry* Imperial Period.]

BIBLIOGRAPHY

Levy, Dore J. "Cai Yan." In *Women Writers of Traditional China: An Anthology of Poetry and Criticism*, edited by Kang-i Sun Chang and Haun Saussy, pp. 22–30. Stanford, Calif.: Stanford University Press, 1999.

Idema, Wilt, and Beata Grant. *The Red Brush: Writing Women of Imperial China*. Cambridge, Mass.: Harvard University Asia Center, 2004. See pp. 112–119.

LISA RAPHALS

CAMA, MADAME BHIKAJI (1861–1936), Indian revolutionary who mentored Indian nationalists abroad and helped publicize the Indian independence struggle internationally through speeches and her journals *Bande Mataram* and *Talwar*. Born into a wealthy Parsi family of social reformers, she married Rustomji Cama in 1885. Because of his pro-British sympathies, however, she soon took the unusual step of leaving him. In 1902 Cama left India for Europe, traveling to Germany, Scotland, and Paris before spending several years in London. She eventually returned to Paris, where she lived for most of the rest of her life. Contact with Shyamji Krishna Verma inspired her to join other Indian revolutionaries abroad. She devoted herself to the movement, sending revolvers concealed in Christmas toys to patriots in India and facilitating communication among Irish, Russian, Egyptian, and German nationalists in Europe.

At the 1907 International Socialist Congress in Stuttgart, Germany, Cama publicized the Indian struggle by unfurling the Indian national flag and highlighting the conditions of those "who are undergoing terrible tyrannies under the English Capitalism and British Government" (quoted in Kaur, p. 108). This trip was followed by a speaking tour of the United States aimed at rallying support for the Indian independence struggle. Cama returned to London in 1908 and is credited with authoring the manifesto of the revolutionary movement, legitimizing the use of force to combat colonial tyranny. Numerous copies of the manifesto were distributed in India. According to colonial documents, the British government believed that Indians regarded her as a reincarnation of the goddess Kali.

Concerned by the British move to clamp down on seditious writing, Cama founded the monthly *Bande Mataram* in 1909 and became identified with another nationalist publication, the *Talwar*. The former was associated with Vinayak Damodar Savarkar, whose writings Cama helped publish and smuggle into India. In recent years Savarkar has been acknowledged as the father of the Hindutva movement, a virulent form of Hindu nationalism that has a legacy of violence against religious minorities. Savarkar's sectarianism was at odds with Cama's espoused commitment to religious pluralism and internationalism. Yet in spite of her belief in religious tolerance, Cama's prescriptions for the anticolonial struggle, like those of many other Indian nationalists during that period, explicitly drew on Hindu mythology. Her internationalism was firmly rooted in a view of the coexistence of nations. As she explained, "The world is my country, every human being is my relation. But to establish internationalism in the world there must be Nations first" (quoted in Kumar, p. 46).

Along with other prominent nationalist women, Cama symbolically invoked maternal power as an important resource in the anticolonial struggle. Addressing the 1910 Egyptian National Congress in Brussels, she commented on the absence of Egyptian women, reminding delegates "the hand that rocks the cradle is the hand that moulds the character. That soft hand is the chief factor in the national life" (quoted in Kumar, p. 50). In other speeches Cama urged Asian men abroad to eschew foreign brides for Asian wives. Such betrothals would uplift Asian women by making them more progressive and, ultimately, benefit Asian countries, she claimed.

At the age of seventy-four and in failing health, Cama finally returned to India, where she died shortly thereafter.

[*See also* Hinduism; India; Nationalism; *and* Terrorism.]

BIBLIOGRAPHY

Jayawardena, Kumari. *Feminism and Nationalism in the Third World.* London: Zed Books, 1986.

Kaur, Manmohan. *Role of Women in the Freedom Movement, 1857–1947.* Delhi: Sterling, 1968.

Kumar, Radha. *The History of Doing: An Illustrated Account of Movements for Women's Rights and Feminism in India 1800–1990.* New Delhi: Kali for Women, 1993.

PURNIMA BOSE

CAMPOAMOR, CLARA (1888–1972), Spanish feminist, suffragist, and lawyer of Republican ideology. Clara Campoamor Rodriguez was born in Madrid into a liberal and progressive family of modest means, and she worked from girlhood to support herself. At age thirty-two she began to study for a bachelor's degree and followed that with law school, supporting herself financially by collaborating on the newspaper *La Tribuna*. In 1925, she applied for admission to the Colegio de Abogados (Bar Association). She was a member of the Academia de Jurisprudencia y Legislación (Academy of Jurisprudence and Legislation), where she was intensely active, giving lectures while focusing her attention on the juridical situation of Spanish women. In 1929 she presided over the congress of the International Women's Suffrage Alliance held in Berlin. In 1931 she created the Unión Republicana Femenina (Women's Republican Union).

When the Miguel Primo de Rivera dictatorship (1923–1930) ended, she joined the Radical Party and in 1932 was elected as Madrid representative to the Cortes Constituyentes (Constituent Courts). With twenty-one other representatives, she formed a commission to work on a new constitution. At that point, Clara Campoamor became a key feminist leader. She fought effectively and successfully to eliminate discrimination on the basis of gender, arguing for the legal equality of men and women. Along with the Socialist representative Victoria Kent, she argued rationally and devotedly in support of universal suffrage for women—although Kent, who was a Socialist, and some Republicans feared that the political participation of women would cause the Republic to swing to the right because women would be influenced by the Church and by right wing politicians. Clara Campoamor won the right to vote for Spanish women, supported by a majority of the Partido Socialista Obrero Español (PSOE; Spanish Socialist Workers' Party), some of the Republicans, and a minority of the right. Manuel Azaña, who served as president of the Spanish Republic from 1936 to 1939, wrote in his *Memorias* (1939) of Clara Campoamor's effectiveness in the famous parliamentary debate.

Spanish women voted in the general elections of 1933, which were won by the Confederación Española de Derechas Autónomas (a right-wing party). The Left blamed its loss on Clara Campoamor, and the election was her political demise. She abandoned the Radical Party and expressed her desire to join the Republican Left, but her application was denied. She did not join the Popular Front, the leftist government elected by a large majority in 1936. That majority included the women's vote, but no one offered Campoamor any apologies. In June 1936 she published *Mi pecado mortal: El voto femenino y yo* (My Mortal Sin: The Women's Vote and Me), an admirable though subjective political statement in which she described her parliamentary struggles. She continued to champion equal rights for women and published two other books, *El derecho femenino en España* (Women's Rights in Spain; 1936) and *La situación jurídica de la mujer española* (The Juridical Situation of Spanish Women; 1938).

She spent the Spanish civil war as an exile in Paris and later lived in Buenos Aires, earning a living by writing biographical essays and giving lectures. Prevented from returning to Spain during the dictatorship of General Francisco Franco (1939–1973), she settled in 1955 in Lausanne, Switzerland, where she worked in a law office. She died in Lausanne in 1972.

[*See also* International Woman Suffrage Alliance; Spain and Portugal; Suffrage; *and* Suffragettes.]

BIBLIOGRAPHY

Fagoaga, Concha. *Clara Campoamor, la sufragista española.* Madrid: Dirección General de Juventud y Promoción Socio-Cultural, Subdirección General de la Mujer, 1981.

Keen, Judith. "Strange Bedfellows: Feminists, Catholics, and Anti-clericals in the Enfranchisement of Spanish Women." *Australian Feminist Studies* 17, no. 38 (2002): 165–175.

Mangini, Shirley. *Women's Voices from the Spanish Civil War.* New Haven, Conn.: Yale University Press, 1995.

MARIA ISABEL CABRERA BOSCH
Translated from the Spanish by Matthew Miller

CANADA. Canada originated as a homeland for diverse communities of First Nations peoples with many different gender regimes. Beginning in the seventeenth and eighteenth centuries, a similarly heterogeneous collection of white settlers—at first from France, Great Britain, and the United States—asserted sovereignty. Black and Asian arrivals were far fewer and remained a small minority until the late twentieth century. In 1867, in a confederation of British colonies (the original four became provinces, subsequently joined by six more provinces and three territories), Canada became a nation with a dominant white majority and a parliamentary democracy that operated in English and French within the British Empire. In the nineteenth century women did the majority of unpaid work. Although Queen Victoria was the nation's sovereign from 1837 to 1901 and a few women exercised authority as native, religious, social, and cultural leaders, as a group they wielded significantly less power than similarly situated men and were vulnerable to oppression. This discrepancy fueled the first feminist wave that emerged soon after confederation in 1867.

Families. As L. M. Montgomery's *Anne of Green Gables* (1908) reminded readers, family forms have always been diverse, but during the twentieth century the heterosexual nuclear family was the most common. Common-law unions increased steadily, with Quebec, the only province with a French-speaking majority and the Civil Code rather than the Common Law leading the way. In 2001, 14 percent of all families were common-law. By the end of the century same-sex couples were also gaining marital rights. As laws liberalized, divorces increased dramatically. Widowed, divorced, or deserted, women have always headed a large majority of one-parent families.

Canadians regularly practiced contraception, but in 1892 it became illegal to advertise or sell birth control. After World War I organizations such as Ontario's Birth Control Society and British Columbia's Parents' Information Bureau emerged to face legal prosecution even as they won public support. A Canadian version of the international eugenics movement also appeared, with legislation in Alberta (1928) and British Columbia (1933) that often resulted in sterilizing minority and Aboriginal women. Planned Parenthood of Canada emerged in 1961. In 1969 the federal government legalized birth control and made limited provision for abortion despite continuing resistance from religious conservatives. In 1988 the Supreme Court, in a decision written by Bertha Wilson, struck down legislation limiting access to legal abortions, although access to abortion remains uneven across the country.

In the past, most teenaged mothers married; very few surrendered babies for adoption. Today more women choose abortion or single motherhood. Teen pregnancy is viewed increasingly negatively, although rates are lower than in the United States and more comparable to those in Australia and Great Britain. The number of childless women decreased and, after a period of increasing fertility rates after World War II, fertility rates dropped considerably among women born at the beginning of the twentieth century to a historic low of 7–8 percent among women born in 1927–1936 (the mothers of the baby boom). By 1997 the fertility rate was less than half what it had been in 1959. Aboriginal women have significantly higher fertility and infant mortality rates.

Health. The welfare state expanded after World War II, with public hospital insurance and Medicare joining old-age pensions, unemployment insurance, and family allowances. As a result, a girl born in 1997 could expect to live into her eighties. Although Canada now has North America's best public health care, inequality ensures different outcomes. In particular, infectious and chronic illnesses ravage poor and Aboriginal communities. HIV and other sexually transmitted diseases remain significant, as do eating disorders among the young and arthritis and osteoporosis among the elderly. Depression and mental illness correlate strongly with marginalization. Sexual assault, energizing feminists throughout the twentieth century, remains common. Aboriginal women and those with disabilities have been especially vulnerable. Prostitutes routinely risk sexual assault and murder. They have not been alone. When New Democratic Party (NDP) Member of Parliament Margaret Mitchell raised the topic of wife battering in 1980, her predominantly male colleagues laughed. Domestic violence is much less trivialized today but frequently goes unreported. Annual events commemorate the murder of fourteen women at the L'École Polytechnique de Montréal by a male antifeminist on 6 December 1989. In 1993 Canada pioneered the recognition of gender persecution as a basis for refugee claims. But in the 1990s neoliberal provincial and federal governments threatened public health by slashing counseling centers and women's shelters.

In the face of frequent efforts by male doctors to assert a monopoly, women have tried to manage treatment of themselves and their communities. By the last decades of the twentieth century, legalization of midwives, women's massive entry into medicine, and a vibrant women's health movement supplied new promise.

Education. Girls and women experience informal and formal education differently from similarly situated males. In Quebec the slow introduction of compulsory education and clerical power reduced options for many years. Black and Aboriginal children regularly entered effectively segregated institutions well into the twentieth century. Not until after World War II was high-school graduation taken for granted, even by more privileged European Canadians. The rates of enrollment in tertiary education are higher among women than among men.

Like its predecessor, feminism's Second Wave valued education. In 1920 women represented 16.3 percent of university undergraduates; this increased to 20.8 percent in 1945 and 58 percent in 2001. First Nations women were more likely than such men to possess postsecondary credentials but remained underrepresented relative to other women. Male advantage, visible in the persistence of a masculinist canon and an overwhelmingly male professorate, survived in higher education, as did racism and homophobia. From the 1970s, however, women's studies and feminist scholarship offered alternatives.

Unwaged and Waged Work. Women perform about two-thirds of unpaid domestic work, including elder and child care, a share persisting since data were first collected in the 1960s. Men benefit in the labor market, as elsewhere, from this division. The percentage of women in the labor force increased from 14.4 percent in 1901 to 24 percent in 1951 to 55 percent in 1999. Although World War II increased wives' employment, the young, single, and childless continued to be the most likely wage earners until the 1960s. By century's end most mothers of preschoolers worked outside the home. In 1999 women constituted almost half of doctors and dentists and more than one-third of managers (although largely at the bottom ranks of these occupations). Most remained teachers, nurses, and clerical, sales, and service workers. Significant "firsts" include Carrie Derick as full professor (at McGill University) in 1912, Elsie Gregory MacGill as an aeronautical engineer in 1929, Elinor Black as head of a medical school department (at the University of Manitoba) in 1951, Lois M. Wilson as moderator of the United Church, Canada's largest Protestant denomination, in 1980, and Roberta Bondar as an astronaut in 1992.

By the 1990s women's labor-force participation almost matched men's. Single-earner families with a male breadwinner were the exception. Women were, however, more likely to work part-time and experience nonstandard conditions and low wages. In 1967 full-time women employees earned 58 percent of men's incomes; in 1997 it was 72 percent. Recent immigrants, members of First Nations, and women of color suffered lower incomes and higher unemployment. Differences in human capital and career choices explained less than one-half of the gender wage gap. Lower lifetime earnings, limited private pension plans, and discriminatory legal regimes compromised future security.

In 1900 very few women were unionized, but in 2000 unionization, concentrated in the public sector, almost equaled men's. Unionization reduced the gendered wage gap and improved security. In the late twentieth century, unions tackled parental leave, pay equity, and sexual harassment, and legislation enshrined pay and employment equity in some jurisdictions.

Social Security. Children and their mothers were the first objects of social welfare initiatives. In the early twentieth century, feminist activists demanded recognition of women's primary role as parents through Mothers' Pensions, also known as Mothers' Allowances. This maternalist interpretation of citizenship floundered during the Great Depression of the 1930s, to be superseded by an emphasis on rights flowing from paid employment. By World War II waged labor was the preeminent basis for social security. Postwar prosperity was succeeded by the "rediscovery" of poverty in the 1960s. In 1971 Canada developed a limited system of public paid maternity leave, adding parental leave in 1990. Such leaves, like sickness benefits, were tied to the employment insurance system. Women's greater likelihood of part-time and interrupted labor-force participation and lower wages limited their protection.

With so many female wage earners, the need for child care has been pressing. Governments briefly made limited provision during World War II but quickly retreated. In 1996, 300,000 day-care spaces were available but 900,000 families needed openings. Motivated by nationalist pronatalism and an active feminist lobby, Quebec quadrupled regulated spaces in the 1990s.

By the end of the twentieth century, cuts to the welfare state and neoliberal restructuring reduced social services and eroded employment. In 1997 women became disproportionately disentitled under an employment insurance system that favored standard full-time, full-year work. Public-sector job loss disproportionately injured unionized and higher-paid workers, while forcing more caring labor onto women. Such developments further divided rich and poor.

Political Action. Early feminists won reforms in regard to child custody, education, and married women's property rights. The Woman's Christian Temperance Union pioneered in condemning alcohol abuse, violence, and economic and political dependence. In 1893 the National Council of Women was created and in 1910 began to champion suffrage. In Quebec, the Fédération nationale St.-Jean-Baptiste, founded as a feminist umbrella organization in 1907, treaded warily in the face of clerical suspicion. Suffragists such as Nellie L. McClung, Carrie Derick, Helena Gutteridge, Edith Archibald, and Marie Lacoste-Gérin-Lajoie were diverse and often radical, but most were European in origin and middle class with limited awareness of others' perspectives. The first municipal suffrage successes came in the 1870s, but hard-fought provincial victories, beginning in the west, waited until World War I. In 1925 Newfoundland was the last province to acquiesce except for Quebec, which resisted until 1940. Military nurses and female relatives of servicemen voted federally in 1917, and a still incomplete federal franchise came in 1918. Japanese and Chinese Canadians waited until the 1940s, Doukhobors until the 1950s, and Aboriginal people until 1960.

Although twentieth-century women proved to be active lobbyists, women's political parties have been rare. Agnes Campbell Macphail of the United Farmers of Ontario, later of the Co-operative Commonwealth Federation, became the first woman elected to the House of Commons (in 1921) and shortly thereafter a noted feminist, pacifist, and prison reformer. In 1930 Liberal Cairine Reay Wilson became the first female senator, soon campaigning to admit refugees from Nazi tyranny. Conservative Member of Parliament Ellen Louks Fairclough became the first female federal cabinet minister—secretary of state—in 1957. Jeanne-Mathilde Benoît Sauvé served as Canada's first female governor-general (1984–1990); later came Adrienne Poy Clarkson, the second woman and the first Chinese

Canadian Politics. Agnes Campbell Macphail, the first woman to become a member of the Canadian parliament, 1921. KELSEY STUDIO/LIBRARY AND ARCHIVES CANADA, C-006908

Canadian (1999–2005), and Michaëlle Jean, a Quebecer of Haitian origin, in 2005. In 1982 Bertha Wilson became the first female judge in the Canadian Supreme Court, and in 1999 Beverley McLachlin the first woman chief justice. In 1975 Rosemary Brown became the first black Canadian to seek the leadership of a federal party, the NDP. In 1988 Liberal Ethel Blondin-Andrew became the first aboriginal woman member of Parliament. Audrey McLaughlin was the first female leader of a national party, the NDP, in 1989. In 1993 Conservative Kim Campbell became prime minister.

At the provincial level, when the suffrage activist Louise Crummy McKinney of the Non-Partisan League and the military dietitian Roberta MacAdams, one of two Soldiers' Representatives, were elected in Alberta in 1917, they became the British Empire's first female legislators. In 1921 Liberal Mary Ellen Smith, minister without portfolio in British Columbia, became the first woman in the Empire to hold ministerial office. In 1991 British Columbia Social Crediter Rita Johnston was the first female provincial premier and Inuvialuit Nellie Cournoyea, as premier of the Northwest Territories, the first Aboriginal woman to head a provincial or territorial government. In 1994 Quebec Liberal Fatima Houda-Pepin became the first Muslim woman elected to a legislature.

Between the suffrage and modern feminist movements, women remained active, winning constitutional recognition as persons (1929), demanding a federal Women's Bureau of Labour (1954), and securing some equal-pay legislation in the 1950s. The 1960s brought the Fédération des femmes du Québec, L'Association féminine d'éducation et d'action sociale, the Committee on Equality for Women, and the Royal Commission on the Status of Women (RCSW). In the 1970s Ottawa and provinces set up advisory councils on the status of women. The Quebec Council produced *Pour les Québécoises: Égalité et indépendance* (1978), a report that invoked sovereigntist principles. In the 1980s women demanded recognition in the federal Charter of Rights and Freedoms, and Native women achieved greater equality under a revised Indian Act.

In the 1960s women's liberation appeared in Canadian universities. Their own histories of oppression inspired French-speaking and Aboriginal activists. In 1966 Le Front de libération des femmes de Québec embraced independence for the province and women. Feminist caucuses also appeared in unions. In 1986 Shirley Carr became the first female president of the Canadian Labour Congress. In the 1960s long-standing peace activists associated with the Women's International League for Peace and Freedom and the Voice of Women (La Voix des femmes) collaborated with younger women such as those in the Student Union for Peace Action. Women against Violence against Women (1977) and annual Take Back the Night Marches (from 1981) further challenged oppression.

A 1972 conference on the RCSW initiated the ad hoc committee that became the National Action Committee (NAC), Canada's leading national representative of organized feminism at the end of the twentieth century. In the 1980s and 1990s Aboriginal activists such as Jeannette Armstrong, women of color such as Sunera Thobani, the first head of the NAC, and organizations such as the National Organization of Immigrant and Visible Minority Women of Canada and the Disabled Women's Network challenged ableism, heterosexism, racism, and classism in the women's movement. Leading feminist groups publicly supported lesbian rights and, with less certainty, transgendered women. In 1996 the Canadian Human Rights Act prohibited "sexual orientation" as a basis of discrimination. Since 1985 the Women's Legal Education Action Fund has used the charter to advance women's rights.

Cultural Production. Throughout the century, artists including Emily Carr, Frances Loring, Florence Wyle, Doris McCarthy, Pitseolak Ashoona, Rita Letendere, Joyce Wieland, Mary West Pratt, and Alanis Obomsawin articulated important visions. Music and art festivals and bookstores celebrated female companionship. The writers Daphne Marlatt, Dionne Brand, Joy Kogawa, Lee Maracle, and Nicole Brossard and the musicians Buffy Sainte-Marie,

Maureen Forrester, k. d. lang, Susan Aglukark, Sarah McLachlan, and Pauline Julien evoked the complicated nature of women's lives. Some, such as the writer Margaret Atwood, the pianist and singer Diana Krall, and the pop singers Shania Twain and Céline Dion, starred internationally. Always central to cultural production, women emerged as front-liners at the close of the twentieth century, reminding others of the centrality of female contributions.

Assessment. Issues facing Canadians at the dawn of the twenty-first century resemble those before their foremothers. Despite significant gains inequality remains rooted in the unequal distribution of power and resources. Canadian women have gained political rights, yet they remain greatly underrepresented, with just over 20 percent of the House of Commons in 2007. Although women reaped educational advances, most work in a segregated labor market and full-time wage earners receive 72 percent of the pay of male counterparts. Unpaid domestic and caring labor rests largely in female hands. For a century, poverty rates have been highest among Aboriginal women, those of color and with disabilities, and single mothers. But feminist activism and cultural production survive, even as globalization, the North American Free Trade Agreement, and the ascendancy of neoliberalism have deepened the gulf between women and men, rich and poor.

[*See also* Contraception; Education; Labor; *and* Suffrage.]

BIBLIOGRAPHY

Atlantis: A Women's Studies Journal 30, no. 1 (2005). A special issue on historical reflections of feminism and the making of Canada.

Backhouse, Constance. *Petticoats and Prejudice*. Toronto: Women's Press, 1991. An erudite treatment of the nineteenth century by a legal scholar.

Bashevkin, Sylvia B. *Welfare Hot Buttons: Women, Work, and Social Policy Reform*. Toronto: University of Toronto Press, 2002. A trenchant comment on social policy by a feminist political scientist.

Boyd, Susan B. *Child Custody, Law, and Women's Work*. Oxford and New York: Oxford University Press, 2003. A scholarly treatment by a feminist legal scholar.

Buss, Helen. *Mapping Our Selves: Canadian Women's Autobiography in English*. Montreal: McGill–Queen's University Press, 1993. A rare scholarly overview.

Clio Collective, *Quebec Women. A History*. Toronto: Women's Press, 1987. A broad-ranging scholarly feminist treatment.

Gleason, Mona, and Adele Perry, eds. *Rethinking Canada: The Promise of Women's History*. 5th ed. Don Mills, Ontario, and New York: Oxford University Press, 2006. A best-selling feminist collection.

Kinnear, Mary. *A Female Economy: Women's Work in a Prairie Province, 1870–1970*. Montreal: McGill–Queen's University Press, 1998. An impressive overview by a feminist historian.

Mitchinson, Wendy. *The Nature of Their Bodies: Women and Their Doctors in Victorian Canada*. Toronto: University of Toronto Press, 1991. A scholarly feminist treatment of Victorian Canada.

Pickles, Katie, and Myra Rutherdale, eds. *Contact Zones: Aboriginal and Settler Women in Canada's Colonial Past*. Vancouver, Canada: University of British Columbia Press, 2005. A broad-ranging scholarly feminist collection.

Prentice, Alison, Paula Bourne, Gail Cuthbert Brandt, Beth Light, Wendy Mitchinson, and Naomi Black. *Canadian Women: A History*. 2nd ed. Toronto: Harcourt Brace Canada, 1996. A broad-ranging scholarly feminist treatment.

Smart, Patricia. *Writing in the Father's House: The Emergence of the Feminine in the Quebec Literary Tradition*. 2nd ed. Toronto: University of Toronto Press, 1991. The perspective of a leading feminist literary scholar.

Stout, Madeleine Dion, and Gregory D. Kipling. *Aboriginal Women in Canada: Strategic Research Directions for Policy Development*. Ottawa: Status of Women Canada, 1998. A critical overview of problems facing Aboriginal women.

GILLIAN CREESE AND VERONICA STRONG-BOAG

CANO, MARÍA (1887–1967), socialist and labor activist. Cano was born María de los Angeles Cano in Medellín, Antioquia, Colombia, the daughter of Rodolfo Cano and Amelia Márquez, an educated and politically radical couple related to journalists, teachers, and artists. She grew up in an unconventional environment that triggered her intellectual and artistic inclinations. Using the pseudonym Helena Castillo, she published literary pieces in the magazine *Cyrano* (1921–1923). She also joined Maria Eastman and Fita Uribe in writing articles and poetry about women in the journal *El Correo Liberal* (Liberal Mail). This early stage of her literary work, characterized by romantic and subjective themes, was soon replaced by efforts to promote opportunities for the working class to enjoy reading and literature. She argued for a system of public libraries for the poor and offered herself as a reader for those who could not read.

Working at the public library of Medellín, Cano became acquainted with the wretched living condition of workers and developed deep feelings of solidarity and commitment to them. In Medellín she was designated La Flor del Trabajo (the Flower of Workers) on 1 May 1925 (International Workers' Day) as a recognition of her dedication to the working class. Cano took seriously the responsibilities bestowed by the title and began a frenzied public career as an advocate of the workers' cause that soon made her a national personality.

Cano engaged in public campaigns promoting the betterment of workers and became an effective public speaker. The key themes of her speeches were social equality, popular education, and justice. Her activities were widely acclaimed by the workers but were resented by the elite. In 1925 she began a series of seven national tours to mobilize the workers in economic enclaves such as the banana zone in the Magdalena River region, the oil fields in the mid–Magdalena River region, and the mining zones in Segovia and Remedios (Antioquia). She rallied against the international owners of the banana, oil, and mining companies and criticized the national government for relinquishing its sovereignty to foreign powers while eluding the defense of the workers, who were ill paid and abused by such companies.

Cano radicalized the workers' organizational activities. In 1926 she took an active part in the labor movement as vice president of the Third National Conference for Workers. On that occasion she was declared La Flor del Trabajo de Colombia (the Flower of All Workers of Colombia) by the National Congress. In the same event the Partido Socialista Revolucionario (PSR; Socialist Revolutionary Party) was founded. This was the first time a woman played a central role on the Colombian labor and political scene.

Cano's national prominence began to decline after 1930 because of internal divisions and confrontations between the Socialist Party and the newly founded Communist Party. She left Bogotá in late 1930, returned to Antioquia, and continued working on behalf of the lower classes. In 1947, at age eighty, she retired from her job in the county library and lived the rest of her life quietly at home. Cano was the first Colombian woman to speak openly about the rights of the "common people," the rights of workers to fair salaries, the right to strike, and justice and equality.

[*See also* Labor, *subentry* Unions, Protests, and Strikes; *and* Socialism.]

BIBLIOGRAPHY

Torres Giraldo, Ignacio. *Maria Cano, apostolado revolucionario.* Bogotá, 1988.

Velázquez Toro, Magdala. *Maria Cano.* Bogotá, 2005.

GUIOMAR DUEÑAS-VARGAS

CAPITALISM. Capitalism is an economic system in which owners of property control the production and distribution of goods and services for sale and use wealth accumulated from profits to employ laborers to produce these goods for wages. As it evolved, the system passed through stages of commercial capitalism and protoindustry before reaching its better-known, nineteenth-century form of industrial capitalism. Capitalism expanded across Europe and the United States, and in the twentieth century it took shape in many countries as so-called welfare-state capitalism. Carried by multinational corporations, by the twentieth-first century it expanded into new areas of the world as global capitalism. Though capitalism's effect on women's lives varies according to a woman's age, marital status, race, ethnicity, regional location, nationality, and wealth, it has played a determining role in the history of women. Each stage of capitalism brought changes whose relative costs and benefits for women provide material for major scholarly debates.

The Traditional Family Economy. Prior to the urbanization of the nineteenth and twentieth centuries, most women—like most men—participated in a household-based system of agricultural production, supplemented by hand manufacture of surplus goods for local markets. Smaller numbers of women made their livings producing articles and implements in family-based workshops governed by guilds that established gender-specific rules for production and distribution. A tiny stratum of aristocratic and wealthy women enjoyed opportunities for education and leisure, but like others of their sex they suffered from frequent childbearing and gender-based social constraints.

For the majority, the old system was characterized by a mutually sustaining relationship of production and reproduction in which women participated in growing and processing foods, making clothing, and manufacturing goods for household consumption while also bearing and rearing children who over time increased the family labor force. Historically, women's work was defined by a hierarchical division of labor determined by attitudes and customs regarding proper gender roles. Women typically worked in occupations associated with providing food and clothing, in retail trade, or in caretaking and cleaning services. Overall they earned wages of one-half to two-thirds those paid to men.

Commercial Capitalism. In the early modern period of European expansion overseas and the concurrent growth of national and international markets, demand for household production increased, providing new opportunities for women to add to family wealth through fabrication for the market of items such as thread, cloth, and small implements. Beginning in England and Belgium in the late eighteenth and early nineteenth centuries, the rapid spread of cotton textile industries, where large-scale production first took place, led to extensive demand for low-paid female (and child) labor. Merchants and manufacturers drew on women's traditional skills in spinning, weaving, and sewing, first in the putting-out system (cottage industry) and later in rural and urban workshops and factories. In some areas of Europe, cotton manufacturing declined as a source of employment for women later in the nineteenth century, but by the end of the twentieth century the demand for (cheap) female labor had advanced across the globe, providing women with substitute employment for opportunities lost in agriculture and small-scale trade.

Women's work in the enlarged market economy contributed in important ways to the accumulation of the capital that enabled new, large-scale commercial enterprises to flourish. This process benefited many women by providing paid employment, while also making accessible attractive and useful products. However, as the example of the cotton textile industry illustrates, the benefits for some came at the expense of others. Industrialists who could sell cotton fabrics at far lower prices than silk and woolen cloth helped many women clothe themselves and their families. But they did so by exploiting the productive and reproductive labor of slaves to increase the output of the raw materials needed to supply textile factories.

The new technologies in agriculture and manufacturing that transformed and relocated much home-based labor created a dilemma for many workers. By separating work for subsistence from its household setting and family control, industrialization and urbanization turned most men and women into wage earners working for capitalists. The prototypical example of this process, famously termed "proletarianization" by Karl Marx (1818–1883), has been the male factory worker reduced to owning nothing but his labor power. For women these shifts created an often neglected and still unsolved problem of how to combine their productive and reproductive work. The separation between home and work constitutes perhaps the most important gender-specific effect of the capitalist system on women's lives.

Industrial Capitalism. Early industrial capitalist expansion increased the demand for female labor even as it also elicited resistance to it. The physical separation of work and family that created conflict for women, along with exploitative conditions in many workshops and factories, encouraged withdrawal from the labor force for women who could afford it. It also contributed to the idealization of home and family life as a refuge from the workplace. Middle-class respectability came to require a male income sufficient to support a family, with a non-wage-earning wife being a marker of successful masculinity. Increasingly, capitalist class differentiation reflected this highly gendered "ideology of domesticity" that ascribed to women, protected from economic competition, greater moral force than men. Later generations of women drew on this attribution to claim rights to participate in public and political affairs.

The impact of these changes on women first captured widespread attention in the mid-nineteenth century, with both representatives of newly forming labor organizations and also social reformers lamenting what they termed "the industrialization of women." While the elimination of guilds in the early industrial period had left many working men with little protection against pressures of the marketplace, the craft associations and unions that men later developed to defend their interests in many male-dominant trades had few counterparts in women's trades. Like the medieval guilds, the unions rarely offered support for women workers and sometimes actively protested their participation in industrial work, on grounds of wage competition or assumptions about "appropriate" gender roles. Capitalism, in this view, corrupted family relations with monetary interests.

The situation of women workers, especially in urban settings where they lacked traditional family and community support and typically earned less than subsistence wages, elicited extensive concern and a broad alliance of men to "protect" women by placing legal limitations on their workplace options. For the French historian Jules Michelet, the term for female laborer, *ouvrière*, was an "impious, sordid" word, "unknown before this age of steel." Depicting women workers as victims of exploitation by rapacious bosses, male workers—concerned also to reduce competition from lower-paid women workers and to minimize the loss of personal status and domestic services—began to call for a "family wage," that is, a wage sufficient for a man to support a family. "Who would wash the husband's socks and salt his soup?" if wives left their homes for other pursuits, they asked. Already fearful of a declining population, some organized French workingmen called for restricting women's work outside the home, at least until they reached the age of forty, preferably after having had four children. Adopted first by early socialist parties, the call for "equal pay for equal work" initially reflected the assumption that it was primarily because of women's low wages that they were employed in industry at all.

By the late decades of the nineteenth century, legislation in most industrialized countries restricted the hours and conditions of women's nondomestic wage labor. Some women, especially if employed in noxious industries, benefited substantially. An important concomitant effect, however, was to eliminate women from most factory work and from newer industries where additional legislation soon led to limited hours for all and improved wages and working conditions, while concentrating women in labor-intensive, low-skilled "sweatshop" production and other unregulated employment known today as the "informal economy."

Explaining "Women's Place." From the late eighteenth century, political economists and historians have sought to explain the secondary place of women under capitalism. Influenced by Enlightenment-based beliefs in the power of human reason and the perfectibility of human society, some early economists and social thinkers offered—to counter inherited religious explanations—materialist rationales for women's subordinate position. The Scottish economist Adam Smith (1723–1790) saw in the commercial capitalism of his day an evolving historical stage that provided new opportunities for women, who, by earning income, could enhance their authority and improve their status relative to men. The French economist Jean-Baptiste Say (1767–1832) explained women's secondary position in the economy as the result of a "natural wage" based on women's lesser needs; not only did men require greater personal sustenance, but they, unlike women, Say assumed, bore responsibility for the support of a family.

Historians' attempts to evaluate the effects of capitalism on women date from the second half of the nineteenth century, when they joined social reformers and novelists in calling attention to the conditions of deprivation in which many poor women and their families lived. In the early twentieth century, two now classic accounts, Alice Clark's *The Working Life of Women in the Seventeenth Century* (1919) and Ivy Pinchbeck's *Women Workers and the Industrial Revolution* (1930), initiated what is known in women's history as the "golden age" controversy. Focusing on England, where the changes began, this debate raises the question of whether in the precapitalist, preindustrial, largely rural, subsistence-level economy where women's contributions were essential to family survival, women enjoyed a higher status and greater degree of equality with men, based on their mutual dependence, than they did at a later date once the products of female labor became available commercially and more women faced a one-sided dependency on men's wages.

To some extent the answer varies with women's marital status. Single women experienced greater constraints in a traditional, family-based labor economy where they lacked a home and wifely position of their own, and under capitalism they gained opportunities for employment and enhanced status along with income earned from wages. For married women the process was reversed: they lost status when under capitalism much of their traditional work was relocated to factories or workshops, with food, clothing, and shelter readily available for purchase, and they could contribute less to their family's income and well-being. For Clark the increased dependence of wives signaled diminishing social importance along with increasing idleness. Pinchbeck, in contrast, examining in detail women's work in agriculture (hoeing turnips, for example), industry (machine spinning), and trade (including white-collar jobs), stressed the miserable conditions in which most women lived in rural England prior to the agrarian and industrial revolutions. In her view, factory employment represented a major improvement over agricultural labor. Pinchbeck highlighted the better hygiene, improved standards of living, wider opportunities, and enhanced social value that women enjoyed following the Industrial Revolution.

Historians of women sometimes frame the debate about the status of women and their work under capitalism in terms of "continuity versus change." Have changes associated with capitalism brought women better employment opportunities and higher rewards, or does women's work, whatever it may be, continue for the most part to be undervalued and ill-compensated because of its very association with the "second sex"? In support of the latter view, historians point to the preindustrial origins of a dual labor market, one in which women were assigned secondary status, were given fewer opportunities for apprenticeship, and were limited to a narrow range of irregular, seasonal, low-paid employment. They also note the persistent clustering, from the 1200s to the 1900s, of most women workers in lower-skilled, lower-paid, lower-status occupations.

Many studies of women and capitalism reflect a Marxist perspective according to which "relations of production" determine class consciousness and social relations. In this view, women's subordination results from the institution of private property and the privatized family designed to ensure the transmission of this property to "legitimate" heirs—an institution that also restricts women's roles in production. Only a socialist revolution that transfers property to a collectivity, draws women into "social production," and provides for the needs of all persons could overcome women's economic and social dependence on individual men. Although early socialist critics of laissez-faire capitalism—such as the Irish writers Anna Doyle Wheeler and William Thompson and the Frenchmen Charles Fourier, Henri Saint-Simon, and Pierre Leroux—thought that, following "natural laws," history would evolve toward a more harmonious society better attuned to women's allegedly less individualistic, less competitive nature, these thinkers, derided by Karl Marx as "utopian," had little impact on capitalist society. Their ideas, including the Frenchwoman Flora Tristan's 1843 proposal that workingmen organize a "universal union" to replace capitalist exploitation of labor and the concomitant degradation of workingwomen, bore little fruit. Socialist visions of a male-dominant family giving way to a more egalitarian "great human family" disappeared in the politics of labor parties seeking votes of men who held conventional attitudes about women.

Since the beginnings of women's studies, many scholars have borrowed Marxist terminology to analyze women's dual roles in production and reproduction, and the linkages between them, as central to understanding women's condition under capitalism. Historians and feminist theorists note that Marxist concepts, including proletarianization and the economic determinism that reduces women to their roles as wage earners, obscure the importance of women's unwaged work in the home and fail to consider the noneconomic aspects of women's subordination in family and society. Seeking more satisfactory explanations, many locate women's subordination in a pervasive gender-based system, often called "patriarchy," that changes over time and place but intersects with capitalism to privilege men in the economy, education, politics, sexual relations, and many social institutions.

But it is important to note the ways that many women benefited from changes associated with capitalist development. Capitalism brought in its train more widespread literacy, enhanced educational opportunities, improved standards of housing, and cheaper and more varied clothing and household furnishings, as well as the improved nutrition and public hygiene that led to reduced infant and maternal mortality and greater longevity. For single women especially, new employment options allowed for greater independence from family and community constraints—although these options also produced greater vulnerabilities, because most women's wages remained insufficient to ensure a comfortable, independent living. This point has been made in studies ranging from that of the French economist Dr. Louis-René Villermé (1782–1863) in the 1840s—who famously observed that women factory workers turned to prostitution for the "fifth quarter of the day," as a means to supplement their meager wages—to that of historians of women such as Joan Wallach Scott and Louise Tilly in their *Women, Work, and Family* of 1978. Married women in industrial societies benefited especially from dramatic decreases in the frequency of childbearing, which, coupled with increased life expectancy, allowed them far more life choices. Some scholars argue that by earning wages, women gained greater power within families.

Changing Women's Status. By devaluing women's productive work and removing the better-off women from the workplace and increasing their educational opportunities, industrial capitalism also created the conditions for the emergence of organized women's movements, beginning in Europe in the late eighteenth century and spreading across the globe into the twenty-first. From their earliest stages, women's rights advocates called for changing relations between the sexes in employment as well as in personal status; revising marriage laws to increase women's authority over their children, their earnings, and their property; admitting women to full citizenship; and giving women a larger voice in society. By the late twentieth century many of these demands had been fulfilled in leading capitalist countries. Women of the middle- and upper-income strata now enjoy many economic benefits and personal privileges associated with capitalist development. Some women enjoy access to education and professional life, control their own financial affairs, participate fully in civic and cultural activities, and transcend the limitations imposed on earlier generations. Others, disproportionately women of color, continue to labor long hours for little pay in occupations unprotected by labor organizations or legislation. They also often lack equal access to education, housing, health care, and other costly benefits available in capitalist society.

Capitalist expansion and the continuing demand for stereotypical women's work has drawn vast numbers of women all over the world into the paid labor force, in many places repeating more recently conditions experienced by women in Europe in earlier periods of economic development. Ester Boserup in her landmark 1970 study *Women and Economic Development* pointed to the declining status of many women that accompanied the introduction of "Westernization" or capitalism. Imported ideas about "appropriate" tasks for women and new technologies that replaced the instruments and methods typically used by women with others used by men (for example, substituting the plow for the hoe), along with new laws regulating land tenure that favored men by designating them heads of household and new corporate enterprises that displaced native collective associations, all worked to the economic disadvantage of women.

This process has expanded in ensuing years, accelerated by the globalization of capitalist production. In emerging market economies, women purveyors who engage in selling and trading goods in local marketplaces and female entrepreneurs who produce small goods—both traditional female occupations—lose out in competition with male entrepreneurs from overseas and with multinational corporations. As labor-intensive capitalist production moves from more industrialized to less industrialized countries, women provide a low-paid-labor force for assembly plants in garment, electronics, and other industries, both in large factories and small, decentralized settings where housewives and mothers repeat the practice of piecework for long hours and low pay that accompanied industrialization and the growth of factories in Europe. In many impoverished countries these wage-earning opportunities constitute the only means of livelihood available to women, who, it is estimated, now make up 70 percent of the world's poor.

The continuing socioeconomic inequality of women under capitalism has been highlighted by economic changes that followed the fall of Communism in Russia and Eastern Europe. As socialist regimes built their industrial economies in the decades following the two world wars, demographic and economic needs impelled them to draw most women into the labor force. Though these regimes provided women with enhanced educational and employment opportunities, they also assigned women most of the burdens of domestic life. They failed, however, to produce the consumer goods designed to alleviate household drudgery and improve the quality of personal life that became readily available in most capitalist countries. Though their promise to reduce domestic labor by socializing housework fell before other priorities, socialist governments did offer partial relief for women's "double burden" by supporting social services addressed to their familial responsibilities. Women constituted the majority of both providers and recipients of this assistance. In the 1990s, during the rapid transition to market economies, most such services disappeared. Facing disproportionate unemployment, many women fell victim to a burgeoning traffic in commercial sex. In place of the socialist call for women to serve the state through paid labor and civic participation came propaganda that encouraged retreat, including idealization of the Victorian woman-at-home model family and government incentives to raise low birthrates. Attacks on women's rights to work and to reproductive choice were accompanied by admiration for stereotypical "feminine" fashions and styles of behavior.

The ideology of separate spheres and gendered limitations on women's work still support capitalism by assigning to women, rather than to men, to employers, or to communities, the primary burden of unpaid work caring for dependent children, the ill, and the elderly. The "maternal dilemma" that arose centuries ago when under capitalism women's traditional work was relocated from the household persists today, aggravated by the decline of welfare states and concomitant trends toward the privatization of public services. Capitalism has brought many changes to women's lives but also supports continuities in women's status.

[*See also* Communism; Industry and Industrialization; *and* Socialism.]

BIBLIOGRAPHY

Clark, Alice. *The Working Life of Women in the Seventeenth Century*. London: Routledge, 1919.

Frader, Laura L., and Sonya O. Rose, eds. *Gender and Class in Modern Europe*. Ithaca, N.Y.: Cornell University Press, 1996.

Kuhn, Annette, and AnnMarie Wolpe, eds. *Feminism and Materialism: Women and Modes of Production*. London: Routledge and Kegan Paul, 1978.

Pinchbeck, Ivy. *Women Workers and the Industrial Revolution, 1759–1850*. London: Routledge, 1930.

Tilly, Louise A., and Joan W. Scott. *Women, Work, and Family*. New York: Routledge, 1978.

MARILYN J. BOXER

CAPITAL PUNISHMENT. *See* Criminality.

CARIBBEAN REGION. The Caribbean was the first point of contact for European exploration and conquest in the Americas. Records from Spanish conquistadores reveal that indigenous women often put up fierce resistance to European encroachment, sexual exploitation, and enslavement. As the population of Amerindians dwindled, Europeans replaced their captive labor force with enslaved Africans. By the start of the nineteenth century, primarily Africans and Europeans populated the Caribbean colonies. The power dynamics of maintaining slavery forged a rigid social hierarchy based on race and gender.

Political Involvement in the Nineteenth Century. Although traditional, patriarchal ideas subordinated women to men, restricted their work to the domestic sphere, and barred them from formal political participation, women were not passive about politics. Women from all classes and races demonstrated their support for political autonomy in a variety of ways. Puerto Rican and Cuban women, primarily from the middle and upper classes and of European descent or racially mixed, joined the early the struggles for independence. For women of African descent, full emancipation and equality were just cause for political action.

Early examples for the Spanish Caribbean highlight women's engagement in politics. In protest to Napoleon's occupation of Spain in 1807, Cuban women cut their hair, an obvious contrast to traditional Spanish styles and a symbol of their ideological support for reform and the French Revolution. During the early insurgencies, Creole women also organized and hosted sociocultural, intellectual gatherings, called *tertulias* or *veladas*, in support of the separatist movements. For instance, María de las Mercedes Barbudo coordinated meetings in Puerto Rico until she was forced into exile in 1823. In Cuba, Pilar Poveda, a free women of African descent, was charged with holding meetings in her home in support of the 1843 Conspiración de la Escalera (Conspiracy of the Ladder), involving free people of color, slaves, and British abolitionists to end slavery and Spanish rule.

Women were key actors during the politically charged events of the 1860s. The abolition of slavery by 1838 in the Anglophone colonies granted former slaves the right to vote, but property restrictions limited their eligibility. These tensions erupted during the 1865 Morant Bay rebellion in Jamaica. Although women did not hold formal positions among the insurgents, they were involved in the organizational network and in direct protest. Women such as Sarah Johnson, Caroline Grant, Rosanna Finlayson, and Ann Thompson participated in meetings, marched in protest, raided stores for weapons, and took part in the attack.

When Puerto Rico and Cuba renewed their claims to independence in 1868, women proved instrumental to the movement. As wives, mistresses, or companions, they supplied clothing and food, cared for the wounded, buried the dead, served as guides in familiar territory, acted as spies relaying information about Spanish troops, and participated in combat. In Puerto Rico, Lola Rodríguez de Tió penned the revolutionary anthem, and Mariana Bracetti stitched the banner of Lares. In Cuba, Mariana Grajales, Ana Betancourt, and Emilia Casanova, all married to well-known military or literary figures, organized women's clubs and raised funds to help support Cuba's independence movement. Caribbean women's actions during rebellions and independence movements in the nineteenth century demonstrated that they could no longer be categorized as weak or harmless, and they stimulated women—as well as some men—to reconsider traditional thinking about the subordination of women.

Haiti. A Haitian woman fills out her voting ballot in Port-au-Prince, November 2000. REUTERS/ KIMBERLY WHITE

Societal Challenges to Women's Equality. Formidable obstacles blocked women's aims to increase their independence. Many men and women opposed gender equality for women on the grounds that it threatened family stability. These societies often considered education for women unnecessary, unfeminine, and ultimately dangerous because it took them away from the traditional domestic arena and exposed them to new ideas that had the potential to erode the family structure. The British colonies stressed the traditional role of women's "service" and resisted the promotion of women's rights. Those in the Spanish Caribbean shared that outlook, emphasizing a gendered division of labor and authority.

Issues of race and class also created tension in women's pursuit of equality. By the end of the nineteenth century, outspoken elite and middle-class women, typically white or of light complexions and increasingly of primarily African descent in the Anglophone areas, led the fight for gender equality and opportunities for women. These women frequently promoted the idea that women should remain in their homes, even though their work as activists forced them away from their families. Rather, they emphasized legal, political, and educational reforms that mainly benefited women of their social status. Activities aimed at working-class women were typically in the realm of charity, with little input from the recipients.

In response, working-class women forged their own voice in the women's movements of the Caribbean. This sector of women, typically poor, underemployed, having limited education, and of African descent, engaged in plantation or domestic wage labor. With the shift from slave to free labor in the 1840s and 1850s, businesses encouraged the migration of indentured workers from India and China. Though the majority of these immigrants were men, wives and single women from these countries added to the ranks of working-class women, often as agricultural laborers and household servants, particularly in Trinidad, Jamaica, Guyana, and Cuba. The increasingly industrialized economy brought poor women into the cities where they worked in factories for low wages and long hours. The brutal working conditions that existed throughout the region caused some women from the working class to establish their own organizations for economic parity.

Despite these differences, women of all sectors pushed for reforms, particularly in education. The reforms gained new support because of their focus on strengthening the family by instructing women on raising children to be good citizens and transmitting respectable cultural values. Some countries perceived educating women as one distinct way to promote national and imperial progress in the Caribbean. With increased access to education, employment opportunities and the right to vote became pivotal issues in the struggle for gender equality.

Organizations. The earliest organizations established by women were social organizations promoting self-help, education, and employment. They focused primarily on offering economic relief to women in the form of charitable programs, such as the Lady Musgrave Self-Help Society of Jamaica founded in 1879 and the Trinidad Home Industries and Women's Self-Help Association in Trinidad and Tobago founded in 1901. These groups enabled upper-class women to support employment for poor craftswomen by helping develop local industries. Activities connected to social work and charity enabled early women's organizations and their members to gain prestige. Moreover, these kinds of selfless endeavors were seen as legitimate activities for women and thus did not challenge the status quo.

Suffrage organizations. The most prominent women's organizations emerged in support of woman suffrage. Women in the English-speaking islands initiated protests for enfranchisement in the 1840s. Their activism coincided with male protests to remove property requirements for suffrage. Moreover, politicians campaigned on issues important to women and the community at large, such as health care, small businesses, and sexual exploitation, knowing that they could sway male voters. Women's influential, if silent, participation, however, did occasionally erupt into active protest. The Jamaicans Ann Warren and Juliana Rogers took part in riots following suspicious election results in 1852. In 1895 and 1901 the Cuban club Esperanza del Valle requested that the government enact voting rights for women, but to no avail. Despite their lack of access to the formal right to vote, women had a clear understanding of the high stakes of politics.

In the early twentieth century, women in the region and the hemisphere forged national and international alliances to press for woman suffrage. Cuba's Women's Suffrage Committee, formed in 1912, served as the launching pad for the more politicized organizations that emerged in the tense atmosphere of government corruption and repression in the 1920s. Jamaican women renewed their call for universal suffrage without regard to gender or wealth. When women gained the right to vote in the United States in 1920, feminists in the Caribbean intensified their efforts. They made extended connections at the First International Feminine Conference, held in Argentina in 1910, and at the Inter-American Women's Conference in Panama in 1926. Though these congresses sometimes revealed international tensions surrounding race, class, and notions of civilization, in many instances they stimulated politicization.

Influenced by these events, Puerto Rico established its first suffrage association, the Suffragist Social League, in 1921, formerly known as the Feminine League formed in 1917 by Ana Roqué de Duprey. Ideological disagreements led Roqué and Isabel Andreu de Aguilar to form the Association of Women Suffragists in 1924 to advocate for enfranchisement without restrictions.

In Cuba, Pilar Jorge de Tella and Ofelia Domínguez Navarro united the nation's diverse feminist organizations under the Cuban Committee for the Defense of Women's Suffrage. The Feminist National Alliance emerged in 1928 but ultimately split into those supporting suffrage through reform and those supporting a revolutionary approach.

In Jamaica in the 1930s, Amy Bailey, Una Marson, and Amy Jacques Garvey asserted that women's achievements in education and business justified their access to political participation. They called for granting universal suffrage, at the time restricted from working-class men and women. In the same decade, activists in the Dominican Republic established Dominican Feminist Action to advocate for women's enfranchisement. Despite the early alliance between the Trujillo regime and Dominican Feminist Action, the government delayed woman suffrage. By 1942 all women in Puerto Rico (1932), Cuba (1934), and the Dominican Republic (1942) had achieved the right to vote.

As women in the neighboring islands were enfranchised, British Caribbean feminists increased their demands to obtain full suffrage rights. By 1964 women in the English-speaking territories gained the right to vote in Jamaica and Bermuda (1944), Trinidad and Tobago (1946), Barbados (1950), Antigua and Barbuda, Dominica, Grenada, Saint Kitts and Nevis, Saint Vincent and the Grenadines (1951), Guyana (1953), Saint Lucia (1954), and the Bahamas and Belize (1964). The Caribbean Women's Conference of 1953 held in Trinidad and Tobago and the Caribbean Women's Association, established subsequently, encouraged women's full and active participation in political, as well as socioeconomic, aspects of society.

A new cadre of professional women entered the workforce by the late 1960s, challenging traditional stereotypes and transforming women's societal roles. Cuba's successful social revolution set a new standard by reframing women's public positions in society and promoting gender equality through free health and child care, education, and subsidized housing. Trinidad's League of Women Voters worked to educate female constituents about their political, social, and economic rights and responsibilities. These advances ushered women into public office. Felisa Rincón de Gautier served as the first female mayor in Puerto Rico (San Juan) from 1946 to 1969 and Beryl Archibald Crichlow was elected mayor in Trinidad and Tobago (San Fernando Borough Council) from 1949 to 1950. Voters selected Elmira Minita Gordon as the first woman governor of Belize in 1981. Mary Eugenia Charles became the first female head of state in the Caribbean as Prime Minister of Dominica from 1980 to 1995.

Labor organizations. Increasing industrialization by the late nineteenth century brought an unprecedented number of women into the workforce. They constituted a significant proportion of both agricultural labor and labor in the textile industries. The massive expansion of women in the workforce, particularly during the two world wars, added new dimensions to working-class women's rights, bringing labor organizing to the forefront.

As early as 1899 the Liberty Federation of Workers in Puerto Rico worked to educate and organize female laborers against economic exploitation and for suffrage. The activist Louisa Capetillo spoke on behalf of needlework and tobacco workers. Jamaicans such as Catherine McKenzie demanded representative taxation, adding that the government could not expect women to pay taxes without gaining the privileges that their taxes helped support. In Cuba the Women's Labor Union focused on improving working conditions, advocating women's equality through revolutionary change rather than through reform.

Political unrest galvanized workers, and strikes broke out around the region in the 1930s. In some areas, workers gained a new voice. In Trinidad and Tobago, Elma Francois organized seaman and waterfront laborers, and a union emerged to address female domestic workers. Lucy Stroder established unions for commercial and industrial workers in Grenada. In contrast, the Dominican Republic's government dismantled the labor movement's socialist wing, implemented tight governmental controls on remaining unions, and fostered disunity among Dominican workers. Unions did not become significantly active again until the mid-1960s.

National organizations dedicated to the rights of working women emerged by the 1950s. Daphne Campbell formed the Jamaica Women's Assembly in 1953 to make working-class women more aware of their rights and to raise their social status. Phyllis Shand Allfrey founded the Dominica Labor Party in 1955 and influenced the formation of the Women's Guild, which championed the island's labor movement. The success of Cuba's social revolution in 1959 enhanced the position of women in the workforce by guaranteeing wage equity, instituting a variety of social programs, and establishing the Federation of Cuban Women in 1960 to foster women's causes and issues.

Despite national claims for workers' rights, labor organizations often gave little voice to the working-class women. Few held leadership positions in unions or were national organization officers. By the 1950s and 1960s many feminist leaders held positions in the government, removing them from the realities of poor and working-class women. Indeed, numerous feminist organizations were co-opted by the government, which refocused their activities back into the domestic sphere and neglected working-class issues.

Moreover, despite their increasing numbers in the workforce, women in the Caribbean continued to be regarded primarily as supplementary breadwinners. Discrimination based on gender persisted throughout the region. Moreover, a distinct feminization of labor resurfaced in the 1950s and 1960s. Trinidadian authorities recast working-class wives and daughters in an idealized male-headed household and viewed labor, particularly in the agricultural industry, as an extension of their duties as homemakers. In Barbados, clerical work lost its initial status for women as employers rationalized sedentary, repetitive, and detailed tasks as best suited for women who were characterized as docile, patient, and dexterous. The phenomenon reproduced itself throughout the region as companies sought to increase profits from cheap labor pools.

A brief resurgence of labor unions during the 1970s and1980s enabled Trinidadian women to form the National Union of Domestic Employees. Jamaica and the Dominican Republic secured minimum wage reforms. Nevertheless, politics and globalization interfered with establishing sweeping grassroots movements, dislodging middle- and working-class women's issues from the political arena. Ultimately unions were dismantled in the Dominican Republic. By the 1980s, competition in the free-trade zones had fostered a large working-class labor pool forced to work in dangerous conditions for low wages. As local male employment opportunities waned, women's employment rate accelerated rapidly in order to meet the rising economic demands of increasingly female-headed households. This pattern continued into the 1990s, setting the stage for new challenges to women's social, economic, and political involvement for the remainder of the twentieth century.

Women and Society at the End of the Twentieth Century. The Decade for Women, declared by the United Nations in 1975, set the stage for optimism. Women were recognized for their critical roles in international labor, national politics, and grassroots leadership. By the 1980s, activists legislated changes designed to end remaining inequalities. Laws protecting women against domestic violence and sexual harassment were enacted. Regional organizations, including Women and Development (WAND), the Women's Bureau of the Caribbean Community and Common Market (CARICOM), and the Caribbean Association for Feminist Research and Action (CAFRA), fostered cross-cultural support. Area and international events on women's education, health care, literature, athletics, and science helped to articulate national agendas, redefine organizational and recruitment methods, and validate gender ties. Increasingly, activists prioritized fighting oppression based on race, class, and sexual orientation, as well as fighting health epidemics. In 1992 the Dominican Republic held its first international meeting to build a political organization that would illuminate issues particularly relevant for women of African descent. Recognition of the region's high rates of HIV/AIDS among women prompted the Caribbean conference on HIV/AIDS held in Barbados in 2000.

Idealistic laws designed to address family dynamics, such as Jamaica's amendments to several laws governing the rights of unmarried parents, have often created contradictions and reproduced inequalities. Cuba's "Special Period" of economic crisis in the 1990s, implemented after the collapse the Soviet Union, eroded employment, health care, and education, renewing prostitution and black-market activities in order to obtain daily necessities. Despite higher levels of education, Caribbean women continue to cluster at the lower sectors of society in terms employment, wages, political representation, and access to social resources, making them vulnerable to gender-based violence and harassment.

In response to these critical issues, women in the Caribbean have continued to assert their political influence, joining the growing ranks of female leaders in the Americas. In 1997 Janet Jagan became the prime minister of Guyana and voters elected Pearlette Louisy the governor of Saint Lucia. From 2000 to 2004 Milagros Ortíz Bosch served as the first female vice president of the Dominican Republic. In 2006 voters elected Portia Simpson-Miller the prime minister of Jamaica.

[*See also* Alonso, Alicia; Anacaona; Codes of Law and Laws, *subentry* Latin America; Espín, Vilma; Feminist Encounters of Latin American and Caribbean Women; First Feminine Congress of the Pan-American League; First International Feminine Congress in Buenos Aires; Gómez de Avellaneda, Gertrudis; Machismo and Marianismo; Peláez, Amelia; *and* Toledo, Maria de.]

BIBLIOGRAPHY

Bailey, Barbara. "The Caribbean Experience in the International Women's Movement: Issues, Process, Constraints, and Possibilities." In *Gender in the 21st Century: Caribbean Perspectives, Visions, and Possibilities*, edited by Barbara Bailey and Elsa Leo-Rhynie, pp. 626–654. Kingston, Jamaica: Ian Randle, 2004.

Freeman, Carla. "Designing Women: Corporate Discipline in Barbados's Off-Shore Pink-Collar Sector." *Cultural Anthropology* 8, no. 2 (May 1993): 169–186.

López Springfield, Consuelo, ed. *Daughters of Caliban: Caribbean Women in the Twentieth Century*. Bloomington: Indiana University Press, 1997. See the essays by Carollee Bengelsdorf (pp. 229–258), Mary Johnson Osirim (pp. 41–67), and Lizabeth Paravisini-Gebert (pp. 3–17).

Matos Rodríguez, Félix V., and Linda C. Delgado, eds. *Puerto Rican Women's History: New Perspectives*. Armonk, N.Y.: M. E. Sharpe, 1998. See the essays by María de Fátima Barceló-Miller (pp. 126–142) and Félix V. Matos Rodríguez (pp. 62–82).

Reddock, Rhoda E. *Women, Labour, and Politics in Trinidad and Tobago*. London: Zed Books, 1994.

Reddock, Rhoda E., and Jasmine Huggins. "Agriculture and Women's Place: The Impact of Changing National Policies on Women's Agricultural Work in Trinidad and Tobago." In *Gender: A Caribbean Multi-Disciplinary Persective*, edited by Elsa Leo-Rhynie, Barbara Bailey, and Christine Barrow, pp. 324–346. Kingston, Jamaica: Ian Randle, 1997.

Sánchez Korrol, Virginia. "Women in Nineteenth- and Twentieth-Century Latin America and the Caribbean." In *Women in Latin America and the Caribbean: Restoring Women to History*, by Marysa Navarro and Virginia Sánchez Korrol, pp. 59–106. Bloomington: Indiana University Press, 1999.

Shepherd, Verene A., ed. *Women in Caribbean History: The British-Colonised Territories*. Princeton, N.J.: Markus Wiener, 1999.

Shepherd, Verene A., Bridget Brereton, and Barbara Bailey, eds. *Engendering History: Caribbean Women in Historical Perspective*. New York: St. Martin's Press, 1995. See the essays by Swithin Wilmot (pp. 279–295), Verene A. Shepherd (pp. 233–257), and Linnette Vassell (pp. 318–336).

Stoner, K. Lynn. *From the House to the Streets: The Cuban Woman's Movement for Legal Reform, 1898–1940*. Durham, N. C.: Duke University Press, 1991.

MICHELE B. REID

CARPENTER, MARY (1807–1877), British educational and social reformer whose well-publicized domestic and imperial work made her a role model for late Victorian British feminists. Inspired by Unitarian reformist principles, Mary Carpenter's philanthropic activities covered a host of social issues, most notably the establishment of secular "ragged" and reformatory schools for destitute children and juvenile offenders. Carpenter's imperial reform work, too, attracted a great deal of notice. Her *Six Months in India* (1868), a report on Indian women, is considered a particularly rich source for understanding women's relationship to empire. In heightening English public interest in Indian women, the book linked Carpenter with the challenge of colonial reform, a link solidified in 1870 when she founded the National Indian Association to promote social reform, including female education, in India.

The story of Carpenter's interest in India constitutes a fascinating instance of the ideological ambivalence of white women toward both Indian customs and the imperialist enterprise. Carpenter respected Indians well enough to support their resistance to Christian proselytization and was sharply critical of the social and educational politics of the colonial government. Yet she could not escape racist and Christian assumptions and vocabularies. Similarly, though Carpenter's accounts of Indian women appeared to be "ethnographic," few realized that linguistic and cultural barriers had minimized Carpenter's contact with the women she was writing about and that her representations were mediated by English-educated Indian men with whom she more deeply identified.

However, in bringing colonial issues within the ambit of "social duty" and thereby within the domain of middle-class English women's lives, Carpenter considerably enlarged the public sphere for British women. Her evaluations of Indian women's potential for progress along Western lines carried great weight, encouraging English women to consider themselves as educators of Indian women and, as such, equal participants in shouldering the moral burden of empire. Thus Carpenter's public career provides evidence that white women's gradual emancipation in their own lives was crucially framed by their involvement in campaigns against such colonial issues as slavery, *sati*, and women's education.

This link between the genesis of British feminism and imperialism in the nineteenth century appears ironic to contemporary scholars of both. Carpenter's plans for ameliorating Indian women's condition glossed over English women's own subordination to the Christian British patriarchy. More orthodox than most Unitarians, Carpenter failed, unlike her more radical Victorian peers, to articulate gender and class inequities in Britain itself. Her awareness of obstacles to English women's emancipation did increase in the years she campaigned for Indian women, but, ultimately, her work on behalf of both Indian and British women effected limited change.

[*See also* Education; Great Britain; Imperialism and Colonialism; India; *and* South Asia, *subentry* Colonial Period.]

BIBLIOGRAPHY

Burton, Antoinette. *At the Heart of the Empire: Indians and the Colonial Encounter in Late-Victorian Britain*. Berkeley: University of California Press, 1998.

Burton, Antoinette. *Burdens of History: British Feminists, Indian Women, and Imperial Culture, 1865–1915*. Chapel Hill: University of North Carolina Press, 1994.

Burton, Antoinette. "Fearful Bodies into Disciplined Subjects: Pleasure, Romance, and the Family Drama of Colonial Reform in Mary Carpenter's Six Months in India." In *History and Theory: Feminist Research, Debates, Contestations*, edited by Barbara Laslett, Ruth-Ellen B. Joeres, Mary Jo Maynes, Evelyn Brooks Higginbotham, and Jeanne Barker-Nunn, pp. 224–253. Chicago: University of Chicago Press, 1997.

Carpenter, Joseph Estlin. *The Life and Work of Mary Carpenter*. London: Macmillan, 1879. Reprint. Montclair, N.J.: Patterson Smith, 1974.

Carpenter, Mary. *Six Months in India*. 2 vols. London: Longmans, Green, 1868.

Watts, Ruth. "Breaking the Boundaries of Victorian Imperialism or Extending a Reformed 'Paternalism'? Mary Carpenter and India." *History of Education* 29, no. 5 (2000): 443–456.

SANDHYA SHETTY

CARSON, RACHEL (1907–1964), American biologist, writer, and environmentalist. Rachel Carson was raised in Springdale, Pennsylvania, in the Allegheny River watershed, and displayed talents in biology and literature from an early age. She earned a master's degree in zoology from Johns Hopkins University in 1932 and engaged in fieldwork at the Marine Biological Laboratory at Wood's Hole, Massachusetts, and at West Southport, Maine, where she kept a summer home. During World War II she worked for the U.S. Fish and Wildlife Service.

Carson is best known for *Silent Spring* (1962), a touchstone of contemporary environmentalism. She was already an established natural historian thanks to *Under the Sea-Wind* (1941), *The Sea around Us* (1951)—which won the National Book Award in 1952—and *The Edge of the Sea* (1955). She began to research the effects of pesticides when large numbers of songbirds were reported dead in Massachusetts and New Hampshire during the summer of 1957 in the wake of aerial spraying. *Silent Spring* was the result, a synthesis of scientific research, literary narrative, and political rhetoric condemning the uncontrolled use of pesticides, especially chlorinated hydrocarbons such as DDT. A best seller, the book generated a public outcry that caused John F. Kennedy to convene the President's Science Advisory Committee (1963), whose report vindicated Carson's analysis in the face of harsh criticism from the chemical industry.

Though widely regarded as the foundation of the contemporary U.S. environmental movement, Carson's work on pesticides remains controversial because of DDT's effectiveness against mosquito-borne malaria. Caricatured by opponents as a "high-priestess of Nature" and a "hysterical" woman, Carson never advocated the elimination of pesticides from general use. Instead, she recommended the integration of biological and chemical controls on insect pests. Behind her pragmatism lay a critique of the idea of the control of nature, which she described in *Silent Spring* as a product of the "Neanderthal age of biology and philosophy." Her recommendation that technology and natural processes evolve in dialogue has not been fully assimilated by her detractors or advocates.

In the United States, the legacy of *Silent Spring* includes the formation of the Environmental Protection Agency and the passage of the Toxic Substances Control Act (1976). Her work had an immediate impact on the larger Anglophone world, especially the United Kingdom, and *Silent Spring* has been widely translated. The antitoxics and environmental justice movements, as well as ecofeminism, social ecology, and deep ecology, show strong traces of Carson's influence. In her immediate historical context she belongs with Murray Bookchin (1921–2006), Herbert Marcuse (1898–1979), and Aldo Leopold (1887–1948) as a theorist of environmental destruction and preservation. In the history of women's leadership in global environmentalism, she is the peer of Ishimure Michiko (b. 1927), the Japanese writer-activist; Gro Harlem Brundtland (b. 1939), the Norwegian prime minister and advocate of sustainable economic development; and Wangari Maathai (b. 1940), founder of the Green Belt Movement in Kenya. Carson's most prominent disciple is Albert Gore Jr., former vice president of the United States, whose *Earth in the Balance* (1992) was inspired by *Silent Spring*.

[*See also* Brundtland, Gro Harlem; Ecofeminism; *and* Maathai, Wangari.]

BIBLIOGRAPHY

Lear, Linda. *Rachel Carson: Witness for Nature.* New York: Henry Holt, 1997. The definitive critical biography.

Smith, Michael B. "'Silence, Miss Carson!': Science, Gender, and the Reception of Silent Spring." *Feminist Studies* 27 (Fall 2001): 733–752. Examines the misogynist rhetoric used against Carson before, during, and after the publication of *Silent Spring*.

ANTHONY LIOI

CASELY HAYFORD, ADELAIDE (1868–1960), Sierra Leonean Pan-Africanist, feminist, and educator. Born Adelaide Smith into elite Krio (Creole) society in Sierra Leone, she moved with her family to England in 1872. Educated in both England and Germany, she was a prominent member of the emerging elite of the African diaspora. She became deeply affected by and attracted to many Western, middle-class, and feminist notions of womanhood at the same time that she was influenced by international currents of Pan-Africanism. In 1903, she married and moved to Ghana with Joseph E. Casely Hayford (1866–1930), a lawyer, journalist, politician, and founder of the National Congress of British West Africa, a moderate anticolonial organization. Their daughter, Gladys, became an internationally known poet. Permanently separating from her husband in 1914, Casely Hayford settled in Freetown, Sierra Leone. Paradoxically, her seemingly rootless life up until that time may have come both from a sense of alienation from elite African and European cultures and from widespread connections throughout the African diaspora.

Indeed, in 1920, after futile attempts to open a school for girls and young women using connections from her brief presidency of the Ladies' Division of the Freetown branch of the Universal Negro Improvement Association (UNIA), Marcus Garvey's international Pan-African organization, Casely Hayford left Africa for a two-and-a-half-year stay in the United States. Hosted by black churches, colleges, women's clubs, and other political and social organizations, she traveled extensively around the United States to learn from the self-help efforts of African Americans and to raise funds. She came to know some of the most influential African Americans of the time, including W. E. B. Du Bois (1868–1963) and Paul Robeson (1898–1976). Her most important contacts were with black women educators. For example, at the 1920 convention of the National Association of Colored Women (NACW) in Indianapolis, Indiana, she met Nannie Burroughs (1879–1961), a founder the Women's Convention of the National Baptist Convention. Burroughs invited Casely Hayford and her niece, Kathleen Easmon, to her National Training School for Women and Girls. Both Burroughs and Margaret Murray Washington (1865–1925), widow of Booker T. Washington (1856–1915), served on the American Advisory Board for the Girls' Vocational and Industrial Training School, which Casely Hayford opened in Freetown in 1923.

This school taught girls to be proud of their African heritage—even though Casely Hayford herself looked down on non-Krio Sierra Leoneans. Based on an ideology of bourgeois cultural nationalism, the school trained girls to be good wives and mothers living in companionate marriages. Influenced by the international feminist movement, the school also aimed to help its students gain economic self-sufficiency.

During a second trip to the United States in 1927, Casely Hayford joined the Circle of Peace and Foreign Relations, an organization led by the black educator and feminist Addie Hunton (1875–1943) that helped fund and organize the Fourth Pan-African Congress in New York City in 1927. She also collaborated with the African American sculptor Meta Vaux Warrick Fuller (1877–1968) to write and produce *The Answer* (a play that tried to help black Americans better understand Africa) at black churches to raise money for Casely Hayford's school. Finally, the Harlem Renaissance poet Langston Hughes (1902–1967) first published "Mista Courifer," her most anthologized short story.

[*See also* Diasporas; Feminism; Harlem Renaissance; National Association of Colored Women; *and* West Africa.]

BIBLIOGRAPHY

Blair, Barbara. "Pan-Africanism as Process: Adelaide Casely Hayford, Garveyism, and the Cultural Roots of Nationalism." In *Imagining Home: Class, Culture, and Nationalism in the African Diaspora*, edited by Sidney J. Lemelle and Robin D. G. Kelley, pp. 121–144. London and New York: Verso, 1994.

Cromwell, Adelaide M. *An African Victorian Feminist: The Life and Times of Adelaide Smith Casely Hayford, 1868–1960.* Washington, D.C.: Howard University Press, 1992. The most authoritative source on Casely Hayford.

Desai, Gaurav. "Gendered Self-Fashioning: Adelaide Casely Hayford's Black Atlantic." *Research in African Literatures* 35, no. 3 (2004): 141–160.

E. FRANCES WHITE

CASSATT, MARY (1844–1926), American-born Impressionist painter. Mary Cassatt was born into an affluent family in Allegheny, Pennsylvania, and was raised in Philadelphia. Her father, Robert S. Cassatt, was a stockbroker and her mother, Katherine Kelso Johnston, also belonged to a banking family. They disapproved of their daughter's inclination for painting but allowed her to take classes at the Pennsylvania Academy of the Fine Arts in Philadelphia, which she did between 1861 and 1865, during the Civil War. After the war, in 1866, Cassatt left for Paris to study painting, but she had to return home when the Franco-Prussian War broke out in 1870.

Once the war was over she went back to Europe on commission from the Archbishop of Pittsburgh. She remained in Europe as an American expatriate for many years. She traveled in Italy, Spain, and the Netherlands and eventually settled down in Paris in 1874, joining a group of U.S.-born artists who searched for inspiration in the propitious French artistic world. Cassatt befriended two of the most notable painters of her day: Camille Pissarro and Edgar Degas, who was a source of friendship and support for many years.

Although she exhibited in the traditional Paris Salon in 1872, she later became affiliated with the Impressionists and exhibited in their salon for the first time in 1879. She was the only American-born painter to exhibit with this group and had her first solo show in 1891. The 1890s were Cassatt's most active artistic years, and according to art critics, the works she produced in this decade are her most original. Among them was a large mural entitled *Modern Woman* for the 1893 World's Columbian Exposition in Chicago; the mural was mysteriously lost after the exposition closed. This triptych represented women pursuing fame and enjoying the products of science and art, appropriate themes for a visionary view of women's future. She persuaded her banker brother and some of her friends to purchase works by French Impressionists and was instrumental in having Impressionism accepted in the United States.

Cassatt was a strong and independent woman. She traveled alone and broke into a field dominated by men. By remaining single she defied expectations of conjugality. She knew what she wanted to paint and how she would paint it, and despite her association with the Impressionists, she developed her own style. She is known as a painter of women and children in domestic scenes and in quotidian activities. In this sense, hers was a feminine world. Although her subjects did not praise or proclaim female submission, nothing in her choice of them indicates rebellion or subversion of established rituals. Her domestic orientation reflects the contemporaneous role of women, but her personal choice as a painter denied a total acceptance of conventional female roles. Hers was a paradoxical world of dignified subjects subtly asserting their individuality.

Cassatt was also a letter writer, and her letters provide good insight into her feelings as a person and as an artist. She was depressed by the outbreak of World War I and by her declining health, including the loss of her sight to cataracts. Despite these problems, she showed more than a passing interest in woman suffrage and arranged for a show of her paintings to support the movement. When she died near Paris in 1926 she had already received recognition in the United States. As years passed, her art gained in appreciation, and today her paintings are among those most highly paid for in international art markets.

[*See also* Art and Architecture.]

BIBLIOGRAPHY

Barter, Judith A., ed. *Mary Cassatt: Modern Woman*. New York: Art Institute of Chicago with H. N. Abrams, 1998.

Pollock, Griselda. *Mary Cassatt: Painter of Modern Women*. London: Thames & Hudson, 1998.

ASUNCIÓN LAVRIN

CASTE AND CASTE SYSTEMS. The caste system is a system of social stratification in which categories of people are ranked in a hierarchy reflective of ideological values and beliefs. In this system—which is widely prevalent in rural India—the hierarchy is kept intact through four factors: birth, which determines occupation; endogamous marriages; segregation of individuals through the concepts of purity and pollution; and cultural beliefs tied to hierarchy and separation.

Two common terms used in writings on caste are *varna* and *jati*. *Varna* refers to the four great status divisions of society found in the ancient Brahmanical text *Manusmriti*: *brahmana* (priest), *kshatriya* (warrior), *vaisya* (trader), and *sudra* (peasant). Later a fifth *varna*, referring to the group of persons outside caste society, was added; this *varna* has variously been called the "untouchables," *harijans*, and *dalits*. *Jati* refers to hereditary groups within which the members traditionally assigned an occupation must marry. But *jatis* are many, and their rank order is ambiguous because they vary from region to region.

Evolution of the Caste System. Many scholars have tacitly accepted that caste divisions in society are a uniquely Indian feature and that Indian society has remained largely unchanged. However, it is now believed that caste divisions may have taken several centuries to crystallize, and caste rigidity may be a more recent phenomenon of the colonial period. Now it also is widely accepted that over the centuries the power of the priestly class was challenged from several quarters. The Jain agnostics, Buddhists, *bhakti* (devotional) saints, and numerous cults were groups that questioned Brahmanical influence in the lives of ordinary people and wanted to reconstruct society on a more humane basis. A challenge to Brahman power is also evident from the fact that many ruling dynasties—the Nandas, the Mauryas, the Kalingas, and the Guptas—did not arise from a Kshatriya background, although they eventually took on a more conservative garb. The Brahmans in India could not impose any rigid uniformity on the practices of Hinduism at a national level. In some regions in the south, in central India, and in Orissa, Brahmans were often compelled to give in to dissenting and heterodox cults, which were then eventually incorporated into Hinduism.

Gender and Modern Social Stratification. Even though all Indian women confront patriarchal arrangements, the specific nature of discrimination varies according to their position in the class and caste hierarchy. Thus extensive regional disparities arise in gender relations when hierarchies of class, caste, and ethnicity intersect the hierarchies of gender.

Large sections of *dalit* (downtrodden) castes remain landless and have only their labor to sell. Class and caste correspond when women of these castes and tribal women work for low wages. In middling artisan castes, women's weaving, pottery, and food preservation consolidate the occupational continuity of these caste groups and the complex processes of their craft. Women provide gender-differentiated services among the service castes of barbers, washermen, and water carriers. Notions of the "pure" and "impure" among castes are related to the occupations that each performs and the nature of the physical contact maintained with each other. Low-caste women deal with midwifery, disposing of waste, and washing dirty clothes, while low-caste men mostly deal with sweeping and scavenging. As one goes up higher up on the social scale, the correlation among class, "pure" caste, and gender hierarchies is marked by greater invisibility of women's bodies and labors but also by greater access to education, wealth, symbolic power, and professional opportunities. Thus an upper-caste woman, regardless of her seclusion, has greater access than a lower-caste man to education, employment, and economic resources.

However, gender roles and identities emerge from, and in turn determine, the nature of caste society. Within each caste, women are seen as sources of pollution and as intrinsically less pure than men. This implies that women never attain the purity of men within their own castes because of the self-pollution resulting from their bodily processes during menstruation and childbirth. But then again the purity of women is crucial to maintaining the blood purity of lineages and the position of the family within the wider caste hierarchy.

All castes have evolved particular practices related to food, domestic rituals—the daily care of family deities—and marriage rites. Women of all castes are expected to reproduce these by domestic labor: through modes of dressing, child-rearing practices, undertaking fasts, organizing *pujas* (prayers), and performing rituals within the household. In doing so they simultaneously preserve traditions in which food, leisure, education, and sanctity of space are allocated differently to boys and to girls. Socialization in gender and caste order is then reproduced on a larger scale outside the home.

In many parts of modern rural India, the caste system is sustained by the power of the upper castes to enforce caste-based codes and norms within the village. One of the principal means of enforcing caste rules across urban and rural units is through endogamous rules of marriage. For a match to be suitable, bride and groom must be drawn from broadly the same caste. This stabilizes the principles of caste hierarchy while reaffirming male control over reproductive powers of women in maintaining the boundaries between castes. The pressures of endogamy compel many families to arrange marriages of the young. Since marriages are also transactions in wealth and caste status, they abide by the system of dowry.

Religious strictures against the remarriage of widows historically marked upper-caste status and have been linked to the practice of immolation (sati). But among the middling *jat* castes, in parts of northern India, custom encouraged the widow to cohabit with the brother-in-law. These differences between castes are linked to the role that *jat* women play in agricultural and household work. While maintaining control over the sexuality of *jat* women, this custom maintained land structures intact within the family.

The coexistence of prohibitions against marriage outside the caste and the persistence of sexual violence against lower-caste women is key to understanding the profound anxieties about caste in modern India. *Dalit* or lower-caste women are subjected to triple disadvantages: as women, as lower castes, and as lower-caste women. Upper-caste men always have sexual access to lower-caste women, given their material advantages and resources. In recent years many brutal killings of couples who transgress caste norms have taken place for the community's honor.

The caste system has, to a large extent, been transformed, but the way that caste impinges on gender relations and the way that gender relations constitute the caste system are very complex. They are related to the way that gender roles emerge from the structures and processes of the caste system and get implicated in the class stratification and multiple patriarchies of Indian society.

[*See also* Age of Consent and Child Marriage; India; Widows and Widowhood; *and* Widow Suicide.]

BIBLIOGRAPHY

Chakravarti, Uma. *Rewriting History: The Life and Times of Pandita Ramabai.* New Delhi, India: Kali for Women with the Book Review Literary Trust, 1998.

Chen, Martha Alter. *Perpetual Mourning: Widowhood in Rural India.* New Delhi, India: Oxford University Press, 2000.

Chowdhry, Prem. *The Veiled Women: Shifting Gender Equations in Rural Haryana, 1880–1990.* New Delhi, India: Oxford University Press, 1994.

Geetha, V., and S. V. Rajadurai. *Towards a Non-Brahmin Millennium: From Iyothee Thass to Periyar.* Calcutta, India: Samya, 1998.

Gupta, Dipankar. *Social Stratification.* New Delhi, India: Oxford University Press, 1991.

VIDHU VERMA

CASTELLANOS, ROSARIO (1925–1974), prominent Mexican intellectual, feminist pioneer, and writer. One of the best-known intellectual figures in modern Mexico, Castellanos was at the center of the cultural, political, and literary debates of her time. Her vocation as a writer was a fervent and committed exercise in critical expression.

She was born in Mexico City on 25 May 1925 and returned there at age sixteen after spending her childhood and adolescence in the heavily indigenous state of Chiapas, an experience that strongly influenced her writing. She died on 7 August 1974 in Israel, where she had been Mexico's ambassador since 1971 and a professor at the universities of Tel Aviv and Jerusalem. Her master's thesis "Sobre cultura femenina" (On Feminine Culture) traced the epistemological roots of a feminist conscience that had to do with the relations among gender, culture, and oppression, a constant in her more than twenty works.

She graduated in philosophy and letters from the Universidad Nacional Autónoma de México (UNAM) in 1950 and went to Spain on a scholarship. Upon her return she worked for a time in Chiapas, first as a promoter of culture for the Instituto de Ciencias y Artes in Tuxtla Gutiérrez and then at the Centro Coordinador del Instituto Indigenista in San Cristóbal de las Casas. In the late 1950s she returned to Mexico City and worked for the Instituto Nacional Indigenista, and in the early 1960s she became the press director at UNAM, where she was a well-known professor of comparative literature. She was also a visiting professor of Latin American and Mexican literature at the universities of Wisconsin, Indiana, and Colorado in the United States.

As a writer, professor, cultural essayist, and defender of the rights of women and the rights of indigenous people, Castellanos synthesized in her work stimulating critical thinking on gender, power, knowledge, ethnicity, and culture. She wrote in all the genres, including poetry, essay, narrative, short story, and theater, and she collaborated energetically on cultural supplements for the principal newspapers of Mexico and on foreign academic journals.

Her work demonstrates an intense passion for and devotion to the incisive word. In her essays she evinces admiration for Gabriela Mistral, Emily Dickinson, Simone de Beauvoir, Virginia Woolf, and Simone Weil, among other women authors. Castellanos influenced the Mexican and international cultural spheres with her defiant writing that questioned the dominant hegemonic ideology that perpetuates oppression, social injustice, and exclusion and denies women a space of their own, and she denounced the burden of difference and inequality that have enslaved the indigenous subject and condemned it to a condition of timeless subalternity.

In the most important indigenist narrative trilogy of Mexico, known as the *Ciclo de Chiapas* (Chiapas Cycle)—which includes *Balún Canán* (1957; English trans., *The Nine Guardians*), *Ciudad Real: Cuentos* (1960; English trans., *The City of Kings*), and *Oficio de tinieblas* (1962; English trans., *The Book of Lamentations*)—she offers a representation of the indigenous subject that goes beyond its exploitation, poverty, and marginalization, dismantles the social hypocrisy of the dominant oligarchies of the landowners, unmasks language as an instrument of oppression, and examines the power relationships in a feudal microcosm drawn from her autobiographical, testimonial, ethnographic, and aesthetic-cultural knowledge. Her trilogy offers a reference point and historical perspective that exposes the conditions and causes that led to the emergence of the Zapatista movement in Chiapas in 1994.

The eminent Mexican writer Elena Poniatowska described Castellanos as an author dedicated to the use of the biting word as an instrument of critical reflection and as endowed with an inquisitive irony that allowed her to see what reality occludes. The well-known Mexican poet José Emilio Pacheco has suggested that Castellanos went beyond her historical moment by making each of her works into the raw material of a lucid and mordant consciousness that demonstrated more clearly than anyone else in her time the double condition of oppression of Mexican women.

A pioneer of Mexican feminist critical thought, Rosario Castellanos deconstructed the Mexican sociocultural reality from the viewpoint of gender, dismantled the cultural domestication of women, and questioned the significance of the symbolic cultural indicators of gender such as servitude, passivity, obedience, subjugation, docility, resignation, and self-denial. She engaged in a dialogue with international feminism by proposing in her works the implementation of a humanist feminism that permitted the establishment of relationships of equality between the genders, "another way of being more human and more free" for women, while fighting for human rights and denouncing the marginalized condition of indigenous people, enslaved and perpetually excluded from the Mexican national project.

Castellanos won the Mexican Critics Award (1957), the Chiapas Prize (1958), the Xavier Villaurrutia Prize (1961), the Sor Juana Inés de la Cruz Prize for Literature (1962), the Carlos Trouyet Prize (1967), and the Elías Sourasky Prize (1972).

[*See also* Literature *and* Mexico.]

BIBLIOGRAPHY

Ahern, Maureen, ed. *A Rosario Castellanos Reader: An Anthology of Her Poetry, Short Fiction, Essays, and Drama*. Austin: University of Texas Press, 1988.

Castellanos, Rosario. *The Book of Lamentations*. Translated by Esther Allen. New York: Penguin, 1998.

Castellanos, Rosario. *The Nine Guardians*. Translated by Irene Nicholson. Columbia, La.: Readers International, 1992.

MAGDALENA MAIZ-PEÑA
Translated from the Spanish by Matthew Miller

CASTILLO Y GUEVARA, SOR FRANCISCA JOSEFA (1671–1742), colonial Colombian nun, author of a noted spiritual autobiography. The writing produced in Spanish American convents was one of the most important forms of women's literature of the colonial era, principally because nuns were from social elites and hence better educated than other women. They wrote a variety of religious literature of which their *vitae*, or spiritual life writings, are the most interesting to the modern reader. The best-known spiritual autobiography is that of the Mexican nun Sor Juana Inés de la Cruz, but the second most famous account is that of Sor Francisca Josefa Castillo y Guevara, known as Madre Castillo. Selections from her work have appeared in many anthologies of Spanish American literature.

Francisca was born in 1671 to an upper-class family in the city of Tunja, in the viceroyalty of New Granada (present-day Colombia). She was literate and knew some Latin. She had a genuine religious calling and, contrary to her family's wishes, joined the Franciscan convent of Santa Clara. Tunja is an austere, gray city, yet the interior of her convent, which is still extant, glows with crimson and gold, an indication of its wealth and prestige.

For upper-class women of the colonial era there were usually only two life choices: marriage or the convent. Upon professing, nuns took vows of poverty, chastity, obedience, and perpetual enclosure. A confined community of women with different degrees of religious vocation often led to psychological tensions, and these are very evident in Madre Castillo's posthumously published autobiography, *Su vida* (Her Life), which tells of being verbally and even physically abused by other sisters. In spite of this, she was elected abbess three times and was a competent administrator of the convent's assets. Her religious feelings fluctuated from constant fear of the Devil to the burden of her demanding and authoritative confessor to times of mystical joy when she sensed oneness with Christ, her "bridegroom." Another feature of her autobiography is her relation of potently erotic dreams, such as seeing herself clad in a red gown, with unbound hair so long it reached the floor, and devils playing with and tangling the ends thereof. One senses how painful the act of personal writing was to her and how dangerous she felt such an activity might be if Satan were guiding her pen. Only after much anguish was she finally convinced that what she had written was neither hers nor the Devil's, but Christ speaking through her.

Madre Castillo also wrote a series of religious meditations, the *Afectos espirituales* (1694–1728, published 1843; Spiritual Affections), in which her narrative voice was much less anguished because she was serving God instead of foregrounding her own person. *Su vida* is an excellent example of Spanish American conventual writing, little of which was published during its time. Madre Castillo's manuscript was saved from oblivion because after her death in 1742 the nuns gave it to her family, who had it published in Philadelphia in 1817.

[*See also* Juana Inés de la Cruz, Sor.]

BIBLIOGRAPHY

McKnight, Kathryn Joy. *The Mystic of Tunja: The Writings of Madre Castillo, 1671–1742*. Amherst: University of Massachusetts Press, 1997.

Schlau, Stacey. "Madre Castillo." In *Spanish American Women Writers: A Bio-Bibliographical Source Book*, edited by Diane Marting, pp. 156–164. New York: Greenwood Press, 1990. In spite of being somewhat dated, this is still an excellent source book for Spanish American women writers.

NINA M. SCOTT

CATHER, WILLA (1873–1947), American novelist. Born in Virginia, Cather moved with her family to Nebraska in 1883 and is best known as a novelist of the American prairie. However, her life history and literary output belie this characterization. As a student at the University of Nebraska she published short stories and poems and worked as a journalist. This experience earned her a position at the *Home Monthly* magazine in Pittsburgh, Pennsylvania. When the magazine failed, she stayed in Pittsburgh, first returning to newspaper journalism and then teaching high school. For several years she lived in the family home of Isabelle McClung, a young society woman. In 1906, Cather moved to New York City to join the editorial staff of *McClure's* magazine. She lived in Manhattan for the rest of her life but traveled widely in the United States and Europe and adopted a series of rural locations north of New York City as summer writing retreats. Cather shared a home in New York for thirty-seven years with Edith Lewis, a magazine editor and advertising copywriter.

Cather's first novel, *Alexander's Bridge* (1912), appeared shortly after she began a leave of absence from her editorial duties at *McClure's*. Both critics and Cather herself dismissed her first novel as a pale imitation of Henry James, but her second novel, *O Pioneers!* (1913), featuring an immigrant Swedish heroine in Nebraska, established her reputation as a novelist of the American West. Cather never returned to magazine editorial work, although a series of articles she wrote for *McClure's* on opera singers led to *The Song of the Lark* (1915), a novel about a Swedish American girl from Colorado who achieves success as an opera singer in Europe and New York. Cather's most autobiographical novel, *My Ántonia* (1918), presents its Bohemian immigrant heroine through the eyes of Jim Burden, an orphan from Virginia sent to live with his grandparents in Nebraska. Cather valued the cosmopolitanism that

Willa Cather. Frontispiece from *The Song of the Lark*, 1915. PRINTS AND PHOTOGRAPHS DIVISION, LIBRARY OF CONGRESS

European immigrants brought to the Great Plains. These novels were soon translated into the languages spoken by those immigrants—Czech, Swedish, Norwegian, French, and others—and they found enthusiastic readers around the world.

Beginning with *My Ántonia*, Cather's novels often feature male protagonists. She modeled Claude Wheeler, the protagonist of the Pulitzer Prize–winning *One of Ours* (1922), on a younger cousin stifled by farm life in Nebraska who found meaning and purpose fighting in France during World War I. Critics widely read Godfrey St. Peter, the protagonist of *The Professor's House* (1925), as expressing Cather's own disaffection with modern American culture.

Cather's literary imagination increasingly turned to the past in her later years. Two historical novels—*Death Comes for the Archbishop* (1927), set in nineteenth-century New Mexico, and *Shadows on the Rock* (1931), set in seventeenth-century Quebec—focus on moments of transition in European colonial projects in North America. She turned to her own family's southern history in her last published novel, *Sapphira and the Slave Girl* (1940). Although she was attacked as conservative and backward-looking by leftist critics beginning in the 1930s, Cather has increasingly been recognized as an important modernist writer who experimented with literary form.

Although Cather positioned herself in opposition to modern commercialism and a tradition of popular women's writing, she published short stories and serialized a novel—*Lucy Gayheart* (1935)—in women's magazines in the 1920s and 1930s. When she died from a brain hemorrhage at the age of seventy-three, she was working on a novel set in medieval France.

[*See also* Literature, *subentry* Fiction and Poetry.]

BIBLIOGRAPHY

O'Brien, Sharon. *Willa Cather: The Emerging Voice* (1987). Reprint. Cambridge, Mass.: Harvard University Press, 1997. An influential feminist biography that focuses on Cather's life to 1913, with an emphasis on her gender identity and sexuality and establishing the basis for reading her as a lesbian writer.

"The Willa Cather Archive." http://www.cather.unl.edu. Contains the full text of Woodress's biography, as well as numerous other resources documenting Cather's life and works.

Woodress, James. *Willa Cather: A Literary Life*. Lincoln: University of Nebraska Press, 1987. The standard critical biography, covering the entire span of Cather's life.

MELISSA J. HOMESTEAD

CATHERINE DE MÉDICIS (1519–1589), queen mother and regent during the French Wars of Religion. Born into the powerful Florentine Medici family, Catherine married the future King Henry II of France in 1533. When he died in 1559, Catherine's son, Francis II, acceded to the throne. A sickly boy of fifteen, he relied heavily on his mother's advice. Her control over royal policy continued when Francis II died and his brother Charles IX came to the throne at the age of ten. She remained influential in determining policy under a third son, Henry III, until her death.

Despite her energy and good intentions, Catherine was unable to rule France effectively. Her attempt to effect reconciliation between Protestants and Catholics in France pleased neither faction. Seeking concord between the two religions on theological grounds, she organized the Colloquy of Poissy late in the summer of 1561. However, the colloquy failed because Protestants and Catholics viewed each other as heretics. Catherine originally believed that a reform of the Catholic clergy would be sufficient to restore unity to the church, but the theological differences between the two religions went beyond questions of abuse and corruption. Both sides sought conversion (or death) of the other. Compromise was out of the question.

When theological unity proved impossible, Catherine pursued a policy of religious toleration for the Protestant minority. The Edict of January 1562 granted Protestants the right to worship in the countryside but not in the towns. Catholics throughout the realm considered toleration abhorrent. In particular, a faction of nobles led by the Guise family took it upon themselves to defend the Catholic faith against Protestants. On the other side, Protestants aimed for more than toleration; they wanted control over the government. The fact that many of the highest nobles, even princes of the blood, adhered to the Protestant cause made the eruption of civil war in 1562 almost inevitable.

Contemporaries viewed Catherine with suspicion. As an Italian, she was seen as deceitful and amoral. In the popular imagination she was known—deservedly or not—for her frequent use of poison as a means of assassination. She also appeared to switch sides, one day seeking an alliance with ultra-Catholic Spain, the next seeking rapprochement with the Protestants. For example, when she could not marry her daughter, Margaret, to Philip II of Spain, she decided to marry her to Henry IV (Henry of Navarre), the leader of the Protestants. During the wedding festivities, Catherine apparently sanctioned the assassination of Gaspard de Coligny, the king's closest Protestant adviser. The attack against Coligny led to a general massacre of more than five thousand Protestants in the city of Paris and in the provinces. Catherine has often been blamed for this incident, the Saint Bartholomew's Day Massacre of 1572, but historians today tend to see it more as a spontaneous popular uprising than a calculated plot.

Catherine aimed primarily to reestablish the authority of the monarchy and to create stability in the realm, a difficult task in any regency government. In a situation where the high nobility still adhered to warrior values and was divided along sectarian lines, this task proved to be impossible.

[*See also* France *and* Monarchy.]

BIBLIOGRAPHY

Knecht, R. J. *Catherine de' Medici.* London: Longman, 1998.

Sutherland, N. M. *Catherine de Medici and the Ancien Régime.* London: Historical Association, 1966.

REBECCA BOONE

CATHERINE II OF RUSSIA (2 May 1729 O.S.–6 November 1796 O.S.; r. 1762–1796), empress of Russia. Catherine II (the Great) was born Sophie Auguste Frederike, Princess of Anhalt-Zerbst, in the Prussian Baltic Sea port city of Stettin (now Szczecin, Poland). Related to the royal houses of Sweden, Denmark, and Russia, Catherine was brought to Russia in 1744 by the empress at the time, Elizabeth, as the prospective bride for Duke Karl Peter Ulrich of Holstein-Gottorp, grandson of Peter the Great and heir to the Russian throne. She converted to Russian Orthodoxy the same year (adopting the name Ekaterina [Catherine] Alekseevna) and married the duke (at that point Grand Duke Peter) in 1745.

The next seventeen years as grand duchess were among the most difficult of Catherine's life. Her marriage to Peter was an unhappy one and afforded little protection against the intrigues forever swirling about her at court. Having failed in her primary duty of producing an heir, Catherine, upon the order of the empress, took a lover, chamberlain Sergei Saltykov, and finally gave birth to a son, Paul (who ruled as Paul I, 1796–1801), in 1754. Although she had no legal claim to the throne, Catherine believed that one day she would rule Russia and began preparing herself by reading extensively, learning the language, history, and customs of her adopted homeland, and ingratiating herself with powerful figures at court.

The grand duke ascended the throne as Tsar Peter III following the death of the empress Elizabeth in December 1761 O.S. The tsar's decision to pull Russia out of the Seven Years' War, combined with a series of ill-planned reforms and his erratic behavior, quickly gave birth to powerful opposition among members of the court and the guards' regiments. In response to fears that the tsar was planning to lock her in a convent and install his mistress in her place, Catherine, with the backing of Grigory Orlov (1734–1783), her lover at the time; Orlov's brothers; and the capital's guards' regiments, seized power on 28 June 1762 O.S. The tsar was abandoned by his supporters, arrested, and murdered soon thereafter at a suburban palace. Although Catherine did not order his killing, she was not blind to its necessity if she were to hold power.

The first years of her reign witnessed a series of reforms and attempts to impose order on a chaotic, poorly managed governmental apparatus that would characterize her entire rule. In 1763, Catherine reorganized the Senate in an attempt to reinvigorate the neglected central administration. Around this time she issued two manifestoes encouraging foreigners to settle in Russia to help develop its fledgling manufacturing industries and to boost its agriculture. She secularized the property of the Russian Orthodox Church as part of her strategy to replenish the treasury's empty coffers. In 1767, she convened the Legislative Commission to devise a new legal code, for which she wrote her famous Instruction (*Nakaz*), which drew heavily from the writings of major Enlightenment thinkers such as Cesare, Marquis of

Catherine II of Russia. An anonymous eighteenth-century painting. MUSEUM OF HISTORY, MOSCOW/BILDARCHIV PREUSSISCHER KULTURBESITZ/ART RESOURCE, NY

Beccaria (1738–1794) and Charles-Louis de Secondat, Baron of Montesquieu (1689–1755).

The outbreak of war between Russia and Turkey in 1768, followed by a devastating plague in Moscow in 1771 and the Pugachev Rebellion two years later, forced Catherine to put her reforms aside until the successful completion of hostilities with Turkey, marked by the Treaty of Kuchuk Kainardji, in 1774. The subsequent dozen years saw a number of major reforms inspired by her German cameralist beliefs: the Provincial Reform (1775) and the Police Ordinance (1782) were implemented, improving local government and the administration of the cities, and charters to the nobility and towns (1785) were issued stipulating for the first time the rights of the country's social and political elite and urban dwellers. Catherine granted private persons the right to establish printing presses and promoted the education system through a variety of initiatives. In 1783, the Crimea was annexed and Russia's southern territories were developed.

A second war with the Ottoman Empire (1787–1792) and another with Sweden (1788–1790) ended this second phase of reforms. Although Russia won the former and held the latter to a draw, the wars placed a heavy burden on the country's finances. By 1791, Catherine had become preoccupied with the French Revolution, which she used to justify the final partitions of Poland in 1793 and 1795 and to clamp down on perceived dissent at home by rescinding the right of private presses and establishing strict censorship in late 1796, just months before her death.

Catherine is rightly considered one of Russia's greatest rulers whose reign marked a period of rare social, political, economic, and cultural development. She greatly expanded the size of the Russian empire, transforming the country into a world power, and fostered a spirit of toleration at home. A prolific writer and patron of the arts imbued with boundless energy and optimism, she ushered in a flowering of Russian culture and intellectual life without which the major artistic achievements of the nineteenth century would not have been possible. As a ruler, she sought to govern through consensus, not coercion—rare in the Russian context—and viewed her ministers as valued partners in the administration of the state.

Throughout her reign Catherine was the object of criticism and calumny, chiefly from foreign observers motivated by unease over the rise of Russian power and the mistaken belief that the empress's reforms were mere window-dressing intended to enhance Catherine's reputation in Europe as an enlightened monarch. Criticism of Catherine was informed by the pervasive notion that women were by their nature more susceptible than men to vanity, voluptuousness, and the temptations of flattery, of which the empress was deemed a prime example.

To her critics, Catherine's numerous lovers and favorites (twelve over five decades) offered the best proof of her wanton depravity. The lurid tales of her private life amount to nothing more than slander intended to destroy the reputation of a woman who wielded with such confidence power traditionally reserved for men and who refused to conform to traditional notions of womanly behavior.

[*See also* Monarchy *and* Russia and Soviet Union.]

BIBLIOGRAPHY

Alexander, John T. *Catherine the Great: Life and Legend.* New York: Oxford University Press, 1989. The best biography of Catherine in English.

De Madariaga, Isabel. *Russia in the Age of Catherine the Great.* 2nd ed. London: Phoenix, 2002. A pioneering work first published in 1981 that still offers the best, most complete picture of Catherine and her reign.

Dixon, Simon. *Catherine the Great.* Harlow, U.K., and New York: Longman, 2001. An exceptionally insightful and accessible study of Catherine's use of power.

Smith, Douglas, ed. and trans. *Love and Conquest: Personal Correspondence of Catherine the Great and Prince Grigory Potemkin.* DeKalb: Northern Illinois University Press, 2004. The first English translation of Catherine's remarkable correspondence with her famous lover, secret husband, and most trusted minister.

DOUGLAS SMITH

CATHERINE OF SIENA (1347?–1380), Catholic saint and mystic, Dominican Order tertiary, co-patron of Italy, and Doctor of the Church. Catherine Benincasa of Siena experienced intensities of individual piety and direct exchange with God that many women have emulated but few have achieved in the seven centuries since her death at the age of thirty-three on 30 April 1380. In her final months the saint-to-be added dehydration to the severe regimen of self-starvation and bodily mortification she had practiced for years, bringing about a death she welcomed as the only way she could finally achieve full union with her spiritual bridegroom Jesus Christ, who had been crucified at that same age. She recognized how difficult a spiritual path she had pursued and even wrote warnings in a scolding tone to tell others not to attempt to imitate her ways. No matter how strange or misguided we moderns may find her choices, they made exquisite sense to her, in her own time and place. She aimed to achieve her individual salvation for all of eternity, adding considerable sacrifice in her lifetime to atone for her earthly father's sins and later for the errors of misguided churchmen. Along the way she achieved a reputation as a living saint, but there were others who thought her to be in league with the devil. In 1375 she became the first woman to experience stigmata, the wounds of Jesus's crucifixion, an empowering sign of grace, visible in her lifetime only to herself, that fortified her greatly in her work to reform the church.

From modest beginnings as the twenty-third child of a Sienese dyer who died when she was still a teenager—an event that seems to have triggered her choice to reject the cloister in favor of a life of intense spirituality in the secular world—Catherine rose to become an ambassador, initially from the papacy to the Tuscan cities of Pisa and Lucca and later as an envoy of the Florentines, who sent her to France with an entourage of followers. Her peace mission on behalf of Florence failed, but she achieved a resounding victory on another front when she successfully urged Pope Gregory XI (r. 1370–1378) to return the papacy from Avignon to its original foundation in Rome. In 1378 she served as the dying pope's emissary to Florence, managed to get herself embroiled in local politics, and barely escaped an assassination attempt during the textile worker uprising

Saint Catherine of Siena. Painting by Andrea Vanni, late fourteenth century. S. DOMENICO, SIENA, ITALY/SCALA/ART RESOURCE, NY

known as the Ciompi revolt. The Great Schism ensued, during which time there were two elected pretenders to the papacy, but Catherine gave all her efforts to the Roman claimant, Urban VI (r. 1378–1389), working successfully to reconcile him with political authorities in Rome. Historians have disputed how much causal weight to assign Catherine in these events, and they have been quick to point out some of her diplomatic shortcomings, but she never had any doubt about the primacy of her role and the ultimate success of her endeavors, which of course she always attributed to God's will. Both visual and written evidence testify abundantly to the enormous charisma this woman must have exuded as she spoke before male princes and popes, exhorting them in no uncertain terms to undertake what God had told her they should do. Nearly four hundred of her letters survive, dictated to a team of scribes and then sent to various political leaders throughout Christendom. She also wrote on occasion to her mother and to her brothers, always urging them to put salvation first and usually apologizing for being too busy to write more often.

Many Catholic saints are known for their prodigious charity, good works, and miracles. While Catherine certainly qualified for sainthood according to these criteria, her greatest strengths were in her intense, highly personal, and mystical relationship with God. She believed in the spiritual value of pain and suffering, just as Jesus had sacrificed himself for humankind's redemption, and she had little interest in praying for supernatural interventions to alleviate earthly needs, all of which she considered trivial or else impediments to spiritual perfection. As with the worldly activities documented so thoroughly in her letters, we have her own writings, collected in the *Dialogue of Divine Providence*, as the best evidence of the quality of her religiosity. She managed, just barely, to stay within the bounds of orthodoxy, in part with the aid of her confessor and adoring biographer, Raymond of Capua (1330–1399), whose work paved the way for Catherine's canonization eighty years after her death. But the reality is that her mystical experience needed no priestly interventions and her message is unequivocally one of personal responsibility for salvation in a way that foreshadows theological viewpoints not put in writing by Christian men for another two centuries. Catherine of Siena is evoked by Catholic feminists today as an inspirational model for their efforts to gain an authoritative voice within the church.

[*See also* Christianity; Religion; *and* Spiritual Leaders, *subentry* Nuns and Abbesses.]

BIBLIOGRAPHY

Caffarini, Thomas Antonii de Senis. *Libellus de Supplemento: Legende Prolixe Virginis Beate Catherine de Senis*. Edited by Giuliana Cavallini and Imelda Foralosso. Rome: Edizioni Cateriniane, 1974. Biographical material by one of Catherine's early confessors and a champion of her canonization.

Catherine of Siena. *The Dialogue*. Translated by Suzanne Noffke. New York: Paulist Press, 1980. English translation of *Il Dialogo della Divina Provvidenza ovvero Libro della Divina Dottrina*, authoritatively edited by Giuliana Cavallini in 1968.

Catherine of Siena. *The Letters of St. Catherine of Siena*. Translated by Suzanne Noffke. Binghamton, N.Y.: Medieval and Renaissance Texts and Studies, 1988. Contains letters 1–88 of the six-volume authoritative Italian edition published between 1913 and 1922. The project continues with Noffke's translations under the title *The Letters of Catherine of Siena*. 2 vols. Tempe, Ariz.: Arizona Center for Medieval and Renaissance Studies, 2000–2001.

Catherine of Siena. *Le Orazioni*. Edited by Giuliana Cavallini. Rome: Edizioni Cateriniane, 1978; Siena: Cantagalli, 1993. A collection of prayers attributed to Catherine of Siena, with editions in Italian and Latin.

Fawtier, Robert. *Sainte Catherine de Sienne: Essai de critique des sources*. 2 vols. Paris: E. de Boccard, 1921–1930. The critical foundation for all modern studies of Catherine of Siena.

Hilkert, Mary Catherine. *Speaking with Authority: Catherine of Siena and the Voices of Women Today*. New York: Paulist Press, 2001.

Raymond of Capua. *The Life of St. Catherine of Siena*. Translated by George Lamb. New York: P. J. Kennedy, 1960.

RUDOLPH M. BELL

CATHOLICISM. *See* Christianity.

CATT, CARRIE CHAPMAN (1859–1947), American and international woman suffragist, who was born and raised in the Midwest. As president of the National American Woman Suffrage Association (NAWSA) in the final campaign to amend the federal constitution, Carrie Clinton Lane Chapman Catt deserves much credit for the passage of the Nineteenth Amendment in 1920. Catt also led the International Woman Suffrage Alliance from 1904 to 1923.

Catt entered the suffrage movement as an organizer for the Iowa Woman Suffrage Association and came to national attention in 1890. A critic of the movement's inefficiencies, outmoded political culture, and marginal social standing, she gained the authority to put her ideas into action within a few years. Victories for woman suffrage in Colorado (1893) and Idaho (1896) were, at the time, credited to her talent. To Susan B. Anthony (1820–1906), contemplating retirement from the presidency of the NAWSA in 1900, Catt was her obvious successor.

Catt's first presidency lasted only four years. The illness of her husband as well as her own exhaustion were valid reasons to retire, but, despite retirement, she was not idle. She established an international presence, traveling abroad for meetings of the IWSA and, in 1911–1912, circumnavigating the globe to encourage suffragists in Africa and Asia. She would later tour South America in 1923. Catt also used the years from 1904 to 1915 to build up a remarkable political machine in New York, the birthplace of suffrage agitation and the nation's most populous state. Though voters defeated woman suffrage in New York in 1915, Catt's tight discipline again offered a national model, and victory followed in 1917.

Catt resumed the presidency of the NAWSA in 1915, replacing Anna Howard Shaw (1847–1919). So disorganized and demoralized had the association grown in her absence that Catt had free rein to set the conditions of her return. She remade the organization into a modern interest group capable of breaking resistance to equal suffrage. Militant suffragists, influenced by the British suffrage movement, had split away to form the Congressional Union to revive the federal suffrage amendment, use bolder tactics, and hold all Democrats responsible for the party's failure to pass the amendment. To Catt, they were an unruly force that frightened the elites and mainstream politicians she courted. With her hand-picked executive board, she imposed her "Winning Plan," restoring the fight for a federal amendment and centralizing decisions about state campaigns. Once the amendment passed in Congress, Catt led the effort for its ratification by three-quarters of the states.

Catt married twice, the first time in 1885 to Leo Chapman, owner of a newspaper in Iowa, who died a year after their marriage. In 1890, she married George Catt, an engineer with sufficient wealth to support her long after his death in 1905. The lengthiest of her partnerships was that with Mary Garrett Hay (1857–1928), and the two women are buried side by side in New York City. Catt died on 9 March 1947 at her home in New Rochelle, New York.

Catt was, and still is, assailed for her antidemocratic leadership and exclusive focus on the vote. There is no doubt that someone of her political acumen was needed to overcome opposition to woman suffrage at the center of American politics, but historians recognize how radicals, labor unions, and feminists (all groups spurned by Catt) contributed to many victories that were billed by contemporaries as exclusively hers.

[*See also* Anthony, Susan B.; International Woman Suffrage Alliance; Nineteenth Amendment; Shaw, Anna Howard; Suffrage; *and* United States, *subentry* Modern Period.]

BIBLIOGRAPHY

Bosch, Mineke, ed. *Politics and Friendship: Letters from the International Woman Suffrage Alliance, 1902–1942.* Columbus: Ohio State University Press, 1990. Includes many letters by Catt.

Fowler, Robert Booth. *Carrie Catt: Feminist Politician.* Boston: Northeastern University Press, 1986. Work by a political scientist that looks closely at Catt's American leadership.

Van Voris, Jacqueline. *Carrie Chapman Catt: A Public Life.* New York: Feminist Press at the City University of New York, 1987. An uncritical but thorough biography.

Ann D. Gordon

CELIBACY

This entry consists of two subentries:

Overview
Comparative History

Overview

Celibacy, the unmarried state, is generally discouraged in orderly societies. Heterosexual marriage ensures the reproduction of children and the transmission of wealth and status to preserve the existing hierarchy. Propertied people exert a variety of pressures upon their children to marry correctly, and they are usually supported by the laws of the larger community. Only young people without property or position are left to drift into loose sexual arrangements, including concubinage, prostitution, or transitory couplings. Occasionally, as in ancient Rome, a small number of women may be set aside as consecrated virgins for some religious purpose. Beyond that, Rome expected its citizens to marry and reproduce from puberty onward, with short respites for widows to ensure the paternity of their children. The frequent repetition of imperial legislation to this effect suggests broad resistance either in favor of wider sexual laxity or abstinence.

Medieval Europe. European civilization since the Middle Ages has been relatively hospitable to celibacy. Outside of the hereditary aristocracy and the great merchant families where elder sons and important heiresses were betrothed by their parents at very early ages (sometimes even at birth), the "European marriage pattern" is characterized by a high percentage of celibate young women and men seeking to establish themselves economically before founding a household, leaving a fairly high proportion of individuals unmarried for life. This practice may have been rooted in the land assignment policies of great estate owners in the early Middle Ages, who discouraged the subdivision of peasant holdings and tended to refuse permission to marry until a holding was open for them. Sources, however, are far too sparse to allow this hypothesis to be satisfactorily tested. In the late eleventh and twelfth centuries, peasant refugees from the overpopulated countryside began to swell the urban populations. Observers saw too many unmarried women and framed female celibacy as a *Frauenfrage*, or woman question.

The "woman problem" was aggravated by papal decrees of 1059 imposing celibacy on the clergy and eventually invalidating their marriages. Schools and universities were accessible only to men in clerical orders, closing most professions to women while even college-educated men who did not enter the priesthood tended to remain celibate.

Secular elements of medieval society also imposed a lengthy professional training period on young men while excluding women from the mysteries of most crafts and professions. Women without dowries from their parents might earn money from domestic service, prostitution, and low-level crafts such as spinning and eventually save enough to make them attractive marriage partners, but they would be celibate well into their twenties. Grossly inadequate economic opportunities pushed many into prostitution or made them dependent upon charity. As a result, celibate men tended to prosper while impoverished celibate women were viewed as a social problem.

Chaste Celibacy. In the latter half of the twentieth century, popular usage gradually redefined celibacy as abstinence from sexual activity—which ancient sources called *encrateia*. Outside the Roman elite, sexual renunciation characterized first-century religious groups anticipating the end of the world. Jewish sources reveal the sexually abstinent Essenes in the Dead Sea region and encratic communities of women and men called Therapeutae in Egypt. The Pauline letters, the earliest Christian documents on record, confront with considerable suspicion and hesitation the problem of men and women who wished either to remain unmarried or to live together without sexual relationships. Sources from the first three centuries refer to communities of Christian virgins living in every section of the Roman world. Prelates like Cyprian of Carthage undertook to lay down rules for their behavior, aware that their disobedience to parents and civil authorities who wished to impose marriage on them stoked the hostility of pagans toward the new religion. Eventually, Christians came to see the virgin martyr as the most vivid emblem of Christian virtue in the face of pagan persecution, but they remained reluctant to endorse a theology that condemned the norms of licit sex and procreation. Encratites, who preached that no one could be saved unless they renounced and denounced sexual activity, were condemned as heretics by the leaders of the early church, and even more modest claims that sexual abstinence was morally superior to marriage were resisted.

Encrateia, or chaste celibacy, provoked a crisis in the classical gender system. In the first millennium of the Christian era, Romans commonly situated individuals of either sex on a continuum ranging from completely manly (self-controlled, temperate, potent) to utterly effeminate (undisciplined, soft, fluid, excessive in temper and behavior, impotent). Women were defined as failed men, but individuals were awarded their share of manliness on the basis of their social position and behavior. Noble women who acted prudently as their husbands' deputies were recognized as more manly (or virtuous) than lower-class, powerless men. Roman women were seen as more manly than barbarian men. But Roman women, by virtue of the subjection imposed by marriage, could never be the equal of Roman men. Only the very small number of Vestal Virgins who remained unmarried after completing their service could qualify for full manhood, which the Roman government recognized by giving them "the right of three children"—full rights as independent citizens usually awarded to fertile women who had done their reproductive duty to the state.

Christian virgins and widows who vowed never to marry or enter into any sexual relationship challenged this social hierarchy. If they remained unmarried, they escaped the subjection to husbands that reduced all Roman women to less manly status. Their sexual integrity suggested a potency that outreached that of the sexually disciplined Roman paterfamilias. Even Christian authors were profoundly disturbed by the implications of women who claimed that they were not women and need not wear the veil that symbolized womanly modesty and subservience. In his tract "On the Veiling of Virgins," the early Christian theologist Tertullian (c. 155–230) introduced the idea of consecrated virgins as brides of Christ, demanding that they veil themselves and behave with the discretion that befitted the wives of such a husband.

This formulation was successful in denying the claims of celibate, encratic women to the manliness that was expected to characterize Christian clergy and gradually led to a concept of gender based on ontological opposition between women and men rather than a continuum of manliness. This theory has been used to justify the Catholic priesthood's monopoly of the sacraments. However, it also allows formulation of a concept of "womanliness" that opened up new horizons for celibate women in the religious professions. The assignment of nurturing, charitable instincts to the feminine gender justified women who wished to occupy a more public role within the Christian society. Encratic women continued to live in their own homes or in small groups in urban environments, supporting one another and the poor through their local churches. After the legalization of Christianity in the fourth century, encratic women and men formed monastic communities in the Near East and Europe that traditionally organized a broad range of social services for the secular community. Christian monasticism, as well as Buddhist forms of celibate religious devotion, now exists globally, and its offer of an encratic alternative to marriage is attracting growing numbers of women.

The Unmarried State in Modern Times. As nuns, celibate women opened up the "womanly" professions of teaching, nursing, and broader social services. Within their orders, they have traditionally fulfilled administrative tasks from which women were excluded in the secular world. Until the second half of the twentieth century nuns were the models for all professional women, who were expected to remain unmarried as long as they continued working. Nonreligious celibate women, in the older sense of the term, have now become increasingly numerous in most Western populations, and they supply a model to the developing world. With the introduction of effective birth control, glamorous and ambitious celibate women supply a positive image in popular media that offsets the impoverished single mothers chastised in political rhetoric.

[*See also* Christianity; Hinduism; Judaism; Spiritual Leaders, *subentry* Nuns and Abbesses; *and* Virginity.]

BIBLIOGRAPHY

Hajnal, J. "European Marriage Patterns in Perspective." In *Population in History*, edited by David V. Glass and David E. C. Eversle, 101–143. London: Edward Arnold, 1965.

McNamara, Jo Ann. *Sisters in Arms: Catholic Nuns through Two Millennia*. Cambridge, Mass.: Harvard University Press, 1996.

McNamara, Jo Ann. "An Unresolved Syllogism: The Search for a Christian Gender System." In *Conflicted Identities and Multiple Masculinities: Men in the Medieval West*, edited by Jacqueline Murray, pp. 1–4. New York: Garland, 1999.

Rubin, Gayle. "The Traffic in Women: Notes on the 'Political Economy' of Sex." In *Toward an Anthropology of Women*, edited by Rayna R. Reiter, pp. 157–210. New York: Monthly Review Press, 1975.

Tertullian. "On the Veiling of Virgins." In *The Ante-Nicene Fathers*, vol. 4. Edited by Alexander Roberts and James Donaldson, pp. 27–38. Grand Rapids, Mich.: Eerdmans, 1976.

JO ANN MCNAMARA

Comparative History

The practice of celibacy among women is found throughout the world at different points in history, for a variety of reasons, and for different lengths of time in a woman's life. For example, it is quite common for a woman to undergo a period of sexual abstinence during her menstrual period or after childbirth. Female shamans in Korea and Japan undergo limited periods of celibacy in order to purify themselves for various rituals. However, in contemporary use, the word "celibacy" usually refers to abstinence from all sexual activity for a sustained period of time, most often within a religious tradition. Buddhism and Christianity are two global religions that have spread the practice of female celibacy around the world throughout their history.

Celibacy in South Asian Traditions. The record of Buddhist nuns first unfolds in a body of teachings known as the *Collection on Discipline*, the *Vinayapiṭaka*, which is part of the canonical writings of the Theravada school of Buddhism. The story begins with Mahāprajāpatī, the woman who had raised Gautama Buddha after his mother died when he was seven days old. Upon her husband's death, Mahāprajāpatī heard a dharma talk given by the Buddha and was present in Kapīlavaṣtu when five hundred noble men entered the *sangha*—the order of ordained followers of the Buddha. Mahāprajāpatī and the wives of these five hundred men approached the Buddha to ask if they could join the Buddha's order as women who had taken up the robes. The Buddha refused their request, and his retinue moved on to Vaiśāli. Mahāprajāpatī led the five hundred women to Vaiśāli and had barbers cut their hair; they gave up their fine clothes for ochre-colored robes. With bare heads, bare feet, and their new robes, Mahāprajāpatī again asked the Buddha if they could join the order. The Buddha again refused, and then Ānanda, his longtime devoted attendant, asked him a third time on Mahāprajāpatī's behalf. The Buddha consented to Ānanda's request and agreed to ordain the women as nuns. But, the Buddha warned, the time that his teachings would be known on earth would no longer be one thousand years but only five hundred, as a result of allowing these women into his *sangha*. Furthermore, these women had to follow an additional eight rules that monks did not have to obey. These rules included the following injunctions: the most senior nun was junior to the most newly ordained monk, the ordination of nuns requires the presence of both monks and nuns, and nuns must live adjacent to a monastery—they could not live apart from monks. The story of Mahāprajāpatī provides us with the mythological history that made it possible for lay Buddhist women to become nuns, or *bhikṣunis*.

Following this story that appears in the canonical literature of the Theravada tradition, there is ample evidence to document the presence of *bhikṣunis* throughout the Indian Subcontinent and Southeast Asia. As Buddhism spread north into Central Asia and east into China, and also east and south into the countries of Southeast Asia, monks, and some nuns, were among those to spread the teachings of Gautama Buddha. There are travelogues written by Chinese Buddhists that speak of the ongoing presence of nuns in South Asia throughout the first millennium of the Common Era; that is, until the tenth or eleventh centuries. One of the earliest of these Chinese pilgrims visited northern India and Sri Lanka at the end of the fourth century C.E. Fa-hien explained that it was the custom of Buddhist monks to make offerings to the stupa of Śāriputra, who was one of the two chief disciples of the Buddha. The *bhikṣunis*, Fa-hien explains, honor the stupa that memorialized Ānanda—the monk who had interceded on their behalf with the Buddha. Other Chinese texts tell the story of how nuns from Sri Lanka brought the lineage of nuns to China in 429 and 434 C.E.

In Sri Lanka, the order of *bhikṣuni* was established by Sanghamittā, the daughter of King Aśoka in the third century B.C.E. Sanghamittā's brother, Mahinda, had been the first to arrive in Sri Lanka to bring the news of Buddhism, but he was approached by a young woman named Anulā who wanted to take up the ordained life as a woman. Mahinda immediately sent for his sister, who arrived with a branch of the *bodhi* tree (the tree under which the Buddha sat when he became enlightened) and soon participated in the ordination ritual for Anulā and her companions. The last inscription we have regarding the order of nuns in Sri Lanka is attributed to King Mahinda V (r. 982–1029), who is said to have built them a large residence during his reign. The *bhikṣuni sangha* was a substantial presence in the tenth century. However, the order of the nuns disappears along with the order of the monks in eleventh-century Sri Lanka. King Vijayabāhu began to solicit help from the Burmese to reestablish the order of monks in the late eleventh century, but the record makes no mention of any attempts to reestablish the order of nuns. Buddhism disappeared from India in the same period, and the nuns along with the religious tradition. As a result, there is no official lineage of Buddhist nuns in South and Southeast Asia today, although there are strong revival movements in the Theravada Buddhist countries of Sri Lanka, Thailand, and Myanmar.

In Mahāyāna Buddhism, the lineage of the order of the nuns remained intact and some schools of Buddhist nuns have a history of close to two millennia. Mahāyāna Buddhism is established in Tibet, Nepal, China, Korea, and Japan as well as in Southeast Asia. At the start of Buddhism's migration into China in the early centuries of the first millennium, the practice of celibacy among both men and women did not blend readily with the traditional Confucian emphasis on family life. Nonetheless, the order of monks and nuns was eventually established in China and spread to Korea and Japan, although there are branches of Buddhism that permit Buddhist monks (men) to be married. The practices undertaken by Buddhist nuns in East Asia are much the same as those followed by nuns in the early period of Buddhist history: they live in nunneries, adjacent to monasteries, and subject to the authority of monks. At the same time, we have texts written by men that document the relative independence of Buddhist nuns, in South Asia as well as in China and Japan.

The lives of Buddhist celibate women, described in a text translated into English (by K. R. Norman and Caroline Rhys Davids) as *Poems of Early Buddhist Nuns (Therīgāthā)*, follow similar patterns. There is often some kind of personal crisis, or longing, that leads to their renunciation of marriage and home life. We get glimpses of their experiences and lives as nuns, as well as their religious practices and attainments. The lives of the nuns are, almost by definition, not typical lives of Indian women in the fifth, fourth, and third centuries B.C.E.; renunciation in Buddhism requires one to leave the home and to enter a state of homelessness; this is as compelling an image for monks as it is for nuns.

The women tell stories of leaving home upon the death of a child or husband; many women describe how unsatisfactory their married lives were, for a variety of reasons that range from a physically abusive husband to a pervading sense of discontent. A few nuns avoided marriage altogether in their insistence upon living a life of renunciation. Other women describe how they lived as prostituted women, sometimes as upper-class courtesans and sometimes not. Subhā, a smith's daughter, tells how she heard the dharma (the teaching of the Buddha) and realized the truth of the teaching on the four noble truths. A successful courtesan says that she woke up one day with a powerful sense of disgust for her physical body and joined the order of nuns. The common element among these women's stories is that their crises propelled them to take up the celibate life in pursuit of the truth of the Buddha's teachings.

Jains, in both the Śvetambara and Dīgambara sects, also have orders of nuns. In the Śvetambara sect, there are far more nuns than monks, although nuns occupy a lower status than monks. In the formative period of classical Hinduism, 200 B.C.E.–200 C.E., there were women who studied and taught alongside male renouncers, and scholars have begun to document the lives of celibate Hindu women, as for example, in the essays collected by Karen Pechilis in *The Graceful Guru* (2004). Buddhist nuns live a life in accordance with the rules for wandering monastics, which were established for the various schools of renouncers, groups that included women as well as men, that wandered throughout the Ganges Valley in the sixth and fifth centuries B.C.E. Because the structure of Hindu renouncers, or *sannyasi*s, is more fluid and flexible than the organization of Buddhist or Jain monks or nuns, it is difficult to trace a single lineage for Hindu nuns, or even to call Hindu women who take on the life of a *sannyasini* (renouncer) by the title of "nun," although that is as proper a title as it is for Buddhist or Jain female renouncers. In all of these cases, women choose to live a celibate life in pursuit of the religious truths of the tradition in which they take their vows. The fundamental similarities between the practices stem from the history that Hinduism, Jainism, and Buddhism share on the Indian Subcontinent.

Celibacy in China. In China, Buddhism influenced the development of Daoism, which in turn shaped the growth of Buddhism. As a result, when the Buddhist orders of nuns were established in China, there were also Daoist orders of nuns, although there is great diversity among Daoist female adepts, nuns, and priestesses—and celibacy was not undertaken by all such female Daoist practitioners. One incarnation of the Chinese Buddhist goddess Guanyin is Maoshan, whose story was first recorded in the seventh century C.E. She escaped the dictates of her father by leaving her home and lived a life of religious renunciation for many years. Having attained enlightenment, she then rescued her father and revealed herself to be Guanyin, the "great goddess of mercy." This story has a wide circulation, and

Maoshan is considered to be the role model for women who wish to take up a life of celibate religious devotion in popular Chinese traditions.

Celibacy is undertaken in these traditions for different reasons, depending on the religious tradition in which the vows are taken. In Hinduism, Buddhism, and Jainism, celibacy is practiced as a means to focus one's attention on the path to salvation or enlightenment. Sexual attraction is a distraction that draws one's time, attention, and efforts away from the necessary meditations on enlightenment. The reasons for rejecting the practices of sexuality are not doctrinally different for women than they are for men in these traditions, although the actual rules for Buddhist celibacy are slightly different for male monks and female nuns in a way that reflects the greater social restrictions placed on women. In Daoism, however, celibacy is an act sometimes undertaken in search of the ultimate goal of immortality, and it is not as common a practice as it is in the renouncer traditions of Hinduism, Buddhism, and Jainism.

Celibacy in Christian Traditions. While the rules for female celibacy were similar in Christian and Buddhist orders—one should wear robes, be modest (which often involved shaving the head or wearing a veil), and avoid contact with the opposite sex—the development of the practice in each religion was quite distinct. In Christianity, celibacy as a religious ideal was not as embedded in the cultures of the Mediterranean as it was in the cultures of northern India in the middle of the first millennium B.C.E. onward. Celibacy was not a practice common to Judaism, although there were Jewish sects that pursued that ideal vigorously in the early centuries of the first millennium. Celibacy was practiced by women devoted to the worship of Vesta, the goddess of the hearth in ancient Rome, and there may be a historical relationship between the Vestal Virgins and the cult of virginity that later emerged in Christianity in the third and fourth centuries C.E.

Celibacy for men or women did not emerge as a clear form of religious practice at the beginning of the Christian tradition as it did in Buddhism and Jainism. The ideal of a young virgin devoted to the worship of God, for life, unfolded in the late third century. One of the earliest instances of Christian women who wished to live a celibate life was the subject of a tract written by Tertullian, perhaps as early as 205 C.E., who rejected the possibility that women could escape the shame of sexuality by devoting themselves to celibacy—despite the fact that women did stand, unveiled, before congregations in proclamation of their devotion to a celibate lifestyle. Female celibacy in Christianity is an embodiment of pure and stainless devotion to Christ. In Buddhism, female celibacy is undertaken to deliberately remove attachment to the body. Despite the different theological reasons that support the practice of female celibacy, and the relative freedom accorded women who live in communities of other celibate women, female celibacy is bound by the prevailing social attitudes toward women throughout history and around the world. A 2001 study by the anthropologists Elisa Sobo and Sandra Bell has begun to examine the cross-cultural variations of celibacy, both male and female, and the intersections with conceptions and practices of human sexuality.

[*See also* Buddhism; Central Asia, *subentry* Ancient Period; China, *subentry* Ancient Period; Christianity; Deities, *subentry* Goddesses; Hinduism; India; Japan; Judaism; Korea; Nepal; Shamanism; South Asia, *subentry* Ancient Period; Southeast Asia, *subentry* Ancient Period; Spiritual Leaders, *subentry* Nuns and Abbesses; Sri Lanka; Tibet and Bhutan; *and* Virginity.]

BIBLIOGRAPHY

Cahill, Suzanne. "Performers and Female Taoist Adepts: Hsi Wang Mu as the Patron Deity of Women in Medieval China." *Journal of the American Oriental Society* 106, no. 1 (1986): 155–168.

Hirakawa, Akira, Karma Leshke Tsomo, and Junko Miura. "The History of Buddhist Nuns in Japan." *Buddhist-Christian Studies* 12 (1992): 147–158.

Irwin, Lee. "Divinity and Salvation: The Great Goddesses of China." *Asian Folklore Studies* 49, no. 1 (1990): 53–68.

Khandelwal, Meena. *Women in Ochre Robes: Gendering Hindu Renunciation.* Albany: State University of New York Press, 2004.

McNamara, Jo Ann. *Sisters in Arms: Catholic Nuns through Two Millennia.* Cambridge, Mass.: Harvard University Press, 1996.

Norman, K. R., and Caroline Rhys Davids, trans. *Poems of Early Buddhist Nuns (Therīgāthā).* Oxford: Pali Text Society, 1989.

Pechilis, Karen, ed. *The Graceful Guru: Hindu Female Gurus in India and the United States.* New York: Oxford University Press, 2004.

Sobo, Elisa J., and Sandra Bell. *Celibacy, Culture, and Society: The Anthropology of Sexual Abstinence.* Madison: University of Wisconsin Press, 2001.

Tsai, Kathryn Ann, trans. *Lives of the Nuns: Biographies of Chinese Buddhist Nuns from the Fourth to Sixth Centuries.* Honolulu: University of Hawaii Press, 1994.

CAROL S. ANDERSON

CENTRAL AFRICA

This entry consists of two subentries:

1500–1900
Twentieth Century

1500–1900

Women in Central Africa, a large region that encompasses 3 million square miles, experienced vast historical change between 1500 and 1900. Historical knowledge about societies and women in this region is limited because of the challenges of accessing source materials. To reconstruct the period prior to the seventeenth century, scholars analyze a combination of oral sources—foundation myths, lineage genealogies, historical linguistics, and material culture. This body of evidence tells more about the idealized perceptions of women in Central African societies than about quotidian dynamics.

Between the sixteenth and nineteenth centuries, more detailed oral histories and written sources authored by Africans and Europeans result in more comprehensive knowledge about the lives of individual women. Gender relations and women's statuses in Central Africa were not monolithic but were characterized by fluid sociopolitical relationships. Historical transformations resulted from regional and global political, religious, social, and economic forces. Agricultural innovations, the creation of states, increased trade, regional and global use of slaves, and the onset of colonial conquest altered the historical landscape of the lives and perceptions of women in Central Africa. Most research on Central Africa in this period focuses on societies that consolidated into the states of the Kongo, Lunda, Luba, Shona, and Ovimbundu.

1500–1600. Though encompassing hundreds of ethnolinguistic groups, Central African societies commonly belong to the Bantu language family, and by 1500 inhabitants of the region shared common but not identical traditions of sociopolitical organization. Physical environments varied among woodland, desert, savanna, and forest. Decentralization remained the nearly ubiquitous form of sociopolitical organization with the exception of Great Zimbabwe, which existed from about the 1400s. Most societies, such as the Shona and Lunda, were patrilineal. Other Central African societies, such as parts of the modern-day Democratic Republic of the Congo (Zaire) and Cameroon, were matrilineal. In such societies, men relied on the fecundity of their sisters for wealth, and relationships between husbands and brothers-in-law and between sister's sons and maternal uncles were crucial. Over the course of centuries, Central African societies migrated and settled throughout the region in search of rain, better land, or game or to escape conflict or war. Fishing was crucial to the survival of communities near waterways in places such as the Democratic Republic of the Congo, and mining and cattle herding were crucial in South Central Africa. Nevertheless, farming remained a central occupation around which many Central African peoples organized their households and societies. Low population density was endemic throughout the region, and people were a vital resource.

Structures of societies. Within the Bantu cosmology of wealth in people, women played crucial and varied roles in their societies. Central African settlements ranged from ten to hundreds of people and were composed of several households headed by "big men" (*vansina*). A "big man" was usually a senior man who lived in a polygamous household with kin, clients, and other dependents. Such extended households were the building blocks of villages composed of groups of fathers and sons or brothers and nephews linked by marriage. Men and women inhabited distinct physical and social spaces. Men and women did not often work, eat, occupy their leisure time, or engage in religious ceremonies together. In a polygamous household, the husband, each wife, and the wife's children would have their own home group in a common homestead. In the Bantu tradition, a wealthy man was one who had many people under his patronage—wives, clients, friends, and dependents. An older man with many female dependents held power over other men because he could offer or withhold access to women.

Kingdom of Matamba. Nzinga, Queen of Matamba, 1582–1663. Photographs and Prints Division, Schomburg Center for Research in Black Culture, New York Public Library, Astor, Lenox and Tilden Foundations

Women's status fluctuated based on marital status, fertility, age, individual talent, and religious faculties. Marriage was the key relationship through which households made alliances and was also the key relationship in determining a woman's status. A woman without a husband or children was regarded with ridicule. Senior men, uncles, fathers, or brothers often decided when and whom women would marry. Parents betrothed a girl as early as infancy, but it was not until after menstruation that a marriage could be consummated. Older women in the husband's household raised the girl until she came of age.

Marriage. Marriage brought together two exogamous groups who sought to forge political alliances and social relationships and build wealth. Marriage occurred in many different forms: woman exchange, marriage by capture, and most frequently marriage by bride-wealth. A senior man from the groom's family remitted the agreed upon bride-wealth to a senior man in the bride's family. In the period before Atlantic trade, bride-wealth was composed of goods valued by a given society—iron in Gabon, cattle, grain, and hoes among the Shona, copper or squares of raffia in Cameroon. The remittance of bride-wealth conferred the physical transfer of a woman and her labor, sexual access, and future children from her natal home to that of her husband. The practice of levirate, in which a widow married a man in her husband's household, ensured that married women remained within their husband's lineage.

Married women had numerous ways in which to negotiate their relations with their husbands and husbands' kin. A new wife was an individual of low status when she first moved to her husband's home. She was expected to respect and obey her husband, to grow and cook food, to maintain a home, and to bear children. She completed tasks assigned to her by her husband, his more senior wife or wives, his mother, and his sisters. Yet wives had recourse to address dissatisfaction with husbands. Wives privately criticized husbands and, through gossip and songs, publicly shamed a husband into changing behavior. Wives also expressed dissatisfaction by refusing to do the tasks socially expected of them, for instance, not cooking or withholding sexual services. Marriage did not end a woman's relationship with her family of birth but established a network of obligations and exchanges between the groom's and the bride's families. Marriage obliged the husband to provide services when the wife's family requested. A woman sought refuge with her natal family to negotiate displeasure or request a divorce. Though women's families often wished for the marriage to last, their families were also key negotiators in ensuring wives' well-being.

Within extended households, the crucial building blocks of Central African societies, wives could also influence men and maintain power over other women. Women's fertility was crucial. The more children a woman bore, the more her household and community held her in esteem. Among the Shona, a woman received her own cooking stones the first time she bore children. As grandmothers and mothers-in-law, older women were responsible for educating grandchildren regarding the social expectations and morals of their societies. As Bantu societies esteemed the elderly, younger men and women were expected to address older women with deference and provide them with labor. Older, postmenopausal women often interceded in family decisions and voiced opinions in the company of men. Senior wives and older women also exercised control over the labor of daughters-in-law, junior wives, and children.

Gendered division of labor. Women and their labor were significant to the economic activities and sustenance of Central African societies. The household was the basic unit of economic and social reproduction, and a gendered division of labor delineated distinct and complementary tasks for women and men. Men participated in agricultural production by clearing fields of heavy brush and in some societies by assisting women at harvest. Among the Kongo, male and female contributions to the evening meal give a sense of the gendered division of labor: women brought the food, and men brought the wine. Women in Central African societies were responsible for nearly all agricultural production, and men were responsible for arboriculture. Chiefs and male leaders assigned individual husbands with control over land, and their wives farmed it.

Women spent their days from sunrise until midday planting, weeding, and maintaining fields of cereals such as millet and sorghum, root crops such as yams, and bananas. Women also maintained smaller household gardens of greens and medicinal plants for family consumption. In the afternoon women and older girls also pounded grain or yams and cooked food. Women made pots and dishes or wove baskets. Women were exclusively responsible for the care and education of children, for collecting water and firewood, for cleaning homes and homesteads, and in some societies for brewing beer.

Slave women. It is difficult to ascertain details on slaves' lives in this period, but some Central African societies did have slaves. Pawnship was how many female slaves entered into servile relationships. Along the Zambezi River valley in East Central Africa, a poor man might pawn a female dependent to a wealthier man in exchange for food or resources. The woman who was pawned labored for the wealthier person, and such arrangements might also grant sexual access and custody of any children born. Pawns sometimes became slaves if the debtor could not repay the debt.

Women's influence. Women in Central Africa exercised power and influenced their societies through informal, indirect, and distinct channels. Evidence does not demonstrate that women in much of Central Africa exercised formal political power. In some Shona chiefdoms, women held political power as influential mothers, sisters, or counselors to rulers. Women were not inheritors of male power but wielded authority on their own over courts or people. Additionally, such female auxiliaries were consulted before rulers made significant decisions.

Women significantly influenced individual and collective actions in their communities through health and healing. As the primary food gatherers, women often possessed specialized knowledge of which plants or roots healed specific ailments. Only women could be present at births, and postmenopausal women who acted as midwives were highly respected. Women and men consulted female healers on how to alleviate illness and pain, treat infertility, and increase sexual ability. Yet Central African cosmologies thought of ailments as having spiritual as well as physical causes.

Spiritual beliefs. Spiritual beliefs shaped the quotidian lives of people and also allowed individual and collective women to influence their societies. Bantu religions believed that higher gods and ancestral spirits of the deceased intervened in the daily lives of the living. Creation myths of individual societies included female ancestors who used their sexuality and fertility to found lineages. Though creation myths prescribed the moral and social taboos that societies should follow, women who broke sexual taboos founded societies. Female healers were often also diviners who consulted the spirit world. Such individuals were respectively referred to as *nganga*. Men and women wishing to see why they were ill or had experienced a misfortune or were seeking luck in an endeavor consulted a *nganga*. The *nganga* communicated with spirits and prescribed the proper sequence of actions that the person should follow to mitigate harm. A *nganga* sought to bring rain in times of drought or victory in times of war.

Postmenopausal women were especially esteemed as communicators with ancestral spirits. Women attained the highly respected positions of spirit mediums who shaped collective social and political action. A spirit medium was a person who had been possessed by an ancestral spirit and prescribed warnings or directions for the community. Women's links to spiritual worlds were demonstrated in material culture. Chokwe and Luba, societies located in the modern-day Democratic Republic of the Congo, produced sculptures of stools, divination bowls, and people replete with images of female figures.

Central African religious beliefs left individual women vulnerable to social ostracism. Individuals accused others of harnessing spirits to cause harm by practicing "witchcraft." Thus widows were often accused of having caused the deaths of their husbands, and co-wives accused each other of having caused infertility or children's illness. As the ability to communicate with the spirits allowed some women to attain power, it also left room for their societies to punish individual women who had attained too much influence.

Women's societies. Women's societies, sometimes secret, allowed women collectively to shape the actions of their societies and maintain power over other women. Men were forbidden to witness the gatherings of women's societies at the risk of death or bringing harm to the community. Communities usually designated places in the forest or in the bush as reserved for women. One purpose of such societies was for married women to initiate pubescent girls in rites of passage, sexual education and health, and roles as wives and mothers. Women's organizations held ceremonies seeking a fruitful harvest, rain, and success in war. Along the Sudanese border, women's secret societies formed across settlements, allowing women to form regional networks beyond their households. At community-wide gatherings, women's societies issued directives to resolve community conflict or to ridicule individuals' behavior.

1600–1900. Between the seventeenth and nineteenth centuries decentralized groups consolidated into larger kingdoms and ushered in an era of increased wealth, war, insecurity, and transformation. Though centralized states were the exception, this political innovation impacted the entire region and the daily lives of its inhabitants. The consolidation of some Central African societies reached its height in the kingdoms of Kongo by the sixteenth century, Lunda, Luba, and Lozi by the eighteenth century, and Ovimbundu by the nineteenth century. At the same time the expansion of trade drew the region into global economic systems. Europe, the Americas, and North and East Africa increasingly sought Central African slaves and goods. Central African leaders sought imported goods, such as guns and cloth, and regional items, such as local cloth, copper, iron, and salt, and circulated slaves for internal use. Each region specialized in particular products for regional and international trade, and Central African elites accumulated immense wealth. Yet as states battled each other to control territory, trade, and people, ordinary citizens struggled to search for security. Religious change also accompanied trade as Central Africans adapted Christianity and Islam into existing and varied Bantu religious beliefs. By the late nineteenth century, encroaching European colonialism further shifted socioeconomic relations and impacted women's lives.

The combination of internal and external transformations provided some opportunities for individual women to attain socioeconomic and political power but also resulted in increased stratification between privileged and less privileged women. Nonelite women were vulnerable to enslavement, social dislocation, and compelled migration. Some elite women took advantage of moments of flux to claim direct political power. Other elite women capitalized upon traditional avenues to women's power to lead sociopolitical movements.

The consolidation of states resulted in political, social, economic, and spatial change that impacted gender relations and the differentiation of women's status. Kings and their counselors used terror, convoked war, and promoted themselves as communicators with spirits to compel people to follow them. Social stratification meant distinctions between elites and commoners. In the Kongo, people were differentiated according to class, occupation, household, and kin group. Basic divisions were between those who lived in the country and those who lived in town, those who farmed or gathered raw materials and those who controlled the distribution of goods. Nearly four-fifths of Kongo's inhabitants lived in rural areas and farmed, collected, and produced surpluses as tribute for the elite who lived in towns. By the 1600s those who lived in rural areas also paid taxes to elites in local currency. The elite owned slaves whom they used as farmers and traders.

Among the Lunda, kings and their counselors established the royal court as the point of attraction and exchange between leaders and subject groups. Leaders maintained control by manipulating patron-client exchanges. Commoners owed kings tributes of food and raw materials, and kings distributed iron, copper, and imported cloth. Though imported goods were indicators of wealth, the ideal of wealth in people continued to guide how Central African societies formed sociopolitical relationships. Women of varied socioeconomic statuses were critical to their societies.

Marriage. Marriage and sexual access to women remained key in consolidating the power of men and in determining a woman's social status. Extended households remained the basic social unit, and marriage was a key social contract that brought people together. In rural areas, households connected by marriage ties formed villages. Bride-wealth remained the key exchange through which families contracted marriage. In a society such as that of the Kongo, which had a well-developed monetary system by the 1600s, bride-wealth consisted of local currency rather than goods. In the nineteenth century, bride-wealth payments increasingly were composed of imported goods. Men who had greater access to these items obtained more wives. Multiple wives increased a man's prestige and wealth, and women's labor produced goods that could be sold. Warrior leaders used marriage to fuse new empires and solidify trading ties.

The creation myth of the Lunda in the 1600s attributed its genesis to the marriage of a Luba hunter to a Lunda princess. In the late nineteenth century a trader warrior named Msiri destabilized and conquered kingdoms in what is now the southeastern Democratic Republic of the Congo. Msiri married the niece of an Angolan trader to cement ties with established Ovimbundu arms suppliers. Msiri and his advisers sought to synthesize this new empire of multiple ethnic groups by aligning men with concubines of varied ethnicities. These concubines were likely women who were slaves.

Slave women. Central Africans enslaved in the Americas in the sixteenth through nineteenth centuries were mainly men, yet Central Africans enslaved in Africa and exported into Arab regions were mainly women and children. Local demands for women fueled the internal slave trade, and throughout Africa female slaves cost more than male slaves. Among the Chokwe in the mid-nineteenth century, merchants and hunters sold ivory for women, who became slave wives in the societies who obtained them. Along trading networks of East Central Africa, women from Malawi, the Kafue Valley, and the Gwembe Valley were sold at the high rate of one woman per tusk. Slaves were usually outsiders who came from a different region than their masters, but they also came from the local region. A woman or girl became a slave in several manners. In addition to pawnship, women became slaves through kidnapping, as payment of fines, as part of the booty of war, and as reward for soldiers. At the conclusion of wars, victors often killed men or sold them into the Atlantic slave trade and retained women.

Slave women performed the same tasks as nonslave women. Female slaves completed essential labor. They worked in agriculture, domestic labor, and craft work. They also bore children that increased their masters' lineages and ensured the continuity of kin groups. Slave women were often slave wives. Masters married them or granted them to followers and sons. A wealthy man might prefer a slave wife because he avoided the obligations owed to the kin of a nonslave woman, purchasing a slave woman might cost less than marrying a nonslave woman with bride-wealth, and any children born from the union were more likely to be loyal to him. Social mobility and some measure of independence were possible for female slaves. Some exceptional slave women traders amassed wealth and owned their own slaves. Among the Bakongo in the Kongo and the Mpongwé of Gabon, a slave woman's children could become free persons or leaders in their societies. Whether a slave woman was married to her master or to another slave, the master retained control over her mobility and that of her children. Among slave and nonslave women, farming remained the most prevalent way most women in Central Africa organized their labor.

Gendered division of labor. Most Central African societies maintained a gendered division of labor in which women, slave and nonslave, were the primary farmers. The period after 1600 witnessed an agricultural revolution, and women farmers were key to the innovation. In the seventeenth century two new crops, maize and cassava/manioc, dominated agricultural production and replaced millet and sorghum to become staples in Central African diets. Additionally, farmers planted pumpkins, beans, and yams. As the primary farmers, women adapted these New World crops to African soils. Women completed all stages of production, from clearing brush to harvesting to preparing raw products into meals or for travel. Cassava in particular provided more food security. Its yields continued for up to two years, the root could be left in the ground until needed, and farmers developed methods for preserving the harvested manioc for months at a time. In the nineteenth century in what is now the middle Democratic Republic of the Congo, women farmers produced nearly all of the cassava that town dwellers ate. These New World crops required more labor. As many men in interior and coastal societies focused more on trade, women assumed agricultural tasks, such as clearing fields, that had previously been completed by men.

The expansion of the Atlantic and Indian oceans trading system along the coasts and interiors in Central Africa resulted in increased workloads for women farmers. Greater population consolidation and global market demands for African agricultural products meant that farmers had to produce greater yields. Townspeople and caravans of slaves and traders traveling across the continent needed to be fed. International markets demanded raw agricultural products, such as groundnuts, palm oil, and tobacco. In a transformation in the gendered division of labor, some male slaves began to engage primarily in agricultural labor. For villagers in kingdoms such as Lozi, Lunda, and Luba, women, slaves, and refugees grew crops in plantations and villages around royal areas.

In the fluid and volatile sociopolitical milieu of nineteenth- through twentieth-century Central Africa, some elite women leaders exercised formal political and economic control. Elite women in households with slaves oversaw the labor of girl and female slaves and controlled the distribution of the produce. Elite women benefited with more leisure time, assistance in labor-intensive tasks, and time to participate in other economic endeavors, such as trading. One Lozi tradition speaks of an eighteenth-century queen who was so wealthy that she bathed in milk. The kingdom of the Kongo had numerous instances of governing women. Female members made up the council that balanced the king's power. The queen mother assisted at political gatherings and influenced her son's decisions. The queen controlled her own land and bequeathed land to followers of her choosing.

Some unmarried women in the Kongo headed their own households of slaves and governed provinces. Amid civil wars and conflicts over succession in the kingdom, in 1624 a woman of a royal family named Nzinga (also written Njinga) claimed power over the state of Ndongo. Political and social strife forced her to flee, and she created her own state in the region of Matamba. Nzinga claimed and legitimized her power based on kinship ties and religious beliefs and at times aligned herself with European missionaries and merchants. When she died in 1621 the state maintained a thriving economy in goods and people.

Increased presence of Europeans. The increased presence of Europeans, the spread of Christianity, and the beginnings of colonial conquest also transformed women's place in Central Africa from 1500 to 1900. Interacting with Portuguese missionaries who reached their shores in the fifteenth century, leaders of the Kongo in 1491 declared Christianity to be the state religion. Though Central African economies were firmly entrenched in global economic systems by 1900, few Europeans traveled beyond the coast. This began to change in the nineteenth century as technological advances allowed Europeans traveling in Africa to survive diseases such as malaria. Religious revivals in nineteenth-century Europe and the United States resulted in the increased presence of Christian missionaries throughout Africa.

In the nineteenth century, religious revivalism also expanded into an antislavery movement. European states banned the slave trade and sent naval ships to patrol African coasts along the Atlantic and Indian oceans. European merchants also sought to control access to African goods, and numerous European adventurers and African guides mapped the African continent and established protectorate treaties with individual chiefs. From 1885 to 1890, European countries settled on who could lay claim to which regions of Africa. By the beginning of the twentieth century several European states had established colonies in the region and were poised to expand further. Individual African women negotiated European expansion with precolonial avenues for women's power.

Some African women tapped into their precolonial positions as communicators with the spirit world to negotiate social change. Since the 1500s the Kongo had maintained diplomatic relations with several European countries, permitting Catholic Portuguese priests residency and sending the sons of royalty to be educated in Europe. Christian emphasis on male priests and pastors as direct communicators with deities eroded African women's power, yet African Christians practiced a syncretic Christianity. The Kongolese continued to believe that *nganga* could communicate with ancestral spirits as well as saints to bring about harm or good to their societies. The church condemned such practices as witchcraft. Yet in 1702 a woman of modest but elite birth named Kimpa Vita claimed to have been possessed by Saint Anthony. Within a few years she attracted thousands of followers and began to ordain her own priests, known as little Anthonys. This sociopolitical movement sought to end the cycle of civil wars in the Kongo and to ordain a new king. Kimpa Vita's claims of direct communication with deities threatened the power of the current leaders and the church. In 1706 priests and the royal council condemned her as a heretic and burned her at the stake.

At the close of the nineteenth century increased European expansion in Central Africa contributed to further sociopolitical chaos but also created opportunities for some women to raise their social status or influence their societies.

Women, particularly former slave women, were often the first to convert to Christianity and sought refuge in missionary settlements. Around mission stations in what is now the southeastern Democratic Republic of the Congo, women who had been slaves, such as a Luba woman named Bwanika, became employees of the church and community activists. As in the Kongo, women elsewhere in Central Africa could obtain power in their roles in traditional religions. A Shona woman named Charwe, a spirit medium, played a role in inspiring the First Chimurenga, the 1896–1897 Ndeble/Shona uprising against British colonial rule. Charwe was possessed by the ancestral spirit named Nehanda, who had war-making power. British officials executed Charwe for murder, though historians debate whether or not she was guilty.

By the dawn of the twentieth century women in Central African societies exercised multiple and differentiated roles in their societies. As mothers, wives, farmers, traders, political leaders, healers, and spiritual guides, women were crucial to their families and societies. Yet women of different sociocultural groups varied in their capacities to maintain control over their own mobility, labor, and social status.

[*See also* Africa; Imperialism and Colonialism; Kinship; Marriage; Matriarchy; Slavery; *and* Slave Trade.]

BIBLIOGRAPHY

Beach, D. N. "An Innocent Woman, Unjustly Accused? Charwe, Medium of the Nehanda Mhondoro Spirit, and the 1896–97 Central Shona Rising in Zimbabwe." *History in Africa* 25 (1998): 27–54.

Berger, Iris, and E. Francis White. *Women in Sub-Saharan Africa: Restoring Women to History*. Bloomington: Indiana University Press, 1999.

Birmingham, David, and Phyllis M. Martin, eds. *History of Central Africa*. Vol. 1. London: Longman, 1983.

Bucher, Henry. "The Mpongwé of the Gabon Estuary: A History to 1860." PhD diss., University of Wisconsin, 1977.

Dangarembga, Tsitsi. *Nervous Conditions*. New York: Seal, 2004.

Heywood, Linda Marinda. *Contested Power in Angola, 1840s to the Present*. Rochester, N.Y.: University of Rochester Press, 2000.

Hilton, Anne. *The Kingdom of Kongo*. Oxford: Clarendon Press, 1985.

Martin, Phyllis M. *The External Trade of the Loango Coast, 1576 – 1870: The Effects of Changing Commercial Relations on the Vili Kingdom of Loango*. Oxford: Clarendon Press, 1972.

Miller, Joseph C. "Nzinga of Matamba in a New Perspective." *Journal of African History* 16 (1975): 201–216.

Reefe, Thomas Q. *The Rainbow and the Kings: A History of the Luba Empire to 1891*. Berkeley: University of California Press, 1981.

Reefe, Thomas Q. "The Societies of the Eastern Savana." In *History of Central Africa*, Vol. 1, edited by David Birmingham and Phyllis M. Martin, pp. 160–204. London: Longman, 1983.

Roberts, Mary Nooter, and Allen F. Roberts, eds. *Memory: Luba Art and the Making of History*. New York: Museum for African Art, 1996.

Robertson, Claire C., and Martin A. Klein, eds. *Women and Slavery in Africa*. Portsmouth, N.H.: Heinemann, 1997. See especially Susan Herlin Broadhead, "Slave Wives, Free Sisters: Bakongo Women and Slavery c. 1700–1850" (pp. 160–184) and Robert Harms, "Sustaining the System: Trading Towns along the Middle Zaire" (pp. 95–110).

Schmidt, Elizabeth. *Peasants, Traders, and Wives: Shona Women in the History of Zimbabwe, 1870–1939*. Portsmouth, N.H.: Heinemann, 1992.

Thornton, John K. *The Kingdom of Kongo: Civil War and Transition, 1641–1718*. Madison: University of Wisconsin Press, 1983.

Thornton, John K. *The Kongolese Saint Anthony: Dona Beatriz Kimpa Vita and the Antonian Movement, 1684–1706*. Cambridge, U.K.: Cambridge University Press, 1998.

Vansina, Jan. *Paths in the Rainforests*. Madison: University of Wisconsin Press, 1990.

Wright, Marcia. *Strategies of Slaves and Women: Life-Stories from East/Central Africa*. New York: L. Barber, 1993.

Rachel Jean-Baptiste

Twentieth Century

> On a day-to-day basis, it is the women, not the men, who shoulder the worries of bringing up children . . . of getting home on time to attend to their household responsibilities and getting up before dawn the following morning to begin the grind again.
>
> (Urdang, p. 233)

The history of Central African women in the twentieth century is largely the history of incompatibility between what they did within and outside provisioning. Women alone processed and cooked food, while men took part in food production to varying degrees, and women played roles in the public realm, politics, and religion. Women experienced varying levels of subordination and autonomy. But gender-based struggles were not only inconclusive in Central Africa; they also came in many forms, as can be seen from the diversity of the region's principles of descent, inheritance, and marriage contracts.

Although known to anthropologists as the "matrilineal belt," Central Africa also featured patrilineal systems at the time of the region's conquest by the Belgians, British, and French in the late nineteenth century. Each system had varied configurations and structured gender differently. The patrilineal regimes of the early twenty-first century's Democratic Republic of the Congo (DRC; called the Belgian Congo from 1908 to 1960 and later Zaire) differed from those of Cameroon, the Central African Republic (CAR), and the Republic of the Congo. There also were great differences between the matrilineal regimes of the DRC, Malawi, and Zambia. Moreover, the fact that in both the matrilineal and patrilineal systems some women held important public offices led them to respond to the economics of imperialism, colonial politics, and Christianity differently from women who did not hold such offices.

Women in Politics and Religion. From the beginning, European missionaries led an aggressive campaign against African religion—and women's roles in it—by denouncing its priestesses, female mediums, healers, and teachers as agents of the devil. These attacks, which went hand in hand with economic change, resulted in the transformation of some cultural institutions and the decline of many others, like *chisungu* initiation schools for girls in Zambia. As the young were deprived of the social and technical skills needed for their survival as adults, the old female ritual specialists also lost their influence and prestige. Thus although formerly differentiated on the basis of religious expertise, Central African women now joined male-led mainstream Christianity and the ubiquitous separatist movements as a homogeneous group of obedient followers. In that context, Alice Lenshina Mulenge (c. 1924–1978) of Zambia takes on great significance in the religious history of Central Africa. In the mid-1950s this illiterate woman founded the Lumpa Church. Her success in both rural and urban areas frightened the male-dominated—and heavily mission-educated—United Nationalist Independence Party (UNIP), who violently repressed the movement. As in religion, so in twentieth-century politics: women were only good enough to serve as obedient followers.

Little is known about women's involvement in Central African political movements of the twentieth century. Nationalist historians wrote before the advent of gender studies, and when scholars began to investigate the history of women in the late 1970s, nationalism had fallen from grace as a field of serious research. As a result there are large gaps in what is known about women's anticolonial politics except for the national liberation movements of the 1970s and 1980s. Did the female religious leaders of Central Africa play the same role that Shona female mediums did in Zimbabwe? There the women took a leading role in organizing the revolt against British settlers in 1896–1897. How did oppressed women such as slaves react to the imposition of colonial rule?

Whatever their initial responses, though, women lost under European rule. Colonial officials routinely replaced aging or dead female chiefs and heads of villages with men, creating all-male political bodies that were insensitive if not openly hostile to the interests of women. Events during the worldwide depression of the early 1930s illustrate this point. Asked by British officials what to do with single women and widows who failed to pay their hut taxes, all-male councils of chiefs in Malawi recommended that such women be forced to marry. In that same period, men's voices became even louder when educated male elites created pressure groups like the organizations of the *évolués* in the DRC, native associations in Malawi, and welfare societies in Zambia. Taxed like men, women remained an invisible group, limited to hidden forms of resistance throughout the interwar period. World War II opened opportunities for both rural and urban women to express their discontent.

As the late Susan Geiger has shown for Tanzania, women's invisibility in the nationalist literature does not mean that they were peripheral to the struggle. Women fought hard for independence, not merely responding to the propaganda of male agitators, but acting on the basis of their direct experiences of colonial oppression. In the cities, married women became the indirect object of capitalist exploitation because they worked in the precarious informal sector to supplement the low wages of their husbands. They subsequently rallied behind their men engaged in labor union action. Meanwhile, cash-crop agriculture helped generate rebellion among rural women. From Cameroon in the north to Malawi in the south, colonial administrators imposed what they called "agricultural betterment" programs after World War II. The intensified labor demands of these programs, and especially their emphasis on export crops rather than food production, drove rural women to become involved in political parties like the Malawi Congress Party (MCP), UNIP in Zambia, and the Mouvement National Congolais (MNC) in the DRC. All major political parties formed women's branches that helped mobilize women in protest actions.

Colonial officials reacted violently, killing, imprisoning, and humiliating female activists. To put down an uprising against a collaborating chief, for instance, members of the Police Mobile Force in Malawi in 1959 applied *chitedze* leaves (which cause severe itching) to women's private parts. Women paid dearly for political independence, but for a whole range of reasons only a tiny group of them gained positions of leadership in the newly independent states. In the 1960s and 1970s this tiny group included women like Petronella Kawandeai, a member of UNIP's central committee in Zambia; Rose Chibambo, a junior minister in Malawi's ministry of social welfare; and Dorothy Njeuma, vice minister in Cameroon's ministry of national education and later head of the University of Yaoundé I in Cameroon. Whatever their level of education, women held these junior offices at the discretion of their male patrons. Like their predecessors, Africa's postcolonial states had little room for independent-minded rural or urban women.

Life in the City. In Central Africa, women started moving to the cities when men did, at the beginning of the twentieth century. Some women followed their husbands, but many others migrated as singles looking for new opportunities, often against the dictates of their parents, chiefs, and the colonial administration. In the late 1920s these rebels found an unexpected ally in the bourgeoning copper-mining industry of the DRC and Zambia. To stabilize the labor force, companies encouraged their male employees to bring their wives to the towns.

Recruiters for the Union Minière du Haut Katanga (UMHK) in the DRC were so determined to keep their men that they advanced money for marriage payment (bride-price). The resulting migration, which also included large numbers of single women, hit another peak after World War II when the reconstruction of war-torn Europe increased the demand for African products like copper. Cities on the copper belt of the DRC and Zambia entered the postcolonial era as powerful magnets for rural dwellers. Even Lusaka, Zambia's sleepy administrative capital, doubled its population from a quarter of a million in the 1960s to half a million by the early 1970s. A decade later, men and women were represented in more or less equal numbers in most cities of Central Africa, with some urban centers like Brazzaville (in the Republic of the Congo) having more women than men. But the numeric parity concealed a disquieting occupational and economic imbalance that resulted in part from women's lack of formal education.

Because of their Victorian upbringing, European missionaries, the main providers of Western education during the colonial era, did not consider women's education to be a priority. They focused on educating boys, whom they regarded as the breadwinners and transmitters of modernity. To be sure, this bias was more pronounced in some Christian churches than in others. Scottish missionaries in Malawi admitted a significant number of girls into their schools—to create proper wives for their educated men. At the time of Malawi's independence in 1964, then, only a small group of educated women existed, including a few, like Maud Kanweka Nanthambwe, who had earned their bachelor's degrees outside the country. In contrast, the Roman Catholic Church in the DRC did next to nothing to educate women besides teaching them how to recite the rosary. Of the one and a half million children in (mostly primary) schools in 1958, only twenty thousand were girls, so that at independence in 1960, the Belgian Congo listed one woman, Sophie Kanza, with a high school diploma.

This sex imbalance in primary and high schools, which was also typical of other Central African countries, meant that boys, rather than girls, benefited from the free university training available during the early years of independence. When national policy makers and the international community began to stress the importance of educating women in the 1980s, girls faced another hurdle: paying for college education. Under the structural adjustment programs (SAPs) of the World Bank and International Monetary Fund (IMF), university students had to pay fees. The era of free college education had bypassed women. The millions of bright daughters of the poor could not earn a university diploma. As in the past, they formed the core of the informal work sector.

Entering the cities with nothing but rural skills, both married and single women learned to survive as petty traders, beer brewers, and domestics. In cities like Lusaka, female seekers of domestic jobs often had to compete with men. They faced less competition, however, when adapting their village-based expertise in the food sector. Everywhere women sustained a flourishing market in cooked food. Women from Brazzaville flocked to Kinshasa (in the DRC; called Léopoldville prior to 1966) to cultivate food for the African population of that city; their sisters in Zambia grew vegetables and gathered mushrooms and honey for sale. Enterprising women of Kisangani (northeast of Kinshasa; formerly Stanleyville) traded fish, rice, and beans from down the river with cloth, radios, and other manufactured goods. In 1972 they created the Association des Femmes Commerçantes (Business Women's Association), and one of them was subsequently elected to the regional committee of the Kisangani Chamber of Commerce. High inflation, which diminished the value of men's earnings, combined with SAPs to increase the importance of the so-called informal sector in most cities. Women who made a living as prostitutes also faced new challenges in the last two decades of the twentieth century.

Prostitution in Central Africa developed as an integral part of urban growth, recruiting mostly young women in need of money to support themselves and their relatives back in the village. With time, prostitution became a highly differentiated occupation, featuring not only the low-paid night streetwalkers and workers in hotels and bars but also mistresses, courtesans, and part-timers who conducted their business from their own homes to supplement income from other activities like petty trade. In some cities of the DRC and the Republic of the Congo, prostitutes created clubs for mutual support and for improving their services. On the eve of independence Kinshasa had an estimated population of four thousand "free women." These were the women who in the 1980s became the earliest victims of the HIV/AIDS pandemic, which has killed untold numbers after subjecting the victims to new forms of poverty. Ill and unable to work, some prostitutes return to their villages to spend their last days with their relatives.

Cash-crop Agriculture. The countryside to which these unfortunate women returned starting in the 1980s was nothing like the villages their predecessors had left at the beginning of the century. Much had changed as a result of labor emigration and, in particular, the revolution in export production: cocoa and coffee in Cameroon and the Republic of the Congo; cotton in the CAR, the DRC, and Malawi; maize in Zambia; and tobacco in the CAR. In some countries, like the DRC, overt political pressure had coerced peasants into the cash-crop regime, and in others,

African Coffee Farms. A woman spreads harvested coffee beans to dry in the sun at the Kibubuti coffee farm in Kiambu, Kenya, February 2004. REUTERS/Antony Njuguna

like Malawi and Zambia, villagers had started export production to pay their taxes. But as the century progressed, purely economic forces maintained the momentum in cash-crop agriculture.

Regardless of the exact pressures, however, villagers everywhere faced often insurmountable difficulties integrating the new crops into the existing systems of food production. It was not easy to accommodate cash crops because, among other things, in some regions there was only one growing or wet season, and nearly everywhere villagers tilled the land without the benefit of new technologies. The twentieth century can thus be characterized as a period of new rural tensions and experiments in the uses of domestic labor.

Africans developed many techniques to grow cash crops, with each method reflecting such factors as the precolonial sexual division of labor, state intervention, and the nature of the crops in question. Perennials like coffee exploited peasants' labor differently from annuals like cotton, maize, and rice. But the same crop could affect women's involvement differently, depending on the preexisting division of labor in food production. In some areas of the DRC the superimposition of cotton on a cassava culture dependent almost exclusively on female labor shaped women's engagement with the export crop differently than it did in Malawi. There cotton competed with millet, sorghum, and maize in what had been for all practical purposes a gender-neutral system of production. Finally, as the following examples suggest, different government policies often complicated women's participation in cash-crop agriculture.

When intercropping was permitted by colonial governments, in Malawi before 1951 and in the DRC after 1954, villagers grew cotton and food crops in the same field. Intercropping minimized the labor and land requirements of the cash crop. Besides, this method tended to conserve the preexisting sexual division of labor, making it easier for single women to raise the cash crop. Cotton divided men and women most sharply when, under government pressure, villagers raised cotton and food crops in different fields—in the DRC before 1954 and in Malawi after 1951. Everywhere the demand for separate cotton fields engendered intense struggles that pitted wives against their husbands.

Although cash cropping increased women's workload, women did not as a rule benefit from their hard work. Only single women, widows, and wives of migrant workers—women in atypical marital situations—managed to control the money made from export production. By contrast, women in regular marriage situations became dependent laborers, working for their husbands. And new technologies did not, it would seem, make much difference in this pattern of female labor use. The plow in Zambia relieved men of their traditional responsibilities of cutting down trees, but by allowing them to open larger fields, it demanded more labor hours from their wives in nonmechanized operations such as seeding, harvesting, and weeding. Men emerged as the real winners.

The cash-crop economy improved the economic position of men in a general pattern of rural differentiation, in part because of preexisting gender hierarchies but mainly because of colonial social engineering. The British in Malawi and Zambia recognized only the husband as the registered grower, with the right to sell the cash crop. For the Belgians and French, the legal unit of labor coincided with the *homme adulte valide*—the healthy adult male. The wives who spent long and hard hours in their husbands' fields of cash crops had no legal existence in the colonial world. Predictably, women everywhere spearheaded the resistance to modernization programs that increased their workload, subordinated them to men, made rural capitalists out of their husbands, and threatened food security.

Gender-sensitive agrarian history shows that there were two sides to the story of the relationship of export production and the food economy. One part of the equation shows how the introduction of cash crops exposed villagers to the vagaries of the international market, diverted their labor and land resources from the food sector, and helped the spread of less labor-intensive crops and of new crop diseases. The other and equally important element of the equation directs attention to the impact of the food-first principle on commodity production in these partially monetized systems. Food cultivation seriously affected export production, although, as usual, the impact varied with time and place. Under weak or indirect forms of state intervention, villagers often enjoyed partial autonomy and devoted more of their resources to food production at the expense of cash cropping.

The triumph and failure of the food-first principle provides one explanation for the ups and downs of the cash-crop economy. The key actors in this dynamic were women. In Malawi's cotton-growing areas, women have consistently acted and portrayed themselves as the defenders of the food economy against the dictates of their husbands and the state. As Elizabeth Anthuachino and her friends eloquently told this researcher in 1996:

> Yes, there are usually intense fights, sir; people fight as they prepare their fields. A wife would say, asking the husband, telling him that we should start planting sorghum, because we want to start eating sorghum early. But the husband would not agree, saying he wants to start with the cotton fields. He would say, "look at what others are doing," and that is when [the wife would say], let's split, you go to the cotton field, and I go to take care of the sorghum; the two would go to different fields, without reaching an agreement.

The resulting separation represented a historic development in the context of Malawi's traditional systems of food production.

The Janus Face of the Food Economy. Though women played essential roles in food production, they did not carry the entire burden alone. They shared with men in varying degrees the labor that went into food cultivation. Aka and Bambuti women of the CAR and DRC, for example, collected roots and fruits while their men hunted. Among settled agriculturalists, the division of labor tended to be task specific. Though in some regions of the DRC men did not return to their cassava fields after clearing the bush, in Malawi men planted, weeded, and harvested cereals alongside their women. Both women and men supported in varying degrees the great agricultural transformations of the twentieth century, as when they adopted new crops and abandoned old cereals. Finally, women also exercised considerable latitude in decisions regarding the sharing of stored food with neighbors and visitors. For all practical purposes, one can say that although never irrelevant, gender did not always predict an individual's task in food production. Gender-based struggles would, however, assume critical historical significance in provisioning.

Provisioning was an all-female domain everywhere in precolonial and colonial Central Africa. Women alone ground, pounded, and turned grain and tubers into flour, and they alone prepared the daily meal. After a couple worked together in the field, it was not uncommon that the husband would rest while the wife began her second job in food processing. Nor was this the whole story. In some societies women were also expected to reserve for the men the better components of the daily meal, particularly the scarcer but protein-delivering relish, stew, or side dish. Provisioning defined gender difference in a radical way.

Although critically important in organizing women's daily lives, provisioning has not received enough attention from historians of Africa. The oversight is partly because of the absence of sources on the subject, but it is mainly because of history's focus on events or on periods marked by singular features. By training, historians cannot easily deal with routines. It is hard to pinpoint turning moments in these repetitive processes, and daily routines assume the aura of a natural order. Even the enlightened leaders of the Frente de Libertaçao de Moçambique (FRELIMO; Mozambique Liberation Front), who aggressively tried to integrate women as the equals of men in the public sphere, moved hesitantly to desexualize homemaking. And the rising group of "modern" women—female professionals and wives of the bourgeoisie—has not helped this desexualizing process, either. These women have saved themselves from the grind of household labor, but not by encouraging their husbands' participation in the drudgery. Rather, they have bought their freedom by employing poor men and especially women as their substitutes, against the backdrop of new differentiation among women. As in many other parts of the globe, in Africa provisioning seems to be impervious to change.

The author's research on colonial Malawi suggests that, notwithstanding its appearances, provisioning is a social construct subject to historical change for at least three reasons. First, the regime's conditions of reproduction have not remained the same. As has been seen, key institutions that once introduced young women formally to the skills of homemaking disappeared in some places and became less effective in others during the colonial era. Furthermore, oppressive systems of provisioning foment internal dissent, creating potential rebels ready to avail themselves of every opportunity for freedom. In that way the otherwise tradition-respecting rural women in Malawi responded with great enthusiasm to the introduction of motorized grinding mills. They flocked to the machines in large numbers and, by making their husbands pay for the service, indirectly forced men to make a contribution to food processing. Finally, the quotidian chores of food processing, cooking, and eating do not lie outside history. They form essential building blocks of linear time, and without them, the better-researched transitions in agriculture, economics, and politics come into view with manifold errors and distortions.

[*See also* African Liberation and Nationalist Movements; Agriculture; Imperialism and Colonialism, *subentry* Modern Period; Missionaries; Mulenge, Alice Lenshina; *and* Nationalism.]

BIBLIOGRAPHY

Chauncey, George, Jr. "The Locus of Reproduction: Women's Labour in the Zambian Copperbelt, 1927–1953." *Journal of Southern African Studies* 7, no. 2 (April 1981): 135–164.

Coquery-Vidrovitch, Catherine. *African Women: A Modern History*. Translated by Beth Gillian Raps. Boulder, Colo.: Westview Press, 1997. English translation of *Les Africaines: Histoire des femmes d'Afrique noire du XIXe au XXe siècle*, first published in 1994.

Geiger, Susan. *TANU Women: Gender and Culture in the Making of Tanganyikan Nationalism, 1955–1965*. Portsmouth, N.H.: Heinemann; Oxford: Currey; Nairobi, Kenya: E.A.E.P.; Dar es Salaam, Tanzania: Mkuki Na Nyota, 1997.

Hewlett, Barry S. *Intimate Fathers: The Nature and Context of Aka Pygmy Paternal Infant Care*. Ann Arbor: University of Michigan Press, 1991.

Likaka, Osumaka. *Rural Society and Cotton in Colonial Zaire*. Madison: University of Wisconsin Press, 1997.

Mandala, Elias C. *The End of Chidyerano: A History of Food and Everyday Life in Malawi, 1860–2004*. Portsmouth, N.H.: Heinemann, 2005.

Richards, Audrey. "Some Types of Family Structure amongst the Central Bantu." In *African Systems of Kinship and Marriage*, edited by A. R. Radcliffe-Brown and Daryll Forde, pp. 207–251. London and New York: Oxford University Press, 1951.

Urdang, Stephanie. *And Still They Dance: Women, War, and the Struggle for Change in Mozambique*. New York: Monthly Review Press, 1989.

Wright, Marcia. "Technology, Marriage, and Women's Work in the History of Maize-Growers in Mazabuka, Zambia: A Reconnaissance." *Journal of Southern African Studies* 10, no. 1 (October 1983): 71–85.

ELIAS MANDALA

CENTRAL AMERICAN COUNTRIES. The countries of Central America gained independence from Spain in 1821 (comprising the modern-day nations of Guatemala, Honduras, El Salvador, Nicaragua, and Costa Rica). Later Panama became independent from Colombia in 1903, and the former colony of Belize from Great Britain in 1981.

Despite political and military instability, during the nineteenth century agricultural exports increased, particularly coffee production and exports in Costa Rica by the 1830s, El Salvador by the 1850s, and Guatemala by the 1860s. The expansion of coffee production transformed land patterns, labor relations and markets, and business and financial organizations. Family labor, and women in particular, increasingly participated in diverse types of tasks related to coffee production, such as gathering, cleaning, and selecting coffee; making carrying crafts for coffee; and other supplementary activities.

Though there were intense fights against land privatization during the nineteenth century, it implied in most of the cases the expropriation of communal proprietors and small and medium producers—most of them from Indian origin—and the formation of great *latifundios*, mainly in Guatemala, El Salvador, Honduras, Nicaragua, and, to a lesser degree, Costa Rica. Consequently, Indian population, and women in particular, were the great losers of this process of land privatization and concentration.

Along with this development of agricultural export production based on coffee, cattle and sugar production also had important roles in the economies of Nicaragua and Honduras. Besides since late nineteenth century in Costa Rica, Honduras, and Nicaragua, banana export production was mainly controlled by transnational corporations such as United Fruit Company and Chiquita Brands. In addition, cities emerged in which an urban culture and semi-industrial economy developed. The expansion of the modern state since the mid-nineteenth century created bureaucratic apparatuses (justice, education, health, police, and military).

Although most women worked in rural areas, they increased their incorporation in the urban labor market, mostly in the service sector, retail stores, and domestic industries of beverages, cigars, and textiles. Women from middle and popular sectors had the possibility to access education and training in occupations "proper for their sex," such as telegrapher, telephone operator, typist, typographer, nursery worker, and teacher (these being some of the few professions acceptable for women). Other important changes were introduced with liberal reforms, but in Guatemala, El Salvador, Honduras, and Nicaragua their implementation was delayed because of great political and military instability until the 1870s and 1880s, except in the case of Costa Rica, which was able to consolidate reforms early, gradually, and successfully during the nineteenth and early twentieth centuries.

Nineteenth-Century Reforms. Liberal reforms significantly modified women's rights and conditions. Despite progressive changes toward women's equality before the law, however, conditions of inequality in women's real rights continued, expressed in legal practices and procedures and in usage and customs. But four crucial changes in women's rights are notable from this period: 1) promotion of access to education; 2) introduction of civil marriage, separation, and divorce; 3) elimination of husband's authority; and 4) the right of married women to exercise paternal authority.

Women's right to education was eventually widened with the intent of schooling women to play their role as mothers and wives and preparing them to join the labor force in the occupations mentioned before. But contrary to common belief, success in reducing literacy gaps was greater by gender than by geographic location, mainly in the case of urban women, and less so for farm and Indian women in rural areas. On the other hand, in comparison to Nicaragua and El Salvador, the more successful early advances in education in Costa Rica made it possible to increase and level the rates of literacy by gender and region as of 1906–1915. In Costa Rica, the literacy gender gap reduced in the cities from 10.1 to 1.4 percent, and in rural areas from 15.3 to 0.6 percent, between born dates of 1885 and before and born dates as of 1906–1915. Also, in Nicaragua the literacy gender gap reduced in the cities from 2.6 to 2.0 percent, and in the rural areas from 10.6 to 1.5 percent. El Salvador had almost the same tendencies as Nicaragua, and the most important advance in literacy rates was between 1916 and 1930, but literacy rates remained stagnant after this period.

There were some unsuccessful attempts in Guatemala to enact civil marriage and divorce in 1837–1840, while in El Salvador civil divorce was enacted in 1880–1881. However, except for Panama (1917), the Central American countries were the first to effect civil binding divorce in Latin America: Costa Rica in 1888; Guatemala, El Salvador, and Nicaragua in 1894; and Honduras in 1898. Nonetheless, in Latin America, Costa Rica was the first country to successfully consolidate the reform to civil binding divorce in 1888, and Guatemala was the first one to decree civil marriage by mutual consent in 1894.

At the same time, the rights of married women were legally strengthened by the introduction of a reform that recognized their juridical capabilities to freely administer, acquire, give, sell, mortgage, and inherit their possessions and to appear in a trial without a husband's consent. This reform was first approved in Costa Rica (1888), and then in El Salvador (1902), Nicaragua (1904), Honduras (1906), Panama (1914), and Guatemala (1926).

The Twentieth Century. The debate over civil and political rights for women that began in the late nineteenth century in Central America was characterized by the implementation of social policies strengthening the "social and scientific maternity" model, which paved the way for greater access to education for women. The women's organizations that emerged during this period were mainly philanthropic. After 1920, however, women's organizations increased in number and the suffragist movement began in earnest within a framework of growing sociopolitical effervescence, including the formation of workers organizations and movements and the struggles to overthrow dictatorships.

However, after the overthrow of the Guatemalan dictator Manuel Estrada Cabrera (8 April 1920) and the coup d'état of Carlos Herrera Luna (6 December 1921), there was an unsuccessful attempt to reintroduce the Central American Federation (1824–1839), which was supported in 1920–1921 by Guatemala, El Salvador, and Honduras, but Costa Rica and Nicaragua rejected it. The Political Constitution of the Central American Federation (9 September 1921) introduced for the first time ever the failed reforms of feminine suffrage for married women and widows over 21 years old and spinsters over 25 years old who were literate and owners of proper rents as indicated in electoral law, and women having access to public posts, but not to popular elected posts.

After the overthrow of C. Herrera Luna in 1921, women lost their possibility to vote. Nevertheless, Guatemalan women's organizations increased by the 1920s, among the best known were the Gabriela Mistral Society (1925), the Guatemalan Feminine Pro-Citizenship Union (1945, headed by the nation's first female lawyer, Graciela Quan), the chapter of the International Democratic Federation of Women (1945), the Guatemalan Feminine Alliance (1951), the Feminine Anti-Communist Central (1952), and the Civic Alliance of Feminine Associations (1960).

Women played an active role in demonstrations that succeeded in overthrowing the dictatorship of Jorge Ubico on 1 July 1944, ending an authoritarian presidency that had begun in 1931. That was the beginning of a new and, unfortunately, brief democratic period in Guatemala under the revolutionary governments of Juan José Arévalo (1945–1951) and then Coronel Jacobo Árbenz (1951–1954). Early in 1945, the revolutionary government approved suffrage for literate women. It was not until 1965 that Guatemalan women achieved the universal right to vote, which made Guatemala the last country in Latin America to approve that reform.

In El Salvador, Prudencia Ayala was a principal feminist leader of the 1920s and 1930s. She declared herself presidential candidate for the Great Feminist Salvadoran Party and founded the newspapers *Feminine Redemption* and the *Tecleño Feminine Circle.* An important role was also played by the Democratic Feminine Front with its newspaper *Democratic Woman* (headed by Matilde Elena López), the Association of Democratic Women of El Salvador with the publication of *the Feminist Tribune* (1945, directed by Rosa Amelia Guzmán and Ana Rosa Ochoa), and the Salvadoran Feminine League (1947) with its publication of the *Feminine Herald* (1948, headed by Ana Rosa Ochoa). During the 1940s, Salvadoran women participated intensively in newspapers' debates, in demonstrations, and, in 1944, the overthrow of the dictator Maximiliano Hernández Martínez (who had been in power since 1931). After the fall of Hernández Martínez, Salvadoran women successfully pressed for elimination of the constitutional literacy restrictions to universal suffrage that denied the vote to 80 percent of women.

In Honduras, the most influential organization was the Society of Feminine Culture (1927, headed by Visitación Padilla). Honduran women played a vital role in the movements to overthrow the dictatorship of Tiburcio Carías (1933–1948) and in subsequent efforts to build a democratic regime. In this brief period of "imposed peace" during the 1940s, calls for woman suffrage increased, although previously feminists had opposed it, because they believed that political repression can put at risk social and family stability, and women's priority was to fight for building a democratic regime rather than the female vote. Finally, universal suffrage was decreed in November 1955 and ratified in the Constitution of 1957.

In Nicaragua, the Liberal Party controlled by the Somoza family stayed in power for more than forty years (1937–1979), in great measure because of the support it received from the women's and feminist movements. The Liberal Party used different strategies to attract women's participation and support, such as declarations in favor of giving women the vote in 1916 and 1944, the founding of the Feminine Wing of the Liberal Party (1936), and inviting the active participation of women speakers such as Josefa Toledo de Aguerri, Antonia Rodríguez, and Nicolasa Sevilla in political campaigns.

Josefa Toledo, a teacher and leader of the Nicaraguan feminist movement and later a leader of the Feminine Wing of the Liberal Party, presented the first proposal for women's suffrage to the congress in 1939. The Constitution of 1950 granted women's suffrage, but political turmoil meant that politicians would not authorize women to exercise it until 1964. In the face of this situation, women organized, and they gained the right to exercise suffrage in 1957. The Liberal Party deliberately removed all mention of feminists from its propaganda and created the Feminine Wing of the Liberal Party in 1955, which replaced and appropriated independent women's organizations and gave the party greater control over women voters—whose cooperation helped the Liberal Party to carry the elections in 1957, 1963, 1967, and 1974. Olga Núñez de Saballos led the electoral campaigns and mobilization of women for the party.

Costa Rica and Panama shared the experience of having early evolutions of feminist and suffragist movements. In Costa Rica, the first women's group was the Ladies of Saint Vincent de Paul, a Catholic charitable organization founded in 1878. Other philanthropic and activist organizations flourished before 1930. Among them were the Vicentine Ladies, who supported philanthropic activities such as the creation of hospices for orphans (1887–1912); the Women's Committees of Anti-Alcoholic Propaganda (1912); and the Anti-Venereal League (1922).

The campaign for feminine suffrage in Costa Rica was influenced by the electoral reforms of 1913, 1925, 1927, and 1946. The political crisis that began with Federico Tinoco's coup d'état in 1917 led to women's active participation in overthrowing Tinoco's dictatorship in 1919 and launched the discussion of women's suffrage before the congress. The development of the workers' movement in the early twentieth century and the foundation of the Reformist Party in 1923 were likewise events that stimulated greater participation of women in political struggles. The Feminist League, founded in 1923 and serving as a chapter of the International League of Iberian and Hispanic-American Women, held suffrage campaigns between 1925 and 1947 and maintained strong relations with other international feminist and suffragist movements. At its head was Costa Rica's first woman lawyer, Ángela Acuña Braun, who had gone to high school in England and had witnessed feminist development in England and the United States.

The League lacked strong support from women but had the endorsement of important politicians and intellectuals. In Costa Rica's polarized sociopolitical atmosphere of the 1940s, the League joined efforts with those of other women who demanded equal and electoral rights, such as the Women's Union of the Town (founded in 1947). A constitutional amendment of 20 July 1949 granted universal women's suffrage. A new era began with the formation of grassroots movements such as the Women's Organization Carmen Lyra (1949), which in 1952 became the Alliance of Costa Rican Women and which from its beginnings has been allied with the communist Popular Vanguard Party (banned from participating in elections from 1949 to 1975).

Panama existed after independence as part of Colombia, until breaking away (with U.S. help) to become an autonomous republic in 1903. The United States continued

Panama. Mireya Moscoso of the Arnulfista Party raises her hands in triumph after being elected Panama's first woman president in May 1999. REUTERS

to maintain a strong influence on the country because of its control of the Canal Zone, granted by Panama in exchange for U.S. investment to complete the canal, which was formally opened in 1914. In spite of periods of political repression, Panamanian women had greater access to education earlier than women in other Central American countries, and they participated actively in defending their civil and political rights and founding a variety of organizations. Among the first women's organizations in Panama was the Federation of Women's Clubs of the Canal, founded in 1907 and supported by the General Federation of Feminine Clubs (headquartered in New York City). The federation in Panama grew to include 58 organizations by 1913, with a total of approximately 695 affiliated women.

Under U.S. influence, debates over the role of feminism gained great weight in Panama during the 1920s and 1930s. The Feminist Group Renovation (FGR) was founded in 1922 under the direction of Panama's first woman lawyer, Clara González, and was tied with the school-workshops project created by Julia Palau in that same year for the education of working-class girls. The FGR became the Feminist National Party in 1923, the first feminist party in Central America, with strong ties to international and U.S. feminist and suffragist movements. Also in 1923, the educator Esther Neira de Calvo founded the National Society for the Progress of Women, an organization that opposed women's suffrage and had support from conservative politicians.

Universal women's suffrage was ratified in Panama's Constitution of 1946, making it the first Central American country to grant women the vote. Two reforms allowed Panamanian women voting and electoral rights previous to the constitutional ratification of women's suffrage: the Constitution of 1941 authorized municipal suffrage limited to literate women, and Decree No. 12, of 2 February 1945, called voters to the election of a National Assembly and allowed both women and men to vote and to present their candidacies as legislators. Two women—Esther Neira de Calvo and Gumersinda Páez—were elected to the National Assembly in 1945, and they were reelected for the New Legislative Assembly of 1946–1948.

Assessment. Central American women formally achieved full citizenship or the universal right to vote in the following order: 1) Panama (1945/1946); 2) Costa Rica (1949); 3) El Salvador (1950); 4) Nicaragua (1950); 5) Honduras (1955/1957); and 6) Guatemala (1965). Nevertheless, at the beginning of the twenty-first century, women in these nations are still not able fully to exercise their political citizenship. They continue to be discriminated against in the processes of selection and election to positions of power. With the exception of Costa Rica and Panama, Central American countries continue to have problems with voter registration and electoral fraud, problems that most greatly effect illiterate, indigenous, and low-income populations, particularly women.

Conversely, according to the report by UNIFEM (2003), women have increased participation and access to power in Costa Rica (46.1 percent), Panama (28 percent), Honduras (23.5 percent), and El Salvador (18.4 percent), but they also diminished in Nicaragua (27.6–25.4 percent) and Guatemala (22.8–17.3 percent). Reforms of electoral quotas for women have also had an important impact in Costa Rica (1996, 40 percent), Panama (1997, 30 percent), and Honduras (2000, 30 percent). The 2007 *Global Database of Quotas for Women* reports the following ranking of congresswomen representation: Costa Rica (38.6 percent), Honduras (23.4 percent), Panama (16.7 percent), El Salvador (16.7 percent), Nicaragua (15.2 percent), and Guatemala (8.9 percent). The top three countries in the world of congresswomen representation are Rwanda (48.8 percent), Sweden (47.3 percent), and Costa Rica (38.6 percent). Finally, it is important to mention that two women presidents were elected: Violeta Barrios de Chamorro (b. 1929) as president of Nicaragua between 1990 and 1996, and Mireya E. Moscoso (b. 1946) as president of Panama between 1999 and 2004.

Central American countries—again excepting Costa Rica and Panama—have been deeply affected by political turmoil and periods of dictatorship. In the wake of such circumstances, women lag behind in education and literacy, especially in heavily indigenous countries such as Guatemala. According to the 2003 report by UNIFEM and data by UNESCO, the rate of universal literacy of women between 15 and 24 years old in 2003 was as follows: Guatemala (around 74 percent), El Salvador (around 88 percent), Nicaragua (around 89 percent), Honduras (around 91 percent), Panama (around 97 percent), and Costa Rica (around 99 percent).

Women throughout Central America are underrepresented in the formal labor market and in professions requiring higher education. Women congregate in the service sector of the economy, with domestic service being the predominant form of employment for poor and indigenous women. Self-employed women are often street vendors. In the 1990s, however, the number of women employed as urban professionals, technicians, and trade employees expanded significantly. Panama and Costa Rica have the largest percentage of women working as professionals and technicians.

In El Salvador, Guatemala, and Honduras, by contrast, a history of dictatorships, military domination, and internal civil wars has left vast numbers of women in poverty and affected their lives in other ways, subjecting them to loss of life or a virtual absence of human rights. Maternal mortality in these three countries is over 20 per 1,000.

[*See also* Civil War, *subentry* Central America; Codes of Law and Laws, *subentry* Latin America; Feminist Encounters of Latin American and Caribbean Women; First Feminine Congress of the Pan-American League; Guatemala; Indigenous Cultures; Inter-American Commission of Women; International League of Iberian and Hispanic-American Women; *and* Pan American Conference of Women of 1922.]

BIBLIOGRAPHY

Chinchilla, Norma Stoltz. "Feminism, Revolution, and Democratic Transitions in Nicaragua." In *The Women's Movement in Latin America: Participation and Democracy*, 2d ed., edited by Jane S. Jaquette, pp. 177–196. Boulder, Colo.: Westview Press, 1994.

González, Victoria. "From Feminism to *Somocismo*: Women's Rights and Right Wing Politics in Nicaragua, 1821–1979." PhD diss., Indiana University, 2002.

González, Victoria. "Josefa Toledo de Aguerri (1866–1962) and the Forgotten History of Nicaraguan Feminism, 1821–1955." MA thesis, University of New Mexico, 1996.

González, Victoria. "Somocista Women, Right-Wing Politics and Feminism in Nicaragua, 1936–1979." In *Radical Women in Latin America. Left and Right*, edited by Victoria González and Karin Kampwirth, pp. 41–78. University Park: Pennsylvania State University Press, 2001.

Marco, Yolanda. "El movimiento sufragista en Panamá y la construcción de la mujer moderna." In *Historia de los movimientos de mujeres en Panamá en el siglo XX*, edited by Fernando Aparicio, Yolanda Marco, Miriam Miranda, and Josefina Zurita, pp. 45–132. Panama City: Instituto de la Mujer de la Universidad de Panamá, 2002.

Mérida, Alba Cecilia. "Mujer y Ciudadanía: Un Análisis desde la Antropología de Género." Licenciatura thesis, Universidad de San Carlos de Guatemala, 2000.

Molina, Iván. "La Alfabetización Popular en El Salvador, Nicaragua y Costa Rica (1885–1950)." In *La Estela de la Pluma. Cultura Impresa e Intelectuales en Centroamérica Durante los Siglos XIX y XX*, by Iván Molina, pp. 61–131. Heredia: EUNA, 2004.

Monzón, Ana Silvia. *Rasgos históricos de la exclusión de las mujeres en Guatemala*. Guatemala City: Sistema de Naciones Unidas, 2001.

Navas, María Candelaria, and Liza María Domínguez. "Las organizaciones de mujeres en El Salvador y sus aportes a la historia sociopolítica (1957–1999)." In *Mujeres, gênero e historia en América Central durante los siglos XVIII, XIX, y XX*, edited by Eugenia Rodríguez, pp. 135–144. San José, Costa Rica: UNIFEM, Plumsock Mesoamerican Studies, 2002.

Rodríguez, Eugenia. "La lucha por el sufragio femenino en Costa Rica (1890–1949)." In *Un siglo de luchas femeninas en América Latina*, edited by Eugenia Rodríguez, pp. 87–110. San José, Costa Rica: Editorial Universidad de Costa Rica, 2002.

Rodríguez, Eugenia. "Movimientos de mujeres y feministas en América Central (1890–1965)." In *Historia de las mujeres en España y América Latina*, vol. 4, edited by Isabel Morant, pp. 553–575. Madrid: Ediciones Cátedra, 2005.

Rodríguez de Ita, Guadalupe. "Participación política de las mujeres en la primavera democrática guatemalteca (1944–1954)." *Diálogos Revista Electrónica de Historia* 5, nos. 1–2 (March–August 2004). Special issue, "Historia, política, literatura y relaciones de género en América Central y México (siglos XVIII, XIX y XX)." Edited by Eugenia Rodríguez.

EUGENIA RODRÍGUEZ-SÁENZ

CENTRAL ASIA

This entry consists of two subentries:

Ancient Period
Modern Period

Ancient Period

Ancient Central Asia encompasses the loosely defined steppes (plains) from west of the Caspian Sea eastward to include modern Kazakstan, Kyrgyzstan, Uzbekistan, Tadjikstan, and Turkmenistan. Because of the lack of major geographical confines, southern Russia and Ukraine have at times been an extension of Central Asia. Before modern boundaries were established, western China's Xinjiang Province, known as Turkistan, was also culturally and economically integral to Central Asia. Northern Afghanistan, known as ancient Bactria, served as a fulcrum between Central Asia proper and cultures in Iran to the west. Siberia, in north Central Asia, is largely in Russia. It extends from the Ural Mountains to the Pacific Ocean and from the Arctic Ocean to central Kazakstan and the boundaries of China and Mongolia.

During the Paleolithic (Old Stone Age) and Mesolithic (Middle Stone Age) periods, hunting, fishing, and gathering populations living in small groups who occupied the lands adjacent to the great rivers and their tributaries in Central Asia and southern Siberia. In addition to food gathering and food preparation, the productive labors of women during childbearing years, such as spinning, weaving, sewing, making lithic (stone) tools, and producing pottery, were jobs compatible with child-rearing. Those not with children were seminal to food gathering and production, and in some contexts they also hunted. With each climatic change, migrating populations brought innovations into Central Asia that are reflected in the archaeology, although it is not possible to single out specific women or to do more than generalize on their important roles in society during these long epochs. It is important, however, to understand in broad strokes the development of civilizations in order to view women's activities within the societies.

From hunting and gathering, societies banded together to build small villages that were supported by primitive agriculture and rudimentary animal husbandry. These developed into larger cultural centers, primarily in oases and along rivers and their deltas. The Neolithic (New Stone Age) Revolution saw the rise of larger cultural centers and the further dissemination of new ideas. The transitional periods in Central Asia and Siberia do not conform to those of the Near East and the Mediterranean, where urbanization took hold and technologies developed, or to those of Europe, where these concepts spread.

During the Bronze Age some urbanization and metallurgical developments occurred east of the Ural Mountains. Archaeological research reveals that a severe drought throughout the central steppe from the Don River east through the southern Ural steppes caused populations to withdraw, probably to the south, for about two hundred years (1000–800 B.C.E.). Kurgans (burial mounds) began to reappear in the steppes at the beginning of the Early Iron Age, indicating that, for the most part, the essentially sedentary people returned to the steppes only to begin to exchange their agricultural economy for that of nomadism. In the steppes nomadism involved trailing increasingly larger herds of sheep, goats, horses, and camels farther out into the steppes to follow green pastures in a northerly then southerly direction during eight to ten months of the year. They returned, however, to sheltered homes along riverbanks during the coldest winter months. In the Altai Mountains of southern Siberia and western Mongolia and the Tian Shan of southern Kazakstan and western China, nomads practiced migration in a much smaller sphere, sheltering during winter below great stone outcroppings that radiated solar heat.

Although Greek and Achaemenid Persian historians have provided meager information about Central Asian nomadic cultures, little was recorded about Siberia until nineteenth-century ethnographers penetrated the region. Thus in the latter region the role of women is primarily deduced from indirect sources associated with archaeology. As an example, impressing woven fabric into damp clay produced negative designs on pottery. The woven textile, in this case fishnet, the technique, and perhaps other industries, such as fishing, are revealed. Petroglyphs (images cut or pecked in stone), pictographs (images painted on stone), and a plethora of burial artifacts reveal social and economic statuses as well as religious and cultic activities. Among the more static populations, ethnographic and mythological studies are tools that also provide glimpses into this hazy past.

Paleolithic and Mesolithic Periods in Central Asia. Systematic and durable colonization by Neanderthals of most of the benign ecological regions of Central Asia encompassing Uzbekistan, the Caucasus, and the Crimea began after the inception of the last ice age, c. 120,000 B.P. (before present). A second population wave of thin and sporadic settlements was noted after 65,000 B.P. The Neanderthals were primarily big game scavengers, and their social structure suggests that bands were made up of parental groups consisting of the mother and one or more children and subsistent groups from which to draw mating partners. Some Neanderthal burials indicate a limited ritual life. Artifacts from between 100,000 and 40,000 B.P. from Teshik-Tash in Uzbekistan indicate a similarity to those from the Near East, especially Palestine.

Ancient Central Asian Sculpture. A female figurine with a circle-dot motif along the hip and thigh and a triangle indicating the pudenda, Yalangach-depe, Turkmenistan, Namazga II period, c. 4000 B.C.E. COURTESY OF JEANNINE DAVIS-KIMBALL

In southern Siberia, however, because of the ice barrier, the more than twenty-eight Paleolithic sites located primarily along rivers are dated much later than those in Uzbekistan and the Caucasus. In unforested Siberian regions, scavenged mammoth, rhinoceros, and deer bones formed the structures of subterranean houses. A carved statuette dated c. 25,000 B.P. displays Arctic clothing similar to that used by Inuit (Eskimos) in the early twenty-first century. These waterproof protective garments are known to be the handiwork of women. Olga Sofer's research dating to c. 20,000 B.P. in southern Russia reveals mammoth-bone dwellings about 80 square meters (861 square feet) in size that housed up to ten people. No doubt at least partially the work of women, some structures had carefully prepared hearths as well as bone and ivory ornaments.

Paleolithic and Mesolithic Periods in Siberia. Beginning in the Paleolithic period and continuing through time, petroglyphs illustrated women's rituals, portable tentlike housing, and large deer. Only the female line was recognized; ancestry was established through the maternal side, and a man entered the woman's clan. Siberian tribal kinships developed from group mating. Matriclans were created, and women had charge of the clan's domestic economy. They were the collective labor required to stalk and scavenge large animals, hunt fowl, and gather edibles. Women were also responsible for artistic creativity: sewing, weaving, and decorative methods. Their position was reflected in artifacts, superhuman females who were mistresses of natural phenomena. Representations of the spirits as well as human females were carved from bone, ivory, and serpentine.

At this time there appeared small corpulent female figurines, known as Venus figures, that were crafted with special emphasis on sexual attributes implying fertility. Other female figurines represented ancestors and deities. Drawing upon ethnography, three female Siberian deities are described as Pinga, the spirit of the earth; Hilla, the spirit of the air; and Sedna, the sovereign spirit, mistress of the sea and all its inhabitants. Ayysyt, a female Yakut deity who seems to have originated during the matriclan era, is the goddess of childbirth. Men could not be present during her postpartum rituals, which included a sympathetic magic ritual in which a young girl shot an arrow into the image of a deer, a ritual animal that has long endured in Siberia and on the steppes.

Siberian female shamans were known by a single term, *udagan*, indicating that their roots were in Paleolithic Siberia (male shamans had many different names throughout Siberia). Special female shaman rituals to augment animal fertility and hunting in which the entire family was involved lasted many days. A second part of the ritual was performed before the matrilineal clan deity. The economy, lifestyle, rituals, and cultic and religious beliefs of Paleolithic Siberians were a circumpolar tradition that extended throughout northern Canada and Alaska.

Mesolithic Period in Central Asia. Mesolithic populations engaged in fishing, hunting, and gathering lived around the Caspian Sea shores, along the now dry Uzboi River southwest of the Caspian, and in caves to the east. Caves and open sites have been excavated in the Fergana Valley (Uzbekistan and adjoining areas) and in campsites in the eastern Pamirs. Goats and sheep were domesticated, but desert conditions impeded agricultural development. Several sites in the heart of Central Asia—Tajikistan, Turkmenistan, and Uzbekistan—dating from 30,000 to 40,000 B.P. reveal deliberate burials, indicating a belief in the afterlife. From a comparative analysis of caries in teeth, it appears that the population increased grain consumption.

It can be deduced from this information that women milked the sheep, making cheeses for consumption immediately and later in the year, and that those not giving birth or caring for infants gathered wild edibles.

Neolithic Period in Central Asia. During the Neolithic Revolution, in addition to pastoralism, agriculture developed c. 6000 B.C.E. as a second economic base in the southern Turkmenistan Djeitun culture. Houses were constructed of daubed and painted clay brick and averaged 20 to 30 square meters (215 to 323 square feet), each large enough for a single nuclear family. The women's domain of this egalitarian society, revealed by the similarity of houses throughout the cultural region, included rooms with large rectangular hearths, storage pits, and floors painted red or black. Each family separately performed domestic activities, for example, processing skins, woodworking, and preparing food. A painted pottery tradition developed for storage vessels, and modeled animal figurines were often pierced, indicating ritual practices. Without specialized trades, women were charged not only with domestic tasks but also with pottery production and leather working. It is estimated that three workers from each family were needed to harvest sufficient grain for each season, requiring women to assist in agriculture as well as in certain aspects of animal husbandry. Religious issues and sympathetic magic were yet another part of their domain.

Toward the end of the sixth millennium, agriculture spread to the wooded steppes north of the Black Sea, to the Ukraine, to the north Caucasus, and ultimately into Central Asia. Beginning c. 4000 B.C.E. in southern Turkmenistan, animal husbandry, now including large cattle, led to permanent settlements. Houses contained many rooms. In Djeitun and the Namazga I settlement, artists painted pottery with new motifs, revealing artistic achievement. The majority of the archaeological finds from these sites are baked clay spindle whorls and pottery, both belonging to the traditionally assigned women's work.

Agricultural development in southern Turkmenistan was comparable to that of Jarmo and Tepe Guran in the Iranian Zagros Mountains and Al Ubaid in southern Mesopotamia. Population growth indicated migrations, and surplus commodities stimulated long-distance exchange with the Near East, where similarities exist with pre-pottery Jericho in the Levant. During the Djeitun period later Neolithic cultural changes were similar to those in the Teheran Oasis and Sialk in northern Iran.

By 4000 B.C.E. the Cucuteni-Tripolye culture, with its distinctively large and prolific painted pottery, had developed in Romania (Cucuteni) and throughout the Ukraine (Tripolye). This was an egalitarian society with many tiny villages (the village moved when the soil was depleted for farming) as well as cities with up to two thousand houses. Cultic ceremonies in which women are depicted dancing are among the motifs on the pottery; the majority of the clay figurines probably devoted to fertility rituals are of females.

Neolithic Period in Siberia. The diffusion of the bow and arrow and the appearance of polished tools, pottery, and other inventions point to the development of two related ethnic groups, one in the Arctic and the other in southern Siberia. From Baikal to the Lena River fine lithic blades and pottery forms decorated with small mesh fishnet designs (the original net made from a fibrous plant) share commonalities. During sympathetic magic hunting rituals, the shaman sought the ancestress, who referred the shaman to a female elk, who then allowed a certain number of animals to be caught. Female elk in magical actions are the subjects of many petroglyphs. Ancient artifacts decorated with mother-of-pearl were among women's offerings at the petroglyphic sites.

The Neolithic Yakutia (Republic of Sakha) had connections with Baikal, the Far East, northeastern Asia, and possibly North America via the Bering Strait. Siberian burial rituals, featuring the veneration of elk and deer, have striking parallels with those of Karelia in northwestern Europe.

Chalcolithic Period in Central Asia. Around 4000 B.C.E. at Yassi-depe in Turkmenistan, cultic architecture was composed of a two-room shrine in the center of the village. The walls were decorated with polychrome frescoes and several wooden pillars; one room had a hearth. A collection of about one hundred female figurines from Geoksyur Oasis reveals that the emphasis was on reproductive issues. Around 2500 B.C.E. newcomers appeared, and extended families now occupied multiroom houses, some with shrines and a central hearth. Pottery painting styles became more elaborate, and female figurines with bird faces indicate the worship of anthropomorphized deities. Male statuettes occur only infrequently.

In northern Afghanistan, known as ancient Bactria, from the Paleolithic through the Neolithic period, cultural developments were similar to those of the Bactria Margiana archaeological cultures (BMAC). Animal domestication, pottery production, and increased agriculture began around 4500 B.C.E. and continued through the Bronze Age. Women's roles were essentially the same as those in the BMAC.

Bronze Age in Siberia (3000–1000 B.C.E.). Copper and bronze tools and weapons signaled the advent of the Bronze Age, in which burials also contained evidence of women's work in the form of sewing and decoration kits. These included bone and copper needles preserved in cases carved from antler, bone awls for leather punching, small chalcedony blades, and mother-of-pearl and copper decorative discs. Decorative motifs on clay vessels became more complex with applied ridges and stamped designs.

A larger mesh applied throughout the bodies of clay vessels emulated textile designs. To the east, Baikal potters developed a unique thicker-walled pottery with stamped repeat textile patterns applied around the rim.

Petroglyphic art along the middle Lena reveals representations of horned animals and horned shamanic individuals, most likely females; the latter served as intermediaries between earth and the otherworld. Shamans continued to play out tribal myths relating to elk and deer that have come down to recent times. A Siberian Tavgi tribal shaman relates: "When I came in I saw on the left two seated naked women. Both of these women had branching antlers on their heads. Both were covered with hair like reindeer." The story continues to relate that the women give birth to two fawns, one to be sacrificed for the forest people, the other for those of the steppes. The cult of theriomorphic deities (deities with animal forms) reached it highest development with the flowering of the matrilineal clan. It seems that during the Late Bronze Age the leading religious roles and the pantheon passed from women to men, and the division of labor between female sorcerers and male hunters was replaced by male shamans and male hunters. This was a radical change from the social order of the previous epoch. However, the influential roles of women were not entirely lost—they surface as warriors, priestesses, and warrior priestesses during the Early Iron Age in Central Asia.

Carved or pecked cliff drawings in Scandinavia show remarkable art forms that relate to cultures of western Siberia east to Yakutia. The most striking are scenes of cultic representations of cervids (deer, elk, and moose) executed with "skeletal" partitions.

Bronze Age in Central Asia. During the Early Bronze Age, agricultural cultures continued to develop in the BMAC and became more homogeneous. Homes contained many rooms, and the domestic quarters were equipped with storerooms containing large ceramic vessels. The ceramic industry was more varied. Of note are smaller vessels decorated with birds—probably a fertility related motif—and others with heraldic goats before a tree. The latter motif was a popular ancient Near Eastern design and is represented in the Luristan bronzes from the Zagros Mountains in western Iran. Around 1500 B.C.E. the larger BMAC sites were abandoned, and cultural decay set in.

The period from 2200 to 2000 B.C.E. marks the beginning of thriving activity in northern Afghanistan. At the site of Sapallitepa, great houses contained suites of rooms occupied by extended families. These were self-contained with bread ovens and kilns. After the area was abandoned, it became a cemetery. Female burials outnumbered those of males 3 to 2, with the wealth concentrated in the female tombs. Moreover, prestige and administrative items, such as seals, were found only in female burials. These cultural innovations separate the Bactrian culture from that of Mesopotamia; some evidence suggests that it was a Central Asian tradition that emerged again with the nomadic Iron Age. Compartmentalized "stamp seals" feature a female riding a lion, a motif that takes on significance as it migrates westward into Anatolia during the subsequent millennia. Corpulent female statuettes carved from green chlorite and white limestone do not seem to represent mythical beings; they may have represented high-ranking women. These and other artifacts relate northern Bactria to the Elamite culture in southern Iran.

From at least the Bronze Age, western China culturally belonged to Central Asia. Beginning around 2000 B.C.E. women's work par excellence was expressed in clothing and containers made from wool felt and in a great variety of exquisite textiles woven from woolen yarns. Women were buried with seeds of grain, and one had a winnowing basket placed on her chest, items that reveal the female role not only in basketry weaving but also in food production in agricultural villages. These normally unpreserved artifacts were excavated from desiccated oasis burials in the vicinity of the Taklimakan Desert in western China.

In the Tian Shan, northeast of Ürümqi, the capital of Xinjiang Province, a great petroglyph delicately carved into a limestone grotto provides the most graphic illustration of a fertility ritual dance performed during the Bronze Age. Larger-than-life-size females are the principal protagonists, while half-size males attempt copulation. The magnitude of the scene indicates it was executed over vast time, leading to the conclusion that the ritual itself endured for perhaps millennia. The stylization of the dancing females is similar to the female images painted on Cucuteni-Tripolye pottery. The dance and ritual seem to have been introduced into western China by migrants from eastern Europe.

Early Iron Age in Central Asia. Cultural ideologies, probably present in the Bronze Age, became stressed during the Iron Age, providing archaeologists with new materials for determining the statuses of nomadic women. A change in the economic status brought about by increased wealth from animal production as well as raiding and trading resulted in disposable income, which was used to acquire articles denoting status. The dynamic belief in the otherworld required that some of the wealth became mortuary relics for various tribes and confederacies known in Greek and Achaemenid Persian written sources, such as the Scythians, Sauromatians, Sarmatians, and Saka.

Between 1000 and 800 B.C.E. Central Asian agriculturists began driving their small herds farther from villages, exchanging the toil of tilling for less labor-intensive herding. Perhaps because of the preexisting tradition of female primacy as noted among the Bactrian and Siberian Bronze Age populations or perhaps because of the change in lifestyle, historical accounts and archaeological evidence reveal that

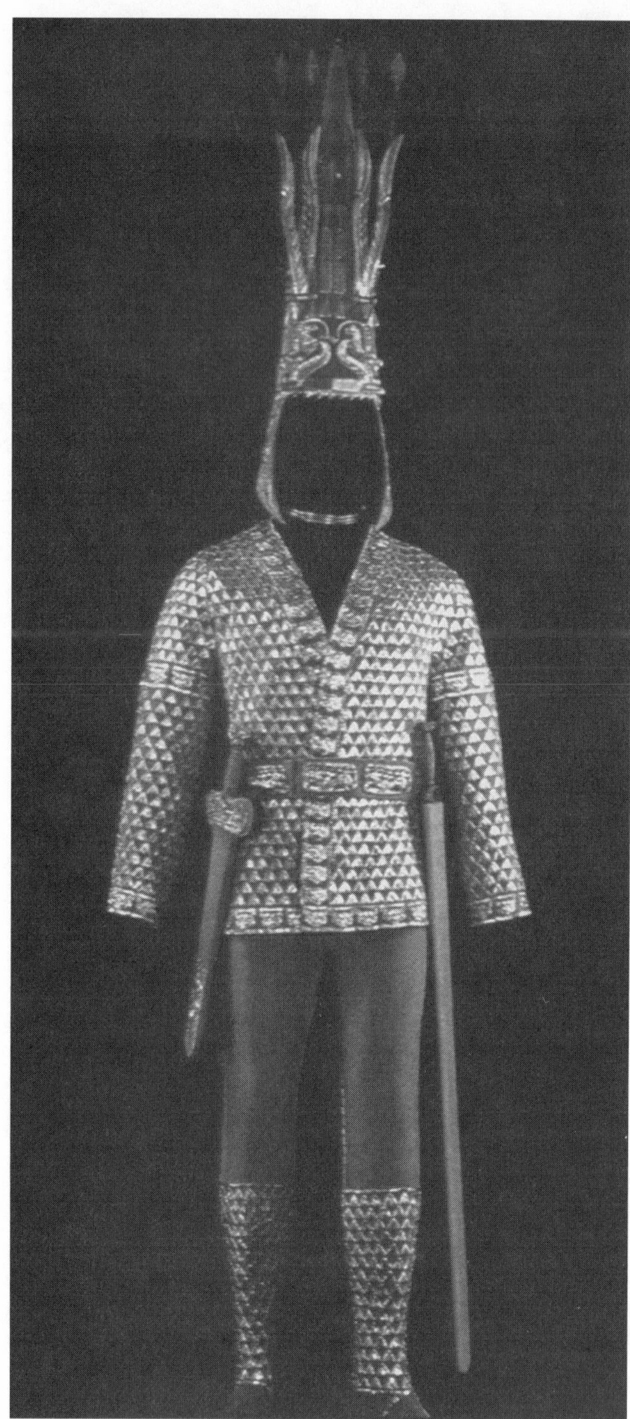

Female Warrior. A reconstruction of an Issyk warrior priestess, Kazakhstan, c. 450 B.C.E. COURTESY OF JEANNINE DAVID-KIMBALL

nomadic women retained much of the supremacy enjoyed during earlier eras. Renate Rolle has noted the wealth of Scythian women in burials. Among the Sauromatians, the earliest sixth-century B.C.E. kurgans were almost exclusively constructed for females of high status and were later reused by Sarmatian nomads (fourth to second centuries B.C.E.).

Excavations by an team of Americans and Russians of over 150 Sauromatian and Sarmatian burials at Pokrovka in the southern Urals revealed that, in addition to child-bearing, child rearing, house maintenance, and food preparation, some women were warriors, as determined by armament in their burials. Other female burials contained mirrors and cultic artifacts, revealing priestesses. A few women of exceptionally high status combined the role of warrior with that of priestess. These women's positions in the nomadic society were found throughout the Central Asian sphere. A few succinct examples reveal the geographic extent of Early Iron Age women of high status.

At Issyk in southern Kazakstan, a Saka tomb at the edge of a large (tsar) kurgan was discovered by a plowing farmer. Kemal Akishev excavations revealed that the deceased had been buried with clothing encrusted with gold and an elaborate headdress decorated with plaques relating to fertility rituals. A ceremonial gold dagger and a ceremonial sword were thought to belong to a "young warrior," but as earrings, large beads, and a silver mirror were also included for the trip to the otherworld, they reveal the physically small personage to have been a warrior priestess.

On the Ukok Plateau in southern Siberia, Natalia Polosmak excavated a frozen priestess bearing a mirror and symbols of fertility. S. I. Rudenko's excavations of the massive Pazyryk kurgans, also in southern Siberia, contained frozen burials of high-ranking personages, including females, several of whom were princesses or priestesses. Because permafrost had prevented the deterioration of organic materials in these burials, the elaborateness of the women's work in felt, woven textiles, and worked leather also reveal ritual beliefs that include fantastical griffins and masked sacrificial horses. In one burial an elaborate felt tapestry of six repeated panels depicts a priestess receiving a male dignitary who seems to be seeking her advice.

Viktor Sarianidi's spectacular excavations at Tillya Tepe in northern Afghanistan included five high-ranking females and a male belonging to the nomadic Yüeh-chih confederacy that had been driven from western China. The iconography and types of artifacts included in the twenty thousand gold objects from the burials revealed three priestesses and two warrior priestesses. The objects buried with the male were of the same types as those with the warrior priestesses, indicating that he was a warrior priest, possibly either a eunuch or a transvestite, who had assumed the intuitive attributes of the priestesses.

[*See also* History of Women; Matriarchy; *and* Shamanism.]

BIBLIOGRAPHY

Barber, Elizabeth Wayland. *The Mummies of Ürümchi*. New York: Norton, 1999.

Barber, Elizabeth Wayland. *Women's Work: The First 20,000 Years; Women, Cloth, and Society in Early Times*. New York and London: Norton, 1994.

Belenitsky, Aleksandr. *Central Asia*. Translated from the Russian by James Hogarth. Archaeologia Mundi series. Geneva: Nagel, 1968.

Christian, David. *A History of Russia, Central Asia, and Mongolia*. Vol. 1: *Inner Eurasia from Prehistory to the Mongol Empire*. Oxford and Malden, Mass.: Blackwell, 1998.

Davis-Kimball, Jeannine. "Enarees and Women of High Status: Evidence of Ritual at Tillya Tepe (Northern Afghanistan)." In *Kurgans, Ritual Sites, and Settlements: Eurasian Bronze and Iron Age*, edited by Jeannine Davis-Kimball, Eileen M. Murphy, Ludmila Koryakova, and Leonid T. Yablonsky, pp. 29–239. BAR International series, 890. Oxford: Archaeopress, 2000. Analyzes the Tillya Tepe finds, with illustrations and a chart.

Davis-Kimball, Jeannine. "Fertility Rituals: The Kangjiashimenzi Petroglyphs and the Cucuteni Dancers." In *Material, Virtual, and Temporal Compositions: On the Relationships between Objects*, edited by Dragos Gheorghiu, pp. 27–44. BAR International series, 953. Oxford: Archaeopress, 2001. Analyzes the specific details of the petroglyphs and their sources.

Davis-Kimball, Jeannine, and Leonid T. Yablonsky. *Kurgans on the Left Bank of the Ilek: Excavations at Pokrovka 1990–1992*. Berkeley, Calif.: Zinat, 1995.

Davis-Kimball. Jeannine, with Mona Behan. *Warrior Women: An Archaeologist's Search for History's Hidden Heroines*. New York: Warner Books, 2002. A new perspective on the histories of dominant women in Eurasian societies written for the general public.

Davis-Kimball, Jeannine, Vladimir A. Bashilov, and Leonid T. Yablonsky, eds. *Nomads of the Eurasian Steppes in the Early Iron Age*. Berkeley, Calif.: Zinat, 1995. Only complete coverage in English on the archaeology of Eurasian nomads from southern Europe to Mongolia.

Gero, Joan M., and Margaret W. Conkey, eds. *Engendering Archaeology: Women and Prehistory*. Oxford: Blackwell, 1991. Particularly valuable for reaccessing women's work in prehistory.

Ligabue, Giancarlo, and Sandro Salvatori, eds. *Bactria: An Ancient Oasis Civilization from the Sands of Afghanistan*. Venice: Erizzo, 1988.

Lillie, M. C. "Mesolithic and Neolithic Populations of Ukraine: Indications of Diet from Dental Pathology." *Current Anthropology* 37, no. 1 (1996): 135–142.

Masson, V. M., and V. I. Sarianidi. *Central Asia: Turkmenia before the Achaemenids*. Translated and edited with a preface by Ruth Tringham. Ancient Peoples and Places, vol. 79. London: Thames and Hudson, 1972.

Okladnikov, A. P. *Yakutia before Its Incorporation into the Russian State*. Edited by Henry N. Michael. Montreal and London: McGill–Queen's University Press, 1970. Detailed study of the Yakuts in southern Siberia.

Rolle, Renate. *The World of the Scythians*. Translated from the German by F. G. Walls. Berkeley and Los Angeles: University of California Press, 1989. English translation of *Die Welt der Skythen*, first published in 1980. Best popular work in English on the Scythians.

Sarianidi, Viktor. *The Golden Hoard of Bactria: From the Tillya-tepe Excavations in Northern Afghanistan*. New York: Abrams, 1985. Picture book and catalog of excavations.

JEANNINE DAVID-KIMBALL

Modern Period

For millennia Central Asia has contained a mix of nomadic pastoral and settled agricultural societies, with a minority of the population living in urban areas. The majority of Central Asians were and are Muslims, excepting small Jewish and Christian communities, but the boundaries of women's lives have been determined as much by their cultural lifeways as by Islamic law. Women's lives in the modern period have also changed enormously because of powerful influences from Russia, China, and, since 1992, newly independent governments.

Central Asia is bounded by the Caspian Sea and Ural Mountains to the west, northeastern Iran (Khorāsān) and northern Afghanistan to the south, the Pamirs and Tian Shan mountains to the east, and the Siberian steppe to the north. The region encompasses the five republics created by the Soviet Union (Uzbekistan, Turkmenistan, Tajikistan, Kazakhstan, and Kyrgyzstan), as well as Xinjiang Province in western China, northeastern Iran, and northern Afghanistan. The region has been inhabited by Iranian, Turkic, and Mongol peoples for more than two thousand years. The modern period began in 1500 when the Uzbek Shaybani Khan conquered the last Timurid rulers of Bukhara, Samarqand, and Herāt. Within one hundred years the relatively stable kingdoms of Bukhara and Khiva emerged under Uzbek dynastic rule; the khanate of Qŭqon claimed independence from Bukhara in the eighteenth century.

Nomadic and Settled Societies. From 1500 until well after the colonial conquests of the 1860s the major social divide was between nomadic Turkmen, Kyrgyz, and Kazakh tribes and Uzbek and Tajik farmers and town dwellers. The labor of nomadic women was vital to group survival, and they could not be encumbered by heavy robes and veils or restricted from such activities as riding horses. Keeping women in seclusion from male nonrelatives was similarly impractical. The tribes were patriarchal in structure, with the honor of the oldest male representing that of the entire group. Parents arranged marriages primarily on the basis of advantageous economic ties, giving less weight to the personal desires of their children. Marriages involved several varieties of gift exchange between the families, including *qalin* (bride-wealth), a gift

Traditional Dress. Dressed in traditional clothing and jewelry, a woman stands on a woven carpet at the entrance to a yurt, early twentieth century. PRINTS AND PHOTOGRAPHS DIVISION, LIBRARY OF CONGRESS

from the groom to compensate the bride's family for loss of labor, and/or *mahr*, given directly by the groom to the bride. One of the functions of *mahr* was economic insurance in case of divorce. A woman could request divorce, in which (rare) case the *mahr* as well as part of the *qalin* remained with her.

Gift-giving customs often meant that poor men could not afford to marry until they were in their thirties, when generally they would take a wife just past the age of puberty. Otherwise men and women were married off by the age of fifteen. The goods exchanged in this way might include the family yurt (a mobile home), livestock, household equipment, and clothing or jewelry, property that the bride could pass on to her children. Nomadic women could not inherit property from their families, even though Islamic law allowed daughters to inherit—albeit they were allowed to inherit only a smaller amount of family wealth than their brothers received. This was one of several areas in which Turkic tribal custom outweighed Islamic law. Sometimes a prospective groom and his friends would symbolically abduct a bride with whom arrangements had been made previously, and genuine bride abduction was occasionally used to settle property disputes between clans.

Nomadic women could wield power in the clan as marriage brokers or property holders or through relationships to high-status men. In a few cases foreign travelers noted the considerable political influence of clan chiefs' widows. Kazakh and Kyrgyz songs and epic poetry depicted women as strong heroes and villains, as in the epic *Forty Maidens*.

The lives of Uzbek, Tajik, and Jewish women in settled communities were determined largely by their class status and sex. Wealthy women did not need to work and lived in seclusion from public society. Polygyny was most often practiced in wealthy urban families. It was not uncommon for middle-aged men to take additional wives who were barely in their teens. Settled families of all classes also exchanged *qalin* and *mahr* upon marriage. Housing consisted of an outer courtyard and eating area and an inner living and sleeping area (the *ichkari*), to which women retreated when male guests arrived.

When women left their homes they wore the *paranji*, a large cloak, and the *chachvon*, a thick veil that completely covered the face. Jewish women also veiled in public to avoid harassment. The head-to-toe covering that so horrified Western observers in the later nineteenth century was actually part of Central Asians' response to conquest. Until the 1870s respectable urban women wore cloaks in public but left their faces open; this style of dress could still be seen in Tashkent into the early twentieth century. Lower-status urban women and preadolescent girls were less restricted. Girls could run and play uncovered in public, and female merchants traveled alone and unveiled to sell household goods to secluded wives. Even when confined to their homes, women could earn income through weaving or raising silkworms. Village women, like their nomadic counterparts, dressed modestly but practically as they worked their fields.

Few people needed a high level of literacy. Elite culture was rooted in Persian literature and music, even though most Central Asians spoke Turkic languages. Below the elite level, learning was passed on orally, with an emphasis on the ability to recite prayers and poetry from memory at the appropriate times. Girls received basic—and occasionally higher—education, although they did not study advanced Islamic law. Sex-segregated schools were the norm, but boys and girls below the age of puberty could study together in elementary schools (*maktabs*). Even though traditional learning was mostly rote memorization, some girls did achieve true literacy. A small group of elite women in nineteenth-century Qŭqon, including the khan's wife Mohlaroyim Nodira and a woman named Dilshod, gained regional fame through their Persian and Turkic poetry. Dilshod taught girls for more than fifty years and wrote a memoir in which she proudly discussed the poetic talents of her students.

Female teachers, called *otins* in the Fergana region and *khalfa* or *bibi khalifa* farther west, were considered suitable wives for clergy, which created a small class of educated families. *Otins* usually passed on their learning and their schools to their daughters or protégés. In the 1890s the English traveler Annette Meakin spoke with women in several Central Asian towns who could write as well as read prose and poetry and who continued their studies after marriage. Meakin observed a school in Samarqand run by the local Islamic judge's mother-in-law, who herself came from a line of learned women. Not all the women she met were so pious, however. In the city of Margilan, Meakin was entertained by two upper-class women who read aloud from a book that she found shockingly immoral. Prostitution existed in Central Asia before the Russians arrived; once Russian soldiers were garrisoned there, the government legalized brothels. A majority of local prostitutes came from the indigenous population, although precise numbers are not available.

Imperial Rule. The Manchu Qing dynasty of China incorporated the northwest Turkic territory (inhabited by Uighurs, Kazakhs, and Kyrgyz) into their empire in 1765; the area became Xinjiang Province in 1884. The British army advanced into Afghanistan from India in the 1840s but was driven back, settling for influence over the Mohammadzai dynasty of emirs, who had ties to the emirs of Bukhara. The Russian Empire conquered the steppe regions by the 1840s and the khanates of Central Asia in the 1860s, retaining Bukhara and Khiva as rump protectorates while dismantling the khanate of Qŭqon in 1876. They divided the remaining territory into the northern Steppe province and the province of Turkistan, both under military governors-general. British and Russian agents were also active throughout the region during their "Great Game" rivalry for dominance over Asia.

Although Central Asians had lost control over their political and economic lives, the imperial powers were not interested in engineering social change. Neither Great Britain nor China had enough local authority to effect significant changes in women's lives. The Russians, who wanted to maintain a stable society to facilitate economic exploitation, barred Christian missionaries on the grounds that they would only antagonize Muslims. They banned the slave trade and imposed Russian law in criminal cases but made no attempt to change social and religious customs, because they believed that simple exposure to a "superior" civilization would cause Central Asian culture to die naturally. In the first decades of Russian rule such exposure came through the establishment of a small network of schools for natives—which added Western methods of teaching literacy and arithmetic in native languages to the standard *maktab* curriculum, as well as instruction in Russian—and medical clinics, although very few girls or women were recorded as attending either.

The pace of change increased in the 1880s when new railroad lines brought more Russians to Central Asia and commercial cotton and silk production began to dominate the economy. Tashkent, Bukhara, and other cities acquired Russian settlements that introduced Western theater, newspapers, vodka, and other innovations to delight and horrify the indigenous population. Small numbers of women began to work in new cotton and silk factories; the 1897 census reported that 10.7 percent of women in the Fergana region were employed, mostly in textile production. The same census found that 2–10 percent of Turkistani women were literate in their own language (with the highest rates in the cities) and barely 1 percent were literate in Russian.

Another outside catalyst for change came from Volga and Crimean Tatar intellectuals, who in turn were influenced by Muslim reform movements in Egypt and the Ottoman Empire. Tatars, who had been subjects of the Russian Empire for centuries, came to Central Asia as translators and cultural intermediaries for the Russians. Possibly the first Turkic nurse-midwife in Tashkent, in the early twentieth century, was a Kazakh woman who had trained in the Tatar capital Kazan. Like many women, she came to Central Asia to work with her husband, who was a physician.

Some Tatar women in Bukhara and Turkistan opened schools for girls based on the principles of the *Jadid* ("new method") Muslim educational reform movement, which emphasized phonetic reading and basic sciences over recitation. The *Jadid* movement was founded in the 1880s by a Crimean Tatar educator named Ismail Bey Gaspirali, who believed that phonetic literacy and linguistic unity were the tools that would free Turkic peoples from Russian domination. His ideas attracted male intellectuals in Central Asia, and the first *Jadid* schools opened in Turkistan in 1893. Uighur traveling merchants also brought *Jadid* and Western-style schools to Xinjiang, although the number of girls who studied there is unknown. The *Jadid*s favored education for women, with the limited aim of training enlightened mothers to raise a new generation of Muslim patriots. Local *Jadid*s opened several schools for girls, but up to 1917 few families allowed their daughters to attend.

The Russian revolution of 1905 removed most state censorship over the press, which created space for new journalism and literature. The dominant theme of the new writing by and about women was that justice and the health of the Muslim *millat* (nation) would best be served by giving more women better education. Reformist Tatar women, including Gaspirali's daughter Şefika, published several newspapers that lamented the ignorance of Central Asian women and called for education and greater freedom. At least one woman in Qŭqon agreed; she wrote a passionate letter to the newspaper *Alem-i-Nisvan* (Women's World) in 1906 decrying the illiteracy and oppression she saw around her.

Central Asian newspapers also ran debates on the "woman question" that included comments from women themselves, who demanded respect and access to education. Male *Jadid*s wrote poetry and plays that attacked polygyny, abusive marriages, and above all the injustice of denying women education. On the other side, conservatives argued that teaching girls to read and write would corrupt their piety and their morals, because among other things a girl who could write might ask a man to meet with her in secret. Both reformers and traditionalists tended to make women the symbols of community health and values, placing a heavy burden on people who still had little control over their own lives.

By the outbreak of World War I in 1914 a small percentage of women in Central Asian cities had learned enough from *Jadid* and Russian schools to engage with the political and social issues of their day. Most women, however, were focused on the ordinary tasks of surviving and caring for their families in increasingly difficult economic conditions. Politics and daily life came together explosively in the summer of 1916 when the Russian military tried to draft Central Asian men for labor service behind the lines of the eastern front. Central Asians throughout Turkistan and the Steppe province rioted against the unprecedented call-up, and for the first time the rioters included women. Although some women were heard to protest having their economic providers taken from them, the motives of most of the rioters remain opaque. The Russians put down the antidraft riots with great brutality; a few Uzbek women were killed, wounded, or arrested. In the steppes tens of thousands of Kazakh and Kyrgyz nomads fled across the border to Xinjiang, where many froze or starved to death. By the beginning of 1917 the riots had ended, but Central Asia was far from peaceful.

Revolution, War, and Shock Modernization. The period from 1917 to just after World War II was one of profound and often violent change across Central Asia. War was a major catalyst for this change, but a drive for rapid modernization, pursued by revolutionary regimes in Turkey, Persia/Iran, Afghanistan, and Central Asia, was an even bigger factor.

In China the Qing dynasty collapsed in 1912, and people in Xinjiang were caught up in decades of war pursued by Chinese Nationalist, Communist, warlord, and Japanese and Soviet interests. Two independent eastern Turkistan republics were formed and destroyed; the second was absorbed into the People's Republic of China (PRC) in 1949. Through the upheavals of the 1940s one Kazakh woman, Kadvan (also written as Hadewan) Hanim, wife of Alin Wang, acquired political power through her pro-Nationalist Chinese husband. After the Communists seized control she switched sides and maintained a secure berth for her family well into Mao Zedong's rule.

In Afghanistan the northern regions absorbed thousands of Turkmen, Uzbek, and Tajik refugees fleeing from the Bolshevik Revolution and civil war of 1917–1921. Well into the 1930s entire nomadic tribes moved across the Soviet–Afghan border in response to Communist pressure. Meanwhile Amanullah Khan (r. 1919–1929) began his reign with a successful two-year war for independence from Great Britain. In 1923 he initiated an ambitious reform program intended to make Afghanistan a modern nation while still respecting Islamic law. The reforms included restrictions on polygyny, the banning of child marriage, and the opening of public schools for girls. Conservative clergy responded by organizing an armed revolt, which caused the king to retreat for a few years. He intensified his secularization campaign again in 1927–1928. Amanullah's wife, Queen Soraya, toured Europe unveiled and publicly argued that all Afghan women should be unveiled and educated. New and stronger armed resistance led to Amanullah's abdication in January 1929 and a brief civil war. Further reforms for women were delayed by decades.

V. I. Lenin's All-Russian Communist Party (the Bolsheviks), which stabilized its control over Central Asia by 1920, intended to make all Central Asians modern, scientific, practical-minded atheists within a few generations. Bolshevik activists saw women as both the primary targets and the means of engineering this revolution; Gregory Massell argued in 1974 that the party wanted women to serve as a "surrogate proletariat" because Central Asia did not have a working class in the European sense. Women themselves were both actors and victims in the Soviet shock modernization campaign. They had to navigate among intense pressures from the state, their families, and larger social forces such as changing economic conditions. By the 1930s women, like all other citizens of the Soviet Union, found that the terms of their liberation had been subordinated to the economic needs of the state.

The Bolsheviks used law, education, and political organizations to transform women's lives. In late 1917–1918, Soviet law made church and mosque separate from and subordinate to the state and gave women rights equal to those of men. The state opened thousands of secular primary schools and guaranteed all children the right to basic education in their native languages, although it accommodated Islamic values by allowing sex-segregated schools. Teacher-training and midwifery schools were also opened, and women were encouraged to enroll.

The Communist Party had a women's division, the Zhenotdel, and several hundred Uzbek women joined the party or its youth league (the Komsomol). This activity was more impressive on paper than in reality, however, because Soviet power was quite weak in Central Asia. Several thousand women and girls attended Soviet schools, but this was out of a total population of almost five million. In 1920 the midwifery program graduated ten native midwives, who made up less than 2 percent of the total enrollment. In 1926 the Tashkent women's teacher academy graduated only fourteen certified teachers out of six hundred enrolled students.

Soviet laws banning polygyny or allowing women the right to demand divorce were ignored or, in the case of polygyny, not promulgated in areas where they would arouse serious opposition. For example, the Turkmen Soviet Socialist Republic, formed in October 1924, had tougher legal restrictions on divorce than did the Russian or Ukrainian republics. In politics, nomadic Turkmen women had to be bribed to participate in local government, and at that only older women were willing to speak in public. Some reformist Uzbek and Tajik women began to unveil in the early 1920s, but they were too few to spark a broad liberation movement. Most Zhenotdel activists in Central Asia were Russians. Traditional practices turned out to be more resilient in the face of revolution than the Bolsheviks had expected.

In March 1927 the party launched a massive assault against all "crimes of traditional life" (known in Russian as *byt* crimes), which was intended to liberate women and deeply restructure Central Asian society. The Zhenotdel staged public demonstrations in the Uzbek, Tajik, and Kyrgyz regions (the Soviet republics were created in 1924, 1929, and 1936, respectively) in which women burned their veils and demanded freedom. In the Turkmen Soviet Socialist Republic women did not have the *paranji* to burn, but the party attempted to prosecute perpetrators of bride abduction and other *byt* crimes.

Throughout Soviet Central Asia the party promoted women in local government positions, encouraged them to divorce abusive husbands, and arrested men who married teenagers or accepted bride-wealth for their daughters. It was inspiring revolutionary theater, but, typically for the Soviets, no preparations had been made for women whose families threw them out or whose relatives and neighbors beat, raped, or murdered them. Many thousands of women were assaulted or killed as the party discovered that it could not force local courts to prosecute men who were upholding Islamic values.

For most Central Asian men and women, modest dress and behavior and the subordination of women to men in marriage were ordained by God, and they feared God more than they feared the Bolsheviks. Even child marriage, which the state prosecuted more vigorously than any other traditional practice, had been modeled by the prophet Muhammad. Communist propaganda campaigns that proclaimed women's liberation and scientifically explained the health threats posed by early marriage and the veil, but were not accompanied by adequate medical clinics, schools, or economic alternatives for women, could disrupt society but not fundamentally restructure it. By the early 1930s the Soviets had to abandon shock tactics. In theory they continued to liberate women through quieter means, but deeper changes were wrought in women's lives by industrialization and collectivization, the purges, and the slow but steady strengthening of Soviet school and court systems than by overt revolution.

Postwar Development. The period from 1945 until the 1980s was a time of relative stability for most Central Asians. With the incorporation of Xinjiang into the PRC in 1949, political borders were settled. Joseph Stalin's death in 1953 ended the purges, along with the accompanying chaos and fear. From 1931 to 1973, Afghanistan was governed by a semiconstitutional monarchy, which presided

Uzbek Agriculture. The corn-growing brigade leader A. G. Nee at the Sverdlov Collective Farm in Tashkent Oblast, Uzbek Soviet Socialist Republic, July 1960. Photograph by K. Razykov. PRINTS AND PHOTOGRAPHS DIVISION, LIBRARY OF CONGRESS

over very gradual and partial modernization. In 1959 the Afghan prime minister, in active cooperation with younger clergy, declared that keeping women veiled and secluded from public society was un-Islamic. Despite some protests, from this point until the 1979 Soviet invasion, elite urban Afghan women were able to obtain higher education and some political power. Some even became cabinet ministers. In rural areas, however, the government's influence remained weak.

For the Chinese Communist Party, the Turkic peoples of Xinjiang presented more of a national separatist threat than a religious or ideological one. Over several decades the PRC created schools with required Mandarin-language instruction, party organizations, and economic infrastructure designed to modernize and assimilate the indigenous people. They also vigorously promoted the immigration of Han Chinese, who by the 1980s equaled the Uighurs in numbers. The party never attempted the kind of radical assault on Islam or on traditional lifeways that the Soviets had, although the Cultural Revolution (1966–1976) caused at least as much destruction. The party also did not pursue the Soviet policy of giving minorities significant local political control, which limited incentives to assimilate into Han culture.

Settled Uighurs were quicker to send their children to the new schools than were the nomadic Kazakhs and Kyrgyz, but in general girls gained significant access to elementary education in Mandarin and in their native languages, especially after Mao's death in 1976. Girls were probably less likely to receive postelementary education, but enrollment data broken down by gender are not available. The settling of nomads and increased urbanization among Uighurs were the greatest forces for change during this period, but they were not accompanied by a significant movement of women into the paid workforce or changes in their family roles.

Women in Soviet Central Asia experienced the furthest-reaching effects of stability and gradual economic improvement. As elsewhere the urban upper classes participated the most in cultural and economic change, but the majority rural population participated much more than it did in Afghanistan or Xinjiang. The development of a distinctly Soviet Central Asian childhood and the promotion of women in the workforce impelled women into the modern world, for better and for worse.

Even before Stalin's death the Soviet Union developed extensive programs for children, including summer camps, after-school clubs, and a repertoire of songs and games that emphasized the importance of a Western-style nuclear family to socialist society. Girls as well as boys played sports, went on hiking trips, and learned to play Western and Central Asian musical instruments. They also attended school in greater numbers and for longer periods as time went on. By the 1950s almost half of all fourth-graders were girls, although that proportion dropped a great deal in the higher grades because parents often removed their daughters once they reached adolescence and marriageable status. The Soviets made early marriage and polygyny illegal, but they never entirely eliminated these and other family customs.

Nikita Khrushchev initiated massive school reforms in 1958 that drew more Central Asian girls into systematic education than ever before. The new program emphasized mathematics and science, improved language instruction in Russian and local languages, and provided for specialized athletic and artistic schools for gifted Central Asian as well as Russian children. Children of workers and collective farmers received polytechnical instruction in addition to the standard curriculum. By the 1970s one-third of the students entering higher education were women.

Greater access to education and job training did not, however, give women social or economic equality, despite Soviet guarantees of such in the law. The Central Asian preference for large families, combined with Soviet underproduction of such laborsaving devices as washing machines, meant that most women's labor was required at home. Although some women became doctors, lawyers, or professors, working women were overwhelmingly relegated to less-skilled and lower-prestige jobs in food processing, textiles, and teaching. Collective farms in the Soviet cotton-monoculture system notoriously forced women and children to pick cotton by hand while men operated the machinery. Women could hold local party or government office but very rarely did they wield any real power. Ironically, as the percentage of women in higher education increased, Moscow relaxed its political and economic control over the republics, including its enforcement of gender-equity laws. This left Central Asian women facing a decline in economic and political opportunities just as they were acquiring the skills to exploit those opportunities.

Post-Communist Deterioration. Though most of the world rejoiced at the 1991 fall of Communism in the Soviet Union and the liberalization movement that Deng Xiaoping started in the PRC in 1978, Central Asian societies have seen their standards of living, political conditions, and public health decline alarmingly. Women have endured the brunt of this decline. The most horrifying collapse was in Afghanistan, where the Soviet retreat in 1989 led to civil war among ethnic and religious groups, culminating in the Taliban's taking power in 1996. The Taliban, a party composed of religious students, was dominated by ethnic Pashtuns from the Afghan south who had never happily accepted modernizing Kabul governments. They instituted extraordinarily harsh repression of women—even the Islamic Republic of Iran criticized them—banning women's education, forcing women out of their jobs, and confining them to their homes unless covered by the burqa, a head-to-toe cloak with a mesh screen for the eyes. An unknown, but large, number of Afghan women and girls were beaten, stoned, tortured, or driven to suicide under Taliban rule. The United States–led overthrow of the Taliban in November 2001 has provided some relief for women in central Afghanistan, but most of the country is still controlled by regional warlords who have not made improvement of women's lives a priority. Political instability and catastrophic economic collapse have eclipsed all other concerns.

The emergence of the five Soviet Central Asian republics as independent states in January 1992 deepened the PRC's worries about national separatism among their own Turkic populations. Beijing intensified economic and political integration with—or, according to Uighur nationalists, absorption of—Xinjiang. Chinese policies created a self-sustaining cycle: economic liberalization and new trade connections between Xinjiang and Central Asia brought greater wealth and an infusion of new cultural ideas. Uighurs wanted more political power to protect their economic development, which threatened Han dominance. Strengthening Beijing's control led to increased Uighur resentment and violence.

Inevitably women have been caught up in this cycle. In 1993–1994, Rebiya Kadir, a Uighur mother of eleven who built her own multimillion-dollar firm, founded the Thousand Mothers Association, a mutual-aid society to promote women-owned businesses and combat drug abuse among Uighur youth. Kadir's activities eventually posed a political challenge to Beijing, leading to a harsh prison term and exile for her and much of her family. She became a leading activist for Xinjiang's independence. Another conflict between Turkic women and the state has been over birthrates. Although the PRC's one-child policy is somewhat flexible for non-Han peoples, Uighur and Kazakh birthrates have been higher than the state desires. Reports of forced abortions and sterilizations among Turkic women have come out of Xinjiang since the 1980s, but the population has continued to increase at a steady rate.

The independent Central Asian republics have fared differently from one another since 1991, with Kazakhstan in the most prosperous condition and Tajikistan in the poorest. Uzbekistan and Turkmenistan have become brutal dictatorships, and Kyrgyzstan has drifted among varying degrees of freedom. In March 2005, Kyrgyzstan had a revolution to install a more representative government, but the results have been ambiguous. All the republics have declined economically since the end of Soviet support, and women's social and working conditions have declined with them. Though the streets of any major Central Asian city are full of women in stylish clothing going to school or work or shopping, women's employment has been dropping along with state child-care subsidies. Access to quality education and health care is possible only through privileged networks or bribery, and in many rural areas it cannot be had at all. The former president for life of Turkmenistan, Saparmurat Niyazov, largely destroyed the education and health-care systems of his country, and the social infrastructure of Tajikistan has never recovered from the civil war of 1992–1997.

In many areas, urban as well as rural, pressure on women to show their rejection of the Soviet past by behaving in "traditional" ways has increased. The return of bride abduction— with or without the consent of the bride—has been observed in Kazakhstan and Tajikistan, and polygyny and child marriage are more openly practiced. Poor young women have increasingly been forced to marry for economic advantage, and divorce, even from an abusive husband, remains deeply shameful. Poverty has also caused a noticeable increase in prostitution and sex trafficking, which, combined with rising rates of intravenous drug use, has led to a rapidly spreading AIDS epidemic. Women have been politically active in trying to improve their lives, particularly in Uzbekistan, but in recent years this has gotten very dangerous. Nodira Hidoyatova, a leader of the Uzbek opposition's Sunshine Coalition, was sentenced in 2005 to ten years in prison for scantily documented financial crimes, then unexpectedly released early. The Uzbek government is currently unwilling to tolerate any political plurality, even as general living conditions deteriorate. Central Asians are not in the desperate straits that Afghans are, but their priorities are becoming increasingly focused on the basics of survival for themselves and their children.

Not So Isolated. Although the great powers of the modern era have looked at Central Asia as a backwater, the region has been decisively influenced by global political and economic patterns. No generalization can adequately cover the historical experiences of Central Asian women, whose lives changed as much in the twentieth century as those of European women did in the nineteenth. Many more women are educated and have at least limited access to economic and political power. Their life expectancies are longer, and their infant mortality rates are lower. They know enough about modern political ideals to expect justice, stability, and economic support from their governments—and to be bitterly disappointed when those expectations are unfulfilled. They have also endured multiple wars and bloody dictatorships, which are as much a product of the modern era as are concepts of human rights, including those of women.

[*See also* Afghanistan; China, *subentry* Modern Period; Divorce; Education; Inheritance; Islam; Marriage; Nepal; Nomads; Pastoralism; Prostitution; Russia and Soviet Union; Seclusion; Tibet and Bhutan; *and* Zhenotdel.]

BIBLIOGRAPHY

Allworth, Edward A., ed. *Central Asia: One Hundred Thirty Years of Russian Dominance, a Historical Overview.* 3d ed. Durham, N.C.: Duke University Press, 1994.

Anderson, Barbara A., and Brian D. Silver. "Ethnic Differences in Fertility and Sex Ratios at Birth in China: Evidence from Xinjiang." *Population Studies* 49, no. 2 (1995): 211–226.

Bacon, Elizabeth E. *Central Asians under Russian Rule: A Study in Culture Change.* Ithaca, N.Y.: Cornell University Press, 1980.

Benson, Linda, and Ingvar Svanberg. *China's Last Nomads: The History and Culture of China's Kazaks.* Armonk, N.Y.: M. E. Sharpe, 1998.

Black, Cyril E., Louis Dupree, Elizabeth Endicott-West, Daniel C. Matuszewski, Eden Naby, and Arthur N. Waldron. *The Modernization of Inner Asia.* Armonk, N.Y.: M. E. Sharpe, 1991.

Chadwick, Nora K., and Victor Zhirmunsky. *Oral Epics of Central Asia.* Cambridge, U.K.: Cambridge University Press, 1969.

Edgar, Adrienne Lynn. "Bolshevism, Patriarchy, and the Nation: The Soviet 'Emancipation' of Muslim Women in Pan-Islamic Perspective." *Slavic Review* 65, no. 2 (2006): 252–272.

Edgar, Adrienne Lynn. *Tribal Nation: The Making of Soviet Turkmenistan.* Princeton, N.J.: Princeton University Press, 2004.

Kamp, Marianne R. *The New Woman in Uzbekistan: Islam, Modernity, and Unveiling under Communism.* Seattle: University of Washington Press, 2006.

Keller, Shoshana. "Going to School in Uzbekistan." In *Everyday Life in Central Asia: Past and Present,* edited by Jeff Sahadeo and Russell Zanca, pp. 246–263. Bloomington: Indiana University Press, 2007.

Keller, Shoshana. *To Moscow, Not Mecca: The Soviet Campaign against Islam in Central Asia, 1917–1941.* Westport, Conn.: Greenwood Press, 2001.

Keller, Shoshana. "Trapped between State and Society: Women's Liberation and Islam in Soviet Uzbekistan, 1926–1941." *Journal of Women's History* 10, no. 1 (1998): 20–44.

Khalid, Adeeb. *The Politics of Muslim Cultural Reform: Jadidism in Central Asia.* Berkeley: University of California Press, 1998.

Lubin, Nancy. *Labour and Nationality in Soviet Central Asia: An Uneasy Compromise.* Princeton, N.J.: Princeton University Press, 1984.

Luong, Pauline Jones, ed. *The Transformation of Central Asia: States and Societies from Soviet Rule to Independence.* Ithaca, N.Y.: Cornell University Press, 2004.

Martin, Virginia. "*Barïmta*: Nomadic Custom, Imperial Crime." In *Russia's Orient: Imperial Borderlands and Peoples, 1700–1917,* edited by Daniel Brower and Edward J. Lazzerini, pp. 249–270. Bloomington: Indiana University Press, 1997.

Massell, Gregory J. *The Surrogate Proletariat: Moslem Women and Revolutionary Strategies in Soviet Central Asia, 1919–1929.* Princeton, N.J.: Princeton University Press, 1974.

Meakin, Annette M. B. *In Russian Turkestan: A Garden of Asia and Its People.* London: George Allen, 1903.

Michaels, Paula A. *Curative Powers: Medicine and Empire in Stalin's Central Asia.* Pittsburgh, Pa.: University of Pittsburgh Press, 2003.

Millward, James A. *Eurasian Crossroads: A History of Xinjiang.* New York: Colombia University Press, 2007.

Nawid, Senzil K. *Religious Response to Social Change in Afghanistan, 1919–1929: King Aman-Allah and the Afghan Ulama.* Costa Mesa, Calif.: Mazda, 1999.

Northrop, Douglas. *Veiled Empire: Gender and Power in Stalinist Central Asia.* Ithaca, N.Y.: Cornell University Press, 2004.

Starr, S. Frederick, ed. *Xinjiang: China's Muslim Borderland.* Armonk, N.Y.: M. E. Sharpe, 2004.

Tapper, Nancy. *Bartered Brides: Politics, Gender, and Marriage in an Afghan Tribal Society.* Cambridge, U.K.: Cambridge University Press, 1991.

SHOSHANA KELLER

CHARLOTTE (1840–1927), princess of Belgium and empress of Mexico as the consort of Ferdinand Maximilian von Habsburg; the fourth child of King Leopold I and Queen Louise Marie d'Orléans of Belgium. After her mother's death in October 1850, Charlotte's father groomed her for exercising political power.

From age sixteen, royal suitors pursued Charlotte (born Marie Charlotte Amélie Augustine Victoire Clémentine Léopoldine on 7 June 1840). She married Maximilian on 27 July 1857. As Austria's governor general of the Italian kingdom of Lombardy-Venetia, Maximilian turned to Charlotte—now known as Carlota—for support. Despite the couple's efforts, Emperor Franz Josef recalled Maximilian in early 1859 after Piedmont-Sardinia, allied to France, invaded and annexed Lombardy.

Blamed for the territorial loss, Maximilian and Charlotte embarked for Brazil in the fall of 1859, but Charlotte took ill and remained on Madeira while Maximilian continued unaccompanied. She wrote about the experience in *Un hiver a Madère, 1859–1860* (A Winter in Madeira) and *Souvenirs de voyage à bord de la "Fantaisie"* (Memories of Travel aboard the *Fantaisie*), published in Vienna in 1861 and 1863, respectively. Rumors of marital discord circulated; conflicting reports ascribe frigidity to Charlotte and homosexuality to Maximilian. Having fallen from favor in Vienna, Maximilian sought out vacant crowns in Greece or Mexico, where local conservatives sought to install a monarchy to unite the country. At Charlotte's insistence, Maximilian accepted the Mexican throne. The couple entered Mexico City on 12 June 1864.

Despite initial success, by early 1865 the empire foundered. Maximilian's liberalism alienated Conservatives. He decreed freedom of religion, carried out fiscal reforms, issued a civil code, built up infrastructure, abolished debt peonage, created labor legislation, restored community lands to Indian villages, and stimulated education.

While Maximilian toured the country, Charlotte looked after affairs of state, presided over the cabinet, received diplomats, drafted reports and legislation on immigration projects, and oversaw the creation of a new constitution. She set a precedent for the involvement of the wives of rulers in politics. She urged women to concern themselves with public affairs and pushed elite women to support institutions of social welfare, education, and the arts. She surprised courtiers with her knowledge of Mexico, particularly history and art.

In July 1866, as Maximilian's rule faced increasing military resistance by Liberals, Charlotte traveled to Europe to secure French military support and to improve relations with the church. Failing on both accounts, she broke down at the Vatican, confiding in Pius IX that she feared for her life. Charlotte locked herself into her hotel for five nights, until her family transferred her to Miramar Castle—the retreat near Trieste, Italy, she and Maximilian had built after their wedding—and placed her under medical treatment on 10 October 1866. On the afternoon of 18 October, Maximilian received a telegram explaining the situation; by evening, he resolved to abdicate, but Conservatives prevented it. Without French support, Liberals gained the upper hand in the battlefield, capturing Maximilian on 15 May 1867 at Querétaro. He was subsequently tried and was executed on 19 June 1867. Meanwhile, Charlotte's brother Leopold II secured her interests and arranged her return to Belgium. By mid-1868, her depression worsened and she was sequestered in Bouchout Castle, where she remained until her death on 19 January 1927. Her tragic story has been the subject of countless works of fiction.

[*See also* Mexico.]

BIBLIOGRAPHY

Michael, Prince of Greece. *The Empress of Farewells: The Story of Charlotte, Empress of Mexico*. New York: Atlantic Monthly Press, 2002. The author obtained unparalleled access to Belgian Royal Archives, and he presents a theory about Maximilian's homosexuality and the abuse that Charlotte suffered over 1866–1867 from the Austrians.

Ratz, Konrad, ed. *Correspondencia inédita entre Maximiliano y Carlota*. Mexico City: Fondo de Cultura Económica, 2003. Includes an insightful introduction and annotations.

Weckmann, Luis, ed. *Carlota de Bélgica: Correspondencia y escritos sobre México en los archivos europeos (1861–1868)*. Mexico City: Porrúa, 1989. Lists many of Charlotte's memoranda, studies, and private papers that have eluded scholars.

VICTOR M. MACIAS-GONZALEZ

CHEKHOVA, MARIA (1866–1937), Russian educator and feminist activist. Maria Aleksandrovna Argamakova Chekhova was born 18 January 1866 to a gentry family in Saint Petersburg. Her maternal and paternal grandfathers were teachers, as was her father. She began her pedagogical career even before completing her training as a teacher, establishing her own school in 1889. In the following year she married a fellow educator, Nikolai Chekhov. The couple initially carried out their populist ideals as rural teachers and, in 1891–1892, as famine-relief volunteers. After moving to Moscow in 1904 with their five children, they became active participants in the liberation movement, seeking an end to autocratic rule, democratic reforms, civil rights, national autonomy, and a parliament elected by universal suffrage and the Teachers' Union.

A cofounder of the *Soiuz ravnopraviia zhenshchin* (Women's Equal Rights Union) in February 1905, Chekhova served as its secretary and, along with her husband, as a member of the organization's central bureau. The union's general goals were equal rights and especially voting rights, considered the first step to women's liberation. Chekhova's ties with the provinces aided the organization in its outreach. By 1906 the union boasted a membership of eight thousand to ten thousand and chapters in cities and towns throughout the Russian Empire. Chekhova served as editor of the organization's journal, *Soiuz zhenshchin* (Union of Women), from 1907 to 1909.

In addition to her involvement with the Women's Equal Rights Union, Chekhova taught courses for workers and helped found the first Moscow children's club. She organized campaigns to submit a petition for woman suffrage to the Second Duma (an elected legislative assembly) and participated in the 1908 First All-Russian Women's

Congress aiming to publicize all aspects of women's status in society and to promote united action for equal rights and the Congress to Combat Prostitution (21–25 April 1910), convened to highlight the problems of prostitution and to combat the trafficking in women.

When the Women's Equal Rights Union disintegrated and its journal ceased publication in December 1909, Chekhova found a new venue for her feminist activity as president of the Moscow branch of the *Liga ravnopraviia zhenshchin* (League for Women's Equal Rights). She helped organize a congress on women's education in Saint Petersburg from 26 December 1912 to 4 January 1913, the last major feminist congress before the 1917 Revolution, which focused on the gains made and the barriers to further progress in women's education. With other feminists she lobbied the very conservative Third and Fourth Dumas, winning modest victories in legislation pertaining to passports, marriage, and inheritance.

After the February 1917 Revolution, Chekhova was among the feminists who successfully pressed the provisional government to grant women full suffrage. On 20 July 1917 Russia became the first major country to do so. Chekhova was on the league's electoral list for the Constituent Assembly, along with the league's president, Poliksena Shishkina-Yavein, the historian Ekaterina N. Shchepkina, the political activist Ekaterina D. Kuskova, the historian and zemstvo (provincial assembly) statistician Alexandra Yefimenko, and Alexandra M. Kalmykova, a supporter of "legal Marxism."

Maria Chekhova and her husband remained in Russia after the Bolshevik Revolution, and Nicholas Chekhov became a prominent Soviet educator. With independent feminist organizations banned, Chekhova devoted herself to educational activity and her family. Her memoirs, never published, are in the Moscow City Historical Archive. She died in Moscow in 1937.

[*See also* Feminism *and* Russia and Soviet Union.]

BIBLIOGRAPHY

Edmondson, Linda. *Feminism in Russia, 1900–17.* Stanford, Calif.: Stanford University Press, 1984.

Ruthchild, Rochelle Goldberg. "The Russian Women's Movement 1859–1917." PhD diss., University of Rochester, 1976.

Stites, Richard. *The Women's Liberation Movement in Russia: Feminism, Nihilism, and Bolshevism, 1860–1930.* Princeton, N.J.: Princeton University Press, 1978; rev. ed., 1991.

ROCHELLE GOLDBERG RUTHCHILD

CHEN DUANSHENG (1751–c. 1796), poet and *tanci* novelist. Chen Duansheng was born in Qiantang (Hangzhou), Zhejiang Province, China. Her father, Chen Yudun, and her uncle Chen Yuwan were scholar-officials. She and her two sisters, Chen Qingsheng and Chen Changsheng, were serious poets, but most of Duansheng's own poetry has been lost; thus she is known today for her *tanci, Zaisheng yuan* (Karmic Bonds of Reincarnation). *Tanci,* plucking rhymes, belongs to the popular literature of storytelling and singing. Although Chen Duansheng's grandfather Chen Goushan (1702–1772), a famous literary man, supported women's education and advocated the development of female talent, he despised the genre of *tanci.* Thus Chen Duansheng had to write *Zaisheng yuan* in secret. The historian Chen Yinke (1890–1969) considered Duansheng's *tanci,* with more than a thousand pages in poetic form, comparable to Greek and Hindu epics. Because of its intricate plots and complex characterization typical of monumental fiction, the author and historian Guo Moruo (1892–1978) compared it to the English and French novels of the eighteenth and nineteenth centuries, such as those by Sir Walter Scott (1771–1832) and Stendhal (1783–1842).

Zaisheng yuan has also been generally accepted as a significant feminist work, portraying a cross-dressed woman who escapes a forced marriage, passes all imperial examinations, and manages state affairs successfully as the prime minister. *Zaisheng yuan* consists of twenty volumes, each containing four chapters. Chen Duansheng began to write it at the age of eighteen and had finished sixteen volumes by the age of twenty when her mother died. Chen's mother had been her first reader and literary guide, and grief over the loss of her mother almost ended Duansheng's literary career.

When she was twenty-three, Chen Duansheng married Fan Tan, a man who was later exiled for allegedly asking a substitute to take the imperial examination for him. Chen Duansheng seemed to have enjoyed moments of happiness with her husband, and she had a son and a daughter by him. But she became increasingly depressed because of his exile and because she was denied opportunities in society as a woman. After her husband's death she wrote the seventeenth volume of *Zaisheng yuan,* in which the protagonist Meng Lijun refuses marriage and the restoration of her proper gender role after the revelation of her sexual identity. By doing so, Meng defies the power of the emperor, her father, and her husband. Chen left her novel open-ended and unfinished.

Although the manuscript of *Zaisheng yuan* had been well circulated, it did not appear in print until the female scholar Hou Zhi adapted and published it under the title of *Jingui jie* (A Woman Hero) in 1821. About another twenty years later, the female poet Liang Desheng was inspired as well as disturbed by the unfinished *Zaisheng yuan* and added the last three volumes, letting Meng Lijun abandon her male attire to marry her betrothed, even though he had already acquired three concubines. Liang's ending reveals the power of the entrenched patriarchal tradition on women. Even Hou Zhi, in *Zaizao tian* (Re-creation of Heaven), her sequel to *Zaisheng yuan*, employs a notorious figure of vanity and ambition as the daughter of Meng Lijun to undermine female power, symbolized by the only woman emperor in Chinese history, Wu Zetian. Such attempted revisions of *Zaisheng yuan* mark Chen Duansheng's radical voice as especially controversial. The political as well as aesthetic value of her work has attracted wide critical attention in both China and the West.

[*See also* China, *subentry* Imperial Period; Liang Mengzhao; Qiu Xinru; Tao Zhenhuai; Wang Yun; Wu, Empress; *and* Wu Zao.]

BIBLIOGRAPHY

Sung, Marina H. *The Narrative Art of Tsai-sheng-yüan: A Feminist Vision in Traditional Confucian Society*. San Francisco: Chinese Materials Center Publications, 1994.

Wu, Qingyun. *Female Rule in Chinese and English Literary Utopias*. Syracuse, N.Y.: Syracuse University Press, 1995. Chapter 3 analyzes *Zaisheng yuan* and compares it with Lady Florence Dixie's *Gloriana; or, The Revolution of 1900.*

QINGYUN WU

CHEN SHU (1660–1736), a famous Chinese painter of the Qing dynasty. Chen Shu is a notable representative of the female artists who constituted a significant minority voice in the scholarly art world of late imperial China. A daughter of the scholar-official class, she was born into an old and respected family in the Xiushui district of Jiaxing Prefecture, Zhejiang Province. As a child she not only learned to sew, but also was instructed in the classics and studied painting and calligraphy. A fortunate marriage into the Qian family of nearby Haiyan allowed her to continue pursuing her training and developing her talent. Her father-in-law, Qian Ruizheng (1620–1702), a noted calligrapher and painter, appreciated her painting, and her husband, Qian Lunguang (1655–1718), added poetic inscriptions to some of her paintings, suggesting that the couple shared artistic interests. Chen's husband did not advance through the official ranks and earned only a teacher's salary, but the family associated with leading members of the literati and enjoyed entertaining, even when doing so strained the family purse. Chen Shu contributed by pawning her clothing and selling her jewelry and paintings. Like many scholarly artists she sometimes realized a profit from her art, but she was not a professional painter.

The White Cockatoo. Hanging scroll by Chen Shu, 1721. THE METROPOLITAN MUSEUM OF ART, NEW YORK

Chen Shu painted a range of subjects: figures, landscapes, small scenes, flowers, plants, birds, and insects. In figure painting she preferred edifying historical themes and religious subjects. In landscape painting she followed the conservative so-called Orthodox School tradition of Wang Shimin (1592–1680) and Wang Hui (1632–1717), who based their works on the landscape styles of old masters. She particularly favored the style of the Yuan-dynasty master Wang Meng (c. 1308–1385), and she executed a number of hanging scrolls in his manner. She also found inspiration in the Ming-dynasty Wu School of Suzhou. Her small scenes sketched in light colors recall Wu School paintings in their mildness and idealization of life in the lower Chang (Yangtze) River region. Like her landscapes, Chen Shu's flower paintings range from hanging scrolls in old styles to small sketches from life. A number of young people, family, and friends developed their painting skills under Chen Shu's tutelage. Later artists—especially but not exclusively her female descendants—learned from her paintings.

Most Chinese women painters slipped into the shadows of art history, with many dropping from sight completely. The most famous exception, the Yuan-dynasty painter and calligrapher Guan Daosheng (1262–1319), was one of Chen Shu's models. Other exceptions nearer Chen's own time were the accomplished flower painters Wen Shu (1595–1634), Ma Quan (eighteenth century), and Yun Bing (eighteenth century). Chen Shu differs from these women not only in her artistic range but also in not being related or married to a famous male artist. However, the stature that she attained was not wholly the result of her artistic accomplishments and influence on other painters; it also was the result of the filial piety and worldly success of her son Qian Chenqun (1686–1774), who attained high rank and served close to the throne. He secured an honorific title for his mother, composed a eulogizing account of her life, and presented a number of her paintings to the Qianlong emperor (r. 1735–1796). This art-loving monarch, known for lavish displays of filial regard for his own mother, received Chen Shu's paintings with enthusiasm and often inscribed them. Many of her works formerly in the Qing imperial collection are now in the National Palace Museum in Taipei.

[*See also* Art and Architecture, *subentry* Artists and Architects, *and* China, *subentry* Imperial Period.]

BIBLIOGRAPHY

Gates, M. J. "Ch'en Shu." In *Eminent Chinese of the Ch'ing Period (1644–1912)*, edited by Arthur W. Hummel, p. 99. Washington, D.C.: United States Government Printing Office, 1943.

Weidner, Marsha. "The Conventional Success of Ch'en Shu." In *Flowering in the Shadows: Women in the History of Chinese and Japanese Painting*, edited by Marsha Weidner, pp. 123–156. Honolulu: University of Hawai'i Press, 1990.

Weidner, Marsha, et al. *Views from Jade Terrace: Chinese Women Artists 1300–1912.* Indianapolis, Ind.: Indianapolis Museum of Art; New York: Rizzoli, 1988. See pp. 16, 24–26, 57–58, 60, 62, 117–120, and 145.

MARSHA WEIDNER

CHICAGO, JUDY (b. 1939), prominent feminist artist. Born Judy Cohen in Chicago (which inspired her adopted name), she studied at the University of California, Los Angeles, from 1960 to 1964. In 1971 she cofounded with Miriam Schapiro the Feminist Art Program at the California Institute of the Arts in Valencia. The program's large-scale collaborative project *Womanhouse* (1971–1972) reclaimed a Los Angeles mansion as a space in which twenty-one women artists presented and performed work related to domestic tasks and female identity.

A prolific painter, sculptor, and author who has received numerous awards and honors, Chicago may perhaps remain best known for *The Dinner Party*, now considered an icon of feminist art. Chicago began the work in 1974 "to teach a society unversed in women's history something of the reality of our rich heritage" (*Beyond the Flower*, p. 45). Though her initial plan was a series of plates hung on a wall, Chicago soon conceived of the work in the context of a dinner table, representing the private domestic space to which women had long been relegated. Thinking as well of Leonardo da Vinci's *Last Supper*, Chicago envisioned the work as a dinner party at which famous historical women would be honored. Chicago's research for *The Dinner Party* is considered groundbreaking; it predates later investigations into female-centered belief systems and matriarchal cultures, as well as later scholarship on women artists such as Artemisia Gentileschi who were prominent in their era but who had been largely forgotten by art historians.

The Dinner Party consists of a massive (48 feet on each side) triangular table—evoking the ancient symbol of the female—at which thirty-nine place settings are arranged, each honoring a historical or mythical figure, from ancient history through the twentieth century. Each wing of the table holds thirteen settings, which include an embroidered runner, a ceramic plate with motifs suggesting the identity of the honoree, a napkin, utensils, and a chalice. The settings are arranged chronologically, beginning with the "Primordial Goddess" and proceeding through women's historical decline in power, through the suffrage movement—and toward a reclamation of political and artistic freedom—and ending in a setting for the artist Georgia O'Keeffe. Below the table the names of 999 other women are inscribed in gold on a while tile floor.

Not only does the work celebrate female historical and mythical figures, it deliberately employs "women's arts," such as china painting and embroidery, that were once diminished by their association with the domestic sphere. A collaborative piece on which more than one hundred volunteers labored, *The Dinner Party* subverts the notion of the singular male genius. In addition, it employs a distinctly female iconography of vaginal imagery, which on the dinner plates rises to increasing prominence as Chicago traces women's progress through the ages.

The work opened in 1979 at the San Francisco Museum of Modern Art, followed by a nine-year international tour. In 2001 the philanthropist Elizabeth Sackler purchased *The Dinner Party*; it was shown at the Brooklyn Museum in 2002 and since March 2007 has been permanently installed at the Elizabeth A. Sackler Center for Feminist Art at the Brooklyn Museum.

Chicago has worked on several other individual and collaborative pieces, including the *Birth Project* (1980–1985), *Powerplay* (1982–1987), and *Resolutions: A Stitch in Time* (1994–2000), which combines needlework and painting. Her numerous books include *The Dinner Party: A Symbol of Our Heritage* (1979), *Beyond the Flower: The Autobiography of a Feminist Artist* (1996), and *Fragments from the Delta of Venus* (2004). Considered one of the most prominent feminist artists of our time, Chicago is the first living artist whose papers have been included in the Arthur and Elizabeth Schlesinger Library on the History of Women in America at Radcliffe College, Harvard University.

[*See also* Art and Architecture.]

BIBLIOGRAPHY

Chicago, Judy. *Beyond the Flower: The Autobiography of a Feminist Artist*. New York: Viking, 1996.

Levin, Gail. *Becoming Judy Chicago: A Biography of the Artist*. New York: Harmony Books, 2007.

Lippard, Lucy, Edward Lucie-Smith, and Viki Thompson Wylder. *Judy Chicago*. New York: Watson-Guptill, 2002.

DOROTHY BAUHOFF

CHIEFS, FEMALE. "Women as chiefs" is for many an anomalous, unusual, or unnatural image. Yet global history is replete with records of women who were chiefs in various ways. The two dominant images are those of chiefs of traditional tribal groups and those of leaders of civil services—chief of police, fire chief—and political leaders, such as heads of governments. In some postcolonial societies that share in Western history there are clashes between traditional chieftaincies and later developments toward democracy.

The Significance of Chiefs. The authority, responsibilities, and functions of tribal chiefs in different regions are comparable to each other. Tribal rule in Cameroon provides a model for a general understanding of the derivation of authority and its exercise, as well as the roles and functions of chiefs. In the Northwest Province of Cameroon the chief derived authority from the myths and rituals of the tribal confederacy. These conferred an incontrovertible power upon the chief, who symbolized the unity of the community and represented the link between the present and the ancestors. The chief was often the communal landlord, and the land itself was a link between the people and the ancestors. The chief functioned as priest, political and military leader, and exemplar of the regulatory codes that ensured the well-being of the people. There were also councils of chiefs when more complex tribal systems were organized, with chiefs recognized as being less or more meritorious. Primordial foundations, sacred embodiments, and linkage of present and past generations were, similarly, foundational authorizations for the functions of Scottish clan chiefs.

As traditional nation-states developed democratic systems, severe fissures often occurred in the relationship between new and traditional structures. Fiji's Great Council of Chiefs, which existed from 1997 to 2007, is an example of a combination of traditional clan structure and the development of a republican structure of governance. The Great Council of Chiefs functioned as an electoral college and in this and other ways sustained the respectful inclusion of ancient traditional leadership within Fiji's democratic institutions. In Botswana's House of Chiefs, the upper chamber of the parliament, representation is based on territory rather than on tribe or ethnicity. In the early twenty-first century, the unusual female chief finds new opportunities for expression and in some instances builds on very old traditions of definitive female leadership.

Female Chiefs. Popular depictions and many studies of traditional chieftaincies tend to focus especially on male leadership of warring tribes and thus obscure the length and antiquity of women's participation in tribal defense and leadership, as well as the cultural, religious, and social aspects of governance and women's able leadership. Historically, female chiefs have distinguished themselves in all areas. Little known is Guatara Mico, once leader of more than thirty-nine Native American chiefs of tribes in the southwestern United States. One of the best-known female leaders is the Queen of Sheba—called Makeda in Ethiopian tradition—depicted in the Tanakh and the Old Testament of the Bible for her relationship with Israel's King Solomon.

Others from classical antiquity include Queen Su-bad of Ur (now in Iraq; c. 2420 B.C.E.), Queen Athaliah of Southern Judea (842–837 B.C.E.), Queen and Admiral Artemisia I of Karia-Halikarnassos and Kos (480 B.C.E.), Arsinoe II of Ptolemaic Egypt (316–270 B.C.E.), Queen Cleopatra Berenice of Egypt (81–80 B.C.E.), the Candace dynasty of Ethiopia, and countless others who were highly influential when they governed at various levels of administration as surrogate rulers, corulers, and independent rulers. Queen Eyleuka of Ethiopia, who ruled for approximately forty-five years (c. 4530–3240 B.C.E.), has the earliest attestation. There were female Islamic rulers such as al-Hurra al-Malika of Yemen (eleventh century C.E.), who had the Khutba (Muslim Friday prayers) said in her name—the ultimate proof of sovereignty. Other women also played roles in the geographic spread of Islam. Ingrid Mattson, a Canadian convert to Islam, was elected as the first female president of the largest Muslim group in North America in 2006.

Assessment. Throughout history there have been queen rulers. In the last century the countries that were earliest with female leaders were not among the more prominent Western countries. In 1960, Sirivamo Bandaranaike of Sri Lanka became the world's first elected female prime minister, and in 1974, Isabel Perón of Argentina became the first female president. In 2007 there were five women prime ministers—in Germany, Jamaica, New Zealand, Mozambique, and the Netherlands Antilles—and eight women presidents—in Chile, Finland, Ireland, Israel (acting), Latvia, Liberia, the Philippines, and Switzerland. Only Monaco and Saudi Arabia have never had a female member of government in at least a subministerial position. There is one female assistant vice minister in the Vatican, and in 1999 Sweden became the first country to have more female ministers than male. In 2007 the Finnish government was 60 percent female. These women continue a tradition of female chiefs, as old as recorded history, who have fulfilled all the duties of chiefs in various ways and conditions, in every kind of tribe, confederate, and nation-state.

[*See also* Indigenous Cultures *and* Monarchy.]

BIBLIOGRAPHY

Abbott, Nabia. "Pre-Islamic Arab Queens." *American Journal of Semitic Languages and Literatures* 58, no. 1 (January 1941): 1–22. Seminal in presenting from scant sources a comprehensive introduction to two dozen influential and ruling women in ancient Mesopotamia and the Arabic world.

Christensen, Martin K. I. "Worldwide Guide to Women in Leadership." http://www.guide2womenleaders.com. Provides well-researched, exhaustive, and up-to-date lists of global women leaders from antiquity to the present; useful as starting points for further research.

Fleischmann, Ellen L. *The Nation and Its "New" Women: The Palestinian Women's Movement, 1920–1948.* Berkeley: University of California Press, 2003. A comprehensive history of the contributions of women in the Palestinian response to English colonialism and Israelite settlement; its use of sources reveals both the challenges and the possibilities in constructing women's roles in history.

Jameson, Anna Brownell. *Memoirs of Celebrated Female Sovereigns* (1832, 1880). Boston: Adamant Media Corporation, 2001. Narrates the lives of twelve female leaders from ancient Mesopotamia to nineteenth-century Europe; singular among similar publications for its historical and geographical span.

Saxonhouse, Arlene W. *Women in the History of Political Thought: Ancient Greece to Machiavelli.* New York: Praeger, 1985. Provides a survey of political theorists from Plato to the early sixteenth century, with useful assessments and explorations of the implications of their thoughts for women's roles in public life.

Thomas, Sue, and Clyde Wilcox, eds. *Women and Elective Office: Past, Present, and Future.* 2d ed. New York: Oxford University Press, 2005. A study of women's performances in elected office in the United States, with limited but useful attention to the history of women's participation at various levels.

ALTHEA SPENCER MILLER

CHILD, LYDIA MARIA (1802–1880), writer and abolitionist. Born Lydia Maria Francis in Medford, Massachusetts, and largely self-educated, Child combined a deep commitment to racial justice with a love of books and writing.

As a young woman Child argued that Native Americans should be integrated into American society. Her first novel, *Hobomok, a Tale of Early Times* (1824), told the story of a love affair between a Puritan woman and an Indian man and was quite well received. Two years later Child became the editor of the *Juvenile Miscellany*, the country's first successful children's magazine.

In 1833 Child published her *Appeal in Favor of That Class of Americans Called Africans*, the first extensive study of slavery and emancipation. Putting American slavery into a global context, and relying heavily on Caribbean history, Child argued that slavery hurts everyone it touches—slaves, obviously, but also slave owners, who are degraded by its cruelty, and free whites, who are impoverished by the inefficiencies of a slave economy. Immediate emancipation, she concluded, is the best and safest path for all concerned. Widely read and debated, Child's *Appeal* was often credited with turning abolitionism into a movement.

Child devoted her next ten years to the abolitionist cause. She became the editor of the *National Anti-Slavery Standard* (and the first woman to edit a political newspaper), and she wrote numerous books, articles, and pamphlets. She was dismayed, however, by the divisions and altercations that plagued the movement, and in 1843 she resigned from the *Standard* and vowed never again to belong to any organization.

Child eventually wrote or edited fifty-eight books. She published novels and short stories, domestic advice manuals and abolitionist tracts, poetry and biographies, one of the first women's histories (*The History of the Condition of Women, in Various Ages and Nations*, 1835), and a three-volume history of the world's religions (*The Progress of Religious Ideas*, 1855). She supported herself with her writing, as her husband, David Lee Child, an abolitionist whom she married in 1828, proved constitutionally incapable of making money.

Child was always ambivalent about promoting the rights of women. She preferred to do what she thought right rather than talking about its propriety. But she always believed women should be able to do anything that helps the human race, and by the 1850s that included voting.

Child returned to national attention after John Brown's attack on Harpers Ferry in 1859. Herself a pacifist, Child argued that the North should secede from the South in order to peacefully separate itself from the stain of slavery and deprive slave owners of the federal troops necessary to keep slaves in line. But she also believed that Brown and his followers were heroes, and her letters praising him were widely reprinted in Southern newspapers as well as in the abolitionist press.

During and after the Civil War, Child sought the full and equal integration of black people into American society. Among other things, she wrote and distributed a textbook, *The Freedmen's Book* (1865), that promoted literacy, active citizenship, and pride in black history.

[*See also* Abolition and Anti-Slavery Movement; Grimké, Angelina Emily; Grimké, Sarah; *and* Stone, Lucy.]

BIBLIOGRAPHY

Karcher, Carolyn L. *The First Woman in the Republic: A Cultural Biography of Lydia Maria Child.* Durham, N.C.: Duke University Press, 1994.

Kenschaft, Lori J. *Lydia Maria Child: The Quest for Racial Justice.* Oxford and New York: Oxford University Press, 2002.

LORI KENSCHAFT

CHILDREN

This entry consists of two subentries:

Overview
Comparative History

Overview

The experience of childhood in world history has unfolded in three main stages, corresponding to the three main economic frameworks within which human cultures and institutions have developed: hunter-gatherer, agricultural, and industrial. In hunter-gatherer—and also in nomadic—economies, children had relatively few assigned work functions until they approached adolescence. For this reason, and because of resource constraints and the demands of recurrent travel, birthrates were kept low, mainly by prolonged lactation. Children's play was valued and often involved interaction with adults.

Agricultural societies depended more heavily on children's labor: they served as assistants from about age five, then as major contributors to the family economy during the teenage years. Birthrates went up, although there was still concern about overburdening families with too many children. On average, upper-class families had higher birthrates than the majority of the population. With the advent of more elaborate class structures and of the written word, a minority of children attended school or received tutoring. Obedience and discipline were emphasized for children in all groups.

Although reliant on child labor for a time, industrial societies quickly moved to make education, rather than work, the primary component of childhood. This was accompanied by a marked decline in birthrates but also in child death rates. By the twentieth century, many industrial societies also began focusing on children as consumers, presenting elaborate arrays of goods and entertainments for adults to give to children or for children to acquire directly.

Not surprisingly, each major version of childhood emphasized different gender components. In hunter-gatherer societies, children were relatively undifferentiated in their early years. Shared play was common. Important rites of passage marked the achievement of more adult status, and here gender distinctions were also marked. Boys had to demonstrate appropriate courage and skills in hunting or (in nomadic groups) ridership. Introduction of girls to the functions of womanhood was quite different.

Agricultural societies characteristically emphasized gender differences at an earlier age, after a few years of undifferentiated infancy and early childhood in which, among other things, styles of dress were shared. Early work tasks saw boys assisting men in the family, and girls aiding their mothers and other women. This provided work service and training alike. Gender distinctions were amplified by more formal work assignments, including apprenticeships for many boys, during the teenage years. Schooling was also characteristically gender separated, and far more boys were educated than girls. Education was closely linked to religious or bureaucratic service, which helped explain the disproportionate attention to boys. Individual girls did, however, receive education, based in part on parental indulgence.

The evolution of industrial societies has generally tended toward a reduction of gender differences. In early industrial Europe or Japan, for instance, boys and girls in schools were subjected to different curricula, with much emphasis on domestic skills and virtues for girls. Gradually, however, differences diminished, and boys and girls were expected to achieve in the same subject areas at least until the level of higher education. Gradually as well, initial disproportions in higher education, favoring men, yielded to more equal entry. By the later twentieth century, in many industrial societies more women than men entered higher education.

Anti-Child-Labor Movement. Children in a child-labor demonstration, New York, May 1909. PRINTS AND PHOTOGRAPHS DIVISION, LIBRARY OF CONGRESS

Industrial societies did, however, attempt to maintain gender distinctions in some other ways. It was in the early twentieth century, for example, that the United States introduced the idea of pink colors for baby girls, blue for boys. Major differences in dress continued, although here, too, by the later twentieth century clothing could be more gender neutral. Consumer toys were often gender specific, and global consumerism emphasized the importance of female sexuality, with major reverberations in childhood. Sports interests, however, initially taken as an important boundary between the two genders in childhood, increasingly became less gendered as sports participation by girls gained in many societies.

Cultural Parameters. Individual societies also have cultural styles, alongside their economic frameworks, that have been highly relevant to children's sense of gender. Confucian ideals in China, for example, though emphasizing strict manners and obedience overall, placed great value on privileging sons. A leading traditional manual, written by an upper-class woman in Han China, urged that boy babies be placed at the side of the parental bed but girls at the feet, so they would learn their inferiority early on. Later the practice of foot-binding literally constrained many girls, particularly in the cities. Ideas about gender in classical India, though also privileging boys, did not encourage such formal initial differentiations.

Early civilizations differed also on the more basic subject of child preference. Many early civilizations practiced infanticide as a means of birth control, with disproportionate focus on girls. Sons were seen as more vital to family futures, and of course reducing the female population was also an effective means of birth control. In China and the Mediterranean, female infanticide was extensive before and during the classical period, although Egypt, as a river-valley civilization, did not indulge the practice, and India, with greater emphasis on the religious sanctity of life, also discouraged the practice.

The widespread world religions—Buddhism, Christianity, and Islam—effected some changes in the gendered quality of childhood. All the religions combated infanticide, with considerable effect; Muhammad specifically attacked the practice, in the Qurʾan. By urging that females and males were spiritually equal, the religions could also encourage more educational attention to girls—although boys remained privileged. Different family structures also affected childhood. The European-style family, developing in the later Middle Ages and stressing a relatively late marriage age, made nuclear households the norm and probably increased the demands on child labor for both boys and girls.

Global Patterns in the Modern World. Worldwide, child labor intensified during the seventeenth and eighteenth centuries in response to population growth, new export opportunities (for example, for Chinese goods such as silks and porcelains), and the spread of commercial slavery in the Atlantic. Industrial societies over time have largely accepted the modern model of schooling and consumerism for children. The United States moved more rapidly toward coeducation, in primary and secondary schools, than did western Europe, although European patterns changed after World War II. Chinese birth-control policies, adopted after 1978, led to a growing number of single-child families. In the countryside some families seem to have responded to the one-child policy with renewed emphasis on female infanticide; Chinese orphanages were often filled with nine girls for every boy. But many families, with their one child a daughter, began to pay more attention to girls' educational experiences and opportunities.

Economic and cultural globalization in the late twentieth century spread new standards for children. Both Japanese and American consumer exports emphasized the cuteness of the young child, whether girl or boy. International agencies spread new ideas about children's rights, including the right to education, and most societies—including the United States, belatedly in 2005—banned capital punishments for children. At the same time a number of societies, exposed to newly rigorous standards for the female body disseminated through Western television and films, experienced a rise in eating disorders as girls attempted feats of slenderness.

Regional differences remained important in the experience of childhood, based in part on major differences in living standards. Worldwide, child labor declined and primary education had spread to about 88 percent of the relevant age-group by the year 2000, but child workers increased in number in South and Southeast Asia. Economic pressures in several regions drove many girls into sexual servitude, sometimes as part of the spread of international tourism. Civil strife drove children in many regions into refugee camps or worse, again in contradistinction to the officially promoted international standards.

The current variations in the contemporary conditions of children are at least as great as ever before in the human experience, despite global connections and some dominant patterns of change. Gender patterns among children reflect dominant economic frameworks, but they also reflect a complex host of regional cultural features.

[*See also* Adoption; Female Life Cycle; Gender Preference in Children; *and* Gender Roles.]

BIBLIOGRAPHY

Ariès, Philippe. *Centuries of Childhood: A Social History of Family Life*. Translated by Robert Baldick. New York: Alfred A. Knopf, 1962. A classic study, often and persuasively disputed but still very challenging; it helped open the field to historical research.

Colón, A. R., with P. A. Colón. *A History of Children: A Socio-Cultural Survey across Millennia*. Westport, Conn.: Greenwood Press, 2001.

Fass, Paula, ed. *Encyclopedia of Children and Childhood: In History and Society*. 3 vols. New York: Macmillan, 2004.

Stearns, Peter N. *Childhood in World History*. London: Routledge, 2005.

On specific societies, see Avner Gil'adi, *Children of Islam: Concepts of Childhood in Medieval Muslim Society* (New York: St. Martin's Press, 1992); Ping-chen Hsiung, *A Tender Voyage: Children and Childhood in Late Imperial China* (Stanford, Calif.: Stanford University Press, 2005); and Tobias Hecht, ed., *Minor Omissions: Children in Latin American History and Society* (Madison: University of Wisconsin Press, 2002).

Alicia Smallbrock

Comparative History

Comparative work on the history of childhood is—perhaps appropriately—in its infancy. Significant insights are available, but systematic comparative categories remain to be developed. Regional coverage is also uneven: Chinese history is increasingly well served, but much less is available on India, to take one example.

Some existing findings are tantalizing. Visitors to ancient Egypt, for example, were astounded that the Egyptians did not practice infanticide, as was routine in Greece and elsewhere—but we do not know why customs varied so strongly. Possibly the greater reliability of Nile-based irrigation enhanced economic security, which in turn relieved the kinds of pressures on families that generated substantial infanticide. Egyptian culture, though patriarchal, held women in somewhat higher esteem than was true in most early civilizations, and since infanticide bore particularly on females, this cultural distinction might have played a role.

Cultural distinctions of uncertain origin often play a role in variations in childhood. Many groups in West Africa viewed twins as possessed by evil spirits and even put them to death. The general notion of identifying bad omens in a newborn was quite widespread in agricultural societies, but specific foci varied greatly from one region to the next. Particular customs associated with childbirth, including uses of "white" magic to promote fertility, were also culturally determined.

Huge differences emerged in the experiences of children in hunting and gathering and nomadic societies, on the one hand, and agricultural societies on the other. Groups that had to move frequently, in search of game or grazing land, maintained low birth rates. Food supplies were uncertain, and children could play little useful work role at least until their teenage years. Studies have shown, for example, that mothers who gather grains and nuts are less productive when accompanied by children—even if the latter try to help—than when working on their own. Travel itself constrained family size, for it was difficult to take more than one fairly young child in transit. Hunting and gathering and nomadic societies almost invariably attempt to limit birth rates by prolonged periods of lactation, ranging up to four or five years, among other methods.

Agricultural societies contrasted greatly. The reliability of food supplies in general improved, and more important, the work services of children became vital to the family economy. Young children, to be sure, could provide only modest useful work, but their training helped prepare more substantial contributions during adolescence. Small wonder that birth rates increased notably with the full advent of agriculture. Most families in agricultural societies (apart from the upper class, which often afforded larger broods) aimed for five to seven children, on the assumption that up to 50 percent would die fairly early and leave a remainder adequate to the task of providing family labor without overwhelming resources. Obviously, devices like infanticide came into play when calculations were surpassed by reality. Peasant families still sought to limit births and provide some spacing, using lactation as one device, but at shorter intervals—often up to only eighteen to twenty-four months.

The distinction between nomadic and agricultural childhoods also applied to the duration of childhood. Most nomadic and foraging societies introduced some passage to adulthood, particularly for boys, in the early teenage years. In agricultural societies religious ceremonies might recall this, establishing a kind of spiritual adulthood, but in practice childhood or at least pre-adulthood was encouraged far longer; it was vital to maintain labor services of older children, which meant that it was important to retain some sense of dependency, if not outright childhood, into the late teens or even beyond.

Among agricultural civilizations, comparison returns strongly to cultural issues, along with some impressive similarities based on the family labor requirements for children. Attitudes and behaviors toward children in classical (Han dynasty) China and the Roman Empire showed some striking parallels. In neither society did people writing about their lives dwell on childhood or suggest any particular pleasures in that stage of life. In both, attitudes toward young children were tentative, and deaths of young children occasioned little notice or commemoration. At the same time, also in both, there was considerable disdain for childish adolescents and a positive esteem for children who could act like adults—something for which the Romans had an approving term, *puer senex*. Most strikingly, though consistent with the work obligations expected of most children, both societies placed a high premium on obedience, and on discipline and manners that would instill obedience. Even upper-class school children, though not held to work in the conventional sense, were expected to show diligence, particularly in memorization.

Differences did emerge, of course, with reference to particular cultures. Chinese Confucianism insisted on more elaborate hierarchies among children, by age and gender, than were common in Rome, and much more detailed ceremonial manners, at least in the upper classes. The Chinese had a particular belief in the educability of children before birth, which could lead to considerable attention to conversations with the fetus and a particular kind of attention to the mother. A number of historians have emphasized the intense bonds that Chinese mothers tried to forge with their children, particularly boys; in upper-class households with several wives or concubines, mothers might insist on this bond as a means of emotional self-expression and assurance of future care. Roman maternal ties, in more diffuse households, seem to have been less fervent on average.

Children's Games. A Roman relief from the sarcophagus of a child, c. 100–300 C.E. KUNSTHISTORISCHES MUSEUM, VIENNA/ERICH LESSING/ART RESOURCE, NY

Chinese socialization materials focus particularly strongly on different treatments between boys and girls; one very durable manual (by a woman, Ban Zhao) urged that infant girls be placed at the foot of the parents' bed, boys at its side, to indicate status differences from the outset. Roman distinctions were also considerable, but less structured. In both cases, in point of fact, some girls in the upper classes received formal education, but this was much more likely for boys.

Childhood in classical India may have differed more strongly from the Chinese and Roman patterns. In the long term, historians of India have emphasized the contrast between highly indulgent early childhoods and strict religious discipline associated with Hinduism or Buddhism, imposed on early adolescents and particularly boys. Whether this emerged in full force during the classical period is, however, unclear, though the greater religious orientation of Indian culture at that point is obvious. Mothers, also, seem to have been surrounded by greater care and celebration than was true in China. All the classical civilizations were patriarchal and emphasized major distinctions between boys and girls, but the particular expressions of this division varied with the culture. Chinese recommendations that boy babies be placed at the side of the parents' bed, but girls at the feet—to inculcate hierarchy immediately—were not paralleled in Rome or in India.

World Religions. The greater spread of world religions, before and during the postclassical period, raises new issues of comparison based on cultural norms. There were some shared impulses. Christianity, Buddhism, and Islam all opposed infanticide, on grounds that children had souls—this was particularly pronounced in Islam. The same principle also encouraged new admonitions about parental care for children. Religion also promoted new types of schooling (qualified, however, by economic levels and political stability) and probably encouraged an expansion of education, though schooling was often based on memorization.

While all the major religions discouraged infanticide, some also provided facilities for abandonment of unwanted children. Death rates were high in this category, and concerns about the treatment of orphans began to emerge, certainly in western Europe by the time of the Middle Ages. Furthermore, the world religions all recognized that females as well as males had souls, and all offered some spiritual expressions for women—for example, in the convents of Christianity or Buddhism. Educational and status differences between boys and girls nonetheless remained considerable.

Both Christianity and Islam religions praised good parenting and urged the moral training of children. Both encouraged religious schooling, though Islam moved faster here if only because the Middle East was long more prosperous than Christian Europe. But the two religions differed markedly in their theoretical approach to children. For Christians, children were tainted by original sin, and of course an important set of sacraments and rituals were directed toward this issue, beginning with baptism. Many versions of Christianity emphasized children's sinfulness and the importance of using fear of death and punishment to discipline them appropriately. Islam differed in presuming children's innocence. During the postclassical period, many Muslim authorities urged against harsh punishments for children and even debated the validity of corporal discipline of any sort. In contrast, European emphasis on severity was noteworthy, a subject of remark, for example, by Native Americans when they encountered European settler families in the seventeenth and eighteenth centuries.

European distinctions may have been compounded when, from the fourteenth century onward, western Europe began to generate a distinctive family structure based on relatively late marriage and considerable nuclearity (if only because the overlap with grandparents was usually limited, given age of marriage and first births). This system placed great emphasis on mother's work and may have limited attention to young children. By the seventeenth century many European children, in the homes of artisans and peasants, were swaddled and hung on hooks, to free up their mother's labor. In Asia maternal attention to young children was greater, if only because most families operated in an extended framework where labor could be provided by a greater variety of family members. African practice also differed, for while women performed a greater variety of agricultural tasks, they typically carried young children with them, cementing mutual bonds. The possibility of European distinctiveness and its relationship to the kinds of reforms in the treatment and perception of children that began to be discussed by John Locke and others in the seventeenth century offer intriguing targets for further analysis.

The Effects of Industrialization. The advent of industrial society and the growth of closer global contacts, from the early nineteenth century onward, generate three kinds of comparative vantage points for childhood. First, a number of key changes began to spread widely, from an initially western European base. Comparison here focuses on significant differences in timing, which shapes history and contemporary experience alike. Second, common trends blended with different traditions to produce significant variants around broadly shared patterns. Third, some societies introduced distinctive individual innovations, which were not widely imitated.

Timing differentials were crucial around basic trends such as birth and death rate reduction and the replacement of work with schooling. Industrialization encouraged a birth rate reduction in the Western world, as children's labor became less essential and school obligations and costs turned them from economic assets to liabilities. By 1900 the infant death rate was falling as well. Similar patterns developed in Russia under communism, in Japan by 1950, in Latin America by the 1970s. By 2000 birth rates were dropping in every region, but some regions were just launching the process, whereas in others the demographic transition, with resultant small families and sibling sets, was well established.

Timing differentials were augmented by some contrary regional developments. In South and Southeast Asia, child labor increased in the decades around 2000, from 6 million to 9 million children—even though governments encouraged schooling. Economic pressures and traditional assumptions presumably combined here, even though child labor worldwide dropped from 6 percent to 3 percent of the total labor force. Disease and famine brought child death rates up in Africa in the same period, again bucking larger global trends. There were other variants beyond timing. Several societies, like Russia and Japan, relied heavily on abortion for birth rate

Working Children. Sri Lankan children picking tea at Talawakele, near Nuwara Eliya, c. 1903. PRINTS AND PHOTOGRAPHS DIVISION, LIBRARY OF CONGRESS

control, whereas other methods predominated in western Europe and Africa.

Several societies dealt with particular regional issues during the nineteenth and twentieth century. In western Europe, an old practice of sending children out to a wet nurse, designed to free up working mothers or coddle aristocratic families, became widely attacked on grounds of health and emotional distance, and it gradually declined. Midwifery was also attacked by physicians with greater impact than in some other societies. Latin America inherited from the colonial period a high rate of illegitimate births, despite official endorsement of European ideals of sex within marriage. Community care and family flexibility responded to the illegitimacy rates, so that few children were untended.

The decline of child labor plus other dislocations required new policies concerning orphans and their placement, in many societies. Trans-regional adoption developed as one response at the end of the twentieth century, amid considerable dispute.

Global influences and in some cases growing urban prosperity prompted widespread attention to children as consumers, from the late nineteenth century onward. Child-oriented consumer holidays gained ground—including Christmas even in Muslim and Chinese regions. The notion of celebrating birthdays spread as well, along with widespread translations of the American "happy birthday" jingle. Again, however, both timing and degree varied with different economic and urban levels and differences in prior culture.

Industrialization and mounting consumerism tended, on the whole, gradually to reduce (though hardly eliminate) gender differences in children and their socialization. A crucial change came beginning in the nineteenth century, when modern educational systems were opened to girls as well as boys, initially at the primary levels and then beyond. The need to train workers and even more the sense that an educated citizenry depended on literate, patriotic mothers motivated this significant development. Furthermore, the decline of child labor reduced this early differentiator as well—all children, increasingly, were to be sent to school. These changes could be modified, of course, by different investments—girls often went to school for shorter periods of time than boys in the earliest industrial decades, though that tended to alter later on. Different curricula were often prescribed, with training for girls emphasizing family skills. And new differentiations—like the idea of pink for girls, blue for boys, introduced in the United States in the 1920s—or separate extracurricular activities could enhance symbolic distinctions. But an overall pattern did tend to emerge that softened the emphasis agricultural societies had placed on gender distinctions. In many societies, even clothing styles crossed gender lines for children by the twentieth and twenty-first centuries.

International agencies helped spread ideas about treating children as individuals, and Western influences had encouraged this in some places earlier. But this message was often modified by cultural tradition. Japan opted eagerly for Western-style education after 1872 but then pulled back in the 1880s to emphasize the importance of obedience and group harmony, the latter still a distinctive quality in Japanese education compared to American or even Chinese. Middle Eastern families after World War II devoted growing attention to individual education, even for girls, but continued to instill the importance of family identity and obligation.

The idea of adolescence was another important variable. Developed in the nineteenth-century West, at a time when older children were increasingly bound to school and in which issues of sexual behavior received new attention, the concept had only loose applicability to other societies. In Africa, work obligations for older children maintained a more traditional sense of a period of youth stretching from the mid-teens well into the twenties—a period neither child nor adult. Historians and anthropologists continue to debate comparative issues around the relevance of adolescence.

Economic conditions shaped other differences in the experiences of older children. In the advanced industrial societies after World War II, rates of university attendance reached a virtual majority. But poorer societies, despite eagerness for education, simply could not afford this. China in 2003 took the bold step of assuring 15 percent of the age group access to higher education, but obviously the comparative difference remained considerable.

Innovations did not stem from the West alone. Japan, by the 1920s, shared with the United States leadership in the development of the most creative toys, or at least the most widely popular, in global markets. Apparently toy design meshed with Japanese artistic and game traditions to provide this surge. Communist societies, though fading by 2000, introduced changes as well. Along with the shorter-lived fascist countries, they pioneered in introducing extensive youth groups, for indoctrination and some labor service. This distinctive organizational experience was crucial for several generations in countries like Russia and China.

Wars caused distinctions as well. The late twentieth century saw conflicts in Africa and parts of Southeast Asia highlight the role of heavily armed boy soldiers—at a time when societies in the rest of the world stressed the importance of keeping children out of conflict.

A comparative perspective on childhood in 2000 would probably stress the huge differences in the timing of changes in birth and death rates, and educational levels, above all, even though similar basic trends may be at work. But other regional distinctions, including some new ones as in leadership of availability children's gadgets, must be considered as well. Economic variables must be combined with new-old blends of variations in cultural standards.

BIBLIOGRAPHY

Burguière, André, Christiane Klapish-Zuber, Martine Segalen, and Françoise Zonabend, eds. *A History of the Family*. Vol. 1: *Distant Worlds, Ancient Worlds*. Cambridge, Mass.: Harvard University Press, 1996.

Colón, A. R., with P. A. Colón. *A History of Children: A Sociocultural Survey across Millennia*. Westport, Conn.: Greenwood, 2001.

Fernea, Elizabeth Warnock, ed. *Children in the Muslim Middle East*. Austin: University of Texas Press, 1995.

Hsuing, Ping-chen. *A Tender Voyage: Children and Childhood in Late Imperial China*. Stanford, Calif.: Stanford University Press, 2005.

Hartman, Mary. *Households and the Making of History: A Subversive View of the Western Past*. New York: Cambridge University Press, 2004.

Kinney, Anne Behnke. *Representations of Childhood and Youth in Early China*. Stanford, Calif.: Stanford University Press, 2004.

Kirschenbaum, Lisa. *Small Comrades: Revolutionizing Childhood in Soviet Russia, 1917–1932*. New York: Routledge, 2001.

Rawson, Beryl. *Marriage, Divorce, and Children in Ancient Rome*. Oxford: Oxford University Press, 1991.

Scheper-Hughes, Nancy, and Carolyn Sargent. *Small Wars: The Cultural Politics of Childhood*. Berkeley: University of California Press, 1998.

Seabrook, Jeremy. *Children of Other Worlds: Exploitation in the Global Market*. London: Pluto Press, 2001.

Stearns, Peter N. *Childhood in World History*. New York: Routledge, 2006.

Uno, Kathleen. *Passages to Modernity: Childhood and Social Reform in Early Twentieth Century Japan*. Honolulu: University of Hawai'i Press, 1999.

PETER N. STEARNS

CHILE. Chilean women and gender relations were affected by global trends such as movements for independence from Spain, the rise of liberalism and liberal conflicts with conservatives, the growth of working-class movements and leftist parties, reforms in the Catholic Church, industrialization and urbanization, the advent of the welfare state, and the Cold War.

The Early Republic. Women were active in Chile's independence struggles—which began in 1810 with Chile's declaration of autonomy and lasted until total independence in 1818—and then in the politics of the early republic, as members of kinship groups aligned with political factions.

The brokering of marriages among the elite of the early republic helped cement political, social, and economic ties among prominent families and secured political stability. Few women had access to formal schooling beyond the primary school level, but some elite girls attended private religious and secular schools. Elite women also sponsored literary and philosophical salons. The first state-sponsored normal school for girls was set up in 1854 by the Catholic Society of the Sacred Heart of Jesus, and women were permitted to attend the University of Chile in 1877. A state-funded vocational school for girls was set up in 1889.

After the promulgation of the Rerum Novarum, Catholic women formed the Liga de Damas (Ladies' League) in 1912. The Liga sought to relieve the suffering of poor women through charitable works and to improve the moral condition of a society they viewed as having been corrupted by modern entertainments and crass consumption. Secular women formed the Círculo de Lectura (Reading Circle) and the Club de Señoras (Women's Club) in 1915. The Círculo de Lectura was founded by the feminist and educator Amanda Labarca, who had become familiar with similar groups during her studies at Columbia University in New York City. Both the Círculo and the Club sought to make women into modern, enlightened mothers and wives. Secular women advocated for women's rights and reform of the civil code but took a cautious attitude about the controversial subject of women's suffrage. In the 1920s the Partido Cívico Femenino (Women's Civic Party) called for granting women greater civil and political rights.

Industrialization and Working-class Women. As the Chilean economy industrialized in the late nineteenth and

Chilean Suffrage Movement. A Chilean broadsheet advocating women's right to vote, 1937. COURTESY OF ASUNCIÓN LAVRIN

early twentieth centuries, increasing numbers of working-class men and women labored for wages, and many of the income-generating activities women performed within the home (laundering, sewing, food preparation) came to be seen as nonproductive extensions of women's domestic work. Scholars hypothesize that the apparent decline in women's workforce participation evident in Chile's 1930 census was due principally to a new definition of what constituted "work" and not to a real decline in women's income-generating activities.

Industrialization provided the impetus for the first organizations of working women. Urban working women—including laundresses, seamstresses, and workers in textile and shoe industries—formed mutual-aid societies and groups affiliated with anarchist resistance societies. A fledgling "worker feminism" advocated for women's rights as wage workers but also saw women's work outside the home as undesirable, arguing that in a socialist utopia women would not need to work outside the home. Women in coal-, nitrate-, and copper-mining communities participated in activities organized by all-male labor unions and formed female auxiliaries that pressed for improved working conditions for male relatives. Catholics, including women in the Liga, countered socialist women's organizing by creating and stewarding non-Marxist labor organizations for working women.

Women in the countryside had fewer opportunities for paid labor. Although entire families worked as resident laborers on large haciendas, the labor of women and children was controlled by male household heads. Temporary laborers were almost exclusively men. Lack of employment opportunities drove many women, including those from indigenous communities, to seek work as domestic servants in the cities. Throughout the twentieth century, between 25 and 40 percent of all women wage earners were employed in domestic service.

Rise of the Welfare State and Feminism. After 1925, public and private welfare measures increasingly sought to mitigate the worst excesses of capitalist modernization, and health and welfare agencies promoted a pro-natalist agenda that privileged women's roles as mothers. They also promoted a family wage system that privileged male work, justifying improved benefits and wages for men by arguing that men needed to support families. Working-class women consequently saw their employment opportunities reduced.

At the same time, the state stimulated new employment opportunities for middle-class women in fields such as teaching, nursing, and social work. These middle-class women formed the backbone of the vibrant feminist movement that flourished in the 1930s and 1940s. Among the most important organizations were the Unión Femenina de Chile (Chilean Women's Union), Comité Pro-Derechos de la Mujer (Women's Rights Committee), Movimiento Pro-Emanicipación de la Mujer Chilena (MEMCh; Movement for the Emancipation of Chilean Women), Acción Nacional de Mujeres (National Women's Action), and Federación Chilena de Instutciones Femeninas (FEChIF; Chilean Federation of Women's Institutions), along with many other smaller groups of different political orientations. Working-class housewives participated in consumers' committees that were eventually organized into a state-orchestrated Asociación de Dueñas de Casa (Housewives' Association).

A revision of the civil code in 1934 expanded women's civil rights, granting shared parental control over children, but men remained the legal heads of households. Women also gained the right to vote in municipal elections in 1934, but only literate women would exercise that right. Women were granted the right to vote in national elections in 1949. Leaders of women's groups argued that, as mothers, women deserved special rights and protections, and professionals within the organizations often derived authority and recognition from their presumed ability to address the needs of working-class women. At the same time, prominent leftist feminists such as Marta Vergara and Elena Caffarena articulated a radical critique of the relation between women's subordination in marriage and in the workplace.

The feminist movement broke apart after 1947 as a result of anti-Communist legislation imposed by the United States and backed by President Gabriel González Videla. During the 1950s and 1960s the main venues for women's social and political participation were the mothers' centers that had grown out of the consumer movement. Mothers' centers were organized by political parties across the spectrum, and beginning around 1965 they were recognized and promoted by the state.

Cold War and Beyond. Until the 2006 presidential election in which Michelle Bachelet became the first woman president of Chile, Chilean women consistently voted for the political parties of the Right in greater numbers than men did. However, women's votes varied starkly by social class, and as more working-class women registered to vote from 1950 to 1970, the gender gap between men and women narrowed. Right-wing women were vocal opponents of the leftist president Salvador Allende, who was elected in 1970, and were supporters of the military coup that brought General Augusto Pinochet to power in 1973.

A resurgence of organized feminism occurred during Pinochet's military dictatorship (1973–1990), when social movements emerged in the place of banned political parties. In 1979 the feminist intellectual Julieta Kirkwood and other middle-class women formed a Círculo de Estudios de la Mujer (Women's Studies Circle) under the aegis of the Academy of Christian Humanism, an organization affiliated with the Catholic Church. At the same time, women from poor neighborhoods organized to oppose the military government, advocate for human rights, and secure the subsistence of their families. Middle-class feminists worked hand in hand with groups of working-class women. A national plebiscite voted Pinochet out of power in 1988, but women were not fully incorporated into the national political agenda in the ensuing years.

Paradoxically, by restructuring the economy and creating new agro-export and service sectors, the military dictatorship increased employment opportunities for women, leading to a rise in Chile's historically low workforce participation rates for women. The proportion of households headed by women rose and family wage policies that excluded women from the workforce gave way in Chile's new neoliberal economy. Chileans celebrated the election of Michelle Bachelet as an important milestone in Chilean history and women's history.

[*See also* Allende, Isabel; Codes of Law and Laws, *subentry* Latin America; Feminist Encounters of Latin American and Caribbean Women; Suárez, Inés de; *and biographies of women mentioned in this article.*]

BIBLIOGRAPHY

Hutchison, Elizabeth Quay. *Labors Appropriate to Their Sex: Gender, Labor, and Politics in Urban Chile, 1900–1930.* Durham, N.C.: Duke University Press, 2001.

Kirkwood, Julieta. *Ser política en Chile: Las feministas y los partidos.* Santiago, Chile: Facultad Latinoamericana de Ciencias Sociales, 1986.

Lavrin, Asunción. *Women, Feminism, and Social Change in Argentina, Chile, and Uruguay, 1890–1940.* Lincoln: University of Nebraska Press, 1995.

Power, Margaret. *Right-Wing Women in Chile: Feminine Power and the Struggle against Allende, 1964–1973.* University Park: Pennsylvania State University Press, 2002.

Rosemblatt, Karin. *Gendered Compromises: Political Cultures and the State in Chile.* Chapel Hill: University of North Carolina Press, 2000.

Tinsman, Heidi. *Partners in Conflict: The Politics of Gender, Sexuality, and Labor in the Chilean Agrarian Reform, 1950–1973.* Durham, N.C.: Duke University Press, 2002.

Verba, Ericka. "The Círculo de Lectura de Señoras and the Club de Señoras of Santiago, Chile: Middle- and Upper-class Feminist Conversations (1915–1920)." *Journal of Women's History* 7, no. 3 (Fall 1995): 6–33.

Vicuña, Manuel. *Labelle époque chilena.* Santiago, Chile: Sudamericana, 2001.

KARIN ALEJANDRA ROSEMBLATT

CHINA

This entry consists of three subentries:

Ancient Period
Imperial Period
Modern Period

Ancient Period

The received textual tradition on the history and status of women in Chinese antiquity includes the Five Classics, historical narratives, and philosophical and ritual works. As new resources become available, scholars are in a new position to explore the history and status of women in Chinese antiquity. Shang oracle-bone inscriptions, Zhou bronze inscriptions, and silk and bamboo texts from the Qin and Han dynasties supplement information from the received textual tradition.

Archaeological evidence suggests the emergence of several important characteristics of gender relations in Neolithic (c. 5000–1766 B.C.E.) and Shang (c. 1766–1045 B.C.E.) China, before the emergence of a specifically "Chinese" culture: (1) the importance of kinship for both men and women, (2) that at least elite women had ritual status as ancestresses and received religious cult, but (3) that women held lower status than men of corresponding rank. This was part of a pattern of reinforcing the authority of males over females, including a preference for male progeny. Some elite women had power and influence, but they were the exception.

With the growth of a specifically Chinese culture during the Eastern Zhou dynasty (770–221 B.C.E.), these broad tendencies received more specific expression through the development of a detailed ritual system that maintained kinship relations through notions of filiality. These notions applied to both men and women. This ritual system also specified that ancestral cult be offered to both men and women, but with important hierarchical gender distinctions that elevated the status of men over women. Rituals and child-rearing practices, including ritual prescriptions for the subordination of women to men, reinforced the authority of men over women. Nonetheless, limited evidence of social practices suggests that norms for these rituals were often disregarded in practice.

The Neolithic and Shang Periods. Neolithic and Shang mortuary evidence provides some data on sex ratios, vital statistics, and marriage patterns, and divination inscriptions also offer perspectives on the status of women in the late Shang dynasty (c. 1200–1045 B.C.E.). The names of royal women such as Fu Hao (late thirteenth century B.C.E.), whose tomb was excavated in 1976, appear in a wide range of divinations concerning childbirth, illness, dreams, military affairs, and ancestral cults. Ancestresses were also important figures in schedules of ritual sacrifice. Temple names, the generous cults that some consorts received, and the existence of a few temples dedicated to royal consorts all attest to the early importance of royal consorts. Oracle bone inscriptions also provide some information on the late Shang marriage system, including the relative status of royal consorts and the lineage groups of the Shang state.

The Neolithic period. Mortuary evidence and statistics based on excavated cemeteries are notoriously difficult to interpret, as are regional and local differences before the emergence of a single Chinese culture. Despite many hermeneutic difficulties, there is suggestive archaeological evidence that from the late Neolithic through the late Shang periods the political and economic status of women was consistently lower than that of men. The evidence also suggests that from the earliest times the status of both men and women greatly depended on kinship.

A preponderance of males in excavated Neolithic cemeteries suggests differential treatment of men and women as early as the fifth millennium B.C.E. Less clear is what led to this preponderance of males. It may be that female infanticide was practiced, that more girls than boys died in childhood and were not given formal burials, that more women than men died between the ages of twenty and thirty through childbearing and harsh conditions, or that at the time of death women were denied important funerary rituals (Keightley, pp. 7–9).

Mortuary evidence also provides some information on social identity. Some mortuary evidence suggests that allegiance to natal kin took precedence over marriage ties. Grave goods indicate a division of labor along gender lines as early as the sixth millennium B.C.E. Such goods also reflect increasing wealth, social differentiation, and a declining status of women and children in favor of adult men, all associated with the intensification of agriculture. Axes and other grave goods suggest that men received more ritual attention than women. Trends involving differential status based on sex, such as the increasing presence of emblematic tools symbolizing male authority, continued in the late Neolithic and Early Bronze Age (c. 2200–1700 B.C.E.). The Shang also practiced human sacrifice exclusively of male prisoners.

Late Shang inscriptional evidence (1200–1045 B.C.E.). Evidence from oracle-bone inscriptions shows that late-Shang kings had polygamous relations with multiple recognized consorts. Although use of the title "lady" (*fu*) was extensive, evidence from ancestral cults indicates that royal polygamy was much more limited. At least some royal consorts held considerable power (such as the prerogative to consecrate shells and bones used for divination) and ritual status (such as being worthy of having divinations performed on their account). One example is Lady Xi, whose name appears on some scapulae and tortoise plastrons used in divination during the reign of Wu Ding (r. 1324–1265 B.C.E.), the twentieth Shang king. Diviners described the birth of a son or daughter as "good" or "not good," as distinct from "fortunate" or "unfortunate," possibly according to whether the baby lived or died. Finally, it is clear that a woman's status derived in part from marriage alliances.

Also, ancestresses were believed to play a political and social role after death. Women became ancestresses in the same way that men became ancestors: by burial rituals, the acquisition of a temple name, and receiving ancestral cult according to schedule. Yet ritual attention to women was limited. Only the consorts of kings in the main line of royal descent (both the sons and fathers of kings) received regular ancestral cult, and the consorts of the same king received cult in the order of their deaths. Even then, their status was subordinate to that of the king. Consorts received only four of the five rituals accorded to kings. They did not receive prayers for rain and harvest and thus had no jurisdictional link with agriculture. Prayers for progeny were directed to ancestresses, yet the divination was performed in the temple of her husband. According to archaeological evidence (Keightley, p. 43), late Shang ancestor cult was directed to ancestors over ancestresses by a ratio of 5 to 1.

On the basis of the evidence above, David Keightley argues that late Shang society was patriarchal, with elite women playing important but limited roles. He argues that the presence of clan names that include the graph for "woman" do not provide evidence for an earlier matriarchal society, contrary to what has been argued elsewhere. Marxist historians and others have also posited that there existed archaic matriarchies and goddess worship in prehistoric China (Mann, pp. 838–839). Keightley, by contrast, concludes that from the late Neolithic period through the late Shang dynasty, the political and economic status of women was inferior overall to that of men. Fewer women received burial rites (including secondary burial) or became ancestresses. When they did, their tombs were smaller than those of their male counterparts, and their authority was more limited. They received regular cult only through their husbands, and only when they had produced royal sons.

From the Zhou to Qin Dynasties. Textual sources for the condition of women in family, social, and political life during the Zhou dynasty (1045–221 B.C.E.) are indirect and present disparate, sometimes conflicting, information. From the time of the *Yi jing* (Book of Changes), religious and philosophical works consistently stressed the cosmological importance of women as the yin component of the complementary pair yin and yang, but they differed on what such complementarity meant.

Yin and yang. The Chinese systems of correlative cosmology that took stable form during the Han dynasty (206 B.C.E.–220 C.E.) prominently included a binary system based on the correlate pair yin and yang. Yin-yang correlations provided a powerful and flexible conceptual schema to describe the political, human, and natural worlds. They became the conceptual bases of early scientific thought in astronomy, medicine, music, and divination. Early Chinese views of yin and yang went through at least four distinct stages. Before the fourth century B.C.E., they referred to the shady and sunny, or north and south, sides of a hill. In fourth century B.C.E. works such as the *Zuo zhuan* (Zuo Annals), they refer to two of six "stuffs" *(qi)*. By the beginning of the third century B.C.E., they were understood as the two *qi* behind the differentiations of pairs of opposites, but with considerable variation in detail. It is in this sense that yin and yang appear in many works of philosophy of the Warring States period (475–221 B.C.E.). They emerged as the ultimate polarity in newly developed cosmological thinking. Finally, after the Qin unified China in 221 B.C.E., yin and yang began to appear in the systematic correspondences of correlative cosmology (Raphals, *Sharing the Light*, pp. 139–168).

For present purposes, the important point is that, initially, yin-yang polarities were relatively nonhierarchical, and yin and yang were not used in analogy with either heaven and earth or male and female. Even when yin and yang entered philosophical discourse as the basic polarity, it was not analogous either to gender (male and female) or to the hierarchy of heaven and earth. Hierarchical analogies between yin and yang on the one hand and male and female on the other became prevalent only in the first century B.C.E., with the growth of correlative cosmology. Indeed, some early yin-yang and gender analogies stressed either that yin and yang are composed of the same stuff (*qi*) or that they are equivalent in their capabilities. Others stressed differences between male and female modes (such as the cock and hen of the early Han manuscripts excavated at Mawangdui, Hunan), but with no hierarchical distinction. The explicitly hierarchical yin-yang male-female analogies of the first century B.C.E. came to dominate the tradition to such an extent that earlier yin-yang and gender analogies were all but ignored.

Ritual prescription and social practice. Ritual works such as the *Li ji* (Book of Rites) gave prescriptions for social behavior that emphasized gender segregation into inner and outer spheres of family and political life. Historical narratives such as the *Zuo zhuan* (Zuo Annals), *Guoyu* (Discourses of the States), *Shiji* (Historical Records), and *Lienü zhuan* (Biographies of Exemplary Women) provide a picture of the activities of women that diverges considerably from the prescriptions of ritual texts. There are important differences between the values and prohibitions of the classics and what we know of the practices of traditional Chinese society in such areas as the subordination of women to men; childhood training; marriage (and its humble cousin concubinage); gender segregation by restricting women to the inner quarters; social separation through names, titles, and ranks; and intellectual separation through education and expertise. There is evidence that women could advise husbands and sons; exert some autonomy within the household; exercise some choice in marriage, divorce, and remarriage; move or work outside the home; receive honorific titles and other honors; function as the intellectual equals and counterparts of men; and gain recognition for erudition and expertise.

Female subordination. Evidence for the inferior status of women dates from the earliest layers of the archaeological record. This subordination is codified and theorized in the *Book of Rites*. It articulates the doctrine of the three obediences (*sancong*): the obedience of women to their fathers as girls, to their husbands as wives, and to their sons as widows. From birth, girls were taught humility and obedience, and the relation of husband and wife was considered analogous to that of ruler and minister.

Evidence of social practice presents a more complex picture. Indeed, an important function of a minister was to advise and even reprimand a ruler. There is considerable evidence of the influence of women over their husbands and sons. Historical narratives describe husbands consulting their wives on domestic matters and women advising and instructing grown sons and husbands about both family matters and affairs of state. They also describe mothers instructing children, and wives controlling subordinates and concubines.

The situation of mothers was particularly complicated. Although inferior to their sons in the gender hierarchy, they were superior in the age hierarchy, and mothers retained at least some authority even over sons who had grown to become rulers and officials. Legendary queens instructed their sons to become virtuous kings and wise ministers. They include the mother of Hou Ji, the inventor of agriculture, and the mothers of the founding rulers of the Shang and Zhou dynasties. There are also records of maternal instruction extended to grown sons, and of maternal instruction on government and statecraft to rulers and high officials. Perhaps the most famous example is Meng Mu, the mother of the Confucian philosopher Mencius. Her moral and practical instruction to him as a child spurred him to study, but even when Mencius was an adult, she continued to advise, and criticize, his behavior.

Widowhood aggravated this tension between age and gender hierarchies. Norms of filiality gave a widow authority within the family, but norms of gender subordination dictated obedience to her son. The extreme case was an empress dowager, who was nominally the family head and a potential regent for the throne, with the power to designate a royal heir and to betroth or dethrone a child emperor. In this case, filiality was at odds with imperial sovereignty. The typical resolution was for the empress dowager to withdraw from court, but to continue to wield psychological power and control over royal marriages and appointments of male relatives. Wives thus began their marriages in weak positions but could gain considerable power if they outlived their husbands.

Childhood. Some evidence for the upbringing of girls during the Zhou dynasty comes from the Five Classics, which show girls as marked by inferior status and taught subordination from birth. The *Shi jing* (Book of Odes) describes boys as sleeping on beds, wearing robes, and playing with scepters, whereas their sisters lie on the ground, wear shifts, and play with tiles (Ode 189). The *Book of Rites* gives rules for the education of children. It describes the proper ages for particular instructions but does not explicitly restrict education according to gender:

> At age six [children] are taught the names of the numbers and the cardinal points. At seven boys and girls do not [sit on] the same mat or eat together. At eight, when they go in and out of doors and gates, proceed to their mats, and eat and drink, they must follow behind their elders, and they begin to receive instruction in deference. At nine they are taught the numbering of the days. At ten they go to an outside master and stay with him and sleep outside [the home]. They study writing and calculation.
>
> (*Li ji*, 12; author's translation)

Instruction in writing and calculation presumably applied to boys, but the *Book of Rites* makes no such specification. The *Book of Rites* does specify that after the age of ten, girls do not go out. Female instructors taught them to be docile and obedient and instructed them in women's work: hemp production, sericulture, weaving, preparing food, and assisting in sacrifices (*Li ji* 1: 479). The text specifies the skills that girls were required to learn, but it does not prohibit them from learning others. An important point here is that education was a family matter. Some elite families educated their daughters and produced scholars such as the historian Ban Zhao and the poet and scholar Cai Yan. Others, the vast majority of the populace, probably did not.

Marriage. For both men and women, filiality was central to a marriage system in which neither spouse had a choice and the parents of the husband chose his wife. A wife's primary obligation was to her husband's parents. As wives, women had no say in their children's marriages, but as widowed grandmothers, they could control their grandchildren's marriages. Again, historical narratives suggest regional differences and more flexibility in practice: they provide examples of women defying their families' choices of husbands or orders to leave (or not to leave) existing husbands, and examples of women remarrying.

An important gender distinction involved the availability of divorce and the acceptability of remarriage. The dominant expectation was monogamy for women and serial polygyny for men. Theoretically, men could divorce their wives on grounds of disobedience to parents-in-law, barrenness, adultery, jealousy, incurable disease, loquacity, or theft, with exceptions based on periods of mourning for the woman's parents, the woman's lack of natal kin, or wealth acquired during the marriage. In practice, divorces occurred for political, economic, and social reasons, and women sometimes left husbands either to return to their families or to marry other men. Remarriage was the norm for both men and women at all socioeconomic levels, and widows who refused remarriage were the exception.

Although monogamy was the norm in ancient China, from the earliest times concubinage was a legally and socially accepted alternative among rulers and the elite. Women became concubines by being sold by their impoverished families or by being kidnapped and sold. Some came from wealthy or elite families, but these were the exception. Although concubinage was legally recognized, it was not marriage, and that had important implications. Legal marriage required a betrothal and a wedding ceremony; concubinage did not. Concubines held lower

Meng Mu and Mencius. Meng Mu at her loom holding a knife while her son, the Confucian philosopher Mencius, stands bowed behind her. From the Ming edition of Gui Fan. COURTESY OF LISA RAPHALS

status within the family than that of wives, and there were prohibitions against elevating a concubine to the status of wife. The children of concubines also held inferior status. Finally, wives were entitled to ancestral cult and held ranks through the titles and positions of their husbands. Concubines were entitled to none of these things (Ch'ü, pp. 44–48).

Separate spheres and women's work. The *Book of Rites* also set out rules for gender relations at the domestic level. These regulated the use of space, possessions, and physical contact between inner and outer. For example, men and women should not sit together, touch hands, or share a clothing stand, towel, or comb. Moreover, there should be no communication between unmarried men and women. Mourning and bathing rules specified that men and women do the same things, but in distinct ways or locations. The perceived need for such prohibitions suggests a high level of contact between the sexes. The courtyard design of wealthy homes provided opportunities for both visual and auditory contact between the sexes in the course of daily family life.

Weaving, regarded as women's work, was typically done within the home for use within the home. Even aristocratic women weaved and spun. Weaving and sericulture also provided a livelihood for widows and poor women, such as Mencius's mother.

There is also evidence that women engaged in family occupations such as farming and crafts. Women performed or supervised sacrifices and practiced divination and medicine. There are accounts of a woman of the Ji clan of Lu offering sacrifice when mourning her son, Wenbo, minister of Lu, and of another woman of Lu who returned to her parents' home to oversee ancestral sacrifices. Women appear in the *Zuo Annals* as both subjects and objects of divination. They personally performed or interpreted divination and prognostication, including military prognostication, physiognomy, and yarrow divination.

Other professions for women were exercised primarily outside the home. Girls trained to sing and dance found employment as entertainers in wealthy homes. Although their social status was low, some female entertainers became wives of powerful men and advanced their families—for example, the mother of the first Qin emperor (r. 221–210 B.C.E.).

There are also records of court offices staffed by women, who thus worked outside their homes. The *Zhou li* (Rites of Zhou) lists a variety of offices connected with the inner quarters of the court, some of them clearly held by women. In some cases, two complementary officials performed analogous tasks in the interior (women's quarters) and exterior (men's sphere)—for example, cooks and store masters (*Tcheou-li*, pp. 79–83 and 127–129). Some titles clearly designated women—for example, maids of the inner chambers, imperial concubines, female incantators, and female annalists (charged with writing; *Tcheou-li*, pp. 153–159).

These women officials were distinct from male officials concerned with the inner quarters. For instance, the (male) administrator and petty officers of the interior assisted the empress in sacrifices and rituals, provided instructions, and carried out her orders. The concierge and the palace eunuchs regulated comings and goings to and from the inner quarters. Other male officials, such as the director of women's work, the director of silk and thread, and the director of hemp, managed the manufacture and distribution of clothing (*Tcheou-li*, pp. 141–153 and 159–170). Though the dating of the *Book of Rites* and the *Rites of Zhou* is problematic, these sections nonetheless suggest that from Zhou times there were regulations of some form for ordering the inner quarters, at least at court, and for restricting conduct within the family.

These texts provide evidence that women moved freely outside their homes to work, visit their natal families, and talk to their neighbors. There are also attested cases of women inheriting property, controlling profitable businesses, and participating at court, though without rank. Elite and royal women received titles and exercised indirect political influence, including intrigue.

Within elite families, rituals for the distinctive treatment of children began at birth and established the importance of boys and the insignificance of girls. Boys' clothing, playthings, and treatment within the family reflected their future social roles as officials and rulers. Girls were prepared for women's work: weaving, preparing food, and assisting at ceremonial functions. Funerary rituals also specified shorter terms of mourning for women than for men of equivalent rank.

Name, rank, and social identity. Naming practices also established and maintained these distinctions. Texts of Eastern Zhou (770–221 B.C.E.) indicated a broad pattern of gender distinctions through names. For males, clan name (*xing*) and lineage name (*shi*) defined identity, rank, and position within patrilineages in Eastern Zhou society. Men also had other names, such as personal names (*ming*) and courtesy names (*zi*). By contrast, female personal names and natal names were usually suppressed after marriage. Unmarried daughters used personal names given by their parents (personal names of daughters appear in the *Zuo Annals* and the *Historical Records*), but Eastern Zhou wives did not retain these personal names.

A married woman was known by one of the names of her husband or his family, clan, or state, sometimes combined with her original nickname (*zi*), but never by the personal name given to her by her family. Names acquired through marriage included various combinations of several elements. Most names came from the husband or son—the husband's state, clan, or lineage name; the husband's rank; the husband's posthumous name; the son's rank; and the husband's clan name—which were combined with a sobriquet designating a special occurrence or special good conduct. The elements that came from the wife were a personal nickname and, in rare cases, a woman arrogating a posthumous name to herself. The overall result of these naming practices was to reinforce male identity and make women identify with their husbands' families. Without personal names, women were without rank.

The *Book of Rites* also makes clear that a woman's rank derived from that of her husband, not from herself or her natal family. Its description of the marriage ceremony specifies that husband and wife eat the same sacrificial meat, to show that they have the same rank. Thus did the wives, mothers, and sisters of rulers and the wives of officials hold rank and such court titles as empress, empress dowager, and princess. The rank of the wives of officials depended on, and was derived from, that of their husbands. For example, the title "court lady" (*mingfu*) was applied to the wives of upper-level officials.

There are some records of rulers awarding ranks, special honorary titles, and related emoluments to women, but such cases are rare. One of the most interesting cases is of a woman, a contemporary of Confucius (551–479 B.C.E.), who took her name from the powerful Ji clan of Lu. She received the title "sedate lady" (*jing jiang*). Little is known of her, but she is praised by Confucius and in the *Book of Rites* for her understanding of ritual and the distinctions between men and women and between superior and inferior. In one account, her son, the official Wenbo of Lu, a student of Confucius, was sent to Confucius by his mother (Raphals, *Sharing the Light*, pp. 92–98). The *Biographies of Exemplary Women* gives several accounts of titles awarded to women. Honored women include the Mother Teacher of Lu (chapter 1, story 12); the Honorable Lady (chapter 2, story 7); the Public-Spirited Aunt of Lu, who prevented an invasion by the state of Qi (chapter 5, story 6); the Righteous Mother of Qi, who impartially preferred the son of her husband's prior wife to her own (chapter 5, story 8); and Illustrious Bequest, a title posthumously awarded to a woman who died protecting the king from invading Qin soldiers (chapter 5, story 11). She also received the mourning rites of a minister, and her brother received rank and financial reward.

Political activity and technical expertise. Despite a statement in the *Book of Rites* that "men must not speak of internal affairs; women must not speak of external matters" (*Li chi*, 1: 454), there is considerable evidence that the activities of women of all classes overlapped considerably with those of their male relatives. There are accounts both of women who participated in the intellectual and political lives of their states and of girls who learned the skills of their fathers. There are accounts of women who gave instruction outside their homes and were recognized for their wisdom, technical expertise, and erudition. They participated in political life, both by actual presence at court and by indirect influence. Accounts of female expertise include expertise in agriculture, archery, astronomy, divination, ferrying, funerary rites, and physiognomy, as well as general skills of prediction, interpretation, quotation of poetry, knowledge of ritual, and composition of eulogies and petitions. Many of these accounts appear in "Skill in Argument," the sixth chapter of the *Biographies of Exemplary Women*.

The *Biographies of Exemplary Women* also presents both elite and commoner women as active political agents. For example, the wife of Duke Wen of Jin helped her husband regain his throne (chapter 2, story 3). Another woman remonstrated (unsuccessfully) with her husband regarding the succession (chapter 3, story 8), and Guan Zhong of Qi consulted his concubine on affairs of state (chapter 6, story 1), and his patron Duke Huan of Qi discussed military campaigns with his wife (chapter 2, story 2), as did King Wu of Chu (chapter 3, story 2). Wives and sisters also advised their male relatives on accepting office (chapter 2, stories 13–15, and chapter 3, story 12.) There are also accounts of daughters of craftsmen and lower-level officials who learned their fathers' or husbands' skills in archery and navigation (chapter 6, stories 3 and 7).

Such early accounts of female expertise and activity outside the home are reinforced by accounts from the Han dynasty (206 B.C.E.–220 C.E.) of women with knowledge of medicine. A medical casebook from the Han dynasty, recorded in the *Historical Records*, describes a female slave who was expert in the arts of the "prescription master" (*fangshi*) of the Han court. A physician observed a maid who was ill with an injured spleen and was told that this woman was skilled in secret formulas (*fang*), was capable in several arts, and used the newest methods (Sima Qian, p. 105; Raphals, *Sharing the Light*, pp. 180–181).

Other accounts from Qin and Han legal records show women presenting arguments both at court and in administrative proceedings. A memorial submitted by the daughter of a physician persuaded the Han emperor Xiaowen (r. 180–157 B.C.E.) to rescind a harsh law on mutilating punishments (Liu Xiang, chapter 6, story 15, and Sima Qian, p. 105; Raphals, "Arguments by Women"). Legal texts excavated from Zhangjiashan, Hubei Province, include a treatment of exemplary decisions of difficult cases (*Zouxianshu*) that includes discussions of the legal status of women. In one case a female slave who surrendered to Han forces after the fall of the Qin neglected to register herself as a free commoner. Subsequently, her former master sought to reclaim her through legal procedures in order to sell her. The question of whether she could have registered herself suggests that she potentially held legal status as a free individual who was no one else's property (Raphals, "Arguments by Women").

In summary, texts from the Zhou dynasty portray women as of great cosmological and social importance, but also as social and intellectual inferiors in nearly all contexts. The conduct and choices of both men and women during the Zhou dynasty were subordinated to the interests of their families and the constraints of their social class. But beyond this, women were consistently subordinated to men and male authority in such matters as marriage, raising children, and being mothers and widows. Custom rather than law prohibited women from holding office or engaging in crafts or professions beyond what was considered women's work. Women represented an important economic base as farmers and preparers of food, and as producers of silk and other textiles used for quotidian and ritual purposes. Finally, despite this inferior status, they had far more freedom for initiative than might be apparent.

In the Zhou period, powerful semi-mythological female figures were incorporated into Chinese patriarchy and politics through stories of order and chaos, inner and outer, and the gender distinctions and divisions of labor that created the early Chinese social order. Strikingly, the Zhou construction of gender was an evenhanded one. It portrayed women as the equals of their male counterparts. Whether in narratives of destructive concubines or of sage wives or mothers, women are conspicuously present in Zhou historical narratives, and their moral influence is consistently used to explain moral and political outcomes (Mann, p. 845). These historical narratives portray women as political and intellectual agents within their society rather than as passive victims of it. They depict female intellectual and moral influence as central to the success or failure of states and dynasties, and they show women as possessing a wide variety of expertise and social mobility. They thus present alternatives to the narrow inner and outer courtly view of received historiography.

[*See also* Ban Zhao; Cai Yan; Concubinage; Fu Hao; Lü Zhi, Empress Dowager; *and* Meng Mu.]

BIBLIOGRAPHY

Ban Gu. *Han shu* (Standard History of the Han Dynasty). Partially translated by Homer H. Dubs as *History of the Former Han Dynasty*. 3 vols. Baltimore: Waverly Press, 1938–1955.

Ch'ü, T'ung-tsu. *Han Social Structure*. Edited by Jack L. Dull. Seattle: University of Washington Press, 1972.

The Ch'un Ts'ew with the Tso Chuen. Translated by James Legge. Volume 5 of *The Chinese Classics*. Reprint. Hong Kong: Hong Kong University Press, 1960. A translation of *Chunqiu* (The Spring and Autumn Annals) and the *Zuo zhuan* (Zuo Annals).

Dull, Jack L. "Marriage and Divorce in Han China: A Glimpse at 'Pre-Confucian' Society." In *Chinese Family Law and Social Change in Historical and Comparative Perspective*, edited by David C. Buxbaum, pp. 23–74. Seattle: University of Washington Press, 1978.

Ebrey, Patricia Buckley. "Women, Marriage, and the Family in Chinese History." In *The Heritage of China*, edited by Paul Ropp, pp. 197–223. Berkeley: University of California Press, 1990.

Elvin, Mark. "Female Virtue and the State in China." *Past and Present* 104 (August 1984): 111–152.

Holmgren, Jennifer. "Myth, Fantasy, or Scholarship: Images of the Status of Women in Traditional China." *Australian Journal of Chinese Affairs* 6 (July 1981): 147–170.

Keightley, David N. "At the Beginning: The Status of Women in Neolithic and Shang China." *Nan nü* 1 (1999): 1–62.

Li chi: Book of Rites. Translated by James Legge. Reprint. New Hyde Park, N.Y.: University Books, 1967. A translation of the *Li ji*.

Liu Dehan. *Dong Zhou funü wenti yanjiu* (Research on the Problem of Women in the Eastern Zhou). Taipei: Taiwan xuesheng shudian, 1990.

Liu Xiang. *Lienü zhuan* (Biographies of Exemplary Women). Translated by Albert Richard O'Hara as *The Position of*

Women in Early China According to Lieh nu chuan. Taipei, Taiwan: Mei Ya Publications, 1971. This translation is problematic, but it is the only one available. Some passages are translated and discussed in Raphals, *Sharing the Light*.

Mann, Susan. "Presidential Address: Myths of Asian Womanhood." *Journal of Asian Studies* 59, no. 4 (November 2000): 835–862.

Raphals, Lisa. "Arguments by Women in Early Chinese Texts." *Nan nü* 3, no. 2 (2001): 157–195.

Raphals, Lisa. *Sharing the Light: Representations of Women and Virtue in Early China*. Albany: State University of New York Press, 1998.

Sima Qian. *Shiji* (Historical Records). Partially translated by Burton Watson as *Records of the Grand Historian of China, Translated from the Shi chi of Ssu-ma Ch'ien*. New York: Columbia University Press, 1961.

Le Tcheou-li, ou rites des Tcheou. Translated by Édouard Biot. Reprint. Taipei, Taiwan: Ch'eng Wen, 1975. A translation of *Zhou li* (The Rites of Zhou).

Thatcher, Melvin P. "Marriages of the Ruling Elite in the Spring and Autumn Period." In *Marriage and Inequality in Chinese Society*, edited by Rubie Watson and Patricia Buckley Ebrey, pp. 25–38. Berkeley: University of California Press, 1991.

LISA RAPHALS

Imperial Period

Any account that purports to discuss Chinese women over a period of two millennia will necessarily blur over important distinctions of era, location, political position, and economic status that profoundly shaped the lives of individual Chinese women. That said, it is possible to identify both the fundamental cultural conceptions and the changing ideas and institutions that provided the basic context of women's lives in the imperial period. The account that follows is divided into two main sections. The first section discusses certain cultural ideals and ideas that, for most of the imperial period, conditioned how people thought about the role of girls and women in family and society. It then shows how these ideas played out in practice by tracing the various stages of a woman's life cycle and by considering the exceptional circumstances of royal women. The second section then considers the broad historical shifts in both ideas and institutions that changed attitudes toward women over time.

Basic Cultural Parameters. The imperial period inherited from classical times certain understandings of how the world worked and of the proper roles of men and women therein. During the consolidation of the Chinese imperial system under the Han dynasty (206 B.C.E.–220 C.E.), scholars worked to systematize early cosmological ideas and ethical precepts that had been developed by the philosopher Confucius and his followers in the preimperial era. The Confucian system they developed presupposed that society and the cosmos interpenetrated in such a way that social relations both mirrored and helped sustain the proper workings of the natural world. Within this framework, the family was understood to be the foundation of a properly ordered society, and the proper functioning of the family was understood to depend on the maintenance of correct hierarchical relationships therein. In this formulation, the central relationship in the family was that between husband and wife, for it was their interaction that produced new life, just as the interaction of the cosmological forces of yin and yang had produced the universe. Although there is some evidence that yin and yang had been understood in preimperial times as essentially equal and complementary forces (and not necessarily correlated with gender relations), in the writings of Han scholars yin and yang were explicitly correlated with gender roles, with yang clearly superior to yin (Raphals). Yang, the male principle, was associated with light (especially the sun), warmth, power, positive action; yin, the female principle, was associated with darkness, dampness, and weakness. Accordingly, Han writers expected husbands to take the dominant, controlling role in the husband-wife relationship. The husband's relation to his wife was like that of heaven and earth: her role was to be respectful and compliant to his wishes. In the eyes of Han ritualists, a woman was to be obedient throughout her life. They formulated the doctrine of the "Three Obediences," according to which a daughter was to be obedient to her father, a wife to her husband, and a widow to her son.

Closely associated with ideas of yin and yang in early imperial theorizing about gender roles were the concepts of inner and outer. Well before the imperial era, classical texts had stipulated that women belonged to the inner realm: a woman's duties were to prepare food and clothing for the household and to care for the young and the elderly within it. Women were not to concern themselves with affairs outside the home. In its most extreme formulation, this was taken to mean that women should not even be seen in public, but rather should remain cloistered within the home. The concepts of inner and outer also implied the physical separation of men and women, even within the home. Accordingly, women should be confined to the inner quarters, separate from the more public rooms where men received guests. Among most of the population, of course, separate rooms for men and women were an unaffordable luxury, but the general principle, that women should be kept out of sight and have as little as possible to do with non-kin males, was widely accepted.

The ideal of inner and outer was also reflected in political thinking. In the classics, the failure to maintain separation between men and women was associated with lack of civilization and with political chaos. This view continued to be articulated throughout the imperial period. The involvement of women in government affairs, in particular, was seen as a sure sign of the impending demise of the state.

In the realm of statecraft more generally, the ideal of separate spheres for men and women was articulated as "Men plow; women weave." Confucian policy makers felt that society should be composed of self-sufficient households in which men farmed to feed the family and women spun and wove to provide the family's clothing. The commercialization of the Chinese economy from the ninth century on meant that, over the course of the imperial period, reality departed further and further from this ideal. Still, the ideal remained sufficiently powerful that, in the early twentieth century, women who were forced by economic circumstances to leave home to labor in factories felt that doing so compromised their virtue (Lisa Rofel, *Other Modernities: Gendered Yearnings in China after Socialism* [Berkeley: University of California Press, 1999]).

In addition to yin and yang and inner and outer, ideas about women and gender in the imperial period were also profoundly shaped by ideas about, and the demands of, ancestor worship and the related concept of filial piety (respect for elders, especially parents). Early in Chinese history, the authority of rulers was believed to originate in the power of deceased ancestors, and the continued success of those rulers to depend on pleasing the ancestors with ritual sacrifice. Since descent in early Chinese society was reckoned through the male line, ritual experts insisted that only sacrifices made by direct male descendants would be acceptable to the ancestors. By the early imperial period, ideas about the importance of ancestor worship had spread to the population at large and had been reinforced by Confucian ethicists. In popular thinking, deceased ancestors were believed to have the power to affect, positively or negatively, the fortunes of their living descendants, and thus it was incumbent on any prudent individual to try to keep the ancestors happy. Meanwhile, Confucius himself, while refusing to speculate about the supernatural existence of the ancestors, had insisted that sacrificing to the ancestors "as if they were present" was a central duty of any virtuous man. To Confucius, such ritual sacrifice was vital to inculcating the virtue of filial piety, upon which proper family relations depended. Confucius's followers articulated a significant logical extension of this train of thought: since failure to produce a male heir to carry on the sacrifices would doom the ancestors to extinction, the greatest unfilial sin a man could commit was to fail to produce a male heir to carry on the sacrifices.

The imperative to produce a male heir and the demands of filial piety had important ramifications for attitudes toward women in Chinese society. To begin with, the imperative to produce male heirs meant that, from the perspective of the Chinese family as an institution, daughters were simply not as important as sons. In conjunction with ideas about filial piety, which, in the most extreme understanding, gave parents virtually the power of life and death over their children, this meant that girls were much more likely than their brothers to be abandoned at birth. Ideas about filial piety were also interpreted to mean that sons were responsible for supporting their aging parents, and by extension, that adult sons should reside with their parents until the parents' deaths. Thus a newly married couple generally did not form a new household of their own; rather, upon marriage a woman was expected to join the household of her husband (or, more accurately, of her mother-in-law). She was expected to transfer her filial sentiments to her husband's parents and patriline, worshipping his ancestors, and, if she was fortunate, producing male descendants for them. When she became an ancestor herself, she in turn could expect to be worshipped by those descendants and their wives. The upshot of this system was that, unlike sons, daughters were widely regarded as being only temporary members of their natal families.

The imperative to produce sons was also associated with another important feature of Chinese family life, polygyny or concubinage. Contrary to the popular image, throughout most of the history of imperial China, a man could have only one legal wife at a time. As in most societies before recent times, marriage was generally an alliance contracted between families, and children (both boys and girls) were expected to acquiesce in their parents' choice. A wife's entry into her husband's household was marked by established ritual proceedings (including worship of his ancestors and the presentation of at least a token dowry), and her legal status as wife could be altered only by death or by formal divorce. Because of the family relationships involved, divorce was a step not lightly taken, and classic ritual texts enjoined both men and women to remain faithful to a deceased spouse. Still, if a man lost his first wife, he was able to take a successor wife, whose legal status was identical to that of his first wife.

Concubines, however, had a status distinctly inferior to that of wives. Legally, they were not allowed to succeed to the position of wife, even if the legal wife died. Unlike marriage to a wife, a relationship with a concubine did not involve kinship connections with her natal family. In fact, while a concubine was legally regarded as "married" to her master, a man who kept a concubine but had no legal wife was regarded as "unmarried." In the early imperial era, regulations stipulated that taking a concubine was a perquisite of noble or official rank (with men of higher rank permitted as many as nine, and those of low ranks only one). And even in later imperial times, taking a concubine was in theory a last resort for men who had reached the age of forty without producing an heir. In practice, however, these rules do not seem ever to have been enforced. Wealthy and noble households tended to include numerous female servants and slaves, any one of whom might be "favored" by the master. If he chose, and especially if a

Life at the Imperial Chinese Court. *Night Revels of Han Xizai*, by Gu Hongzhong, c. 906–960 C.E. NATIONAL PALACE MUSEUM, TAIWAN, REPUBLIC OF CHINA

she bore him a child, such a woman could be raised to the status of concubine, and her children regarded as legitimate. Alternatively, her child could be legitimized but her own status left unaffected. In general, only men of relative affluence could afford to keep a concubine, although one study of the period from the late nineteenth to early twentieth centuries suggests that as many as 30 percent of ordinary farmers had concubines (James Watson). Still, ordinary families were significantly affected by the markets in women that the practice of concubinage created. The heads of poor families were always aware that, in times of crisis, the sale of an attractive daughter (or even a wife) into concubinage could be a lucrative option.

In sum, ideas about yin and yang and inner and outer, the demands of ancestor worship and of producing male heirs, and the marriage system with its attendant institution of concubinage all combined to shape the roles and options available to Chinese women in the imperial era. It should be stressed, however, that all these principles were normative. Although they influenced what people thought was right or proper, the behavior of real people diverged from these principles at least as often as it upheld them.

The Life Cycle. A useful way to explore how women's lives were constrained by the parameters discussed above is to look at how the effect of these parameters varied over the course of a woman's life cycle.

Daughters. The reaction of a Chinese family to the birth of a baby girl varied tremendously according to their economic circumstances and her place in the birth order. If she were her parents' first child, in any but the poorest families her birth would be welcomed, perhaps not quite as joyously as the birth of a son, but with joy nonetheless. In a family that already had several sons, the birth of the first girl might likewise be deeply desired: the imperative for male heirs notwithstanding, ordinary Chinese families seem to have wanted at least one girl among their offspring. Mothers in farming families understood that daughters could be useful in minding siblings or helping with household chores; and once his duty to produce male heirs was satisfied, a father could look forward to a more affectionate relationship with a daughter than he could have with his sons. Yet in the very poorest families, or in families with several daughters and no sons, the birth of a girl could be a disappointment, if not a calamity. Baby girls born into such circumstances might be quietly disposed of, through infanticide or, if they were luckier, through adoption.

Many families reared their daughters with great affection and tenderness. Upper-class parents had the luxury of doting on their daughters, cherishing them for their quick wits or amiable dispositions. Such daughters might well be educated along with their brothers, for although there was no public outlet for women's learning, it was generally held that education enhanced moral virtue, and didactic texts for women were extremely popular. It was not unusual for upper-class daughters to repay their parents' affections by providing assistance to their natal families even after they had been married out into another patriline. In lower-class families, where resources were scarce, girls tended to receive a somewhat smaller share of those resources than their brothers: whereas expensive medicine might be purchased to treat a sick son, a daughter might have to get by on home remedies. In a marginal family, resources invested in a son were considered as investments in the family's future, whereas money spent on a daughter would only serve another patriline. By the same token, after marriage a daughter in a marginal family had few resources with which to help her natal family, even if she wished to. While even poor families might try to help their relatives by marriage when they could, frequent interaction and close relationships between families related by marriage were much more common among the well-to-do.

Wives and daughters-in-law. Whether the family was wealthy or poor, when a daughter reached adolescence, her parents began to think about finding her a husband, or more accurately, a mother-in-law. It was assumed that virtually every girl would marry: female infanticide and the custom of concubinage meant that there were never quite enough women to go around, and only by marrying and producing children could a woman hope to become an ancestor herself. Although a very small number of women became Buddhist nuns or remained unmarried because of illness or for other reasons, the percentage of never married women in imperial China was extremely low in comparison to many other cultures.

In some cases, a daughter's betrothal was taken care of early in her life, when her parents agreed on an appropriate match with the child of a friend or relative. Marriage with anyone of the same surname was forbidden by law and custom, but marriage with maternal cousins, though not always legal, was a common practice. If an early betrothal had not been arranged, matchmakers would be consulted when a girl turned fifteen or sixteen, with an eye to locating an appropriate match. Once a suitable boy was identified, the negotiations would begin. For most farming families, procuring a bride was a major expense, for the bride's parents expected to be compensated for the effort and costs of rearing her. If the negotiations were successful, the betrothal rituals would be completed, and when the appointed day came, the girl would be transferred, with as much ceremony as her family could afford, to the home of her new husband. Although women were sometimes acquainted with their prospective husbands before marriage, as in the case of cousins, in many cases husband and wife were complete strangers to one another.

Once in her husband's home, a bride's life was shaped as much or more by her role as daughter-in-law as by her role as wife. As daughter-in-law she was expected to rise early to wait upon her mother-in-law and, in all but the wealthiest families, to help cook the meals and do household chores. The newest daughter-in-law had the lowest status of any member in the household, and as a stranger to the household routines, her lot was an unenviable one. Moreover, she could not count on her husband's support: newlyweds were expected to behave with great circumspection toward one another, and in any family conflict, filial duty demanded that the husband always take his mother's side against his wife.

In some parts of China, the tensions of the daughter-in-law's relocation to her in-laws' home was eased by customs that encouraged frequent and extended visits to her natal family for the first few years of marriage. Similarly, in upper-class families, particularly when a woman's father was a person of some eminence, married daughters and their families often lived for extended periods of time with her parents, so that her husband could benefit from the advice and connections of his father-in-law. Finally, in many parts of the country the custom of "little daughters-in-law" (*tong yang xi*) was common: young or even infant girls were adopted and reared by their prospective in-laws. Although such marriages were regarded as less prestigious than marriage between adults, they were popular because they saved the husband's family the considerable bride-price required to secure an adult woman and because a mother-in-law could train a little daughter-in-law from a tender age, inculcating a level of filial obedience that she was unlikely to obtain from an adult bride.

Mothers. By the time a woman gave birth to a child, the most trying phase of her life as a daughter-in-law was behind her. By now she was familiar with family routines and had established a place for herself within the family hierarchy. By producing a child, even a girl, she had demonstrated her fertility and potential to produce an heir. And if she had managed to produce a son, the expense and effort the family had extended to secure her was repaid, and her future place on the ancestral altar was assured. For the first month after childbirth, a new mother could expect to be pampered to the best of the household's ability, and her natal family would also send special foods for her and gifts for the infant. Thereafter child-rearing would be added to the burdens of her daily responsibilities, to be sure, but in this matter she would have the willing assistance of her mother-in-law, as well as the comforting assurance that she had fulfilled her duty as a daughter-in-law.

In well-to-do households, a wet nurse was commonly hired to feed the newborn, and most day-to-day child-rearing would fall on the shoulders of a servant or nanny. Still, an educated mother might participate in the early instruction of her children, and she would be expected to socialize her daughters into such women's work as embroidery, the making of cloth shoes, and other needlework appropriate to their station.

Mothers-in-law. As a woman's children matured, she could begin to look forward to the day when she would be a mother-in-law running her own household. Despite the cultural ideal that all living members of a patriline would share a single household, in practice the deaths of her husband's parents would almost always precipitate a dissolution of the household that the woman had lived in since her marriage. Her husband and his brothers would divide the family property into equal shares (his sisters having long since married out), and she, her husband, and the couple's children would form a nuclear family, but only until it was time to bring in a daughter-in-law for the couple's eldest son.

In this stage of her life, a woman found herself at long last on the receiving end of the cultural demand for filial piety. Injunctions that a woman should obey her sons notwithstanding, a mother who had reared her sons well could expect their deference and filial attentions. If her relationship with her husband was a good one, she could expect that he too would take her views into account in family decision making. And even if her relationship with her husband was poor, her children's respect and affection for her allowed her greater authority in the household than she had had as a mere daughter-in-law. It was now her role to train new daughters-in-law in family routines and to help rear the next generation of her descendants.

Royal women. As in any society, women who belonged to the royal household led lives that were different in important ways from those of ordinary women. From the very beginning of the imperial period, the imperial household included not only the empress, but also hundreds of palace women. Some of the latter were servants engaged in preparing food and clothing and otherwise attending to the needs of the imperial family; others were musicians and entertainers; still others were imperial consorts or concubines of various grades. In general, women in the palace were cloistered: the emperor and imperial children were the only noneunuch males allowed to move among them.

From the perspective of the male officials of the bureaucracy, the empress, as the emperor's legal wife, was ideally a woman selected from among the families of high-ranking ministers. In practice, however, virtually any woman who captured the emperor's fancy (especially if she managed to produce a son) might hope to become empress. This meant that some of the women who became Chinese empresses came from poor commoner and even slave backgrounds. Having obtained the favor of the emperor, an empress, and for that matter lesser consorts as well, were in a position to obtain ranks and honors for the men of their natal families. At several points in the Han dynasty, consort families became powerful enough to threaten the central government. Later dynasties were more careful to prevent consort families from accumulating influence, but their intimate access to the throne meant that empresses themselves could be significant centers of power at court. This was especially the case when, after an emperor's death, his widow was able to dominate his young son or nephew on the throne.

One famous case was that of the notorious Wu Zetian, or Empress Wu, of the Tang dynasty (618–907). Originally a concubine in the harem of Emperor Taizong (r. 627–649), Wu retired to a convent upon Taizong's death, whence she reportedly caught the eye of Taizong's successor, Emperor Gaozong (r. 650–683). Only a few years after she entered Gaozong's harem, he deposed his first empress and put Wu in her place. When the emperor's health failed in 660, she ruled in his stead, and after his death she placed one and then another son on the throne. In 690 she had her second son deposed and took the unprecedented step of declaring herself emperor. Wu ruled as emperor for another fifteen years, until a palace coup deposed her in 705, when she was over eighty years old. The only woman in Chinese history with the audacity to have herself declared emperor, Empress Wu was excoriated by traditional Chinese historians, who condemned her admittedly ruthless political machinations and accused her of all manner of iniquitous conduct. Yet the empire prospered during the nearly fifty years of her rule.

The same cannot be said of another famous royal woman, Empress Dowager Cixi of the Qing dynasty (1644–1911). Like Wu Zetian, Cixi began her career as an imperial concubine, in this case in the harem of the Xianfeng emperor (r. 1850–1861). She bore the emperor's only son, who, after his father's death in 1861, was named emperor and reigned as the Tongzhi emperor (r. 1862–1875). With the accession of her young son to the throne, Cixi was elevated to the rank of Empress Dowager, in spite of the fact that she had been only the concubine of his father. By ensuring that a series of infant emperors were placed on the throne after her own son died, Cixi remained the central power at the Qing court from 1861 until her death in 1908. Shrewd but narrow-minded and ignorant of affairs outside the court, she is widely regarded as having hampered China's attempts to modernize in the face of Western encroachment in the late nineteenth and early twentieth centuries, with ultimately disastrous effects for the dynasty and, indeed, the whole imperial system.

Historical Shifts. This discussion thus far has presented a largely ahistorical picture of Chinese women's lives over a period of more than two millennia. While certainly much of the rhetoric conditioning Chinese women's lives remained remarkably similar over the course of this span, Chinese society as a whole changed dramatically over 2,000 years, and these changes had significant repercussions on women's lives and gender relations. The following paragraphs trace a few of the most significant developments in Chinese women's history during the imperial period.

Women in markets and markets in women. Between the ninth and twelfth centuries, China underwent a commercial revolution that was to have a profound effect on virtually all aspects of Chinese society. Economic growth and expansion of the population led to the proliferation of urban centers, the development of commercialized agriculture, and the articulation of long-distance trading networks. Although economic growth seems to have suffered a setback in the late fourteenth and early fifteenth centuries, by the early sixteenth century it had recovered, and thereafter growth continued steadily until the early nineteenth century.

Tang Court Dancer. A figurine of a dancer in fashionable dress, c. 650, Xi'an, China. THE METROPOLITAN MUSEUM OF ART, NEW YORK

The commercialized economy created new roles and opportunities for women. Women provided the main labor for tea picking and sericulture, producing tea and silk for a luxury market that ultimately extended throughout the world. Even women's domestic production of fibers and cloth was increasingly tied to the market: rather than simply clothe their families, women in later imperial China often sold thread they had spun, for use in commercial enterprises that weaved cloth on a larger scale. Thus, even when women's labor remained largely within the household, their labor could contribute significantly to household incomes.

The expansion of urban centers also created new opportunities for women. Wives of petty shopkeepers and restaurant proprietors assisted their husbands in running family businesses, and widows might take over as proprietresses in their own right. The proliferation of urban pleasure quarters beginning late in the Tang dynasty (618–907) created new demands for female entertainers, and from that time down to the end of the imperial period, high-class courtesans, skilled in music or dance and often highly literate, provided expensive and exclusive entertainment for officials and wealthy merchants alike.

The commercial revolution, in combination with changes in government recruitment early in the Song dynasty (960–1279), most notably the expansion of the examination system for recruiting government officials, contributed to both the expansion of, and a change in the nature of, the educated elite in China. This shift too had important ramifications for markets in women. To begin with, the elite marriage market was altered. Whereas during the Tang dynasty elite marriages were arranged largely on the basis of illustrious ancestry, during the Song dynasty and later, current status and even future promise became far more salient criteria. A high-ranking official might marry a daughter to the son of a similarly ranked colleague, yet he might choose instead a young man who had shown his promise by attaining a high mark in the recruitment examinations. Similarly, the head of a locally prominent family might choose as a son-in-law a talented local scholar, in hopes that the young man might eventually raise the family to office-holding status. In this environment, an ambitious elite family seeking a daughter-in-law tended to look for a woman who could be relied on to run the household efficiently, managing the household affairs so that her husband would be free to concentrate on his studies. Similarly, a woman who had sufficient education so that she could provide her sons with an elementary education, giving them a head start in the competition for examination success, was more desirable than a woman who was illiterate.

The expansion of the elite also meant an expanded market for maids, cooks, nannies, and various other types of serving women to serve in elite households. Of particular importance here was a fad, first seen late in the Tang and popular throughout the Song, for "household courtesans" (*jia ji*). Like their sisters in the pleasure quarters, these women (and girls) were trained in music, singing, or dancing, and were sometimes literate. Unlike upper-class wives, who did not socialize with their husband's friends, household courtesans were routinely brought out to entertain, pour wine, and banter with their masters' guests. Not infrequently such women also became their masters' concubines. Although upper-class households in earlier periods had also kept troupes of entertainers, those women typically had slave status. The expanding economy of the late Tang and Song undermined strict class distinctions, however, and household courtesans in the Song were usually indentured servants, often hired on short-term contracts, rather than slaves.

The proliferation of such women in Song households significantly complicated family relationships, especially when they gave birth to children. It was in this context that Song moralists began to call for reestablishing Confucian morality. Central to the demands of these neo-Confucian moralists were the restraint of physical desire and strict regulation of the family. In the eyes of these moralists, concubinage was legitimate for the production of descendants, not for the satisfaction of desire, and they emphasized the role of concubines as mothers (Neil Katkov, "The Domestication of Concubinage in Imperial China" [PhD thesis, Harvard University, 1997]). The ideas of the neo-Confucians gained gradual acceptance over the course of the Song and Yuan (1260–1368) dynasties, and by the Ming dynasty (1368–1644), the flaunting of household courtesans was no longer socially acceptable. Although men still enjoyed taking attractive young concubines, such concubines were increasingly held to wifely standards of behavior. No longer did men write poetry teasing their friends' concubines or praising their musical skills, as they had in the late Tang and Song periods.

Another long-term effect of the popularity of public and household courtesans in the late Tang and Song was the spread of the practice of foot-binding. Foot-binding appears to have originated with tenth-century courtesan-dancers, who bound their feet to form upward curves. Over the next few centuries, foot-binding gradually became fashionable among upper-class women, who often imitated the latest styles of the entertainment quarters. Bound feet did indeed restrict women's movement, but the oft-repeated notion that foot-binding was introduced by neo-Confucian moralists of the Song dynasty to keep women at home has no basis in fact. Although those moralists did want women to stay home and out of sight, they did not approve of foot-binding, with its erotic associations. On the contrary, in the few instances where Song and Yuan moralists mention foot-binding, they praise women who did *not* bind their feet.

In spite of moralists' injunctions, by the fourteenth century the practice of foot-binding had become quite common, at least among upper-class women. It appears that styles of binding changed over the centuries. Rather than the upward-bowed foot seen in some Song paintings, by Ming times the foot was usually curved downward, with the toes folding under the foot. Foot-binding seems only gradually to have been adopted by lower-class families, and women of some groups (women of ethnic groups such as the Hakka and women of the lowest classes) never bound their feet. The ruling house of the Qing dynasty (1644–1911) was ethnically Manchu, and Manchu women did not bind their feet. Though the Qing government early on attempted to outlaw foot-binding among Chinese women as well, they were unsuccessful in enforcing the ban.

Western missionaries arriving in China in the nineteenth century were appalled by foot-binding, and by the early twentieth century Chinese intellectuals had adopted that attitude, seeing the practice as a symbol of the oppression of Chinese women. Progressive families of the nineteenth century sometimes refrained from binding their daughter's feet, and successive Chinese governments of the twentieth century were ultimately successful in eradicating the practice. While, from our twenty-first-century perspective, it is easy to decry the practice of foot-binding, we can understand the longevity of the custom better if we recognize that foot-binding was a technique adopted by women (or imposed on their daughters) as a means of enhancing beauty. Women's poetry from the Ming and Qing dynasties shows that women took pride in their beautifully bound feet, which were at once symbols of femininity and discipline. Exquisitely embroidered shoes for bound feet became an important element of women's culture, and women sent shoes to each other as tokens of esteem and affection.

Widow fidelity. The period between the late Song and Yuan dynasties also saw a dramatic hardening of attitudes toward the remarriage of widows. The notion that a woman should remain faithful to a deceased spouse had been idealized in the classics, and faithful widows who chose death or disfigurement over remarriage were prominent among the exemplary women celebrated in didactic texts for women, such as the influential *Lienü zhuan* (Biographies of Exemplary Women), compiled in the Han (206 B.C.E.–220 C.E.). Still, despite this ideal, throughout the early imperial period and into the Song dynasty, remarriage of widows was common practice, even among the elite. From the mid-Song on, a number of factors conspired to change attitudes toward widow fidelity. Early in the Song, neo-Confucian moralists had urged a return to strict standards of marital fidelity, suggesting that neither men nor women should remarry on the death of a spouse (men, if they needed someone to run their households and produce children, were urged to take concubines rather than remarry). Although these injunctions were little heeded in practice, a political crisis in the mid-Song led both to increased government emphasis on exemplary behavior of all types and, after the Song regime lost nearly half its territory to non-Chinese invaders from the north, to a near obsession with the virtue of loyalty. Repeatedly in the latter half of the Song, women who had died rather than submit to rape by invading soldiers were held up as models for men, who were urged to be similarly loyal in the face of political chaos. By the late Song period, faithful widows who refused to remarry were appropriated for the same purpose, their loyalty to their deceased husbands' families explicitly held up as models for men's loyalty to the state.

With the Mongol conquest of the Song dynasty in 1279, the figure of the faithful widow became a more and more significant element in both government and elite culture. The Mongol rulers of the Yuan dynasty were persuaded by their Chinese advisors that celebrating exemplary behavior with government awards and tax remission would help the new regime establish legitimacy while improving the morality of the populace. By the early fourteenth century the government found itself besieged with requests for such awards. Complaining that too many of these requests came from families scheming to avoid tax levies, the Yuan government in 1304 issued strict new regulations limiting awards for "faithful widows" to women who had been widowed before age thirty and remained unmarried at least until age fifty. In spite of government efforts to reduce the number of officially honored faithful widows, however, the discourse of fidelity only proliferated through the Yuan dynasty, as the fathers, brothers, and sons of elite faithful widows began celebrating the virtuous behavior of their daughters, sisters, or mothers by compiling collections of poetry in their honor. These collections, initially used as a means to celebrate government awards, came to serve many other functions. They could also be a means for a son to demonstrate his own filiality, for a family to extend its local moral reputation, and for neo-Confucian moralists to propagandize their fundamentalist Confucian agenda. The popularity of faithful-wife compilations increased exponentially, with the result that by the end of the Yuan, faithful widowhood had begun to become the central symbol of female virtue.

At the same time, albeit for almost completely unrelated reasons, major changes in women's property rights during the Yuan also came to favor widows who did not remarry. Up through the Song, customary practice was that widowed women returned to their natal families, taking their dowries (and often their children) with them. If a widow were to remarry, her parents (or, after their deaths, the widow herself) negotiated the new marriage. These customs were drastically at odds with Mongol principles of marriage and property exchange, which called for widows (and their property) to be kept in the husband's family by means of levirate marriage (that is, the widow was expected to marry her husband's younger brother or nephew). To Chinese eyes, by contrast, levirate marriage was nothing short of incestuous. The Mongol takeover of China thus precipitated a long period of negotiation and renegotiation of marriage and property laws, as Mongol rulers and their Chinese advisors strove to reconcile the two very different systems. The compromise ultimately reached was that if a widow remarried, her dowry property remained with her deceased husband's family, and the right to negotiate her remarriage rested with her deceased husband's parents. These changes reduced both widows' autonomy and their financial incentives for remarriage.

The Ming dynasty adopted both Yuan marriage laws and Yuan practices of rewarding faithful widows. Thus, what is sometimes called the "cult of widow chastity" grew apace over the course of the fifteenth and sixteenth centuries, in extreme cases even taking the form of widow suicide. Although the Manchu rulers who founded the Qing dynasty (1644–1911) strongly opposed this most extreme form of widow fidelity, they continued to issue government awards for faithful widowhood more generally. During the Qing dynasty the ideal of widow fidelity came to be widely accepted even among the lower classes, and among the upper classes was extended (albeit not without controversy) even to unmarried girls whose fiancés had died (Weijing Lu, "True to Their Word: The Faithful Maiden Cult in China, 1650–1850." [PhD dissertation, University of California, Davis, 2001]). The demand for widow fidelity is sometimes taken as emblematic of Confucian oppression of women, but the decision to remain faithful was not necessarily forced on women. On the contrary, whether inspired by romantic affection for a deceased spouse, by the relative autonomy of action a widow could enjoy, or simply by the respect and social approbation accorded to faithful widows, not a few women chose faithful widowhood over the active opposition of their parents and/or parents-in-law.

Women's education and literacy. The late imperial period saw a steady expansion of women's literacy. To a large extent this mirrored a more general rise in literacy concomitant with economic development.

Throughout imperial history, many girls in upper-class families had been educated as a matter of course. Although women's work of cooking and housekeeping did not require literacy, as early as the Han dynasty explicit arguments were made for the importance of educating women. Didactic texts explicitly for women were composed as early as the first century C.E., when Ban Zhao (c. 45–116 C.E.), the highly literate daughter in a family of historians and an accomplished historian in her own right, composed *Nü jie* (Admonitions for Women) for the moral edification of her daughters. Ban's text was copied and recopied down through the centuries. Women in the dominant elite families between the Han and Tang were often literate, and the names and some works of a small number of the most celebrated were transmitted through the centuries. In part because of notions that women belonged to the inner realm and should be kept out of the public eye, however, very few works by women from this period have survived.

One important aspect of the commercial revolution of the ninth through eleventh centuries was the development of block-printing technology. The increased availability of books that this made possible was undoubtedly an important factor in the Song expansion of the educated elite noted above. During the Song dynasty both the development of entertainment culture (with its literate courtesans) and the development of neo-Confucianism (with its advocacy of moral education for men and women) favored the education of women, albeit in different directions. In part because of the model presented by courtesans, Confucian moralists were adamant that women of their class should confine themselves to moral learning, and in particular should eschew poetry, with its associations of desire and romance. In spite of such injunctions, however, elite Chinese women did write poetry, and once again a few works by the very best poets survive from the Song and Yuan. Still, it was not until the revitalization of the economy in the mid-sixteenth century, with its associated printing boom, that women's writings began to be preserved in much greater numbers. By the late sixteenth and early seventeenth centuries, a veritable flood of works by Chinese women appeared in print (Widmer and Chang; Chang and Saussy), so women's literacy must have been both widespread and highly esteemed in this period. In the bitterly competitive society of the late Ming, where men's learning was often seen simply as an instrument of getting ahead in the examination system, women's learning was regarded as pure, free of the taint of crass ambition. At the same time, men's publication of the writings of their female relatives or neighbors could serve to extend both the family's and the region's prestige. For women themselves, literacy became the foundation of social networks that, even while based in cloistered inner quarters, connected women across great distances as they exchanged poetry and letters. By the mid-seventeenth century, a number of women were anthologizing other women's writings in large collections, many of which survive to this day.

Late imperial stirrings of feminism. Ironically, by the late nineteenth and early twentieth centuries, the long tradition of women's literacy in China was largely forgotten, or at least discounted, by those who sought to modernize China. When the Qing government found itself unable to resist European, American, and eventually Japanese incursions, some Chinese intellectuals concluded that Confucian social attitudes were to blame for China's weakness. Prominent among their complaints was the cloistered and subservient role of women in Chinese society. Struck by the public presence and (to Chinese eyes) high status of women in European and American societies, Chinese reformers began to advocate radical change in the treatment of Chinese women. They created anti-foot-binding societies, in which members promised to marry each other's "big-footed" sisters and daughters. They called for an end to cloistering and for women to be educated for public roles in society. Elite families began to send their daughters to modern-style schools in China, or even abroad to Japan.

While elite men and women began to agitate for change in social attitudes toward women, the lives of women in poor families near modernizing coastal cities were changing in different ways. Incipient industrialization and rapid urbanization drew girls out of the family setting into factories and the booming entertainment and sex industries of cities such as Guangzhou and Shanghai. Although the effects of these changes on society at large were not to be felt until well after the end of the imperial era, new forces created by the globalizing economy were already beginning to undermine traditional gender roles.

In late 1911 the Qing dynasty was brought down by an almost bloodless revolution. After more than two thousand years, the Chinese imperial era was brought to an abrupt and unceremonious end. In the twentieth century, war and political revolution were to bring wrenching change to virtually all aspects of Chinese life, not least to the lives of women. Still, in spite of a century of revolutionary rhetoric in China advocating the equality of men and women, many of the basic attitudes toward women and gender roles developed in imperial times remain surprisingly influential and continue to shape the behavior of men and women in China even today.

[*See also* Ban Zhao; Chen Duansheng; Cixi, Empress Dowager; Foot-Binding; Gu Taiqing; Huang Yuanjie; Liu Shi; Lü Zhi, Empress Dowager; Mulan; *Nüshu*; Qiu Xinru; Shen Shanbao; Shen Yixiu; Shuangqing; Su Sanniang; Taiping Rebellion; Tao Zhenhual; Wang Duan; Wang Duanshu; Wang Yun; Wu Zetian, Empress; Wu Zao; Xue Tao; Yu Xuanji; Yun Zhu; *and* Zhu Shuzhen.]

BIBLIOGRAPHY

Bernhardt, Kathryn. *Women and Property in China, 960–1949.* Stanford, Calif.: Stanford University Press, 1999. Traces shifting property regimes for women from the tenth to the mid-twentieth centuries.

Birge, Bettine. *Women, Property, and Confucian Reaction in Sung and Yüan China (960–1368).* Cambridge, U.K.: Cambridge University Press, 2002. Examines the impact of the Mongol occupation of China on women's property law.

Bossler, Beverly. " 'A Daughter Is a Daughter All Her Life': Affinal Relations and Women's Networks in Song and Late Imperial China." *Late Imperial China* 21, no. 1 (June 2000): 77–106. Shows the importance of kinship connections through women to Chinese social life from the eleventh through nineteenth centuries.

Carlitz, Katherine. "Shrines, Governing-Class Identity, and the Cult of Widow Fidelity in Mid-Ming Jiangnan." *Journal of Asian Studies* 56, no. 3 (August 1997): 612–640. Shows how the construction of shrines to faithful widows (especially widow suicides) was part of a larger movement by upper-class men to Confucianize the religious landscape of the fifteenth and sixteenth centuries.

Chang, Kang-i Sun, and Haun Saussy, eds. *Women Writers of Traditional China: An Anthology of Poetry and Criticism.* Stanford, Calif.: Stanford University Press, 1999. The first major anthology of English translations of Chinese women's writing, containing poetry by nearly 150 authors, as well as literary criticism of women's work by both male and female writers. The anthology covers virtually the entire imperial period, from 206 B.C.E. to 1911 C.E., but is especially rich with respect to the sixteenth to eighteenth centuries.

Ebrey, Patricia Buckley. *Family and Property in Sung China: Yuan Ts'ai's Precepts for Social Life.* Princeton, N.J.: Princeton University Press, 1984. A translation, with commentary, of a twelfth-century Chinese manual for family life. Provides extremely valuable insights into the conflicts and concerns that shaped the lives of well-to-do families in this period.

Ebrey, Patricia Buckley. *The Inner Quarters: Marriage and the Lives of Chinese Women in the Sung Period.* Berkeley: University of California Press, 1993. Describes the lives of elite women in the eleventh to thirteenth centuries.

Elvin, Mark. "Female Virtue and the State in China." *Past and Present* 104 (August 1984): 111–152. Traces the involvement of the Chinese imperial state in the promotion of female virtue, especially widow fidelity, from the Han through the later imperial period.

Idema, Wilt, and Beata Grant. *The Red Brush: Writing Women of Imperial China*. Cambridge, Mass.: Harvard University Asia Center, 2004. A massive compilation of translations of Chinese women's writing from the imperial period, enhanced by extended introductory and biographical information.

Judd, Ellen R. "Chinese Women and Their Natal Families." *Journal of Asian Studies* 48 (1989): 525–544. Twentieth-century anthropological work uncovers "delayed transfer" marriage patterns in northern China. This research undercuts the received view that Chinese wives moved to their husband's households upon marriage. Provides an important corrective to normative images of male-centered Chinese kinship.

Kinney, Anne Behnke. *Representations of Childhood and Youth in Early China*. Stanford, Calif.: Stanford University Press, 2004. Examines childhood, family, and gender norms operative during the Han dynasty.

Ko, Dorothy. *Every Step a Lotus: Shoes for Bound Feet*. Berkeley: University of California Press, 2001. A richly illustrated discussion of foot-binding and its material culture. Shows the importance of foot-binding to women's culture and identity in the Ming and Qing dynasties.

Ko, Dorothy. *Teachers of the Inner Chambers: Women and Culture in Seventeenth-Century China*. Stanford, Calif.: Stanford University Press, 1994. A revolutionary study of women's lives in the late Ming and early Qing dynasties. One of the first scholarly monographs in English to make extensive use of Chinese women's own writings to explore women's culture and women's communities. This study effectively exploded long-held myths about the position of women in traditional China.

Lu Weijing. "Uxorilocal Marriage among Qing Literati." *Late Imperial China* 19, no. 2 (December 1998): 64–110. Demonstrates the popularity of uxorilocal marriage as a means of social strategizing among the Qing elite.

Mann, Susan. *Precious Records: Women in China's Long Eighteenth Century*. Stanford, Calif.: Stanford University Press, 1997. A landmark study that shows the central importance of women in society and government in the high Qing period.

Nie Zeng Jifen. *Testimony of a Confucian Woman: The Autobiography of Mrs. Nie Zeng Jifen, 1852–1942*. Translated by Thomas L. Kennedy. Athens: University of Georgia Press, 1993. The autobiography of the daughter of one of nineteenth-century China's most eminent officials, Zeng Guofan. Reveals details of the daily lives of women in eminent families of the late Qing period, including their sub rosa involvement in the politics of the day.

Pruitt, Ida. *A Daughter of Han: The Autobiography of a Chinese Working Woman*. Stanford, Calif.: Stanford University Press, 1967 (1945). The autobiography of a poor woman of the late nineteenth and early twentieth centuries, as recorded by Ida Pruitt. Provides rare look into the experiences and attitudes of a lower-class Chinese woman at the end of the imperial era.

Raphals, Lisa. *Sharing the Light: Representations of Women and Virtue in Early China*. Albany: State University of New York Press, 1998. Shows the evolution of gender constructs from the classical to early imperial periods. Also examines how early imperial didactic texts were deployed in later imperial China.

Sommer, Matthew H. *Sex, Law, and Society in Late Imperial China*. Stanford, Calif.: Stanford University Press, 2000. This study, based on an examination of legal archives from the Qing dynasty, shows how ideas about sex and gender played out among the lower classes.

Stockard, Janice E. *Daughters of the Canton Delta: Marriage Patterns and Economic Strategies in South China, 1860–1930*. Stanford, Calif.: Stanford University Press, 1989. An early study of "delayed transfer" marriage in southern China, showing that late-nineteenth-century marriage practices in this region were often radically different from received norms.

Theiss, Janet M. *Disgraceful Matters: The Politics of Chastity in Eighteenth-Century China*. Berkeley: University of California Press, 2004. Based on legal archives, this study shows how ordinary Chinese women in the Qing dynasty manipulated ideals of chastity to their own ends.

Waltner, Ann Beth. *Getting an Heir: Adoption and the Construction of Kinship in Late Imperial China*. Honolulu: University of Hawai'i Press, 1990. Examines the ideals and practices of adoption in the late imperial period, showing that practice often strayed far from the ideal.

Watson, James L. "Transactions in People: The Chinese Market in Slaves, Servants, and Heirs." Chapter 9 in *Asian and African Systems of Slavery*, edited by James L. Watson, pp. 223–250. Berkeley: University of California Press, 1980. Traces the interactions and overlap in Chinese markets for slaves, servants, concubines, and heirs, showing how kinship relationships for women in Chinese families differed from those of men.

Watson, Rubie S. "Wives, Concubines, and Maids: Servitude and Kinship in the Hong Kong Region, 1900–1940." In *Marriage and Inequality in Chinese Society*, edited by Rubie S. Watson and Patricia Buckley Ebrey, pp. 231–255. Berkeley: University of California Press, 1991. An anthropological study of concubinage as practiced in South China in the late nineteenth and early twentieth centuries. Shows the fluidity of status between maids and concubines, and the important distinctions between these two groups and wives.

Widmer, Ellen, and Kang-i Sun Chang, eds. *Writing Women in Late Imperial China*. Stanford: Stanford University Press, 1997. A wide-ranging collection of essays about women's lives in the Ming and Qing dynasties, based for the most part on women's writings. The scholarship in this volume essentially introduced the study of gender into the field of Chinese literary studies.

Wolf, Margery. *Women and Family in Rural Taiwan*. Stanford, Calif.: Stanford University Press, 1972. Based on fieldwork in a Taiwanese village in the 1950s, this work provides critical insights into the dynamics of rural Chinese family life, and especially the role of women therein.

BEVERLY BOSSLER

Modern Period

Though the lives of women at the time of the 1911 Revolution, which overthrew the Qing dynasty in China, varied greatly according to class, region, and family, a few generalizations can be made. Women's lives were defined largely by their roles as daughters, wives, and mothers. Most girl children still had their feet bound—a painful process that limited their mobility and tended to keep them close to home. Newly set up schools for girls had begun to cater to the lucky few, and some girls learned to read at home, but the vast majority were illiterate. Marriages were arranged, and the bride joined her husband's household usually while still in her teens. The women of the poor often worked in the fields or in handicrafts and family businesses. Elite women were more likely to be secluded in their households, spending their time on household tasks, child care, and spinning, weaving, and sewing. Very few worked outside the home. Property was transmitted through the male line, although a woman could sometimes assert rights over her dowry. Sons were considered much more desirable than daughters, and families that fell on hard times might abandon female infants and sell girl children as maids or child daughters-in-law. Women, especially older women, might have considerable authority within the domestic sphere, but few had any role outside it.

Early Women's Movements. The struggle to improve women's status in twentieth-century China was linked closely to the growth of nationalism and the struggle for modernity. Even before the overthrow of the Qing dynasty in 1911, reformers had begun to advocate education for women on the grounds that it would strengthen the nation. Although many more boys than girls attended school, the number of girls receiving an education from government and mission schools gradually increased, and girls' schools proved an effective recruiting ground for political and feminist movements. Some women took part in the 1911 Revolution both in support roles and as combatants. In 1912, Tang Qunying, a woman veteran of the revolution, founded the Chinese Suffrage Society, which, in addition to agitating for the vote, demanded an improved position for women in the family and an end to foot-binding, concubinage, child marriages, and prostitution.

The May Fourth Movement, a dynamic and eclectic campaign for a comprehensive reassessment and reform of China's traditional culture that began in 1915 and continued into the 1920s, treated the "woman question" as a major issue. At first, radical men such as Chen Duxiu, the founder of the influential journal *Xin qingnian* (New Youth), and the May Fourth Movement writers Hu Shi and Lu Xun were the most prominent figures exposing women's oppression and in particular attacking the Confucian cult of female chastity.

Later during the May Fourth Movement, women themselves wrote and organized around such demands as equality of the sexes, free-choice marriage, and coeducation. Whereas male thinkers tended to advocate women's emancipation as a necessary step toward the modernization of China, women more often advocated a feminist agenda for its own sake. Women were admitted to higher education in 1920, and this change, together with the rapid development of girls'

Chinese Foot-binding. Woman with bound feet reclines on a chaise longue, China, early twentieth century. PRINTS AND PHOTOGRAPHS DIVISION, LIBRARY OF CONGRESS

schools, produced women determined to break into careers and public life. Although only a small minority in the total population, independent professional women became a highly visible urban group.

By the mid-1920s various approaches had developed within the women's movement. Some women continued to put their energies into women's organizations that pursued exclusively feminist goals. These organizations tended to emphasize suffrage and reform through legislation as long-term goals but were often also involved in welfare work. Organizations such as the Chinese Young Women's Christian Association and the Christian Women's Temperance Union were active in the big cities, especially in Shanghai, trying to help young working women and reporting on the problems of child labor, poor housing, and public health.

Other women chose to work within the Nationalist Party (Guomindang) or the Communist Party, the two dominant political organizations to emerge from the period of the May Fourth Movement. Both were committed to gender equality and both set up women's sections to mobilize women and work on women's issues. During the united front between the two parties (1924–1927), Cai Chang, Deng Yingchao, Xiang Jingyu, and other women Communists worked in the Nationalist Central Women's Department, led by He Xiangning, a veteran revolutionary who had been a member of the inner circle of Sun Yat-sen (Sun Yixian). Based in Guangzhou, it mobilized women around marriage problems, the right to divorce, the abolition of concubinage, and employment for women. In Shanghai, female party activists worked for improved working conditions and education for women workers.

The Central Women's Department also trained female political workers, many of whom were attached to the Nationalist armies during the Northern Expedition, a northward march from Guangzhou to the Chang (Yangzi) River valley launched in 1926 to subdue the warlords in central and northern China. Seeking to carry the revolution north, women propagandists attempted to organize women's unions in all the villages and towns that they passed through. Their work was not easy. In villages where women's feet were still bound and peasant women rarely left their homes, the natural feet, bobbed hair, and military uniforms of the women propagandists often caused astonishment and even horror. In 1927, when the united front broke down, this work was abandoned. The Communists went underground or fled to rural areas, and the Nationalists became much less radical on gender issues.

Pronounced differences in strategies and priorities emerged among different groups of feminists in the 1920s. Liberal feminists rejected the Marxist idea of class struggle and tended to devote their energies either to self-fulfillment as career women or to welfare work among the poor. In the long term they hoped for change through constitutional methods. The revolutionary left rejected this position. Xiang Jingyu, the most prominent of the women Communists until her execution by a warlord in 1928, published critiques of "narrow bourgeois feminism," arguing that women could be liberated only through a thoroughgoing revolution that totally altered the economic and political system. Yet until 1927 there was a lot of overlap among these different groups. They shared some ideals of the May Fourth Movement, and their activities were not in fact completely distinct: women moved from one group to another and had friends and acquaintances in other groups. In the 1930s the split between the Nationalist Party and the Communist Party was reflected in their diverging policies toward women.

Women in Republican China. The Nationalist government, which was based in Nanjing from 1928 to 1937 and in Chongqing during the Japanese occupation from 1938 to 1945, gradually moved away from social radicalism. In 1931 it enacted a civil code containing family law that drew on various European codes. It was premised on the idea of a patrilineal family that would normally be headed by a man. There were, however, gains for women. They had the same inheritance rights as their brothers and were entitled to choose their own husbands. Divorce by mutual consent was permitted. The grounds for divorce were drawn up on the principle of equality. For example, adultery was a ground whether it was committed by a man or a woman. However, the law clearly broke with the principle of equality in two areas. Unless a married couple elected for a separate-property regime, the man had the right to manage and control the property that his wife brought into the marriage. A woman regained control over her property only in the event of a divorce. In any conflict over the children, the husband, as head of the family, had the right to decide.

The new code was based on the model of a conjugal family based on a voluntary union of husband and wife. It reflected and gave legal force to trends that were already to some extent under way in the urban areas, where economic change and the employment and education of women were influencing family forms and mores. But it had little relevance to rural areas, where the vast majority of Chinese still lived within traditional family structures, and the Nationalist Party made little effort to popularize the law there.

The New Life Movement, launched by the Nationalist Party in 1934 to produce "social regeneration," was avowedly antifeminist. In some respects it rehabilitated Confucian attitudes. Chinese women were urged to cultivate chastity and a proper appearance, to manage their households well, and to show wifely devotion and maternal love. Vigilantes even patrolled public places rebuking women who wore cosmetics or whose clothing was considered inappropriate. Mayling Soong (Song Meiling), the American-educated wife of Chiang Kai-shek (Jiang Jieshi), the Nationalist Party leader, involved herself enthusiastically in the movement, preaching the importance of women in maintaining virtue, service, and hygiene for the nation. She organized schools to teach young women literacy skills and train them in sanitary living and modern household skills.

Chiang's marriage to Mayling Soong had been politically useful because she was the younger sister of Sun Yat-sen's widow, and the connection strengthened Chiang's claim to the leadership of the Nationalist Party. After their marriage in 1927, the leader and his beautiful, sophisticated wife were portrayed as an ideal modern couple—a skillful presentation considering that Chiang was much older and was twice divorced and that they were childless. Mayling Soong's role personified Nationalist Party ambivalence toward women. On state and diplomatic occasions and in her New Life Movement activities, she claimed a public role as a consort that was alien both to Chinese tradition, in which women did not occupy public space, and to the May Fourth model of the independent woman. Able, assertive, and opinionated, always fashionably dressed and coiffed, a smoker, and looked after by servants, Mayling was also the antithesis of the submissive, modest, frugal housewife upheld by the New Life Movement.

Many changes for women in the 1920s and 1930s were related more to economic change than to government policy. Despite the increasing ambivalence of the Nationalist Party toward women's roles, in China's great cities, especially in Shanghai, some May Fourth goals were being realized. Young educated women were increasingly able to develop careers as doctors, lawyers, teachers, writers, and journalists. Feminists continued to work to improve the

Mayling Soong. c. 1940. PRINTS AND PHOTOGRAPHS DIVISION, LIBRARY OF CONGRESS

lives of women through education and welfare work. They ran literacy classes, trained women for employment, helped slave girls and deserted women, and urged women to use their new political rights. Economic change created fertile ground for these activities. The growth of factories, especially textile mills, produced a demand for a young female workforce. In the 1930s, two-thirds of the factory labor force of Shanghai was female. Pay and conditions were lamentable, but the young rural women who came into the cities to work forged new ways of living away from their families. The cities also developed a new consumer culture, in which women were highly visible. Department stores, magazines, and advertising promoted the idea of the comfortable home and fashionable clothing as desirable ways to achieve modernity. In response to the spread of new ideas, foot-binding came to a gradual end in all but remote rural areas, where it was finally eradicated only after the Communist victory in 1949.

The invasion of northeast China by the Japanese in 1931 and the outbreak of war between China and Japan in 1937 created new priorities for women. Women's national salvation associations were formed to organize boycotts of Japanese goods, support for the Chinese army, and donations for the war effort. The dislocations of war had an impact on everyone, especially the rural poor. Gender inequality probably meant that women suffered disproportionately from poverty and malnutrition; infant and maternal mortality was high; and, as always when times were hard in China, many girl children were the victims of infanticide or were sold as maidservants, prostitutes, or child brides.

Women in the Communist Areas. From the late 1920s on, the Chinese Communists continuously controlled and administered small base areas in rural China. Thus they were in a position to translate their ideas on women into law and action. Yet their priority was survival and, if possible, expansion of their power. They were therefore reluctant to do anything that might prove socially divisive and erode their sources of support, and their policy toward women tended to become less radical over time as it became clear that radical policies incurred the hostility of male peasants.

Marriage laws were enacted in the Jiangxi Soviet Republic in 1931 and 1934 and in various Communist areas in north China from 1939 on. These varied in detail, but all stressed free-choice marriage, the principle of monogamy, and equality of the sexes. There was a clear tendency for these laws to be informed less by radical idealism and more by experience. Divorce was freely available under the Jiangxi marriage laws, whereas later Communist marriage laws set out limited grounds on which divorce could be requested. Later laws dealt with practical problems such as the responsibility for child support after divorce. Documents from the 1940s tend to downgrade the whole problem of women's oppression within the family, urging women cadres to drop useless sloganizing about free-choice marriage and sex equality in favor of building flourishing and harmonious families.

Economic work became a more important theme in the Communist women's movement. Women leaders such as Cai Chang and Deng Yingchao followed the party line by arguing that the way to liberate women was to involve them in economic work, teach them agricultural skills, and mobilize them to spin, weave, and produce uniforms for the army. Communist land-reform policies entitled women to allocations of land on equal terms with men. Land reform had been suspended during the war years but was undertaken again from 1946, and cadres were urged to ensure that women's names were included on the land deeds.

Women in the Communist areas, like women elsewhere, suffered from a double burden of economic work and household work, and their difficulties were often blamed on their own backwardness rather than on their oppression. Critical feminist voices were silenced in the interests of unity. Ding Ling, a famous woman writer who had left Shanghai to live and work in the Communist capital of Yan'an, was severely criticized for an article about

Communist treatment of women that she published in the *Jiefang ribao* (Liberation Daily) in 1942.

The fear of alienating male peasants, the priorities of a predominantly male leadership, and the constant military danger to Communist areas certainly constrained Communist policy toward women before 1949. However, there were certain achievements. The message of sexual equality and the reform of family relationships was heard in the rural areas almost for the first time. Tens of thousands of rural women were recruited by women's associations to work for the war effort. This brought them into contact with people outside their own families and gave them a new vision of themselves and their potential.

Women in the People's Republic. When the Communist Party came to power in mainland China, it sought to implement measures already tested in the base areas across the whole country. Policies that were expected to contribute to establishing the equality of the sexes were land reform and collectivization, the implementation of a new marriage law, and the mobilization of women for employment or community activity.

The land-reform program gave women the right to own land in their own names. However, because this in effect would have meant breaking up the holdings of the peasant household, it was rarely carried out. Men and women counted equally in the calculation of how much a household would receive, but women usually did not receive individual land titles. Land reform was soon followed by the collectivization of agriculture, under which the private ownership of land was abolished. All land belonged to the collective, and when the harvest was divided, remuneration was made on the basis of work contributed to the collective. Again, hopes that this would improve the position of women were largely unfulfilled. Rural cadres were predominantly men who valued men's labor higher than women's. The nurseries and canteens that were supposed to relieve women of some of their domestic work proved unpopular and uneconomic, and few survived. The system of collective farming increased women's contacts outside their immediate families and made some of the work they did more visible, but it brought them fewer benefits than had been expected.

The priority still given to family reform in the construction of the new society is reflected in the fact that the Marriage Law of the People's Republic, promulgated on 1 May 1950, was the second law announced by the new government. Drafted by the party women's committee, led by veterans such as Deng Yingchao and Cai Chang, the law followed familiar lines, with an emphasis on equality, monogamy, and free choice. It was consciously more

Chinese Military. Female soldiers in rifle practice, c. 1937–1945. Prints and Photographs Division, Library of Congress

radical than any laws since the marriage laws of the early 1930s in the Jiangxi Soviet. In particular, it allowed divorce when one party insisted on it, even if the other was opposed—a point fought for by Deng Yingchao against considerable opposition. All the energies of the Communist women's organization, the All-China Women's Federation, were mobilized for the implementation of the new law. Books, comic strips, pamphlets, plays, and films were produced to publicize it and to expose and condemn the "feudal" oppression of women.

The marriage law was not popular among men or even among older women, particularly in the countryside. There were complaints that it amounted to a divorce law and that it favored women over men. Women who sought divorce often suffered violence from their husbands or in-laws. Tens of thousands of women are reported to have been killed over marriage-related issues in the first years of the People's Republic. The worst effects occurred when women tried to assert their right both to divorce and to a share of the family land. The backlash was so severe that the campaign to enforce the marriage law was cut back. Neither the new marriage law nor collectivization challenged the patrilocal marriage system, which put women at a fundamental disadvantage in Chinese society. Women came as strangers to their new villages, whereas men remained where they were born, and hence it was men who controlled the collective structures.

The party accepted the Marxist view that women were oppressed because they were excluded from production. A campaign to employ women was therefore launched, and women became an important part of the urban workforce all over China. This did not mean that they achieved equality. They were disproportionately allocated work in lower-paid employment, such as textiles and light industry, or in neighborhood-run workshops, which offered fewer benefits than state industry. Usually the husband's employer provided accommodation at or near his place of work, which meant that women were more likely than their husbands to have to endure long commutes to their workplaces.

The All-China Women's Federation was the leading organization pressing for measures that would benefit women. From 1949 to 1957, its most powerful years, following what was then the party line, it attempted to draw progressive non-Communist figures into its work. Not only was Sun Yat-sen's widow, Ching Ling Soong (Song Qingling), made its honorary president; in addition, He Xiangning, the former head of the Nationalist women's organization, and survivors of the May Fourth Moment such as Liu Wang Liming of the Woman's Christian Temperance Union and Deng Yuzhi of the Young Women's Christian Association were on its standing committee. Unfortunately, most of these women were to suffer severely during the Cultural Revolution.

Perhaps more effective than the measures specifically designed to improve women's lives were the changes in living standards, education, and health brought about after 1949. Living standards were low before the economic reforms: most household gadgets were unavailable, food and clothing were rationed, and even running water was a privilege enjoyed only in advanced urban areas. However, improvements in the supply and distribution of food meant that the majority lived better than they had during the long years of war and civil strife (a notable exception being the famine years from 1959 to 1961).

In the field of health, improved nutrition, together with the introduction of preventive health measures and a focus on maternal and child welfare, brought infant and maternal death rates down dramatically. Life expectancy for women improved from about 40 years in 1950 to 51 in 1957, 65.3 in 1980, and 73 in 2000 (adjusted figures from J. Banister, *China's Changing Population* [Stanford, Calif.: Stanford University Press, 1987]; the figure for 2000 is from the 2000 census). Female life expectancy was only one year more than that for males in 1950, but the gap had increased to 3.7 by 2000.

The expansion of education was of special benefit to women, because women before 1949 had been overrepresented among those with no schooling. Table 1 shows how women have increased their share in enrollment at each level of education. Women have not yet achieved equality with men, however, even in primary school enrollments. Though the differences are by no means negligible, the improvement is impressive by the standards of the developing world. The figures should be seen in the context of the proportion of all children in school. Primary school enrollment grew from about 25 percent of the appropriate age-group in 1950 to 98 percent by the end of the century. Secondary school enrollment was 3 percent of the appropriate age-group in 1950. By 2005 the great majority of children in China had at least some years of secondary schooling. Education has put hundreds of millions of women into a better position to realize their full potential.

The height of insistence on gender equality in China was the period of the Cultural Revolution (1966–1976).

TABLE 1. *Female share of enrollment in primary, secondary, and tertiary education (%)*

	1951	1958	1974	1985	1995	2002
Primary	28	38.5	43.7	44.8	47.3	47.2
Secondary	26.6	31.3	38.1	40.2	44.8	46.7
Tertiary	22.5	22.3	33.8	30.0	35.4	44.0

SOURCES: Quanguo Funü Lianhe Hui, *Zhongguo funü tongji ziliao 1949–1989* (Beijing: Zhongguo Tongji Chubanshe, 1991), and Guojia Tongji Ju, *Zhongguo tongji nianjian 2003* (Beijing: Zhongguo Tongji Chubanshe, 2003).

Chairman Mao's aphorism "What men can do, women can do" was used to justify the presence of women in male-dominated fields such as engineering and aviation and to insist on the right of women in the mining industry to do underground work, from which they had been excluded by health and safety legislation. The percentage of women in all levels of education rose, and women were catapulted into leading positions in many institutions.

Yet despite the vocal support given to equality during the Cultural Revolution, the idea of women's special interests was rejected, and the need for women's organizations was denied. The All-China Women's Federation came under heavy attack and ceased all activity in 1968. Leading members such as Cai Chang and Deng Yingchao had steered a difficult path between the women's movement and the Communist Party, on the one hand keeping women's issues on the party's agenda and recruiting women activists to work for it, and on the other trimming the goals of May Fourth Movement feminism where it was judged necessary in the pragmatic interests of the party. Now they were forced to make self-criticisms of their "bourgeois attitudes" and to see their life's work negated. The All-China Women's Federation was accused of opposing gender interests to class interests, of making too much of family problems, and of distracting women from politics. Ironically, because she had never been involved with the women's movement, the insistence on equality during the Cultural Revolution became associated with its most prominent woman leader, Jiang Qing, Mao Zedong's wife. After Mao's death and Jiang Qing's fall, her personal unpopularity helped ensure that the ideals of equality upheld during the Cultural Revolution were discredited.

Women after the Economic Reforms. After the death of Mao Zedong in 1976, China introduced economic reforms that included liberalization of the economy, the restoration of markets and a private sector, and efforts to attract foreign investment. The changes produced extraordinarily rapid economic growth and had profound impacts on society.

In rural areas, collective land was distributed once more to peasant households. Each family could farm its holding for its own profit, and the revival of private markets made it possible to sell agricultural surplus and the products of cottage industries. The response to the new incentives was a significant increase of agricultural output. Moreover, this output was produced with less labor than in the past. Households redirected surplus labor into rural industry, trade, transport, and construction work and into labor migration to the urban areas.

Under the new system, women's access to land again became a problem. Land was distributed to the household on a per capita basis. Women theoretically received their own share, but it was managed by the patrilocal household, so women could not own or control it as individuals. The patrilocal marriage system undermines gender equality in relation to land. Attempts to give women plots in their new villages upon marriage while withdrawing their plots in their natal villages created such frequent redistributions and were so disruptive that they have been widely abandoned. As in the past under private ownership, women's access to land usually depends on their relationships with their fathers or their husbands.

Many young rural women migrate to the cities, where they work in factories, sweatshops, and restaurants, or as domestic servants. They tend to work long hours in hard conditions but earn far more than they could in their villages. Some enjoy having money to spend on themselves; others remit money back to their families or save to set up small businesses. Although their lives can be hard and lonely, migration gives women a small window of independence between childhood and marriage. Most return to the rural areas to marry in their early to middle twenties. Once married, they usually remain in the villages to care for their children and to farm. Their husbands, by contrast, are likely to continue to undertake seasonal or even long-term migration in search of better wages. The result is that although women do not ultimately control the land, in many regions they perform the bulk of farm labor.

In urban China there have been winners and losers among women in the period of economic reform. The expansion of commercial activity and the creation of much office employment created many white-collar opportunities for women. On the other hand, cutbacks and closures in the old state-owned industries have led to large-scale layoffs. Women tend to be selected as the first to go. The idea that men are more able than women is still widespread, despite many years of Maoist education to the contrary. So many political ideas of the Maoist past have now been discredited, the idea of sex equality may have suffered by association. Whatever the reason, many employers openly discriminate against women in hiring practices, and women's confinement to the lower-paid sectors of the labor market is rarely even challenged. The Law to Protect Women's Rights, enacted in 1992, seems to have done little to help. Indeed, by requiring women to retire five years earlier than men and by encoding maternity leave and special treatment during menstruation and pregnancy, the law may even have strengthened the image of women as difficult employees.

The one-child family policy, introduced in 1980, limited Chinese couples to one child. Women have undoubtedly suffered from the invasive and sometimes coercive methods used to enforce the policy. The burden of contraception has fallen mainly on women, and women commonly have to undergo abortions or sterilizations that they do not really want. The cultural imperative to have a son can cause immense difficulties when the only child permitted turns out to be female. Disappointed husbands and in-laws sometimes punish the mother. The sex ratio of boys to girls began to rise in the early 1980s—an indication of infanticide and concealed female births. The rules were then relaxed to allow many rural families to have a second child, and sex-selective abortion, although illegal, was facilitated by new technology. The sex ratio of infants under one year of age was 111 boys to 100 girls in the 1990 census and had climbed to 119 in the 2000 census, much higher than the biological norm of 105 or 106. Lowered fertility has at least meant that women are no longer burdened with frequent pregnancy and large families, but the impact of China's population policy has revealed how fundamental the preference for boys remains.

The marriage law has been amended twice in the reform period, once in 1980 and once in 2001. The new texts reflect a view of law as a means of dealing with social problems rather than as a way of revolutionizing society. The 1980 law reflected the state's concern with population control and with the burden of social welfare. It specifically prohibited female infanticide, imposed a duty on all married couples to practice family planning, and contained a greatly increased emphasis on the obligation of individuals to support their dependent children or grandchildren and their elderly parents or grandparents. New clauses in the law of 2001 deal with the problems of married people who cohabit with third parties, of domestic violence, of the abduction of women and coerced marriages, and of alimony and child support.

The modest gains in living standards achieved in Maoist China have been dwarfed by advances after Mao's death. People in urban and rural areas have lives that are incomparably richer in material terms than those of their parents and grandparents. Shopping is easy, and everything is available if you have the money. Consumerism is a powerful force in contemporary China and has transformed how women live in many respects. In the cities, this means fashionable and varied clothing, comfortable furniture, and many household amenities, such as better cooking facilities, easy-to-clean surfaces, refrigerators, and washing machines.

Some new market-related phenomena would grieve the feminists of the past. The media and advertisements commodify women as sex objects or portray them in domestic roles. Local governments sponsor beauty competitions. Prostitution is rife. Young women from poor rural regions are tricked into sex work or even trafficked against their will. Businessmen and officials bond or seal agreements in hostess and karaoke bars, a male business world in which women cannot function on equal terms. Wealthy businessmen and officials set up young women in apartments. This is sometimes referred to as the reemergence of concubinage, but in fact concubinage probably offered women more protection than its modern-day equivalent does.

Although women are still clearly far from equal in China, much progress has been made in the last century. Some efforts of the state to empower women have met with little success, but advances in education and health care have enabled women to take a much more active role in the economy and society than was open to them in the past, and their health and life expectancy have shown remarkable gains.

[*See also* Ching Ling Soong; Communism; Deng Yingchao; Ding Ling; Fang Junying; Foot-Binding; Gender Preference in Children; Jiang Qing; Kang Keqing; Mayling Soong; *Nüshu*; Rape of Nanjing; Taiwan; Wang Anyi; White Terror; Wu Yi; Xiang Jingyu; Yang Zhihua; *and* Zhang Jie.]

BIBLIOGRAPHY

Bossen, Laurel. "Women and Development." In *Understanding China*, edited by Robert R. Gamer, pp. 309–339. Boulder, Colo.: Lynne Rienner, 2003. Useful and accessible overview of Chinese women in the twentieth century, informed by the most recent research.

Croll, Elisabeth. *Endangered Daughters: Discrimination and Development in Asia*. London: Routledge, 2000. A pathbreaking comparative study of daughter discrimination in Asia that shows why it is on the rise and why sex ratios are becoming more distorted in favor of boys despite economic growth and the generally improved status of women.

Davin, Delia. *Internal Migration in Contemporary China*. Basingstoke, U.K.: Macmillan, 1999. An overview of the significance of rural-urban migration in the postreform era, with two chapters that focus on gender.

Diamond, Norma. "Collectivization, Kinship, and the Status of Women in Rural China." In *Toward an Anthropology of Women*, edited by Rayna Reiter, pp. 372–395. New York: Monthly Review Press, 1975. A pioneering and influential essay that shows how the impact of the patrilocal marriage system in China held women back at all stages of their lives under collectivization.

Evans, Harriet. *Women and Sexuality in China: Dominant Discourses of Female Sexuality and Gender since 1949*. Cambridge, U.K.: Polity Press, 1997. A comprehensive analysis of the discourse on women's sexuality in China after 1949 that shows why gender relations are of central importance for the revolutionary state.

Gilmartin, Christina. *Engendering the Chinese Revolution: Radical Women, Communist Politics, and Mass Movements in the 1920s*. Berkeley: University of California Press, 1995. The best study of Chinese women activists and the Communist movement in China in the 1920s.

Honig, Emily. *Sisters and Strangers: Women in the Shanghai Cotton Mills, 1919–1949*. Stanford, Calif.: Stanford University Press, 1986. A study of the formation of female textile workers, their living and working conditions, and their gradual politicization.

Honig, Emily, and Gail Hershatter. *Personal Voices: Chinese Women in the 1980's*. Stanford, Calif.: Stanford University Press, 1988. A wonderfully readable account of urban Chinese women in the first postreform decade, with chapters on growing up, dress, courtship, marriage, family relations, divorce, work, violence, and feminist voices.

Jacka, Tamara. *Rural Women in Urban China: Gender, Migration, and Social Change*. Armonk, N.Y.: M. E. Sharpe, 2006. An ethnographic study of the lives of female migrants in China at the end of the twentieth century and the beginning of the twenty-first century.

Jacka, Tamara. *Women's Work in Rural China: Change and Continuity in an Era of Reform*. Cambridge, U.K.: Cambridge University Press, 1997. An examination of the gendered division of labor in rural China under reform; explains why that division persisted even while considerable shifts in the boundaries of the division were taking place.

Meijer, M. J. *Marriage Law and Policy in the Chinese People's Republic*. Hong Kong: Hong Kong University Press, 1971. A study of the development of marriage law in twentieth-century China. Includes chapters on Republican and early Communist law.

Milwertz, Celia. *Accepting Population Control: Urban Chinese Women and the One-child Family Policy*. Richmond, U.K.: Curzon, 1997. A study of the implementation of the one-child policy in urban China, with a strong focus on the experience of individual women.

Wang Zheng. *Women in the Chinese Enlightenment: Oral and Textual Histories*. Berkeley: University of California Press, 1999. A comprehensive study of the Chinese women's movement in the 1920s and 1930s that rescues non-Communist feminism from obscurity; includes moving interviews with surviving activists.

West, Jackie, Zhao Minghua, Chang Xianqun, and Cheng Yuan, eds. *Women of China: Economic and Social Transformation*. New York: St. Martin's Press, 1999. A collection of essays on Chinese women that covers women's complex and varied experiences of economic reform.

DELIA DAVIN

CHISHOLM, SHIRLEY (1924–2005), politician, women's rights advocate, first African American woman elected to the U.S. Congress, and candidate in the Democratic Party primary for the U.S. presidency in 1972. Shirley Anita St. Hill Chisholm served as a legislator from Brooklyn, New York, for nearly twenty years, first in the New York State Assembly, and then as a member of the U.S. Congress. She was a vocal advocate for an activist government to redress economic, social, and political injustices, and she frequently used her national prominence to bring attention to racial, gender, and class-based inequalities.

Chisholm was born in Brooklyn on 30 November 1924, the first of four daughters born to Ruby Seale and Charles St. Hill, who were immigrants from Barbados. Economic challenges compelled Chisholm's parents to send the girls to live with their maternal grandmother in Barbados for six years. In 1934, they returned to Brooklyn, where Chisholm lived for much of her life.

A strong student, Chisholm attended Brooklyn College from 1942 to 1946. On campus, she developed her oratorical skills in the Debate Society. At the same time, her membership in the Harriet Tubman Society and the Political Science Society stimulated her racial and political consciousness. Her leadership skills began to attract attention, and one of her professors suggested she enter politics.

Shirley Chisholm. PRINTS AND PHOTOGRAPHS DIVISION, LIBRARY OF CONGRESS

Upon graduation, Chisholm began a career in early childhood education. Between 1946 and 1964, she rose from a position as a teacher's aide to a consultant to the New York City Division of Day Care, where she supervised ten day care centers. She also attained a master's degree in early childhood education from Columbia University in 1952.

Chisholm's participation in politics began in 1953 when she worked with a group of activists to fight racial discrimination in the local political structure. In 1960 she joined an insurgent organization, the Unity Democratic Club (UDC), which did a significant amount of political education and organizing. With the UDC's backing, Chisholm ran successfully for the State Assembly, in 1964. Once in office, she fought for legislation to address racial and sexual discrimination, poverty, and unemployment.

Chisholm's political acumen and her ambition were manifested in her successful campaign for the U.S. Congress in 1968 in which she defeated the civil rights leader James

Farmer. The first black woman elected to that position, Chisholm's victory was touted as an important milestone. She remained consistent in her political vision and used her position in Congress to address social, political, and economic injustices. She also joined with the twelve other African American members of Congress to formally establish the Congressional Black Caucus in 1971.

Chisholm was a women's rights advocate. In Congress, she fought for women's issues including the Equal Rights Amendment (ERA). She was also an officer in the National Organization for Women (NOW), the honorary president of the National Association for the Repeal of Abortion Laws (NARAL), a cofounder of the National Women's Political Caucus, and a cofounder of the National Political Congress of Black Women.

In 1972, Chisholm ran for the U.S. presidency. She entered a number of Democratic Party primaries and secured enough delegates to participate in the party's national convention. After her defeat, she returned to Congress, where she served her district until 1982, winning every election with a significant majority of the vote.

After her retirement as a legislator, Chisholm taught at Mount Holyoke College and was a visiting scholar at Spelman College. In 1993, she was inducted into the National Women's Hall of Fame. That same year, President Clinton nominated Chisholm as ambassador to Jamaica, but she declined the position because of poor health. Chisholm died in Florida on 1 January 2005.

[*See also* Abortion, *subentry* Politics; Civil Rights Movement; *and* Equal Rights Amendment.]

BIBLIOGRAPHY

Brownmiller, Susan. *Shirley Chisholm: A Biography*. Garden City, N.Y.: Doubleday, 1970.

Chisholm, Shirley. *The Good Fight*. New York: Harper and Row, 1973.

Chisholm, Shirley. *Unbought and Unbossed*. Boston: Houghton Mifflin, 1970.

Haskins, James. *Fighting Shirley Chisholm*. New York: Dial Press, 1975.

JULIE GALLAGHER

CHŌ KŌRAN (1804–1879), Japanese poet, painter, and calligrapher. The daughter of a country samurai from the village of Sone in Mino Province (present-day Gifu Prefecture), Chō Kōran learned to read and write Chinese when she was a child. She delved into the study of Chinese poetry, which was unusual for women of her day, becoming a pupil of the well-known poet Yanagawa Seigan (1789–1858). Kōran married Seigan when she was seventeen. As both mentor and husband he was a key figure in her unconventional life.

The intellectual couple led a rather bohemian lifestyle, spending years on the road and journeying as far as Shikoku and Kyushu in western Japan. They relied on the hospitality of a network of scholars, poets, and patrons, and the opportunities to associate with other Sinophiles further stimulated Kōran's interest in Chinese arts. After returning briefly to Mino, they eventually settled in Kyoto. There Kōran took lessons in *bunjinga*, or Chinese literati painting, from Nakabayashi Chikutō, and she became a skillful painter in the genre known as "four gentlemen" (bamboo, orchid, plum, chrysanthemum). Earlier she had dabbled in bird and flower painting, but now she began to turn more to ink landscapes. By 1830 Kōran had made a name for herself and was listed in the *Heian jinbutsu shi* (Record of Heian [Kyoto] Notables) as a specialist of *bunjinga*.

In 1832 the wandering couple moved to Edo (present-day Tokyo), where Seigan set up a private school. Kōran became recognized for her talents there, too. An illustration of one of her ink bamboo paintings was included in the *Hyaku meika gafu* (Album of Calligraphy and Painting by One Hundred Artists), published in 1837, and she had a book of her poems published in 1841, *Kōran kōshū* (Selected Poems by Kōran).

The couple made their living largely through Seigan's lectures and poetry lessons, but part of their income came from selling Kōran's paintings. The couple left Edo in 1845 and moved to Ōgaki, where Kōran began learning how to play the Chinese *qin*, a seven-string zither instrument beloved by the literati. A year later Kōran and Seigan returned to live in Kyoto, where they remained for the rest of their lives. During the second half of her life, Kōran wrote many poems, which were published posthumously as a volume titled *Kōran ikō* (Posthumous Manuscripts of Kōran; included in vol. 4 of [*Yanagawa*] *Seigan zenshū* by Tominaga Chōjo, 1958). She often inscribed poems on her paintings as well. The total number of her extant poems is around four hundred.

While living in Edo, Kōran and Seigan had begun to associate with men who were promoting government reforms in the face of aggression from the West. The unsympathetic shogunate tried to repress these reformers, and in 1858 many of their friends who sought to restore imperial sovereignty were arrested. Seigan died suddenly of cholera, but Kōran was taken captive and imprisoned for six months. After being released, Kōran, aided by her husband's pupils, opened a private school, where she taught Chinese poetry to women.

As the wife of a distinguished poet, Kōran had always been in Seigan's shadow, but after his death Kōran continued to evolve as a poet and painter in her own right. Fully committed to the arts, she remained active in literary and artistic circles well into her seventies.

[*See also* Art and Architecture, *subentry* Artists and Architects; *and* Japan.]

BIBLIOGRAPHY

Fister, Patricia. "The Life and Art of Chō Kōran." In *Flowering in the Shadows: Women in the History of Chinese and Japanese Painting*, edited by Marsha Weidner, pp. 265–293. Honolulu: University of Hawai'i Press, 1990.

PATRICIA FISTER

CHRISTIANITY. Like all religious traditions, Christianity has been used to both strengthen and question existing gender structures, providing ideas about hierarchy as well as complementarity and equality. Christian officials and authorities have attempted to create and enforce uniformity through specific religious texts, patterns of worship, clerical personnel, court systems, and alliances with political leaders, but individuals and groups have often chosen to interpret divine will and authoritative teachings regarding gender differently than have church leaders. This has created great variety within Christianity at any given time, and even more diversity over the two millennia of Christianity's existence.

The Early Church. Christianity is based on the teachings of Jesus of Nazareth, called the Christ (a Greek translation of the Hebrew word "Messiah" meaning "anointed one"), who was apparently executed by the Romans about 30 C.E. and is believed by most Christians to have been resurrected from the dead three days later. Jesus's teachings and life story are recorded in the first four books of the New Testament, called the Gospels, written several decades after his death. (Christians regard Hebrew scripture as also being authoritative, and label this the "Old Testament," though Christian groups differ as to exactly which books should be included in the Old Testament.) Women figure prominently in the Gospels, listening to and speaking with Jesus; in two of the Gospels (Mark and Matthew) they are the first to see Jesus after his resurrection and were told to give the good news (which is what the word "Gospel" means) to his other followers.

Women took an active role in the spread of Christianity, preaching, acting as missionaries, and being martyred alongside men. Early Christians expected Jesus to return to earth again very soon, and so taught that his followers should concentrate on this Second Coming. Because of this, these early Christians believed, marriage and normal family life should be abandoned, and Christians should depend on their new spiritual family of cobelievers; early Christians often met in people's homes and called each other brother and sister, a metaphorical use of family terms that was new to the Roman Empire in which Christianity developed. This made Christians seem dangerous to many Romans, especially when becoming Christian actually led some young people to avoid marriage, viewed by Romans as the foundation of society and the proper patriarchal order.

Not all Christian teachings about gender were radical, however. Many of Jesus's early followers, particularly the Apostle Paul whose letters make up a major part of the New Testament, had ambivalent ideas about women's proper role in the church. Paul asserted that "in Christ there is neither male nor female" (Galatians 3:28), but he forbade women to preach. Women were gradually excluded from holding official positions within Christianity. Both Jewish and classical Mediterranean culture viewed female subordination as natural and proper, so that in limiting the activities of female believers Christianity was following well-established patterns, in the same way that it soon patterned its official hierarchy after that of the Roman Empire.

Some of Christianity's most radical teachings about gender also came to have negative consequences for women. In the first centuries of Christianity, some women embraced the ideal of virginity and either singly or in communities declared themselves "virgins in the service of Christ." This was threatening to most church leaders, who termed such women, at best, "brides of Christ"; that is, in a dependent relationship with a man. Some of these leaders also advocated a life of virginity for men, which led to a strong streak of misogyny in their writings, for they saw women and female sexuality as the chief obstacles to this preferred existence; because they wrote far more than women and their writings were preserved more frequently, their opinions came to be much more influential than those of the women who chose virginity.

The most important theologian in the Western Christian Church, Saint Augustine of Hippo (354–430), linked sexuality clearly with sin by viewing sexual desire as the result of disobedience to divine instructions by Adam and Eve, the first humans. The condition of sinfulness was passed down, in Augustine's opinion, through sexual intercourse, so that even infants were tainted with this original sin. Christian scripture offered positive comments about marriage and procreation—Jesus himself had blessed a wedding with a miracle—so that Augustine could not reject them completely, but he and later Christian writers clearly regarded virginity as the preferred state of existence and particularly condemned any sexual activity that could not lead to children, such as homosexual acts or masturbation.

Christianity became the official religion of the Roman Empire in the fourth century. It also gradually spread beyond the boundaries of the Roman Empire, northward into Germanic- and Celtic-speaking lands, eastward into Persia and the southwest coast of India, and southward into Ethiopia. Women were often active in spreading Christian ideas, especially within their own families, and

Christianity and Sexuality. An excerpt from *Der Jungfrauspiegel*, a twelfth-century German manuscript, depicting the Christian hierarchy of womanhood and the associated heavenly rewards in accordance with levels of abstinence on earth, with virgins at the top, widows in the middle, and married women at the bottom. RHEINISCHEN LANDESMUSEUM, BONN, GERMANY

women's monastic communities were under the leadership of female abbesses; Jesus's mother Mary became an important figure of devotion, as did female as well as male saints.

Outside of women's monasteries, however, all Christian officials were men, who were increasingly expected to follow a distinctive life pattern, though this differed slightly in various branches of Christianity. In Europe and the Mediterranean area, Christianity split into two main branches, the Orthodox Church of eastern Europe and the Roman (Catholic) Church of western Europe, an event later termed the Great Schism. In eastern Europe, married men could become priests, though in some orthodox churches a man who was unmarried when ordained as a priest was expected to remain unmarried, and married priests could not move up the church hierarchy and become bishops. In Ethiopia (Coptic Church) and India (Malabar or St. Thomas Church), married men were also accepted into the priesthood, though celibate and ascetic monks rather than priests provided the intellectual and political leadership in the church. In western Europe, Roman church councils in the twelfth century, particularly the Second Lateran Council of 1139, forbade all priests to marry and declared clerical marriages that did exist invalid, driving priests' wives and children from their homes; at the same time they condemned homosexual activities more sharply. The policy of clerical celibacy proved difficult to enforce, and for centuries priests and higher officials simply took concubines. (Though in doing this they were technically "celibate," a word that actually means "not married" rather than "chaste.")

Medieval and Reformation Christianity. The spread of Islam in the seventh and eighth centuries separated Indian and Ethiopian Christianity both geographically and intellectually from European Christianity and put most of the traditional centers of Christianity, such as Jerusalem and Alexandria, under Muslim control. The majority of Christians lived in Europe, where highly educated philosophers developed more complex theology and the church became an important political and economic institution.

In the twelfth and thirteenth centuries, Scholastic philosophers attempted to bring together Christianity and the teachings of the Greek philosopher Aristotle into one grand philosophical system. Saint Thomas Aquinas (c. 1225–1274), the most brilliant and thorough of the Scholastics, synthesized classical and Christian ideas about women, stating in the *Summa Theologica*, his major work, that women's inferiority was not simply the result of Eve's actions, but was inherent in her original creation. The opinions of the Scholastics were expressed not only in complex philosophical treatises, but were communicated more broadly through public sermons and university lectures.

In the thirteenth century, church councils expanded the power of priests, decreeing that they had the power to absolve sins through confession and to change bread and wine into the body and blood of Christ to be consumed by believers during the Eucharist, the central ritual of Christianity (a transformation termed "transubstantiation"). Thus priests, who were all male, had powers that no woman (or nonordained man, including kings) had, a situation that continues to the present day within Roman Catholicism. The special powers of the priest make the conflict over the ordination of women especially heated within Roman Catholicism, with many observers predicting that the Catholic Church will admit married men as priests long before it ordains women.

In western Europe until the sixteenth century and in eastern Europe until the twentieth century, the most powerful and in many ways independent women in Christianity were the abbesses of certain convents, who controlled large amounts of property and often had jurisdiction over many individuals. Convents had widely varying levels of religious devotion and intellectual life; many were little more than dumping grounds for unmarriageable daughters, while others were important centers of piety and learning. In addition to living in convents, a number of women in the late Middle Ages lived in less structured religious communities, supporting themselves by weaving, sewing, or caring for the sick.

During the early sixteenth century, long-standing criticism of Western Christianity led to a rupture in the church, later termed the Protestant Reformation. Protestant reformers differed on many points of doctrine, but they uniformly rejected clerical celibacy and agreed that the clergy should be married heads of household. Thus there was no separate religious vocation open to women, who were urged to express their devotion within the family as "helpmeet" to their husband and guide to their children. Protestantism proclaimed family life as the ideal for all men and women, an ideal communicated through sermons, hymns, and printed books; unmarried people of both sexes were increasingly suspect.

Like Christianity itself, the Protestant Reformation both expanded and diminished women's opportunities. During early decades when a decision to break with the Catholic Church was being made by a particular area or group, women and men who did not have formal theological training tried to shape religious institutions through preaching, religious riots and other sorts of popular actions, and writing pamphlets. Women's preaching or publishing religious material stood in direct opposition to the words ascribed to Saint Paul (1 Timothy 2:11–15), which ordered women not to teach or preach, and once Protestant churches were institutionalized, polemical writings by women (and untrained men) largely stopped. Women continued to write hymns and devotional literature, but these were often published posthumously or were designed for private use. Women's actions as well as their writings in the first years of the Reformation upset political and religious authorities. Many cities prohibited women from even getting together to discuss religious matters, and in 1543 an Act of Parliament in England (the Act for the Advancement of True Religion) banned all women except those of the gentry and nobility from reading the Bible, and upper-class women were prohibited from reading the Bible aloud to others.

Once the Reformation was established, most women expressed their religious convictions in a domestic, rather than public, setting. They prayed and recited the catechism with children and servants, attended sermons, read the Bible or other devotional literature if they were literate, served meals that no longer followed Catholic fast prescriptions, and provided religious instruction for their children. The Protestant rejection of celibacy had a great impact on female religious, both cloistered nuns and women who lived in less formal religious communities. In most areas becoming Protestant, monasteries and convents were closed; nuns got very small pensions and were expected to return to their families.

The response of the Catholic Church to the Protestant Reformation is often described as two interrelated movements, one a Counter-Reformation that attempted to win territory and people back to loyalty to Rome and prevent further spread of Protestant ideas, and the other a reform of abuses and problems within the Catholic Church. Women were actively involved in both movements, but their actions were generally judged to be more acceptable when they were part of a reform drive; even more than the medieval Crusades, the fight against Protestants was to be a masculine affair. The Council of Trent, the church council that met for three periods between 1545 and 1563 to define what Catholic positions would be on matters of doctrine and discipline, reaffirmed the necessity of cloistering for all women religious, though enforcement of this decree came slowly. The only active apostolate left open to religious women was the instruction of girls, and that only within the convent. No nuns were sent to the foreign missions for any public duties, though once colonies were established in the New World and Asia cloistered convents quickly followed.

Scholars differ sharply about the impact of Protestantism on women. Some see it as elevating the status of most women in its praise of marriage, while others see it as

The Annunciation. Painting by Sandro Botticelli, c. 1485, depicting the archangel Gabriel's revelation to Mary that she will conceive God's son, Jesus Christ. Uffizi, Florence/Erich Lessing/Art Resource, NY

limiting women by denying them the opportunity for education and independence in monasteries and stressing wifely obedience. Still others see it as having little impact, with its stress on marriage a response to economic and social changes that had already occurred, not a cause of those changes.

Worldwide Christianity. The Protestant Reformation occurred concurrently with the beginning of European colonization, which took Christianity around the world. Indeed, the conversion of indigenous people was one of the primary justifications for conquering new territories. Christian officials tried to impose European gender patterns—monogamous marriage, male-headed households, limited (or no) divorce—on newly encountered cultures, but where these European patterns conflicted with existing ones they were often modified, and what emerged was a blend of indigenous and imported practices. In some areas, such as the Andes of South America and the Philippines, women had been important leaders in animistic religions, and they were stronger opponents of conversion than were men; in other areas, women became fervent Christians. Most scholars of colonization and imperialism view the activities of Christian authorities and missionaries as leading to a sharpened gender hierarchy, for religious leaders paid little attention to indigenous women's activities and either misunderstood or opposed women's power. They were also complicit in the establishment and maintenance of racial hierarchies, regulating marriage and other types of sexual activities so as to maintain boundaries. In the immediate postcolonial period, Christianity was often rejected as a remnant of the colonial past, but this began to change in the late twentieth century, and the formerly colonial world now has the fastest-growing Christian churches.

The spread of Christianity around the world was accompanied by even more diversity in gender patterns. Protestantism continued to splinter into more and more groups, some of which became increasingly liberal and activist on social and intellectual issues, working to end slavery, reform prisons, improve working conditions, and expand schooling. Many of these groups allowed women to assume leadership roles, become clergy and missionaries, and eventually gain formal theological training. This began with groups that did not have an ordained clergy, such as the Quakers, and groups that emphasized personal conversion, direct communication with God, and moral regeneration, such as the Methodists. Western women served as missionaries in Asia and Africa, established Sunday schools, preached in prisons, and worked for social changes that they believed would make society more godly and moral, such as the abolition of slavery and temperance. African and Asian women also worked as teachers, medical workers, and missionaries sponsored by Protestant groups; generally these groups, and the women active in them, cooperated with colonial authorities, though sometimes they served as centers of resistance.

Beginning in the middle of the twentieth century, women were admitted as students at many seminaries and developed feminist Christian theology. Individuals and groups created gender-inclusive liturgies, rituals, prayers, and texts and promoted institutional changes that gave women greater access to official positions. By the end of the century, seminaries in the United States were training more women than men to be clergy. Some Protestant denominations, or individual churches within them, became even more tolerant on gender issues, allowing not only women but also actively practicing homosexuals as clergy.

In the early twentieth century, conservative Protestants responded to changes that were going on in many denominations, including a widening role for women, with a movement termed "fundamentalism," which downplayed more complicated issues of doctrine and largely supported a conservative social agenda. In the United States, this came to focus in the 1980s on the issues of abortion, gay rights, prayer in schools, and what were labeled "traditional family values." Fundamentalist groups often broke from the Protestant denominations that had developed in previous centuries to form nondenominational community churches, though some denominations contained a fundamentalist and a liberal wing within themselves. Many fundamentalist groups emphasize the importance of maintaining patriarchal power structures in the church, home, and community, though the wives of prominent preachers sometimes share leadership with their husbands.

The Roman Catholic Church was similarly split between liberals (and radicals) and conservatives in the twentieth century. Women were important voices in the "liberation theology" that called for radical social change, and both nuns and lay women claimed larger roles for themselves within Catholicism, working as teachers and aid workers throughout the world. The church allowed these more active roles and relaxed rules on enclosure (the cloistering of women) and the wearing of distinctive religious dress, but it refused to consider the issue of female ordination or a relaxation of the official prohibition on birth control and homosexuality.

In the early twenty-first century, Christian groups, both traditional and nondenominational, gained their largest number of converts in formerly colonial areas; in 2000, nearly two-thirds of the world's Christians lived outside Europe and North America. These churches appeal to people whose cultural values are shaped by animism, Hinduism, Buddhism, and various other religions, and the norms they are establishing in regard to gender also draw on many traditions, with churches often deciding individually how they will handle issues such as polygamy, child marriage, remarriage of widows, and other issues in which local traditions conflict with traditional Christian teachings. Because Christianity is declining in importance in Western society—except for the United States—it is clear that what is regarded as "traditional" in Christianity may also change, and that because of migration, these debates will be played out not only in the former colonies, but in Europe and North America as well. Most of the world's religions—not only Christianity—have a fundamentalist wing, which advocates stronger gender distinctions and hierarchy, and a more liberal wing, which advocates greater gender egalitarianism. At the beginning of the twenty-first century, fundamentalism is more politically and socially powerful within Christianity, Hinduism, and Islam, but the gender implications of this fundamentalism also evoke strong criticism, and more liberal adherents of these faiths search their texts and traditions for less restrictive messages.

[*See also* Celibacy; Eve; Feminism; Imperialism and Colonialism, *subentry* Modern; Mary; Missionaries; *and* Spiritual Leaders, *subentry* Nuns and Abbesses.]

BIBLIOGRAPHY

Børresen, Kari Elisabeth, ed. *The Image of God: Gender Models in Judaeo-Christian Tradition*. Minneapolis: Fortress Press, 1995. First published 1991 by Solum Forlag. Covers biblical through contemporary Christianity.

Clark, Elizabeth A. *Ascetic Piety and Women's Faith: Essays on Late Ancient Christianity*. Lewiston, N.Y.: E. Mellen Press, 1986. Discusses the early church.

Coon, Lynda L., Katherine J. Haldane, and Elisabeth W. Sommer, eds. *That Gentle Strength: Historical Perspectives on Women in Christianity*. Charlottesville: University of Virginia Press, 1990.

Greaves, Richard L., ed. *Triumph over Silence: Women in Protestant History*. Westport, Conn.: Greenwood Press, 1985. Includes essays covering the sixteenth through the twentieth century.

Hawley, John Stratton, ed. *Fundamentalism and Gender*. New York: Oxford University Press, 1994. Includes essays on Christianity as well as other world religions.

Karant-Nunn, Susan C., and Merry E. Wiesner-Hanks, eds. and trans. *Luther on Women: A Sourcebook*. Cambridge, U.K., and New York: Cambridge University Press, 2003. Martin Luther's writings on women, marriage, and sexuality.

King, Ursula, ed. *Feminist Theology from the Third World: A Reader*. Maryknoll, N.Y.: Orbis Books, 1994.

Mack, Phyllis. *Visionary Women: Ecstatic Prophecy in Seventeenth-Century England*. Berkeley: University of California Press, 1992. Discusses Quaker and other radical women.

Marshall, Sherrin, ed. *Women in Reformation and Counter-Reformation Europe: Public and Private Worlds*. Bloomington: Indiana University Press, 1989.

McNamara, Jo Ann Kay. *Sisters in Arms: Catholic Nuns through Two Millennia*. Cambridge, Mass.: Harvard University Press, 1996.

Newman, Barbara. *From Virile Woman to WomanChrist: Studies in Medieval Religion and Literature*. Philadelphia: University of Pennsylvania Press, 1995. Traces changes in the gender strategies of religious women in medieval Christianity.

Pagels, Elaine. *Adam, Eve, and the Serpent*. New York: Random House, 1988. Introduction to ideas of original sin in Christianity, written for a wide audience.

Roper, Lyndal. *The Holy Household: Women and Morals in Reformation Augsburg*. Oxford: Clarendon Press; New York: Oxford University Press, 1989. Analyzes the impact of the Protestant Reformation in one city.

Ruether, Rosemary Radford. *Christianity and the Making of the Modern Family*. Boston: Beacon Press, 2000. Traces Christianity's changing ideas about the family, especially since the Protestant Reformation; by a leading Christian feminist theologian.

Ruether, Rosemary Radford, and Rosemary Skinner Keller. *Women and Religion in America*. 3 vols. San Francisco: Harper & Row, 1981–1986. Multivolume documentary history of women's religious contributions in America from colonial times to the present.

Schulenburg, Jane Tibbetts. *Forgetful of Their Sex: Female Sanctity and Society, ca. 500–1100*. Chicago: University of Chicago Press, 1998. Analyzes the way women created and manipulated ideals of female sanctity.

Warner, Marina. *Alone of All Her Sex: The Myth and the Cult of the Virgin Mary*. London: Weidenfeld and Nicolson, 1976. Uses visual and textual evidence from the first century to the twentieth.

Wiesner-Hanks, Merry E. *Christianity and Sexuality in the Early Modern World: Regulating Desire, Reforming Practice*. London and New York: Routledge, 2000. Traces the spread of Christian sexual and marital ideas and practices around the world from 1500 to 1750.

MERRY E. WIESNER-HANKS

CHRISTINA OF SWEDEN (1626–1689), queen of Sweden. Christina inherited the throne in Sweden from her father, the Protestant champion Gustavus Adolphus (r. 1611–1632), who was shot in battle when she was six years old. She signed the Peace of Westphalia in 1648, ending the Thirty Years' War, and she brought European scholars, book collections, and ballet dancers to Stockholm until her abdication in 1654.

Interested in Neoplatonism, Christina had slowly turned to Universalism in the Catholic form. In 1648, she secretly approached two Jesuits in the Portuguese embassy, and in 1651 she took the decisive step of sending a letter to the polymath Jesuit Athanasius Kircher (1602–1680) in the Collegio Romano. He sent her his treatise on music, *Musurgia Universalis* (Rome, 1650), and welcomed her to the eternal city. The covert and successful operation to convert her resulted in a great propaganda victory for the Jesuits and the Catholic Church.

The French ambassador Pierre-Hector Chanut brought the famous philosopher René Descartes (1596–1650) to Christina's court in Stockholm in 1649. Descartes died there some months later. They did discuss his philosophy, but Christina said she already had seen his ideas in the philosophies of the skeptic Sextus Empiricus (fl. c. 200 C.E.)

Christina of Sweden. Surrounded by her court, the queen listens to Descartes give a lecture on geometry. Painting by Louis Michel Dumesnil, early eighteenth century. Chateaux de Versailles et de Trianon, France/Réunion des Musées Nationaux/Art Resource, NY

and in Plato (c. 429–c. 347 B.C.E.). Descartes tried to persuade her to abandon her Greek readings but could not gain lasting influence over her. The philosopher Gottfried Wilhelm Leibniz (1646–1716) visited Christina in Rome in 1689 and in 1702 wrote an essay, "On the Doctrine of a Single Universal Spirit," revealing that Christina was a believer in the world soul, not so much as described in Plato, but, surprisingly, as in the work of the Arabic rationalist Averroës (c. 1126–1198).

Christina converted to Catholicism in a public ceremony at Innsbruck in 1656 (she had converted privately in Brussels in 1655), followed by a triumphant entry into Rome through the gate of Piazza del Popolo. She started a learned academy in Palazzo Farnese in her own accommodations there in 1656 and later in her own palace Villa Riaro (now Palazzo Corsini). Her Accademia Reale was part of her extensive cultural program, which also included concerts, poetry, opera, and theater.

She plotted with Cardinal Mazarin (1602–1661) to become Queen of Naples in 1657. Her plans were betrayed by the Marquise Monaldesco, whom she had executed in the Fontainebleau castle, on loan from the French king. Supported by Pope Alexander VII (r. 1655–1667), Christina went back to Rome and settled there permanently. In 1667, she ran as a candidate for the elective throne in Poland, but was not chosen. While preparing her Polish campaign in Hamburg, she worked on alchemy with the famous heretic Giuseppe Francesco Borri. She had a laboratory in her palace and collected some thirty alchemical manuscripts, among them the contemporary compilation *Veritas Hermetica* and the famously illustrated *Rosarium Philosophorum*.

A lasting legacy of her reign is the library of 2,200 manuscripts and 4,500 printed books that she left to her heir and companion Cardinal Decio Azzolino (1623–1689). The manuscripts were bought by the Vatican and are now housed in Biblioteca Vaticana as *Codices reginenses graeci et latini* (Greek and Latin Codices of the Queen) She is one of only four women who have been buried in Saint Peter's Basilica.

Christina's abdication and conversion gave support to the Catholic faith but were viewed by critics as political acts. Her retention of her royal title in the cultural world caused debate about the role of abdications in relation to absolute royal power.

[*See also* Monarchy.]

BIBLIOGRAPHY

Åkerman, Susanna. *Queen Christina of Sweden and Her Circle: The Transformation of a Seventeenth-Century Philosophical Libertine.* Leiden, the Netherlands, and New York: E. J. Brill, 1991.

Arckenholtz, Johan. *Mémoires concernant Christine, reine du Suède* . . . 4 vols. Amsterdam and Leipzig: P. Mortier, 1751–1760.

Stolpe, Sven. *Drottning Kristina.* 2 vols. Stockholm: Bonnier, 1960–1961. English translation, *Christina of Sweden*, edited by Sir Alec Randall. Translation of the abbreviated German version. London: Burns and Oates, 1966.

Susanna Åkerman

CINEMA

This entry consists of three subentries:

Feminist Theory and Criticism

From the earliest days of film, women assumed a prominent place on screen. In the primitive cinema, for instance, spectators viewed Thomas Edison's vision of Fatima the belly dancer, Georges Méliès's depictions of disappearing soubrettes, and Louis Lumière's portrayals of rural maids feeding doves. In all these cases—be they films, fantasy, or documentary—the representation of women axiomatically followed cultural stereotypes—the sexpot, the passive female, the farm girl—that were prevalent in the silent cinema at large. Even in the pre-cinema era, as Linda Williams has described in *Hard Core*, gender lines were drawn. When Eadweard Muybridge took his serial photographs of naked or scantily clad men and women, the men were shown executing athletic moves or muscular work while the women were shown sweeping floors or getting out of bed. Thus "greater sexuality already culturally encoded in the woman's body [fed] into a new cinematic power" (Williams, p. 39). Reflecting this, when feminist film criticism and theory first emerged in the 1970s and 1980s, critics focused on readings of the "image" of women in cinema. The title of Sumiko Higashi's book *Virgins, Vamps, and Flappers* (1978) makes this approach clear. She examines Lillian Gish as a Victorian heroine, Mary Pickford as America's sweetheart, Theda Bara as a vampire, and Joan Crawford as the New Woman.

Reconceptualizing Women in Film. Eventually critics became impatient with the "images" approach because it often labeled representations as either retrograde (the showgirl, the dumb blonde, the temptress) or progressive (the career woman, the adventuress, the tomboy), foregrounding a film's plot and ignoring its style and special status as a medium. Some sought to historicize the stereotypes. In her book *The Wages of Sin*, Lea Jacobs investigated the troubled position of the "fallen woman"—in *Back Street* (1932), *The Easiest Way* (1931), *Baby Face* (1933), and *Blonde Venus* (1932)—and attempts by Hollywood's Production Code and the Motion Picture Producers and Distributors of America to censor her depiction. Although some have seen the image of the fallen woman as "subversive" of bourgeois values, Jacobs cautions against this assumption (pp. 24–25).

Feminists also tried to revise the accepted valence associated with certain screen images. Thus although early on the figure of the mother was devalued as overly sentimental and traditional, eventually E. Ann Kaplan (in *Motherhood and Representation*) and Lucy Fischer (in *Cinematernity*) questioned women's own colonized dismissal of such a central female role. Seeking to address the mother's discourse "from within," Kaplan examined "resisting" maternal melodramas such as *Stella Dallas* (1937), in which a strong mother–daughter relationship exists and the mother refuses the "'classic' patriarchal . . . position" (p. 170). Fischer then expanded the discussion of motherhood beyond the constraining boundaries of film melodrama, investigating documentaries such as *The Ties That Bind* (1985), crime films such as *White Heat* (1949), horror films such as *Rosemary's Baby* (1968), and comedies such as *The Kid* (1921), demonstrating the historic ubiquity of the maternal discourse.

Furthermore, in a deconstructionist move, feminists began reading texts "against the grain"—surfacing unexpected messages in ostensibly "obvious" portrayals. For instance, although the actress Jane Russell is seen as a sexual object in *Gentlemen Prefer Blondes* (1953), she is not a passive receptacle of male lust. Rather, in the ship

Film Celebrities. Marilyn Monroe in front of Niagara Falls, 1953. New York World-Telegram and the Sun Newspaper Photograph Collection, Library of Congress

gymnasium sequence, she sings "Ain't There Anyone Here for Love?" to the U.S. Olympic team and is actively desirous of a horde of men.

Beyond applauding or chastising female on-screen roles, critics also began to question whether, in the male-authored cinema, women were present at all. Claire Johnston deemed woman only the "pseudo center of the filmic discourse"—a mere projection of the male artist—not so much female as "non-male." She also noted how the discourse surrounding women in the cinema is one of myth that "transmits and transforms the ideology of sexism and renders it invisible" (quoted in Kay and Peary, p. 409). For example, Orson Welles's *The Lady from Shanghai* (1947), which takes place on or near the ocean, casts the female protagonist as a Lorelei or Siren who lures men to their destruction. Other critics, including Mary Ann Doane, explored the notion of femininity as "masquerade"—even as experienced by women. As she notes, "The masquerade, in flaunting femininity, holds it at a distance. Womanliness is a mask which can be worn or removed" (in Kaplan, ed., p. 427).

Discovering Women Filmmakers. Building on these debates, scholars began to explore the existence of women directors in the history of cinema, many of whom had been ignored or neglected. Andrew Sarris, for instance, in his 1968 list of prestigious auteurs, included none in his pantheon. Dorothy Arzner is not mentioned at all, and Ida Lupino is included under the dismissive category of "Oddities, One-Shots, and Newcomers." To remedy this, Annette Kuhn in *Queen of the 'B's* researched the work of Lupino, admitting that, although important, it has sometimes been a "disappointment" to feminist critics because the actress-director "unapologetically cast herself as a man's woman" and did not evince the "kind of stylistic innovation that might be construed as a female voice" (p. 5). Judith Mayne in *Directed by Dorothy Arzner* examined the career of this pioneering Hollywood filmmaker, exploring the feminist aspects of such films as *Craig's Wife* (1936), *Christopher Strong* (1933), and *Dance, Girl, Dance* (1940), as well as Arzner's lesbianism and the manner in which her masculine look was treated within the film community and press.

Scholars also looked toward female filmmakers in other parts of the world. In *Brazilian Cinema*, Ellen Munerato and Maria Helena Darcy de Oliveira wrote that they were saddened to find that only twenty feature films in Brazil had been directed by women and that their plots generally focused on "amorous relations in which the women characters form part of triangles" (in Johnson and Stam, p. 345). Considering the same terrain in *The New Latin American Cinema*, Zuzana Pick examined the contemporary artists Valeria Sarmiento, Mayra Segura, Mayra Vilasis, Ann Rodriguez, and Maria Luisa Bemberg, all of whom "reject social realism in favor of modernist strategies, to evaluate the impact of address on sexual difference and on the social constructions of identity" (p. 69). Turning to non-Western film, Shuqin Cui observed how "the international reception of [mainland] Chinese cinema has been largely confined to films made by the so-called fifth generation of [male] film directors. . . . By contrast, little attention has been given to the subject of women's films in China. Compared to the films of their male counterparts, the works of women directors evince scant interest in macronarratives or allegorical models" (p. 171). Among the films she discusses are Hu Mei's *Army Nurse* (*Nuer Lou*, 1985), Zhang Nuznxin's *Sacrified Youth* (*Qingchun Ji*, 1985), and Li Shaohong's *Blush* (*Hong Fen*, 1994).

Writing about the Hong Kong director Ann Hui, Elaine Yee-lin Ho notes how her recent films "fracture the patriarchal determinations of old and also chart recognizable passages toward a horizon of the 'modern' in which utopian ideals of equality, compassion, and sociality are never lost sight of" (p. 182). Feminist critics also revisited the work of established male auteurs. In *The Women Who Knew Too Much*, Tania Modleski concentrates on the films of Alfred Hitchcock, concluding that he is "anything but exemplary of Hollywood cinema" and that his work "invokes typical patterns of male and female socialization . . . only to reveal the difficulties inherent in these processes—and to implicate the spectator in [them]" (p. 13).

Veering away from narrative or popular cinema, some feminist critics have also investigated the work of women in the avant-garde or feminist counter-cinema. In *Points of Resistance*, Lauren Rabinovitz considers women artists in New York from 1943 to 1971, focusing on Maya Deren, Shirley Clarke, and Joyce Wieland. She finds that all were trailblazers in a man's world and that all had begun careers in other art forms before turning to film. Finally, and most centrally, all "consistently articulated positions for a refusal of the male gaze" in their work (pp. 5, 6, and 10).

In *Shot/Countershot*, Lucy Fischer counterposes works by experimental women filmmakers (for example, Yvonne Rainer, Laura Mulvey, Kathy Rose) against those of canonical male directors, demonstrating how, in an intertextual gesture, the women's work "rewrites" masculine texts. Hence, for instance, she contrasts Ingmar Bergman's film *Persona* (1966), which constitutes a rather unsympathetic portrait of an actress in crisis, with Mai Zetterling's *The Girls* (*Flickorna*, 1968), which paints a far more sympathetic portrait of performing women. Similarly, in *To Desire Differently*, Sandy Flitterman-Lewis considers the films of Germaine Dulac, Marie Epstein, and Agnès Varda, each of whom worked outside the mainstream system in different historical periods. She finds that each filmmaker made a contribution to the development of film language and helped establish a "viable feminist tradition for an alternative cinematic practice" (p. 25). Finally, in *Women and*

Experimental Filmmaking the editors Jean Petrolle and Virginia Wright Wexman describe how women avant-garde artists "respond to a patriarchal context fraught with voices and images that describe the world from a masculinist perspective." Nonetheless, they "have not necessarily followed feminist agendas," nor have they "been comfortable . . . being categorized as feminist filmmakers" (pp. 1–2).

Exploring Genre and Gender. The complex relation between genre and gender has also been considered by feminist theorists. When movies first turned to narrative, melodrama immediately proved the favored form and usually involved an innocent heroine savaged by an evil male villain. Although over many decades melodrama's parameters have changed, it has remained a popular paradigm, especially with female audiences. Reflecting this, such scholars as Marcia Landy and Christine Gledhill have edited entire volumes on the topic. Others, including Mary Ann Doane, have concentrated on the subgenre of "woman's film," which focuses on romance and family drama as viewed from a female perspective. In *The Desire to Desire*, Doane examines the means by which female sexual passion is simultaneously highlighted and thwarted in such works from the 1940s as *The Spiral Staircase* (1946), *Humoresque* (1946), and *Now, Voyager* (1942) and concludes that the genre "does not provide us with an access to a pure and authentic female subjectivity, much as we might like it to" (p. 4).

Though most writing on melodrama has concentrated on American and British cinema, some has investigated the genre in an Asian context. Teresita Herrera and Wimal Dissanayake wrote, "In the world of Filipino melodrama, the female is generally constructed as a symbolic product of patriarchal desire. The female becomes an object of male gaze as her subjectivity is denied, and any attempt to destabilize this widely circulated image results in her being stigmatized as treacherous, sinister, and possessed of an unassuageable sexual appetite" (p. 218).

Many critics attended to women's genres, but others investigated those directed toward men. As noted above, Linda Williams analyzed pornography in *Hard Core*, taking as one of its major problematics the "invisibility" of female pleasure in comparison with the highly photogenic male member. Moreover, she draws surprising parallels between pornography's sex scenes and the musical's production numbers. In *Men, Women, and Chain Saws*, Carol Clover explores contemporary American horror films that feature women: slasher, occult, and rape-revenge movies such as *Friday the 13th* (1980), *Carrie* (1976), and *I Spit on Your Grave* (1978). As she notes, the films' "subject matter alone guarantees [their] cultural conservatism" (p. 15). Finally, turning their attention to the nonfiction genre in *Feminism and Documentary*, Diane Waldman and Janet Walker argue that it is this form that can best explore issues of race, class, nation, and gender, even though documentaries have been largely ignored by feminist scholars.

Scrutinizing the Female Performer. Concentrating on another aspect of women and film, some critics have highlighted the star personae of major actresses. In *Most Beautiful Woman on the Screen*, Michaela Krützen writes about Greta Garbo's style of "non-acting," concluding that it is precisely that which "allows the ideal presentation of beauty, her central characteristic as a star" (p. 26). Thus facial expression would only "distract from the face itself" (p. 27). On a different note, Fischer in *Designing Women* finds Garbo an art deco icon of the 1920s and 1930s, one who visually and dramatically signals the danger of the newly liberated female. Lending the question of stardom the framework of nationality, Ginette Vincendeau in *Stars and Stardom in French Cinema* writes about Brigitte Bardot, Jeanne Moreau, Catherine Deneuve, Juliette Binoche, and other actresses. She notes Bardot's status as an emblem of "youth: jazz and pop music" in addition to bold sexuality (p. 90).

Surfacing Theoretical Issues. In the late 1970s and early 1980s feminist film criticism moved beyond a focus on the themes and trajectories of screen narrative to more conceptual planes. Questions were asked about how the film form itself contributed to the portrayal of women and how stylistic tropes affected the spectator. Furthermore, the notion of a universal viewer came under assault with gender emphatically inserted into the equation. In "Visual Pleasure and Narrative Cinema," Laura Mulvey took a psychoanalytical approach to filmic construction, arguing that the articulation of the camera's "gaze" was a paramount feature of screen discourse. Focusing on female screen characters as viewed by the camera, Mulvey speculated that the apparatus favored a sexualized, "voyeuristic" look at them as seen from the perspective of an ideal male spectator. According to her, women constituted eroticized spectacles that arrested narrative development and functioned in a fetishistic fashion to ward off male fear of the "castrated" female body.

E. Ann Kaplan and other feminist critics later questioned whether the gaze was, in fact, always male and called for attention to the existence and interests of the female audience. Furthermore, Mulvey herself revised her theory in an "afterthought" to her original essay, arguing—through a discussion of *Duel in the Sun* (1946)—for the manner in which female viewers might in fact be able to identify with active male screen heroes rather than be forced to connect exclusively with inert screen heroines. Building on this, in *Alice Doesn't*, Teresa de Lauretis theorized female spectatorship as "doubled"—a "twofold process of identification sustaining two distinct sets of identifying relations"—thus releasing woman from a monolithic transvestite stance (p. 144).

Marlene Dietrich. A motion picture advertisement for Hermann Sudermann's *The Song of Songs*, 1933. PRINTS AND PHOTOGRAPHS DIVISION, LIBRARY OF CONGRESS

Feminist work on psychoanalysis and film continued with the publication of such books as Gaylyn Studlar's *In the Realm of Pleasure*, which argued for a "masochistic aesthetic" in the filmic collaborations between Josef von Sternberg and Marlene Dietrich. Arguing against Mulvey's position that women on screen are always in the subordinate position, Studlar saw the characters that Dietrich played as dominatrixes, subjugating their male lovers. Thus in *The Blue Angel* (*Der Blaue Engel*, 1930) Lola Lola rules and ruins the life of an impotent Professor Rath. Janet Walker's *Couching Resistance* investigates the institution of psychiatry, both within American culture and as represented in such films as *Whirlpool* (1949) and *The Three Faces of Eve* (1957). Applying aspects of "apparatus theory" to the realm of sound, Kaja Silverman in *The Acoustic Mirror* likened the spectator's perception of voice-over narration in film to the maternal voice perceived by the infant in utero. She then proceeded to read its use in *Diva* (1981), *Journeys from Berlin* (1980), and *Riddles of the Sphinx* (1977). Also subjecting sound to feminist analysis, Amy Lawrence in *Echo and Narcissus* examined women's voices in classic Hollywood cinema to argue that "sound is conflated with the feminine" and that "both sound and woman . . . have been made Echo to a vain and self-absorbed Narcissus" (p. 111).

Foregrounding Sexual Orientation and Race. Reflecting developments in gay liberation, theorists also began to protest the "compulsory heterosexuality" of cinema scholarship; hence the field of lesbian film studies flourished. In *Deviant Eyes, Deviant Bodies*, Chris Straayer sought to introduce a "queer viewpoint into feminist film theory" and to "raise questions and propose strategies that reveal subtexts and subversive readings . . . more complex . . . than the patriarchal heterosexual system assumes" (p. 2). Rather than questioning whether the gaze is male, she is more concerned with whether it is heterosexual and applies this investigation to films with lesbian heroines, transvestite protagonists, and themes of motherhood.

Similarly, the field's focus on white femininity was challenged as feminist critics began to consider the fate of black women on screen. Pearl Bowser along with Jane Gaines—who also wrote *Fire and Desire*, on African Americans and cinema—and Charles Musser published *Oscar Micheaux and His Circle*, a study of the renowned director of all-black "race movies" from the 1910s through the 1940s. In writing about *The Symbol of the Unconquered* (1920), Bowser (with Louise Spence), notes how "race solidarity and self-reliance" are themes that run throughout Micheaux's early works.

Investigating Gender and Nation. A historical turn in film studies led feminist scholars to consider more concrete aspects of women's relation to the screen, including the connection between gender and nation. In *Fascism in Film*, Marcia Landy observes that in Italian cinema between 1931 and 1943 "many narratives involving women serve to enact a disciplinary process on the female, couched not as discipline but as redemption." This "entrapment" of female characters within the drama demonstrates "an affinity with . . . the fascist attempt to [symbolically] imprison women" within patriarchal culture (p. 75). Likewise, in their introduction to *Off Screen: Women and Film in Italy*, Giuliana Bruno and Maria Nadotti note that Italian feminist theory gives priority to questions of "fascination and female desire," leading it to interrogate the female film critic's "own pleasure in the attempt to grasp the relationship between the spectator's gaze and critical-scientific scrutiny" (p. 13).

Lynn Attwood writes of women in Russian film in *Red Women on the Silver Screen*, surveying its history from the teens through the contemporary era. Speaking of Dziga Vertov during the revolutionary period, she notes that although his wife (Yelizaveta Svilova) was his film editor, none of his early works focused on women, an indication that female emancipation is seen as a low priority in socialist ideology (p. 32). In *Nationalising Femininity*, Christine Gledhill and Gillian Swanson consider "women, the home front and cultural representation [in Britain] during the Second World War," simultaneously relating women's position then to pre- and postwar reality (pp. 1–3). Looking toward non-Western and Third World cinema, in *With Open Eyes: Women and African Cinema* about gender in 1970s and 1980s Algerian film, Ratiba Hadj-Moussa finds that many works suggest "the incapacity of female characters to accomplish their objectives or to fulfill their desires" (in Harrow, p. 58).

Similarly, Shahla Lahiji wrote that although cinema might have helped achieve feminist goals, "Instead, the picture the film industry painted of the Iranian woman, in its more charitable version, amounted to no more than a seal of approval on reactionary and prejudiced attitudes according to which women had . . . to behave as second-class citizens whose main duty was to reproduce the human race, to live within the four walls of their homes and to keep house for their husbands" (in Tapper, p. 216). In *African Cinema: Politics and Culture*, Manthia Diawara finds that contemporary films show that "while African men have accepted progress in certain areas of modernism, they are regressive when it comes to giving up male privileges" (p. 144).

Finally, as Isolde Standish observes in *A New History of Japanese Cinema*, whereas World War II films stressed masculinity and sexual repression, postwar Japanese films (made during the U.S. occupation) promoted amorous themes, romanticized female characters, and favored the act of kissing. Thus women were reinscribed "into passive roles of containment within narratives of heterosexual romance" (p. 164). As for Indian film, Lalitha Gopalan discusses in *Cinema of Interruptions* how contemporary movies have seen an escalation of violence, one strain of which involves "lady avengers" (p. 35). She seeks to place these works in the context of Indian censorship regulations pertaining to the portrayal of sexual intercourse, rape, and sadomasochism.

Exploring the same topic in *National Identity in Indian Popular Cinema*, Sumita Chakravarty examines the courtesan figure, which "as historical character and cinematic spectacle is one of the most enigmatic . . . to haunt the margins of Indian cultural consciousness. . . . [She is] at once celebrated and shunned, used and abused, praised and condemned" (p. 269). Finally, writing on Chinese cinema in *Women through the Lens*, Shuqin Cui investigates how "woman acts as a visual and discursive sign in the creation of the nation-state" in twentieth-century China (p. xi), noting the way that the newer socialist system "transforms woman from a 'ghost of old society' into a 'master of the new state'" (p. xiii).

Documenting Female Spectators and Material Culture. Other writers concentrated on the ties between female spectators and material culture, chronicling the influence of film fashion on consumer behavior and probing the relation between the department store and cinema screen. In 1990, Jane Gaines and Charlotte Herzog edited *Fabrications*, in which Gaines traced the relation between costume and narrative—a theme that Fischer later extended in *Designing Women*—Herzog examined the fashion show as articulated in a variety of movies, and Maureen Turim investigated the "sweetheart line," a particular fashion look that dominated the image of American female style that emerged between 1947 and the mid-1950s in such films as *June Bride* (1948), *All About Eve* (1950), and *A Place in the Sun* (1951).

Focusing more on reception studies and the question of who actually attended the cinema, Kathy Peiss in *Cheap Amusements* considers working women and leisure in turn-of-the-century New York, with movies as one form of entertainment. Similarly, Lauren Rabinovitz in *For the Love of Pleasure* investigates the nature of early female film viewership in Chicago and concludes that women were a substantial part of the nickelodeon audience. Shelley Stamp's *Movie-Struck Girls* examined the female audience in a slightly later era; she established that women's presence in theaters was actively solicited by exhibitors to make the cinema more middle-class. Nonetheless, she finds women favoring some contentious genres: serials, white-slave narratives, and suffragist dramas.

In *Joyless Streets*, Patrice Petro explores women film spectators in Weimar Germany through the era's popular press—women's magazines, illustrated publications, and journals—to focus on issues of androgyny. Taking an ethnographic approach and frustrated by the "lack of interest in actual cinema spectators in film studies" (p. 35), Jackie Stacey in *Star Gazing* questioned British women film viewers of the 1940s and 1950s about their recollections of such actresses as Joan Crawford, Rita Hayworth, Bette Davis, and Lauren Bacall. For *An Everyday Magic*, Annette Kuhn interviewed British women about their moviegoing experience in the 1930s and concluded that "cinema was a more potent force in women's lives than in men's." Furthermore, she found that the names of certain film stars—Ginger Rogers and Deanna Durbin—came up repeatedly.

Some feminist critics have also investigated the male stars who appeal to women. Miriam Hansen in *Babel and Babylon* determined that the allure of the "Latin Lover" Rudolph Valentino in the 1920s drew on his ethnic otherness, his ambiguous sexual identity, and his feminized beauty. She concludes: "Beckoning with the promise of sexual—and ethnic-racial—mobility, the Valentino figure appealed to those who most keenly felt the need, yet also the anxiety of such mobility" (p. 268).

[*See also* Feminism *and* Performing Arts, *subentry* Popular Arts.]

BIBLIOGRAPHY

As evidence of the coming of age of the scholarly field of feminist film studies, anthologies of critical work began to be published, including Karyn Kay and Gerald Peary's *Women and the Cinema: A Critical Anthology* (New York: Dutton, 1977); Patricia Erens's *Sexual Stratagems: The World of Women in Film* (New York: Horizon Press, 1979) and *Issues in Feminist Film Criticism* (Bloomington: Indiana University Press, 1990); Diane Carson, Linda Dittmar, and Janice Welsch's *Multiple Voices in Feminist Film Criticism* (Minneapolis: University of Minnesota Press, 1994); and E. Ann Kaplan's *Feminism and Film* (Oxford and New York: Oxford University Press, 2000). Journals dedicated to the topic began to be published in the 1970s, including *Women and Film*, *Frauen im Film*, and *Camera Obscura*. Encyclopedias and dictionaries include *Women's Companion to International Film* (London: Virago, 1990) and *Women in Film: An International Guide* (New York: Fawcett Columbine, 1991), both edited by Annette Kuhn and Susannah Radstone; *The St. James Women Filmmakers Encyclopedia* (Detroit, Mich.: Visible Ink Press, 1999), edited by Amy Unterburger; and *Women Film Directors: An International Bio-critical Dictionary* (Westport, Conn.: Greenwood Press, 1995), edited by Gwendolyn Audrey Foster.

Attwood, Lynne. *Red Women on the Silver Screen: Soviet Women and Cinema from the Beginning to the End of the Communist Era*. London: Pandora, 1993.

Bowser, Pearl, Jane Gaines, and Charles Musser, eds. *Oscar Micheaux and His Circle: African-American Filmmaking and Race Cinema of the Silent Era*. Bloomington: Indiana University Press, 2001.

Bowser, Pearl, and Louise Spence. *Writing Himself into History: Oscar Micheaux, His Silent Films, and His Audiences*. New Brunswick, N.J.: Rutgers University Press, 2000.

Bruno, Giuliana, and Maria Nadotti, eds. *Off Screen: Women and Film in Italy*. New York and London: Routledge, 1988.

Chakravarty, Sumita S. *National Identity in Indian Popular Cinema, 1947–1987*. Austin: University of Texas Press, 1993.

Clover, Carol. *Men, Women, and Chainsaws: Gender in the Modern Horror Film*. Princeton, N.J.: Princeton University Press, 1992.

Cui, Shuqin. *Women through the Lens: Gender and Nation in a Century of Chinese Cinema*. Honolulu: University of Hawai'i Press, 2003.

De Lauretis, Teresa. *Alice Doesn't: Feminism, Semiotics, Cinema*. Bloomington: Indiana University Press, 1984.

Diawara, Manthia. *African Cinema: Politics and Culture*. Bloomington and Indianapolis: Indiana University Press, 1992.

Doane, Mary Ann. *The Desire to Desire: The Woman's Film of the 1940s*. Bloomington: Indiana University Press, 1987.

Fischer, Lucy. *Cinematernity: Film, Motherhood, Genre*. Princeton, N.J.: Princeton University Press, 1996.

Fischer, Lucy. *Designing Women: Cinema, Art Deco, and the Female Form*. New York: Columbia University Press, 2003.

Fischer, Lucy. *Shot/Countershot: Film Tradition and Women's Cinema*. Princeton, N.J.: Princeton University Press, 1989.

Flitterman-Lewis, Sandy. *To Desire Differently: Feminism and the French Cinema*. New York: Columbia University Press, 1996.

Gaines, Jane. *Fire and Desire: Mixed-Race Movies in the Silent Era*. Chicago: University of Chicago Press, 2001.

Gaines, Jane, and Charlotte Herzog, eds. *Fabrications: Costumes and the Female Body*. New York: Routledge, 1990.

Gledhill, Christine, and Gillian Swanson, eds. *Nationalising Femininity: Culture, Sexuality, and British Cinema in the Second World War*. Manchester, U.K.: Manchester University Press, 1996.

Gopalan, Lalitha. *Cinema of Interruptions: Action Genres in Contemporary Indian Cinema*. London: British Film Institute, 2002.

Hansen, Miriam. *Babel and Babylon: Spectatorship in American Silent Film*. Cambridge, Mass.: Harvard University Press, 1991.

Harrow, Kenneth W., ed. *With Open Eyes: Women and African Cinema*. Amsterdam and Atlanta, Ga.: Rodopi, 1997.

Herrera, Teresita, and Wimal Dissanayake. "Power, Pleasure, and Desire: The Female Body in Filipino Melodrama." In *Melodrama and Asian Cinema*, edited by Wimal Dissanayake. Cambridge, U. K., and New York: Cambridge University Press, 1993.

Higashi, Sumiko. *Virgins, Vamps, and Flappers: The American Silent Movie Heroine*. Saint Albans, Vt.: Eden Press Women's Publications, 1978.

Ho, Elaine Yee-lin. "Women on the Edges of Hong Kong Modernity." In *At Full Speed: Hong Kong Cinema in a Borderless World*, edited by Esther C. M. Yau, pp. 177–206. Minneapolis and London: University of Minnesota Press, 2001.

Jacobs, Lea. *The Wages of Sin: Censorship and the Fallen Woman Film, 1928–1942*. Madison: University of Wisconsin Press, 1991.

Johnson, Randal, and Robert Stam, eds. *Brazilian Cinema*. Expanded ed. New York: Columbia University Press, 1995.

Johnston, Claire, ed. *The Work of Dorothy Arzner: Towards a Feminist Cinema*. London: British Film Institute, 1975.

Kaplan, E. Ann. *Motherhood and Representation: The Mother in Popular Culture and Melodrama*. New York and London: Routledge, 1992.

Krützen, Michaela. *The Most Beautiful Woman on the Screen: The Fabrication of the Star Greta Garbo*. New York: Peter Lang, 1992.

Kuhn, Annette. *An Everyday Magic: Cinema and Cultural Memory*. London: I. B. Tauris, 2002.

Kuhn, Annette, ed. *Queen of the 'B's: Ida Lupino behind the Camera*. Westport, Conn.: Greenwood Press, 1995.

Landy, Marcia. *Fascism in Film: The Italian Commercial Cinema, 1931–1943*. Princeton, N.J.: Princeton University Press, 1986.

Lawrence, Amy. *Echo and Narcissus: Women's Voices in Classical Hollywood Cinema*. Berkeley: University of California Press, 1991.

Mayne, Judith. *Directed by Dorothy Arzner*. Bloomington: Indiana University Press, 1994.

Modleski, Tania. *Women Who Knew Too Much: Hitchcock and Feminist Theory*. New York and London: Routledge, 2005.

Mulvey, Laura. *Visual and Other Pleasures*. Bloomington: Indiana University Press, 1989.

Peiss, Kathy. *Cheap Amusements: Working Women and Leisure in Turn-of-the-Century New York*. Philadelphia: Temple University Press, 1986.

Petro, Patrice. *Joyless Streets: Women and Melodramatic Representation in Weimar Germany*. Princeton, N.J.: Princeton University Press, 1989.

Petrolle, Jean, and Virginia Wright Wexman, eds. *Women and Experimental Filmmaking*. Urbana: University of Illinois, 2005.

Pick, Zuzana M. *The New Latin American Cinema: A Continental Project*. Austin: University of Texas Press, 1993.

Rabinovitz, Lauren. *For the Love of Pleasure: Women, Movies, and Culture in Turn-of-the-Century Chicago*. New Brunswick, N.J.: Rutgers University Press, 1998.

Rabinovitz, Lauren. *Points of Resistance: Women, Power, and Politics in the New York Avant-Garde Cinema, 1943–71*. Urbana: University of Illinois Press, 1991.

Sarris, Andrew. *American Cinema, Directors and Directions: 1929–1968*. New York: Dutton, 1968.

Silverman, Kaja. *The Acoustic Mirror: The Female Voice in Psychoanalysis and Cinema*. Bloomington: Indiana University Press, 1988.

Stacey, Jackie. *Star Gazing: Hollywood Cinema and Female Spectatorship*. New York and London: Routledge, 1994.

Stamp, Shelley. *Movie-Struck Girls: Women and Motion Picture Culture after the Nickelodeon*. Princeton, N.J.: Princeton University Press, 2000.

Standish, Isolde. *A New History of Japanese Cinema*. Continuum: London, 2005.

Straayer, Chris. *Deviant Eyes, Deviant Bodies: Sexual Re-Orientations in Film and Video*. New York: Columbia University Press, 1996.

Studlar, Gaylyn. *In the Realm of Pleasure: Von Sternberg, Dietrich, and the Masochistic Aesthetic*. Urbana: University of Illinois Press, 1988.

Tapper, Richard, ed. *The New Iranian Cinema: Politics, Representation, and Identity*. London: I. B. Tauris, 2002.

Vincendeau, Ginette. *Stars and Stardom in French Cinema*. London: Continuum, 2000.

Waldman, Diane, and Janet Walker, eds. *Feminism and Documentary*. Minneapolis: University of Minnesota Press, 1999.

Walker, Janet. *Couching Resistance: Women, Film, and Psychoanalytic Psychiatry*. Minneapolis: University of Minnesota Press, 1993.

Williams, Linda. *Hard Core: Power, Pleasure, and the "Frenzy of the Visible."* Berkeley: University of California Press, 1999.

LUCY FISCHER

Laws and Privileges

In 1896, a one-minute film titled *The Kiss* created a scandal in some circles in the United States: it showed the faces of two adults, a smiling woman and her masculine lover (sporting a giant moustache), who were seen in a close-up, and were about to kiss each other. Then the kiss, a mutually consenting one, occurred, and lasted for many seconds. Some at the time were shocked, since people did not then kiss in public, but a few decades later, the same film was often seen as inoffensive or even funny. That short film was directed by William Heise and featured May Irwin and John C. Rice; the actors, who were romantically involved, did not "pretend" to love each other. This anecdote demonstrates how rules, social norms, and taboos about moving pictures evolve and change over time and in different social contexts.

A Tacit Rule: The Hays Code. The years from 1896 to 1930 saw little official control regarding morals and norms in films in the United States. In Hollywood, the Motion Picture Production Code (known as the "Hays Code") introduced strict rules regarding morality and permissiveness in movies, starting on 31 March 1930. Some groups and leagues had been protesting against risqué films, and asked local and federal authorities to control the morals of the film industry. But to avoid severe legislation by the U.S. government, Hollywood's major studios agreed to comply to their own set of norms, and asked William Hays (current president of the Motion Picture Producers and Distributors of America, or MPPDA) to write these moral rules. For instance, the Hays Code clearly stated that seduction or rape "should never be more than suggested," that "sex hygiene and venereal diseases are not subjects for motion pictures," and that "scenes of actual child birth, in fact or silhouette, are never to be presented" (Maltby, pp. 593–597). The Hays Code was not censorship per se; it was rather a way for the movie industry to avoid more severe measures that might be taken by the government that would have limited the circulation of movies. Hollywood thus essentially censored itself.

This change in rules explains why some film experts refer to "pre-code" movies, which were produced or written before the Hays Code entered into force, and which featured situations that were later to be avoided. For instance, although she was dressed, Jean Harlow (Harlean Carpenter) was braless in a scene from *Red Dust* (1932), directed by Victor Fleming. Some scenes in pre-code movies featured nudity, like *Sign of the Cross* (1932), by Cecil B. DeMille, and *Roman Scandals* (1933), directed by Frank Tuttle. Other deviant themes were also present in pre-code movies, for example, in Ernst Lubitsch's *Trouble in Paradise* (1932), which glorified thieves, both men and women. There was adultery in melodramas like Robert Z. Leonard's *The Divorcee* (1930) or Alfred Green's *Baby Face* (1933), and *The Story of Temple Drake* (1933), directed by Stephen Roberts, centered around the rape of the title character.

Since the code was often challenged, in 1968 the industry replaced it with the Motion Picture Association of America (MPAA) ratings system, which is still in use at the beginning of the twenty-first century.

Privileges for Women Directors. Very few directors (male or female) have had the chance to get an unlimited budget to shoot a film; however, German director Leni Riefenstahl (1902–2003) was given full license to create two controversial documentaries about the Nazi era, *Triumph des Willens* (*Triumph of the Will*, 1935), a propaganda film of Nazi Party rallies in Nuremberg, and the documentary *Olympia* (1938), about the 1936 Berlin Olympic Games.

In Canada, some institutional strategies helped women create more films about their points of view. In 1971, the

National Film Board of Canada (NFB), a federal cultural agency within the Canadian government, created a unique and innovative program dedicated to women's and feminist approaches, the Challenge for Change program, as well as a studio expressly for women, called Studio D. But of all Canadian women filmmakers, Francophone directors were the most dynamic and prolific; they had their own program from 1971, called "En tant que femmes" (which translates roughly to "Women's Perspectives"). Among memorable titles (mostly documentaries), *Le temps de l'avant* (1975), directed by Anne Claire Poirier, was one of the first feature films made by a woman about abortion. Poirier also directed the first feature film made by a woman about rape, *Mourir à tue-tête* (*A Scream from Silence*, 1979), which had an international audience.

In Canada, Bonnie Sherr Klein directed a documentary titled *Not a Love Story: A Film about Pornography* (1981), in which she argued that pornography was not a matter of regulation, but a problem of representations. Most critics appreciated the movie and the interviews with porn actresses. Some observers were shocked by the fact that one director of pornographic movies using women was actually a woman, and some academics criticized Klein's lack of distance from her subject: her documentary featured the making of some sexually explicit scenes.

Many Kinds of Censorship. Controversy did not only touch specifically women's issues. A short documentary on the nuclear industry, *If You Love This Planet* (1982), directed by Terre Nash, was labeled in the United States as "political propaganda," although it was not banned. The initial idea was simple: the director was aware of a public conference with Dr. Helen Caldicott, the founder and president of "Physicians for Social Responsibility," so she simply filmed the lecture, which was given at SUNY Plattsburgh. The film was edited to include some stock shots of the Hiroshima bombing from 1945 and excerpts from some of President Ronald Reagan's movies from the 1940s.

For many decades, India has produced the highest number of feature films every year, about double the number produced in the United States. However, even in the twenty-first century in India, strict rules apply regarding morals. Indian audiences may watch a foreign woman naked in a movie, but some will protest if that naked woman is Indian. Canadian scholar Thomas Waugh has studied the case of the Canadian film *Masala* (1991), directed by Srinivas Krishna, which was refused by the 1992 International Film Festival of India because it includes a sex scene featuring Southern Asian actors.

May women still watch everything anywhere in term of moving images? Hannah Davis wrote an ethnographical essay in which she examined the attitudes and comments of a group of six Moroccan women who were watching, for the first time, a clandestine pornographic videocassette made in France, in a Moroccan house, in 1990. Most of them were shocked, but curious enough to watch until the end. The access of women to movies and filmmaking is still changing and can remain limited, according to cultures, networks, and contexts.

[*See also* Abortion; Adultery; Feminism; Rape; Sexuality; *and entries on countries and regions mentioned in this article.*]

BIBLIOGRAPHY

Aitken, Ian, ed. *Encyclopedia of the Documentary Film*. New York: Routledge, 2006.

Davis, Hannah. "Des Femmes Marocaines et *La Chaleur de Saint-Tropez*." *Les Cahiers de l'Orient* 20 (1990): 191–199.

Dudrah, Rajinder Kumar. *Bollywood: Sociology Goes to the Movies*. New Delhi, India, and Thousand Oaks, Calif.: Sage Publications, 2006.

Jones, Derek, ed. *Censorship: A World Encyclopedia*. London and Chicago: Fitzroy Dearborn, 2001.

Lever, Yves. *Histoire générale du cinéma au Québec*. 2nd ed. Montreal: Boréal, 1995.

Maltby, Richard. *Hollywood Cinema*. 2nd ed. Malden, Mass.: Blackwell, 2003. Includes all the articles from the Hays Code from 1933; see pp. 593–597.

Waugh, Thomas. "Home Is Not the Place One Has Left: or, *Masala* as 'A Multi-cultural Culinary Treat'?" In *Canada's Best Features: Critical Essays on 15 Canadian Films*, edited by Eugene P. Walz, pp. 253–272. Amsterdam and New York: Rodopi, 2002.

YVES LABERGE

Producers

It is not too much to say that women invented the narrative cinema. Director Alice Guy shot the first scripted film in France in 1896 for producer Leon Gaumont; it was titled *La Fée aux choux*, or *The Cabbage Patch Fairy*. The running time of this film was a mere sixty seconds, and it depicted a young couple "finding" their newborn baby in the cabbage patch (much in the same manner that American babies are supposedly "delivered" by the stork). After this film, Guy went on to direct hundreds of one-reel shorts for Gaumont, including some of the first films with synchronized sound and hand-stenciled color, before moving to the United States in 1907 and founding her own film production company, Solax, in 1910.

In her films during this period, Guy developed the close-up, the two-shot, the use of intercutting for suspense, narrative compression, the deep-focus shot, and the use of a stock company of actors for her films, as well as pioneering a more natural style of acting in her films. Later, others would take the credit for Guy's contributions to the grammar of the cinema. Guy's *A House Divided* (1913), for example, is a superb domestic farce that offers a satiric and light comedic vision of marriage. Its plot hinges on a series of mistakes and coincidences that lead a husband and wife to unjustly suspect each other of infidelity. Her other films ranged from horror films to domestic dramas in such one-reel shorts as *The Pit and the Pendulum* (1913), *A Terrible Night* (1913), *The Face at the Window* (1912), *A Fool and His Money* (1912), and *Canned Harmony* (1912). Sadly, of the hundreds of films that Guy produced, only a handful survive, the others victims of nitrate decomposition and historical neglect, and it was only in the 1970s that historians generally began to acknowledge Guy's influence on the early days of filmmaking, along with that of her colleagues.

Guy continued to direct films until 1920, but she was far from alone in the early days of cinema. Margery Wilson, whose films included *Insinuation* (1922), *The Offenders* (1922), and *That Something* (1920); Ida May Park, who directed *The Risky Road* (1918), *Broadway Love* (1918), and *The Grand Passion* (1918); Dorothy Davenport Reid, who tackled drug addiction and gambling in such films as *The Woman Condemned* (1934), *The Road to Ruin* (1934), *Sucker Money* (1933), and the tragic romance *Linda* (1929); along with Hanna Henning, Gene Gauntier, Grace Cunard, Julia Crawford Ivers, Ruth Stonehouse, and a score of other pioneering women produced, wrote, acted in (and performed stunts for) their own directorial efforts in the exciting first decades of the dawn of cinema.

Director Cleo Madison began as an actor for Universal Studios. By 1916, she was directing and starring in her own two-reel productions. *Her Defiance* (1916) is noteworthy for its feminist depiction of an early American heroine who is abandoned by her lover. When her family arranges a wedding for her with a much older man, the young woman refuses to comply with the arranged wedding. Instead, she bears an illegitimate child and goes to work as a cleaning woman in order to support herself and her child. Lois Weber directed the deeply felt domestic drama *The Blot* (1921), in which a poorly paid college professor is unable to support his family, forcing his wife to steal a chicken from a neighbor's yard to provide food for their sick daughter. It is worth noting that all these films were substantial box-office successes; in the early days of cinema, women were welcome behind the camera. But as sound was introduced in 1927, and cinema became a mature industry, the chances for women filmmakers became increasingly scarce.

The Wilderness Years. With mainstream cinema forcing women out of the director's and producer's chairs, independent cinema—low-cost, experimental filmmaking—became a more popular vehicle of personal expression. In France, the independent filmmaker Germaine Dulac created *The Seashell and the Clergyman* (1928), a surrealist film from a script by Antonin Artaud. Dulac also directed *The Smiling Madame Beudet* in 1922, an early film that examines the plight of women in patriarchal society. Married to a chauvinistic martinet, Madame Beudet conjures images of imaginary young lovers, while murder rages in her heart. Fed up with her husband's threats to shoot himself every time he gets angry with her, Madame Beudet replaces the blanks in his revolver with real bullets. In the United States, filmmaker Maya Deren picked up on the work of Dulac and began to make her own dreamlike films, including *Meshes of the Afternoon* (1943), in which Deren also starred, followed by the personal and poetic short films *Witch's Cradle* (1944), *At Land* (1944), *A Study in Choreography for Camera* (1945), *Ritual in Transfigured Time* (1946), *Meditation on Violence* (1948), and her last completed film, *The Very Eye of Night* (1958).

Dorothy Arzner was one of the few women who directed major Hollywood films from 1930 to 1950, including the groundbreaking *Christopher Strong* (1933), which featured Katharine Hepburn as a world-famous aviator whose love life brings about her ruin. Arzner's last film was *First Comes Courage* (1943), a wartime drama dealing with the Norwegian Resistance. Between 1943 and 1949, no women made feature films in Hollywood. It was not until the actress Ida Lupino directed the taboo-breaking *Not Wanted* (1949), dealing with unmarried pregnancy, that women began to regain their footing in the industry. Lupino followed this film with *Outrage* (1950), the first feminist film on rape; *Hard, Fast, and Beautiful* (1951), in which a mother is willing to ruin her daughter's life by driving her to tennis stardom, thereby furnishing the mother with the financial security she longs for; and *The Hitch-Hiker* (1953), one of the first serial killer films, along with many television projects. Through sheer persistence, Lupino managed to push the gates of filmmaking open again, and other women followed in the 1960s and 1970s.

During this period, although women were not employed as directors, they were often used as film editors or negative cutters. Legendary figures Dede Allen, Verna Fields, and many others used editing as a springboard to increased power within the industry. As technical workers, women were usually assigned to such tasks as wardrobe, script clerk, and costuming. Throughout the world, the segregation of the sexes on movie sets was a sad fact of life, and only a few women, such as Virginia Van Upp, rose to the ranks of producer. After being a writer on *Cover Girl* (1944), she worked as an associate producer on *Affair in Trinidad* (1952), and as producer on *Gilda* (1946), all of which were directed by men. Dorothy Arzner quit the industry and only much later directed Pepsi commercials at the behest of her friend, the actress Joan Crawford. Lupino was the lone woman filmmaker in 1950s Hollywood who managed to put her individual signature on her work despite continual front office interference.

The Promise of the Present. In more recent years, the Anglo-African filmmaker Ngozi Onwurah (*The Body Beautiful*, 1991) and the African/Indian lesbian Pratibha Parmar (*Warrior Marks*, 1993) have created personal feminist films that have reached a wide international audience. The black British director Maureen Blackwood (*The Passion of Remembrance*, 1986), the Indian director Gurinder Chadha (*Bahji on the Beach*, 1993), the Chinese filmmaker Christine Choy (*Who Killed Vincent Chin?*, 1988), the French director Claire Denis (*Beau Travail*, 1999), and the African American filmmakers Kathleen Collins (*Losing Ground*, 1982), Zeinabu Irene Davis (*Cycles*, 1989), Leslie Harris (*Just Another Girl on the I.R.T.*, 1992), and Darnell Martin (*I Like It Like That*, 1994) have created compelling films that examine the issues of race, gender, and social expectations that women face in contemporary society. In Hollywood, the directors Tamra Davis (*Guncrazy*, 1992), Alison Anders (*Gas Food Lodging*, 1992), Kathryn Bigelow (*Near Dark*, 1987), Jane Campion (*The Piano*, 1993), Stacy Cochran (My New Gun, 1992), Nora Ephron (*This Is My Life*, 1992), Jodie Foster (*Little Man Tate*, 1991), Maggie Greenwald (*The Ballad of Little Jo*, 1993), Penny Marshall (*A League of Their Own*, 1992), and Nancy Savoca (*Household Saints*, 1993) entered mainstream filmmaking with a vengeance, forever breaking down the barrier between men and women as filmmakers. In addition, contemporary women avant-garde filmmakers such as Beth B., Storm De Hirsch, Holly Fisher, Jill Godmilow, Yoko Ono, and Monika Treut have made significant contributions to the development of film as an experimental medium, and the future of women in film seems assured.

As producers, directors, and industry power brokers, such women as Lili Fini Zanuck, a director/producer, Sherry Lansing, chair of Paramount Pictures' Motion Picture Group from 1992 to 2005, Amy Pascal, co-chair of Sony Pictures Entertainment, and producer Laura Ziskin have all left their mark on commercial filmmaking. Throughout the world, directors such as Algeria's Assia Djebbar, Argentina's Maria Luísa Bemberg, Canada's Alanis Obomsawin, Belgium's Chantal Akerman, Mexico's Matilde Landeta, India's Mira Nair, Poland's Asgnieszka Holland, Senegal's Safi Faye, and Vietnam's T. Minh-ha Trinh have made films that simultaneously entertain audiences and enlighten them to the social injustices of contemporary society. The future of women in film will always be precarious, if only because of the ever-rising cost of filmmaking, but with such a rich history of filmmaking, women will continue to find the ways to back their projects and get them before the public. If the films of the twentieth century are any indication, women as filmmakers in the twenty-first century will continue to have an ever-increasing voice within the worldwide industry of the cinema.

BIBLIOGRAPHY

Foster, Gwendolyn Audrey. *Women Film Directors: An International Bio-Critical Dictionary*. Westport, Conn.: Greenwood, 1995.

Kuhn, Annette, and Susannah Radstone, eds. *The Women's Companion to International Film*. Berkeley: University of California Press, 1994.

Seger, Linda. *When Women Call the Shots: The Developing Power and Influence of Women in Television and Film*. New York: Henry Holt, 1996.

Slide, Anthony. *Early Women Directors*. New York: Da Capo Press, 1984.

Unterburger, Amy L. *The St. James Women Filmmakers Encyclopedia: Women on the Other Side of the Camera*. Detroit, Mich.: Visible Ink Press, 1999.

GWENDOLYN AUDREY FOSTER

CITIZENSHIP

This entry consists of two subentries:

Overview
Comparative History

Overview

"Citizenship is multiple and various," writes the feminist philosopher Marilyn Friedman. "It can be an identity; a set of rights, privileges, and duties; an elevated and exclusionary political status; a relationship between individuals and their states; a set of practices that can unify—or divide—the members of a political community; and an ideal of political agency" (p. 3). The elements and processes that make up citizenship not only change over time but, importantly, are inflected by gender. Modern feminists have taken a dual approach to citizenship, on the one hand criticizing its discrimination against women, in both theory and practice, and on the other seeking to use it as a platform for gender equality.

Liberal Rights and Feminist Critiques. The concept of citizenship is firmly rooted in Western political thought, with a genealogy that may be traced from the city-states of ancient Greece through the Enlightenment and the French Revolution to the present day. Many modern discussions draw on an important series of essays by the British political theorist T. H. Marshall, *Citizenship and Social Class* (1950), in which he argued that citizenship entails both privileges and responsibilities, distributed equally among all who are eligible. Marshall divided citizenship into three components: civil, political, and social. He claimed that the three types of rights are linked; that is, individuals must have access to social citizenship—health care, social insurance, education, and the like—in order to participate in the market and enjoy full civil and political citizenship.

Though generally accepting the ideals articulated in the liberal definitions, feminists have faulted Marshall as well as most of his male predecessors—John Stuart Mill would be the notable exception—for ignoring the ways in which citizenship has, both historically and theoretically, been gendered male, thus depriving women of citizenship's rights as well as excusing them from its duties. Many feminists have focused on women's containment within the family—and the conflation of the family with the private sphere—as the source of their exclusion. Feminist critiques of Western liberal theory have pointed out that Western thinkers, beginning with Plato and proceeding through Aristotle, Jean-Jacques Rousseau, Thomas Hobbes, and Georg Wilhelm Friedrich Hegel, regarded men not merely as individuals but also as the heads of households, all of whose members—women, children, and often servants or slaves—they were empowered to represent in public. The historian Joan Landes, examining the era of the French Revolution, has shown how the rise of the bourgeois family in eighteenth-century France relegated women to the private sphere, thus curtailing the cultural and political power they had managed to amass in the salons of the Old Regime, while thrusting men into the center of the new liberal polity and civil society.

Women's exclusion from the public sphere meant that the rights of citizenship became concentrated in men's hands. To be sure, as other historians have demonstrated, women continually sought ways to breach the public-private divide; nevertheless, in most Western societies they remained, until the twentieth century, "second-class citizens," lacking formal political and civil rights.

Similarly, though accepting Marshall's tripartite model as a powerful rationale for modern welfare states, feminist theorists have criticized it for implicitly portraying the typical citizen as a male breadwinner, thus overlooking the ways in which social citizenship has been designed to meet the needs of men—through policies such as worker's compensation, social insurance, employment-based pensions, and so forth—but not those of women, such as child care, caregivers' allowances, and the like. They point out that the traditional assignment of military service—regarded as one of the primary duties of citizenship—to men also discriminates against women. Although it entails risk, soldiering often brings with it public recognition, potentially a route to public office, as well as concrete rewards in the form of veterans' benefits, for which women are generally ineligible, except indirectly as dependents. By contrast the work of reproduction conventionally assigned to women, though sometimes cast as service to society, seldom brings with it the same kinds of recognition and benefits.

Expanding the Concept of Citizenship. Feminist theorists have expanded Marshall's tripartite model to highlight and accommodate other dimensions of citizenship. The historian Alice Kessler-Harris, for example, calls for adding the concept of economic citizenship to cover rights such as occupational choice (including caring work), "wages adequate to the support of self and family," freedom from discrimination, access to education and training, and other supports "necessary to sustain and support labor force participation" (p. 159). Some political theorists argue for sexual citizenship: protection of intimacy, sexuality, and reproduction, including the freedom to reproduce (or not) under self-chosen conditions, to express sexual preferences and identities, and to pursue sexual pleasure and fulfillment. Sexual citizenship would also entail decoupling the rights of social citizenship from marriage.

Still other scholars have drawn attention to the cultural dimensions of citizenship, pointing to the ways in which homogenizing national myths, anthems, and public rituals can efface ethnic and racial—as well as sexual and gender—differences, depriving minorities and subordinated groups of the right to recognize or represent themselves in popular culture as well as in public discourses. This is not exclusively a women's issue, but feminist scholars, perhaps hypersensitive to the dynamics of exclusion, have been at the forefront in addressing it. The psychologist Aída Hurtado, for example, finds that Chicana feminists shape their culture around the simultaneous loss of their own "land, language, and knowledge" and affirmation of their own group allegiance (in Friedman, ed., p. 125). Moreover, she notes, whereas most Western feminists implicitly accept the individualism embedded in liberal concepts of citizenship, Chicanas are more likely to seek collective rights—"a space to congregate with others," rather than "a room of one's own."

Transnational Perspectives on Citizenship. Hurtado is but one of many contemporary feminists who, working from a transnational perspective, point to the "Westocentric" (to use a term coined by Nira Yuval-Davis) roots of most conceptualizations of citizenship—even feminist ones. This bias obscures national differences in the configuration of citizenship. The anthropologist Suad Joseph, for example, explains that in the Middle East, citizenship is shaped by the "kin contract," which prioritizes familial rights and responsibilities over relationships to the state. Individuals are thereby insulated from direct rule of, as well as from access to the protections and privileges afforded by, the state, which often works through families to exercise its power. Although women and men are equally bound by the kin contract, families' patriarchal structures and values restrict women's citizenship more than men's. Joseph concedes that the kin contract is not dissimilar to the concept of the male-headed household in Western liberal theory, but, she maintains, widespread public acceptance of the politicization of the family and the familialization of the state in the Middle East make it distinctive.

Migration, political shifts, and globalization also have an impact on access to citizenship rights. Because of the seldom-questioned linkage between citizenship and nation-states—themselves imagined constructs often based on a specific group identity—migrants, refugees, ethnic and religious minorities, and indigenous populations of settler societies have typically been excluded from full citizenship. A nonresident mother working temporarily in the Netherlands, for example, cannot transfer Dutch child benefits to the offspring she has left behind in Indonesia.

Moreover, gaining citizenship is often predicated on gendered and heteronormative criteria that privilege male over female claims when it comes to "naturalizing" spouses and honoring child custody rights and that exclude same-sex couples altogether. Because women often have greater access to citizenship rights in regional or subnational entities on the one hand, or in extranational bodies such as the European Union or NGOs on the other, many transnational feminists call for recognition of the rights of groups as well as individuals and invoke a human rights discourse as a means of transcending the exclusivity of citizenship based on nation-states.

[*See also* Civil Society; Human Rights; Migration; Refugees; *and* Suffrage.]

BIBLIOGRAPHY

Citizenship Studies 5, no. 3 (2001). Special issue on sexuality and citizenship including articles by Anna Marie Smith, Bryan Turner, and Eileen Richardson.

Friedman, Marilyn, ed. *Women and Citizenship*. New York: Oxford University Press, 2005. Friedman's introduction is a useful theoretical overview; the volume includes essays by Aída Hurtado, Suad Joseph, Joan Scott, and Iris Young.

Kessler-Harris, Alice. "In Pursuit of Economic Citizenship." *Social Politics* 10, no. 2 (2003): 157–175. Part of a special forum on "Economic Citizenship" also including Barbara Hobson and Jane Lewis.

Landes, Joan. *Women and the Public Sphere in the Age of the French Revolution*. Ithaca, N.Y.: Cornell University Press, 1988. Important historical study of gender and the evolution of political rights.

Lister, Ruth. *Citizenship: Feminist Perspectives*. 2d ed. New York: New York University Press, 2003. Clear and cogent feminist critique of citizenship in its many dimensions.

Yuval-Davis, Nira. "Women, Citizenship, and Difference." *Feminist Review*, no. 57 (Autumn 1997): 4–27. Part of a special issue called "Citizenship: Pushing the Boundaries."

SONYA MICHEL

Comparative History

Women's relationship to the state and their access to political standing and civil rights have been central issues in defining citizenship in human history. From Athenian democracy and the Roman Republic to the modern European Union, the rights and obligations of citizenship have been accorded first to property-owning men and have been denied or only partially extended to others, including women of the same class, education, nativity, and race. For this reason the British feminist Virginia Woolf in *Three Guineas* (1938) argued that women have a tenuous relationship to the state, one that might best be severed, because nation-states are engines for patriarchal oppression and violence.

Early feminists writing in the wake of the American and French revolutions had no doubt that women had contributions to make to the nation-state; the question was what form the contributions would take. Did women have status and rights as equally participating citizens or only as second-class subjects, as direct beneficiaries of rights and obligations or only as derivative recipients of the privileges of civil membership? Though citizenship was and is masculine in its origins and cultural construction, women have asserted their equality as citizens in countries of their birth and adoption. Active participants in political movements, women have claimed rights in and fulfilled obligations to nation-states and have democratized them.

Over the centuries, women's exclusion from formal citizenship has been rooted in perceptions of their biological and social differences from men. Both social assumptions about the separation of public and private and women's primary-care responsibilities disqualified women from political life. Meaningful citizenship, in which the citizen actively participates in civic governance, is of relatively recent origin and became widespread only in the twentieth century. When different nations first created governments based on the participation of citizens, rather than the obedience of subjects, their constitutions grounded political standing in property ownership and military service. Women were thus excluded from citizen participation not only for cultural reasons but also because they lacked resources for civic membership. This was particularly true for married women, who lacked property rights in countries with common-law traditions or with civil laws based on the Napoleonic Code. Even in the twenty-first century, when property and military service are no longer prerequisites for citizenship, family obligations and the private-public divide continue to underwrite the exclusion of women from public life.

The democratic revolutions in the seventeenth and eighteenth centuries, struggles for independence in the nineteenth century, and national liberation struggles in the twentieth century developed the ideas and practices of citizenship. Despite the universalist claims of these political movements, "democracy" and "citizenship" have been gendered terms throughout world history. In granting "universal" suffrage, states have generally allowed only men to vote. Expanding the scope of rights and privileges of citizens almost always created inequalities along gender lines. As second-class citizens, women have found their participation truncated by their exclusion from the rights and obligations of citizenship.

The primary vehicle for women's claims to full citizenship have been revolutions, struggles for national independence, and social movements for the rights of women. The movements for women's suffrage and women's rights in the nineteenth and twentieth centuries argued for equal citizenship for women, basing their arguments on universal claims for human rights and on particular assertions of women's differences from men. As recently as the 1990s, when Frenchwomen struggled for political equality in parity in the number of candidates running for office, women have worked within both traditions—human rights and assertions of differences—to press for women's right to equal representation and full participation.

The Emergence of Citizenship in Political Life. Citizenship has had varied meanings in world history and in contemporary political debate. T. H. Marshall, a political theorist, defined citizenship as full membership in the community of the nation. This sense of national belonging was thought to override particular class, ethnic, and religious identities. Citizenship signifies the political participation of equals, with the rights and obligations pertaining to citizens. It is a public category that stands in contrast to the private realm. Because it mirrors the public-private divide of Western cultures, citizenship has been central to Western political theory and practice. Nations and political movements in the East and West have claimed equal citizenship, at least for citizens of native birth or parentage, as a political goal. Throughout most of world history, these rights and obligations have been the exclusive preserve of men—in particular, men of the propertied class. During this same history, women have derived some protections of citizenship from their relationships to male citizens, albeit at the cost of personal dependence. Though age, racial, ethnic, class, and religious differences have also come into play, gender continues to be the dominant means by which citizens are included in or excluded from the rights and obligations of citizens.

The earliest forms of citizenship were found in the Greek city-states of Sparta and Athens. In Sparta, men of the elite citizenry received land and slave labor in compensation for their service to the state. In Rome, citizens and their families received marriage and trade rights as well as military and judicial protections. Citizenship further evolved in the city-states of medieval Europe and Renaissance Italy. Male citizens of these city-states had obligations that required them to serve in the military, pay taxes, and participate in government, as well as rights to political voice and social stature. Citizenship was bolstered by the ideal of civic virtue (*aretē* in Greek, *virtus* in Latin), which underwrote service to the state. Civic virtue, as practiced in the Greek city-states and Florence at the height of its power, was associated with the masculine pursuit of public life and military service. In the beginning, then, citizenship, as an idea and a practice, created a privileged class, male citizens, whose families derived social standing and material gain from their place in society. At the same time, citizenship excluded women and others—discriminated in racial, ethnic, class, and religious terms—as unfit for the virtuous life of public service.

Marshall's theory of citizenship evolved to include not merely such basic rights as voting and office holding in modern democracies but also rights and obligations in two other arenas, the law and the economy. On the basis of British experience, Marshall argued that British citizenship evolved over three centuries to establish and foster new rights. British male citizens in the eighteenth century received new civil rights, judicial protections, and economic freedom of contract. The market revolution led to the gradual emancipation of men from the bonds of debt, indenture, and apprenticeship, and in the political sphere there arose new obligations of expanded taxation, conscripted military service, and jury duty. In France and later in other European states, reforms freed peasant men from the land, created new state obligations, and opened the door for expanded participation in civic and economic life. These reforms left in place traditional kinship obligations, the constraints on married women in particular.

Modern ideas and practices of citizenship were first developed in the nation-states born of the English Civil War and the American and French revolutions. By the late eighteenth century, the struggle against British colonial rule in the Americas and widespread political dissent in France gave rise to revolution. As political movements, the American and French revolutions reconceptualized the relationship between the state and its male citizens, enshrining equal citizenship, personal freedom, and solidarity among men as the basis for republican government. Taking inspiration from the ancient Greek democracies and the Roman Republic and drawing on the thought of the Enlightenment philosophers John Locke, Jean-Jacques Rousseau, and others, the American and French republics tried to re-create the conditions of democratic citizenship with widespread property ownership, political participation, and service among equals. But they based national citizenship on the unfree labor of dependents—that is, the family labor of women and children and, in the United States, slave labor.

In the nineteenth century, universal male suffrage became the standard of modern nationhood. In 1848, France became the first nation to grant all native-born men the right to vote without property qualifications. Britain gradually expanded suffrage to include not only propertied men but also wage-earning men. The revolutions of 1848 and other political reform movements created similar pressures elsewhere to integrate all male citizens into the political process. Italy, Sweden, Denmark, and several Germanic states (including Prussia and the Austrian Empire) experimented with democracy, gradually increasing the size of the electorate and expanding the political rights of adult men. Independence movements in Greece, the Balkans, and Latin America similarly put universal male suffrage on the political agenda. Also, by the twentieth century the parliamentary reforms instituted in Russia opened the door for broader political participation.

By the late nineteenth century, industrialized nations began to create new state entitlements for their citizens in an effort to stabilize economies and build political loyalties. Faced with the risks of mass production and the instability of capitalism, male workers and their political organizations pushed for increased state intervention in the economy and social insurance for the unemployed, the injured and disabled, and the elderly. Most nations extended rights to social insurance, medical care, and pensions to native-born males. According to Marshall, the expansion of citizenship rights created greater social cohesion in industrial nations but also helped to reproduce class inequality. Yet there was a more pervasive denial of citizenship rights to women and greater gender inequality in countries where citizenship was gendered male—a point overlooked by Marshall.

For women worldwide, the road to citizenship was considerably less well developed than that for men. As late as 1940 more than half the world's women lived in nations that denied them the right to vote, for reasons that ranged from women's family obligations and their lack of property to the difficulty of achieving rights for a disenfranchised and largely disempowered majority. Yet citizenship comprises more than political power and the right to vote. Women were excluded from citizenship rights in every arena of state action. Women lacked access not only to the vote but also to fundamental civil rights to property and equal treatment, economic opportunities that came from equal citizenship, and social entitlements to income security, health care, and pensions.

Women and Citizenship in World History. Throughout the West, wherever a common-law tradition existed, women's legal rights were truncated by the law of coverture. Based on the argument that married women were absorbed into the legal person of their husbands, coverture denied married women generally the right to own property, possess their wages, and have custody of their children. Lacking legal personhood, women could not sue or sign contracts. Some suggested that women were not accorded such rights because they were generally unable to represent themselves in the political arena. The French civil code of 1804 also denied married women property rights, while guaranteeing such rights, including inheritance rights, to single women. This further subordinated women within marriage. Throughout Europe and Latin America, this code underwrote women's legal inequality wherever it was adopted. It would take more than a century before women were granted full legal status.

Whatever other protections national citizenship might entail, women lacked civil citizenship rights until the passage of married women's property acts in the nineteenth century. Beginning in the 1840s, women in the United States petitioned states to redress women's inequality by granting married women property rights. On a state-by-state basis they were given the right to hold property in their own names, and states gradually granted women wage and parental rights as well. Yet married women continued to lack access to independent credit and faced discrimination in banking, insurance, and pensions until the civil rights laws of the 1960s. In Great Britain, John Stuart Mill pressed his arguments for women's independence in the reform acts of the 1860s, and the Married Women's Property Act put limited rights into law in 1882. Elsewhere in Europe, prohibitions against married women inheriting or owning property were gradually repealed. In France, married women did not achieve full legal equality until the reforms of the 1960s and 1970s.

In the Pacific, customary law kept women in many cultures propertyless. Married women in Australia and New Zealand had to push for reform of common-law rights. Despite Westernization, Japan denied women property and parental rights in its 1898 civil code. In India, once a British colony, dower rights—the right to a portion of the deceased husband's estate—left young brides vulnerable to murder. In most of sub-Saharan Africa and areas of the Middle East, even at the beginning of the twenty-first century, women could not own property independently of fathers or husbands or have equal parental rights. Indeed, in societies where Sharia (Islamic law) governs social relations, women lack many civil rights, including the right to have custody of children and to divorce their spouses without severe penalties.

Women's Participation in Politics. Beyond legal standing, women's political rights were debated and contested in the democratic revolutions of the eighteenth and nineteenth centuries. In challenging the customary bases of political authority, the American and French revolutions put into play not only the rights of men but also rights of women to speak in public, join political organizations, petition, and vote. Though women supported the revolutionary movements—putting at risk not just their livelihoods but also their lives in protests against illegal authority, unjust taxation, and the cost of bread—the new governments did not honor their political participation by according them equal rights. On the contrary, the protests of the disorderly women of Paris, the activism of their political clubs, and the outspoken demands of the feminist Olympe de Gouges sparked a national law prohibiting women's political organization.

Not surprisingly, women of this revolutionary generation published such tracts as *On the Equality of the Sexes* (Judith Sargent Murray, 1790) and *The Declaration of the Rights of Woman* (Olympe de Gouges, 1791). Seeking to contest as well as further the legacies of the American and French revolutions, the English feminist Mary Wollstonecraft wrote *A Vindication of the Rights of Woman* (1793) to challenge the social and educational underpinnings of women's subordination. In 1848 when the world's first women's rights convention met in Seneca Falls, New York, women's call for equal citizenship echoed the words of the American Declaration of Independence. Women protested against the unjust authority of men over women and against their exclusion from political citizenship.

Over the next century, women organized suffrage movements and political organizations to fight for women's rights worldwide. Women's right to vote, often paired with other electoral and political reforms, elicited friendly but unenthusiastic support from political parties, trade unions, and temperance organizations. It also provoked opposition from those who saw women as socially conservative and politically fractious. Antisuffragists imagined that if women participated in politics, either women would ruin politics or politics would corrupt women, demoralize men, and undermine the family. The governments of France and Japan fought equal political citizenship for women not merely by denying women the vote but also by denying them the right to organize politically, assemble publicly, or even petition their own governments for redress of wrongs. In 1890 the Japanese parliament passed a law that made it illegal for women, soldiers, police, and teachers to hold or attend political meetings or to form political organizations. Japanese women had to wait until 1922 to attend political meetings.

The exclusion of women from political life may well explain the international popularity of the Woman's Christian Temperance Union—ostensibly not a political organization—and the support of the international union for women's political rights. At the same time, European women on the margins of the West—the Pitcairn Islands (1838), the Cook Islands and New Zealand (1893), and South Australia (1894)—early on gained the right to vote. Their access to political office, however, came only slowly in the course of the twentieth century.

In the United States, after the 1848 Seneca Falls convention came other women's rights conventions. Within a few years, women's advocates had embraced an agenda of property laws, parental rights, equal participation in religion, dress reform, and even the right to retain family names. Expanding the definitions of citizenship to encompass women's right to "solitude of self" (to use Elizabeth Cady Stanton's words), the founding generation of American suffragists sought to reform not only women's place in society but also democracy as a whole. In 1869 the state of Wyoming granted women the right to vote. A few western states followed, and other state legislatures granted women municipal and school-district suffrage before the twentieth century. By 1915 other states had given women the right to vote. It was not until 1920, however, that the U.S. Congress and the states passed and ratified a federal amendment granting women the right to vote. Yet the amendment did not give all women access to the vote or create de facto universal suffrage because there were laws on the books disenfranchising African Americans and other racial minorities until the Voting Rights Act of 1965.

Historically, women have had no guarantee to citizenship in their own name. In the United States, though women who married American men automatically became American citizens and sometimes lost citizen rights in their country of birth, a 1907 law denied American women the same right to confer American citizenship on their husbands. Instead, if a woman married a foreign citizen, she could restore her American citizenship only by petitioning for naturalization. In 1922 the Cable Act restored some of married women's rights to citizenship.

In Great Britain, women could not transmit their citizenship to their children. In many other countries of the world, marriage with noncitizens cost women their rights, including the ability to own property. In the beginning of the twenty-first century, women migrants who lacked the proper papers, access to resources, or even a right to citizenship in their own country were sometimes at risk of being stateless and lacking any government protection. Such women had to act transnationally even when they had no overt reason to do so.

Progress on women's political rights was far slower in other countries. In Great Britain, changes were incremental. For instance, women were granted municipal suffrage in 1869, and women over thirty gained the right to vote in 1918. Another decade would pass before Great Britain had universal suffrage. Finland and Norway granted women the right to vote after the turn of the twentieth century; other European countries, such as Germany, enfranchised women after World War I. In France, the fervor of women's revolutionary politics and their continuing support for republicanism did not gain them the right to vote. French electoral politics, fear of women's conservatism and their Catholic loyalties, and an imbalanced sex ratio appear to have blocked women from gaining the right to vote until the government of Charles de Gaulle enfranchised women in 1944. As French feminists have pointed out, by that time women in Palestine, some Latin American nations, parts of China, and most of Europe already had the vote and gained at least a foothold as equal political citizens.

Japanese women received the vote under the Japanese constitution ratified during the American occupation. In Switzerland (1971) and South Africa (1994), women received the vote only after numerous campaigns or long struggles for liberation.

The Future of Women's Citizenship. In the new global political economy—in which regional and ethnic identities vie with global ones over political and cultural resources—states, political movements, and individuals have sought to redefine citizenship both as a universal category and as a gender-differentiated one. Scholars and political activists have sought to expand the idea of citizenship to claims for rights to personal and economic autonomy by incorporating the concepts of "intimate citizenship" and "economic citizenship." Furthermore, in Western states, concern over the right to privacy prompted women in some countries to demand equal rights for such sexual minorities as gays and lesbians.

Women's demands for equal citizenship have grown to encompass the social entitlements that social democracies passed in the twentieth century. Pensions for mothers and provisions for maternal health care and leave have often left women with inadequate support. To give one example, family allowances in Britain were originally given not to women but to men. Hence women's unequal access to health care, pensions, and social insurance (for the unemployed, the injured and disabled, and the elderly) have become the focus of activists' political efforts. Yet women also have other barriers to full participation.

Another strategy for women to gain full citizenship—that is, to participate fully in the economic and political life of society—is to seek child care, parental leave, and income support. Yet women argue for these rights in the context of democratic political systems in which they have only a small portion of the total number of parliamentary seats. They occupy few, if any, cabinet posts, and they head relatively few governments at either the local or national level. Though women have made gains in women's representation in the U.S. Congress, the British and Australian parliaments, and the French Assembly, such gains must be seen against a backdrop of general political weakness for women worldwide. Women's fight for equal national citizenship in all its dimensions remains an ongoing struggle.

[*See also* Civil Society; Democracy; Dowry; Gouges, Olympe de; Married Women's Property Acts; Parity; Property Rights; Suffrage; *and* Wollstonecraft, Mary.]

BIBLIOGRAPHY

Blacklock, Cathy, and Jane Jenson, eds. "Citizenship in Latin America." Special issue. *Social Politics* 5, no. 2 (Summer 1998).

Daley, Caroline, and Melanie Nolan, eds. *Suffrage and Beyond: International Feminist Perspectives*. New York: New York University Press, 1994.

Friedman, Marilyn, ed. *Women and Citizenship*. Studies in Feminist Philosophy. New York: Oxford University Press, 2005.

Gardner, Martha. *The Qualities of a Citizen: Women, Immigration, and Citizenship, 1870–1965*. Princeton, N.J.: Princeton University Press, 2005.

Heater, Derek. *A Brief History of Citizenship*. New York: New York University Press, 2004.

Isenberg, Nancy. *Sex and Citizenship in Antebellum America*. Chapel Hill: University of North Carolina Press, 1998.

Joseph, Suad, ed. *Gender and Citizenship in the Middle East*. Syracuse, N.Y.: Syracuse University Press, 2000.

Kerber, Linda K. *No Constitutional Right to Be Ladies: Women and the Obligations of Citizenship*. New York: Hill and Wang, 1998.

Lister, Ruth. *Citizenship: Feminist Perspectives*. 2nd ed. New York: Palgrave Macmillan, 2003.

Marshall, T. H. *"Citizenship and Social Class" and Other Essays*. Cambridge, U.K.: Cambridge University Press, 1950.

Pateman, Carole. *The Sexual Contract*. Stanford, Calif.: Stanford University Press, 1988.

Rose, Sonya, and Kathleen Canning, eds. *Gender, Citizenship, and Subjectivities*. Oxford: Blackwell, 2002.

Scott, Joan Wallach. *Only Paradoxes to Offer: French Feminists and the Rights of Man*. Cambridge, Mass.: Harvard University Press, 1996.

Sinha, Mrinalini. *Gender and Nation*. Women's and Gender History in Global Perspective Series. Washington, D.C.: American Historical Association, 2006.

Yuval-Davis, Nira, and Pnina Werbner. *Women, Difference, and Citizenship*. New York: Zed Books, 1999.

ELIZABETH FAUE

CIVIL DISOBEDIENCE. Civil disobedience as a term, concept, and practice has a long history. Western and Eastern philosophers and religious figures from Plato, John Locke, and Socrates to Indian dharma practitioners have developed the concept's meaning. Generally it is an act of resistance that posits a higher law that is superior to the laws of the state. It is an intentional refusal to abide by law or regulation in order to get some concession from a controlling power, usually a government. It aims to disrupt. Civil disobedience authorizes the individual to follow conscience before state law if such law is deemed unjust.

Origins. One of the figures most closely associated with the idea is Henry David Thoreau (1817–1862). He coined the phrase in his essay "Civil Disobedience" (1849) and was particularly concerned with conscience and moral questions of legal authority and legitimacy. If the individual perceived the state or state law to be unjust and in conflict with his or her conscience, then appropriate civic response involved noncompliance. State held no meaning or power without the consent of the governed.

Another individual associated with civil disobedience and its application was Mahatma Gandhi (1869–1948). Inspired by the Sikh philosopher and reform activist Ram Singh, Gandhi first used civil disobedience in 1906 to defy the South African government and demand that rights be restored to the Indian immigrant community. Others often referred to his use of civil disobedience as "passive resistance." Gandhi built on the concept by adding his own criteria, among them the insistence on nonviolence, a commitment to a living truth, and a devotion to volunteer community or social work.

The Practice. Many independence movements have used civil disobedience to effect social change. Women have figured prominently in these efforts in many places, including India, South Africa, Great Britain, and the United States.

Indian women participated in organized civil disobedience efforts and achieved historical distinction for their commitment to national independence during the early decades of the twentieth century. Women picketed foreign cloth shops and liquor stores to disrupt sales. Sometimes their defiance included interposing their bodies between store entrances and prospective customers. In defiance of colonial authority, their spinning and weaving of khaddar (khadi) allowed boycotting of foreign cloth. Women also led processions, at which leaders delivered rousing speeches. They boycotted government ceremonies and the like. Significantly they participated in the 1930 Salt Satyagraha, a demonstration march in protest of the British salt tax. The women joined others in producing and selling salt, a violation of the colonial law that allowed only the British government to control the production and sale of salt. Women formed organizations to facilitate their participation, among them the Desh Sevika Sangh, the Ladies Picketting Board, and the Nari Satyagraha Samiti.

South African women led the way in using civil disobedience to strike blows at apartheid. In the early 1950s the Federation of South African Women (FSAW) renewed campaigns against passes (identification documents) and breathed new life into their national liberation movement. They rejected the apartheid regime's plan to extend passes to women. Such passes were already mandatory for men. In August 1956 twenty thousand women marched on Union buildings in Pretoria to protest the pass laws because passes restricted their movement and labor. For the next two years women moved around the country forming new branches of the FSAW and organizing anti-pass demonstrations. Thousands were arrested.

Of course civil disobedience was not a weapon used solely by the colonized against colonial powers. Activists used the tactic to change the balance of power within Western societies as well. Originating in the 1860s, the British woman suffrage movement used civil disobedience to dramatic effect during its most militant phase beginning in 1903. Suffragists held marches and numerous public demonstrations. The British suffragists of the Women's Social and Political Union chained themselves to the gates of Parliament and went on hunger strikes when they were jailed. They resisted law in the hundreds of thousands, winning the vote for women over age thirty in 1918 and for all women in 1928. Their successful use of mass action inspired activists in other countries. Inspired by the work of the WSPU founders Emmeline and Christabel Pankhurst, militant U.S. suffragists led by Alice Paul used similar tactics—arrests, imprisonment, hunger strikes, White House demonstrations—to help win the vote during a critical phase. Gandhi witnessed the defiance of WSPU protesters when he traveled to London in 1906, and their bold resolve influenced his approach to securing Indian rights in South Africa and fighting against British colonialism in India. Hoping to inspire other Indians during his London trip, Gandhi wrote enthusiastically about suffragists and their tactics in a newspaper article, "Deeds Better Than Words."

The social and political landscape shifted dramatically beginning in the United States in the mid-twentieth century, when women antiwar activists, labor activists, student activists, environmentalists, and feminists used civil disobedience to focus public attention on their causes, in most cases with much success. The most vivid and sustained example included protests waged by African American civil rights activists. In December 1955 the middle-aged seamstress Rosa Parks defied segregation law when she declined to give up her seat to a white male passenger on a city bus in Montgomery, Alabama. Her arrest touched off the Montgomery Bus Boycott and marked the emergence of the civil rights leader Martin Luther King Jr., who best articulated the entire movement's philosophy of nonviolent direct action. For 381 days, the Women's Political Council and others organized a boycott observed by the majority of the city's fifty thousand black citizens, who stayed off the buses until courts outlawed segregated transportation. Many other women followed Parks in using individual acts of passive resistance to spark mass action. In February 1960 college students began using sit-ins to defy local laws and customs that required racial separation at lunch counters, in bus terminals, and in other public places. Growing to nearly fifty thousand protestors in over thirty communities in seven states, sit-in encounters between activists, law enforcement, and segregationists were often violent and captured international headlines. Women such as Ruby Doris Smith Robinson and Diane Nash earned much respect for their willingness to use their bodies to challenge unjust laws, enduring beatings and imprisonment repeatedly.

In the late twentieth century, civil disobedience became an effective grassroots weapon among environmental activists around the world. In 1977, Wangaari Maathai launched the nonviolent Green Belt Movement to combat deforestation in her native Kenya and to provide women leadership opportunities. While encouraging people to reforest through growing trees, Maathai also led demonstrations into forest areas where she confronted a stubborn government and eager developers. Although she was severely beaten and jailed for her campaigns, Maathai succeeded at getting communities to plant over 20 million trees, and the Green Belt Movement is now in thirty African countries. In 2004 she earned the Nobel Peace Prize for her work.

Toward the end of the twentieth century and the beginning of the twenty-first century, women peace activists built on a long tradition of feminist pacifism and applied civil disobedience in creative ways in response to conflicts in the Middle East. In 1988 the Israeli women's peace movement (Women in Black) began using nonviolent protests to call for an end to violent conflict between Israelis and Palestinians. Their initial protest was simple. They stood at a major traffic intersection in Jerusalem for an hour each week, dressed in all black, and held a black sign that read "End the occupation." Their audience included Israeli officials, the Israeli public, and the entire international community. The movement spread to include other women's peace organizations and resulted in the Coalition of Women for Peace, which included Israeli and Palestinian women who marched with banners calling for peace. The Persian Gulf War (1991) and the second Iraq war revived feminist antiwar activism in the United States, where the women of Code Pink, the Granny Peace Brigade, and United for Peace and Justice have marched, held vigils, and confronted public officials to press the claim for peace.

[*See also* Apartheid; Civil Rights Movement; Suffragettes; Women's Liberation; *and biographical entries on women mentioned in this article.*]

BIBLIOGRAPHY

Chatterjee, Manini. "1930: Turning Point in the Participation of Women in the Freedom Struggle." *Social Scientist* 29, nos. 7–8 (July–August 2001): 39–47.

Henning, Melber. "The Virtues of Civil Courage and Civil Disobedience in the Historical Context of Namibia and South Africa." *Politikon* 28, no. 2 (2001): 235–244.

Jayawardena, Kumari. *Feminism and Nationalism in the Third World*. London: Zed Books, 1986.

Kuumba, M. Bahati. "'You've Struck a Rock': Comparing Gender, Social Movements, and Transformation in the United States and South Africa." *Gender and Society* 16, no. 4 (August 2002): 504–523.

Mayhall, Laura E. Nym. "Defining Militancy: Radical Protest, the Constitutional Idiom, and Women's Suffrage in Britain, 1908–1909." *Journal of British Studies* 39, no. 3 (July 2000): 340–371.

Thapar, Suruchi. "Women as Activists, Women as Symbols: A Study of the Indian Nationalist Movement." *Feminist Review* 44 (summer 1993): 81–96.

CHANA KAI LEE

CIVIL RIGHTS MOVEMENT. The civil rights movement was an organized effort to end decades of racial segregation, political exclusion, and economic marginalization. Although it was a full-scale effort most commonly associated with the southern United States, other regions of the country were involved directly and indirectly. It followed decades of organized responses to inequality and vulnerability. Following emancipation, African Americans formed churches, schools, and secular organizations to respond to the challenge of new freedom. Organizations such as the National Association of Colored Women supported various race and gender causes, including temperance, suffrage, and antilynching during the early twentieth century. The engine of the movement was African American women's participation, although it was not as visible as the more male-dominated leadership prominent in churches and well-established organizations like the National Association of Colored People (NAACP) and later the Southern Christian Leadership Conference (SCLC).

Women's leadership was mostly witnessed from behind the scenes. The mass movement included women as strategists, participants, and moving orators. The movement focused on major areas of American life, including education, politics, public accommodations, and employment, and resulted in landmark court decisions (often with women as lead plaintiffs) and legislation.

Education. Segregated education stifled racial progress. African American women educators had long argued that racial liberation depended on quality education. The chronology of their work long preceded the movement, thereby shaping the movement's direction once it developed. The Charleston native Septima Poinsette Clark (1898–1987) defined civil rights activism as providing a useful education to the poor, particularly those living on the impoverished South Sea Islands of South Carolina.

Clark knew discrimination in education as a student and teacher. In 1916 she began her teaching career on John's Island, where social and economic conditions were wretched. African Americans comprised a large, exploited plantation workforce. Poverty, illiteracy, malaria outbreaks, and high infant mortality severely limited life chances. With an expansive view of education's role and value to society, Clark focused first on teaching adults and children the basics. She gained valuable experience about working with "the folk," whatever their station, and this informed her civil rights activism decades later. Clark and others believed that citizenship education was critical to racial progress. Citizenship education taught individuals how to read and write simple documents, how to balance checkbooks, and how to vote. An educated citizenry was an empowered citizenry.

In the 1950s and 1960s Clark and others performed "literacy and liberation" training in various settings and by stealth because of violent opposition to teaching blacks about their rights as citizens. She set up several hundred "citizenship schools" throughout the region. Some operated in kitchens, in beauty parlors, and under trees. Between 1957 and 1970 over eight hundred citizenship schools operated. In 1964, a peak year of activity for all phases of the movement, nearly two hundred schools were in operation.

Clark's activism also included advocating for pay equity for African American teachers. Joining her in this effort was another highly respected civil rights advocate from the Palmetto State, Modjeska Simkins (1899–1992), a prominent educator and community activist. Simkins helped Clark win victories in the struggle to equalize teachers' salaries in Charleston in 1944 and in the state capital of Columbia in 1945. Simkins distinguished herself as a fierce NAACP activist in the 1940s and 1950s. Most notably she was important to the NAACP lawsuit *Briggs v. Elliot* that challenged school segregation in South Carolina. This case became the first of five cases that resulted in the landmark *Brown v. Board of Education* in May 1954.

Other women made their movement contributions in desegregating education. Included among them were individuals who challenged segregated higher education. In 1956 the young, shy Autherine Lucy became the first African American to enroll at the University of Alabama (Tuscaloosa). Her admittance and attempt to enroll was one chapter in a string of successful challenges directed at higher education by the NAACP in the 1940s and 1950s. However, Lucy's stay was shortened when the university expelled her allegedly for safety reasons. Vivian Malone, amid a showdown between the avowed white supremacist governor George Wallace and federal troops, made the second attempt to attend in 1963. She succeeded and became the first African American to graduate from the University of Alabama. In 1961 Charlayne Hunter became one of two black students to desegregate the University of Georgia.

Of the high-profile battles between southern states and the federal government, the 1957 desegregation of Central High School in Little Rock, Arkansas, was the most dramatic. Nine African American students (six were teenage girls), under the leadership of the NAACP activist Daisy Bates, forced the implementation of the *Brown* decision. On the students' first attempt, Governor Orval Faubus called out the state national guard to prevent them from entering Central High in September. In October, President Dwight D. Eisenhower federalized the Arkansas National Guard, thereby removing them from Faubus's control. Eisenhower then sent the 101st Airborne Division to protect the black students and to allow implementation of *Brown*. This case made international headlines.

As a woman civil rights leader, Bates held a public role, but her behind-the-scenes work typified women's leadership for the entire movement. She prepared the students psychologically and spiritually for the daily challenge of going to school. She organized the logistics of their daily entry into and exit from Central High and the afternoon briefings, where students shared their experiences and received encouragement from Bates and other organizers. She intervened and wrote letters to the U.S. president, state officials, and clergy. She also set up security patrols for herself, the students, and their families. She tended to every detail, including dealing with the large media coverage of events.

Mass Direct Action. Education and the courts composed one battleground for racial protest; public accommodations included another. "Tearing down the walls of Jim Crow," as some activists referred to their central aim, took its most dramatic expression in challenges to segregated transportation and lunch counters. There too women led. They strategized, they put their bodies on the front lines, they went to jail, and they experienced all forms of harassment and persecution. Their involvement crossed class, age, and religious divides.

The most well known of these figures remains the Alabaman Rosa Parks, whose defiance on 1 December 1955 started the Montgomery bus boycott, the 381-day protest against segregated city buses. A seamstress by trade and a devoted NAACP activist, Parks refused to give up her seat on a bus to a white patron. The bus driver called the police and had Parks arrested when she declined to move after repeated requests. Parks, a middle-aged woman, became an important symbol of courage. Black Montgomerians took heart and followed her defiance by refusing to ride the bus, many choosing to walk several miles to work

Misc.

POLICE DEPARTMENT
CITY OF MONTGOMERY

Date 12-1-55 19

Complainant J.F.Blake (wm)

Address 27 No.Lewis St. Phone No.

Offense Misc. Reported By Same as above

Address Phone No.

Date and Time Offense Committed 12-1-55 6:06 pm

Place of Occurrence In Front of Empire Theatre (On Montgomery Street)

Person or Property Attacked

How Attacked

Person Wanted

Value of Property Stolen Value Recovered

Details of Complaint (list, describe and give value of property stolen)

We received a call upon arrival the bus operator said he had a colored female sitting in the white section of the bus, and would not move back.

We (Day & Mixon) also saw her.

The bus operator signed a warrant for her. Rosa Parks,(cf) 634 Cleveland Court.

Rosa Parks (cf) was charged with chapter 6 section 11 of the Montgomery City Code.

Warrant #14254

THIS OFFENSE IS DECLARED:
UNFOUNDED ☐
CLEARED BY ARREST ☐
EXCEPTIONALLY CLEARED ☐
INACTIVE (NOT CLEARED) ☐

Officers F. B. Day
D. W. Mixon

Division Patrol Time 7:00 pm 12-1-55

Rosa Parks. The police report on the arrest of Rosa Parks, charging her with "refusing to obey the orders of a bus driver," December 1955, Montgomery, Alabama. Records of the U.S. District Courts, National Archives, Southeast Region (Atlanta)

instead. However, Parks became more than a symbol. Along with involvement in the legal case that accompanied the protest, she made several practical contributions to one of the most successful civil rights campaigns of the era. Daily she helped oversee an alternative transportation system to offer rides to blacks needing to go across town for work or other purposes. She organized a food and clothing distribution effort for those who were fired for their participation in the boycott. In retrospect, she came to be called the "mother of the civil rights movement" for starting it all.

Although Parks's defiance triggered the protest, Jo Ann Gibson Robinson, Mary Fair Burks, and other community women of distinction had contemplated and established a base for ultimately attacking segregated transportation several years prior to Parks's arrest. In 1946 Burks formed the Women's Political Council (WPC), which started documenting the humiliation and abuse endured by black riders. Parks had known these abuses all too well. Not only were black patrons separated in the last ten rows of a bus, but spiteful racist drivers often drove off after black riders boarded at the front to pay their fares and before they could reenter through the back door, which was the custom. Bus drivers cursed black passengers for no apparent reason other than the color of their skin. The WPC distributed the initial call for a boycott in the wee hours of the morning by going house to house and issuing notices to stay off the buses the following day. The WPC was involved in the administrative affairs of the Montgomery Improvement Association (MIA), the nearly all-male organization that became the leadership face of the boycott. Historically the Montgomery bus boycott is known as the point at which a young, gifted preacher named Martin Luther King Jr. entered the movement and gave it a powerful orator and informed proponent of civil disobedience or nonviolent direct action. The WPC played a critical role in MIA and in King's success. WPC made a mass movement possible through its networking, through its informed advice about how to mobilize a community, and through its practical help in raising funds by creative means, including bake sale competitions between different neighborhoods of women.

While King is most often credited with giving the movement a strategy informed by nonviolent direct action, the most ingenious movement strategist and tactician was the highly experienced Ella Baker, a native of North Carolina with social activist roots that stretched back to the Depression era, when she organized workers. Baker was regarded by many, including her detractors, as a mastermind. While she worked with the NAACP during the 1940s, traveling around the South documenting the impact of Jim Crow and material deprivation, she often felt hemmed in by the bureaucracy of the organization and its inability to imagine social change in broader, more radical ways. Baker often found herself among the prominent male leaders in the movement, and ironically her contributions to their success often made them more famous and pushed her nearer the margins. Her role in pivotal movement moments, such as the founding of SCLC, King's organizational base, is often overlooked. The idea of a regional organization of local affiliate organizations was her idea, and she helped get SCLC off the ground, although she was never given any permanent position in the organization.

Baker remained loyal to her own vision as she moved further away from "the preachers." Her intelligent vision kept her focused on the areas with most potential for the movement. In 1960 she noticed the power and momentum generated by student protests that began as a sit-in movement in February 1961, when four African American students protested a segregated lunch counter at a Woolworth's store in Greensboro, North Carolina. This first protest lasted several days and garnered much attention for the violent white reaction and arrests that resulted. Eventually the students were joined by others, and a wave of similar protests occurred. By the end of the month the sit-in movement had reached over thirty communities in seven states. By April some fifty thousand participants had "sat in" somewhere in the South.

Baker saw the need to harness this energy and institutionalize the wave of activity. She called a meeting at her alma mater, Shaw University in North Carolina. A diverse group of student activists from all over showed up. The result was the formation of the Student Nonviolent Coordinating Committee (SNCC), the powerful youth-led organization that took the movement into another gear. Baker not only facilitated the group's founding but protected it from cooptation by the "adult" organizations with which she had been involved (SCLC and the NAACP). More important, she influenced the group's thinking about leadership. She got the college students to think about becoming their own leaders, instead of waiting for others to lead them, and to see validity in it. She challenged the notion of a messianic leader who would come and complete the task of social transformation. Similarly she encouraged them to see the rural folks whom they would help organize in the same way. At every turn she reminded the students and her peers that strong people do not need strong leaders. While this introduced a tension between established civil rights organizations and the youth, it also kept the main energy of the movement focused in a radical direction. Her intervention was crucial to keeping the movement alive.

Moreover, Baker's example and her guidance helped develop a cadre of young women leaders who became a new face for civil rights activism. Baker inspired the likes of Ruby Doris Robinson of Atlanta and Diane Nash of Nashville, two women who redefined the idea of "courage" and "defiance" in mass challenges like the 1961 Freedom Rides, where activists took on interstate bus segregation with extremely violent results. Still, they succeeded when the federal government ended segregation on interstate buses and in terminal facilities.

Voter Registration. Ending segregation in education and public accommodations were necessary steps taken in the march toward freedom. However, black southern citizens still remained locked out of mainstream politics. Some argued correctly that African Americans could never protect gains in other areas without full participation in the political process. Dating back to the end of Reconstruction, black women and men were effectively disfranchised by a series of laws and extralegal measures, including poll taxes, literacy clauses, and the threat of violence. A substantial number of blacks were too poor to pay poll taxes in consecutive years (a requirement), and most registrars were blatantly discriminatory in deciding who "passed" literacy tests given at county courthouses. Others knew that some blacks had been killed for trying to exercise their constitutional right. The result was that the majority of southern states had black registration in the single digits even though these states had sizable black populations.

The movement addressed this through a massive voter registration campaign that peaked in 1964. A significant figure in this movement was the Mississippi native Fannie Lou Hamer, who along with Baker, Annie Devine, and Victoria Gray helped found the Mississippi Freedom Democratic Party in April 1964. In that same year SNCC and Hamer waged an intensive effort to register blacks in the state with the worst figures for black registration: Mississippi. Joining them in this effort were a large number of white students, including women who became inspired to seek equality for their sex. Through her inspirational speeches, her campaigns for office, her field canvassing for registrants, her many trips taking the fearful but committed to county courthouses, and her constant appeals to the U.S. Congress, Hamer helped register over eighty thousand potential voters. While some SNCC members debated the effectiveness of voter registration work in comparison to daring, attention-getting civil disobedience campaigns, everyone knew that voter registration was extremely dangerous. Local law enforcement jailed voter registration organizers, and many employers fired them from jobs. On one occasion in 1963, Hamer and her coworkers were beaten, sexually molested, and tortured in a rural Mississippi jail based on mere suspicion of "agitating." Women civil rights activists knew that sacrifice and danger knew no gender bounds.

Legacy and Consequences. The civil rights movement began and ended at different times and in different places. Some movement activity stretched into the mid-1970s, although most historians agree that the main efforts had ended by the late 1960s. In many urban areas in the North, Midwest, and West "the movement" had refocused on black power with an emphasis on separatism and race pride. Indisputably, the civil rights phase of the black freedom struggle changed the country in significant ways. It resulted in landmark court cases like *Brown v. Board of Education*. It pressured the government to pass major pieces of legislation, such as the 1964 Civil Rights Act, which outlawed various forms of discrimination, including that having to do with sex, and the 1965 Voting Rights Act, which provided federal referees in southern states where registration numbers were lowest, thereby changing the political landscape in the region and ultimately the entire country. Without the involvement of women, this momentous expansion of democracy would not have happened. By the 1960s the movement included larger numbers of other racial communities and other marginalized groups (the disabled, lesbians, and gays). Soon the civil rights movement overlapped in theme and chronology with other movements, some inspired directly by their civil rights experiences, such as the gay liberation movement, the

Selma-to-Montgomery March. Harlem residents gather in New York to show their support for the civil rights march in Alabama, 1965. DIANA DAVIES/SOPHIA SMITH COLLECTION, SMITH COLLEGE

Chicano movement, the Native American movement, the Asian American movement, the free speech movement, and the antiwar movement.

[*See also* Baker, Ella; Clark, Septima Poinsette; Hamer, Fannie Lou; National Association of Colored Women; *and* Parks, Rosa.]

BIBLIOGRAPHY

Bates, Daisy. *The Long Shadow of Little Rock: A Memoir.* Fayetteville: University of Arkansas Press, 1987.

Carson, Clayborne. *In Struggle: SNCC and the Black Awakening of the 1960s.* Cambridge, Mass.: Harvard University Press, 1981.

Clark, Septima. *Ready from Within: Septima Clark and the Civil Rights Movement.* Edited with an introduction by Cynthia Stokes Brown. Navarro, Calif.: Wild Tree, 1986.

Collier-Thomas, Bettye, and V. P. Franklin, eds. *Sisters in the Struggle: African American Women in the Civil Rights–Black Power Movement.* New York: New York University Press, 2001.

Crawford, Vicki L., Jacqueline Anne Rouse, and Barbara Woods. *Women in the Civil Rights Movement: Trailblazers and Torchbearers, 1941–1965.* Brooklyn, N.Y.: Carlson Publishers, 1990.

Fleming, Cynthia Griggs. *Soon We Will Not Cry: The Liberation of Ruby Doris Smith Robinson.* Lanham, Md.: Rowman and Littlefield, 1998.

Lee, Chana Kai. *For Freedom's Sake: The Life of Fannie Lou Hamer.* Urbana: University of Illinois Press, 1999.

Moody, Anne. *Coming of Age in Mississippi.* New York: Dell, 1968.

Ransby, Barbara. *Ella Baker and the Black Freedom Movement: A Radical Democratic Vision.* Chapel Hill: University of North Carolina Press, 2003.

Robinson, Jo Ann Gibson. *The Montgomery Bus Boycott and the Women Who Started It: The Memoir of Jo Ann Gibson Robinson.* Knoxville: University of Tennessee Press, 1987.

CHANA KAI LEE

CIVIL SERVICE. Civil service is government work to provide a range of state services that include administering the state's taxation policies and financial accounts, implementing laws and justice, attending to the upkeep of state property including harbors, roads, and buildings, and overseeing public health, education, and other programs for citizens. Not all governments provide all of these services, nor have they done so in a uniform way over time. It was only with the development of the modern nation-state that civil service has generally expanded to be so encompassing and that women have come to play an influential role in staffing it.

The Chinese Exam System. One common denominator of civil service work is that it is based on merit, often displayed by taking an exam, and that advancement takes place through the demonstration of merit and along a path of steps and grades. The prototype for this type of merit-based civil service, with its regular procedures and examinations, is China. In China, from the Song dynasty (960–1279) into the early twentieth century, the civil service examination system provided Chinese men with their only entryway into official positions. This had profound consequences for Chinese society because it meant that the only way to secure and maintain elite status was through a high degree of literacy in the classical corpus that was the basis of the exam. By custom, women were not allowed in the examination compounds, but the premium placed on literacy led many families to seek daughters-in-law who were themselves highly literate so they might oversee the early education of their sons.

The rapid growth of book publishing in the sixteenth and seventeenth centuries led to intensified competition in the examination system and to the growing literacy of women in China's elite. Young boys and girls were most often educated by their mothers. As they reached puberty the boys would move on to a professional tutor or senior male relative who performed the same function. The girls might continue to study with their mother or other female relatives, though by the eighteenth century some young women studied with famous male teachers, thereby scandalizing conservative Confucian critics. In the Qing dynasty (1644–1911), more than thirty-six hundred women published books under their own names. Some critics argued that women wrote better poetry than men precisely because their talents could be freely developed, with an emotional spontaneity unhampered by the constraints of examination competition. Other critics argued that the publication of women's emotional poetry was both shameful and highly dangerous.

A popular theme in Chinese novels, short stories, and dramas was the talented woman who in male disguise took and passed the civil service examinations and went on to a successful political career as a high official. There were far more female-authored fantasies about Chinese women scholars passing exams in male disguise than about such women warriors as Mulan. In one famous example from the eighteenth century, Wang Yun wrote *Dreams of Glory*, in which a woman dreamed such a scenario—and married three other women in the process—before waking to discover that it was all a dream. Wang Yun expressed in some of her poetry her deep frustration at not being able to compete in the civil service examinations. Her happiest poems, however, come in the celebration of her son's examination success, which she clearly saw as a reflection on her own abilities and a guarantee of her family's future.

Civil Service Opens to Women. Several major changes in modern society throughout the world opened the doors of civil service to women. The first was the institution of public school education from the nineteenth century on. Educated women who could pass the required public examinations could find jobs in these schools. Even in colonial situations, local women had an opportunity to rise in status and earn their living. For instance, in the Philippines, where 97 percent of women came to be literate, women passed the tests and took teaching posts wherever the government sent them. In France the civil service offered good jobs after a law in 1881 made public schooling secular, free, and obligatory. Women from the middle and lower-middle classes suddenly had a respectable way to become valued state employees, provided that they could prove themselves competent and pro-republican—not monarchist.

Women's civil service employment also grew with the expansion of government during the wars of the twentieth century, when government jobs increased and when women had the choice of entering a wider variety of occupations. In Great Britain women held 33,000 civil service jobs in 1911 but 102,000 by 1921. Even noncombatant countries were affected: in 1918, Spanish women were allowed in the civil service for the first time, and in 1920 women in Denmark were guaranteed equal pay in civil service positions except for cost-of-living increases; in 1958 equal cost-of-living benefits were mandated.

Still another opening of civil service jobs occurred with the expansion of the welfare state after 1945. Although many nation-states offered pensions to veterans and old-age and disability insurance to men from the late nineteenth century on, the full-blown welfare state providing maternity care, day care, family allowances, and national health services was born on a practical level in Sweden in the 1930s as a way to promote population growth. The Bolshevik Revolution saw the establishment of many of these services after 1918, but they functioned badly or fitfully because of the civil war and the competing drive for industrialization, which gobbled up state resources. After World War II other European countries, including those in the Soviet bloc, began providing these benefits to replenish the population and to fight fascism. Many of these institutions were staffed by women civil servants functioning in office work, health care, and day care. This has led many people to observe the feminine nature of the welfare state at the grassroots level and to conclude that women were hired in part to lessen the cost of the new obligations that the government was taking on.

There have been civil service careers that break out of these categories. After receiving her MA in zoology at Johns Hopkins, the U.S. scientist Rachel Carson (1907–1964) worked part-time writing articles for magazines, and she also worked for the U.S. Bureau of Fisheries (now the U.S. Fish and Wildlife Service), writing the scripts for its radio program *Romance under the Waters*. In 1936 she became the first woman to take and pass the civil service exam, after which the Bureau of Fisheries hired her to write a variety of publications as one of its biologists. Meanwhile, Carson published her own books on the ocean, notably *The Sea around Us* (1951). As she wrote her well-received books, she became the chief editor of all publications for the U.S. Fish and Wildlife Service, resigning in 1952 to write full time; she published her classic *The Silent Spring* in 1962.

Barriers to Entry and Promotion. Despite the opportunities, in general the civil services do not fully accept women on equal terms. For instance, before 1946, Frenchwomen were generally not admitted to the administrative branches of the civil service because they were seen as not able to reason. Instead they tended "to privilege their personal life over public affairs," as one administrator put it (quoted in Allwood and Wadia, p. 233, note 23). Advancement occurred less rapidly for women than it did for men, or not at all. Women also received lower pay and fewer promotions and, as in the French case, were confined to certain branches of the civil service.

The first and most important characteristic of civil servants in the upper reaches of government across all continents was and is that they are male. Numerous studies have shown that masculinity is a better determinant of upward mobility in the civil service than are class, family connections, prior experience of the family in government, reputation of a university diploma, or any other factor. Although there may be a greater number of women than men in civil service positions, only the smallest fraction in the upper levels will be women. In France, where women were allowed to enter the civil service freely only with the constitution that went into effect in 1946, their numbers in health and social services grew rapidly with the development of the postwar welfare state so that in 1999 they constituted 56.9 percent of the civil service. However, men constituted 90 percent of the upper levels of the bureaucracy as a whole—a pattern that is consistent across the European Union. In the late twentieth century the EU investigated the conditions of women's recruitment into the upper levels of the civil service, determining a series of measures to remedy the gross imbalance.

The lack of women in high civil service positions also occurs in recently created revolutionary states, such as the postcolonial states of Africa. In Nigeria and Zambia, for instance, women were at the forefront of agitation for independence, forming a Women's Brigade of the United National Independence Party in Zambia and fighting the colonial government in Nigeria throughout much of the colonial period. But the one-party states and military governments that often succeeded the imperial powers rarely made women important officials until women began protesting their exclusion from the newly independent bureaucracy. In Zambia in 1974, two women but sixty-five men were district governors; in 1983 one woman was a district governor and ninety-two men were. In 1974 one woman was a cabinet minister, and twenty-two men were. By 1983 there were no women cabinet ministers. In most instances in the Zambian civil service women constituted 10 percent or less of officials. In some West African states, in contrast, women held as many as 20–25 percent of positions.

The careers of individual women demonstrate that even when women do reach high administrative levels in the civil service, their positions concern administering social programs, especially for women and families. Ginko Sato, the Japanese assistant vice minister of labor in 1990, attended the University of Tokyo, Cornell University, and the London School of Economics. Her career until she became assistant vice minister of labor included positions in the women's and young workers' department of the ministry, director of the industrial homework division, director of the women's division, director of the women workers' division, and director general of the Women's Bureau. Like Ginko Sato, highly placed women civil servants rarely have responsibilities in administering ministries of finance, justice, or military affairs.

Women also work unpaid behind the civil service scenes, creating the infrastructure for successful male careers. In countries like Japan, women play important roles in molding the highest reaches of the civil service by maintaining their family's status and social networks along which the male civil servant advances in his career. Women not only perform household tasks but also take responsibility for family finances and for determining advantageous marriages that will allow the next generation to start on a career with advantages, with credentials, and possibly at an even higher level.

Civil Service Activism and Its Results. Women in the civil service of various countries have been active for reform and equality. One example comes from the United Kingdom, where government typists and clerks joined forces in 1916 to create the Federation of Women Civil Servants, which contributed to the passage in 1919 of the Sex Disqualification Act. Although this was to reform the conditions under which women worked, it created special ranks and grades for women. During World War II, British women agitated to receive the same benefits that their male counterparts did. Winston Churchill threatened to have them all arrested as traitors. The women civil servants in Britain continued their activism after the war, contributing to the rise of the feminist movement.

Reformers elsewhere have targeted civil service gender policies for their activism, which has led to many reports on women in the civil service. In 1973 the Irish government repealed parts of a 1956 law that forced women to leave their civil service jobs upon marriage. A 2002 report of the Association for Civil Rights in Israel pointed to the underrepresentation of women in managerial civil service positions, but it especially noted that Arab and Druze women were even more drastically underrepresented, with the government taking no account of the discrimination.

Progress in civil service advancement occurred in Europe in 2005 when Catherine Day, an Irish bureaucrat, was chosen amid sharp competition from men to head the civil service department of the European Union. The bureaucracy of the European Union itself consisted of 48 percent women at the time, but only 12 percent of the top civil servants were women, with women (after Day's appointment) heading only six of the EU's thirty-five major departments. However, in China, where the modern civil service might be said to have started, women in 1995 held only 20 percent of all civil service jobs and very few upper-level ones.

[*See also* Citizenship; Civil Society; Parity; Wang Yun; *and* Welfare State.]

BIBLIOGRAPHY

Allwood, Gill, and Khursheed Wadia. *Women and Politics in France 1958–2000*. London: Routledge, 2000.

Elman, Benjamin A. *A Cultural History of Civil Examinations in Late Imperial China*. Berkeley: University of California Press, 2000.

Mann, Susan. *Precious Records: Women in China's Long Eighteenth Century*. Stanford, Calif.: Stanford University Press, 1997.

Parpart, Jane L., and Kathleen A. Staudt, eds. *Women and the State in Africa*. Boulder, Colo.: Lynne Rienner, 1989.

Rothacher, Albrecht. *The Japanese Power Elite*. New York: St. Martin's Press, 1993.

BONNIE G. SMITH

CIVIL SOCIETY. The term "civil society" is commonly used today to refer to a sphere or space apart from both the home and the state where debate and discussion can freely occur. Civil society has a long and complicated history, throughout most of which it was associated with men. Invented in seventeenth- and eighteenth-century Europe as a key concept of enlightened political theory by thinkers such as John Locke, Adam Smith, Charles-Louis de Secondat, the baron of Montesquieu, and Immanuel Kant, civil society underwent considerable revision at the hands of Alexis de Tocqueville and Karl Marx.

Though promising harmony and cooperation, civil society's utopian tone, feminist critics now point out, was belied by its being primarily a plan developed by men for men; women were only marginally involved in the debates as either interlocutors or subjects. Because participation in civil society was commonly limited to the politically mature, responsible citizen who acted independent and free, women—along with nonwhite men, non-Christians, and non–property owners—were routinely excluded.

In twentieth-century political theory, civil society went into eclipse, only to emerge around the 1980s as a key category in the antidictatorial critique in socialist Eastern Europe and in liberation movements in Latin America and South Africa. Civil society also gained new life through the work of the German philosopher Jürgen Habermas, who not only provided a historicized account of its development but also linked it to what he called the "public sphere"—the site of critical public debate whose utopian potential is realized when participants develop "communicative competence."

Feminist Critiques. Nowadays the term "civil society" is widely used the world over by exponents of diverse political stripes. Yet, or perhaps because of this, its definition remains unstable. Is it a utopian political norm, a descriptor for concrete historical practices, or an analytical concept? Does it refer to a recognizable social space—a field that includes self-organized initiatives, associations, federations, movements, and networks that are attributed neither to the state sphere and its institutions nor to the market, and that are also not located in the so-called private sphere, which generally refers to the family? Or does it refer to the voluntary activities of particular social actors—those who are self-organized, autonomous, and emphasize communication, publicity, and the willingness and ability to deal peaceably with conflict? Does civil society take one form or many?

Feminist scholars have fueled this debate by challenging the mainstream political theorists who sought to generalize the developmental path of a few western European civil societies—or more precisely, that of one social stratum and one sex in these civil societies—as the universal pattern. Feminist historians have argued that in the "enlightened past," civil society was never an inclusive and just social sphere positioned among the market, the state, and the family, but rather was a social sphere that was strictly exclusive. This was because the white, male, middle-class struggle for civil, political, and social citizenship as a precondition for a flourishing civil society was closely related to the processes of state- and nation-building. The exclusion of women from the public sphere, state institutions, and political rights was consolidated by the introduction of universal conscription, allowing military service to become the precondition for political participation.

Historical Exclusions. The enlightened distinction between public and private helped define and naturalize civil society, like politics in general, as an exclusively male sphere, with the family as the complementary female "other." As members of households, women—along with children and servants—were to be represented in public by the male head; they had no rights of their own. Women were admitted into civil society only far enough to be bound by its laws, but not so far that they could evade continuing subordination to men. Even when the concept of civil society has been broadened to include women or has been formulated in seemingly gender-neutral terms, it continues to regard women's interests as "particular," especially when they pertain to the gendered division of labor, and thus as inimical to the presumed universality of civil society.

Yet as feminist historians have shown, the voluntary associations that constituted the building blocks of civil society were themselves more prone to discriminatory practices than were the publicly scrutinized institutions of the state, a tendency that persists to this day. Though commonly linked to men, such associations offered many women their initial entrée into civil society and a means of engaging politically with the state. Despite an often acute sense of their own political exclusion, female association members often ended up engaging in discriminatory practices of their own. These historical patterns suggest that in order for a democratic civil society to flourish, a strong state may be necessary to guarantee political equality and universal access to basic civil, political, and social citizenship rights.

Whereas mainstream political theorists insist that civil society lies outside the family—specifically, between the family and the state—many feminist theorists contend that the family should be integrated more systematically into the analysis of civil society. In their view, the family and kinship networks are important not only for the organization of civic and political associations but also as basic institutions for raising children with the virtues needed by actors in civil society. Rejecting the historically constructed separation between civil society and the family and the assignment of the family to the so-called private sphere, feminists argue that this dichotomy obscures our view of both civil society's gender-segregated structure and its manner of functioning, as well as the family's potential contributions to civil society. Indeed, the political theorists Jean Cohen and Andrew Arato have urged us to think of the family as one of civil society's key institutions, "one that, if conceived of in egalitarian terms, could have provided an experience of horizontal solidarity, collective identity, and equal participation to the autonomous individuals comprising it—a task deemed fundamental for the other associations of civil society and for the ultimate development of civic virtue and responsibility with respect to the polity."

Ongoing Problems of Exclusivity. Queer theorists, however, take issue with the very idea of privileging the family in relation to civil society, because doing so almost invariably implies a heterosexual relationship, usually formalized through marriage. This, in turn, argues the queer literary scholar Eric O. Clarke, is linked to "the proprietary codes that (inappropriately) shape publicity practices" and exclude or marginalize gays and lesbians. By these codes he means "the heterosexist tenor of the bourgeois familial morality defining proper civic personhood and universal humanity" and "the relegation of erotic experience, which has largely shaped a queer sense of self and collective belonging, to the proprietary privacy of the intimate sphere." Clarke also points out that when gays and lesbians do gain entry to the public sphere (for example, through gay marriage), it is only by conforming to a "heteronormative standard." "These heroically bland affirmations," he writes, "pay for admission with immiserating disavowals." To be sure, here Clarke is discussing the public sphere, not civil society, but it is easy to see how the same restrictions would play out in both.

Closely allied to the feminist and queer critiques of civil society is that of postcolonial studies, which challenges the Eurocentric perspective of the Western debate, with its focus on the tension between an autonomous individual, usually thought of as male, and the state and includes only open, secular institutions based on voluntary membership. This perspective, according to postcolonial scholars, fails to do justice to the ways in which non-European societies achieve social integration, safeguard civility, and exercise solidarity. Taken together, the feminist, queer, and postcolonial critiques call for greater attention to the gendered, social, sexualized, and racialized borders of actually existing civil societies, in particular to processes of inclusion and exclusion not just through discourses but also through the social, political, and cultural practices that create meaning and shape perception and thus also action—including disruption and even violence.

Given the strength and range of feminist critiques of civil society, one may well ask whether feminism needs civil society. Many feminist scholars believe that, with some modification, the concept can be useful. First, civil society must be conceptualized more from its borders. From a gender perspective, the boundaries between civil society and the private sphere are particularly problematic. The family should be recognized as a key institution of civil society, albeit with sensitivity toward its heteronormative implications. Second, civil societies must be historicized and analyzed in their specific contexts but also as competing entities within a single national or transnational context. Third, feminist scholars must develop a nonnormative comparative and descriptive perspective on civil societies that is open to differences in political and social structures and experiences. In regard to these points, the contributions of two feminist philosophers are extremely useful: Iris Marion Young's description of the public as "messy" and Nancy Fraser's notion of "multiple publics." Finally, feminist scholars must integrate into their analysis the various negative tendencies of civil society and must conceive of civil society as an open historical project.

[*See also* Citizenship; Civil Rights; *and* Human Rights.]

BIBLIOGRAPHY

Calhoun, Craig, ed. *Habermas and the Public Sphere*. Cambridge, Mass.: MIT Press, 1992. Important reflections on Habermas's concept, including feminist perspectives by the philosophers Nancy Fraser and Seyla Benhabib and the U.S. historian Mary Ryan.

Chambers, Simone, and Will Kymlicka, eds. *Alternative Conceptions of Civil Society*. Princeton, N.J.: Princeton University Press, 2002. Contains important critiques of classical theories, including Anne Phillips, "Does Feminism Need a Conception of Civil Society?"

Clarke, Eric O. *Virtuous Vice: Homoeroticism and the Public Sphere*. Durham, N.C.: Duke University Press, 2000. Queer perspective on civil society and the public sphere.

Cohen, Jean L., and Andrew Arato. *Civil Society and Political Theory*. Cambridge, Mass.: MIT Press, 1992. Comprehensive synthesis of classical and critical concepts.

Einhorn, Barbara, and Charlotte Sever. "Gender and Civil Society in Central and Eastern Europe." *International Feminist Journal of Politics* 5, no. 2 (2003): 163–191. Points to gendered limitations of the new civil societies in post-Communist Europe.

Fraser, Nancy. "Rethinking the Public Sphere: A Contribution to the Critique of Actually Existing Democracy." *Social Text*, no. 25/26 (1990): 56–80. Feminist critique of Habermas.

Ginsborg, Paul. "Family, Civil Society, and the State in Contemporary European History: Some Methodological Considerations." *Contemporary European History* 4 (March 1995): 249–273. Makes the case for including the family in conceptualizations of civil society.

Habermas, Jürgen. *The Structural Transformation of the Public Sphere: An Inquiry into a Category of Bourgeois Society*. Translated by Thomas Burger. Cambridge, Mass.: MIT Press, 1989. First published in German in 1965. A somewhat abstruse but important historicization of the concepts of civil society and the public sphere.

Hann, Chris, and Elizabeth Dunn, eds. *Civil Society: Challenging Western Models*. New York: Routledge, 1996. Important collection of postcolonial critiques.

Keane, John. *Civil Society: Old Images, New Visions*. Stanford, Calif.: Stanford University Press, 1998. An important overview of theoretical trends.

Pateman, Carole. *The Disorder of Women: Democacy, Feminism, and Political Theory*. Cambridge, U.K.: Polity Press, 1989. Foundational feminist critique of Western political theory.

Young, Iris Marion. "State, Civil Society, and Social Justice." In *Democracy's Value*, edited by Ian Shapiro and Casiano Hacker-Cordón, pp. 141–162. New York: Cambridge University Press, 1999. Nuanced feminist critique of classical Western concepts.

KAREN HAGEMANN AND SONYA MICHEL

CIVIL WAR

This entry consists of three subentries:

United States
Russia
Central America

United States

The American Civil War of 1861 to 1865 culminated a period of growing sectional tension. Historians continue to debate the causes and meaning of the conflict and recently have turned their attention to how gender shaped the war and, conversely, how the war shaped gender.

In the North, middle-class ideology granted women an autonomous sphere of influence in the domestic arena. From the 1820s some of these women began challenging the legal power of husbands to deny wives control over their income, wages, property, bodies, and children. In contrast, the gender ideology of Southern planters granted women no separate sphere and subordinated white women and black slaves to the authority and power of male heads of households and slave masters. These differences influenced sectional politics as political parties endorsed diverse gender roles and family practices. Democrats in both the North and the South upheld the patriarchal model of male rights and female dependence, whereas the moderately antislavery parties—Liberty (1840), Free Soil (1848), and Republican (1854)—debated women's roles and adopted abolitionist views of slavery as an institution contrary to the formation of proper families.

Women's Work for the War. Once the war began, gender ideology structured women's work for the war on the home front. In the North, where women had considerable experience with benevolent and moral-reform associations, activists quickly organized to aid soldiers. They knitted socks and gloves, rolled bandages, collected supplies, and raised funds. Gradually this activity was rationalized and centralized through the U.S. Sanitary Commission and its primary auxiliary, the Women's Central Association of Relief. Some female volunteers became paid professionals in state and local branches of the association. Southerners, in contrast, vociferously debated the limits of female civic activism. Women generally conducted themselves within boundaries set by male opinion-makers. In cities, churches sponsored volunteer aid societies and soldiers' relief associations, bringing women together to raise funds or sew uniforms, cartridge bags, and bandages. On the Southern home front, women's efforts tended to be individual rather than collective and local rather than sectional.

Nursing bridged the home and war fronts. Dorothea Dix received a military commission as the Union army's first superintendent of women nurses, with authority to select and place her charges in military hospitals. Volunteers struggled against the popular belief that their natural delicacy hindered them in coping with battlefield conditions, and as single women they faced suspicion about the propriety of working closely with men whose separation from home might have undermined their morals. To counter these fears Dix accepted only women over thirty-five who displayed good conduct, serious disposition, neatness, sobriety, and an industrious work ethic. She believed that nurses required no training because nature had prepared women to be helping hands. By July 1862 the need for nurses had grown beyond the supply of volunteers, so the army offered wages to entice a broader range of recruits. Nurses came to see themselves as professionals with career potential, which promoted conflicts with military surgeons and threatened the male monopoly on medical practice.

Southern elite women undertook nursing only in the company of male relatives, leaving white women of lesser social status, slaves, and free blacks to fill the need. Popular opinion depicted nurses as masculinized, either because of their attraction to such work or as a result of the work. The Confederacy began recruiting nurses late in 1862, remunerating them for their labor. Protected from lusty soldiers by marital or widowed status, elite women such as the sixty-year-old Alabama widow Sophia Calmer Bibb turned homes and schools into hospitals. President Jefferson Davis so admired Bibb's efficiency that he permitted her to supplement her dwindling medical supplies from military warehouses. She generated considerable controversy, however, by providing the same care to prisoners of war as to Confederate soldiers.

Some 450 women served in the military. Of the 250 who have been identified, 70 percent fought for the Union and 30 percent for the Confederacy, in ranks from private to major. They enlisted and fought as men, transforming their gender by adopting male dress, demeanor, body mechanics, and behaviors, such as drinking, smoking or chewing tobacco, cursing, gambling, fistfighting, and even womanizing, to obscure their sex. Evidence suggests that some men ignored these soldiers' sex so long as they could count on the quality of their soldiering. Women occasionally recognized and protected each other by serving and bunking together. The majority were discovered as casualties or by accident. Women often went to war with family. The sisters Mary and Mollie Bell enlisted and served together. Others fought alongside fathers, brothers, or husbands. Their motives for enlisting included a desire to accompany loved ones or to take revenge for those lost in war, patriotism, adventure, good pay, and escape from the constraints on women in civilian society. Whatever their reasons for enlisting, women, like men, stayed out of duty and comradeship.

Slave women accompanied Confederate troops as laundresses and cooks. Those fleeing their masters sought refuge in contraband camps under the command of the Union army. Serving the troops facilitated their release from harsh camp conditions and prevented commanders from returning them to slavery. After the war, reconstituting families and establishing black familial, marital, and parental prerogatives drove slaves to embrace emancipation as much as a transformation of labor relations. White racism and black masculinity combined largely to subordinate black women to men, encasing their urban entrepreneurship in marital households and subjecting rural women to the labor discipline of male household heads. Nevertheless many black women contested returning to husbands' and fathers' assumption of privilege and power, relying upon their own household economies to support themselves.

Long-Term Results. Wartime changes in gender ideology and relations rarely overturn patterns of dominance and subordination permanently. As the Southern fiction of slave servility and natural dependence dissolved, the subordination of white women remained as the one dependency upon which white men constructed their sense of independence. Northern victory ended slavery with its overlapping categories of kinship and property that had constrained Southern white women's access to the domestic rights acquired by Northern women. Reconstructed state legislatures except South Carolina's eased laws regulating women's place in the family to permit divorce, maternal custody of children, and married women's right to control their own wages. Expanded private rights helped win white Southern women's public support for a postwar, postslavery social order that augmented white male supremacy. The "protection" of dependent white women by white men became a pretext for terrorism of black women and men, as well as a mechanism for upholding white racial supremacy.

Historians disagree about war's effect on Northern gender ideology. Older notions of female benevolence competed with new ideas of public service in wartime, debates over paying wages to nurses, centralizing the corporate functions of soldiers' aid for purposes of efficiency, associating benevolence with public government rather than private charity, and using funds for administrative as well as charitable purposes. This has led some historians to emphasize continuity, arguing that roles remained consistent with prewar assumptions of gender difference, and has led others to assert that war reinforced emerging ideas of greater gender similarity.

A lasting contribution of the war stems from the rules governing military conduct, drafted for the Union army by Francis Lieber, a professor at Columbia University. In April 1863 the secretary of war issued General Orders No. 100, charging federal forces to distinguish between combatants and noncombatants, protect women, and guard the "sacredness of domestic relations" in hostile territory. The Lieber Code prohibited wanton violence against all persons and defined rape as a crime subject to penalty of death. It served as a model for the Hague and Geneva conventions, as well as for recent international treaties defining rape as a war crime.

[*See also* Abolition and Anti-Slavery Movement; Barton, Clara; Civil Rights Movement; Dix, Dorothea; Healing and Medicine; Military; Racism; Rape; Slavery; *and* United States, *subentries* Nineteenth Century *and* Modern Period.]

BIBLIOGRAPHY

Blanton, DeAnne, and Lauren M. Cook. *They Fought like Demons: Women Soldiers in the American Civil War.* Baton Rouge: Louisiana State University Press, 2002.

Clinton, Catherine, and Nina Silber. *Divided Houses: Gender and the Civil War.* New York: Oxford University Press, 1992. An anthology describing how the Civil War transformed gender roles and attitudes toward sexuality among Americans.

Faust, Drew Gilpin. *Mothers of Invention: Women of the Slaveholding South in the American Civil War.* Chapel Hill: University of North Carolina Press, 1996.

Hartigan, Richard Shelly, ed. *Lieber's Code and the Law of War.* Chicago: Precedent, 1983. An introduction to, and the full text of, the Union Army's General Orders No. 100 governing its conduct toward enemy soldiers and civilians.

Leonard, Elizabeth D. *All the Daring of the Soldier: Women of the Civil War Armies*. New York: W.W. Norton and Company, 1999.
Leonard, Elizabeth D. *Yankee Women: Gender Battles in the Civil War*. New York: W. W. Norton and Company, 1994. How the wartime nurse Sophronia Bucklin, the physician Mary Walker, and the aid worker Annie Wittenmyer challenged the gender ideology of their day.

LEE V. CHAMBERS

Russia

The civil war in Russia (1918–1920) was a contest for political power between Reds (Bolsheviks), Whites (monarchists and others), and Greens (independent peasant groups). Battles ranged over European Russia and Siberia, causing women of all social classes to suffer from hunger, cold, disease, and deprivation. Roughly a million men died in combat, with three times that many men and women dying from epidemics and some 5 million from the famine of 1921–1922. Seven million children were left orphaned and wandering the city streets and railways by 1922. Millions of women were left without breadwinners.

Yet the civil war was also a time of changing gender norms, both because of larger social processes taking place (urbanization and deurbanization, changing landholding patterns in the villages, changing work in the cities) and because of the new commitments made in the February Revolution of 1917, which brought down the tsar, and the October Revolution, which brought the Bolsheviks to power.

Women's potential for service in the military was a hotly debated topic from the moment of the war's outbreak in spring 1918. In March 1918 the Communist Party called for universal training of the adult population without distinction of sex. In practice this meant obligatory military training for males with voluntary training for only a few women workers and peasants.

The exact number of women serving in the Red and White armies is unknown. Soviet sources (much prone to make legends out of women's involvement) claim that in general women served in a range of positions directly associated with the war: as telephone operators, spies, supply agents, translators, secretaries, switch controllers on the railroads, and local police. The 1920 census recorded a figure of 66,000 women in the Red Army (2 percent of the total). Of these some 60 percent were in administrative work behind the lines, while 40 percent were in medical work, mostly nursing, both behind the lines and at the front. Some 50,000 women trained as "Red sisters," nurses who not only brought physical comfort to the wounded but also presents and propaganda from the party and the Soviet state. Overall some one hundred women were awarded medals for bravery (out of fifteen thousand total medals).

However, quite a number of Bolshevik women, some of them well known in Soviet history, did play prominent roles in the army, including Evgeniia Bosh (1879–1925), Larisa Reisner (1895–1926), and Rosalia Zemliachka (1876–1947). Bosh was notorious for ordering the violent suppression of rebellions in Penza, southwest of Moscow; in Astrakhan, on the Caspian Sea; and in Gomel, Belarus. Reisner became an icon of the revolution and the civil war, a symbol of Bolshevik flamboyance, serving as a commissar in the Red fleet, spying behind the lines of the White Army, and writing articles praising the revolution. Zemliachka gained notoriety for her masculine attire and her alleged participation in the cold-blooded mass execution of White forces in the Crimea at the end of the war.

Women made some gains during this period. Peasant women increased their representation in the village assemblies. Often the younger generation, the sons who had fought in the Red Army and their wives, were able to break away from the older generation and form their own households, a net gain for women because of the oppressive controls otherwise exerted by their mothers-in-law. Women in the cities formed an increasing part of the workforce. Their overall percentage of the total industrial workforce had already increased from 25 percent in 1913 to 40 percent in 1917. By 1920 women constituted 46 percent of labor in heavy industry; in the city of Petrograd, women made up 65 percent of all civilian jobs. Despite their access to paychecks, women workers found that the civil war brought intense hardship in the absence of reliable sources of both food and fuel, only partially offset by new Bolshevik policies on equal rights in work and in marriage. Terrible material scarcity crippled state-sponsored efforts to relieve women's domestic burdens.

Special propaganda efforts were made to appeal to women workers and peasants more generally to spread the word about the new regime and help win the civil war. Several prominent women in the Bolshevik Party, including Nadezhda Krupskaia (1869–1939), Inessa Armand (1874–1920), and Alexandra Kollontai (1872–1952), served on so-called agitation trains and boats that traveled the country. Women were targeted in part because men were in such short supply. Yet even more important was the perception that women possessed certain qualities that made them indispensable. In general, it was alleged, they could influence the mood of society, "setting the tone" of vigilance and fighting instead of despair. They could shame their menfolk, making them feel embarrassed to appear on the streets when they should be at the front. They could provide caring hands and tender hearts that would remind male soldiers of the benefits of Soviet power. Their sharp eyes would ferret out swindling and mismanagement.

The civil war affected the nascent Women's Section of the Communist Party, known as the Zhenotdel, in a number

Russian Civil War. A Bolshevik female regiment, 1919. AKG-IMAGES

of ways. It legitimized the call for women's participation in public activities on the grounds that the Bolshevik state was protecting women and hence had a right to ask for their participation in return. The military culture forced the Women's Section to put national priorities first—helping the Red Army, fighting against desertion, trying to obtain food and fuel for the population. At the same time, however, the chaos of the civil war benefited the Women's Section as women workers and peasants increasingly turned to it for assistance in obtaining scarce resources, finding job training, and settling disputes at the local level.

Paradoxically the Russian civil war mobilized women both on the front and at home on the grounds of their new equality yet appealed to women in terms that continued to uphold stereotypes of women as the managers of the home and as those who could present the caring side of the regime. While the regime promulgated ideas of women's equality, it had few resources to implement actual services. The real gains in terms of numbers of child care centers and so on would have to wait until the post–civil war years.

[*See also* Armand, Inessa; Communism; Kollontai, Alexandra; Krupskaia, Nadezhda; Russia and Soviet Union; *and* Zhenotdel.]

BIBLIOGRAPHY

Clements, Barbara Evans. *Bolshevik Women.* Cambridge, U.K.: Cambridge University Press, 1997.

Clements, Barbara Evans. "The Effects of the Civil War on Women and Family Relations." In *Party, State, and Society in the Russian Civil War*, edited by Diane P. Koenker, William G. Rosenberg, and Ronald Grigor Suny. Bloomington: Indiana University Press, 1989.

Goldman, Wendy Z. *Women, the State, and Revolution: Soviet Family Policy and Social Life, 1917–1936.* Cambridge, U.K.: Cambridge University Press, 1993.

Stites, Richard. *The Women's Liberation Movement in Russia: Feminism, Nihilism, and Bolshevism, 1860–1930.* Princeton, N.J.: Princeton University Press, 1978.

Wood, Elizabeth A. *The Baba and the Comrade: Gender and Politics in Revolutionary Russia.* Bloomington: Indiana University Press, 1997.

ELIZABETH A. WOOD

Central America

Three Central American nations—Guatemala, El Salvador, and Nicaragua—suffered political upheaval, civil warfare, and attempted revolution throughout the twentieth century because of conflict over land, because of the control of political life and economic wealth by local elites, because of the exploitation of ethnic populations, and because of the continual interference of the United States in what it believed to be its legitimate sphere of influence. Nationalist and socialist movements, led by Farabundo Martí in El Salvador and Augusto Sandino in Nicaragua, were violently crushed by the armed forces in the early 1930s, and Guatemala's first social democratic government was overthrown in a coup backed by the U.S. Central Intelligence Agency in 1954. All three nations underwent decades of repressive rule, under the dynasty of the Somoza family in Nicaragua and under military-backed oligarchies in El Salvador and Guatemala.

Revolution and Its Aftermath. This era of repression led to the formation of armed, left-wing revolutionary groups in Central America in the 1960s and 1970s. The Frente Sandinista de Liberación Naciona (FSLN; Sandinista National Liberation Front) overthrew the dictatorial regime of Anastasio Somoza Debayle on 19 July 1979. However, the revolutionary Sandinista government was ousted in the 1990 elections, after several years of civil conflict with the contras, a U.S.-backed counterrevolutionary movement. In El Salvador, the Frente Farabundo Martí de Liberación Nacional (FMLN; Farabundo Martí National Liberation Front) fought the government to a stalemate, and the conflict ended in a cease-fire and peace accord in 1992. The Unidad Revolucionaria Nacional Guatemalteca (URNG; Guatemalan National Revolutionary Unity) guerrilla forces were weaker, so a U.N.-sponsored peace process ended the civil war in 1996.

Women constituted around a third of active participants in the three Central American movements, counting those who fought or lived at the front—in the liberated zones and clandestinely—or who provided essential support services, such as safe houses, communications, and logistics. The FMLN had 40 percent female membership (30 percent combatants and 20 percent leadership), whereas the URNG had 14.8 percent women combatants and 25.2 percent women political cadres. Women flocked into the FSLN between 1977 and 1979, and they led several successful military operations.

The high rate of female participation in each of these revolutionary groups was the result of a number of factors that freed women from traditional roles. The growth of agro-exports forced men to migrate in search of agricultural labor, creating many female-headed households that then migrated to the urban centers, where women entered the labor market and became involved in urban social movements linked to the progressive wing of the Catholic Church. As the emergent guerrilla movements shifted their strategy away from small cells of rural-based combatants to a mass mobilization strategy, the women members and leaders of these urban groups acted as a crucial bridge that enabled the revolutionary movements to communicate their message to, and garner support from, urban civil society. Compared to male militants, women militants tended to be more highly educated, to come from families with some tradition of resistance, and, if young, to enter through student politics.

At least 120,000 women were widowed in Guatemala, their husbands the victims of military or paramilitary executions. Many also suffered sexual assault at the hands of the army or local civil-defense patrols. Resultant shame and community rejection led to a loss of self-esteem and often of livelihood, because women lacked formal rights to their dead husband's land and could retain access only with the support of their family or community.

Counterinsurgency campaigns destroyed hundreds of Maya villages in Guatemala and displaced around one million people internally, a situation that drove between 100,000 and 200,000 to migrate, mainly illegally, to the United States and drove up to 350,000 over the border to Mexico. Of the 45,000 registered refugees, most were women with children, as was the case with the 31,000 registered Salvadoran refugees who migrated to Honduras. Up to a fifth of El Salvador's 8 million population migrated, mostly to the United States. Half were women, many of whom took work as domestics and who in the early twenty-first century continued to contribute significantly to an annual U.S. $2.5 billion in remittances sent back to El Salvador, keeping many communities afloat. In Nicaragua, women lost their husbands and sons on both sides of the conflict.

Women were underrepresented and had little influence on the peace accords, with gender issues regarded as secondary to demobilization and eventual power sharing. In Nicaragua, demobilized contras, Sandinista soldiers, and unemployed agricultural workers all competed for land tenure, and women were sidelined, even though legislation under the Sandinistas gave women equal rights to land ownership. In El Salvador, women were initially treated unequally when land was allocated to former combatants, and they encountered more problems than men did in obtaining loans, technical assistance, and voter registration cards. In Guatemala, senior women in the URNG and the Assembly of Civil Society succeeded in getting gender issues incorporated into the peace accords; four of the seven substantive agreements included women's equality. However, reintegration programs responded to the presumed needs of single male combatants, with no provision for women, orphaned children, and other war victims. Most demobilized FMLN women went back to domestic work, were disadvantaged in the labor market, suffered health problems related to posttraumatic stress, and found reintegration into their families very difficult.

Women's Postrevolutionary Organizations. Women within the revolutionary movements responded by forming independent groups, such as the Asociación de Mujeres por la Dignidad y la Vida (Association of Women for Dignity and Life; known as Las Dignas) in El Salvador, to pursue a feminist agenda within their parties and the new governments. Advocacy groups such as the Coordinadora Nacional de Viudas de Guatemala (CONAVIGUA; National Coordinating Committee of Guatemalan Widows), set up in 1988, campaigned to claim compensation for husbands killed in the counterinsurgency.

Women even formed coalitions across ideological lines. In Nicaragua, Las Madres del Héroes y Mártires (Mothers of the Heroes and Martyrs) joined forces with the mothers of dead contras to press for the rights of low-income peasant women. Feminists and conservatives in El Salvador lobbied on gender quotas for electoral lists, responsible paternity, and new legislation and social services to address domestic violence. In Nicaragua, when the new government cut support for day care, domestic violence services, family planning, and marriage counseling and urged a return to "traditional" family values, women mobilized to retain the gains in gender equality won under the Sandinistas. The Coalición Nacional de Mujeres (National Women's Coalition) supported women's candidacies, agreed on a minimum agenda for the political parties, and won special women's police stations. Women in the FSLN and FMLN were also able to persuade their parties to institute internal gender quotas (30 percent and 35 percent, respectively), which resulted in a significant rise in female representation in the legislature.

Women's direct and indirect involvement in the revolutionary movements, as well as in the human rights and advocacy groups that emerged to counteract the terrible toll exacted by the civil wars, thus gave birth to a newly confident and autonomous Central American women's movement that has been able to secure gender-positive policies and legislation, even in inauspicious postconflict contexts.

[*See also* Central American Countries; Feminist Encounters of Latin American and Caribbean Women; Guatemala; Indigenous Cultures; Menchú, Rigoberta; Migration; Mothers of the Plaza de Mayo; Refugees; *and* War.]

BIBLIOGRAPHY

Green, Linda. *Fear as a Way of Life: Mayan Widows in Rural Guatemala*. New York: Columbia University Press, 1999. Looks at the impact of war on indigenous women.

Kampwirth, Karen E. *Feminism and the Legacy of Revolution: Nicaragua, El Salvador, Chiapas*. Athens: Ohio University Press, 2004. Examines gender equality after civil war.

Kampwirth, Karen E. *Women and Guerrilla Movements: Nicaragua, El Salvador, Chiapas, Cuba*. University Park: Pennsylvania State University Press, 2002. A study of the reasons why women join guerrilla groups, based on more than two hundred interviews with women combatants and militants, looking at both structural and personal factors.

Luciak, Ilja A. *After the Revolution: Gender and Democracy in El Salvador, Nicaragua, and Guatemala*. Baltimore: Johns Hopkins University Press, 2001. A comprehensive study of women's campaign for gender equality in three postconflict revolutionary movements.

Menchú, Rigoberta. *I, Rigoberta Menchú: An Indian Woman in Guatemala*. Translated by Ann Wright. London: Verso, 1984. Autobiographical account by Nobel Peace Prize winner of the Guatemalan army's repression of the indigenous community, which became controversial when the anthropologist David Stoll questioned the veracity of some of its details.

Metoyer, Cynthia Chavez. *Women and the State in Post-Sandinista Nicaragua*. Boulder, Colo.: Lynne Rienner, 2000. How gender equality was rolled back after 1990.

FIONA MACAULAY

CIXI, EMPRESS DOWAGER (1835–1908), the last powerful ruler of the Chinese Qing dynasty (1644–1911). As he lay dying at the hands of the unifier of the Manchu tribes in the early seventeenth century, the leader of the Yehe-Nara clan vowed that a woman would avenge his clan. The vow came true in 1851 when the future Empress Dowager Cixi entered the Forbidden City and was designated a concubine of the fifth rank to the Xianfeng emperor (r. 1850–1861). Upon the birth of the emperor's only son, her son, she moved up in the ranks. When the emperor died in 1861, her son at the age of five became the Tongzhi emperor (r. 1862–1875). With the help of Prince Gong, the Xianfeng emperor's brother, and others, Cixi staged a coup d'état and overthrew the five-man regency that her husband had established. As Empress Dowager Cixi ("motherly and auspicious"), she served as coregent with the Empress Dowager Ci'an ("motherly and calming"; 1837–1881), the first wife of the Xianfeng emperor, who had no male children and never really exercised much power. Although there had been other empress dowager regents in Chinese history, criticisms and regulations of this practice began in 107 C.E. One regulation was that these female regents had to rule behind a curtain during imperial audiences. They could not rule openly or ascend the throne, in the way that Queen Victoria of England (r. 1837–1901) did.

As was also true of Queen Victoria, several men, most notably Prince Gong (1833–1898) and the Manchu bannerman Ronglu (1836–1903), advised and supported Cixi's rise to power. When the Tongzhi emperor died, he was succeeded by Cixi's nephew, the three-year-old Guangxu emperor (r. 1875–1908), whose legitimacy of succession was questioned. By this time China was in decline because of external wars with Britain, France, Germany, and Japan, as well as because of internal turmoil caused by secret societies, the Taiping Rebellion and other rebellions throughout the country, natural catastrophes, and social and economic dislocations. British merchants and Western missionaries, the growth of Western imperialism and capitalism, global trade issues, and corruption in government all worsened the situation. In 1898 the Guangxu emperor reached maturity, and Cixi retired to the Summer Palace, but she kept informed about the events in court. The death of Prince

Empress Dowager Cixi of China. Painted in 1903 by Katherine A. Carl for the Louisiana Purchase Exposition in Saint Louis. FREER GALLERY OF ART AND ARTHUR M. SACKLER GALLERY ARCHIVES, SMITHSONIAN INSTITUTION, WASHINGTON, D.C./PHOTOGRAPHER XUNLING, NEGATIVE SC-GR 247

Gong in 1898 and the urgent need for reform opened the door for Kang Youwei (1858–1927) and others to persuade the emperor to order radical changes in the government. Known as the 1898 Hundred Days of Reform, the program was a threat to many holders of power. The conservative faction assisted in a coup d'état in September 1898 that reestablished Cixi's regency for the third time and confined the emperor to the palace because of "illness."

The natural disasters, ever-increasing foreign imperialism, and other problems contributed to the rise of the antiforeign Boxers, who were defeated by foreign troops in 1900. Cixi, who had fled to the West with the court, ordered one of her supporters, the accomplished diplomat Li Hongzhang (1823–1901), to negotiate a peace treaty with the foreign powers. When she returned to Beijing, Cixi implemented some reforms and interacted with some of the foreigners. This did not stem the tide of rebellion and eventual revolution in 1911. Cixi died on 15 November 1908, one day after the Guangxu emperor himself died. Her last act, on 14 November 1908, was to install Puyi, the last emperor of the Qing dynasty.

Cixi was interred, surrounded by gold and gilded-bronze ornaments, in the Dingdongling tomb complex in a lavish site with temples, gates, and pavilions, covered with gold leaf. In July 1928 the local warlord and Guomindang general occupied her tomb and stripped the complex of its ornaments, opened Cixi's coffin, threw her corpse on the floor, and stole all of the jewels.

In contrast to the long reign of Queen Victoria, which saw the expansion of the British Empire, Cixi's reign saw a dramatic decline in the power and prestige of China. Both women saw sweeping institutional reforms in domestic and foreign policies and growing trade relations. Both women also experienced a lessening of power as others gradually took over. Both women painted and were patrons of the arts. Cixi also founded, in 1906, the Beijing Zoological Garden, later the first zoo to breed the giant panda. In the opinion of some scholars, Cixi's actual power surpassed that of Queen Victoria, even though Cixi ruled for a shorter period of time (forty-seven years to Victoria's sixty-four). Confucian historians, opposed to females in political power, and foreign writers, especially British adventurers and diplomats in China, have portrayed Cixi's three regencies in a negative light and blamed her for the fall of the Manchu Aisin-Goro clan's Qing dynasty (1644–1911).

[*See also* Boxer Uprising; China, *subentry* Imperial Period; *and* Taiping Rebellion.]

BIBLIOGRAPHY

Chung, Sue Fawn. "The Much Maligned Empress Dowager: A Revisionist Study of the Empress Dowager Tz'u-hsi (1835–1908)." *Modern Asian Studies* 13, no. 2 (1979): 177–196.

Seagrave, Sterling, and Peggy Seagrave. *Dragon Lady: The Life and Legend of the Last Empress of China*. New York: Knopf, 1992.

Warner, Marina. *The Dragon Empress: Life and Times of Tz'u-hsi, 1835–1908, Empress Dowager of China*. New York: Macmillan, 1972.

SUE FAWN CHUNG

CLARK, SEPTIMA POINSETTE (1898–1987), educator and civil rights leader. Septima Poinsette Clark was born in Charleston, South Carolina, the daughter of Peter Porcher Poinsette, a caterer, and Victoria Warren Anderson; she married Nerie Clark in 1920 and had one surviving child, a son; Nerie Clark died in 1925. Clark taught in South Carolina schools from 1916 to 1956 and for many of those years she also belonged to the local chapter of the National Association for the Advancement of Colored People (NAACP). When the Charleston school board found out about her NAACP membership, however, they demanded that she sever her ties to the organization. She refused. The board quickly fired her, and almost immediately Myles Horton of the Highlander Folk School, an interracial and nontraditional school in Tennessee, hired her, first as the school's director of workshops and later as its director of education. In this capacity Clark developed citizenship classes that were designed to prepare black adults, the vast majority of whom were both poor and politically powerless, to register to vote. The work was tedious, as Clark explained: "In '56 and '57 night after night I sat down and wrote out a citizenship education program which would help illiterates to learn to read and write, so they could register to vote" (Morris, p. 152).

Clark's program proved to be enormously popular and before long requests for classes were pouring into Highlander. As she traveled around the South setting up these classes, Clark was especially vulnerable because of the determined segregationist opposition to these efforts. Regardless of how dangerous her travels became, however, Clark was always careful to dress the part of the middle-class school teacher she had been for so many years. Clark's middle-class demeanor notwithstanding, she always displayed a great deal of sensitivity to the plight of the poor, and she was determined to make sure that they recognized their own worth.

Despite the difficulties and the dangers she faced, Clark's commitment never wavered; but as she worked tirelessly, first at Highlander, and later with the Southern Christian Leadership Conference (SCLC), she received little public recognition for her efforts. Yet, whether she received public recognition or not, Septima Clark's work was a critical part of the civil rights struggle of the 1960s. Her middle-class existence never limited her vision, and her notion of civil rights transcended social and economic class. Because of her efforts, there was a dramatic rise in the number of black registered voters in the South. Her work had an impact on the balance of political power in many southern communities and also set the stage and provided a positive example for future leaders.

[*See also* Baker, Ella; Civil Rights Movement; Hamer, Fanny Lou; *and* Parks, Rosa.]

BIBLIOGRAPHY

Morris, Aldon D. *Origins of the Civil Rights Movement: Black Communities Organizing for Change*. New York: Free Press, 1984.

Young, Andrew. *An Easy Burden: The Civil Rights Movement and the Transformation of America*. New York: HarperCollins, 1996.

CYNTHIA GRIGGS FLEMING

CLASS

This entry consists of two subentries:

Overview
Comparative History

Overview

Class as a concept to locate human beings in society arose in the era of the French Revolution of 1789 as an alternative to the hierarchical division of the former regime that divided people into the three orders (or estates)—clergy, nobility, and commoners—legal distinctions that were abolished by the revolutionary government. As citizens of a future society that freed them from being just subjects of a monarch and promised them liberty and equality, people would be more properly categorized on grounds that reflected their functions in agriculture, commerce, and industry, especially their relationship to property and to the power and authority that wealth conferred. Class in its modern sense of a social stratum of persons who share certain characteristics of economic position and social identity was linked to the market-driven status of men and ascribed to members of their families. It was neither gender nor race neutral.

As a category, class has been used both heuristically to explain social positions and practices and descriptively as an element of personal identity. Most class analysis and politics has tended to ignore women, whose status was generally determined by their relationships to their fathers or husbands. But women's lives as individuals are vitally affected by material conditions that vary with socioeconomic position. Class determines access to choices, comforts, even children. It affects degrees of health and well-being, including nutrition and medical care, access to birth control, literacy, even life expectancy. Class ascription, for men and family as well as for women, also depends on women's behavior; in nineteenth-century Europe, for example, whether or not a woman was employed outside the home came to define middle-class family status.

Postrevolutionary societies included only a tiny group with inherited titles—the aristocracy—and a small stratum of landowners, or gentry. Increasing numbers of persons who with the expansion of commerce and industry owned nonlanded wealth came to be known as "bourgeoisie," a term originally used to designate residents of townships (or burghs) but now applied to property holders, including professional practitioners and skilled craftsmen who owned the tools of their trade and managed their own workshops. All others made up a vast pool of less skilled agrarian and industrial workers, persons who owned only their labor power. This group included large numbers of men and women who made their living as domestic servants, an occupation that into the twentieth century surpassed others in providing employment for women who worked outside their own homes. Class analysis, however, typically ignores domestic work, including the unpaid labor of women as wives and mothers.

Since the mid-nineteenth century, when Karl Marx published his landmark analysis of political economy, *Das Kapital* (1867; English trans., *Capital*), and organized the International Workingmen's Association to prepare for a class struggle of propertyless workers that he designated "proletarian" against property owners that he labeled "bourgeois," the language of class and interpretations of class relationships have reflected a Marxian philosophy of history. In this view, society moves forward through a succession of conflictual stages toward a "classless" society. Even those who reject this interpretation of historical progress through class struggle tend to define class in materialistic terms, in which class is an attribute of individuals based on the assumed existence of economic structures, and class consciousness reflects individuals' relationship to the means of production. For Marx, in the era of industrial capitalism, the two main classes were the owners of property and the laborers who worked for them, the "bourgeoisie" and the "proletariat." Alternatively, the main class divisions might be labeled aristocracy, middle class, and working class, or expanded to include upper and lower segments of the latter two. Or they might be collapsed into two, owners and working class, rich and poor. In any case, the "quintessential worker" was male: farmer, factory worker, miner, craftsman, or unskilled laborer.

When applied to women, the standard terminology of class presents major conceptual difficulties. Until second-wave feminist scholars of the late 1960s and the 1970s encouraged social thinkers to include women in their studies, the unit of analysis for questions of class was the family, and class was defined by the dominant male's position. Using the female individual as the basis of analysis raises new questions. What determines a woman's class? Is it established at birth by the status of her father? Does it change with marital status? How is it affected by her own economic activity? The importance of these questions is complicated by historical studies that show the important role that female workers played in early capitalist accumulation and development, demonstrating, for example, how many women, especially the poor and women of color, always worked for pay or how as wives they contributed substantially to family enterprises attributed to men alone. Furthermore, since the late twentieth century, middle-class married women have entered the paid labor force en masse.

An interpretation of class that includes women points to several other ways in which women impact concepts of class. Explanatory schemes based on men's occupations in Europe in the early industrial period often neglect the place of employees in the occupations that proliferated to serve the increasingly large-scale manufacturing and distribution centers and the new public institutions of later industrial times. The invention of the typewriter and standardization of recordkeeping offered opportunities as office clerks, and the establishment of great department stores to purvey ready-to-wear and relatively low-priced goods to growing urban populations required sales work that drew large numbers of young, increasingly literate, women into paid employment. The expansion of public education attracted many women to teaching. This created a so-called new class of workers, sometimes described as "petit bourgeois," that by the mid-twentieth century had become overwhelming female and does not fit neatly into the class models formulated earlier.

Nor do class definitions apply easily to other huge categories of women workers, employees in the sweatshops of the garment and other industries and purveyors in small-scale trade, frequently of food products or household implements. Millions of women labor in their own homes or so-called family workshops, where they perform piecework for subcontractors, often on a seasonal basis, usually earning low pay despite long hours. These types of employment proliferated in European cities at the turn of the twentieth century, as an adjunct to factory production, and they persist around the world today, now described as the "informal economy." Despite their numbers, these workers often remain outside class analysis, neither bourgeois nor proletarian. Conventional class designations also ignore the importance of women's roles as consumers of an increasing variety of manufactured goods and as managers of households in ways that serve to achieve and maintain the class status of their families. Class analysis also needs to take note of the wealthier women whose education, leisure, and philanthropic traditions have provided them with opportunities to enter the "public sphere," to campaign for various causes, ranging from the abolition of slavery, prohibition of prostitution, and women's rights to patriotic pursuits.

Definitions of class have broadened over recent decades to encompass aspects of social experience relegated by Marx (and other early political economists) to secondary importance. New formulations, drawing on the testimony of workers themselves, underscore the importance of everyday life in families and communities in the creation of class consciousness. Derived from behavior and social life, class necessarily includes relationships of gender that themselves reflect social definitions of femininity and masculinity.

Historians have now demonstrated how cultural assumptions about class and gender work together to influence ideas and customs that affect both home and workplace. For example, the demand for a "family wage" that arose in the mid-nineteenth century reflected both workingmen's fears of competition for jobs with lower-paid female labor and their desire for upward mobility into a middle class marked by full-time housewives. Having a wife at home became a marker of successful masculinity, reflecting an ideal of "separate spheres" that assigned market activity as well as engagement in public and political life to men and confined women to a "private" realm of domestic life, which was alleged to be better attuned to women's nature. Women's sexual and social behavior also served as proxies for class. Class attribution and consciousness thus reflected moral as well as economic considerations.

As a leading category of social analysis, class reached its apogee in the 1970s. In the 1980s, new approaches based on gender and ethnicity began to replace class as a dominant analytic tool. Historians challenged the view of causality that identified the Industrial Revolution as a great divide in the human experience of class and gender. In the 1990s following the collapse of Communism, with its heritage of Marxist ideology in Russia and Eastern Europe, some questioned whether "class" any longer had relevance as a theoretical construct. Others sought to reformulate it to include women. Postmodernists also challenged conventional forms of class analysis by emphasizing language and linguistic practices as more than representations of experience, seeing them as important factors in the production of the cultural knowledge and power once accorded exclusively to economic structures. The practice of reducing the economy to material forces and reducing class to supposedly objective criteria, discounting cultural, political, and ideological factors, is now considered by many analysts to be untenable. Today notions of class reflect the complex, interrelated effects not only of gender but also of ethnicity, race, nationality, and other attributes on individual and group consciousness, and include the recognition that individuals have multiple, overlapping, and changing experiences of class.

[*See also* Domestic Service; *Origin of the Family, Private Property, and the State, The*; *and* Food.]

BIBLIOGRAPHY

Dimant, Robert and Chris Nyland, eds. *The Status of Women in Classical Economic Thought*. Cheltenham, U.K., and Northampton, Mass.: Edward Elgar, 2003.

Hall, Catherine. *White, Male, and Middle Class: Explorations in Feminism and History*. New York: Routledge, 1992.

Hall, John R., ed. *Reworking Class*. Ithaca, N.Y.: Cornell University Press, 1997.

Neale, R. S., ed. *History and Class: Essential Readings in Theory and Interpretation*. Oxford: Blackwell, 1983.

Rose, Sonya O. "Proto-Industry, Women's Work and the Household Economy in the Transition to Industrial Capitalism." *Journal of Family History* 13, no. 2 (1988): 181–193.

Ryan, Mary P. *Cradle of the Middle Class: The Family in Oneida County, New York, 1790–1865*. Cambridge, U.K., and New York: Cambridge University Press, 1981.

Scott, Joan Wallach. "Women in *The Making of the English Working Class*." In her *Gender and the Politics of History*. New York: Columbia University Press, 1988.

Thompson, E. P. *The Making of the English Working Class*. London: Victor Gollancz, 1963.

MARILYN J. BOXER

Comparative History

Women's historical experience of "class" includes a vast range from privilege to poverty. Conventionally defined on the basis of men's occupations and wealth, women's class position reflected the status of their male-dominated families. In the past century, many women in some societies have attained a class position based on their individual achievement. This development varies widely depending on rural or urban setting, nationality, religion, and other factors. It reflects both changing economies that opened new educational and employment opportunities to many women and also feminist success in challenging women's prior legal status as perpetual minors subject to male tutelage. For many others, however, age-old systems of female subordination continue to define class experience on the basis of gender.

European Origins. As a way of dividing society into social strata, class rankings reflect gradations of socioeconomic and political power as they appeared in nineteenth-century Europe, where political economists developed analytical frameworks appropriate to a new era of industrial capitalism. Although reinterpreted more recently to include powers derived from education and cultural knowledge as well as from material goods, concepts of class nevertheless continue to reflect this origin. As Europe expanded, missionaries, colonial officials, and industrialists carried across the globe ideas, attitudes, and customs drawn from European experience that affected the ways women experienced class position, economic development, and concomitant changes in gender relations. A comparative study that includes the class experiences of women outside Europe and the countries included in the "West" draws on this vocabulary of class, but it also raises the question of how well such concepts fit many societies in the contemporary world.

The paradigmatic case for analyzing the class position of women in the past and observing changes over several centuries of commercial and industrial capitalist development has been England, where the agrarian and industrial revolutions that brought about these changes first took place. Following the agrarian revolution of the seventeenth and eighteenth centuries, during which the consolidation of small landholdings and tenancies into larger, more productive units of cultivation deprived vast numbers of people of traditional means of subsistence, class divisions deepened. Some women, related to men of high economic achievement, found themselves enjoying new leisure and opportunities. Although they played an increasingly important (though underappreciated) economic role as consumers, the loss of women's traditional productive activities and the ideology that consigned and confined them to unpaid domestic work left these women dependent on the productivity of men. Many others, lacking adequate support—especially large numbers of young women—migrated from the countryside, often to become domestic servants in urban areas. Others survived through employment in textile mills or eked out a minimal living in industrial homework. To borrow the formulation of the historian Gerda Lerner, "the lady" experienced economic development a world apart from the "mill girl."

Class Effects of Separation of Home and Work. The resulting model of middle-class family life, often associated with the Victorian age, had its origins with the separation of home and work. Beginning in the early modern period, guildsmen in textiles, garment making, and other crafts distinguished between their own professional work in public settings and labor performed by women at home, which they considered "nonprofessional." Having a "nonworking" wife became a mark of successful masculinity, and the role of "housewife" became a status symbol of meritorious femininity. Some middle-class French women who sewed for pay at home kept their shutters closed to hide their labor.

This middle-class, gendered division of labor gave rise to an ideology of separate spheres, which had as its corollary a pattern of paid labor that concentrated poorer women in low-paid, labor-intensive industries, generally performing tasks seen as extensions of female domestic chores. By the 1830s and 1840s, most wage-earning women worked in domestic service or, especially if married, in a few trades such as sewing linens, dressmaking, and millinery. Since women worked outside the home for pay only if they could not afford to stay home, their wage labor was considered temporary and provided little security or opportunity for advancement. Paying many women less than subsistence wages, this system supported maximum capital accumulation. To assist the least fortunate, especially in their maternal roles, public welfare agencies later took on many formerly familial (that is, patriarchal) functions. By the late decades of the nineteenth century, protest against the unregulated exploitation of female and child laborers in industry led to passage of legislation designed to protect them by limiting the conditions of their work. Marginalizing women workers in factories, these laws had the collateral effect of exacerbating their exploitation in unregulated, "sweatshop" labor.

As the power of private, family production gave way to large-scale, male-dominated industry, women of the wealthier classes enjoyed new choices. Like French women of the "leisure classes," they might cling to traditional roles centered on childbearing, family, and religious rituals. They could fill their days with educating their children, planning social gatherings, or performing acts of charity, such as creating crèches for less fortunate working mothers. The introduction of electricity and public health measures such as running water, and the invention of household appliances, reduced the burden of household chores for those who could afford them and led to improved health and life expectancy for all, but these things spread more slowly in poor neighborhoods than in rich ones. Public education systems brought enhanced opportunities for education, an important factor in reducing women's fertility.

Other wealthier women, enjoying access to both education and household help, could seek new roles in public affairs, often as extensions of traditional female roles as caregivers. Writers such as Elizabeth Gaskell (1810–1865), a minister's wife, called attention to the condition of the poor in industrial cities, such as the sufferings that she depicts in *Mary Barton* (1848). Set in Manchester in the "hungry forties," Gaskell's novel portrays two extremes in women's class experience. She contrasts workers uprooted from the idyllic green countrysides of their birth to dwell in the cold hovels of smoke-blackened cities, where their children die of malnutrition, with well-fed mill owners' daughters who fuss about perfume and flowers. Drawing on religious convictions, some women of Gaskell's class formed antislavery and prison reform associations. Still others supported colonial ventures by organizing female emigration societies and creating nursing associations to tend the ill in West Africa and other parts of the British Empire, judging applicants for the new profession on the basis of "ladylike" appearance and manners. German women of similar situation served patriotic goals by sewing flags and staffing soup kitchens. Feminist movements, which women's literacy and leisure made possible, arose in most countries of Europe and North America, and they campaigned with considerable success for more equitable treatment in education, employment, family status, public policies, and the law. In the so-called second wave of feminism in the 1960s and 1970s, women demanded personal freedoms and educational and employment opportunities equal to those of men, as well as greater representation in decision making. In the early twenty-first century, transnational feminist networks encourage new women's movements on a global scale.

As bearers of class and national identity, women reformers and professional workers served as conduits of middle-class values to working-class families at home and to whole populations abroad. Gender relations based on the middle-class model spread to all parts of the world, following on the heels of advancing capitalism, socialist revolutions, and national liberation movements. Under the influence of European expansion, both capitalist and socialist regimes brought change to largely agrarian economies, disrupting traditional family authorities and tribal powers and determining women's varied experiences of class. The class position of women today reflects not only relationships with men, family, and law, but increasingly also the practices of multinational corporations that represent "global capitalism."

Global Expansion. Case studies drawn from around the globe show many similar effects of changing economic conditions on women's class experiences. Recurring themes include a shift from a family or household-based system of production to a mercantile or industrial economy; the emergence of increased class disparity, in which the term "housewife" represents a symbol of class status; the concentration of economic power in men's hands; the use of low-paid female workers as a "reserve labor force" that fluctuates with demand; the migration of girls and young women to urban areas for employment, especially as domestic servants; the continuing role of textile and garment-making industries as the dominant source of demand for female employment, accompanied by the proliferation of sweatshops; the persistence of racialized class disparities; and an increase in commercialized sex work. On the other hand, improvements in public

Soup Kitchens. Volunteers *(right)* stir pots to feed impoverished families. "Soup kitchen Strousberg at the Dorotheenstraße in Berlin," by Otto Brausewetter, 1870. AKG-IMAGES

health, educational opportunities, and nontraditional, higher-status employment for a privileged minority frequently follow. In most industrial nations, reformers of both sexes (often with widely different aims), male workers, and defenders of the status quo combine political strengths to enact "protective legislation" that restricts female employment. Feminists of many nationalities strive to improve the overall status of women in male-dominated societies.

Capitalist expansion on a global scale brought class-defining developments to women of all continents. Depicted at the international exposition in Paris in 1889, the middle-class model was transported to Algeria and Tunisia, where colonists taught indigenous Muslim women lessons in home economics, hygiene, and thrift as practiced in France, believing that they would also shed their veils and adopt what the French considered superior, "modern" standards of class behavior. By the mid-twentieth century, the word "housewife" had entered the Malay language. In the 1980s a leftist government in West Bengal assumed that married women worked for pay only to supplement men's earnings, in home-based occupations such as needlework seen as extensions of domestic chores.

The transformation of women's economic activity also reached Latin America. In Argentina in the first half of the nineteenth century, most woolen fabrics were produced at home by provincial women who spun yarn on wooden spindles and weaved coarse flannels on handlooms. Following the introduction of railways into interior regions in the 1870s, the introduction of machine production and increasing imports from abroad led to a new division of labor in which women's work was degraded. As women became "deskilled," many moved into textile factories in Buenos Aires, working for a burgeoning export market in which Argentinean wool increasingly supplemented or supplanted more expensive European products. The spread of sewing machines and the subdivision of labor into smaller operations requiring less skill and paid on a piecework basis became the preferred method of manufacture, often taking place at home or in sweatshops. Women thus became part of a working class. In Oaxaca, Mexico, women weavers faced similar losses in status and income. The marginalization of women workers in this way was a worldwide phenomenon, in which the degradation of working women's skills helped maximize profits and make cheaper products available to consumers, while pushing women into the proletariat or working class.

But efforts to institutionalize class divisions based on imported normative standards encounter cultural differences that make a single model of development and class ascription untenable. In some societies, economic and political power may depend more on inherited position than on wealth. In Africa, for example, not "class" in its European sense, but rather kinship systems determine individual status. Gender, birth order, and age, along with family lineage, all play important roles. In some sub-Saharan countries, women traditionally exercised power as "queen mothers" or tribal chiefs. Elderly women served as mediators and judges in resolving disputes. Women's work traditionally included agricultural labor that seemed inappropriate feminine behavior to colonists. In Ivory Coast (Côte d'Ivoire), where Baulé women were the primary producers of crops, colonizers bypassed women and attributed controlling interests in land to men. They reinforced West African patriarchy by designating men as heads of household for census and tax purposes, and they registered family or tribal land ownership in male names. They further marginalized women by introducing implements wielded by men, the male-driven plow replacing the women's handheld hoe. When cash crops grown for distant markets replaced food for local consumption as the chief source of employment, they also displaced many women who earned their livings as purveyors and traders in local marketplaces. In Lagos, Nigeria, Yoruba women's market associations lost power to large, overseas operations. Elsewhere in Nigeria, the Igbo "Women's War" of 1929, led by rural women, drew many thousands into a revolt protesting a census of women and rumored taxation by colonial administrators, showing the continuing power of indigenous women. Some Igbo women used their domination of trade in palm oil to gain wealth and status in international import-export markets. African women's economic behavior often conflicted with European class and gender ascriptions.

The dominant effects of changing structures of gender roles in production and marketing, however, have been "deskilling" and the concentration of working women in relatively few occupations, where supply exceeds demand for labor, creating the "industrial reserve army" foreseen by Karl Marx in the mid-nineteenth century. This facilitates what today is termed "labor flexibility," a major factor in reducing costs of production and increasing the profitability of investments. A comparative study of female employment and unemployment in Japan and Germany in the 1990s found that "flexibility" in the labor market was provided disproportionately by female workers. In many countries of Asia, Europe, and North America, a dramatic increase in the labor force participation of middle-class as well as working-class married women in the late twentieth century greatly expanded the "buffer labor force." It also challenged the attribution of class status based on the unemployed housewife model.

By the late twentieth century, global capitalism had produced a global labor market, including pools of low-paid women workers that, parallel to the earlier European experience, were concentrated in industrial homework for the textile and garment-making industries. In Mexico City, the garment industry employed some twenty to twenty-five thousand seamstresses, mostly working at home. Others made toys and plastic implements or assembled small electronic appliances such as irons and radios, while men worked on larger devices. Since the 1960s *maquilas*, or plants for assembling electronic and other consumer objects for export, have opened in Mexico and other countries in Latin America, including Colombia, the Dominican Republic, Guatemala, and Nicaragua, because female labor can be hired in these places for low wages and limited benefits. In the presence of this vast pool of labor, costly protections established by law or union contract can be avoided. The "feminization of poverty" runs parallel to the accumulation of capital. Class disparities among women persist, with indigenous, black, and mixed race women among the poorest.

The migration of women from countryside to cities, accompanied today by movement from poorer to richer nations, is another pattern that now appears on a global scale. In some cases, migrant women, whose employment options are limited by cultural and linguistic factors as well as gender, find opportunity in industrial homework. In Britain, women of South Asian heritage constitute a ready pool for labor for subcontractors. In other instances, they provide domestic service, often enabling women with higher earning potential to pursue their own employment outside the home or to participate in public affairs. In capitalist Chile, women of the middle and upper classes became free to enter politics. By the late 1960s, many women with university education served in public administrative offices in Chilean cities, usually employing other, less-advantaged women to serve as surrogates in their domestic roles. Similarly, in revolutionary Nicaragua in 1982, middle-class women strove to write a new constitution that would advance women's rights. Their working-class country women sustained a long strike against *maquila* industries. In Thailand in the 1980s, women who migrated from agricultural areas to become the primary work force for labor-intensive industries gained new salable skills and new concepts of workers' rights that led them to conduct major strikes in textile plants. Women organized grassroots labor movements also in Bangladesh, the Philippines, Chile, and Nigeria.

Class distinctions, however, may count for less than other differences. For example, in recent years, Filipinas of middle-class as well as working-class background have moved to Taiwan, whose government legalized the import of labor in 1992. While in the past migration has served to expose poor, untrained, young women to middle- or upper-class standards of consumption and behavior, in this instance the immigrant workers often equal their employers in education and class status. Racialized cultural differences constitute the primary dissimilarity.

The lack of opportunity for other well-paid employment has also augmented the numbers of women drawn into the sex trade. Illegal trafficking in persons, largely women and children, has increased along with other forms of mobility, especially between eastern Europe and the West. According to a 2002 report, more than 175,000 women from former Communist countries in eastern Europe, along with others from Southeast Asia, West Africa, and China, are drawn into the commercial sex trade each year, pushed by the loss of employment in public services that followed the collapse of Communist regimes and pulled by the promise of better employment opportunities.

If, as some critics suggest, feminism, by encouraging nontraditional roles for women, has served as an "unwitting midwife" to industrial and postindustrial capitalism, it has also demanded ameliorative efforts. The Communist regime in China, whose socialist heritage included a commitment to improve the female condition, sponsored party work to enlist neighborhood women and organize housewives. This "state feminism" transformed women, who were "subaltern by both gender and class," into "speaking subjects." Women ranging from prostitutes and barmaids to sixty- and eighty-year-olds who rarely left home were reported to parade in Shanghai on International Women's Day in 1951. The United Nations' naming of 1975 as the International Year of the Woman and the recognition of women's rights as "human rights" at its Beijing conference in 2000 gave impetus to efforts to improve the status of women on a global scale. Transnational feminist networks now call attention to the inequalities suffered by women as a result of market-driven trends as well as of traditional gender norms.

Although concepts of "class" derived from nineteenth-century Europe can be applied to women only with reservations, feminist movements are frequently denigrated on an alleged class basis. Dismissed by leftist critics as "bourgeois" at the turn of the twentieth century in Europe, this dubious class construction soon spread to Asia and Latin America, appearing in China and Vietnam, Brazil, Chile and Peru, and elsewhere. Today changing the status of women sometimes encounters resistance as a form of Western imperialism.

[*See also* Capitalism; Communism; Industry and Industrialization; *and* Socialism.]

BIBLIOGRAPHY

Benería, Lourdes, and Martha Roldán. *The Crossroads of Class and Gender: Industrial Homework, Subcontracting, and Household Dynamics in Mexico City*. Chicago: University of Chicago Press, 1987.

Chuku, Gloria. *Igbo Women and Economic Transformation in Southeastern Nigeria, 1900–1960*. New York: Routledge, 2005.

Davidoff, Leonore, and Catherine Hall. *Family Fortunes: Men and Women of the Middle Class, 1780–1850*. Chicago: University of Chicago Press, 1987.

Hanawalt, Barbara, ed. *Women and Work in Preindustrial Europe*. Bloomington: Indiana University Press, 1986.

Lerner, Gerda. "The Lady and the Mill Girl: Changes in the Status of Women in the Age of Jackson." In her *The Majority Finds Its Past: Placing Women in History*. New York: Oxford University Press, 1979.

Rose, Sonya O. *Limited Livelihoods: Gender and Class in Nineteenth-Century England*. Berkeley: University of California Press, 1992.

Smith, Bonnie G. *Ladies of the Leisure Class: The Bourgeoises of Northern France in the Nineteenth Century*. Princeton, N.J.: Princeton University Press, 1981.

MARILYN J. BOXER

CLEOPATRA VII (69–30 B.C.E.; r. 51–30 B.C.E.), the final and best-known pharaoh of the Ptolemaic dynasty of ancient Egypt. Cleopatra VII was the third child of Ptolemy XII (r. 80–51 B.C.E.), who was called Auletes (the Flute Player). Following Egyptian pharaonic tradition, she was the presumed daughter of Auletes' sister and wife, Cleopatra V, but she was, in fact, the biological daughter of an Egyptian concubine.

Cleopatra was the product of two woman-affirming cultures. Ancient Egyptian metaphysics embraced inclusive dualism ("both/and") and gender complementarity. All women were considered to carry the divine within them, no matter their social class or status. They and all roles associated with them were highly valued. The ancient Macedonian culture of which the Ptolemies were a part had a similar attitude toward women, especially toward those of the ruling class. Consequently, Cleopatra was raised in two traditions that nurtured her intellect, self-reliance, and self-confidence.

Cleopatra was born and educated in Alexandria, a city literally at the crossroads of trade and cultural channels among Africa, Asia, and Europe. Her education followed the same curriculum as that of daughters of pharaohs centuries before her, and it put great emphasis on scholarship. Because of Macedonian influence, Cleopatra's curriculum probably included the canonical works of Greek literature. She learned mathematics and sciences, including astronomy and medicine, from the Egyptian masters in Alexandria at the time. Photinus, an expert in mathematics, titled one of his works *The Canon of Cleopatra*. By all accounts Cleopatra's intellectual abilities were remarkable, and as a young girl she revealed an extraordinary gift for foreign languages. According to the Greek historian Plutarch (c. 46–after 119 C.E.), Cleopatra rarely used an interpreter and was fluent in several Afro-Asiatic languages including Ethiopian, Hebrew, and Arabic. She was also considered a gifted artist and musician.

When Auletes died in 51 B.C.E., Cleopatra, then eighteen, became the pharaoh, the seventh Cleopatra. Following pharaonic tradition, her male copharaoh was her younger brother Ptolemy XIII (r. 51–47 B.C.E.), who was twelve years old. As pharaoh, Cleopatra VII became the "Daughter of Isis" and "Mistress of the Two Lands," reigning autonomously over Upper and Lower Egypt. The challenge that Cleopatra faced was daunting. Her father had left the governing infrastructure of Egypt in shambles; famine and political unrest made the situation worse, as did the deflation of the Egyptian currency. Most important, Egypt had become more dependent on Rome. Furthermore, Cleopatra had to contend with family intrigues to dethrone her and the manipulation of her copharaoh by advisers hostile to her.

Cleopatra proved that she was up to the challenge. She devalued the currency by one-third to increase exports essential to the Egyptian economy. She won over the Egyptians by allying with them culturally and restoring ancient Egyptian religious rites. She also addressed Egypt's foreign affairs: she was determined to avoid war with Rome, which had spread its imperialistic wings into Asia Minor and Africa.

Cleopatra dealt with Rome through a series of goodwill gestures, but she miscalculated by supporting Pompey the Great (Gnaeus Pompeius Magnus; 106–48 B.C.E.) in his rivalry with Julius Caesar (100–44 B.C.E.). This support angered the Alexandrians, and that anger combined with family political intrigues to encourage a revolt against her. She was forced to leave Alexandria; while she was away, Pompey was assassinated in Egypt. Cleopatra's future now depended on Julius Caesar.

Caesar summoned Cleopatra and Ptolemy XIII to negotiate their differences. After initial wariness, Cleopatra decided to go to Alexandria. Fearing her brother's spies, she arrived secretly late at night and was smuggled into Caesar's apartments. Both her ingenuity and her beauty impressed him. The point at which Cleopatra, twenty-one, and Caesar, fifty-two, became lovers will never be known, but their relationship began because of political expediency. Caesar supported Cleopatra's bid to regain the pharaohship, and in 47 B.C.E. Cleopatra was the ruler of Egypt, ostensibly coruling with a younger brother, Ptolemy XIV, until 45 B.C.E. In fact, however, she shared the reins of power with Caesar. In that year Cleopatra gave birth to her first child, Ptolemy Caesar (later Ptolemy XV; r. 44–30 B.C.E.), nicknamed by the Alexandrians "Caesarion." In 46, Cleopatra accompanied Caesar to Rome.

After Caesar's assassination in 44 B.C.E., Cleopatra returned to Egypt to deal with more family plots and more famine. Rome was never far from her thoughts, and she showed great foresight in not choosing sides between Octavian (Gaius Julius Caesar Octavianus, later the Roman emperor Augustus; r. 27 B.C.E.–14 C.E.), Caesar's grandnephew and adopted son, and Mark Antony (Marcus Antonius; c. 83–30 B.C.E.), Caesar's first lieutenant. When Cleopatra met Mark Antony at Tarsus in 41 B.C.E., she was twenty-eight and even more astute as a politician than she had been upon meeting Caesar. She once again entered into a sexual relationship to establish a political alliance. Although history fixates on the seemingly endless parties and pleasures in which Cleopatra and Antony indulged, Cleopatra never lost sight of the main point of her relationships with Romans: autonomy for Egypt. It is a challenge to assess the validity and objectivity of some of these stories about Antony and Cleopatra because the stories are found in texts by authors who often had political agendas.

In 40 B.C.E., six months after Antony had left Egypt, Cleopatra gave birth to twins: Cleopatra Selene (Moon) and Alexander Helios (Sun). In 37, Cleopatra and Antony married according to an Egyptian rite. By now the relationship between Antony and Octavian was very strained, despite the marriage of Antony to Octavian's sister, Octavia. As a result of Antony's marriage to Cleopatra, Octavian began a smear campaign against Cleopatra, the effects of which still reverberate today. No attack was too unseemly, and by 32 B.C.E. Rome had declared war against Cleopatra. Following the Battle of Actium in 31 B.C.E., the fate of Cleopatra was sealed. Upon the erroneous report that Cleopatra was dead, Antony fell on his sword. He was taken to Cleopatra and died in her arms. Cleopatra, not wanting to experience the humiliation of Octavian's triumphal procession, committed suicide with two of her most devoted servants. The legend of Cleopatra asserts that it was the bite of an asp that killed her, but it is not certain that that was the method Cleopatra used. She was thirty-nine.

Soon after her death, Octavian destroyed nearly all her likenesses. The result has been that throughout modern times both popular culture and historical scholarship have debated endlessly the question of her beauty (or lack of it) and of her ethnic and racial heritage. This, in turn, has caused the neglect of the political, economic, and intellectual accomplishments of Cleopatra. The debate is important, nonetheless, as a barometer of the prevalent racial and gender discourse.

Though it is misleading to apply modern racial classifications to Cleopatra, the symbolic identification that many women of color (particularly African Americans) feel with Cleopatra is understandable. Cleopatra's treatment at the hands of men of the dominant group, her demonization in the historical record, the erasure of her intellect in discussions of her, and the obsession with her appearance are all issues to which women of color, in particular, can relate.

Cleopatra remains a historical enigma. Was she a brilliant political strategist or a brainless sex addict? Clearly she learned early to mold her persona to please whoever was in power. She presented herself to Julius Caesar as a doe-eyed innocent in need of a mentor. For Antony, she became his fantasy come to life: wealthy, beautiful, and confident. She was a woman in control of her own sexuality. It is this fact that made her such a threat to the rigid patriarchy that was so prevalent in Rome.

[*See also* Egypt, *subentry* Ancient Period; Europe, *subentry* Roman Empire; *and* Monarchy.]

BIBLIOGRAPHY

Flamarion, Edith. *Cleopatra: The Life and Death of a Pharaoh.* Translated by Alexandra Bonfante-Warren. New York: Harry Abrams, 1997.

Grant, Michael. *Cleopatra.* London: Weidenfeld and Nicolson, 1972.

Haley, Shelley P. "Black Feminist Thought and the Classics: Re-membering, Re-claiming, Re-empowering." In *Feminist Theory and the Classics*, edited by Nancy Sorkin Rabinowitz and Amy Richlin, pp. 23–43. New York: Routledge, 1993. Discussion of the relevance of Cleopatra to black women in America.

Hamer, Mary. *Signs of Cleopatra: History, Politics, Representation.* London and New York: Routledge, 1993. Traces the influence of Cleopatra in later centuries.

Hughes-Hallett, Lucy. *Cleopatra: Histories, Dreams, and Distortions.* New York: Harper and Row, 1990.

Plutarch. *Fall of the Roman Republic: Marius, Sulla, Crassus, Pompey, Caesar, Cicero—Six Lives.* Translated by Rex Warner. Revised edition with introduction and notes by Robin Seager. Harmondsworth, U.K., and New York: Penguin, 1972. See especially the lives of Caesar and Cicero.

Plutarch. *Makers of Rome, Nine Lives: Coriolanus, Fabius Maximus, Marcellus, Cato the Elder, Tiberius Gracchus, Gaius Gracchus, Sertorius, Brutus, Mark Antony.* Translated by Ian Scott-Kilvert. Harmondsworth, U.K., and Baltimore: Penguin, 1965. See especially the lives of Mark Antony and Brutus. Both these compilations are made from biographies in Plutarch's *Parallel Lives.*

SHELLEY P. HALEY

CLITORIDECTOMY. *See* Female Genital Mutilation.

CLOTILDA (c. 475–545), queen of the Franks who converted her husband, King Clovis, from paganism to Roman Catholicism. She was the daughter of Chilperic, the Catholic king of the Burgundians, and his wife, Cartena. Clotilda married Clovis in 492.

The decline of the Roman Empire and the barbarian invasions of the fifth and sixth centuries left western Europe with limited administrative organization. The formal hierarchy of the Catholic Church, through its system of established bishoprics, was able to some extent to fill that void. The conversion of the settled populace of Gaul to Catholicism was nearly complete by the time of Clotilda, but the majority of the barbarian tribes that invaded the region practiced Arianism, a form of Christianity that denied the divinity of Jesus. Some groups, including the Franks, continued to embrace paganism. The relationship between church and state was very much in flux, and the preeminence of Catholicism was by no means assured at the end of the fifth century. Clovis was a conspicuously successful warrior-king, and his conversion was instrumental in establishing the church-state relationship that came to characterize European political and religious history.

Clotilda was a fervent Catholic, and her efforts to bring Clovis to her faith were patient but insistent. Over the objections of the king, she had their first child baptized, but the boy died shortly thereafter. Undeterred, Clotilda had their second child baptized as well. He, too, sickened soon after his baptism but recovered. Though Clovis made no apparent attempt to restrict his wife's religious practices, he saw no reason to embrace them.

It was not until he was engaged in an especially intense battle with the Alemanni tribe in 496 that Clovis reconsidered his faith. Facing imminent defeat he called upon "Clotilda's God" and promised to be baptized if that god would grant him victory. A seemingly miraculous turn of fortunes allowed Clovis to rally his troops and vanquish his enemy. Upon confessing his pledge to Clotilda, it was she who summoned Bishop Remi of Rheims to instruct the king in his new religion and to perform his baptism. The Frankish people quickly followed their king's example.

Clovis's conversion to Catholic Christianity established the first formal link between church and state that is typically associated with historical notions of European kingship. Equally important was the bond he succeeding in creating with the people he had subjugated. By acknowledging their religion as the true faith he eased the assimilation of the Frankish people into Gaulish culture. The subsequent military successes of Clovis enhanced and spread the influence of both the Catholic Church and the Franks through much of northern Europe. The Holy Roman Empire, created three centuries later under Charlemagne, had its roots in Clovis's conversion and the inextricable link between church and state initiated by Clotilda.

Clotilda lived for another thirty-four years after her husband's death in 511. She was a generous benefactor to the church, and it is for this, coupled with her history-making role in the conversion of her husband and his people to Roman Catholicism, that she is venerated as a popularly declared saint.

[*See also* Christianity.]

BIBLIOGRAPHY

Harrison, Dick. *The Age of Abbesses and Queens: Gender and Political Culture in Early Medieval Europe.* Lund, Sweden: Nordic Academic Press, 1998.

Pernoud, Régine. *Women in the Days of the Cathedrals.* Translated and adapted by Anne Côté-Harriss. San Francisco: Ignatius Press, 1998.

AMANDA S. QUINBY

CODES OF LAW AND LAWS

This entry consists of eleven subentries:

Overview
Ancient Greek and Roman Law
China
Europe
International Law
Islamic Law
Japan
Latin America
Medieval Roman and Canon Law
Russia
South and Southeast Asia

Overview

In almost all of the world's major legal systems, women have historically stood in a different, and inferior, relation to law than have men, and this has been true along three axes: women have not authored laws to the extent that men have, women have been regarded as essentially different from men, and women have been subordinated to men's interests.

Women Have Not Authored Laws to the Extent That Men Have. Laws are man-made rules, and women have simply not been part of the ruling elites that have drafted them. As a result, women have lacked the authority both to define the content of law and also to shape its meaning through subsequent interpretation.

In democratic political systems, women's lack of legal authority has been a direct consequence of women's comparative lack of political power. In democratic countries with civil law (such as in Europe), in which law

U.S. Supreme Court. Sandra Day O'Connor sworn in as a justice of the Supreme Court by Chief Justice Warren Burger as her husband John O'Conner *(center)* looks on, September 1981. COURTESY OF THE RONALD REAGAN PRESIDENTIAL LIBRARY

is codified and in which legislative assemblies draft and pass codes of law, the absence of women's representation in those assemblies has translated directly into an absence of authorial responsibility for laws. In "common law" legal systems (Great Britain, the United States, Canada, New Zealand, and Australia), in which some legal rules are partly or totally produced by judges through the course of opinion writing, the result has been similar although through a less direct route. In the common-law world, women have not been well represented in the political branches of government, in the judiciary, or, until recently, in the legal professions from which judges are drawn. In legal systems embedded in nondemocratic regimes, the exclusion has been even more extensive: women have not shared in the customary devolutions of power that confer appointed or inherited legal authority. The consequence of this lack of authority in both democratic and nondemocratic regimes is that law has not had its roots in the expression of women's will, has not well served women's interests, and has not inured to women's benefit.

Women Have Been Regarded as Essentially Different from Men. Historically, and again in virtually all legal systems, lawmakers have understood women's objective nature—what a woman is—to be fundamentally different from men's, resulting in very different forms of legal regulation and hence very different forms of regulated life. In family law systems worldwide, for example, laws creating and then regulating what it means to be a "wife" have been either subtly or drastically different from laws defining and regulating what it is to be a husband, father, or son. Thus wives, by virtue of various rules of family law, property law, and public law still in force in many legal systems today and until recently in others, have been barred from owning property, cannot enter into contracts in their own name, and have no rights to be free of forced sex or some measure of disciplinary violence imposed upon them by their husbands. In legal systems derived from English common law, until well into the nineteenth century, married women had no legal existence at all apart from their husbands by virtue of the doctrine of "coverture": the wife's legal being was literally merged with that of her husband. In many legal systems where family law is explicitly derived from or dependent upon religious law, divorce is less available to women than to men, and women and men have drastically different rights and duties within the marriage. In those Arab law systems that draw from Islam, for example, wives may have enforceable rights to the economic support of their husbands, but they also have correlative duties of obedience and sexual submission. These rights and duties are not typically reciprocal.

At the same time, laws governing public life have historically excluded women from some measure of participation in various forms of work or civil society. In the West, until well into the twentieth century, laws and legally sanctioned private employment practices barred women from actively pursuing professional careers or trades, from voting, from running for office, from serving in the military, and from participating on juries. Even when employment practices have been relaxed, permitting some participation of women in the world of work, and antidiscrimination laws passed, so as to prevent blatantly discriminatory hiring, employers nevertheless remain legally empowered to pay women less for comparable work and expose their female employees to greater risk and vulnerabilities than their male employees. These laws effectively precluded women worldwide from generating substantial income and from having any presence in the public sphere, at the same time that family law regimes have limited women's power within the family and their control over its assets.

Through sanctions of this sort, family law, estate law, and public law have accordingly created different objective forms of life for women and men. The combined effect of the rules governing relations and distributions of property within the family, and then barring opportunities for work outside of it, has been the impoverishment of women as a class, worldwide. Without property, and without a way to generate income, legal limits on women's mobility and productivity have first confined women to the domestic, familial sphere and then rendered women dependent upon men within that private sphere—creating private hierarchies of dependency rather than webs of interdependency between equals. Women, across widely disparate legal and political systems, are less educated, less productive, less practiced in the arts of war, less capable in the building crafts and practical engineering, less accomplished in all spheres of culture, and less involved in the worlds of scientific discovery and in practical invention.

These differences in both the law and the objective forms of life to which those laws lead typically have been justified by either perceived or real differences between female and male nature. Women, the world's legal philosophers, jurists, and legislators have argued, by virtue of biology, nature, God's will, or their own choice are simply more inclined to family life, more nurturing of children, more domestic, and more emotional—and thus less autonomous, less powerful, less political, less rational, less intellectual, and less culturally inclined than men. This ideology of natural difference undergirding legal difference has been reinforced, of course, by parallel perceptions and claims of difference in the cultural, religious, and social norms that govern nonlegal life.

Women Have Been Subordinated to Men's Interests. Along the third legal axis, women historically have not received the full benefits of legal protections against intimate and sexual violence, and consequently, women have not been as safe as men in their intimate or domestic lives. Legal systems worldwide have always contained some sort of prohibition on murder and private assault; yet legal systems worldwide, at the same time, have failed to fully criminalize men's violent assault against their wives, female relatives, or sexual intimates. In Anglo-American legal systems, for example, the doctrine of chastisement, by which the state allowed the husband and father of a family to use moderate corporal punishment to discipline, or chastise, their wives, remained fully in force until the beginning of the nineteenth century. Even today in a number of countries (both Eastern and Western), the murder of an adulterous or sexually promiscuous woman by a male relative, although a crime, is often excused or mitigated because of the injury to his or his family's honor occasioned by the victim's misbehavior (in some Arab and South American countries) or, alternatively (in the common-law world), by the perpetrator's jealous passion that may have been inflamed by the victim's adultery.

As important, women have received only erratic protection against violent rape, even while their voluntary sexual expression has been rigorously regulated. Marital rape, for example, is far more often legitimated, rather than criminalized, by law. Outside of marriage, states have likewise failed to criminalize some violent rapes between some men and some women; have failed to enforce criminal sanctions that do exist against rape; have enforced those sanctions only arbitrarily or only in such a way as to single out disfavored classes of men; or have perversely punished the female victim, rather than the male perpetrator, for the violation of the woman's sexual chastity, particularly where that chastity is viewed as an essential part of her family's or man's honor or property. The result of this lack of protection against intimate and sexual violence has been the construction of one very large class of people—women—who must survive under the rule of two sovereigns who hold the power of the sword over them: the state and its official system of laws, on the one hand, and a man, and his authority, delegated by the state and to which she is subjected, to impose a private law and back it up with force.

Challenging the Inferior Position of Women in Law. Roughly from the eighteenth century to the beginning of the twenty-first, feminist lawyers and activists have challenged all three prongs of this disparate and inferior position of women in law, and with considerable success. Law itself, particularly when coupled with political agitation and educational and cultural reform, has been the vehicle for doing so. In constitutional democracies such as the United States, constitutional "higher law" commitments to equality have provided feminist lawyers one tool by which to challenge state law that differentiates between women and men on the grounds of difference. Thus the legally differential treatment of women in estate law, in public law, in employment law, and in property law, and the differential rights and responsibilities of women and men in public life, have all been attacked as violations of various constitutional commitments, and with striking success, in countries with established constitutional traditions. Laws prohibiting or excessively regulating access to abortion and contraception have been struck as violative of constitutional protections of liberty, privacy, or autonomy.

In a number of states, feminists have been able to fashion legal rights for women—such as a right to be free of sexual harassment at work—by resort to ideals, such as "equality" or "human dignity," that are drawn from their countries' constitutions, common law, or cultural norms. Inadequate protection against violence has been construed, with some success, as a "civil rights violation" and challenged accordingly. In countries in which international law is regarded as binding upon domestic legal regimes, feminists have employed its commands—notably, treaties guaranteeing equal rights of women—to challenge and strike inegalitarian domestic law. In systems of mixed secular and religious law, such as in some Asian and Arab legal systems, secular legalist ideals have been used to challenge discriminatory or damaging religious norms, and religious ideals have been called upon to challenge discriminatory legal interpretations. In countries with new constitutions, and in countries currently drafting constitutions, some measure of women's representation and participation in democratic legislative assemblies is often guaranteed.

Finally, as women's participation in lawmaking grows, legislation explicitly designed to promote women's interests has become increasingly a central, rather than a peripheral or incongruous, part of law's warp and woof. Thus with women's participation in lawmaking on the rise, laws in many countries now protect women's rights to nondiscrimination in labor markets, ensure women's economic security at the time of divorce, ensure mothers of young children economic well-being when those mothers are excluded from remunerative labor because of child-raising responsibilities, and protect women against sexual violence in the home and elsewhere. Law itself, once a primary source of women's inequality, is also now, at times, a shield against harmful or discriminatory private practices, as well as a sword with which to rectify private and public injustices.

[*See also* Adultery; Citizenship; Civil Society; Inheritance; Patriarchy; Property Rights; Rape; Suffrage; *and* Violence.]

BIBLIOGRAPHY

Abu-Odeh, Lama. "The Reform of Egyptian Family Law." *Vanderbilt Law Review* 37 (2004): 1043–1146. An extensive history and comparative analysis of the various influences—Westernization, Islam, and feminism—on contemporary Egyptian family law.

Brownmiller, Susan. *Against Our Will: Men, Women, and Rape.* New York: Simon and Schuster, 1975. One of the first publications to focus the attention of American feminists on rape as an instrument of the social control of women.

Coontz, Stephanie. *Marriage, a History: From Obedience to Intimacy; or, How Love Conquered Marriage.* New York: Viking, 2005.

Ginsburg, Ruth Bader. "Sex Equality and the Constitution: The State of the Art." *Women's Rights Law Reporter* 14 (Spring–Fall 1992): 361–366. A good explication of how the U.S. Constitution's Fourteenth Amendment has been used to further sex equality. The author became an associate justice on the U.S. Supreme Court.

Kittay, Eva Feder. *Love's Labor: Essays on Women, Equality, and Dependency.* New York: Routledge, 1999. Kittay looks at the inequality and dependency that women suffer by virtue of their caretaking roles and at various legal responses to that inequality.

MacKinnon, Catharine. *Sex Equality.* New York: Foundation Press, 2001. This casebook presents legal materials, primarily from the United States but also from Europe, South America, and Africa, on all aspects of women's lives and women's equality and inequality affected by legal regimes.

MacKinnon, Catharine. *Toward a Feminist Theory of the State.* Cambridge, Mass.: Harvard University Press, 1989. This early and now classic book presents a powerful, controversial argument that the point of patriarchy worldwide is the control of women's sexuality and that that control is largely validated, but can also be challenged, through law.

Mill, John Stuart. "The Subjection of Women." *Three Essays.* London and New York: Oxford University Press, 1975. A classic essay by a nineteenth-century feminist and founder of liberalism that assesses women's subordinate position and its causes in marriage, family, and the home, in England and elsewhere.

Nussbaum, Martha. *Women and Human Development: The Capabilities Approach.* New York: Cambridge University Press, 2000. A philosophical defense of liberalism and a critique of multiculturalism that also contains a detailed and subtle comparative account of Indian and U.S. constitutionalism. The author explores how each country's constitution has differently constructed family and religious life and explores the impact of those laws and traditions on women.

Siegel, Reva, and Catherine MacKinnon, eds. *Directions in Sexual Harassment Law.* New Haven, Conn.: Yale University Press, 2004. This volume of essays contains discussions of the varied origins of sexual harassment law in the United States, France, Germany, Israel, and Japan.

ROBIN WEST

Ancient Greek and Roman Law

Systems of law in the ancient world were created by men for men. As a result, women had virtually no public voice or public role, especially in the legal systems of ancient Greece and Rome, and their status was determined not by social or economic position but by their sex and position in the life cycle (unmarried maiden, wife, widow). Even though women played at best a passive role in the creation and development of ancient law codes, they could not be ignored completely. Consequently, laws governing family relations, marriage and divorce, inheritance, and sexual crimes such as rape and adultery came to be the primary loci where legal attention to women appears.

Women in Ancient Greek Law. The texts for understanding the laws of the poleis (city-states) of ancient

The Laws of Gortyn. An ancient Greek legal text, c. 400 B.C.E. GORTYN, CRETE, GREECE/ERICH LESSING/ ART RESOURCE, NY

Greece are scarce: papyrus and stone fragments; the laws of Athens—attributed to Draco (c. 625 B.C.E.), Solon (c. 550 B.C.E.), and lawmakers of the fifth and fourth century B.C.E.—inscribed on stone stele in the Athenian Agora; the laws of Gortyn, a Dorian polis on Crete, also inscribed in stone; the analysis of Greek legal systems by classical philosophers such as Plato, Aristotle, and Xenophon; and a number of speeches prepared by sophist rhetoricians such as Lysias and Demosthenes for litigants engaged in suits before the Athenian Assembly or Areopagus Council. In addition, the Roman historian Plutarch (c. 46–c. 120 C.E.) wrote biographies of the creators of law in ancient Greece, but the temporal distance between Plutarch and his subjects renders him a problematic source. In all of these contexts, women exist only as passive subjects of the law and are more or less invisible in many circumstances. This is particularly true for the laws of Athens, about which modern historians have the most information, although much is both speculative and debated.

Respectable women in Athens were neither seen nor heard, and they were subject to the perpetual tutelage of a *kyrios* (guardian/lord): first their fathers, then their husbands, and finally their sons or brothers. Athenian female citizens had the same legal status as children, the insane, and the mentally incompetent. They were not permitted to control any real property, and their dowries—primarily movable goods and cash—were controlled by their husbands. The only way a female could inherit family property was as an *epikleros*, a daughter who acted as the conduit for family property. If a daughter was the only possible heir, her father was legally obligated to divorce her from her husband, marry her to his closest male relative (who also had to divorce his wife), and ensure that she became pregnant as frequently as necessary until a male heir for the father was born. That grandson then became heir to the family's property.

Athenian laws regarding marriage and divorce inevitably favored men over women. Men arranged their own marriages once they came of age at twenty-one, but girls' marriages were arranged by their fathers. A man could divorce his wife by the simple expedient of sending her back to her natal family and returning her dowry. The father of an *epikleros* could compel his daughter to divorce her husband, as mentioned above. Fathers, it seems, could also initiate divorce proceedings for their daughters without their permission. Although this seems to have occurred only rarely, this paternal privilege might in fact have protected women in unhappy marriages because a father could negotiate an almost immediate remarriage for his daughter, which would preserve the social respectability essential to Athenian women.

Though women did have the right to initiate divorce proceedings against their husbands, they needed compelling reasons for divorce, such as charges of impiety or neglect. In addition, a woman seeking a divorce had to appear before the *eponymous archon* (the head of the government) and charge her husband with the offense. Once she was before the archon, nothing prevented her husband from contesting her charge or even disrupting the proceedings by the simple expedient of bodily removing her from the court, as Alcibiades is said to have done when Hipparete, his wife, appeared before the archon to sue him for divorce (Plutarch). Even if a woman successfully secured a divorce, her status as a respectable woman was compromised: she had to abandon her dowry, and unless her father could negotiate an immediate remarriage, she lost her ability to participate in the religious activities that marked her as respectable.

Athenian women's respectability occupied the legal system in ways beyond the problem of divorce. Of particular concern for a woman's respectability were sexual crimes, especially rape and adultery or seduction. Rape was prosecuted not as a crime of violence against a specific female victim but rather as a crime against that woman's respectability—she was considered shamed—and against the woman's *kyrios* (husband, father, son, or brother). Indeed, the *kyrios* was treated as the real victim of rape, for the penalty for rape was a monetary fine—based on the woman's legal status as citizen, resident alien, or slave—paid to the *kyrios*. Seduction and adultery, considered far more serious crimes, again emphasized the victimization of the woman's *kyrios*. In this situation, both participants were seen as perpetrators, but they suffered different penalties. If the lovers were caught, especially in the act, the wronged *kyrios* could kill the male seducer with impunity, as demonstrated in a famous speech by Lysias, "On the Murder of Eratosthenes," created for a husband charged with the murder of his wife's lover. In the speech, the wronged husband, Euphiletos, presented his murder plot as a reasonable solution to redressing the social stigma of cuckoldry. "Eratosthenes seduced my wife and corrupted her . . . he brought shame on my children and insulted me by entering my house. . . . I did not commit this deed . . . for any other advantage except revenge, as the law allows" (Lysias 1 at Diotima).

On the other hand, instead of killing his adulterous wife, the cuckolded husband was required to divorce her, and she lost both her dowry and her respectability. Seduction was seen as more serious than rape because, according to Lysias, a woman hates her rapist, but an adept seducer turns the woman's affections away from her husband.

If the sources for women in the laws of Athens are sparse, those for women in legal systems in the rest of Greece are scarce indeed. The main sources for understanding the legal system of the Spartan Peloponnesus are the laws of Gortyn, Xenophon's fourth-century B.C.E. treatise on the constitution of the Lacedaemonians (the people of the Peloponnese, controlled by and connected to Sparta), Aristotle's *Politics*, and Plutarch's "Life of Lycurgus." The literary and philosophical texts are not useful in this context because they emphasize the unique status of Spartan women to dramatize the differences between Sparta and Athens and are not reliable as sources for women's actual legal status. The Gortyn law code provides more concrete evidence and demonstrates that Athenian law was not necessarily the norm in ancient Greece.

In Gortyn, women could inherit land and other property from both their natal families and their husbands, and they could dispose of their own property by testament. If a daughter was the sole heir, she was required to marry her paternal uncle in a system seemingly similar to the Athenian *epikleros* system. Unlike in Athenian law, however, if her uncle was unacceptable to her and the family could not come up with a solution, she was permitted to marry another of her choosing so long as he was a member of the family, and she still received a portion of the inheritance and control of her portion. Spartan women had control of their dowries, although these were embedded in the marital estate until the marriage ended through death or divorce, but unlike men, a woman was not permitted to adopt a man as her heir. Divorce, too, seems to have been more egalitarian: a judge presided over the settlement, and the woman was permitted to retain her dowry and whatever "she has woven" if the husband was found to be at fault (Law IV). Unlike Athenian law, the laws of Gortyn considered rape and adultery to be roughly equivalent crimes and assigned monetary fines for both. Both are clearly considered to be crimes against the family rather than crimes against specific women.

Women and Roman Law. The evidence from Roman republican and imperial codes of law is much more comprehensive than that from ancient Greece. From the Laws of the Twelve Tables (c. 450 B.C.E.) to the Corpus Juris Civilis (Body of Civil Law, c. 550 C.E.), Roman law developed over an eleven-hundred-year period into a thoroughly organized and institutionalized legal system, complete with lawyers, law courts, judges, and clearly defined litigants. Moreover, Roman law intersected with virtually every aspect of the Roman citizen's life, and a substantial amount of juridical literature is devoted to the status and role of women in Roman society.

The central institution of Roman society was that of the paterfamilias, the male head of the household, who exercised sovereign authority over all other members of the family, including sons, unmarried daughters, and servants. Like Athenian women, Roman women were under perpetual tutelage to some male authority figure: fathers, husbands, sons, or other male relatives who assumed the status of paterfamilias. They could not make wills, sign contracts, engage in trade, or appear in the law courts unless they were accompanied by a "tutor," who oversaw the activity. Such tutelage limited female activity. Nevertheless, late in the empire (first century B.C.E.–sixth century C.E.), tutelage was largely pro forma, and women engaged in many activities, such as acting as municipal patrons—wealthy elites who paid for the building of monuments and temples and sponsored entertainments such as gladiatorial games, sporting contests, and theatrical productions—and owning and managing considerable property, all activities that women of the republic (510 B.C.E.–first century B.C.E.) found closed to them.

Early in the republic, the paterfamilias also had absolute authority over his wife and the wives of his sons through the practice of marriage "with *manus*" (guardianship). In this form of marriage, the bride's position in her natal family was transferred to her family by marriage, and she became, in the eyes of the law, the daughter of her husband, with status equivalent to her own children. As a member of her husband's family, a wife could inherit property from her husband's estate, and after his death her sons were obligated to maintain her as a member of their own families. However, marriage with *manus* also meant that divorce was nearly impossible to obtain and that women could not inherit from their fathers estates beyond their dowries.

Later in the republic a new form of marriage developed: marriage without *manus*. In this form of marriage the bride remained a part of her natal family and technically under the tutelage of its paterfamilias. There were significant social advantages to marriage without *manus*. Divorce was more easily obtained, and a woman could be freed from the authority of her paterfamilias, a situation that grew more common later in the empire. Yet marriage without *manus* made women's lives less secure in some ways, especially because they had no legal status in their husbands' families, to which their own children belonged. Marriages became more legalistic overall, with dowries becoming increasingly inflated and with the property a widow could receive diminishing to only a small portion of her late husband's estate (the *donatio propter nuptias*). Nevertheless, since males substantially profited more from marriage without *manus*, it became the most popular form of marriage.

Changes in republican-era marriage laws continued to be made throughout the imperial era, beginning with the Lex Julia (Julian Law) of Augustus (r. 27 B.C.E.–14 C.E.), which was designed to promote marriage and the procreation of legitimate children. Under the Lex Julia a woman could be freed from tutelage if she gave birth to at least three children within marriage (four if the woman was a freedwoman). Augustus tried to limit divorce and to prevent people from adopting adults as heirs instead of marrying. The popularity of the flexible arrangements of the late republic, however, seems to have rendered these limitations ineffective, as were later attempts to reimpose the severe Augustan marriage legislation.

As in other aspects of Roman civil law, women were at a fundamental disadvantage in the Roman system of inheritance. They could not make wills without the permission of their tutors—husband, father, or hired representative—and they could not inherit land by testamentary bequest from either their husbands or their fathers. Instead, women had to rely on the absence of a will to inherit the standard share for a daughter from their fathers (if married without *manus* or unmarried) or husbands (if married with *manus*). Although these restrictions were eased by late in the empire, the discomfort of the jurists with female access to land and female independence is evident in the Corpus Juris Civilis, Emperor Justinian's massive compilation of Roman law from the earliest texts to his reign (527–565). Even at that late date, the liberalization of female status begun more than five hundred years before was viewed with suspicion. There is, for example, an extended discussion of laws forbidding women from drinking wine and a certain approval of Cato the Elder's conviction that women caught drunk should be executed on the spot.

Roman laws concerning violence against women were concerned far less with the woman as victim and far more with the effect on the woman's male kin. Rape was embedded in a larger category of crimes of *raptus*, which included abduction, assault, and rape. In all circumstances the crime was considered to be directed against the woman's paterfamilias, not against her. Indeed, female victims of *raptus* were considered shamed beyond redemption. Later in the empire, *raptus* was used as a means to force a reluctant father to marry his daughter to her abductor or rapist. This interpretation of the law—that the "punishment" for the crime of *raptus* was that the abductor had to marry the victim—persisted as a part of the definition of rape in medieval canon law.

The Influence of Greek and Roman Law. Although the fragmented sovereignty among the numerous poleis in ancient Greece limited the influence of their individual legal systems, Greek legal ideas did endure in the Hellenistic kingdoms of Syria, Egypt, and Macedonia and in Greek Sicily and southern Italy. Contact with other cultures, especially that of Egypt, which was much less restrictive of female activity, seems to have softened the classical period's extreme regulation of female activity, and this moderation was transmitted to Roman law when Rome conquered the Hellenistic kingdoms at the end of the republican era. Roman law lasted far longer than any other system in the West, spreading throughout Europe in the Middle Ages and forming the basis of the canon law of the Christian church in the West.

[*See also* Europe, *subentries* Ancient Greece *and* Roman Empire.]

BIBLIOGRAPHY

Cantarella, Eva. *Pandora's Daughters: The Role and Status of Women in Greek and Roman Antiquity*. Translated by Maureen Brown Fant. Baltimore: Johns Hopkins University Press, 1986.

Clark, Gillian. *Women in Late Antiquity: Pagan and Christian Lifestyles*. Oxford: Clarendon Press, 1994. One of the few general studies of women in the late Roman Empire, especially useful for comparing the early and late Roman empires to see the changes that followed the legalization of Christianity.

"Diotíma: Materials for the Study of Women and Gender in the Ancient World." http://www.stoa.org/diotima/anthology/eratosthenes.shtml. A Web site specifically about women in ancient history.

Gardner, Jane F. *Women in Roman Law and Society*. Bloomington: Indiana University Press, 1991. An essential text for understanding women's position in Roman social and legal culture.

Halsall, Paul, ed. "Internet Ancient History Sourcebook." http://www.fordham.edu/halsall/ancient/asbook.html. An extremely useful collection of sources in translation, maps, images, and links.

Johnston, David. *Roman Law in Context*. Cambridge, U.K.: Cambridge University Press, 1999. A careful study of the Corpus Juris Civilis and its application late in the Roman Empire.

Lefkowitz, Mary, and Maureen Fant, eds. *Women's Life in Greece and Rome: A Source Book in Translation*. Rev. ed. Baltimore: Johns Hopkins University Press, 1992. A comprehensive collection of sources, organized by subject.

Pomeroy, Sarah B. *Goddesses, Whores, Wives, and Slaves: Women in Classical Antiquity*. New York: Schocken Books, 1994.

LINDA E. MITCHELL

China

For centuries, the close relationship between law and Confucian morality in imperial China gave rise to Confucianized law, in which women occupied a conspicuously inferior position (Ch'ü). The subordinate legal status of women derived in large part from the Confucian emphasis on the patriline, with its strict gender and generational hierarchy. The earliest Chinese legal code to survive in full, the Tang code, for example, meted out gradations of punishment according to age, gender, and social status. Despite severe legal restrictions, Chinese women during the Han, Tang, and Song dynasties enjoyed a certain amount of autonomy and benefited from substantial property rights and protections, at least in customary practice. These customary rights and privileges were curtailed after the Mongol invasion and occupation of China in the thirteenth and fourteenth centuries. Mongol rule was succeeded by the Ming dynasty, which directed a strong Confucian reaction and resurgence of patrilineal principles.

Late Imperial Law, 1368–1911. In imperial China, the "Three Obediences" (*san cong*) exhorted daughters to obey their fathers, wives to obey their husbands, and widows to obey their sons. Yet these moral and legal prescriptions did not go unchallenged. First, actual legal practice often departed from the state's representation of the law. A substantial number of female plaintiffs appealed to the legal system to resolve disputes and seek redress, though female litigants were expected to rely upon male relatives to serve as proxies. Second, there arose some informal institutions, like the uterine family and women's communities, which defied some of the harshest patrilineal measures.

As marginal members of the patriline, women's claims to manage and inherit property under late imperial law were mainly residual and conditional. Their claims depended upon the presence or absence of men, namely brothers (biological or adopted), husbands, or male agnatic kin. Inheritance took place under one of two processes, both of which adhered to the father-son logic associated with the continuity of the patriline. First, when a man had a birth son or sons, the system of household division mandated equal division among the sons. Second, when a man did not have any birth sons, patrilineal succession required him to adopt a male heir for ritual and economic purposes. Under this regime of male inheritance, a woman could at most claim a dowry for an unmarried daughter or provision for maintenance in old age in the case of a widowed mother, usually in money or movable goods, not land. Scholars disagree about whether a half-share law was in place earlier during the Song dynasty (960–1279), allowing daughters to inherit even in the presence of sons, but during the Song, widows and daughters were entitled to full inheritance in the absence of sons, in other words, when the patriline faced extinction. This ability to inherit by default was curtailed in 1369, however, when the early Ming state imposed mandatory nephew succession: when a man died without a son, one of his nephews had to be appointed as his heir postmortem. Beginning in the middle of the Qing dynasty (1770s), widows who refused to remarry earned greater latitude to reject nephews they disliked and to choose one more to their liking—a reflection of the higher legal standing accorded to chaste widows and concubines.

Like property law, late imperial family law was designed to promote the continuity of the patriline. Laws on marriage, for instance, provided for parents or elder family members to arrange a marriage, regardless of the individual bride's or groom's wishes. Moreover, the law conceived of marriage primarily as the acquisition of a daughter-in-law by the groom's patriline. The marital residence was patrilocal unless otherwise agreed upon. Important divergences included marriage resistance, delayed transfer of the bride, and postmarital dual residence. Technically, the law prohibited polygamy but permitted the taking of concubines, ostensibly to support the continuity of the patriline: a man who had reached a certain age could increase his chances of having a son. But the custom of concubinage was not limited to older, sonless men.

Late imperial law also featured several kinds of divorce, most of which served the unilateral interests of the husband's patriline. First and most notoriously, the law established seven conditions under which a husband's family could expel a wife. A wife could be ousted if she failed to give birth to a male child, committed adultery, disobeyed her parents-in-law, spoke excessively, stole, was given to bouts of jealousy, or suffered from an incurable illness or loathsome disease. But these seven conditions were curbed by three limitations: a husband could not divorce a wife if she had already observed the mourning rites for her parents-in-law, if she had no natal family to return to, or if the husband's family was poor at the time of marriage and had since prospered. These protections from expulsion did not apply, though, to a woman guilty of adultery. Another type of divorce mandated dissolving marriages between close same-surname relatives or other prohibited groups. A wife could also apply for permission to remarry under certain narrowly defined circumstances, such as severe injury to the wife (at least a broken bone or tooth) or abandonment of at least three years by a husband fleeing after committing a crime, engaging in rebellion, or as a result of famine. Finally, the law permitted divorce by mutual consent.

Criminal law too safeguarded the interests of the patriline. Sexual transgressions by a wife or widow posed the greatest threat of adulterating the patriline and consequently had to be strictly regulated. For example, a married woman was guilty of adultery when she engaged in sexual relations with any man other than her husband. But a married man was not guilty of adultery when he engaged in sexual relations with his concubine, his maid, a courtesan, a prostitute, or other woman of low status. He was guilty of adultery only if he had sex with a married woman, thus infringing upon another man's patriline. To better protect the purity of the patriline, penalties for rape were systematically increased from penal servitude in the Tang and Song codes to death in the Ming and Qing codes. Additional legislation expanded official valorization of female chastity, providing for payments of silver and the construction of shrines for widows who maintained their chastity over long periods of time (over twenty years) and for women who committed suicide rather than submit to rape.

In matters not pertaining to the patriline, women and men were generally subject to the same criminal penalties. For certain crimes, the law even permitted women (as well as the elderly and the disabled) to convert their punishments into monetary fines. However, for crimes rooted in poverty, such as wife- or daughter-selling or forced prostitution, the law offered little protection. At most, women exercised what Huang refers to as "passive agency," degrees of consent and resistance to the abuses against them.

Republican Law, 1911–1949. In conjunction with both the movement to abolish extraterritoriality and the New Culture Movement, reformers in the late nineteenth and early twentieth centuries proposed dramatic changes in the Chinese legal system. In outward form, modern Chinese law represented an instrument of progressive social change. The adoption of such Western legal principles as individualism (especially the notion of individual property), monogamy, and equality (especially the notion of individual rights) did not unequivocally enhance the position of Chinese women. Although the Republican Civil Code of 1929–1931 ushered in formal gender equality, women's gains in legal status were often offset by losses of informal power.

Under the Republican Civil Code, wives and husbands, daughters and sons, mothers and fathers, grandmothers and grandfathers, and sisters and brothers enjoyed equal property and inheritance rights. However, to implement a regime of individual property, the Nationalist government reclassified family property as the father's personal property. The new inheritance law also provided for compulsory portions, but property owners who wished to maintain patrilineal traditions could resort to inter vivos gift transfers to circumvent the principle of gender equality.

Republican family law departed from imperial law in several respects. The revered place of the patriline in Chinese law was replaced with greater importance attached to the individual and conjugal unit. Lawmakers introduced freedom of marriage and divorce and redefined marriage as the consensual union of an individual wife and husband. Moreover, legal recognition of concubines was withdrawn, and as a result, monogamy replaced polygyny. Perhaps most significantly, divorce provisions were revised to accord with gender equality. Wives and husbands were granted equal rights to divorce, annulment, and marital separation. Divorce by mutual consent remained an option as well.

The first women lawyers and judges emerged during the Republican period. Zheng Yuxiu, for instance, trained as a lawyer in Paris and helped draft the Republican Civil Code. The Chinese women's movement also successfully campaigned for the right to vote and the right to a quota of legislative representatives. However, women's exercise of their new-found formal rights was limited by regional variation, class biases, low levels of education, and the widespread persistence of Confucian patriarchal attitudes and practices. Rural areas were especially resistant to change.

Socialist and Postsocialist Law, after 1949. Gender equality was a central promise of socialist law. Shortly after the establishment of the People's Republic of China, the Chinese Communist Party enacted the Marriage Law of 1950 (revised in 1980 and 2001). It upheld freedom of marriage and divorce, first introduced under the Republican Civil Code, but with an important difference being that the Communist Party also carried out a mass campaign to educate the public about the new laws. The Communist Party also banned concubinage and other feudal practices outright. During the socialist era, divorce, however, was not as easily obtained as the written laws suggest. Parents continued to influence decisions, and newly organized work units also exercised authority over marriage and divorce decisions. Resistance to female-initiated divorces ran high, especially among male peasants, who constituted the core constituency of the Communist Party.

In other areas as well, socialist law promised emancipation but had mixed effects upon women. The Communist Party upheld gender equality in its property law, but the collectivization of land ownership beginning in the 1950s limited inheritable property mostly to houses and household items, and this circumstance favored inheritance by sons, who were not required to change residence upon marriage. Moreover, with the advent of the one-child policy in the late 1970s, the state legally and physically intruded upon women's reproductive lives in new ways, forcing women to limit their families.

[*See also* China *and* Courtesanship, *subentry* Comparative History.]

BIBLIOGRAPHY

Bernhardt, Kathryn. *Women and Property in China, 960–1949*. Stanford, Calif.: Stanford University Press, 1999.

Ch'ü, T'ung-tsu. *Law and Society in Traditional China*. Paris: Mouton, 1961.

Diamant, Neil J. *Revolutionizing the Family: Politics, Love, and Divorce in Urban and Rural China, 1949–1968*. Berkeley: University of California Press, 2000.

Ebrey, Patricia Buckley. "Shifts in Marriage Finance from the Sixth to the Thirteenth Century." In *Marriage and Inequality in Chinese Society*, edited by Rubie S. Watson and Patricia Buckley Ebrey, pp. 97–132. Berkeley: University of California Press, 1991.

Edwards, Louise. "From Gender Equality to Gender Difference: Feminist Campaigns for Quotas for Women in Politics, 1936–1947." *Twentieth Century China* 24, no. 2 (April 1999): 69–105.

Glosser, Susan. *Chinese Visions of Family and State, 1915–1953*. Berkeley: University of California Press, 2003.

Huang, Philip C. C. *Code, Custom, and Legal Practice: The Qing and the Republic Compared*. Stanford, Calif.: Stanford University Press, 2001.

Johnson, Kay Ann. *Women, the Family, and Peasant Revolution in China*. Chicago: University of Chicago Press, 1983.

Macauley, Melissa. *Social Power and Legal Culture: Litigation Masters in Late Imperial China*. Stanford, Calif.: Stanford University Press, 1998.

Sommer, Matthew H. *Sex, Law, and Society in Late Imperial China*. Stanford, Calif.: Stanford University Press, 2000.

Tai, Yen-hui. "Divorce in Traditional Chinese Law." In *Chinese Family Law and Social Change in Historical and Comparative Perspective*, edited by David C. Buxbaum, pp. 75–106. Seattle: University of Washington Press, 1978.

Theiss, Janet M. *Disgraceful Matters: The Politics of Chastity in Eighteenth-Century China*. Berkeley: University of California Press, 2004.

Wolf, Margery. *Women and the Family in Rural Taiwan*. Stanford, Calif.: Stanford University Press, 1972.

MARGARET KUO

Europe

Liberal accounts of European legal systems since the Renaissance highlight the move from serfdom to representative democracy and the ending of brutal physical punishments for convicted criminals. It is easy to assume a similar steady improvement in the status and power of women, from subservience in eras when legal writers openly declared wives to be "under the rod" of their husbands to the substantial rights and relative freedoms that female citizens enjoy today. The reality, however, is more complex than this progressive narrative suggests. Each of the key changes that characterize this historical period—the move from customary law to law codified by statute, from customary inheritance to freedom of choice for testators, and from languages of duties to languages of rights—had negative as well as positive effects on women. In addition, laws did not always match practice, so that some women suffered more and others gained more than formal laws prescribed.

Customary Law and Roman Law. In 1500, Europe was broadly divided in two in terms of secular law. Customary law held sway in the north and west, from northern France and England to Scandinavia, while in the south, particularly in Italy, southern France, Spain, and Portugal, written law influenced by Roman models had been modifying custom since the thirteenth century. Customary laws, whether local custom or broad-based custom such as the English common law, favored men more than women. For example, primogeniture governed inheritance among elites in much of France, England, Scandinavia, and Italy, channeling lands to the eldest male, and in all regions laws offered husbands substantial powers over the lives, property, and bodies of their wives. However, the rights that custom did extend to women—such as the ability for daughters to inherit in the absence of sons, for married women to carry on certain trades independently from their husbands, or the entitlement of widows to claim dower—were remarkably durable. The nature of dower varied from region to region, both in quantity (from an interest in a third or a half or all of a late husband's lands or goods) and in duration (either lasting for life or ending if a widow remarried), but dower applied to all widows equally. In short, customary rights were limited in extent, but they were universal in application. In addition, the nature of custom—which was usually local, often unwritten, and affirmed by the community through juries of tenants or civic leaders—fostered exceptions and accommodations that many women exploited.

In areas influenced by Roman law, legal codes regularly made women subject to male guardians for matters involving property or law: fathers supervised daughters, husbands supervised wives, and uncles or other male guardians supervised widows. In practice, however, widows can be found in Italy wielding virtually the same control over their property as widows in France or the German states.

Dowries were more crucial to marriage in these regions than in the north, but contests over dowry resources more often pitted family against family than men against women. Everywhere in Europe women's legal status was tied to their marital status, with marriage itself the greatest restrictor of female autonomy. Custom, statute, and practice not only limited wives' rights and freedoms but also conspired to prevent single or widowed women from holding public office on the grounds that they might one day marry.

The Rise of Centralized Government. In the sixteenth and seventeenth centuries ruling monarchs and state and civic authorities across Europe increased the roles they played in government and the provision of justice. Court systems expanded, and levels of litigation rose dramatically, reaching astonishing levels in England and Spain. The passing of legislation and regulations also increased, amounting in many regions to a codifying of law. Lawmakers in the German states, northern France, and the Low Countries turned more and more to Roman law to replace, modify, or supplement custom. In many areas the influence of patriarchal concepts of Roman law, such as paterfamilias (the male head of the household) and *patria potestas* (the male head's power), appears to have strengthened the already considerable authority of fathers and husbands. At the same time, more and more individuals sought ways to evade customary practices. This process could be positive for women—for example, in England the development of trusts provided a means for married women to retain control over property that would otherwise have passed to their husbands—but more often it served to undermine women's rights and access to power. Increasing freedom of disposition meant that husbands could disinherit wives, and fathers could disinherit daughters, or at least ensure that they did not gain control of lands.

All over northern Europe paternalistic systems dominated by custom gave way to more individualistic systems characterized by contractual thinking, where women's rights were only as good as individual written agreements allowed. Experienced and wealthy widows enjoyed an enhanced ability to negotiate their futures and protect their property if they remarried. However, many poorer widows saw their customary rights trampled by domineering patriarchs employing crafty lawyers. For example, widows' automatic rights to dower increasingly were replaced by jointures, agreements negotiated at the time of marriage that in most cases were less generous than dower. Overall it appears that more women suffered than gained in this move from limited but universal entitlements and protections to what amounted to a marketplace of privileges and property rights. They did not, however, give up their entitlements quietly, and thousands of women fought for their rights in court, many of them finding ways to enjoy in practice rights that laws denied them in theory.

Criminal Law and Moral Regulation. As rulers, lawmakers, and other authorities moved to centralize power and to play a greater role in government, they intruded more into the private lives of citizens and subjects. Church and state authorities made increasing use of laws and regulations to control or discipline populations, punishing more individuals for crimes and for moral offenses such as fornication and adultery. Women who did not conform to prescribed ideals of female behavior, such as unmarried women who gave birth to illegitimate children, suffered considerably. In most areas prosecutions for infanticide and witchcraft overwhelmingly targeted women, reflecting a sense that "unruly" or "unnatural" women posed a threat to the community. However, apart from these particular offenses, women were underrepresented in criminal prosecutions. Historians used to explain this by reference to the "chivalry thesis," the assumption that male prosecutors, judges, and juries took pity on women and were hesitant to accuse, prosecute, convict, or punish female offenders. Certainly, in many European regions women took part in riots and popular protests under the widespread belief that they were less likely than men to be prosecuted, and in many systems husbands were held partly or wholly responsible for their wives' actions. However, it now appears that European legal systems rarely offered special treatment to women accused of crimes, and women who flouted expectations about acceptable feminine behavior fared worse in court than men did. An indication of the patriarchal underpinnings of European criminal law can be seen in the English law of homicide, under which a husband who killed his wife was guilty of murder, but a wife who killed her husband was guilty of petty treason, a crime against the state.

Revolution and Individual Rights. In the eighteenth century the process of passing statutes and codifying laws continued to erode customary and common law and to impose a legal uniformity that was less tolerant of exceptions. The language of rights also became more influential, culminating in the political upheavals of the French Revolution. Despite the determination and advocacy of vocal women across Europe, the transformations that turned subjects into citizens largely bypassed women. Lawmakers followed political philosophers in regarding the household as exempt from the argument that political authority relied on the consent of the governed, choosing to regard women as dependants rather than bearers of individual rights. Advocates of representative government, for example, rarely considered political (and legal) emancipation for women.

Many regions reacted to the threat of revolution by tightening existing laws. In England, for example, a new conservatism saw common-law judges undo the recent gains that married women had made in asserting their legal individuality separate from their husbands by reaffirming that a husband's legal identity eclipsed his wife's. Even in France, the minor improvements in women's status enacted after the Revolution were swept away by the Civil Code Napoléon, enacted in 1804, that emphasized the rights of men at the expense of women, especially wives. As article 213 made clear, "the husband owes his wife protection: the wife owes her husband obedience." In the hustle and bustle of day-to-day life, strong-willed European women continued to exercise independence and play active roles in local and national market economies, but those without the resources to secure increasingly expensive legal services were noticeably disadvantaged.

The exclusion of women from a developing culture of individual rights could not last. Across Europe the later nineteenth and early twentieth centuries witnessed slow advances in married women's rights to property, to protection from violence, to divorce, and to custody over children, and in married and later single women's right to vote. The peeling away of centuries of prejudicial laws and judicial attitudes owed much to the ideology of liberalism, but the battles to change these laws were hard fought rather than inevitable, advocated by feminist critics and reformers who in many instances had fewer rights and less access to legal process than women had enjoyed in previous centuries.

[*See also* Dower Systems; Europe; Great Britain; Inheritance; Legitimacy and Illegitimacy; Marriage; Married Women's Property Acts; *and* Primogeniture.]

BIBLIOGRAPHY

Erickson, Amy Louise. *Women and Property in Early Modern England.* London and New York: Routledge, 1993. Focuses on property but includes detailed analyses of Britain's complex system of competing legal jurisdictions and the uses that women made of it.

Heuer, Jennifer Ngaire. *The Family and the Nation: Gender and Citizenship in Revolutionary France, 1789–1830.* Ithaca, N.Y.: Cornell University Press, 2005. Demonstrates the Revolution's positive as well as negative effects on women's rights.

Holcombe, Lee. *Wives and Property: Reform of the Married Women's Property Law in Nineteenth-Century England.* Toronto: University of Toronto Press, 1983. A detailed study of the dynamics of legislative reform in the English context.

Hufton, Olwen. *The Prospect before Her: A History of Women in Western Europe.* Vol. 1: *1500–1800.* New York: Knopf, 1996. A magisterial overview of change and continuity in European women's lives, emphasizing the effects of social status.

Kuehn, Thomas. *Law, Family, and Women: Toward a Legal Anthropology of Renaissance Italy.* Chicago: University of Chicago Press, 1991.

Staves, Susan. *Married Women's Separate Property in England, 1660–1833.* Cambridge, Mass.: Harvard University Press, 1990.

Wiesner, Merry E. *Women and Gender in Early Modern Europe.* 2d ed. New York: Cambridge University Press, 2000. Chapter 1, "Ideas and Laws regarding Women," covers all aspects of this topic and includes a comprehensive annotated bibliography.

TIM STRETTON

International Law

International law refers to the body of rules and principles governing relations among nations (called "states" or "states parties" in international law jargon) and many relations involving international organizations or persons that concern more than one country, including international human rights. Though men's domination of society and the subordination of women are embedded within international law, women have nevertheless sometimes been able to use international law to improve their role and status. International law legitimates the continued oppression of women, but to do so effectively it must also moderate and reduce this oppression to one degree or another.

Family and Citizenship. Rules concerning family and citizenship typically affect women more adversely than they do men, even if the provisions are formally sex neutral. The reality that basic principles of international law were established in a male-dominated milieu is reflected in the standard supposition that most questions regarding family are domestic issues and are thus not appropriate for international regulation.

Marriage and citizenship. Traditionally upon a woman's marriage many countries conferred the nationality of the husband upon the wife and withdrew the woman's own nationality—summarily depriving her of citizenship although she had done nothing wrong or socially undesirable. This practice remained common until the 1957 United Nations Convention on the Nationality of Married Women, which allowed women to retain their nationality but also left it easier for the wife to acquire the husband's nationality than the reverse.

Today most countries grant preferential immigration status to the spouse of their own nationals, thus encouraging marriage and therefore the various formal and informal disabilities for women associated with marriage. These provisions also facilitate the frequently exploitative and demeaning practice of "mail-order brides."

Child custody and the Hague Convention. The Hague Convention on the Civil Aspects of International Child Abduction (entered into force in 1980) is an international agreement whereby the signing countries agree to give effect to the custody determinations made by another signatory to the convention. One important purpose of the convention was to stop estranged fathers who were kidnapping their children and leaving the country, and generally to reduce the incidence of noncustodial parents transporting their child to another jurisdiction in order to obtain legal custody in the alternative jurisdiction.

One seriously negative effect of the convention as it is enforced, however, is that custodial parents, usually women, have found themselves restricted from international travel because the other parent uses such travel as grounds to claim a violation of the convention, usually on the basis that the travel interferes with visitation rights. Also, insufficient provision is made to protect mothers who have fled a country to escape domestic violence or religious persecution from being forced by the Hague Convention to return to that country to litigate custody.

Sources of International Law. Sources of international law are primarily treaties or conventions, binding upon the countries that sign them; customary international law, binding upon all states; general principles of law, also binding on all; and court decisions and the teachings of "the most highly qualified publicists." In addition, resolutions of the General Assembly of the United Nations, activities and codes of conduct adopted by international non-governmental organizations (NGOs), and declarations and programs of actions worked out at various global summits or conferences form what is often referred to as "soft" international law, not formally binding upon countries unless and until the resolution, code, or declaration becomes part of customary international law, but nevertheless influential and useful for interpreting treaties and for pressuring governments and individuals to act in accordance with the declarations.

Treaties: CEDAW. A treaty of particular importance to women is the Convention on the Elimination of All Forms of Discrimination against Women (CEDAW), drafted in the late 1970s by the U.N. Commission on the Status of Women (established 1946) and adopted by the General Assembly in 1979. CEDAW requires countries to "take all appropriate measures," including legislation, to end discrimination against women, to advance women through affirmative measures, and to combat gender stereotypes and negative gender ideology. It has been called the "central and most comprehensive document for the advancement of women." Though CEDAW is considered to be binding on countries that have ratified it, sanctions for violation are very limited. Every five years ratifying countries must submit a report outlining their efforts at compliance to the Committee on the Elimination of Discrimination against Women. An effort to respond to the inadequacy of enforcement mechanisms resulted in an Optional Protocol, adopted in 1999, which allows individuals to submit complaints to the committee and provides an investigation procedure.

Feminist critics rightly note that CEDAW "recognizes discrimination against women as a legal issue but is premised on the notion of progress through good will, education and changing attitudes and does not promise any form of structural, social or economic change for women" (Charlesworth and Chinkin, *Boundaries of International Law*). Other criticisms include that the convention fails to address specifically violence against women, a criticism at least partially met by the Declaration on the Elimination of Violence against Women of 1993.

Customary law. The advantage of customary law is that it applies to all countries. To establish international customary law, however, requires a uniform and consistent practice and what is called *opinio juris sive necessitates*, or the belief by states that the practice is required. These requirements limit the value of customary law in forcing a change to the existing status quo and thus limit its value to women regarding the most persistent forms of mistreatment.

Other sources. The World Conference on Human Rights, held in Vienna in 1993, and the Fourth World Conference on Women, held in Beijing in 1995, both issued important declarations that provide a good example of "soft" law. The Vienna Declaration and Programme of Action identified inadequacies in the existing human rights system for women and declared that the human rights of women were "an inalienable, integral and indivisible part of universal human rights" and should form "an integral part of the United Nations human rights activities" (section I, paragraph 18). The Beijing Platform for Action described women's empowerment and participation as equals in all spheres of life to be an essential component for world peace. NGOs played an important part in both of these meetings, and their role in such events has been steadily increasing.

The U.N. System and the Rise of Human Rights. The U.N. system and the rise of human rights offer further examples of international law serving women's interests but at the same time being limited by the gendered quality of international law. Specifically, several treaties oblige countries to protect the interests of women. Yet treaties are a limited source of international law insofar as they are voluntary, based on the consent of individual governments; moreover, the process of giving consent has largely excluded women. In addition, the treaty process reinforces voluntarism by allowing individual governments to limit their obligations under treaties through reservations, understandings, and declarations (RUDs).

United Nations. The Charter of the United Nations (1945) includes among its goals the promotion of human rights and fundamental freedoms for all, without distinction as to race, sex, language, or religion. Yet, even in the twenty-first century women are marginalized in the United Nations, with women almost completely absent from the senior levels of decision making within the organization. The U.N.'s response has been a policy of "gender mainstreaming"—integrating the concerns of gender into all the organization's activities and spreading responsibility for gender issues throughout the organization. However, feminist commentators have identified as a "conceptual limitation" the fact that "gender" is assumed to mean women, "leaving male gender identities unexamined." Thus, gender mainstreaming "requires women to change, but not men" (Charlesworth and Chinkin, *Boundaries of International Law*, p. 196). The categories used to compartmentalize and analyze the work of the United Nations—security, peacekeeping, human rights, and economic development—are largely defined by male experience and illustrate the marginalization of women.

Human rights. The rising importance of human rights since World War II has challenged basic traditional notions of international law as involving relations between nations. Insofar as human rights law asserts an international interest in the way governments treat their own people, it raises a profound challenge to notions of state sovereignty and autonomy. The major human rights documents date from 1948—the Universal Declaration of Human Rights (UDHR)—and from 1966—the International Covenant on Economic, Social, and Cultural Rights (ICESCR) and the International Covenant on Civil and Political Rights (ICCPR). These have now been joined by the Convention on the Rights of the Child (entered into force in 1990) and CEDAW.

Gender-Based Violence and Abuse. Gender-based violence and abuse, in the areas of trafficking, domestic violence, and war crimes, are partially and incompletely addressed by international law.

Trafficking in women. To the extent that sexual intercourse has been socially constructed to benefit men, many men seek to commoditize sex through prostitution. The high demand for prostitution and the large sums of money available to those who control and manage it have contributed to a major social and political problem of trafficking in women.

International laws addressing the issue began with 1904 and 1910 conventions against trafficking in women for purposes of prostitution. The 1949 convention for the Suppression of the Traffic in Persons and of the Exploitation of the Prostitution of Others was drafted by the U.N. Commission on the Status of Women and forbids pimping, procurement, and buying sex, but not prostitution itself. The U.N. Conference on Women held in Nairobi in 1985 identified prostitution as a "form of slavery imposed on women by procurers" and noted that prostitution "stems from women's dependence on men." More recently, Article 6 of CEDAW requires states to take measures "to suppress all forms of traffic in women and exploitation of prostitution of women."

Domestic violence, crimes of passion, crimes of honor. In many countries men are empowered to abuse women with whom they claim a sexual or family relationship. In the West, notions of family privacy and assumptions about men's reactions to sexual competition or sexual rejection have led governments to deny the protection that is usually given to their residents to the victims of crimes that are committed by a male family member or that can be characterized as a crime of passion. In some countries in the Middle East and elsewhere, the idea that a family's honor is affected by the sexual morality or assumed sexual morality of its women members has led to a similar result.

War crimes. The international law on war crimes has traditionally focused attention primarily upon the treatment of combatants and thus omitted most of the harms done to women. The Fourth Geneva Convention (1949), however, obliged states involved in international armed conflict to protect women "against any attack on their honour"—rape or enforced prostitution. During the 1990s feminists were able gradually to shift the focus away from men protecting the honor of their women to the direction of recognizing violence as an attack upon women and women's integrity.

Though most war crimes have been addressed by ad hoc tribunals, such as in Nuremberg and Tokyo after World War II and, more recently, tribunals dealing with the former Yugoslavia and with Rwanda, in 1998 the permanent International Criminal Court (ICC) was established, with jurisdiction over such crimes against women. Although the U.S. government has been working to undermine the court's functions and jurisdiction, it remains to be seen whether the rest of the world will effectively resist these efforts and make the court fully functional.

[*See also* Convention on the Elimination of All Forms of Discrimination against Women; Declaration on the Elimination of Violence against Women; Human Rights; Prostitution; Rape; United Nations; *and* War.]

BIBLIOGRAPHY

Charlesworth, Hilary, and Christine Chinkin. *The Boundaries of International Law: A Feminist Analysis*. Manchester, U.K.: Manchester University Press, 2000. The best book-length feminist analysis of international law.

Charlesworth, Hilary, Christine Chinkin, and Shelley Wright. "Feminist Approaches to International Law." *American Journal of International Law* 85, no. 4 (1991): 613–645. Foundational feminist critique of international law.

Cook, Rebecca J., ed. *Human Rights of Women: National and International Perspectives*. Pennsylvania Studies in Human Rights. Philadelphia: University of Pennsylvania Press, 1994. Classic collection introducing the notion of women's human rights.

Dallmeyer, Dorinda G., ed. *Reconceiving Reality: Women and International Law*. Washington, D.C.: American Society of International Law, 1993. Collection of articles from the first conference focusing on women and international law—includes materials on war crimes, theory, trafficking, and many other topics.

Enloe, Cynthia H. *Bananas, Beaches, and Bases: Making Feminist Sense of International Politics*. London: Pandora Press, 1989.

Enloe, Cynthia H. *Police, Military, and Ethnicity: Foundations of State Power*. New Brunswick, N.J.: Transaction Books, 1980.

Frances E. Olsen

Islamic Law

The phrase "Islamic law" can refer to a variety of things, including the specific prescriptions of the authoritative sacred texts of the Qurʾan and Sunnah (the exemplary conduct of Muhammad, reported in the Hadith literature); manuals of jurisprudence written by legal scholars from a variety of legal schools (*madhahib*; sing. *madhhab*); judicial practice in various times and places; or the codified laws of modern Muslim-majority nation-states, where Islamic family law "has become for most Muslims the symbol of their Islamic identity, the hard irreducible core of what it means to be a Muslim today" (An-Na'im, p. xi). The status and power allocated to women vary considerably between and within each of these types of law.

Sources and Development of Islamic Law. Relying on the Qurʾan and the Sunnah, the exemplary conduct and dicta of the prophet Muhammad (c. 570–632), Muslim jurists developed a complete and complex series of rules regulating all aspects of Muslim life. The Qurʾan devotes a significant proportion of its specific injunctions to modifying, usually to women's benefit, seventh-century Arabian customs regulating family life, especially in provisions for inheritance, witnessing, marriage, and divorce. Local customary practices, which varied over time and throughout the vast Muslim empire, influenced both the development of law and its application, leading to both diversity of opinions among the legal schools and, at times, distinctions between the theoretical writings of the jurists and the usual practice of the courts.

The Quʾran. A folio from a Mamluk Quʾran, c. 1400–1500 C.E., M.843, f. 2v. THE PIERPONT MORGAN LIBRARY, NEW YORK/ART RESOURCE, NY

Female rights in marriage, divorce, inheritance, and child custody were generally distinct from and/or lesser than male rights in the same areas, although the extent of male privilege has varied dramatically both in classical jurisprudence and modern law. Additionally, the extent to which individual women were able to circumvent legal restrictions through their own initiative depended on both individual qualities and social prestige and wealth. In other areas, such as worship, property rights, and criminal law, women had essentially the same rights and obligations as men, although some of these could be circumscribed in practice.

Worship. The scope of Islamic jurisprudence is broader than "law" in the modern Western sense and includes, like Jewish Halacha, ritual practices. Women's obligations with regard to Islam's five pillars (profession of faith, prayer, alms, fasting, and pilgrimage) are essentially the same as men's, although there are restrictions on fasting and prayer during menstruation. (Apart from a prohibition on intercourse, there are no other legal taboos associated with menstruation. Jurists discuss menstruation as they regulate matters such as the waiting period after divorce, which, as its purpose is to determine paternity, is calculated on the basis of menstrual cycles.) Women are required to pay *zakat*, or alms, on their own wealth. Finally, the obligation to make pilgrimage to Mecca once in a lifetime, assuming one is capable, is an obligation for women just as for men, though women are expected to be chaperoned by a husband or closely related male relative such as a father, uncle, or son. For those thinkers who consider jihad an essential duty, women are considered exempt.

Classical and medieval thinkers, and many modern ones, understand a wife to have a duty of obedience to her husband. Nonetheless, they are in agreement that this duty can never override a woman's religious obligations; a woman must disobey her husband if he orders her to disobey God.

Property. Female rights to property ownership are legally guaranteed, whether the property is gifted, inherited, or earned. A dower (*mahr* or *sadaq*) is legally due to the wife herself at marriage, and females inherit from husbands and kin. Despite the fact that women's property rights are fiercely defended by jurists and consistently enforced by judges, they have at times been overlooked in practice. Fathers sometimes claim their daughters' dowers according to custom, and females may be shut out of their legally due inheritance (usually, but not always, half the share going to a male who has the same relationship to the deceased), particularly when the property at stake is land rather than money or movable goods. Sometimes, women may be actively thwarted when they seek to press their property claims while in other instances, as Annelies Moors has noted, women forgo claiming rights to dower or inheritance in order to enhance husbands' or brothers' obligations toward them.

Even married women—who elsewhere have suffered restrictions on their personhood—retained their legal capacity as proprietors. While a minority of classical jurists, from the Maliki legal school, held that a married woman could not alienate more than one-third of her property without her husband's permission, the majority of jurists agreed that a woman's property rights were not affected by her marital status.

Not only can women own property, they can also buy, sell, and manage it. In various times and places, including Mamluk Egypt, upper-class women have served as custodians of family property trusts. Court records from the Ottoman period show that women, particularly from the lower classes, transacted business themselves, appearing before judges to press claims. Upper-class and noble women, for whom seclusion was normal practice, often used an agent (*wakil*) to represent them before the courts.

Criminal Law. In classical Islamic law, male and female transgressors are treated the same way, although the *diya* (compensation for injury or homicide paid to the victim or victim's kin) for a female is usually half that for a male. In Iran, one of the few nations to implement the practice in its modern law, the law's provisions have meant that in some cases of deliberate murder of a female by a male, the family must pay half the male's blood money in order to have him executed.

Illicit sex, or *zina*, historically rarely punished through formal channels, was defined in classical law as consensual intercourse outside a lawful union. (A union permitting sex could be either marriage or slave concubinage, although the universal illegality of slavery now makes moot a man's legal entitlement to have sex with his own unmarried female slave by right of possession.) A legal double standard pertains clearly with regard to the number and type of lawful sex partners a man or woman could have: men were allowed four wives (supplemented, under Ja'fari Shiite law, with an unlimited number of "temporary," or *mut'a*, wives) while women are restricted to one husband. The double standard disappears, however, with regard to legal punishment for illicit sex outside those boundaries: both men and women are subject to punishment for illicit sex, either flogging in the case of a never-married individual or stoning when the offender was or had been married. Both punishments apply equally regardless of gender.

There are two gender-related differences with regard to these punishments: women cannot serve as any of the four witnesses (who must have actually seen the act of illicit intercourse) required for the sexual act to be punished, and women are, in a minority view (again held by the Maliki), to be punished on the basis of pregnancy outside a valid marriage (while men are not). Colonial law and modern identity politics have often resulted in the worst of both worlds for Muslim women, with prosecutions occurring without the premodern loopholes and stringent standards of evidence that made conviction extremely difficult.

Marriage, Divorce, and Custody. In classical jurisprudence, marriage is a consensual contract between two parties. Most jurists held that a female's father or other close male relative had to serve as *wali*, or guardian. Some allowed him to contract the marriage over her objections if she had not been married before; others prohibited this once she had attained majority, and the Hanafi legal school and the Ja'fari Shiites even allowed women past the age of majority to make their own contracts.

Marriage was unilaterally dissolvable by the husband through an extrajudicial procedure known as *talaq*. A wife could not prevent her husband from exercising this right, but she could seek to secure it for herself as well under certain circumstances, such as if her husband took another wife or attempted to relocate her away from her hometown. Women were also entitled to divorce for cause, which required them to make a case in court. Grounds for judicial divorce ranged from long-term abandonment to nonsupport to cruelty. Additionally, marriages could be dissolved by a negotiated settlement, *khul'*, where a woman repaid her dower and might also waive other financial claims.

Islamic law treated legal guardianship and physical custody separately. A father was always his children's legal guardian, although some held that he could appoint the mother to succeed him in the event of his death. After divorce or widowhood, custody of young children passed invariably to the mother, with the obligation of support on the father. The legal schools differed over the age at which custody reverted to the father. Some held that boys as young as two should remain with their fathers; girls might remain with their mothers until age seven in some views or until puberty. In practice, custody arrangements were more flexible and evidence suggests that some mothers retained custody even after remarriage when in theory custody should have passed to other maternal relatives. This was more often the case when women agreed to waive the right to support from the children's father.

Colonial and Postcolonial Reforms. Colonial and postcolonial nation-states reformed marriage and divorce laws in a variety of ways while supposedly maintaining their religious character; these reforms included several measures designed to increase the range of state supervision over marriage, thus creating requirements for registration where previously there had been none. The most important reforms came in three areas: raising the age of marriage, especially for girls; altering divorce regulations to restrict or, rarely, abolish unilateral male divorce and provide further options for women to seek divorce; and restricting or, as in Tunisia and Turkey, abolishing polygamy.

The codification process and the implementation of standardized marriage contracts in many nations resulted in the removal of some flexibility from the law. Reformers in Egypt and Iran, among other nations, have attempted to work within the system by advocating the inclusion of various stipulations to protect female rights on the preprinted marriage contracts. Morocco's 2003 reform of the Moudawana, which governs family law, on the basis of "justice and equality" has resulted in one of the most egalitarian frameworks for marriage and divorce. It retains the theoretical permissibility of polygamy, while surrounding its practice with numerous restrictions.

Overall, there have been two tendencies in movements to reform family laws. Some activists have argued that any accommodations with regard to Islamic law represent a capitulation, advocating instead secularism as the only responsible path for attaining women's rights. Others suggest—either out of religious commitment or strategic reasoning—that reforms must be justified on the basis of religious language and logic. Women's activist organizations, including the international network Women Living under Muslim Laws and the Malaysian group Sisters in Islam, have adopted a practical "best practices" model in attempting to promote female rights within diverse legal settings. In other settings where Muslims live as minorities, Muslims have debated the usefulness of Islamic legal tribunals as a parallel mediation and arbitration system. While some Muslim women support these endeavors, others argue that civil legal systems best embody the spirit of Islamic legal protections for women.

[*See also* Adultery; Divorce; Islam; Marriage; *and entries on countries and regions mentioned in this article*.]

BIBLIOGRAPHY

An-Na'im, Abdullahi A., ed. *Islamic Family Law in a Changing World: A Global Resource Book*. London and New York: Zed Books; distributed in the United States by Palgrave, 2002.

Mir-Hosseini, Ziba. *Islam and Gender: The Religious Debate in Contemporary Iran*. Princeton, N.J.: Princeton University Press, 1999.

Moors, Annelies. "Debating Islamic Family Law: Legal Texts and Social Practices." In *Social History of Women and Gender in the Modern Middle East*, edited by Margaret L. Meriwether and Judith E. Tucker, pp. 141–176. Boulder, Colo.: Westview Press, 1999.

Moors, Annelies. *Women, Property, and Islam: Palestinian Experiences, 1920–1990*. Cambridge, U.K., and New York: Cambridge University Press, 1995.

Rapoport, Yossef. *Marriage, Money, and Divorce in Medieval Islamic Society*. Cambridge, U.K., and New York: Cambridge University Press, 2005.

Sonbol, Amira El Azhary, ed. *Women, the Family, and Divorce Laws in Islamic History*. Syracuse, N.Y.: Syracuse University Press, 1996.

Spectorsky, Susan A., ed. and trans. *Chapters on Marriage and Divorce: Responses of Ibn Hanbal and Ibn Rahwayh*. Austin: University of Texas Press, 1993.

Tucker, Judith E. *In the House of the Law: Gender and Islamic Law in Ottoman Syria and Palestine*. Berkeley, Calif.: University of California Press, 1998.

Tucker, Judith E., ed. *Arab Women: Old Boundaries, New Frontiers*. Bloomington: Indiana University Press, 1993.

KECIA ALI

Japan

The laws of a country at any time may advantage or disadvantage women, but other factors have to be considered: the availability and strength of courts, the disposition of magistrates and judges, local custom, and local conditions. Research increasingly finds exceptions to the rules, which indicate a general tendency to ignore or circumvent the law whenever it is deemed inconvenient to the family or community concerned. In addition, the position of women in Japan has to be evaluated in relation to infanticide, marriage, divorce, child custody, abortion, labor, and property.

The first attempts to move from local and customary law began with the Taika Reforms (645; first edict, 646), and continued with the first national census and registration of 670, the Kōgonen-jaku; the Asuka-Kiyomihara Code of 689; and the Taihō Code of 701, which was replaced by the 718 Yōrō Code, promulgated in 757. These codes created a Chinese-style state meant to extend imperial control of men and matériel through direct taxation of grain, textiles, corvée, and military service. Every six years, households were allocated land: every free male aged six and over received 0.25 acres; every female one-third of that. Because females received land from the government but were not taxed, they were valued for more than their labor in the fields. Since families did not want to lose their girls, existing forms of matrilocal marriage were confirmed and entrenched.

Women were permitted to inherit upon the death of the head of the household. The widow received two shares, the children of the legal wife or wives received two shares, and the children of concubines one share. This division became increasingly important to the upper classes of peasantry and gentry, as ownership of reclaimed land was permitted beginning in 723 with the Sanze Isshin no Hō (Law of Three Generations or a Single Lifetime), while in 743 the

Konden Eisei Shizai Hō permitted permanent possession. This reclaimed land became the basis for the development of private estates. In 800 the last census was carried out. To evade taxation, especially military service and the much-abused corvée duty, peasants absconded to private estates, where they negotiated better terms for their labor. Under the principle of partible inheritance, women inherited income from private estates. Hence, the more land held privately, the more women in the gentry and upper classes benefitted. Although women were ineligible for many of the offices of the bureaucracy, there were many positions in imperial palaces and households of great nobles funded by the income from such estates.

By 1200 about half the land under cultivation in Japan was non-taxable private land. The shift of so much land to private status was accompanied by a shift from rule by the imperial bureaucracy to relationships based on patronage. This culminated in rule by a warlord, Minamoto Yoritomo (1147–1199), who founded the Kamakura Shogunate (1185–1333).

To adjudicate suits between and involving the Minamoto vassals, a court was established. To aid the court judges, the Jōei Goseibai Shikimoku, or Formulary for the Shogun's Decision of Lawsuits, was drawn up in 1232. The shogunate was most concerned with receiving services from those vassals who had been granted offices. The salaries of these offices were paid in land, outright fiefs, and positions as stewards (*jitō*) on private estates. Under the principle of partible inheritance, parents, specifically the father, had the right to bestow the family estate, in part or in whole, upon the children of both sexes. Thus, women inherited Minamoto vassalages. Although a woman might send her husband and sons off to guard duty or war, it was she herself who corresponded officially with the government. Enfeoffed women could lose their estates only if their husbands committed crimes of a premeditated sort, such as treason, but a wife or concubine given fief land by her husband and subsequently divorced could not be forced to return the estate unless she had she had been divorced for a serious reason. Women widowed and left childless were confirmed in their right to adopt children, to whom they could transmit fiefs and vassalages of the house of Minamoto.

Under the Ashikaga shogunate (1336–1573), the Kenmu Shikimoku of 1336 and Tsuikahō (a supplement) addressed government, land, and the new economy. The codes established by the imperial government and the shogunate remained in effect as far as they could be enforced until the complete fragmentation of the country after the Ōnin War of 1467–1477. Following a tradition of leaving family injunctions (*kakun*, such as the *Asakura Toshikage jūshichikajō* [1480] and the *Hōjō Sōun nijūikkajō* [c. 1495]), local warlords, great and small, signaled their absolute right to rule by establishing codes for their own domains (*bunkokuhō*), such as the Imagawa Kana Mokuroku (1526), and the Kōshū Hatto no Shidai (after 1547) of the house of Takeda. Meant to control vassals, such codes had little to say about women except for specifying the lord's right to approve marriages and to determine succession. After the fall of the Kamakura shogunate in 1333, a contract to provide military services in exchange for land became the principal form of land possession, and women gradually lost the right to inherit land. In the latter part of the sixteenth century, especially after 1582, national cadastral surveys (surveys of land for tax purposes) registered the names of men responsible for working the fields. As the nobility became impoverished by the confiscation of their estates, women received less and less. Centuries of violence and government by a military class established patriarchy as entrenched custom.

The Tokugawa regime (1603–1867) followed the sixteenth-century tradition of issuing edicts, to the military (Buke Shohatto, six between 1615 and 1715), to the nobility (Kinchū narabi ni Kuge Shohatto, 1615), and a series of ad hoc edicts (*ofuregaki*), of which there are four compilations. The shogunate sought to maintain hierarchy, status, and control of vassals. Except for the requirement that domain lords keep their principal wives and children in Edo (now Tokyo) and the ban of women from the stage, there was little legislation that directly affected women as women. A ban on abortion was issued in 1647, and most domains had policies against abortion to keep up the number of agricultural workers. Guidelines for magistrates, the Kujikata Osadame-gaki of 1742 and the Kajō Ruiten of 1767—stressed the dangers of crimes against one's master, of unbridled female sexuality, and of neglect in the care of children. And yet women are known to have ignored the laws. Whatever the nature of society prescribed by the authorities, barring natural disasters and dire poverty, women fared as well under the Tokugawa as they ever did: women in all classes married more than once, kept their dowries if divorced, initiated divorce (by seeking sanctuary in a temple or official house), assumed headships of houses, inherited households by adopting grooms, and earned their own living in a variety of trades. Around 15 to 20 percent of women were functionally literate, and many managed grade schools. Though married women lost a husband to a mistress, concubine, or prostitute, this hardly affected their marriages.

Conditions for women worsened drastically as Japan modernized its legal codes on the model of the French and German systems, the result being first the Old Civil Code, in 1890, and then its replacement, in 1896. To make all men available for military service, the new government enfranchised men and created a national system of households, like the old military households, headed by men and replicating the system of absolute authority represented by the emperor over his family, the people of Japan. The codes that limited the world of Japanese women were the Civil Code (Minpō, 1896), the Commercial Code (Shōhō, 1899), and the Criminal Code (Keihō, 1907). Women were barred from succession to the throne (by the Meiji Constitution of 1889–1890), were not legal persons, could not own property independently of their husbands, could not vote, could not join political associations (until 1922), and lost their children to their husbands in the cases of divorce, which they could not initiate. Infanticide and abortion were made illegal, and family planning was suppressed to create a large workforce and large army. To pay the new taxes paid by peasants instead of landowners, peasant girls worked and died by the scores in the silk mills, which earned the foreign currency to pay for the nation's navy. The young were subordinated to the old, and women to men. Women of all classes were subjected to the *ie*, the multigenerational house, and to the absolute authority of its head.

Most of the inequalities were mitigated by the post-war 1947 Constitution of Japan. With the abolishment of the patrilineal house (*ie*) and the authority of its head (as well as the growth in wealth, which makes independence possible), women were free to marry to form nuclear families. Even though they are woefully underrepresented in government, women may vote (under the 1945 Election Law), inherit property (although there are women who refuse, since they have already received their dowries), and manage their own property.

A woman may sue for divorce but may not marry for six months after the divorce. A woman who does faces discrimination in the registration of the child's birth and messy legal proceedings to establish the child's parentage. Mothers are usually awarded custody of children upon divorce.

Birth control was not permitted until the 1948 Eugenic Protection Law permitted abortion. Yet the Maternal Protection Law (Botai Hogo Hō, 1996) permits abortion only for rape or for severe health or economic reasons, and only with the permission of the husband. For birth control, women relied principally on condoms, the rhythm method, diaphragms, and intrauterine devices (1974). Birth control pills were not generally available until 1999.

Despite the 1985 Equal Employment Opportunity Law for Men and Women and a revision of 1997, women still face discrimination in hiring, firing, and pay in the twenty-first century. The 1947 Labor Standards Law grants maternity leave and allows nursing on the job, while the 1991 Child Care Leave Law grants either the mother or father of a child under one a year's leave. But there is little in the way of child care.

Although the constitution and laws grant women status fully equal with that of men, it is the courts that have the greatest influence. For example, in 1999 a woman brought a charge of rape against a governor of Osaka. The court permitted her to testify from behind a screen and then awarded the plaintiff $110,000 in damages. In 2001 the Law for the Prevention of Spousal Violence and Protection of Victims was passed, making the fine for hitting a wife or former wife $10,000.

[*See also* Aristocracy, *subentry* Comparative History, *and* Japan.]

BIBLIOGRAPHY

Grossberg, Kenneth, ed. *The Laws of the Muromachi Bakufu*. Translated by Kenneth Grossberg and Kanamoto Nobuhisa. Tokyo: Monumenta Nipponica, Sophia University, 1981.

Haley, John Owen. *The Spirit of Japanese Law*. Athens: University of Georgia Press, 1998.

Hall, John Carey. *Japanese Feudal Law*. Washington, D.C.: University Publications of America, 1979. First published 1911.

Wigmore, John Henry, ed. *Law and Justice in Tokugawa Japan: Materials for the History of Japanese Law and Justice under the Tokugawa Shogunate 1603–1867*. Tokyo: University of Tokyo Press, 1985.

S. A. THORNTON

Latin America

Women in Latin America have achieved important victories in the field of legal rights. By the dawn of the twenty-first century the majority of Latin American countries had enacted legislation intended to guarantee equal status to men and women and, most important, to help women overcome the subordinate gender role that the law has traditionally given them. Modern constitutional provisions have recognized the importance of women's status by guaranteeing them the same rights as men, and statutory legislation has specifically targeted some of the most critical problems that Latin American women have traditionally faced in the fields of political rights, reproductive rights, labor conditions, family status, domestic relationships, health, and education, to name a few.

Outside the state's apparatus, numerous non-governmental organizations have emerged at the local and international levels to advance and protect women's rights. Multilateral entities like the Organization of American States (OAS), the Inter-American Commission of Human Rights (IACHR), the United Nations Food and Agriculture Organization (FAO), and the World Health Organization (WHO) have also established a myriad of initiatives to this end.

Latin American women can hardly be treated as a homogeneous group. The region comprises twenty countries with different social, political, and economic realities, where social stratification, race, economic status, and gender have each played roles in affecting women's status. Also there are significant differences across national legal systems, as well as in each nation's legal cultures—that is, in the attitudes and perceptions that its citizens have toward the law. However, some common traits can still be identified.

Most of the region was once dominated by Spanish and Portuguese colonizers, who during more than two centuries transplanted their legal, political, and social structures from Europe to the heterogeneous colonies of the New World. As a result Luso-Hispanic laws and legal principles were regularly applied across the territories, thus creating a relative uniformity throughout the different colonies. Whereas the Portuguese monarchy controlled Brazil, the Spanish kingdom of Castile ruled over the rest of the territories in South and Central America.

In the case of the Spanish provinces, an extensive corpus of legislation largely based on Visigoth, Roman, and canon law was applied during colonial times and, in many instances, mixed with local regulations. The most relevant codes were the Siete Partidas promulgated by Alfonso X El Sabio in 1265, the Ordenamiento de Alcalá of 1348, Leyes del Toro of 1505, Nueva Recopilación de las Leyes de Castilla of 1567, Recopilación de las Leyes de Indias of 1680, and Novísima Recopilación de las Leyes de España of 1805. In the case of the Brazilian territory, the most influential legislation was the Código Philipino, ou Ordenacoes e Leis do Reino de Portugal, compiled by Philip II in 1603. All these texts contained detailed provisions pertaining to the status of women, mainly dealing with their legal capacity, property rights, family relations, and criminal justice. And even though authority among Spanish colonies was largely decentralized, women experienced similar challenges and enjoyed more or less the same benefits throughout the region.

The ideas advanced by the French Revolution and some of the principles set forth by the Code Napoléon (1804) also influenced the legislators of the early Latin American republics during the nineteenth century. The most salient impact was with respect to the regulation of women's rights in areas like civil marriage and divorce, the age of majority, and the institution of entails. As a consequence of the separatist movements that resulted in the establishment of independent Latin American states, the young nations also developed their own unique legal framework and created institutions not previously found in Spanish or French law.

Another shared characteristic of Latin American women is that their status has been affected by the preponderant role that the Roman Catholic Church played throughout the region during colonial times. By extensively regulating family life and having exclusive control over the institution of marriage, the religious hierarchy contributed to the preservation of the patriarchal model that traditionally enabled men to hold greater economic, social, and political power. The colonial legal and social structures, largely modeled after the church's moral views of the family, placed women in a subordinate, semiautonomous, and unequal position with respect to men, and on occasion their behavior was far more scrutinized than that of men. One typical example of such disparate treatment is adultery. Even though both men and women had the duty to remain faithful to each other during marriage, the adultery committed by a woman usually carried a far more severe sanction than that committed by a man.

Marriage has traditionally had an important place in the lives of Latin American women. On the one hand, marriage has usually allowed women to achieve higher social and moral positions, economic security, and status; but it has also brought important limitations to their legal sphere. Early-twenty-first-century legislation throughout the region places emphasis on guaranteeing equality among men and women, and most reform efforts have focused on expunging the discriminatory provisions that established female subordination as a rule. To this end, most countries have now abolished the rules that vested familial authority in men. They have also eliminated the laws that restricted the legal capacity of married women, and prevented them from making decisions regarding the well-being of their children. However, some remnants of colonial legislation can still be found within a number of countries. In Chile, for example, men are in charge of administrating not only marital property but also their wives' personal assets. Married women cannot fully exercise their rights and are subject to significant restrictions to transfer and administer their own property. A similar situation exists in the Dominican Republic where the husband is still seen as the head of the household, and as such is the only one who decides the family's legal domicile, and the transfer and administration of community property, among other things. In most countries it is the wife who adopts her husband's family name.

One of the most important achievements of the republican codes of the nineteenth century was the secularization of marriage and the regulation of divorce, which took away from the church the exclusive jurisdiction over this area and contributed to the separation between the religious authority and the secular state. Despite being criticized by the church, states viewed divorce as a solution for women so that they could get out of oppressive marriages and regain their individual freedom. Central American countries led the way in this respect: all of them had adopted civil divorce by the end of the nineteenth century, whereas their South American counterparts took much longer. By the beginning of the twentieth century in South America, only Uruguay, Ecuador, and Venezuela had adopted divorce laws. The rest of the countries in the region followed slowly, Chile being the last one to pass a divorce law, in 2004.

Legal Capacity. In the early twenty-first century in most Latin American countries, legal majority is acquired at the age of eighteen. This represents a gradual decrease from the age of twenty-one that civil codes established until the twentieth century and from the age of twenty-five at which full capacity was acquired when colonial and early republican legislation was in force. Legal majority is what allows citizens to vote, to enter validly into contractual obligations, to bequest, to marry without parental permission, and in general to exercise rights and fulfill obligations of any kind.

Even though the provisions that institute full legal capacity apply to men and women equally, some exceptional gendered rules are still in effect that establish different age requirements for women to exercise certain rights. The most common rule of this kind is the one that sets a specific minimum age for a woman to marry (with parental consent). For women the minimum age varies between twelve and sixteen, whereas for men the minimum age varies between fourteen and eighteen.

At least in formal terms, women in the early twenty-first century enjoy the same legal rights as men in matters of testamentary freedom, inheritance, and administration of their property. This reflects a significant change from the traditional legal regime that prevailed in Latin America until the first half of the twentieth century, which gave men a dominant role over their wives' patrimonial rights.

Property Rights. In the colonial period and even after the establishment of the republican era, Latin American women faced important limitations in their ability to access and control their property. Women were always entitled to own, acquire, and bequeath property, but its administration was always in the hands of the male head of their household. The institution of *patria potestas* gave men the right to exercise extensive powers over the person and property of his family members and especially over women, who were thought of as fragile and weak.

During marriage, men were called to administer their wives' private assets, including the dowry and *arras* (groom's wedding gift to his wife). But the law also created mechanisms to prevent the misappropriation of the wife's estate and to protect it from the husband and his creditors. Women used these remedies to protect their economic interests and to counterbalance the power granted to men. Early Latin American civil codes preserved the patriarchal model, and it was not until the mid-twentieth century that gender-progressive legislation made the transition from a male-dominated family structure to a dual-headed one. The result was that women gained control over their own assets and began sharing authority with their husbands.

Another important aspect of the property rights of women is referred to as the marital patrimonial regime. Statutory regulations on marriage estates in Latin America have always oscillated between full or partial community (*gananciales*) and total separation of property. Full community was typical of Brazil, and partial community was typical of other South American countries that followed the principles of colonial legislation, whereas separation of property was an innovation established by Central American countries as a default regime during the early twentieth century. The separation-of-property regime was considered a victory in the sphere of women's rights, since it allowed them to manage their own assets without their husbands' consent. South American countries still give preference to the partial-community regime, according to which all property acquired after the celebration of the marriage is deemed common and therefore subject to the administration of both spouses and all that was acquired before the marriage belongs to each spouse individually.

[*See also* Divorce; Marriage; *and* Property Rights.]

BIBLIOGRAPHY

Aviel, JoAnn Fagot. "Political Participation of Women in Latin America." *Western Political Quarterly* 34 (1981): 156–173.

Crotty, Patricia McGee. *Women and Family Law: Connecting the Public and the Private*. New York: Peter Lang, 1998.

Deere, Carmen Diana, and Magdalena León. "Derechos de Propiedad, herencia de las esposas e igualdad de género: aspectos comparativos entre Brasil e Hispanoamérica." *Revista Estudos Feministas*, Florianópolis 9, no.2, 2001.

Deere, Carmen Diana, and Magdalena León. "Liberalism and Married Women's Property Rights in Nineteenth Century Latin America." *Hispanic American Historical Review* 85 (2005): 627–678.

Díaz, Arlene J. *Female Citizens, Patriarchs, and the Law in Venezuela, 1786–1904*. Lincoln: University of Nebraska Press, 2004.

Gauderman, Kimberly. *Women's Lives in Colonial Quito*. Austin: University of Texas Press, 2003.

Kanowitz, Leo. *Women and the Law: The Unfinished Revolution*. Albuquerque: University of New Mexico Press, 1969.

Mirow, Matthew C. "Borrowing Private Law in Latin America: Andrés Bello's Use of the Code Napoleón in Drafting the Chilean Civil Code." *Louisiana Law Review* 61 (2001): 291–239.

Mirow, Matthew C. *Latin American Law: A History of Private Law and Institutions in Spanish America*. Austin: University of Texas Press, 2004.

Seed, Patricia. *To Love, Honor, and Obey in Colonial Mexico: Conflicts over Marriage Choice, 1574–1821*. Stanford, Calif.: Stanford University Press. 1998.

MANUEL A. GÓMEZ

Medieval Roman and Canon Law

The mass migration of Germanic people into western Europe from the late fourth century C.E. fractured the unity of the Roman Empire. By 600 the western half of the empire had been divided into individual Germanic kingdoms of varying size and ethnic composition, the eastern half of the empire had been transformed into a largely Greek-speaking autocracy (the Byzantine Empire), and the southern Mediterranean, from North Africa to Syria, was poised to be appropriated first by a resurgent Persian Empire and then by the Islamic Umayyad Empire.

The political, geographic, and ethnic fragmentation of the former Roman Empire extended to systems of law and justice. The Germanic conquerors of Italy and Spain maintained their own customary laws but mandated that the Roman population continue to be governed under Roman law. In Frankish Gaul, Germanic and Roman systems of law competed and intertwined, with the south being dominated by Roman legal traditions and the north by Germanic, local, and customary law.

The Roman law most closely associated with the early medieval West was not the Corpus Juris Civilis (Body of Civil Law), compiled by the command of Emperor Justinian about 550 C.E., but instead an earlier compilation under Emperor Theodosius II. The Theodosian Code was the only Roman law in the West until the twelfth-century rediscovery of Justinian's Digest (part of the Corpus Juris Civilis), which revolutionized the development and codification of law in western Europe and in particular led to the codification of the laws of the Christian church, referred to as canon law. Thus the legal position of women in the medieval West varied, sometimes significantly, according to location, but it always reflected to some extent the traditional liabilities that women experienced under Roman law.

Medieval Marital Law. A miniature marriage scene from the "Magnus Eriksson Code of Law," Sweden, c. 1450. UNIVERSITY LIBRARY, UPPSALA, SWEDEN/BRIDGEMAN-GIRAUDON/ART RESOURCE, NY

Byzantine Law. The Eastern Roman Empire, called the Byzantine Empire after 600, had never stopped operating under the Corpus Juris Civilis. This was added to in every imperial reign in books of laws known as Novellae (New Laws), written in Greek after 600 but still recognizably Roman in construction. Since Byzantine law was fundamentally based on late Roman imperial law, the legal status of women did not change significantly from the norms of the sixth century. Although aristocratic women and women in the imperial family sometimes commanded great power, even ruling as empresses at key times, the traditional restriction of women from public life and the traditional hostility against independent women persisted. The greater influence of Greek culture in the Byzantine Empire also contributed to hardened attitudes about relegating women to the domestic sphere, to the requirement that respectable women—that is, women who were not prostitutes, entertainers, or slaves—be entirely veiled, and to a growing tension between ideology and the economic need of some women to work in public to survive and care for their families.

Like the earlier Roman civil law, Byzantine law relates to women almost entirely in the contexts of marriage, legitimacy, and inheritance. Although women experienced significant restrictions on their public capacities—they could not act as witnesses, hold administrative office, or be involved in banking, for instance—they were permitted to own property and could both inherit land and grant it to others without male oversight. Changes in marriage laws in the eighth century made marriage a privileged state for women and emphasized the partnership between husbands and wives. The ability to inherit and maintain property gave wealthy and aristocratic women tools to influence the political milieu and gave poor women the capacity to be self-sufficient. Byzantine law, like most medieval legal systems, often emphasized social status over gender—a circumstance that gave some women an advantage but significantly restricted the vast majority.

The lack of clear separation between imperial law and the law of the Byzantine church (canon law) also affected women's lives. Although Roman legal traditions emphasized the need for all women to be married and made divorce relatively easy to obtain, Christian traditions privileged celibacy over marriage, discouraged both divorce and remarriage, and condemned public roles for women except as subordinates of males. In the Byzantine Empire, the Christian norms became embedded into the legal system. As a result, convents for nuns were controlled by the state, it became difficult for women to gain control over their marriages, and most public roles that had appeared in the late Roman Empire disappeared.

One possible exception to the restriction of women's public roles in both Roman and Christian law was the role of empress in the Byzantine state, both as wife of an emperor and as female heir to the imperial throne. From the time of the infamous empress Theodora, wife of and coruler with Justinian I, the position of empress (or *basilissa*) transcended legal boundaries against female public activity. Even so, the power of empresses was viewed with suspicion. The great Byzantine historian Michael Psellus supported the rule of sister-empresses Zoë and Theodora (active 1042–1056) but still objected to the notion of female rule. In his *Chronographia*, Psellus describes the problems inherent in female rule: "for the first time in our lives we saw the transformation of a *gynaeconitis* [women's quarters] into an emperor's council chamber. . . . To put it quite candidly . . . neither of them was fitted by temperament to govern. They neither knew how to administer nor were they capable of serious argument on the subject of politics" (Psellus, Book 6).

Medieval Canon Law. In the West, the institutionalization of the Christian church in the later Roman Empire led to the establishment of an extensive bureaucracy, complete with sophisticated administration, with the pope as head. The development of canon law marks a logical step in the papacy's program of operating as sovereign ruler in the West. Canon law served within the church to govern the lives of priests, monks, and nuns and in the society at large to oversee places where religious and secular life intersected: birth, marriage, and death. As a result, the church could regulate the activities of the medieval populace even when challenged by local custom, state legal systems, and Roman civil law.

The relationship between canon and local law became far more complex because both systems regulated many of the same phenomena. Local laws regarding marriage and remarriage, the legitimacy of children, divorce, widowhood, inheritance, even the definition of rape, differed from region to region. Canon law defined and regulated exactly the same issues. The debate over which system would have precedence in a given region occupied both secular- and canon-law jurists for hundreds of years.

Although most canon-law regulations involved members of the clergy, with only about a tenth of the contents of the Corpus Juris Canonici (Body of Canon Law) overseeing the activities of laypeople, canon-law courts were often busy with litigation over the secular issues in which women figure prominently. These can be broken down into a few general categories: marriage and divorce, inheritance and legitimacy, violence against women (including rape), and heresy.

Marriage and divorce. Unlike Roman civil law, Byzantine law, and most Germanic customary law (including English common law), the canon marriage law states that consent between the interested parties is the only requirement for a legal marriage. Medieval people seem to have been well aware that canon law drastically differed from local law in this regard, and clandestine marriages seem to have been relatively common. Cases of disputed marriages were heard in the Christian courts, presided over by bishops, including cases in which civil litigants disputed the existence of a valid marriage in the context of another suit.

The church also determined whom a woman or man could marry. Before 1215 the canon laws of consanguinity identified close kin as people related within seven degrees of kinship (that is, people with great-great-great-great-great-grandparents in common, on either the paternal or maternal side). After the Fourth Lateran Council of 1215, the degree of consanguinity was reduced to four generations (sharing any great-great-grandparent on either side). Definitions of consanguinity also included people related not by blood but by affinity: godparents, stepfamilies, and so on. Individuals of these relationships, too, were restricted from being marriage partners. The canon laws of consanguinity ran counter to local and civil law, both of which allowed considerably more flexibility in marriage arrangements.

The most important law regarding marriage categorized marriage as a sacrament akin to the Eucharist or the ordination of priests and thus indissoluble. Here, too, the church found itself in conflict with the needs of the emerging kingdoms of the High Middle Ages. In the secular world, couples were united in marriage to produce legitimate—and preferably male—children to maintain the integrity of family property. Therefore it was imperative for the landowning population in particular to be able to dissolve marriages between people who were incompatible or infertile. The church, on the contrary, determined that the indissolubility of marriage outweighed all other considerations, including consanguinity.

One example of the priority of marriage and the primacy of the canon laws of marriage presents all the issues in a nutshell. In 1314, John de Warenne, Earl of Surrey, sought to divorce his wife, Joan of Bar, on the grounds of both consanguinity and incompatibility. Both William and Joan detested each other and refused not only to engage in conjugal relations but even to live together. William had acquired a mistress, Maud de Nerford, and they had had a number of children together, whom William hoped to legitimate. Although royal pressure was brought to bear on the pope, the discovery of a papal dispensation approving the marriage between John and Joan (they were close cousins) meant that a divorce was impossible. In the end the children of John and Maud were never legitimated, and the earldom of Surrey was surrendered to the Crown after his death. Thus the tension between the church's attempts to control the laity by designating marriage as a sacrament and the lay population's need for a more flexible system of marriage could have significant political overtones.

The effects of the canon laws of marriage on medieval women were both positive and negative. On the one hand the indissolubility of marriage protected women from being abandoned; on the other hand it also forced women to remain in abusive marriages without any hope of amelioration. Even though women could try to have their marriages dissolved on the grounds of impotence or, sometimes, life-threatening abuse, their success depended on having powerful male supporters and, usually, the acquiescence of their husbands.

Inheritance and legitimacy. Canon law also conflicted with local, customary, and common law in the matter of legitimating children, which had an effect on the inheritance of estates. Most Germanic customary law, including English common law, identified children as legitimate whose parents were married at some time. Therefore if a man had illegitimate children but then married the mother of his children, they would become legitimate and therefore eligible for inheritance. The church, on the other hand, refused to consider children born out of wedlock to be legitimate, even if the parents subsequently married. Therefore only children born within a church-sanctioned marriage could be considered heirs to property. In addition, if the papacy approved the dissolution of a marriage, any children born to the couple could be declared illegitimate on the grounds that a valid marriage had never actually taken place. The controversies surrounding the accession of King Richard III of England (r. 1483–1485) illustrate this problem. The legality of King Edward IV's marriage to Elizabeth Woodville was disputed, and their children were as a result declared illegitimate. This made Richard the only legal heir to the throne.

The effects of canon laws regarding valid marriages on women could be profound. Concubines had no hope that their children would be legitimated, and the danger of a wife's children being delegitimated following a divorce could perpetuate an unhappy marriage.

Violence against women. The canon-law status of women as victims of male aggression or control, though not all that different from similar categorizations in secular legal codes, nevertheless created significant differences in the substance of charges and forms of punishment mandated. A good case in point is the different definitions of rape found in secular and canon law. Secular law, such as Roman civil law, defined rape as a crime against the male head of the household because the rapist gained illegal control over the female's procreative abilities. The punishment for rape in most secular systems was punitive indeed: castration or death.

The church, in contrast, defined rape as a crime of violence perpetrated specifically against a woman. Though this might seem far more enlightened to our modern sensibilities than the secular definition of rape, the punishment deemed most appropriate for a convicted rapist was that he had to marry his victim in order to redeem her. To make matters worse, the church did not recognize marital sex as anything but consensual, so the victimized woman thus faced a lifetime of continued abuse. When the widowed countess Alice de Lacy was abducted by Sir Hugh de Frene in 1336, not only was she forced to marry him, but the bishop of Lincoln chastised her for failing to keep the vow of chastity that she had made after her second husband, Ebulo Lestrange, had died.

Heresy. Although both women and men were subject to canon laws regarding heresy, women were far less frequently prosecuted for heretical activities, and the kinds of activities for which women were prosecuted often differed from those usually attributed to men. One reason for the difference is the obvious chasm between male and female power within the church hierarchy. Women were not permitted to attend universities or cathedral schools, and most medieval heresies originated in those intellectual communities. Women were not permitted to preach, so even if they followed a religious heresy, they were less likely to be charged than male followers because female minds were considered more malleable and liable to suggestion. Generally, only women perceived as challenging the church's authority, such as the mystic Hildegard of Bingen, were in danger of being charged with heresy.

Two specific circumstances are exceptions to the above characterization: female participation in radical heretical groups (such as the Cathars, Lollards, or Beguines) and female challenges to the accepted social order, especially the appropriation of male clothing and male roles. Women were prosecuted for heresy in these circumstances, but unlike the trials of the Knights Templar, the prosecutions were targeted specifically at leaders or at individual women rather than at entire groups: Beatrice de Planisoles, the thirteenth-century noblewoman who supported the Cathars of Languedoc (see Le Roy Ladurie); Marguerite Porête, the leader of the Beguines of Paris, who was burned as a heretic in the late thirteenth century; and Joan of Arc, who was prosecuted in the fifteenth century primarily because she wore men's clothing and appropriated male social and political roles.

Although women were occasionally prosecuted for witchcraft in the Late Middle Ages (it was one of the charges levied against Joan of Arc but was secondary to the heresy of wearing men's clothing), such prosecutions most frequently occurred on a local level and were caught up in typical community disputes, such as those between neighbors in which one party was alleged to have cursed the other's cows or children. Most often it was not investigated through the Christian courts.

Assessment. The relationships among medieval Roman, Byzantine, and canon law have to do with their origins: Roman law arose as the civil law of the Roman Empire, canon law arose from biblical strictures as interpreted by the church fathers, and Byzantine law arose from the integration of Christianity into profoundly secular political and legal systems. Byzantine law integrated doctrinal and theological issues into the civil codes concerning marriage and remarriage, legitimacy and inheritance, and violence against women as part of the seamless integration of the religious with the political in Byzantine administration. The fragmentation of political authority and the competition among different authoritative bodies in the medieval West led to a similar fragmentation of legal authority and competition among legal codes. Canon law addressed this fragmentation in a more universal way than local, customary, and common codes of law, but its jurisdiction was nonetheless limited by the competing legal systems of the medieval western kingdoms and city-states. Indeed, the universal application of canon law lasted only as long as Catholic Christianity could claim universal jurisdiction over western Europeans. Once the Lutheran and Calvinist separations had been completed, the primacy of canon law was broken.

[*See also* Europe, *subentry* Medieval Period, *and* West Asia, *subentry* Roman and Byzantine Periods.]

BIBLIOGRAPHY

Amt, Emilie, ed. *Women's Lives in Medieval Europe: A Sourcebook*. New York: Routledge, 1992. The best collection of sources for medieval women's history, organized by subject.

Brundage, James A. *Law, Sex, and Christian Society in Medieval Europe*. Chicago: University of Chicago Press, 1987. A comprehensive study of the effect of canon law on sexuality and marriage in the Middle Ages, although issues specific to women are not fully explored.

Brundage, James A. *Medieval Canon Law*. London: Longman, 1995. A general text providing a useful introduction to the issues of canon law.

Kuehn, Thomas. *Law, Family, and Women: Toward a Legal Anthropology of Renaissance Italy*. Chicago: University of Chicago Press, 1991. Virtually the only book-length text on women and medieval civil law. Places the legal issues in the context of Italian Renaissance culture.

Le Roy Ladurie, Emmanuel. *Montaillou: The Promised Land of Error*. Translated by Barbara Bray. New York: G. Braziller, 1978.

Mitchell, Linda E., ed. *Women in Medieval Western European Culture*. New York: Garland, 1999. A general study organized by subject, with particular emphasis on integrating the Byzantine world into the Middle Ages. Of particular use are "Women in Byzantine Society," by Angeliki Laiou, and the section on women and law.

Sheehan, Michael M. *Marriage, Family, and Law in Medieval Europe: Collected Studies*. Edited by James K. Farge. Toronto: University of Toronto Press, 1996. The collected essays of the foremost expert on medieval canon laws of marriage. More accessible than most texts on legal history, but still technical.

LINDA E. MITCHELL

Russia

In the imperial period, the legal codes affecting women had a paradoxical character. Beginning in the eighteenth century, family law became more restrictive, explicitly subordinating women to men and rendering divorce very difficult and separation illegal; in the second half of the nineteenth century, jurists revising criminal law denied women agency and restricted their civil status under the influence of Western ideas about women's special nature. Yet in this same period, Russian women, married as well as single, gained and exercised more substantive rights to property than did their counterparts to the west. The Bolshevik takeover in 1917 swept these paradoxes away, only to replace them with others. Regarding law as a tool of social engineering, the Bolsheviks sought to equalize women's civil status with men's; at the same time, their provisions for and, subsequently, mandating of women's childbearing role reinforced women's exceptional status.

Family Law. By law and custom, Muscovite Russia was patriarchal, subordinating women to men and the young to their elders. Peter the Great (r. 1682–1725), author of far-reaching changes in public and private life, eased the second but not the first of these conditions. In 1702 he altered the Muscovite custom wherein marriages were contracted by the parents or by close relatives of the parties. His decree required a six-week betrothal period before the wedding, enabling the couple to become acquainted; the betrothed gained the right to terminate the engagement. A decree of 1722 explicitly forbade forced marriages and required both bride and groom to avow their freely given consent to their union. Parental permission remained a requirement. But during Peter's reign, only a man could rid himself of an unwanted spouse by placing her in a nunnery. Adulterous wives were sentenced to forced labor, whereas men who murdered their wives were merely flogged with the knout. Developments after Peter's death further buttressed men's marital authority over women. In 1782, for the first time, civil law articulated women's responsibility to obey their husband; the 1832 Digest of Laws transformed this into an obligation to render "unlimited obedience" to him.

During the course of the eighteenth century, strictures on marital dissolution tightened. The Russian Orthodox Church steadily increased its authority over marriage and divorce, ending the ability of parish priests to grant divorce certificates and making divorce virtually inaccessible to the Russian Orthodox faithful, even in cases of severe wife abuse. In 1819, a decision by the Senate, Russia's highest judicial body, forbade the separation of spouses. The internal passport, necessary to take a job, enroll in school, or reside more than roughly thirty miles (forty-eight kilometers) from a husband's ascribed place of residence put teeth in this decision, requiring a wife to gain her husband's permission for a separate passport. Although Senate decisions chipped away at this law, allowing abused peasant wives to obtain a passport without their husbands' permission (1888 and thereafter), and then wives of townsmen (1912), only in 1914 did all married women gain the right to obtain their own passport on request.

Property Law. Women's subordinate status in law coexisted, sometimes uneasily, with their legal right to own and manage property, which Russian wives, as well as single women and widows, enjoyed. In the course of the eighteenth century, the prior trend toward restricting women's right to inherit was reversed and women's rights to immovable property became more secure. To be sure, patrimonial property laws continued to privilege male heirs. Nevertheless, a law of 1731 not only permitted nobles to bestow land on a widow or marriageable daughter as dowry, but invested women with full rights of ownership of their estates. A decree of 1753 formalized married women's separate control of property and granted them the freedom to dispose of assets without their husband's consent. Thereafter, many noble families acted to secure their daughters' right to property in land in the form of the dowry. In such cases, she bore responsibility for collecting taxes, supplying serf recruits, and fulfilling other obligations connected with the ownership of land. In subsequent decades, noblewomen actively defended their legal prerogatives, pressing claims to inheritance and control over property during marriage. When they did, courts often found in the women's favor, suggesting widespread acceptance of women's right to property. Noblewomen's right to own and manage property was gradually extended to women of other social groups. It was mirrored in the customary laws that governed peasant life, which granted men almost exclusive right to land, but recognized women's dowry and the property acquired through her labor as inalienably hers. Courts had difficulty resolving the tension between women's right to property and their subordination according to marital law. Faced with complaints of husbands' violence in pursuit of wives' property, courts proved more responsive to property crimes than to crimes against women's persons.

Criminal Law. Criminal law targeted women who erred sexually, but otherwise made little distinction between men and women before the second half of the nineteenth century. Decrees of 1721 and 1736 extended state control over women's sexuality by specifying punishments for women and girls convicted of "loose," "debauched," or "dissolute" behavior, and, in 1800, by enjoining the police to pick up "vagrant maids of dubious character" suspected of harboring venereal disease. Decrees of 1843, targeting mainly women of the lower orders, culminated the trend by subjecting alleged prostitutes to state regulation. Otherwise, the law distinguished between individuals according to social standing (*soslovie*), not gender. Thus, men and women of the lower orders might be flogged in public and tortured under interrogation, while, from the late eighteenth century, the privileged were exempt from these physical abuses. This changed in 1863, when the growing association of women with motherhood and the domestic sphere resulted in an edict exempting all women from corporal punishment, except for those in exile; these gained immunity in 1893.

The 1917 Revolution and After. After 1917, the Bolsheviks used law as a means to transform women's civil status and equalize it with men's. The Family Code of 1918 ended women's subordination to men within the family. Marriage was secularized. Divorce became easily obtainable at the request of either spouse. Employing self-consciously gender-neutral language, the law allowed "spouses" to retain their nationality upon marriage and request support from the other if unable to work. The law promised equal pay to women if their work equaled men's "in quantity and in quality." The Land Code of 1922 entitled women to an equal right to own land and other property and equal participation in village self-government. When unmarried women who had borne children in unregistered unions swamped courts with alimony suits, the state revised the law of 1918, which had made no provision for such unions. The Family Code of 1926 extended rights to women in unregistered unions and further simplified divorce procedures.

Other laws sought to protect and foster motherhood. The Labor Code of 1918 granted laboring women eight weeks of paid maternity leave before and after childbirth; women engaged in mental labor gained six. The code also denied women the right to work at night, or where conditions might be dangerous to their health. A law of 1920 made abortion legal if performed by a physician, while referring to abortion as a serious "evil," necessitated only by difficult conditions. Subsequent legal changes aimed to ensure childbearing. The Family Code of 1936 recognized only registered marriages, made divorce more complicated and expensive, and prohibited abortion except when childbearing threatened the mother's life or health. It provided financial incentives to women who bore more than six children and raised both the level of child support and the penalties for men who failed to pay it. These trends intensified in 1944, with a new family code that made divorce still more difficult and deprived people in unregistered unions of legal benefits and access to housing. The law restored the distinction between legitimate and illegitimate children that had been abolished in 1918. It barred women from bringing paternity suits, and, at the same time, was unabashedly pronatalist, taxing single people and married couples with fewer than three children, while also making unmarried mothers eligible for additional financial support from the state.

These rigid strictures eased following the death of Joseph Stalin in 1953. In 1955, abortion was legalized. In December 1965, a new divorce law simplified procedures and reduced costs. Divorce rates doubled between 1963 and 1974 due to judges' favorable responses to divorce applications; by 1978 a third of all marriages ended in divorce—with women initiating most divorces. The Basic Principles of Family Law of 1968 permitted paternity suits and enabled mothers to eliminate the blank space on the birth certificate of an out-of-wedlock child. At the same time the government increased incentives for childbearing. In 1981, it introduced partially paid leave for working mothers until the child reached the age of one, in addition to the fully paid maternity leave (fifty-six days before and after childbirth). In 1987, it added two more weeks to maternity leave, increasing it to seventy days after the birth, and extending the period of partially paid maternity leave to eighteen months.

State-sponsored efforts to foster women's productive and reproductive roles ended with the collapse of the Soviet Union. The new focus of lawmakers was the family and the need to revitalize it. Their efforts led to a 1992 bill on the "Protection of the Family, Motherhood, Fatherhood, and Childhood," which proposed to make the family, rather than the individual, the basis of many civil rights, such as owning an apartment or a plot of land. The bill would have required women with children under fourteen to work no more than thirty-five hours a week. The women's movement successfully mobilized to defeat the bill. As a result of concern with the family, Russian law continues to mandate paid maternity leave; now, however, payment has become the responsibility of the enterprise as well as the state.

[*See also* Abortion; Divorce; Labor, *subentries* Overview *and* Types of Labor and Labor Systems; Marriage; *and* Russia and Soviet Union.]

BIBLIOGRAPHY

Engelstein, Laura. *The Keys to Happiness: Sex and the Search for Modernity in Fin-de-siècle Russia.* Ithaca, N.Y.: Cornell University Press, 1992.

Goldman, Wendy Z. *Women, the State, and Revolution: Soviet Family Policy and Social Life, 1917–1936.* Cambridge, U.K., and New York: Cambridge University Press, 1993.

Lapidus, Gail Warshofsky. *Women in Soviet Society: Equality, Development, and Social Change.* Berkeley: University of California Press, 1978.

Marrese, Michelle Lamarche. "Gender and the Legal Order in Imperial Russia." In *The Cambridge History of Russia,* vol. 2, *Imperial Russia, 1689–1917,* edited by Dominic Lieven, pp. 326–343. Cambridge, U.K., and New York: Cambridge University Press, 2006.

Marrese, Michelle Lamarche. *A Woman's Kingdom: Noblewomen and the Control of Property in Russia, 1700–1861.* Ithaca, N.Y., and London: Cornell University Press, 2002.

Schrader, Abby M. *Languages of the Lash: Corporal Punishment and Identity in Imperial Russia.* DeKalb: Northern Illinois University Press, 2002.

Wood, Elizabeth A. *The Baba and the Comrade: Gender and Politics in Revolutionary Russia.* Bloomington: Indiana University Press, 1997.

Worobec, Christine D. *Peasant Russia: Family and Community in the Post-emancipation Period.* Princeton, N.J.: Princeton University Press, 1991.

BARBARA ALPERN ENGEL

South and Southeast Asia

The interaction between women and the law and the legal rights enjoyed by South Asian women have largely been determined by the extent to which Hindu law has been applied by the state. Hindu legal code is derived from religious commentaries known as the *dharmasastras*. The most orthodox of the *dharmasastras* was the *Manu smriti*, which was relied upon heavily, particularly during the colonial period, in the process of determining the legal rights of Hindu women. Manu's interpretation of women's property rights, for instance, held sway throughout most of the precolonial and colonial periods. Manu identifies six types of property that women can legally possess as gifts given (1) during the marriage ceremony, (2) during the bridal procession, (3) "in token of love" (presumably by her husband), (4) by her mother, (5) by her father, or (6) by her brother. Although Manu did not intend this to be an exhaustive list, it has been treated as such during the modern period. Hindu legal code derived from the *Manu smriti* also insists that women be under the guardianship of men at all times. During infancy and childhood she must be under the control of her father; a married woman falls under the purview of her husband; a widow must be controlled by her sons.

Hindu legal code, then, grants women few rights. Fortunately, however, the living law in South Asia does not coincide precisely with normative prescription. During the ancient and precolonial periods, law on the subcontinent was adjudicated through local (caste or village) *panchayats*, or local councils, which were generally composed of five or more village elders or caste authorities (women were not strictly excluded from membership). While paying due attention to religious and state law, *panchayats* nonetheless tended to administer such law according to local custom, usages, practices, and most importantly, their own ideas of what was appropriate in a given situation and within a particular community. Penal, religious, and civil law, as applied by *panchayats*, was fluid and adaptable and varied greatly from region to region. Most scholars agree that women fared better under this system, as the severe dictates of normative law were tempered by local custom. Panchayats, however, were increasingly marginalized as the Anglo-Indian judiciary grew in power, jurisdiction, and popularity, especially with respect to civil law.

The British began administering law on the subcontinent as early as the seventeenth century, and by the late eighteenth century they had established the principles of "noninterference" and religious pluralism with respect to the "personal laws" governing the Hindu and Muslim communities. What this meant in real terms is that South Asian Hindus and Muslims would "continue" to be governed by textually derived religious code when it came to matters such as divorce, marriage, adoption, and inheritance. Disputes over personal matters, which disproportionately affect women, began to be determined by a strict reading of religious text during the British colonial period. Women lost many of the advantages afforded them by the *panchayat* system and felt the unmediated effects of orthodox Hindu legal code.

In addition to bolstering scriptural law, the British, acting in concert with native elite men, instituted a number of legal reforms to improve the condition of women. Nineteenth-century Indian society was consumed by debate and discussion over these reforms, which included the abolition of widow burning (1821), the Hindu Widows' Remarriage Act (1856), the Age of Consent Act (1891), and the prohibition of female infanticide (1870). Women, however, did not participate in these debates and benefited little from the reforms. Indeed scholarly consensus holds that women's legal rights and freedoms were increasingly restricted during the colonial period owing to the strict application of religious code and landholding policies that favored men.

Women, however, were not merely victims of colonial legal policies. They also took advantage of the newly developing Anglo-Indian court system to voice protests and win small battles, especially with regard to the possession of property. Women litigants were not uncommon in the courts of the Raj, and the judgments they received tended to vary a great deal from region to region.

Religious pluralism and the strict application of religious law represented a severe break, as opposed to a seamless continuity, for native Indians, but it nonetheless became the hallmark of the Indian legal system during both the colonial and the postcolonial periods. The independent Indian state, despite its firm commitment to the principles of secularism, continues to adjudicate personal law based on Hindu and Muslim religious law, leaving Indian women, Hindu and Muslim alike, with little legal recourse when faced with injustices in divorce, marriage, inheritance, and maintenance rights.

The legal status of women in precolonial Southeast Asia was high. Only in Vietnam was the status of women conspicuously lower. This high status was due to *adat* law (indigenous customary law), which governed kinship and sexual relationships. Divorce could be easily obtained by both partners, and remarriage was legal. There were laws allowing a woman extramarital sexual relations during the prolonged absence of her husband. Premarital sex was not considered an offense; pregnancy required marriage, however. *Adat* law also permitted temporary marriages, wherein foreigners lived with local women and provided support for them and their offspring; upon termination of the marriage the children remained with their mother. Criminal law applied equally to men and women.

Some women were allowed to participate in military and political activity. In Vietnam women famously led resistance forces against the Chinese. There were female military corps in Java and Siam; Burma, Patani, and Aceh on occasion had female rulers. Indeed from 1641 to 1699 Aceh was ruled by four queens until a fatwa (legal decree) declared that allowing female rulers violated Islamic law.

The spread of certain major religious traditions in Southeast Asia led to the deterioration of women's legal position; their physical mobility outside of the home and their sexual expression were also restricted. New regulations emphasized a woman's duties to husband and family. In the Muslim Malay Archipelago and the southern Philippines, *adat* law now coexisted with Islamic law, which allowed *talak* divorce for men (declaration of divorce without witnesses or courts) and made divorce for women difficult; however, women were able to remarry once they were widowed or divorced. Confucian laws in Vietnam were softened by customary Vietnamese laws. On the Buddhist mainland, stricter laws were integrated into more tolerant local practices. In Burma, however, most of the old *adat* law supporting consensual marriage, easy divorce and remarriage, and equal property and inheritance rights has been maintained until the early twenty-first century.

As the number of foreign men in Southeast Asia increased with the advent of modern colonialism, prostitution replaced temporary marriage and its legal benefits. Colonial laws often reduced women's autonomy and legal status as *adat* law became subordinated to "modern" legal codes. The introduction of Roman law into the Philippines reduced the legal rights of indigenous women, particularly in regard to children, property, and divorce. In the Dutch East Indies marriages between Dutch men and Javanese women were permitted but only if the latter converted to Christianity. If Dutch men recognized their illegitimate children, the children were given European legal status; this meant that mestizo children could be taken away from their mothers and put in orphanages to ensure that they would be raised as Europeans. Colonial laws also forbade relations between white women and indigenous men in order to uphold white prestige and superiority.

During the struggle for independence, many new laws affecting women's legal status were proposed. The Indochinese Communist Party promoted equal pay, inheritance rights, free choice in marriage and divorce, and an end to polygamy. Some Indonesian women's organizations promoted the importance of *adat* versus Islamic law and pressed their husbands (and the Dutch colonial state) to support monogamy and equal rights to divorce. In the Philippines women's organizations founded during the American occupation actively sought the franchise and achieved it in 1937. Thai legal reforms deprived secondary wives of legal protection and made it more difficult for women to obtain a divorce and enter contracts independently of their husbands. However, the same reforms ended polygamy and prohibited husbands from physically punishing their wives.

As newly independent Southeast Asian governments sought to extend state control over families and secure social stability in the late twentieth century, women were pushed back into the home. General Suharto of Indonesia made the promotion of women as mothers and housekeepers a key element of his New Order (1966–1998). The same period brought a reforming trend in most of Southeast Asia, however, as new family and marriage laws recognized the rights of women to free choice in marriage, to have custody of their children, and to inherit property. Yet divorce is still illegal in the Christian Philippines.

[*See also* Divorce; Dowry; Hinduism; Imperialism and Colonialism; India; Islam; Marriage; Philippines; *and* Prostitution.]

BIBLIOGRAPHY

Agarwal, Bina. *A Field of One's Own: Gender and Land Rights in South Asia*. Cambridge, U.K.: Cambridge University Press, 1994.

Agnes, Flavia. *Law and Gender Inequality: The Politics of Women's Rights in India*. Oxford: Oxford University Press, 1999.

Chandra, Sudhir. *Enslaved Daughters: Colonialism, Law, and Women's Rights*. New Delhi: Oxford University Press, 1998.

Dhavan, Rajeev, ed. *Law and Society in Modern India*. New Delhi: Oxford University Press, 1989.

Kumar, Nita. *Women as Subjects: South Asian Histories*. Charlottesville: University of Virginia Press, 1994.

Mommsen, W. J., and J. A. de Moor. *European Expansion and Law: The Encounter of European and Indigenous Law in Nineteenth and Twentieth-Century Africa and Asia*. Oxford: Berg, 1992.

Nair, Janaki. *Women and Law in Colonial India: A Social History*. New Delhi: Kali for Women, 1996.

Ramusack, Barbara N., and Sharon Sievers, eds. *Women in Asia: Restoring Women to History*. Bloomington: Indiana University Press, 1999. Extensive bibliography on women in Asia from premodern times to the late twentieth century with a separate introduction to each subsection.

Ray, Bharati, ed. *From the Seams of History: Essays on Indian Women*. New Delhi: Oxford University Press, 1995.

Reid, Anthony. *Southeast Asia in the Age of Commerce, 1450–1680*. Vol. 1, *The Lands below the Winds*. New Haven, Conn.: Yale University Press, 1988. Extremely valuable work on precolonial culture in Southeast Asia with special recognition of female agency when present.

Sangari, Kumkum, and Sudesh Vaid, eds. *Recasting Women: Essays in Colonial History*. New Delhi: Kali for Women, 1989.

Sivaramayya, Bhamidipati. *Matrimonial Property Law in India*. New Delhi: Oxford University Press, 1990.

Stoler, Ann Laura. *Carnal Knowledge and Imperial Power: Race and the Intimate in Colonial Rule*. Berkeley: University of California Press, 2002.

Williams, Rina Verma. *Postcolonial Politics and Personal Laws: Colonial Legal Legacies and the Indian State*. New Delhi: Oxford University Press, 2006.

SINA HILDEGARD MACHANDER AND NITA VERMA PRASAD

CO-EDUCATION. *See* Education.

COLLECTIVIZATION. In agriculture, collectivization involves the pooling of privately owned parcels of land to form large-scale agricultural units that are then farmed by the members of the collective. Land becomes the property of the collective, and the income that members receive is wholly dependent on their work contribution. In the past, collectives were often preceded by cooperatives, in which members received a dividend based on the land and resources they had contributed as well as payment for their work.

Historically collectivization has been implemented by socialist regimes with centrally planned economies. Such regimes justified collectivization on ideological grounds; they saw the collective ownership of land as desirable and equitable. Planners also believed that collectivization would increase efficiency. They argued that by pooling their resources farmers would be better able to afford modernization, mechanization, and technical aid. Larger fields would mean better land use. With higher productivity and efficiency, agricultural resources, primarily labor, capital, and raw materials, could be released to support industrialization.

The earliest large-scale collectivization was carried out hastily in the Soviet Union during the first five-year plan (1928–1932). After the 1917 Revolution, land had been distributed to the peasants, establishing a system of small-scale peasant farming. Despite land reform, considerable differences remained between the *kulaks* (rich peasants) at the top and the poorest at the bottom. The campaign to establish collectives was combined with *dekulakification*, a process in which *kulaks*, or sometimes ordinary peasants who opposed the collectives, were deprived of their land and homes, and exiled, imprisoned, or even killed.

Coercive collectivization was fiercely resisted. Mass demonstrations were organized, private property was defended, and government officials were attacked. Peasants slaughtered and ate their animals rather than allow them to be taken away. The ensuing shortage of draft animals and the general disruption of collectivization put harvests at risk. Hungry peasants stole grain from the *kolkhoz* (collective) whenever they could, leaving the collectives unable to fulfill their obligation to supply grain to the state. State officials carried out seizures of grain, which culminated in a mass famine in the grain-producing regions in 1932–1933. Recovery was gradual. By the outbreak of World War II, agricultural yields had only just recovered, and the livestock population took until the 1950s to regain its former levels.

The *kolkhoz* had been established for only about a decade when the Soviet Union entered World War II. In the period leading up to the war, industrialization was already the priority for investment and attention. The Soviet Union needed to gain strength and to catch up with advanced countries. The war necessitated an even greater focus on industry and armaments, a priority that was continued in the Cold War years. Neglected and deprived of investment for so long, agriculture was still a backward sector when the economic reforms of the 1980s swept away the collectives.

The pattern of collectivization in China was similar in some respects. As in the Soviet Union, collectivization was preceded by a land redistribution that established an economy of small owner-occupiers. Collectivization was justified on ideological grounds, but it was also hoped that the system would allow the state to extract a surplus from the agricultural sector in support of industrialization. Until 1957 the approach was careful and gradual. Peasant households were drawn first into "lower" and then "higher" cooperatives in which there were still different degrees of private ownership and enterprise. Finally, in 1958, hundreds of millions of peasant households were swept into communes (large-scale collectives). Perhaps because the Chinese revolution had rural roots and could command more loyalty from the peasants, the process of collectivization met less resistance than it had in the Soviet Union. Still, the establishment of the communes was followed by a terrible agricultural crisis. Although yields fell dramatically for three consecutive years, the state failed to reduce grain procurement. The result was a famine in which more than 30 million died.

Responding to this crisis, communes were reduced in size beginning in 1961. Many of their functions were delegated to subdivisions of the commune known as production brigades and teams, and efforts were made to improve work incentives—a perennial problem in collective agriculture. As China recovered from its economic crisis, more attention was given to modern inputs. The irrigated area was increased, investment was made in chemical fertilizers, and modern, high-yield seeds were developed. Agriculture achieved modest annual growth.

Viewed as a whole, the period 1952–1978 during which collectivization was implemented saw worthwhile achievements in China's agriculture. The output growth rate of 2.9 percent per annum was higher than the population growth rate of 2 percent. Food availability improved, and, with the terrible exception of the famine years 1959–1961, there was an end to hunger as a large-scale problem. Voluntary or very cheap labor was used to construct huge irrigation works. Agriculture contributed to industrialization by supplying cheap food to the towns and exports to earn foreign exchange to buy industrial plant and raw materials from abroad. But per capita food availability in China at the time of collectivization was lower than in the Soviet Union in 1928. Inevitably this support for industry was extracted from a poor rural economy at the expense of commune members. Rural standards of living rose very little, and the system failed to provide peasants with sufficient incentives.

In 1978 a reassessment of agricultural policy resulted in the introduction of dramatic reforms. Under the new household-responsibility system, rural households regained responsibility for farming the land they were allocated, making crop choices and marketing produce. Communes were abandoned and collective institutions dismantled; free markets were restored. In the five years that followed, the agricultural growth rate averaged 7.4 percent a year while the population growth rate averaged only 1.3 percent. The result was a considerable improvement in rural living standards.

Women under Collectivization. One of the social benefits of collectivization was supposed to be an improvement in the position of women. According to Marxist theory, women's exclusion from social production accounted for their oppression. Dependent on men, they were burdened with domestic work and reproduction within the family. Once land passed into collective ownership, the theory held, women would have equal access to the means of production and their productive work would be properly rewarded. Furthermore, domestic burdens would be greatly reduced by the introduction of communal child care and the provision of canteens. With economic equality, the balance of power between men and women would change and full equality could be established. However, reality did not see these ideals achieved.

Soviet women. Women were prominent as both organizers and participants in the peasant protests against grain seizures in the 1920s. Historians argue that this was

Collectivization. Farmers harvest flax on a collective in the Mari Autonomous Soviet Socialist Republic. PRINTS AND PHOTOGRAPHS DIVISION, LIBRARY OF CONGRESS

because they could expect to be punished less severely than men, but it was probably also related to their determination to feed their families. Once collective agriculture was established, women continued to be responsible for subsistence agriculture in addition to housework. They kept poultry and cultivated the plots that peasant families retained to grow vegetables for their own use. This limited the time they could spend working for the collective, a fact recognized in the *kolkhoz* rules, which required fewer hours of labor from women. They therefore earned less than men. The Soviet Union industrialized rapidly during the 1930s, and millions of male peasants were drawn into the towns. By 1939 the female workforce in agriculture was 58 percent of the total. Yet domestic responsibilities and traditional attitudes still excluded most women from all but heavy unskilled agricultural labor. Only 8 percent of combine and tractor drivers and 3 percent of farm managers were female. The war changed this. By 1943 women made up 70 percent of all collective farmers, more than 50 percent of the combine and tractor drivers, and even 12 percent of farm managers. But women's authority was associated with the emergency and suffering of the war years. They headed their own households if their husbands had been killed or were away fighting or in prison, and they got good jobs when all the men were away. It is hardly surprising that the postwar restoration of normality included the restoration of the gender hierarchy.

With the enormous loss of men's lives during the war and the absorption of men into industry, women remained important in the agricultural labor force to the end of the collective period in the 1980s. The progress of mechanization and technology created more skilled jobs in agriculture. But because these jobs went primarily to men, women's representation in farm management actually fell during the postwar years. By the end of the 1950s, 23 percent of rural women and 30 percent of rural men had received some sort of secondary education, yet women found skilled jobs in significant proportions only in raising livestock and dairy work.

Most rural women remained in the lowest-paid jobs of a backward sector of the economy. Cooking, fetching fuel and water, and laundering clothes were still immensely labor intensive in the poor countryside. Women's response to overwork and poverty, in European Russia at least, was family limitation. Anxious to compensate for wartime population losses, the Soviet government introduced policies to encourage large families. These were largely ignored, and in the 1960s the birthrate began a new decline. In the last years of collectivization the reaction of many young rural women to their lack of prospects in agriculture was a resolve to move to the city.

China. Collectivization in China was accompanied by claims that it would liberate women. The lives of rural women were highly circumscribed. They had few contacts outside the family circle, rarely attended school, and entered arranged marriages usually when still in their teens. Authority within the family was based on gender and, to a lesser extent, age. Work in the collective fields was expected to give formerly secluded women contacts outside the family. Economic independence conferred by their earnings would give them a role equal to that of men in the family, the village, and the collective. Their domestic burdens would be eased by the establishment of nurseries and canteens.

In reality the gains were more limited. Unpopular and economically unviable, most canteens closed after a year or two. Rural nurseries were only a little more successful—most working women preferred to leave small children with relatives. Chinese women continued to be burdened by the time-consuming work of preparing food, making clothes and shoes, and caring for children. They also cultivated vegetables and raised poultry and pigs on the family plots. They worked shorter hours for the collective than men, and their jobs tended to be less well paid. Men plowed and did work that involved machinery; women hoed, weeded, and transplanted and picked tea and cotton. Despite campaigns and protests led by the All-China Women's Federation, women were far from achieving equal pay. Moreover, their earnings, like those of other members of the household, were paid to the (male) household head.

Women were rarely appointed to managerial roles or trained for technical ones. The marriage system also contributed to work discrimination. As marriage was patrilocal and village exogamy was observed, a woman normally left her own brigade or work team upon marriage, when she joined her husband's household. Women were therefore seen as temporary residents in their natal villages but as

Chinese Popular Communes. Mao Zedong with peasants from Guangdong, twentieth century. SNARK/ART RESOURCE, NY

untried newcomers in their new homes. Their teams were unlikely to recommend them for education, technical training, or preparation for leadership posts. By contrast, young men had a network of male kin in their home village to support and promote them. Village cadres selected them for training because they would remain in the village.

Some women became team leaders, but this was unusual. Often they were women who had made exceptional marriages that allowed them to stay in the village where they had grown up. However, there were some real gains in this period. Women became much less restricted to the home. The expansion of education meant that most attended school for at least some time. Later, in the fields and at production and political meetings, they mixed with people from outside their families. Education increased their confidence and competence. All units were required to have women cadres to safeguard women's interests and campaign for health and marriage issues. As the development of women's education had more effect, female accountants, teachers, and medical workers began to appear. Peasants gradually became accustomed to seeing women with some authority.

Worried by high levels of population growth, the government started to encourage family limitation beginning in the 1960s. The 1970s saw a rapid decline in the total fertility rate, from 4–5 children per woman at the beginning of the decade to 2.7 at its end. (By 2000–2005 it had dropped to 1.8). This, probably more than any other factor, eased the work burdens and improved the quality of life for rural women in China.

Other countries. Other countries under Communist governments have experimented with collective agriculture, including the Eastern European countries over a fifteen-year period after World War II, Cuba after its 1959 revolution, Vietnam from the 1960s, Cambodia under the Khmer Rouge in 1975, and Laos after the establishment of the Pathet Lao government in 1975. Each had its own particular conditions and problems. In most of Eastern Europe, collectivization followed the imposition of Communist regimes by the Red Army, whereas Cuba's reorganization of agriculture was based on the voluntary principle and preserved diversity. Cooperatives, state farms, and private smallholders all coexisted. Vietnam, Cambodia, and Laos, all poor peasant economies, collectivized in conditions of serious devastation and disruption brought about by war. In all these countries except Cuba collectivization has been abandoned.

Assessment. Collectivization was proposed as a way of dealing with highly unequal land distribution, technical backwardness, and rural poverty. In most cases it was accompanied by increases in production, but these were often disappointingly small. Technological backwardness usually remained a problem because investment was siphoned off to industry, leaving agriculture with insufficient funds. It was often implemented in very difficult conditions, which no doubt contributed to its lack of success.

For women collectivization had both negative and positive aspects. Along with others in rural society, women suffered the horrors of violence, famine, and poverty that were often associated with the start of collectivization. The suppression of private markets that usually accompanied collectivization put an end to peasant women's sales of sideline products such as eggs, surplus vegetables, and handicrafts. On the positive side, collectives in most regions improved women's access to land and paid work (an exception is Laos, where women's customary land rights were largely ignored by the state during the period of collectivization and the land redistribution that followed it). Women benefited from the expansion of education and health in the collectivized countryside and thus might be drawn into public roles. Moreover, collectives campaigned against the abuse of women. The selection of target issues depended on the local culture; they included male alcoholism, domestic violence, forced marriage, trafficking in women, and female infanticide. The success of these campaigns was limited, but collective institutions provided a useful vehicle by which to raise such issues.

The problems that women faced under collectivization—the double burden of work in and outside the home, subordination, domestic violence, and poverty—had their roots in the social structures of precollective rural society. Collectivization did not cause these problems, but neither did it solve them. In particular, it failed to mount an effective challenge to female subordination within the peasant family. The sexual division of labor remained largely intact. Women who were wholly responsible for domestic work and childbearing could not compete on equal terms with men. Where women's lives did improve, the major factors were peacetime; rising prosperity; and access to income, education, health care, and the means to control fertility. These much-prized conditions are not guaranteed by collectivization any more than they are by the operation of the free market.

[*See also* Agriculture; China, *subentry* Modern Period; *and* Russia and Soviet Union.]

BIBLIOGRAPHY

Bridger, Susan. *Women in the Soviet Countryside: Women's Roles in Rural Development in the Soviet Union*. Cambridge, U.K.: Cambridge University Press, 1987. Well-researched monograph that covers every aspect of rural women's lives in the Soviet period.

Davin, Delia. "Chinese Models of Development and Their Implications for Women." In *Women, Development, and Survival in the Third World*, edited by Haleh Afshar, pp. 30–52. London: Longman, 1991. Compares the impact of collectivization on women in China with that of the household-responsibility system that followed it.

Jacka, Tamara. *Women's Work in Rural China: Change and Continuity in an Era of Reform*. Cambridge, U.K.: Cambridge University Press, 1997. Thoughtful analysis of continuity and change in the sexual division of labor in China's rural areas.

Lapidus, Gail Warshovsky. *Women in Soviet Society: Equality, Development, and Social Change*. Berkeley: University of California Press, 1978. Comprehensive study of women in Soviet society.

Meurs, Mieke. *Many Shades of Red: State Policy and Collective Agriculture*. Lanham, Md.: Rowman and Littlefield, 1999. The introduction and the conclusion offer a balanced reassessment of collective agriculture. The chapters include case studies of collectivization in Russia, Bulgaria, Hungary, China, and Cuba. Women are given only passing attention.

Pine, Frances. "Uneven Burdens: Women in Rural Poland." In *Women in the Face of Change: The Soviet Union, Eastern Europe, and China*, edited by Shirin Rai, Hilary Pilkington, and Annie Phizacklea, pp. 57–78. London: Routledge, 1992.

Stubbs, Jean. "Women and Cuban Smallholder Agriculture in Transition." In *Women and Change in the Caribbean: A Pan-Caribbean Perspective*, edited by Janet H. Momsen. Bloomington: University of Indiana Press, 1993.

Tinker, Irene, and Gale Summerfield, eds. *Women's Right to House and Land: China, Laos, Vietnam*. Boulder, Colo.: Lynne Rienner, 1999.

Wiegersma, Nancy. *Vietnam: Peasant Land, Peasant Revolution; Patriarchy and Collectivity in the Rural Economy*. Basingstoke, U.K.: Macmillan, 1988.

DELIA DAVIN

COLONIALISM. *See* Imperialism and Colonialism.

COMMUNES. Women have participated in the formation and governance of communes—also known as voluntary communities or intentional communities—for centuries. In general, the term "commune" indicates many types of organizations of people, including cities, towns, and villages, that in places around the world are commonly called "communes." Throughout history, however, people have founded their own communes based on ideological principles or shared practices of living. For instance, women mystics and nuns have joined together in communities such as those of the Beguines of Europe, who hoped to put themselves outside the jurisdiction of the clergy and secular government in order to live separate and holy lives. At the secular end of the spectrum, people around the world have settled in anarchist, feminist, and ecological communities in order to live out a particular set of values. Thus those living in communes have a sense of separation from the normal existence and values of the vast majority of people.

The Quest for Utopian Living. In modern times communes have formed around utopian ideas, religious faith, or a secular mission to bring about revolutionary change, especially in terms of family, work, and sexual life. In 1772, "Mother" Ann Lee became head of an English religious group called the Shaking Quakers that had split off from the regular Quakers to lead their distinctive way of communal life. Moving to the North American colonies in 1774, they eventually settled in some nineteen communes across the United States. The Shakers banned sexual relationships even among their married members, while undertaking collective agriculture and crafts. Their distinctive family ways meant that they had to recruit among outsiders, but eventually the communes all failed after making notable experiments in work, worship, and the regulation of behavior between the sexes.

After the French Revolution the West was alive with enthusiasm for creating perfect living spaces independent of ordinary society. Adhering to the ideas of the Comte de Saint-Simon, groups of intellectuals, professionals, and workers organized a commune in Paris in the 1830s based on principles of scientific production, shared work, and fraternal affection. Soon the commune's ideology had turned into a quasi religion, featuring a spiritual father whose prerogatives involved sexual access to the commune's women. Submitting to the men in the group but also imbibing the general ideology of equality, women participants soon organized themselves to write critically about their past exploitation and potential liberation by founding a journal called *La femme libre* (The Free Woman). These women formed a feminist cohort in the revolution of 1848.

A second important commune was Brook Farm, founded in 1841 in Massachusetts and associated with the ideas of utopian socialists such as Saint-Simon and Charles Fourier, who proposed detailed plans for the organization of communes or "phalansteries." Other model communities such as Fruitlands were founded in the area, and as in Paris, ideas of shared work, rational planning, and group living motivated participants. Important intellectuals such as Margaret Fuller, Caroline Dall, and Louisa May Alcott developed in the orbit of these communes, many of them becoming critics of gender relations that they saw there. As Louisa May Alcott observed of the 1840s, "in those days communities were the fashion . . . [and each] member was allowed to mount his favorite hobby and ride it to his heart's content." But her story of the experience, "Transcendental Wild Oats," showed men spinning out their wild ideas while women did the work (*The Independent*, 18 December 1873). Despite this type of experience, utopian socialist communes spread around the world after the middle of the nineteenth century.

Other communal experiments had more overtly industrial or religious goals. The English industrialist Robert Owen and his son Robert Dale Owen set up a utopian community in New Harmony, Indiana, around ideas for reforming work and family life. The son joined with Frances Wright, the founder of another commune at Nashoba, Tennessee, in her experiment with creating gender and racial equality through education and peaceful communal living. At about the same time, utopian religious impulses led Joseph Smith to establish his community of Mormons in 1830; ultimately the community settled near Great Salt Lake, Utah. The Mormon belief in polygamy was another aspect of the founding of new sexual and gender relationships that so characterized the founding of communes and utopian communities.

Politics and the Commune. More politically motivated were the communes formed by young Russians after the liberation of the serfs in 1861. Seeing the grip of the aristocracy loosening in the countryside, young people—many from noble families—escaped from their parents' domination of their personal lives to join communes. Young noblewomen had the additional motivation of escaping unwanted marriages determined by their parents, and in joining communes they took up hard work, which many had never known before. In further rejection of the ostentatious aristocratic lifestyle, they wore austere clothing and cut their hair short. Many sought out workers and peasants to aid and to politicize for what they believed was an imminent peasant revolution.

Ashrams in Central and South Asia have served as healing communities, with individuals entering these communities for a temporary period or for a lifetime. In 1895, Gauri Ma (Mataji Gauri Mata Puri Devi) founded an ashram in northern Calcutta (now Kolkata) where women could live communally and devote themselves to a spiritual life. The most famous ashram was that founded by Mahatma Gandhi in Ahmedabad, which was designed to flout British values of commercialism, militarism, and colonial oppression. There men and women lived out their commitment to truth telling, celibacy, and work and devoted themselves to acquiring the discipline necessary to practice nonviolence. Gandhi's unusual relationships with the "sisters" in his ashram have become the object of discussion, but the attraction of Asian philosophies has led to the creation of ashrams around the world, many founded or funded by women patrons. More recently many Asian ashrams offer temporary shelter to abused and impoverished women and are run by off-site volunteers.

The Commune and the Evolution of Consciousness. In 1926, Mirra Alfassa, born in 1878 of an Egyptian mother and a Turkish father, migrated to Pondicherry, India, to create with her followers an ashram around Sri Aurobindo, a famed sage and holy man. The Sri Aurobindo Ashram was devoted to promoting the evolution of individual consciousness and advancing forms of collective life. In 1968, after the death of Sri Aurobindo, The Mother, as Mirra Alfassa was now called, established another, more ambitious project called Auroville—an expanded commune intended eventually to accommodate fifty thousand people. In thirteen volumes The Mother explained the ways in which humanity would evolve into a different species. Auroville would be the incubator of this evolution through careful planning of agricultural spaces for organic gardening, an industrial ring for cooperative crafts, and at its center the "Peace Area, comprising the Matrimandir and its gardens, the amphitheatre with the Urn of Human Unity that contains the soil of 121 nations and 23 Indian states, and a lake to help create an atmosphere of calm and serenity." The creation of Auroville in southern India was endorsed by both UNESCO and the Indian government. The Mother died in 1973, but Auroville still exists.

Auroville was created during a new outburst of communal living that erupted in the 1960s with the backing of the global student, feminist, and environmental movements. In many of these communes "hippies" likewise sought to develop a new form of consciousness. Though many women joined communes with men, feminist separatists set up women-only communes. In some cases they still maintain them. These communes were part of a general move toward new family patterns, with the nuclear family becoming the minority household form. People shared property, sexual partners, and children and professed to reject middle-class values. They experimented with drugs, wrote poetry and songs, and tried to develop new ways for humans to relate to one another.

In all communes the exploitation of women by men and even of women by other women has been noted, despite many other benefits. The official rejection of hierarchy often led to the leadership of tyrannical men or occasionally of powerful women. At the extreme, some recent communes have had a sinister, even murderous side and have led to the exploitation of women members in particular. Asahara Shōkō, leader of the Aum Shinrikyo cult and communes, which let out deadly sarin gas in the Tokyo subway in 1995, not only forced his members to submit to drugs, brainwashing, and torture but held many women members in sexual slavery.

[*See also* Communism; Socialism; *and* Utopian Communities.]

BIBLIOGRAPHY

"Auroville: A Universal City in the Making." http://www.auroville.org.

Braunstein, Peter, and Michael William Doyle, eds. *Imagine Nation: The American Counterculture of the 1960s and '70s.* New York: Routledge, 2002.

Echols, Alice. *Shaky Ground: The Sixties and Its Aftershocks.* New York: Columbia University Press, 2002.

Foster, Lawrence. *Women, Family, and Utopia: Communal Experiments of the Shakers, the Oneida Community, and the Mormons.* Syracuse, N.Y.: Syracuse University Press, 1991.

Moses, Claire Goldberg, and Leslie Wahl Rabine, eds. *Feminism, Socialism, and French Romanticism.* Bloomington: Indiana University Press, 1993.

Sargisson, Lucy, and Lyman Tower Sargent. *Living in Utopia: New Zealand's Intentional Communities.* Aldershot, U.K.: Ashgate, 2004.

BONNIE G. SMITH

COMMUNICATIONS AND MEDIA. Debates about women, gender, and communications technology tend to revolve in various ways around the question of representation, whether in the sense of the depiction of women in media texts or in the sense of how women are represented in the production and consumption of the media.

Images of Women. Second Wave feminism from the 1960s was highly critical of the prevailing images that belittled, caricatured, or victimized women, proposing that the mass media was deeply implicated in the patterns of discrimination operating in society. Content analyses of mainstream media and advertising tended to show that men were represented as dominant, active, and authoritative, while women were represented as subservient, passive, domesticated, or sexualized. The analysis was not always very sophisticated—these representations were often seen as directly shaping men's behavior, as well as duping women into certain forms of oppressive femininity.

A fairly unsophisticated notion of media effects was particularly evident in some of the high-profile debates about whether there is a causal relation between pornography and acts of sexual violence against women, debates that culminated in the so-called sex wars of the 1980s, in which cultural feminists such as Andrea Dworkin and Catharine MacKinnon were ranged against anticensorship, so-called pro-sex feminists such as Carol Vance and Gayle Rubin. However, while the methodology of this early work has been widely criticized, it was nevertheless important in putting the disclosure and condemnation of sexism firmly on the research, policy, and public agenda.

Through the 1970s and 1980s much feminist media criticism was concerned with identifying how the media was an ideological tool in producing and reproducing the patriarchal hegemony, an approach that also drew attention to the counter-hegemonic possibilities of resistance as both consumers and producers.

Women as Media Producers. One of the strategies offered for redressing the balance in favor of women was to argue for greater access to the means of production of media images, on the rather problematic assumption that women as producers of their own images would inevitably produce more positive and representative public images of women. Alongside demands for more women to be involved in the media industries came calls for a new feminist aesthetic that might subvert or deny the male gaze and in its place offer authentic, believable, and positive images of women, often within new narrative forms. In some instances these demands came together in the production of innovative films for and by women, distributed at a grassroots level as an alternative means of information and education that would inspire and provoke debate about women's issues. In contrast to this often quite didactic approach, other producers were more concerned about exploring visual pleasures and fantasies for women, or simply establishing a presence for women within the mainstream.

Women as Media Consumers. Within the academy, too, the meeting of feminism and cultural studies began to focus attention on the forms of popular media that were widely consumed by women or were commonly associated with them—like melodramas, soap operas, romance novels, and women's magazines—and that had, not least because of their status as "women's genres," been marginalized, ridiculed, or entirely neglected by academic and other critics. These studies were in part an expression of the feminist adage that "the personal is political," and important work was done in unpacking the textual complexities of feminine narratives and the everyday practices of media consumption in the home.

It was suggested, for example, by both Tania Modleski and Michèle Mattelart that the formal properties of the daytime soap opera as a never-ending but interruptible and low-status genre worked to complement and reinforce the patterns of housework experienced by its audience and to hook them in to the commercial logic of the schedule. Work by Hermann Bausinger and James Lull began to examine the "politics of the living room" and who had control of the remote control. However, the concentration on entertainment and popular culture eventually encountered some criticism for tending to reinscribe the conventional gendered division of public and private, in regarding women primarily as consumers rather than as citizens.

Women, News Media, and the Public Sphere. In thinking about citizenship, news and current affairs conventionally occupy a privileged place because of the role that they are perceived to play in allowing citizens to participate in an informed way in the democratic process. Historically and philosophically in the Western tradition, the model of what Jürgen Habermas calls the bourgeois public sphere, which still colors the organization of modern public life, assumes and prescribes a universal distinction between rational public aspects of human nature and emotional private ones. The prerequisites for participation in the public sphere have conventionally therefore included impartiality, detachment, and reasoned argument. Everything else, including partisan or particular interest, emotion, or desire, was consigned to the private realm. These distinctions both expressed and reinforced perceived gender differences, and they were accordingly organized hierarchically to validate reason over emotion, impartiality over partiality, political news over human interest, documentary over entertainment, and so on.

Recognizing this, feminist criticism faces a dilemma over news and current affairs, which has conventionally been perceived as a masculine domain. One of the obvious ways of countering the masculinity of the news has been to insist on a fairer proportion of women involved in making and presenting the news. This is an argument based both on a concern for equity and on the assumption that the involvement of women would change the nature of news and make it more accessible to women. The dilemma for feminists making such an argument is that it gets caught up in essentialist arguments about masculine and feminine spheres of interest. Either women learn to read and make the news like men, in which case the feminist critique of impartiality and universal rationality remains unanswered, or the involvement of women inspires more human-interest stories or prioritizes processes over events, which again serves to reproduce traditional notions of a gendered separation of interests.

The issue is further complicated because the increasing attention given to human-interest stories has coincided not only with the increase in the number of women journalists involved in production but also with the increasing commercial and ratings pressure on news organizations. It is commonplace to suggest that television news, for example, has undergone a dumbing down or tabloidization, with the emphasis widely on more populist "infotainment." Underpinning this kind of criticism is the belief that when news is permeated with private-sphere values—or is "feminized"—it loses its traditional social and political functions.

Media by Women and for Women. Another strategy has been to develop separate women's media, whether newspapers, radio stations, or Web-based networks. Carving out a separate space within the public sphere for women as citizens in all their diversity can be read as a pragmatic response to the prevailing prejudices and institutional arrangements that act as obstacles to women's participation, although the creation of a space for women as women might serve to perpetuate conventional notions of separate spheres. There is a growing number of international organizations devoted to monitoring and promoting women's representation in the media, such as the International Women's Media Foundation (IWMF), the Women's International News Gathering Service (WINGS), Women in Media and News (WIMN), and the Feminist International Radio Endeavour (FIRE). Links to national organizations can be found through the International Network for Gender Media Watchdogs (INGMewa).

Women, New Media, and Development. The democratizing potential of the communications media is becoming a central concern in the modernization policies of developing countries and of the various NGOs working to promote women's rights. Gender-sensitive media training initiatives are now widespread. The Platform for Action announced at the 1995 U.N. Fourth World Conference on Women in Beijing, China, declared the intention to "increase the participation and access of women to expression and decision-making in and through the media and new technologies of communication" and to "promote a balanced and nonstereotyped portrayal of women in the media" throughout the developing and developed world.

However, one interim review five years after Beijing by WomenAction 2000 reported that although there were widespread indications of increasing numbers of women entering the media professions (not least in Asia and Latin America), women's access to decision making and policy remained limited, and female media practitioners still faced discrimination in the workplace. The review was even less positive about the trends in media content and representations of women, where negative and pornographic images were on the increase—trends that it linked to the absence or inconsistent implementation of national media codes.

Five years following that report, another U.N. report acknowledged that the development of information and communication technologies (ICTs) has enabled more women to be involved in knowledge sharing, networking, and electronic commerce but that widespread poverty and illiteracy, including computer illiteracy, among women continue to impede development. The new media technologies have a paradoxical relationship to the concerns of gender and development, enabling international communication and exchange while at the same time being beyond the reach of many women and so widening the gap between the information rich and the information poor. Women who are involved in working for fair representation in and on the media are campaigning for reforms in legislation and regulation of ownership and control, as well as for access and content, while exploiting the possibilities enabled by the new technologies and the global village.

The anonymity of the Internet has been celebrated by Donna Haraway and Sadie Plant, among others, as a potentially gender-blind public space where users can produce or perform new kinds of selves and circumvent conventional barriers to equal participation, not least in blurring the boundaries between nature and culture, human and machine, gendered individuals and genderless cyborgs. For others, such as Dale Spender, the hyperbole surrounding this latest communication technology ignores historical comparisons with the introduction of older media and fails to understand both information technology and women as embedded in existing social relations. Tellingly, one of the conclusions of the Beijing +10 report by the U.N. Economic and Social Council Commission on the Status of Women is that traditional media such as print and radio need to be enhanced, particularly in rural areas around the world, as local sources of information and as sites where women and girls can begin to participate in media and communications technology.

[*See also* Popular Culture *and* Soap Operas.]

BIBLIOGRAPHY

Dines, Gail, and Jean M. Humez, eds. *Gender, Race, and Class in Media: A Text-Reader*. 2d ed. Thousand Oaks, Calif.: Sage, 2003.

Haraway, Donna J. *Simians, Cyborgs, and Women: The Reinvention of Nature*. New York: Routledge, 1991.

Prasad, Kiran, ed. *Communication and Empowerment of Women: Strategies and Policy Insights from India*. New Delhi, India: Women Press, 2004.

Ross, Karen, and Carolyn M. Byerly. *Women and Media: A Critical Introduction*. Oxford: Blackwell, 2006.

Ross, Karen, and Carolyn M. Byerly, eds. *Women and Media: International Perspectives*. Oxford: Blackwell, 2004.

Shivdas, Meena M., comp. "Alternative Assessment of Women and Media Based on NGO Reviews of Section J, Beijing Platform for Action." Coordinated by Isis International-Manila on behalf of WomenAction 2000. http://www.womenaction.org/csw44/altrepeng.htm.

Spender, Dale. *Nattering on the Net: Women, Power, and Cyberspace*. North Melbourne, Australia: Spinifex, 1995.

U.N. Division for the Advancement of Women. "The United Nations Fourth World Conference on Women, Platform for Action: Women and the Media." September 1995. http://www.un.org/womenwatch/daw/beijing/platform/media.htm.

Zoonen, Liesbet van. *Feminist Media Studies*. London: Sage, 1994.

KATE LACEY

COMMUNISM

This entry consists of two subentries:

Overview

Karl Marx (1818–1883) did not specifically address the broad public discussion over women's status—legal, cultural, and political—that by the mid-nineteenth century was known as "the woman question." Yet Marxist theory that the economic domain formed the basis upon which social, cultural, and moral practices were built offered a way of rethinking women's place in society by drawing attention to its economic determinants. Marxist thought showed, among other things, that far from being ahistorical or "natural," women's position in society and in the family was subject to historically determined economic forces. At the same time it primarily focused on relations of production, not on relations of gender. While the Marxist tradition has produced an extraordinarily rich set of theoretical and practical tools for understanding the place of women in society and culture, feminist thinkers and activists have struggled with the formidable task of articulating gender relations with economic relations. This article will provide an overview of Marx's thinking on the place of women and of some of the complex expansions of and interventions in that thinking since Marx wrote.

The Classic Theory and Early Elaborations. In *The German Ideology* (1846; reprint, 1970) Marx hints at an analysis of the status of women in capitalist society, noting that "the nucleus" of the first form of private property lies in the family, "where the wife and children are slaves of the husband." In the *Communist Manifesto* (1848; reprint, 1998) Marx and his collaborator Friedrich Engels (1820–1895) critique bourgeois marriage by claiming that it "is really a system of wives in common . . . . It is self-evident

Clara Zetkin. The leader of the German Social Democratic Party, May 1894. INTERNATIONAL INSTITUTE OF SOCIAL HISTORY

that the abolition of the present system of production must bring with it the abolition of the community of women springing from that system, i.e., of prostitution both public and private." Linking the two realms—the public sphere of the marketplace and the private one of the domestic—that were by the middle nineteenth century frequently conceived as distinct and autonomous from one another, Marx and Engels argue that this division is itself an effect of industrial capitalism. Under capitalism the bourgeois wife exchanges her body, in the form of its reproductive ability as well as in the form of her unwaged labor in the home, for material security; this, they claim, makes her little different from the prostitute, who openly sells her body in streets and brothels.

Earlier in the *Manifesto* Marx and Engels point out that lower-class women have a different experience under capitalism. Capitalism's effects on the proletarian family structure are devastating. As women and children, cheap labor for factory owners, entered the workforce in larger numbers, the family unit was destroyed. The fundamental attention is on capitalism's extraction of value from labor. Human beings become things whose differences from one another can only be represented in terms of the amount of surplus value the capitalist can extract from their labor. The central category of analysis is economic class; capitalism impacts different classes, and therefore women, in different ways.

August Bebel's influential *Woman under Socialism* (1879; repr. 1971) was the first extensive discussion of the role of women by a Marxist. Under capitalism, Bebel (1840–1913) argues, even bourgeois women are proletarianized in so far as they are obliged to exchange their bodies and labor for survival and have few if any civil rights. On the one hand, women are a means of production—they produce children, thereby securing for the propertied class legitimate transmission of property and for the nonpropertied a supply of workers—and on the other hand, women are a form of low- or unwaged labor.

For Bebel, following Marx's theory of historical change, the moment of women's freedom is resolutely in the future, after capitalist society ends. Women's enslavement to bourgeois marriage and to social mores restricting sexuality and their exclusion from educational and public institutions are all to be understood as superstructural, that is, as determined by the capitalist mode of economic organization. The future freedom of women envisioned by Bebel is broad and optimistic. In his final chapter, "Women in the Future," he foresees the emergence of women's full civil, social, educational, and sexual freedom after the victory of socialism. With the abolishment of private property, marriage will no longer be needed to secure legitimate heirs; with free education, "the woman of the future is socially and economically independent, she is no longer subjected to even a vestige of domination or exploitation, she is free and on a par with man and mistress of her destiny" (Bebel). In Bebel's Utopian vision, however, women's education will still require "some modifications demanded by difference of sex and sexual functions." Although he never describes these modifications, he implies that traditional household divisions of labor will in some measure be retained even under socialism, evidently because he believed them to be rooted in nature rather than capitalism.

Engels's *The Origin of the Family, Private Property, and the State* (1884; repr. 1942), written in the immediate aftermath of Marx's death, draws from Marx's own notes, particularly those Marx had made on the anthropologist Lewis Morgan's *Ancient Society* (1877). Morgan's ideas on a matrilineal origin for human society and his depiction of a stateless primitive society where all property is held in common, suggesting an early form of communist social organization, had greatly interested both Marx and Engels. Engels follows Morgan in depicting prehistoric societies; for him, private property brought the crucial shift, where mother right was overthrown in favor of patrilineal descent to ensure that men's property was passed on to legitimate heirs. "The overthrow of mother-right was the world-historic defeat of the female sex," Engels writes. Women, "reduced to servitude," were the first group to be oppressed.

Thereafter the patriarchal family structure emerged. Engels's privileged example is the Roman family, in which the man had power of life and death over his wife, children, and slaves, vestiges of which persisted into the nineteenth century. In order to achieve the reproduction of legitimate offspring who will inherit the father's property, women's sexuality must be subjected to forms of social, legal, and political control. Thus while culture vaunts the ideal of sexual love as central to marriage, such love has had little to do with the institution of monogamy. Indeed, Engles argues that monogamous marriage brings the first sexual antagonism in history; monogamy "appears as the proclamation of a conflict between the sexes entirely unknown . . . in prehistoric times." The emergence of monogamy inaugurates an epoch in which "the well-being and development of one group are attained by the misery and repression of the other."

Modern prostitution supplements bourgeois marriage. Men in bourgeois society practice a mode of informal polygamy, where many women are held in common, so to speak, while each man has a single official wife for himself. Engels points out that the social condemnation of prostitution most frequently is directed at women, thereby signaling the real stakes of marriage: as long as they ensure legitimate heirs, men can enjoy full sexual freedom, constrained only by nominal social prohibitions. Engels unveils the culture of middle- and upper-class European life as laden with hypocrisy and false moralities; in this he joins any number of nineteenth-century writers. But where he and Marx differ from their contemporaries, socialist or not, is that they locate the fundamental framework of these hypocrisies in the economic sphere through a radical and coherent analysis of the ways social relations are themselves shaped inside and out by relations of production.

One of the contradictions of capitalism, according to Engels, is that the proletarian family is comparatively free of the kinds of gender oppression that beset the middle and upper classes. To the extent that marriage is a means of controlling property, proletarian households are not in the strict sense "monogamian," Engels points out. There is no property to control. With a large percentage of women performing waged labor, the husbands have lost a hold on traditional male dominance, and as a result of these factors, authentic sexual love can at present only exist among the working classes. As later feminist thinkers pointed out, however, in Engels's representation of the proletarian household, there is little room for explaining domestic violence against women except as a residual effect of an ancient system of property control that impacts the working-class couple only obtusely.

The importance of *The Origin of the Family*, however, should not be underestimated. In this work gender oppression appears as a major force in history and culture. Engels develops the ways gender oppression is structurally bound to the institution of private property, making clear that it is only with the eradication of this institution and the emergence of a new form of social organization—communism—that gender oppression can cease. Like Bebel, Engels is optimistic that "we are now approaching a social evolution in which the hitherto existing economic foundations of monogamy will disappear just as certainly as will those of its supplement—prostitution." He envisions a moment when women will be fully emancipated and when authentic sexual relations between men and women will be possible.

Women in Workers' Movements. Marx had provided a way to theorize the specific interests of proletarian women that proved vital not only in analyzing the situations of women in capitalist societies but in contesting some of the dominant preoccupations of middle-class feminism. Bebel's and Engels's elaborations had suggested that working-class women's interests were not aligned with those of their bourgeois sisters and that furthermore, as V. I. Lenin later put it, proletarian women were important to the success of any communist revolution. While the Marxist theory of historical progression may seem, in one view, to argue for the necessary deferral to a later day of political, social, and cultural issues pertinent to women's status, in another view, it makes the role of women, particularly proletarian women, central to that historical transformation. Socialist and communist women, like Clara Zetkin, Alexandra Kollontai, and Emma Goldman, made it clear that no revolution was possible without the full participation of women workers.

In Germany the revolutionary activist and writer Zetkin contested sexism within socialist and revolutionary circles, arguing against those who saw women workers as a competitive threat, since women were cheaper to hire and, according to popular wisdom, more submissive to authority. Against those who saw women's work as presenting unfair competition to men's work by potentially lowering wages, she pointed out that to pit male workers against female workers was to miss the point. Women's labor as well as men's was exploited by capitalists who appropriated it to produce wealth for themselves. In an 1896 speech titled "Only in Conjunction with the Proletarian Woman Will Socialism Be Victorious," she traced the ways class differences determine the kind of oppression women undergo. Zetkin argues that the proletarian woman's struggle, like that of her male counterpart, is explicitly with the capitalist: "Therefore, the liberation struggle of the proletarian woman cannot be similar to the struggle that the bourgeois woman wages against the male of her class . . . . It must be a joint struggle with the male of her class with the entire class of capitalists" (Zetkin). In this speech Zetkin argues that the participation of women in revolutionary action is essential; she critiques bourgeois feminism by insisting that women are divided by class; and she demands that proletarian men see women of their class as comrades in struggle, not as competitors or enemies.

Zetkin was joined by the Russian Alexandra Kollontai in attacking bourgeois feminism and in organizing and promoting the interests of women workers and their full emancipation. These women and others in Europe and America were strongly influenced by their early reading of Bebel and Engels. They focused on a range of issues, from working conditions and women's unwaged labor within the home to universal suffrage free of restrictions based on gender or conditions of property ownership. Where some of their male contemporaries were content to read Marxist theory as deferring the question of women's emancipation until after the revolution and others insisted that women's emancipation would be from waged labor altogether and would ultimately entail their "natural" resubjection to male authority within the home, revolutionaries like Zetkin and Kollontai believed that women had a central role to play in history as it was currently unfolding and that they must be in the vanguard of revolutionary change.

Marxism and Feminism. In the second half of the twentieth century, forms of Marxist feminism sought to address the gaps that seemed to arise from a purely Marxist analysis of women's social position. While this trend was no doubt influenced by women's personal experiences in socialist and communist organizations, it was also determined by historical shifts in labor and a broader reexamination of Marxist historiography. More women were entering the labor force, starting with their recruitment as replacement workers in heavy industry during World War II. In the years after the war, increasing mechanization of the home reduced the need for the kind of hard domestic labor that had been the norm in earlier times. If the contention, derived from Marx and advanced by Engels and generations of communist revolutionaries, that economic independence would emancipate women was correct, why was it that as more women achieved some degree of economic independence they seemed in some ways no closer to full emancipation? What of Russia and China, where ostensibly communist economic systems were in place and where women's gains seemed small compared to the Utopian visions of nineteenth-century thinkers? Would it be necessary to defeat capitalism globally before those visions could be realized?

In the United States and Britain women of the New Left realized they had to create new methods of analysis that explicitly developed gender as a distinct category. As Heidi Hartmann put it, the "marriage between Marxism and feminism" had become an "unhappy one" (Hartmann). Some radical feminists saw gender as a more fundamental category than class. Other feminists continued to ground their thinking in Engels's insights in *The Origin of the Family*, retaining the Marxist insistence that all forms of gender oppression are understandable in terms of the contradictions of capitalism. More recent theorists and historians in the Marxist feminist tradition have focused on the place of women in an era of global capitalism, examining new forms of economic struggle around the world and articulating class exploitation with race, ethnicity, and national identity.

[*See also* China; Class, *subentry* Overview; Cuba; Domestic Violence; *Origin of the Family, Private Property, and the State, The*; Feminism; Goldman, Emma; Kollontai, Alexandra; Labor, *subentry* Unions, Protests, and Strikes; Matriarchy; Marx, Eleanor; Patriarchy, *subentry* Comparative History; Prostitution; Russia and Soviet Union; *and* Zetkin, Clara.]

BIBLIOGRAPHY

Bebel, August. *Woman under Socialism.* Translated by Daniel De Leon from the 33d ed. of *Die Frau und der Sozialismus.* New York: Schocken, 1971.

Davis, Angela Y. *Women, Race, and Class.* New York: Vintage Books, 1983.

Engels, Friedrich. *The Origin of the Family, Private Property, and the State.* New York: International Publishers, 1942.

Hartmann, Heidi. "The Unhappy Marriage between Marxism and Feminism." In *Women and Revolution: A Discussion of "The Unhappy Marriage between Marxism and Feminism,"* edited by Lydia Sargent. Boston: South End, 1981.

Kollontai, Alexandra. *Selected Writings.* Translated by Alix Holt. New York: Norton, 1980.

Marx, Karl, and Friedrich Engels. *The Communist Manifesto.* New York: Signet, 1998.

Marx, Karl, and Friedrich Engels. *The German Ideology.* New York: International Publishers, 1970.

Marx, Karl, and Friedrich Engels. *The Marx-Engels Reader.* 2nd ed. Edited by Robert Tucker. New York: Norton, 1978.

Price, Ruth. *The Lives of Agnes Smedley.* Oxford and London: Oxford University Press, 2005.

Vogel, Lise. *Marxism and the Oppression of Women.* New Brunswick, N.J.: Rutgers University Press, 1983.

Zetkin, Clara. *Selected Writings.* Edited by Philip Foner with a foreword by Angela Davis. New York: International Publishers, 1984.

SARA MURPHY

Comparative History

Communist parties around the world committed themselves to the Soviet program of women's emancipation. This article will consider the ways in which ideology was translated into policy and practice. The similarities between the experiences of dozens of Communist parties operating in very different cultures are quite striking, both because most parties adopted the Soviet program and because patriarchal resistance to gender change played out in similar ways. The differences are also instructive, however, for they shed light on the political, cultural, and temporal influences on Communist praxis regarding reforms for women.

The Soviet Program. The Soviet program had its roots in a German Social-Democratic platform developed in the 1890s that called for civic and legal equality for women, equal educational and employment opportunities, regulations to protect the health of working women, and social services to relieve working women's domestic burdens. In the 1900s the Russian Social-Democratic Labour Party (RSDLP) committed itself to this list of reforms. After the Bolshevik wing of the RSDLP seized power in 1917, it developed a program of women's emancipation based on Marxist theory and the German agenda. Revised laws legalized divorce and established women's legal equality, the education and employment available to women were vastly expanded, and support services (health care, day care, and low-cost cafeterias at work sites) were funded. Female Bolsheviks also established the Zhenotdel (Women's Department) within the Communist Party to mobilize women's support and to enlist women in enacting the reforms. The Zhenotdel soon asserted itself as a lobby for womens' emancipation within the party.

People's Republic of China. Newly trained members of the Red Guard stand holding copies of *The Little Red Book*, a collection of quotations from Mao's speeches and writings, 1966. AKG-IMAGES/ ZHOU THONG

The limitations of the Soviet approach quickly became apparent. All Communists believed that women's emancipation depended on the construction of socialism, and the construction of socialism in Russia in turn required rapid industrialization. Party leaders debated how to build the economy until the late 1920s when, in an atmosphere of rising international tensions, they chose to emphasize military spending and heavy industry at the expense of social programs, among them the social programs most beneficial to women.

Communist leaders saw themselves as women's benefactors, bringing enlightenment and liberation to the backward female population. Their motives were ethical and utilitarian: they believed that women should be freed from patriarchal controls, and they hoped that freeing them would increase support for the party. Millions of women flowing into the labor force would also hasten the pace of industrialization. The party leaders and most of the rank and file were not as committed as the activists of the Zhenotdel, however, to gender equality within the family. By the mid-1930s the regime had backed away from calls to equalize the roles of husbands and wives and had endorsed instead the contemporary European conception of the nuclear family, in which wives bore the primary responsibility for housework and child care. Party propaganda declared that Soviet women had been given full equality with men. In return, they were to serve their country at home and in the workplace. The Zhenotdel raised no protest; it had been abolished in 1930.

Soviet programs for women bore considerable fruit by the end of the 1930s. The literacy of peasant females under the age of forty-nine increased 40 percent between 1926 and 1939; in the cities female literacy was more than 90 percent. Women were employed throughout the urban workforce. Day-care centers and cafeterias were being funded. There were shortfalls, however. The government had outlawed abortion and made divorce more difficult to obtain in order to encourage population growth. Women worked the so-called double shift, doing their paid labor eight to ten hours a day, then coming home to care for their families. Public services were woefully inadequate, particularly in rural areas where most of the population lived. But even with these major limitations, the Soviet program of women's emancipation was one of the most progressive in Europe.

From the 1920s onward, Communist parties that affiliated with Moscow committed themselves to following the Soviet example. What happened over the rest of the century was shaped by (1) the parties' political environments, (2) cultural influences, and (3) the time period in which the parties operated. In reality these three clusters of influences were intertwined, but for purposes of analysis they will be discussed separately.

Political Environments. The Communist parties' political environments can be roughly categorized as follows: underground parties and guerrilla movements, single-party regimes, and multiparty states. Each situation affected Communist policies and practices regarding women.

Underground parties and guerrilla movements. Outlawed parties needed all the help they could get, and most were quite happy to enlist women. Typically, women constituted small minorities (10–15 percent) of full-time members; many more helped out part-time. They organized and led cells, wrote and distributed broadsides, held illegal meetings, maintained communication and supply networks, and did housekeeping for men. In guerrilla wars in Angola, Namibia, Guinea-Bissau, Mozambique, Zimbabwe, Nicaragua, Cambodia, Vietnam, and elsewhere, women served as spies and combat troops.

A few female members of underground parties rose to positions of leadership during the underground period. The South African Communist Party elected women to its central executive committee, as did the Russian, the Chinese, and the Cambodian parties. The most powerful women were often the partners of high-ranking men. Vladimir Lenin and Nadezdha Krupskaia were only the first of many such couples. More commonly, women held office in women's organizations charged with cultivating support among women, or they served in the lower ranks of party organizations.

Communist women remembered the underground as a time of great hardship that was redeemed by the shared dedication, comradeship, and egalitarianism of the party. Most women who joined such movements were young, and they found the experience intensely liberating, for they often had more political authority and more job opportunities, so to speak, in the underground than they had had in the larger society from which they had come. Some resented the influence of patriarchal ideas within the movement—they wanted to fight as equals, not do the cooking and laundry—but the price of acceptance was not to question too loudly. As women, they were under pressure to prove to the men that they belonged there; as guerrilla fighters they learned to follow orders and be loyal to their comrades.

For the Chinese Communist Party and many others, the period of underground stretched into decades. Leadership was primarily a male prerogative, but women were integrated into the movement's lower ranks, and that in itself was a significant departure from local customs. Russian, Chinese, Angolan, and other Communists testified that the experience of men and women fighting together weakened gender stereotypes, thereby strengthening the parties' commitment to gender reforms.

Single-party regimes. From China to Poland, women's participation in governing Communist parties was strikingly similar. Women constituted a greater percentage of party members than in the underground years—usually 20–30 percent after the parties consolidated their regimes. Female Communists specialized in education and other social services, and they worked in women's organizations modeled on the Zhenotdel. These groups cultivated support among the female population, taught women about their new rights and responsibilities, enlisted them in various projects, and assisted in the implementation of policies aimed at women.

Some of the Communist women's organizations—the Organização da Mulher Moçambicana (Organization of Mozambican Women) and the Women's League of Zimbabwe, for example—spent most of their time raising money for the party and singing the praises (literally) of the male leaders. Other groups worked hard to draw attention to women's issues within the party. In the late 1980s the Asociación de Mujeres Nicaraguenes Luisa Amanda Espinoza (Luisa Amanda Espinoza Association of Nicaraguan Women) organized farm-worker unions to provide day-care centers, maternity benefits, and laundries. Communist women's groups were most likely to be effective advocates for women's programs in the early years of Communist rule, before bureaucratization set in. These were also the years when revolutionary enthusiasm was highest, making it possible for the women's organizations to rally the most support for experiments such as communal laundries and day-care centers.

Some Communist women's organizations grew into well-established institutions. By the mid-1990s the All-China Women's Federation employed 98,000 full-time staffers and many more volunteers across the country, and the Federación de Mujeres Cubanas (Federation of Cuban Women) counted more than 80 percent of the island's female population between the ages of 14 and 65 among its members. Such organizations enlisted women in volunteer work, counseled them on social services and job training, and ran educational programs. They also propagated the party line, and sometimes they lobbied the party leaders for attention to women's problems.

Working within a ruling Communist party both limited and empowered women's organizations. They were required to follow instructions from the male leadership (as were women in most political parties in the twentieth century). Furthermore, they were Communists, loyal to their organization and eager to win the leadership's favor. The concentrated power of Communist dictatorships meant, however, that when the women's organizations were working with the backing of the leadership, particularly the most powerful leaders, they could accomplish a great deal.

Communist parties ruling in single-party states around the world achieved many of the same changes in women's lives as had the Soviet regime. They declared women's equality in national constitutions and improved their status in civil and criminal law. They expanded educational opportunities. In Bulgaria, for instance, female enrollment in the universities rose from one-third of students in the late 1930s to one-half in 1965. In Poland, women received 27 percent of the doctoral degrees awarded between 1970 and 1974. Health care, particularly maternity and pediatric medicine, improved under Communist governments. Cuba achieved the lowest levels of infant and maternal mortality in Latin America in the 1990s.

Communist parties also energetically promoted the movement of women into the paid labor force by establishing affirmative-action programs in training and employment. In Eastern Europe, the percentage of women in the labor force rose from roughly one-third in 1950 to one-half in 1970. In China by the early 1980s, 90 percent of urban women aged twenty to thirty-nine were employed outside the home. Gender ideas affected employment opportunities and choices in markedly similar ways across the Communist world: women tended to work in fields such as education, health care, food production, clerical services, and textile manufacturing. Most held lower-paying, less-skilled jobs, but there were unconventional opportunities, too, in engineering, architecture, and other professions. In Cuba, for example, by 1990 women constituted 48 percent of physicians and 69 percent of dentists.

As in the Soviet Union, day care and the other services that could lighten women's domestic burdens lagged behind. The double shift persisted because Communist governments set the same economic priorities as the Soviets, because, like the Soviets, they ruled poor countries, and because they endorsed motherhood as one of women's highest callings. The veneration of maternity had considerable support from ordinary folk, female and male. In southern Africa, motherhood even became a rallying cry as Communist liberation movements called for women to rise up and fight to free their children from oppression. This praise for loving mothers did not have to mean that women should wash the dishes and defer to their husbands, but in practice it worked out that way, in both Communist and non-Communist states.

In many parts of the world, the family values endorsed by Communist parties were emancipating. In China, for example, where traditions granted older men almost complete control over their female kin, the party decreed that parents could no longer force their children into marrying against their will. Communist parties also worked to cut the power of clan leaders and tribal chiefs, who were enforcers of patriarchal norms, and they outlawed the most abusive traditional practices such as polygamy, child marriage, forced marriage, dowry and bride-price, foot-binding, genital mutilation, and ritual gang rape.

Over time, Communist programs and propaganda changed gender ideals. In the Soviet Union, Eastern Europe, China, and Cuba, the principles that women should enjoy legal and civil equality and that they should be educated and participate in the paid labor force gained widespread acceptance. Polls conducted in the late decades of the twentieth century reported that women in Communist-ruled countries believed that working outside the home fostered their self-esteem. For their part, men declared that they supported their wives' independence.

Multiparty states. Communist parties in Western Europe, southern Africa, India, and East Asia participated in multiparty states, joining coalitions with other parties and holding national and local offices. To succeed in this political environment, Communists had to be more responsive to public opinion than did those holding dictatorial power. They were also more subject to influences from the larger society than were Communists in one-party states.

Until the 1970s, most Communist parties in multiparty polities advocated the Soviet line, which marked them as progressive even in Western Europe, let alone the more patriarchal cultures of Asia and Africa. They also established women's organizations that conducted recruitment efforts among working-class women and held demonstrations from time to time. In South Africa in the 1950s, for example, Communist women active in the trade-union movement organized strikes. Working with members of the newly formed African National Congress and the Congress of Democrats, they also formed the multiethnic Federation of South African Women, which held protests against apartheid in 1955 and 1956 that drew tens of thousands of women to Pretoria.

The development of Second Wave feminism in the 1960s challenged Communist parties operating in multiparty regimes. The new generation of feminists accepted much of the Marxist analysis about women's subordination, but they also criticized economic determinism as inadequate for explaining the persistence of patriarchy. Rather, the feminists argued, gender should be given its theoretical due. Feminists in Western Europe and North America also organized campaigns to outlaw discriminatory employment practices, reform marriage laws, extend access to contraceptives, and legalize abortion. Their successes in building public support and winning reforms shoved Communists onto the defensive. In an effort to maintain their standing within the Left, many parties reluctantly adopted some feminist principles and programs.

South Africa and Italy are instructive examples. In the 1980s South African female Communists worked with other activists in developing strategies for liberating women that drew heavily on international feminist theory and practice. When democratic government came in the early 1990s, the collaboration continued. Communist women joined the Women's Lobby, which played an important role in shaping the new constitution.

In Italy, the Communist Party (the largest in Western Europe) kept to the Soviet line on women's emancipation into the 1970s, years after feminist groups had become active across the country. Leading Italian Communists dismissed feminism as bourgeois and kept their distance from campaigns to legalize divorce and abortion. The pressure on the leadership began to build from within the party itself, however, as a new generation recognized that the old guard was out of touch politically. By the end of the 1970s the party leadership had acknowledged the legitimacy of attending to gender discrimination and was making an effort to recruit women. In the 1980s they introduced quotas for female office-holding within the party. Newly promoted women in turn lobbied the leaders to take more progressive stands on women's issues.

Communist parties operating in multiparty regimes had to respond to shifts in public opinion in order to maintain political support. Furthermore, party leaders could not control members' access to information, which enabled female Communists in Western Europe, Latin America, Africa, and Asia to bring feminist ideas and agitation into the parties themselves. This was true even when the Communists held considerable governing power. A case in point is the Communist Party of India (Marxist), or CPI(M), which in the late 1970s was elected to rule West Bengal, the Indian state containing Calcutta (now Kolkata). Thereafter the Paschim Banga Ganatantrik Mahila Samiti (PBGMS), the West Bengal branch of the CPI(M)'s All India Democratic Women's Association, grew into a mass organization. By 1990 it enrolled 2 million members, of whom 60,000 to 80,000 were activists, working on literacy campaigns among women, supporting female producer cooperatives, and providing counseling and legal assistance to victims of domestic violence.

The CPI(M) took its programs and analysis of gender subordination from the Soviets, but it was influenced by the need to cultivate popular support. When the PBGMS could demonstrate that female voters were in favor of particular programs, such as literacy campaigns, the party leadership was more likely to extend funding. Furthermore the PBGMS drew ideas and strategies from India's vibrant feminist movement, even while condemning feminism as bourgeois. This combination of activist women within the ruling party and empowering political conditions made the PBGMS an effective organization. Consequently, the Communist party of West Bengal compiled a better record of reforms for women than the more centrist governments of other Indian states.

The limitations common to all Communist parties constrained the CPI(M). Its male leadership required the PBGMS to hew to the party line, particularly to the proposition that women's subordination derived from economic structures. When feminists across India publicized the evils of domestic violence, particularly the murder of young wives by their in-laws, the PBGMS avoided discussing the persistence of patriarchal values within the family. It condemned the abuse of women and assisted those victims who sought its help, but its leaders also trivialized domestic violence as the deviant behavior of a few overstressed working-class men.

This refusal to consider gender as an independent variable was common among Communist parties worldwide. It derived partly from Marxism's economic determinism and from the influence of patriarchal norms on Communists themselves. Indeed, local gender ideas and practices were often as important as Marxism and the political environment in shaping party behavior.

Cultural Influences. Patriarchy was the most important cultural influence affecting the programs and behavior of Communist parties around the world. Strongly patriarchal cultures weakened the Communists' commitment to gender change and limited their ability to carry out even those reforms they favored. The starkest example is Afghanistan, where a Communist government took power in the late 1970s. Afghanistan had a century-long history of liberal governments expanding women's legal rights and educational and employment opportunities, only to be overthrown by more conservative regimes that repealed the reforms. In the 1980s the pattern repeated itself. A Communist government, backed by Soviet troops, declared women's legal equality with men, prohibited child marriage, and encouraged women to take jobs outside the home, particularly in medicine and education. Mujahideen rebels condemned the changes as corrupting, anti-Islamic, and Soviet-inspired. After the Soviet Union withdrew its army, Mujahideen governments repealed the laws and programs and required that all women veil themselves in public. This reaction intensified when the Taliban took power in 1996 and instituted a reign of terror against women. Women were prohibited from working outside the home, stoning as a punishment for adultery was authorized, and Taliban youths circulated through the streets harassing women for a myriad of infractions.

Communist reforms for women elsewhere also provoked strong responses. In the 1920s women in the Central Asian republics of the Soviet Union were killed by their relatives for associating with Zhenotdel workers. Thousands of Chinese women who sought divorces under a revised marriage law in the early 1950s were beaten, murdered, or driven to suicide. Defenders of patriarchal institutions also had less violent means at their disposal: families simply forbade female members from attending meetings, going to school, or taking jobs outside the home. Neighbors and communities shamed or ostracized women who challenged gender norms. Male leaders of families, clans, and communities let Communists know that they did not welcome the new ideas about women, and then they used their power to intimidate women's organizations and block the implementation of reforms. The more powerful the local leaders (as in Afghanistan, South Yemen, and Angola), the less the Communists were able to achieve.

Women, particularly older, rural women, who constituted a substantial percentage of the female population in most countries with Communist governments, also rejected the Communists' call to liberation. They were pressured to stay within the established order by their menfolk, of course, but they acted out of their own loyalties and self-interest as well. Senior women in Chinese families, for example, exercised considerable power over junior women. They did not appreciate the "speak bitterness" campaign of the early 1950s, during which Communists encouraged daughters-in-law to criticize publicly their mothers-in-law. Women in many other cultures saw, quite rightly, that the Communists were trying to undermine their authority over younger women and attenuate their ties to their sons. Such meddling with custom threatened women's security, for older women depended on the support of their children.

Furthermore, Communists did not usually offer much to such women. Those parties that followed the Soviet program most strictly made few effective efforts to improve the lot of peasants. Their programs were designed for urban, particularly working-class, women. Reforms in family law proposed in the Soviet Union and China, for example, worked well among the nuclear families in the cities but conflicted with the traditional inheritance practices of the countryside. The Communists' all-purpose solution to women's problems—namely, joining the paid labor force—made little sense to female peasants who were already working full-time on the land or to older, lower-class urban women who did not have the strength for long hours of grueling factory work. The Chinese Communists did a better job of reaching out to the peasantry than did many other Communist parties, but even they had little power to improve rural women's condition substantially, and by the mid-1950s they turned from criticizing rural patriarchs to working with them. The lesson to women was all too often that Communists asked a lot and offered little. They decided that it was better to defend the arrangements that one trusted and enjoy the benefits and protections of their familiar world.

Female Communists were as unable as male to overcome the resistance of poor women, in part because they were not poor themselves. Most female Communists, particularly those who held leadership positions in women's organizations, were educated people from the cities who had trouble communicating with more traditional women. Communist women's organizations in South Africa, Nicaragua, India, and Bangladesh made headway among the peasantry by appealing to younger women, but even their main successes came in the cities, where patriarchal controls were weaker, women's options beyond the family greater, and the cultural gap between Communist women and poor women smaller.

Time Period. Finally, Communist efforts and public responses were affected by the time period in which they occurred. In the early and mid-twentieth century, when the Soviet Union was a shining model (and stern taskmaster), Communists around the world adhered more strictly to its program of women's emancipation. The parties under direct Soviet control, those in Eastern Europe, were the most orthodox; they also faced the least resistance from their people, because they were working within European cultures where the gender values endorsed by the Soviet program were already familiar. In Asia and Africa, Communist parties took the Soviet program into cultures where its notions about women were far more alien and where resistance was consequently more formidable. The process was roiled still further in the second half of the twentieth century by the development of two competing ideologies, feminism and ethno-religious nationalism. The demise of the Soviet Union itself then strengthened the influence of both these ideologies on Communist parties.

Second Wave feminism and the Soviet collapse. Communist women worldwide were influenced by Second Wave feminism. When the Soviet Union launched perestroika in the 1980s, those women were further encouraged to take a more ecumenical attitude toward feminist thought and to speak up more vigorously within their parties. Even the Soviet Women's Committee, which had barely said a critical word in decades, began to inveigh against the unequal lot of Soviet women. In 1988 a similar discussion began in the Chinese press.

After the dissolution of the Soviet Union in 1991, some Communist parties were abolished, and others regrouped to compete for votes in newly founded democracies. Most of the remaining Eastern European Communists continued to condemn feminism, but they also strongly supported the benefits program for women—day care, pensions, medical services—that were under threat of being privatized by cost-cutting governments. This advocacy gained the Communists of Poland, Russia, and Bulgaria considerable support among elderly women. In a poignant reversal of older patterns of resistance, gray-haired grandmothers marched in Moscow carrying banners that proclaimed their loyalty to the Communist Party.

In China and Vietnam, by contrast, the Communists maintained their political power while permitting the development of private enterprise. In the new world of booming trade and increased consumerism, the two parties stressed women's responsibilities to maintain family values, but they responded differently to women's needs. The Vietnamese Communist Party, perhaps because it had been at war through most of its history, had put a lower priority on women's programs than other Communists and had developed no strong women's organizations. When it legalized free markets in the late 1980s, the results for women were very similar to those in Eastern Europe after Communist parties lost power. Female unemployment rose, funding for social services fell, and the regime laid still greater stress on women's domestic responsibilities in the emerging social order.

The Chinese took a different course. There Communist women's organizations had a far longer and more active history. In the 1980s the leaders of the All-China Women's Federation studied the ideas of international feminism but kept their distance from it. Instead, they adopted the strategy pioneered by the Zhenotdel so many decades before: they argued that women would be able to contribute more to China's economic development if they were freed from the burdens of the double shift. The federation also called on the party to make good on its promises to liberate women from patriarchal controls. This application of orthodox ideas to new realities produced a series of victories—laws guaranteeing women's rights, strengthened administrative control over benefits programs, literacy campaigns, and training programs for women working in agriculture. The federation sponsored schools where party workers and academics could study women's situation, while academics organized women's studies programs at several universities. One of the great successes of this careful activism was the hosting in 1995 of a U.N.-sponsored conference on women. In Beijing, delegates from around the world, many of them feminists, conducted an uncensored and influential debate on women's emancipation.

Ethno-religious movements. The last decades of the twentieth century also saw the rise of ethno-religious movements that generated powerful opposition to Communist reforms for women. Two of the most important were Hindu fundamentalism and Islamism, both of which preached that their people had been corrupted by outside, particularly Western, influences. As a remedy they proposed a return to traditional values. Women were seen to play a central role in this redemption, for Islamists and Hindu nationalists asserted that women were entrusted with rearing the next generation in the true faith. They could fulfill that sacred mission only by devoting themselves entirely to family life. Taking a leaf from the Communists' book, Islamist and Hindu nationalist parties organized women's groups to spread the word, and they made many converts among the professional and business elites. In India in the 1990s, female members of a Hindu organization, Shiv Sena, marched in support of traditional Indian customs, including sati, the immolation of widows. They also participated in violent attacks on Muslims.

Some Communist parties facing such nationalist movements, the Indian CPI(M) for example, denounced the patriarchal values of their opponents. Weaker parties, such as the one in Sudan, played up the veneration of motherhood and backed away from efforts to reform the family. These attempts at conciliation rarely staved off powerful Islamist movements. The Sudanese Communists were crushed after a military coup in 1971. In South Yemen in the 1970s, the Communist government enacted significant reforms in family law but then enforced the new laws sporadically. Their restraint did not mollify their powerful Islamist neighbor to the north, Saudi Arabia; it accused the South Yemen government of betraying Islam, pointing specifically to the new family law. In 1990 the Communists bent to the pressure and merged with the government of North Yemen. The resulting republic of Yemen subscribes to Islamic family law, although it does permit women to vote.

Assessment. Communists did not, as they had promised, abolish gender inequality, but they did make substantial improvements in women's legal, educational, and employment status around the world. They also promoted notions of female equality and condemned the worst patriarchal abuses. Their programs were copied by liberal and socialist governments, and their ideas influenced Second Wave feminism. The achievements of communism's flawed version of women's emancipation look better still in light of what has happened in nations where Communist rule ended in the 1990s. In eastern Europe, successor regimes permitted huge rises in female unemployment, cut funding for day care and other social services, and imported heavily sexualized images of women to promote capitalist-style consumerism. The fate of women in countries governed by non-Communist authoritarian parties, especially Islamist ones, was still worse. Communist regimes were also authoritarian, sometimes brutal, but their program of reforms for women remains one of their more positive contributions to social change in the twentieth century.

[*See also* Capitalism; Feminism; Labor; Russia and Soviet Union; Socialism; *and* Zhenotdel.]

BIBLIOGRAPHY

Basu, Amrita, and C. Elizabeth McGrory. *The Challenge of Local Feminisms: Women's Movements in Global Perspective.* Boulder, Colo.: Westview Press, 1995.

Eley, Geoff. *Forging Democracy: The History of the Left in Europe, 1850–2000.* Oxford: Oxford University Press, 2002.

Ellis, Deborah. *Women of the Afghan War.* Westport, Conn.: Praeger, 2000.

Geisler, Gisela. *Women and the Remaking of Politics in Southern Africa: Negotiating Autonomy, Incorporation, and Representation.* Uppsala, Sweden: Nordiska Afrikainstitutet, 2004.

Jancar, Barbara Wolfe. *Women under Communism*. Baltimore: Johns Hopkins University Press, 1978.
Kruks, Sonia, Rayna Rapp, and Marilyn B. Young, eds. *Promissory Notes: Women in the Transition to Socialism*. New York: Monthly Review Press, 1989.
Metoyer, Cynthia Chavez. *Women and the State in Post-Sandinista Nicaragua*. Boulder, Colo.: Lynne Rienner, 2000.
Padula, Alfred, and Lois M. Smith. *Sex and Revolution: Women in Socialist Cuba*. New York: Oxford University Press, 1996.
Pettus, Ashley. *Between Sacrifice and Desire: National Identity and the Governing of Femininity in Vietnam*. New York: Routledge, 2003.
Ray, Raka. *Fields of Protest: Women's Movements in India*. Minneapolis: University of Minnesota Press, 1999.
Wolf, Margery. *Revolution Postponed: Women in Contemporary China*. Stanford, Calif.: Stanford University Press, 1985.

BARBARA EVANS CLEMENTS

COMNENA, ANNA (1083–c. 1153/54), Byzantine princess and author. The daughter of Emperor Alexius I Comnenus and Empress Irene, Comnena was born in Constantinople (present-day Istanbul, Turkey), the capital of the Byzantine Empire, which included much of the eastern Mediterranean, Asia Minor, and the southern Balkans from the fourth to the fifteenth centuries. In Comnena's time Constantinople was one of the richest and most vibrant cities in the world, and it became the target of the Crusaders in the first expansion of Europe toward the east (late eleventh century through early thirteenth century). Comnena received a remarkable education in Greek rhetoric and philosophy; this was an education unusual for Byzantine women in general but increasingly possible for women of Comnena's social status. She was active in Byzantine political court life, and she followed closely her father's career, especially his dealings with foreigners and his treatment of Byzantine political and religious dissidents. After her father's death in 1118, Comnena plotted against her brother John II Comnenus to obtain the imperial throne for her husband, Nicephorus Bryennius. She failed and retired for the remainder of her life to a Constantinopolitan nunnery dedicated to the Virgin Mary and founded by her mother Irene.

Comnena was proud of both her aristocratic origins and her erudition. She was a patron of contemporary intellectuals who wrote, among other things, commentaries on Aristotle. Most important, she wrote a lengthy and highly sophisticated work, the *Alexiad*, a history of the career of her father Alexius. In the *Alexiad*, written twenty years after Alexius's death, Comnena eulogizes her father and his policies. She also describes in detail the First Crusade (1095–1099) and offers vivid portraits of Western foreigners as well as powerful women like her mother Irene and her grandmother Anna Dalassene. The text belongs in the context of twelfth-century Byzantine writing, a period of creative revival of classical Greek literature. Comnena employed highly rhetorical and archaic Greek, insisted on emotional reactions in imitation of Greek tragedy, and evoked Homer's epic poetry (the title *Alexiad*, for example, is a conscious echo of the *Iliad*).

Comnena's contemporaries either praised her beauty, self-mastery, and learning or criticized what they regarded as her masculine aspirations. Modern scholarship has found in Comnena both a typical and an atypical woman of an androcentric age who conformed to as well as challenged the demands of a society dominated by men. She is one of the few secular women historians of the Middle Ages and premodern female Greek writers whose texts have survived.

[*See also* Literature, *subentry* Personal and Private Narratives.]

BIBLIOGRAPHY

PRIMARY WORKS

Comnena, Anna. *The Alexiad*. Translated by Edgar Robert Ashton Sewter. London and New York: Penguin, 2003.
Comnena, Anna. *Annae Comnenae Alexias*. Edited by Diether R. Reinsch and Athanasios Kambylis. Berlin and New York: de Gruyter, 2001. The most recent edition of the original Greek text of the *Alexiad*.

SECONDARY WORKS

Buckler, Georgina. *Anna Comnena: A Study*. London: Oxford University Press, 1929. The only monograph on Comnena; an old but still useful work.
Gouma-Peterson, Thalia, ed. *Anna Komnene and Her Times*. New York and London, 2000. An excellent collection of essays on different aspects of Comnena's life and writings and their historical and cultural contexts.
Talbot, Alice-Mary, ed. Bibliography on Women in Byzantium, 2004. Dumbarton Oaks, Byzantine Studies. http://www.doaks.org/WomeninByzantium.html. A regularly updated Web site with an annotated bibliography on Byzantine women and related matters.

STRATIS PAPAIOANNOU

COMPANY OF MARY, THE. The Catholic female teaching order the Company of Mary was founded by Jeanne of Lestonnac (1557–1640), the niece of the French man of letters Michel de Montaigne. Raised in a family of Calvinist leanings that encouraged learning for women, she married Gaston de Montferrant, baron of Landiras, and had eight children, five of whom survived. In 1603, after her husband's death, when she was forty-six, Jeanne chose to enter the Catholic Order of Cister in the city of Tolouse. The demanding Cistercian regime did not suit her, and after leaving the convent she spent three years in retreat. In 1606 she decided to found a religious order dedicated to educating women following the pedagogic model of the Jesuit order, under whose guidance she remained during the foundational process. The order was approved by the cardinal of Bordeaux, the city where the order's first house would be sited, and on 7 April 1607, Pope Paul V approved the order under the name of Company of Mary, Our Lady.

The Order of Mary followed a life dedicated to studying as a personal goal and teaching women as a social objective. The rules of the order were finally completed in 1638. Those professing in it were trained to teach, and the convents would receive boarders as well as sustain a public school for poor girls. The Order of Mary spread through France in the first half of the seventeenth century, but after mid-century, when the number reached thirty houses, the pace of foundations began to decline, partly because of a law approved in 1689 whereby the real estate property of the convents was forcibly sold to collect taxes for the crown. Despite the slow economic decline and arrested expansion, by 1792 the order had fifty-one convents in France.

At its peak the order also began founding nunneries in Spain and Spanish America. Nine convents were founded in Spain before 1760. In the New World the first convent was in Cap Français (today's Haiti, 1733), a French colony. In Spanish America the order founded the houses of Mendoza (today's Argentina, 1780), Mexico City (1754), and Santa Fé de Bogotá (today's Colombia, 1783). Three more convents were founded in Mexico before its independence from Spain: Irapuato (1804), Aguascalientes (1807), and New Enseñanza in Mexico City for Indian women (1811).

In 1789, French revolutionary authorities closed down all convents and sold their properties. In 1806, Napoleon Bonaparte restored the order, which began a period of reconstruction of former houses. Mother Thérèse Duterrail (1759–1834) was a central figure in this task. In 1828 she initiated the cause for the beatification of the order's founder. The order expanded with the foundation of three houses in Italy between 1828 and 1834 and one in England in 1895. Internal problems of jurisdiction plagued the order in the nineteenth century. The house of Rome, founded in 1834, and the house of Bordeaux, founded in 1607, fought for the honor of being considered the First House. One of the most contested issues was whether the girls admitted to the conventual schools should adopt the enclosure the nuns followed. The house of Bordeaux dropped this rule in 1846, creating a conflict with other houses of the order that did not accept it. The weak economic situation of many houses led the pope to void the order's original commitment to free education to poor girls in 1838. This curtailed the services originally envisioned by Jeanne de Lestonnac.

The secularization of education adopted by many countries in the nineteenth century affected the fate of all the order's houses. In Spain the number of nuns rose from 264 in 1859 to 1,091 in 1900. In France in the same period, the number rose from 520 to 1,491. In Spanish America, secularization meant the expulsion of the nuns from their convents in Colombia in 1861 and Mexico in 1867. However, in both countries the nuns were able to refound their schools and begin their educational services by the last quarter of the nineteenth century. The house of Mendoza (Argentina) thrived and was able to found a new one in Chile (1868). Even so, the number of religious remained small. It was 141 in 1859 and 195 in 1900, despite the foundation of a house in Chile. The French convents were badly hurt by the legislation separating church and state. In 1904 all cloistered convents were suppressed and their properties sold. Many nuns left France to live in houses established in other countries or to found new ones.

The order continued to expand in the early twentieth century with houses in Belgium and Holland. The beatification of Jeanne de Lestonnac by Pope Leo XIII in 1900 was a boost to the order. On 12 March 1921, Pope Benedict XV authorized the foundation of a generalate, or central government, for the order that altered the form of government established since the seventeenth century. The foundational 1606 document—known as the *abrégé*—approved by Jeanne de Lestonnac established a new independent order, but at that time Pope Pius V determined that the nuns should be under the jurisdiction of the local bishop or archbishop and not under a mother superior (general superior) common to all the convents. The 1638 rules established autonomy in all the houses' government. The 1921 papal establishment of a generalate intended to maintain unity and uniformity in the observance of the religious life as well as strengthen the order during a period of intense anticlerical feeling.

The generalate, and its site in Rome, created a split among the houses. Many of them resisted assimilation to the generalate and remained separate as a congregation. In November 1956 the two branches reunited, with papal approval. Nuns, under a mitigated vow of enclosure, were free to move around the world in their apostolic and educational tasks. The crowning event in the history of the order was the canonization of Jeanne de Lestonnac by Pope Pius XII on 15 May 1949. Today the Company of Mary has houses in Central Africa, the United States, Japan, Italy, England, the Netherlands, Brazil, Colombia, Chile, and Cuba.

[*See also* Spiritual Leaders, *subentry* Nuns and Abbesses, *and* Ursulines.]

BIBLIOGRAPHY

Foz y Foz, Pilar. *Archivos históricos Compañía de María Nuestra Señora*. Vol. 1: 1607–1921. Rome: Tipografía Políglota Vaticana, 1989. Vol. 2: 1607–1921. Rome: Tipografía Vaticana, 2006.

Foz y Foz, Pilar. *Las enseñanzas iberoamericanas, 1754–1820*. Bogotá, Colombia: Consejo Episcopal Latinoamericano, 1988.

Foz y Foz, Pilar. *Mujer y educación en Colombia, siglos XVI–XIX: Aportaciones del colegio de la enseñanza, 1783–1900*. Bogotá, Colombia: Academia Colombiana de Historia, 1997.

Foz y Foz, Pilar. *La revolución pedagógica en Nueva España, 1754–1820: María Ignacia de Azlor y Echeverz y los colegios de la enseñanza.* 2 vols. Madrid, Spain: Instituto Gonzalo Fernández de Oviedo (C.S.I.C.), 1981.

Hoesl, Paula. *In the Service of Youth: St. Jeanne de Lestonnac, Wife, Mother, and Foundress.* London: Sands, 1950.

ASUNCIÓN LAVRIN

CONCUBINAGE

This entry consists of two subentries:

Overview
Comparative History

Overview

The term "concubinage" is used to describe a range of relationships. Historically, some form of concubinage can be found in most societies, and it is still widely practiced today. The essential characteristic of concubinage—what makes it distinct from other relationships like marriage or betrothal—is the cohabitation of a man and a woman in a long-term sexual relationship without the promise of legal marriage. What differs in each case is the role of the concubine within the household, her legal and social status, and the larger intellectual justifications and perceptions of the institution.

Types of Concubinage. Most commonly, a concubine is a woman who provides sexual and/or reproductive services to a man of higher social standing in whose household she resides. In some cases, concubinage is monogamous; that is, concubine and concubinator live together in a quasi-marriage that is the locus of emotional and sexual intimacy in their lives. Women in these relationships can often be accused of adultery if they have sexual relations with additional male partners. Men in these relationships who take additional sexual partners do so on a clearly temporary basis, such as with prostitutes. In theory, neither partner is married to someone else. If they are, that union has dissolved in practice.

The reasons why a couple would live as husband and wife yet not marry are rooted in social, cultural, and legal mores governing marriage. Either one or both of the partners may be legally barred from marrying. Class, religious, or ethic differences may make their marriage socially inappropriate. One partner, usually the male, may wish to have a companion without the legal and property complications of marriage. The couple may wish to marry but perhaps cannot afford the costs of the rites and rituals required to legitimate their union. Lastly, they may not recognize the power of others to marry them. In this case, the classification of concubinage by the state can be at odds with the subjectivity of the couple.

In addition to monogamous concubinage is the widespread practice of plural concubinage, in which a concubine may be just one of several women providing sexual and reproductive functions to a male who presides over the household. A concubine may cohabit with a legal wife (or wives), with several other concubines, or both. In royal or imperial households, concubines could number in the thousands. Though their duty was to provide sexual pleasure and sons to the male head of household, they also served as status markers. Possessing concubines required and demonstrated wealth. Plural concubinage is most common in patriarchal cultures that place enormous emphasis on the production of sons. Hence concubinal children further increased the status of the male head of household, marking him as fertile, dutiful, and, in some cases, blessed in a specifically religious sense. In many societies, plural and monogamous concubinage coexisted.

Though the broad structures of concubinage are easily mapped out, determining which relationships count as concubatory is more difficult. It is useful to distinguish formal and informal concubinage. In formal concubinage, the relationship has juridical status or social recognition as a unique institution. It is defined positively in law or custom. The concubine is recognized as having a specific status to which are inhered certain rights and obligations. The Roman institution of *concubinatus*, which was defined juridically as well as in practice, is an example of formal concubinage. Informal concubinage is the attachment of the term to relationships that look like concubinage but are not recognized as distinct by those societies in which they occur.

Even with formal concubinage, however, certain classification can be difficult largely because it requires a clear definition of marriage. Concubinage and marriage are generally considered to be mutually exclusive institutions. Concubinage is like marriage but is not marriage. Yet religious and legal formulations of marriage historically have been unstable or inconsistent. For example, some medieval European theologians considered a concubinatory couple married if they had "marital affection" for each other. Hence in the eyes of some church officials in twelfth-century Europe, a couple living in concubinage could become married simply by agreeing between themselves to be so. This formulation was rejected by others, leaving a couple to doubt whether they were married or living in sin. Marriage, moreover, is as much an institution of practice as it is of law, giving local custom definitional privilege. The confusion persists even in highly literate and juridical societies. A cohabiting couple in modern-day Massachusetts who meet certain requirements can find themselves in a common-law marriage after a certain number of years.

The social and cultural values that underpin concubinage have to be understood within the multiple contexts of the status of women, attitudes toward sex and sexuality, the construction of social hierarchies, and marriage. With the

European Depictions of Concubinage in Asia. *The Harem*, a painting by John Frederick Lewis, c. 1850. VICTORIA & ALBERT MUSEUM, LONDON/ART RESOURCE, NY

exception of concubinage as an alternative marriage, it tends to occur in societies in which male sexual activities are not expected to be limited to the marital bed, and it also tends to exist in societies in which women are valued less than men and hence can legitimately be considered sexual or reproductive servants. These inequalities are usually inscribed in both law and custom such that a concubine's rights, formal or informal, stem only from her position as mother or lover rather than from her status as a human being.

Concubinage also is inclined to reinforce class hierarchies because it pairs women of lower rank with men of higher rank. The concubinatory rather than marital nature of these relationships reflects and reinforces the subordinate class status of the concubine. Plural concubinage is found mainly in patrilineal societies in which a primary function of marriage is both the production of male children and the exchange of property. The concubine is flexible within this system. She can be brought into the household to produce sons, or her position as concubine can automatically illegitimate her children, excluding them from inheriting any portion of their father's estate.

Voluntary and Involuntary Concubinage. In twenty-first-century parlance, "concubine" refers either to a mistress or to a sex slave. Historically and currently, not all concubinal relations are equally oppressive to women who enter into them; voluntary concubinage should be distinguished from involuntary concubinage. In the latter, a woman is sold, usually by her family. As a concubine, she is rarely a slave, at least legally; indeed, the fact of becoming a concubine often freed women from slave status. In the household hierarchy concubines stood above slaves and paid servants but below the legal wife (in cases of plural concubinage). Yet in practice, the life of an involuntary concubine may look very much like that of a slave. She is often subject to abuse by both her master and his legal wife. She can, in many societies, be arbitrarily expelled from the household or sold again. Concubinal rape was rarely considered a crime.

With voluntary concubinage a woman enters into the relationship freely. In cases in which concubinage is an alternate marriage, gender relations in the household usually reflect prevailing gender relations, hence concubinage is more onerous in that it denies women many of the rights, privileges, and status of wives. The notion of free choice, however, must be qualified. Societies in which concubinage is practiced often have fewer social and economic opportunities for women, coercing some into accepting concubinal status as part of a survival strategy.

Though the structure of concubinage is supported by and in turn maintains the inferior status of women, there are still varying degrees of female agency within the institution. Since concubinage tended to bring women of lesser fortune and status into wealthier households, it was clearly a way for some women to improve their life circumstances. Moreover, voluntary and involuntary concubines have historically been able to use their positions as mothers or favorite lovers to gain power within the household, taking over finances and living spaces and even dictating inheritance arrangements. In cases where the concubine was bound to a political ruler, power within the household could translate into real political power.

[*See also* Celibacy; Marriage; *Nüshu*; Patriarchy; Prostitution; Single Women; Slavery; *and* Taiping Rebellion.]

BIBLIOGRAPHY

Andaya, Barbara Watson. "From Temporary Wife to Prostitute: Sexuality and Economic Change in Early Modern Southeast Asia." *Journal of Women's History* 9, no. 4 (1998): 11–34.

Andaya, Barbara Watson, ed. *Other Pasts: Women, Gender, and History in Early Modern Southeast Asia*. Honolulu: Center for Southeast Asian Studies, University of Hawai'i, 2000.

Engels, Dagmar. *Beyond Purdah? Women in Bengal 1890–1939*. Oxford: Oxford University Press, 1996.

Jones, Eric Alan. "Wives, Slaves, and Concubines: A History of the Female Underclass in Dutch Asia." PhD diss., University of California, Berkeley, 2003.

Ko, Dorothy, Jahyun Kim Haboush, and Joan R Piggott, eds. *Women and Confucian Cultures in Pre-Modern China, Korea, and Japan*. Los Angeles: University of California Press, 2003.

Rawson, Beryl. "Roman Concubinage and Other de Facto Marriages." *Transactions of the American Philological Association* 104 (1974): 279–305.

Rawson, Beryl, ed. *The Family in Ancient Rome: New Perspectives*. London: Routledge, 1986.

Yasutaka, Teruoka. "The Pleasure Quarters and Tokugawa Culture." In *Eighteenth Century Japan: Culture and Society*, edited by C. Andrew Gerstle, pp. 3–29. Sydney, Australia: Allen and Unwin, 1989.

NINA KUSHNER

Comparative History

The keeping of concubines has been common almost everywhere, existing throughout history in societies with both strong and weak marriage traditions, although its significance has varied across cultures. Both formal and informal concubinage have been part of the fabric of pre- and postcolonial societies in Central and South America, Africa, and much of Asia. Although the spread of Christianity and Islam, as well as shifting economic structures, has informed modern meanings and constructions of concubinage, it continues to be widely practiced.

Ancient Near East. Concubinage was a fairly common practice among the peoples of Mesopotamia, where, as in many ancient societies, the primary purpose of marriage—which was patrilineal and patriarchal—was the production of offspring. Concubinage increased the odds of successful reproduction without the consequent social destabilization of divorce and remarriage. Concubinage took several forms. The practice of a barren wife providing her husband with a slave girl (or handmaiden) for the purposes of procreation is well documented in many surviving law codes and legal documents.

The custom is also described in the Bible, where the Hebrew term for a concubine is *pilegesh*. In the book of Genesis, Sarah, unable to conceive children, gives her handmaiden Hagar to her husband, Abraham, in the hopes of reproducing through her. Hagar gives birth to Ishmael, who is eventually cast off when Sarah gives birth to her own child, Isaac. Hammurabi's code similarly allowed for women who could not legally or biologically have children to provide a slave to their husbands for this purpose. The status and rights of the concubine were not uniform across the region. In becoming a concubine, a woman generally lived in the household of her concubinator and ceased to be a slave. Yet most contemporary legal codes tried to preserve a social hierarchy among the household women, elevating a concubine above slaves but not granting her the status of a wife. Concubinal children were generally legitimate and entitled to a share of the inheritance, although they could be displaced by children born subsequently to the legal wife. As in many other societies, concubinage could also serve as a status marker, especially

Macaconas. A gold figurine of one of the *mamaconas* or "chosen women," the concubines of the Inca emperor, c. 1430–1532 C.E. ETHNOLOGISCHES MUSEUM, STAATLICHE MUSEEN ZU BERLIN, BERLIN/ WERNER FORMAN/ART RESOURCE, NY

for royalty, who often kept harems. The biblical King David was said to have ten concubines.

The distinction between a *pilegesh* and a wife was further clarified in later Jewish law, though there was no consensus on the question. A *pilegesh* was defined in the Babylonian Talmud as a woman dedicating herself to a particular man with whom she lived without *kiddushin* (betrothal) or *ketubbah* (a marriage contract), two of the rites constituting a legal marriage. There is, however, little evidence of a continuation of the practice of concubinage among Jews in the Talmudic period and afterward.

Greece. The Greek word most commonly translated as concubine is *pallake* (plural, *pallakai*). There is little evidence in the Greek corpus regarding her status or role, leading to the possibility that *pallakai* were not socially, legally, or culturally significant. Most evidence comes from ancient Athens and describes a *pallake* as a woman who lived in a permanent (or long-term) relationship with a man to whom she had not been given by *engue*. *Engue* was a form of contract in which a dowered woman was transferred by her male guardian (*kyrios*) to her husband, who became her new *kyrios*. She then became part of her husband's household (*oikoi*). Being married by *engue* meant that the children of this union were legitimate (*gnesioi*) as opposed to illegitimate (*nothoi*). However, the meanings of *engue*, *gnesioi*, and *nothoi* shifted over time.

Attic sources from the seventh century B.C.E. suggest that concubines could be taken for the explicit purpose of bearing "free children." A father could legitimize any child born from such a union. In the fifth century B.C.E., this was no longer possible. Laws governing citizenship in Athens became increasingly restrictive. Only children born to Athenian citizen mothers given to their Athenian citizen fathers by *engue* were legitimate and hence could participate in the political life of the polis, inherit, and become full-fledged members of various kinship groupings. At this time a *pallake* was a merely a member of an *oikos*. Her children were not legitimate, and she could be dismissed from the household at any time—unlike a wife who had to be divorced and her property returned to her.

A *pallake* could be a woman of almost any social status. Some Athenians did give their daughters to other *oikos* as *pallakai*, negotiating the terms. Most concubines, however, were probably slaves, freedwomen, or foreigners and hence legally prohibited from marrying Athenian citizens. Some scholars argue that *heteras* (often slaves, freedwomen, or foreigners) who cohabitated with their lovers became their *pallakai*. Others argue that *heteras* could not be *pallakai*, because the latter were essentially servile but *heteras* were not.

The emotional content of concubinal relationships seems to have varied greatly. In some cases they were clearly companionate. Literary sources suggest that *pallakai* and their children were sometimes established in the same household as the legal wife, thereby creating a parallel family. In other instances, men separated their wives and concubines by space, procuring the *pallake* and her children separate lodgings, or by time, beginning a concubinal relationship only after being widowed. Despite the possibility for emotional intimacy, concubinal unions were not clearly or legally separated from those of master and slave, hence bringing into question the respectability of *pallakai*.

Rome. The definition and meaning of Roman concubinage (*concubinatus*) remains a subject of scholarly debate. Because concubinage was considered a marriage-like institution, the debate in part stems from questions over what constituted a legal marriage and the degree to which legal impediments to marriage actually invalidated marriages. Roman sources, most of which come from the second and third centuries, offer two definitions of concubinage. In the less common usage, found mainly in literary texts, *concubinatus* referred to any extramartial sexual relationship, most often that between a wealthy or politically powerful man and a woman of low social origins kept for sexual service. The marital status of the man was irrelevant. More usually, *concubinatus* concerned a sort of a quasi-marriage in which the couple did not marry either because legal or social impediments prevented them from doing so or because they chose not to. In these cases neither partner—but especially the woman—was considered to be married.

In general, a marriage was valid if the couple had both the capacity to marry (*conubium*) and the intent to do so. During the republic, certain classes of people (close blood relatives, for example) were prohibited from marrying by law. Augustan marriage law in the first century C.E. disqualified more groups from marrying, or from marrying each other. Soldiers, for example, could no longer marry during their service. Senators and their progeny could not marry freedmen or freedwomen or those of "lowly origins." But soldiers did take "wives," even if the unions were not legally recognized. In living together, they engaged in *concubinatus*.

In some cases, the impediment to marriage was not capacity but intent. This could occur when a man was young and not ready for marriage or, later in life, after he had had children, was widowed, and did not want the inheritance complications that would arise from another marriage. The children of a concubine were not legitimate. Neither she nor they became heirs, nor did a concubine bring a dowry into the relationship. Emperor Augustus had a concubine before he married. Emperor Vespasian had one after the death of his wife. In each case, the *concubina* was chosen because she was ineligible for marriage. This was a common practice among the propertied classes. Evidence from epitaphs suggests that these relationships, like many Roman marriages, were emotionally intimate and based on conjugal love and affection. The Augustan marriage laws (Lex Julia and the Papia Poppeae) increased the legal standing of concubinage as an institution, but confusion in the laws led to several centuries of interpretative debates.

Christian Europe. Early Christian and patristic thinkers established a sexual ideology that, at least in theory, could not support concubinage as a legitimate institution. The apostle Paul accorded sexual intercourse within marriage a sacred status, one that helped to unite husband and wife spiritually and physically. Consequently, he denounced all other forms of sexual union. Despite these teachings, early Christians accepted *concubinatus* as social practice in the second and third centuries.

In the fourth and fifth centuries, patristic writers, especially Saint Augustine, further developed Christian sexual ideology, laying the groundwork for later medieval teachings. They progressively conceptualized sexual pleasure as impure and sinful and hence dangerous to human salvation. Collectively, they further limited the parameters of legitimate sexual activity to that which took place in marriage for the explicit purposes of reproduction. Even then, argued Augustine, sexual activity should be curtailed in duration and frequency. Sexual acts outside of marriage were increasingly considered serious sins requiring substantial penance.

Despite these teachings, fourth-century patristic writers embraced contradictory stances on concubinage. Some argued that the church should recognize concubinatory unions as alternative forms of marriage, since they were often created by legal impediments. Others rejected concubinage because it endorsed sexual activity outside of marriage. Both Augustine, who had had concubines before converting to Christianity, and Jerome, who was hostile to most forms of sexuality, fully condemned the institution, claiming that its sole purpose was the gratification of sexual desire. Based on the idea that concubinage was legalized fornication, the fifth-century church made efforts to abolish it but was unsuccessful and eventually fell back to the position of trying to keep concubinage monogamous.

In the legal arena, Christian emperors improved the status of the concubine. Emperor Justinian in his great sixth-century code, the Corpus Iurus Civilis, granted to concubines and their children the sorts of property and inheritance rights usually reserved for wives. He brought the institution of *concubinatus* closer to marriage, but he also repeated the Christian injunction that concubinage must be permanent and monogamous.

Concubinage continued to be a problem for Christian theologians and canon lawyers throughout the Middle Ages. Almost all condemned any arrangement that led to polygyny—either plural concubinacy or the keeping of concubines by married men—although nonmonogamy continued to be a common practice among the propertied elite. But the status of monogamous concubinage remained ambiguous. Complicating matters was the evolving definition of marriage. In the twelfth century, church teachings retained the Roman notion that marriage was made by the principle of marital affection, which allowed the Christian emperor Gratian, in one of the first great textbooks of canon law, *Concordia discorfantium canonum* (c. 1140; English trans., *A Harmony of Conflicting Canons*), to argue that concubinage was a form of marriage.

A few decades later, Pope Alexander III clarified marriage law by stating that a valid marriage had to be contracted between people who were free to marry each other and who exchanged consent—or the promise of consent, if that promise was consummated by sexual intercourse. Although the church urged couples to marry in front of witnesses, those who did not, and engaged in what was called clandestine marriage, were still legally married. This meant that a couple engaged in concubinage, for whom there were no legal impediments to marriage, would be married if they simply claimed they were. Later theologians tried to work out this problem by forcing concubines to formalize their relationship.

Concubinage was not just a religious problem, determining questions of sin and salvation. As in Roman law, concubine, wife, and their respective children had different property and political rights in medieval Europe, enforced by both church courts and municipalities. The increasing hostility of the church to concubinage in the fourteenth and fifteenth centuries led many municipalities to penalize it or outlaw it outright. The church followed suit and fully condemned it in 1514. Monogamous concubinage continued to be a common practice in Christian societies through the early modern and into the modern era.

China. Officially, a formal concubine system was a basic part of the Chinese family economy from ancient times. The Chinese term for concubine, *qie*, referred to a woman who resided with a married man and his legal wife. The man had exclusive access to the body of the concubine, her children by him were legitimate, and the position of the concubine was legally defined. In terms of rights and status within the household, the concubine fell somewhere between the paid servants and the legal wife. The way in which concubine status is measured, however, has been the subject of scholarly contention, focused on whether her separation from her own family and her inability to marry into her new one separated her from the kinship systems that helped to shape status in ancient and early modern China. Her status was certainly equally dependent on law and social convention. What is also clear is that the concubine's legal standing and social status shifted over the course of the imperial era and then changed drastically in the twentieth century.

Confucian ideas of filial piety and ancestor worship provided the intellectual foundations of the institution. A concubine enabled a husband to have more sons. From the Song period (960–1279), a man who was at least forty-one years old could take a concubine, provided that he had no sons. As in so many other societies, concubines and concubinage also served as status markers. Generally, concubines came from families of lower social status, some of whom might have been too poor to provide their daughters with the dowries necessary for marriage, and perhaps so poor that they needed the income derived from selling her (the custom of *mooi-jai*). The possession of a concubine, and of sons by her, added to the status of the head of household. Some emperors had hundreds of concubines.

The legal condition of the concubine improved over the course of the imperial era. In the Song era, concubines were legally distinguished from wives and did not have the basic rights of inheritance or even a guarantee that they would not be suddenly expelled from the household. Giving birth to sons could stabilize a concubine's position in the household and attach her to her master's kin network. A concubine did have the right, should she outlive both her master and his legal wife, to become the legal guardian of her children and their inheritance.

During the Ming period the differences between concubine and wife became less clear. In principle, what separated them was that the wife underwent a ceremony of Six Rites—various betrothal and nuptial rituals. That she went through this ceremony (or went though it first) marked her as a legal wife or main wife, while the concubine, who entered the household with little or no ceremony, came to be known as a minor wife. The shift in language indicates that the concubine was beginning to be seen in marital terms in both legal and literary sources. In the Republican period, beginning in 1912, official legislation abolished concubinage, changing the status of the concubine from minor wife to a member of the household. Despite this ruling, the practice continued into the Communist era.

Regardless of the era, the position of the concubine within any particular household in China was precarious. Though her vulnerability could be lessened by the birth of a son, she was never fully secure without the sustained goodwill of her husband-master. Individual concubines were sometimes able to translate this goodwill or affection into power within the household, including control of finances and, when possible, inheritance. When such concubines belonged to the emperor, power in the household could translate into power in government. The most famous example of this was Cixi, a low-ranking concubine of the Emperor Xianfeng, who in 1865 bore his only son. At the age of six this boy became the Tongzhi emperor. Cixi remained involved in state affairs, often dominating the government as sole regent until her death in 1908.

[*See also* Celibacy; Cixi, Empress Dowager; Codes of Law and Laws; Marriage; *Nüshu*; Patriarchy; Prostitution; Single Women; Slavery; *and* Taiping Rebellion.]

BIBLIOGRAPHY

Brundage, James A. *Law, Sex, and Christian Society in Medieval Europe*. Chicago: University of Chicago Press, 1987.

Ebrey, Patricia. *The Inner Quarters: Marriage and the Lives of Chinese Women in the Sung Period*. Berkeley: University of California Press, 1993.

Jaschok, Maria. *Concubines and Bondservants: The Social History of a Chinese Custom*. London: Zed Books, 1988.

Just, Roger. *Women in Athenian Law and Life*. London: Routledge, 1989.

McGinn, Thomas A. J. "Concubinage and the Lex Iulia on Adultery." *Transactions of the American Philological Association* 121 (1991): 335–375.

Tran, Lisa. "Concubines under Modern Chinese Law." PhD diss., University of California, Los Angeles, 2005.

Treggiari, Susan. "Concubinae." *Papers of the British School at Rome* 49 (1981): 41–69.

Treggiari, Susan. *Roman Marriage: Iusti Coniuges from the Time of Cicero to the Time of Ulpian*. Oxford: Clarendon Press, 1991.

NINA KUSHNER

CONSUMPTION. "I Am Woman, Hear Me Shop," shouted the headline of an article in the 14 February 2005 online edition of *Businessweek*. The essay went on to lay out how "female consumer power is changing the way companies design, make and market products." Contemporary American women, although their salaries are still only 78 percent of those earned by their male peers, do most of the shopping and make most of the purchasing decisions, the author noted. Are women's identities in fact defined by shopping, as the title implies? And what kind of power does the consumer actually wield? How has the place of consumption in women's lives, and its accompanying power, changed over time?

Since time immemorial, women have borne fundamental responsibility for provisioning their households. They have acquired the food from which they have prepared meals, as well as the wool, yarn, fabric, or readymade garments that clothed themselves and their families. Moreover, they often found, decorated, and maintained their dwellings. Whether in the drought- or disease-induced famines that plagued medieval and early modern Europe and continue to devastate Africa, or in the privations accompanying wars, or in the omnipresent quiet struggle of the poor, the challenge of ensuring the everyday subsistence and comfort of the household has fallen most heavily on women.

This obligation has not always been, or only been, a burden. Women have also used their purchasing power as a political tool and as a means of communication, self-expression, and even self-realization. Most dramatically, in times of shortage they have rioted, smuggled, and stolen to ensure a supply of food and other necessities. Less spectacularly, they have petitioned governments, fought for credit, and found ingenious ways of giving fourth and fifth lives to tattered remnants of shoes and blankets. And they have

Wartime Consumption. An official shows shoppers how to use War Ration Book Two when purchasing processed foods, February 1943. Photograph by Alfred T. Palmer. PRINTS AND PHOTOGRAPHS DIVISION, LIBRARY OF CONGRESS

boycotted goods produced or sold under unacceptable conditions.

Women have also sometimes simply enjoyed the sensuous and sociable aspects of the acquisition and use of goods. From time to time a woman has taken pleasure in the touch of a fabric, the new form a dress could give her body, the elegance a curtain bestows on a window, the heady aroma of spices in a market, or the sheen of a perfect eggplant. Discussions with friends and sellers could be equally satisfying. Goods provided a basis for conversation, whether to locate the best buy or highest quality, crow over a bargain or ruefully admit an extravagance, haggle with a merchant, or pass on consumer skills to the next generation. Goods also communicate for their owners and users. By decorating their homes in a certain manner or wearing certain clothes or accessories, women gave others clues about their income, class, social and ethnic origins, sexual orientation, political positions, and religion. Consumption has not been women's only work, nor has it been only women's work, but particularly since the mid-eighteenth century it has played a particularly important role in women's lives, and women have been deeply influential as consumers.

Consuming in Times of Shortage. It is only since the middle of the twentieth century, and even then only for a minority of the world's population, that adequate food, clothing, and shelter could be relied upon. Throughout most of history, food shortages due to natural or human causes have been the norm. Taxation, low wages and high prices, and war are the familiar means by which humans have caused great hunger, homelessness, and destitution. These very different causes of scarcity have been met with appropriately different responses.

In early modern Europe, when the price of necessities was set by the state, women would petition the monarch when they found supplies low or prices too high. When those petitions failed, the women often took to the streets, seizing the bread and flour or other goods they needed to feed or warm their families. The unregulated prices of so-called free markets have posed similar challenges to poor households, and here, too, women have taken recourse to both political mobilization and direct action. In both the past and the present, when raw materials for clothing and housing have been unavailable, women have scavenged and sometimes stolen, building dwellings from mud, cardboard boxes, oil drums, or plastic garbage bags. Clothes can be recycled, coats can be lined with newspapers, and tires can provide the soles of shoes. Pawnshops have long been used creatively—an object not immediately required is pawned to provide the money with which to acquire another object, which is then used to redeem the first. In modern states that have welfare systems or receive international aid, women have figured out ways to get the most from these always insufficient resources. These are the responses to natural catastrophe or everyday poverty; war produces its own challenges in provisioning.

War virtually always brings shortages with it. Whether in the context of siege warfare—when cities were encircled and the inhabitants literally starved out—or of the destruction of fields, dwellings, and workshops and factories as a strategy of war, or of the diversion of food, clothing, metal, and heating fuel to the front, war has brought radical deprivation. Those hardships have inspired ingenuity. Women invented recipes for unfamiliar (and often unappetizing) foodstuffs. Some urban women learned to recognize wild edible plants. Others honed their social and bargaining skills to persuade rural dwellers to trade or sell their chickens, hams, or butter. Inventiveness was not limited to food. Women also created new forms of clothing and heating, or they trafficked in ration cards or traded cigarettes for other needed goods. Women's demonstrated capacities as wartime consumers have sometimes brought them political recognition after peace returned. Historians have persuasively argued, for example, that women's wartime contributions, as consumers as much as as producers, were critical in gaining them political recognition and extended rights after World Wars I and II.

Although goods are commonly scarce for substantial portions of the world's population, the last two hundred and fifty years have seen a vast increase in possibilities for abundance, to the point where many would argue that the twentieth century was dominated by consumption and consumerism.

Consuming in Times of Plenty. Although women played a crucial role in the acquisition and use of goods far earlier than the modern period, one of the characteristics of modernity is the invention of the female consumer. The avant-garde of this movement was western Europe, but it spread rapidly, if very unevenly, across the globe. With an increasing separation of workplace, state, and home came a new ideal for women: homemakers. A fundamental task for homemakers was the appropriate acquisition and use of goods. Rather than worrying about supplying enough nutritional calories to their families, women were tasked with organizing tasty and attractive meals. Rather than fighting to keep warm or dry in winter and cool in summer, women were to provide the appropriate clothes needed by members of their family in their daily tasks. Homes and gardens also needed careful attention, of course. Through their labor as consumers, women would serve the nation by maintaining and transmitting national taste—which was understood as the bedrock of national identification—and by providing a market for domestic products.

The media used to teach consumer practices varied by period. In the nineteenth century, etiquette books, fashion and decorating magazines, cookbooks, and books on the domestic arts, along with the new department stores, played crucial roles in modeling bourgeois consumption. Novels and the theater, whatever their subject matter, also provided guidance. Advertisements in shop windows, in newspapers, in catalogs, and on the sides of trams and buildings all encouraged purchases and suggested what could be bought. This barrage of incitement to consume also produced anxiety, however, as the identification of a new disorder, kleptomania, indicates.

Kleptomaniacs were defined as people, almost entirely women, who stole because of desire rather than because of need. They were so aroused by the appeal of advertisements that they could not resist their call. This sense of the power of things, for both good and bad, encouraged social scientists and social workers to intervene in the world of modest consumerism. In evening classes, social workers taught native working-class and immigrant women how to consume appropriately—a model that was later extended to colonial subjects in the twentieth century when both mass media and the mass market radically expanded and changed the world of consumerism.

In the twentieth century, first radio and then cinema, television, and the Internet entered the cultural world. Though nineteenth-century cultural media (fiction, museums, and the theater) kept the commercial at arm's length, that changed in the twentieth century. Radio first developed sophisticated advertisements, but with film the linkage between art and consumption was most thoroughly elaborated. The clothing worn by stars, in modified form, was promoted for sale in stores. Women viewers were directly encouraged to emulate their admired stars by adopting their appearances and ultimately their lifestyles. Women were encouraged to devote their lives to consumption, but to do so appropriately. Bourgeois women's role as consumers was to ensure political stability through the reproduction of national taste, to domesticate men by tying them to comforts of the home, and to consolidate class identities and differences through material resemblance and dissemblance. Working-class and

Consumerism in China. A salesperson helps a mainland Chinese woman to browse through a catalog at a Giorgio Armani store in Hong Kong, September 2002. REUTERS/Bobby Yip

colonial women, in turn, were to consume according to their class and station.

Women consumers also found themselves enrolled in other political struggles. During the Cold War, for example, West Berlin was used as a showcase of what capitalism could bring to consumers, particularly women consumers, and the world's fairs were designed to disseminate a message of plenty. Governing regimes in the Soviet Union responded by promising greater production of consumer goods and at times increasing access to goods from the West.

To say that women were the target of aggressive campaigns to influence their spending habits is not to say that they were passive victims of consumerism. Women often derived pleasure from buying and using things, and they used those things to express themselves and communicate. Women have used goods to express rejection of existing sexual, gender, race, and class norms and to invent other norms. Though wealth made such creative and pleasurable use of things easier, such use was not limited to the wealthy or even the middle class, historians have demonstrated. By the nineteenth century and more broadly in the twentieth, working-class women also engaged in leisure shopping and commercial entertainments. Even slaves in the antebellum South used goods creatively, though their autonomy and access to markets was obviously limited. There is no question that consumption came to play a central role in women's lives. The outcome of that role was not entirely predictable, however, nor did it always serve the interests of either the state or capitalism.

Political Uses of Consumption. The dependence of the market and the nation-state on consumers, in combination with women's increased sense of themselves as consumers, created the possibility of political mobilization around consumption. Following in the footsteps of their French cousins, who rioted for food and petitioned the king for bread, women in colonial America were instrumental in the boycotts that helped spark the American Revolution. A key difference between the two movements, however, was that whereas French women mobilized around their right to consume, the American boycotts were an organized refusal to consume one item and substitution of another. American colonists wore homespun instead of imported silk or drank coffee instead of tea. Boycotts rarely entailed absolute privation and thus were a product of consumer society.

This strategy was used again as part of the struggle for racial justice on both sides of the Atlantic. In the 1810s and 1820s women in the antislavery movement organized a boycott of slave-produced products, most notably sugar. A little more than a century later, African Americans demanded the right to equal access to consumption. Sitting in at lunch counters or retail establishments that refused to serve blacks and sitting in whites-only sections of buses and trains, African Americans demonstrated the symbolic importance of consumption in contemporary life.

From the late nineteenth century through the present, women have used their consumer power to try to improve the lives of both the producers and consumers of goods in various ways: consumer cooperatives, boycotting clothes made by nonunion labor, campaigns to eliminate the objectification of women in advertisements, and the early-twenty-first-century campaigns against various aspects of globalization, to name a few. Such engagement indicates the power of women as consumers but also the continued and, one could argue, increasingly problematic place of consumption in women's (and others') lives. For example, to buy things, women are going into ever increasing debt, which they often cannot service. Those things turn out not to provide the advertised happiness or comfort but rather to be just things. As consumers, women have power, but only if they seize it.

[*See also* Body Adornment and Clothing; Capitalism; Class; Domesticity; Food Riots; Poverty; *and* War.]

BIBLIOGRAPHY

Auslander, Leora. *Taste and Power: Furnishing Modern France.* Berkeley: University of California Press, 1996.

Breen, T. H. *The Marketplace of Revolution: How Consumer Politics Shaped American Independence.* Oxford: Oxford University Press, 2004.

Carmeli, Yoram S., and Kalman Applbaum. *Consumption and Market Society in Israel.* Oxford: Berg, 2004.

Cohen, Lizabeth. *A Consumer's Republic: The Politics of Mass Consumption in Postwar America.* New York: Alfred A. Knopf, 2003.

Davis, Belinda. *Home Fires Burning: Food, Politics, and Everyday Life in World War I Berlin.* Chapel Hill: University of North Carolina Press, 2000.

De Grazia, Victoria, ed. *The Sex of Things: Gender and Consumption in Historical Perspective.* Berkeley: University of California Press, 1996.

Kidd, Alan, and David Nichols. *Gender, Civic Culture, and Consumerism: Middle-Class Identity in Britain, 1800–1940.* Manchester, U.K.: Manchester University Press, 1999.

Lynch, Annette. *Dress, Gender, and Cultural Change: Asian American and African American Rites of Passage.* Oxford: Berg, 1999.

Russell, Mona L. *Creating the New Egyptian Woman: Consumerism, Education, and National Identity, 1863–1922.* New York: Palgrave Macmillan, 2004.

Sato, Barbara. *The New Japanese Woman: Modernity, Media, and Women in Interwar Japan.* Durham, N.C.: Duke University Press, 2003.

Strasser, Susan, Charles McGovern, and Matthias Judt, eds. *Getting and Spending: European and American Consumer Societies in the Twentieth Century.* Cambridge, U.K.: Cambridge University Press, 1998.

Sussman, Charlotte. *Consuming Anxieties: Consumer Protest, Gender, and British Slavery, 1713–1833.* Stanford, Calif.: Stanford University Press, 2000.

Yellin, Emily. *Our Mothers' War: American Women at Home and at the Front during World War II.* New York: Free Press, 2004.

LEORA AUSLANDER

CONTAGIOUS DISEASES ACTS. The British contagious diseases acts allowed police and medical inspection of women suspected of prostitution in garrison and port towns in both Britain and its colonies. After the debacle of the Crimean War (1853–1856) and the Indian Mutiny (1857–1858), the health of British troops became a source of escalating alarm. In particular, the widespread venereal disease among soldiers and sailors concerned the military leadership and government. In 1859 the infection rate of British soldiers in India was 359 per 1,000 hospital admissions. A strong empire required a strong military. Because venereal disease was regarded as a by-product of prostitution, legislation was enacted to control and regulate women who engaged in prostitution. The acts were presented as a public health measure that would secure the health of the military and thereby the strength of the empire.

Origins. The earliest contagious diseases act, passed in 1857 in Hong Kong, required brothels to be registered with the authorities and prostitutes to be regularly examined—and hospitalized if found to be infected with venereal disease. By 1870 such acts were enforced in more than a dozen British colonies. The colonial acts required brothel keepers to register the women in their employ; brothels were therefore the focus of inspection and regulation. The registered women were typically not permitted to have non-European clients. In 1864 and 1866 the British Parliament passed contagious diseases acts that applied to eleven garrison and port towns in England and Ireland, and in 1869 they were extended to eighteen communities. The British acts were directed at streetwalkers. The police were to identify women working as prostitutes, require them to undergo medical examination by a military doctor, and enforce the confinement of infected women in a hospital for up to nine months. When released, the women were to submit to regular medical examinations. It was difficult for a woman to have her name removed from the register. The acts contributed to a process that placed prostitutes in an identified professional class of social outcasts. They reflected a new interventionist approach to social problems and fostered new kinds of relationships between the state and hospitals as well as creating substantial new powers for the recently formed police force. The campaign to repeal the acts was to shape the feminist movement, the public debate about sexuality, the role of the state in public health, the regulation of the poor, and relations between colonizer and colonized.

The acts were justified as a public health measure directed at prostitutes, but the reality was more complicated. There was no clear definition of prostitution in the legislation, and the disputes between women and those who enforced the acts demonstrate that they did not share an understanding of the term. The women who fell under the acts' provisions in Great Britain were typically in their twenties, were employed in poorly paid occupations, and took to prostitution in times of unemployment. Prostitution was temporary, transitional, and episodic work. Many women left prostitution when they settled with one man, but, like many working-class couples, they often did not legally marry. Others considered separation from a husband and cohabitation with another man to be the equivalent of divorce and remarriage. Marriage was one of the few ways for a woman to have her name removed from the register of prostitutes, but these less formal alliances did not meet the standards of the authorities. Many women actively resisted the requirements of the acts by fleeing the police, refusing examination, and complaining to magistrates. Women decried the rough treatment by police, who made no secret of the names of registered women. The doctors were so rough that some women preferred prison to the pain and humiliation of examinations. One woman complained that it was particularly hard to be put before a magistrate who had been her client the previous week.

Repeal Efforts. The first organization formed to agitate for the repeal of the contagious diseases acts was established in 1869. A separate organization, the Ladies National Association for the Repeal of the Contagious Diseases Acts, was formed in 1870, with Josephine Butler as its leader. It was highly unusual for middle-class women to speak publicly about sexuality, prostitution, or venereal disease, and the campaign was sharply criticized by the press and members of the government. The Ladies National Association pioneered forms of public protest not previously used by women's groups. Hostile mobs attacked speakers at public meetings. One member of Parliament told Butler that the government did not know what to do with "the revolt of the women" (Walkowitz, p. 113). The activists were overwhelmingly middle-class women married to wealthy industrialists or merchants and committed to a wide range of social reforms. They regarded prostitution as the unfortunate consequence of the restrictions on women's education and employment, inadequate wages, and the sexual double standard that allowed men access to "fallen" women while "respectable" women were to remain ignorant of these realities. The contagious diseases acts, the repealers noted, degraded one group of women and allowed police, medical men, and clients unfettered access to them. The repeal campaign was organized at both local and national levels. Many activist women also campaigned for woman suffrage, employment rights, access to education, and medical reform—all critical feminist issues and all involved with securing rights for women that would diminish the appeal of prostitution. The repeal movement served as a training ground where women learned to speak in public, write for the press, organize petitions, and create other means of public protest. In addition, it broadened the theoretical understanding of women's rights to include sexuality, and it encouraged cross-class alliances. Many British women also campaigned for the repeal of the colonial acts.

The repeal effort was deeply influenced by the movement for the abolition of slavery and its adherence to principle. For example, repealers argued that if prostitution was morally wrong, then the state was wrong to condone it by regulation. The acts violated women's constitutional rights by detaining and imprisoning them on hearsay without a trial and thus enslaved women. Even if the acts succeeded in lowering the incidence of venereal disease, repealers maintained, they were still wrong in principle.

The British acts were repealed in 1886. The repeal movement continued to agitate for repeal in the colonies. The British government had little enthusiasm for further agitation. In some colonies the acts were repealed or no longer enforced. However, in others, notably Hong Kong and India, administrators argued vigorously for the need to uphold the acts. Registered women formally complained in petitions and letters and evaded the requirements of the law when they could. Years of debate ensued, fueled by wider disagreements about the division of power in the colonial government. The colonial acts were repealed through the 1890s but in most cases were replaced by other restrictions on brothels and state regulation of contagious diseases, including venereal disease. Medical treatment of venereal disease changed after the 1905 discovery of the microorganism that caused syphilis and the subsequent improvements in treatment. The most effective treatments were reserved for British soldiers, but the claim that the regulation of prostitution was a medical necessity for imperial strength lost force when medical treatment improved. The regulation of sexuality continued in other forms. In Britain, the Criminal Law Amendment Act of 1885 raised the age of consent for girls and increased police powers over brothels and streetwalkers.

[*See also* Butler, Josephine; Disease and Illnesses; Healing and Medicine; *and* Prostitution.]

BIBLIOGRAPHY

Levine, Philippa. *Prostitution, Race and Politics: Policing Venereal Disease in the British Empire.* New York and London: Routledge, 2003. A study of the contagious diseases acts in the British colonies.

McHugh, Paul. *Prostitution and Victorian Social Reform.* London: Croom Helm, 1980. A study of the contagious diseases acts from a political perspective.

Walkowitz, Judith R. *Prostitution and Victorian Society: Women, Class and the State.* Cambridge, U.K.: Cambridge University Press, 1980. A groundbreaking study that considers the contagious diseases acts in the context of the history of sexuality and feminism.

PAMELA J. WALKER

CONTRACEPTION

This entry consists of two subentries:

Overview and Comparative History

Evidence from antiquity demonstrates that contraception is not a modern invention but a practice deeply embedded in the history of the societies that produced the three world monotheisms. The biblical figure Onan incurred God's wrath by refusing the command to impregnate his brother's widow. He copulated with her but withdrew before ejaculation, spilling his semen on the ground (Genesis 38:9). While Onan represents the ubiquitous efforts by men to control their fertility, women sought female-controlled methods. Ancient Egyptian papyri describe vaginal contraceptive plugs. Some contained materials with spermicidal properties such as lactic acid; others were intended physically to block the passage of sperm into the uterus. Similar formulas appeared in Greek and Roman texts. In the fourth century, Christian authorities cited Onan's fate in forbidding the separation of coitus from procreation, but their efforts to police sexuality were limited by human rebelliousness and the availability of contraceptive knowledge in popular culture and non-Christian sources.

In the ninth century, al-Jahiz, one of the first great prose writers in Arabic, declared that the difference between man and other animals is that only man practices withdrawal when he does not want children. Islamic law sanctioned contraception, and discussions of withdrawal and of intravaginal female methods were frequent in the Arab literature through which the cultures of antiquity were transmitted to the West. Recipes for contraceptive suppositories and pessaries were deliberately lost in translation by Christian scholars during the Middle Ages, but knowledge of withdrawal and other rational contraceptive strategies survived as folk practices that were rediscovered and publicized by Western freethinkers following the political and social ferment of the late eighteenth century.

The men who synthesized Christian theology and built the Roman Catholic Church in late antiquity were profoundly influenced by Greek philosophies that renounced the material world for an ideal world of the spirit. They believed celibacy to be the best sexual status, grudgingly accepted the necessity of procreation, and conceded the legitimacy of coitus only as a means to procreation. They declared all nonprocreative sexuality illicit, and their sex-negative vision heaped scorn on women, who were viewed as temptresses capable of leading men away from the path to salvation through renunciation of physical desire.

Birth-Control Advocacy. A hooked rug, undated. DOROTHY HAMILTON BRUSH PAPERS, SOPHIA SMITH COLLECTION, SMITH COLLEGE

Men and women, acting in their perceived interests, practiced many forms of fertility control, but they persisted in this clandestine behavior despite the aggressive hostility of social leaders. Christian sexual morality shaped the development of a European marriage system that curbed population growth through late marriage and the inability of a large percentage of adults to acquire the capital necessary to meet the expectation that married couples would establish an independent household. Thomas Malthus, a clergyman and political economist, made reproductive decision making an important part of formal social thought through the six editions of his *Essay on the Principle of Population* (1798–1826). Malthus attacked the so-called poor laws that provided subsistence for the indigent on the grounds that recipients responded to public assistance by having additional children whom they could not support. As a Christian moralist, Malthus argued that the poor could be saved from misery only by "moral restraint" in the form of sexual abstinence, and he shunned contraception within marriage.

Contraception in the Nineteenth Century. Freethinkers and political radicals in the West included advocacy of contraception as part of their efforts to demystify nature and to promote social justice for the working classes. Ironically, these iconoclasts became known as neo-Malthusians despite the fact that Malthus abhorred their secular arguments and contraceptive methods. Francis Place, a self-taught English workingman, proposed in 1822 that withdrawal or use of a vaginal sponge might better serve the needs of working people than moral restraint. In handbills that were given away in the streets of industrial cities, he explained that sex could be separated from procreation.

Charles Knowlton, an American physician, combined blunt materialism with Yankee will to find better technology in his *Fruits of Philosophy* (1832), one of the new marriage manuals that proliferated in the emerging mass commercial economies of the West. Knowlton advocated spermicidal douching with a vaginal syringe on the grounds that withdrawal required too much sacrifice of male pleasure. The commercial promotion of "feminine hygiene" douches in the twentieth century gave Knowlton's method a longer life than might be expected after 1885, when Wilhelm P. J. Mensinga, a German physician and professor of anatomy, described a spring-loaded rubber vaginal diaphragm that became the mainstay of medical contraception until the marketing of the anovulant birth-control pill in 1960. Nineteenth-century medical leaders were more prominent in campaigns to criminalize abortion, to manage unhappy women through ovariotomy, and to warn the public of the dangers of masturbation than they were in contraceptive research. Purity crusades against commercial vice led to harsh obscenity laws that failed to distinguish between smut and information on abortion or contraception, with the result that contraception remained a matter of self-help for individuals.

By the early nineteenth century a long-term decline in fertility had begun in parts of Western Europe and North America. Twentieth-century social scientists often erred in associating this demographic transition to lower fertility with declines in infant mortality. Deaths in childhood remained high until vast improvements in sewerage and water systems, followed by the spread of the germ theory of disease, brought rapid decline in infant mortality in the early twentieth century. The nineteenth-century decline in fertility was the result of married women having fewer children despite the high risk that the children they did have might die. Husbands and wives' motives for limiting children might differ, but cooperation between spouses was often a significant factor in their ability to limit their families.

Many specific social groups—including French peasants and aristocrats, members of the emerging business class in the United States, workers in capital-intensive industries where women and children were no longer employed, and market-oriented farmers in developing regions where land prices were rising—began to have fewer children by employing old methods such as abstinence and withdrawal and new practices that depended on the availability of new products such as rubber syringes, diaphragms, cervical caps, condoms, and spermicides. Contraceptors sought to protect the integrity of their families in economies where children were no longer necessary hands for household production but expensive dependents who required expensive schooling. New rationales for marriages that emphasized romantic love proved contradictory in market economies where the desire for erotic expression and higher standards of living had to be reconciled with the rising expense of dependent children. Despite the almost universal opposition of religious authorities and social elites, married adults pursued their self-interests by limiting family size, although the relative roles of contraception, abortion, and sexual repression in the process cannot be estimated with certainty.

Birth-Control Clinics. Iconoclastic medical men published descriptions of contraceptive regimens of many kinds, but no systematic clinical studies were conducted to identify the safest and most effective methods, and most professional leaders shunned the topic except to warn against the grave dangers of family limitation. In 1925, Morris Fishbein, editor of the *Journal of the American Medical Association*, included contraception as a topic in his book *Medical Follies* and denied that effective or safe contraceptive practice was possible, while implying that those who tried it risked cancer and madness. This diatribe from the leader of a science-based profession accounts for the important role that radical feminists later played in the rediscovery and refinement of contraceptive practice.

In 1923, Margaret Sanger opened the Birth Control Clinical Research Bureau in New York and managed to keep it open despite a police raid in 1928. Sanger began her public career as a socialist, labor organizer, and protégée of the anarchist Emma Goldman, but before World War I she had decided to narrow her focus to women's reproductive health issues. She believed that the first step toward women's liberation was to gain access to reliable contraception, and that required challenging the obscenity laws by publishing information and providing services. The closing of her first women's advice center in 1916 resulted in a court decision that implied that doctors might give contraceptive advice for the cure or prevention of disease. In response Sanger campaigned for legislation that would support the medicalization of contraception and mobilized the resources required to establish her doctor-staffed birth-control clinic in 1923.

Although Sanger was bitterly criticized by rival feminists in the 1920s and by Second Wave feminists in the 1970s for making birth control a matter of access to medical services, her pragmatic strategy allowed her to reach some important goals. Under the medical direction of Hannah Stone, the clinical research bureau became the primary source of data that refuted the claims of Fishbein and other conservative medical leaders. Stone proved that the vaginal diaphragm, used with spermicidal jelly, is a safe and effective contraceptive. The Sanger-Stone clinic provided training in contraception for hundreds of physicians, and it was the model for the nationwide network of more than three

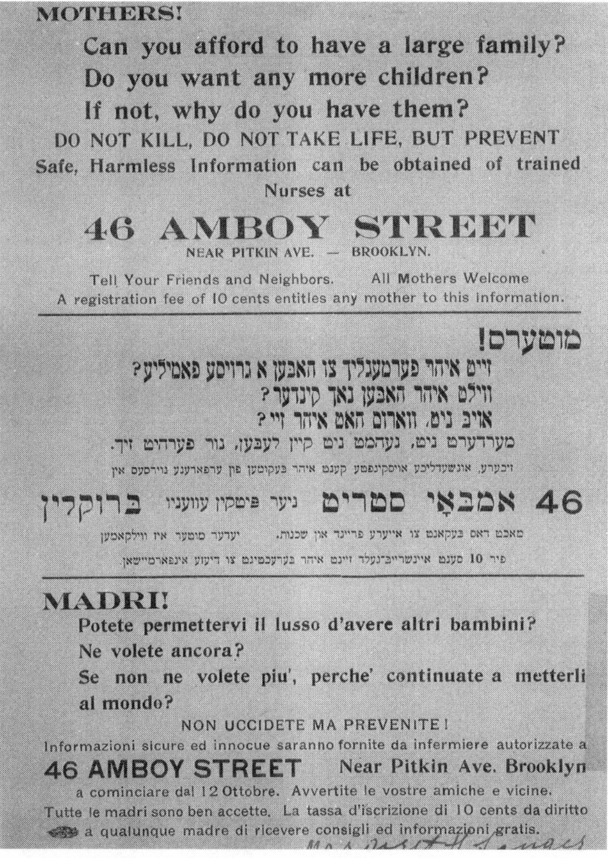

Birth-Control Clinics. A flyer for Margaret Sanger's family planning clinic, 46 Amboy Street, Brownsville, Brooklyn. MARGARET SANGER PAPERS, SOPHIA SMITH COLLECTION, SMITH COLLEGE

Margaret Sanger. In her clinic with a patient, early twentieth century. GEORGE GRANTHAM BAIN COLLECTION, LIBRARY OF CONGRESS

hundred clinics that Sanger and her feminist allies had established by 1936, when Stone won a federal court decision that established the right of physicians to receive contraceptive supplies. In 1937 the American Medical Association recognized contraception as a legitimate service that should be included in the medical curriculum.

The women who funded and staffed birth-control clinics in the 1930s embraced the vaginal diaphragm as a female-controlled method that commanded some medical support. Education in methods used by men, such as condoms and withdrawal, was not offered, and critics noted that, whatever the theoretical effectiveness of the diaphragm, many clinic patients stopped using the method after a brief period, and others, socialized in a genital-shy culture, were psychologically or anatomically incapable of using it.

New Concerns as Justification of New Methods. In the 1930s birthrates in the Western democracies were declining and often fell below the level needed to maintain the existing population. Contraceptive research was not a high priority for scientists or governments. After World War II the Cold War and the discovery of a population explosion in the Third World provided a powerful rationale for the development of new contraceptive methods. Alan F. Guttmacher, an obstetrician on the medical advisory committee of the Population Council (founded in 1952), an American foundation interested in promoting population control abroad, surveyed the effectiveness of Third World family-planning programs and concluded that the effort to control world population growth would fail unless new methods could be discovered that were inexpensive, highly effective, and capable of delivery through mass public health campaigns.

In the 1930s Ernst Grafenberg, a German physician, developed an intrauterine device (IUD) consisting of a flexible coil of wire that prevented conception when placed in the uterus. This method had been shunned by Guttmacher on the grounds that it might lead to pelvic inflammatory disease, but with the advent of antibiotics and the "population bomb" Guttmacher decided that the IUD might be the technological fix required for the success of mass family-planning programs in the Third World. Thanks to new flexible plastic materials, the IUD could be inserted in the uterus without dilation of the cervix, and the method proved highly effective in the worldwide clinical trials that the Population Council sponsored. In the late 1960s IUDs of nearly 100 percent effectiveness were developed by embedding copper in the plastic coils. As of the early twenty-first century the IUD is the most widely used reversible contraceptive in the world, but it has been generally rejected by women in United States, where the Dalkon Shield, a defective IUD promoted by commercial interests that were not part of the Population Council project, caused septic shock among users. Successful lawsuits against the manufacturer of the Dalkon Shield encouraged class-action litigation against the makers of all IUDs, and in 1985 the major American pharmaceutical firms withdrew their IUDs from the market, despite their demonstrated safety and effectiveness, because liability issues threatened their assets.

In the 1950s the perceived perils of population growth provided impetus for experiments with hormonal contraceptives. During the 1920s rapid advances in knowledge of the mammalian reproductive system, subsidized by the U.S. National Research Council's Committee for Research in Problems of Sex, encouraged pursuit of physiological approaches to contraception. Identification of the sex hormones and their role in the female ovulatory cycle made it possible to predict when the brief period of fertility would occur. The rhythm method, calling for periodic abstinence around the middle of a menstrual month, won approval from Roman Catholic authorities but became known as "Vatican roulette" because of the variability in the ovulatory cycles of individuals. By the 1940s steroid chemists had begun to synthesize sex hormones, which proved a mainstay for a science-based and capital-intensive pharmaceutical industry. Relatively inexpensive synthetic hormones were widely prescribed to treat the symptoms of menopause and other gynecological disorders by the early 1950s, but the use of these designer molecules to prevent contraception seemed problematic to most industry leaders because such powerful therapeutic agents had never been given to healthy persons, and association with contraception might threaten their most lucrative products.

The effort to develop a birth-control pill was mobilized by Margaret Sanger, who recruited Gregory Pincus of the Worcester Foundation for Experimental Biology by introducing him to Katharine Dexter McCormick, an old feminist ally and heir to the International Harvester fortune. McCormick provided the funds that Pincus needed to realize her dream of a female-controlled method that was divorced from sexual intercourse, but Pincus often cited the perceived world population crisis as justification for a radical experiment in hormone therapy. The marketing in 1960 of what became known as the "the pill" brought contraception from "messy gadget" notoriety into mainstream biomedical science. In 1963, John Rock, the Roman Catholic gynecologist who had led the clinical trials of the pill, proclaimed in *The Time Has Come* that, thanks to the pill, contraception was compatible with natural-law theology. Rock's optimism proved illusory when the 1968 papal encyclical *Humanae vitae* rejected the pill and all "artificial" contraception, but by then a majority of married Catholics were practicing contraception.

Roughly 120 million women used various versions of the pill between 1960 and 2000, but its popularity was challenged by reports of side effects and by Second Wave feminists who pointed out that women were absent from the expert panels that made decisions about its safety and that it placed the whole burden of contraception on women. The emerging women's health movement challenged male medical condescension and demanded more collaboration with female patients in health-care decision making. The package inserts now included with all prescription drugs in the United States were developed, despite the opposition of organized medicine, in response to lobbying by women concerned about undisclosed side effects of oral contraception. The pill played a key role in changing sexual values between 1960 and the early 1980s, when the acquired immunodeficiency syndrome (AIDS) epidemic brought renewed anxiety about sexually transmitted disease, but the pill found greatest acceptance among women in the affluent West rather than in the population-control programs that provided crucial justification for hormonal contraception.

An Endless Frontier. In the last decades of the twentieth century, foundations and governments continued a capital-intensive search for better contraceptive technology. One of the key figures in this multidisciplinary and international effort was Sheldon Segal, who served as director of the biomedical research division of the Population Council and later as a director of population sciences at the Rockefeller Foundation. In 1970, Segal organized the International Committee for Contraception Research (ICCR), a worldwide network of medical researchers such as the Brazilian gynecologist Elsimar Coutinho, who developed the long-lasting injectable contraceptive regimen that was first marketed in the United States in 1993 as Depo-Provera.

The ICCR's ability to sponsor clinical trials of new contraceptives in multiple international sites proved essential as requirements for the approval of new drugs became more stringent. In the early 1970s Segal's research team worked with medical-grade plastics supplied by Dow Corning in an attempt to develop a removable plug for reversible closure of the vas deferens in men. The search for a reversible vasectomy turned into a decades-long quest for an "under the skin pill" for women when Segal learned that oil-soluble dyes slowly diffused out of the plastic. Steroid hormones are also oil soluble. Exploiting synthetic "super progestins" that were becoming available, Segal managed to broker agreements with Dow Corning and the Wyeth Corporation that allowed him to combine a delivery system of Dow plastic with a Wyeth progestin in a nonprofit effort to provide a radical advance in birth control.

After ten years of extensive testing and acceptance by authorities abroad, a subdermal implant with five-year effectiveness was introduced in the United States in 1991 with the trade name of Norplant. Segal was appalled by the controversies that immediately erupted when a California state judge offered a female drug addict the choice of jail or Norplant. While ethical issues festered, successful class-action suits against Dow Corning for its breast implants inspired a rash of product-liability suits against Norplant's manufacturer. By 1997 twenty-five thousand of the million Norplant users in the United States had been recruited by lawyers competing for class-action certification. After spending $40 million to defend Norplant successfully from claims of harm, Wyeth discontinued the product in 2002. Subdermal implants remained popular in Europe, where the Organon Company of the Netherlands successfully marketed Implanon. The proliferation of commercial-sector innovations in hormonal contraception included Lovelle, a pill that delivers its hormones through absorption by the vaginal wall, with the advantage that the hormones do not pass through the liver. A contraceptive skin patch, Ortho Evra, was marketed in 2002.

Feminists viewed these innovations with suspicion, but Segal worked with women's health advocates to develop emergency contraception that could be employed after a rape or unprotected coitus. It had been established in the 1960s that a large dose of a conventional birth-control pill would cause sloughing of the uterine lining and thus prevent the implantation of a fertilized egg, but manufacturers resisted endorsement of this off-label use because the raging controversy over abortion might threaten their profitable sale of contraceptives. An alternative was provided with the independent development of Plan B, a "super progestin" powerful enough to induce shedding of the uterine lining without an estrogen component. In 2006 controversy raged over the hesitancy of the U.S. Food and Drug Administration to approve Plan B for nonprescription or over-the-counter sale despite broad scientific agreement about its safety and effectiveness.

Another approach to postcoital contraception was provided by mifepristone, a progesterone-receptor modifier that prevents progesterone, the hormone of gestation, from carrying out its natural function in the uterus and thus terminates pregnancy. After the French company that developed RU-486, the first of these contragestational agents, declined to risk the investment required to market their molecule in the United States, the Population Council assumed the burden, with the hope that the 2000 FDA approval of RU-486 would provide an alternative for women who might be deprived of access to safe surgical abortion as a result of the country's changing legal climate.

In 1972, Segal published the article "Contraceptive Research: A Male Chauvinist Plot?" in response to oft-repeated charges that reproductive biology was dominated by men who lacked interest in sharing the burden of contraception with women. Although the grant-making committees in the field pursued reversible vasectomy, a male vaccine, a male implant system, and a male pill, Segal argued that it was more difficult to disrupt spermatogenesis safely than to attack the vulnerable sites in the process of ovulation and gestation. There was a pressing political need for a modern male contraceptive, but science was proving impotent in the short run.

The prospect for a male pill brightened when scientists at the Chinese Academy of Medical Sciences reported that gossypol, the pigment that gives cottonseed a yellowish color, was a potent antifertility agent for men. Hopeful of an Asian breakthrough in a field that was dominated by Westerners, the Rockefeller Foundation sponsored a major effort to identify the contraceptive agent in gossypol and to conduct standardized trials of its effect, but the effort foundered on issues of toxicity, and the search for a safe male pill continued on many fronts. Most of the promising leads involved methods that would appeal to affluent men in committed relationships, and control of their fertility did not justify high-risk regimens.

In 1994, Susan Benoff of New York University suggested that nifedipine, a calcium-channel blocker widely used to reduce blood pressure, caused sterility in men by preventing sperm maturation. However, funding agencies concluded that this line of investigation posed unacceptable risks for healthy men, and Benoff moved on to other problems.

In the early twenty-first century vast improvements in contraceptive technology have enhanced the reproductive autonomy of many women and contributed to the worldwide decline of fertility, but debates still rage over the costs and goals of contraception. Most governments support access to contraception for their citizens, and there is a dramatic international convergence of total fertility rates (the number of children born over the reproductive life of the average woman).

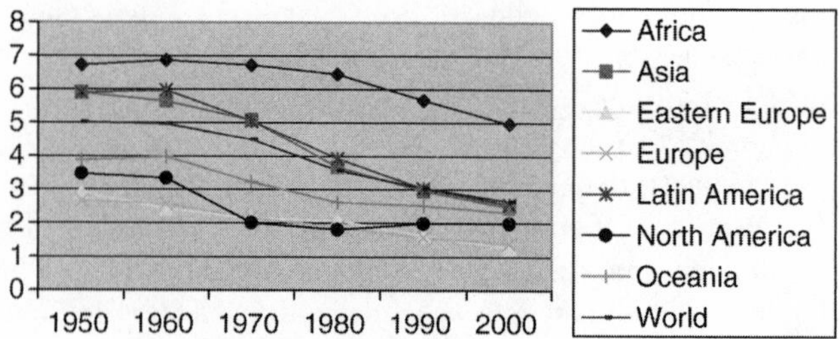

FIGURE 1. Total Fertility Decline SOURCE: United Nations World Population Database: 2002 Revision (http://esa.un.org/unpp/index.asp?panel=2).

[*See also* Abortion; AIDS; Demography; Hormones; Jacobs, Aletta; Non-Governmental Organizations; *and* Sanger, Margaret.]

BIBLIOGRAPHY

Bullough, Vern L. *Sexual Variance in Society and History*. Chicago: University of Chicago Press, 1976. A wide-ranging history of sexuality that includes contraceptive practice and contrasts the "sex-negative" West with the rest of humanity.

Chesler, Ellen. *Woman of Valor: Margaret Sanger and the Birth Control Movement in America*. New York: Simon and Schuster, 1992. The best biography of Sanger.

Clarke, Adele E. *Disciplining Reproduction: Modernity, American Life Sciences, and "The Problems of Sex."* Berkeley: University of California Press, 1998. Analyzes the rise of endocrinology and places contraceptive research in a broad context.

Cook, Hera. *The Long Sexual Revolution: English Women, Sex, and Contraception: 1800–1975*. New York: Oxford University Press, 2004. Provides a nuanced argument for the importance of the pill in the evolution of sexual behavior and values.

Himes, Norman E. *Medical History of Contraception*. Baltimore: Williams and Wilkins, 1936. The first attempt at a comprehensive history of contraceptive practice, it still stimulates thought.

Marks, Lara V. *Sexual Chemistry: A History of the Contraceptive Pill*. New Haven, Conn.: Yale University Press, 1991. The most comprehensive account of the pill and its impact.

McLaren, Angus. *A History of Contraception: From Antiquity to the Present Day*. Cambridge, Mass.: Basil Blackwell, 1990. A comprehensive account of the social and political contexts that shaped contraceptive practice in the West.

Musallam, B. F. *Sex and Society in Islam: Birth Control before the Nineteenth Century*. Cambridge, U.K.: Cambridge University Press, 1983. Examines the extensive discussions of contraception in Arab literatures.

Oudshoorn, Nelly. *The Male Pill: A Biography of a Technology in the Making*. Durham, N.C.: Duke University Press, 2003. The search goes on, but if they make it, will he take it?

Segal, Sheldon J. *Under the Banyan Tree: A Population Scientist's Odyssey*. New York: Oxford University Press, 2003. An insider's account of modern contraceptive research.

Tone, Andrea. *Devices and Desires: A History of Contraceptives in America*. New York: Hill and Wang, 2001. A good account of the commercial culture of nonmedical contraception.

Watkins, Elizabeth Siegel. *On the Pill: A Social History of Oral Contraceptives, 1950–1970*. Baltimore: Johns Hopkins University Press, 1998. Strong on the dialectic between women activists and the medical establishment.

JAMES W. REED

Politics

Anthropologists studying human reproduction in premodern cultures have found that the desire for children is not an innate human drive but an acquired motive that must be reinforced by social rewards and punishments sufficient to overcome the wish to avoid the pain of childbirth and the burdens of parenthood. The process of social reproduction has always involved struggle among the competing interests of men, women, and social authorities, who usually discouraged contraception in the belief that it violated natural law or deprived society of human capital.

Thomas Malthus brought contraception into modern political economy with his *Essay on the Principle of Population* (1798). He attacked welfare for the indigent on the grounds that their numbers always grew with increases in subsistence. As a Christian moralist he regarded contraception within marriage as a sin and argued that only "moral restraint" in the form of sexual abstinence and late marriage could save the poor from the "positive checks" imposed on their numbers by famine, disease, and war. Ironically, nineteenth-century radicals and free thinkers, who began the movement to promote fertility-limiting practices in the interests of the working poor, became known as "neo-Malthusians."

From Voluntary Motherhood to Birth Control. By the early nineteenth century a long-term decline in fertility had begun in parts of Europe and North America. Reductions in marital fertility, which were the result of an earlier decline in childbearing, alarmed social conservatives. Physicians, concerned about frequent requests for abortion by married women, organized successful campaigns to criminalize induced abortion, while other middle-class reformers conducted purity crusades against commercial vice. In the United States, the Comstock Act (1873), a strengthened federal obscenity law, allowed no distinction between smut, abortifacients, or contraceptives; all were prohibited. In 1877 the British free thinker Annie Besant was prosecuted for republishing an American marriage manual that recommended contraceptive douching. Besant's trial inspired radical neo-Malthusians all over Europe.

During the nineteenth century most leaders of the first civil rights movement for women were wary of the propaganda of neo-Malthusians. Rather than directly challenge pronatalist values, they advocated "voluntary motherhood," or the right of married women to decide whether to have coitus, and they feared that contraception might provide new rationales for traditional male sexual prerogatives. In the early twentieth century suffragists dissociated themselves from birth control, believing that its advocacy might hurt their principal goal. The anarchist Emma Goldman and socialist women began to articulate a new feminist vision in which women and men struggled as partners against wage slavery and sexual repression. The term "birth control" was coined in a 1914 issue of *The Woman Rebel*, a militantly feminist journal published in New York by Margaret Sanger. Sanger became the preeminent champion of reproductive autonomy for women through her campaigns to abolish the obstacles to contraceptive practice.

Sanger offered contraception as an alternative to abortion. Like her British competitor Marie Stopes, Sanger realized that political success depended on playing down the issue of sexual freedom. Although Sanger and Stopes celebrated the sexual joys of marriage in their advice books, the compelling official justification for their work was to bring modern contraception to the poor women who suffered from the effects of high-risk fertility-control methods. Sanger, alienated by the male chauvinism of some radical colleagues, became convinced that women needed a distinctive voice representing them as an interest group in the struggle for social justice. The cause of reproductive autonomy for women could not wait, she argued, for the socialist revolution.

Sanger and her sister, both trained as nurses, provided the contraceptive instruction offered in Sanger's first clinic, opened in 1916. Following her arrest and imprisonment, she appealed her case and won a clarification of New York State law. The Crane decision implied the right of doctors to provide women with contraceptive advice for "the cure and prevention of disease." Sanger interpreted the Crane decision as a mandate for doctor-staffed birth-control clinics and began lobbying for doctors-only legislation that removed legal prohibitions on medical advice. This pragmatic concession was bitterly opposed by Mary Ware Dennett, Sanger's chief rival for leadership of the American birth-control movement in the 1920s, but Sanger bested Dennett in their struggle for the allegiance of the society women who provided the capital needed for the cause. In 1923, Sanger opened a doctor-staffed clinic, which served as a model for a nationwide network of more than three hundred birth-control clinics established in the 1930s.

As a political opportunist, Sanger became a fellow traveler in the eugenics movement, which flourished in the United States from the late 1890s until World War II. Eugenicists, obsessed by the declining fertility of the upper classes, sought to encourage high birthrates among the "fit" and to prevent the "unfit" from reproducing. Sanger was contemptuous of the pronatalist aspects of the eugenics agenda but was willing to make common cause with eugenicists in promoting contraception and sterilization for the poor. By the 1930s population studies in the United States and Britain were institutionalized through a marriage of convenience between birth controllers and eugenicists that served both interests well until the Nazi campaign of racial purification exposed the hellish potential of hereditarianism. Under the Nazi "racial hygiene" program, Aryan women were forbidden to use contraception, while Jews and other "inferior" groups had generous access to it.

In the 1930s Sanger conducted a major lobbying campaign to remove the provisions regarding contraception from the Comstock Act. The effort failed because the idea of reproductive autonomy for women was literally a joke among male legislators at a time when the birthrate had fallen below the level needed to maintain the existing population. In *United States v. One Package of Japanese Pessaries* (1936), however, Sanger won a major revision in federal law with a ruling that physicians had a right to receive contraceptive materials. *One Package* set the stage for a 1937 resolution by the American Medical Association that recognized contraception as an ethical medical service.

Family Planning and the Demographic Imperative. On the eve of World War II the limits of the birth-control movement seemed to have been realized. A majority of married people in the West practiced some form of fertility control, but there was widespread concern about the low birthrate and little support for public subsidy of services. In 1942 the Birth Control Federation of America changed its name to the Planned Parenthood Federation of America as part of a public relations campaign to dispel popular association with feminism. After World War II influential social scientists provided a new rationale for birth control by drawing attention to rapid population growth in the Third World and by arguing that the United States risked losing the Cold War because economic development compatible with capitalism might be impossible if means were not found to curb birthrates.

John D. Rockefeller III became the leader of the revived movement to promote fertility control. In 1952 he founded the Population Council, which subsidized the development of demographic research in the United States and foreign universities. By the late 1950s the council was providing technical assistance to India and Pakistan for family-planning programs, and belief in the demographic imperative to lower birthrates in the Third World had become part of U.S. natural security doctrine. The first obstacle to lowering birthrates was the high failure rates of conventional barrier contraceptives. The council invested heavily in the clinical testing, improvement, and statistical evaluation of intrauterine devices (IUDs), which became a mainstay of Asian population-control programs in the 1960s. The council's budget swelled with contributions from the U.S. Agency for International Development and the Ford Foundation.

The successful marketing of the birth control pill in 1960 aroused hopes among liberal Catholics that their church would accept hormonal methods of contraception. Hope turned to disaffection when the papal encyclical *Humanae vitae* (1968) confirmed traditional teachings, but by then a majority of married Catholics were using artificial contraceptives.

A series of federal court decisions based on the right to privacy removed legal prohibitions on contraception in the United States. *Griswold v. Connecticut* (1965) struck down a law that prohibited contraceptive practice among the married, and *Eisenstadt v. Baird* (1972) established right of the unmarried to contraceptives. As President Lyndon Johnson's War on Poverty legislation emerged from Congress in 1964, a number of planned-parenthood groups successfully applied to the Office of Economic Opportunity for funds, and the Social Security Amendments of 1967 specified that at least 6 percent of expanding maternal and child health care funds be spent on family planning services. The Foreign Assistant Act of the same year removed contraceptives from the list of materials that could not be purchased with funds from the Agency for International Development (AID). Arguments for coercive population-control programs gained attention through the efforts of the Dixie Cup tycoon Hugh Moore, who founded the Population Crisis Committee and spent lavishly on full-page newspaper advertisements warning of the ticking "population bomb." Rockefeller was appalled by Moore's scare tactics, but Moore had the means to hire high-powered lobbyists. The pro-family-planning caucus in the U.S. Congress included environmentalists, War on Poverty Democrats, and demographic-imperative Cold Warriors.

From 1966 to 1978 the American effort to promote population control abroad was dominated by Reimert T. Ravenholt, MD, head of the AID's population division. With an academic background in public health, Ravenholt had great faith in the mass delivery of biomedical technology. Convinced that the Third World masses needed and wanted his product, Ravenholt relentlessly pushed a "supply side" approach to family planning in which foreign governments were induced to accept massive supplies of new contraceptives without much attention to their other needs. Doubts over whether client states had health care systems adequate to the task of monitoring the side effects of IUDs and hormonal drugs were suppressed, and a blind eye was turned to coercive practices in many countries where the ruling elites ruthlessly recruited "acceptors" into their goal-driven population-control programs. Beginning in 1970 with congressional hearings on side effects of oral contraceptives, Second Wave feminists challenged the male-dominated medical and population establishments.

Ravenholt's "body count" mentality encountered mounting resistance from an emerging international women's health movement.

Reproductive Rights and Challenges to Population Control. In 1970 the Republican president Richard Nixon appointed Rockefeller chairman of the Commission on Population Growth and the American Future, but in 1972 Nixon repudiated the commission's recommendations on sex education and abortion law reform because they had become intensely controversial. By the late 1960s feminists were successfully challenging state laws that limited access to abortion. In 1973 the U.S. Supreme Court attempted to forge a new consensus in *Roe v. Wade*, which recognized the right of abortion on demand during the first trimester of pregnancy. The court's decision added fuel to an escalating firestorm of controversy as Roman Catholic leaders found common cause with Protestant fundamentalists and social conservative critics of the welfare state in a "right-to-life" and "family values" movement.

From the Left, groups such as the Committee to End Sterilization Abuse (founded in 1974) charged that disproportionate numbers of Hispanic and black women were sterilized in Medicaid and War on Poverty health care programs. The lack of adequate ethical guidelines in government-funded program gave legitimacy to complaints by the women's health movement that the American health care establishment had gone radically wrong in its high-tech, top-down, paternalistic approach to reproductive health issues.

Rockefeller, under the influence of his aide Joan Dunlop, a leftist feminist with a background in urban policy, began to have serious doubts about the population establishment that he had founded. At the 1974 United Nations World Population Conference, held in Bucharest, Rockefeller delivered an address that stressed reproductive rights over population control. The AID, as the primary sponsor of the United Nations Fund for Population Activities, had expected that the Bucharest Conference would rally foreign governments for population control. Instead it provided a forum for criticism of U.S. hegemony. A delegate from India captured headlines by declaring "Development is the best contraceptive." The Chinese delegation said that population was not a problem under socialism.

Ironically, India and China became world leaders in aggressive population control during the 1970s, in part because of U.S. foundation programs that brought thousands of the most promising students from the developing world to the United States and that subsidized research centers abroad. A new generation of scientists and technocrats in economics, demography, and the reproductive life sciences eventually had an influence on state policies all over the world. In India and China, overzealous bureaucrats, eager to meet government fertility-reduction goals, routinely abused the reproductive rights of the poor through forced sterilization and abortion.

In 1978 the People's Republic of China launched both its market-oriented economic reform era and its unique one-child policy. The one-child policy required that after a first birth, the mother had to have an intrauterine device inserted. If a woman had two children, she or her husband was required to be sterilized. All pregnancies that had not received prior official approval were to be aborted. Despite great suffering and considerable resistance in rural areas, dramatic declines in fertility paralleled a rapid increase in per capita income. At the 1984 World Population Conference in Mexico City, most non-Western representatives assumed the demographic imperative to manage fertility in the interests of economic development, while the conservative administration of Ronald Reagan sent representatives who declared population growth "a neutral phenomenon" in economic development. The administration's "global gag rule" on information about abortion in domestic or foreign maternal health programs led to the withdrawal of funds from the International Planned Parenthood and United Nations programs, but it also provided powerful incentives for the population establishment to find common cause with feminist critics.

At the 1994 International Conference on Population and Development, held in Cairo, activists in the women's health movement enjoyed the support of the administration of Bill Clinton and outmaneuvered conservatives to forge a new consensus on population policy. The program of action from the Cairo conference shunned demographic objectives and proposed a broad agenda of women's issues. Margaret Sanger's original vision of birth control as the cutting edge of female liberation was refurbished after decades of erosion by eugenic and demographic-imperative thinking. The privacy-rights doctrine articulated in U.S. Supreme Court decisions and the reproductive rights emphasized in the Cairo Consensus were challenged by New Right coalitions of Catholics, evangelicals, and neoliberal economists.

The neoliberal economists, whose ranks included the Nobel Prize winner Gary Becker, embraced population growth. They argued that Malthusians underestimated humans' technological and organizational ingenuity. Human beings were "the ultimate resource" because population growth drives innovation and creates economies of scale. Neoliberals insisted that the market should determine the optimal number of children and recognized no demographic imperative as justifying government programs of population control.

Scholars on the Left also contributed to the deconstruction of family planning as population control. A new generation of anthropologists, informed by the academic discipline of women's studies, became major voices in scholarly journals such as the *Population and Development Review.* These Third Wave feminists brought an ethnographic turn to demography that demonstrated the rationality of women's fertility decisions and the basic irrelevance of modern contraceptives without accompanying advances in women's education, health care, and incomes. Betsy Hartmann, an anthropologist at Hampshire College, gained a wide audience for the Left-feminist critique with her muckraking *Reproductive Rights and Wrongs: The Global Politics of Population Control and Contraceptive Choice* (1987). New ethical guidelines were developed for family-planning programs. Even Chinese policy makers declared their desire to move on to enhancement of female reproductive health rather than maintain a single-minded concentration on fertility control, but deep social divisions remained between "pro-choice" and "pro-life" advocates.

In the early twenty-first century the neoliberal embrace of population growth displaced Malthusian concerns over the carrying capacity of the earth. Free marketeers, politicians of the right, the Vatican, and fundamentalist Protestants were united by faith in immutable natural laws that they believed were immune to social engineering. For Third Wave feminists, the arguments of social conservatives were trumped by their primary commitment to equality for women, which could be achieved only when they possessed the right to control their fertility.

[*See also* Abortion; Demography; Gender Preference in Children; *and* Sanger, Margaret.]

BIBLIOGRAPHY

Buss, Doris, and Didi Herman. *Globalizing Family Values: The Christian Right in International Politics*. Minneapolis: University of Minnesota Press, 2003. A good guide to the activities of the Christian right in the international arena.

Critchlow, Donald T. *Intended Consequences: Birth Control, Abortion, and the Federal Government in Modern America*. New York: Oxford University Press, 1999. The best account of political events in the United States that shaped international policy.

Dixon-Mueller, Ruth. *Population Policy and Women's Rights: Transforming Reproductive Choice*. Westport, Conn.: Praeger, 1993. A useful account of the genesis of the women's international health movement.

Eager, Paige W. *Global Population Policy: From Population Control to Reproductive Rights*. Burlington, Vt.: Ashgate, 2004. A political scientist's account of the organization of the Cairo Consensus.

Krause, Elizabeth L. *A Crisis of Births: Population Politics and Family-Making in Italy*. Belmont, Calif.: Wadsworth, 2005. One of the many feminist ethnographies that influenced the discipline of demography and opinion on family-planning programs.

McLaren, Angus. *A History of Contraception: From Antiquity to the Present Day*. Cambridge, Mass.: Blackwell, 1990. The most comprehensive and nuanced social history of birth control.

Simon, Julian. *The Ultimate Resource 2*. Princeton, N.J.: Princeton University Press, 1996. An example of economic thought regarding population from a leading proponent of growth.

James W. Reed

CONVENTION ON THE ELIMINATION OF ALL FORMS OF DISCRIMINATION AGAINST WOMEN. The United Nations Convention on the Elimination of All Forms of Discrimination against Women (CEDAW) is an international treaty that promotes the human rights of women, legal and political equality between men and women, women's reproductive rights, and an end to all discrimination against women. The Commission on the Status of Women (CSW), established in 1946, worked since the end of World War II to draft a document that would specifically set forth the human rights of women. In March 1967 the CSW presented the Declaration on the Elimination of Discrimination against Women to the United Nations General Assembly, and it was adopted in November 1967. However, because the declaration was only a statement of moral intent, the CSW realized that it needed a more binding agreement that would hold the contractual force of a treaty.

In the 1970s the Economic and Social Council of the United Nations invited member states to submit recommendations on the document and to open a dialogue within their countries on women's needs and desires for the agreement. The United Nations declared 1975 to be International Women's Year, promoting equality between men and women. The affiliated World Conference in Mexico City allowed for open discussion of many of the issues that were incorporated in the convention against discrimination, including women's access to education, jobs, and international development resources. After the conference the CSW created a draft of the convention, sending copies to various governments and U.N. agencies for evaluation.

The final draft of the convention argues that without equality for men and women, the eradication of racism, poverty, and war cannot occur. The convention further emphasizes that discrimination against women hinders social progress and development. It states that all women should be able to participate in elections and in the formulation and implementation of government policy. Furthermore, women should have control over their own nationality, the same educational and career opportunities as men, the right to social security and maternity leave, and other social and health benefits. The convention strongly emphasizes that women should have the same legal capacity as men, including equal control over marriage rights and the right to choose a spouse freely.

Several aspects of the convention have been controversial, particularly those that conflict with national or religious laws, including women's right to choose their residence and to enter freely into marriage or divorce. In addition, some antifeminist groups have argued that the convention is merely promoting a radical feminist agenda. Despite these controversies, the United Nations General Assembly adopted the convention in 1979, and it was submitted for ratification at the 1980 World Conference on the United Nations Decade for Women in Copenhagen, Denmark. The convention entered into force on 3 September 1981, and as of 2006 nearly 90 percent of United Nations members were party to the convention, although some states have chosen to ratify the treaty with reservations. A 1999 Optional Protocol allows women and organizations to denounce CEDAW violations directly to CEDAW. The convention is the most comprehensive international treaty specifically to address the human rights of women.

[*See also* Declaration on the Elimination of Violence against Women; Human Rights; *and* United Nations.]

BIBLIOGRAPHY

Rehof, Lars Adam. *Guide to the Travaux Préparatoires of the United Nations Convention on the Elimination of All Forms of Discrimination against Women.* Dordrecht and Boston: M. Nijhoff, 1993. Details the discussions around the drafting of CEDAW, including specific countries' reservations and suggestions for changes in style and content.

United Nations Convention on the Elimination of All Forms of Discrimination against Women. http://www.un.org/womenwatch/daw/cedaw/. The United Nations CEDAW Web site is the best resource for information on the convention. It includes its history, the full text of the document, a lists of signatories, and information on all of the debates and issues surrounding the treaty.

DARCIE S. FONTAINE

COOPER, ANNA JULIA (1858?–1964), African American civil and women's rights activist. Anna Julia Haywood Cooper was one of most prolific reformers of the twentieth century. Believed to have been born on 10 August 1858 in North Carolina, she was the daughter of a slave named Hannah Stanley; she believed her mother's owner, Fabius J. Haywood, to have been her father. At an early age Cooper learned to read and write and developed a passion for learning. In 1867 she entered St. Augustine's Normal School, where she tutored students and protested the exclusion of women from some courses. At St. Augustine's she also met George C. Cooper, a native of the West Indies. Fourteen years her senior, George Cooper was a teacher and theology student. The pair married in 1877, and George Cooper died two years later.

Following her husband's death, Cooper continued to pursue her education. She entered Oberlin College in Ohio in 1881 and graduated in 1884. From 1884 to 1887 she taught at St. Augustine's, became head of the modern languages department at Wilberforce University in Ohio, and earned a master's degree from Oberlin College.

Like most African American female reformers, Cooper was dedicated to racial uplift and the promotion of women's rights. In 1892 she told a group of clergymen, "Only the BLACK WOMAN can say when and where I enter . . . then and there the whole Negro race enter me." This affirmation guided Cooper and inspired her to participate in reform that fostered positive black images and defended the reputations of African American women. In 1892 she wrote *A Voice from the South by a Black Woman of the South*, a compelling ideological view of black politics, women's movements, and American race relations. She also participated in organizations that promoted race and gender advancement. She was a member of Alexander Crummell's American Negro Academy and cofounder of the Colored Woman's League (1892) in Washington, D.C. Cooper also spoke at national and international conferences on the status of blacks and women. At the Women's Congress in Chicago in 1893 she presented a paper, "Needs and Status of Black Women," and she spoke at the first Pan-African Conference in London in 1900.

In 1902 Cooper became the principal of the M Street High School in Washington, D.C. She succeeded Robert H. Terrell, husband of Mary Church Terrell, after he was appointed to a judgeship by President Theodore Roosevelt. Under Cooper's leadership (1902–1906), the school became a symbol of excellence. After retiring from teaching, Cooper—at age sixty-seven—earned a PhD in Latin from the Sorbonne in Paris, becoming the fourth black woman to earn a doctoral degree. On 15 June 1930 she became the second president of Frelinghuysen University, a school in Washington, D.C., dedicated to educating working-class blacks. In 1951 she privately published *Personal Recollections of the Grimke Family and the Life and Writings of Charlotte Forten Grimke.* After a lifetime of race and gender activism, Cooper died in Washington, D.C., on 27 February 1964.

[*See also* Bethune, Mary McLeod; Burroughs, Nannie Helen; *and* National Association of Colored Women.]

BIBLIOGRAPHY

Baham, Eva Semien. "Anna Julia Haywood Cooper, A Stream Cannot Rise Higher than Its Source: The Vanguard as the Panacea for the Plight of Black America." PhD diss., Purdue University, 1997.

Hutchinson, Louise Daniel. *Anna J. Cooper: A Voice from the South.* Washington, D.C.: Smithsonian Institution Press, 1981.

Loewenberg, Bert James, and Ruth Bogin, eds. *Black Women in Nineteenth-Century American Life: Their Words, Their Thoughts, Their Feelings.* University Park and London: Pennsylvania State University Press, 1976.

LASHAWN HARRIS

CORN MOTHER. Singular or plural and also known simply as Mother, Corn Mother is a central figure in creation stories among the Hopi and Pueblo nations, located primarily in northeastern Arizona and the Rio Grande Valley of New Mexico. These indigenous peoples consider Corn Mother as sacred. Although rarely portrayed in drawings or as kachinas (Hopi ancestral spirits often represented by carved dolls), she is represented as an ear of corn, particularly among the Keresan-speaking peoples including those at Zia, Santa Ana, San Felipe, Santo Domingo, Cochiti, Acoma, and Laguna. In Keresan towns, as well as at Zuni and San Juan, ears of corn are guardians of infants. At Isleta, ears of corn are said to be "born" rather than "created." Unadorned or elaborate, such sacred corn accompanies an individual or an entire pueblo throughout life.

The Hopi generally perceive a male sky and a female earth, although both sky and earth have male and female aspects. Two complementary Hopi metaphors refer to people as corn and to corn as females. Corn and people share similar characteristics and stages of the life cycle from birth through attainment of spiritual perfection after death. Young corn plants, referred to as "maidens," are associated with unmarried girls. However, when ears of corn develop, they and the Mothers become associated with womanhood, fertilization, and rain. Consequently, both corn and the earth are referred to as "Mother."

Corn Mother's role is important in differing versions of Hopi and Pueblo creation stories of when people emerged from the underground dark world. These stories relate that the Mothers came up into the world with the people. For instance, in the Keres version the Mother, Iyatiku, lives at Shipap where the first people emerged. After her son found the sun, she and her sister chose clans—hence the Nantsiti (Sun Clan) and the Iyatiku (Corn Clan). At Jemez a similar creation story is told while holding or ritually "breathing" from a "mother," or ear of corn. Zia creation stories also describe how Iyatiku went into daylight only long enough to provide people with agriculture. The Isleta creation story accounts for remembrance of the Mother in curing illness. She is also remembered during childbirth, when women present at a birth do not turn their backs to doorways so as to symbolize the Mothers who did not turn back at the emergence from the underworld.

In the naming ritual for Hopi kachina cult initiation, corn is referred to as "mothers" because Corn Mother created the kachinas as well as the *koshare* (clowns to entertain during times of sadness). She remains beneath to receive the dead back into the underworld. In Isleta, a black Corn Mother serves one of the four corn divisions by officiating at deaths. Pueblo leadership also recalls Iyatiku, such as at Keresan towns where chiefs represent her. She is said to have taught finger counting to chiefs at Acoma so that they could count kachinas upon their arrival at Acoma. Although Corn Mother has the attributes of an earth mother, in most Pueblos the earth is referred to separately in prayer.

[*See also* Indigenous Cultures, *subentry* North America, *and* Religion.]

BIBLIOGRAPHY

Black, Mary E. "Maidens and Mothers: An Analysis of Hopi Corn Metaphors." *Ethnology* 23, no. 4 (October 1984): 279–288.

Parsons, Elsie Clews. *Pueblo Indian Religion*. 2 vols. Lincoln: University of Nebraska Press, 1996.

DIANA M. MENESES

CORREIA, MÃE AURÉLIA (1810?–1875?), slave trader and merchant. Mãe Aurélia Correia was a prominent trader in the nineteenth century in the Upper Guinea Coast, a region that historically stretched from the Senegal region to Sierra Leone. Correia traded in slaves, rum, and agricultural products. She also owned several hundred slaves. Correia's background is shrouded in mystery. As is the case with many women in history, records tended to ignore her. Europeans and Luso-Africans referred to Mãe Aurélia Correia as "Queen of Orange," which is the largest island of the Bijago archipelago, situated off the coast of present-day Guinea-Bissau. Although evidence proving that she was from the Bijago islands is problematic, Correia does appear to have had some ancestral ties to the islands. She resided in Bissau or on Bolama Island. From her name we can draw some hints. "Mãe" means "mother" in Portuguese and is used as sign of respect in most African societies today. "Aurélia" means "gold" in Old Portuguese. Thus her name connotes respect and a sense of wealth. Moreover, "Correia" was a common surname for Luso-Africans in the Upper Guinea Coast. Luso-Africans usually had mixed African and European ancestries, Portuguese in this case; others were Africans who had assimilated some European cultural worldviews.

In addition, Correia was also referred to as Nhara Aurélia. The title *nhara* was used in the Guinea-Bissau area for women traders and comes from the Portuguese word *senhora*. In the Gambia valley, these women were called *senora*, and in the Senegal region they were called *signares*. Thus these women traders were very well established in the Upper Guinea Coast. *Nharas* were cultural brokers and traders between the Portuguese and Africans; they were multilingual and multicultural. Usually they were married to outsiders, such as Europeans and Cape Verdeans, who were not familiar with the customs and ways of local African societies. *Nharas* used their position as cultural brokers to amass wealth and to help their families, and they tended to dress in elaborate clothing and jewelry that corresponded to their status in society.

Mãe Aurélia Correia was related to Nhara Júlia da Silva Cardoso, another wealthy woman merchant. While living with Nhara Júlia, Nhara Aurélia was trained and educated about commerce. Nhara Júlia is less remembered in history than Mãe Aurélia is, but Nhara Júlia was also a truly accomplished merchant in her own right. Nhara Aurélia had a Cape Verdean husband, Caetano Nozolini, a trader and military officer from the island of Fogo. They were successful slave traders, which caught the attention of the British as the British were trying to abolish the slave trade with the Portuguese-British mixed commissions. Nhara Aurélia and her husband had great influence and power in the commerce of the Geba and Grande rivers and the islands of Bijago. They owned large estates on the coast, especially in Bolama, on which slaves worked to produce peanuts. Peanut cultivation in the 1830s resulted in massive movements of migrant workers to plantations in West Africa. In the 1830s the British navy attacked Bolama Island to free slaves working on the plantations.

[*See also* Slave Trade.]

BIBLIOGRAPHY

Brooks, George E. "A Nhara of the Guinea-Bissau Region: Mãe Aurélia Correia." In *Women and Slavery in Africa*, edited by Claire C. Robertson and Martin A. Klein, pp. 295–319. Portsmouth, N.H.: Heinemann, 1997.

Havik, Philip J. *Silences and Soundbites: The Gendered Dynamics of Trade and Brokerage in the Pre-Colonial Guinea-Bissau Region*. Münster, Germany: Lit, 2004.

LUMUMBA HAMILCAR SHABAKA

COSMETICS. Cosmetics are natural or man-made substances employed to protect, color, or scent the skin or hair. Humans have used cosmetics since the Stone Age. Tribal societies, small and sometimes nomadic, painted their bodies and faces to indicate social status, rank, sexual maturity, and age; to camouflage hunters stalking game; to frighten enemies in battle by wearing "war paint"; to represent the tribal totem, the protective animal or bird spirit of the tribe; to define the roles of performers in rituals; and to protect the body against evil spirits.

History of Cosmetics. In ancient Egypt both men and women painted their faces and dyed their hair as adornment, as a screen against the sun and insects in the hot climate, to spiritualize the external body, and to protect against the "evil eye." They used henna, a plant dye, to color hair and paint designs on hands and kohl, a blackening agent made from crushed metals like malachite, to line eyes and darken eyebrows. Such practices spread throughout the Middle East, typified by Jezebel, the biblical Hebrew temptress who painted her face and is still a symbol of deceitful women.

The city states of ancient Greece and the early society of Rome emphasized a natural look, although courtesans (known as hetaerae in Greece) wore heavy makeup, as did Etruscan and Cretan women, while respectable women, confined to their homes, dyed their hair blonde. By the fifth century B.C.E. the commercial trade around the Mediterranean included face powder and hair dye. With the consolidation of the Roman Empire in the first century B.C.E., well-to-do citizens adopted the cosmetics and frequent bathing of the Middle East, which were associated with luxury.

Many early civilizations, including Egypt, China, and Babylonia, prized perfumes for medicinal and spiritual properties as well as pleasant aromas. In China and Japan, perfumes developed along with incense. Perfumers, who used a range of herbs (some with therapeutic value), sometimes functioned as doctors. In 2000 B.C.E. Egyptian priests

Cosmetics. A Japanese woman paints her lips. A woodcut print by Utamaro Katagawa, c. 1794. PRINT COLLECTION, MIRIAM AND IRA D. WALLACH DIVISION OF ART, PRINTS AND PHOTOGRAPHS, NEW YORK PUBLIC LIBRARY, ASTOR, LENOX AND TILDEN FOUNDATIONS

distilled essential oils like balsam and cedar, creating a process still used in modern perfume making. The word "cosmetics" comes from the name of Roman slaves (*cosmetae*), who bathed their masters in perfume.

By 1500 B.C.E. upper-class women in China and Japan used white rice powder on their faces, shaved and plucked their eyebrows, and painted their teeth gold and black. Women in India used perfumed powders, accented their eyes with kohl, and painted designs on their faces and hands with henna. A small black circle in the middle of the forehead indicated high caste. The Kama Sutra (c. 300 C.E.), the famed Indian sex guide, recommended that both women and men wear cosmetics to please their partners. In non-European countries, however, makeup practices generally remained traditional and unchanging over the centuries, just as women—and men—wore traditional dress. In Europe cosmetic use varied over time.

With the rise of Christianity, an ascetic religion, in the first century C.E. and the dissolution of the sophisticated Roman state in the fifth century C.E., the use of cosmetics in Europe declined. By the twelfth century, however, Christian crusaders who fought in the Middle East to reclaim Jerusalem from the Muslims brought back to Europe Eastern cosmetics and ideas of cleanliness. Although the practice of frequent bathing did not take hold in Europe until the nineteenth century, the rise of the cult of courtly love, which spiritualized women, and the growth of a merchant class by the fourteenth century brought into vogue blonde hair and a face painted white with eyebrows plucked out. The white face indicated, as it would over the centuries, both youth and elite status, since peasants (both men and women) worked in the fields and thus had tanned skin. In Europe it also signified the purity of Christianity, identified with the "light" of God against the "darkness" of the devil, and of lighter-skinned Europeans over darker-skinned Arabs and Semites. Painting the face white also covered the skin blemishes produced by epidemic diseases like smallpox and syphilis.

The secularism of the Italian Renaissance of the sixteenth century, combined with European exploration, conquest, and increased wealth, expanded the use and variety of cosmetics. Eye makeup regained its popularity; coloring the eyelids and the teeth became voguish. Venice was the center of cosmetic production; Catherine de Médicis of Florence, the wife of Henry II of France, brought these fashions to France; Elizabeth I of England introduced them to England. Elizabeth made her own cosmetics and obtained ingredients like carmine from her far-flung empire. Carmine, made from the crushed bodies of the cochineal insect, remains the major dye in red lipstick.

Chemists, cosmetic makers, and peddlers sometimes sold cosmetics in Europe and elsewhere, although most women made their own. Recipes for face creams and rouge were passed down from mother to daughter in family recipe books. Many well-to-do women in Europe used a cream called ceruse, which had a lead base that whitened the skin but was poisonous. Face creams containing lead and arsenic, also toxic, remained available through the nineteenth century, despite warnings in beauty manuals and women's magazines of their danger.

The use of cosmetics in early modern Europe reached an apogee among the French aristocracy of the eighteenth century. They painted their faces white, rouged their cheeks, and wore small patches, called *mouches*, on their faces to cover pockmarks on the skin. Women also wore cloth plumpers in their mouths to attain the full checks that were fashionable and put moleskin covers over their eyebrows. Both men and women wore white wigs, and aristocratic and well-to-do women had their hair arranged into towering headdresses. People did not bathe much; the wealthy used heavy perfumes to conceal body odor.

Glamour during Modernization. By the nineteenth century the advent of Romanticism, which emphasized the natural, and Victorianism, which emphasized restraint, brought a reaction against the use of cosmetics, especially among the middle classes of England and the United States, which were rapidly expanding in size with the growth of commerce and industry. Heavy cosmetics were now associated with prostitutes. Only face cream, to soften skin, and powder, to cover blemishes, were acceptable. Perfumes, often diluted into cologne or toilet water, were delicate—rose, gardenia, and lavender. The middle-class preoccupation with cleanliness brought an increased demand for soap. Entrepreneurs, often peddlers who brewed soaps and face creams in their kitchens, marketed their wares. Some of these small enterprises grew into major firms. Colgate, Palmolive, Peet was an amalgamation of local companies. The bookseller David Hall McConnell founded the California Perfume Company in 1886, when he discovered that the perfume samples he gave away were more popular than his books.

As the century progressed, cosmetics became more widely available, often sold in local drugstores. Unlike the aristocracy in early modern Europe, men did not wear them. The United States was the world leader in manufacturing cosmetics, but by the end of the nineteenth century U.S. wholesale drug suppliers offered dozens of foreign as well as domestic cosmetics. French firms dominated the perfume industry: Guerlain was founded in 1828 and Boujois in 1863. By the end of the century both firms had branched into cosmetics, given the increased demand.

Cosmetic entrepreneurs were often women. Helena Rubenstein, who turned her Polish mother's homemade face cream into a multimillion-dollar business, opened her first salon in Australia in 1902 and then expanded into New York, London, and Paris. Elizabeth Arden opened a salon on Fifth

Avenue in New York in 1910, and by 1938 she had opened salons in major cities worldwide. Madame C. J. Walker, an African American entrepreneur from Indianapolis, turned the hair-straightening product she invented into a huge business in the United States. She supplied beauty products to women owners of local black beauty parlors.

The cosmetics business expanded in line with new inventions. Manicuring, which developed out of chiropody (medical care of the feet), dated from the 1840s. Electrolysis was invented in the 1880s. Deodorants first appeared in the 1890s, as did rudimentary cosmetic surgery, especially face peeling. In 1906 Charles Nessler invented an electric machine to put "permanent" waves into hair. In 1909 the French chemist Eugene Schueller developed the first safe commercial hair dye, which he marketed through the company he founded, the French Harmless Hair Coloring Company, later renamed L'Oreal. In 1915 cylindrical metal tubes were invented, the basis of the modern lipstick. In 1917 Cutex marketed the first nail polish. The Maybelline Company introduced mascara in 1919. Kurlash, the first eyelash curling device, was invented in 1923.

By the turn into the twentieth century, heavy cosmetics were back in fashion in Europe and the United States. Actresses like Sarah Bernhardt in France, Lillie Langtry in England, and Lillian Russell in the United States—all of whom used makeup and endorsed commercial brands—were becoming celebrities. Women in general copied their look. The imperialism of the late nineteenth century stimulated a vogue for "the Orient," including the heavy makeup of Eastern women. Heavy perfumes once again came into vogue. As women left the home for work or to participate in women's organizations, they needed to look up-to-date. The "New Woman" of the age sometimes wore makeup as an act of rebellion against Victorianism. In 1906 the federal Pure Food and Drug Act made the use of lead and arsenic in cosmetics illegal in the United States. By 1910 beauty parlors had appeared in Europe and the United States, and department stores sold cosmetics over the counter.

In this era the advent of modernization in Europe, which spread around the world along trade routes and imperial paths, brought into existence small elites in most non-Western countries. These elites often followed Western practices in dress and behavior. In 1872 Shiseido, among the leading cosmetic firms in the world, was founded as the first Western-style pharmacy in Japan.

The mass expansion of the cosmetic industry in the West dated from the 1920s. Cosmetics were heavily advertised as up-to-date and sexy, in line with the "sexual revolution" of that decade. By the mid-1920s cosmetics firms ranked second behind food companies in the amount of money spent on advertising, and they expanded the percentage of their budgets spent on advertising over the course of the twentieth century. As skirts became shorter and hair was bobbed, the face became more prominent, leading to an increased use of mascara and eye shadow. As leisure expanded and women discarded voluminous Victorian bathing suits to expose their skin, suntanned skin became the mode, overturning the centuries-long preference for white skin. The French couturier Jean Patou created the first suntan lotion in 1928. Cosmetic surgery increased in popularity in the 1920s, especially as its techniques became more sophisticated to deal with the extensive facial injuries suffered by soldiers during World War I.

The popularity of bobbed and curled hair in the 1920s resulted in a large increase in beauty parlors. Such businesses used the Nessler "permanent wave" machine to curl hair before switching to chemical hair-curling lotions after their invention in 1927. The Hollywood cosmetician Max Factor built a major business on makeup he developed for use in the movies. The movie stars, whose perfect "glamour" look was achieved through makeup, influenced women in general. Charles Revson founded Revlon in 1930, concentrating on colored nail polish. In 1931 Almay marketed the first hypoallergenic products, designed to be safe on sensitive skin. In 1932 the chemist Lawrence Gelb created a more permanent and less caustic hair dye than what was available; he founded Clairol to market it. By 1932 three thousand face powders and several hundred rouges were sold. In 1938, as a result of a national increase in skin diseases due to the rise in the use of cosmetics, the U.S. Congress passed a second Pure Food and Drug Act that prohibited using any dangerous substances in making cosmetics. In 1939 the California Perfume Company became Avon, and Avon ladies began selling the company's products, now including cosmetics, door-to-door. By 1950 1.5 million Avon ladies were selling Avon products door-to-door in one hundred countries.

From the 1940s on cosmetic innovations continued to appear. In 1938 Volupte introduced the lip liner pencil. In 1941 aerosols were developed, paving the way for hair spray. Army chemists during World War II discovered lanolin, the basis of modern skin creams. In 1944 a Miami Beach pharmacist developed sunscreen to protect soldiers in the South Pacific. Home permanents were first marketed in the early 1950s.

In Europe and the United States heavy makeup remained in fashion through the 1950s: bright red for lipstick and heavy accents for eyes. Extensive advertising on the part of Clairol and the popularity of a number of actresses with peroxided hair, especially Marilyn Monroe, brought bleached blonde hair into fashion. The 1960s witnessed the advent of the civil rights and black power movements, the rebellion of youth, and the Second Wave feminist movement. A natural look came into vogue. Pale lipstick was the norm, although heavy mascara and eye shadow—in addition to new thick false eyelashes—remained the fashion for eyes. Hair was worn long and straight, although the appearance of the militant black movement, with its slogan "Black Is Beautiful," changed individuals' perceptions of blacks worldwide and eventually led to vogues for frizzy hair and then braided cornrows.

During the post–World War II period, the cosmetics business evolved from a loose association of entrepreneurs into a multimillion-dollar industry dominated by multinational corporations. Its growth was fueled by sophisticated advertising and marketing techniques, the conversion of war factories after World War II into domestic production, and the growing size and wealth of modernizing populations. New cosmetic companies appeared. Estée Lauder marketed her company by training saleswomen in department stores to do cosmetic makeovers on their customers. Market expansion was a common marketing strategy of all the cosmetic companies. In 1943 Helena Rubenstein launched the first men's cosmetic line, called Gourielli. In 1961 Cover Girl makeup appeared; it was the first brand sold in grocery stores and targeted to teenagers. By the 1980s cosmetic companies were targeting ever younger girls, including five- and six-year-olds.

Five trends characterized the history of cosmetics during the last few decades of the twentieth century. The first was the expansion of the narcissism and product identification of the U.S. population in particular and the modernized world population in general, leading to vast expansion in cosmetic sales. The second was increased marketing of cosmetics in drugstores, grocery stores, and on the Internet. The third was the marketing to men of aftershave lotions, deodorants, hair sprays, and hair dyes. The fourth was the growing power of the multinationals and their market penetration into rapidly modernizing nations, such as China and Korea. The fifth was the increasing popularity of surgical techniques for body enhancement, such as breast implants, liposuction (the surgical removal of fat from the abdomen), and permanent eyeliner.

In the twenty-first century the American cosmetics industry totals over $20 billion in sales yearly. Products heavily advertised in print and on television dominate it. The painted face is in vogue, and the fashionable look requires the use of many products, including foundation to mask skin flaws, blush on cheeks, and lips lined with black and painted red. Eye shadow, eyeliner, and mascara are used. Given trends in the use of cosmetics over the twentieth century, it is doubtful that such practices will change without a return to Victorianism or a radical revolution producing a natural look.

[*See also* Bernhardt, Sarah; Catherine de Médicis; Christianity; Civil Rights Movement; Cosmetic Surgery; Elizabeth I of England; Imperialism and Colonialism, *subentry* Modern Period; Personal Services, *subentry* Beauticians; *and* Walker, Madam C. J.]

BIBLIOGRAPHY

Angeloglou, Maggie. *A History of Make-up*. London, 1970. The best general history of makeup, primarily in the West, from ancient times to the present.

Banner, Lois. *American Beauty*. New York, 1983. A general history of attitudes toward and practices concerning beauty in the United States with considerable attention to cosmetics.

Basten, Fred E., Robert A. Salvatore, and Paul A. Kaufman. *Max Factor's Hollywood: Glamour, Movies, and Make-up*. Los Angeles, 1995. Illuminates the importance of the movies in general and the Max Factor company in particular in spreading a vogue for cosmetics throughout the world.

Castelbajac, Kate de. *The Face of the Century: 100 Years of Makeup and Style*. Edited by Nan Richardson and Catherine Chermayeff. New York, 1995. Covers the twentieth century in some detail, mostly England and the United States.

Peiss, Cathy Lee. *Hope in a Jar: The Making of America's Beauty Culture*. New York, 1998. A history of the cosmetics industry in the United States as a force behind women's advance with attention to African American cosmetics entrepreneurs.

Riordan, Teresa. *Inventing Beauty: A History of the Innovations That Have Made Us Beautiful*. New York, 2004. Explores material culture collections and patents to uncover technological innovations in the beauty and cosmetics industries.

Woodhead, Lindy. *War Paint: Madame Helena Rubinstein and Miss Elizabeth Arden; Their Lives, Their Times, Their Rivalry*. Hoboken, N.J., 2003. The story of the lives and rivalry of the twentieth century's greatest cosmetic entrepreneurs.

LOIS BANNER

COSMETIC SURGERY. Cosmetic surgery emerged at the beginning of the twentieth century. In addition to the beauty parlors and hairdressers that were springing up across the United States and Europe, cosmetic "salons" where people could have their faces "lifted" and their noses "corrected" were established. Advertisements appeared in daily newspapers for surgeons expounding the wonders of cosmetic surgery. While many of these early cosmetic surgeons operated on the fringes of the medical establishment and were not taken seriously by established medical professionals, who regarded them as untrained charlatans ("irregular doctors"), these "beauty surgeons" nevertheless developed many of the techniques that are still employed in cosmetic surgery.

Plastic surgery, which includes both cosmetic or aesthetic surgery and reconstructive surgery, is much older. The first rhinoplasty (nose reconstruction) was reported as early as 1000 B.C.E. in India, where a thief's nose might be cut off as a form of punishment or, in the case of an adulterous Hindu wife, bitten off by her wronged husband. Gaspare Tagliacozzi, often called the "father of plastic surgery," wrote the first book about plastic surgery in 1597; he gave an illustrated account of his successful reconstruction of a

Cosmetic Operations. Chie Hirata, age twenty-three, shows a picture taken of her two months before she had plastic surgery at Jujin Hospital, the oldest Japanese medical institution to offer plastic surgery, 1999. REUTERS/Toshiyuki Aizawa

young nobleman's nose that had been sliced off during a duel. Plastic surgery was not practiced on a broad scale until the nineteenth century, when the discovery of antisepsis and anesthesia made operations safer and thus more feasible. However, it was not until the beginning of the twentieth century that plastic surgery—and in particular cosmetic surgery—became a popular medical specialty. This new popularity was the result of two separate but related developments.

The first development was World War I and the large numbers of soldiers with facial damage, burns, and lost limbs that required reconstructive surgery. This gave surgeons the opportunity to practice their surgical techniques and gain experience in performing cosmetic operations. The previous negative associations of bodily deformity with syphilis or divine retribution for sins committed were dispelled by the image of the noble and deserving soldier disfigured in the defense of his or her country. For the first time cosmetic surgery became *salonfähig,* acceptable for the wider public.

The second development was the emergence of a mass beauty culture. Cultural prohibitions against women in particular trying to look younger and more attractive were dropped, and a ubiquitous ideology of self-improvement emerged. The tools for achieving beauty became more democratic as well and were available to all women, regardless of their socioeconomic circumstances.

Twenty-First-Century Cosmetic Surgery. Cosmetic surgery is the fastest-growing medical specialty around the world. Millions of people flock to cosmetic surgeons each year to have their faces "lifted," their eyelids "corrected," their breasts "enhanced," or their tummies "tucked," as the operations are euphemistically called. New techniques and devices proliferate, joining older interventions and allowing more sophisticated interventions in bodily appearance: earlobe tucks, botex injections to eliminate frown wrinkles, belly-button enhancements, and vulva reductions. Once associated with celebrities as the "happy few" who could afford it, cosmetic surgery is increasingly available to ordinary people with modest incomes. Moreover it has rapidly become a multibillion-dollar global industry. While cosmetic surgery is often associated with the United States, the globalized ideal of feminine beauty and the widespread deployment of medical technologies have made it increasingly popular in other parts of the world as well. Cosmetic surgery has increased exponentially throughout Europe and is also on the rise in China, Japan, and Korea. It is estimated that one in three Korean girls desires cosmetic surgery. The high incidence of procedures to create a "double eyelid" or to build up the bridge of the nose suggest that women of Asian descent are under pressure to alter their bodies in compliance with a Western beauty ideal. Cosmetic surgery has become commonplace among affluent women in parts of South America. In Brazil, breast reductions are in great demand—a relic of Brazil's history of slavery and the common association of large breasts with poverty and "looking too black." In contrast, upper-class women in Argentina tend to prefer breast augmentations, thereby fulfilling what is regarded as a desirable balance between the erotic and the European ideal of feminine beauty (Gilman). South America, along with South Africa, Thailand, and Israel, have also become popular among an international clientele that is interested in combining affordable cosmetic surgery interventions with a vacation in an exotic location.

Controversies. Cosmetic surgery is not only popular, it also evokes controversy and dissent. Given the pain and the myriad side effects associated with most operations, cosmetic surgery invariably raises the question whether surgery that is, strictly speaking, medically unnecessary should be performed for the sole purpose of enhancing appearance. The medical profession is in the position of having to justify performing dangerous surgical interventions on otherwise healthy bodies. Debates have emerged concerning whether cosmetic surgery is essentially "frivolous," a "luxury" reserved for those who can afford it, or necessary for the patient's (psychological) welfare and well-being. Cosmetic surgery is also costly. While most operations are performed in private clinics, there has been discussion about which operations should be covered by medical insurance. In the wake of a rapidly aging population and the state's inability to meet even basic health care needs, it is difficult to justify funding expensive surgery for what is regarded as a luxury problem. Controversies have also emerged concerning the risks and side effects associated with cosmetic surgery. Most operations have side effects ranging from pain and bruising to infection, scarring, permanent numbness, and serious disabilities, including embolisms, blood clots, immune disorders, or even death. The highly publicized side effects of silicone breast implants and their insufficient testing before being released on the market led to numerous malpractice suits and class actions. Ultimately this resulted in their being abolished in the United States except for reconstructive purposes (following mastectomies for breast cancer) or under controlled conditions.

Cosmetic surgery has been controversial because it is unnecessary, expensive, and risky, and critical scholars in the humanities and social sciences have depicted cosmetic surgery as an expression of consumer capitalism. It reproduces the cultural fantasy that the human body can be endlessly transformed, allowing the individual to create the body and the self of his or her dreams. This intoxication with the body's "makeability" denies the material constraints of embodiment (including the body's mortality) and promotes an illusion that the avenue to happiness lies through the alteration of the body.

Medical ethicists have explored the normative implications of cosmetic surgery. In addition to the issue of whether surgery purely for "enhancement" is desirable, the issue of "informed consent"—the mainstay of ethical medical practice—has come under scrutiny. It has been argued that, given the cultural pressures on patients to meet the ideals of feminine beauty, it is debatable whether cosmetic surgery can ever be a "choice." Indeed it has increasingly become a moral imperative for individuals to seek surgery to achieve an acceptable appearance. Cosmetic surgery often involves compliance with cultural norms that are themselves problematic. More generally, cosmetic surgery raises philosophical issues concerning the limits of technology and how far it should go in altering the "natural" body. Does the surgical transformation of the body increase a person's chances of a "good life" and, more generally, a society's prospects of a better future?

Women and Cosmetic Surgery. Feminists have been the most outspoken critics of cosmetic surgery. Women are not only the primary recipients of nearly every form of cosmetic surgery, but the practice itself reproduces discourses of gendered inferiority, instructing women that their bodies are never good enough: too fat, too flat-chested, too old, or too "ethnic." Many feminist scholars have devoted attention to the phenomenon of cosmetic surgery. The feminist critique of cosmetic surgery takes gender and the culture of femininity as a starting point. Cosmetic surgery is implicated in the production and reproduction of femininity, whereby symbolically woman as sex is idealized as the incarnation of physical beauty, while most ordinary women are rendered drab, ugly, loathsome, or fearful bodies. Women are lulled into believing that they can gain control over their lives through continued vigilance over their bodies and are trapped in the hopeless race for the perfect body. Cosmetic surgery, along with the cosmetic industry, advertising, and the media, belongs to the disciplinary regime of the feminine beauty system, which includes the procedures, rituals, and technologies drawn upon by individual women in their everyday lives to meet the contemporary cultural requirements of feminine appearance. While cosmetic surgery is part of the continuum of beauty practices for body improvement and maintenance (like leg waxing, exercise, dieting, and makeup), it is by far the most pernicious. It is the site par excellence for disciplining and normalizing the female body, for literally "cutting women down to size."

One of the primary debates within feminist scholarship on women's involvement in cosmetic surgery has focused on the practices and technologies of cosmetic surgery as well as the discourses of feminine inferiority that it sustains without undermining women who choose to undergo cosmetic surgery. Whether women are treated as blinded by the lures of consumerism, oppressed by patriarchal ideologies, or inscribed within the disciplinary discourses of femininity, the feminist critique of cosmetic surgery has tended to relegate the woman who has cosmetic surgery to the role of "cultural dope," as mindlessly marching to the beat of a hegemonic beauty system that polices, constrains, and inferiorizes her. It is difficult to view her as an agent who, at least to some extent, actively and knowledgeably gives shape to her life, albeit under circumstances that are not of her own making. Feminist scholars have struggled to find ways to combine a critique of cosmetic surgery with a more nuanced and respectful understanding of women's suffering with their bodies and their reasons for viewing cosmetic surgery as an acceptable way to alleviate this suffering. This has often required a kind of feminist "balancing act," whereby the comfort of the easy solution—whether it is "just say no" or "just do what you want"—is avoided in favor of an ongoing willingness to grapple with the complexities and contradictions that cosmetic surgery evokes.

Future Directions. The field of cosmetic surgery continues to expand and change, and indeed the end is nowhere in sight. Technologies have developed to such an extent that they offer ever more sophisticated interventions in bodily appearance. Whereas women continue to be the primary targets of cosmetic surgery, other groups are also targets for the "surgical fix." Pectoral implants and penile enhancements for men with "locker room anxiety," eyelid corrections for Asian American teenagers in search of a more Western appearance, leg lengthening for dwarfs, and facial surgery for Down syndrome children have become cosmetic surgery interventions.

These new developments raise several additional issues of concern for feminists. First, feminists need to explore the use of cosmetic surgery not only to regulate femininity but also to eliminate forms of embodied "difference." Cosmetic surgery has historically been deployed to minimize or eliminate physical signs of ethnicity that marked individuals as "other" than the dominant racial or ethnic groups. Sander L. Gilman has provided a detailed study of the historical use of rhinoplasty (nose corrections) in the first half of the twentieth century in Germany to eliminate visible signs of ethnicity among Jews who wanted to become assimilated into the dominant Aryan society. Cosmetic surgery became a kind of "passing." The media promotes cosmetic surgery as a neutral technology equally available to any person for realizing the body of her or his dreams. However, in reality it continues to be used to "normalize" bodies to meet a hegemonic white, Western, affluent, heterosexual, able-bodied ideal. In view of these developments, it remains important that the phenomenon of cosmetic surgery—its incidence, the kind of operations performed, the recipients who are targeted—be viewed against the backdrop of structured, systemic social inequalities that impinge upon individuals' embodied experiences as well as on the acceptability of cosmetic surgery as a "solution" to their problems with their appearance.

Second, cosmetic surgery is increasingly a global commodity. Medical tourism has enabled individuals from affluent countries in the West to combine international travel with inexpensive elective surgical procedures. "Safari" packages to developing countries combine a medical procedure with the "fun" of a vacation. For many poor countries, cosmetic surgery has become a part of their development strategy, a way to attract wealthy tourists. Aside from the potential risks of medical care in so-called Third World locales, cosmetic surgery tourism promotes an ideal of consumerism and upper-class celebrity lifestyles in non-Western contexts. The hegemonic beauty ideal that is disseminated favors white, Western beauty while diminishing the bodies of poor, non-Western women of color. Given the globalization of cosmetic surgery, it is important to explore cosmetic surgery not only through the lens of "race," ethnicity, and class but also to show how it is implicated in and works to sustain globally structured hierarchies of power.

[*See also* Cosmetics; Feminism; *and* Health.]

BIBLIOGRAPHY

Blum, Virginia L. *Flesh Wounds: The Culture of Cosmetic Surgery*. Berkeley: University of California Press, 2003.

Bordo, Susan. *Unbearable Weight: Feminism, Western Culture, and the Body*. Berkeley: University of California Press, 1993.

Davis, Kathy. *Dubious Equalities and Embodied Differences: Cultural Studies on Cosmetic Surgery*. Lanham, Md.: Rowman and Littlefield, 2003.

Davis, Kathy. *Reshaping the Female Body: The Dilemma of Cosmetic Surgery*. New York: Routledge, 1995.

Gilman, Sander L. *Making the Body Beautiful: A Cultural History of Aesthetic Surgery*. Princeton, N.J.: Princeton University Press, 1999.

Gimlin, Debra L. *Body Work: Beauty and Self-Image in American Culture*. Berkeley: University of California Press, 2002.

Haiken, Elizabeth. *Venus Envy: A History of Cosmetic Surgery*. Baltimore and London: Johns Hopkins University Press, 1997.

Jacobson, Nora. *Cleavage: Technology, Controversy, and the Ironies of the Man-made Breast*. New Brunswick, N.J.: Rutgers University Press, 2000.

Morgan, Kathryn Pauly. "Women and the Knife: Cosmetic Surgery and the Colonalization of Women's Bodies." *Hypatia* 6 (1991): 25–53.

Parens, Erik, ed. *Enhancing Human Traits: Ethical and Social Implications*. Washington, D.C.: Georgetown University Press, 1998.

Wolf, Naomi. *The Beauty Myth: How Images of Beauty Are Used against Women*. New York: Morrow, 1991.

Young, Iris Marion. *Justice and the Politics of Difference*. Princeton, N.J.: Princeton University Press, 1990.

KATHY DAVIS

COTTAGE INDUSTRY. *See* Production Systems.

COURTESANSHIP

This entry consists of two subentries:

Overview
Comparative History

Overview

The English word "courtesan" has its roots in the court culture of Renaissance France and the northern Italian city-states. The French *courtisan* and the Italian *cortigano* referred to someone attached to the court of a prince, usually the *curia*, the court of the pope (the papal prince).

By the middle of the sixteenth century the definition of the word had shifted. Now feminine, it referred at times to a woman attached to a court, but more regularly it was used to describe a "court-mistress" or type of elite prostitute who emerged in this period. These sixteenth-century definitions attempted to distinguish the courtesan from the whore. Problematically, "whore" (and its many synonyms such as "strumpet") was not clearly defined in this period, either in dictionaries, literature, legal texts, or general usage.

Modern-day denotations of "courtesan" retain the sixteenth-century meaning; "courtesan" is an elite prostitute catering to men of high social standing, especially those attached to a royal court. While this definition is accurate, it is also incomplete. Those occupational groups that have been translated as "courtesan"—including the hetaera (ancient Greece), the *ganika* and *tawaif* (ancient and precolonial India), the *cortigiana onesta* (Renaissance Italy), the geisha (Japan), and the *chang* and *ji* (ancient and early modern China) did cater to the same type of clients. However, they form a group and were differentiated from prostitutes by several other factors: the services they offered, the ambiguity of their status, and their accomplishments in and importance to the arts.

The Worlds of the Courtesan. Courtesans were distinguished by the nature of their clientele, who were of high social standing or had significant wealth but were not necessarily attached to a court. In fact, courtesan cultures flourished in some societies, such as ancient Greece, in which there were no courts. Courtesans were also distinguished by the number of their clients. In principle, the body of the prostitute was accessible to all. In contrast, a courtesan had fewer clients and, at least in theory, she was able to choose them. Through generous patrons, the courtesan could accrue sufficient wealth to establish her own household. The most successful courtesans became famously wealthy. Cross-culturally, courtesans are often depicted as the most independent women of their day, in part because they lived in societies in which few women were educated and rarely headed their own households. Yet this independence should not be overestimated. Most courtesans lived in times and places where women lacked full legal personalities and were unable to own real property. Moreover, the ability to practice their profession often depended on the mood of local governments who could and did place crippling restrictions on the actions of courtesans, sometimes banning them outright. The freedom to be selective, which differentiated a courtesan from a whore, made a courtesan more desirable, respectable, and alluring, but this freedom was limited to the very few who had reached the top of their profession. Economic necessity would make such selectivity implausible for most. Moreover, the power dynamic in such selection is illusory. While clients may have applied to courtesans for their services, these were powerful men in patriarchal societies in which women, especially those practicing prostitution, had few rights.

The job of the courtesan can perhaps best be described as providing pleasure, rather than sexual services, although

Courtesanship in Japan. *Courtesans of the Tamaya House.* Painting by Utagawa Toyoharu, c. 1780, depicting the courtesans' daily routines. British Museum, London/Art Resource, NY

the sale of sex was an important component of what they did. Geisha and kisaeng, existing mainly in early modern and prewar Japan and Korea respectively, are sometimes considered courtesans. However, such a designation is controversial; it assumes a fundamental relationship with prostitution that many argue is misleading. But even among courtesans, sexual commerce was enmeshed in a larger series of exchanges that included elevated conversation, companionship, and artistic performance. The parameters governing courtesan prostitution served to deemphasize it, making the courtesan an ambiguous figure: simultaneously dishonorable as a prostitute and respectable as an artist. While a few famous courtesans embraced their role as elite prostitutes, most actively cultivated the image of respectability, emphasizing their accomplishments as artists while downplaying and in some cases denying their involvement in prostitution. Some, like the hetaerae of ancient Greece, achieved this by taking payment in gifts, rather than cash. Others, like the *cortigiana onesta* used their literary skills to defend themselves in print against attacks on their honor and to make clear the difference between themselves and prostitutes. Even their name, "honest courtesans," was part of this larger campaign. Yet, courtesans had to be clearly identifiable in order to attract clients. Their distinctive clothing, their frequenting of exclusively male social and intellectual circles, and their use of public spaces off-limits to respectable women advertised their sexual availability.

The respectability of courtesans could be enhanced or diminished by state policies. In some of the states of precolonial India, the courtesanal position of *ganika* was an officially sanctioned position. Women chosen to be courtesans underwent state-sponsored training, and because of their service to the state were given a pension upon retirement. In China, state policy mediated between the courtesan as debased (*jian*) and the courtesan as artist. Official courtesans were recognized as musicians by belonging to the "register of musicians," but at the same time, their dishonorable status disqualified them from having intimate relationships with officials. In Renaissance Italy, state policy accentuated the dishonor of courtesanship; some city-states ghettoized courtesans together with prostitutes and forced them to wear distinguishing clothing—in particular, a yellow veil that was considered a mark of ignominy.

Unofficial attitudes toward courtesans were similarly organized around celebrating the courtesan as artist and denigrating her as prostitute. Some of the most vicious attacks, like that made by the Italian writer Pietro Aretino in his *Dialogues* (1534), depicted courtesans pornographically. He also showed them as heartless mercenaries. Moralists and satirists frequently accused courtesans of feigning emotion in order to infatuate their clients for greater financial gain. This image of the unprincipled courtesan is linked to a broader critique of luxury. Courtesans, especially in ancient Greece and early modern Europe, were considered dangerous to the health of the state. Critics worried that men patronizing courtesans would not have sufficient funds to fulfill their duties as fathers and citizens.

Courtesans as Subjects and Creators of Art. At the same time courtesans were denigrated, they were also the subject of enormous fascination. Of particular interest to writers and painters was the tension between the courtesan's professional obligations and her personal desires. The genre of the courtesan romance was well developed in the Chinese tradition, in which love stories were woven around the poems sent between a courtesan and her lover. These love stories may have reflected a real dynamic. Courtesan cultures tended to emerge in highly homosocial societies, those in which socializing was limited to members of the same sex. Marriage, especially among the class of men who patronized courtesans, was generally a financial and strategic partnership, not a locus of love, friendship, and sexuality. Hence courtesans were often the only women with whom upper-class males could experience emotional and sexual intimacy. The courtesan romance was also a significant literary theme in the nineteenth century, even as companionate marriages became increasingly common. The most famous work of this type in the Western canon was Alexander Dumas's *La dame aux camélias* (1848; English trans., *Lady of the Camelias*), which Giuseppe Verdi turned into the opera *La traviata* (1853). Fact and fiction overlap in the multiple tellings of this story. It was supposedly based on the life of a real courtesan, and nineteenth-century courtesans modeled for paintings of the work's protagonist, Marguerite Gautier. Fascination with courtesans extended beyond their private or imagined romances. Courtesans were celebrities in many societies. What they wore started fashion trends.

Defenders of courtesans extolled both their beauty and their artistic accomplishments. Courtesans in every society were expected to possess numerous amatory and artistic skills that together formed the entertainment package they offered. The courtesan's basic skills in the arts generally included the ability to play an instrument, sing, dance, recite poetry, and engage in witty and refined conversation. Beyond this, skills were culturally dependent. The *ganika*, for example, were expected to have proficiency in dozens of other areas as varied as the martial arts, building construction, and magic. In China courtesans also learned chess, wine, games, and calligraphy. Many of the hetaerae were philosophers and masters of rhetoric. What is increasingly emphasized in scholarship on courtesans, however, is the degree to which courtesans not only performed art, but created it. Across cultures, they composed music, choreographed dances, wrote poetry and prose works, and even invented new literary and musical genres. In doing so, they

Nana. Édouard Manet's depiction of Nana, the courtesan from Émile Zola's popular novel, 1877. HAMBURGER KUNSTHALLE, HAMBURG, GERMANY/BILDARCHIV PREUSSISCHER KULTURBESITZ/ART RESOURCE, NY

were often among the most important women artists of their time. In some cultures, they alone had the right to perform certain dances and songs, which made them culture bearers.

In the eighteenth and nineteenth centuries the relationship between the "*grandes horizontales*," whom contemporaries identified as courtesans, and the arts loosened. Although some of these women were actresses and singers, mastery of the arts was no longer a prerequisite for the title, raising the question of whether these women could properly be called courtesans. Modern conventions of marriage and the advancement of women's rights have made courtesanship largely obsolete. In almost all cultures, the role of the woman artist has been divorced from that of prostitute. In some cases, women performers have retained the titles once given to courtesans, these tend now to refer mainly to their status as singers and dancers, rather than the ways in which artistic performance was linked to a certain social status and sexual service.

[*See also* Geisha; *Kisaeng*; *and* Prostitution, *subentry* Comparative History.]

BIBLIOGRAPHY

Feldman, Martha, and Bonnie Gordon, eds. *The Courtesan's Arts: Cross-Cultural Perspectives*. New York: Oxford University Press, 2006. Most complete examination of courtesans in print, with articles on ancient Athens, Renaissance Italy, pre- and post-colonial India, and Japanese geisha. Concentrates especially on the ways in which courtesans produced culture.

NINA KUSHNER

Comparative History

Courtesans were highly educated women whose role was to provide certain forms of pleasure to elite men in the societies in which they resided. These included sexual services, conversation, and perhaps most significantly performance in dance, music, and poetry. The tension between these services reflected the esteem in which courtesans were held, simultaneously lauded as artists and debased as prostitutes.

Ancient Athens. The archetype of the courtesan in Western culture is the hetaera of the Greek city-states, especially Athens, in the fourth and fifth centuries B.C.E. Despite the impact of the hetaera on later courtesan cultures, scholars emphasize the difficulty of determining exactly who hetaerae were and what they did. *Hetairai*, loosely translated as female companions, was not always clearly distinguished from *pallakai*, concubines, and *pornai*, common prostitutes.

Hetaerae were some of the many entertainers hired to work at symposia, the male drinking parties that were the center of elite social life in this period. Their job was to provide witty conversation, flirt with and flatter the symposiasts, be good company, and possibly have sex with guests at the end of the evening. Such work required an extensive education.

Hetaerae were sometimes slaves, but more often they were freedwomen. Though they could not own property, they headed their own lavishly furnished households or shared them with other hetaerae. It was in these homes that they received clients, including leading illuminati, with whom they were believed to have discussed politics and philosophy. The most successful among the hetaerae were the *megalomisthoi* or "big-fee hetaerae," who amassed significant wealth. The fortune of the hetaera Phyrne was so great that she alone was able to pay for the rebuilding of the walls of Thebes after they were destroyed by Alexander the Great. Some big-fee hetaerae were maintained as mistresses by wealthy and often high-status patrons. Aspasia was the lover of Pericles and supposedly trained him in rhetoric.

Although hetaerae did sell sex, they actively differentiated themselves from *pornai* in ways that emphasized respectability and refinement. For example, whereas a *porne* could not refuse a customer, the reputation of the hetaera was based on her selectivity. Her selectivity enabled her to frame her sexual commerce, in some cases, as friendship. In a broader sense, hetaerae filled the space of heterosexual sociability left vacant by the construction of contemporary gender roles. Marriage in this period was for the purposes of alliance and procreation, rather than a locus of sexual or emotional intimacy. Elite women had very little freedom; respectability hinged on a guarantee of their chastity, which in turn led to their seclusion at home, mainly within the women's quarters. They were poorly educated. Elite men socialized with other male citizens, and the proper love object was considered to be an adolescent boy of the same class. Recreational sexual activity also took place between elite men and slaves or prostitutes, many of whom were also slaves. Prostitution was a well-developed industry in ancient Greece.

Hetaerae were celebrated for their style, learning, intelligence, and wit. They were also commonly attacked in contemporary writings. The seductive powers of a hetaera were thought to be dangerous, able to make a man abandon his traditional responsibilities.

There were hetaerae in Greece and then Rome in later centuries. However, these courtesans never achieved the same sort of prominence or cultural importance that their counterparts in the fourth century B.C.E. did.

Renaissance Italy. Courtesans and a rich courtesan culture reemerged in city-states of northern and central Italy during the Renaissance (late fifteenth century). Their emergence at that moment can be attributed to a number of factors, including increased female access to education, the role that courtly women played in the development in the arts, and dowry inflation, which prohibited some women from marrying. Many courtesans were the daughters of courtesans. Others came from impoverished but respectable families of middling social status.

As the Italian word *cortegiana,* or "courtesan," suggests, these women aspired to the ideal of the courtly woman, and like her, they had a broad education. They learned to read, speak, and write in Latin, Italian, and other languages. They could compose music, sing, and accompany themselves on the lute or keyboard instruments. They were required to recite and write poetry, converse wittily, and even engage in philosophical debate. Some were trained in painting and art. The most accomplished poets and composers among them were the most accomplished women artists and intellectuals of the era. These included the Venetian poet Veronica Franco and the Roman poet and composer Tullia d'Aragona. Like many of the most famous courtesans, Tullia hosted an important salon.

Detractors and moralists equated courtesans with street prostitutes, often depicting them in pornography. Courtesans defended themselves vigorously, emphasizing their own refinement, intellectual accomplishments, and virtue. They called themselves *courtegiane honorate*, or "honest courtesans," to differentiate themselves from lower-class prostitutes who also used the term *cortegiane.* A few, such as Tullia d'Aragona, never acknowledged selling sexual

Hetaerae. *Phyrne before the Tribunal,* by Jean-Léon Gérôme, 1861. Phyrne's lawyer rips off her clothes to reveal her beauty and prove that she is Aphrodite's representative and attendant on Earth. HAMBURGER KUNSTHALLE, GERMANY/BILDARCHIV PREUSSISCHER KULTURBESITZ/ART RESOURCE, NY

services, presenting herself exclusively as a poet instead. Those who did acknowledge selling sexual services, such as Veronica Franco, considered prostitution part of a larger set of integrated performances that were required of them. Like the hetaerae, the *courtegiane honorate* staked out an ambiguous territory in which they represented themselves as both respectable and sexually available.

The freedom to practice this profession was dependant upon the changing mood of governments and the protection of powerful patrons. Rome regularly expelled all courtesans. Florence, another center of courtesan culture, increasingly regulated the practice throughout the sixteenth century, requiring courtesans to wear a yellow veil. The city-state of Venice, the third center, was the most tolerant of all and consequently was the most attractive to courtesans, twelve thousand of whom were officially registered as *cortegiane*.

Like the hetaerae, Renaissance courtesans were celebrated intellectuals and artists, fashion trendsetters, and, in Venice, tourist attractions. Yet they were perceived as having the ability to destroy marriages and fortunes.

Renaissance courtesan culture declined in the seventeenth century, in part because of the Counter-Reformation, with its renewed emphasis on piety and chastity and its more negative valuation of women. Courtesan culture moved north to Paris and then to London.

Eighteenth- and Nineteenth-Century France and England. Although there were a number of women in seventeenth-century France and England who were considered courtesans, it was not until the middle of the eighteenth century that a significant courtesan culture developed. This culture was qualitatively different from that of the Renaissance. The special link between literary, conversational, and musical skill and discreet prostitution that had characterized the culture of hetaerae and the *courtegiane honorate* was severed. Although they were often called courtesans, elite prostitutes in this period were not necessarily well educated. They were expected to be charming, lively, and charismatic, not artistic or well read. Intellectual work became the exclusive preserve of the Enlightenment *salonnières*—who had no ties to prostitution.

Gone as well was the special emphasis on refinement and virtue, although elite prostitutes, called demimondaines, did cloak their sexual availability by packaging it with other offerings. In theory, a demimondaine was a professional mistress who sold her company, affections, and body in exchange for being maintained by a patron in a long-term relationship. In practice, many demimondaines earned a good portion of their income by selling sex alone. Moralists, social commentators, and novelists depicted demimondaines in the eighteenth century as heartless, manipulative women who would feign love in order to pull whatever money they could from their patrons, bankrupting many in the process. This was not a baseless criticism. Conspicuous consumption dominated Enlightenment courtesan culture, and demimondaines were largely defined by their luxurious lifestyle.

One aspect of the Renaissance connection between the arts and prostitution remained, although it was entirely transformed. The demimonde was fully integrated into the world of the performing arts, specifically the opera (which included ballet at this time) and to a lesser degree the theater. But whereas Renaissance courtesans achieved virtue and respectability through their artistic and intellectual accomplishments, the demimondaine's connection to the theater was based on the dishonor that inhered to women who appeared in public on the stage. Not all demimondaines were theatrical performers, but most singers and dancers were demimondaines.

The professionalization of the performing arts in the nineteenth century weakened this link. The most famous courtesans of the day, now called the *les grandes horizontales*, were no longer actresses, dancers, and singers, though many had connections to the world of the arts. Instead their identity was rooted in a particularly elegant and lavish lifestyle with which the public was fascinated. Demimondaines were celebrities. Newspapers reported their comings and goings. Crowds gathered to watch the most famous courtesans ride in Hyde Park in London or attend the races at Longs Champs in Paris. What they wore set fashion trends. The figure of the tragic, virtuous courtesan replaced that of the heartless gold digger in an ever-increasing number of plays, operas, and novels written about them. The nineteenth century is often considered a golden era for courtesans. During the French Second Empire (1852–1870), the twelve most powerful were called *la garde* (the guard, or watch).

Courtesan culture in the West died out at the beginning of the twentieth century. It was made obsolete by the expectation of a companionate marriage based on a fulfilling sex life.

India. Courtesan culture was in evidence in northern India from the sixth century B.C.E. Ancient Hindu, Buddhist, and Jain texts on law, statecraft, ritual, and pleasure and works of mythology and literature all attest a hierarchy of prostitutes based on education. At the top was the *ganika*, also later called the *tawa'if*. By the second century, the sixth section of the *Kamasutra*, "On Courtesans," reported that a courtesan had to master sixty-four arts and sciences. Jain texts from the sixth century list dozens of additional skills, including combat, chemistry, architecture, and augury.

Ganikas, like courtesans in other cultures, entertained men of the elite with both artistic performance and sexual services. The arts were such an important part of their work that at least by the eighteenth-century, both contemporaries and scholars considered these women culture bearers. They were and still are instrumental in the development of certain forms of dance, music, and poetry. As artists, they were active participants in elite culture, integrated and supported by courts through the mid-nineteenth century, at which point British colonial rule disrupted traditional social alignments. In the ancient period, *ganika*s often had specific official functions: participating in victory celebrations, waiting on the king, and sometimes working as spies for the government. Through the nineteenth century, *ganika*s and *tawa'if*s were often able to choose their own clients. Much is made in ancient texts of the prices they charged, prohibitive to all but nobility, royalty, and rich merchants. Like the "big-fees" and *les grandes horizontales*, they lived opulently.

Courtesanship was regulated in India, though the nature of regulation varied regionally and over time. In the ancient period, texts on politics and statecraft position *ganika*s as state employees who received their training for free, paid taxes, and received a pension upon retirement. Each town was supposed to have a chief courtesan, "the ornament of the city," who policed prostitution and selected which girls to train as *ganika*s. In other cases, courtesans were attached to courts and lived in self-regulated communities managed by women who had retired from the profession. Some of these communities have survived into the present.

Attitudes toward *ganika*s through the mid-nineteenth century seem to have been more positive than in other societies. Some scholars argue that this view reflected their role as custodians of Indian high culture. Courtesan sexuality also was celebrated in some texts, and *ganika*s were often depicted as generous and charitable. Yet in these same texts, many of which are from the ancient period, their position as unchaste women made them impure and hence unable to perform certain ritual functions reserved for wives.

The special status of courtesans was challenged by the British, who collapsed all prostitutes into a single category. By the nineteenth century, *ganika*s and *tawa'if*s were lumped with other "singing and dancing girls" for bureaucratic purposes. Local rulers worked with the British to ostracize courtesans, while encouraging respectable women to carry on the courtesans' artistic traditions. After the Indian Rebellion in 1857, some courtesans were forced to work as prostitutes in British regimental brothels servicing military personal. British rule reduced the power of courtesans and the esteem in which they were once held, though this was true in some regions more than in others. In parts of northern India, *tawa'if*s are still musicians and dancers, but they are no longer courtesans. They engage in lower-level prostitution to supplement their income. In other areas, such as in Lucknow, the *tawa'if* community survived colonial rule and Indian independence.

Scholarship on the Lucknow community provides a window into the subjective world of the courtesan, which, at least in this case, was female-dominated. The culture of this community reversed traditional gender values, celebrating a much more positive view of women than the dominant culture did. Daughters born to *tawa'if*, for example, were given greater wealth and resources than were sons. According great value to both women and the profession of *tawa'if* has enabled the Lucknow community to empower its own members, many of whom had fled situations of domestic violence or extreme poverty, a function of the limited opportunities of women. The scholarship on Lucknow raises the question of whether courtesan communities in other societies challenged traditional values associated with gender roles and similarly translated their success into a greater subjective sense of self-worth.

China. Like the *ganika* and hetaera, Chinese courtesans were distinguished from prostitutes because of their accomplishments. From the fifth and sixth centuries on, there are records of famous courtesans who entertained not only with music, songs, and dance but also by mastering the ornaments of literati culture—zither, chess, wine games, poetry, painting, calligraphy, and refined, witty conversation. Mastery of such skills, often prized above beauty, sometimes meant that a courtesan was less sexually available, although it also played a standard part in the game of seduction.

Usually associated with an independent establishment in an urban setting wherein her choices and accessibility were in varying degrees negotiable, the courtesan could nevertheless overlap with the female singer and entertainer kept inside the palace (*gongji*) or the confines of rich and powerful families (*jiaji*) as the property of the emperor or her master. A courtesan was often born or sold into that station, but an elite or even aristocratic woman could have been reduced to that status because her family belonged to a vanquished dynasty or an ousted faction in court or simply got into political troubles, and as such she retained the allure of what might otherwise have been inaccessible.

Courtesanship was regulated by the state in China. Regulation was organized around the idea of maintaining distinctions between the "debased" (*jian*) and the "respectable" (*liang*), as well as the idea that "women of pleasure" could serve the "public good." Official courtesans belonged to registers of musicians (*yueji*) and were directly and indirectly controlled by the government through the bureau of music instruction (*jiaofang*). The institution of the bureau, founded by Emperor Yang of Sui (r. 605–618), lasted for more than a thousand years. Official courtesans could be summoned for performance in state celebrations. During the Song and Ming dynasties, official courtesans entertained and performed at social gatherings. The system of official courtesans was brought to an end during the Qing dynasty (1644–1911). By 1655, eunuchs had permanently replaced female entertainers in the bureau of music instruction. However, private courtesans (*siji*), who had always coexisted with official courtesans despite statutes of prohibition, continued to flourish. In the Song, Ming, and Qing periods, there were periodic decrees prohibiting prostitution and forbidding liaisons between officials and courtesans, but these decrees were widely ignored.

The relationship between patron and courtesan encompassed many gradations of sexual, romantic, and intellectual intimacy. With arranged marriages—whereby husband and wife first met at their wedding—being the norm in premodern China, friendship (with or without nuances of romantic tension) between men and women might be possible only in the courtesans' world. Countless anecdotes, poems, songs, stories, novels, and plays trace the contours of the courtesan romance. As a collective object of desire, the courtesan also defined the relationship between men. Courtesans functioned as gifts in a system of exchange involving patronage and service.

New art forms often first emerged or became popular in the pleasure quarters. Song lyrics in the tenth century, dramatic arias in the thirteenth and fourteenth century, the *kun* operatic style in the sixteenth century, and the sentimental courtesan novel in the nineteenth century were all cultural innovations rooted in the pleasures and passions of the courtesans' world. Like European courtesans, those in China were also sartorial fashion trend setters.

Courtesans in China were lauded for their talents and beauty; at the same time, they were treated as mere pleasure objects of their patrons. Their favors could be purchased, yet they were routinely praised as unattainable immortals (*xian*) and goddesses (*shennü*) or were extolled for their fierce loyalty. The lore of courtesans celebrates the passionate, unconventional, and independent spirit that defied prescribed roles and sometimes even gender boundaries. She consorted with elite men, sometimes as intellectual equals, and could reclaim respectability through marriage (*congliang*). Yet, classified as "debased" (*jian*), her status as object of desire and sexual exploitation inflicted shame and degradation.

[*See also* Geisha; *Kisaeng*; Liu Shi; Marriage; *and* Prostitution.]

BIBLIOGRAPHY

Bhattacharji, Sukumari. "Prostitution in Ancient India." *Social Scientist* 15, no. 2 (February 1987): 32–61.

Davidson, James. *Courtesans and Fishcakes: The Consuming Passions of Classical Athens*. London: HarperCollins, 1997.

Faraone, Christopher A., and Laura K. McClure, eds. *Prostitutes and Courtesans in the Ancient World*. Madison: University of Wisconsin Press, 2006.

Henry, Madeleine M. *Prisoner of History: Aspasia of Miletus and Her Biographical Tradition*. New York: Oxford University Press, 1995.

Hickman, Katie. *Courtesans: Money, Sex, and Fame in the Nineteenth Century*. New York: HarperCollins, 2003.

Idema, Wilt, and Beata Grant, eds. *The Red Brush: Writing Women of Imperial China*. Cambridge, Mass.: Harvard University Asia Center, 2004.

McClure, Laura K. *Courtesans at Table: Gender and Greek Literary Culture in Athenaeus*. New York: Routledge, 2003.

Oldenburg, Veena Talwar. "Lifestyle as Resistance: The Case of the Courtesans of Lucknow, India." *Feminist Studies* 16, no. 2 (Summer 1990): 259–287.

Rosenthal, Margaret F. *The Honest Courtesan: Veronica Franco, Citizen and Writer in Sixteenth-Century Venice*. Chicago: University of Chicago Press, 1992.

Rounding, Virginia. *Grandes Horizontales: The Lives and Legends of Four Nineteenth-Century Courtesans*. London: Bloomsbury, 2003.

Storoni, Laura Anna, ed. *Women Poets of the Italian Renaissance: Courtly Ladies and Courtesans*. Translated by Laura Anna Storoni and Mary Prentice Lillie. New York: Italica Press, 1997.

Widmer, Ellen, and Kang-i Sun Chang. *Writing Women in Late Imperial China*. Stanford, Calif.: Stanford University Press, 1997.

NINA KUSHNER AND WAI-YEE LI

COUSINS, MARGARET (1878–1954), Irish suffragist who was active in the Indian women's movement. Margaret Gillespie Cousins, an Irishwoman, participated in both the movement for Irish suffrage and the Indian women's movement, recording many of these experiences in *We Two Together* (1950), coauthored with her husband, James Cousins. She became active in Ireland during the early twentieth century, when the nationalist, labor, and women's movements were gaining momentum. Along with Hanna Sheehy Skeffington, Cousins founded the Irish Women's Franchise League (IWFL) in 1908 as a militant alternative to the more sedate Irish Women's Suffrage and Local Government Association. Employing a wide range of tactics in their campaign, the IWFL gave open-air speeches in Dublin and the countryside, heckled politicians, shattered the windows of government buildings, and published newspaper articles in support of suffrage.

Both Cousins and Sheehy Skeffington were nationalists, believing that women's franchise had to be included within Home Rule for Ireland. As a member of a 1910 women's deputation to gain interviews with London politicians, Cousins was sentenced to a monthlong prison term in Holloway Goal for her part in lobbing potato missiles and flowerpot shards at the windows of the residences of government dignitaries. In contrast to this experience, which she described as "a living death," she seemed energized by her later one-month imprisonment for suffragist activities in Tullamore, an Irish jail, in 1913. In addition to refusing to cooperate with prison authorities during an initial one-night incarceration at Mountjoy Jail, Cousins and her suffragist companions successfully campaigned to change their classification from common prisoners to political prisoners by going on hunger strike.

In 1913 Cousins left Ireland, eventually going to India in 1915, where she spent the next forty years and helped to galvanize the women's movement. Within a year of her arrival, she began hosting "tea-parties" for ladies, which evolved into the Abala Abhivardini Samaj (Weaker Sex Improvement Society). Eventually, in 1917, the organization merged with the Tamil Women's Association to become the Women's Indian Association headquartered in Madras (now Chennai). Members presented government officials with resolutions passed by local chapters on women's franchise, the prevention of child marriage, and inheritance rights for women. These activities were publicized in *Stri Dharma*, under Cousins's editorship. In 1927 she founded the All India Women's Conference (AIWC) to address the educational needs of children and women. The fifty-eight delegates to the first AIWC session in Poona envisioned education as the means to self-actualization "for the service of humanity." They drafted resolutions on school curricula, the need for compulsory primary education and schools for the disabled, the creation of gender-segregated facilities for girls under purdah, and the need to raise the age of consent; and they called for the use of the vernacular as an instructional medium. The AIWC still exists.

Unlike many other British women activists of her era, such as Eleanor Rathbone, Cousins represents an early and exemplary case of international feminist solidarity for her ability to establish egalitarian relationships with Indian women. The younger Indian colleagues whom she mentored, including Kamaladevi Chattopadhyay and Muthulakshmi Reddi, regarded her with fondness and respect.

[*See also* India.]

BIBLIOGRAPHY

Bose, Purnima. "Feminist-Nationalist Individualism: Margaret Cousins, Activism, and Witnessing." In her *Organizing Empire: Individualism, Collective Agency, and India*. Durham, N.C.: Duke University Press, 2003.

Candy, Catherine. "Relating Feminisms, Nationalisms, and Imperialisms: Ireland, India, and Margaret Cousins's Sexual Politics." *Women's History Review* 3 (1994): 581–594.

Ramusack, Barbara N. "Cultural Missionaries, Maternal Imperialists, Feminist Allies: British Women Activists in India, 1865–1945." *Women's Studies International Forum* 13 (1990): 309–321.

Purnima Bose

CO-WIVES. Polygyny prevails in many societies, especially in Africa. But the experiences of co-wives differ starkly because regulations, values, and the agency of women create diverse cultural and legal frameworks in which co-wives operate. In addition, the exact number of co-wives in African societies is difficult to obtain because of differing forms of polygyny and problems with data collection.

No generalization about co-wives in Africa can adequately capture the variety of practices across the continent. Yet among the underlying patterns that emerge are the importance of agriculture in most polygynous societies and its associated labor requirements. The connection between marital form and economic system is not automatically or intrinsically linked to male dominance. Indigenous cultural values were either reinforced by intrusions, as in the case of Islam in societies in the Sahel and in East and West Africa, or contested through Christianity in West, Central, and southern Africa.

Co-Wives in Africa. Historically, being a co-wife in West African societies such as the Ga in what is now Ghana entailed considerable independence. Because responsibilities were shared among co-wives, senior wives especially were not restricted to matrimonial duties, which allowed for economic, cultural, and in some settings political and ritual activities. Thus seniority structured the relationships among co-wives and gave the senior wife more freedom and power.

Besides the positions of spouses within the group, the spatial arrangements of polygyny enabled or restricted co-wives, depending on whether they were based on compounds of matrilineal kin or on virilocal housing principles. In settings with spatially separated residences, co-wives often had a self-controlled economic space as well, with relations within the household or hearth-hold shaped not by pooling but by exchange. Such regulations allowed co-wives in West and East African settings to keep considerable private possessions after marriage.

Though having several co-wives could be a symbol of male power and wealth, the dissociation of biological sex and social gender in some cultures enabled women to obtain male status and decide on their inheritance, as the Igbo institution of female husbands demonstrates. Having gained sufficient material wealth, a woman could marry other women and claim their children. This concept was expanded by Ahebi Ugbabe, who in the 1880s skillfully played on political crisis and power imbalances in Igboland (now southeastern Nigeria), using colonial and indigenous attempts to conquer her homeland. She made herself the first and only female king of Enugu-Ezike and performed her acquired "manhood" by taking numerous wives, some of whom were abducted from their home communities.

The disruptive impact of colonialism—which favored male institutions and re-gendered the economic sphere by privileging males for public offices and socially recognized productive activities while confining females to private reproductive work—significantly changed the experiences of co-wives. The resulting gender-biased socioeconomic development proved unfavorable to co-wives and deprived them of their economic and political base, which previously had secured them varying degrees of independence from their husbands. Trajectories of this can still be identified in the ongoing dissolution of extended family structures, especially but not only in urban centers all over Africa.

Monogamous nuclear family structures are both the cause and the result of the decline of polygyny. As resource allocation based on kin, social capital, and social relations is replaced by a monetary economy, the strategic importance of extended kinship declines. As a result of the eroding economic independence of co-wives, being a co-spouse carries fewer opportunities to retain economic autonomy and share domestic work. Given the deepening gender imbalances with regard to economic activities, being a co-wife can result in dependence on a man who may not be able to act as sole provider for all of his wives. In the light of this development, becoming a co-wife appears increasingly less favorable. Despite this general trajectory of changes in the economic sphere, there are a number of cultural and pragmatic reasons for women in various African cultures to demand the continuity of polygyny and thereby secure the advantages that especially middle-aged women can earn from being co-wives.

Representations in oral and written literature. The complex forms of representation of co-wives can be illustrated using West African and Sahelian oral literature. In the Xaxar genre of Senegalese Wolof, derogatory wedding songs mocking new co-wives articulate rivalry between co-wives and establish a hierarchy that secures both greater work shares for junior wives and greater independence for senior wives. These practices can be read as female complicity in the hegemonic practice that makes senior wives accomplices in female subjugation. At the same time the songs are public performances that transgress conventions of female politeness and passivity. They provide opportunities for creative expression that can be marked by ridicule, mockery, and violent vocabulary; that is, behaviors for which women are usually sanctioned are here performed in public. The ensuing cathartic effect releases tension in a potentially conflicting situation.

In Niger Zarma culture, a new co-wife is welcomed through a competitive dialogue sung and danced by groups of women in corresponding age-groups or positions as first and second co-wives. This symbolic competition ends with a demonstrative unification of all spouses during which they guarantee each other mutual support as co-spouses.

African women's literary engagement with polygyny has been shaped by the general controversy around the institution. This allows two contrasting readings of modern representations of co-wives, as shown in Mariama Bâ's *Une si longue lettre* (1979; English trans., *So Long a Letter*, 1981). Modernists who view polygyny as an oppressive practice in a primordial, static "African" culture read the book as condemnation voiced by aggrieved women who refuse to submit to it. Scholars who criticize the underlying dichotomy of "modernity" and "tradition" differentiate between the cultural norm, which in this case is shaped by African and Islamic laws, and its practice in postindependence urban Senegal, which does not necessarily comply with cultural norms. A focus on the specificity of the story casts co-wives and men as self-determined actors who appropriate custom or refuse such appropriation that emphasizes co-wives' duties but omits their rights. *So Long a Letter* thus is exemplary of accounts of the experiences of co-wives facing a decline in polygamous arrangements that adhere to the cultural norms of the institution and an upsurge of its masculinized version, in which male privileges are retained while the rights of co-wives are eroded.

Legal situations. The legal situations of co-wives vary considerably between and within African subregions. Though polygyny is allowed in most North African states—only Tunisia prohibits polygamy legally—despite the Islamic base of most North African societies, it is rarely practiced there; a 1988 source noted that Egypt had the highest rate of polygamy in the region, at 8 percent. Regulations in Egypt, Libya, Algeria, and Morocco make consent of the first wife mandatory for the addition of co-wives.

In East Africa, polygyny is legally prohibited only in Ethiopia, although the practice is common there. In Uganda, Tanzania, and Kenya, lobbying by women's rights organizations has improved the legal situation of co-wives, who now have to agree to their husbands' decision to marry another wife. Uganda still grapples with the need to define the relationships among the five different legal types of marriage—namely, customary, civil, Christian, Islamic, and Hindu. Many southern African countries operate with a dual legal system of British-style common and customary law in which co-wives are recognized.

The African diaspora. Among the Saramaka Maroons, co-wives exist as part of marital systems that were retained and re-created based on the various West and Central African cultures of origin of the fugitive slaves that established independent communities in Suriname. Even though African diasporan cultures are by necessity alterations of their origins, the preservation of matrilineality and polygyny in Suriname points to the high value that Africans ascribed to the institution when confronted with different gender hierarchies in the plantation slavery system.

Mormon Polygamy. Mormon polygamy provides an opportunity to observe polygyny controversies and the agency of co-wives in a predominantly monogamous Western society. It has been the focus of intense study that has reinforced two conflicting readings of polygamy—that is, as either an institution of patriarchy or a regulation that allows for considerable independence of co-wives. Historically the controversy surrounding Mormon polygamy delayed the admission of the Mormon state of Utah into the United States and led clerics to grant suffrage to women in Utah in hopes of keeping polygamy. Even though most Mormon marriages were monogamous, the controversy waged well beyond the abolition of polygamy in Utah.

[*See also* Bâ, Mariama; Codes of Law and Laws, *subentry* Islamic Law; *and* Marriage.]

BIBLIOGRAPHY

Achebe, Nwando. "'And she became a man': King Ahebi Ugbabe in the History of the Engu-Ezike, Northern Igboland, 1880–1948." In *Men and Masculinities in Modern Africa*, edited by Lisa A. Lindsay and Stephan F. Miescher. Portsmouth, N.H.: Heinemann, 2003.

Amadiume, Ifi. *Male Daughters, Female Husbands: Gender and Sex in an African Society*. London: Zed Books, 1987.

Bâ, Mariama. *So Long a Letter*. Translated by Modupé Bodé-Thomas. London: Heinemann, 1981.

Esonwanne, Uzo. "Enlightenment Epistemology and 'Aesthetic Cognition': Mariama Bâ's So Long a Letter." In *The Politics of (M)othering: Womanhood, Identity, and Resistance in African Literature*, edited by Obioma Nnaemeka. London: Routledge, 1997.

Moore, Henrietta L. *Feminism and Anthropology*. Cambridge, U.K.: Polity, 1988.

Mullings, Leith. "Women and Economic Change in Africa." In *Women in Africa: Studies in Social and Economic Change*, edited by Nancy J. Hafkin and Edna G. Bay. Stanford, Calif.: Stanford University Press, 1976.

Nnaemeka, Obioma. "Urban Spaces, Women's Places: Polygamy as a Sign in Mariama Bâ's Novels." In *The Politics of (M)othering: Womanhood, Identity, and Resistance in African Literature*, edited by Obioma Nnaemeka. London: Routledge, 1997.

Solway, Jacqueline S. "Affines and Spouses, Friends and Lovers: The Passing of Polygyny in Botswana." *Journal of Anthropological Research* 46, no. 1 (1990): 41–66.

White, Douglas R. "Rethinking Polygyny: Co-wives, Codes, and Cultural Systems." *Current Anthropology* 29, no. 4 (1988): 529–572.

Takyiwaa Manuh and Joshua Kwesi Aikins

CRAWFORD SEEGER, RUTH (1901–1953), American classical music composer and folk song arranger and collector. Ruth Crawford was born in East Liverpool, Ohio, on 3 July 1901, the daughter of Clark Crawford, a Methodist minister, and Clara Graves Crawford. After numerous moves the family settled in Jacksonville, Florida, where Ruth spent her adolescence and began her piano studies. Upon graduation from high school she taught piano in a local school, then attended the American Conservatory of Music in Chicago, where she lived through the 1920s. She quickly developed into a superb pianist and began her career as a composer, coming under the influence of European modernists. During the later 1920s she created a number of complex compositions, full of dissonance, such as "Five Preludes for Piano," "Music for Small Orchestra," and her best-known early composition, "Sonata for Violin and Piano." In late 1929 she moved to New York City, where she joined a group of the country's foremost composers.

She soon met Charles Seeger, a modernist composer and political maverick. She became the first woman to win a Guggenheim Fellowship in composition and created her most important work, "String Quartet 1931." She married Seeger in late 1932 and continued her modernist musical career, although her developing radical politics led her to such compositions as "Sacco, Vanzetti" and "Chinaman, Laundryman," which reflected her interest in the Chinese revolution and the exploitation of immigrant labor. The birth of her son, Michael, in 1933, with three daughters to follow, soon led her away from classical composition.

In 1936 the Seegers moved to Washington, D.C., where Charles Seeger worked for the government, and they became involved in the burgeoning folk music movement. She soon began work on transcriptions for a folk song book by John and Alan Lomax, *Our Singing Country* (1941), and a second one for them, *Folk Song U.S.A.* (1947). But her real interest now was in promoting this music for children, first expressed in her collection *American Folk Songs for Children* (1948). It was followed by *Animal Folk Songs for Children* (1950), *American Folk Songs for Christmas* (1953), and *Let's Build a Railroad* (1954). Her own children were immersed in folk music, with two, Mike and Peggy, developing careers as professional musicians. Although Ruth Crawford Seeger never abandoned her vocation as a classical composer, and her earlier works were still performed, she used her musical skills mostly to arrange and publish a wide range of folk songs before her death on 18 November 1953. In subsequent decades she has been recognized as a female pioneer in modernist music, and the publication of *The Music of American Folk Song and Selected Other Writings on American Folk Music* (2001) well documents her sophistication in understanding and arranging folk music. Crawford Seeger had a remarkable, influential musical career, connecting classical training and composition with the promotion and shaping of folk music, particularly for children.

[*See also* Music.]

BIBLIOGRAPHY

Allen, Ray, and Ellie M. Hisama, eds. *Ruth Crawford Seeger's Worlds: Innovation and Tradition in Twentieth-Century American Music*. Rochester, N.Y.: University of Rochester Press, 2007. An edited collection based on a conference on Ruth Crawford Seeger's life and musical contributions.

Seeger, Ruth Crawford. *"The Music of American Folk Song" and Selected Writings on American Folk Music*. Edited by Larry

Polansky and Judith Tick. Rochester, N.Y.: University of Rochester Press, 2001.
Tick, Judith. *Ruth Crawford Seeger: A Composer's Search for American Music.* New York: Oxford University Press, 1997. The most complete study of Seeger's life.

RONALD D. COHEN

CRESSON, ÉDITH (b. 1934), French Socialist politician, first woman prime minister of France, and European Union commissioner for science and education. Édith Campion was born 27 January 1934 in Boulogne-Billancourt (near Paris) to an affluent family. She graduated from the prestigious School of Higher Commercial Studies and earned her doctorate in demography. In 1959 she married Jacques Cresson, a Peugeot executive. Her belief that the bourgeoisie collaborated in the French deportation of Jews in World War II and her "boredom" with her middle-class upbringing led her to join the Socialist Party in 1965.

Cresson was elected mayor of Thuré in 1977, to the European Parliament in 1979, and to the National Assembly in 1981. In 1983 she won the mayoralty of Châtellerault (a conservative city southwest of Paris). After François Mitterrand's election to the presidency in 1981, he appointed Cresson the first woman minister of agriculture. The French farmers, a conservative and traditionally masculine political group, treated "the Perfumed One" with contempt, staging protests and showering her with rotten tomatoes. Cresson raised the French farmers' income by 10 percent in 1982. In 1984 Cresson became the minister of industrial restructuring and external trade and strayed from Socialist doctrine by revamping the country's steel industry and urging tax cuts for businesses. She even rode a French motor scooter to work every day to show that she considered them superior to Japanese models.

On 15 May 1991 Mitterrand appointed Cresson the country's first woman prime minister. She had difficulty passing bills for social reform because of the social problems she inherited and the decline of the Socialist Party. She also drew negative international attention by insisting that Japan was bent on world domination. Television journalists declared Cresson's appointment a "real catastrophe" because she did not possess the "necessary qualities." Cresson, on the other hand, complained that women politicians were judged not on their policies (as men were) but on "the details of their person"—their dress, jewelry, and smile. Yet she revealed her support of these same gender stereotypes by once insisting that Englishmen were "not interested in women as women" because they did not look at women in the streets and that this indicated that they were "a little maimed."

Cresson's relationship with Mitterrand (which was stereotypically rumored to be intimate) became the focus of a popular television program that used satirical puppets to mock politicians. In 1991 the show introduced a Cresson-inspired puppet—a slavish and sex-mad feline that panted after Mitterrand, licking his boots. Within a month Cresson's approval rating dropped from two-thirds to less than half. The Socialists began to see Cresson as a liability and in April 1992 asked for her resignation.

Cresson became the European Union commissioner for science and education in 1995 but was forced to resign in 1999 on charges of mismanagement and nepotism. Some analysts speculate that internal political instabilities caused the European Union to crack down on Cresson, since the commission had had a history of "waste and misuse" long before Cresson's involvement. Later in her career, Cresson emphasized that what she had learned from her political experiences was that all women in leadership positions suffer varying degrees of "denigration" due to an omnipresent sexism in politics, and that "polishing one's image" is more important than constant, hard work for women politicians.

[*See also* France.]

BIBLIOGRAPHY

Liswood, Laura A. *Women World Leaders: Fifteen Great Politicians Tell Their Stories.* San Francisco: Pandora, 1995. Traces the commonalities of fifteen women political figures: their values, experiences, triumphs, tragedies, mistakes, and accomplishments in an honest look at women in positions of power. The book was made into a videorecording in 2003.
Ramsay, Raylene L. *French Women in Politics: Writing Power, Paternal Legitimization, and Maternal Legacies.* New York: Berghahn Books, 2003. A fascinating assessment of the power of writing on women's power in politics. Cresson is included thematically in several chapters, and there is also an interview with her, with a thought-provoking interpretation by the author.
Schemla, Elisabeth. *Edith Cresson: La femme piégée.* Paris: Flammarion, 1993.

CYNTHIA SHARRER KREISEL

CRIMINALITY. Throughout history women have engaged in criminal activity, most notably theft but also murder and other violent crimes. Women's criminality has in general been lower than that of men, hovering in the modern period at around a tenth of all criminal activity. In many cases women have been accomplices to men's crime, whether victimless or violent. Often, acting on their own, they have stolen and engaged in fraud to gain property. Where prostitution is criminalized, they constitute the vast majority of those arrested for sexual solicitation. With greater globalization, the rate of conviction for crimes by women has been growing, as has activism around women's imprisonment. This has occurred despite a general decline in crime in many parts of the world. Thus, whereas in 1970 there were 5,600 women held in U.S. prisons, in 2001 there were 161,200. This trend holds worldwide.

Women's Criminality. Women's crime has in general involved the theft of property, with men constituting the vast majority of violent criminals. In early modern times, theft generally targeted subsistence items such as wood, food, fodder, and items of clothing—crimes testifying to the want that poor women experienced. Women have also been pickpockets, smugglers, carriers of stolen goods, and brewers of illegal alcohol. A study of 2,424 Mexican women prisoners in the early twenty-first century showed 36 percent serving time for "offenses against health," which included drug charges, 33 percent for theft, and 18 percent for murder or assault. In contemporary India, by contrast, some 76 percent of women prisoners in the north of the country were serving time for murder, which may indicate the nature of punishment rather than the ratio of violent to nonviolent crime.

Whereas crimes of property are generally attributed to women's poverty, women's less frequent violent crime has involved family members, especially abusive husbands and other male relatives. In these crimes, women have resorted to weapons such as guns, machetes, and swords and to poison. Although physical abuse by husbands leads women to murder, where polygamy is practiced, co-wives are common murder victims as well, oftentimes because tensions were great and a husband took the new wife's side. "If this woman had never been brought into the home," one convicted murderer reported of the unwanted co-wife, "I would never have gone through all this" (Tibatemwa-Ekirikubinza, p. 128). Witchcraft also provoked women to murder. As one Ugandan murderer explained the killing of her stepmother: "She had cursed me to suffer throughout my life. As a result my three attempts at marriage were all frustrated. On the day of the crime I went to contact [her] in order that she revokes the curse on me, but she was rude.... I grabbed a hoe and struck her" (Tibatemwa-Ekirikubinza, p. 192). Among other relatives, women have killed unwanted children in great numbers throughout history, with strangulation, throwing into wells, burning, exposure, and other techniques playing a role in the murder of minors.

With the criminalization of drugs in the modern period and more concerted enforcement of antidrug laws in the late twentieth century, women's apprehension for drug-related crimes and other offenses characterized as morality offenses has increased. Women are particularly suspect as carriers of illegal drugs for the male dealers in their families. Other moral issues such as global sex trafficking have also targeted women. In regions such as Europe where immigration is a political issue, police target women of color on the charge of participating in global sex trafficking.

Although there has always been monitoring of women's sexuality by religious and secular authorities, the criminalization of women's private sexual behavior continues—often for purposes that have little to do with actual religious law. For instance, in Pakistan the state announced in 1979 a series of regulations allegedly stemming from Islamic law. However, the *zina* laws, said to concern morality, often seemed to be used to intimidate women. Parents whose daughters married in defiance of their families' wishes were often imprisoned for *zina* offenses, and although 95 percent of cases were eventually dismissed, imprisonment lasted for years. Even after marrying a husband of her father's choice, one young bride found herself in jail because her mother had wanted a different marriage and had her daughter jailed for *zina* or adultery. In another case, a young worker escaped from an abusive employer, who then charged a woman janitor and coworker with *zina*—or leading a young person to be disobedient and thus immoral. "Now my husband and I are both in jail," the "offender" reported (Sudbury, p. 93).

Some women have engaged in crime for political reasons, assassinating leaders of opposing political groups and engaging in mass murder for political reasons. In the Russian Empire, women assassinated government officials after the emancipation of the serfs in 1861 in hopes of provoking the overthrow of the government. The most daring attack involved the assassination of Tsar Alexander II in 1881—a plot headed in large part by Sofia Perovskaia, who was executed with other assassins in 1881. About a century later, in 1991, the Tamil Tiger Thenmuli Rajaratnam, known as Dhanu, killed Rajiv Gandhi, the former prime minister of India, in a suicide attack. The Tamils, an ethnic group in Sri Lanka, consider themselves an independent nation, and when Gandhi sent soldiers into the neighboring country to put down the Tamils, four of Dhanu's brothers were killed in the offensive and she herself was gang-raped. Between 1960 and the 1980s women participated in a range of terrorist activities protesting the Vietnam War, the erosion of democracy, and the tightening grip of multinational corporations. After the Russian invasion of Chechnya in the 1990s, women participated in attacks on Russian civilians, taking hostages in schools and blowing up planes. A fifth of suicide bombers in the early twenty-first century are women.

Crimes and Punishments. Where countries are multiracial, minority status can lead to greater criminality, perceptions of criminality, and incarceration for crime. For instance, in Australia, Aboriginal women constitute 30 percent of women in prisons, whereas they make up only 2 percent of the population. In U.S. federal prisons in 1999, one-third of women were Latina, mostly incarcerated on drug charges. In New York State, Latinas were more likely to be imprisoned by the state for drug-related crimes than were white women offenders, and they received longer sentences than did men who had been convicted of more serious crimes.

Class was an additional ingredient that shaped the profile of women criminals, with poor women generally constituting the vast majority of the prison population. Even as the "science" of criminology advanced, professionals as late as the 1960s claimed to see criminality in qualities such as appearance, saying of one homely girl, for example, that her "whole posture and facial expression suggest nervousness, dull intellect and the possibility of anti-social attitudes" (Cox, p. 145).

These attitudes affect rates of conviction and types of punishment or incarceration; moreover the punishment of crime has varied over time. Before modern times, a convicted criminal was often not incarcerated, receiving instead whippings and other corporeal punishment. What might appear to the modern observer to be leniency testifies instead to the need for all hands to be used in subsistence economies, and for adults to remain alive to tend for their children and other relatives. People were charged for their imprisonment, and women were the least likely to be able to pay. In general corporal punishment declined over the years, with fines and incarceration rising, and in the early twenty-first century the rates of female incarceration were rising more rapidly than those for men.

In the modern period women criminals were exported or exiled as well as incarcerated, especially through indenturing and transportation to other parts of the world. The British, for example, sent women criminals to penal colonies in Australia, where they formed the basis for populating the continent with whites. Louise Michel, a famed French activist during the Paris Commune of 1871, was sent into exile for her participation in that uprising against the French state. Although many indentured Asian women in the nineteenth and twentieth centuries simply accompanied their husbands to the Caribbean and other places to keep the family together, other women were forced into transport as punishment for indigence and prostitution.

Understanding Women's Criminality. In early modern times criminals were said to live in a state of sinful disobedience, whether by breaking the laws of a god, the codes of a sacrosanct family, or the rules governing a theocratic society. In the Western Judeo-Christian tradition, however, women were seen as inherently more sinful because "woman was the first to fall"—a reference to Eve's temptation of Adam. Religious law determined many punishments based on the profiling of witches, heretics, adulterers, and other criminal women, seeing in them sinfulness and unholiness. By the nineteenth century in the West, concerns about criminality had turned to finding the scientific origins of criminality in women and men alike. The development of the field of criminology followed.

Theorists determined that although both sexes could be criminal, the crimes of women were far worse than those of men. Generally, theorists of the new "science" of criminology believed, women committed far fewer crimes than men because their natural tendency to nurture and care simply precluded criminal behavior. However, the woman who did resort to crime was in the most debased category: "more uncivilized than the savage, more degraded than the slave, less true to all natural and womanly instincts than the untutored squaw of a North American Indian tribe," as one English criminologist commented in 1866 (quoted in Zedner, p. 43). Once the eugenics movement became powerful, from the late nineteenth century on, female crime came to be seen as particularly dangerous to the nation as a whole, undermining its strength through the breeding of potentially criminal children and thus weakening the race.

From the beginning of the twentieth century, young girls' potential for criminality became a heated topic in the West, as psychologists, social workers, and sociologists all looked for the sources of criminality in general. Through the century, investigators of adolescent criminality focused on girls' sexuality, especially promiscuity, nascent nymphomania, and homosexuality. In Japan the "modern girl" was on the one hand praised for putting aside tradition and on the other hand criminalized for the disruption she caused with her sexual freedom and consumerism. As women achieved the vote, the focus on adolescents intensified. Theorists of girls' criminality in advanced consumer societies across the world focused on their unbridled desires, fostered by indulgent parents or a permissive society. As one British commentator put it in the 1960s: "Everyone knows how the good-looking girl is first petted and spoiled by kindly uncles and by munificent friends of the family; and soon, quite pardonably, begins to cultivate a coy appealing look for every visitor. . . . from thence it is no long step to soliciting, with dumb demureness, the passing stranger in the street" (Cox, p. 146).

Notorious Criminals. Women have also been notorious criminals and murderers—for example, Bonnie Parker (1910–1934), who teamed up with Clyde Barrow (1909–1934) to kill more than a dozen people in a criminal spree that lasted from 1932 until their deaths in 1934. Far more celebrated was Phoolan Devi (1963–2001), who belonged to a *dacoit* gang (rural outlaw gang) in India. Her attempts to kill the murderers of her lover in 1981 led to a rampage of killings before she finally turned herself in to authorities. Admired by many as their "bandit queen" who avenged the abuse of women and who gave to the poor, Phoolan Devi was elected to parliament in 1996, two years after her release from prison, but was later assassinated.

Such women became the heroines, or antiheroines, of journalists, authors, and filmmakers. The Paquin sisters, domestic servants who murdered their employers and gouged out their eyes in France in the 1930s, were made legendary not only by the newspapers but by the famed psychoanalyst Jacques Lacan, members of the surrealism movement, the philosopher and novelist Simone de Beauvoir, and the novelist and dramatist Jean Genet. Among other famed women criminals were the guards in Nazi extermination and concentration camps and the four assistant nurses in the Lainz city hospital outside Vienna who killed scores of elderly patients in the 1980s.

Contemporary Policy Issues. Treatment of women in prisons has become one of the major policy debates of the twenty-first century. The People's Republic of China professes to provide appropriate custodianship for women criminals, including access to women doctors and other professionals. The penal system allows visitation rights for women and their minor children. There is also concern about the skyrocketing number of women criminals and prisoners, which some view as the result of globalization. Students of criminology believe that more sophisticated methods are now being used globally and that the need to show results in such endeavors as the war on drugs and the war on terrorism has led to the incarceration of increasing numbers of women, who are less dangerous and far easier to catch because they front for their male associates, often involuntarily.

Women have long been involved in prison activism aimed at reforming the conditions under which women were sentenced and incarcerated. European women in the nineteenth century organized a number of charities to visit women prisoners and their children. Because women receive less education and health care in prisons than men do, and because of women's special concern for the welfare of their children, activists have worked to improve access to training and to provide support for families. In the early twenty-first century, a range of organizations and numerous individuals are prison activists on behalf of women, resulting in pardons for those receiving overly harsh sentences, the mass release of women prisoners, and the reduction of sentences.

[*See also* Domestic Violence; Marriage; Piracy and Smuggling; Prostitution; Sciences, *subentry* Social Sciences; Sexuality; Violence; Witchcraft; *and entries on countries, regions, and women mentioned in this article.*]

BIBLIOGRAPHY

Belknap, Joanne. *The Invisible Woman: Gender, Crime, and Justice.* 3d ed. Belmont, Calif.: Thomson Wadsworth, 2007.

Cox, Pamela. *Gender, Justice, and Welfare: Bad Girls in Britain, 1900–1950.* Houndmills, U.K., and New York: Palgrave Macmillan, 2003.

Ozo-Eson, Philomena I. *Patterns, Trends, and Control of Female Criminality in Nigeria: A Sociological Analysis.* Ibadan: University Press Nigeria, 2004.

Rublack, Ulinka. *The Crimes of Women in Early Modern Germany.* New York: Oxford University Press, 1999.

Saxena, Rekha. *Women and Crime in India: A Study in Sociocultural Dynamics.* New Delhi: Inter-India Publications, 1994.

Shapiro, Ann-Louise. *Breaking the Codes: Female Criminality in Fin-de-siècle Paris.* Stanford, Calif.: Stanford University Press, 1996.

Skaine, Rosemarie. *Female Suicide Bombers.* Jefferson, N.C.: McFarland, 2006.

Sudbury, Julia, ed. *Global Lockdown: Race, Gender, and the Prison-industrial Complex.* New York: Routledge, 2005.

Tibatemwa-Ekirikubinza, Lillian. *Women's Violent Crime in Uganda: More Sinned Against than Sinning.* Kampala, Uganda: Fountain, 1999.

Zedner, Lucia. *Women, Crime, and Custody in Victorian England.* New York: Oxford University Press, 1991.

BONNIE G. SMITH

CRUSADES. The Crusades, a type of holy war in which participants believed that they were fighting on God's behalf, were a series of military campaigns fought by medieval Catholic Christians against peoples who, they believed, threatened their Christian faith. These opponents included Muslims on the Iberian Peninsula and in the Middle East, pagans of the Baltic region, Greek Orthodox Christians, and Christian heretics such as Cathars and Hussites. Catholics who wished to join a crusading expedition would take a religious vow and wore on their clothes the Christian symbol of the cross. They believed that God would reward their service with indulgences—that is, by canceling the punishment due them for their past sins, disobedience to God's will. Those who could not take part in person could get the same reward by making a monetary donation.

From the late eleventh century until the sixteenth century, crusading made an impact on all sectors of European society. Any Catholic Christian could accompany a Crusade and win a Crusade indulgence: warriors and their servants, young and old, men, women, and children from every social class. Some wealthy noblewomen accompanied their husbands. Eleanor of Aquitaine accompanied King Louis VII of France on the Second Crusade (1147–1149), Berengaria of Navarre accompanied King Richard I of England on the Third Crusade (1190–1192), and Margaret of Provence accompanied King Louis IX on his crusade to Egypt (1248–1254). Others, such as Countess Alice of Blois in 1288, traveled without their menfolk and financed warriors from their own resources. Crusading was the most honorable form of warfare for medieval Catholic Christian warriors. Noncombatants also played an important supportive role, collecting and preparing food, looking after the sick, and taking water to the troops on the battlefield. Both men and women acted as traders, selling food to the army, or as craftspeople, manufacturing armor and weapons. Noncombatants also gave spiritual support, praying for the warriors.

Yet the presence of women in a crusading army could disrupt military discipline. When crusades failed, the women of the crusading army were often blamed, because (critics claimed) they led the male warriors into sin, bringing God's wrath down upon the crusaders. Popes and preachers tried to discourage noncombatants from going on the Crusades, but without success. Women wanted to play their part in this service for God, even though their society and culture did not normally permit them to take part in military action.

Historians have questioned whether women could be true crusaders if they did not fight. James Brundage has shown that medieval canon lawyers did acknowledge that women's crusading vows were valid. Less clear is whether women crusaders actually took part in military action. Medieval Catholic commentators did not mention Christian women fighting on Crusade battlefields, but Muslim writers claimed that women crusaders fought against them in the field. Helen Nicholson has argued that these Muslim writers' descriptions of Christian women warriors were intended to demonstrate Christian barbarity rather than to depict actual events.

Whatever their military role, Catholic women also played a crucial role in the expansion and continuation of the Crusades by encouraging their menfolk to take crusading vows and by maintaining family traditions of crusading. Certain female Christian saints, including Christ's mother the Virgin Mary, were the focus of crusaders' special religious devotion.

Not all women involved in crusading acted voluntarily. Women who lived in the regions where the Crusades took place could not avoid military events. In the early thirteenth century the English monk Thomas of Beverley wrote of how his elder sister Margaret had been trapped in Jerusalem when the city was attacked by Sultan Saladin of Egypt in 1187; she had donned makeshift armor and brought water to the defenders while being bombarded by Saladin's siege engines. Women were also found among the crusaders' opponents. In 1420 women of the Hussite heretics of Bohemia fought in defense of their capital city, Prague, against the crusaders who had come to destroy them.

Like medieval Christians, Muslims preferred that their women not fight except in cases of great need, and so it is difficult to find contemporary accounts of Muslim women playing a military role against the Christian crusaders. However, in November 1249, after the death of Sultan al-Salih Ayyub of Egypt, his widow Shajar al-Durr coordinated the successful Egyptian defense against the Crusade of King Louis IX of France.

[*See also* Eleanor of Aquitaine *and* Europe, *subentry* Medieval Period.]

BIBLIOGRAPHY

Brundage, James. *Medieval Canon Law and the Crusader.* Madison: University of Wisconsin Press, 1969.

Edgington, Susan B., and Sarah Lambert, eds. *Gendering the Crusades.* Cardiff, U.K.: University of Wales Press, 2001.

Geldsetzer, Sabine. *Frauen auf Kreuzzügen: 1096–1291.* Darmstadt, Germany: Wissenschaftliche Buchgesellschaft, 2003.

Gerish, Deborah. "Gender Theory." In *Palgrave Advances in the Crusades*, edited by Helen J. Nicholson. New York: Palgrave Macmillan, 2005.

Nicholson, Helen. "Women on the Third Crusade." *Journal of Medieval History* 4 (1997): 335–349.

HELEN J. NICHOLSON

CUBA. Existing historiography has long favored the stories of Cuba's male revolutionary heroes. The poetic meditations of José Martí, the probing ideology of Ernesto "Che" Guevara, and the progressive social policies of Fidel Castro are known worldwide. Less familiar are the struggles and contributions of the many women whose actions likewise shaped the trajectory of Cuban history over the last hundred years. From the unknown slave woman to the mythologized revolutionary heroine to the industrious female entrepreneur of the "Special Period," Cuban women have sustained and often reinvented the social, economic, cultural, and political life of their nation. In recognition of these important contributions, historians, feminist scholars, and international political activists have begun the important work of building up a history of women's experiences that enriches and often challenges our understanding of Cuban society past, present, and future.

Women in Pre-independence Cuba, 1868–1898. Women's lives in nineteenth-century Cuba were defined largely by their commitments to home, family, and work. In urban areas, popular attitudes about the link between female public labor and sexual immorality discouraged most white women from working outside the home; thus, they frequently chose to roll cigars and cigarettes from home as part of the putting-out system. Female slaves worked not only on sugar, coffee, and tobacco plantations, but also as domestic servants, cooks, and laundresses in cities and towns. With the abolition of slavery in 1886, some freedwomen continued to work in and around plantations or in rural areas, often combining traditional cultivation with wage labor, but most migrated to urban areas. Concerns about the increasing number of female laborers entering Havana in search of work prompted colonial authorities to regulate prostitution as early as 1873. Throughout the 1880s and 1890s, the majority of female labor outside the home was in domestic service occupations, but increasing numbers of women entered the island's booming tobacco industry. These female tobacco factory workers aligned themselves with the island's burgeoning anarchist labor movement and mobilized against unfair wages and sexually abusive foremen.

In addition to their familial duties, women's lives in nineteenth-century Cuba were marked profoundly by the nation's protracted struggle for independence from Spain.

Between 1868 and 1898, the Cuban people mobilized on multiple fronts to capsize colonial authorities and establish an independent republic. While some Cuban women defended the Spanish system as part of the island's cultural heritage, many others supported the rebel cause both on and off the battlefield. Mariana Grajales famously sacrificed several sons to the Ten Years' War (1868–1878), and Ana Betancourt publicly demanded that women's rights be incorporated into the national blueprint for revolutionary change; thousands of women contributed to the independence process in ways that did not garner such widespread public acclaim. Off the battlefield, women in Cuba and abroad formed patriotic clubs whose fund-raising efforts lent much-needed support to beleaguered insurgent forces. Peasant women in rural areas (*guajiras*) sheltered, fed, and provisioned rebels with coffee, honey, and candles. In the insurgent camps, freed slaves (*libertas*) and the wives of rebels operated secret workshops to produce war goods, cultivated fields, cooked meals, cared for stock animals, washed and repaired clothing, and staffed hospitals for the sick and wounded. In addition to these more traditional female duties, women risked their lives as couriers and armed combatants (*mambisas*). One woman, Paulina Ruiz, achieved the rank of captain within the rebel forces. With the end of Spanish rule in Cuba in 1898, women hoped that their important contributions to the independence struggle would secure their rights to the vote, public education, and divorce. Instead, women were disappointed to discover that such rights, much like a truly independent status for their country, would prove elusive.

Women after Cuban Independence, 1898–1952. With the signing of the Treaty of Paris in 1898, Cubans of every class, race, and gender faced a world of new possibilities but also great economic and social uncertainty. Women's issues were largely sidelined early in the twentieth century as Cubans focused on stabilizing the domestic political situation under U.S. tutelage. By the second decade of the twentieth century, however, women were playing a more visible role in all spheres of public life, including politics and labor. The number of women entering the waged labor force in Cuba increased significantly between 1899 and 1919, as one out of every two Cuban women was widowed by the war and many more were left destitute and geographically dislocated. As in the nineteenth century, Afro-Cuban women provided the bulk of the female labor force in Cuba, working primarily as laundresses, domestic servants, and vendors. Most nurses, teachers, and clerical workers were white women. Increased immigration from Spain between 1899 and 1943 further threatened Afro-Cuban women's tenuous access to work, even in the service and manufacturing occupations where they had traditionally found employment.

By 1920, years of political corruption, social unrest, and economic decline prompted the creation of feminist groups composed primarily of elites who hoped to mobilize Cuban women as mothers. Conservative and leftist activists found significant common ground on issues of female suffrage and protective labor legislation but differed on the issue of rights and protections for illegitimate children. Notwithstanding these internal divisions, Cuban feminists organized three national women's congresses (1923, 1925, and 1939) and won significant victories, including a revised property rights law (1917), a no-fault divorce law (1918), and the right to vote (1934). Furthermore, the Cuban constitution of 1940—which prohibited sexual discrimination in employment and guaranteed women equal pay for equal work—represented some of the most progressive labor legislation in the Western Hemisphere. This new body of legislation was a tremendous victory for feminists, but hardly a guarantee of real social change. Assured that the new constitution would protect their rights to full equality, women's organizations in the 1950s shifted their interests toward social philanthropy, education, sports and leisure activities, and the arts rather than issues of gender reform. Waning vigilance on the part of feminists allowed many employers to disregard Cuba's progressive legislation and maintain a working environment that offered few protections to female employees. Furthermore, most women's organizations were decidedly out of sync with the daily struggles of the Afro-Cuban female population and did little to address enduring patterns of racism.

The first half of the twentieth century also witnessed the development of Cuba's international tourism industry. By the 1950s, U.S. tourists were traveling to Cuba in droves, drawn to the intoxicating mix of the foreign and the familiar offered by the island's bars, cabarets, casinos, and brothels. Even though prostitution had been officially deregulated in Cuba since 1913, the island's prostitution industry flourished into the 1950s, as young men from the United States came in search of exotic encounters in Havana brothels. Cuba soon became known as a "Latin Las Vegas," where state authorities courted mass foreign tourism, U.S. corporate interests, and organized crime to the detriment of the Cuban populace. The corruption, exploitation, and extreme economic stratification that became the cornerstones of Cuban politics and society by the 1950s eventually provided the justification for revolutionary change in 1959.

Women and the Cuban Revolution, 1953–1959. On 10 March 1952, Fulgencio Batista y Zaldívar seized control of the Cuban government via a military coup d'état. In reaction to the illegality of Batista's actions, university students, workers, and women began mobilizing in protest. Three young Cuban women, Aida Pelayo, Olga Sánchez, and Carmen Castro Porta, organized a clandestine group of female dissidents they christened the Martí Women's Civic Front (FCMM, Frente Cívico de Mujeres Martianas). The FCMM was a heterogeneous conglomeration of Cuban women consisting of laborers, housewives, professionals, and employees of local businesses. Members of the organization distributed anti-Batista propaganda, housed fugitive insurgents, transported arms and explosives, and even published their own daily newspaper, *News and Commentaries*. When guerrilla forces under the command of Fidel Castro attacked the Moncada military barracks in Santiago de Cuba on 26 July 1953, only two women, Haydée Santamaría and Melba Hernández, were allowed to join their male compatriots as nurses. Both women were eventually captured, tortured, and imprisoned for seven months. The assault on the Moncada barracks was an unequivocal military disaster, which led to the imprisonment of twenty-seven of the male rebels in the Presidio Modelo (Model Prison) on the Isle of Pines. During this stage of the revolution, the FCMM smuggled messages between the disconnected leadership and the urban units, including fragments of Castro's first ideological platform, "History Will Absolve Me." In addition to printing and distributing nearly ten thousand copies of the revolutionary manifesto, members of the FCMM successfully lobbied the Cuban state for the release of the imprisoned male revolutionaries in the summer of 1955. In an attempt to consolidate his revolutionary forces after his release from prison, Castro requested that the FCMM merge with his embryonic 26 July Movement (M-26-7).

Following Castro's release from prison, his guerrilla forces relocated to Mexico and began strategizing the next phase of the revolution. In the absence of the male leadership, women once again emerged as crucial organizers of the effort. Celia Sánchez Manduley became the most influential and visible female leader of the Cuban Revolution during this period. An adept organizer with an intimate knowledge of the eastern provinces and their people, Sánchez mobilized a considerable clandestine force that smuggled automatic weapons into the Sierra Maestra in preparation for Castro's return to Cuba in November 1956. Following the arrival of the male revolutionary forces from Mexico, only a few women, namely Sánchez, Vilma Espín, Hernández, and Santamaría, continued to wield significant power within the revolutionary forces. Initially reluctant to accept females as military equals, the male leadership eventually recognized the significant contributions of their female compatriots-in-arms. In September 1958, Castro approved the organization of a fourteen-member female combat platoon known as the "Mariana Grajales Women's Platoon" that not only served as Castro's personal security detail in the Sierra Maestra, but also participated in at least ten encounters with Batista's army. The creation of the women's platoon did not eradicate a more traditional division of labor along gender lines within the rebel camp, as the Marianas were expected to cook and sew in addition to undertaking combat duties.

Women in Post-Revolutionary Cuba, 1959–1990. With the triumph of the revolution in January 1959, Cuban women continued to push for recognition as an important arm of the revolution. In 1960, the revolutionary government responded to these demands by approving the creation of an official organization of Cuban women known as the Federation of Cuban Women (FMC) with Espín as president. The FMC would eventually become the largest women's organization in the history of Latin America, boasting millions of official members. In a speech delivered on 9 December 1966, Castro encouraged Cuban women to become a "revolution within the Revolution," and charged the FMC with mobilizing women in support of the revolutionary government. To this end, the FMC mounted extensive literacy campaigns, created night schools for domestic servants and former prostitutes, organized volunteer work brigades, lobbied for better female health care (including abortions), and provided job training to enable Cuban women to enter the national labor force. The FMC also organized national congresses every five years at which Cuban women could celebrate accomplishments and air grievances.

By the mid-1970s, Cuban women began to complain that incorporation into the labor force required them to shoulder the double burden of full-time employment and regular household chores. Hoping that a reduction of household responsibilities would enable greater numbers of women to enter the workforce, the Cuban government passed the Working Women's Maternity Law (1974) and the Family Code (1975). The maternity law granted working mothers eighteen weeks paid maternity leave, while the Family Code obligated Cuban men to share equally in all household tasks and child-care duties. Despite their new legal right to demand an equitable distribution of household labors and even divorce an uncooperative mate, many Cuban women complained that the legislation was largely ineffective. Aside from continuing problems at home, many women entering the labor force encountered sexual discrimination based on their reproductive role. Viewing all women as potential future mothers, employers often refused to place women in jobs that might harm their reproductive capabilities. Likewise, women found that they were placed in jobs more suited to their "female characteristics" (for example, manual dexterity), which were often lower paid, lower status, and the first jobs to be eliminated in a financial crisis. Thus, while the FMC was designated as the representative body of Cuban women, it faced real limitations to its ability to effect social change within the home and within the labor sector. At the beginning of the twenty-first century, the FMC has faced stern criticism from its own members who feel that women's issues are ultimately subsumed within the larger goals of the revolutionary state.

Despite these concerns about the institution's lack of autonomy from the party, the FMC remains the only legally permitted women's organization on the island. In November 1994, a group of Cuban women in communications organized an independent feminist group called MAGÍN to address contemporary issues of gender inequality in Cuba, but state authorities forced the group to disband shortly after its founding.

Cuban Women Face New Challenges, 1990–Present. No single event has impacted contemporary Cuban society more than the dissolution of the Soviet Union in 1989. With the collapse of its primary foreign trade partner, Cuba's import-export power was reduced by over 80 percent. This economic shock was exacerbated by the continuation of U.S. economic sanctions against the island. By the early 1990s, Cuba was plunged into a "Special Period" characterized by a series of wide-ranging economic cutbacks intended to help stabilize the island's rapidly deteriorating economic situation. Acute shortages in food, gasoline, medicine, and many basic goods forced the Cuban state to embrace international tourism as a means to regenerate the domestic economy. The sharp increase in foreign arrivals to the island during the 1990s prompted the development of a dynamic informal economy sustained in large part by female entrepreneurship. The Cuban state responded to this shift in economic activities by legalizing the possession of U.S. dollars in 1993. At the same time, it imposed a series of hefty taxes intended to exert state control over household income levels, prevent sharp economic stratification within Cuban society, and bolster state coffers. Drawn by the promise of greater access to dollars, many professional women—especially those who spoke English—left their occupations to pursue work in the informal sector. Commercial activities geared toward the island's booming tourism industry, such as renting homes to tourists, food vending, operating non-state restaurants, producing handicrafts, and engaging in sex tourism, became commonplace. Other Cuban women made the difficult choice to emigrate (legally or illegally) to the United States and other countries in search of greater economic opportunity. In light of Cuba's continued political, economic, and social challenges, Cuban women will undoubtedly continue to develop strategies to confront the issues facing their families and their country in the years to come.

[*See also* Labor; Marriage; Socialism; *and* War.]

BIBLIOGRAPHY

Castro, Fidel, Vilma Espín, and others. *Women and the Cuban Revolution: Speeches and Documents*. Edited by Elizabeth Stone. New York: Pathfinder Press, 1981. An invaluable collection of primary documents relating to women's roles in the Cuban Revolution that includes excerpts from important speeches and full-text reproductions of key legislation relating to women and the family.

Haney, Richard. *Celia Sánchez: The Legend of Cuba's Revolutionary Heart*. New York: Algora, 2005. The only existing English-language biography of Cuba's revolutionary heroine, this text is based in part on information gleaned from a series of personal letters penned by Sánchez herself.

Maclean, Betsy, ed. *Haydée Santamaría*. Melbourne and New York: Ocean Press, 2003. A concise biography that weaves together interviews, poetry, speeches, and personal correspondence to shed light on the events and tragedies of the revolutionary heroine's life.

Maloof, Judy, ed. and trans. *Voices of Resistance: Testimonies of Cuban and Chilean Women*. Lexington: University Press of Kentucky, 1999. A collection of interviews with thirteen important women whose actions shaped the political, cultural, and social topographies of their respective countries.

Molyneux, Maxine. "State, Gender, and Institutional Change in Cuba's Special Period: The Federación de Mujeres Cubanas." In *Hidden Histories of Gender and the State in Latin America*, edited by Elizabeth Dore and Maxine Molyneux, pp. 291–321. Durham, N.C.: Duke University Press, 2000. An insightful analysis of the development of, and contemporary challenges faced by, Cuba's only officially recognized women's organization.

Prados-Torreira, Teresa. *Mambisas: Rebel Women in Nineteenth-Century Cuba*. Gainesville: University Press of Florida, 2005. The first book-length study of the women who contributed to Cuba's struggle for independence from Spain as combatants, arms smugglers, and nurses during the nineteenth century.

Puebla, Teté, and Mary-Alice Waters. *Marianas in Combat: Teté Puebla and the Mariana Grajales Women's Platoon in Cuba's Revolutionary War, 1956–58*. New York: Pathfinder, 2003. A general discussion of women's participation in the Cuban Revolution from the 1950s to the present based on interviews with the highest-ranking woman in Cuba's Revolutionary Armed Forces.

Randall, Margaret. *Cuban Women Now: Interviews with Cuban Women*. Toronto: Women's Press and Dumont Press Graphix, 1974. A collection of interviews with a diverse array of Cuban women that speaks to the complex and often contradictory impact of the Cuban Revolution on women's daily lives. This text should be read alongside Randall's later analysis of women's experiences in contemporary Cuban society, *Women in Cuba: Twenty Years Later* (New York: Smyrna Press, 1981).

Smith, Lois M., and Alfred Padula. *Sex and Revolution: Women in Socialist Cuba*. New York: Oxford University Press, 1996. The first book-length assessment of the successes and failures of the revolutionary state in advancing gender equality in Cuba through legislation and social programming in the second half of the twentieth century.

Stoner, K. Lynn. *From the House to the Streets: The Cuban Woman's Movement for Legal Reform, 1898–1940*. Durham, N.C.: Duke University Press, 1991. Drawing on in-depth archival research, interviews, and periodical sources, this is the only book-length study of the development of the early feminist movement in Cuba.

TIFFANY THOMAS-WOODARD

CULTURAL EXCHANGE. Cultural mixture has occurred for millennia, and the exchange of ideas, everyday practices, food, clothing, music and art, and popular culture continues to take place. Women's involvement in these exchanges has been brisk, ranging from the travel of Japanese women artists to discover the techniques of Russian icon painting to the sporting of clothing designs from around the world. Women integrated new kinds of food into their families' diets, and they gained some of their political ideas from around the world. While adopting foreign religious beliefs and scientific ideas, they also facilitated cultural exchange by serving as translators, guides, collectors, and travelers.

Religion. The spread of world religions in ancient and medieval times found women active in this form of cultural exchange. The Chinese and Japanese became Buddhist nuns as that religion entered their region from South Asia. The Korean queens Chong-Hui and Sohye were great patrons of translations of Buddhist works, a common form of women's royal patronage. Women in Europe adopted the Christian religion, which came from the Middle East, and in so doing surrendered many of their beliefs in polytheism, forest gods, and other spirits. Africans became devotees of Islam, which originated in the Arabian Peninsula, and later African American women adopted this religion on the other side of the Atlantic. Women served as Christian and Buddhist missionaries, often traveling thousands of miles to promote religious conversion. In the early modern period, Latin American native women adopted Catholicism, surrendering an array of Native American religious practices or sometimes integrating both sets of beliefs.

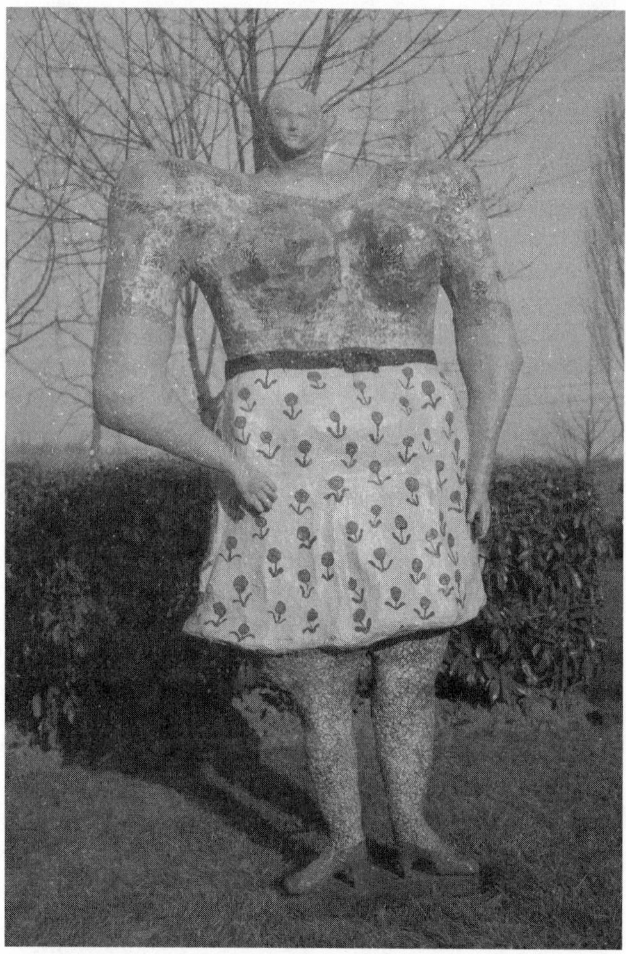

Die Waldaff. Sculpture by Niki de Saint-Phalle, 1962. © 2007 Artists Rights Society (ARS), New York, Musée National d'Arte Moderne, Centre Georges Pompidou, Paris/Réunion des Musées Nationaux/Art Resource, NY

Clothing. The exchange of clothing has been ubiquitous, crossing oceans, deserts, and continents. In the Tang dynasty Chinese women enjoyed Turkish fashions, sporting baggy "harem" pants and snug jackets. Influenced by the tightly bound ballet shoes of Persian dancers, Chinese women began binding their feet, using a variety of techniques—most of them painful—to modify the foot. European and American women from the mid-seventeenth century onward chose brightly colored cottons from India and China for their clothes and household linens and gradually loosened their corsets to look more natural, as the prints of Japanese, Chinese, and other Asian women showed them to be. High-quality Asian cottons such as muslin and a variety of styles borrowed from western Asia and elsewhere also allowed Western women to attain the kind of cleanliness that other peoples already practiced.

In the mid-nineteenth century, American feminists, like earlier Chinese ladies, adapted the Turkish harem pants to make the "bloomer"—a reform fashion that was one precursor of slacks. Western women also delighted in East Asian fans and umbrellas, and by the end of the nineteenth century they were even wearing kimonos, a loosely fitting garment that signaled their desire for less constricting dress. At about this time African and Polynesian women were adopting Western fashions—an event that frustrated painters such as Paul Gauguin who were traveling the world to find "authentic" and "natural" women. A later stage in the cultural exchange in garb came when "Western" styles, which were earlier borrowings from other parts of the world, were taken up by women around the world. In twentieth-century west Asia, many Muslim women unveiled and discarded other traditional garments in an attempt to be more modern and comfortable. Contests over what women's "authentic" garb should be were sometimes heightened as global exchange accelerated in the late twentieth century.

Health and Medicine. Cultural exchange occurred in some of the most intimate matters of everyday life. In the twentieth century, Western missionaries insisted that African and west Asian women abstain from traditional practices of genital cutting, and this has become a global issue. Simultaneously, however, women in other parts of the world were fascinated by and even adapted genital cutting. Marie Bonaparte, the early French psychoanalyst, had genital surgery three times and wrote about practices of cutting in the Middle East. Women also exchanged ideas on childbirth techniques, with many practices for "natural childbirth" such as rhythmic breathing coming from Buddhist instructions for meditation. This occurred even while childbirth in many parts of the world became medicalized along the lines of European and American standards. As this occurred, many women practitioners of traditional medicine lost their jobs because of scientific cultural exchange.

Translators and Guides. Women served as intermediaries in cultural exchange among traders and conquerors. One common practice was for conquerors to intermarry with women of vanquished peoples—especially royal and noble women. The Mongols demanded Chinese and Korean royal women and commoners for wives and concubines, which not only cemented countries politically but also facilitated the transfer of culture. Women also served as translators and guides to conquerors, using their linguistic and local knowledge on behalf of the dominant parties. Many of these women have disappeared from history as individuals, but others are legendary.

Doña Marina (c. 1500–1527), also known as Malinche and La Lengua (the tongue), interpreted for Hernán Cortés during his conquest of Mexico and became highly valued by the Spanish because of her knowledge of several local languages. Her ambivalent reputation, like that of other translators, stems from her role in Cortés's conquest of Montezuma, for she served as the intermediary and carried messages to the Aztec ruler. Malinche also bore one of Cortés's many illegitimate children as well as other children by her Spanish-born husband.

In the mid-seventeenth century the Khoikhoi Eva used her knowledge of Dutch and Portuguese to aid Dutch and other migrants at the Cape of Good Hope, while in the early nineteenth century the Shoshone Sacagawea assisted the Lewis and Clark expedition by serving as guide. She also exchanged survival skills including healing practices and knowledge of underground food sources with the expeditionary team and taught them secrets of the region's topography. Diplomatic customs also passed back and forth.

Translations and Literature. Women have excelled for centuries in providing more formal translations of literary classics, holy scriptures such as the Bible, and advice and journalistic writings. Translations circulated in various East Asian, European, and other languages to introduce women to models of behavior. For instance, Korean women learned of Chinese heroines who practiced Confucian virtues, while late in the nineteenth century in an attempt to combat Japanese imperialism translators offered them models from the West such as Joan of Arc and Madame Roland. In the twenty-first century, literary translation in the global age with its tens of thousands of new editions of books from other cultures has expanded as a means for women to earn a living.

Feminist writers of literature and history intermingled stories of women from other cultures with their own to make a composite activist message. In 1921 the Korean author Na Hye-Sok published the poem "A Doll's House," picking up on the themes of women's liberation from the family and establishment of an independent character. Women writers in Egypt, India, and Japan were among those using connections not only to fire their feminist thinking but also to fire their nationalism. They traveled to discover the latest news about women's education, politics, and cultural life and to return those ideas to their own societies. Early in the twentieth century many of these feminist writers created national versions of the Western "new woman."

Meanwhile, feminist writers in the West latched on to ideas from around the world, shaping their ideas of gender. Many of the most famous incorporated the idea of gender transformations over millennia through reincarnation—a concept central to Asian religion. Most famous among these was Virginia Woolf's *Orlando* (1928), the story of gender metamorphosis over centuries of history. The protagonist begins as an aristocratic young man, whose opening scene has him wildly striking his sword at the head of a Moor that is hanging from the rafters of the family home. Orlando matures to stride boldly across the stage of early modern history, encountering an array of colorful characters. However, by modern times the protagonist, while remaining the same self, has changed physically into a woman. Time rushes by a core self, although the reader will soon grasp that there is nothing to that core. Woolf's delightful novel, cerebral and whimsical, captures the essential belief in reincarnation common among the literati and feminists. More than any other work it demonstrates the casting off of bodies and biological sex across the centuries with the core self, or atman, remaining intact to live out one's karma in progressive lives. The writers Katherine Mansfield and Selma Lagerlof, the Nobel laureate, were but two of many others displaying similar ideas.

Philosophy, Music, and Dance. From the United States to England and Russia, adherents of the ideas of Madame Blavatsky held meetings to discuss the advanced ideas emanating from South and East Asia; they chanted and meditated together. To facilitate the kind of lifestyle that Hinduism and Buddhism in particular advocated, they set up vegetarian restaurants and resorts in Saint Petersburg, Vienna, and elsewhere. The professional violinist Aleksandra Unkovskaia regularly contributed articles analyzing the music of Wagner and other avant-garde composers according to the Asian ideas of "color-sound" that passed through collaborators of Madame Blavatsky.

Western women's practice of hypnotism, meditation, and a variety of Eastern and African therapies and martial arts gained ground.

Modern dance developed because of women's participation in cultural exchange. The American dancer Isadora Duncan was among the first to imitate the steps and bearing of "primitive peoples" from around the world. In Germany the dancer Mary Wigman took up modern dance just before World War I—a form that she also contributed to by taking ideas from non-Western models. She studied the Noh plays and danced wearing Japanese masks, white, gaunt, and expressive. Wigman investigated the dance forms of other cultures, including Native Americans, and worked to capture their theoretical and inner essence.

Modern dance in the United States developed from the same non-Western influences, with women at the forefront of this movement. Before World War I, Ruth St. Denis and Ted Shawn packed arenas and concert halls around the world. Among their first productions was *The Legend of the Peacock*, begun in 1909, about an overly ambitious wife of a raja whose scheming condemns her to reincarnation as a peacock. St. Denis choreographed striking works such as *The Japanese Spear Dance*, a violent, acrobatic dance performed to great acclaim around the world. A regular at the performance of the *Black and Gold Sari* when it was danced in Calcutta (now called Kolkata) in the mid-1920s, according to Jane Sherman in *The Drama of Denishawn Dance*, Rabindranath Tagore tried to get the university there to hire St. Denis to teach dance in India as a way of reviving traditions that the British had worked to destroy. The Denishawn school of dance trained other legends in modern dance, including Martha Graham.

In Asia, women musicians learned to play the new instruments that traveled the Silk Road. In the West, popular culture such as jazz, reggae, hip-hop, and other forms built on cultural mixture evolved because of the participation of women such as Ella Fitzgerald and Billie Holiday. In classical music the Polish composer and percussionist Marta Ptaszynska (b. 1943) absorbed the global culture around her, even though said to be behind an Iron Curtain in the Soviet Empire. In 1986 she composed *Moon Flowers*, a work for cello and piano, to celebrate the astronauts killed when the spaceship *Challenger* exploded. Drawing on Asian art and Zen philosophy for her inspiration, she also composed "Concerto for Marimba and Orchestra" and used lights as an integral part of her musical works. The Russian composer Sofia Gubaidulina used multicultural sounds, incorporating electronic music but also making human sounds such as cries, whispers, and screams part of her work; some of this was inspired by her interest in world religions.

Environmentalism. By the end of the twentieth century women were active as environmentalists and "deep" ecologists, participating in a Western movement that was heavily influenced by cultural borrowings from Asia and Africa. Much environmentalist thinking had arisen over the course of the nineteenth century—inspired by such thinkers as Henry David Thoreau and Leo Tolstoy, whose interest in Asian thought was profound. Petra Kelly, who participated in the founding of the German Green Party, was among those who sought to understand the fundamental processes of the natural world and, on the basis of the oneness of all life, to let them be. Integrating ideas from Tantric Buddhism into her position, Kelly preached that rather than protecting nature and righting the wrongs committed against the environment, deep ecologists wanted people to stand lovingly aside, ending their struggle to conquer an unconquerable force. Activists such as Wangari Maathai of Kenya were important leaders in devising practices to resolve environmental issues that influenced the world.

[*See also* Body Adornment and Clothing; Buddhism; Christianity; Dance, *subentry* Modern and Professional; Foot-Binding; Islam; Kelly, Petra; Literature; Midwifery; Music; Religion; Sacagawea; *and* Woolf, Virginia.]

BIBLIOGRAPHY

Burton, Antoinette M. *At the Heart of the Empire: Indians and the Colonial Encounter in Late-Victorian Britain.* Berkeley: University of California Press, 1998.

Dixon, Joy. *Divine Feminine: Theosophy and Feminism in England.* Baltimore: Johns Hopkins University Press, 2001.

Hyun, Theresa. *Writing Women in Korea: Translation and Feminism in the Colonial Period.* Honolulu: University of Hawai'i Press, 2004.

Kartunnen, Frances E. *Between Worlds: Interpreters, Guides, and Survivors.* New Brunswick, N.J.: Rutgers University Press, 1994.

Pendle, Karin, ed. *Women and Music: A History.* Bloomington: Indiana University Press, 1991.

Yoshihara, Mari. *Embracing the East: White Women and American Orientalism.* Oxford and New York: Oxford University Press, 2003.

BONNIE G. SMITH

CUMMINGS-JOHN, CONSTANCE (1918–2000), Sierra Leonean anticolonial activist, feminist, and politician. Born Constance Agatha Horton into Sierra Leone's elite Krio (Creole) society, she attended missionary and colonial schools in Freetown. At seventeen she went to England to attend Whiteland College, an affiliate of London University. Then in 1936, she took up a six-month fellowship at Cornell University in the United States. Her stays abroad exposed her to critiques of Western imperialism, colonial rule, and racism. In London on Sundays she was drawn to Hyde Park, where speakers such as Marcus Garvey held sway. There she met and was influenced by the Sierra Leonean radical labor organizer and journalist I. T. A. Wallace-Johnson (1895–1965). Wallace-Johnson introduced Cummings-John to important Pan-Africanists and anticolonial activists such as George Padmore, C. L. R. James, and T. R. Makonnen. During her fellowship at Cornell University, she traveled to black schools in the South, Hampton and Tuskegee institutes, and was influenced by both the racism of the "Jim Crow" South and the black self-help ideology that responded to that racism.

In 1937 she married Ethan Cummings-John, and they returned to Freetown, where Constance Cummings-John become the principal of the African Methodist Girls' Industrial School. After her radicalization in England and the United States, she found Sierra Leone's political culture too conservative. Fortunately her political ally Wallace-Johnson returned to Freetown soon after Cummings-John did. She joined his newly established branch of the West African Youth League (WAYL), a radical group that used mass mobilization tactics and gave women a central role. This was just the opportunity Cummings-John needed. With WAYL backing in 1938, the twenty-year-old Cummings-John won a stunning victory in Freetown council elections. During this period she began building an alliance with Sierra Leone's market women, whom she called on successfully during the decolonization period. Cummings-John held her council seat until 1942, when she was unseated.

After lying low during World War II, Cummings-John returned to the United States in 1946 and stayed there for five years. She supported herself by working in hospitals as a nurses' aide, and she joined several internationally focused organizations, including the American Council of African Affairs (ACAA), on whose executive committee she served. Led by the actor, orator, singer, and well-known Communist Paul Robeson, the ACAA supported mass action against colonial rule. Cummings-John recalled being pelted with eggs and tomatoes by anti-Communist demonstrators for speaking as a member of the ACAA. She returned to Freetown in 1951 and began setting up a school named for Eleanor Roosevelt, whom she had met while in the United States. This venture was greatly influenced by Adelaide Casely Hayford (1868–1960), a fellow Krio who founded her own school in 1923.

Cummings-John played a central role in Sierra Leone's decolonization politics. She joined the party that represented the Protectorate (non-Krio) peoples of Sierra Leone, the Sierra Leone People's Party (SLPP), and served on its executive committee. With the support of her relative Mabel Dove-Dunquah, an activist and writer from the Gold Coast (later Ghana), Cummings-John and other Freetown women founded the Sierra Leone Women's Movement (SLWM), whose goals were to improve the status of all Sierra Leone women and to seek representation on governing bodies that were concerned with education, social welfare, and the economy. With market women as their main constituency, the movement turned out some twenty thousand women for its first demonstration against inflation. Three years after its founding, the SLWM had two thousand dues-paying members in Freetown and three thousand in the Protectorate.

Cummings-John was one of the most popular politicians in decolonizing Sierra Leone. In 1957 she stood for a seat in the general election for the newly created house of representatives and won the most votes, but this time the Krio political elite forced her to resign even before she took her seat. In 1958 she was elected to the Freetown Municipal Council, again with the most votes. In 1966 Sierra Leone's first prime minister, Albert Margai, appointed her mayor of Freetown.

In the unstable and rapidly shifting power dynamics that characterized Sierra Leone since its independence, Cummings-John was charged by her old rivals, the Krio political elite, with misuse of public funds during a coup d'état while she was abroad at a Women's International Democratic Federation meeting. She thought it best not to return to Freetown and decided to settle in London. There again she became politically active, joining the Labour Party and the Campaign for Nuclear Disarmament.

Cummings-John made two attempts to resettle in Freetown, first from 1974 to 1976 and again in 1996, when her political party, the SLPP, was back in power. Each time she returned to London because of Sierra Leone's instability. She died in London on 21 February 2000.

[*See also* African Liberation and Nationalist Movements; Democracy; *and* West Africa, *subentry* Twentieth Century.]

BIBLIOGRAPHY

Adi, Hakim, and Marika Sherwood. "Constance Cummings-John." In *Pan-African History: Political Figures from Africa and the Diaspora since 1787*, pp. 29–33. London: Routledge, 2003. Short, accurate summary of Cummings-John's life.

Cummings-John, Constance Agatha. *Constance Agatha Cummings-John: Memoirs of a Krio Leader*. Introduction and annotation by LaRay Denzer. Ibadan, Nigeria: Sam Bookman, 1995. Introduction is carefully researched and authoritative.

Denzer, LaRay. "The Influence of Pan-Africanism in the Career of Constance A. Cummings-John." In *Pan-African Biography*, edited by Robert A. Hill, pp. 137–160. Los Angeles: African Studies Center, University of California, Los Angeles, 1987.

Spitzer, Leo. *The Creoles of Sierra Leone: Responses to Colonialsim, 1870–1945*. Madison: University of Wisconsin Press, 1974. The best book on the Krio elite but with little focus on women.

Spitzer, Leo, and LaRay Denzer. "I. T. A. Wallace-Johnson and the West African Youth League." *International Journal of African Historical Studies* 6 (1973): 413–452, 565–601. Authoritative source on Cummings-John's early political mentor.

White, E. Frances. *Sierra Leone's Settler Women Traders: Women on the Afro-European Frontier*. Ann Arbor: University of Michigan Press 1987. History of Krio market women, many of whom were organized by Cummings-John.

E. FRANCES WHITE

CURIE, MARIE (1867–1934), Polish-born French physicist. Few women in science have attained the iconic status of Marie Sklodowska Curie, who with her husband, Pierre Curie (1859–1906), discovered the radioactive elements polonium and radium. She was born on 7 November 1867 in Warsaw, Poland, to Wlasdislaw Sklodowski and his wife Bronislawa, the youngest of five children. She, like her sisters, studied at a girls' schools in Warsaw, where lessons were conducted in Russian as well as Polish. Banned from Warsaw University because of her sex, she studied at the clandestine "Flying University." After completing her course work at the age of eighteen, she took a position in the provinces as a governess, saving half her salary to send her oldest sister, Bronia, to Paris to study medicine.

In the fall of 1891, Marie Sklodowska joined her sister in Paris to study for a science degree at the University of Paris, Sorbonne, passing three years later with high marks in physics and mathematics. After she began graduate studies in physics, a friend introduced her to a brilliant young physicist, Pierre Curie, who was the head of the laboratory at the School of Industrial Physics and Chemistry and with whom she found she shared social and scientific ideals. Shortly before their marriage in 1895, Pierre finally completed his doctorate and was made a professor of physics at his school.

For her graduate thesis, at Pierre's suggestion, Marie began to study spontaneous radiation emitted by uranium compounds, which had recently been discovered by the physicist Henri Becquerel (1852–1908). Finding that the radiation was related to the amount of uranium in the compound and was therefore an atomic property of the element, she proposed the term "radioactivity." Analyzing uranium ores, she found an indication that highly radioactive, unknown elements remained after the extraction of uranium. Pierre put aside his own study of crystals to join her in measuring the new elements, using his invention, the piezoelectric quartz electrometer.

The two spent many hours in the laboratory. By July 1898, they announced the discovery of polonium (named in honor of Marie's native land) and then, in December of the same year, radium. They still needed to refine and extract the new elements in sufficient quantities to place them in the atomic table. Obtaining large amounts of pitchblende, with the help of the Austrian Academy of Sciences, and working in a leaky shed where they refined the ore, Pierre Curie investigated the physical properties of radium while Marie performed chemical experiments to produce pure radium salts. By 1900 they had produced papers pointing out the chemical and physical properties of radium, including its brilliant luminosity. With Becquerel, they were awarded the Nobel Prize in Physics in 1903, the first husband and wife team to be so honored. Pierre was offered a professorship at the University of Paris, Sorbonne, in 1903, and Marie was made head of the university's new laboratory.

Marie Curie. In her laboratory, 1912. OXFORD SCIENCE ARCHIVE, OXFORD/HIP/ART RESOURCE, NY

In 1906, Pierre, whose health was already fragile from his exposure to radiation, was killed by a horse-drawn cart in the streets of Paris. Marie, now left with two daughters—one nine years old and one eighteen months old—struggled to further refine the chemistry of the new elements, supported in her personal life and scientific work by scientific friends. She took over Pierre's position at the Sorbonne and his small laboratory, and she made it her project to obtain the more suitable radiation laboratory they had envisioned.

In late 1910, Marie Curie endured an unsuccessful candidacy before the esteemed Paris Academy of Sciences, from which all women were then excluded. During the next year her close relationship with the physicist Paul Langevin (1872–1946) led to savage attacks on Curie from the right-wing Parisian press. In the midst of the 1911 scandal over her personal life, however, she was awarded a second Nobel Prize, this time in chemistry.

During World War I, Marie and her seventeen-year-old daughter Irène (1897–1956) set up a mobile X-ray unit that aided surgeons close to the battlefield in locating bullets and shrapnel in soldiers' wounds. Marie's younger daughter, Ève (b. 1904), became a journalist and later wrote a celebrated biography of her mother, *Madame Curie* (1937). Marie, who had suffered from various illnesses as a result of her long exposure to radioactivity, died of aplastic pernicious anemia on 3 July 1934.

[*See also* Joliot-Curie, Irène, *and* Science, *subentry* Natural Sciences.]

BIBLIOGRAPHY

Curie, Ève. *Madame Curie*. Translated by Vincent Sheean. Garden City, N.Y.: Doubleday, 1937.

Curie, Marie. *Pierre Curie*. Translated by Charlotte and Vernon Kellogg. With an introduction by Mrs. William Brown Meloney and autobiographical notes by Marie Curie. New York: Macmillan, 1923.

Goldsmith, Barbara. *Obsessive Genius: The Inner World of Marie Curie*. New York: Norton, 2005.

Quinn, Susan. *Marie Curie: A Life*. New York: Simon and Schuster, 1995.

Joy Harvey

CUTTING. *See* Female Genital Mutilation.

CZECH REPUBLIC. Before 1918, the region that forms today's Czech Republic was part of the Habsburg Monarchy. In the nineteenth century, women in the Czech lands had few rights or economic opportunities. Like the Napoleonic Code used in other parts of Europe, Habsburg civil law gave a husband complete jurisdiction over his wife's body and property. Wives could not get a job without their husband's permission and did not even have the right to keep their own earnings. Women had no access to secondary education and were considered unfit for professional positions. Middle-class women were expected to marry, not to work. Peasants and lower-class women toiled in the fields or factories, but remained economically dependent on their husbands or fathers. Women of all classes were forbidden to vote or even join political organizations.

The Czech women's movement first emerged in the mid-nineteenth century and was closely connected to the Czech nationalist movement. The first women's organizations, established in the 1860s and 1870s, were influenced by the work of female nationalist writers, including Božena Němcová (1820–1862), Karolina Světlá (1830–1899), and Sofie Podlipská (1833–1897), who urged Czech women to support their nation by developing their own capabilities. Accordingly, many early Czech women's groups were dedicated to women's education. Prominent examples include the American Ladies' Club, established in Prague in 1865 to expose women to modern (or "American") feminist ideas, and the Ženský výrobní spolek český (Czech Women's Industrial and Commercial Training Association) founded by Světlá and Podlipská in 1871.

The Czech women's movement gained more strength in the 1890s during a long campaign to open university education to women. It was headed by the energetic and capable Eliška Krásnohorská (1847–1926). Krásnohorská's efforts resulted in the first gymnasium (secondary school preparing students for university) for women in the Habsburg Monarchy. The school, called Minerva, opened in Prague in the fall of 1890. Minerva's successful students helped put pressure on Habsburg officials, who finally allowed women into university humanities departments in 1897 and medical schools in 1900. These new educational opportunities enabled some middle-class women to find professional work and a new economic independence outside of marriage.

Feminists and Democrats. Around the turn of the century, several groups with a more overtly feminist orientation formed in the Czech lands, including the Ženský klub český (Czech Women's Club), established in 1903, and the Zemská pokroková organizace žen na Moravě (Moravian Progressive Women's Organization), which had ten branches by 1910. Both espoused a version of feminism that was deeply inspired by the Czech professor and nationalist Tomáš Garrigue Masaryk (1850–1937). Under Masaryk's influence, Czech feminists developed an emphatically egalitarian ideology, causing them to largely reject the maternalist thinking common to many women's groups in Europe during the late nineteenth and early twentieth centuries. Czech feminists also took from Masaryk an unshakeable faith in democracy as the way to liberate not only women, but the entire Czech nation.

Although most Czech feminists were middle class and often worked as teachers or journalists, many were attracted to the growing socialist movement in the Czech lands, which had its own vibrant women's movement by the turn of the century. The relationship between Czech socialist and bourgeois feminist leaders was generally amicable, and groups like the Czech Women's Club included both. This ability to cooperate across political lines was unusual compared with other European women's movements that lasted through 1945.

After 1905, Czech feminists turned their attention to the issue of suffrage, creating the Výbor pro volební právo žen (Committee for Women's Voting Rights) led by a young schoolteacher, Františka Plamínková (1875–1942). Although the committee started with only twelve members, they were able to gain support for their cause by convincing nationalist politicians that women's fight for the vote was part of the Czech nationalist struggle against the Habsburg regime. In 1912, Czech suffragists were able to convince three Czech political parties (the Czech National Socialists, the Progressives, and the Young Czechs) to publicly protest women's inability to vote by running a female candidate in a replacement election for a provincial assembly seat. Their candidate, the nationalist writer Božena Vitková-Kunětická (1862–1934), won the election, although she was not allowed to take office. Her victory, while only symbolic, cemented the partnership between Czech feminists and nationalists.

The Women's Movement in Independent Czechoslovakia. Czechoslovakia became independent in 1918. The democratic Czechoslovak government, led by President Tomáš Masaryk, immediately granted women suffrage and included a guarantee of women's equality in its constitution. However, Czech activist women soon discovered that they would still have to fight to see that equality realized. Plamínková created the Ženská národní rada (Women's National Council) for this purpose in 1923. The WNC was a nonpartisan federation of existing women's groups dedicated to fighting for women's rights. It also represented Czechoslovakia in groups like the International Council of Women and the Alliance for Women's Suffrage. The WNC fought to see women and men treated on equal terms in the workplace, in civil law, and in the family. Until its demise during World War II, the WNC continued to portray its work as an integral component of Czech nationalism, dedicated to building an egalitarian democracy.

Alongside the WNC, a wide range of Czech women's groups existed during the decades between World Wars I and II, including professional organizations, housewives' associations, religious groups, and party auxiliaries. This expansion inevitably led to conflict. One of the largest groups was the Svaz katolických žen a dívek (Federation of Catholic Women and Girls) which claimed over 300,000 members in 1936. Its leaders emphasized women's special social role as mothers and rejected the decidedly anti-maternalist stance of the WNC. The two groups battled each other over issues such as divorce (legal in Czechoslovakia after 1918) and women's place in the working world. Another divisive issue was abortion. Social Democratic and Communist women, led by Social Democrat Betty Karpíšková (1881–1942), campaigned heavily for legal abortion in Czechoslovakia, but in vain. They were opposed by Catholics, and also by many middle-class feminists.

The Communist Era and Beyond. During World War II, the Germans occupied the Czech lands. Most women's organizations stopped meeting, and many feminist leaders, including Plamínková and Karpíšková, were killed. After the end of the war, one of the survivors, a lawyer named Milada Horáková (1901–1950), tried to revive the democratic Czech feminist tradition by founding a new nonpartisan federation, the Rada československých žen (Council of Czechoslovak Women). The Communist seizure of power in 1948 ended this attempt. Horáková, who resisted the Communist regime, was arrested and executed for treason in 1950. After 1948, the women's movement in the Czech lands was controlled by the Czechoslovak Communist Party, which allowed few women into its leadership circles. Claiming that women had achieved equality and did not need their own organizations, Communist leaders abolished the party's women's commission in 1952.

After the fall of the Communist regime in 1989, Czech women were again free to associate as they pleased. However, women's groups have been slow to form in the new Czech Republic, created in 1993 by the peaceful dissolution of Czechoslovakia. While Czech women have not yet recreated the vibrant movement of the 1920s and 1930s, some events at the beginning of the twenty-first century, such as the founding of the department of Gender Studies at the Charles University in Prague in 2004, show that the contemporary movement continues to grow.

BIBLIOGRAPHY

Burešová, Jana. *Proměny společenského postavení českých žen v první polovině 20. století*. Olomouc, Czech Republic: Palacký University, 2001. A solid survey of Czech women's organizations during the first half of the twentieth century, including both feminist and Catholic groups.

David, Katherine. "Czech Feminists and Nationalism in the Late Habsburg Monarchy: 'The First in Austria.'" *Journal of Women's History* 3, no. 2 (1991): 26–45.

Feinberg, Melissa. *Elusive Equality: Gender, Citizenship, and the Limits of Democracy in Czechoslovakia*. Pittsburgh: University of Pittsburgh Press, 2006. The only book-length study of gender politics in Czechoslovakia in English.

Heitlinger, Alena. *Women and State Socialism: Sex Inequality in the Soviet Union and Czechoslovakia*. Montreal: McGill–Queen's University Press, 1979. A sociological study of women's place in Communist society.

Neudorflová, Marie. *České ženy v 19. století: Úsilí a sny, úspěchy i zklamání na cestě k emancipaci*. Prague: Janua, 1999. Comprehensive overview of nineteenth-century Czech women's organizations.

MELISSA FEINBERG